Barcode in Back

D1221481

FILM AND TELEVISION MUSIC

A GUIDE TO BOOKS, ARTICLES, AND COMPOSER INTERVIEWS

COMPILED AND EDITED BY

WARREN M. SHERK

The Scarecrow Press, Inc.
Lanham, Maryland • Toronto • Plymouth, UK
2011

SCARECROW PRESS, INC.

Published in the United States of America
by Scarecrow Press, Inc.
A wholly owned subsidary of
The Rowman & Littlefield Publishing Group, Inc.
4501 Forbes Boulevard, Suite 200, Lanham, Maryland 20706
www.scarecrowpress.com

Estover Road
Plymouth PL6 7PY
United Kingdom

British Library Cataloguing in Publication Information Available

Library of Congress Cataloging-in-Publication Data

Sherk, Warren M.
  Film and television music : a guide to books, articles, and composer interviews / compiled and
editor by Warren M. Sherk.
       p. cm.
  Includes bibliographical references and index.
  ISBN 978-0-8108-7686-6 (cloth : alk. paper)
  1. Motion picture music–History and criticism–Bibliography. 2. Television music–History and
criticism–Bibliography. I. Title.
  ML128.M7S545 2011
  016.7815'4—dc22   2010010109

♾️™ The paper used in this publication meets the minimum requirements of
American National Standard for Information Sciences—Permanence of
Paper for Printed Library Materials, ANSI/NISO Z39.48-1992.
Manufactured in the United States of America.

To Dianne

Contents

Foreword

Music is an essential component of film and television productions, but for those wishing to study this critical element, there has, up to now, been very limited information about available resources in books, periodicals, theses, and dissertations. The only book-length bibliography on the subject, *A Comprehensive Bibliography of Music for Film and Television*, compiled by Steven D. Wescott, was published in 1985. *Film and Television Music: A Guide to Books, Articles, and Composer Interviews* rectifies this by providing a comprehensive and indispensable resource tool for a critical century's worth of information on all aspects of motion picture and television music.

The entries in *Film and Television Music* assist researchers by providing thoughtful and succinct synopses of the contents of books and articles from the silent era to the digital age. With the aid of a detailed index, one will be able to find the works that deal with sociological or aesthetic aspects, practical suggestions for composing, a practicing musician's treatise on music for accompanying films in 1913, or a television rehearsal and studio pianist's experiences with variety shows in the 1960s and 1970s. Other topics covered include the evolution of music supervision, theory and application, legal agreements and sample contracts for music, soundtracks, music for sci-fi and fantastic cinema, the music of Walt Disney cartoons, songs written for films, opera on film, source music, studio musicians, late twentieth-century music in German cinema, analyses of the music in specific films, and biographical material and career profiles on multitudes of composers. Also covered are click tracks, music in Hong Kong films, a 1909 compilation of piano music for films, silent-era discussions of theater organists and their repertoire, and synchronization of music via computer.

Warren Sherk is uniquely qualified to author this work. Recipient of an advanced degree in music composition, he has done extensive orchestration and arranging for films. He has also published articles on various aspects of film music, reviewed film music books, and given presentations on film music at various conferences. For more than two decades Warren has worked at the Margaret Herrick Library of the Academy of Motion Picture Arts and Sciences, where he is currently the archivist in charge of the music and recorded sound holdings and is also the special collections database archivist. He edited and compiled *The Films of Mack Sennett: Credit Documentation from the Mack Sennett Collection at the Margaret Herrick Library*, published by Scarecrow Press in 1998, a book detailing the holdings in the library's massive Mack Sennett collection of papers and photographs. A dedicated and diligent researcher, Warren has brought all his talents to bear in the creation of this new work. While he was able to ferret out a good portion of the material for this book from the holdings of the Margaret Herrick Library, he researched multiple major holdings elsewhere, pulling together a massive amount of information that does not exist in any other source. *Film and Television Music: A Guide to Books, Articles, and Composer Interviews* is a work that will prove invaluable to present and future generations of researchers.

Linda Harris Mehr
Director
Margaret Herrick Library
Beverly Hills, California

Acknowledgments

I would like to extend heartfelt thanks to Linda Harris Mehr, director of the Margaret Herrick Library, for her encouragement and support. In compiling this work, I relied on the library's knowledgeable staff of librarians, including Don Lee, Susan Oka, Lucia Schultz, and Lea Whittington, who assembled and cataloged the library's comprehensive collection of books and periodicals. For their expertise and guidance, I often turned to my colleagues in Special Collections: Joe Adamson, Val Almendarez, Laurie Asa-Dorian, Catherine Butler, Anne Coco, Bob Dickson, Barbara Hall, Chen Mei, Howard Prouty, Jenny Romero, and Leah Smith. Thanks also to systems librarian Zoe Friedlander and to library staffers Sandra Archer, Stacey Behlmer, Allison Berntsen, Jeanie Braun, Russ Butner, Pat DeFazio, Mark Frerking, Lisa Gall, Harry Garvin, Jane Glicksman, Russell Good, Sue Guldin, Tony Guzman, Jessica Holada, Mona Huntzing, Elizabeth Kim, Kristine Krueger, Michele Lane, Andrea Livingston, Janet Lorenz, Mary Mallory, Dan Miller, Kathryn Reesman, Brad Roberts, Vionnette Sellers, Matt Severson, Mary Anne Thomas, Faye Thompson, Michael Tyler, Jonathan Wahl, Greg Walsh, Libby Wertin, Galen Wilkes, and Mary Jeanne Wilson.

At the UCLA Music Library, Stephen Fry (emeritus), Gordon Theil, and Bridget Risemberg went above and beyond the call of duty, as did Steve Hanson, Sandra Garcia-Myers, Ned Comstock, and John Brockman of USC's Cinematic Arts Library. The Film Music Society has worked tirelessly toward preserving the music and memories of some of our most fertile minds; thanks to the society's producing director, Marilee Bradford, and board member Jon Burlingame for their contributions, and to composer Christopher Young for keeping the society afloat during a rough patch and for access to his personal library, care of his assistant, Samantha Barker. The late Clifford McCarty selflessly shared with me his holograph typed manuscript, "Film Music in America: A Bibliography." Film historian and editor Anthony Slide was the first to suggest the publication of this work after my previous Scarecrow Press book, *The Films of Mack Sennett*, was published in 1998. I also wish to thank my editor at Scarecrow, Stephen Ryan, for his patience and tenacity as I labored to deliver this book. Production editor Sally Craley ably guided the book through the production process and proofreader Nancy Styrett conformed and corrected the text.

To those who have shared their knowledge and appreciation of film and television music, I am grateful to Gillian Anderson, Rudy Behlmer, Jeff Bond, David Bondelevitch, Lance Bowling, Ross Care, Alfred Cochran, Ray Colcord, Maurizio Corbella, Annette Davison, Robin Esterhammer, Dan Foliart, Peter Franklin, Hubai Gergely, Daniel Goldmark, Claudia Gorbman, Arthur Hamilton, Sanya Henderson, Paul Henning, Roger Hickman, Howard Hilliard, Christopher Husted, Jeongwon Joe, Preston Neal Jones,

Kathryn Kalinak, the late Fred Karlin, Lukas Kendall, Robert Kosovsky, Randall D. Larson, Neil Lerner, Martin Marks, Gary Marmorstein, Kathleen Mayne, Michael McDonagh, Denise McGiboney (Music Librarian, Free Library of Philadelphia), John W. Morgan, Hans Offerdal, Michael Pisani, Jeannie Pool, Nick Redman, Robert Reneau, Bill Rosar, Michael Scarbrough, David Schecter, Linda Schubert, Rachel Segal, Jeff Smith, Steven Smith, Craig Spaulding, William Stromberg, Jack Sullivan, Robert Townson, Steve Vertlieb, James Westby, Dirk Wickenden, James Wierzbicki, and H. Stephen Wright. Thanks to those who support film music preservation through performances and recordings of their family legacies: Susan Sukman McCray, Dylan and Abigail North, Susanna Moross Tarjan, John Waxman, and especially Olivia Tiomkin Douglas.

My first piano teacher, Betty Schmuck, had a love of music that included film and television themes. From her, starting at age twelve, I learned to play Henry Mancini's "The Pink Panther," Miklós Rózsa's "Spellbound" concerto, Richard Rodgers's "Victory at Sea," and Richard Addinsell's Warsaw concerto, among other classics. I owe her a debt of gratitude for her musical influence. To my mother, Jean Brunk, for her love and support, and for the use of her Apple Macintosh back in 1984, on which I laid the groundwork for this book, thanks always.

Finally, this work would not have been possible without the support of two individuals. More than twenty years ago, Linda Mehr put her faith in an eager but inexperienced UCLA work/study student. Patrick Russ, a top music orchestrator and my good friend, opened the door to my participation as a union musician in numerous film and recording ventures over the past fifteen years, which has helped make it financially possible to devote the countless hours to putting together this volume.

Introduction

Film and Television Music: A Guide to Books, Articles, and Composer Interviews is an authoritative reference work that represents a comprehensive listing of books and articles on the subject of film and television music. It is the culmination of years of work spent finding, accessing, and compiling the thousands of entries found within these pages.

Film, film music, and television music are all essentially twentieth-century arts. *Film and Television Music* attempts to aid those studying or writing about film and television music by documenting writings on the subject, particularly in books, dissertations, and film and music magazines published from 1906 through 2005. It is aimed at scholars, teachers, students, composers, fans, and others interested in finding out more about the rich history of film and television music.

The year 1906 brought movies to the masses in the form of the nickelodeon. It was also the year that *Views and Film Index* became the first American trade paper devoted exclusively to motion pictures, running an editorial that declared, "Many exhibitors are prone to overlook the importance of music as an essential to the success of the show." From *Views and Film Index* to the *Cue Sheet*, this book documents one hundred years of writings devoted to the subject of film and television music and its practitioners. The past fifteen years have witnessed an explosion of books and articles on every aspect of film music. Composer interviews, film music guidebooks, critical studies, anthologies, mass-market books, and an assortment of magazines and fanzines flooded the market. In recent years, the dramatic shift away from print journals to online journals and the Internet as a content provider became commonplace by around 2006, prompting this book's cutoff date of 2005.

While this work reflects my interest in dramatic music composed for American films and those who create it, it also embraces a diverse range of material on television music, songwriters, musicals, source music, session musicians, and other topics. Included are analytical, critical, historical, and theoretical writings by composers, academics, historians, musicians, students, and fans. Disciplines range from critical studies to sociology and everything in between.

Criteria for Inclusion

Books and articles must be in English and have some substantive discussion of music for inclusion. Preference is given to composer interviews, biographies, and writings by composers. Excluded are newspaper articles, soundtrack reviews, book reviews, obituaries, concert programs, concert reviews, liner notes, electronic journals, oral histories, most general-interest articles or news items, and resources in languages other than English.

Exceptions include material that has been translated into English and any form of material (newspaper articles, liner notes, and so on) reprinted in a book or magazine.

As a result, the film industries of the United States, Canada, the United Kingdom, Australia, and India receive the most coverage. In the case of India, with a film industry that rivals that of the U.S., only selected material has been included, particularly articles from mainstream non-Indian journals such as *Popular Music*. Timely news items regarding the music business, scoring assignments, and so on are not specifically included. Although there is considerable information on session musicians, on-screen performers are generally not covered, with some exceptions for overlapping material from genres such as jazz, opera, and musicals.

Methodology and Sources

I first began collecting bibliographic entries in the early 1980s as an undergraduate music student at the University of Arizona, and continued during my graduate studies at UCLA in the mid-1980s. The project gradually evolved from a bibliography of bibliographies into an indispensable reference and research tool. Leads from soundtrack and fan magazines were pursued, columns devoted to film music were sought out (it seems the first or last occurrence of a column is rarely announced), and a single bibliographic reference often led to other articles within the cited periodical.

This work benefits from bibliographies compiled by Rick Altman, Gillian Anderson, Irene Kahn Atkins, Stephen M. Fry, Claudia Gorbman, Martin Marks, Clifford McCarty, Robert U. Nelson, Walter H. Rubsamen, Ronald H. Sadoff, Winston Sharples, Robynn J. Stilwell, Tony Thomas, Steven Wescott, H. Stephen Wright, and many others.

In addition to the books and articles in my personal collection, I searched the holdings of libraries across Southern California. First and foremost among these is the Academy of Motion Picture Arts and Sciences Margaret Herrick Library in Beverly Hills, California. The library—my place of employment for the past twenty-five years—contains one of the nation's great collections of film books and magazines written in English. Material was consulted at UCLA; the University of California, Santa Barbara; the University of Southern California (USC); the Film Music Society; the public libraries of Los Angeles, Santa Monica, Beverly Hills, and Culver City; and the Brand Library in Glendale, California. Bookstores up and down the West Coast, from Powell's Books in Portland to Wahrenbrock's Book House in San Diego—even Borders and Barnes & Noble—were helpful resources. I gathered numerous listings from the personal libraries of orchestrator Patrick Russ and composer Christopher Young. Online sources include the Search Inside! feature on Amazon.com, Google Book Search, WorldCat, and online book catalogs for the Margaret Herrick Library, the Library of Congress, California Digital Libraries, the British Library, and the British Film Institute. I used proprietary or subscription-based databases such as InfoTrac OneFile (Thomson Gale), JSTOR, Questia Online Library, and Proquest. Additional reference sources include *Books in Print, Film Literature Index, The New Film Index: A Bibliography of Magazine Articles in English, 1930–1970, The International Index of Music Periodicals* (IIMPFT online, published by Chadwyck-Healey), *International Index to Film Periodicals* (FIAF, accessed via Proquest and on CD-ROM), *Retrospective Index to Film Periodicals, 1930–1971*, and the *RILM Abstracts of Music Literature* (thanks to NISC and BiblioLine).

Note to the Reader

Having worked extensively in music prep for motion pictures and as an archivist in a library devoted to documenting and sharing the history of motion pictures, I hope that my own background and experience, as well as my familiarity with the subject and those who have written about it, has added value to this compilation. I was not able to locate and review each and every citation; however, I did examine the vast majority of books and periodicals listed in these pages. Those I was unable to locate may contain inaccuracies. My goal in putting together this work was to provide context, background, accuracy, and breadth of coverage, and to bring an awareness of this vast literature to a larger audience and foster interest in neglected topics and individuals.

Guide to Using This Book

The material is organized in eleven sections. Information is organized by the book or periodical that contains the material cited.

Books on Film and Television Music

Books are listed alphabetically by author. Criteria for inclusion include publications whose primary subject matter is film and/or television music, to which the entire or a substantial portion of the work must be devoted. Publication details include the title; publisher; year of publication; publication history, including editions or reprints; and number of pages. Forewords or introductions written by a film composer are noted. The annotation may include a synopsis of the content, the background of the author, and the source of material. Backmatter, including bibliographies, filmographies, discographies, and indexes, is noted.

Academic Dissertations and Theses

Dissertations are listed alphabetically by author. Preference for inclusion is given to those whose work appears elsewhere in this volume, particularly when the dissertation led to a published book or journal articles. Sources consulted include the California Digital Libraries and WorldCat Dissertations and Theses databases. In most cases, the publication details were then confirmed by the online library catalog for the university at which the dissertation was completed. Publication details include the title, form (dissertation or thesis), university granting the degree, year of publication, and number of pages (pages are traditionally leaves, or one-sided typescript). Since the page counts are from library catalog records, they follow the librarian standard of counting pages from one to the end, disregarding frontmatter pagination. Therefore the page counts may differ from those in RILM, which does include frontmatter pagination. Bibliographies, a requirement for such works, are not noted. The terms *dissertation* and *thesis* were extracted from library catalog records and may not be used consistently.

Composer Biographies

Books are listed alphabetically by the subject's name. Criteria for inclusion include autobiographies and biographies whose primary subject matter is film and/or television music. Books for concert composers were selected if they contain coverage of the subject's film music. Publication details include the title; publisher; year of publication; publication history, including editions or reprints; and number of pages. If the entire book is devoted primarily to film music, then the total page count is given. Otherwise, only that portion of the book devoted to a composer's film work is noted.

Songwriter and Lyricist Biographies

Books are listed alphabetically by the subject's name. Selections are biased toward those songwriters who worked under the studio system and/or those who wrote songs specifically for films. Publication details include the title; publisher; year of publication; publication history, including editions or reprints; and number of pages. Biographies of songwriters tangentially related to films can be found in the section "Books with Material on Film and Television Music."

Books with Material on Film and Television Music

Books are listed alphabetically by author. Publication details include the title, publisher, and year of publication. In most cases, specific page numbers are cited for topical material. The book's total page count follows the date of publication if specific pages are not given. Most entries cite a relevant chapter or section of the book.

Music for the Accompaniment of Silent Films

This chronological list of music compilations, albums, or folios contains selected works issued from 1909 to 1928 for the accompaniment of silent films. In general, the selections represent compilations in common use, those with music by composers of interest, or those put together by persons of interest. Performance or instructional manuals from the era that contain textual material are listed in the books section, as are catalogs that list music for performance, such as Julius S. Seredy's *Motion Picture Music Guide to the Carl Fischer Modern Orchestra Catalogue.*

Film Music Periodicals

Publications devoted exclusively to the topic are listed alphabetically by periodical title. For each publication a brief history is given. Issues are then listed chronologically, with articles following in the order that they appear. The bulk of the entries are for articles, essays, interviews, and reports. In general, book reviews, news items, obituaries, and soundtrack reviews are omitted. Interviews that are in question-and-answer format are referred to as "Interview," whereas an "Interview-based article" contains running text. Publications are generally found under their current or last published title, with the exception of *Film and Television Music*, found under its more familiar title, *Film Music Notes*. The following publications are included in this chapter.

CinemaScore (1979–1987)
The Cue Sheet (1984–2005)
Film Music (1998–2005)
Film Music Notebook (1974–1978)
Film Music Notes (1941–1951), followed by *Film Music* (1951–1956) and *Film and TV Music* (1956–1958)
Film Score Monthly (1990–2005)
Fistful of Soundtracks: The Movie Music Magazine (1980–1981)
From Silents to Satellite (1990–1993)

Hollywood Scores (1992)
The Journal of Film Music (2002–2005)
Main Title (1974–1977)
Music from the Movies (1992–2005)
New Zealand Film Music Bulletin (1973–1999)
Reel Music (2001–2002)
The Score (ASMA, 1944–1953)
The Score (SCL, 1986–2005)
Sound Track: Music n' Movies, Music in Movies (2005)
Soundtrack! The Collector's Quarterly (1975–2002), includes *SCN: Soundtrack Collector's Newsletter*
The Swiss Film Music Society Newsletter (1993–)

Composer Society Journals and Newsletters

Publications devoted largely to the music of a single composer are listed alphabetically by periodical title. For each publication a brief history is given. Issues are then listed chronologically, with articles following in the order that they appear. As it was beyond the scope of this book to list each issue of every journal, selected issues and articles are given. In most cases, the issues selected were based on availability. The following publications are included in this chapter.

ALBEDO: Vangelis International Appreciation Society
Bax Society Bulletin [Arnold Bax]
The Bernard Herrmann Society Journal
The Bruce Broughton Society Journal
Cantina Band [John Williams]
The Creel [Alan Rawsthorne]
Dreams to Dreams [James Horner and others]
Erich Wolfgang Korngold Society Newsletter
International Filmusic Journal [John Barry]
Journal Into Melody [Robert Farnon and others]
Legend [Jerry Goldsmith]
Max Steiner Music Society publications: *The Max Steiner Annual* (1967–1976), *The Max Steiner Journal* (1977–1980), and *The Max Steiner Music Society News Letter* (1965–1976)
The Miklos Rozsa Appreciation Music Society Journal
The Miklos Rozsa Cult Quarterly Newsletter
Movie Music [Jerry Goldsmith]
Musica sul Velluto [Ennio Morricone]
Noise: Notes from Mark Isham
Pro Musica Sana [Miklós Rózsa and others]

Film and Media Periodicals

Periodicals are organized alphabetically by title, with the selected articles listed chronologically. Country of origin is in parentheses following the periodical title. A brief annotation regarding the publication contains relevant information, usually the intended audience and place of publication. In many cases, the information is from the publication.

International Film, Radio, and Television Journals (Greenwood Press, 1985), edited by Anthony Slide, was consulted. Where applicable, columns and special issues are listed after articles.

A&E Monthly (US)
Action (US)
After Dark (US)
Afterimage (UK)
afterimage (US)
American Cinematographer (US)
American Cinemeditor (US)
American Classic Screen (US)
American Film (US)
American Film Institute Report (US)
American Premiere (US)
Angles (US)
Animation Journal (US)
Animation Magazine (US)
Animation World Magazine (US)
Animatrix (US)
Author and Composer (US)
Back Stage (US)
The Big Trail (US)
Blackhawk Film Digest (US)
Boxoffice (US)
The British Film Academy Journal (UK)
British Film Review (UK)
British Journal of Photography (UK)
Broadcast (UK)
Bulletin of the Academy of Motion Picture Arts and Sciences (US)
Business Screen (US)
Cahiers du Cinéma in English (US)
Camera Obscura (US)
Canadian Film Weekly (Canada)
Canadian Film Weekly Yearbook (Canada)
Cantrills Filmnotes (Australia)
CBC Times (Canada)
Channels of Communications (US)
CineAction (Canada)
Cineaste (US)
CineFan (US)
Cinefantastique (US)
Cinegram Magazine (US)
Cinema (US, 1947)
Cinema (US, 1962–1976)

Cinema and Theatre (UK)
Cinema Arts (US)
Cinema Canada (Canada)
Cinema Chronicle (USSR)
Cinema in India (India)
Cinema Journal (US)
Cinema Papers (Australia)
Cinema Quarterly (UK)
Cinema Studies (UK)
The Cinema Studio (UK)
Cinema TV Today (UK)
Cinema Vision India (India)
Cinema Year Book of Japan (Japan)
Cinemacabre (US)
Cinémas: Revue d'Etudes Cinematographiques (Canada)
Cinemaya: The Asian Film Quarterly (India)
Cinemusic and Its Meaning (US)
Classic Images (US)
Close Up (UK)
Contemporary Cinema (UK)
Contemporary Theatre, Film, and Television (US)
Cue (US)
Decision (US)
DGA News (US)
Dialogue on Film (US)
Disney Magazine (US)
The Disney News (US)
The Distributor (US)
Documentary News Letter (UK)
Dramatic Mirror (US)
Edison Kinetogram (US)
Emmy (US)
Entertainment Weekly (US)
European Journal of Communication (US)
Everyones (Australia)
Exhibitors Daily Review (US)
Exhibitors Herald (US)
Exhibitors Herald and Moving Picture World (US)
Exhibitors Trade Review (US)
Exposure Sheet (US)

Fangoria (US)
Film (UK)
Film and Philosophy (US)
Film Careers (US)
Film Comment (US)
Film Criticism (US)
Film Culture (US)
The Film Daily (US)
The Film Daily Yearbook of Motion Pictures (US)
Film Directions (UK)
Film Dope (UK)
Film Heritage (US)
Film History (US)
The Film Index (US)
Film Industry (UK)
Film International (Iran)
Film International (Sweden)
Film Library Quarterly (US)
Film Monthly Review (UK)
Film News (US)
Film Quarterly (US)
Film Reader (US)
Film Review (UK)
Film Spectator (US)
Film Studies (UK)
Film West (Ireland)
Filmfax (US)
Filmmaker (US)
Filmmakers Newsletter (US)
Filmplay Journal (US)
Films: A Quarterly of Discussion and Analysis (US)
Films and Filming (UK)
Films Illustrated (UK)
Films in Review (US)
Films of the Golden Age (US)
Films on Screen and Video (UK)
Flickers Magazine (UK)
Focus on Film (UK)
Focus on Fox (US)
Funnyworld (US)
G-Fan (Canada)
Gore Creatures (US)
Griffithiana (Italy/US)
Harlequinade (US)
Historical Journal of Film, Radio, and Television (UK)
Hitchcock Annual (US)

Hollywood (US)
Hollywood Creative Directory (US)
Hollywood Daily Screen World (US)
Hollywood Filmograph (US)
Hollywood Movie Music Directory (US)
Hollywood Music Industry Directory (US)
Hollywood Quarterly see *Film Quarterly*
The Hollywood Reporter (US)
Hollywood Review (US)
Hollywood Spectator (US)
Hollywood Studio Magazine (US)
Hollywood Who's Who (US)
Image (US)
Indian Cinema (India)
Inside Facts of Stage and Screen (US)
International Documentary (US)
International Film Annual (US)
International Film Festival Magazine
International Motion Picture Almanac (US)
International Review of Educational Cinematography (Italy)
International Television and Video Almanac (US)
Iris (US and France)
Jones' (US)
Journal of Communication (US)
Journal of Film and Video (US)
Journal of Film Preservation (Brussels)
Journal of Popular Film and Television (US)
Journal of the University Film Association, Journal of the University Film and Video Association, Journal of the University Film Producers Association see *Journal of Film and Video*
Jump Cut (US)
Kinematograph Weekly (UK)
Kinematograph Year Book, Film Diary and Directory (UK)
LA 411 (US)
The Last Word (US)
Leonard Maltin's Movie Crazy (US)
Lion's Roar (US)
Literature/Film Quarterly (US)
Lumiere (Australia)

The Media Project, Inc. (US)
Metro (Australia)
Metro-Goldwyn-Mayer Studio Club News (US)
The M-G-M Record (US)
Midnight Marquee (US)
Millimeter (US)
Monthly Film Bulletin (UK)
Motion (Canada)
Motion Picture Almanac see *International Motion Picture Almanac*
Motion Picture Classic (US)
Motion Picture Herald (US)
Motion Picture Magazine (US)
Motion Picture Mail (US)
Motion Picture Music and Musicians (US)
Motion Picture News (US)
Motion Picture News Studio Directory (US)
Motion Picture Review Digest (US)
Motion Picture Story Magazine (US)
Motion Picture Studio Insider (US)
Motography (US)
Movie (UK)
Movie Collector Magazine (UK)
Movie Maker (UK)
Movie Pictorial (US)
Movieline (US)
MovieMaker (US)
Movies Now (US)
Movietone News (US)
Moving Image (US)
Moving Picture News (US)
Moving Picture World (US)
National Board of Review Magazine (US)
The New Hungarian Quarterly (Hungary)
The New Movies (US)
The Nickelodeon (US)
Now (US)
Onfilm (New Zealand)
On Location (US)
On Writing (US)
Outre (US)
Paramount Artcraft Progress-Advance (US)
Paramount Progress (US)

Paramount Studio News (US)
Penguin Film Review (UK)
The Perfect Vision (US)
Photoplay (UK)
Photoplay (US)
Photoplay Studies (US)
Picture Show (UK)
The Picturegoer (UK)
Polish Film (Poland)
Post Script (US)
POV: Point of View Magazine (US)
Pratfall (US)
Premiere (US)
Publix Opinion (US)
Quarterly of Film, Radio and Television see *Film Quarterly*
Quarterly Review of Film and Video (UK)
Quarterly Review of Film Studies (US)
Radio Personalities (US)
Reel Life (US)
Reel West (Canada)
RKO Studio Club News (US)
Rob Wagner's Script (US)
Roxy Theatre Weekly Review (US)
Scarlet Street (US)
Screen (UK)
The Screen (US)
Screen Education (UK)
Screen Facts (US)
Screen International (US)
The Screen Writer (US)
Screenland (US)
Shadowland (US)
Showtime in Walthamstow (UK)
Sight and Sound (UK)
The Silent Picture (UK/US)
Silver Screen (US)
The Silver Sheet (US)
SMPTE Journal (US)
Soviet Film (Russia)
Spaghetti Cinema (US)
Star Trek: The Next Generation (US)
Star Trek Voyager (US)
Star Wars Insider (US)
Starlog (US)
Starlog Science-Fiction Explorer (US)
Step (US)
Stills (UK)

Take One (Canada)
Talking Screen (US)
TCI (US)
Technical Bulletin (US)
Television and New Media (US)
Television Quarterly (US)
Theatre Arts (US)
Today's Film Maker (US)
The Triangle (US)
T.V. Guide (US)
24 Images (Canada)
Twilight Zone Magazine (US)
Universal City Studios Club News (US)
The Universal Weekly (US)
University Film Study Center Newsletter (US)

Variety (US), includes *Variety Weekly* and *VLIFE* (*Variety* supplement)
Variety International Film Guide (UK)
The Velvet Light Trap (US)
Venice (US)
Vertigo (UK)
Video Magazine (US)
Videomaker (US)
Views and Film Index (US)
Vitagraph Bulletin (US) and *Vitagraph Life Portrayals* (US)
Vitaphone News (US)
Warner Club News (US)
What's Happening in Hollywood (US)
Wide Angle (US)
World Film News (UK)

Music Periodicals

Periodicals are organized alphabetically by title, with the selected articles listed chronologically. Country of origin is in parentheses following the periodical title. A brief annotation regarding the publication contains relevant information, usually the intended audience and place of publication. Where applicable, columns and special issues are listed after articles.

The Absolute Sound (US)
Acoustic Guitar (US)
Acta Musicologica (Switzerland)
African Music (South Africa)
American Composer's Alliance Bulletin (US)
American Harp Journal (US)
American Music (US)
American Music Research Center Journal (US)
American Music Teacher (US)
The American Organist (US)
American Record Guide (US)
ASCAP in Action (US)
ASCAP Today (US)
Asian Music: Journal of the Society for Asian Music (US)
Australasian Music Research (Australia)
Australian Musical News (Australia)
Band Wagon (UK)
BBC Music Magazine (UK)
Beethoven Forum (US)
Berklee Today (US)

Billboard (US)
Black Music Research Journal (US)
Black Perspective in Music (US)
Bluegrass Unlimited (US)
BMI Bulletin (US)
BMI: The Many Worlds of Music (US)
Brio (UK)
British Journal of Ethnomusicology (UK)
British Music: Journal of the British Music Society (UK)
British Music Society News (UK)
British Music Yearbook (UK)
British Musician (UK)
Cadenza (US)
Cambridge Opera Journal (UK)
The Canadian Composer (Canada)
Canadian Folk Music Bulletin (Canada)
Canadian Musician (Canada)
Canadian Review of Music and Art (Canada)
Canadian University Music Review (Canada)

The Canon: A Musical Journal (Australia)
Capitol News (US)
Capitol Record see *Capitol News*
Cassettes and Cartridges (UK)
Centerstage (US)
Chinese Music (US)
Church Music (UK)
Cine-Technician (UK)
Cinema Organ Society Newsletter (UK)
Civiltà Musicale (Italy)
Classic CD (UK/US)
Classical Music (UK?)
Classics (UK)
Clavier (US)
CLGA's Report (US)
Co-Art Turntable (US)
College Music Symposium (US)
Composer (UK)
The Consort: The Journal of the Dolmetsch Foundation (UK)
Contemporary Keyboard (US)
Contemporary Music Forum (US)
Contemporary Music Review (UK)
Context: A Journal of Music Research (Australia)
Crawdaddy (US)
Creem (US)
Crescendo International (UK)
Crescendo & Jazz Music (UK)
Cum Notis Variorum (US)
Current Musicology (US)
Czech Music (Czech Republic)
The Diapason (US)
Discourses in Music (Canada)
Down Beat (US)
Ear (US)
Electronic Age (US)
Electronic Musician (US)
The Elgar Society Journal (UK)
Empire (UK)
Ethnomusicology (US)
The Etude (US)
European Meetings in Ethnomusicology (Romania)
Ex Tempore (US)
Fanfare (US)
Film and Television Music Guide (US)
Film and TV Music Yearbook (UK)

Finnish Music Quarterly (Finland)
Folk Roots (US)
The Gramophone (UK)
Guitar Player (US)
High Fidelity (US)
Hinrichsen's Musical Year Book (UK)
The Horn Call (US)
The Hymn Society of Great Britain and Ireland Bulletin (UK)
Indian Musicological Society (India)
Indiana Theory Review (US)
Institute for Studies in American Music Newsletter (US)
The Instrumentalist (US)
Interdisciplinary Humanities (US)
Interdisciplinary Studies in Musicology (Poland)
International Journal of Music Education (US)
International Journal of Musicology (Switzerland)
International Music Guide (UK/US)
International Musician (US)
International Review of the Aesthetics and Sociology of Music (Republic of Croatia)
International Who Is Who in Music (US)
International Who's Who in Classical Music (US)
International Who's Who in Popular Music (US)
Irish Musical Studies (Ireland)
Jacobs' Orchestra Monthly (US)
Jazz Educators Journal (US)
Jazz Journal International (UK)
Jazz Magazine (US)
Jazz Research Proceedings Yearbook (US)
The Jazz Review (US)
Jazz Times (US)
Jazziz (US)
JEMF Quarterly (US)
Journal of the American Musicological Society (US)
Journal of the Association for Recorded Sound Collections (US)
Journal of the Cinema Organ Society (UK)

The Journal of Country Music (US)
Journal of Music Therapy (US)
Journal of Musicological Research (UK)
The Journal of Musicology (US)
Journal of Popular Music Studies (US)
Journal of the Royal Musical Association (UK)
Journal of the United Kingdom branch of the International Association of Music Libraries, Archives and Documentation Centres (UK)
Juilliard Review (US)
Kastlemusick Monthly Bulletin (US)
Keyboard (US)
Keyboard Classics (US)
Kurt Weill Newsletter (US)
Latin American Music Review/Revista de Musica Latinoamericana (US)
Leonardo Music Journal (US)
Life with Music (US)
Listen to Norway (Norway)
Living Music (US)
The Los Angeles Record (US)
Mechanical Music (US)
Melody (US)
Melody Maker (UK)
The Metronome (US)
Mix Magazine (US)
Modern Music (US)
Monthly Musical Record (UK)
Motion Picture and Television Music Credits Annual (US)
MP/TV Music Credits Bulletin (US)
Music Analysis (UK)
Music and Letters (UK)
Music and Musicians (UK)
Music and Musicians International (UK)
Music and the Arts (US)
Music Clubs Magazine (US)
Music Connection (US)
Music Educators Journal (US)
Music in Art (US)
Music in Education (UK)
Music Journal (US)
Music Journal Annual (US)
Music News (US)
Music Parade (UK)

Music Perception (US)
Music Reference Services Quarterly (US)
Music Research Forum (US)
The Music Review (UK)
The Music Scene (Canada)
Music Supervisors' Journal (US)
Music Survey (UK)
Music Teacher (UK)
Music Theory Spectrum: The Journal of the Society for Music Theory (US)
Music Tracks Newsletter (US)
Music Trade News (US)
The Music Trade Review (US)
Music U.S.A. (US)
The Music World (US)
Musica e Storia (Italy)
Musical Advance (US)
Musical America (US)
Musical Courier (US)
The Musical Digest (US)
Musical Express (UK)
Musical Leader (US)
Musical News (UK)
Musical News and Herald (UK)
The Musical Observer (US)
Musical Opinion (UK)
The Musical Quarterly (US)
Musical Standard (UK)
The Musical Times (UK)
The Musical Woman: An Interdisciplinary Perspective (US)
The Musician (US)
Musicologica (Czechoslovakia)
Musicology (Australia)
MusicWorld (US)
NARAS Journal (US)
The New Music Review and Church Music Review (US)
New Sound (Yugoslavia)
New Zealand Listener (New Zealand)
Notes: Quarterly Journal of the Music Library Association (US)
On Tape (US)
Opera (US)
Opera, Concert, and Symphony (US)
Opera News (US)
The Opera Quarterly (UK)
Optic Music (US)

The Organ (UK)
Organised Sound (UK)
Ovation (US)
Overture (US)
Pacific Coast Musician (US)
Penguin Music Magazine (UK)
Perfect Beat (Australia)
Performing Arts (US)
Performing Arts Annual (US)
Performing Arts at the Library of Congress (US)
Performing Arts: Broadcasting (US)
Performing Arts: Motion Pictures (US)
Performing Right (UK)
Perspectives of New Music (US)
Piano & Keyboard (US)
Piping Times (UK)
Playback (US)
Playon (US)
Popular Music (UK)
Popular Music (US)
Popular Music & Society (US)
Proceedings of the Royal Musical Association see *Journal of the Royal Musical Association*
Psychology of Music (US)
Psychomusicology (US)
Pulse! (US)
The Ragtimer (Canada)
Recording Engineer/Producer (US)
Records and Recording (UK)
Rock and Roll in the Movies (US)
Rolling Stone (US)
Royal College of Music Magazine (UK)
RTS Annual (US)
RTS Music Gazette (US)
Sangeet Natak: Journal of Indian Music, Dance, Theatre (India)
The School Music News (US)
Schwann Opus (US)
The Score and I.M.A. Magazine (UK)
Screen Songs (US)
Selected Reports in Ethnomusicology (US)
Show Music (US)

Sheet Music Magazine (US)
The Sinfonian (US)
Sing Out (US)
Song Hits Magazine (US)
Songwriter Magazine (US)
Songwriters Guild of America News (US)
Songwriter's Market (US)
Songwriters Musepaper (US)
Sonneck Society Newsletter (US)
Sound Illustrated (UK)
Sound Waves (US)
Sounds Australian (Australia)
The Soundtrack Collector
The Southern California Music Record (US)
Sruti: India's Premier Music and Dance Magazine (India)
Stereo Review (US)
The Strad (UK)
Swedish Journal of Musicology [Svensk tidskrift för musikforskning] (Sweden)
Symphony (US)
Symphony News (US)
Tempo (UK)
Tempo (US)
Theatre Organ (US)
Theatre Organ Bombarde see *Theatre Organ*
Theatre Organ Review (UK)
Three Oranges (UK)
The Tibia see *Theatre Organ*
Twentieth-Century Music (UK)
21st Century Music (US)
Vierundzwanzigsteljahrsschrift der Internationalen Maultrommelvirtuosengenossenschaft (VIM) (US)
The Violinist (US)
Wagner (UK)
Women & Music (US)
Words & Music (Canada)
The World of Music (Germany)
Yearbook of the International Folk Music Council (US)

General Interest and Other Periodicals

Publications are listed alphabetically by title. Country of origin is in parentheses following the periodical title. In general, this survey of articles is meant to convey the breadth of publications that have covered film music.

The Advocate (US)
Africa Today (US)
American (US)
American Hebrew (US)
American Heritage (US)
American Journal of Psychoanalysis (US)
American Scholar (US)
Annali di Sociologia (Italy)
Annals of the American Academy of Political and Social Sciences (US)
ARSC Journal (US)
Arts (US)
Arts and Architecture (US)
Arts and Decoration (US)
Arts Magazine (US)
Atlantic (US)
Atlantic Monthly (US)
Asian Art and Culture (US)
Audience Magazine (US)
Audio Magazine (US)
Ballet Review (US)
BAM (US)
Black Creation (US)
Booklist (US)
Bookman (UK)
Boston Magazine (US)
California Arts and Architecture (US)
California Life (US)
Callaloo (US)
Canadian Psychology (Canada)
Canzona (New Zealand)
Carte Blanche (US)
Catholic Digest (US)
The Chesterian (UK)
Christian Science Monitor Magazine (US)
The Chronicle of Higher Education (US)
Collier's (US)
Commentary (US)
Commonweal (US)
Contemporary Review (US)

Coronet (US)
Cosmopolitan (US)
Creative Art (US)
Critical Inquiry (US)
Current Biography (US)
Current Opinion (US)
Details (US)
Direction (US)
Discovery (US)
Dynamics (US)
The Economist (US)
Eighteenth-Century Life (US)
Empirical Studies of the Arts (US)
Entertainment, Publishing and the Arts Handbook (US)
The Epigram (US)
Esquire (US)
The European Legacy (US)
Everyweek Magazine (US)
The Force of Vision: Inter-Asian Comparative Literature (Japan)
Friends of the Harold B. Lee Library Newsletter (US)
Frontier (US)
Good Housekeeping (US)
GQ (US)
Grand Street (US)
Harper's Bazaar (US)
Harper's Magazine (US)
Harvard Library Bulletin (US)
Health (US)
Holiday (US)
Human Behavior (US)
The Illustrated London News (UK)
International Journal of Instructional Media (US)
Interview (US)
ITA Journal (US)
The Journal of Aesthetics and Art Criticism (US)
Journal of American Culture (US)
Journal of Australian Studies (Australia)

Journal of European Studies (UK)
Journal of General Psychology (US)
Journal of Popular Culture (US)
Journal of the Copyright Society of the U.S.A. (US)
The Journal of Value Inquiry (US)
Keynote (UK)
L.A. Weekly (US)
Labor History (US)
Ladies Home Journal (US)
Liberty (US)
Library of Congress Information Bulletin (US)
Library of Congress Newsletter (US)
The Listener (UK)
Literary Digest (US)
The Lone Hand (Australia)
Look (US)
Los Angeles Magazine (US)
Maclean's (Canada)
Macworld (US)
Magazine of Art (US)
Marketing Theory (US)
Meanjin (Australia)
Memory and Cognition (US)
The Mentor (US)
Michigan Academician (US)
Michigan Quarterly Review (US)
Military Chaplains' Review (US)
The Mississippi Quarterly (US)
Mosaic (Canada)
Nation (US)
National Identities (UK)
The New Criterion (US)
The New Republic (US)
New Statesman and Nation (UK)
New Theatre (US)
New West Magazine (US)
New York (US)
New York Times Magazine (US)
New Yorker (US)
News from The Fleischer Collection (US)
Newsday (US)
Newsweek (US)
North American Review (US)
The Observer Magazine (US)
The Open Space Magazine (US)
Opportunity (US)

Orange County Illustrated (US)
Our Time (UK)
The Outlook (US)
The Pacific Spectator (US)
PC/Computing (US)
Peanuts Collectors Club Newsletter (US)
People (US)
People Weekly (US)
Philosophy and Literature (US)
Playboy (US)
Popular Culture in Libraries (US)
Pynchon Notes (US)
Q (US)
Quadrant Magazine (Australia)
Quarterly Journal of the Library of Congress (US)
Radio Times (UK)
RCA News (US)
Readers Digest (US)
Recorded Sound (UK)
The Reporter (US)
Research in African Literatures (US)
Ritz (UK)
The Sackbut (UK)
Salmagundi (US)
Saturday Review (UK/US)
School and Society (US)
Science Digest (US)
Scientific American (US)
Scone (US)
Scop (US)
Seven Arts (US)
Shakespeare Quarterly (US)
SIGUCCS Newsletter (US)
South Atlantic Quarterly (US)
The Southern Quarterly (US)
Southwest Review (US)
The Spectator (UK)
Stage: The Magazine of After-Dark Entertainment (US)
Stanford Humanities Review (US)
Stanford Magazine (US)
Studies in the Literary Imagination (US)
Style (US)
Talkabout (UK)
TASCAM User Guide (US)
Teaching Music (US)

Technology and Culture (US)
The Theatre (US)
The Thousand Eyes Magazine (US)
Time (US)
Time Out (UK)
Time Out (US)
Today (US)
Town and Country (US)
Twentieth Century (UK)

UCLA Librarian (US)
University of Hartford Studies in Literature (US)
Urban Life (US)
Vanity Fair (US)
Woman's Home Companion (US)
World Psychology
Yale French Studies (US)

Chapter 1

Books on Film and Television Music

Adorno, Theodor, and Hanns Eisler.
  Composing for the Films. London and Atlantic Highlands, N.J.: Athlone Press, 1994.
  171 pp. ill.
Topics include prejudices and bad habits, function and dramaturgy, new musical resources (techniques used in the works of Schoenberg, Bartók, and Stravinksy), sociological aspects, aesthetics, the composer and the moviemaking process, and suggestions and
conclusions. Appendixes include a report on Eisler's Film Music Project at the New
School for Social Research and a composition by Eisler. Originally published in 1947
under Eisler's name only. This edition includes an introduction by Graham McCann and
an index. See Eisler, *Composing for the Films*, for the book's publication history.

Ahern, Eugene A.
  What and How to Play for Pictures. Twin Falls, Idaho: News Print, 1913. 61 pp.
Believed to be the first published treatise on the subject, written by a Midwestern musician. The manual contains general music recommendations for accompanying films,
based on the author's experiences. One of only two music books cited in the first published motion picture bibliography in *Motography* in 1916; the other is Lyle C. True's
How and What to Play for Moving Pictures.

Alberti, Bob.
  Up the Ladder and Over the Top: Memoirs of a Hollywood Studio Musician. Hilton
  Head Island, S.C.: privately printed, 2003. 178 pp.
Autobiography of a television rehearsal and studio pianist who specialized in music vari-
ety shows in the 1960s and 1970s, including work at NBC and for Steve Allen and Bob
Hope, see esp. pp. 87–154.

Altman, Rick.
  The American Film Musical. Bloomington and Indianapolis: Indiana Univ. Press,
  1987. 386 pp.
A film studies professor analyzes the structure and style of the American film musical
genre, subdivided into the fairy tale, show, and folk musical.

Altman, Rick, ed.
  Genre, The Musical: A Reader. BFI Readers in Film Studies. London: Routledge,
  1981. 228 pp.

Anthology of critical articles on the musical, written since 1975, from publications such as the *Quarterly Review of Film Studies*. Also includes original essays by Jim Collins, Martin Sutton, and Alan Williams. Written from an academic perspective, as indicated by the subject index entries: Freudian psychology, ideology, the spectator, and a woman's place in the musical. Introduction and postscript by Altman; "Vincente Minnelli," by Thomas Elsaesser, 8–27; "George Sidney: Artificial Brilliance/The Brilliance of Artifice," by Alain Masson, 28–40; "Some Warner Musicals and the Spirit of the New Deal," by Mark Roth, 41–56; "Art and Ideology: Notes on *Silk Stockings*," by Robin Wood, 57–69; "The Image of Woman as Image: The Optical Politics of *Dames*," by Lucy Fischer, 70–84; "Show-Making," by Dennis Giles, 85–101 (originally appeared in *Movie*, Spring 1977); "Segmenting/Analysing," by Raymond Bellour, 102–33; "Toward Defining a Matrix of the Musical Comedy: The Place of the Spectator Within the Textual Mechanisms," by Jim Collins, 134–46; "The Musical Film and Recorded Popular Music," by Alan Williams, 147–58; "The Self-Reflective Musical and the Myth of Entertainment," by Jane Feuer, 159–74; "Entertainment and Utopia," by Richard Dryer, 175–89; "Patterns of Meaning in the Musical," by Martin Sutton, 190–96; "The American Film Musical: Paradigmatic Structure and Mediatory Function," 197–207; "The Hollywood Musical: An Annotated Bibliography," by Jane Feuer, including "serious" (not journalistic) entries, 208–15.

American Film Institute.
>   *Film Music*. Factfile number 8. Washington, D.C.: American Film Institute/National Education Services, 1977. 24 pp. Frederick, Md.: University Publications of America, 1984. 23 pp.

One of the earliest resources listing contacts for film music clubs, music guilds and associations, schools offering courses in film music, soundtracks, production music, films on film music, and oral history programs. Bibliography lists books and periodicals. Edited by Diana Elsas, compiled with special assistance from Win Sharples Jr., an AFI administrator and film professor with a background in sound and film editing, and son of composer Winston Sharples.

Anderson, Gillian B., comp.
>   *Music for Silent Films 1894–1929: A Guide*. Washington, D.C.: Library of Congress, 1988. 182 pp. ill.

The introduction by Anderson, a music specialist, offers insight into the musical presentation of silent films, including information on Hugo Riesenfeld, cue sheets, compiled and original scores, and music played during the shooting of silent films. Music scores and/or cue sheets in collections at the Library of Congress and the Museum of Modern Art are listed by film title in 1,047 annotated alphabetical entries. Appendixes contain a list of microfilmed scores in the Library of Congress music collection and the Museum of Modern Art music collection (on permanent loan to the Library of Congress Music Division); film scores at the University of Minnesota in the Arthur Kleiner Collection; cue sheets in the George Eastman House in Rochester, New York; film scores at the New York Public Library Music Division; and film scores at the Federation Internationale des Archives du Film in Brussels, Belgium. Bibliography and index.

Anderson, Gillian B., comp., and H. Stephen Wright, ed.
>   *Film Music Bibliography I*. Foreword by David Raksin. Hollywood: Society for the Preservation of Film Music, 1995. 171 pp.

A retrospective supplement to Wescott's *A Comprehensive Bibliography of Music for Film and Television* (1985), compiled by a music specialist and edited by a music librarian and associate professor. New citations, additions to Wescott's citations, and corrections to Wescott's citations supplied by Clifford McCarty. Many of the new entries are from the first 14 volumes of *The American Organist* (circa 1918–1930) and the first 10 volumes of *Film Music Notes* (1941–1951). Entries are relevant to the silent and early sound era, including organ accompaniment of silent films, and opera performed on film and television. A shorter, preliminary version appeared in *Music Reference Services Quarterly* in 1993. Name/subject and film title indexes.

Appelbaum, Stanley.
    The Hollywood Musical: A Picture Quiz Book. New York: Dover; London: Constable and Company, 1974. Approx. 150 pp.
More than 200 photographs from Culver Pictures musicals from 1927 to 1960, with questions keyed to stills and arranged by composers, performers, and so on. Film and performer indexes.

Atkins, Irene Kahn.
    Source Music in Motion Pictures. Rutherford, N.J.: Fairleigh Dickinson Univ. Press; London and Toronto: Associated Univ. Presses, 1983. 190 pp. ill.
Covers the visual, narrative, and musical elements of source music (music from a seen or implied onscreen source, such as a phonograph or radio). Historical perspectives and three types of source music (songs in films of the American past, opera and classical music composed for specific films, and ethnic source music) are examined. Discusses music by composers John Green and Nelson Riddle in relation to songs; George Gershwin, Bernard Herrmann, Erich Wolfgang Korngold, and Oscar Levant in relation to concert music composed for films; and Bronislaw Kaper in relation to ethnic music in films. Extensive annotated bibliography of music and sound in motion pictures (pp. 128–85) and index. Partially based on Kahn's thesis, "Source Music in the Dramatic Motion Picture." Daughter of songwriter Gus Kahn, the author was a music and sound effects editor. She also conducted a number of oral histories, including one with Hugo Friedhofer for the American Film Institute, part of which was published in Linda Danly's biography of the composer.

Aumack, Sheryl.
    Song & Dance: An Encyclopedia of Musicals. Newport Beach, Calif.: Sea-Maid Press, 1990. 462 pp.
Alphabetical listing of musicals ca. 1933 to 1987, by film title with cast and credits, songs, brief synopses, and soundtrack recordings. Indexes include shows and performers, choreographers, and songs and songwriters.

Aylesworth, Thomas G.
    History of Movie Musicals. London: Hamlyn; Greenwich, Conn.: Bison Books, 1984. 256 pp. ill.
    Broadway to Hollywood: Musicals from Stage to Screen. Twickenham, U.K.: Hamlyn; New York: Gallery Books, 1985. 256 pp. ill.
A general history first published under the former title and republished a year later under the latter title. Decade-by-decade historical summaries from the 1920s to 1980s, illustrated

with some 400 photographs. Composers include George Gershwin, Richard Rodgers, and Sigmund Romberg. Index.

Aziz, Ashraf.
> *Light of the Universe: Essays on Hindustani Film Music.* New Delhi: Three Essays Collective, 2003. 127 pp.

A monograph with five essays: "Noor Jahan: Portrait of a Female Indo-Pakistani Artist," "Lyrical Griefwork: The Genius of Sajjad Hussain," "Shailendra: The Lyrical Romance of Suicide," "Baiju Bawra: Musical Reaction or Revolution?" and "The Female Voice in Hindustani Film Songs."

Babington, Bruce, and Peter William Evans.
> *Blue Skies and Silver Linings: Aspects of the Hollywood Musical.* Manchester, U.K.; Dover, N.H.: Manchester Univ. Press, 1985. 258 pp. ill.

Film theory readings of ten selected musicals from 1933 to 1979.

Barnes, Jennifer.
> *Television Opera: The Fall of Opera Commissioned for Television.* Woodbridge, Suffolk; Rochester, N.Y.: Boydell Press, 2003. 124 pp.

Three case studies of works by Gerald Berry, Benjamin Britten, and Gian Carlo Menotti. Genesis, production, and filming techniques are discussed within their historical contexts. Examines formats, including live broadcasts, videotape, and filmed operas, along with techniques indigenous to television. Includes a list of operas commissioned for television (more than 50 original operas were commissioned from 1951 to 2002 in the United States and the United Kingdom), collections that house recordings or reference materials, and a bibliography.

Barrios, Richard.
> *A Song in the Dark: The Birth of the Musical Film.* New York and Oxford: Oxford Univ. Press, 1995. 493 pp. ill.

A film historian, musician, and writer chronicles the development of sound technology, including films, songwriters, and performers from 1926 to 1934. Discography and index.

Bazelon, Irwin.
> *Knowing the Score: Notes on Film Music.* New York: Van Nostrand Reinhold, 1975. 352 pp. ill. New York: Arco, 1981.

A treatise on film scoring written from the perspective of a composer of concert music and documentary films. The book grew out of "Music for Motion Pictures," a course Bazelon taught at the School of Visual Arts in New York. Topics include a short history of film music, the contemporary concert composer in films, and the technique and aesthetics of film scoring. The last half of the book includes interviews (and musical examples in reduced or full score) with John Barry, Richard Rodney Bennett, Elmer Bernstein, Paul Glass, Jerry Goldsmith, Bernard Herrmann, Gail Kubik, Johnny Mandel, Alex North, David Raksin, Leonard Rosenman, Laurence Rosenthal, Lalo Schifrin, Bernardo Segáll, and John Williams. Index.

Bell, David.
> *Getting the Best Score for Your Film: A Filmmakers' Guide to Music Scoring.* Los Angeles: Silman-James Press, 1994. 112 pp. ill.

Aimed at filmmakers, this work, written by a film and television composer, explains the function of underscore; choosing and communicating with the composer; spotting, composing, and recording; orchestrators and arrangers; the roles of music supervisor and music editor; and using songs. Business aspects covered include ASCAP, BMI, the musician's union, package deals, and music budgets.

Benjamin, Ruth, and Arthur Rosenblatt.
Movie Song Catalog: Performers and Supporting Crew for the Songs Sung in 1460 Musical and Nonmusical Films, 1928–1988. Jefferson, N.C.: McFarland, 1993. 352 pp.
Alphabetical listings by film title. Each entry includes songwriters, songs, performers, and basic information about the film. Compiled by a husband (architect) and wife (novelist and book editor) who share a passion for movie songs. Sources include reference works; research at libraries, archives, and performing rights societies; and films and soundtracks. Performer, songwriter, and song indexes.

Berg, Charles Merrell.
An Investigation of the Motives for and Realization of Music to Accompany the American Silent Film, 1896–1927. New York: Arno Press, 1976.
This facsimile of Berg's 1973 University of Iowa thesis covers antecedents of film music and topics from cue sheets to compiled and original scores. Documents the reasons for music, including neutralizing distracting sounds and silence, for continuity, and for illustrating the picture. Techniques covered include music for identifying characters and subjects, for establishing atmosphere, and to reflect actions, emotions, and moods. Bibliography.

Bernstein, Charles.
Film Music and Everything Else! Music, Creativity and Culture as Seen by a Hollywood Film Composer. Beverly Hills, Calif.: Turnstyle Music, 2000. 131 pp.
Essays contain the composer's musings on a myriad of subjects, including the creative process, inspiration, originality, teaching, and his remembrances of Georges Delerue. Most of the material was previously published in Bernstein's "Musical Shares" column in *The Score*, the quarterly newsletter of the Society of Composers and Lyricists.

[Bernstein, Elmer.]
Elmer Bernstein's Film Music Notebook: A Complete Collection of the Quarterly Journal, 1974–1978. Sherman Oaks, Calif.: Film Music Society, 2004.
Facsimile reprint, in one volume, of the composer's 1970s film music journal. Foreword by Jon Burlingame, introduction by Bernstein, and a newly created errata and index. For contents, see the entry herein under "Film Music Periodicals." From 1974 to 1978, members of Bernstein's Film Music Collection received issues of this journal along with a rerecorded LP of film music by a composer featured in that issue. While president of the Film Music Society (FMS) in the 1990s, Bernstein granted permission to publish the journal in one volume. After no known masters of the journal were found to exist, pristine copies in the possession of longtime FMS trustee Jack DeNault were used for scanning.

Betts, Tom.
>   *The European Western: A Compilation by Composer.* N.p.: privately printed, n.d.,
>   ca. 1990. Unpaginated (loose-leaf).

Includes films released from the late 1950s to circa 1990. Sources include fellow collectors and the Margaret Herrick Library. The typical entry, listed alphabetically by composer, includes alternate titles, director, composer, and, if applicable, song titles and discography. Ennio Morricone has 35 entries and Bruno Nicolai has 26. Includes title indexes and selected bibliography, including citations for a private pressing of Robert Bahn's "A Compilation of Italian Soundtracks" (1986) and G. Roger Hammonds's "Recorded Music for the Western Film" (Sound Track Album Retailers, 1983). The third revision of this unpublished work is available at the UCLA Music Library. Betts publishes and edits *Westerns...All'Italiana,* a quarterly fanzine on Italian Westerns that reviews soundtracks by Ennio Morricone, Bruno Nicolai, Riz Ortolani, and others.

Beynon, George W.
>   *Musical Presentation of Motion Pictures.* New York: G. Schirmer, 1921. 148 pp. ill.

Music director Beynon's manual on musical accompaniment discusses the evolution of picture music; the music library's contents and classification; scores and cue sheets; and the proper presentation of pictures, including the theme and how to use it, songs as themes, the choice of incidental music, and fitting music to image. The chapters on playing the picture include topics such as orchestral balance and the use of silence. Biographical sketches of music directors John Arthur, S. M. Berg, Carl Edouarde, Nat W. Finston, Erno Rapée, Hugo Riesenfeld, Alois Reiser, and Francis J. Sutherland. Sketches reprinted in *Film History* 14:1 (2002).

Bloom, Ken.
>   *Hollywood Song: The Complete Film and Musical Companion.* 3 vols. New York:
>   Facts on File, 1995. 1504 pp.

Credits, songs, and notes for nearly 7,000 films, including musical shorts, documentaries, and animated films. Includes some names of singers who dubbed lyrics and often includes songs written for a film but not necessarily used. Bloom reviewed an estimated 15,000 cue sheets at the major Los Angeles-area studios, supplemented by secondary sources including sheet music, production records, ASCAP, and BMI records. Bloom is president of a New York-based record company. Vol. 1: Films (A to L); Vol. 2: Films (M to Z); Vol. 3: Chronology (1922–1990; bulk 1928–1989), personnel index, song index.

Boer, H. J. de, and M. van Wouw.
>   *The Ennio Morricone Musicography.* Amsterdam: MSV, 1990. Ring-bound, 521+
>   pp.

Lists concert music (1954–1988); film music (1961–1990); various compositions, including music for theater, radio, television, as well as songs; arrangements (1959–1985); improvisations; oddities; and discography. Includes "A Short Biography," by Martin van Wouw; "An Interview with Willem Breuker," by de Boer; "Morricone One and Two," by Roberto Scollo; "Some Thoughts About Morricone's Arrangements," by Gary W. Radovich. Name and title index. Van Wouw founded an Ennio Morricone Society called Musica sul Velluto, also known as MSV, that began publishing a fanzine devoted to the composer in 1980.

Bond, Jeff.
> *The Music of Star Trek: Profiles in Style*. Los Angeles: Lone Eagle Publishing, 1998.
> 219 pp. ill.

A critical and historical overview of television and film music for Paramount's *Star Trek* franchise, written by the former managing editor of *Film Score Monthly*. Interviews with Paul Baillargeon, David Bell, Jay Chattaway, Alexander Courage, Don Davis, Cliff Eidelman, Gerald Fried, Jerry Goldsmith, Joel Goldsmith, Ron Jones, Dennis McCarthy, Leonard Rosenman, Garry Sackman (music editor), and Fred Steiner. Cue sheets (for original and tracked cues), episode production guide, music sketches, scoring schedule, and discography.

Borodkin, Maurice M.
> *Borodkin's Guide to Motion Picture Music*. [Chicago]: privately printed, 1928. Unpaginated.

Music selections for the accompaniment of motion pictures. Lists more than 6,000 music numbers classified into 150 categories from Agitatos to Witches. Each one-line entry lists the title, number assigned by the publisher, note, composer, and publisher. Borodkin assigned a unique number to each musical piece, thereby allowing a music director to file an entire library in consecutive numerical order, to simplify the task of compiling a score. Author was a music librarian.

Bradley, Edwin M.
> *The First Hollywood Musicals: A Critical Filmography of 171 Features, 1927 through 1932*. Jefferson, N.C.: McFarland, 1996. 386 pp. ill.

Film-by-film listing of early sound musicals, with cast and credits, songs, and short essays. Appendixes include silent features inspired by Broadway musicals and selected short subjects, 1928–1932. Contains some material on Dimitri Tiomkin's early ballet music for films. Bibliography.

Brophy, Philip.
> *100 Modern Soundtracks*. London: British Film Institute, 2004. 262 pp.

An alphabetical compilation of international titles, from *Akira* to *The Wrong Man*. The author, an Australian composer and sound designer, "guides the reader through an alternative cinema canon of the 'ear' of sonically exciting and remarkable films." Music, sound, and sound design are discussed. Ironically, this book is part of the BFI Screen Guide series, a series of monographs each devoted to a single film, in which music and sound design are rarely mentioned.

Brophy, Philip, ed.
> *Cinesonic: The World of Sound in Film*. North Ryde: Australian Film, Television
> and Radio School, 1999. 266 pp. ill.

Complete proceedings of the first Cinesonic International Conference on film scores and sound design, held in 1998. Includes "Composing with a Very Wide Palette" (Howard Shore in conversation); "Music for the Films of Joel and Ethan Coen" (Carter Burwell in conversation); "I Scream in Silence: Cinema, Sex and the Sound of Women Dying," by Philip Brophy; "Reeling in the Years: American Vernacular Music and Documentary Film," by David Sanjek; "The Legacy of Modernism: Film Music, Fassbinder, Kluge, and Political (After) Shock," by Caryl Flinn, includes material on Peer Raben; "Sound Music in the Films of Alain Robbe-Grillet," by Royal S. Brown; "Ornament, Entrance and the Theme Song," by Will Straw; "Nickelodeon and Popular Song," by Rick Altman. Brophy is an Australian director and composer and the founder and director of Cinesonic.

Brophy, Philip, ed.
  Cinesonic2: Cinema and the Sound of Music. North Ryde: Australian Film, Television and Radio School; St. Leonards, Australia: Allen & Unwin, 2000. 224 pp. ill.
Complete proceedings of the second Cinesonic International Conference on film scores and sound design, held in 1999. Includes "Reinventing Film Scores" (David Shea in conversation); "My Aisles of Golden Dreams: The Beauty of Supermarket Soundtracks," by Joseph Lanza; "Scenic Darkness: Towards an Aesthetic of Jazz in Film Noir," by John Conomos; "Scoring the Other: Musical Coding of Indians in the Western," by Claudia Gorbman; "The World Heard: Music, Nature, Film," by Evan Eisenberg; "How Sound Floats on Land: The Suppression and Release of Folk and Indigenous Musics in the Cinematic Terrain," by Philip Brophy.

Brophy, Philip, ed.
  Cinesonic3: Experiencing the Soundtrack. Sydney: AFTRS Publications, 2001. 236 pp.
Complete proceedings of the third Cinesonic International Conference on film scores and sound design, held in 2001. Includes "Revolutionizing Cinema: Or, How I Put Rock 'n' Roll in the Movies," (Jack Nitzsche in conversation); "Jack Nitzsche: In Memoriam," by Philip Brophy; "*Mallboy*: A Case Study of Sound and Music for an Australian Feature" (Vince Giarrusso, Fiona Eagger, and Philip Brophy in conversation); "Musical Mutations: Before, Beyond and Against Hollywood," by Adrian Martin; "Taking Music Supervisors Seriously," by Jeff Smith; "Redeemed by Ludwig Van: Stanley Kubrick's Musical Strategy in *A Clockwork Orange*," by Krin Gabbard; "Listening for Identifications: Compiled vs. Composed Scores in Contemporary Hollywood Films," by Anahid Kassabian.

Brown, Royal S.
  Overtones and Undertones: Reading Film Music. Berkeley: Univ. of California Press, 1994. 396 pp.
A film studies professor and *Fanfare* writer and critic explores the aesthetics of film music in various essays. The interaction between a film and its score is examined in the context of narrative film music for American and European films, including classical and source music. Particular attention is given to *Double Indemnity* (Miklós Rózsa), *Laura* (David Raksin), *Pierre le fou* (Antoine Duhamel), *Psycho* (Bernard Herrmann), *The Sea Hawk* (Erich Wolfgang Korngold), *Shadow of a Doubt* (Dimitri Tiomkin), and *Vivre sa vie* (Michel Legrand). Interviews with John Barry, Bernard Herrmann, Maurice Jarre, Henry Mancini, David Raksin, Miklós Rózsa, Lalo Schifrin, and Howard Shore, some of which were originally published in *Fanfare*. Other previously published material, often revised for this volume, includes "Herrmann, Hitchcock, and the Music of the Irrational." The latter appears in *Alfred Hitchcock's* Psycho: *A Casebook*, edited by Robert Kolker (Oxford: Oxford University Press, 2004). Concludes with an outline, "How to Hear a Movie," intended as a guide for writers, students, and listeners. Bibliography and index.

Bruce, Graham.
  Bernard Herrmann: Film Music and Narrative. Ann Arbor, Mich.: UMI Research Press, 1985. 248 pp. ill.

Revision of the author's 1982 New York University thesis, Chapters include "A Tradition of Music for Film," "Herrmann: Film Music and Narrative Structure," "Herrmann: Orchestral Color and Narrative," "Herrmann and Hitchcock: The Sound of Suspense," "*Vertigo*," and "*Psycho*." Filmography, discography, and bibliography.

Brunswick-Balke-Collender Co.
    Brunswick Mood Accompaniment Library & Motion Picture Cue Service. Chicago: Brunswick-Balke-Collender, n.d. Unpaginated.
A catalog of 500 disc recordings used in theaters equipped with a nonsynchronous device, or player, to supply musical accompaniment for motion pictures, usually newsreels, short subjects, educationals, and comedies. The device is a Vitaphone-like system from the late 1920s that was also used to provide intermission music. Includes directions for use, such as how to select records and how to use the provided cue sheets. Cue sheets include cue number, title or action, catalog number, and optional substitutes. When the record and recording branch of Brunswick-Balke-Collender was purchased by Warner Bros. in 1930, what remained became Brunswick Billiards, the pool table and bowling equipment manufacturer.

Buhler, James, Caryl Flinn, and David Neumeyer, eds.
    Music and Cinema. Hanover, N.H.; London: Univ. Press of New England, 2000. 397 pp. ill.
Anthology in five parts, introduced by the editors. Buhler is a professor of music, Flinn a professor of film studies, and Neumeyer a professor of music theory. Bibliography and index.
    Part 1: Leitmotif: New Debates and Questions
    "*Star Wars*, Music, and Myth," by James Buhler, 33–57; "Richard Wagner and the Fantasy of Cinematic Unity: The Idea of the *Gesamtkunstwerk* in the History and Theory of Film Music," by Scott D. Paulin, 58–84; "Leitmotifs and Musical Reference in the Classical Film Score," by Justin London, 85–96.
    Part 2: Beyond Classical Film Music
    "Songlines: Alternative Journeys in Contemporary European Cinema," by Wendy Everett, 99–117; "Strategies of Remembrance: Music and History in the New German Cinema," by Caryl Flinn, 118–41; "Kansas City Dreamin': Robert Altman's Jazz History Lesson," by Krin Gabbard, 142–57.
    Part 3: Style and Practice in Classical Film Music
    "Music, Drama, Warner Bros.: The Cases of *Casablanca* and *The Maltese Falcon*," by Martin Marks, 161–86; "Tonal Design and the Aesthetic of Pastiche in Herbert Stothart's *Maytime*," by Ronald Rodman, 187–206; "Finding Release: 'Storm Clouds' and *The Man Who Knew Too Much*," by Murray Pomerance, 207–46; "That Money-Making 'Moon River' Sound: Thematic Organization and Orchestration in the Film Music of Henry Mancini," by Jeff Smith, 247–71.
    Part 4: Gender, Ethnicity, Identity
    "Ultrasound: The Feminine in the Age of Mechanical Reproduction," by Michelle Lekas, 275–94; "Designing Women: Art Deco, the Musical, and the Female Body," by Lucy Fischer, 295–315; "Disciplining Josephine Baker: Gender, Race, and the Limits of Disciplinarity," by Kathryn Kalinak, 316–35.
    Part 5: Methodological Possibilities

"Inventing the Cinema Soundtrack: Hollywood's Multiplane Sound System," by Rick Altman, with McGraw Jones and Sonia Tatroe, 339–59; "Film Music: Perspectives from Cognitive Psychology," by Annabel J. Cohen, 360–77.

Burcher, Suellen, comp.
Dramatic Music. Catalogues of Australian Compositions, vol. 5. Sydney: Australia Music Centre, 1977.
The section "Media Music: Film, Television and Radio" (pp. 27–126) contains listings by composer for feature films, documentaries, animated films, and television series. The composer-supplied information usually includes project title, producer, director, date, duration, and occasionally instrumentation. Composer's birth year is often given. Composers include Don Banks, Tristram Cary, George Dreyfus, Trevor Jones, Sven Libaek, Brian May, Bruce Smeaton, and Robert Young.

Burlingame, Jon.
Sound and Vision: 60 Years of Motion Picture Soundtracks. New York: Billboard Books, 2000. 244 pp. ill.
Begins with a brief history of movie soundtrack recordings followed by soundtrack listings. Focus is on dramatic underscores, arranged alphabetically by composer. A typical entry contains a short biographical sketch with annotated listings of noteworthy soundtracks. Song scores and compilation scores are arranged by film title. Illustrated with photographs of composers and album covers. Composer and film indexes and bibliography. Author is a writer, journalist, and authority on television music.

Burlingame, Jon.
TV's Biggest Hits: The Story of Television Themes from "Dragnet" to "Friends." New York: Schirmer Books, 1996. 338 pp. ill.
Based on extensive interviews with composers and supplementary research. Organized into chapters on the birth of television music, cop and detective shows, Westerns, fantasy and science fiction, dramas, sitcoms, action-adventure, documentaries and news programs, prime-time animation, and made-for-TV movies and miniseries. Discography is in the form of a suggested listening list that corresponds to the chapter genres. Index.

Burn Corp.
Soundtrack Paradise: Soundtrack Chronicle, 1939–1996: Europe Version. Japan: Burn Corp., n.d., ca. 1997. 208 pp.
Photographs of 2,000 LP and singles covers for soundtracks released in France, Germany, Italy, Japan, and Scandinavia. As reviewed in *Soundtrack* (March 1998), the inclusive years are given as 1959 to 1996, whereas the book's cover appears to read *1939–1996.* Publisher planned to produce two similar books on American and Japanese soundtracks.

Burt, George.
The Art of Film Music: Special Emphasis on Hugo Friedhofer, Alex North, David Raksin, Leonard Rosenman. Boston: Northeastern Univ. Press, 1994. 266 pp.
A composer and music professor examines the practical and aesthetic aspects of film scoring. Aimed at filmmakers and composers interested in the creation of music for dramatic films, the book goes beyond the fundamentals to address point of view and musical style, retaining musical intensity under dialogue, starting music less obtrusively on a cut,

perception of time as it relates to the composer, and point of release. Six chapters cover music's role in conjunction with story, characterization, dramatic line, the sequence as a unit, the function of silence, and practical matters. In-depth analyses of the homecoming scene from *The Best Years of Our Lives* (Hugo Friedhofer), the apartment scene from *Laura* (David Raksin), and the climactic scene from *East of Eden* (Leonard Rosenman) are the focus of "The Sequence as a Unit." The chapter "Practical Matters" is a summary view from spotting through dubbing. Considerable material from interviews with Ernest Gold. Music examples, bibliography, and index.

Burton, Jack.
   The Blue Book of Hollywood Musicals: Songs from the Sound Tracks and the Stars Who Sang Them Since the Birth of the Talkies a Quarter-Century Ago. Watkins Glen, N.Y.: Century House, 1953. 296 pp. ill.
Covers a 25-year period from 1927 to 1952. Films are arranged chronologically by year, then alphabetically in four categories: musicals, feature films with songs, Western films with songs, and full-length animated films with songs. Song names and credits are derived from the annual volumes of *Film Daily Year Book* and the *Motion Picture Almanac* and from ASCAP cue sheets. A short introduction precedes each year's listings. Film title index only. With *The Blue Book of the Tin Pan Alley* (1951) and *The Blue Book of Broadway Musicals* (1952), this book completes a trilogy on popular music.

Carlin, Dan, Sr.
   Music in Film and Video Productions. Boston: Focal Press, 1991. 173 pp. ill.
A veteran music editor examines the music process from preproduction through postproduction. Topics include fundamentals of film sound and music, prescoring, playbacks, live recording on the set, the composer, the music editor, the scoring stage, the dubbing stage, rerecording and sweetening, cue sheets, tracking, and sync licenses. Index.

Carter, G. Roy.
   Theatre Organist's Secrets: A Collection of Successful Imitations, Tricks and Effects for Motion Picture Accompaniment on the Pipe Organ. Los Angeles: privately printed, 1926. Unpaginated.
The author, an organist, compiled and published this rare 20-page pamphlet to share ways of spicing up the theater organist's arsenal. In the introduction, Carter claims the organ is the "perfect accompaniment to the Silent Drama" as "it can do all and much more than a large orchestra, greatly surpassing it in power and grandeur and even variety of tone.... An audience will often be more favorably impressed by the organist who takes advantage of appropriate situations for putting in some clever trick or effect than by one who might possibly be a better musician buts lets these scenes pass unnoticed." Carter then suggests musical effects ranging from imitating animal sounds to simulating musical instruments like the banjo. Each effect includes organ settings and notated music samples. The pamphlet was reprinted by the American Theatre Organ Society, with a foreword by organist Tom B'hend, as a souvenir for its 1968 national convention. It was also reportedly reprinted by *Console* magazine. G. Roy Carter, a Los Angeles-area organist in the 1920s, is unrelated to organist Gaylord Beach Carter.

Chandler, Ivan.
   The Music Copyright Guide for Television and Film Production. 2nd ed. London: Producers Alliance for Cinema and Television, 1997. 85 pp.

A British music supervisor and PACT consultant offers advice and guidance on licensing music.

Christlieb, Don.
> *Recollections of a First Chair Bassoonist: 52 Years in the Hollywood Studio Orchestras*. Edited by Anthony Christlieb and Carolyn Beck. Foreword by David Raksin. Los Angeles: Christlieb Products, 1996. 152 pp. ill.

Contains biographical material on the session musician. Personal anecdotes on working with some 70 composers, arrangers, and music directors devote about a paragraph to each individual in approximate chronological order. Recollections of Bernard Herrmann, Alfred Newman, and Franz Waxman are slightly longer. Christlieb's musings on around 60 fellow instrumental musicians are arranged by instrument. An appendix lists composers alphabetically, with film titles listed chronologically for scores on which Christlieb played. Some contain orchestration credits, particularly for Arthur Morton. Contains recording session photographs by Christlieb and composer sketches (drawings) by his son, Anthony. Index.

Cima, Alex.
> *Click Tables in Beats Per Minute and Frames Per Beat*. Fullerton, Calif.: Neuron Music, 1988. 460 pp.

Unable to locate a copy. Presumably this is comparable to other click books, with charts for converting time to film frames and vice versa.

Citron, Marcia J.
> *Opera on Screen*. New Haven, Conn.: Yale Univ. Press, 2000. 295 pp. ill.

A professor of musicology surveys the origins and development of screen opera, including significant works. Investigates the relationship between sound and image, lip-synching, the disembodied voice, and filmed opera's influence on stage operas.

Cockshott, Gerald.
> *Incidental Music in the Sound Film*. London: British Film Institute, 1946. 8 pp.

This pamphlet contains the British composer's essay on aesthetics and current trends, which discusses incidental music as unobtrusive servant, musical excellence as a distraction to the viewer, congruity of style, and the excessive use of music.

Cohan, Steven, ed.
> *Hollywood Musicals: The Film Reader*. London: Routledge, 2002. 212 pp.

This anthology, in four parts, examines how musicals achieved cultural currency, representation of sexual differences, reading "straight" entertainment, and the significance of race and ethnicity. Each part is introduced by the editor, an English professor. Bibliography is rich in recent critical studies entries covering the genre. Index.
> "Introduction: Musicals of the Studio Era," by Steven Cohan, 1–15
> Part 1: Generic Forms
> "Entertainment and Utopia," by Richard Dyer, 19–30, originally published in *Movie* (Spring 1977); "The Self-Reflective Musical and the Myth of Entertainment," by Jane Feuer, 31–40; "The American Film Musical as Dual-Focus Narrative," by Rick Altman, 41–51; "Busby Berkeley and the Backstage Musical," by Martin Rubin, 53–61.

Part 2: Gendered Spectacles
"Sexual Economics: *Gold Diggers of 1933*," by Patricia Mellencamp, 65–76; "Pre-Text and Text in *Gentlemen Prefer Blondes*," by Lucie Arbuthnot and Gail Seneca, 77–85; "'Feminizing' the Song-and-Dance Man: Fred Astaire and the Spectacle of Masculinity in the Hollywood Musical," by Steven Cohan, 87–101.
Part 3: Camp Interventions
"Judy Garland and Camp," by Richard Dyer, 107–13; "'Working Like a Homosexual': Camp Visual Codes and the Labor of Gay Subjects in the MGM Freed Unit," by Matthew Tinkcom, 115–28; "Feminist Camp in *Gold Diggers of 1933*," by Pamela Robertson, 129–42; "'The Lady in the Tutti-Frutti Hat': Carmen Miranda, A Spectacle of Ethnicity," by Shari Roberts, 143–53.
Part 4: Racial Displacements
"Dancin' in the Rain," by Carol J. Clover, 157–73; "New Deal Blackface," by Michael Rogin, 175–82; "Beautiful White Bodies," by Linda Mizejewski, 183–93.

Cohen, Daniel.
    Musicals. New York: Gallery Books, 1984. 80 pp. ill.
A largely pictorial tribute to movie musicals in the form of a historical overview. Filmography and index.

Consumer Guide, with Phillip J. Kaplan.
    The Best, Worst & Most Unusual: Hollywood Musicals. New York: Beekman House, 1983. 158 pp. ill.
Synopses and background information. Categories include backstage, show biz, Americana, fairy tales, faraway places, and rock 'n' roll.

Cooper, David.
    Bernard Herrmann's The Ghost and Mrs. Muir: *A Film Score Guide*. Scarecrow Film Score Guides, no. 5. Lanham, Md.: Scarecrow Press, 2005. 167 pp. ill.
Chapters on Herrmann's career prior to the 1947 film; Herrmann's film scoring technique; the literary, filmic, and critical contexts of the score; overview of the score as musical text; and analysis and readings of the score. Bibliography and index. Author is a senior lecturer in music.

Cooper, David.
    Bernard Herrmann's Vertigo: *A Film Score Handbook*. Film Score Guides, no. 2. Westport, Conn.: Greenwood Press, 2001. 157 pp.
A critical studies perspective on Herrmann's career prior to *Vertigo* that also focuses on his musical style in *Vertigo*, the production of the film's musical and sonic text, and an analysis and reading of the score. Includes music examples and detailed cue analysis.

Coyle, Rebecca, ed.
    Reel Tracks: Australian Feature Film Music and Cultural Identities. Sydney: John Libbey; Eastleigh, U.K.: John Libbey Publishing; Bloomington: Indiana Univ. Press, 2005. 257 pp. ill.
Focuses on music in recent mainstream Australian films.
    "Introduction: Film Music Mnemonics...Australian Cinema Scores in the 1990s and 2000s," by Rebecca Coyle, 1–18.
Part 1: Musical Identities

"Soundscapes of Surf and Steel: *Blackrock* and *Bootmen*," by Shane Homan, 21–34; "New-Age Ned: Scoring Irishness and Masculinity in *Ned Kelly*," by Helen O'Shea, 35–47; "Hauntings: Soundtrack Representations of Papua New Guinea in *To Have and to Hold* and *In a Savage Land*," by Philip Hayward, 48–58; "*Hei-fen* and Musical Subtexts in Two Australian Films by Clara Law," by Tony Mitchell, including music by Davood Tabrizi, 59–73; "Lost in Music: Popular Music, Multiculturalism and Australian Film," by Jon Stratton, 74–93.
Part 2: Musical Sounds
"Scoring: Sexuality and Australian Film Music, 1990–2003," by Bruce Johnson and Gaye Poole, 97–121; "'Christ Kid, You're A Weirdo': Aural Construction of Subjectivity in *Bad Boy Bubby*," by Melissa Iocco and Anna Hickey-Moody, 122–36; "The Sound of Redemption in *Chopper*: Rediscovering Ambience as Affect," by Mark Evans, 137–46; "Sounds of Australia in *Rabbit-Proof Fence*," by Marjorie D. Kibby, 147–57; "Untangling *Lantana*: A Study of Film Sound Production," by Rebecca Coyle, including music by Paul Kelly, 158–74.
Part 3: Musicscapes
"Moon Music: Musical Meanings in *One Night the Moon*," by Kate Winchester, 177–88; "Transcendent Voices: Choral Music in *Paradise Road*," by Jude Magee, 189–202; "Musical Intertextuality in *The Bank*," by Michael Hannan on Alan John's score, 203–17; "Carl Vine's Score for *beDevil*," by Catherine Summerhayes and Roger Hillman, 218–27; "The Composer as Alchemist: An Overview of Australian Feature Film Scores, 1994–2004," by Michael Atherton, 228–40.

Coyle, Rebecca, ed.
Screen Scores: Studies in Contemporary Australian Film Music. Sydney: Australian Film, Television and Radio School, 1998. 247 pp. ill.
Anthology of case studies on particular films that explore how music can amplify filmic themes. Appendix features a discography (pp. 217–31) by Saffron Upton for films produced and/or filmed in Australia from 1927 to 1996 (bulk 1950s–1990s).
Part 1: Music and Textual Identity
"Creating a Sonic Character: Non-Diegetic Sound in the *Mad Max* Trilogy," by Ross Harley, including material on Brian May, 16–28; "The Violence of Sound: *Romper Stomper*," by Toby Miller, 29–38; "Emotional Times: The Music of *The Piano*," analysis of Michael Nyman's score by Theo van Leeuwen, 39–48; "Avant-Garde Meets Mainstream: The Film Scores of Philip Brophy," by Philip Samartzis, 49–64.
Part 2: Musical Associations
"Sound, Cinema and Aboriginality," by Marj Kibby and Karl Neuenfeldt, 66–77; "Music and Camp: Popular Music Performance in *Priscilla* and *Muriel's Wedding*," by Catharine Lumby, 78–88; "Italo-Australian Cinematic Soundscapes," by Tony Mitchell, 89–105; "*Shine*: Musical Narratives and Narrative Scores," by Fiona Magowan, 106–23.
Part 3: Directors and Film Music
"Sound and Author/Auteurship: Music in the Films of Peter Weir," by Bruce Johnson and Gaye Poole, 124–40; "Sonic Semaphore: Music in the Films of Yahoo Serious," by Rebecca Coyle, 141–63; "Life in the Bush: The Orchestration of Nature in Australian Animated Feature Films," by Michael Hill, 164–80.
Part 4: Film Industry
"Film Music Costs and Copyright," by Mark Evans with Raelene Lawrance and Kerryn Welsh, 181–96; "Screen Composition in Australia: The Work of Martin Armiger,"

by Michael Hannan and Jude Magee, 197–210; "Music for Film: A Composer's View," by Jan Preston, 211–16.

Craggs, Stewart R.
  Soundtracks: An International Dictionary of Composers for Film. Aldershot, U.K.; Brookfield, Vt.: Ashgate, 1998. 345 pp.
Composers listed alphabetically, with complete or partial film credits and year of release. British and European composers are well represented. Contains little or no biographical information (typical entry reads "British composer"). A selected list of classical music used in film (pp. 208–20). Film title index. Compiled by a professor of music bibliography and former librarian who has compiled and written numerous bio-bibliographies on 20th-century British composers from Arthur Bliss to William Walton.

Craig, Warren.
  The Great Songwriters of Hollywood. San Diego: A. S. Barnes; London: Tantivy Press, 1980. 287 pp.
Brief biographies, with songs listed chronologically by film title, of the following songwriters/lyricists: Harold Adamson, Harold Arlen, Irving Berlin, Nacio Herb Brown, Johnny Burke, Sammy Cahn, Sam Coslow, Walter Donaldson, Al Dubin, Ray Evans, Sammy Fain, Dorothy Fields, Arthur Freed, Ira Gershwin, Mack Gordon, Gus Kahn, Jerome Kern, Burton Lane, Jay Livingston, Frank Loesser, Jimmy McHugh, Johnny Mercer, Jimmy Monaco, Ralph Rainger, Harry Revel, Leo Robin, Jule Styne, James Van Heusen, Harry Warren, Ned Washington, Paul Francis Webster, and Richard Whiting.

Darby, Ken.
  Hollywood Holyland: The Filming and Scoring of The Greatest Story Ever Told. Metuchen, N.J.: Scarecrow Press, 1992. 282 pp. ill.
An insider's view of the creation of Alfred Newman's music from 1962 to 1965 for the George Stevens film. The author, a longtime Newman associate and vocal arranger, bases his account on personal experience supplemented by journal entries and tape recordings. Includes information on music editor George Brand and arrangers Hugo Friedhofer, Jack Hayes, Leo Shuken, and Fred Steiner. Includes "About Ken Darby," by Page Cook (pp. xiii–xxx); "Interlude," by Fred Steiner (1987) (pp. 153–61).

Darby, William, and Jack Du Bois.
  American Film Music: Major Composers, Techniques, Trends, 1915–1990. Jefferson, N.C.: McFarland, 1990. 605 pp. ill. Reprint, McFarland, 1999.
Chapters on the transition from silents to sound, studio arrangements, the 1940s and 1950s, foreign composers, the 1960s and 1970s, and the 1980s. Chapters on each of the following composers contain a short biography and musical analyses with thematic material: Elmer Bernstein, Hugo Friedhofer, Jerry Goldsmith, Bernard Herrmann, Erich Wolfgang Korngold, Henry Mancini, Alfred Newman, Alex North, Miklós Rózsa, Max Steiner, Dimitri Tiomkin, Franz Waxman, John Williams, and Victor Young. Bibliography and index. The authors hold doctorates in English and Humanities.

D'Arc, James V., and John N. Gillespie, comps. and eds.
  The Max Steiner Collection: MSS 1547. Provo, Utah: Brigham Young University, 1996. 89 pp. ill.

This booklet is a register of the collection at BYU, with a scope and content note and container list for Steiner's music sketches, scores, recordings, scrapbooks, and photographs. Introduced by D'Arc, curator of BYU's Film Music Archives. "Max Steiner: Vienna, New York, and Finally Hollywood," by Tony Thomas, 5–20; "A Max Steiner Chronology," with emphasis on his early years, by Edward A. J. Leaney, 23–31. Filmography by Clifford McCarty.

Daubney, Kate.
 Max Steiner's Now, Voyager: *A Film Score Guide.* Film Score Guides, no. 1. Westport, Conn.: Greenwood Press, 2000. 112 pp. ill.
Chapters on Steiner's musical background, his technique of film scoring, historical and critical context of *Now, Voyager,* the film's music and its context, and an analysis of the score. Bibliography and index. The author is a music lecturer whose doctoral thesis was on Steiner.

Davis, Richard.
 Complete Guide to Film Scoring: The Art and Business of Writing Music for Movies and TV. Boston: Berklee Press; Milwaukee: Hal Leonard, 1999. 378 pp. ill.
The Berklee College of Music approach to film scoring, written by a Berklee professor, composer, and orchestrator. Five parts: the history of film music, production (spotting, music prep, recording), the music (creating, syncing, and more), the business (publishing, copyrights, royalties), and interviews. Interview subjects include Elmer Bernstein, Terence Blanchard, Alf Clausen (a Berklee alumnus), Cliff Eidelman, Danny Elfman, Richard Gibbs (a Berklee alumnus), Elliot Goldenthal, agents Michael Gorfaine and Sam Schwartz, Mark Isham, Michael Kamen, Mark Mancina, David Newman, David Raksin, Lolita Ritmanis, William Ross, Alan Silvestri, Mark Snow, Richard Stone, and Shirley Walker. Index.

Davison, Annette.
 Hollywood Theory, Non-Hollywood Practice: Cinema Soundtracks in the 1980s and 1990s. Aldershot, U.K.; Burlington, Vt.: Ashgate, 2004. 221 pp.
Revised version of the author's Ph.D. dissertation for the University of Sheffield. Examines alternative scoring and soundtrack practices in films produced outside of Hollywood or at its margins, first through historical practices, then through four case studies. Chapters 1–3 discuss classical Hollywood film scoring, post-classical scoring, and alternatives to classical scoring. Case studies include analysis of the soundtracks for Jean-Luc Godard's *Prénom: Carmen,* including the use of Beethoven quartets; Derek Jarman's *The Garden*; Wim Wenders's *Der Himmel über Berlin,* including Western art music, rock music, and circus music; and David Lynch's *Wild at Heart.* Earlier versions of the essays on Jarman and Wenders were published in *Indiana Theory Review* and in Scanlon and Waste's *Crossing Boundaries* (2001). The author is a British professor with a background in film music theory and analysis.

Denisoff, R. Serge, and William D. Romanowski.
 Risky Business: Rock in Film. New Brunswick: Transaction Publishers, 1991. 768 pp.
A history of the genre written by two professors, both with backgrounds in American popular culture. Index and bibliographic notes.

Deutsch, Didier C., ed.
> *MusicHound Soundtracks: The Essential Album Guide to Film, Television, and Stage Music.* Detroit: Visible Ink Press, 2000. 872 pp.

This updated guide is arranged alphabetically by film title. Forewords by Lukas Kendall ("The Purist Point of View") and Julia Michels ("The New Age of Soundtracks—Behind the Scenes"). Composers, conductors, and lyricists are indexed. Editor is a soundtrack producer.

Deutsch, Didier C., ed.
> *VideoHound's Soundtracks: Music from the Movies, Broadway, and Television.* Foreword by Lukas Kendall. Detroit: Visible Ink Press, 1998. 1024 pp.

More than 2,000 soundtrack recordings arranged alphabetically by film title. A typical entry includes music credits, track titles and lengths, and a paragraph-length review. Indexed by film title, composer, producer, orchestrator (credits for the latter are drawn primarily from compact disc recordings and rerecordings), conductor, performer, and song title. With contributions from Jeff Bond, Andy Dursin, Gary Graff, Chuck Granata, David Hirsch, Lukas Kendall, Marc Kirkeby, Randall D. Larson, Paul Andrew MacLean, and Jerry Thomas. Editor is a soundtrack producer.

Dickinson, Kay, ed.
> *Movie Music, The Film Reader.* London: Routledge, 2003. 207 pp.

Anthology, in four parts, of previously published essays from books and periodicals. Each part begins with an introduction by the editor. Bibliography and index.
> Part 1: The Meanings of the Film Score
> "The Language of Music: A Brief Analysis of *Vertigo*," by Kathryn Kalinak, 15–23; "Prejudices and Bad Habits," by Theodor Adorno and Hans [*sic*] Eisler, 25–35; "Why Music? The Sound Film and Its Spectator," by Claudia Gorbman on the functional role of music, including for pleasure and bonding, 37–47; "Reforming 'Jackass Music': The Problematic Aesthetics of Early American Film Music Accompaniment," by Tim Anderson, 49–60.
> Part 2: The Place of the Song
> "Banking on Film Music: Structural Interactions of the Film and Record Industries," by Jeff Smith, 63–81; "Cinema, Postmodernity and Authenticity," by Lawrence Grossberg, 83–97; "*The Silences of the Palace* and the Anxiety of Musical Creation," by Anastasia Valassopoulos, 99–108; "Must You Remember This? Orchestrating the 'Standard' Pop Song in *Sleepless in Seattle*," by Ian Garwood, 109–17.
> Part 3: The Formal Politics of Music on Film
> "Whose Jazz, Whose Cinema?" by Krin Gabbard, 121–32; "The Animation of Sound," by Philip Brophy, 133–42; "Pop, Speed, Teenagers and the 'MTV Aesthetic,'" by Kay Dickinson, 143–51.
> Part 4: Crossing Over into the Narrative
> "Gender, Power, and a Cucumber: Satirizing Masculinity in *This Is Spinal Tap*," by Carl Plantinga, 155–64; "Manufacturing Authenticity: Imagining the Music Industry in Anglo-American Cinema, 1956–62," by Keir Keightley, 165–80; "A Madonna 'Wanna-Be' Story on Film," by Lisa Lewis, 181–90.

Donnelly, K[evin] J.
> *Pop Music in British Cinema: A Chronicle.* London: BFI Publishing, 2001. 274 pp.

Films are listed chronologically, grouped by decade from the 1950s through the 1990s. Mostly features and B movies, including short plot outlines; director, producer, screenwriter, and music credits; and year of the film's registration in the United Kingdom. Compiled from the author's own experience and from journals, films and videos, and soundtracks. A useful historical summary precedes each decade. Musical artists, film directors, and film titles are indexed. Began as the author's doctoral thesis for the University of East Anglia.

Donnelly, K[evin] J.
　　The Spectre of Sound: Music in Film and Television. London: BFI Publishing, 2005. 192 pp.
Focuses on the emotional and manipulative power of film music. Topics include horror music; popular music in film; ethnicity in European, Irish, and American film music; television stock music, and "Soundtracks without Films." The use of concert music in *The Shining* is examined in detail (pp. 36–54). "Music on Television 2: Pop Music's Colonization of Television" includes material from the author's "Tracking British Television: Pop Music as Stock Soundtrack to the Small Screen," published in *Popular Music* (October 2002). The author's keen observations and analyses are supplemented by his exemplary use of the existing literature from academia to psychology.

Donnelly, K[evin] J., ed.
　　Film Music: Critical Approaches. New York: Continuum, 2001. 214 pp. ill.
"Introduction: The Hidden Heritage of Film Music: History and Scholarship," by K. J. Donnelly, 1–15; "Analytical and Interpretive Approaches to Film Music (I): Analyzing the Music," by David Neumeyer and James Buhler, 16–38; "Analytical and Interpretive Approaches to Film Music (II): Analyzing Interactions of Music and Film," by James Buhler, 39–61; "'In the Mix': How Electrical Reproducers Facilitated the Transition to Sound in British Cinemas," by Michael Allen, 62–87; "*King Kong* and Film on Music: Out of the Fog," by Peter Franklin, 88–102; "The Dies Irae in *Citizen Kane*: Musical Hermeneutics Applied to Film Music," by William H. Rosar, 103–16; "The Documentary Film Scores of Gail Kubik," by Alfred W. Cochran, 117–128; "Embracing Kitsch: Werner Schroeter, Music and *The Bomber Pilot*," by Caryl Flinn, 129–151; "Performance and the Composite Film Score," by K. J. Donnelly, 152–166; "Sound and Empathy: Subjectivity, Gender and the Cinematic Soundscape," by Robynn J. Stilwell, 167–187; "'Would You Like to Hear Some Music?': Music In-and-Out-of-Control in the Films of Quentin Tarantino," by Ken Garner, 188–205. Bibliography and index.

Dorricott, I[an] J., and Bernice Allan.
　　Exploring Film Music. 3 vols. Sydney: McGraw-Hill, 1998.
A secondary-education textbook presenting music concepts in the context of film music. Sections on evoking time and place, conveying character or ideas, creating mood, and expressing emotions. Australian music and films are presented throughout. Styles include ethnic, folk, jazz and ragtime, marching band, rock, and electronic music. The complete package includes the textbook, a supplementary score reading and performance book, a teacher's manual, and two compact discs. Dorricott, a composer and teacher, has written a number of versions of *Listen to the Music* for McGraw-Hill's Australian education division that are widely used in that country.

Druxman, Michael B.
> *The Musical: From Broadway to Hollywood.* South Brunswick, N.J.: A. S. Barnes; London: Thomas Yoseloff Ltd., 1980. 202 pp. ill.

Explores the production histories of 25 musical adaptations from 1949 to 1977. Title index.

Duncan, Dean.
> *Charms That Soothe: Classical Music and the Narrative Film.* New York: Fordham Univ. Press, 2003. 211 pp.

Examines the use of serious (concert) music in film. Chapters include "Interdiscipline and the Place of Classical Music in Film Studies," "Film Music and the Musical Community," "Sound Montage and Counterpoint Analogies," "Narration, Program, and Narrative," "Interpreting Classical Music in Film," and "Summary, Conclusions, and Implications." Topics include the aesthetics of Theodor Adorno, Hanns Eisler, and Hans Keller; music in the films of directors Sergei Eisenstein and Jean-Luc Godard; the use of Beethoven's music; counterpoint; film music's place in the *Grove* dictionary; and film music's relation to program music (concert music intended to suggest nonmusical ideas).

Dunne, Michael.
> *American Film Musical Themes and Forms.* Jefferson, N.C.: McFarland, 2004. 215 pp. ill.

Topics include Depression-era musicals, blackface, rock music, musical biopics, intertextual musicals. Bibliography and index. Author is a professor of English.

Egorova, Tatiana K.
> *Soviet Film Music: An Historical Survey.* Translated by Tatiana A. Ganf and Natalia A. Egunova. Australia: Harwood Academic Publishers, 1997. 311 pp. ill.

Historical survey and analysis of Russian film music from 1917 to 1991. Topics include silent films, the transition to sound, the role of music in creating a mythicized image of socialism, song films, musicals, ideological functions, and composer–director collaborations (Eisenstein and Sergei Prokofiev, Kozintsev and Dmitri Shostakovich, Tarkovsky and Edward Artemyev). Other composers discussed include Edison Denisov, Isaak Dunayevsky, Sofia Gubaidulina, Aram Khachaturian, Alfred Schnittke, and Georg Sviridov. Notes, filmography, and index.

Ehrenstein, David, and Bill Reed.
> *Rock on Film.* New York: Delilah Books, 1982. 275 pp. ill.

Historical survey includes chapters on beach rock, the Beatles, soundtrack rock, and the rockumentary. Alphabetical list of nearly 500 films, with cast, synopses, and songs for each. Index of musicians, music industry figures, rock movies, and significant songs.

Eisler, Hanns.
> *Composing for the Films.* New York: Oxford Univ. Press, 1947. 165 pp. London: Dennis Dobson, 1951. 165 pp.

A theoretical and practical guide covering the function of film music, new musical resources, sociological aspects, aesthetics, and the composer and the moviemaking process. The original German text was written by Eisler and Theodor Adorno in 1944 and was an outgrowth of Eisler's Film Music Project at the New School for Social Research and Adorno's Princeton Radio Research Project. The 1947 edition, translated into English and edited by Eisler, George Macmanus, and Norbert Guterman, contains significant changes from the 1944 text and Adorno withdrew his name prior to publication. In 1949, *Komposition für den Film* was published in Germany with revisions to the text. The first edition of *Komposition für den Film,* citing Eisler and Adorno as co-authors, was published in Germany in 1969. It was based on the original 1944 German text version with deletions by Adorno of Eisler's earlier changes. No English translation of this version exists (save for the postscript by Adorno, "Zum Erstdruck der Originalfassung," pp. 212–13, see next entry). A critical edition of *Komposition für den Film* was published in Germany in 1977 as part of the *Complete Works of Hanns Eisler.* There is also a 1994 Athlone Press edition (see Adorno and Eisler, *Composing for the Films*). Eisler was a composer and critic and Adorno's background was in sociology and philosophy.

Eisler, Hanns, and Theodor Adorno.
> *Composing for the Films; With a Translation of the Postscript from the German Language Edition.* Freeport, N.Y.: Books for Libraries Press, 1971. 169 pp.

Reprint of the 1947 English translation (see previous entry). Contains a translation of the 1969 Adorno postscript. When the manuscript was first published, in 1947—translated into English and edited by Eisler, George Macmanus, and Norbert Guterman—it contained significant changes to the original 1944 text. Just prior to publication, Adorno removed his name and the work was published under Eisler's name only. The original German text was published in 1949, in Germany, as *Komposition für den Film.*

Evans, Mark.
> *Soundtrack: The Music of the Movies.* New York: Hopkinson and Blake, 1975. 303 pp. ill. Reprint, New York: Da Capo Press, 1979.

History, functions, and aesthetics of film music, written by a composer and film aficionado. Chapters on silent films, the coming of sound, the rise of the symphonic score, the Golden Age, special perspectives (animation, ballet, concert music, historical films, jazz, opera, source music, and theme songs), outstanding scores of the 1950s, the emergence of pop music, functions of the film score, and ethics and aesthetics (on concert performances, conductors, orchestration, and session musicians). Draws on material from Hollywood film music insiders, including composer David Raksin, conductor Irvin Talbot, and others. Contains musical examples—usually the first page of a conductor part—and drawings of composers by Marc Nadel. Index.

Faulkner, Robert R.
> *Hollywood Studio Musicians: Their Work and Careers in the Recording Industry.* Chicago: Aldine-Atherton, 1971. 218 pp. Reprint, Lanham, Md.: Univ. Press of America, 1985.

A sociological analysis of freelance musicians, career problems, making it in the studios, skills, hiring structures, and more. Based on extensive interviews, with numerous excerpts; however, the subjects of the interviews are not named. Based on the author's dissertation, "Studio Musicians: Their Work and Career Contingencies in the Hollywood Film Industry" (1968).

Faulkner, Robert R.
> *Music on Demand: Composers and Careers in the Hollywood Film Industry.* Foreword by Fred Steiner. New Brunswick, N.J.: Transaction Books, 1983. 281 pp. ill. Reprint, Piscataway, N.J.: Transaction Publishers, 2003.

A sociological approach to the composer in Hollywood, including career problems and mobility, skills, freelancing, and hiring structures. From the jacket copy: "Interviews with those composers considered to be elite (the ten percent who write almost half the film scores) and those on the industry's periphery (the ambitious freelancers who hope to break in) reveal how they perceive their careers, how they define commercial artistic success, and how they establish, or try to establish, those vital connections with filmmakers." Based on extensive interviews, with numerous excerpts; however, the subjects of the interviews are not named.

Fawkes, Richard.
 Opera on Film. London: Duckworth, 2000. 262 pp. ill.
Chronological history of opera within cinema, written by a film director. One chapter devoted to television. Appendix, "Opera Singers in the Movies" (pp. 210–37). Bibliography and index.

Fehr, Richard, and Frederick G. Vogel.
 Lullabies of Hollywood: Movie Music and the Movie Musical, 1915–1992. Jefferson, N.C.: McFarland, 1993. 366 pp.
Chronological history based on interviews with 21 songwriters—including Hoagy Carmichael, Richard Rodgers, James Van Heusen, and Harry Warren—and lyricists between 1976 and 1988. Appendix includes lists of popular songs from musicals (by year), selected western songs, and songs from Shirley Temple films. Index.

Feuer, Jane.
 The Hollywood Musical. Bloomington: Indiana Univ. Press, 1982. 131 pp. ill. 2nd ed., Bloomington: Indiana Univ. Press, 1993. 154 pp. ill. British Film Institute Cinema Series, Basingstoke, U.K.: Macmillan, 1993. 154 pp. ill.
A film studies perspective of the genre, focusing on the ideological and cultural meanings of musicals. Chapters on mass art as folk art, spectators and spectacles, celebration of the popular song, dream worlds and dream stages, and history of the Hollywood musical: innovation as conservation. Topics include the reflexive song lyric, opera vs. jazz (popular vs. elite), and the popularization of classical music. Based on the author's dissertation. Second edition contains a postscript on 1980s teen musicals and a reinterpretation of the musical from a gay perspective.

Fischer, Carl.
 Carl Fischer Moving Picture Catalog: How and What to Play for Moving Pictures: A Manual and Guide Issued by The Carl Fischer Moving Picture Music Department. New York: Carl Fischer, n.d., ca. 1916. 30 pp.
A catalog of the music publisher's works, aimed at those who play for silent films. Listings and brief interspersed paragraphs provide the musician with a guide to synchronizing picture and music: "Music should never be considered an accompaniment to the motion picture, it should be a *part* of it." Text addresses dramatic and romantic situations, society dramas, improvising, using the music theme, and the effectiveness of effects. Not to be confused with two similarly titled works, Eugene Ahern's *What and How to Play for Pictures* (1913) and Lyle True's *How and What to Play for Moving Pictures* (1914). Most likely related to another Fischer publication from the era, *What to Play for the Movies: A Complete Motion Picture Music Guide for Pianists and Conductors.*

Fisher, Jeffrey P.
> *How to Make Big Money Scoring Soundtracks: Your Complete Guide to Writing and Selling Original Music.* 2nd ed. Westmont, Ill.: Fisher Creative Group, 1993. 218 pp. 3rd ed., with complete revisions, under the title *Cash Tracks: How to Make Money Scoring Soundtracks and Jingles: Your Complete Business Guide to Original Music Profits!* Westmont, Ill.: Fisher Creative Group, 1994. 208 pp. [First edition publication details unknown.]

Vocational guidance focusing on marketing and selling original music. Author is a creator of commercial music, project studio owner, and business consultant.

Fisher, Jeffrey P.
> *How to Make Money Scoring Soundtracks and Jingles.* Emeryville, Calif.: Mix Books, 1997. 144 pp.

Revised edition of *Cash Tracks* (see previous entry). Subjects include finding work, resources, demo tapes, marketing, financial aspects, and the Internet. Serious students would be better off with Richard Davis's *Complete Guide to Film Scoring*.

Flanders International Film Festival.
> *Moving Music: Conversations with Renowned Film Composers.* Tielt: Lannoo Publishers, 2003. 173 pp.

Interviews with 19 composers, published on the occasion of the 30th Flanders International Film Festival, with accompanying compact disc.
> "Foreword," by Jacques Dubrulle; "Of All Stories," by Bart Moeyaert; "Cherishing Film Music," by Bart De Pauw; "Music Is the Soul of a Film," by Samuel Schwartz and Michael Gorfaine; "Georges Delerue," by Geoffrey MacNab and Raf Butstraen; "Elmer Bernstein," by Jon Burlingame; "Elliot Goldenthal," by Ben Van Alboom; "Rachel Portman," by Roel Van Bambost; "David Julyan," by Ben Van Alboom; "John Powell," by Chris Craps; "Hans Zimmer," by Geoffrey MacNab; "Peer Raben," by Raf Butstraen; "Henny Vrienten," by Ruben Nollet; "Patrick Doyle," by Ray Bennett; "Michael Kamen," by Roel Van Bambost; "Howard Shore," by Jan Temmerman; "Gabriel Yared," by Raf Butstraen; "Ennio Morricone," by Patrick Duynslaegher; "Stephen Warbeck," by Roel Van Bambost; "George Fenton," by Jan Temmerman; "Jean-Claude Petit," by Steven De Foer; "Michael Nyman," by Ray Bennett; "Nicola Piovani," by Jan Temmerman; "The Classical Belgians," by Roel Van Bambost; "Belgian Pop Goes Film," by Eddy Hendrix.

Flinn, Caryl.
> *Strains of Utopia: Gender, Nostalgia, and Hollywood Film Music.* Princeton, N.J.: Princeton Univ. Press, 1992. 195 pp.

Explores romantic aesthetic ideology in Hollywood film scores, particularly those of the 1930s and 1940s, and argues that films link music to the sense of a utopian past. Film noir and melodrama are examined in connection with music and nostalgia. Emphasis on authorship, creativity, and femininity. Based on the author's dissertation; some material previously published. Bibliography and index. Some readers have been put off by the theoretical nature of the work and its perceived lack of discussion of the music itself.

Foort, Reginald.
  *The Cinema Organ: A Description in Non-Technical Language of a Fascinating In-
  strument and How It Is Played.* London: Pitman, 1932. 126 pp. ill. 2nd ed., Vestal,
  N.Y.: Vestal Press, 1970. 199 pp. ill.
A prominent British organist offers his personal experience, historical perspective, and
technical knowledge. Topics include pipe and console organs, Wurlitzer organs, effects,
acoustics, silent pictures and interludes, and recording. "A Few Personal Notes," 118–24,
includes biographical notes. Second edition includes "The Man Who Started It All: A
Personal Glimpse of Reginald Foort," by Ben M. Hall, 127–32, and new material by
Foort, primarily his life story from the early 1930s through the 1960s. "The BBC Theatre
Organ," 173–85, contains the author's detailed description of the Compton organ. Discography of Foort recordings prior to 1958.

Fordin, Hugh.
  The World of Entertainment! Hollywood's Greatest Musicals. New York: Double-
  day; New York: Avon, 1975. 566 pp. ill. First paperback ed. published under the title
  The Movies' Greatest Musicals: Produced in Hollywood USA by the Freed Unit.
  New York: F. Ungar, 1984. 566 pp. ill. Unabridged version of the 1975 ed. published
  under the title *M-G-M's Greatest Musicals: The Arthur Freed Unit.* New York: Da
  Capo Press, 1996. 566 pp. ill.
Film-by-film account of the musicals of Arthur Freed, written by a record company executive and producer, that provides a wealth of insider information. Draws on material
from Freed, internal studio documents, and interviews, and on the cooperation of Saul
Chaplin, Alexander Courage, Adolph Deutsch, Johnny Green, and Conrad Salinger,
among others. Considerable material on Nacio Herb Brown and Harry Warren, who
wrote most of the music for Freed's lyrics. Filmography and song catalog.

Francillon, Vincent J., comp. and ed.
  Film Composers Guide. Foreword by Richard Bellis. 3rd ed. Beverly Hills, Calif.:
  Lone Eagle Publishing, 1996. 386 pp.
Credits updated through 1995. See also Steven C. Smith, Vincent Jacquet-Francillon, and
Lone Eagle Publishing for other editions. Contacts for music publishers, film studios,
master use licensing, soundtrack labels, music clearance, and worldwide performing
rights societies. Lists music supervisors and some orchestrators, with some credits.

Francillon, Vincent J., and Steven C. Smith, comps. and eds.
  Film Composers Guide. 2nd ed. Beverly Hills, Calif.: Lone Eagle Publishing, 1994.
  320 pp.
Follows the format and criteria of Smith's first edition, with credits updated through
1993. Foreword by record producer Nick Redman. See also Smith and Lone Eagle Publishing for other editions. Francillon is a composer and a former board member of the
Film Music Society.

Fredericks, Marc.
  The Theory and Practice of Click Tracks. New York: Comprehensive Publications,
  1974. 689 pp.
A click-track book with 145 click charts for 6.0 to 24.0 frames, six conversion charts, and
10 composite master charts. Advocates an all-frame system so that the charts are com-
patible with any film format running at 24 frames per second, including 16mm and

35mm. Nine-page question-and-answer section addresses internal sync points and other technical considerations. Click calculations are by the author, an East Coast composer and arranger experienced in commercial music, including jingles, with at least two film score credits. A later 145-page book by the author, *The Sub-Division of Click Tracks* (United States: Minius Enterprises, 1992), was not examined.

Funnell, John.
    Best Songs of the Movies: Academy Award Nominees and Winners, 1934–1958. Jefferson, N.C.: McFarland, 2005.
Presentation, performance, and historical or biographical insights are included for each song. Appendix includes brief songwriter biographies. Bibliography and index. Author is a retired teacher living in Australia.

Gabbard, Krin.
    Jammin' at the Margins: Jazz and the American Cinema. Chicago: Univ. of Chicago Press, 1996. 350 pp. ill.
Examines race, gender, and sexuality in American jazz films. Topics include historical and ideological moments in specific films (such as the *Jazz Singer* films), jazz biopics, the jazz trumpet as phallic instrument, the state of jazz in film after 1970 (examining *New York, New York* and *Short Cuts*), and the careers of Duke Ellington, Louis Armstrong, Nat King Cole, and Hoagy Carmichael. Bibliography and index.

Garbutt, Matthew, and Gary Ford, eds.
    R.E.D. Soundtracks Catalogue. London: Paulton House / Retail Entertainment Data Publishing, 1995. 336 pp.
Although R.E.D. publishes many CD catalogs, this is the only one devoted solely to film and television soundtracks.

Gelfand, Steve.
    Television Theme Recordings: An Illustrated Discography, 1951–1994. Ann Arbor, Mich.: Popular Culture, Ink, 1994. 332 pp. ill.
Comprehensive discography listing a staggering number of themes released on record. Listed alphabetically by series title. Each theme lists composer and lyricist; recording artist; recording format; record title, label, and number; release date of record; and versions. Introduction includes notes on collecting television themes and an overview of trends in television theme music. Appendixes contain various lists of interest. Of note are *Peter Gunn*, with the most recordings, and Mike Post, with the greatest number of different recorded television themes. Composer, artist, and song title indexes. An earlier 136-page version, *Television Theme Recordings*, also by Gelfand, was published by the Television Music Archives, Bronx, New York, 1985.

George, W. Tyacke.
    Playing to Pictures: A Guide for Pianists and Conductors of Motion Picture Theatres. London: Kinematograph Weekly, 1912. 64 pp. 2nd ed., London: E. T. Heron [publisher of *Kinematograph Weekly*], 1914. 92 pp.
Includes "List of music approximately timed," 78–83; "Suggested appropriate music," 85–89 (page citations from 1914 ed.). Copies available at the British Film Institute Library, London.

Goldmark, Daniel.
    Tunes for 'Toons: Music and the Hollywood Cartoon. Berkeley: Univ. of California Press, 2005.
Chapters include "Introduction: Why Cartoon Music?"; "Carl Stalling and Popular Music in the Warner Bros. Cartoons"; "'You Really Do Beat the Shit Out of That Cat': Scott Bradley's (Violent) Music for M-G-M"; "*Jungle Jive*: Animation, Jazz Music, and Swing Culture"; "Corny Concertos and Silly Symphonies: Classical Music and Cartoons"; "*What's Opera, Doc?* and Cartoon Opera"; "A Brief Conclusion." Two appendixes (pp. 165–69) include reprinted material by, or regarding, Carl Stalling and Scott Bradley. Based in part on the author's dissertation.

Goldmark, Daniel, and Yuval Taylor, eds.
    The Cartoon Music Book. Chicago: A Capella Books, 2002. 320 pp.
Anthology includes new and reprinted articles on a wide range of topics, including film and television music throughout the 20th century. Index.
    <u>Main Title</u>
    "Tunes for Toons: A Cartoon Music Primer," by Neil Strauss, 5–13.
    <u>Part 1: An Episodic History of Cartoon Music</u>
    "Animated Cartoons and Slap-Stick Comedy," by Edith Lang and George West (reprint, *Musical Accompaniment of Moving Pictures*, 1920), 17–19; "Make Walt's Music: Music for Disney Animation, 1928–1967," by Ross Care, 21–36; "An Interview with Carl Stalling," by Mike Barrier, 37–60 (reprint, *Funnyworld*, Spring 1971); "Hidey Hidey Hidey Ho…Boop-Boop-A Doop! The Fleischer Studio and Jazz Cartoons," Jake Austen, 61–66; "I Love to Hear a Minstrel Band: Walt Disney's *The Band Concert*," by David Wondrich, 67–72; "Disney, Stokowski, and the Genius of *Fantasia*," by Charles L. Granata, 73–91; "Music and the Animated Cartoon," by Chuck Jones, 93–102 (reprint, *Hollywood Quarterly*, July 1946); "Classical Music and Hollywood Cartoons: A Primer on the Cartoon Canon," by Daniel Goldmark, 103–14; "Music in Cartoons," Scott Bradley, 115–120 (reprint, *Film Music Notes*, December 1944); "Personality on the Sound Track: A Glimpse Behind the Scenes and Sequences in Filmland," by Scott Bradley, 121–24 (reprint, *Music Educators Journal*, 1947); "*Make Mine Music* and the End of the Swing Era," by Stuart Nicholson, 125–35; "Sublime Perversity: The Music of Carl Stalling," by Will Friedwald, 137–40 (appeared in different form as liner notes to *The Carl Stalling Project*, 1990); "Carl Stalling, Improviser & Bill Lava, Acme Minimalist," by Kevin Whitehead, 141–50; "Raymond Scott: Accidental Music for Animated Mayhem," by Irwin Chusid, 151–60; "Winston Sharples and the 'Inner Casper' (or Huey Has Two Mommies)," by Will Friedwald, 161–67; "An Interview with Hoyt Curtin," by Barry Hansen and Earl Kress, 169–72; "Rock 'n' Roll Cartoons," by Jake Austen, 173–91; "'Put One Note in Front of the Other': The Music of Maury Laws," by Greg Ehrbar, 193–99.
    <u>Part 2: Cartoon Music Today</u>
    "Merrie Melodies: Cartoon Music's Contemporary Resurgence," by Elisabeth Vincentelli, 203–6; "An Interview with Mark Mothersbaugh," by Daniel Goldmark, 207–17; "Robots, Romance, and Ronin: Music in Japanese Anime," by Milo Miles, 219–24; "An Interview with Richard Stone, Steve Bernstein, and Julie Bernstein," by Daniel Goldmark, 225–38; "An Interview with Alf Clausen," by Daniel Goldmark, 239–52; "I Kid Because I Love: The Music of *The Simpsons*," by Will Friedwald, 253–62; "An Interview with John Zorn," by Philip Brophy, 263–67; "Rhapsody in Spew: Romantic Undertones in *The Ren & Stimpy Show*," by Joseph Lanza, 269–74.

End Title
"A Very Visual Kind of Music: The Cartoon Soundtrack Beyond the Screen," by John Corbett, 279–87; "Cartoon Music: A Select Discography," by Greg Ehrbar, 289–98; "Bibliography," by Daniel Goldmark, 299–305.

Gorbman, Claudia.
  Unheard Melodies: Narrative Film Music. Bloomington: Indiana Univ. Press; London: BFI Publishing, 1987. 190 pp. ill.
A film studies work of theory and analysis that uses semiological, psychoanalytical, and historical approaches to explain the functions of music in narrative cinema. Three films (*Sous les toits de Paris*; *Zéro de conduite*, Maurice Jaubert; and *Hangover Square*, Bernard Herrmann) are analyzed. Some material previously appeared in the author's dissertation, "Film Music: Narrative Functions in French Films." In the author's assessment, her book "introduced a more academic run of film music books in the late 1980s which continues to the present." This groundbreaking work influenced a generation of writers and is arguably the most cited book on film music of the past 20 years.

Gorbman, Claudia, and Warren M. Sherk, eds.
  Film Music 2: History, Theory, Practice. Foreword by Christopher Young. Introduction by Claudia Gorbman. Los Angeles: Film Music Society, 2004. 254 pp. ill.
"Musical Texture as Cinematic Signifier: The Politics of Polyphony in Selected Documentary Film Scores by Virgil Thomson and Aaron Copland," by Neil Lerner, 1–25; "*Deception*'s Great Music: A Cultural Analysis," by Peter Franklin, 27–41; "Jay Livingston and Ray Evans: An Interview," by Arthur Hamilton, excerpted from a Film Music Society oral history, 43–87; "Works of Distinction: The Functional Music of Gail Kubik," by Alfred W. Cochran, 89–111; "Paul Beaver: Analog Synthesist Extraordinaire," by Warren M. Sherk, 113–43; "Linking the Film and Music Industries: Cross-Promotion, the Soundtrack Album, and the Case of United Artists," by Jeff Smith, 145–59, reprinted from Smith, *The Sounds of Commerce* (1998); "The Opera Films of Daniel Toscan du Plantier," by Michel Chion, trans. Claudia Gorbman, 161–67; "*Sense and Sensibility*: Musical Form and Drama in the Film Adaptation," by Robynn J. Stilwell, 169–98, original version published in *Acta Musicologica* (2000); "Film Music on the Internet: The Origin and Assessment of FILMUS-L," by H. Stephen Wright, 199–212; "Teaching Film Music in a Liberal Arts Curriculum," by Michael V. Pisani, 213–44.

Green, Stanley.
  Encyclopaedia of the Musical Film. New York: Oxford Univ. Press, 1981. 344 pp.
More than 1,600 alphabetical entries for films, songs, and personalities. Brief biographical entries for composers and lyricists. Film entries, including releases from approximately 1927 to 1979, feature plot outline, historical notes, brief credits, and songs (including those cut from the film). List of musical biographies based on the lives of classical and popular composers and lyricists (pp. 328–31). Includes title differences between American and British releases (pp. 332–34). Bibliography, discography, and index. Author was a lecturer, film publicist, writer, and editor.

Green, Stanley.
  Hollywood Musicals Year by Year. Milwaukee: Hal Leonard Publishing, 1990. 351 pp. ill. 2nd ed., revised and updated by Elaine Schmidt, 1999. 392 pp. ill.

Historical summaries, songwriter credits, songs, and soundtracks listed for 300 major musicals from 1927 to 1989, compiled primarily from secondary sources. Numerous indexes including composer-lyricist and studio. The last book written by the musical theater historian. Second edition adds material covering the 1990s.

Hagen, Earle.
   Advanced Techniques for Film Scoring: A Complete Text. Los Angeles: Alfred Publishing, 1990. 172 pp. ill.
Current trends in the mechanics of film scoring, edited by the respected television composer and arranger. Part 1, "Composer Aids," revisits click tracks, calculators, and SMPTE time code as synchronization tools. Two chapters on computer synchronization: "Auricle: The Film Composer's Time Processor," by Richard and Ron Grant, and "Cue: The Film Music System," by Rick Johnston. In Part 2, "Multiple-Reel Recording," Alan Silvestri discusses the purpose and psychology of juxtaposing and overlaying multiple reels of music. This is the technique of moving one complete track of music in relation to another (not to be confused with multiple-track recording). Concludes with a short essay by Hagen on composing and conducting. Music examples include a cue by Jerry Goldsmith from *Mephisto Waltz* and Silvestri's main title from *Clan of the Cave Bear*. One compact disc of musical examples.

Hagen, Earle.
   Scoring for Films: A Complete Text. New York: Criterion Music, 1971. 253 pp. ill.
A treatise on the mechanics of film scoring, written by the respected television composer and arranger. Topics include click tracks, converting footage (frames) to time (seconds), free timing, and segues and overlaps. Addresses the psychology of creating music, including approach; when, where, and why to use music; dialogue as counterpoint; and source music. Five composers (Hugo Friedhofer, Jerry Goldsmith, Quincy Jones, Alfred Newman, and Lalo Schifrin) are asked four questions on the composer's contribution, determining start and stop points, playing under dialogue, and picture dictating musical style. Section on the responsibilities of the composer covers prerecords, guide tracks, recording, and dubbing. Contains numerous musical examples from television cues written by Hagen and two seven-inch disc recordings conducted and narrated by Hagen. This book and the author's BMI film-scoring workshop influenced many young Hollywood composers in the 1970s and 1980s, particularly in regard to the technical aspects of synchronizing music to the moving image.

Hagen, Earle.
   Scoring for Films: A Complete Text. Updated ed. Los Angeles: Alfred Publishing, ca. 1989. 254 pp. ill.
The "update" is a compact disc that replaces the original analog disc recordings.

Halfyard, Janet K.
   Danny Elfman's Batman*: A Film Score Guide.* Scarecrow Film Score Guides, no. 2. Lanham, Md.: Scarecrow Press, 2004. 177 pp. ill.
Elfman's musical background, his technique of film scoring, the historical and critical context of the 1989 film, the sound of the score, and analysis of the score. Bibliography and index. Author is a British lecturer.

Hall, Roger L., comp.
  A Guide to Film Music: Songs and Scores. Stoughton, Mass.: PineTree Press, 1997.
  80 pp. 2nd ed, 2002.
A potpourri compiled by a teacher, radio host, musician, and film music buff. Brief chronology of film songs and scores, 1927–1997; suggestions for listening; brief interviews
with Aaron Copland and Virgil Thomson; excerpts from film music literature; and where
to find more information.

Harris, Steve.
  Film and Television Composers: An International Discography, 1920–1989. Jefferson, N.C.: McFarland, 1992. Reprint, Jefferson, N.C.: McFarland Classics, 2001. 302
  pp.
Intended as a sequel to *Film, Television, and Stage Music on Phonograph Records: A
Discography* (see below), with far more material specific to film and television. Nearly
8,000 recordings listed by composer. Soundtracks issued as conventional phonograph
recordings pressed in the United States are favored, as are composers writing original
music. Entries include title, quantity of music (theme, excerpts, score), country of pressing, record format, and record label and number. Compiled from material at specialty
record stores and collections at public libraries and in private hands. Title index. Harris
was a record producer and film and television historian.

Harris, Steve.
  Film, Television, and Stage Music on Phonograph Records: A Discography. Jefferson, N.C.: McFarland, 1988. 445 pp.
Commercial releases of disc recordings from the United States and Great Britain through
1986, listed alphabetically by title and organized by film, television, and stage music.
Entries include title, date, quantity of music (theme, excerpts, score), composer, country
of pressing, record format, and record label and number. Compiled from material at specialty record stores and collections at public libraries and in private hands. Composer
index.

Harris, Steve.
  Recorded Music for Motion Pictures, Television, and the Theater. Los Angeles: A-1
  Record Finders, 1976.
This hard-to-find loose-leaf volume is a precursor to Harris's McFarland books (see pre-
vious entry). The author was employed at A-1 Record Finders, a business specializing in
soundtracks since 1971. Billed as "newly revised" in the introduction, the previous edi-
tion may have been distributed privately. Composer index. A copy is available at the Los
Angeles Central Library.

Hayward, Philip, ed.
  Off the Planet: Music, Sound and Science Fiction Cinema. Eastleigh, U.K.: John
  Libbey; Bloomington: Indiana Univ. Press, 2004.
With music examples. Originally published as the January and July 2003 issues of the
Australian journal *Perfect Beat.*
  "Sci Fidelity—Music, Sound, and Genre History," an introductory survey by Philip
  Hayward, 1–29; "Hooked on Aetherophonics: *The Day the Earth Stood Still*," by
  Rebecca Leydon, on Bernard Herrmann's score and the Theremin, 30–41; "Atomic
  Overtones and Primitive Undertones: Akira Ifukube's Sound Design for *Godzilla*,"

by Shuhei Hosokawa, includes discussion of Ifukube's score, 42–60; "*Forbidden Planet*: Effects and Affects in the Electro Avant Garde," by Rebecca Leydon, on Louis and Bebe Barron, 61–76; "The Transmolecularisation of [Black] Folk: *Space Is the Place*, Sun Ra and Afrofuturism," by Nabeel Zuberi, on Sun Ra, aka Herman Blount, 77–95; "Nostalgia, Masculinist Discourse, and Authoritarianism in John Williams' Scores for *Star Wars* and *Close Encounters of the Third Kind*," by Neil Lerner, 96–108; "Sound and Music in the *Mad Max* Trilogy," by Rebecca Coyle, on music by Brian May and Maurice Jarre, 109–28; "These Are My Nightmares: Music and Sound in the Films of David Cronenberg," by Paul Théberge, on music by Howard Shore, 129–48; "Ambient Soundscapes in *Blade Runner*," by Michael Hannan and Melissa Carey, on music by Vangelis, 149–64; "'I'll Be Back': Recurrent Sonic Motifs in James Cameron's *Terminator* Films," by Karen Collins, on music by Brad Fiedel, 165–75; "Inter-Planetary Soundclash: Music, Technology and Territorialisation in *Mars Attacks!*" by Philip Hayward, on music by Danny Elfman, 176–87; "Mapping *The Matrix*: Virtual Spatiality and the Realm of the Perceptual," by Mark Evans, 188–98.

Hillman, Roger.
   Unsettling Scores: German Film, Music, and Ideology. Bloomington: Indiana Univ. Press, 2005.
Classical music in film, focusing on the New German Cinema of the 1970s and early 1980s. Explores music by Ludwig van Beethoven, Gustav Mahler, and Richard Wagner in the films of Rainer Werner Fassbinder, Werner Herzog, Alexander Kluge, Hans-Jürgen Syberberg, and Luchino Visconti. Author, a native of Australia, specializes in film studies and German studies.

Hemming, Roy.
   The Melody Lingers On: The Great Songwriters and Their Movie Musicals. New York: Newmarket Press, 1986, 1988, 1991, 1995, 1999. 388 pp. ill.
Biographical material, career profiles, and filmographies for Harold Arlen, Irving Berlin, Nacio Herb Brown, Hoagy Carmichael, George Gershwin, Jerome Kern, Frank Loesser, Jimmy McHugh, Cole Porter, Ralph Rainger, Richard Rodgers, Arthur Schwartz, Jule Styne, James Van Heusen, Harry Warren, and Richard Whiting. Bibliography and index. Title is fashioned after Irving Berlin's "The Song Is Ended But the Melody Lingers On."

Henderson, Amy, and Dwight Blocker Bowers.
   Red, Hot & Blue: A Smithsonian Salute to the American Musical. Washington, D.C.: National Portrait Gallery and the National Museum of American History, in association with Smithsonian Institution Press, 1996. 268 pp. ill.
Written by two historians to accompany an exhibition at the National Portrait Gallery. Includes "Light the Lights: Broadway and Hollywood, 1927–1942," 81–137, and "The Heights: Broadway and Hollywood, 1943–1959," 139–97. Bibliography, discography, and index.

Hirschhorn, Clive.
   The Hollywood Musical. New York: Crown, 1981. 456 pp. ill.
A newspaper film critic's year-by-year, film-by-film summaries. Appendixes list fringe musicals, pop musicals, and documentaries. Indexes include film titles, song and music

titles, performers, composers and lyricists, and other creative personnel, including musical directors and orchestrators such as Conrad Salinger.

Hischak, Thomas S.
   The American Musical Film Song Encyclopedia. Westport, Conn.: Greenwood Press, 1999. 521 pp.
A theater professor presents entries on more than 1,800 individual songs from more than 500 musical films, with information on the songs' authors, original singers, initial film appearances, commentary on how the songs were used in the film, subsequent film and stage appearances, and notes on memorable recordings. Contains a selective list of memorable movie songs from non-Hollywood sources, including Broadway and Tin Pan Alley. Bibliography.

Hischak, Thomas.
   Film It with Music: An Encyclopedic Guide to the American Movie Musical. Westport, Conn.: Greenwood Press, 2001. 464 pp.
Entries for films, composers, songwriters, studios, and performers, with a chronological list of the 383 films covered (pp. 367–78).

Hischak, Thomas S.
   Through the Screen Door: What Happened to the Broadway Musical When It Went to Hollywood. Lanham, Md.: Scarecrow Press, 2004. 311 pp.
Examines 176 Broadway and off-Broadway musicals that were made into Hollywood films. All of the stage productions are American except for 10 British musicals popular in New York. Conversely, about a dozen screen musicals adapted for the Broadway stage are discussed. Two appendixes list nonmusical films that became stage musicals and nonmusical plays that became movie musicals.

Hofmann, Charles.
   Sounds for Silents. New York: DBS Publications/Drama Book Specialists, 1970. 1 vol. Unpaginated, ill.
A short historical overview of musical accompaniment for silent films. The author, musical director of the film department at the Museum of Modern Art (MOMA) in New York, often accompanied silent films at the piano. Cue sheets, music examples, illustrations, and the author's list of important musical scores for films from 1908 to 1931. Includes a seven-inch analog disc recording of musical backgrounds composed and performed by the author and recorded at MOMA screenings in the late 1960s.

Houten, Theodore van.
   Silent Cinema Music in the Netherlands: The Eyl/Van Houten Collection of Film and Cinema Music in the Nederlands Filmmuseum. Buren, The Netherlands: Frits Knuf Publishers, 1992. 328 pp. ill.
Documentation of cinema music at the Nederlands Filmmuseum, including that of Ido Eyl, a cinema musician, and the author, a radio producer and silent film specialist. Introduction (pp. 11–57) provides a historical overview with quotations from cinema musicians, documentation of original scores for silent Dutch films, a profile of Eyl with his remembrances, and background on the Eyl/Van Houten collection. Alphabetical listing (pp. 60–304) of composers for around 3,300 works. The latter includes mood music,

classical music arrangements, popular and light music, songs, and some original works. Index of mood music titles.

Huntley, John.
    British Film Music. London: Skelton Robinson, 1947. 247 pp. ill. Reprint, with a foreword by Muir Mathieson. New York: Arno Press, 1972.
History of British film music through 1946. Subjects cover the British musical; music for documentary films; the industrial, animated, and newsreel film; and recording film music. Includes "The Ideal Music Recording Stage," by George Burgess, 145–48; "The Future of British Film Music," by Louis Levy, 149–51; "A Film Recording Session," by Edward Silverman, 152–55; "Film Music Forum," 156–76, contains brief comments on British film music by various composers; "Hollywood Looks at British Film Music," by Margery Morrison, 164–69; "*Henry V*" (analysis) by Stanlie McConnell, 171–76; "Film Music," by Ralph Vaughan Williams, 177–82 (reprint, *Royal College of Music Magazine*); "Aspects of Film Music," by Muir Mathieson, 183–87; biographical index, 189–229; list of British film music orchestras, 229–31; selected list of classical music in British films, 231–32; list of dance bands in British films, 233–34; list of BBC broadcasts on film music, 234–36; list of BBC film music performances, 237–38; recordings of British film music, 239–44. Bibliography.

Huntley, John, and Ronald Reading, comps.
    Music Cue Sheet Index for Silent Films. Sheffield, U.K.: Federation of Film Societies, n.d.
A copy of this 18-page pamphlet can be found at the British Film Institute National Library in London.

Jacquet-Francillon, Vincent, comp. and ed.
    Film Composers Guide. 4th ed. Beverly Hills, Calif.: Lone Eagle Publishing, 1997. 416 pp.
Entries for 2,600 composers and 25,000 films. Last edition to date.

Jastfelder, Frank, and Stefan Kassel, eds.
    The Album Cover Art of Soundtracks. Boston: Little, Brown, 1997. 128 pp. ill.
A visual history of collectible records by a graphic designer and disc jockey, respectively, with nearly 300 color photographs.

Jay, Richard.
    How to Get Your Music in Film & TV: The Music Broker Guide to Soundtrack Licensing and Commissioning. United Kingdom and United States: Music Broker Organisation, 2003. 98 pp. New York: Schirmer Trade Books, 2005.
Guide for songwriters, publishers, and independent record producers looking to place their previously composed or published music in films and television. Tips on marketing, deal making, negotiation, and contracts, as well as the basics of music publishing, record companies, and copyright. Author is director of the U.K.-based Music Broker Organisation.

Jenkinson, Philip, and Alan Warner.
    Celluloid Rock: Twenty Years of Movie Rock. London: Lorrimer Publishing, 1974. 136 pp. ill.

Historical survey of the genre from approximately 1955 to 1973, written by a British television personality and a record producer, respectively. Filmography and index.

Joe, Jeongwon, and Rose Theresa, eds.
   Between Opera and Cinema. New York: Routledge, 2002. 244 pp.
Anthology compiled by a professor of musicology and a music history instructor, respectively. Bibliography and index.
   "From Méphistophélés to Méliés: Spectacle and Narrative in Opera and Early Film," by Rose Theresa, 1–18; "'There Ain't No Sanity Claus!' The Marx Brothers at the Opera," by Michal Grover-Friedlander, 19–37; "*The Tales of Hoffmann*: An Instance of Operality," by Lesley Stern, 39–57; "The Cinematic Body in the Operatic Theater: Philip Glass's *La Belle et la Béte*," by Jeongwon Joe, 59–73; "Why Does Hollywood Like Opera?" by Marc A. Weiner, 75–91; "Opera in Film: Sentiment and Wit, Feeling and Knowing: *The Shawshank Redemption* and *Prizzi's Honor*," by Mary Hunter, 93–119; "Is There a Text in This Libido? *Diva* and the Rhetoric of Contemporary Opera Criticism," by David J. Levin, 121–32; "The Elusive Voice: Absence and Presence in Jean-Pierre Ponnelle's Film *Le nozze di Figaro*," by Marcia J. Citron, 133–53; "Verdi in Postwar Italian Cinema," by Deborah Crisp and Roger Hillman, 155–76; "Chinese Opera, Global Cinema, and the Ontology of the Person: Chen Kaige's *Farewell My Concubine*," by Teri Silvio, 177–97; "Sounding Out the Operatic: Jacques Rivette's *Noroît*," by Mary M. Wiles, 199–222; "Afterword: In Appreciation," by Stanley Cavell, 223–29.

Jonge, Jon de.
   Tune Up the Hoover! Cinema Musicians Tell Their Stories. Blackpool, U.K.: Jon de Jonge, 1994. 48 pp. ill.
A booklet with reminiscences of residents in Lancashire County, northwest England.

Kalinak, Kathryn.
   Settling the Score: Music and the Classical Hollywood Film. Madison: Univ. of Wisconsin Press, 1992. 248 pp. ill.
A film studies professor examines musical, theoretical, structural, and historical questions in the context of the language of music (using Bernard Herrmann's score for *Vertigo* as a model), a theory of film music, the silent film score, and the classical Hollywood film score (epitomized by Erich Wolfgang Korngold's score for *Captain Blood*). Textual analyses of *The Informer* (Max Steiner), *The Magnificent Ambersons* (Herrmann), *Laura* (David Raksin), and *The Empire Strikes Back* (John Williams). Earlier versions of two chapters were previously published. Music examples, bibliography, and index. Based in part on the author's 1982 dissertation, "Music as Narrative Structure in Hollywood Film."

Karlin, Fred.
   Listening to Movies: The Film Lover's Guide to Film Music. New York: Schirmer Books; Toronto: Maxwell Macmillan Canada; New York: Maxwell Macmillan International, 1994. 429 pp. ill.
A historical survey for general audiences, written by the Oscar-winning composer. Six parts cover such topics as composing the music, what to listen for, the studio system and freelancing, songs and soundtrack records. Short decade-by-decade chronology and personal profiles of composers, including how they got started in the business. Bibliography and index.

Karlin, Fred, and Rayburn Wright.
    On the Track: A Guide to Contemporary Film Scoring. Foreword by John Williams.
    New York: Schirmer Books; London: Collier Macmillan, 1990. 856 pp. ill.
The authors, an Oscar-winning composer and a composer-teacher, respectively, explore
the entire compositional process, combining a nontechnical overview of creative aspects
with a technical guide to scoring films. Ten parts focus on preliminaries, conceptualizing,
timings, composing, recording, electronic and contemporary scoring, styles and genres,
songs, the business, and specialized themes. Topics include communicating with filmmakers, temp tracks, spotting, budgets, developing the concept, demonstrating the score,
timing and click tracks, playing the drama, and the effective use of melody, harmony,
rhythm, and orchestration. The authors interview more than 70 composers, lyricists, producers, directors, film and music editors, recording engineers, copyists, contractors, executives, music supervisors, and agents; selected credits and photos accompany each.
Contains a complete click book by Alexander R. Brinkman and more than 150 music
excerpts. Glossary, filmography, bibliography, and index.

Kassabian, Anahid.
    Hearing Film: Tracking Identifications in Contemporary Hollywood Film Music.
    New York: Routledge, 2001. 189 pp. ill.
Chapters on "How Film Music Works"; "How Music Works in Film"; "A Woman
Scored," on popular music soundtracks; "At the Twilight's Last Scoring," on gender,
race, sexuality, and assimilation (a previous iteration appeared in David Schwarz et al.,
Keeping Score, 1997); and "Opening Scores." Films discussed include *Corrina, Corrina*;
Dirty Dancing; *The Hunt for Red October*; and *Mississippi Masala*. Bibliography and
index. Based in part on the author's dissertation. Author is an assistant professor of communications and media studies specializing in popular music, film music, and feminist
theory.

Keller, Hans.
    *The Need for Competent Film Music Criticism: A Pamphlet for Those Who Care for
    Film as Art, with a Final Section for Those Who Do Not*. London: British Film Insti-
    tute, 1947. 23 pp.
Essay by the British music critic on the aesthetic and sociological need for classical film
music criticism to foster awareness and appreciation of music in films. A month after the
essay's publication, Keller apparently started writing anonymous reviews for the BFI.
From November 1947 to November 1948 nearly two dozen appeared in what Christopher
Wintle in *Film Music and Beyond* (2006) refers to as the *Monthly Film Music Bulletin*.

Kendall, Lukas, comp.
    The Soundtrack Club Handbook. Amherst, Mass.: Film Score Monthly, 1991–2005.
Issued free to new subscribers to Kendall's journal *Film Score Monthly* as early as October 1991, with periodic updates. *Club* was dropped from the title around 1994. The handbook's primary purpose was to answer frequently asked questions by the readership
(most frequently asked: why certain soundtracks aren't available on CD). Covers the
history of *Film Score Monthly*, submission guidelines, film music on laserdisc, promos
and bootlegs, music in movie trailers, film music on radio, film music on the Internet,
film music societies, publications covering film music, film composer societies, and some
film music books.

Knudson, Carroll.
  Project Tempo. Los Angeles: privately printed, 1965. 241 pp.
Contains 241 click-track tables for converting film footage (as expressed in frames from
6 to 36) to musical beat numbers. In the moviola era, prior to computers and home studios, this was the bible, the tempo finder, for music editors and composers. Author was a
music editor who received a 1966 Academy of Motion Picture Arts and Sciences Technical Award for this book.

Kobal, John.
  Gotta Sing, Gotta Dance: A Pictorial History of Film Musicals. London: Hamlyn,
    1970. 320 pp. ill.
Includes some material on early sound musicals, the foreign film musical, and the 1930s
through 1950s.

Koerner, Julie.
  Hollywood Musicals. The Life, Times, and Music series. New York: Fried-
    man/Fairfax, 1997. 64 pp.

  Love Songs from Stage and Screen. The Life, Times, and Music series. New York:
    Friedman/Fairfax, 1994. 72 pp.
The Life, Times, and Music series pairs a compact disc highlighting a popular genre with
a booklet that places the music in historical and social context.

Kompanek, Sonny.
  *From Score to Screen: Sequencers, Scores & Second Thoughts: The New Film Scor-
    ing Process*. New York: Schirmer Trade Books, 2004. 172 pp.
An orchestrator and educator synthesizes his experiences into a succinct and practical
manual for anyone involved with preparing music ("music prep") for film or television.
The new film scoring process refers to a generational shift in the way films are scored
today, brought on by the introduction of MIDI (music instrument digital interface) in the
1980s. MIDI changed film music in a fundamental way. Most symphonic scores are now
"pre-scored." The director and/or producer hears a MIDI mockup of each cue; once the
mockup is approved, the music is passed on to an orchestrator. "From MIDI to Live Orchestra" is a must-read for composers and filmmakers interested in traditional orchestral
music, particularly the section on what MIDI cannot do. The new scoring method may
serve to enrich the collaborative process and result in fewer surprises when the music is
recorded. However, there are drawbacks: the process allows for more meddling than in
the past, the orchestrator may be encouraged to replicate the MIDI mockup instead of
exercising his own creative skills, and music played back with samples and synthesizers
may be difficult to reproduce in a live orchestral setting (that is, the music may not sound
the same as the mockup to the director). Discusses the roles of key music prep personnel,
getting started, composing, orchestrating, conducting, recording, copying the music,
preparing for a career in film music, and business aspects and resources.

Kreuger, Miles, ed.
  *The Movie Musical from Vitaphone to "42nd Street," as Reported in a Great Fan
    Magazine*. New York: Dover, 1975. 367 pp. ill.
Anthology of selected articles and illustrations from *Photoplay* magazine, published
between 1926 and 1933. Arranged chronologically by month and year, with feature arti-

cles, publicity, reviews, cast lists, advertising, and more, covering feature and short-subject films and the people who made them, including songwriters. Film and name indexes. Editor is founder of the Institute of the American Musical.

Kreuger, Miles, ed.
> *The Warner Bros. Musical: (1933–1939)*. Palo Alto, Calif.: Stanford Theatre Foundation, 1990. 32 pp.

Pamphlet, with text from the author's as-yet-unpublished magnum opus, *The American Musical Film*.

Kurtti, Jeff.
> *The Great Movie Musical Trivia Book*. New York: Applause, 1996.

In question-and-answer format, with chapters on MGM musicals, from Broadway to Hollywood, fantasy musicals, Americana, and animation. Index. Author is a Walt Disney Imagineering employee.

Lack, Russell.
> *Twenty Four Frames Under: A Buried History of Film Music*. London: Quartet Books, 1997. 368 pp.

Refreshing survey of film music in various guises that delves beyond traditional Hollywood Golden Age scores. Essays on film music aesthetics are divided between the silent and sound eras. Silent-era topics include recorded sound systems, original scores, and presentation of the music. Sound-era topics include film music and narrative sensibility, resistance to sound, formation of film music convention, impact of recording technology, French New Wave and jazz, the rise of pop songs, pop culture and film music, experimental soundtracks, filming musical performance (musicals, opera. and music documentaries), film music and politics, film music and film time, emotional impact, impact of film theory, electronic film music, and Art House cinema and classical music. International in scope and touches on rarely examined topics such as music in Japanese cinema during the early sound era. Index. Author is a television and new media producer and scriptwriter.

Laing, Heather.
> *Gabriel Yared's* The English Patient*: A Film Score Guide*. Scarecrow Film Score Guides, no 1. Lanham, Md.: Scarecrow Press, 2004.

This interesting choice for Scarecrow's first film score guide examines the Academy Award-winning score from the 1996 film. Yared is a Lebanese-born composer who began his career on a number of French films. Chapters cover Yared's musical background, his technique of film scoring, themes and issues in the film, the narrative soundtrack, and the score. Filmography, bibliography, and index. Author is a freelance researcher and writer whose thesis was titled "Wandering Minds and Anchored Bodies: Music, Gender and Emotion in Melodrama and the Woman's Film."

Lang, Edith, and George West.
> *Musical Accompaniment of Moving Pictures: A Practical Manual for Pianists and Organists and an Exposition of the Principles Underlying the Musical Interpretation of Moving Pictures*. Boston: Boston Music; New York: G. Schirmer; London: Winthrop Rogers, 1920. Reprint, New York: Arno Press, 1970. 64 pp.

A performance manual in three parts. "Equipment" covers mental alertness; musical resourcefulness, including thematic development, transition and modulation, and improvisation; and repertoire. "Musical Interpretation" covers features, flashbacks, animation, slapstick comedies, comedy-dramas, weekly news, educationals, and travel views. "The Theatrical Organ" covers technique; "orchestration"; use of tone colors for descriptive purposes, including a two-page chart for specific emotions, moods, and situations; and special musical effects. The material on animation and slapstick comedies is reprinted in Daniel Goldmark and Yuval Taylor, *The Cartoon Music Book* (2002).

Lannin, Steve, and Matthew Caley, eds.
  Pop Fiction: The Song in Cinema. Foreword by Anahid Kassabian. Bristol, U.K.; Portland, Ore.: Intellect, 2005.
Anthology in which each essay examines the use of one song in two or three specific films released from 1965 to 2000. The editors are conversant in audio-visual design, graphic design, and graphic communications.
  "Introduction," by Steve Lannin and Matthew Caley, 9–14; "Garibaldi Fought Here," by Dave Beech, 15–27; "Heavy Rotation," by Matthew Caley, 29–39; "Two Jews Wander through the Southland," by Elizabeth C. Hirschman, 41–45; "The Ambi-Diegesis of 'My Funny Valentine,'" by Morris B. Holbrook, 47–62; "Music, Masculinity and Membership," by Ian Inglis, 63–69; "Fluid Figures: How to See *Ghost*[s]," by Steve Lannin, 71–84; "Reap Just What You Sow," by Miguel Mera, 85–97; "Blond Abjection: Spectatorship and the Abject Anal Space In-Between," by Phil Powrie, 99–119; "Always Blue: Chet Baker's Voice," by John Roberts, 121–27; "From Bond to Blank," by Jeff Smith on the use of "Live and Let Die" in *Grosse Pointe Blank*, 129–37; "Clean Reading: The Problematics of 'In the Air Tonight' in *Risky Business*," by Robynn J. Stilwell, 139–53; "Falling into Coma," by David Toop, 155–61.

Larson, Randall D., ed.
  Film Music Around the World. A CinemaScore special edition. Sunnyvale, Calif.: Fandom Unlimited Enterprises, 1987. Reprint, San Bernardino, Calif.: Borgo Press, 1987. 74 pp. ill.
Excerpted from *CinemaScore*, 1:15 (Winter 1986–Summer 1987). Interviews, often with filmographies.
  Powers, Philip. "Bruce Smeaton." 2–4. Interview with the Australian composer.
  Powers, Philip. "Bill Motzing." 5–6. Interview with the Australian composer.
  Powers, Philip. "Simon Walker." 7–8. Interview with the Australian composer.
  Werba, Marco. "Philippe Sarde." 9–10. Interview with the French composer.
  Werba, Marco. "Pierre Jansen." 11. Interview with the French composer.
  Werba, Marco. "Georges Delerue." 11. Interview with the French composer.
  Larson, Randall. "Jan Rychlik." 12. Profile of the Czech composer.
  Larson, Randall. "Lubos Fiser." 13. Interview with the Czech composer.
  Larson, Randall. "Zdenek Liska." 15–16. Profile of the Czech composer.
  Wolthuis, Julius. "Loek Dikker." 18–19. Interview with the Dutch composer.
  Panuccio, Alessandro. "Angelo Francesco Lavagnino." 20–21. Interview with the Italian composer.
  Werba, Marco. "Nicola Piovani." 22. Interview with the Italian composer.
  Carlin, Dan. "Francesco De Masi." 22. Interview with the Italian composer.
  Werba, Marco. "Stelvio Cipriani." 23. Interview with the Italian composer.

Werba, Marco. "Claudio Gizzi." 24. Interview with the Italian composer.
Douglas, Andrew. "Alessandro Cicognino." 25–26. Profile of the Italian composer.
Larson, Randall. "Trevor Jones." 28–32. Interview with the British composer.
Werba, Marco. "Stanley Myers." 32. Interview with the British composer.
Werba, Marco. "Richard Harvey." 33–34. Interview with the British composer.
Larson, Randall. "Masaru Sato." 35–36. Profile of the Japanese composer.
Douglas, Andrew. "Toru Takemitsu." 37–38. Profile of the Japanese composer.
Larson, Randall. "Akira Ifukube." 39–43. Profile of the Japanese composer.
Schuder, Ralf. "Klaus Doldinger." 45. Interview with the German composer.
Schuder, Ralf. "Hans-Martin Majewski." 46. Interview with the German composer.
Schuder, Ralf. "Rolf Wilhelm." 47. Interview with the German composer.
Schuder, Ralf. "Eugen Thomass." 47. Interview with the German composer.
Larson, Randall. "Film Music of India." 48–50.
Douglas, Andrew. "Soviet Film Music." 51.
Douglas, Andrew. "Theodorakis and Hadjidakis." 52. Profiles of Greek composers
    Mikis Theodorakis and Manos Hadjidakis.
Werba, Marco. "Anton Garcia Abril." 53–54. Interview with the Spanish composer.
Larson, Randall. "Other Spanish Film Composers." 54–56.
Douglas, Andrew. "Film Music Traditions In Brazil." 57.
Douglas, Andrew. "John Neschling." 57. Profile of the Brazilian composer.
Hershon, Robert. "Modern Film Music in Brazil and Argentina." 58. Report.
Lerena, A. "Traditions in Argentine Film Music." 59–60.
Douglas, Andrew. "Chilean Film Music." 61.
Larson, Randall. "Erik Nordgren." 61–62. Profile of the Swedish composer.
Larson, Randall. "Erland Von Koch." 63. Profile of the Swedish composer.
Larson, Randall. "Christopher Komeda." 63. Profile of the Polish composer.
Douglas, Andrew. "Jack Trommer." 63. Profile of the Swiss composer.
Adamson, Colin. "The New Zealand Film Music Scene." 64–65.
Douglas, Andrew. "Films and Film Music in China." 66.
Simak, Steven. "Bill Conti." 67–70. Interview.
Hershon, Robert, and David Kraft. "Mark Isham." 71–74. Interview.

Larson, Randall D.
    Musique Fantastique: A Survey of Film Music in the Fantastic Cinema. Metuchen,
    N.J.: Scarecrow Press, 1985. 592 pp. ill.
Exhaustive historical and analytical survey of music written for science fiction, fantasy,
and horror films. Topics covered include Universal horror films; Japanese, European, and
British (including Hammer) genre films; Roger Corman films; television; electronics; and
the use of classical music. Individual chapters on music by Les Baxter, Bernard
Herrmann, Miklós Rózsa, and John Williams, although any composer who wrote genre
music is likely mentioned in the book. Based on interviews and extensive research, including interpolated material from periodicals devoted to film music and the fantastic
cinema. Covers the 1930s to 1980s, with a chronology of landmark films. An extensive
filmography lists international composers alphabetically. Discography and index. Originally self-published by the author as *A Survey of Film Music in the Fantastic Cinema* in
1980 and available by mail order through Larson's Fandom Unlimited Enterprises. A
1983 expanded version was advertised in *CinemaScore* (no. 10). Author, a fire department supervisor in California, published *CinemaScore* in the 1980s and has written extensively about film music.

Larson, Randall D.
   Music from the House of Hammer: Music in the Hammer Horror Films, 1950–1980.
   Lanham, Md.: Scarecrow Press, 1996. 193 pp.
History and analysis of music written for Hammer Film Productions, with an introduction
by James Bernard and afterword by Harry Robertson. Composers and music directors
include Malcolm Arnold, Edwin T. Astley, Don Banks, Richard Rodney Bennett, James
Bernard, Stanley Black, John Cacavas, Tristram Cary, Marcus Dodds, Don Ellis, Benja-
min Frankel, Paul Glass, Christopher Gunning, John Hollingsworth, Laurie Johnson,
Wilfred Josephs, Elisabeth Lutyens, John McCabe, Philip Martell, Carlo Martelli, Mario
Nascimbene, Monty Norman and David Heneker, Clifton Parker, Franz Reizenstein,
Harry Robinson (Harry Robertson), Leonard Salzedo, Gerard Schurmann, Humphrey
Searle, Roland Shaw, Ivor Slaney, Michael Vickers, David Whitaker, and Malcolm Wil-
liamson. Nonhorror notable composers include Douglas Gamley, Richard Hartley, Alun
Hoddinott, and Gary Hughes. Based on extensive research and some 20 interviews. Fil-
mography, music credits by title, discography, bibliographical references, index.

Lazarou, George A.
   Max Steiner and Film Music: An Essay. Athens, Greece: Max Steiner Music Society,
   1971. 40 pp.
Steiner's life and background, awards, contribution to the art of film music, and critical
views of his film music. Selected bibliography. The author, a longtime resident and
community leader in Greece, is apparently a Steiner fan.

Leinberger, Charles.
   Ennio Morricone's The Good, the Bad and the Ugly: *A Film Score Guide.* Scarecrow
   Film Score Guides, no. 3. Lanham, Md.: Scarecrow Press, 2004. 137 pp. ill.
Morricone's musical background, his technique of film scoring, the historical and critical
context of the 1966 film, the music and its context, and analysis of the score. Bibliogra-
phy, filmography, and index. Author is a professor of music.

Lewis, Edgar J.
   *The Archive Collections of Film Music at the University of Wyoming: A Descriptive
   Guide for Scholars: A Summary Report of an Inspection and Evaluation of Specific
   Collections of Film Music in the Custody of the Division of Rare Books and Special
   Collections, Coe Library, the University of Wyoming.* Laramie, Wyo.: E. J. Lewis,
   1976. 42 leaves.
Information on film music collected by the university during the 1960s and early 1970s.

Limbacher, James L., comp. and ed.
   Film Music: From Violins to Video. Metuchen, N.J.: Scarecrow Press, 1974. 835 pp.
Reprinted articles from *Film Music Notes* (also known as *Film Music* and *Film/TV Music*,
depending on the year), sans the original music examples. Notable for the number of
essays by composers writing about their own music. Part 1 focuses on the early days,
theories and comments, techniques, scoring the dramatic film, the film spectacle, classical music on the screen, and animated films and comedy. Part 2 lists films and their composers, composers and their films, and recorded musical scores (discography).
Bibliography. Index to Part 1. Author is a library audio-visual director.
   "How It All Began," by James L. Limbacher, 13–14; "The Origin of Film Music,"
   by Max Winkler, 15–24; "Don't Shoot the Piano Player," by Jack Shaindlin, 25–28;

"The Art of Composing Music Scores for Films," by Loren G. Buchanan, 29–31; "Is There Any Music at the Movies?" by Paul Kresh, 32–41; "Jazz at the Movies," by Martin Williams, 42–44; "Film Music Comes of Age," by Gordon Hendricks, 45–50; "Facing the Music: Why Movie Scores Are Usually So Awful," by William Wolf, 51–54; "Composing for Films," by Dimitri Tiomkin, 55–60; "The Structure of Film Music," by Jeffrey Embler, 61–65; "Documentary Music," by Louis Applebaum, 66–71; "The Music Mixer," by John Huntley, 72–75; "*The African Queen*," by John Huntley, 76; "*The Bad and the Beautiful*," by William Hamilton, 77–80; "*The Best Years of Our Lives*," by Louis Applebaum, 81; "*Carrie*," by David Raksin, 82–84; "*Champion* and *Home of the Brave*," by William Hamilton, 85; "*East of Eden*," by Leonard Rosenman, 86–87; "*Edge of Doom*," by William Hamilton, 88; "*From Here to Eternity*," by George Duning, 89–90; "*High Noon*," by William Hamilton, 91–92; "*Jeanne Eagels*," by George Duning, 93; "*The Man with the Golden Arm*," by Elmer Bernstein, 94–95; "*The Mudlark*," by John Huntley, 96; "*No Sad Songs for Me*," by George Duning, 97–98; "*Oliver Twist*," by John Huntley, 99–102; "*On the Waterfront*," by William Hamilton, 103–4; "*The Sword and the Rose*," by Clifton Parker, 105; "*The Thief*," by Herschel Burke Gilbert, 106–8; "*The Third Man*," by William Hamilton, 109–10; "*3:10 to Yuma*," by George Duning, 111; "*Treasure Island*," by John Huntley, 112–13; "*What's the Matter with Helen?*" by Page Cook, 114–19; "*The Wild One*," by Leith Stevens, 120–22; "*Christopher Columbus*," by Sir Arthur Bliss, 123; "*Cinerama Holiday*," by Jack Shaindlin, 124; "Music for Historical Films," by Miklós Rózsa, 125–27; "Music for Shakespearean Films," by Sir William Walton, 128–30; "A Note on *Hamlet*," by Muir Mathieson, 131; "*Julius Caesar*," by Miklós Rózsa, 132–35; "*Raintree County*," by John Green, 136–44; "*Salome*," by George Duning, 145–46; "*Quo Vadis*," by Miklós Rózsa, 147–53; "*The Ten Commandments*," by Elmer Bernstein, 154–57; "Classical Composers on the Screen," by James L. Limbacher, 158; "P R K F V," by Sergei Eisenstein, 159–63; "A Time for Bach," by Gene Forrell, 164–65; "Shadow Opera," by Francis Rizzo, 166–72; "New Film Music for New Films," by Mary Ellen Bute, 173–75; "The Ku-Ku Song Man!" by Jim Shadduck on Marvin Hatley, 176–81; "The Movie Cartoon Is Coming of Age," by Otis L. Guernsey Jr., 182; "Notes on Cartoon Music," by Ingolf Dahl, 183–89.

Limbacher, James.
   Keeping Score: Film Music 1972–1979. Metuchen, N.J.: Scarecrow Press, 1981. 510 pp.
Continues and supersedes the author's *Film Music: From Violins to Video* (see previous entry). Contains an alphabetical list of film titles by year of release, a chronological list of films and their composers from 1908 to 1979, and an alphabetical list of composers and their films. Discography is an alphabetical list by title of recorded film and television scores and anthologies. Film composer necrology and bibliography. Introduction has information on the "White House Record Commission," a soundtrack collection for the president of the United States.

Limbacher, James, comp.
   A Selected List of Recorded Musical Scores from Radio, Television, and Motion Pictures. Pamphlet. Dearborn, Mich.: Dearborn Public Library, ca. 1961. 21 pp. 2nd ed., 1962. 31 pp. Supplement to the 2nd ed., 1963. 9 pp. 3rd ed., date and pagination unknown. 4th ed., 1967. 48 pp.

Full scores, suites, and themes from feature films, listed by film title. Also contains listings for music from short subjects, as well as scores, suites, and themes from radio and television. Each entry includes title, studio, release year, composer, and record label and number. Second edition lists film music on 45 rpm and 78 rpm. Composer index. The Dearborn Public Library, where the author is audio-visual director, does not list the first or third editions in its online catalog. Some researchers, including film music accreditation expert Clifford McCarty, have taken issue with inaccuracies in this work due to the author's over reliance on secondary sources.

Limbacher, James, and H. Stephen Wright.
  Keeping Score: Film and Television Music, 1980–1988, with Additional Coverage of 1921–1979. Metuchen, N.J.: Scarecrow Press, 1991. 916 pp.
Lists films and their composers, followed by composers and their films, in the same format as Limbacher's previous books (see above). Film guides, almanacs, and record catalogs are among the authors' sources. Wright's "Recorded Musical Scores: A Discography" (pp. 664–762) lists soundtracks issued on LP or CD in the United States from 1980 through 1987. Film title index.

London, Kurt [Ludwig].
  Film Music: A Summary of the Characteristic Features of Its History, Aesthetics, Technique; and Possible Developments. Translated by Eric S. Bensinger. London: Faber & Faber, 1936. 280 pp. ill. Reprint, New York: Arno Press, 1970.
This history covers the origins of film music, music with the silent film, and the sound film. Topics include gramophone records as accompaniment; technical developments, including sound-on-disc and sound-on-film; synchronization; the theme song craze; orchestration problems for sound films; the microphone orchestra; the problems of acoustics in recording and reproduction; prominent European film composers from Great Britain, Germany, France, Italy, and Soviet Russia and their artistic significance; training the next generation; and the future of the sound film. Photographs, musical excerpts, and index. A Paris publisher originally commissioned this book but went bankrupt before the author delivered the manuscript. The author then sent the text to Moscow, where it was translated into Russian and published in 1937. After the Faber English-language edition was published in 1936, the author was invited to Russia to lecture on film music. This led to his next book, *The Seven Soviet Arts*, which covers music and film but not film music. The author, who holds doctorates in law and music from German universities, later taught in New York, served in the U.S. State Department, headed a university program in Sino-Soviet studies, and was widely published in the field of Russian/Soviet world politics.

Lone Eagle Publishing, comp. and ed.
  Film Composers Directory. 5th ed. Los Angeles: Lone Eagle Publishing, 2000. 406 pp.
Follows the format and criteria of Steven Smith's first edition, with credits updated through 1999. More than 2,500 composers and 25,000 titles. Contacts for agents and managers, music publishers, film studios, master use licensing, soundtrack labels, music clearance, and music supervisors (with some credits). See also previous editions published as *Film Composers Guide* by Smith, Francillon, and Jacquet-Francillon.

Lustig, Milton.
  Music Editing for Motion Pictures. New York: Hastings House, 1980. 182 pp.

A career music editor discusses job responsibilities and takes readers through the process from spotting to tracking. Technical topics include timing, synchronization, and click tracks. Glossary and index.

Luz, Ernst.
   Motion Picture Synchrony: For Motion Picture Exhibitors, Buyers and Orchestras. New York: Music Buyers' Corp., 1925. 64 pp.
In this monograph, a music director explains his system for selecting music to accompany films. A theater's sheet music is color coded according to a corresponding mood, allowing appropriate music to be selected quickly for a specified film by referring to a chart of the desired moods.

Lynch, Dennis.
   Recorded Music for the Animated Cartoon. Cedar Rapids, Iowa: Available from the author, 1983. 101 pp.
Lynch's self-published book covers records originating in the United States, Japan, and Europe, including Disney records. Composer and title index.

Lynch, Richard Chigley.
   Movie Musicals on Record: A Directory of Recordings of Motion Picture Musicals, 1927–1987. New York: Greenwood Press, 1989. 445 pp.
Discography of 666 commercial albums for motion picture musicals, arranged alphabetically by film title and including 6,500 song titles. Performer and composer-lyricist indexes and filmography. Companion volume to the author's *Broadway on Record* (1987).

Lynch, Richard Chigley, comp.
   TV and Studio Cast Musicals on Record: A Discography of Television Musicals and Studio Recordings of Stage and Film Musicals. New York: Greenwood Press, 1990. 330 pp.
A listing of commercially recorded television musicals in the same vein as the author's three previous discographies. Descriptive headings for "Film Score," "Television Production," and "Television Special." Introduction, discography, television chronology, movie musical chronology, and performer index.

MacDonald, Laurence E.
   The Invisible Art of Film Music: A Comprehensive History. New York: Ardsley House, 1998. 431 pp. ill.
A chronological historical survey by a music history professor, based on his research, radio program, and interviews with composers. Topics include music and the birth of film, the evolution of synchronized sound, the dawn of the golden age, World War II and its aftermath, the decline of the studio system, the changing of the guard, the revival of the symphonic film score, the influence of synthesized sound, and into the 1990s. More than 30 biographical sketches. Bibliography, filmography, and index.

Mancini, Henry.
   Case History of a Film Score: The Thorn Birds. Edited by Roy Phillippe. Miami: Northridge Music /Warner Bros. Publications, 2004.
Published ten years after Mancini's death, this work focuses on his music for the 1983 television miniseries and was culled from a mid-1980s unpublished manuscript. Mancini's

colleague, music arranger Roy Phillippe, completed the manuscript and prepared it for publication. Part 1 covers preproduction and traces the genesis of the music from original thematic material, music spotting, instrumentation, and dubbing. Part 2 focuses on the music itself. Music was selected from each of the miniseries' four installments and includes 16 music cues with corresponding music timing sheets (five were re-created for this book) and Mancini's commentary. The latter are paragraph-long synopses of the dramatic action with brief analytical remarks interspersed. Mancini's short score sketches were typeset and checked by Phillippe against the music as heard in the film. A few of Mancini's handwritten sketch pages are reproduced.

Mancini, Henry.
> *Sounds and Scores: A Practical Guide to Professional Orchestration.* Los Angeles: Northridge Music, 1962. 245 pp.

The Oscar-winning composer's guide to orchestrating and arranging commercial music, with typeset musical sketches from *Peter Gunn* and *Mr. Lucky.* Features recorded musical examples performed by Mancini ensembles on three seven-inch discs. Later editions featured the musical examples on one cassette (1973) and on one compact disc (1986).

Mansfield, John.
> *Music and Sound Effects: Sound for Television.* Borehamwood, Hertfordshire, U.K.: BBC Television Training, 1992. 36 pp.

Pamphlet on recording sound for television.

Manvell, Roger, and John Huntley.
> *The Technique of Film Music.* London: Focal Press, 1957. 299 pp. ill. Reprinted in 1967 and 1969. Reprint, New York: Hastings House, 1971. Rev. ed. by Richard Arnell and Peter Day, New York: Focal Press, 1975. 310 pp. ill.

Compiled under the guidance of a committee appointed by the British Film Academy that included William Alwyn, Ken Cameron, Muir Mathieson, and Basil Wright. Chapters on music and the silent film, music in the early sound film, and the function of music in the sound film. Dramatic, animated, documentary, and musical films are covered. Functional music for action, scenic, period, drama, and comedy is analyzed and the emotional aspect of music discussed. Chapter on the music director and sound recordist. Analyses of single cues—from William Walton's *Henry V*, Virgil Thomson's *Louisiana Story*, Miklós Rózsa's *Julius Caesar*, and William Alwyn's *Odd Man Out*—with two or three-stave sketches aligned with a shot breakdown of action and frame enlargements. Excerpts of interviews with John Addison, William Alwyn, Arthur Bliss, Hugo Friedhofer, Elisabeth Lutyens, David Raksin, Miklós Rózsa, and Roman Vlad. An outline of the history of film music from 1895 to 1972 lists principal events and prominent film scores. Critical essays on film music include "A Consideration of Film Music Away from the Screen," by Gerald Pratley, and "Film Music: Speech Rhythm," by Hans Keller, the latter reprinted from *Musical Times* (September 1955). Selected bibliography, musical excerpts, and index. The 1975 revised edition, by a composer and filmmaker, respectively, adds analyses of four films since 1955: *The Devils* (Peter Maxwell Davies), *2001: A Space Odyssey* (classical music), *Second Best* (Richard Arnell), and *Zabriskie Point* (rock music).

Marill, Alvin H.
> *Keeping Score: Film and Television Music, 1988–1997.* Lanham, Md.: Scarecrow Press, 1998. 358 pp.

Continues the series begun by Limbacher, *Keeping Score: Film Music 1972–1979* (1981). Entries primarily cover English-language theatrical and direct-to-video features and made-for-television movies and miniseries. Includes a small number of foreign listings by composers of international status. Listings include films and their composers (by year), composers and their films, soundtracks, and awards. Film title index. Author has written numerous books on film and television.

Marks, Martin Miller.
>   *Music and the Silent Film: Contexts and Case Studies, 1895–1924.* New York: Oxford Univ. Press, 1997. 303 pp. ill.

Opens with an introduction to film music research, including a survey of the literature to 1990. Topics include the origins of film music, compilation and original scores, early American film scores from 1910 through 1914 (listed chronologically in Part 3 of the appendix), music for Kalem films, pioneers of orchestral scores from 1912 through 1914, Camille Saint-Saëns's score for *L'Assassinat du Duc de Guise*, Walter Cleveland Simon's score for *An Arabian Tragedy*, history and analysis of Joseph Carl Breil's score for *The Birth of a Nation*, and Erik Satie's score for *Entr'acte*. Based on primary source materials and publications such as *Moving Picture World*. An extensive revision of the author's 1990 Harvard dissertation, "Film Music of the Silent Period, 1895–1924." Index. Author is a professor of music and a leading authority on music of the silent era, and occasionally provides piano accompaniment to screenings of silent films.

Marmorstein, Gary.
>   *Hollywood Rhapsody: Movie Music and Its Makers, 1900 to 1975.* New York: Schirmer Books; London: Prentice Hall, 1997. 456 pp. ill.

A history of American movie music, written by a Hollywood writer and music buff. Topics include film music before the soundtrack; the invasion of the songwriters; the émigré composers; the careers of Elmer Bernstein, Aaron Copland, Ernest Gold, Bernard Herrmann, Jerome Moross, and Alex North; Fred Astaire and the great songwriters; Columbia, MGM (the Freed unit), Paramount, 20th Century-Fox (Alfred Newman), and Universal (Henry Mancini) studios; the Screen Composers Association and HUAC; westerns; jazz; animation; movie songs; and rock soundtracks. Bibliography and index.

McCarty, Clifford, comp. and ed.
>   *Film Composers in America: A Checklist of Their Work.* Glendale, Calif.: privately printed, 1953. 193 pp. Reprinted as *Film Composers in America: A Checklist of Their Work*, with minor additions and corrections. Foreword by Lawrence Morton. New York: Da Capo Press, 1972. 193 pp.

Contains 163 composer entries, with film scores listed chronologically. The author, a film music accreditation expert, spent the rest of his life turning this checklist into a filmography covering six decades (see below).

McCarty, Clifford, comp. and ed.
>   *Film Composers in America: A Filmography 1911–1970.* 2nd ed. Oxford: Oxford Univ. Press, 2000. 534 pp.

Meticulously researched over 45 years, this book documents the work of more than 1,500 composers, from Robert Armbruster to Josiah Zuro. Extensive research at the seven largest film studios, supplemented by the author's correspondence and interviews with composers, makes this the most reliable and comprehensive work of its kind. Includes features, shorts, independent films, animated films, and documentaries. Supplementary list of screen-credited names who are not composers. Index of 20,000 film titles. The author was a pioneer and leading practitioner in the field of film music accreditation. He sought to document composers' contributions to films based on primary source material, including cue sheets, instead of relying solely on screen credits. Lawrence Morton took an interest early on and helped the author gain access to studio records and composers.

McCarty, Clifford, ed.
> *Film Music 1*. New York: Garland Publishing, 1989. 285 pp. ill. Reprint, Hollywood: Film Music Society, 1998.

"Introduction: The Literature of Film Music," by Clifford McCarty; "The Materials of Film Music: Their Nature and Accessibility," by H. Stephen Wright; "'Tumult, Battle and Blaze': Looking Back on the 1920s—and Since—with Gaylord Carter, the Dean of Theater Organists," by Rudy Behlmer; "Performing with Silent Films," by Dennis James; "What Were Musicians Saying about Movie Music during the First Decade of Sound? A Symposium of Selected Writings," by Fred Steiner; "Stravinsky and MGM," by William H. Rosar; "Max Steiner and the Classical Hollywood Film Score: An Analysis of *The Informer*," by Kathryn Kalinak; "The Music of *Flash Gordon* and *Buck Rogers*," by Richard H. Bush; "Holding a Nineteenth Century Pedal at Twentieth Century-Fox," by David Raksin; "Miklós Rózsa's *Ben-Hur*: The Musical-Dramatic Function of the Hollywood Leitmotif," by Steven D. Wescott; "A Conversation with Bernard Herrmann," by Leslie T. Zador and Gregory Rose (a 1970 interview for the Los Angeles *Free Press*); "The Film Composer in Concert and the Concert Composer in Film," by Eddy Lawrence Manson. Index.

McGehee, Michael.
> *Click Trak Book*. N.p.: Author, 1989.

A musician supplies some 184 click-track tables organized in musical measures. (Most click books are organized by musical beats per minute or by film frames per second.)

McGill, Maude Stolley.
> *Ten Lesson Course in Moving Picture Piano Playing*. Portland, Ore.: Stolley-McGill Publishing, 1916.

Topics include general advice; repertory; playing drama, comedy, military, scenic, tragedy; weeklies; classical music; and more. Reprinted as a column in *Melody* in 1922.

McNally, Keith, and Dorie McNally.
> *McNally's Price Guide for Collectible Soundtrack Records (1950–1990)*. Newhall, Calif.: West Point Records, 1994. 239 pp. ill.

This rare softcover book of LP listings was published at the dawn of the CD age. Included are domestic and foreign commercial releases, special issues, alternate formats (ten- and seven-inch LPs), and television soundtracks. Black exploitation albums are particularly well represented. More than 700 photographs help document the album covers. An introductory essay is complemented by material on collecting foreign records by Wolfgang Jahn. The compilers owned a now-defunct mail-order soundtrack dealership. Some collectors took issue with the book's numerous errors and dealer-centric attitude toward value (affecting which LPs were included).

McVay, Douglas.
> *The Musical Film.* London: A. Zwemmer; New York: A. S. Barnes, 1967. 175 pp.
Chronological survey of musicals seen by the author. Selected bibliography and film title index.

Marshall, Bill, and Robynn Stilwell, eds.
> *Musicals: Hollywood and Beyond.* Exeter, U.K.; Portland, Ore.: Intellect, 2000. 187 pp. ill.
Anthology with an introduction by the editors.
> Music and Structure
> "Emotion by Numbers: Music, Song and the Musical," by Heather Laing; "I've Heard that Song Before: Woody Allen's Films as Studies in Popular Musical Form," by Ken Garner.
> Classical Hollywood Musical Cinematic Practice
> "The Colour of Entertainment," by Richard Dyer; "Jumping on the Band Wagon Again: Oedipus Backstage in the Father and Mother of All Musicals," by Bruce Babington; "'I Keep Wishing I Were Somewhere Else': Space and Fantasies of Freedom in the Hollywood Musical," by Kenneth MacKinnon.
> Star Texts
> "Merry Melodies: The Marx Brothers' Musical Moments," by Ian Conrich; "How Do You Solve a 'Problem' Like Maria van Poppins?" by Peter Kemp; "'A Cutie with More than Beauty': Audrey Hepburn, the Hollywood Musical and *Funny Face*," by Peter Krämer.
> European Musical Forms
> "Queering the Folklore: Genre and the Re-presentation of Homosexuality and National Identities in *Las Cosas del Querer*," by José Arroyo; "Between Nostalgia and Amnesia: Musical Genres in 1950s German Cinema," by Tim Bergfelder; "*Der Kongress Tanzt:* UFA's Blockbuster *Filmoperette* for the World Market," by Horst Claus and Anne Jäckel; "Time, History and Memory in *Les Parapluies de Cherbourg*," by Sylvie Lindeperg and Bill Marshall; "Harnessing Visibility: The Attractions of Chantal Akerman's *Golden Eighties*," by Cathy Fowler; "More than a Pale Imitation: Narrative, Music and Dance in Two Greek Film Musicals of the 1960's," by Lydia Papadimitriou.
> Minority Identities
> "Hardly *Chazans*: *Yentl* and the Singing Jew," by Michele Aaron; "Beach Bound: Exotica, Leisure Style and Popular Culture in Post-war America from *South Pacific* to *Beach Blanket Bingo*," by Bill Osgerby; "*Zero Patience:* AIDS, Music and Reincarnation Films," by Monica Pearl; "From the Vulgar to the Refined: American Vernacular and Blackface Minstrelsy in *Showboat*," by Peter Stanfield; "Memory, Magic and the Musical in Derek Jarman's *The Tempest* and *Edward II*," by Maggie Taylor.
> Youth Cultures
> "'Let's Film the Sound of the Underground?' The Uses of Hip Hop and Reggae in Recent French Films," by Steve Cannon; "Entertainment and Dystopia: The Punk Anti-Musical," by K. J. Donnelly.

Meeker, David.
> *Jazz in the Movies: A Guide to Jazz Musicians 1917–1977.* London: Talisman Books; New Rochelle, N.Y.: Arlington House, 1977. 286 pp. ill.

Compiled primarily from published sources, including periodicals and music reference works. Includes 2,239 entries for films in which jazz musicians either appear on screen or contribute to the soundtrack. Arranged by film title, each entry includes a brief description. Index. Expanded from the author's 89-page illustrated booklet, *Jazz in the Movies: A Tentative Index to the Work of Jazz Musicians for the Cinema* (London: British Film Institute, 1972). Author is associated with the British Film Institute.

Meeker, David.
> *Jazz in the Movies*. New York: Da Capo Press; London: Talisman Books, 1981. Reprint. New York: Da Capo Press, 1982. 336 pp. ill.

Revised edition (see previous entry) updated to 3,724 entries, now including films originally produced for television. Index of jazz musicians.

Meyers, Randall.
> *Film Music: Fundamentals of the Language*. Oslo: Ad-Notam: Gyldendal (ÇAd-Notam Guldendahlë), 1994. 231 pp.

Includes interviews with Toru Takemitsu and Nicola Piovani. Bibliography. Author is an American-born composer residing in Europe.

Mordden, Ethan.
> *The Hollywood Musical*. New York: St. Martin's Press, 1981. 261 pp. ill.

A history written by a professor, historian, writer, and fan of musicals. Topics include defining the musical; early musicals; genres, including dance, comedy, fantasy, and rock; wartime; Americana; and economics. Discography and bibliography.

Morgan, David.
> *Knowing the Score: Film Composers Talk about the Art, Craft, Blood, Sweat, and Tears of Writing for Cinema*. New York: HarperEntertainment, 2000. 313 pp. ill.

A film writer interviews Elmer Bernstein, Carter Burwell, Elia Cmiral, John Corigliano, Mychael Danna, Patrick Doyle, Philip Glass, Elliot Goldenthal, Jerry Goldsmith, Mark Isham, Michael Kamen, Alan Menken, Basil Poledouris, Jocelyn Pook, David Raksin, David Shire, and record producer Robert Townson. Presented in the form of a virtual forum on writing, collaboration, period pieces, orchestration, adaptation, and recording. Interviews conducted in the late 1990s, with the exception of Bernstein (1991) and Goldsmith (1986–1987).

Muir, John Kenneth.
> *Singing a New Tune: The Rebirth of the Modern Film Musical, from* Evita *to* De-Lovely *and Beyond*. New York: Applause Theatre & Cinema Books, 2005.

Focuses on the film musical from 1996 to 2004. Includes material from interviews with directors such as Todd Haynes and Joss Whedon and arranger Dick Hyman (pp. 114–17). Chapters cover the history of the movie musical through the 1980s; the early 1990s; *Evita* to *Moulin Rouge*; *Hedwig and the Angry Inch* to *De-Lovely* and beyond; and the musical on television.

Mundy, John.
> *Popular Music on Screen: From the Hollywood Musical to Music Video*. Manchester, U.K.: Manchester Univ. Press, 1999. 272 pp.

Chapters on the early developments in the relationship between recorded sound and the screen, technological developments in early cinema, musicals of the 1930s to mid-1950s, rock 'n' roll and the youth market, British contributions from the 1930s to 1960s, and popular music and television. Bibliography, selected filmography, and index. Author is a professor of popular music and moving image culture.

Murray, R. Michael.
   The Golden Age of Walt Disney Records 1933–1988. Dubuque, Iowa: Antique Trader Books, 1997. 246 pp. ill.
Discography and price guide for Disney record collectors. Brief introductory essay on the history of recorded Disney music. Lists more than 3,200 disc recordings in formats including LPs, EPs, 45s, and 78s. Filmography of music composers for Disney films. More than 200 color photographs of album covers. Index. Author is a collector and former *Film Score Monthly* columnist.

Nasta, Dominique.
   Meaning in Film: Relevant Structures in Soundtrack and Narrative. Bern, Switzerland; New York: Lang, 1991. 179 pp.
This theoretical treatise on music and sound is a revision of the author's dissertation. Includes a discussion of filmic narrative and expositive, synthetic, and contrastive songs.

Nicholson, Dennis Way, comp.
   Australian Soundtrack Recordings 1927–1996: A Select Discography of Soundtracks and Associated Recordings Relating to Australian Film and Television Productions. The Rocks, Australia: privately printed, 1997. 287 pp. Sydney: Australian Music Centre, 1997. 288 pp.
Lists films alphabetically by title, with soundtrack label, catalog number, and release year.

Northam, Mark, and Lisa Anne Miller.
   Film and Television Composer's Resource Guide: The Complete Guide to Organizing and Building Your Business. Los Angeles: CinemaTrax, 1997. 197 pp. Milwaukee: Hal Leonard, 1998. 199 pp. ill.
Discusses marketing materials; operating a business; finances, contracts, and agreements; and other composer resources. Ready-to-use forms and documents. Topics include resumes, demo tapes, scheduling, cue sheets, budgets, contract terminology, film music terms, and rates. Compiled by the husband-and-wife composing team behind the Film Music Network and *Film Music* magazine.

Osborne, Jerry, and Judith M. Ihnken Ebner, eds.
   The Official Price Guide to Movie/TV Soundtracks and Original Cast Albums. 2nd ed. New York: House of Collectibles, 1997. 860 pp. ill.
Revised edition (see previous entry). More than 11,000 entries for 5,200 films and shows.

Osborne, Jerry, and Bruce Hamilton.
   Movie/TV Soundtracks & Original Cast Albums Price Guide. Phoenix, Ariz.: O'Sullivan Woodside, 1981. 177 pp. ill.
Title above taken from title page; cover reads "Osborne & Hamilton's / Original Record Collectors Price Guide / First edition / Soundtracks & Original Cast." Osborne (a collector)

and Hamilton's (a business manager) first foray into the field of film and television music after producing several pop and rock price guides. Introduction, condition-grading tips, alphabetical listings, composer and conductor index, and dealer's directory. Approximately 4,000 entries listed alphabetically by title, with label, record number, issue year, and price for good and near-mint condition.

Osborne, Jerry, and Ruth Maupin, eds.
   The Official Price Guide to Movie/TV Soundtracks and Original Cast Albums. New York: House of Collectibles, 1991. 663 pp. ill.
Approximately 8,000 entries listed by film or show title. Includes label, record number, issue year, and price. Index includes composers and conductors. Osborne, a collector, incorporated information and material from dealers and collectors worldwide.

Palmer, Christopher.
   The Composer in Hollywood. London: Marion Boyars Publishers, 1990. 346 pp. ill.
The orchestrator and writer draws on his own research, interviews, and musical analysis in discussing Hollywood film music from the 1930s to 1950s through the lives and work of 11 composers: Elmer Bernstein, Bernard Herrmann, Erich Wolfgang Korngold, Alfred Newman, Alex North, Leonard Rosenman, Miklós Rózsa, Max Steiner, Dimitri Tiomkin, Franz Waxman, and Roy Webb. Palmer personally knew and worked with Bernstein, Rózsa, and Tiomkin and was a leading expert on Webb and his music. Throughout the 1970s he wrote extensively about this group of composers in *Film Music Notebook, Crescendo International, Monthly Film Bulletin,* and *Performing Right.* Photographs and musical sketches accompany most of the profiles.

Parish, James Robert, and Michael R. Pitts.
   The Great Hollywood Musical Pictures. Metuchen, N.J.: Scarecrow Press, 1992. 806 pp. ill.
Covers some 350 films, most entries several pages in length. Includes a chronology.

Pattillo, Craig W.
   TV Theme Soundtrack Directory and Discography with Cover Versions. Portland, Ore.: Braemar Books, 1990. 279 pp.
A collector draws on his personal holdings of disc recordings (primarily 45 rpm singles), supplemented by his correspondence with composers, performers, production companies, and television networks. Arranged alphabetically by series title, entries include the composer and/or recording artist of the original television track (regardless of whether the recording was released commercially) as well as cover versions. An alphabetical list of performers follows with record label and number. Other lists include top themes and hits, most recorded themes and artists, and album recordings. Concludes with an alphabetical list of song/theme titles and corresponding series title. Organization is somewhat convoluted and abbreviation-heavy; however, the information is worth the effort.

Pérez Pérez, Miguel Ángel.
   Hollywood Film Music: Cramping the Composer's Style. Alicante, Spain: Departamento de Filología Inglesa, Universidad de Alicante, 2004. 149 pp.
A historical and theoretical monograph including sections on "Silent and Sound Films and the Need for Music," 35–73; "Basic Patterns and Functions of Film Music," 75–116; and "The Evolution of the Language of Film Music in the Golden Age," 119–42.

Prendergast, Roy M.
> *Film Music: A Neglected Art: A Critical Study of Music in Films.* New York: Norton, 1977. 268 pp. ill. First published as *A Neglected Art: A Critical Study of Music in Films.* New York: New York Univ. Press, 1977. 268 pp. ill. 2nd ed., with a foreword by William Kraft, New York: Norton, 1992. 329 pp. ill.

An overview of the history, aesthetics, and techniques of film music. Chapters on music in the silent film; early sound film; 1935–1950; after 1950; cartoons and the experimental animated film; aesthetics; form; synchronization; and dubbing. Examines specific scores by Elmer Bernstein, Leonard Bernstein, Scott Bradley, Aaron Copland, Hugo Friedhofer, Jerry Goldsmith, Bernard Herrmann, Edmund Meisel, Sergei Prokofiev, David Raksin, Miklós Rózsa, and Max Steiner. Author interviews Raksin and Rózsa. Musical examples, bibliography, and index. Author is a music editor and friend of David Raksin.

Preston, Mike, comp.
> *Tele-Tunes: The Book of TV and Film Music: Television and Film Music on Record.* Kidderminster, U.K.: Record Information Centre, 1979.

A seminal work that serves as a reference book of music for films, television programs, and television commercials. Numerous editions followed, some under variant titles, such as *Tele-Tunes: Television and Film Music on Compact Disc, Record and Cassette.* Each edition is basically an annual update compiled and edited by Preston and published by Mike Preston Music since at least 1985.

Preston, Mike, comp.
> *Tele-Tunes 2: The Second Book of TV and Film Music.* First published in Great Britain in April 1979. 2nd ed., Kidderminster, U.K.: Record Information Centre, November 1979. 152 pp. ill. Other selected editions: 1985, 160 pp. 1989, 232 pp. 1990, 264 pp. 1998 (16th ed.), 352 pp. 2003 (last edition to date).

More than 3,000 entries for U.K. productions. Section 1 lists television themes alphabetically by program title, with network (BBC/ITV), title of theme music, composer, recording artist, record label, and record catalog number. Section 2 lists commercial (advertising) themes on record. Section 3 lists film soundtracks alphabetically by title, with composer or artist, record label, and record catalog number. Section 4 lists television and film music awards for 1978–79. Also lists compilation albums and themes that charted in the United Kingdom. After the April 1979 edition the "2" was dropped from the title; the year of the edition was later added (e.g., *Tele-Tunes 1990*), but it is unclear when.

Prokofiev, Sergei.
> *Ivan the Terrible* [transliterated Russian title]. Gamburg [Hamburg]: Sikorski, 1997. 265 pp. ill.

Complete orchestral score (with chorus and soloists) for the 1944 Sergei Eisenstein film. "*Ivan the Terrible* by Prokofiev—Eisenstein," contains historical notes, 26–31; "Commentary" contains notes for each musical number, 246–50; "Suggested Order for Concert Performances," 251–53; "The Manuscript Sources of *Ivan the Terrible*," 253–55. At the time of publication, this was the only extant example of a complete published film score, according to music librarian H. Stephen Wright.

Raksin, David.
  David Raksin Remembers His Colleagues: Hollywood Composers. Los Altos, Calif.:
  Stanford Theatre Foundation, 1995. 47 pp. ill.
Booklet published in conjunction with a film festival honoring 10 composers who scored
films made between 1933 and 1953. Author reminisces about Aaron Copland, Hugo
Friedhofer, Bernard Herrmann, Erich Wolfgang Korngold, Alfred Newman, Miklós
Rózsa, Max Steiner, Dimitri Tiomkin, and Franz Waxman.

Raksin, Ruby.
  Technical Handbook of Mathematics for Motion Picture Music Synchronization. 2nd
  ed. Hollywood: MUSICAID, 1966. 83 pp. Sherman Oaks, Calif.: R-Y Publishing,
  1972. 87 pp. ill.
Primarily a master click chart aimed at composers and music editors. Contains mathematical formulas for converting footage to time and time to footage. Author was a music
editor and the brother of composer David Raksin.

Rapée, Erno.
  Erno Rapée's Encyclopædia of Music for Pictures. New York: Belwin, 1925. 510 pp.
  Reprinted as *Encyclopedia of Music for Pictures*, New York: Arno Press, 1970.
A compilation of music selected for the accompaniment of motion pictures advertised as
being "as essential as the picture." In the introductory material (pp. 7–27), the author
draws on his experience as a music director in focusing on such topics as accompanying
the overture, newsreels, and features; the organ; and how to organize an orchestra. Arranged by classification (from cannibal music to Swiss music), with composer and publisher listed. Music publisher Hans Heinsheimer later wrote that this work classifies
20,000 pieces. A follow-up to the author's *Motion Picture Moods for Pianists and Organists* (1924).

Reay, Pauline.
  Music in Film: Soundtracks and Synergy. London: Wallflower, 2004. 135 pp. ill.
Written from a theoretical perspective, this work presents a historical overview of film
music and addresses textual functions of film music, including an in-depth discussion of
Danny Elfman's score for *Edward Scissorhands*; popular music in film, including a case
study of the score for *Magnolia*; pop stars and rock musicians who have composed film
music; and synergy and commercial functions of film music, including cross-promotion.
Author is a British lecturer in film and media studies.

R.E.D. Publishing.
  The R.E.D. Soundtracks Catalogue. London: Retail Entertainment Data Publishing,
  1995. Unpaginated.
Lists some 6,000 film, show, and television soundtracks from the combined databases of
Music Master and Gramophone, available in the United Kingdom. Listed alphabetically
by title, with composer-artist and distributor indexes. Supersedes a 1990 guide to Music
Master recordings, *Music Master Films & Shows Catalogue*.

Robinson, David.
  *Music of the Shadows: The Use of Musical Accompaniment with Silent Films, 1896–
  1936*. Pordenone, Italy: Le Giornate del Cinema Muto: 1990. 111 pp. ill.

Exhibition catalog distributed at the 1990 Pordenone festival of silent films. Contains an introductory overview, in English and Italian, of the cinema organ, cue sheets and musical suggestions, musical libraries, compiled and composed scores, mechanical music and effects, synchronization and sound films, and mood music on the set. Includes brief biographies of composers and compilers, and notable film scores in chronological order. Supplement to *Griffithiana* (October 1990).

Romney, Jonathan, and Adrian Wootton, eds.
   Celluloid Jukebox: Popular Music and the Movies Since the 50s. London: British Film Institute, 1995. 168 pp.
A collection of essays, including "Pop and Film: The Charisma Crossover," by Ben Thompson, 32–43; "Rock Musicians and Film Soundtracks," by David Toop, 72–81; and "Music as Film," by Mark Sinker, 106–17. Interviews with filmmakers and musicians, including David Byrne and Ry Cooder. Filmography. Editors are a British film critic and head of the British Film Institute, respectively.

Rona, Jeff.
   The Reel World: Scoring for Pictures: A Practical Guide to the Art, Technology, and Business of Composing for Film and Television. San Francisco: Miller Freeman Books, 2000. 272 pp.
Chapters on music for film and television, developing a style, new directions in scoring, setting up a studio, writing and recording the score, beginning a career and career challenges, and making a living. Brief interviews ("perspectives") with Carter Burwell, James Newton Howard, Mark Isham, Basil Poledouris, Marc Shaiman, John Williams, and Hans Zimmer. Interviews with music contractor David Low, composer's agent Cheryl Tiano, music supervisor Chris Douridas, and music executive Robert Kraft. Case studies on the author's scores for film (*White Squall*) and television (*Homicide, Chicago Hope*). Index.

Rosar, William H., and Leslie N. Andersen, eds.
   Union Catalog of Motion Picture Music. Claremont, Calif.: International Film Music Society, 1991. Unpaginated.
The partial realization of Rosar's vision—which originated when he was president of the Society for the Preservation of Film Music (SPFM; now the Film Music Society)—of a nationwide catalog documenting film music scores, sketches, and other primary source material. Rosar left the SPFM in 1990 to form the International Film Music Society; this volume, based on information compiled by the SPFM from the Columbia Studios catalog, was published the following year. The project remains a work in progress. Subsequent editions contain additional material from the David O. Selznick archive at the University of Texas–Austin.

Rose, Edward.
   Soundtrack Record Collectors' Guide. Minneapolis: Dored, 1978. 48 pp. ill.
A guide to building a soundtrack library, written by a soundtrack dealer. Topics include prices, sources, and markets. Soundtracks are listed by composer with the title, label, and label number. Composers are categorized under major (Bernard Herrmann, Alfred Newman, and so on), minor (John Barry, Elmer Bernstein, Jerry Goldsmith, Alex North, John Williams, and so on), or miscellaneous (Les Baxter, Jerome Moross, David Raksin).

Russell, Mark, and James Young.
    Film Music. "Screencraft" series. Boston: Focal Press, 2000. 192 pp. ill.
A coffee-table book for general audiences. Chapters on John Barry, Elmer Bernstein, Danny Elfman, Philip Glass, Jerry Goldsmith, Bernard Herrmann, Maurice Jarre, Michael Nyman, Zbigniew Preisner, Ryuichi Sakamoto, Lalo Schifrin, Howard Shore, and Gabriel Yared. Each chapter includes a biographical sketch and a narrative interview (with the exception of the Herrmann chapter, which features an essay by professor Mervyn Cooke), accompanied by film stills and music score excerpts. Includes a compact disc with a major theme written by each featured composer. Authors are London-based musicians.

Sabaneev, Leonid.
    Music for the Films: A Handbook for Composers and Conductors. Translated by S. W. Pring. London: Sir I. Pitman & Sons, 1935. 128 pp. ill. Reprint, New York: Arno Press, 1978.
Practical and technical advice, originally in Russian, with chapters on sound recording, aesthetics, composition, orchestration, conducting and synchronizing, musical doubling (dubbing singers), montage, mixing, and music for animated cartoons. Author was a Russian composer and critic.

Sackett, Susan.
    Hollywood Sings! An Inside Look at Sixty Years of Academy Award®-Nominated Songs. New York: Billboard Books, 1995. 332 pp. ill.
Chronicles the history of every nominated song from 1934 to 1993. Appendixes list title songs, films from which songs have been nominated, top-charting nominees, and more. Researched by Marcia Rovins. Author is former assistant to *Star Trek* creator Gene Roddenberry.

Sam Fox Publishing Company.
    Classified Catalogue of Sam Fox Publishing Co. Motion Picture Music. Cleveland: Sam Fox Publishing, 1929. 185 pp.
Music in the Fox catalog arranged into more than 120 genres, including agitatos, battle music, erotic, grotesque, Hawaiian, mother, rags, villain, and zanzibar. Title, composer, subtitle, tempo, key, and time signature listed for most compositions, along with the catalog edition in which the music appears. J. S. Zamecnik is credited with many of the compositions.

Sandahl, Linda J.
    Rock Films: A Viewer's Guide to Three Decades of Musicals, Concerts, Documentaries and Soundtracks 1955–1986. New York: Facts on File, 1987. 239 pp. ill. Also published under the title *Encyclopedia of Rock Music on Film: A Viewer's Guide to Three Decades of Musicals, Concerts, Documentaries and Soundtracks 1955–1986*. Poole, U.K.: Blanford Press, 1987. 239 pp. ill.
Entries arranged alphabetically by film title under three categories: musicals, concerts and documentaries, and soundtracks. Musical performers, songs performed, soundtrack songs, and short critiques are included for more than 400 films. Index of film titles, names, and song titles.

Scharf, Walter.
   The History of Film Scoring. Studio City, Calif.: Cinema Songs, 1988. 119 pp.
A decade-by-decade overview of film music, written by the respected composer. Each overview is followed by the author's list of memorable scores and a list of music department staff personnel for each studio. The author also discusses his experiences with the scoring process from screening room to dubbing stage. Includes a short biography of Scharf by Simon Lewis. Filmography of the author's films. Those looking for a comprehensive history would do better elsewhere.

Schelle, Michael.
   The Score: Interviews with Film Composers. Los Angeles: Silman-James Press, 1999. 427 pp.
Interviews with John Barry, Elmer Bernstein, Terence Blanchard, Bruce Broughton, Paul Chihara, John Corigliano, James Newton Howard, Mark Isham, Daniel Licht, Joel McNeely, Thomas Newman, Marc Shaiman, Howard Shore, Shirley Walker, and Christopher Young. Each interview is preceded by a two-page background sketch of the subject, consisting mainly of film credits. Interviews are 20 to 30 pages and organized alphabetically. With the exception of Bernstein and Barry, all the interview subjects started their careers within the last 25 years. Author is composer-in-residence at Butler University's School of Music in Indianapolis.

Schroeder, David.
   Cinema's Illusions, Opera's Allure. New York: Continuum, 2002. 372 pp.
Organized into six parts: "Appropriation of Opera in Early Cinema," "The Film Score," "Cinema Gives Opera the Finger," "Wagner's Bastards," "Cinema as Opera," and "Opera Returns as Cinema." Specific films discussed include *Apocalypse Now*, *Carmen* (including two silent versions), *Citizen Kane*, *E la nave va*, *Hannah and Her Sisters*, *A Night at the Opera*, *Philadelphia*, and *Star Wars*. Other topics include main title music as operatic overture, cinema as grand opera, and film directors' operas. Author is a Canadian professor of music and film studies.

Sciannameo, Franco.
   Nino Rota, Federico Fellini, and the Making of an Italian Cinematic Folk Opera, Amarcord. Lewiston, N.Y.: Edwin Mellen Press, 2005. 108 pp.
This monograph includes a biographical profile of Rota, a discussion of his collaborations with Fellini, an examination of the film *Amarcord*, and observations and analysis of music in the film, including its function.

Screen Music Society.
   Cinema Music as a Profession. London: Torquay, 1925.
Issued, possibly as a pamphlet, by the education section of the Screen Music Society, a 1920s London-based organization. Unable to locate a copy.

Sennett, Ted.
   Hollywood Musicals. New York: Abrams, 1981. 384 pp. ill.
A lavish coffee-table book, organized by decade, paying homage to musicals from 1927 to 1980. Includes some 400 illustrations, with more than 100 in color. Selected bibliography and filmography, musicals listed by studio or company, and index. Author is a specialist in film and the performing arts.

Seredy, Julius S., comp.
>*Carl Fischer Analytical Orchestra Guide: A Practical Handbook for the Profession.* New York: Carl Fischer, 1929. 244 pp.

A compilation of orchestral music in the Fischer catalog, arranged by genre or mood. Lists title, composer, tempo, key, time signature, and duration for most titles, along with the Fischer catalog number and price. Selections are largely 19th-century classical in nature and include works by Beethoven, Liszt, Rachmaninoff, and Verdi. American composers of light classical music, including Chaminade, Herbert, and MacDowell, are also represented. A few pieces by James C. Bradford, Erno Rapée, and other early music directors are listed.

Seredy, Julius S., and Charles J. Roberts and M. Lester Lake, comps.
>*Motion Picture Music Guide to the Carl Fischer Modern Orchestra Catalogue: Indicating All the Themes and Motives Suitable for Motion Pictures, and Showing Their Practical Application to the Screen.* New York: Carl Fischer, 1922. 40 pp.

Short, Marion.
>*Hollywood Movie Songs: Collectible Sheet Music.* Atglen, Penn.: Schiffer Publishing, 1999. 191 pp. ill.

Chapters on the transition to sound, the dawn of the movie musical, the 1930s, 1940s, 1950s, and Hollywood stars featured on song covers. More than 700 color photographs of sheet music covers, each accompanied by an explanatory paragraph, taken largely from the author's collection and supplemented by those from fellow members of the National Sheet Music Society. Many are grouped thematically: film noir, gangster films, and the like. Price guide and index. Author, a collector and musician, also wrote *From Footlights to "The Flickers."*

Skiles, Marlin.
>*Music Scoring for TV and Motion Pictures.* Blue Ridge Summit, Penn.: Tab Books, 1976. 261 pp.

Based on the author's Hollywood film scoring experience from 1936 to 1968. Subjects include mechanics, functional elements, constructing and integrating the score, and relating the score to the story. Appendix, "The Composers Speak Out" includes interviews with Hugo Friedhofer, John Green, David Grusin, Quincy Jones, Arthur Morton, and Alex North. The extensive musical examples are drawn from films scored by the author, including *The Violent Ones* (1967). Index.

Skinner, Frank.
>*Underscore.* Los Angeles: Skinner Music, 1950. 291 pp. ill. Rev. ed. New York: Criterion Music, 1960. 239 pp. ill. Hackensack, N.J.: Wehman Bros., 1960.

Traces the creative process of the composer's 1948 score for *The Fighting O'Flynn* (referred to as *The Irishman*) from assignment, preparation, prerecording, production numbers, themes, first running and cueing, writing the score, checking the picture and recording, and dubbing and preview. Student's summary and orchestration review chapters contain suggestions on orchestration. Includes extensive music examples from the film.

Smalley, Jack.
>*Composing Music for Film.* Los Angeles: JPS Publishing, 2005. 175 p.

The author draws on his background as a film music orchestrator and discusses his approach to harmony and voicings, spotting a film, and writing and laying out a music cue.

Smith, Jeff.
> *The Sounds of Commerce: Marketing Popular Film Music.* New York: Columbia Univ. Press, 1998. 288 pp. ill.

This groundbreaking work is the first comprehensive look at film music marketing and promotion. Topics include structural interactions between the film and record industries, cross-promotion, 1960s pop songs and the compilation score, and theme songs and soundtracks after 1975. Specific composers and films include Henry Mancini ("Moon River" and *Breakfast at Tiffany's*), John Barry (*Goldfinger*), and Ennio Morricone (*The Good, the Bad and the Ugly*). Particularly strong coverage of United Artists. Index. Based in part on the author's 1995 dissertation.

Smith, Robert L.
> *U.S. Soundtracks on Compact Disc: The First Ten Years 1985–1994.* Vineyard Haven, Mass.: Lukas Kendall, 1995. 131 pp.

A price guide to more than 1,500 soundtracks. Introduction includes a short history and current state of the format. Entries arranged alphabetically by film title and include composer, year of release, record label and number, and price. Selected compilation discs are listed by composer. Two appendixes list Varese Sarabande and Bay Cities releases compiled by Jeremy Monitz. Author is a collector and a medical doctor.

Smith, Robert L.
> *U.S. Soundtracks on Compact Disc: Scores for Motion Pictures and Television 1985–1999.* 2nd ed. Culver City, Calif.: Vineyard Haven LLC, 1999. 154 pp.

Expanded to more than 2,400 entries, with improved accuracy, new releases from 1995 to 1999, and revised prices. "Market Report 1999" (pp. xiii–xxi) discusses specialty labels and composer-generated promos.

Smith, Steven C., comp. and ed.
> *Film Composers Guide.* Beverly Hills, Calif.: Lone Eagle Publishing, 1990. 314 pp.

Alphabetical listings divided into two sections: film composers and notable composers of the past. Entries include title, releasing company and date, and contact information. Academy Award and Emmy Award winners and nominees are marked with a star. Lists film, television, and cable feature films and documentaries; television and cable miniseries; and animated film and television features. Index of film titles, agents, and managers. Subsequent editions by Vincent Francillon, Vincent Jacquet-Francillon, and Lone Eagle Publishing. Smith is a television writer and Herrmann biographer.

Smolian, Steven, comp.
> *A Handbook of Film, Theater, and Television Music on Record, 1948–1969.* 2 vols. New York: Record Undertaker, 1970. 64 pp. each.

Discography compiled by a recorded sound preservationist and collector from *Schwann* catalog entries and the author's personal collection, correspondence with record companies, and research at New York area archives and record stores. The first volume contains alphabetical listings by film title, including category, release date, title and composer, label, issue date, and cut-out date. The second volume contains a manufacturer's (label) index and composer index.

Springer, John.
>   *All Talking! All Singing! All Dancing! A Pictorial History of the Movie Musical.*
>   New York: Citadel Press, 1966. 256 pp. ill. *They Sang! They Danced! They Ro-*
>   *manced! A Pictorial History of the Movie Musical.* Rev. ed. Secaucus, N.J.: Carol
>   Publishing Group, 1991. 256 pp. ill.

Coffee-table book illustrated with production stills. Contains a chapter, "Music in the
Background" (pp. 204–17), on underscore (with more production photographs but no
behind-the-scenes photos). Appendix contains the author's personal listing of top songs
from movie musicals.

Stanfield, Peter.
>   *Body and Soul: Jazz and Blues in American Film, 1927–63.* Urbana: Univ. of Illinois
>   Press, 2005. 213 pp.

In-depth look at jazz and blues in film, primarily through the use of popular songs and
performances. Index. Author is a British film studies lecturer.

Stanfield, Peter.
>   *Horse Opera: The Strange History of the 1930s Singing Cowboy.* Urbana: Univ. of
>   Illinois Press, 2002. 177 pp.

Discusses the singing western, including cowboy songs and singers, musical performance
in series westerns, and the use of folk music and jazz.

Staskowski, Andréa.
>   *Movie Musicals.* Minneapolis: Lerner Publications, 1992. 80 pp. ill.

Aimed at young readers, this short volume "discusses the musical film genre and gives
analysis and plot summaries of several notable musicals, including *Top Hat*, *Meet Me in
St. Louis*, *Singin' in the Rain*, *West Side Story*, *Grease*, and *Dirty Dancing*." Bibliographical references and index.

Stemmer, Michael, comp. and ed.
>   *Western Movie Composers: A Selected, Annotated Listing of 2006 Genre Films
>   Shown in Germany.* Berlin: Wiesjahn, 1996. 329 pp.

Entries include discographies. Bibliography and indexes. In English and German.

Stern, Lee Edward.
>   *The Movie Musical.* New York: Pyramid Communications, 1974. 144 pp. New York:
>   Pyramid Publications, 1975. 159 pp. ill.

Aimed at students, this illustrated history of film musicals covers the 1920s through the
1970s. Index.

Stubblebine, Donald J.
>   *British Cinema Sheet Music: A Comprehensive Listing of Film Music Published in
>   the United Kingdom, Canada and Australia, 1916 through 1994.* Jefferson, N.C.:
>   McFarland, 1997. 207 pp.

Alphabetical listing of film titles, including studio, release year, song title, music and
lyric credits, and cover personalities. Indexes for composers and lyricists and song titles.
Author is a sheet music collector.

Stubblebine, Donald J.
  Cinema Sheet Music: A Comprehensive Listing of Published Film Music from "Squaw Man" (1914) to "Batman" (1989). Jefferson, N.C.: McFarland, 1991. 628 pp.
An indispensable work by an East Coast sheet music collector with one of the most complete collections of songs from films. Alphabetical listing of film titles includes studio, release year, song title, music and lyric credits, and cover personalities. Indexes for song titles and for notable composers and lyricists. List of selected thematic cue sheets from the 1920s. Bibliography. Second printing contains corrections.

Sutak, Ken.
  The Great Motion Picture Soundtrack Robbery: An Analysis of Copyright Protection. Hamden, Conn.: Archon Books, 1976. 111 pp.
An entertainment lawyer specializing in copyright law discusses copyright as it relates to motion picture music and soundtrack recordings, with an emphasis on copyrighting soundtracks and soundtrack piracy. A substantial portion first appeared in *Bulletin of the Copyright Society of the U.S.A.* (June 1975).

Swynnoe, Jan G.
  The Best Years of British Film Music, 1936–1958. Rochester, N.Y.: Boydell and Brewer Press, 2002. 256 pp.
Instead of a general history of the period, this work examines specific topics and concentrates on the distinctive characteristics of British film music that set it apart from its American, namely Hollywood, counterpart. Chapters cover a historical perspective of the differences between British and American films; formulas in the classical Hollywood score; a comparison between British and American composers in their approaches to film scoring; British composers' use of themes for narrative development; Arnold Bax's musico-dramatic treatment of *Oliver Twist* (1948); three other attempts at feature-film scoring: *49th Parallel* (1941) by Ralph Vaughan Williams, *The Halfway House* (1944) by Lord Berners, and *Blue Star* (1949) by Grace Williams; dialogue scoring of British films on the 1930s; the impact of World War II on British films and developments in dialogue scoring in the 1940s; a look at British films scored by foreign composers; and the decline of British cinema in the 1950s and its consequences for British film scores. Additional composers featured include William Alwyn, Malcolm Arnold, Ernest Irving, Muir Mathieson, and William Walton. Christopher Palmer is mentioned frequently, as are Miklós Rózsa (for his work with Alexander Korda) and Max Steiner. A filmography lists films included in the text. Appendixes include a 1993 interview with Roy Douglas in the form of a "conversation" with the author; "The True Story of *The Warsaw Concerto*," written by Douglas, who orchestrated Richard Addinsell's score for *Dangerous Moonlight* (1941), which featured that concerto; and the author's 1997 interview with composer Doreen Carwithen. Author, a British composer and pianist, wrote his 1997 dissertation on the subject.

Tagg, Philip.
  Kojak: Fifty Seconds of Film Music: Toward the Analysis of Affect in Popular Music. Göteborg, Sweden: Göteborgs Universitet, Musikvetenskapliga Institutionen, 1979. 301 pp. New York: Mass Media Music Scholars' Press, 2000. 424 pp.
An expanded and radically re-edited translation of the author's thesis for the University of Göteborg Department of Musicology. Includes an exceptionally detailed analysis of

Billy Goldenberg's 1973 theme for the television detective show that discusses melody, harmony, musical message, and complementary visual message, even dissecting the theme's Moog "violin" ostinato and octave portamento. The music is viewed in the context of hundreds of years of previously written music as well as contemporary popular music. An 80-page discussion of background and theory precedes the analysis. Rarely, if ever, has a work of this length been dedicated to less than one minute of music—50 seconds, to be exact. The author has since become an influential voice in film musicology.

Tambling, Jeremy.
    Opera, Ideology, and Film. New York: St. Martin's Press, 1987. 223 pp.
A British professor of literature examines filmed operas and the use of opera in film. Bibliography and index. The author followed this work with *A Night at the Opera: Media Representations of Opera* (London: John Libbey, 1994).

Taylor, John Russell, and Arthur Jackson.
    The Hollywood Musical. New York: McGraw-Hill, 1971. 278 pp.
Collection of essays on the subject. Reference section includes selected filmographies (with credits and song titles) and one-line biographies (with birth date and birthplace) and credits for composers, songwriters, lyricists, and performers. Alphabetical lists of 2,750 song titles and 1,437 film titles.

Thomas, Lawrence B.
    The MGM Years. New York: Columbia House, 1972. 138 pp.
An alphabetical guide, with chronology, to MGM musicals. "The Major Music Men" (pp. 122–23) includes music director or orchestration credits for Saul Chaplin, Adolph Deutsch, Roger Edens, Johnny Green, Lennie Hayton, André Previn, Conrad Salinger, and Georgie Stoll. Other material of interest includes "When a Star Needs a Voice..." (p. 123), a sidebar on dubbed vocals; and "The Art of the Soundtrack Recording" (pp. 130–32), by MGM Records executive Jesse Kaye, which features a discography. Author is an entertainment magazine editor.

Thomas, Tony, ed.
    Film Score: The View from the Podium. South Brunswick, N.J.: A. S. Barnes, 1979.
    266 pp. ill.
Twenty composers speak on film music in their own words: John Addison, William Alwyn, Elmer Bernstein, Aaron Copland, Jerry Fielding, Hugo Friedhofer, Jerry Goldsmith, Bernard Herrmann, Bronislaw Kaper, Erich Wolfgang Korngold, Henry Mancini, Alfred Newman, David Raksin, Leonard Rosenman, Miklós Rózsa, Hans Salter, Fred Steiner, Max Steiner, Dimitri Tiomkin, and Franz Waxman. Drawn primarily from published sources and transcripts of the author's interviews. Discography by Page Cook. Bibliography by Win Sharples Jr. Author was a film historian, record producer, and former writer-producer for the Canadian Broadcasting Corporation.

Thomas, Tony.
    Film Score: The Art & Craft of Movie Music. Burbank, Calif.: Riverwood Press,
    1991. 340 pp. ill. Rev. ed. of *Film Score: The View from the Podium* (see previous
    entry).
This edition adds six composers (and removes William Alwyn): Georges Delerue, Ernest Gold, Alex North, Laurence Rosenthal, John Williams, and Victor Young. Most of the

composers supplied text or allowed previously written material to be used. The author personally met or knew all but Korngold and Young.

Thomas, Tony.
> *Music for the Movies*. South Brunswick, N.J.: A. S. Barnes; London: Tantivy Press, 1973. 270 pp. ill. Reprint, South Brunswick, A. S. Barnes, 1977.

Embraced by film music enthusiasts, this behind-the-scenes look at the craft of film music composition appeared at about the same time as the first Charles Gerhardt-conducted LP recordings in RCA's Classic Film Score series. Contains material on George Antheil, Elmer Bernstein, Aaron Copland, Hugo Friedhofer, Ernest Gold, Jerry Goldsmith, John Green, Bernard Herrmann, Bronislaw Kaper, Erich Wolfgang Korngold, Henry Mancini, Alfred Newman, Alex North, André Previn, David Raksin, Leonard Rosenman, Laurence Rosenthal, Miklós Rózsa, Lalo Schifrin, Max Steiner, Virgil Thomson, Dimitri Tiomkin, Franz Waxman, and Victor Young. Author, a respected film historian and record producer, interviewed or corresponded with each, with the exception of Antheil, Korngold, and Young. Rosenthal and Rózsa contributed commentaries on their music. "The Score of the Scores," by Clifford McCarty, contains a listing of scores by the composers discussed within. Discography and index. This book was influential on a number of nascent film composers in the 1970s, including Christopher Young.

Thomas, Tony.
> *Music for the Movies*. 2nd ed. Los Angeles: Silman-James Press, 1997. 330 pp. ill.

This updated and expanded edition (see previous entry) adds the composers Bruce Broughton, George Duning, Basil Poledouris, John Scott, David Shire, and Herbert Stothart. Also new are Fred Karlin's material on film scoring mechanics and William Alwyn's adapted lecture on aesthetics, the latter of which previously published in *Films and Filming* (March 1959).

Tietyen, David.
> *The Musical World of Walt Disney*. Preface by Richard M. Sherman and Robert B. Sherman. Milwaukee: Hal Leonard Publishing, 1990. 158 pp.

A film-by-film history of songs and scores created for animated features and shorts by George Bruns, Frank Churchill, Sammy Fain, Leigh Harline, Ed Plumb, the Sherman brothers, Paul Smith, Carl Stalling, Oliver Wallace, Ned Washington, and others.

Timm, Larry M.
> *The Soul of Cinema: An Appreciation of Film Music*. Needham Heights, Mass.: Ginn Press, 1998. 179 pp. ill. Upper Saddle River, N.J.: Prentice Hall, 2003. 346 pp.

Textbook with chapter review questions, written by a music professor and musician. A historical survey from 1895 through the 1990s. Topics include the functions of film scoring, music for silent films, music in the early sound film, the rise of the symphonic film score, and women composers. Composers with the most coverage include Elmer Bernstein, Hugo Friedhofer, Jerry Goldsmith, Bernard Herrmann, Maurice Jarre, Alfred Newman, and Franz Waxman. Bibliography and index. The 2003 edition contains significant additions, particularly profiles and interviews.

Tonks, Paul.
> *Film Music*. Harpenden, U.K.: Pocket Essentials; North Pomfret, Vt.: Trafalgar Square Publishing, 2001. 96 pp. Rev. ed., 2003. 96 pp.

A historical overview covering the following subjects: the silent era; "pioneers," including Bernard Herrmann, Erich Wolfgang Korngold, Alfred Newman, Miklós Rózsa, Max Steiner, and Franz Waxman; movie monsters and epics; commercial instincts in the 1960s; international discoveries; John Williams; and a step-by-step guide to creating a score. Does an admirable job of fitting nearly a hundred years of history into 96 pages. Author is the London correspondent for *Film Music* magazine and writes for the British Academy of Composers and Songwriters.

Tootell, George.
> *How to Play the Cinema Organ: A Practical Book by a Practical Player.* London: W. Paxton, 1927. 114 pp. ill.

This primer includes an introduction that outlines the author's background and experience as a theater organist. Chapters on playing the harmonium, Mustel organ, and pipe organ; playing with an orchestra; playing from odd parts; solo playing in the cinema; how to compile a film accompaniment; and the extemporized accompaniment. Musical examples and an appendix with typical examples of music for film scenes. Index. Partially reprinted in *Theatre Organ Bombarde* (April–October 1967).

True, Lyle C.
> *How and What to Play for Moving Pictures: A Manual and Guide for Pianists.* San Francisco: Music Supply, 1914. 24 pp.

Primarily a list of published music, classified by mood, to assist in selecting music to accompany silent film. One of only two music books cited in the first published motion picture bibliography in *Motography* in 1916; the other is Eugene Ahern's *What and How to Play for Pictures.*

Turley, Fred.
> *Mighty Music at the Movies: The Cinema Organ in Sheffield and the Surrounding Area.* Sheffield, U.K.: Sheaf, 1990. 60 pp. ill.

Documents the history of organs and organists in the area around Sheffield, in north-central England. A copy is available at the British Library in London.

Ulrich, Allan, ed.
> *The Art of Film Music: A Tribute to California's Film Composers.* Oakland, Calif.: Oakland Museum, 1976. 40 pp. ill.

Catalog accompanying the museum's film program. Includes an introduction by Ulrich, program notes on the films screened, and seven questions asked of five composers: Elmer Bernstein, Ernest Gold, Lyn Murray, David Raksin, and Fred Steiner.

USC Entertainment Law Institute.
> *Music in Film, Film in Music.* Los Angeles: University of Southern California Law Center and the Beverly Hills Bar Association, 1990. 338 pp.

Handouts, outlines, sample contracts, articles, and related material for the 36th annual USC Entertainment Law Institute's Vic Netterville memorial lectures in 1990. Lectures include "Putting Music in Film," "Film as Ancillary to Music," "Music Clearance Nuts and Bolts," "Soundtracks," and "Music and Film Merchandising/Promotion." Participants include Burt Berman, Universal Pictures music.

Ussher, Bruno David.
>*Music in the Films, 1937–1941.* Edited by G. D. Hamann. Hollywood: Filming To-
>day Press, 2001.

A collection of the author's writings, retyped by Hamann, from the *Los Angeles Daily News*, including his columns "Music in the Films" and "Sounding Board"; the *Hollywood Spectator*, including his column "Music in Current Pictures"; and the *California Eagle*. Documents the period through capsule reviews of music in films, scoring assignments, news, and other topical issues, including coverage of the music branch of the Academy of Motion Picture Arts and Sciences. Beginning 10 years after the introduction of sound, the writings cover a fascinating period in American film history, when an influx of American and European composers to Hollywood led to an abundance of films with full orchestral background scores. Composers receiving the most coverage are Robert Russell Bennett, Aaron Copland, Richard Hageman, Werner Janssen, Erich Wolfgang Korngold, Boris Morros, Alfred Newman, André Previn, Frank Skinner, Max Steiner, Herbert Stothart, Dimitri Tiomkin, Ernst Toch, Franz Waxman, Roy Webb, and Victor Young. Index of names and film titles. The author personally knew and conversed with many of the musicians, wrote program notes for Hollywood Bowl concerts from 1923 to 1945, and was one of the first music reviewers to recognize and acknowledge the importance of film music.

Valkenburg, Robert, comp.
>*Soundtrack Encyclopedia.* Edited by Henk Korevaar and Robert Valkenburg. Lelys-
>tad, Netherlands: Cinemusica, 1985. [196 pp.]

Some 10,000 LP soundtracks listed alphabetically by film title, with release year, composer, label, and label number. Published by the Dutch Centre for Filmmusic. Contributors include Willem Breuker, Cees Eijk, Hans Feenstra, Kees Hogenbirk, Albert Pouw, Sijbold Tonkens, and Julius Wolthuis. Also features a three-page list of compact discs that includes some of the earliest soundtrack CDs for films released from 1980 to 1985 (including reissues of previously released material).

Valkenburg, Robert, ed.
>*Soundtracks on CD: The Official & Complete Encyclopedia.* Lelystad, Netherlands:
>Stichting Cinemusica, 1991. 40 pp.

Entries listed alphabetically by film title, with country of origin, label, and label number. Introduction, "The Rise of the CD-Score," by Cees Eyk, is a short history of soundtracks on CD. Published by the Dutch Centre for Filmmusic.

Vallance, Tom.
>*The American Musical.* New York: A. S. Barnes; London: A. Zwemmer, Ltd.,
>1970. 192 pp. ill.

An alphabetical listing of 500 artists (performers, composers, directors), with short biographies and film credits. Index of song titles and more than 1,750 films.

Ven, Luc Van de, ed.
>*Motion Picture Music.* Mechelen, Belgium: Soundtrack, 1980. 155 pp. ill.

Contains retypeset articles, interviews, and filmographies, some updated and revised, originally published in the first 12 issues of *Soundtrack! The Collector's Quarterly*. The Herrmann, Kaper, and Baxter filmographies were previously unpublished.

"Introduction," by Luc Van de Ven, 5–6; "Mrs. Muir & Mr. Herrmann," by W. F. Krasnoborski, 7–11; "Herrmann on Record," 12–17; "*Taxi Driver*: Herrmann's Last Ride," by W. F. Krasnoborski, 18–20; "A Filmography/Discography of Herrmann," by Ron Bohn and Luc Van de Ven, 21–26; "Omens and Obsessions," by W. F. Krasnoborski, 27–32; "Goldsmith on Record: Anatomy of a Reissue," by John Caps, 33–35; "A Filmography/Discography of Philippe Sarde," by Luc Van de Ven, 36–40; "A Conversation with David Shire," by Tom DeMary, 41–55; "A Filmography/Discography of David Shire," by Tom DeMary, 56–59; "TV Music: Roots and Offshoots," by W. F. Krasnoborski, 60–63; "TV Music: Music Makes All the Difference," by John Caps, 64–68; "A Conversation with Carlo Rustichelli," by Enzo Cocumarolo, 69–77; "A Filmography/Discography of Rustichelli," by Enzo Cocumarolo, James Marshall, and Jean-Pierre Pecqueriaux, 78–88; "Henry Mancini: On Scoring and Recording," by John Caps, 89–92; "A Conversation with Richard Rodney Bennett," by John Caps, 93–104; "A Filmography/Discography of R. R. Bennett," by John Caps and Tom DeMary, 105–7; "*Nicholas and Alexandra*," by John Caps, 108–14; "A Filmography/Discography of Les Baxter," by James Marshall, Ronald Bohn, and Tom DeMary, 115–21; "A Conversation with Bronislau Kaper," by W. F. Krasnoborski, 122–32; "A Filmography/Discography of Bronislau Kaper," by the American Film Institute and Luc Van de Ven, 133–39; "Mario Nascimbene," by James Marshall, 140–48; "*Jaws*," by W. F. Krasnoborski, 149–50; "Williams on Record," 151–52; "*The Towering Inferno*," by W. F. Krasnoborski, 153–55.

Vogel, Frederick G.
Hollywood Musicals Nominated for Best Picture. Jefferson, N.C.: McFarland, 2003. 374 pp. ill.
Examines 38 films through 1991, with production credits followed by an assessive essay.

Walker, Mark, ed.
Gramophone Film Music Good CD Guide. Foreword by Danny Elfman. Harrow, Middlesex: Gramophone Publications Ltd., 1996. 256 pp. 2nd ed., with foreword by John Scott, 1997. 3rd ed. (revised and updated), 1998. 260 pp.
With capsule reviews for more than 400 soundtracks, this composer-by-composer guide includes short biographies (with birth years and, if applicable, death years) of American and some international composers and reviews of selected films. List of addresses for record companies, distributors, dealers, and mail order companies. Index of film titles. Editor started at Gramophone in the discography department and also produced the *Gramophone Musicals Good CD Guide* (1997) covering Broadway musicals and some movie musicals.

Warner, Alan.
Who Sang What on the Screen. North Ryde, Australia: Angus & Robertson Publishers, 1984. 168 pp.
Chapters discuss singers, vocal groups, songs based on classical music, Hollywood choirs, popular songs used in films, title and theme songs, James Bond theme songs, songs inspired by films, television theme songs, singing actors, singers and songs in nonmusicals, vocal dubbing, and songs from musicals. Indexes for song titles, artists, and movie and television programs. Author wrote the "Records" column in *Films and Filming* in the 1970s.

Wescott, Steven D., comp.
   A Comprehensive Bibliography of Music for Film and Television. Detroit: Information Coordinators, 1985. 432 pp.
Entries are organized by subject: history, composers, aesthetics, special topics (including musical performance on film and television, film musicals, and animated sound), and research. The history section is subdivided by decade and includes sections on sound techniques and music for television. Includes citations for reviews of books. Separate bibliographies for more than 100 composers are listed alphabetically. Index of personal names. A monumental work at the time of its publication, this volume has been indispensable to researchers. Its influence, however, has been hampered by limited distribution and availability, lack of the compiler's direct access to the material, and a brief index. The work has since been overshadowed by the enormous amount of literature on film music. Compiler is a musicologist and composer.

Wierzbicki, James.
   Louis and Bebe Barron's Forbidden Planet. Lanham, Md.: Scarecrow Press, 2005. Scarecrow Film Score Guides, no. 4. 185 pp. ill.
The electronically generated score for the 1956 science fiction film is discussed. Chapters cover origins, compositional techniques, historical and critical contexts, the music, and the score. No written score ever existed, making this analysis of particular interest. Bibliography and index. Author is a musicologist.

Williams, John, ed.
   The Magic of Mancini: Melody, Movement, & Mayhem. Foreword by Blake Edwards. Dorset, U.K.: Music from the Movies, 1993. 93 pp. ill.
Sections include "The Henry Mancini Story," by Damian Bull, 14–32; "Douglas Gamley on Henry Mancini," interviewed by John Williams, 34–36; "How I Discovered Henry Mancini," by director Stanley Donen, 37; "Still Happy After All These Years: Henry Mancini in Conversation with Peter D. Kent," 38–46; "*Tom and Jerry–The Movie…*and Mancini!" by Peter D. Kent, 50–56. Others speaking of Mancini include Alan and Marilyn Bergman, Don Black, Howard Blake, Leslie Bricusse, Bob Hathaway, Jack Hayes, John Scott, and Terence Young. Introduction by Williams, filmography by Damian Bull, and discography. Issued as a limited edition paperback from the editor of *Music from the Movies* (not to be confused with the composer).

Williams, John, ed.
   The Magic of Ron Goodwin. Bridport, U.K.: Variations, 1995. 69 pp.
This portrait of the British composer includes Rodney Newton's interview with Goodwin, a chapter on Goodwin's *Frenzy* score, filmography, and discography, from the editor of *Music from the Movies* (not to be confused with the composer).

Williams, John, ed.
   The Music of Benjamin Frankel. Bridport, U.K.: Variations, 1996. 60 pp.
Articles on the composer and his work, from the editor of *Music from the Movies* (not to be confused with the composer).

Williams, John, ed.
   TV Composer Guide: An A to Z of Principal Composers. Dorset, U.K.: Variations, 1995. 200 pp.

Profiles 157 British composers from John Altman to Guy Wolfenden, with credits and contacts. Contains exclusive articles written by 29 composers, including John Altman, Philip Appleby, Evelyn Glennie, Michael J. Lewis, Mike Moran, Jim Parker, Barrington Pheloung, and Francis Shaw. Includes a guide to British television music on compact disc. Other material includes "John Barry: The Television Years," by Jon Burlingame, a Wilfred Josephs retrospective by Derek Elley, and an interview with Laurie Johnson. Advertised as the first of what was to become an annual issue, although there is no evidence that any further issues were published. Williams, editor of *Music from the Movies* and no relation to the composer, did publish a film and telelvision music yearbook.

Wlaschin, Ken.
   Encyclopedia of Opera on Screen: A Guide to More Than 100 Years of Opera Films, Videos and DVDs. New Haven, Conn.: Yale Univ. Press, 2004.
Updated version of the author's 1996 opus, with more than 1,900 entries covering a comprehensive A to Z listing of material related to the subject from 1896 to 2003. Entries on animated opera, first opera films, first operas on film and television, silent films about opera, operas based on movies, and more. Selected bibliography and index.

Wlaschin, Ken.
   Opera on Screen: A Guide to 100 Years of Films and Videos Featuring Operas, Opera Singers and Operettas. Los Angeles: Beachwood Press, 1996.
Entries on operas, singers, films, and performers. Each opera is followed by filmed versions, in chronological order, with a paragraph on the film. "Related films" follows the filmed versions, as do silent-era "early" versions. Personal name entries include Arthur Benjamin (one of the first composers commissioned to create an opera for BBC television), Jerome Kern, Robert Stolz, and Herbert Stothart. The brief entries on film composers usually mention "imaginary" operas, that is, newly composed works for use in a specific film. Standard entries, including "Silent Films of Operas" and "Television Operas," are supplemented by imaginative material such as "Worst Operetta on Film." Author has worked for the American Film Institute and the British Film Institute.

Wojcik, Pamela Robertson, and Arthur Knight, eds.
   Soundtrack Available: Essays on Film and Popular Music. Durham, N.C.: Duke Univ. Press, 2001. 491 pp.
Topics include popular vs. serious music, singing stars, music as ethnic marker, African American identities, contemporary compilations, and gender and technology.
   "Overture," by Arthur Knight and Pamela Robertson Wojcik, 1–15; "Cinema and Popular Song: The Lost Tradition," by Rick Altman, 19–30; "Surreal Symphonies: *L'age D'or* and the Discreet Charms of Classical Music," by Priscilla Barlow, 31–52; "'The Future's Not Ours to See': Song, Singer, and Labyrinth in Hitchcock's *The Man Who Knew Too Much*," by Murray Pomerance, 53–73; "'You Think They Call Us Plastic Now': The Monkees and *Head*," by Paul B. Ramaeker, 74–102; "Real Men Don't Sing Ballads: The Radio Crooner in Hollywood, 1929–1933," by Allison McCracken, 105–33; "Flower of the Asphalt: The *Chanteuse Réaliste* in 1930s French Cinema," by Kelley Conway, 134–60; "The Embodied Voice: Song Sequences and Stardom in Popular Hindi Cinema," by Neepa Majumdar, 161–81; "Music as Ethnic Marker in Film: The 'Jewish' Case," by Andrew P. Killick, 185–201; "Sounding the American Heart: Cultural Politics, Country Music, and Contemporary American Film," by Barbara Ching, 202–25; "Crossing Musical Borders: The

Soundtrack for *Touch of Evil*," by Jill Leeper, 226–43; "Documented/Documentary Asians: Gurinder Chadha's I'm British But—and the Musical Mediation of Sonic and Visual Identities," by Nabeel Zuberi, 244–66; "Class Swings: Music, Race, and Social Mobility in Broken Strings," by Adam Knee, 269–94; "Borrowing Black Masculinity: The Role of Johnny Hartman in *The Bridges of Madison County*," by Krin Gabbard, 293–316; "'It Ain't Necessarily So That It Ain't Necessarily So': African American Recordings of *Porgy and Bess* as Film and Cultural Criticism," by Arthur Knight, 319–46; "'Hollywood Has Taken on a New Color': The Yiddish Blackface of Samuel Goldwyn's *Porgy and Bess*," by Jonathan Gill, 347–71; "Picturizing American Cinema: Hindi Film Songs and the Last Days of Genre," by Corey K. Creekmur, 375–406; "Popular Songs and Comic Allusion in Contemporary Cinema," by Jeff Smith, 407–30; "The Girl and the Phonograph; or the Vamp and the Machine Revisited," by Pamela Robertson Wojcik, 434–54. Bibliography.

Woll, Allen L.
The Hollywood Musical Goes to War. Chicago: Nelson-Hall, 1983. 186 pp.
A professor of history examines the political and social implications of the film musical.

Woll, Allen L.
Songs from Hollywood Musical Comedies, 1927 to the Present: A Dictionary. New York: Garland Publishing, 1976. 251 pp.
Films are listed alphabetically. Indexes for songs and composers/lyricists.

Wright, H. Stephen.
Film Music at the Piano: An Index to Piano Arrangements of Instrumental Film and Television Music in Anthologies and Collections. Lanham, Md.: Scarecrow Press, 2003. 189 pp.
An index to published film and television music for solo piano. Entries arranged by film or television program title. More than 600 listings, culled from 240 anthologies available at public or academic libraries. The compilations and folios in this volume are from 1940 to 2002 (with 1935 being the earliest copyright). The indexed music is primarily in the form of piano arrangements of theme music, in some cases as elaborate as "suites for piano." Most major film composers are represented. Excerpt title index and index of composers. Author is an associate dean and former university music librarian.

Wright, H. Stephen.
Film Music Collections in the United States. Hollywood: Society for the Preservation of Film Music, 1996. 50 pp.
Author was tapped by the Society for the Preservation of Film Music (now the Film Music Society) to document the location of primary source material. Survey forms distributed to film studios and libraries form the basis for the entries, which are listed geographically. First published in the Society's *Cue Sheet*, the remarkably useful information was revised and expanded for this edition.

Yanow, Scott.
Jazz on Film: The Complete Story of the Musicians and Music Onscreen. San Francisco: Backbeat Books, 2004. 314 pp. ill.
Paragraph-long capsule reviews for 1,300 films and television programs that include a jazz musician or singer. Grouped by subject, including jazz on television and Hollywood

movies. Opens with a brief history of jazz on film from 1917 to 1960. Filmography, bibliographical references, and index. Author is a jazz reviewer.

Zager, Michael.
    Writing Music for Television and Radio Commercials: A Manual for Composers and Students. Lanham, Md.: Scarecrow Press, 2003.
A composer draws on his experience composing and arranging jingles, with a discussion of artistic and business aspects of the profession.

Zuckerman, John V.
    Music in Motion Pictures: Review of Literature with Implications for Instructional Films. Technical Report SDC 269-7-2. Instructional Film Research Program. Pennsylvania State College, 1949.
A 17-page paper examining the informational, emotional, and conceptual functions of music and its techniques and applications. The work was inspired by specialists in film, education, and psychology at Pennsylvania State College's film research program, who became interested in improving the power of instructional film through the use of music.

Chapter 2

Academic Dissertations and Theses

Anderson, Milton Carl.
: *The Background Musical Score with Analysis of the Motion Picture* The Dark Corner. MA thesis, UCLA, 1957.

Analysis of Anderson's score for a student film, *The Dark Corner* (UCLA, 1957), including a discussion of the composition, orchestration, and recording techniques. Two volumes; vol. 2 contains the music score for the film.

Arnold, Alison E.
: *Hindi Filmi Git: On the History of Commercial Indian Popular Music.* PhD thesis, University of Illinois at Urbana-Champaign, 1991. 401 pp.

Focuses on the Hindi film song from 1931 to 1955.

Atkins, Irene Kahn.
: *Source Music in the Dramatic Motion Picture.* MA thesis, UCLA, 1978. 131 pp.

Formed the basis for Atkins's book, *Source Music in Motion Pictures* (1983).

Berg, Charles Merrell.
: *An Investigation of the Motives for and Realization of Music to Accompany the American Silent Film, 1896–1927.* PhD diss., University of Iowa, 1973. 311 pp.

Published as a book in 1976 under the same title.

Biancorosso, Giorgio.
: *Where Does the Music Come From? Studies in the Aesthetics of Film Music.* PhD thesis, Princeton University, 2002. 198 pp.

Bias, Rebecca H.
: *From Golden Age to Silver Screen: French Music-Hall Cinema from 1930–1950.* PhD thesis, Ohio State University, 2005. 216 pp.

Examines films that contain music-hall performers, venues, mise en scène, revues, and music-hall songs or repertoire.

Bick, Sally.
: *Composers on the Cultural Front: Aaron Copland and Hanns Eisler in Hollywood.* PhD diss., Yale University, 2001. 390 pp.

Block, Andrew M.
> *Irrational Film Music: Sounds and Techniques in Movies.* MS thesis, Illinois State
> University, 2001. 93 pp.

Discusses music by Danny Elfman and Bernard Herrmann.

Bogart, Betsy Ann.
> *Music and Narrative in the French New Wave: The Films of Agnès Varda and
> Jacques Demy.* PhD thesis, UCLA, 2001. 283 pp.

Bowes, Malcolm Eugene.
> *Eurhythmics and the Analysis of Visual-Musical Synthesis in Film: An Examination
> of Sergei Eisenstein's* Alexander Nevsky. PhD diss., Ohio University, 1978. 208 pp.

Includes a discussion of Sergei Prokofiev's score.

Bozynski, Michelle Carole.
> *Music in Canadian Visual Narrative: Musical Collaborations in Five Films of Atom
> Egoyan and Patricia Rozema.* PhD thesis, University of Toronto, 2004. 401 pp.

Discusses music by Lesley Barber, Mychael Danna, and Mark Korven.

Brownrigg, Mark.
> *Film Music and Film Genre.* PhD thesis, University of Stirling, 2003. 308 pp.

On film scores and soundtracks.

Bruce, Graham Donald.
> *Bernard Herrmann: Film Music and Film Narrative.* PhD diss., New York Univer-
> sity, 1982. 425 pp.

Includes analyses of Herrmann's scores for *Citizen Kane, Obsession, Taxi Driver, Vertigo,* and *Psycho.* Formed the basis for Bruce's book, *Bernard Herrmann: Film Music
and Narrative* (1985).

Carroll, Don.
> *Copland's* Something Wild *and* Music for a Great City: *From Cinematic to Sym-
> phonic Narrative.* PhD diss., University of Southern California, 2000. 293 pp.

Carter, Allen Lance.
> *Interactive Arranging: Techniques of Jazz, Commercial, and Formal Twentieth-
> Century Composition and Their Application to Composing for Film and Television.*
> DA thesis, University of Northern Colorado, 2001. 190 pp.

Chalk, Rosemary A.
> *The Film Music of George Dreyfus:* The Big Island, A Steam Train Passes, *and*
> Break of Day. BA thesis, University of Queensland, 1986.

Discusses the Australian composer's music.

Christophersen, Bjørn Morten.
> *Erich Wolfgang Korngold: Orchestration in Opera and Film.* PhD diss., University
> of Oslo, 2002. 157 pp.

Includes analysis and discussion of the orchestration for cues from several films, primarily *The Sea Hawk,* pp. 85–150. Voluminous music excerpts.

Cochran, Alfred Williams.
> *Style, Structure, and Tonal Organization in the Early Film Scores of Aaron Copland.*
> PhD diss., Catholic University of America, 1986. 512 pp.

Includes analysis of music for *The City* (1939), *Of Mice and Men* (1939), and *Our Town* (1940).

Cochrane, Keith A.
> *George Antheil's Music to a World's Fair Film.* DA thesis, University of Northern Colorado, 1994. 184 pp.

Cohen, Thomas Franklin.
> *How Cinema Changes Music: Metronomes, Maestros, and Composition.* PhD thesis, University of Florida, 2001. 189 pp.

Conway, Kelley.
> *The Chanteuse at the City Limits: Femininity, Paris, and the Cinema.* PhD thesis, UCLA, 1999. 360 pp.

Formed the basis for Conway's book, *Chanteuse in the City: The Realist Singer in French Film* (2004).

Daubney, Katherine Sarah.
> *The View from the Piano: A Critical Examination and Contextualisation of Film Scores of Max Steiner, 1939–1945.* PhD thesis, University of Leeds, 1996. 263 pp.

Daugherty, Florence Anne Millard.
> *Narrative and Nonnarrative Structures in the Film Music of Michael Nyman.* PhD thesis, Florida State University, 1997. 201 pp.

Examines four films, including *Prospero's Books* and *The Piano*.

Doughty, Ruth.
> *Scoring a Black Aesthetic: Music in the Films of Spike Lee.* PhD thesis, Keele University, 2004.

Examines the political and cultural implications of music in Lee's films and analyzes the underscore and songs.

Eastman, Patricia Lynn.
> *The Collateral Relationship between Sound Effects and Music in Selected Media.* MA thesis, San Jose State University, 1994. 252 pp.

Ennis, Frank Robert.
> *A Comparison of Style between Selected Lieder and Film Songs of Erich Wolfgang Korngold.* DMA diss., University of Texas, Austin, 1999. 247 pp.

Evans, Lee.
> *Morton Gould: His Life and Music.* EdD thesis, Columbia University Teachers College, 1978. 375 pp.

Farah, Wanda Therese.
> *The Principle of Counterpoint and Its Expression in Music, Dance, and Cinema.* PhD thesis, University of Texas, Austin, 1985. 425 pp.

Faulkner, Robert R.
> *Studio Musicians: Their Work and Career Contingencies in the Hollywood Film Industry.* PhD thesis, UCLA, 1968. 294 pp.

Formed the basis for Faulkner's book, *Hollywood Studio Musicians: Their Work and Careers in the Recording Industry* (1971; 1985).

Feuer, Jane.
> *The Hollywood Musical: The Aesthetics of Spectator Involvement in an Entertainment Form.* PhD thesis, University of Iowa, 1978. 251 pp.

Formed the basis for Feuer's book, *The Hollywood Musical* (1982; 1993).

Flinn, Carol Ann [Caryl Flinn].
> *Film Music and Hollywood's Promise of Utopia in Film Noir and the Woman's Film.* PhD diss., University of Iowa, 1988. 304 pp.

Formed the basis for Flinn's book, *Strains of Utopia: Gender, Nostalgia, and Hollywood Film Music* (1992).

Fox, Barbara Beeghly.
> *Obsession and Crisis: Film Music and Narrative in* Double Indemnity *(1944),* Laura *(1944), and* Psycho *(1960).* MA thesis, University of Nevada, Reno, 2005. 75 pp.

Discusses music by Miklós Rózsa, David Raksin, and Bernard Herrmann.

Freeman, John.
> *Effect of Familiar Background Music Upon Film Learning.* MA thesis, University of Nebraska, Lincoln, 1953. 44 pp.

The *Journal of Educational Research* published an article by Freeman under the same title in 1959 (vol. 53, no. 3, pp. 91–96).

Gargaro, Kenneth Vance.
> *The Work of Bob Fosse and the Choreographer-Directors in the Translation of Musicals to the Screen.* PhD diss., University of Pittsburgh, 1979. 213 pp.

"The Cinematic Nature of Music in Non-Musical Films," 164–75; "Montage and Music—Rhythmic Harmony," 177–92.

Garwood, Ian.
> *Pop Music and Characterisation in Narrative Film.* PhD thesis, University of Warwick, 1999. 372 pp.

George, Lee.
> *Aspects of Industrial Film Music.* MA thesis, Wayne State University, 1964. 90 pp.

Gengaro, Christine Lee.
> *"It Was Lovely Music That Came to My Aid": Music's Contribution to the Narrative of the Novel, Film, and Play,* A Clockwork Orange. PhD thesis, University of Southern California, 2005. 270 pp.

Gerrero, Richard Henry.
   Music as a Film Variable. PhD diss., Michigan State University, 1969. 110 pp.

Gibby, Trudy B.
   Innovations in American Film Music 1929–1980. MS thesis, Brigham Young University, 1983. 203 pp.

Gilbert, Michael John Tyler.
   Bertolt Brecht and Music: A Comprehensive Study. PhD diss., University of Wisconsin, Madison, 1985. 536 pp.
Documents the views of the playwright Bertolt Brecht concerning the function of music in film.

Goldmark, Daniel Ira.
   Happy Harmonies: Music and the Hollywood Animated Cartoon. PhD diss., UCLA, 2001. 560 pp.
Includes material on Scott Bradley and Carl Stalling. Formed the basis for Goldmark's book, *Tunes for 'Toons: Music and the Hollywood Cartoon* (2005).

Goldsmith, Melissa Ursula Dawn.
   Alban Berg's Filmic Music: Intentions and Extensions of the Film Music Interlude in the Opera Lulu. PhD thesis, Louisiana State University and Agricultural and Mechanical College, 2002. 178 pp.
"Film Music," 95–102.

Goldstein, Lynda R.
   Cultural Interpellations: Popular Song Interpolations in Narrative Film. PhD thesis, Temple University, 1992. 307 pp.

Gorbman, Claudia.
   Film Music: Narrative Functions in French Films. PhD diss., University of Washington, 1978. 219 pp.
Formed the basis for Gorbman's book, *Unheard Melodies: Narrative Film Music* (1987).

Hamilton, James Clifford.
   Leith Stevens: A Critical Analysis of His Works. DMA diss., University of Missouri, Kansas City, 1976. 168 pp.
Contains a brief biography, a study of Stevens's musical and stylistic techniques using selected music excerpts of his scores, and an analysis of the music for *When Worlds Collide* (1951). Filmography, awards, and brief chronology.

Hanlon, Esther S.
   Improvisation: Theory and Application for Theatrical Music and Silent Film. PhD diss., University of Cincinnati, 1975. 176 pp.

Hartmann, Donald Conrad.
   The Don Quichotte à Dulcinée *of Maurice Ravel and the* Chansons de Don Quichotte *of Jacques Ibert: A Study of Two Song Cycles Composed for the Film* Don Quixote, *Which Starred Feodor Chaliapin.* DMA diss., University of Oklahoma, 1994. 111 pp.

Compares two song cycles related to the 1932 film. When Ravel did not produce the music in a timely manner, Ibert stepped in. Ravel ultimately returned to finish the music, which turned out to be his last completed work.

Heine, Erik James.
> *The Film Music of Dmitri Shostakovich in* The Gadfly, Hamlet, *and* King Lear. PhD diss., University of Texas, Austin, 2005. 337 pp.

Detailed analysis of Shostakovich's music for three films.

Heine, Erik James.
> *Musical Recycling: A Study and Comparison of Ralph Vaughan Williams' Film Score for* Scott of the Antarctic *with "Sinfonia Antartica" (Symphony No. 7).* MM thesis, University of Arizona, 2001.

Henderson, Sanya Shoilevska.
> *Alex North: The Life and Career of a Composer.* PhD diss., Novi Sad University, 1998. 302 pp.

Formed the basis for Henderson's book, *Alex North: Film Composer* (2003).

Hilliard, Howard.
> *The History of Horn Playing in Los Angeles from 1920–1970.* PhD diss., University of North Texas, 1999. 73 pp.

Based on interviews with studio horn players Jack Cave, James Decker, Vincent de Rosa, George Hyde, and Gale Robinson.

Hoover, John Gene.
> *The Warner Brothers Film Musical, 1927–1980.* PhD diss., University of Southern California, 1985. 479 pp.

Huckvale, D[avid].
> *Hammerscore: The Influence of Nineteenth-Century Romantic Music on Scores Written for Hammer Film Productions (1957–1980).* PhD diss., Open University (U.K.), 1990. Unpaginated.

The author went on to write a biography of Hammer composer James Bernard.

Joe, Jeongwon.
> *Opera on Film, Film in Opera: Postmodern Implications of the Cinematic Influence on Opera.* PhD diss., Northwestern University, 1998. 324 pp.

Johnson, Jennifer.
> *Developing a Curriculum on Film Composition: African-American Composers' Contributions to Motion Picture Film.* EdD thesis, Columbia University, 1989. 173 pp.

Kaiser, Katherine.
> *A Fluid Conception of Style: A Study of Hanns Eisler's Film Music.* Undergraduate honors paper, Mount Holyoke College, 2002. 88 pp.

Kalinak, Kathryn Marie.
    Music as Narrative Structure in Hollywood Film. PhD diss., University of Illinois, Urbana–Champaign, 1982. 250 pp.
Discusses the uses of music in film and traces the evolution of Hollywood film scoring. Analyses of Erich Wolfgang Korngold's score for *Captain Blood* (1935), Max Steiner's score for *The Informer* (1935), Bernard Herrmann's score for *The Magnificent Ambersons* (1942), and David Raksin's score for *Laura* (1944). Formed the basis for Kalinak's book, *Settling the Score: Music and the Classical Hollywood Film* (1992).

Kassabian, Anahid.
    Songs of Subjectivities: Theorizing Hollywood Film Music of the 80s and 90s. PhD diss., Stanford University, 1993. 193 pp.
Formed the basis for Kassabian's book, *Hearing Film: Tracking Identifications in Contemporary Hollywood Film Music* (2001).

Kilian, Mark Andre.
    The Relationships between Music and Sound Effects in Post 1960 Popular Hollywood Film. MMus thesis, University of KwaZulu-Natal, 1994.
Two volumes; vol. 2 contains composition portfolio.

King, Jeffrey Thomas.
    Music Composition for Film: A Series of Creative Projects Designed as Adjunct Learning Experiences in Lower-Division Music Theory Classes. DA diss., Ball State University, 1977. 539 pp.

Knight, Arthur Lee [Arthur L. Knight III].
    Dis-integrating the Musical: African American Musical Performance and the American Musical Film, 1927–1959. PhD diss., University of Chicago, 1998. 340 pp.
Became the basis for Knight's book, *Disintegrating the Musical: Black Performance and American Musical Film* (2002).

Koegel, John.
    The Film Operettas of Sigmund Romberg. MA thesis, California State University, Los Angeles, 1984. 203 pp.

Kolstad, Michael L.
    Leo Arnaud (1904–1991), Trombonist, Composer, Film Musician: A Biographical Sketch and Catalogue of Musical Works and Films. DMA thesis, University of North Carolina, Greensboro, 1996. 144 pp.

Kraft, James P.
    Stage to Studio: American Musicians and Sound Technology, 1890–1945. PhD thesis, University of Southern California, 1990. 320 pp.
Served as the basis for the author's book *Stage to Studio: Musicians and the Sound Revolution, 1890–1950* (1996).

Kulezic-Wilson, Danijela.
    Composing on Screen: The Musicality of Film. PhD thesis, University of Ulster, 2005.

Music's temporality, rhythm, and kinesis are explored and compared to music in the contexts of the opposing aesthetic choices of the shot and the cut. The main theoretical propositions are tested in the case studies of Jim Jarmusch's *Dead Man* and Darren Aronofsky's *Pi*.

Laing, Heather.
Wandering Minds and Anchored Bodies: Music, Gender and Emotion in Melodrama and the Woman's Film. PhD thesis, University of Warwick, 2000. 356 pp.

Leech, Charles.
The Metasemiotics of Classical Music and Film: The Recontextualisation of Strauss and Wagner in Pop Culture. PhD thesis, Queensland University of Technology, 1999. 83 pp.

Leinberger, Charles Francis.
An Austrian in Hollywood: Leitmotifs, Thematic Transformation & Key Relationships in Max Steiner's 1942 Film Score Now, Voyager. PhD diss., University of Arizona, 1996. 309 pp.

Lek, Robbert Adrianus Jacobus van der.
Diegetic Music in Opera and Film: A Similarity between Two Genres of Drama Analysed in Works by Erich Wolfgang Korngold (1897–1957). PhD diss., University of Amsterdam, 1991. Amsterdam: Rodopi, 1991. 378 pp. Translated from the Dutch, with a summary in Dutch.
The theory of diegetic music in opera and film, vocal diegetic music in film as used in stand-alone performances (examining music from ten films), and vocal diegetic music in film as "Leitmelodie" (examining music from three films).

Lerner, Neil William.
The Classical Documentary Score in American Films of Persuasion: Contexts and Case Studies, 1936–1945. PhD diss., Duke University, 1997. 304 pp.
Topics include defining the classical documentary film score, and music and realism in early cinema theory. Analyses of Virgil Thomson's music for *The Plow That Broke the Plains* and *The River* and Aaron Copland's score for *The Cummington Story*. With music examples. Appendix contains a preliminary list of classical documentary film scores, arranged alphabetically by composer.

Leviton, Lawrence Dana.
An Analysis of Erich Wolfgang Korngold's Cello Concerto and Underscore Written for the Film Deception. PhD thesis, University of Wisconsin, Madison, 1998. 117 pp.

Lias, Stephen.
A Comparison of Leonard Bernstein's Incidental Music for the Film On the Waterfront *and the Subsequent "Symphonic Suite" from the Film*. DMA diss., Louisiana State University, 1997. 246 pp. (Page count includes an original music composition by Lias.)

Lionnet, Leonard.
  Point Counter Point: Interactions between Pre-Existing Music and Narrative Structure in Stanley Kubrick's The Shining. PhD thesis, City University of New York, 2003. 114 pp.

Lipscomb, Scott David.
  Cognition of Musical and Visual Accent Structure Alignment in Film and Animation. PhD diss., UCLA, 1995. 177 pp.
The results of three experiments focusing on the perceived relationship between music and visual images.

Lipscomb, Scott David.
  Perceptual Judgement of the Symbiosis between Musical and Visual Components in Film. MA thesis, UCLA, 1990. 130 pp.

Liu, Yi-Hsin Cindy.
  The Examination of the Appearance and Use of French Horn in Film Scores from 1977 to 2004. DMA thesis, University of Cincinnati, 2005. 83 pp.
Discusses how and why the French horn has been used in Hollywood film scores, particularly in three James Horner scores.

Luna, David Nathan.
  An Investigation of the Film Music of Darius Milhaud. MMus thesis, Hardin-Simmons University, 1995. 92 pp.

Marks, Martin Miller.
  Film Music of the Silent Period, 1895–1924. PhD diss., Harvard University, 1990. 513 pp.
Formed the basis for Marks's book, *Music and the Silent Film* (1997).

May, Daniel Joseph.
  Altered States: *A Discussion of John Corigliano's Film Score.* DMA thesis, Cornell University, 1990. 68 pp.
The author studied with Corigliano and has some film music credits.

McKay, Frances Thompson.
  Movement in Time and Space: The Synthesis of Music and Visual Imagery in Luchino Visconti's Death in Venice *and Stanley Kubrick's* 2001: A Space Odyssey. DMA thesis, Peabody Conservatory of Music, 1982. 270 pp.

McLaughlin, Robert Guy.
  Broadway and Hollywood: A History of Economic Interaction. PhD diss., University of Wisconsin, Madison, 1970. 302 pp. New York: Arno Press, 1974. 302 pp.
"The Economic Importance of Recording Companies" discusses the repercussions of licensing soundtracks from stage musicals made into films, 218–24.

McQuiston, Katherine.
  Recognizing Music in the Films of Stanley Kubrick. PhD thesis, Columbia University, 2005. 326 pp.

Includes a discussion of preexisting music used in *2001: A Space Odyssey* and *A Clockwork Orange*.

Millar, Michael W.
> *Los Angeles Studio Brass Players*. DMA thesis, Claremont Graduate University, 1999. 135 pp.

A historical account based on interviews with Milt Bernhart, Vincent De Rosa, Tommy Johnson, Roy Main, Dick Nash, Uan Rasey, Jeff Reynolds, George Roberts, Jim Self, Phil Teele, Tony Terran, Lloyd Ulyate, and Chauncey Welsch.

Missiras, Michael.
> *Musical Reference, Syntax, and the Compositional Process in Film Music*. PhD diss., New York University, 1998. 180 pp.

Includes discussion of a music cue from Leonard Rosenman's score for *East of Eden* and a jazz-based cue from John Lewis's score for *Odds Against Tomorrow*.

Munro, Eden.
> *The Rock Film: Film Genre and Notions of Authenticity in Rock Music*. MA thesis, Carleton University, Ottawa, 2004. 132 pp.

Napthali, Diane.
> *Music and the Australian Film Industry, 1894–1969: A History*. PhD thesis, University of New South Wales, 1998. 507 pp.

Nasta, Dominique.
> *Meaning in Film: Relevant Structures in Soundtrack and Narrative*. PhD diss., Universite Libre de Bruxelles, 1989.

Published in book form in 1991.

Ng, Jing Fen Brenda.
> *A Study of Contrast in Integration of Film Music with Cinematic Techniques in Two Hollywood Motion Pictures*. BA project, National Institute of Education, Nanyang Technological University, 2005. 63 pp.

Discusses music by Howard Shore for the *Lord of the Rings* film trilogy and by John Williams for *Harry Potter and the Prisoner of Azkaban*.

Nisbett, Robert Franklin.
> *Louis Gruenberg: His Life & Work*. PhD diss., Ohio State University, 1979. 434 pp.

"His Life" contains material on Gruenberg's film work and views on film music, 63–69. "*The Fight for Life*" contains an analysis, with music examples, of Gruenberg's score for this film, 262–88. "Film Music," comprising part of the thematic catalog, contains the principal melodic themes for ten films, 413–25.

North, Joseph H.
> *The Early Development of the Motion Picture (1887–1909)*. PhD diss., Cornell University, 1949. 313 pp. New York: Arno Press, 1973.

"The Exhibitor and His Problems," discusses performance practice and the role of music, with specific examples from early films cited, 73–78.

Nulph, Robert Glenn.
   The Analysis, Application, and Evaluation of Three Critical Methodologies, and the Synthesis of a New Critical Model for Audiovisual Analysis: Case Study, Titanic *(1997).* PhD diss., University of Kansas, 2002. 320 pp.
Develops a methodology for analysis based on writings by Michel Chion, Nicholas Cook, and Claudia Gorbman. The music of James Horner is discussed.

Oblak, Jerica.
   Altered States: Analysis of the Collaboration between Ken Russell and John Corigliano. PhD diss., University of Pittsburgh, 1999. 63 pp.
Analyzes the music in the context of the film.

Offerdal, Hans.
   Contrast and Clarity: A Study of the Compositional Technique of American Composer Jerry Goldsmith with Main Focus on Contrapuntal Treatment. Thesis, University of Oslo, 2002. 264 pp.
Examines instrumental counterpoint in Goldsmith's film scores, with several hundred typeset music examples representing numerous films. In preparing this work, Offerdal was given access to Goldsmith's music scores and sketches and attended scoring sessions in Los Angeles for *The Last Castle.*

Orledge, Robert.
   A Study of the Composer Charles Koechlin (1867–1950). PhD diss., Cambridge University, 1973.
Includes a discussion of Koechlin's film scores. Formed the basis for Orledge's book, *Charles Koechlin (1867–1950): His Life and Works* (1989).

Otter, Kelly Joyce.
   The Role of Music in the Construction of Gender in Gone with the Wind. PhD diss., New York University, 2002. 278 pp.

Perison, Harry D.
   Charles Wakefield Cadman: His Life and Works. PhD diss., Eastman School of Music, University of Rochester, 1978. 474 pp.
"Fox Film Corporation Contract" covers Cadman's short period under contract to the studio in 1929–1930, largely through correspondence with lyricist Nelle Richmond Eberhart, 253–63.

Phillips, Nicola.
   An Investigation of the Role of Music as an Articulator of Narrative Structure in Film. MPhil, University of Cambridge, 1995.
Discusses the narrative functions of film music.

Pinsonneault, Michael.
   Social Dimensions of Hollywood Movie Music. PhD diss., Concordia University, Montreal, 1999. 285 pp.
An analysis of film music and society—theoretical considerations, economics, technology, politics—and the social dimensions of film music content. Discusses the lack of musical censorship of composers writing dramatic underscores, 132–36.

Poché, Bill Joseph.
    Musical Content and Thematic Process in the Star Wars *Concert Suites of John Williams*. MA thesis, San Diego State University, 1995. 174 pp.

Porfirio, Robert Gerald.
    The Dark Age of American Film: A Study of the American Film Noir (1940–1960). PhD thesis, Yale University, 1979.
Material on Miklós Rózsa and jazz, including "Sequence from *The Dark Corner*: Aural Structure—Music and Effects," with music examples by Duke Ellington, Jimmy McHugh, and Harry Ruby, 114–23.

Prado, Sharon S.
    Leigh Harline's Pinocchio: *A Consideration of Music for Films*. MM thesis, University of Cincinnati College, Conservatory of Music, 1984. 180 pp.

Quinto, O. Lenard.
    A Survey of the Use of Music in the Entertainment Film. MM thesis, University of Southern California, 1942.

Raykoff, Ivan.
    Dreams of Love: Mythologies of the Romantic Pianist in Twentieth-Century Popular Culture. PhD thesis, University of California, San Diego, 2002. 460 pp.
Discusses José Iturbi and others, with filmography.

Reece, Nadine Michalscheck.
    On the Piano and Film Music: Advancing toward a Progressive and Relevant Pedagogy. Master's project, Boise State University, 1998. 76 pp.

Reed, Philip.
    The Incidental Music of Benjamin Britten: A Study and Catalogue of His Music for Film, Theatre and Radio. PhD thesis, University of East Anglia, 1987.

Ross, Jonah Zachary.
    Acoustic Graffiti: The Rock Soundtrack in Contemporary American Cinema. PhD diss., University of California, Berkeley, 2003. 161 pp.

Scarbrough, Michael Lee.
    Portrait of a Leading Choral Conductor: The Life and Work of Roger Wagner, 1914–1992. DMA thesis, Arizona State University, 1996. 247 pp.
Describes Wagner's start in the movie industry, 20–22; documents his work in "Movies and Television," 74–83; lists singers in the Roger Wagner Chorale who went on to successful solo careers, such as Marilyn Horne and Marni Nixon, 92–93; includes other references to Wagner's film work.

Schildt, Matthew C.
    Music for Film by American Composers during the Great Depression: Analysis and Stylistic Comparison of Film Scores, 1936–1940, by Aaron Copland, Virgil Thomson, George Antheil, and Marc Blitzstein. [Part 2.] PhD diss., Kent State University, 2005. 208 pp. [Parts 1 and 2.]

Schubert, Linda Katherine.
 Soundtracking the Past: Early Music and Its Representations in Selected History Films. PhD diss., University of Michigan, 1994. 361 pp.
Examines the scores for *The Agony and the Ecstasy* (Alex North); *Becket* and *A Man for All Seasons* (Laurence Rosenthal); *The Private Life of Henry VIII* (Kurt Schroeder); *Quo Vadis?* (Miklós Rózsa); and *The Sea Hawk* (Erich Wolfgang Korngold).

Schwartz, Stanley.
 Film Music and Attitude Change: A Study to Determine the Effect of Manipulating a Musical Soundtrack upon Changes in Attitude toward Militarism-Pacifism Held by Tenth Grade Social Studies Students. PhD diss., Syracuse University, 1970. 75 pp.

Siemers, Robert.
 The Humorous Contribution by the Background Music in Three Classic Warner Brothers Cartoons. DMA thesis, Indiana University, Bloomington, 1997. 52 pp.

Silliman, Thomas Leland.
 Research into the Problems Encountered in a Film Experiment Integrating Abstract Forms and Music. MA thesis, UCLA, 1958. 67 pp.

Simpson, Alexander Thomas, Jr.
 Opera on Film: A Study of the History and the Aesthetic Principles and Conflicts of a Hybrid Genre. PhD diss., University of Kentucky, 1990. 196 pp.

Smith, Irma M.
 Cocteau's Collaborations with Musicians. PhD diss., Pennsylvania State University, 1975. 354 pp.

Smith, Jeff [Jeffrey Paul].
 The Sounds of Commerce: Popular Film Music from 1960 to 1973. PhD diss., University of Wisconsin, Madison, 1995. 442 pp.
Formed the basis for Smith's book, *The Sounds of Commerce: Marketing Popular Film Music* (1998).

Smith, Julia Frances.
 Aaron Copland: His Work and Contribution to American Music: A Study of the Development of His Musical Style and an Analysis of the Various Techniques of Writing He Has Employed in His Work. PhD thesis, New York University, 1952. 648 pp.
Published in book form by Dutton in 1955.

Steiner, Frederick R.
 The Making of an American Film Composer: A Study of Alfred Newman's Music in the First Decade of the Sound Era. PhD diss., University of Southern California, 1981. 441 pp.
Newman's life and film music are examined in the sections "Boy Pianist (1900–14)," "Making a Name (1915–16)," "Getting into Show Business (1917–19)," "The Broadway Years (1920–29)," "Broadway to Hollywood (1930)," The UA [United Artists] Years (1930–39)," "From *Street Scene* to *The Dark Angel*," "*Beloved Enemy* to *The Hunchback of Notre Dame*," and "Analysis of *Wuthering Heights*." Offers insight into the origins of

American film music style and Newman's philosophy. Filmography. See "About Alfred Newman: New Data (and Some Errata)," in the *Cue Sheet* (October 2005) for updates.

Sutton, Martin.
    The Hollywood Musical. MA thesis, University of Exeter, 1976.

Swynnoe, Jan G.
    Brief Encounter: British Composers and the Seventh Art (British Film Music 1930–1960). PhD thesis, University of Wales, Bangor, 2000. 268 pp.
Formed the basis for Swynnoe's book, *The Best Years of British Film Music, 1936–1958* (2002).

Traubner, Richard.
    Operette: The German and Austrian Musical Film. PhD thesis, New York University, 1996. 346 pp.

Tucker, Aubrey S.
    Music from The Red Pony: *Film Music by Aaron Copland*. MM thesis, Rice University, 1989.

Vitale, John L.
    The Effect of Music on the Meanings Students Gain from Film. EdD, University of Toronto, 2002. 296 pp.

Voill, Martin A.
    Science Fiction Film Music after Star Wars *(1978)*. MA thesis, Loyola University, New Orleans, 1990.

Wescott, Steven Dwight.
    Miklos Rozsa: A Portrait of the Composer as Seen through an Analysis of His Early Works for Feature Films and the Concert Stage. PhD diss., University of Minnesota, 1990. 527 pp.
Historical account based on interviews, archival material, and analysis, with emphasis on film noir and historical epics. Wescott was working on this dissertation at the time his landmark book, *A Comprehensive Bibliography of Music for Film and Television*, was published in 1985.

West, Melissa.
    Music, Emotions and the Role of the Body. MA thesis, McMaster University, 1998. 145 pp.
Examines James Horner's music for *Glory*.

Westby, James John.
    Castelnuovo-Tedesco in America: The Film Music. PhD diss., UCLA, 1994. 718 pp.
Mario Castelnuovo-Tedesco, his film music, and his influence on Hollywood composers.

Whalley, Ian Harry.
    Music for the Dream Factory: 1955 to 1985. MSS thesis, University of Waikato, 1991. 102 pp.

A sociological study of the use of rock music in mainstream Hollywood films.

Whitesitt, Linda.
>   *The Life and Music of George Antheil, 1900–1959.* PhD diss. (revised), University of
>   Maryland, 1981. 351 pp.

A cursory look at Antheil's film scores. "Catalogue of Antheil's Music" includes film
and television scores, 250–60.

Widgery, Claudia.
>   *The Kinetic and Temporal Interaction of Music and Film: Three Documentaries of
>   1930's America.* PhD diss., University of Maryland, 1990. 471 pp.

Includes an extensive analysis of Aaron Copland's score for *The City*, 256–315, and
analyses of scores by Virgil Thomson for *The River* and Marc Blitzstein for *Valley Town*.

Wood, Simon.
>   *Scoring the Body: Psychoanalysis, Image Schemata, and the Syntax of the Narrative
>   Film Score.* MA thesis, McMaster University, 1999. 144 pp.

Yeh, Yueh-yu [Emilie Yueh-yu Yeh].
>   *A National Score: Popular Music and Taiwanese Cinema.* PhD diss., University of
>   Southern California, 1995. 263 pp.

Topics include the use of songs in 1970s policy films and romantic melodramas.

Zeliff, Edward David.
>   *Dimitri Tiomkin: An Analysis of Style.* DMA diss., Claremont Graduate University,
>   2002. 52 pp.

A close examination of distinguishing characteristics of Tiomkin's style, including
rhythmic vitality, *sotto voce* scoring, orchestral coloring, melodic invention, boldness and
tenderness, and tempo flexibility. Vocal uses, source music, unusual instrumentation, and
quiet openings and closings are discussed, as are molding influences. With music examples.

Chapter 3

Composer Biographies

William Alwyn
Johnson, Ian.
  William Alwyn: The Art of Film Music. Woodbridge, Suffolk, U.K.: Boydell Press,
  2005. 357 pp.
An evaluation of Alwyn's film music that incorporates biographical and historical elements. Discusses Alwyn's output, film by film, from 1937 to 1963. The author takes Alwyn's writings (in addition to a lecture the composer gave late in his film career) on his philosophy and approach to film scoring and integrates them with his own analysis of the music, one of the book's strengths. Alwyn believed that sound film should draw from stage, not silent film, practices. An entire chapter discusses the support the composer received early in his career from the music director and conductor Muir Mathieson. The William Alwyn Foundation provided a publication grant, and the author was granted access to Alwyn's papers through his widow, Mary Alwyn (née Doreen Carwithen). The author has a background in history and the arts.

David Amram
Amram, David.
  Vibrations: The Adventures and Musical Times of David Amram. New York: Macmillan, 1968. 469 pp. ill. Westport, Conn.: Greenwood Press, 1980. 469 pp. New York: Thunder's Mouth Press, 2001. 498 pp.
Autobiography of the American composer best known for scoring *The Manchurian Candidate*.

George Antheil
Antheil, George.
  Bad Boy of Music. Garden City, N.Y.: Doubleday, Doran and Co., 1945. 378 pp. London and New York: Hurst and Blackett, 1947. 295 pp. New York: Da Capo Press, 1981. 378 pp. With a new introduction by Charles Amirkhanian. Hollywood: Samuel French, 1990. 378 pp.
Contains a chapter titled "Hollywood," pp. 281–368 (1945), on Antheil's experiences in film composing.

Louis Applebaum
Pitman, Walter.
  Louis Applebaum: A Passion for Culture. Toronto: Dundurn Press, 2002. 512 pp.

Biography of the Canadian composer, notable for his documentary film scores.

Malcolm Arnold
Burton-Page, Piers.
> *Philharmonic Concerto: The Life and Music of Sir Malcolm Arnold.* London: Methuen, 1994. 194 pp. ill.

"Rhapsody for Orchestra: or *The Sound Barrier*" contains a survey of Arnold's film music, 44–55; "The Films of Malcolm Arnold" is a list of works, 182–85. The book's title is taken from an Arnold symphony.

Cole, Hugo.
> *Malcolm Arnold: An Introduction to His Music.* London: Faber Music, in association with Faber and Faber, 1989.

"Composer as Illustrator: Film Music" is a survey of Arnold's most popular works, 56–65.

Craggs, Stewart R.
> *Malcolm Arnold: A Bio-Bibliography.* Westport, Conn.: London: Greenwood Press, 1998. 232 pp.

"Works and Performances" has a section on film music; filmography, 62–82. Also contains an alphabetical and chronological list of works.

Jackson, Paul R. W.
> *The Life and Music of Sir Malcolm Arnold: The Brilliant and the Dark.* Aldershot, Hants, U.K.; Burlington, Vt.: Ashgate, 2003.

"Films, 1947–69: 'Solving Jigsaw Puzzles'" offers a survey of Arnold's work, 41–55.

Meredith, Anthony, and Paul Harris.
> *Malcolm Arnold: Rogue Genius: The Life and Music of Britain's Most Misunderstood Composer.* Norwich, U.K.: Thames/Elkin, 2004.

Arnold's music is covered in its historical context, including music for documentaries, 103–8; and music for the films of director David Lean and others, 165–69.

Poulton, Alan J., comp.
> *The Music of Malcolm Arnold: A Catalogue.* London: Faber and Faber, 1986.

"Film Music," 128–57; "Incidental Music for Radio, Television and Theatre," 158–66.

John Barry
Fiegel, Eddi.
> *John Barry: A Sixties Theme: From James Bond to Midnight Cowboy.* London: Constable, 1998. 261 pp. ill.

A music journalist and broadcaster follows Barry's journey from pop star (the John Barry Seven) and arranger (for Adam Faith) to film composer. Includes material from interviews with Barry, lyricist Leslie Bricusse, actor Michael Caine, and director John Schlesinger, among others. Discography and index.

Leonard, Geoff, Pete Walker, and Gareth Bramley.
> *John Barry: A Life in Music.* Bristol, U.K.: Sansom, 1998. 243 pp.

The authors, each a Barry fan and authority, focus on the composer's professional life and accomplishments. Details of Barry's personal life are not covered. Includes chapters on the James Bond films, scores for the films of Bryan Forbes, and music for television, television commercials, radio, and the concert hall. Copiously illustrated with more than 300 photographs (half in color), including album covers. Discography and index.

Richard Rodney Bennett

Seabrook, Mike.
   [*Richard Rodney Bennett*. Scholar Press.]
This book was announced in 1997 and appears in some bibliographies; however, no evidence was found that it was ever published.

Robert Russell Bennett

Ferencz, George J., ed.
   The Broadway Sound: The Autobiography and Selected Essays of Robert Russell Bennett. Rochester, N.Y.: Univ. of Rochester Press, 1999. 356 pp.
First publication of Bennett's autobiography, written in the late 1970s. Topics include playing for silent films, 36–37; New York films, 44–45; experiences in Hollywood; and remembrances of Irving Berlin, Jerome Kern, Cole Porter, Richard Rodgers, and Vincent Youmans. Compiled and edited by a music professor.

James Bernard

Huckvale, David.
   James Bernard, Composer to Count Dracula: A Critical Biography. Jefferson, N.C.: McFarland, 2006.
Includes an examination of Bernard's scores for Hammer films. Music examples, filmography, discography, bibliography, and index. The author, a British freelance lecturer in music and cultural history, wrote his dissertation on music for Hammer film productions. Included herein since it was announced for publication in 2002 (Westport, Conn.: Praeger), though no definitive evidence of its publication by Praeger can be found.

Leonard Bernstein

Bernstein, Leonard.
   The Joy of Music. New York: Simon & Schuster, 1959. London: Weidenfeld & Nicolson, 1968. New York: Simon & Schuster, 1980. New York: Anchor Books, 1994. Pompton Plains, N.J.: Amadeus Press, 2004.
"Interlude: Upper Dubbing, Calif.," written in 1954, is on dubbing the music for *On the Waterfront* (1954), 65–69.

Burton, Humphrey.
   Leonard Bernstein. New York: Doubleday, 1994.
Contains material regarding *On the Waterfront* (1954), 236–38.

Myers, Paul.
   Leonard Bernstein. London: Phaidon Press, 1998. 240 pp. ill.
References Bernstein's film music.

Secrest, Meryle.
  Leonard Bernstein: A Life. New York: Knopf, 1994. New York: Vintage Books, 1995. 471 pp.
Passages on his work in Hollywood.

John Cacavas
Cacavas, John, with Bonnie Becker Cacavas.
  It's More Than Do-Re-Mi: My Life in Music. Philadelphia: Xlibris, 2003. 482 pp. ill.
A prolific arranger and Hollywood film and television composer, Cacavas and his wife, Bonnie, filled this autobiography with anecdotes based on his personal experiences. Material includes "Morton Gould," 151–58; "Meeting Ira [Gershwin]," 202–13; "Hollywood Beckons," 300–306; "The Academy Awards," 307–9; "The Universal Lot," 319–23; "CLGA" (Cacavas served as president of the Composers and Lyricists Guild of America), 340–43; "Rejection," 353–57; "More about TV Movies," 363–72; "Bernard Herrmann," 385–86; "It Could Only Happen in Hollywood," 387–89. Filmography and discography.

Benny Carter
Berger, Morroe, Edward Berger, and James Patrick.
  Benny Carter: A Life in American Music. Metuchen, N.J.: Scarecrow Press, 1982. 2nd ed., in two volumes. Lanham, Md.: Scarecrow Press; The Institute of Jazz Studies, Rutgers University, 2001–2002.
Carter was one of the first black arrangers and musicians accepted by the Hollywood studio system in the 1940s, and later inspired and mentored the young Quincy Jones. Documents his work in film and television.

Aaron Copland
Berger, Arthur.
  Aaron Copland. New York: Oxford Univ. Press, 1953. Reprint, Westport, Conn.: Greenwood Press, 1971. New York: Da Capo Press, 1990.
"Copland and Hollywood," 85–90.

Butterworth, Neil.
  The Music of Aaron Copland. London: Toccata Press, 1985. New York: Universe Books, 1986.
A chronological survey with some references to film music; see especially *The Red Pony* suite, 113–17.

Copland, Aaron, and Vivian Perlis.
  Copland: 1900 through 1942. New York: St. Martin's/Marek, 1984.
"Hollywood," 295–304.

Kostelanetz, Richard, ed.
  Aaron Copland: A Reader: Selected Writings 1923–1972. New York: Routledge, 2004.
Contains the essays "Tip to Moviegoers: Take Off Those Ear-Muffs" (originally published 1949), 104–10; "Second Thoughts on Hollywood" (originally published 1949), 111–17.

Pollack, Howard.
> *Aaron Copland: The Life and Work of an Uncommon Man*. New York: Henry Holt, 1999. Urbana: Univ. of Illinois Press, 2000.

"Music for the Movies and for Keyboard" includes "Copland on Film Music," 336–50. Music for specific films is discussed throughout.

Robertson, Marta, and Robin Armstrong.
> *Aaron Copland: A Guide to Research*. New York: Routledge, 2001.

"Film Scores" contains four capsule reviews of books and dissertations on the composer, 171–73.

Duke Ellington
George, Don.
> *Sweet Man: The Real Duke Ellington*. New York: Putnam, 1981.

"Paris Blues" discusses Ellington's music for the film of the same name, 153–57.

Hasse, John Edward.
> *Beyond Category: The Life and Genius of Duke Ellington*. New York: Da Capo Press, 1995.

References to film appearances and film music, 128–29, 183–85, 248–50, 363–64.

Hugo Friedhofer
Danly, Linda, ed.
> *Hugo Friedhofer: The Best Years of His Life: A Hollywood Master of Music for the Movies*. Lanham, Md.: Scarecrow Press, 1999. 212 pp. ill.

"Introduction," by Tony Thomas, 1–2; "A Portrait of Hugo Friedhofer," by Linda Danly, 3–25; "AFI Oral History," interview by Irene Kahn Atkins, 27–154 [abridged]; "Correspondence with Page Cook," 159–73; "Epilogue," by Gene Lees, 175–84 [abridged from Lees's chapter on Friedhofer in *Singers and the Song* (Oxford Univ. Press, 1987)]; "In Memoriam," by David Raksin, 185–87. Filmography compiled by Friedhofer, Clifford McCarty, and Tony Thomas. Thomas and Danly served as trustees for the Film Music Society; Thomas suggested she take on this project. Friedhofer is Danly's favorite composer; her dog, Hugo, is named after him.

Philip Glass
Glass, Philip, edited and with supplementary material by Robert T. Jones.
> *Music by Philip Glass*. New York: Harper and Row, 1987. New York: Da Capo Press, 1995.

Brief coverage of *Koyaanisqatsi* (1983) and *Mishima* (1985), 203–4.

Albert Glasser
Glasser, Albert.
> *I Did It!!!* Los Angeles, ca. early 1980s.

This unpublished autobiography includes material on Glasser's work in music prep as a copyist at RKO and as an assistant to Dimitri Tiomkin on the "Why We Fight" documentaries made by Frank Capra for the U.S. Army Signal Corps during World War II. A copy of the manuscript is in the book collection of the Margaret Herrick Library at the Academy of Motion Picture Arts and Sciences.

Morton Gould
Goodman, Peter W.
> *Morton Gould: American Salute.* Portland, Ore.: Amadeus Press, 2000. 382 pp. ill.

This biography of the composer, written by a journalist and classical music editor, contains a chapter, "Lenny, and Hollywood," on Gould's brief foray into film music in 1944, 156–70.

Earle Hagen
Hagen, Earle.
> *Memoirs of a Famous Composer–Nobody Ever Heard Of.* Philadelphia: Xlibris, 2000. 336 pp.

Hagen, best known for his work in television, goes behind the scenes in this breezy anecdotal autobiography to reveal that being a commercial composer involves more than just writing music. Chapters cover Hagen's beginnings as a big-band trombonist with Benny Goodman and Tommy Dorsey and as an arranger for CBS television and the Army Air Corps. He details his work under Alfred Newman as a staff arranger and orchestrator at 20th Century-Fox from 1946 to 1952, primarily on musical numbers. Hagen left Fox with Herbert Spencer to forge a career in television music, and his prolific output over the next thirty years is chronicled. He wrote themes and background music for *The Andy Griffith Show, The Dick Van Dyke Show, I Spy, That Girl,* and *The Mod Squad,* among others. His friendships with producers Sheldon Leonard and Ernie Frankel provide perspective on the business side of music. Hugo Friedhofer and Herbert Spencer are profiled through their business relationships and friendships with Hagen. The book clearly delineates and explains the division of labor involved in creating music on demand. Hagen also discusses authoring two textbooks and establishing his BMI film scoring workshop.

Marvin Hamlisch
Hamlisch, Marvin, with Gerald Gardner.
> *The Way I Was.* New York: Charles Scribner's Sons; Toronto: Maxwell Macmillan Canada; New York: Maxwell Macmillan International, 1992. 234 pp. ill.

This memoir includes coverage of Hamlisch's Hollywood career.

Victor Herbert
Waters, Edward N.
> *Victor Herbert: A Life in Music.* New York: Macmillan, 1955. Reprint, New York: Da Capo Press, 1978.

"Motion Pictures and the Irish Operetta" contains a detailed history of the composition and historical significance of Herbert's symphonic score for *The Fall of a Nation* (1916), 484–507; see also "Aftermath and Twilight," 537–40.

Bernard Herrmann
Johnson, Edward.
> *Bernard Herrmann: Hollywood's Music-Dramatist.* Foreword by Miklós Rózsa. Rickmansworth, U.K.: Triad Press, 1977. 60 pp.

This booklet, published as a tribute two years after Herrmann's death, includes a biographical sketch, filmography, catalog of works, discography, and bibliography. Draws on material from a British Film Institute program booklet that included a 1972 interview with Herrmann by Ted Gilling. Contains "Elgar: A Constant Source of Joy," written by Herrmann for the *Edward Elgar Centenary Sketches* (Novello, 1957), 29–31. The author is a British music critic who befriended Herrmann around 1970 and introduced him to Unicorn Records, which released the score for *Psycho*, conducted by Herrmann.

Smith, Steven C.
> *A Heart at Fire's Center: The Life and Music of Bernard Herrmann*. Berkeley: Univ. of California Press, 1991. 415 pp. ill.

Biography based on extensive interviews and research. Herrmann's former wives Norma Shepard, Lucille Fletcher, and Lucy Anderson provided access to papers and photographs along with their own recollections. Other sources include David Raksin and Norman Corwin; the latter collaborated with Herrmann on numerous radio programs. Appendix includes filmography, concert works, radio works, television music, and recordings conducted by Herrmann. Selected bibliography. A groundbreaking work that should set the standard to which all film composer biographies should compare. A journalist and author, Smith is a writer and producer for television and cable.

Arthur Honegger

Halbreich, Harry.
> *Arthur Honegger*. Translated by Roger Nichols. Portland, Ore.: Amadeus Press, 1999. Translation of *Arthur Honegger: Un musicien dans la cité des hommes*, 1992.

The biographical component of this work, titled "Chronicles of a Life," contains numerous references to Honegger's film music as well as a chapter, "Toward the Summit: Claudel and the Cinema," on his 1930s film music, 132–61. "Inventory of Works" contains sections on his piano works, chamber works, art songs, and orchestral works for film. A typical entry includes an informational paragraph, first performance, instrumentation and versions, duration, and composition date. A chapter on incidental music contains a section titled "Music for Film," with an introductory assessment and a chart with film title, composition date, duration of surviving music, and publication information, 523–46.

Spratt, Geoffrey K.
> *The Music of Arthur Honegger*. Cork, Ireland: Cork Univ. Press, 1987.

In the section "Film Scores" is an index to scores mentioned in the text, 495–96. Filmography.

Quincy Jones

Bayer, Linda N.
> *Quincy Jones: Overcoming Adversity*. Philadelphia: Chelsea House Publishers, 2001. 104 pp.

The composer's inspirational life story, targeted at young readers. See "Hollywood Beckons," 51–61; chronology, 94–97.

Horricks, Raymond.
> *Quincy Jones*. Tunbridge Wells, Kent: Spellmount; New York: Hippocrene Books, 1985.

This 127-page monograph contains some references to Jones's film music.

Jones, Quincy.
> *Q: The Autobiography of Quincy Jones*. New York: Doubleday, 2001. 412 pp. New York: Harlem Moon, 2002.

"Frank," on Frank Sinatra, contains material on the composer's film scores, 176–78; "Helter Skelter" covers Jones's Hollywood film scores, 185–200; discussion of the end of his film music career, 209–11. Filmography.

Kavanaugh, Lee Hill.
   Quincy Jones: Musician, Composer, Producer. Springfield, N.J.: Enslow, 1998. 128 pp.
For young adult readers.

Ross, Courtney Sale, ed.
   Listen Up: The Lives of Quincy Jones. New York: Warner Books, 1990. 191 pp.
Described by the *New York Times* as the ultimate multimedia package: a book, a movie, a compact disc, an audiocassette, and a videocassette. Contains an essay by Nelson George.

Erich Wolfgang Korngold
Carroll, Brendan.
   Erich Wolfgang Korngold, 1897–1957: His Life and Works. Paisley, Scotland: Wilfion Books, 1984. 42 pp.
A short monograph by the president of the International Korngold Society, who went on to write a full-length biography of the composer (see next entry). Includes a short biography, commentary on *The Adventures of Robin Hood* (1938), and filmography.

Carroll, Brendan G.
   The Last Prodigy: A Biography of Erich Wolfgang Korngold. Portland, Ore.: Amadeus Press, 1997. 464 pp. ill.
Near definitive biography based on 25 years of research, with full cooperation of the Korngold family and estate. Author is president of the International Korngold Society. "From Vienna to Hollywood: 1934–1944" consists of five chapters on Korngold's film music, 231–314. Complete list of works. Index.

Duchen, Jessica.
   Erich Wolfgang Korngold. London: Phaidon Press Ltd., 1996. 239 pp. ill.
Synthesizes the existing literature on Korngold. Two chapters devoted to Korngold's Hollywood composing career, 149–200. Author is a freelance writer and editor of the magazine *Classical Piano.* Her 1987 thesis covered the musical and dramatic structure of Korngold's opera *Die tote Stadt* (The Dead City). List of works. Selected discography.

Korngold, Julius.
   Child Prodigy: Erich Wolfgang Korngold's Years of Childhood. New York: Willard, 1945. 80 pp.
A booklet containing excerpts from the unpublished memoirs—written in German—of Erich Wolfgang Korngold's father, Julius, a Viennese music critic. Though it was published after the younger Korngold had found success as a film composer, it covers only his pre-adult life, including his training and success as a musical prodigy. The decision to publish only the material on the younger Korngold was no doubt influenced by his fame in America.

Louis Levy
Levy, Louis.
   Music for the Movies. London: Sampson Low, Marston & Co., 1948. 182 pp. ill.

The British composer's memoir incorporates biographical data, anecdotes, information on the process of writing music for films, and some general film music history. As head of a music department servicing both Gaumont British and Gainsborough films, Levy was an influential figure in British film music in the 1930s and 1940s. Index.

Henry Mancini
Mancini, Henry, with Gene Lees.
   Did They Mention the Music? Chicago: Contemporary Books, 1989. 252 pp. ill.
Mancini's anecdotal autobiography discusses his early struggles, his television work at Universal Studios, his lengthy film career, and his personal and family life. Appendix lists awards, film and television credits, and discography.

Lyn Murray
Murray, Lyn.
   Musician: A Hollywood Journal of Wives, Women, Writers, Lawyers, Directors, Producers, and Music. Secaucus, N.J.: Lyle Stuart, 1987. 388 pp. ill.
A collection of Murray's journal entries rather than a biography. Chronicles his professional, personal, and social life from 1947 to 1983. Many of his colleagues are mentioned in multiple entries, including Jeff Alexander, Jerry Fielding, Bernard Herrmann, lyricist Sid Kuller, Louis Lipstone, André Previn, David Raksin, Fred Steiner, Leith Stevens, and Stanley Wilson. Murray served on the Executive Committee of the music branch of the Academy of Motion Picture Arts and Sciences; for a rare insider's view of that period, see p. 373.

Alex North
Henderson, Sanya Shoilevska.
   Alex North: Film Composer: A Biography, with Musical Analyses of A Streetcar Named Desire, Spartacus, The Misfits, Under the Volcano, *and* Prizzi's Honor. Foreword by John Williams. Jefferson, N.C.: McFarland, 2003. 264 pp.
The author, a Macedonian-born musicologist, pianist, and composer who now resides in the United States, wrote her thesis on Alex North for Novi Sad University in 1998. Her studies in the U.S. were sponsored by Dr. Beverly Grigsby of California State University, Northridge. Jeannie Pool, then executive director of the Film Music Society, facilitated Henderson's access to research material, while North's widow, Anna, granted interviews and full access to the composer's studio and music prior to the donation of North's papers to the Margaret Herrick Library. Part One, at just under a hundred pages, is on North's life and career. Details on his early life are from North's brother, Harry; others interviewed include playwright Arthur Miller, David Raksin, dancer Anna Sokolow, and Fred Steiner. Part Two contains astute analyses, with numerous music examples, of the scores for *A Streetcar Named Desire* (1951), *Spartacus* (1960), *The Misfits* (1961), *Under the Volcano* (1984), and *Prizzi's Honor* (1985). Filmography, discography, awards, bibliography, and index.

Stu Phillips
Phillips, Stu.
   "Stu Who?": Forty Years of Navigating the Minefields of the Music Business. Studio City, Calif.: Cisum Press, 2003. 301 pp. ill.
Extensive coverage of the composer's film and television career from the 1960s through the 1980s, 133–241. Sections include "Henry Mancini," 154–56; "Goodbye Records...

Hello Movies," 174–77; "The Russ Meyer Connection," 187–93; "The Glen Larson Years," 205–7; "*Battlestar Galactica*," 215–28; "The Fortuitous Fox Years," 233–36. Filmography.

André Previn
Bookspan, Martin, and Ross Yockey.
  André Previn: A Biography. Garden City, N.Y.: Doubleday, 1981.
See the section titled "The Hollywood Life," 1–96.

Freedland, Michael.
  Andre Previn. London: Century, 1991.
Chapters 4–11 cover Hollywood, 41–165.

Greenfield, Edward.
  Andre Previn. New York: Drake Publishers; London: Allan, 1973.
Previn's film music career is covered on pp. 20–35.

Previn, André.
  No Minor Chords: My Days in Hollywood. New York: Doubleday, 1991. 148 pp. ill.
Previn's anecdotal memoir of his life as a composer and arranger in Hollywood from 1948 to 1964, primarily at MGM.

Previn, André, and Antony Hopkins.
  Music Face to Face. London: Hamish Hamilton, 1971. New York: Scribner's, 1971. 131 pp.
Previn's conversation with Hopkins covers his Hollywood film music career, 47–55, 65–70, including his work with Herbert Stothart, 52–53.

Ruttencutter, Helen Drees.
  Previn. New York: Marek/St. Martin's, 1985. 234 pp. ill.
Cursory coverage of Previn's Hollywood years.

Sergei Prokofiev
Hanson, Lawrence and Elisabeth Hanson.
  Prokofiev: A Biography in Three Movements. New York: Random House, 1964. 368 pp.
Discussion of the composer's film scores, 239–40, 269–70, 294–96.

Jaffé, Daniel.
  Sergey Prokofiev. London: Phaidon, 1998. 240 pp.
Cursory coverage of the composer's film scores.

Nest'ev, I. V.
  Prokofiev. Stanford, Calif.: Stanford Univ. Press, 1960. 528 pp.
Discusses Prokofiev's film scores. Originally published in Russia.

Nice, David.
  Prokofiev: From Russia to the West, 1891–1935. New Haven, Conn.: Yale Univ. Press, 2003.

"Sound and Vision, 1932–4" includes a discussion of Prokofiev's film music, 298–319.

Prokofiev, Sergei, trans. and ed. by Oleg Prokofiev.
> *Soviet Diary, 1927, and Other Writings*. Boston: Northeastern Univ. Press, 1992. 315 pp.

Prokofiev writes about *Lieutenant Kijé* in the autobiographical section, 295–96. Christopher Palmer served as associate editor.

Robinson, Harlow.
> *Sergei Prokofiev: A Biography*. New York: Viking, 1987. New York: Paragon House, 1988. Boston: Northeastern Univ. Press, 2002.

Cursory coverage of his film scores and interest in film.

Alan Rawsthorne
McCabe, John.
> *Alan Rawsthorne: Portrait of a Composer*. Oxford, U.K.: Oxford Univ. Press, 1999. 311 pp.

Contains material on the British composer's film work.

J. A. C. Redford
Redford, J. A. C.
> *Welcome All Wonders: A Composer's Journey*. Grand Rapids, Mich.: Baker Books, 1997. 341 pp.

This autobiography focuses on the composer's journey from Mormonism to Christianity, with references throughout to his musical and spiritual development. For accounts of his film and television career, see "The Hollywood Shuffle," 125–46, and "Music under Mercy," 211–34. Filmography and discography.

Nelson Riddle
Levinson, Peter J.
> *September in the Rain: The Life of Nelson Riddle*. New York: Billboard Books, 2001. 320 pp. ill.

"Hollywood Calling" covers Riddle's early career in radio and television, 63–81. Additional documentation throughout on his film and television work. The author is a jazz publicist who knew Riddle and interviewed friends and family of the arranger, best known for his association with Frank Sinatra.

Miklós Rózsa
Palmer, Christopher.
> *Miklós Rózsa: A Sketch of His Life and Work*. London: Breitkopf and Härtel, 1975. 78 pp. ill.

This monograph contains a short biography and essays on perspective, concert music, and film music; appendixes (a complete list of concert works and filmography), and index. Rózsa supplied the music examples and photographs to the author, who was his orchestrator and friend in the composer's later years.

Rózsa, Miklós.
> *Double Life: The Autobiography of Miklós Rózsa*. Tunbridge Wells, U.K.: Midas Books; New York: Hippocrene Books, 1982. 224 pp. ill. Tunbridge Wells, U.K.:

Baton Press, 1984. Also published as *Double Life: Miklós Rózsa*. New York: Wynwood Press, 1989. 256 pp. ill.

The composer discusses his childhood in Hungary; recounts his early years in Leipzig, Paris, and London; and details his Hollywood career, including his experiences as a staff composer at MGM. List of concert works, filmography, and concert music and film music discographies. The 1989 publication is retypeset, with a preface by André Previn; otherwise it is identical to the 1982 edition.

Walter Scharf

Scharf, Walter, with Michael Freedland.

Composed and Conducted by Walter Scharf. Totowa, N.J.: Vallentine, Mitchell & Co. Ltd., 1988. 231 pp. ill.

Autobiography with anecdotes about the people Scharf worked with and for. Filmography.

Nathaniel Shilkret

Shilkret, Nathaniel.

Nathaniel Shilkret: Sixty Years in the Music Business. Edited by Niel Shell and Barbara Shilkret. Lanham, Md.: Scarecrow Press, 2005. 345 pp.

This anecdotal autobiography, completed around 1965, was edited by the composer's daughter-in-law and her son. Shilkret writes about his lengthy career as a composer and arranger, his work as a music director at RKO from the mid-1930s on, and his conducting career at MGM in the 1940s. Many of his professional associates are discussed, including Nathaniel Finston (also his friend and brother-in-law), Louis Gruenberg, Erno Rapée, and Max Steiner. Filmography, discography, and bibliography.

Dimitri Shostakovich

Fay, Laurel E.

Shostakovich: A Life. New York: Oxford Univ. Press, 2000.

For a discussion of the Russian composer's film scores, see pp. 45–46, 48–49, 246–47, 253–55.

MacDonald, Ian.

The New Shostakovich. Boston: Northeastern Univ. Press, 1990. 339 pp.

Includes a discussion of Shostakovich's film scores.

Riley, John.

Dimitri Shostakovich: A Life in Film. New York: I. B. Tauris, 2005. 150 pp. ill.

The first full-length book in English devoted to the composer's film scores. The films are examined in chronological order and the music is discussed in the context of the film. Covers all of Shostakovich's original film scores, with commentary on the political, social, and personal circumstances surrounding their creation. The author, who has a background in Soviet music and film, believes that Shostakovich's film music legacy may be underappreciated because the composer did not have a long-term association with a notable director (Shostakovich wrote nearly forty scores with twenty-one different directors). Chronology and filmography.

Volkov, Solomon, ed.
> *Testimony: The Memoirs of Dmitri Shostakovich*. New York: Harper & Row, 1979.
> New York: Harper Colophon Books, 1980. 1st Limelight ed., New York: Limelight
> Editions, 1984. 8th Limelight ed., New York: Limelight Editions, 2004.

For Shostakovich's film work, see pp. 148–51 (2004). Translated from the Russian by
Antonina W. Bouis.

Wilson, Elizabeth.
> *Shostakovich: A Life Remembered*. Princeton, N.J.: Princeton Univ. Press, 1994.
> London: Faber & Faber, 1994.

See "Film Scores," in index.

Max Steiner
Steiner, Max.
> *Notes to You*. Unpublished [written between 1963 and 1965].

The manuscript for this autobiography is in the Max Steiner Collection, Arts and Communications Archive, Harold B. Lee Library, Brigham Young University.

William Grant Still
Still, Judith Anne.
> *William Grant Still: A Voice High-Sounding*. Flagstaff, Ariz.: Master-Player Library,
> 2003. 318 pp.

Sixteen essays written by the composer's daughter.

Still, Judith Anne, Michael J. Dabrishus, and Carolyn L. Quin.
> *William Grant Still: A Bio-bibliography*. Westport, Conn.: Greenwood Press, 1996.
> 331 pp.

Contains a biographical sketch, works and performances, writings, bibliography, discography, and preliminary list of arrangements and orchestrations.

Toru Takemitsu
Burt, Peter.
> *The Music of Toru Takemitsu*. New York: Cambridge Univ. Press, 2001.

Includes a brief survey of Takemitsu's film music, 46–49; other films mentioned
throughout the text.

Mikis Theodorakis
Giannaris, George.
> *Mikis Theodorakis: Music and Social Change*. Foreword by Mikis Theodorakis.
> New York: Praeger, 1972. 322 pp.

Primarily a political biography. Brief discussion of Theodorakis's music for Greek films,
140–44.

Virgil Thomson
Hoover, Kathleen, and John Cage.
> *Virgil Thomson: His Life and Music*. New York: T. Yoseloff, 1959. Reprint,
> Freeport, N.Y.: Books for Libraries Press, 1970.

This book takes an unconventional approach: Cage, a twentieth-century concert composer, writes on the music of Thomson, a fellow concert composer who also scored a

handful of influential documentary films; see pp. 176–83, 199–200, 207–14. Thomson granted Cage access to unpublished manuscripts and private recordings. The coauthor, Hoover, discusses Thomson's life, including his film music, 85–90, 102–4. See also "Film Music," in list of works, 273–74.

Dimitri Tiomkin
Elley, Derek.
> *Dimitri Tiomkin: The Man and His Music*. London: British Film Institute, 1986. 86 pp.

This dossier was produced for a British Film Institute retrospective of films with music by Tiomkin at the National Film Theatre in London. Includes "An Interview with Dimitri Tiomkin," with director Curtis Lee Hanson; "Composing for Films," by Dimitri Tiomkin (reprinted from *Films in Review*, November 1951); "The Achievement of Dimitri Tiomkin," by Christopher Palmer. Filmography and discography.

Palmer, Christopher.
> *Dimitri Tiomkin: A Portrait*. London: T. E. Books, 1984. 144 pp. ill.

Organized into three parts: chronology (a biographical essay), perspective (Tiomkin's place in Hollywood and film music history), and landmarks (a musical analysis of Tiomkin's major works, with some music examples). The biographical portion draws heavily from Tiomkin's autobiography (see next entry), with new material covering the 1960s on. The author's analysis in Part 3 is the heart of the work. Photos supplied to Palmer by Olivia Tiomkin Douglas. Palmer befriended Tiomkin in the composer's later years and specialized in arranging concert suites based on Tiomkin's film scores. Principal awards and honors, filmography, and index.

Tiomkin, Dimitri, and Prosper Buranelli.
> *Please Don't Hate Me*. Garden City, N.Y.: Doubleday, 1959, 1961. 261 pp. ill.

Tiomkin's autobiography, written in a conversational style.

Vangelis
Griffin, Mark J. T.
> *Vangelis: The Unknown Man*. Ythanbank, Scotland: privately published, 1994. 92 pp. 2nd ed., U.K.: Infinite Source Ltd., 1997.

Unauthorized biography consisting largely of quotations from previously published articles and interviews. Includes coverage of the composer's film and television work.

William Walton
Kennedy, Michael.
> *Portrait of Walton*. New York: Oxford Univ. Press, 1989. New York: Clarendon Press, 1998.

"War Films, 1939–42," 108–18; material on *Henry V* (1944), 123–26; see also the classified index of works for film music, 330–31 (all pages refer to the 1989 edition).

Lloyd, Stephen.
> *William Walton: Muse of Fire*. Rochester, N.Y.: Woodbridge, Suffolk, U.K.: Boydell Press, 2001.

"A Reel Composer," 147–69; "Films Again—and Radio," 170–94; appendix 3, "Walton and Film Music," contains "Music for Shakespearean Films," by Walton, and "Recording the Music," by Muir Mathieson, 276–80. Mathieson's essay was first published in Brenda Cross, ed., *The Film* Hamlet (1948).

Walton, Susana.
  William Walton: Behind the Façade. New York: Oxford Univ. Press, 1988.
"Music for Films," 87–92; "Laurence Olivier," regarding music for *As You Like It* (1936), *Hamlet* (1948), and *Henry V* (1944), 93–99.

Meredith Willson
Oates, Bill.
  Meredith Willson, America's Music Man: The Whole Broadway-Symphonic-Radio-Motion Picture Story. Bloomington, Ind.: AuthorHouse, 2005. 230 pp.
Includes coverage of Willson's brief foray into Hollywood. The author is a radio enthusiast.

Skipper, John C.
  Meredith Willson: The Unsinkable Music Man. El Dorado Hills, Calif.: Savas Woodbury Publishers, 2000. 288 pp.
"From Broadway to Hollywood to Mason City," on Willson's work in film and television, 143–62. The author is a newspaper journalist.

Eric Zeisl
Cole, Malcolm S., and Barbara Barclay.
  Armseelchen: The Life and Music of Eric Zeisl. Westport, Conn.: Greenwood Press, 1984. 441 pp.
The Austrian émigré contributed music to feature films scored by others in the 1940s and 1950s but never received screen credit. He also wrote music for numerous MGM short films throughout the 1940s. Zeisl's life, career, music, and thematic catalog are covered. The recollections of the composer's widow, Gertrud Susan Zeisl, along with her oral history for UCLA (*Eric Zeisl: His Life and Music*), form the basis of the book. Some anecdotes regarding his film music. Zeisl taught composition theory at Los Angeles City College; Jerry Goldsmith was among his students.

Chapter 4

Songwriter and Lyricist Biographies

Harold Arlen

Jablonski, Edward.
    Harold Arlen: Happy with the Blues. Garden City, N.Y.: Doubleday, 1961. Reprint,
    New York: Da Capo Press, 1986. 286 pp.
"We're Off to See the Wizard" includes material on Hollywood, 99–107. Selected discography includes songs issued on film music soundtracks.

Jablonski, Edward.
    Harold Arlen: Rhythm, Rainbows, and Blues. Boston: Northeastern Univ. Press,
    1996. 426 pp.
"Hooray for Hollywood," 95–107; "The Works of Harold Arlen," including material on film songs, 363–84.

Burt Bacharach

Brocken, Michael.
    Bacharach: Maestro! The Life of a Pop Genius. New Malden, Surrey, U.K.: Chrome
    Dreams, 2003. 319 pp.
Includes material on his collaborations with Hal David.

Irving Berlin

Barrett, Mary Ellin.
    Irving Berlin: A Daughter's Memoir. New York: Simon & Schuster, 1994. 320 pp.
The author writes about her father's Hollywood career.

Bergreen, Laurence.
    As Thousands Cheer: The Life of Irving Berlin. New York: Viking, 1990. 658 pp.
"Hollywood Refuge," 340–67.

Ewen, David.
    The Story of Irving Berlin. New York: Holt, 1950. 179 pp.
Includes an appendix, "Motion pictures for which Berlin wrote the score."

Freedland, Michael.
    Irving Berlin. New York: Stein and Day, 1974. 224 pp. *A Salute to Irving Berlin*.
    Rev. ed. London: W. H. Allen, 1986. 316 pp.
Includes material on Berlin's experiences in Hollywood.

Furia, Philip, with Graham Wood.
  Irving Berlin: A Life in Song. New York: Schirmer Books, 1998. 323 pp.
An English professor and musical theater historian covers Berlin's film songs and his involvement in film production. Songography by Ken Bloom. Index.

Jablonski, Edward.
  Irving Berlin: American Troubadour. New York: Henry Holt, 1999. 406 pp.
Well-documented coverage of Berlin's work in Hollywood, with discussion of individual films.

Sammy Cahn
Cahn, Sammy.
    I Should Care: The Sammy Cahn Story. New York: Arbor House, 1974. 318 pp. ill.
    London: W. H. Allen, 1975. 253 pp.
Autobiography including material on the lyricist's work with his principal collaborators, Saul Chaplin (1933–1942), Jule Styne (1942–1949 and 1953–1954), Nicholas Brodszky (1949–1956), and James Van Heusen (1955–1968). Cahn also wrote *The Songwriter's Rhyming Dictionary* (New York: Facts on File, 1983).

Hoagy Carmichael
Carmichael, Hoagy.
    The Stardust Road. New York: Rinehart, 1946. 156 pp.
Carmichael writes about Hollywood beginning on p. 129.

Carmichael, Hoagy, with Stephen Longstreet.
    Sometimes I Wonder: The Story of Hoagy Carmichael. New York: Farrar, Straus and
    Giroux, 1965. 313 pp.
The songwriter in Hollywood, 192–202, 256–60, 265–66.

Sudhalter, Richard M.
    Stardust Melody: The Life and Music of Hoagy Carmichael. New York: Oxford
    Univ. Press, 2002. 432 pp.
Discusses Carmichael's film songs.

Saul Chaplin
Chaplin, Saul.
    The Golden Age of Movie Musicals and Me. Norman: Univ. of Oklahoma Press,
    1994. 262 pp. ill.
Autobiography covering the songwriter's Hollywood career, including his employment at Columbia Pictures and commentary on his mentor, Morris Stoloff.

Betty Comden
Comden, Betty.
    Off Stage. New York: Simon & Schuster, 1995. 272 pp. ill.
The lyricist's personal memoir.

Sam Coslow
Coslow, Sam.

> *Cocktails for Two: The Many Lives of Giant Songwriter Sam Coslow*. New Rochelle, N.Y.: Arlington House, 1977.

"Tin Pan Alley Goes Hollywood," 95–146; "Hollywood's Golden Age," 147–75; "Hollywood and Tin Pan Alley in the Late Thirties," 205–22.

Howard Dietz

Dietz, Howard.
> *Dancing in the Dark: Words by Howard Dietz*. New York: Quadrangle, 1974. 370 pp. ill.

The lyricist's personal memoir.

Al Dubin

McGuire, Patricia Dubin.
> *Lullaby of Broadway*. Secaucus, N.J.: Citadel Press, 1983. 204 pp. ill.

Biography by the lyricist's daughter.

Vernon Duke

Duke, Vernon.
> *Passport to Paris*. Boston: Little, Brown, 1955.

Includes material on his work for Paramount studios, 238–42, his work in California, 352–64, and his Hollywood career, 479–82.

Edward Eliscu

Eliscu, Edward.
> *With or Without a Song: A Memoir*. Edited by David Eliscu. Lanham, Md.: Scarecrow Press, 2001. 284 pp. ill.

This memoir includes a chapter on the Hollywood blacklist.

Cy Feuer

Feuer, Cy, and Ken Gross.
> *I Got the Show Right Here: The Amazing, True Story of How an Obscure Brooklyn Horn Player Became the Last Great Broadway Showman*. New York: Simon & Schuster, 2003.

Feuer discusses his film scoring work for Republic Pictures, where he served as music director in the 1940s.

Dorothy Fields

Winer, Deborah Grace.
> *On the Sunny Side of the Street: The Life and Lyrics of Dorothy Fields*. Foreword by Betty Comden. New York: Schirmer Books, 1997. 267 pp. ill.

The lyricist's Hollywood career from 1929 to 1968, including her collaborations with Oscar Hammerstein II, Jerome Kern, Jimmy McHugh, and Richard Rodgers, 41–116, 181–85.

George and Ira Gershwin

Ewen, David.
> *George Gershwin: His Journey to Greatness*. Englewood Cliffs, N.J.: Prentice Hall, 1970. Rev. ed. of the author's *A Journey to Greatness*, 1956.

Completely revised and rewritten. "Beverly Hills," on Gershwin's Hollywood years, 266–77.

Ewen, David.
  The Story of George Gershwin. New York: Holt, 1943.
Discussion of the composer's work for motion pictures, 138–40, 163–65.

Furia, Philip.
  Ira Gershwin: The Art of the Lyricist. New York: Oxford Univ. Press, 1996. 278 pp. ill.

Gershwin, Ira.
  Lyrics on Several Occasions: A Selection of Stage & Screen Lyrics Written for Sundry Situations, and Now Arranged in Arbitrary Categories: To Which Have Been Added Many Informative Annotations & Disquisitions on Their Why & Wherefore, Their Whom-For, Their How, and Matters Associative. New York: Knopf, 1959. 362 pp. New York: Limelight Editions, 1997. 384 pp.

Hyland, William G.
  George Gershwin: A New Biography. Westport, Conn.: Praeger, 2003.
"Hollywood," 185–207.

Jablonski, Edward.
  Gershwin. New York: Doubleday, 1987. 436 pp.
Hollywood, 298–323.

Jablonski, Edward, and Lawrence D. Stewart.
  The Gershwin Years: George and Ira. New York: Doubleday, 1958. 313 pp. New York: Doubleday, 1973. 416 pp. New York: Da Capo Press, 1996. 402 pp. ill.
Documentation of the Gershwins' Hollywood period, 155–65, 241–96; "The Gershwin Archives" is of interest, 397-403 (1973). The Da Capo edition is an unabridged reprint of the 1973 edition, with an updated bibliography.

Peyser, Joan.
  The Memory of All That: The Life of George Gershwin. New York: Simon & Schuster, 1993. 319 pp.

Rosenberg, Deena.
  Fascinating Rhythm: The Collaboration of George and Ira Gershwin. New York: Dutton, 1991. 516 pp. ill. Reprint, New York: Plume, 1993. Ann Arbor: Univ. of Michigan Press, 1997. 520 pp. ill.
"*Shall We Dance*: The Gershwins in Hollywood" is based on interviews with Ira Gershwin, 321–69 (1991). Discography, filmography, and index.

Schwartz, Charles.
  Gershwin, His Life and Music. Indianapolis: Bobbs-Merrill, 1973. 428 pp.
"Hollywood Muse," 195–209.

Stewart, Lawrence D.
   The Gershwins: Words Upon Music. New York: Verve Records, 1959. 47 pp. ill.
Some film songs are discussed. Published in conjunction with *Ella Fitzgerald Sings the George and Ira Gershwin Song Books.*

Wood, Ean.
   George Gershwin: His Life & Music. London: Sanctuary Publishing, 1996.
"Hollywood," 219–46.

Haven Gillespie
First, William E., with Pasco E. First.
   Drifting and Dreaming: The Story of Songwriter Haven Gillespie. St. Petersburg,
      Fla.: Seaside Publishing, 1998. 120 pp. ill.
The Tin Pan Alley lyricist's songs have been incorporated into films since the early days of sound. "The Songs of Haven Gillespie," 88–95.

Jay Gorney
Gorney, Sandra K.
   Brother, Can You Spare a Dime? The Life of Composer Jay Gorney. Lanham, Md.:
      Scarecrow Press, 2005.
Includes the chapter "Hollywood, Here He Comes" and a section titled "Hollywood and the Big City." Appendixes include lists of songs in "Jay Gorney in Hollywood," 135–38, covering the years 1929–1945, and "Radio and Television Shows and Songs," 139–40. The author is Gorney's widow.

E. Y. Harburg
Meyerson, Harold, and Ernie Harburg, with Arthur Perlman.
   Who Put the Rainbow in the Wizard of Oz? Yip Harburg, Lyricist. Ann Arbor: Univ.
      of Michigan Press, 1993. 454 pp. ill.
"Foray into Films," 98–100; "*The Wizard of Oz*: Broadway in Hollywood," with numerous lyric excerpts, 119–60. Includes material from interviews with Ira Gershwin, Johnny Green, Burton Lane, Earl Robinson, Phil Springer, Jule Styne, and Dana Suesse. With material on Harburg's collaborators, including Harold Arlen and Jerome Kern. Appendix of film songs, 375–90, and radio and television shows and songs, 391–92. Bibliography and index.

Lorenz Hart
Hart, Dorothy, ed.
   Thou Swell, Thou Witty: The Life and Lyrics of Lorenz Hart. New York: Harper &
      Row, 1976. 191 pp. ill.
"Broadway and Hollywood 1925–1935," see pp. 73–86. Filmography. Hart was married to Lorenz's brother, Theodore.

Nolan, Frederick W.
   Lorenz Hart: A Poet on Broadway. New York: Oxford Univ. Press, 1994. 390 pp. ill.
The lyricist's work is discussed in "Hollywood Bound," 154–66; movies and song titles are indexed, 364.

Jerry Herman
Herman, Jerry, with Marilyn Stasio.
　　Showtune: A Memoir. New York: Donald I. Fine Books, 1996. 277 pp. ill.
"Hollywood Work and Social Life," 209–15.

Al Kasha
Kasha, Al, and Joel Hirschhorn.
　　Reaching the Morning After. Nashville: Nelson, 1986. 187 pp.
Documents Kasha's battle with agoraphobia, the fear of public open spaces. Kasha also struggled with anxiety and depression, which he determines were probably brought on by the abuse he suffered as a child and from his lack of self-confidence despite his phenomenal success. The book documents Kasha's spiritual transformation as he deals with the angst, marital problems, drug addiction, and other fallout from his illness . His conversion from Judaism to Christianity provided his final salvation. Kasha's songwriting career and ascension to fame, shared with his longtime collaborator and friend Joel Hirschhorn—who even shares co-author credit—are a continual side story in the narrative, particularly in regard to songs for (ironically) disaster films such as *The Towering Inferno.* Kasha later wrote *Jesus, Hollywood and Me.*

Jerome Kern
Bordman, Gerald.
　　Jerome Kern: His Life and Music. New York: Oxford Univ. Press, 1980.
Includes "The 'Talkies' and New Producers," 311–33; "Hollywood for Good," 350–76.

Freedland, Michael.
　　Jerome Kern: A Biography. London: Robson Books, 1978. 182 pp. ill. New York: Stein and Day, 1981.

Jack Lawrence
Lawrence, Jack.
　　They All Sang My Songs. Fort Lee, N.J.: Barricade Books, 2004. 320 pp.

Alan Jay Lerner
Jablonski, Edward.
　　Alan Jay Lerner: A Biography. New York: Holt, 1996. 345 pp. ill.
"A New Yorker in Hollywood," on Lerner's work at MGM, 51–69.

Lees, Gene.
　　Inventing Champagne: The Worlds of Lerner and Loewe. New York: St. Martin's Press, 1990. 350 pp.
Discusses their film work.

Lerner, Alan Jay.
　　The Street Where I Live. New York: Norton, 1978. 333 pp. New York: Da Capo Press, 1994.
Autobiography.

Frank Loesser
Loesser, Susan.

A Most Remarkable Fella: Frank Loesser and the Guys and Dolls in His Life: A Portrait by His Daughter. New York: Donald I. Fine, 1993. 304 pp. ill.
"Early Hollywood Years," 22–39; "Back to Hollywood," 58–83.

Johnny Mercer

Bach, Bob, and Ginger Mercer, eds.
Our Huckleberry Friend: The Life, Times, and Lyrics of Johnny Mercer. Secaucus, N.J.: Lyle Stuart, 1982. 252 pp.

A decade-by-decade look at Mercer's songs, organized in a scrapbooklike layout with lyrics, photographs, and memorabilia (provided by Mercer's widow, Ginger), and with some textual documentation. "Johnny Mercer's Movie Contributions" arranges the songs by film title from 1933 to 1971, 245–52.

Furia, Philip.
Skylark: The Life and Times of Johnny Mercer. New York: St. Martin's Press, 2003. 328 pp. ill.
"Hooray for Hollywood," 77–91; on Mercer's time in Hollywood, 180–87, 216–20.

Lees, Gene.
Portrait of Johnny: The Life of John Herndon Mercer. New York: Pantheon Books, 2004.
Chapters 10 through 12, 102–30, and chapters 27 and 28, 270–90, document the lyricist's Hollywood film songs.

Cole Porter

Eels, George.
The Life That Late He Led: A Biography of Cole Porter. New York: Berkeley Publishing, 1967. 447 pp. ill. New York: Putnam, 1967. 367 pp. ill.
Includes entries from a 1936 diary of Porter's days in Hollywood, 131–52.

Ewen, David.
The Cole Porter Story. New York: Holt, Rinehart & Winston, 1965. 192 pp. New York: Crowell, 1966. 192 pp.
Appendix of Porter's film and television music, 169–79.

Grafton, David.
Red, Hot & Rich! An Oral History of Cole Porter. New York: Stein and Day, 1987. 242 pp. ill.
Quotations from numerous Porter associates are organized into a narrative.

Hubler, Richard G.
The Cole Porter Story. Cleveland: World Pub. Co., 1965. 140 pp.
With an introduction by Arthur Schwartz.

Kimball, Robert, ed.
Cole. New York: Holt, Rinehart & Winston, 1971. London: Joseph, 1972. New York: Dell, 1992. Woodstock, N.Y.: Overlook Press, 2000.

Provides the lyrics to Porter's songs along with a brief biographical essay by Brendan Gill. "Chronology of Cole Porter Songs and Productions," 255–67; "Alphabetical List of Cole Porter Songs," 268–80; discography, 281–83 (all pages from the 1992 edition).

McBrien, William.
>   *Cole Porter: A Biography.* New York: Knopf, 1998. 459 pp. ill.

Film work is discussed, 269–70, 289–98, 191–200, 206–9, 226–28, 370–79.

Morella, Joseph, and George Mazzei.
>   *Genius and Lust: The Creativity and Sexuality of Cole Porter and Noël Coward.* New York: Carroll & Graf, 1995. 276 pp. ill.

On Hollywood, 154–59, 186–90; see also individual films listed in index.

Schwartz, Charles.
>   *Cole Porter: A Biography.* New York: Dial Press, 1977. 365 pp. ill.

"Hollywood Resident," 147–60.

Richard Rodgers

Ewen, David.
>   *Richard Rodgers.* New York: Holt, 1957. 378 pp. ill.

Includes "To Hollywood and Back," 134–44, and material on his collaborations with Lorenz Hart and Oscar Hammerstein II.

Green, Stanley.
>   *The Rodgers and Hammerstein Story.* New York: J. Day, 1963. 187 pp. ill.

This dual biography includes "To Hollywood and Back," 66–77, and a complete songography, 171–79.

Hyland, William G.
>   *Richard Rodgers.* New Haven, Conn.: Yale Univ. Press, 1998.

"Hollywood" covers the songwriter's work in movie musicals at MGM, Paramount, and United Artists from 1931 to 1934, 89–100.

Marx, Samuel, and Jan Clayton.
>   *Rodgers & Hart: Bewitched, Bothered, and Bedeviled: An Anecdotal Account.* New York: Putnam, 1976. 287 pp. ill.

Nolan, Frederick.
>   *The Sound of Their Music: The Story of Rodgers and Hammerstein.* New York: Walker, 1978. 272 pp. ill. New York: Applause Theatre & Cinema Books/Hal Leonard, 2002. 326 pp. ill.

John Green was among those interviewed.

Rodgers, Dorothy.
>   *A Personal Book.* New York: Harper & Row, 1977. 188 pp. ill.

Rodgers's wife discusses his work in Hollywood, 107–27.

Rodgers, Richard.
>   *Musical Stages: An Autobiography.* New York: Random House, 1975. 341 pp. ill.

Secrest, Meryle.
> *Somewhere for Me: A Biography of Richard Rodgers.* New York: Knopf, 2001. 457
> pp. ill.

Taylor, Deems.
> *Some Enchanted Evenings: The Story of Rodgers and Hammerstein.* New York:
> Harper, 1953. 244 pp. ill.

Richard M. Sherman and Robert B. Sherman
Sherman, Robert B., and Richard M. Sherman.
> *Walt's Time: From Before to Beyond.* Santa Clarita, Calif.: Camphor Tree, 1998. 252
> pp. ill.

The Shermans' autobiography, in the form of an oversize scrapbook, documents the work
of the songwriting team. The text is illustrated with sheet music, lead sheets, lyrics, record jacket art, photographs, artwork, storyboards, and other ephemera from the brothers'
personal archives. The project-by-project coverage of their entire career includes songs
for films, television, and theme parks; their work for Walt Disney forms the bulk of the
book. There is substantial material on their father, Al Sherman, who was a songwriter and
a piano accompanist for silent films. Also focuses on the Sherman family, which boasts
four generations of songwriters, three of which have written songs for films. Appendix
lists published songs by the Sherman brothers from 1951 to 2000. Index. An early version
of the first chapter appeared in *Variety* under the title "Entering the Kingdom of Walt
Disney" (October 27, 1981).

Stephen Sondheim
Secrest, Meryle.
> *Stephen Sondheim: A Life.* New York: Knopf, 1998. 461 pp. ill.

On his work in Hollywood, 97–100; also includes material on orchestrator Jonathan Tu-
nick.

Jule Styne
Taylor, Theodore.
> *Jule: The Story of Composer Jule Styne.* New York: Random House, 1979. 293 pp.

Includes "The Hollywood Story," 61–129. Author draws on his experiences covering the
Hollywood studio beat as a veteran newspaper reporter.

Henry Tobias
Tobias, Henry.
> *Music in My Heart and Borscht in My Blood: An Autobiography.* New York: Hip-
> pocrene Books, 1987.

Includes sections on Vic Mizzy, 85–86, and on Tobias's brothers, Harry Tobias, 173–76,
and Charlie Tobias, 176–80, who also were songwriters.

Harry Warren
Thomas, Tony.
> *Harry Warren and the Hollywood Musical.* Secaucus, N.J.: Citadel Press, 1975. 344
> pp. ill.

This chronological volume traces the songwriter's career film by film and studio to studio: Warner Bros., Fox, MGM, and Paramount. Copiously illustrated with photos, music

examples, and in some cases, complete songs in sheet music form. "The Harry Warren catalog," 331–41. Index.

Vincent Youmans

Bordman, Gerald.

Days to Be Happy, Years to Be Sad: The Life and Music of Vincent Youmans. New York: Oxford Univ. Press, 1982.

Includes documentation on the New York songwriter's foray into Hollywood at RKO, 129–32, 157–64, 195–204.

Chapter 5

Books with Material on Film and Television Music

Abel, Richard, and Rick Altman, eds.
　　The Sounds of Early Cinema. Bloomington: Indiana Univ. Press, 2001.
Revised papers from the Fifth Biennial Conference of Domitor, an international association dedicated to the study of early cinema, hosted by the Motion Picture Division of the Library of Congress, Washington, D.C., 1998. Essays are on the topic of sound; some also cover music. "That Most American of Attractions, the Illustrated Song," by Richard Abel, 141–55. "Part Five: Film Music" contains five essays: "Domitor Witnesses the First Complete Public Presentation of the [Dickson Experimental Sound Film] in the Twentieth Century," by Patrick Loughney, 215–19; "'A Secondary Action' or Musical Highlight? Melodic Interludes in Early Film Melodrama Reconsidered," by David Mayer and Helen Day-Mayer, 220–31; "The Living Nickelodeon," by Rick Altman, contains a lexicon of misunderstood terms, including *musical cue*, in the context of the period, 232–40; "Music for Kalem Films: The Special Scores, with Notes on Walter C. Simon," by Herbert Reynolds, 241–51; "The Orchestration of Affect: The Motif of Barbarism in Breil's *The Birth of a Nation* Score," by Jane Gaines and Neil Lerner, 252–68.

Adams, Byron, and Robin Wells, eds.
　　Vaughan Williams Essays. Aldershot, Hants, U.K.: Ashgate, 2003.
"Music, Film and Vaughan Williams," by Daniel Goldmark, discusses the composer's film music, including critics' reactions, and takes a close look at *49th Parallel* and *Scott of the Antarctic*, 207–33. Selected bibliography.

Adams, Ramsay, David Hnatiuk, and David Weiss.
　　Music Supervision: The Complete Guide to Selecting Music for Movies, TV, Games, & New Media. New York: Schirmer Trade Books, 2005.
A career guide describing the work of the music supervisor in finding and matching music, primarily in the form of songs, to scenes or images in film and television projects. Topics include the evolution of music supervision, theory and application, tools of the trade, effective placement, cue sheets, and licensing. Music supervisors Jason Bentley and Budd Carr are profiled.

Adelman, Kim.
　　The Ultimate Filmmaker's Guide to Short Films: Making It Big in Shorts. Studio City, Calif.: M. Wiese Productions, 2004.
"Why Music Will Kill You," on the prohibitive expense—to independent filmmakers—of licensing songs, 149–55.

Adler, Larry.
  It Ain't Necessarily So: An Autobiography. London: Collins, 1984. Reprint, New
  York: Grove Press, 1987.
Autobiography of the harmonica virtuoso, with anecdotes regarding his associations with
Hollywood film music. See especially pp. 91–100 and material concerning the score for
Genevieve (1953), 181–85.

Adorno, Theodor W.
  Essays on Music. Selected, with introduction, commentary, and notes by Richard
  Leppert; new translations by Susan H. Gillespie. Berkeley, Calif.: Univ. of California
  Press, 2002.
Leppert's commentary addresses Adorno's film music aesthetic, 365–71.

Agel, Jerome, ed.
  The Making of Kubrick's 2001. New York: Signet Books/New American Library,
  1970.
"Alex North/Film Composer" gives the backstory on North's unused score in the composer's own words, 198–99; reviews of the music, 258–60.

Albertstat, Philip.
  Media Production Agreements: A User's Guide for Film and Programme Makers.
  [London]: Routledge, 1996. 336 pp.
Contains legal agreements and sample contracts covering television music licensing
rights, low-budget composer agreements, and soundtracks.

Alexander, Van.
  First Arrangement. New York: Capitol Songs, 1946. 64 pp.
Introductory method book on arranging for the modern orchestra. Author is a television
composer and arranger.

Alexander, Van, with Jimmie Haskell.
  First Chart. Lynbrook, N.Y.: Criterion Music Corp., 1971.
Update of *First Arrangement* (see previous entry). Discusses instrumentation, voicing,
the contemporary rhythm section, and recording tips. Music examples by the authors,
both television composers and arrangers, and one seven-inch disc recording.

Allen, Richard, and Sam Ishii-Gonzáles, eds.
  Hitchcock: Past and Future. New York: Routledge, 2004.
"Music and Identity: The Struggle for Harmony in *Vertigo*," by Daniel Antonio Srebnick,
149–63.

Allen, Richard, and Murray Smith, eds.
  Film Theory and Philosophy. Oxford: Clarendon Press; New York: Oxford Univ.
  Press, 1997.
"Music in the Movies: A Philosophical Enquiry," by philosophy professor Peter Kivy,
308–28.

Allinson, Mark.
  A Spanish Labyrinth: The Films of Pedro Almodóvar. London: I. B. Tauris, 2001.

"Music and Songs," 194–205.

Almquist, Sharon G., comp.
   Opera Mediagraphy: Video Recordings and Motion Pictures. Westport, Conn.: Greenwood Press, 1993. 269 pp.
A guide to operas on video and laserdisc, as well as soundtracks from film and television productions, compiled by a librarian. Operas listed alphabetically by title. Singers, conductors, composers, and production locations are indexed.

Almquist, Sharon G.
   Opera Singers in Recital, Concert, and Feature Film: A Mediagraphy. Westport, Conn.: Greenwood Press, 1999. 376 pp.
Entries organized by personal name and film title (with performers listed but not indexed). Index of conductors and pianists.

Altman, Rick.
   Silent Film Sound. New York: Columbia Univ. Press, 2004. 462 pp.
Covers sound in the broadest sense, with extensive documentation on the use of music in the early days of cinema. The author, a leading authority on sound practices prior to sound on film, expands on his prior findings and writings. This landmark work encompasses a wide range of interrelated subjects including the Kinetophone, vaudeville, and nickelodeon music. "Music for Films" discusses early film scores, the first published collections of music for films, and musical suggestions. Whether music is improvised, interpolated, or used intermittently, it's discussed in this work, even sparsely documented topics such as training musicians. The final section, "The Golden Era of Silent Film Music," documents the motion picture orchestra; new roles for keyboard instruments, such as Automatic pianos, one-man orchestras, and the cinema organ; cue sheets and photoplay music; and musical practices. Altman draws heavily on archival collections and period journals, from the *American Organist* to *Views and Films Index*.

Altman, Rick, ed.
   Sound Theory, Sound Practice. New York: Routledge, 1992.
"The Sound of the Early Warner Bros. Cartoons," by Scott Curtis, 191–203; see also "Conventions of Sound in Documentary," by Jeffrey K. Ruoff, particularly "Music in Documentary," 226–29. Music is mentioned in several other essays as well.

American Council of Learned Societies.
   Dictionary of American Biography. New York: Scribner, 1964–. Cumulative index complete through supplement 8. New York: Scribner, 1990.
Supplement 8 (1988) includes biographical sketches of Jerry Fielding and Alfred Newman, by Nick Redman and Fred Steiner, respectively.

American Federation of Musicians.
   Directory. Published annually.
Alphabetical listing of contact addresses and phone numbers for members of Professional Musicians, Local 47, published as a service to the membership. Members listed by instrument. Also includes lists of arrangers, composers, conductors, and orchestrators. Many members are or were involved in film music recordings under the jurisdiction of Local 47 in Los Angeles-area film studios. A valuable resource, this directory was used

to locate *Magnetic Monster* composer Blaine Sanford in Hawaii, debunking film music accreditation expert Clifford McCarty's long-held belief that the name was a pseudonym. See also the Recording Musicians Association, Los Angeles Chapter, *Directory.*

American Film Institute.
> *The American Film Institute Catalog of Motion Pictures Produced in the United States.* New York: R. R. Bowker; Metuchen, N.J.: Scarecrow Press; Berkeley: Univ. of California Press, 1971–1999.

The American Film Institute (AFI) catalog documents feature films from 1893 to 1970. Credits, detailed production information, synopses, and notes are provided for some 50,000 films. Indexed by personal name, corporate name, genre, and subject. More than 85 percent of films produced since 1935 have been viewed by the compilers prior to publication. Secondary source material is supplemented by studio records, reviews, and research conducted at Los Angeles-area libraries, including the Margaret Herrick Library. Bound-book versions are published for each decade, with the exception of the 1950s; abridged versions are available online. Editors, contributors, and specialist researchers have included Patricia King Hanson, Alan Gevinson, and Amy Dunkleberger. The AFI is a Washington, D.C.-based organization established by the National Endowment for the Arts in 1967 and dedicated to the advancement and preservation of the art of film, television, and other forms of the moving image. The catalog is compiled from the AFI's Los Angeles campus, which includes a prestigious training facility for young filmmakers.

> <u>1893–1910</u>
> See "Music and musicians" in subject index, 382.
> <u>1911–1920</u>
> Composers such as Joseph Carl Breil and Victor Herbert are listed in the personal
>> name index.
> <u>1921–1930</u>
> Film entries include music score credits, song titles, and composer and lyricist cred-
>> its. Composers such as Hugo Riesenfeld are entered in the personal name index.
> <u>1931–1940</u>
> See "Songwriters and Composers Index," 1123–42. The genre index has listings for
>> musicals, musical comedies, and films with song, 1092–1103. Subject index in-
>> cludes entries for jazz music, 931.
> <u>1941–1950</u>
> See "Songwriters and Composers Index," 1071–1104. The genre index has listings
>> for musicals, musical comedies, and films with song, 1041–51. Subject index
>> includes entries for jazz music, 895, and music and musicians, 926–27.
> <u>1961–1970</u>
> Film entries include music score credits, song titles, and composer and lyricist cred-
>> its. Subject index includes entries for jazz and jazz bands, 829–30, and music
>> and musicians, 863–64.

American Society of Composers, Authors and Publishers.
> *The ASCAP Biographical Dictionary.* 1948–1980.

Established in 1914, ASCAP is the world's largest performing-rights organization.
> <u>First edition</u>
> McNamara, Daniel I., ed.
>> *The ASCAP Biographical Dictionary of Composers, Authors and Publishers.*
>> New York: T. Y. Crowell, 1948. 483 pp.

Biographical entries on ASCAP members, including birth and death dates, education, and selected works.

Second edition

McNamara, Daniel I., ed.

The ASCAP Biographical Dictionary of Composers, Authors and Publishers. New York: Thomas Y. Crowell, 1952. 636 pp.

Includes approximately fifty Los Angeles members of the American Society of Music Arrangers, according to Lawrence Morton.

Third edition

The Lynn Farnol Group, comp. and ed.

The ASCAP Biographical Dictionary of Composers, Authors and Publishers. New York: ASCAP, 1966. 845 pp.

Biographical entries on ASCAP members, including birth and death dates, education, and selected works. Compiled from questionnaires filled out by ASCAP members, supplemented by material from the second edition, the *ASCAP Index* (1964), and other standard reference sources.

Fourth edition

Jaques Cattell Press, compiled for ASCAP.

ASCAP Biographical Dictionary. New York and London: R. R. Bowker, 1980. 589 pp.

Member profiles similar in scope and content to the previous edition, with initial year of ASCAP membership given.

American Society of Composers, Authors and Publishers.

ASCAP Hit Tunes. New York: ASCAP, 1964.

Booklet of hit songs written by ASCAP members, published for the organization's fiftieth anniversary in 1964 (although the songs date back to 1892). Many of the songs are from films; however, no production titles are given, only composer and lyricist credits. Song title index.

American Society of Composers, Authors and Publishers.

ASCAP Index of Performed Compositions. 2 vols. New York: ASCAP, 1952. 2 vols, 1963. 3 vols, 1978.

Alphabetical list of compositions in the ASCAP repertoire that have appeared in the organization's survey of performances. A typical film music entry gives the film title appended by the term *cues* (e.g., DRESSED TO KILL CUES) and the composer(s). Useful for identifying composers who wrote individual cues, particularly when a number of composers contributed music but only one is credited. In *Far Frontier* (1949), for example, in addition to the credited composer, R. Dale Butts, there are original (or stock) cues by John M. Elliott, Foy Willing, and Stanley Wilson. No distinction is made between original, reused, or logo music, or between productions having the same title. ASCAP occasionally issued a supplementary index (e.g., in 1954).

American Society of Composers, Authors and Publishers.

30 Years of Motion Picture Music: The Big Hollywood Hit Tunes Since 1928. New York: ASCAP, ca. 1960. 135 pp.

Lists recordings of Hollywood hit tunes from 1928 to 1959. Arranged chronologically by year, then alphabetically by film title, with artist, record number, and writer/publisher. Title index.

Amfitheatrof, Daniele.
> *Italy–Music and Films*. Pamphlet. Hollywood: Academy of Motion Picture Arts and Sciences, 1949. 11 pp.

The composer reports on a trip to Rome and his participation in the Fourth International Music Conference, in Florence.

Ammer, Christine.
> *The Facts on File Dictionary of Music*. 4th ed. New York: Facts on File, 2004.

"Film Music," 140–41.

Anderson, E. Ruth, comp.
> *Contemporary American Composers: A Biographical Dictionary*. Boston: G. K. Hall, 1976. 2nd ed., 1982.

Includes a number of film composers, including Miklós Rózsa and Dimitri Tiomkin, along with awards, selected works, and other biographical information.

Anderson, Joseph D.
> *The Reality of Illusion: An Ecological Approach to Cognitive Film Theory*. Carbondale: Southern Illinois Univ. Press, 1996.

"Music" discusses the synchrony between music and image, 86–88.

Anderson, Joseph D., and Barbara Fisher Anderson, eds.
> *Moving Image Theory: Ecological Considerations*. Carbondale: Southern Illinois Univ. Press, 2005.

"Background Tracks in Recent Cinema," by Charles Eidsvik, 79–104.

Anderson, Joseph L., and Donald Richie.
> *The Japanese Film: Art and Industry*. Rutland, Vt.: Charles E. Tuttle, 1959. Expanded ed., Princeton, N.J.: Princeton Univ. Press, 1982.

A critical assessment of the film music industry and the "general worthlessness of most Japanese film scores" can be found in the chapter on technique, 341–44 (both editions). Points out the ineffective use of Western classical music. Some individual films and composers are singled out for their worthy contributions to the art.

Anderson, Lindsay.
> *Making a Film: The Story of* "Secret People." London: George Allen and Unwin, 1952. New York: Garland Publishing, 1977.

Anderson's diary documents the creation and recording of music by Roberto Gerhard, a Spanish émigré living in England, for a ballet sequence containing the only original music in the film. Thematic material from the ballet, also adapted as source music, appears in an appendix, "Music," 215.

Andrew, J. Dudley.
> *The Major Film Theories: An Introduction*. London: Oxford Univ. Press, 1976. 278 pp.

Isolated references to music in theories espoused by Rudolf Arnheim, Sergei Eisenstein, and Siegfried Kracauer.

Andrews, Betsy, and Randi Gollin, eds.
  ZagatSurvey Music Guide: 1,000 Top Albums of All Time. New York: Zagat Survey,
  2003.
Around 100 soundtracks, from *Aladdin* to *Woodstock*, are included in this "delicious"
guidebook published by the restaurant survey group. The "informative" entries are based
on the opinions of more than 10,000 "music lovers" who have rated and reviewed the
albums. Peter Gabriel's *Passion* (with his score from *The Last Temptation of Christ*)
leads the pack, outranking the main title from *Star Wars.* Soundtracks hailed as definitive
discs include Prince's *Purple Rain* as "Make-Out" music, *Pink Panther* for "Cocktail
Hour," Vince Guaraldi's *A Boy Named Charlie Brown* for "Sunday Mornings," and
Flashdance or Vangelis's *Chariots of Fire* for "Work-Out."

Apel, Willi, ed.
  Harvard Dictionary of Music. 2nd ed. (rev.). Cambridge, Mass.: Belknap/Harvard
  Univ. Press, 1969. *The New Harvard Dictionary of Music.* Edited by Don Michael
  Randel. Cambridge, Mass.: Belknap Press of Harvard Univ. Press, 1986. *The Har-
  vard Dictionary of Music.* Edited by Don Michael Randel. 4th ed. Cambridge, Mass.:
  Belknap Press of Harvard Univ. Press, 2003.
"Film Music," by Frederick W. Sternfeld, 314–15 (1969); "Film Music," 312–14 (2003).
The original 1944 edition contained no entry for film music.

Appel, Bernhard R., Karl W. Geck, and Herbert Schneider, eds.
  Musik und Szene: Festschrift für Werner Braun zum 75. Geburtstag. Saarbrücken,
  Germany: SDV, Saarbrücker Druckerei und Verlag, 2001.
"Music as Entertainment and Symbol in the Yiddish Cinema from the 1920s and 1930s,"
by John Herschel Baron, 413–28.

Applebaum, Louis.
  A Proposal for the Establishment of a Music Film Library of America. New York:
  World Today, 1948. 15 pp.
A copy is at the California State Library in Sacramento.

Armer, Alan A.
  Directing Television and Film. Belmont, Calif.: Wadsworth, 1986. 2nd ed. (rev.),
  1990.
"The Musical Program," covers photographing musical performances and musicians in
various styles, including classical and rock; dramatizing the music through shot selection
and editing; and other aspects (preparation, and so on), 298–317 (1986).

Arnheim, Rudolf.
  Film. Translated by L. M. Sieveking and Ian F. D. Morrow. London: Faber and Faber, 1933.
A short essay, "Film and Music," focuses on music's role as an integral part of the production or as accompaniment, 270–75. Of interest, as it was written in the days of the
early sound film, when dramatic scores were in their infancy.

Arnold, Denis, general ed.
  The New Oxford Companion to Music. Oxford: Oxford Univ. Press, 1983.
"Film Music," by Peter Gammond, 679; "Theme Song," 1817.

Aros, Andrew A.
   Broadway & Hollywood Too. Diamond Bar, Calif.: Applause Publications, 1980.
This 80-page discography of Broadway musicals and Hollywood soundtracks was written
by an audio-visual librarian and intended as a collection development tool for libraries.
The "Hollywood" section lists forty-four scores that the author felt were representative of
soundtracks, 25–41. Each entry gives the film title and record number, followed by a
short assessive paragraph. Nearly a quarter of these are film musicals that correlate to the
original cast albums listed elsewhere in the discography.

Asherman, Allan.
   The Making of Star Trek II, The Wrath of Khan. New York: Pocket Books, 1982.
"The Music of *Star Trek II: The Wrath of Khan*," on James Horner's score, 211–14.

Asherman, Allan.
   The Star Trek Compendium. New York: Simon & Schuster, 1981. Special 20th-
   anniversary edition, completely revised and updated. New York: Pocket Books,
   1986; 1989.
"The Music of *Star Trek–The Motion Picture*," 185 (1981). Episode-by-episode entries
include composer credits for Alexander Courage, George Duning, Gerald Fried, Sol Kaplan, and Fred Steiner.

Asherman, Allan.
   The Star Trek Interview Book. New York: Pocket Books, 1988.
Interviews with Gerald Fried, 238–42, George Duning, 243–46, and James Horner, 260–
64.

Auiler, Dan.
   Vertigo: *The Making of a Hitchcock Classic*. New York: St. Martin's Press, 1998.
The postproduction chapter covers the genesis and historical background of Bernard
Herrmann's score and the songs, 137–46.

Bachman, Gregg, and Thomas J. Slater, eds.
   American Silent Film: Discovering Marginalized Voices. Carbondale: Southern Illi-
   nois Univ. Press, 2002.
"Sound and the Silent Film," by Maureen Furniss, 115–24, includes a discussion of cue
sheets as aids in musical accompaniment, as well as passages from "An Oral History with
Hans J. Salter," interview by Warren M. Sherk, Academy of Motion Picture Arts and
Sciences, 1994.

Baker, Fred, and Ross Firestone, eds.
   Movie People: At Work in the Business of Film. New York: Douglas, 1972. New
   York: Lancer Books, 1973. Reprint, *Movie People: At Work in the Film Industry*.
   London: Abelard-Schuman, 1973.
"Quincy Jones on the Composer," 147–67 (1972).

Baker, Rhonda.
   Media Law: A User's Guide for Film and Programme Makers. London: Routledge,
   1997.
Material on how to acquire and clear rights, with emphasis on music rights.

Balázs, Béla.
> *Theory of the Film: Character and Growth of a New Art.* Translated by Edith Bone.
> London: D. Dobson, 1952. New York: Roy Publishers, 1953. New York: Dover,
> 1970. New York: Arno Press, 1972.

"Film Music," 235–36; "Musical Forms," primarily on film opera, 275–82 (all 1953).

Bancroft, Shelly, ed.
> *The Use of Music.* London: Association of Independent Producers, 1987. 43 pp.

One of several AIP information packs assembled for members of the group that represented outside contractors supplying programs to the BBC.

Banfield, Stephen, ed.
> *The Twentieth Century.* Vol. 6 of *Blackwell History of Music in Britain.* Oxford:
> Blackwell, 1995.

"Film and Television Music," by David Kershaw, 125–44.

Barber, Richard W., ed.
> *King Arthur in Music.* Cambridge, U.K.: D. S. Brewer, 2002.

"King Arthur in Popular Musical Theatre and Musical Film," by William A. Everett, discusses musical films based on the legend, 145–60.

Barnes, Bernard.
> *From Piano to Theatre Pipe Organ: An Instruction Book Written for the Pianist Who
> Wishes to Become an Efficient Organist.* New York: Belwin, 1928. Reprint, Vestal,
> N.Y.: Vestal Press, undated.

This 70-page booklet includes suggestions and techniques for taking music written for the piano and adapting it to the organ, primarily for motion pictures. "Imitations and Tricks," including dog howls, bees buzzing, and several other motion picture effects, is illustrated with notated music and suggested organ stops, 68–70. The undated reprint is described in various online book catalogs as being issued anytime between the 1950s and the 1970s. Vestal was founded in 1961; the reprint most likely dates from the early 1970s.

Barnet, Richard D., Bruce Nemerov, and Mayo R. Taylor.
> *The Story Behind the Song: 150 Songs That Chronicle the 20th Century.* Westport,
> Conn.: Greenwood Press, 2004.

Brief histories of more than a dozen songs composed for films, including "Boogie Woogie Bugle Boy," "The Continental," "Happy Days Are Here Again," "Love Is a Many-Splendored Thing," "Mona Lisa," "My Heart Will Go On," "Over the Rainbow," "Stayin' Alive," "Streets of Philadelphia," "Tumbling Tumbleweeds," "When You Wish Upon a Star," and "White Christmas." Television is represented by the "Miami Vice" theme and "(Theme from) The Monkees." Unusual entries include "Jack Johnson" (from the similarly named documentary) by Miles Davis and "I Am a Man of Constant Sorrow," the early American song arranged for *O Brother, Where Art Thou?* Entries for songs not specifically written for film, such as "Blue Skies," may contain information on subsequent usage, or popularization, in film. The authors are a professor, audio specialist, and librarian, respectively.

Barnouw, Erik, and S. Krishnaswamy.
   Indian Film. New York: Columbia Univ. Press, 1963. 2nd ed., New York: Oxford Univ. Press, 1980.
"Mighty River of Music," 66–69/70–73; "A Star, Six Songs, Three Dances," 148–60/155–67; "There Are Other Kinds of Music," 199–206/207–13 (all 1963/1980). These three essays document how Indian film songs drew on preexisting musical traditions and material.

Barnouw, Erik, editor in chief.
   International Encyclopedia of Communications. New York: Oxford Univ. Press, 1989.
"Musical, Film," on the origin and evolution of the musical in Hollywood and Bombay, by Barnouw and S. Krishnaswamy, vol. 3, 142–46.

Barrier, Michael.
   Hollywood Cartoons: American Animation in Its Golden Age. New York: Oxford Univ. Press, 1999.
Contains material on synchronization and the music for *Steamboat Willie* (1928), 51–55; on Carl Stalling, see especially 52–55, 338–40; on Leigh Harline, 100–102; and on Scott Bradley, 421–22. References to Frank Churchill and Bert Lewis.

Baskerville, David.
   Music Business Handbook and Career Guide. Los Angeles: Sherwood, 1979; 1981; 1982; 1985; 1990. 6th ed., Thousand Oaks, Calif.: Sage Publications, 1995. 7th ed., Sage, 2001.
"Music in Television," 403–19; "Dramatic Scoring for Motion Pictures and TV," on the craft, hiring practices, and studio musicians, 443–59; "Composer of Dramatic Music," with career descriptions and qualifications, 470–71 (all 2001). "Film Scoring" (1995).

Baumgarten, Paul A., and Donald C. Farber.
   Producing, Financing and Distributing Film. New York: Drama Book Specialists, 1973. 2nd ed. (by Baumgarten, Farber, and Mark Fleischer), New York: Limelight Editions, 1992.
"Music" covers composer compensation, royalties, credit, soundtracks, prerecorded music, synchronization licensing, and rights, 161–76 (1973); 205–23 (1992).

Baxter, Joan.
   Television Musicals: Plots, Critiques, Casts and Credits for 222 Shows Written for and Presented on Television, 1944–1996. Jefferson, N.C.: McFarland, 1997. 204 pp.
Entries are alphabetical by show title, with abbreviated cast and credits, song titles, story synopses, and review excerpts.

Baxter, John.
   The Hollywood Exiles. New York: Taplinger Publishing; London: Macdonald and Jane's Publishers, 1976.
Contains a general overview of European émigré composers, including Hanns Eisler, Eugene Zador, and others, 217–25.

Beardsley, Charles.
  Hollywood's Master Showman: The Legendary Sid Grauman. New York: Cornwall
    Books, 1983. 145 pp.
Includes extensive documentation of the musical prologues at Grauman's theaters in Los
Angeles. Covers organist Jesse Crawford and discusses conductors such as Constantin
Bakaleinikoff and C. Sharpe Minor (Charles Sharpe, also known as Charles Minor).

Beaton, Welford.
  Know Your Movies: The Theory and Practice of Motion Picture Production. Holly-
    wood: Howard Hill, 1932.
"Music," 81–95; "Musicals," 100–106. The chapter on music makes a case for more
synchronized music scores and begins, "Without continuous musical scores sound pictures can not survive."

Beattie, Eleanor.
  A Handbook of Canadian Film. Toronto: P. Martin Associates, 1973. 2nd ed., 1977.
"Music in Films" includes a list of Canadian composers who have scored Canadian films,
as well as profiles of Louis Applebaum, Maurice Blackburn, Robert Fleming, Eldon
Rathburn, and William McCauley, 187–92 (1973). "Film Music Study," 299 (1977).

Beauchamp, Robin.
  Designing Sound for Animation. Amsterdam: Elsevier/Focal Press, 2005.
"Music" contains an overview on various topics, from the role of music to producing an
original or library score, 43–61. Advocates developing a vocabulary for scoring and includes a two-page list of emotional terms, including *boisterous, sweeping,* and *triumphant.* Two case studies document the use of music cues derived from the DeWolf Music
library. Author is a professor of sound design.

Beck, Jerry.
  Pink Panther: The Ultimate Guide to the Coolest Cat in Town. London: DK, 2005.
"The Pink Panther Theme" documents Henry Mancini's theme for the film, 14–15.

Beck, Jerry, ed.
  The Harvey Cartoon History. New York: Harvey Comics, 1997.
"Winston Sharples: Cat and Mouse Melodies and Haunting Refrains," by Will Friedwald.
Reprinted in Daniel Goldmark and Yuval Taylor, *The Cartoon Music Book* (2002).

Beck, Ken, and Jim Clark.
  *The Andy Griffith Show Book: From Miracle Salve to Kerosene Cucumbers: The
    Complete Guide to One of Television's Best-Loved Shows.* New York: St. Martin's
    Press, 1985. Rev. ed., 1995. 2nd ed., 2000.
"Music from Mayberry" recalls some of the songs used as source music in the show,
112–14 (2000).

Behlmer, Rudy.
  America's Favorite Movies: Behind the Scenes. New York: F. Ungar Publishing,
    1982. Reprint, *Behind the Scenes: The Making of...* Hollywood: Samuel French,
    1990.

Includes material from a 1977 interview with Alex North on *A Streetcar Named Desire*. The music of Alfred Newman, Max Steiner, and Dimitri Tiomkin is also discussed in the context of specific films.

Behlmer, Rudy [selected, edited, and annotated by].
　　Inside Warner Bros. (1935–1951). New York: Viking Press, 1985. New York: Simon & Schuster, 1987.
Material from the studio's archives in the form of memos and production records—some involving composers—provides an inside look at moviemaking.

Behlmer, Rudy [selected and edited by].
　　Memo from David O. Selznick. New York: Viking Press, 1972. New York: Grove Press, 1981. Hollywood: Samuel French, 1989. New York: Modern Library, 2000.
Material from the producer's correspondence with Lou Forbes, Bernard Herrmann, Alfred Newman, Max Steiner (*Gone with the Wind*, in particular), Herbert Stothart, and Dimitri Tiomkin.

Bellman, Jonathan, ed.
　　The Exotic in Western Music. Boston: Northeastern Univ. Press, 1998.
"I'm an Indian Too: Creating Native American Identities in Nineteenth- and Early Twentieth-Century Music," by Michael V. Pisani, 218–57.

Bennett, Robert Russell.
　　Instrumentally Speaking. Melville, N.Y.: Belwin-Mills, 1975.
Drawn from his vast experience as an arranger primarily for the New York stage, Bennett's book covers instrumentation and orchestration. "Scoring, It Says Here," covers the film scoring process, 155–57; a few minor Hollywood anecdotes, 121–31.

Benstock, Seymour L., ed.
　　Johann Sebastian: A Tercentenary Celebration. Westport, Conn.: Greenwood Press, 1992.
"The Message of Johann Sebastian Bach in Ingmar Bergman's Cinematic Art," by
Fritz Sammern-Frankenegg, examines the director's use of Bach's music in five films, 45–57.

Berg, A. Scott.
　　Goldwyn: A Biography. New York: Knopf, 1989. New York: Riverhead Books, 1998.
Includes anecdotes on Alfred Newman's music for Goldwyn films.

Bergan, Ronald.
　　Glamorous Musicals: Fifty Years of Hollywood's Ultimate Fantasy. London: Octopus Books, 1984. 160 pp.
Picture book, largely of performers.

Bergfelder, Tim, and Sarah Street, eds.
　　The Titanic in Myth and Memory: Representations in Visual and Literary Culture. London: I. B. Tauris, 2004.

"Riverdancing as the Ship Goes Down," by K. J. Donnelly on music in James Cameron's 1997 film, 205–14.

Bernstein, Abby, ed.
>Fantastic Four: *The Making of the Movie.* London: Titan Books, 2005.

"Making Music," on John Ottman's score, 158.

Betz, Albrecht.
>*Hanns Eisler, Political Musician.* Translated by Bill Hopkins. Cambridge: Cambridge Univ. Press, 1982.

"Practice and Theory: The Project for Film Music" includes material on his documentary film scores and the film music project at the New School for Social Research in New York in the late 1930s and 1940s, 169–82; "Hollywood: A Temporary Refuge," 183–93. Translation of *Hanns Eisler: Musik einer Zeit, Die Sich Eben Bildet* (Munich, Germany, 1976).

Billips, Connie, and Arthur Pierce.
>*Lux Presents Hollywood: A Show-by-Show History of the Lux Radio Theatre and the Lux Video Theatre, 1934–1957.* Jefferson, N.C.: McFarland, 1995.

"Music" includes information on Lux music directors Robert Armbruster, Louis Silvers, and Rudolph "Rudy" Schrager, 64–68. The long-running program featured one-hour radio adaptations of contemporary films. It used specifically composed music, not music from the films being adapted. In the 1990s, PBS had Dimitri Tiomkin's music from the film *It's A Wonderful Life* adapted for a live theatrical version using the radio script.

Blaine, Hal, with David Goggin.
>*Hal Blaine and the Wrecking Crew.* Emeryville, Calif.: Mix Books, 1990. N.p.: Rebeats, 2003.

Autobiography of the studio musician, one of the most recorded drummers of popular music in Hollywood. Includes "Patti Page and the Movies," 47–52.

Blake, Michael F.
>*Code of Honor: The Making of Three Great American Westerns*—High Noon, Shane, *and* The Searchers. Lanham, Md.: Taylor Trade, 2003.

Discusses Dimitri Tiomkin's song and music from *High Noon,* 35–38; *Shane,* including music by Franz Waxman and the song, 120–21, 129; and *The Searchers* song and Max Steiner's music, 159–60, 190–92.

Blakeston, Oswell, ed.
>*Working for the Films.* London: Focal Press, 1947.

"Composer," by composer Gerbrand Schürmann, 169–77. This overview of the writing and recording process is aimed at aspiring composers and begins, "The day may not be too far off when the music that goes in the making of a film will as a matter of course be in the hands of genuine, capable, and conscientious composers."

Bliss, Arthur.
>*Bliss on Music: Selected Writings of Arthur Bliss, 1920–1975.* Edited by Gregory Roscow. Oxford: Oxford Univ. Press, 1991.

Includes "Those Damned Films!" on musical aesthetics, 31–33, reprinted from *Musical News and Herald* (1922); "Film Music," from a 1947 symposium, 186–87, reprinted from John Huntley's *British Film Music* (1947); "Some Answers to Some Questions," on the effect of film music on style, 203; "Writing Music for the Films," 241–43, reprinted from Roger Manvell and John Huntley, *Technique of Film Music* (1957).

Block, Geoffrey, ed.
  The Richard Rodgers Reader. Oxford: Oxford Univ. Press, 2002.
"Not a Few of His Songs Were Left on the Cutting Room Floor," by Stanley Green, 70–78, reprinted from *Films in Review* under the title "Richard Rodgers' Filmusic" (October 1956). The entire final section, "The Composer Speaks, 1939–1971," contains collected writings by Rodgers.

Blok, Vladimir, comp.
  Sergei Prokofiev: Materials, Articles, Interviews. Moscow: Progress Publishers, 1978.
"Music for *Alexander Nevsky*," 34–36, translated from material written in 1939.

Blom, Eric, ed.
  Grove's Dictionary of Music and Musicians. 5th ed. London: Macmillan Press; New York: St. Martin's Press, 1954.
"Film Music," by Ernest Irving, Hans Keller, and Wilfrid H. Mellers, vol. 3, 93–110, covers history; technical procedures; the composer's task; British music: perspective, thematic organization; tonal organization; tonal texture: melodrama, style, prospect; the musical problem; American music; continental music; and film opera and film cartoon; and includes a bibliography. Biographical entries on Bernard Herrmann, Erich Wolfgang Korngold, Miklós Rózsa, and others. Superseded by H. Wiley Hitchcock and Stanley Sadie, *The New Grove Dictionary of American Music* (1986).

Bloom, Ken.
  The American Songbook: The Singers, Songwriters & the Songs. New York: Black Dog & Leventhal, 2005.
This coffee-table book includes a lengthy section, "The Songwriters," with biographies, photographs, and graphic art, 176–312. All major songwriters who wrote for film are included. Also, "Television," 198–99; "Hollywood Songwriters," 256–58.

Bloomfield, Gary L., and Stacie L. Shain, with Arlen C. Davidson.
  Duty, Honor, Applause: America's Entertainers in World War II. Guilford, Conn.: Lyons Press, 2004.
Documents all aspects of Hollywood's involvement in the war effort, from canteens and war documentaries to songs and music, with limited coverage of songwriters.

Bloustein, Gerry, ed.
  Musical Visions. Wakefield, Kent Town, South Australia: International Association for the Study of Popular Music, 1999.
Selected proceedings from the sixth national conference of Australia/New Zealand IASPM in Adelaide, including material on film scores.

Bobker, Lee R.
> *Elements of Film*. New York: Harcourt, Brace & World, 1969. 2nd ed., New York: Harcourt, Brace, Jovanovich, 1974. 3rd ed., 1979.

"The Art of Film Music" discusses the purpose and use of film music, music themes, music and movement, the indirect use of music, and silence, 120–26 (1969), 112–18 (1979).

Boggs, Joseph M.
> *The Art of Watching Films*. Menlo Park, Calif.: Benjamin/Cummings Publishing, 1978. 2nd ed., Palo Alto, Calif.: Mayfield Publishing, 1985. 3rd ed., Mountain View, Calif.: Mayfield Publishing, 1991. 4th ed., 1996. 5th ed. (with Dennis W. Petrie). 2000. 6th ed. (with Dennis W. Petrie). Boston: McGraw-Hill, 2004.

For the educational market. "The Musical Score" discusses film music and its general and specific functions, 189–204 (1985), 217–33 (1991). The book's long life and widespread use in the classroom make it an important source. Originally published as *The Art of Watching Films: A Guide to Film Analysis*.

Bonavia, Ferruccio, ed.
> *Musicians on Music*. London: Routledge & Kegan Paul, 1956. New York: R. M. McBride, 1957. Reprint, Westport, Conn.: Hyperion Press, 1979.

"Film Music," 40–46, reprint of "Film Music," by Ralph Vaughan Williams, *Royal College of Music Magazine* (February 1944).

Bondebjerg, Ib, ed.
> *Moving Images, Culture, and the Mind*. Luton: University of Luton Press, 2000.

"The Sound of Images: Classical Hollywood and Music," by Peter Larsen, 167–85.

Boorman, John, and Walter Donohue, eds.
> *Projections 3: Filmmakers on Film-Making*. London: Faber and Faber, 1994.

"Making Music for *Short Cuts*," by Hal Willner, who produced the music, 81–100.

Boorman, John, and Walter Donohue, eds.
> *Projections 4 1/2: Film-Makers on Film-Making*. London: Faber and Faber, 1995.

"How John Ford and Max Steiner Made My Favorite Movie," by director Samuel Fuller, regarding *The Informer*, 70–71.

Boorman, John, and Walter Donohue, eds.
> *Projections 7: Film-Makers on Film-Making in Association with Cahiers du Cinéma*. London: Faber and Faber, 1997.

"Making Music for *Forbidden Planet*: Bebe Barron interviewed by Mark Burman," 252–63.

Borch, Gaston.
> *Practical Manual of Instrumentation*. New York: C. Schirmer; Boston: Boston Music, 1918.

The author's music was often used to accompany silent films and appears in published compilations for that purpose. This manual compares American and European theater orchestras and discusses the technique of arranging music for performance by diverse ensembles, from a few instruments to many, through "cross-cueing" the individual parts.

Cross-cuing is often used in stock arrangements and school orchestras, where, for example, a bassoon solo may have to be performed by a cello if a bassoon is not available.

Bordwell, David.
  Planet Hong Kong: Popular Cinema and the Art of Entertainment. Cambridge, Mass.: Harvard Univ. Press, 2000.
Some discussion of music in specific Hong Kong films.

Bordwell, David, and Noël Carroll, eds.
  Post-Theory: Reconstructing Film Studies. Madison: Univ. of Wisconsin Press, 1996.
"Unheard Melodies? A Critique of Psychoanalytic Theories of Film Music," by Jeff Smith, includes a brief analysis of Franz Waxman's score for *Love in the Afternoon* (1957), 230–47. "Film Music and Narrative Agency," by Jerrold Levinson, contains a wide range of observations with illuminating examples of music heard in fiction films that does not originate in, or issue from, the fictional world depicted, 248–82.

Bordwell, David, Janet Staiger, and Kristin Thompson.
  The Classical Hollywood Cinema: Film Style & Mode of Production to 1960. New York: Columbia Univ. Press, 1985.
"Music as Destiny" focuses on music for continuity, narrative functions, and reinforcing point of view, 33–35. Music during the transition to sound, 302–3; scattered references throughout to music and musicals.

Bordwell, David, and Kristin Thompson.
  Film Art: An Introduction. Reading, Mass.: Addison-Wesley, 1979. 2nd ed., New York: Knopf, 1986. 3rd ed., New York: McGraw-Hill, 1990. 4th ed., New York: McGraw-Hill, 1993. 5th ed., New York: McGraw-Hill, 1997.
Textbook on film appreciation, criticism, and aesthetics. Music is discussed in the context of the film for *The River* (1938), music by Virgil Thomson, 102–5, 290–91; *A Movie* (1958), classical music, including Respighi, 115–19, 296–97; *A Man Escaped* (1956), classical music, including Mozart, 265–66; and *Citizen Kane* (1941), music by Bernard Herrmann, 283–85. Discussion of sound and music, 250–56, includes *Jules and Jim* (1962), music by Georges Delerue. Also, "Film Music" (bibliography), 272–73 (all 1990).

Born, Georgina, and David Hesmondhalgh, eds.
  Western Music and Its Others: Difference, Representation, and Appropriation in Music. Berkeley: Univ. of California Press, 2000.
"Scoring the Indian: Music in the Liberal Western," by Claudia Gorbman, 234–53. Numerous other references to film music throughout.

Bornoff, Jack, and Lionel Salter.
  Music and the Twentieth Century Media. Florence, Italy: Leo S. Olschki, 1972.
"The Place of Music in Television," primarily concerned with the performance of music, such as opera, 85–88; "From Opera to Music Theatre on Stage, Film and Television," 131–61; and "The Audio-Visual Media," including a brief section on film music, 196–98.

Bornstein, Robert G., comp. and ed.
  Range & Transposition Guide to 250 Musical Instruments, with French, Italian, and German Translations. North Hollywood, Calif.: Holly-Pix Music Publishing, 1964.
Sixty-page guide for film and television composers, compiled by a Paramount studios supervising music copyist.

Bousé, Derek.
  Wildlife Films. Philadelphia: Univ. of Pennsylvania Press, 2000.
Discusses several aspects of music in nature documentaries, including music as an intensifier of content, images set to music, comical uses of music, and the use of wall-to-wall music to retain television viewers.

Bowen, Meirion, ed.
  Gerhard on Music: Selected Writings. Aldershot, Hants, U.K.: Ashgate Publishing Group, 2000.
Contains "Music and Film (1930)," by the Catalan-born composer Roberto Gerhard, 79–80.

Bower, Dallas.
  Plan for Cinema. London: Dent, 1936.
"Opera and Cinema," by the director-producer and sound recordist, 100–119.

Bowers, Q. David.
  Nickelodeon Theatres and Their Music. Vestal, N.Y.: Vestal Press, 1986.
"Theatre Music," 127–89, covers automatic instruments; photoplayers; automatic orchestras, such as Wurlitzer's PianOrchestra or Motion Picture Orchestra (pipe organ orchestra); and theatre pipe organs, including the Wurlitzer Hope-Jones Unit Orchestra. Extensive photo documentation and reproductions of vintage advertisements. Vestal Press published related works by the author, including *Put Another Nickel In: A History of Coin-Operated Pianos and Orchestrions* (1966) and *Encyclopedia of Automatic Musical Instruments* (1972).

Brabec, Jeffrey, and Todd Brabec.
  Music, Money, and Success: The Insider's Guide to the Music Industry. New York: Schirmer Books; Toronto: Maxwell Macmillan Canada; New York: Maxwell Macmillan International, 1994. 2nd ed. (under the title *Music, Money, and Success: The Insider's Guide to Making Money in the Music Industry*), New York: Schirmer Trade Books, 2000.
The second edition contains two chapters, "Music, Money, and Television," 117–65, and "Music, Money, and Motion Pictures," 166–221, that include information on budgets, contracts, licensing, fees, and royalties. Other chapters cover general topics such as performing rights organizations (ASCAP and BMI), copyright, and music publishing. The authors are twin brothers and entertainment lawyers; Todd is vice president and director of membership for ASCAP. ASCAP published a 24-page synopsized pamphlet, *Music, Money, Success and the Movies: The Basics of 'Music in Film' Deals,* in 2001.

Braheny, John.
  The Craft and Business of Song Writing. Cincinnati: Writer's Digest Books, 1988. 2nd ed., 2002.

"Film and Television" covers skills, learning, finding work, and getting paid, 306–11 (2002). Author is a songwriter, music industry consultant, and songwriting mentor.

Brand, Jack.
  Shelly Manne: Sounds of the Different Drummer. Rockford, Ill.: Percussion Express, 1997.
This limited edition biography of the drummer extraordinaire documents his work as a session musician from 1947 to 1991 for film and television scores by Elmer Bernstein, Jerry Goldsmith, Quincy Jones, Henry Mancini, André Previn, John Williams, and others. Filmography by Bill Korst.

Brand, Neil.
  Dramatic Notes: Foregrounding Music in the Dramatic Experience. Luton, Bedfordshire, U.K.: Univ. of Luton Press, 1998.
Focuses on British music for dramatic productions. "Television," 25–27; "Film," 27–31. "Knowing the Score: Interviews" includes Barrington Pheloung, 59–70; Stephen Warbeck, 73–78; Carl Davis, 93–98; John Altman, 101–11; George Fenton, 121–27; and Richard Rodney Bennett, 133–40.

Bratton, Jacky, Jim Cook, and Christine Gledhill, eds.
  Melodrama: Stage, Picture, Screen. London: BFI [British Film Institute] Publishing, 1994.
"Music and the Melodramatic Past of the New German Cinema," by Caryl Flinn, 106–18.

Braudy, Leo.
  The World in a Frame: What We See in Films. Garden City, N.Y.: Anchor Press/Doubleday, 1976. Chicago: Univ. of Chicago Press, 1984.
"Musicals and the Energy from Within," essay on musicals from the 1930s through the 1950s, 139–63 (1976).

Brindle, Reginald Smith.
  Musical Composition. Oxford: Oxford Univ. Press, 1986.
Textbook by the British composer and guitarist. Writing film and television music is discussed in "Practical Applications," 160–63.

Brinkmann, Reinhold, and Christoph Wolff, eds.
  Driven into Paradise: The Musical Migration from Nazi Germany to the United States. Berkeley: Univ. of California Press, 1999.
"A Viennese Opera Composer in Hollywood: Korngold's Double Exile in America," by Brian Gilliam, 223–42.

Broadcast Music, Inc.
  1,000,000 Performances. New York: BMI, 1979.
Lists 361 song hits, many from films, that have been licensed by BMI and performed more than one million times each (that translates into 50,000 hours of airplay for the average three-minute song).

Brode, Douglas, comp.
  Crossroads to the Cinema. Boston: Holbrook Press, 1975.

"What Ever Happened to Great Movie Music?" by Elmer Bernstein, 180–87. Reprinted from *High Fidelity Magazine* (July 1972).

Broekman, David.
> *The Shoestring Symphony*. New York: Simon & Schuster, 1948.

This fictionalized autobiographical novel is based on the author's experiences in Hollywood as a music director and composer from 1928 to 1942, and mentions his music work at Universal, 5–6. The back of the dust jacket contains a worthy biography.

Bronfeld, Stewart.
> *How to Produce a Film*. Englewood Cliffs, N.J.: Prentice Hall, 1984.

"Music on Film" covers music as a creative tool, commercial music libraries, and music editing, 113–21.

Brophy, Philip, ed.
> *Kaboom! Explosive Animation from America and Japan*. Sydney, Australia: Museum of Contemporary Art, 1994.

"No More Mickey-Mousing Around," by David Sanjek. Also, Brophy interviews composer/musician John Zorn. The interview is reprinted in Daniel Goldmark and Yuval Taylor, *The Cartoon Music Book* (2002).

Brownlow, Kevin.
> *David Lean: A Biography*. New York: St. Martin's Press, 1996.

Includes references to the music of Malcolm Arnold and Maurice Jarre.

Brownlow, Kevin.
> *The Parade's Gone By*. New York: Knopf; Berkeley: Univ. of California Press, 1968. New York: Ballantine Books, 1969.

"The Silents Were Never Silent," a short general overview, 337–41 (1968), 384–88 (1969).

Brunette, Peter, ed.
> *Martin Scorsese: Interviews*. Jackson: Univ. Press of Mississippi, 1999.

References throughout to the director's use of music.

Bryant, Clora, and others, including Marl Young, eds.
> *Central Avenue Sounds: Jazz in Los Angeles*. Berkeley: Univ. of California Press, 1998.

Some references to film music, including the experiences of drummer Lee Young, one of the first African Americans to hold a regular studio musician position, 65–70; on Buddy Collette being hired by Jerry Fielding, 159; and the amalgamation of AFM Local 767 with the white Local 47 in the 1950s, due in part to the efforts of Marl Young, interviewed here. The material is drawn from the UCLA Oral History Program.

Buchanan, Larry.
> *It Came from Hunger! Tales of a Cinema Schlockmeister*. Jefferson, N.C.: McFarland, 1996.

The director's autobiography contains a chapter on *Rebel Jesus* (1972) that includes material on Alex North's score.

Buchland, Michael, and John Henken, eds.
   The Hollywood Bowl: Tales of Summer Nights. Los Angeles: Balcony Press, 1996.
"Hollywood and the Bowl," by Lisa Mitchell, highlights movies filmed at the outdoor
amphitheater in Los Angeles, listing some two dozen films from 1928 to 1994 on p. 86.
Also documents concerts of film music, 74–89.

Buckley, P. Kevin.
   *The Orchestral and Cinema Organist; A Popular Treatise on the Use of the Organ
   and the Harmonium in Cinema, Hotel, and Other Bands; With a Simple Introduction
   to the Study of Harmony*. London: Hawkes and Son, 1923.
Aimed at pianists who turned to organ playing by economic necessity at a time when the
organ was fast becoming the accompaniment instrument of choice, and the demand for
cinema organists exceeded the supply. The author, an organist, covers the unique attrib-
utes of the instrument and improvisation. This 40-page pamphlet can be found in the
British Film Institute National Library in London.

Bull, Michael.
   Sounding Out the City: Personal Stereos and the Management of Everyday Life. Oxford: Berg, 2000.
Includes material based on interviews with several ordinary citizens concerning their
personal use of film music as a soundtrack to their lives, 91–95.

Bunting, Alan, comp.
   *The Robert Farnon Discography: Recordings, Compositions, Film Scores, Arrange-
   ments*. Ilminster, U.K.: Robert Farnon Society, 1996.
With cue titles and timings.

Burlingame, Jon.
   *For the Record: The Struggle and Ultimate Political Rise of American Recording
   Musicians within Their Labor Movement*. Hollywood, Calif.: Recording Musicians
   Association, 1997.
A 106-page history of the Recording Musicians Association (RMA), from its roots in the
Musicians Guild to the present. Virtually all Los Angeles session musicians are members
of the RMA, a conference of the American Federation of Musicians' union. Based in part
on interviews with Harold Bradley, Vincent De Rosa, Dennis Dreith, Walt Levinsky, Ted
Nash, Gene Orloff, Uan Rasey, Lloyd Ulyate, and others.

Burrows, Michael.
   Mario Lanza and Max Steiner. St. Austell, Cornwall, U.K.: Primestyle Ltd., 1971.
Biographical material on Steiner compiled by a fan from secondary sources, 22–40.

Burt, Rob.
   Rock and Roll: The Movies. New York: New Orchard Editions; New York: Sterling,
   1986, 1983. 208 pp.

Burton, Humphrey, and Maureen Murray.
   William Walton: The Romantic Loner: A Centenary Portrait Album. Oxford: Oxford
   Univ. Press, 2002.

Contains some scoring stage photographs and film score manuscript pages.

Buscombe, Edward.
    Stagecoach. London: BFI Publications, 1992.
The film's score is discussed in this BFI Film Classics series booklet, 47–49.

Buskin, Richard.
    Insidetracks: A First-Hand History of Popular Music from the World's Greatest Re-
    cord Producers and Engineers. New York: Spike, 1999.
Interviews with Giorgio Moroder, 201–4; Vangelis, 238–41; and Hans Zimmer, 295–301,
include discussions of their film music.

Butler, David.
    Jazz Noir: Listening to Music from Phantom Lady *to* The Last Seduction. Westport,
    Conn.: Praeger, 2002.
"Kind of Jazz: Themes in the Study of Film Noir, Film Music and Jazz," 1–28; "Abso-
lutely Functional? Jazz in 1940s Film Noir," 61–94; "Touch of Kenton: Jazz in 1950s
Film Noir," 95–142; "The Last Syncopation: Jazz in Contemporary Film Noir," 143–86.

Butler, Ivan.
    The Making of Feature Films: A Guide. Harmondsworth, U.K.: Penguin Books,
    1971.
In "The Composer," John Barry, Richard Rodney Bennett, and Dimitri Tiomkin talk
about their working methods and problem solving involved in the preparation and recording of a score, 158–66.

Butterworth, Neil.
    Dictionary of American Classical Composers. 2nd ed. New York: Routledge, 2005.
    Previous edition, *A Dictionary of American Composers*. New York: Garland, 1984.
The 2005 edition contains biographies and credits for concert composers who scored
films, such as George Antheil, Aaron Copland, and Morton Gould; and for a few film
composers who wrote concert music, such as Bernard Herrmann and Miklós Rózsa.

Butterworth, Neil.
    Ralph Vaughan Williams: A Guide to Research. New York: Garland, 1990.
See "Film Scores" for publication details and instrumentation, 30–34; "Film Scores" for a
discography, 155–56; and "Film Music" for a bibliography, 311. Also includes short
biographies on Larry Adler, Ernest Irving, and Muir Mathieson.

Byworth, Tony.
    The History of Country & Western Music. New York: Exeter Books, 1984.
"The New Dimensions of Country" covers the use of country music on television and in
films, 180–99.

Cacavas, John.
    The Art of Writing Music: A Practical Book for Composers and Arrangers of Instru-
    mental, Choral, and Electronic Music as Applied to Publication, Films, Television,
    Recordings, and Schools. Los Angeles [Van Nuys]: Alfred Publishing, 1993.

"Writing Music for Motion Pictures and Television," 113–50; "Writing for Documentary and Industrial Films," 151–59; "An Interview with Morton Gould," 170–72, reprinted from *The Score* (Fall 1991); musical examples from Cacavas's film and television music, including *Kojak*, *Columbo*, and others. Session musician Steve Kaplan contributed a chapter on electronic music.

Cacavas, John.
>   *Music Arranging and Orchestration.* Melville, N.Y.: Belwin-Mills Publishing, 1975.
>   175 pp.
Aimed at music arranging for publication, television composer Cacavas includes his favorite arranging techniques along with autobiographical anecdotes largely culled from his experience as director of publications for a New York music publisher. Copiously illustrated with examples from Cacavas's published arrangements.

Cadbury, William, and Leland Poague.
>   *Film Criticism: A Counter Theory.* Ames: Iowa State Univ. Press, 1982.
Includes discussion of music and iconicity and meaning in music, 27–33.

Callender, Red, with Elaine Cohen.
>   *Unfinished Dream: The Musical World of Red Callender.* London: Quartet Books,
>   1985.
Autobiography of the studio musician George Sylvester "Red" Callender, who played bass and tuba on the scores for *Blazing Saddles*, *A Soldier's Story*, and other films.

Cameron, Evan William.
>   *On Mathematics, Music, and Film.* Pamphlet. Bridgewater, Mass.: Experiment Press,
>   1970.
A 103-page discourse on music as the rhythmic ordering of all things from the author's Boston University MS thesis in film. Also published in *Cinema Studies* (Spring 1970).

Cameron, Evan William, ed.
>   *Sound and the Cinema: The Coming of Sound to American Film.* Pleasantville, N.Y.:
>   Redgrave Publishing, 1980.
"Hollywood Converts to Sound: Chaos or Order?" by Douglas Gomery, see pp. 31–32 for information on the position of the musicians' union; "Bernard Herrmann, Composer," 117–35. The latter was previously published as "The Contemporary Use of Music in Film: *Citizen Kane, Psycho, Fahrenheit 451*," in the *University Film Study Center Newsletter* (February supplement, 1977).

Camm, Frederick James.
>   *Marvels of Modern Science.* London: George Newnes, 1935. Rev. ed., 1938.
"Marvels of the Cinema Organ," focuses on obtaining effects from the instrument, 159–64.

Campion, Jane.
>   *The Making of* The Piano. New York: Hyperion, 1993.
A section on preproduction includes a lengthy quotation from the film's composer, Michael Nyman, 150–51.

Capogrosso, Eric.
The IDC Hollywood Labor Guide. Los Angeles: IDC Services, 1983.
Each volume contains a chapter on the American Federation of Musicians and covers basic motion picture and television agreements, working conditions, and pay scales. Vols. include *The IDC Hollywood Labor Guide* 1981/82, 1983/84, 1984/85, 1986, 1989; *The IDC Labor Guide* 1990, 1991, 1994/95; *The Industry Labor Guide* 1995/96, 1996–97.

Carlton, Joseph R.
Carlton's Complete Reference Book of Music. Studio City, Calif.: Carlton Publications, 1980. 723 pp.
A section on best-known songs and instrumental music includes film scores and songs, with composer and lyricist credits. A section on best-known composers and lyricists includes film composers and lyricists, with name, birth year, nationality, and an alphabetical list of songs and scores. The author, a record producer and music recording executive, compiled the material from personal experience and published sources.

Carpenter, Paul S.
Music: An Art and a Business. Norman: Univ. of Oklahoma Press, 1950.
The chapter "Hollywood Carousel" covers studio staff composers and arrangers, the Academy Awards, mechanics and synchronization, dealing with music directors and executives, deadline pressure, Hollywood hierarchy, and other topics, 40–68. Includes a cost analysis for scoring a mid-1940s film, 141–43. Based on the author's observation of several recording sessions and conversations with Alfred Newman, Herbert Stothart, Roy Webb, and others.

Carringer, Robert L.
The Making of Citizen Kane. Berkeley: Univ. of California Press, 1985. Rev. ed., 1996.
"Music" contains background information on Bernard Herrmann and a brief analysis of his score, 106–9 (1985).

Carroll, Noël.
Mystifying Movies: Fads & Fallacies in Contemporary Film Theory. New York: Columbia Univ. Press, 1988.
Includes a brief discussion of movie music by the film critic.

Carroll, Noël.
Theorizing the Moving Image. Cambridge: Cambridge Univ. Press, 1996.
Contains an essay, "Notes on Movie Music."

Carter, Gaylord Beach.
The Million Dollar Life of Gaylord Carter. Oakland, Calif.: Paramount Theatre of the Arts, 1995.
Autobiography of L.A.'s leading theater organist, who provided organ accompaniment for films at the Million Dollar Theater and other theaters in the mid-1920s. His discussion of the renaissance of silent film screenings from the 1960s through the 1990s is of interest. Compiled and edited from oral histories conducted by Jack Loren in 1969 and Dennis R. Forkel in 1995.

Casper, Joseph Andrew.
    Vincente Minnelli and the Film Musical. South Brunswick, N.J.: A. S. Barnes, 1977. London: Thomas Yoseloff, Ltd., 1977.
"Traditions: The Film Musical," 21–32; "Music," 119–46. The latter examines dramatic motivation, technical positioning and handling, and the exegesis of selected musical numbers.

Chadabe, Joel.
    Electric Sound: The Past and Promise of Electronic Music. Upper Saddle River, N.J.: Prentice Hall, 1997.
This history of electronic music and MIDI contains information on various instruments utilized by film composers, including the theremin, ondes martenot, Moog, Minimoog, ARP, Prophet-5, Yamaha CS-80 and DX-7, Fairlight, E-mu Emulator, and Synclavier.

Chaneles, Sol.
    Collecting Movie Memorabilia. New York: Arco Publishing, 1977.
"Sound Tracks and Other Movie Music," on musicals, personalities, and songs, primarily on 78 rpm discs from 1927 to 1941, 137–54.

Chase, Donald, ed.
    Filmmaking: The Collaborative Art. Boston: Little, Brown, 1975.
"The Composer" includes quotes from Elmer Bernstein, Jerry Goldsmith, John Green, and Alex North from their appearances at American Film Institute seminars, 271–91.

Chase, Gilbert, ed.
    Music in Radio Broadcasting. New York: McGraw-Hill Book, 1946.
"Composing for Radio," by Morris Mamorsky, 47–65; "Arranging Music for Radio," by Tom Bennett, 76–90.

Chávez, Carlos.
    Toward a New Music: Music and Electricity. Translated by Herbert Weinstock. New York: W. W. Norton, 1937. Reprint, New York: Da Capo Press, 1975.
This theoretical work contains references to the possibilities of music in film. See "The Sound Film," 89–121; "Toward a New Music," 166–80.

Childs, Peter, and Mike Storry, eds.
    Encyclopedia of Contemporary British Culture. London: Routledge, 1999.
"Film Music," by Christopher Smith, 198.

Chion, Michel.
    Audio-Vision: Sound on Screen. Edited and translated by Claudia Gorbman. New York: Columbia Univ. Press, 1994.
"Music as a Symbolic Punctuation: *The Informer*," on Max Steiner's score, 49–54. Numerous references to film music, including cadences, counterpoint, and the "value added" by music. Author is a French composer, film critic, and author.

Christlieb, Don.
    Remembrance of Lawrence Morton. Los Angeles: Lawrence Morton Fund of the California Community Foundation, 1987.

Contains "An Autobiographical Sketch by Lawrence Morton," written for a 1979 Hollywood Bowl concert honoring the film music critic's seventy-fifth birthday, 66–67.

Churchill, Sharal.
   The Indie Guidebook to Music Supervision for Films. Los Angeles: Filmic Press,
   2000.
Traditionally, the music supervisor's primary role is to assist filmmakers in the placement of pre-composed music, usually popular songs, in their films. This book reflects the current trend toward expanding that role to include hiring and interacting with composers. (This move brought the music supervisor closer to what was once known as a music director; since then, however, the Directors Guild of America has successfully campaigned to limit the use of the word "director.") Covers preproduction, including the role and responsibilities of the supervisor; production, including negotiating a composer agreement, music placement, and source music; and postproduction, including licensing songs and the soundtrack album. With numerous sample documents.

Citron, Stephen.
   Noël and Cole: The Sophisticates. New York: Oxford Univ. Press, 1993. Milwaukee:
   Hal Leonard, 2005.
Biography of Noël Coward and Cole Porter, with analyses of selected songs.

Clark, Andrew, ed.
   Riffs & Choruses: A New Jazz Anthology. New York: Continuum, 2000. London:
   Continuum by arrangement with Bayou Press, 2001.
Contains a chapter, "All the Usual Pitfalls: Jazz and Film (Cliché, Stereotype, Ambience)," 407–50, that includes "Jazz Digest" (1988) by Kenneth C. Spence; "Questions of Influence in the White Jazz Biopic" (1996) by Krin Gabbard; "Louis Armstrong: The Films" (1994) by Donald Bogle; "*Round Midnight*: An Interview with Bertrand Tavernier" (1986) by Jean-Pierre Coursodon; "At the Movies: Everycat" (1986) by Francis Davis; "Birdman of Hollywood" (1988) by Gary Giddons; "Birdland: Mon Amor" (1988) by Francis Davis; "Films" (1944) by James Agee; "On the Beat in Hollywood" (1944) by Charles Emge; "Is Hollywood Yielding?" (1945) by Jackie Lopez; "*The Sound of Jazz*" (1983) by Whitney Balliett; "*Let's Get Lost*: Baker as Icon" (1989) by Hal Hinson; "*A Great Day in Harlem*" (1995) by James Berardinelli.

Clark, Barbara, and Susan J. Spohr.
   Guide to Postproduction for TV and Film: Managing the Process. Boston: Focal
   Press, 1998. 2nd ed., Amsterdam: Focal Press, 2002.
"Music," 37–38 (1998), 50–52 (2002), and "Music/Scoring," 127–29 (1998), 187–88 (2002), each contain brief definitions and an overview of the process.

Cline, William C.
   In the Nick of Time: Motion Picture Sound Serials. Jefferson, N.C.: McFarland,
   1984.
"Soothing the Savage Beast (The Music)," provides an overview of music for Columbia and Republic serials, 172–78.

Cline, William C.
   Serials-ly Speaking: Essays on Cliffhangers. Jefferson, N.C.: McFarland, 1994.

"The Beat Goes On," a 1986 article on James King's rerecordings of Republic serials, 170–74.

Clute, John, and Peter Nicholls, eds.
>   *The Encyclopedia of Science Fiction*. London: Orbit, 1999.
"Music," by M. Jakubowski, 840–46.

Cocteau, Jean.
>   *Diary of a Film*. Translated by Ronald Duncan. London: Dennis Dobson, 1950. New York: Roy Publishers, 1950.
Contains the French director's diary entry on the recording of Georges Auric's score for *La Belle et la Bête* (*Beauty and the Beast*, 1946).

Coers, Donald V., Robert J. Demott, and Paul D. Ruffin, eds.
>   *After the* Grapes of Wrath: *Essays on John Steinbeck in Honor of Tetsumaro Hayashi*. Athens: Ohio Univ. Press, 1995.
"Of Mice and Music: Scoring Steinbeck Movies," by Robert E. Morsberger, discusses Aaron Copland's score for *Of Mice and Men*, 58–73.

Collins, W. H.
>   *The Amateur Filmmaker's Handbook of Sound Sync and Scoring*. Blue Ridge Summit, Penn.: Tab Books, 1974.
"Scoring" includes how to use music, 48–49; and technical aspects of recording, 53–57.

Connelly, Marie Katheryn.
>   *Martin Scorsese: An Analysis of His Feature Films, with a Filmography of His Entire Directorial Career*. Jefferson, N.C.: McFarland, 1993.
Analysis of eleven films, often with commentary on Scorsese's use of music; see, for example, *The Color of Money*, 120.

Conrich, Ian, and David Woods, eds.
>   *The Cinema of John Carpenter: The Technique of Terror*. London: Wallflower Press, 2004.
"Fast and Cheap? The Film Music of John Carpenter," by David Burnand and Miguel Mera, 49–65.

Conway, Kelley.
>   *Chanteuse in the City: The Realist Singer in French Film*. Berkeley: Univ. of California Press, 2004.
Examines the meaning and traces the use of the female voice in French films, from its roots in the music hall and café-concert. Based on the author's PhD thesis.

Cook, Nicholas.
>   *Analysing Musical Multimedia*. Oxford, U.K.: Clarendon Press; New York: Oxford Univ. Press, 1998. New York: Oxford Univ. Press, 2000.
Includes "Disney's Dream: The *Rite of Spring* Sequence from *Fantasia*," and "Reading Film and Re-reading Opera: From *Armide* to *Aria*."

Cook, Nicholas, and Anthony Pople, eds.
> *The Cambridge History of Twentieth-Century Music.* Cambridge: Cambridge Univ.
> Press, 2004.

Contains discussion of film music in "Music, Text and Stage: The Tradition of Bourgeois Tonality to the Second World War," by Stephen Banfield, 90–122; "Music of Seriousness and Commitment: The 1930s and Beyond," by Michael Walter, 286–306.

Cook, Pam, ed.
> *Gainsborough Pictures.* London: Cassell, 1997.

"Wicked Sounds and Magic Melodies: Music in Gainsborough Melodramas," by K. J. Donnelly, 155–69.

Cooke, James Francis.
> *Great Men and Famous Musicians on the Art of Music: Educational Conferences with Representative Men and Women.* Philadelphia: Theodore Presser, 1925.

"Musical Classics for Millions," by Hugo Riesenfeld, 408–13.

Cooke, Mervyn, ed.
> *The Cambridge Companion to Benjamin Britten.* Cambridge: Cambridge Univ.
> Press, 1999.

"Britten in the Cinema: *Coal Face,*" by Philip Reed, 54–77.

Cooke, Mervyn, ed.
> *The Cambridge Companion to Twentieth-Century Opera.* Cambridge: Cambridge
> Univ. Press, 2005.

"Opera and Film," by Mervyn Cooke, 267–90; "Popular Musical Theatre (and Film)," by Stephen Banfield, 291–305.

Cooper, B. Lee, and Wayne S. Haney.
> *Rock Music in American Popular Culture: Rock 'n' Roll Resources.* New York: Haworth Press, 1995.

Contains a survey of motion pictures, 169–71, and television shows, 171–72.

Cooper, B. Lee, and Wayne S. Haney.
> *Rock Music in American Popular Culture II: More Rock 'n' Roll Resources.*
> Binghamton, N.Y.: Harrington Park Press, 1997. New York: Haworth Press, 1999.

"Horror Films," discusses horror film songs and "rock 'n' horror recordings," 117–44; "Motion Pictures," includes "Motion Picture Bibliography," 205–20.

Copland, Aaron.
> *Our New Music: Leading Composers in Europe and America.* New York: Whittlesey
> House [McGraw-Hill], 1941.

"Music in the Films," 260–75. This chapter is only in the 1941 edition, not in the 1968 revision titled *The New Music.* Chapter is reprinted in Siegmeister, *The Music Lover's Handbook* (1943).

Copland, Aaron.
> *What to Listen for in Music.* Rev. ed. New York: McGraw-Hill, 1957. 2nd rev. ed.,
> 1963. San Francisco: McGraw-Hill, 1988. New York: Mentor, 1999.

"Film Music," on how music can serve the screen, 152–57 (1963), 252–63 (1988). This chapter is not in the 1939 or 1953 editions.

Cornwell, Sue, and Mike Kott.
  The Official Price Guide, Star Trek and Star Wars Collectibles. New York: House of
    Collectibles, 1986. 2nd ed., 1987. 3rd ed., 1991.
Star Trek sheet music, 113–15, and records, tapes, and compact discs, 129–35; *Star Wars* sheet music, 226, and records and tapes, 244–49 (all 1991).

Corwin, Norman.
  Years of the Electric Ear. Interviewed by Douglas Bell. Metuchen, N.J.: Scarecrow
    Press, 1994.
The director discusses his working relationships, primarily in radio, with Bernard Herrmann and Lyn Murray in this oral history for the Directors Guild of America, 99–106.

Courrier, Kevin.
  Randy Newman's American Dreams. Toronto: ECW Press, 2005.
Contains some material on the film music of the composer-songwriter.

Courtnay, Jack, comp.
  *Theater Organ World: Cinema Organists and Their Instruments "Spotted" for Your
    Information by Famous Writers, Artists and Musicians.* London: Theatre Organ
    World Publications, 1946.
Courtnay, a theater organist and music editor of *Kinematograph Weekly*, compiled this anthology of personal recollections of writers, artists, and musicians, including such organists as Reginald Foort and Wilson Oliphant. Primarily focuses on the cinema organ in Britain, with some European material. Many of the articles are only tangentially related to film or film music; however, there are wonderful insights, such as Eugene Stuart Barrie's recollections of the Robert Hope-Jones Wurlitzer in Seattle in 1914. Most of the articles are one or two pages in length. Topics include installations, specifications, and specific organs, for example, the Theatrone, Hammond, and Orgatron. The 216-page illustrated book contains extensive biographical material on members of the London-based Association of Theatre Organists.

Cousins, E. G.
  Filmland in Ferment. London: Denis Archer, 1932.
"The Savage Beast," a contemporary account of the use of music in early sound films, 117–22.

Cox, Bette Yarbrough.
  *Central Avenue—Its Rise and Fall, 1890–c.1955: Including the Musical Renaissance
    of Black Los Angeles.* Los Angeles: BEEM Publications, 1996.
Contains material on choir directors Elmer Bartlett, Jester Hairston, Emmanuel Hall, Hall Johnson, and Frieta Shaw (Johnson). The African American choirs they led contributed choral background music for film scores from the late 1920s on, particularly those by Max Steiner and Dimitri Tiomkin. Includes information on film composers Benny Carter, William "Buddy" Collette, Quincy Jones, and William Grant Still, and on black studio musicians and performers from Local 767 prior to the 1953 merger with the white Local 47.

Of interest are oral histories with Florence Cadrez "Tiny" Brantley, on her experiences as a studio musician (piano accompanist) and at Grauman's Chinese Theater, 113–37; Frieta Shaw Johnson, 157–67; Jester Hairston, 169–82; Verna Arvey Still on her husband, William Grant Still, 213–22; conductor Leroy Hurte, on arranging songs for the Four Blackbirds for motion pictures, 223–29; MGM rehearsal pianist Eddie Beal, 290–91; William "Buddy" Collette, 297–303; and arranger and union activist Marl Young, on how film music played a role in desegregating the union, 317–23. The oral histories were conducted in 1983, with the exception of Hairston's, recorded in 1977–78.

Cox, Stephen.
  It's a Wonderful Life: *A Memory Book*. Nashville: Cumberland House, 2003.
Includes information on Dimitri Tiomkin and his music for the film, 12–14. With additional references to Tiomkin's music, which was partially unused.

Craggs, Stewart R.
  Arthur Bliss: A Bio-Bibliography. New York: Greenwood Press, 1988.

Craggs, Stewart R.
  Benjamin Britten: A Bio-Bibliography. Westport, Conn.: Greenwood Press, 2002.
"Film Music," 88–95.

Craggs, Stewart R., comp.
  Arthur Bliss: A Source Book. Aldershot, U.K.: Scolar Press; Brookfield, Vt.: Ashgate, 1996.

Craggs, Stewart R., ed.
  Arthur Bliss: Music and Literature. Aldershot, U.K.: Ashgate, 2002.
"The Film Music," by Stephen Lloyd.

Craggs, Stewart R., comp.
  Peter Maxwell Davies: A Source Book. Aldershot, U.K.; Burlington, Vt.: Ashgate, 2002.
The British composer's two film scores are included.

Craggs, Stewart R., comp.
  Richard Rodney Bennett: A Bio-Bibliography. New York: Greenwood Press, 1990.
"Film Music," 105–15.

Craggs, Stewart R., comp.
  William Walton: A Catalogue. Oxford: Oxford Univ. Press, 1990.
Revised edition of the author's 1977 work (see next entry), with an introduction by Christopher Palmer.

Craggs, Stewart R., comp.
  William Walton: A Source Book. Aldershot, Hants, U.K.: Scolar Press; Brookfield, Vt.: Ashgate Pub. Co., 1993.
Includes film music and information on manuscript material.

Craggs, Stewart R.
    William Walton: A Thematic Catalogue of His Musical Works. London: Oxford
    Univ. Press, 1977.
This complete catalog of Walton's compositions lists his works chronologically. Fourteen
are film titles and include cues, instrumentation, and location of the manuscript, if
known. A few of the entries cover thematic material.

Craggs, Stewart R., ed.
    William Walton: Music and Literature. Aldershot, U.K.; Brookfield, Vt.: Ashgate,
    1999.
"Film Music," a historical survey by Stephen Lloyd, 109–31.

Craggs, Stewart, and Alan Poulton, comp.
    William Alwyn: A Catalogue of His Music. Hindhead, U.K.: Bravura Publications,
    1985.
With a profile of the composer by Trevor Hold.

Craig, Warren.
    Sweet and Lowdown: America's Popular Song Writers. Metuchen, N.J.: Scarecrow
    Press, 1978. 645 pp.
Short biographies and chronological song credits for songwriters divided into the following categories: before Tin Pan Alley, Tin Pan Alley, and after Tin Pan Alley. Compiled
from secondary sources, including works by Jack Burton, David Ewen, Roger D. Kinkle,
Julius Mattfeld, Nat Shapiro, and Sigmund Spaeth. Song title, production, and name
indexes.

Crenshaw, Marshall.
    Hollywood Rock: A Guide to Rock 'n' Roll in the Movies. New York: HarperPeren-
    nial, 1994. 351 pp.
Includes cast, reviews, synopses, cameos, scenes, songs, and memorable lines from more
than 300 films. Reviews contributed by two dozen rock enthusiasts, including Crenshaw,
a songwriter and recording artist. Appendixes contain short entries for additional rock
films, concert films, and rockumentaries, as well as a rock actors filmography. Performer
index.

Cross, Brenda, ed.
    The Film Hamlet: *A Record of Its Production*. 3rd ed. London: Saturn Press, 1948.
"The Music of Hamlet," by William Walton, 61–62, with a reproduction of one cue in
sketch form; "Recording the Music," by Muir Mathieson, 63–64.

Crouch, Tanja L.
    100 Careers in Film and Television. Hauppauge, N.Y.: Barron's, 2003.
A chapter on sound and music includes material on specific careers in that field. Each
career entry includes an overview, special skills, a typical workday, advice for the job
seeker, and a profile of an industry professional. "Music Editor" (Jeff Charbonneau),
189–92; "Composer" (Steve Dorff), 193–95; "Senior Vice President of Music" (Todd
Homme, DreamWorks), 195–97; "Vice President of Music" (Celest Ray, Aaron Spelling
Productions), 198–200; "Music Clearance" (Julie Butchco, DreamWorks), 200–201;
"Music Supervisor" (Barklie Griggs), 202–4.

Crouch, Tanja L.
  100 Careers in the Music Business. Hauppauge, N.Y.: Barron's, 2001.
"Music for Film, Television, and Advertising, and New Media," 193–209.

Cubitt, Sean.
  The Cinema Effect. Cambridge, Mass.: MIT Press, 2004.
"Total Film: Music," on Sergei Prokofiev's music for *Alexander Nevsky*, 100–129.

Cumbow, Robert C.
  Once Upon a Time: The Films of Sergio Leone. Metuchen, N.J.: Scarecrow Press,
  1987.
"He Not Only Plays—He Can Shoot, Too" analyzes Ennio Morricone's music in the
films of Leone, 199–211; "Well, You Know Music and You Can Count," on the operatic
elements of music in Leone's films, 213–16; other references throughout to music in
Leone's films.

Dagort, Aïda Mulieri.
  Harps Are Not for Angels. Princeton, N.J.: Xlibris, 1997.
The session musician's autobiography includes anecdotes of recording sessions from the
1940s to 1960s with Bernard Herrmann, 210–11; Erich Wolfgang Korngold, 224–29;
Max Steiner, 117–19, 125–29, 131–33; Franz Waxman, 157–58, 197–99; and Victor
Young, 183–85. Film titles and composers are listed in the index.

Dale, Edgar.
  *How to Appreciate Motion Pictures: A Manual of Motion-Picture Criticism Pre-
  pared for High-School Students.* New York: Macmillan, 1933.
"Sound and Music" includes "The Use of Music in Films," 175–76; "The Work of the
Director of Music," 176–77.

Das Gupta, Chidananda.
  Talking about Films. New Delhi: Orient Longman, 1980.
"Music: Opium of the Masses?" 29–39.

Davis, Glyn, and Dickinson, Kay, eds.
  Teen TV: Genre, Consumption, Identity. London: BFI Publishing, 2004.
"'My Generation': Popular Music, Age and Influence in Teen Drama of the 1990s," by
Kay Dickinson, discusses the use of contemporary and noncontemporary popular music
in dramatic television aimed at teens, 97–111.

Davis, Sheila.
  The Craft of Lyric Writing. Cincinnati: Writer's Digest Books, 1985.
"The Anatomy of a Film Song" analyzes the lyrics to "The Shadow of Your Smile" from
The Sandpiper, music and lyrics by Johnny Mandel and Paul Francis Webster, 249–53.
References throughout to film songs, songwriters, and lyricists. Also by the author: *Suc-
cessful Lyric Writing: A Step-By-Step Course and Workbook* (1988) and *The Songwriters
Idea Book: 40 Strategies to Excite Your Imagination, Help You Design Distinctive Songs,
and Keep Your Creative Flow* (1992).

Davy, Charles, ed.
>   *Footnotes to the Film.* New York: Oxford Univ. Press; London: Lovat and Dickson, 1937. Reprint, New York: Arno Press, 1970.

"Music on the Screen," by the French composer Maurice Jaubert, discusses musicals, nonmusicals, and subjective elements, and critiques American film music, 101–15.

Daxl, Heiko, and Ingeborg Fulepp, eds.
>   *Media-Scape 3: Turbulences of Transition.* Zagreb: Media-Scape, 1995.

"CUBASE: The Way to Compose Film Music," by Irena Paulus, on using the computer program in film music composition, 89. From an international symposium on art and audio-visual culture.

Deans, Marjorie.
>   *Meeting at the Sphinx.* London: MacDonald, 1946.

This book, on the making of *Caesar and Cleopatra* (1946), includes "The Music," on the circumstances surrounding the composition of Georges Auric's score, 102, 107.

DeCurtis, Anthony.
>   *In Other Words: Artists Talk about Life and Work.* Milwaukee: Hal Leonard, 2005.

Interviews with rock musicians, country musicians, and motion picture producers and directors; some references to popular music in films.

Dench, Ernest A.
>   *Making the Movies.* New York: Macmillan, 1915.

"Musical Matters in Motion Picture Producing" mentions music played on the set to inspire actors, and songs specially composed for actors, 95–99. One of the earliest books to include substantive material on musical customs on the set and the use of film personalities to promote sheet music sales.

DeNitto, Dennis, and William Herman.
>   *Film and the Critical Eye.* New York: Macmillan, 1975.

A discussion of viewing and interpreting films. "Tracks: Sound and Music," 44–46. The authors often include music in the discussion and analysis of specific films, many helmed by a European—particularly French—or Japanese director.

De Thuin, Richard.
>   *Official Identification and Price Guide to Movie Memorabilia.* New York: House of Collectibles, 1990.

"Sheet Music" lists song titles alphabetically with prices, 354–81.

Dettmar, Kevin J. H., and William Richey, eds.
>   *Reading Rock and Roll: Authenticity, Appropriation, Aesthetics.* New York: Columbia Univ. Press, 1999.

"Musical Cheese: The Appropriation of Seventies Music in Nineties Movies," 311–26.

Devereaux, Leslie, and Roger Hillman, eds.
>   *Fields of Vision: Essays in Film Studies, Visual Anthropology, and Photography.* Berkeley: University of California Press, 1995.

"Narrative, Sound, and Film: Fassbinder's *The Marriage of Maria Braun*," by Roger Hillman, 181–95.

Dickinson, Peter, ed.
   Copland Connotations: Studies and Interviews. Rochester, N.Y.: Boydell Press, 2002.
"Copland on Hollywood," by Sally Bick, 39–54.

Dickinson, Peter, ed.
   Twenty British Composers. London: Chester Music for the Feeney Trust, 1975.
"The Celluloid Plays a Tune," by British composer Alan Rawsthorne, previously published in John Sutro's *Diversion: Twenty-Two Authors on the Lively Arts* (1950).

Dixon, Wheeler Winston, ed.
   Film Genre 2000: New Critical Essays. Albany: State Univ. of New York Press, 2000.
"Of Tunes and Toons: The Movie Musical in the 1990s," by Marc Miller, 45–62.

Doherty, Thomas.
   Teenagers and Teenpics: The Juvenilization of American Movies in the 1950s. Boston: Unwin Hyman, 1988.
Contains material on rock 'n' roll music.

Dolan, Robert Emmett.
   Music in Modern Media: Techniques in Tape, Disc and Film Recording, Motion Picture and Television Scoring and Electronic Music. New York: G. Schirmer, 1967. 181 pp.
This technical manual is organized into sections on recording, films, television, and electronic music. Film topics include preproduction, prerecording, recording playbacks, recording on the set, the film score, preparation, writing and recording the score, and dubbing. There are musical examples in the form of short scores from film and television productions with music by Van Cleave, Aaron Copland, Robert Emmett Dolan, Hugo Friedhofer, Alfred Newman, Alex North, David Raksin, and Dolan himself, a composer and conductor. A survey of the state of electronic music is largely unrelated to film music, with the exception of "Electronic Music Scoring," 171–72.

Dominic, Serene.
   Burt Bacharach, Song by Song: The Ultimate Burt Bacharach Reference for Fans, Serious Record Collectors, and Music Critics. New York: Schirmer Trade Books, 2003.
The Bacharach song oeuvre, including his songs for film, is examined by the author, a music writer.

Doyle, Billy H.
   The Ultimate Directory of Film Technicians: A Necrology of Dates and Places of Births and Deaths of More Than 9,000 Producers, Screenwriters, Composers, Cinematographers, Art Directors, Costume Designers, Choreographers, Executives, and Publicists. Lanham, Md.: Scarecrow Press, 1999.

A number of composers, arrangers, and music directors are included, with no distinction made between underscore composers and songwriters. Many of the composers listed are from the world of popular music and have little or no connection to film. Data compiled from obituaries in the *New York Times, Variety,* and *Hollywood Reporter,* supplemented by research from the California Death Index and Social Security records.

Drazin, Charles.
    In Search of The Third Man. New York: Limelight Editions, 2000.
"The Fourth Man" traces the history of Anton Karas's zither-based score, 95–109.

Dressler, John Clay.
    Alan Rawsthorne: A Bio-Bibliography. Westport, Conn.: Praeger, 2004.
Contains material on the British composer's film work.

Duke, Vernon.
    Listen Here! A Critical Essay on Music Depreciation. New York: Ivan Obolensky, 1963.
The composer-songwriter mentions four film composers he respects, 64–65, and critiques Hollywood music packagers, bombastic orchestrations, television music, and Dimitri Tiomkin, 302–9. A dozen film scores mentioned in the text are indexed, 401.

Dunn, Leslie C., and Nancy A. Jones, eds.
    Embodied Voices: Representing Female Vocality in Western Culture. Cambridge: Cambridge Univ. Press, 1995.
"Deriding the Voice of Jeanette MacDonald: Notes on Psychoanalysis and the American Film Musical," by Edward Baron Turk, 103–19.

Du Noyer, Paul, ed.
    The Billboard Illustrated Encyclopedia of Music. New York: Billboard Books, 2003.
"Film Music and Soundtracks," an overview, 413–15.

Durwood, Thomas, ed.
    Close Encounters of the Third Kind: *A Document of the Film.* Kansas City: Ariel Books, 1978.
Contains quotes from John Williams on the creation of his score for the 1977 film.

Dyer, Richard.
    Only Entertainment. London: Routledge, 1992. 2nd ed., New York: Routledge, 2002.
"Entertainment and Utopia," 17–34 (1992). Originally appeared in *Movie* (Spring 1977).

Earnshaw, Steven, ed.
    Postmodern Surroundings. Amsterdam: Rodopi, 1994.
"Altered Status: A Review of Music in Postmodern Cinema and Culture," by K. J. Don-nelly, 39–51.

Eckstein, Arthur M., and Peter Lehman, eds.
    The Searchers: *Essays and Reflections on John Ford's Classic Western.* Detroit: Wayne State Univ. Press, 2004.
"'Typically American': Music for *The Searchers,*" by Kathryn Kalinak, 109–43.

Edgerton, Gary R., ed.
>*Films and the Arts in Symbiosis: A Resource Guide*. New York: Greenwood Press, 1988.

"Film and Classical Music," by Royal Brown, on the historical development, musical styles, preexisting musical associations, the Leitmotif, Mickey Mousing, and narrative implications, 165–215. Portions later appear in Brown's *Overtones and Undertones: Reading Film Music* (1994). "Film and Popular Music," by Gary Burns, discusses historical development and styles and genres of interaction, 217–42.

Edmonds, Robert.
>*The Sights and Sounds of Cinema and Television: How the Aesthetic Experience Influences Our Feelings*. New York: Teachers College, Columbia Univ., 1982.

"The Characteristics of Music" and "Some Applications of Music" contain terminology, 125–29; "Speech as Music," 130–31; "The Relationship of Music to Pictures," 139–43; the structure of music, 153–54. Author is a professor.

Eisenstein, Sergei M.
>*Film Essays, with a Lecture*. Translated and edited by Jay Leyda. London: Dobson, 1968. New York: Praeger, 1970. Princeton, N.J.: Princeton Univ. Press, 1982.

The film director discusses Sergei Prokofiev, 180–82 (1968).

Eisenstein, Sergei M.
>*Film Form: Essays in Film Theory*. Translated and edited by Jay Leyda. New York: Harcourt Brace, 1949.

The film director discusses film music, 152–53, 177–78.

Eisenstein, Sergei M.
>*Film Form; The Film Sense: Two Complete and Unabridged Works*. Translated and edited by Jay Leyda. New York: Meridian Books, 1957.

See the preceding entry and the next entry.

Eisenstein, Sergei M.
>*The Film Sense*. Translated and edited by Jay Leyda. New York: Harcourt, Brace, 1942. London: Faber and Faber, 1943. 2nd ed., 1947. New York: Harcourt, Brace & World, 1970. Rev. ed., New York: Harcourt Brace Jovanovich, 1975.

On Prokofiev's music for *Alexander Nevsky*, 158ff. (1942).

Eisenstein, Sergei M.
>*Notes of a Film Director*. Compiled and edited by R. Yurenev. Translated by X. Danko. London: Lawrence & Wishart, 1959. Moscow: Foreign Languages Pub. House, 1959.

Contains Eisenstein's 1946 essay, "P-R-K-F-V," on Prokofiev, 149–67.

Eisler, Hanns.
>*Hanns Eisler: A Rebel in Music: Selected Writings*. Edited by Manfred Grabs. New York: International Publishers, 1978; Berlin: Seven Seas, 1978.

"Blast-Furnace Music: Work on a Sound Film in the Soviet Union, 1932," 61–62; "A Musical Journey through America," including his visit to Metro-Goldwyn-Mayer studios in 1935, 90–91; "Hollywood Seen from the Left," including his impressions of a Hollywood music department in 1935, 103–5.

Elsaesser, Thomas, and Michael Wedel, eds.
    A Second Life: German Cinema's First Decades. Amsterdam: Amsterdam Univ. Press, 1996.
"Giuseppe Becce and Richard Wagner: Paradoxes of the First German Film Score," by Ennio Simeon, 219–24.

Elschek, Oskár, ed.
    A History of Slovak Music: From the Earliest Times to the Present. Bratislava: VEDA, 2003.
"Slovak Music of the 20th Century: Film Music," by Juraj Lexmann, translated by Martin Styan, 427–37.

Erlewine, Michael, and others, eds.
    All Music Guide: The Experts' Guide to the Best Recordings from Thousands of Artists in All Types of Music. 3rd ed. San Francisco: Miller Freeman, 1997.
Includes soundtracks.

Erni, John Nguyet, and Siew Keng Chua, eds.
    Asian Media Studies: Politics of Subjectivities. Malden, Mass.: Blackwell Publishing, 2005.
"The Whole World Is Watching Us: Music Television Audiences in India," by Vamsee Juluri, 161–82.

Essoe, Gabe.
    The Book of Movie Lists. Westport, Conn.: Arlington House, 1981.
"Cabaret, Or: There's Music and Laughter in the Air," 133–46, includes "Debbie Reynolds' List of 11 Unforgettable Musical Numbers," "Debbie Reynolds' List of Her 8 Favorite Musicals," "Shirley Jones' List of the 10 Best Movie Adaptations of Broadway Musicals," and "David Rose's List of 9 Memorable Movie Musical Scores."

Essoe, Gabe, and Raymond Lee.
    DeMille: The Man and His Pictures. South Brunswick, N.J.: A. S. Barnes, 1970.
"The DeMille Legend," by Elmer Bernstein, recalls Bernstein's experience with the producer while scoring *The Ten Commandments* (1956), 277–82. Originally appeared in the *Los Angeles Times.*

Etter, Jonathan.
    Quinn Martin, Producer: A Behind-the-Scenes History of QM Productions and Its Founder. Jefferson, N.C.: McFarland, 2003.
Based on the author's interviews with composer Duane Tatro and QM Productions postproduction supervisor John Elizalde, who selected composers and provided music supervision.

Evans, John, Philip Reed, and Paul Wilson, comps.
    A Britten Source Book. Rev. ed. Alderburgh, Suffolk: The Britten Estate, 1987.
"Music for Film" includes manuscript material, instrumentation, and notes, 131–44.

Everett, William A., and Paul R. Laird, eds.
The Cambridge Companion to the Musical. Cambridge: Cambridge Univ. Press, 2002.
"The Melody (and the Words) Linger On: American Musical Comedies of the 1920s and 1930s," by Geoffrey Block, includes musical theater songs, some of which were subsequently used in films, 77–97. "Distant Cousin or Fraternal Twin? Analytical Approaches to the Film Musical," by Graham Wood, 212–30.

Ewbank, Alison J., and Fouli T. Papageorgiou, eds.
Whose Master's Voice? The Development of Popular Music in Thirteen Cultures. Westport, Conn.: Greenwood Press, 1997.
"Music in India: A Look at Something Different," by Usha Vyasulu Reddy, includes a discussion of Indian film music, 98–112.

Ewen, David.
All the Years of American Popular Music. Englewood Cliffs, N.J.: Prentice Hall, 1977.
"The Silent Screen Erupts into Sound" includes material on theme songs, Broadway composers in Hollywood, Leo F. Forbstein, Max Steiner, click tracks, Erich Wolfgang Korngold, and Alfred Newman, 380–408. "The Movies, the Radio, and Now Television: The Early Post-War Years" includes material on Hugo Friedhofer, John Green, Bernard Herrmann, Bronislaw Kaper, David Raksin, Miklós Rózsa, Dimitri Tiomkin, Franz Waxman, and Victor Young, 495–508. "Music Is Heard and Seen: Radio and Television in the Fifties" includes material on television theme music, David Rose, and Henry Mancini, 511–30. "The Hollywood Scene in the Fifties" includes material on theme and title songs, Elmer Bernstein, Ernest Gold, Alex North, André Previn, Leonard Rosenman, and Walter Scharf, 581–93. "The Decline and Fall of the Hollywood Empire" includes material on musicals from Broadway productions, original screen musicals, Jerry Goldsmith, Marvin Hamlisch, Maurice Jarre, Quincy Jones, Fred Karlin, Michel Legrand, Lionel Newman, Laurence Rosenthal, Lalo Schifrin, Richard and Robert Sherman, and John Williams, and the decline in screen music, 760–77. General topics, organized decade by decade, include original background music and scoring, screen biographies of popular musicians, and vocal dubbing.

Ewen, David.
American Songwriters: An H. W. Wilson Biographical Dictionary. New York: H. W. Wilson, 1987.
Profiles more than a hundred songwriters, many of whom made contributions to film, including Harold Arlen, Burt Bacharach, Alan and Marilyn Bergman, Jimmy McHugh, Henry Mancini, Randy Newman, Richard and Robert Sherman, David Shire, and Dimitri Tiomkin.

Ewen, David.
Great Men of American Popular Song: The History of the American Popular Song Told through the Lives, Careers, Achievements, and Personalities of Its Foremost Composers and Lyricists—From William Billings of the Revolutionary War to the "Folk-Rock" of Bob Dylan. Englewood Cliffs, N.J.: Prentice Hall, 1970. Rev. and enlarged ed., 1972.

The three-part section "Song from the Movies" covers Harry Warren, James Van Heusen, and Henry Mancini, 310–46 (1970).

Ewen, David, comp. and ed.
  Popular American Composers: From Revolutionary Times to the Present. New York: H. W. Wilson, 1962.
A biographical and critical guide, with significant coverage of songwriters. Entries are often accompanied by a small photograph and include Harold Arlen, Irving Berlin, Hoagy Carmichael, Con Conrad, Walter Donaldson, Vernon Duke, Sammy Fain, Morton Gould, Johnny Green, Jerome Kern, Burton Lane, Jay Livingston, Frank Loesser, Frederick Loewe, Jimmy McHugh, Alfred Newman, André Previn, Ralph Rainger, Richard Rodgers, Sigmund Romberg, Harold Rome, David Rose, Arthur Schwartz, Raymond Scott, Max Steiner, Jule Styne, Dimitri Tiomkin, Jimmy Van Heusen, Harry Warren, Richard A. Whiting, Meredith Willson, Vincent Youmans, and Victor Young. A 1972 supplement contains updated and/or new entries for Burt Bacharach, Elmer Bernstein, George Forrest, Ernest Gold, John Green, Jerry Livingston, Henry Mancini, and Robert Wright.

Ewen, David, ed.
  American Composers Today: A Biographical and Critical Guide. New York: H. W. Wilson, 1949.
Entries, often accompanied by a small photograph, on George Antheil, Robert Russell Bennett, Leonard Bernstein, Marc Blitzstein, Henry Brant, Mario Castelnuovo-Tedesco, Aaron Copland, Vladimir Dukelsky (Vernon Duke), George Gershwin, Morton Gould, Louis Gruenberg, Bernard Herrmann, Erich Wolfgang Korngold, Gail Kubik, Douglas Moore, Jerome Moross, Alex North, Earl Robinson, Miklós Rózsa, Elie Siegmeister, William Grant Still, Virgil Thomson, and Meredith Willson.

Ewen, David, ed.
  American Popular Songs: From the Revolutionary War to the Present. New York: Random House, 1966.
Entries arranged alphabetically, with anecdotal and historical material on hundreds of film songs. In addition to composer and lyricist credits, the entries often include the name of the performer, popular recordings outside of the film, and later interpolations in other films.

Eyman, Scott.
  The Speed of Sound: Hollywood and the Talkie Revolution, 1926–1930. New York: Simon & Schuster, 1997. Baltimore: Johns Hopkins Univ. Press, 1999.
References throughout to music for silent films and musicals.

Famous Music Corp.
  Combined Famous Music Catalog: The Best of Motion Picture, Standard Songs, Television, Soul Hits. New York: Famous Music, ca. 1970.
Established in 1928 as the music publishing division of Paramount Pictures, Famous Music's catalog contains well over 100,000 copyrights. This 114-page booklet has "a listing categorically and thematically of the most important copyrights in the Famous-Paramount catalogs," and includes a seven-page supplemental listing from February 1971. A copy is at UC Santa Barbara.

Fantle, David, and Tom Johnson.
  25 Years of Celebrity Interviews from Vaudeville to Movies to TV, Reel to Real. Oregon, Wis.: Badger Books, 2004.
The section "Your Hit Parade" contains the following interviews: "Little Miracle," Sammy Cahn, 277–79; "Stardust and Residuals," Hoagy Carmichael, 280–82; "The Art of Perfect Timing," Burton Lane, 283–85; "Still in Tune," Jay Livingston and Ray Evans, 286–88; and "Lullabies and Nightmares," Harry Warren, 289–92.

Farneth, David, with Elmar Juchem and Dave Stein.
  Kurt Weill: A Life in Pictures and Documents. Woodstock, N.Y.: Overlook Press, 2000.
Includes documentation of Weill's film work, letters written in Hollywood, and a chronology. The authors are associated with the Weill–Lenya Research Center, the New York Public Library for the Performing Arts, and the Kurt Weill Foundation for Music.

Fawell, John Wesley.
  The Art of Sergio Leone's Once Upon a Time in the West: *A Critical Appreciation*. Jefferson, N.C.: McFarland, 2005.
Includes "The Leone-Morricone Soundtrack," 169–88; and "The Music of Sound and Dialogue," 189–202.

Fawell, John Wesley.
  Hitchcock's Rear Window: *The Well-Made Film*. Carbondale: Southern Illinois Univ. Press, 2001.
The asynchronous use of music and songs in the 1954 film is examined in "Aural Intrusions," 25–28; "The Rhythm of Sound," 28–31; and "The Rhythm of Sound: One Sequence," 31–34.

Fay, Laurel E., ed.
  Shostakovich and His World. Princeton, N.J.: Princeton Univ. Press, 2004.
Contains "Stalin and Shostakovich: Letters to a 'Friend,'" by Leonid Maximenkov, 43–58, and additional references to Shostakovich's film music throughout the remaining essays.

Feather, Leonard, and Ira Gitler.
  The Encyclopedia of Jazz in the Seventies. New York: Horizon Press, 1976. Reprint, New York: Da Capo Press, 1987.
"A Guide to Available Jazz Films," by Leonard Maltin, 382–86. Organized by performer, with film titles.

Feild, Robert D.
  The Art of Walt Disney. New York: Macmillan, 1942.
The index entry for "Music" includes text references to the Disney music department, 259–63, and suggestions for musical numbers for *Pinocchio*, 177–78.

Feist, Leo.
  Catalog of Copyrighted Musical Compositions. New York: Leo Feist, ca. 1936. 72 pp.

Copyrighted compositions from musical productions owned by Leo Feist, music publisher for Metro-Goldwyn-Mayer, are listed by film title. Song title index.

Felton, Gary S.
   The Record Collector's International Directory. New York: Crown, 1980.
Index includes film score and soundtrack dealers.

Ferencz, George J.
   Robert Russell Bennett: A Bio-Bibliography. New York: Greenwood Press, 1990.
An appendix, "Film and Television Scores/Orchestrations," documents Bennett's work in Hollywood from 1931 to 1958, 184–87.

Field, Mary, and Percy Smith.
   The Secrets of Nature. London: Faber and Faber, 1934.
An in-depth look at the making of this series of short films dealing with natural history, which began production in 1922. Great care was given to the musical accompaniment of these silent and sound films, which featured compiled and original music.

Field, Shelly.
   Career Opportunities in the Music Industry. New York: Facts on File, 1986. 2nd ed., 1990. 3rd ed., 1995. 4th ed., 2000.
Contains job descriptions and duties for the music and recording industries. No material specifically on film music; however, there are brief career profiles for arranger, orchestrator, copyist, session musician, and songwriter.

Fielding, Raymond.
   The March of Time, 1935–1951. New York: Oxford Univ. Press, 1978.
An in-depth look at the history and making of this series of documentary shorts underwritten by Time, Inc. Includes several pages on the music, with information from music director and composer Jack Shaindlin and assistant Robert McBride; see esp. 222–25. Shaindlin, who was interviewed by Fielding, scored the series from 1941 on, following John Rochetti and Louis De Francesco. Bernard Herrmann parodied the *March of Time* music style in *Citizen Kane*'s *Time on the March* newsreel sequence.

Film Federation of India.
   Indian Talkie, 1931–56: Silver Jubilee Souvenir. Bombay: Film Federation of India, 1956.
A number of articles look back at twenty-five years of film music, primarily songs and classical music. "Music of the Movies," by Naushad Ali, mentions the growing use and acceptance of orchestras to accompany films, 99–100; "Mixing Tunes Not Edifying," by K. B. Sundarambal, 100; "Soft Voices that Came of the Sore Throat: Accident that Led to the Saigal Tunes," by R. C. Boral, a music director, mentions the influence of Chaplin and Disney on his use of dramatic music for film, 101; "Perennial Appeal of Classical Music," by Lata Mangeshkar, 102; "Why Film Music Is Popular?" by Gantasala V. Rao, 102; "Meant-to-Hit Songs to Be Made to Order: Limitations on the Film Lyricist," by Pradeep, 103–4; "Trends in Film Music: Warning Against Hybridisation," by Shanker Rao Vyes, 161; "A Song Is Born?" by S. Rajeswara Rao, 161; "Conserve India's Music Heritage: An Appeal to Music Directors," by S. Kanagasabhai, 163.

Finch, Christopher.
  The Art of Walt Disney from Mickey Mouse to the Magic Kingdom. New York: Abrams, 1973. Rev. ed., 1995.
The index in the revised edition includes references to music in the text.

Finler, Joel W.
  The Hollywood Story. New York: Crown, 1988. London: Wallflower Press, 2003.
Historical biographies of nine Hollywood studios: Columbia, Disney (new to 2003 edition), Fox, MGM, Paramount, RKO, United Artists, Universal, and Warner Bros. An "Other Departments" section includes summaries of some of the studios' music departments. In the 2003 edition, a "Creative Personnel" sidebar for each studio lists composers/music directors by name and their inclusive years of service; for example, see United Artists, 252. (The previous edition used graphic charts with year spans for composers and mini Oscars®.) One of the few sources to compile the information in this format; superior to Walter Scharf's lists of music department staffs by decade in *The History of Film Scoring* (1988).

Flinn, Caryl.
  The New German Cinema: Music, History, and the Matter of Style. Berkeley: Univ. of California Press, 2004.
Includes chapters on historical predecessors of melodrama and modernism, including composite scores; "New German Melodrama"; Peer Raben's film music for director Rainer Werner Fassbinder; and music in the films of director Werner Schroeter (an elaboration on "Embracing Kitsch: Werner Schroeter, Music and *The Bomber Pilot*," in K. J. Donnelly's *Film Music: Critical Approaches*, 2001). Among the theoretical topics discussed are the absence or inadequacy of music, fragmentation of music, and music as a substitute for speech. Index.

Flower, John.
  Moonlight Serenade: A Bio-Discography of the Glenn Miller Civilian Band. New Rochelle, N.Y.: Arlington House, 1972.
Film recording sessions are documented beginning on page 283.

Floyd, Samuel A., Jr., ed.
  International Dictionary of Black Composers. 2 vols. Chicago: Fitzroy Dearborn, 1999.
Entries on Duke Ellington, Jester Hairston, Herbie Hancock, Isaac Hayes, Francis Hall Johnson, Wynton Marsalis, William Grant Still, and Stevie Wonder. Brief biographies and music list.

Ford, Andrew.
  Undue Noise: Words about Music. Sydney, Australia: ABC Books, 2002.
"Film Music in Context," 127–30; "The Art of Bernard Herrmann," 131–38. Author is an Australian (Liverpool-born) composer, writer, and radio show host.

Foreman, Lewis, ed.
  Information Sources in Music. Munich: K. G. Saur, 2003.
"Film and Its Music," by David Whittle, discusses reference and research materials.

Foreman, Lewis, ed.
   Vaughan Williams in Perspective: Studies of an English Composer. London: Albion,
   1998.
"The Film Music of Ralph Vaughan Williams," by John Huntley, 176–80.

Forlenza, Jeff, and Terri Stone, eds.
   Sound for Picture: An Inside Look at Audio Production for Film and Television. Em-
   eryville, Calif.: MixBooks/Hal Leonard Publishing, 1993.
"Hans Zimmer and Jay Rifkin, Media Ventures, Los Angeles—Akai DD100 Disk Re-
corder," on *Thelma & Louise*, 28–29; "Music," in the chapter on *Terminator 2: Judgment
Day*, by Tom Kenny, 33–34; "Music," in the chapter on *Malcolm X*, by Tom Kenny, 40–
41; "Original Score Recording," in the chapter on *Beauty and the Beast*, by Tom Kenny,
46–47; "*Twin Peaks*," by Blair Jackson, discusses Angelo Badalamenti's music for the
television series, 110; "CD Production Music and Sound Effects Libraries: A User's
Guide," by George Petersen, 124–25.

Forte, Allen.
   The American Popular Ballad of the Golden Era, 1924–1950. Princeton, N.J.:
   Princeton Univ. Press, 1995.
Analyzes American popular songs (some from films) by Harold Arlen, Irving Berlin,
Hoagy Carmichael, Walter Donaldson, George Gershwin, Johnny Green, Jerome Kern,
Burton Lane, Jimmy McHugh, Cole Porter, Richard Rodgers, Ann Ronell, Jimmy Van
Heusen, Harry Warren, Richard Whiting, Vincent Youmans, and others.

Foss, Hubert, and Noel Goodwin.
   London Symphony: Portrait of an Orchestra. London: Naldrett Press, 1954.
Contains material on director Humphrey Jennings's proposed film on the orchestra, in-
cluding its role in recording film music.

Fox, Deborah.
   People at Work Making a Film. New York: Dillon Press, 1998.
This entry in the author's People at Work book series for children discusses music in the
context of producing a film.

Fraigneau, André.
   Cocteau on the Film: A Conversation Recorded by André Fraigneau. Translated by
   Vera Traill. London: Dennis Dobson, 1954. New York: Roy Publishers, 1954. New
   York: Dover, 1972. New York: Garland Publishing, 1985.
The director Jean Cocteau talks about *La Belle et la Bête* (*Beauty and the Beast*, 1946),
his fondness for accidental synchronization between music and image, and his collabora-
tion with Georges Auric, including "reshuffling" the composer's music, 71–74 (1954).

Franks, A. H.
   Ballet for Film and Television. London: Sir Isaac Pitman and Sons, 1950.
A short catalog of dance and ballet films, most without composer credits, 78–82.

Frascella, Lawrence, and Al Weisel.
   Live Fast, Die Young: The Wild Ride of Making Rebel without a Cause. New York:
   Simon & Schuster, 2005.

"The Composer," on Leonard Rosenman and his score, 223–25; with many references throughout to the music.

Frasier, David K.
>   *Suicide in the Entertainment Industry: An Encyclopedia of 840 Twentieth Century Cases*. Jefferson, N.C.: McFarland, 2002.

Several composers, songwriters, and musicians peripherally connected to film music are mentioned, including Fred Fisher, Richard Goodman, Jerry Overton Jarnegin, Bob Merrill, Caleb Sampson, and Fred Wise. Each entry indicates the method of death and extracts from notes left behind. Darrell Calker's 1964 suicide is overlooked.

Fricke, John, Jay Scarfone, and William Stillman.
>   The Wizard of Oz: *The Official 50th Anniversary Pictorial History*. New York: Warner Books, 1989.

"Scripts, Songs, and Staff," 26–44, contains a discussion of the music, 39–43.

Friedman, James, ed.
>   *UCLA Film and Television Archive Presents Hallmark Hall of Fame: 50, The First Fifty Years*. Los Angeles: The Archive, 2001.

Includes music credits for more than 125 programs produced between 1972 and 2001.

Friedman, Lawrence S.
>   *The Cinema of Martin Scorsese*. New York: Continuum, 1997.

"The Sound(s) of Music: From the Bands to The Band" primarily covers the musical *New York, New York*, 88–112; Scorsese's use of music is mentioned throughout the text.

Friedwald, Will.
>   *Stardust Melodies: The Biography of Twelve of America's Most Popular Songs*. New York: Pantheon Books, 2002.

"The St. Louis Blues," "Body and Soul," and "I Got Rhythm" are among the songs, all but one of which were composed between 1927 and 1938. While none were initially written for a film, their inclusion in countless motion pictures makes this book noteworthy. The author, a frequent contributor to liner notes, gives an extended history of each song and explores the musical and lyric content. The chapter on "As Time Goes By" discusses the use of the song in *Casablanca* and its prior history, 213–41.

Frith, Simon.
>   *Music for Pleasure: Essays in the Sociology of Pop*. New York: Routledge, 1988.

Contains two essays, "Sound and Vision: Ennio Morricone (1981)" and "Pretty Vacant: John Barry (1986)."

Frith, Simon.
>   *Performing Rites: On the Value of Popular Music*. Cambridge, Mass.: Harvard Univ. Press, 1996. Also published as *Performing Rites: Evaluating Popular Music*. Oxford: Oxford Univ. Press, 1998.

A British professor of English discusses film music, including the use of music to communicate feelings and the meaning of music in film (drawing on the work of theorists Claudia Gorbman and Philip Tagg), in "Where Do Sounds Come From?" 99–122.

Frogley, Alain, ed.
  Vaughan Williams Studies. Cambridge: Cambridge Univ. Press, 1996.
"Vaughan Williams and British Wartime Cinema," by Jeffrey Richards, 139–65.

Fruttchey, Frank.
  Something New: 400 Self-Help Suggestions for Movie Organ Players. Detroit, 1916.
Unable to acquire a copy for review. The author was a church organist based at various
times in Michigan, New Jersey, and New York who also wrote *Voice, Speech, Thinking:
A Volume Containing Comment and Statement of Fact Concerning Man's Use of the
Elements of the Universe Wherewith He (Man) Is to Make Intelligible His Act and His
So-Called Thought* (Detroit: Music in America, 1920) and *Delinquent Gods: 2800 Perti-
nent Questions and 2800 Dependable Answers... (A Comment and Criticism of Present
Day Standards of Music)* (Detroit, 1917). A reader of the latter commented, "The voice is
so strident, intense, judgmental and decisive that it's like being spoken to from on high."
Based on that assessment, Fruttchey's 1916 work may be a great find.

Fry, Stephen M., comp. and ed.
  Film, Television, and Radio Music Resources in the UCLA Music Library. Los An-
    geles: UCLA Music Library, 1994.
An eight-page guide to finding aids, particularly for the numerous film and television
composers represented in UCLA's Special Collections. Fry's lifelong appreciation of
film music inspired him in acquiring many of these collections for the university as head
of the Music Library.

Furia, Philip.
  The Poets of Tin Pan Alley: A History of America's Great Lyricists. New York: Ox-
    ford Univ. Press, 1990.
"Hip, Hooray, and Ballyhoo: Hollywood Lyricists," a survey, with strong coverage on
Harry Warren, 231–43.

Gabbard, Krin.
  Black Magic: White Hollywood and African American Culture. New Brunswick,
    N.J.: Rutgers Univ. Press, 2004.
"Robert Altman's Jazz History Lesson," 235–50 (portions appeared in James Buhler et
al., *Music and Cinema*); "Spike Lee Meets Aaron Copland," on the director's use of
Copland's music in his film *He Got Game* (1998), 251–74 (reprinted from *American
Music*). Additional references to film music throughout.

Gabbard, Krin, ed.
  Representing Jazz. Durham, N.C.: Duke Univ. Press, 1995.
"Jammin' the Blues, or, The Sight of Jazz, 1944," by Arthur Knight, includes discussion
of Hollywood jazz, 11–53; "Doubling, Music, and Race in *Cabin in the Sky*," by Adam
Knee, discusses Duke Ellington's performance, 193–204.

Gaines, Jane M., and Michael Renov, eds.
  Collecting Visible Evidence. Minneapolis: Univ. of Minnesota Press, 1999.
"Damming Virgil Thomson's Score for *The River*," by Neil William Lerner, 103–15.

Gaines, Philip, and David J. Rhodes.
Micro-Budget Hollywood: Budgeting (and Making) Feature Films for $50,000 to $500,000. Los Angeles: Silman-James Press, 1995.
"Music," 70–71; "Interview with Chuck Cirino, Composer," 87–96, with his credits, primarily for films directed by Jim Wynorski and Fred Olen Ray, 96–98.

Galbraith, Stuart.
The Emperor and the Wolf: The Lives and Films of Akira Kurosawa and Toshiro Mifune. New York: Faber and Faber, 2002.
Discussion of music by Fumio Hayasaka, Masaru Sato, and Toru Takemitsu, largely in Japanese films.

Gale Research.
Contemporary Musicians. Detroit: Gale Research, 1989–2002.
Biographical essays and chronological career summaries, with selected discographies and bibliographies. Paul Anka (vol. 2), Harold Arlen (vol. 27), Burt Bacharach (vols. 1, 20), Angelo Badalamenti (vol. 17), John Barry (vol. 29), Alan and Marilyn Bergman (vol. 30), Irving Berlin (vol. 8), Leonard Bernstein (vol. 2), Terence Blanchard (vol. 13), Benjamin Britten (vol. 15), David Byrne (vol. 8), Sammy Cahn (vol. 11), Jimmy Cliff (vol. 8), Stewart Copeland (vol. 14), Aaron Copland (vol. 2), Andraé Crouch (vol. 9), African-born composer Manu Dibango (vol. 14), Thomas Dolby (vol. 10), Donovan (vol. 9), session guitarist Duane Eddy (vol. 9), Danny Elfman (vol. 9), Duke Ellington (vol. 2), Maynard Ferguson (vol. 7), Mitchell Froom (vol. 15), Peter Gabriel (vols. 2, 16), Diamanda Galás (vol. 16), Ira and George Gershwin (vol. 11), Glenn Gould (vol. 9), Dave Grusin (vol. 7), Vince Guaraldi (vol. 3), Marvin Hamlisch (vol. 1), Herbie Hancock (vols. 8, 25), George Harrison (vol. 2), Isaac Hayes (vol. 10), Bernard Herrmann (vol. 14), Mark Isham (vol. 14), Quincy Jones (vols. 2, 20), John Kander (vol. 33), Mark Knopfler (vols. 3, 25), John Lennon (vol. 9), Alan Jay Lerner and Frederick Loewe (vol. 13), Frank Loesser (vol. 19), Henry Mancini (vols. 1, 20), Branford Marsalis (vol. 10), Curtis Mayfield (vol. 8), Paul McCartney (vols. 4, 32), Alan Menken (vol. 10), Johnny Mercer (vol. 13), Pat Metheny (vols. 2, 26), Hugo Montenegro (vol. 18), Ennio Morricone (vol. 15), Milton Nascimento (vol. 6), Randy Newman (vols. 4 and 27), Harry Nilsson (vol. 10), Michael Nyman (vol. 15), Van Dyke Parks (vol. 17), Oscar Peterson (vol. 11), Cole Porter (vol. 10), André Previn (vol. 15), Trent Reznor (vol. 13), Lionel Richie (vol. 2), Sonny Rollins (vol. 7), Nino Rota (vol. 13), Carole Bayer Sager (vol. 5), Ryuichi Sakamoto (vol. 18), Peter Schickele (vol. 5), Paul Schütze (vol. 32), Ravi Shankar (vol. 9), Taj Mahal (vol. 6), Tan Dun (vol. 33), Tom Waits (vols. 1, 12), Kurt Weill (vol. 12), John Williams (vols. 9, 28), Paul Williams (vols. 5, 26), music supervisor Hal Willner (vol. 10), Neil Young (vol. 15), and Hans Zimmer (vol. 34).

Gallusser, Werner, and Andrew D. McCredie, direction; and the Australian Musicological Commission, general eds.
Music Librarianship and Documentation: Report of the 1970 Adelaide Seminar. Adelaide, Australia: University of Adelaide Department of Adult Education, 1970.
"The Music Department of the Commonwealth Film Unit," by James McCarthy, on the need to organize the National Music Archives at the National Archives of Australia, Canberra, 75; "The Establishment and Creative Responsibilities of an Australian National Music Archive," by Andrew D. McCredie, including film music, 88–96.

Gammond, Peter, and Peter Clayton.
    Dictionary of Popular Music. New York: Philosophical Library, 1961.
This dictionary of light music and jazz covers an eclectic mix of composers and song-writers, including Richard Addinsell, George Bassman, Elmer Bernstein, Frank Churchill, Eric Coates, Morton Gould, Frank Loesser, Frederick Loewe, Ralph Rainger, Erno Rapée, Richard Rodgers, Raymond Scott, Jule Styne, Harry Warren, and Victor Young. The chronological index (see 1929 to 1959) lists films mentioned in the biographical entries. Topical entries include ASCAP, musical films, and the zither. Gammond is a prolific author of books on a wide variety of music and music styles, particularly jazz. Both authors have a background in music interpretation and criticism, with an emphasis on British music.

Gantim, Tejaswini.
    Bollywood: A Guidebook to Popular Hindi Cinema. New York: Routledge, 2004.
References to film music and songs.

Garcia, Russell.
    The Professional Arranger Composer. 2 vols. New York: Criterion Music Corp., 1954.
Focuses on dance-band arrangements, covering all aspects from harmony, voicings, and form to experimental material. Author, a film and television arranger, originally wrote the text in 1950 for his class at Westlake School of Music in Hollywood.

Garraty, John A., and Mark C. Carnes, general eds.
    American National Biography. 24 vols. New York: Oxford Univ. Press, 1999.
Published under the auspices of the American Council of Learned Societies, the volumes include biographies on Frank Churchill, Leigh Harline, and Herbert Stothart (all written by Linda Danly); Aaron Copland and Bernard Herrmann (by Roger Hall), and Henry Mancini and others.

Gassner, John, and Dudley Nichols.
    Twenty Best Film Plays. New York: Crown, 1943; New York: Garland Publishing, 1977.
"Pare Lorentz's Music Instructions for *The Fight for Life*," by the director of the 1940 documentary scored by Louis Gruenberg, 1082–87.

Gates, Theodore J., and Austin Wright.
    College Prose. Boston: D. C. Heath, 1942. 2nd ed., 1946.
"Hollywood Composer," by George Antheil, 370–84. Originally appeared in *Atlantic Monthly* (February 1940).

Gates, W. Francis, ed.
    Who's Who in Music in California. Los Angeles: Colby and Pryibil, 1920.
This first edition, from the publishers of *The Pacific Coast Musician*, includes biographical sketches for Joseph Carl Breil and Morris Stoloff.

Gautam, M. R.
    The Musical Heritage of India. New Delhi: Abhinav Publications, 1980. Rev. and enlarged ed., New Delhi: Munshiram Manoharlal Publishers, 2001.

Features a lengthy essay on the "Impact of Western Music on Our Film Music," 87–92 (1980). The author, a professor of vocal music, is generally pleased with the impact of Western music on Indian culture but bemoans its influence on music in Indian films. He believes the Westernization of Indian Ragas and folk music for film use corrupts its underlying aesthetic. The author also posits that Indian music cannot be successfully orchestrated because of its unique characteristics, namely the importance of tonic pedal tone and the use of an untempered scale.

Geduld, Harry.
> *The Birth of the Talkies: From Edison to Jolson.* Bloomington: Indiana Univ. Press, 1975.

On the plight of movie theater musicians and the corresponding positive effect on composers, especially in the first two years of talkies, 253–56.

Geduld, Harry M., ed.
> *Film Makers on Film Making: Statements on Their Art by Thirty Directors.* Bloomington: Indiana Univ. Press, 1967.

D. W. Griffith's predictions for film music in the year 2024, 52–53; director Michelangelo Antonioni's comments on the contribution of music to film, 218–19; director Kenneth Anger on his choice of rock 'n' roll for *Scorpio* (1973), 290–91.

Gehring, Wes D., ed.
> *Handbook of American Film Genres.* New York: Greenwood Press, 1988.

"The Musical," by James M. Collins, 269–84.

Gessner, Robert.
> *The Moving Image: A Guide to Cinematic Literacy.* New York: E. P. Dutton, 1968.

"Music on the Sound Track," on good and bad examples of the use of music, often for specific scenes, in films from the 1950s and 1960s, 376–84.

Gibbon, Monk.
> *The Tales of Hoffmann: A Study of a Film.* London: Saturn Press, 1951. Published as
> *The Red Shoes Ballet: The Tales of Hoffmann.* New York: Garland Publishing, 1977.

"Prospero and His Wand," on Sir Thomas Beecham conducting the opera and on choosing the singers, 93–94 (1951).

Gifford, Denis.
> *Chaplin.* Garden City, N.Y.: Doubleday; London: Macmillan, 1974.

"His Musical Career" includes Charles Chaplin's film music compositions and recordings, 126.

Giger, Andreas, and Thomas J. Mathiesen, eds.
> *Music in the Mirror: Reflections on the History of Music Theory and Literature for the 21st Century.* Lincoln: Univ. of Nebraska Press, 2002.

"Film Theory and Music Theory: On the Intersection of Two Traditions," by David Neumeyer, 275–94.

Gillmor, Alan M.
> *Erik Satie.* Boston: Twayne Publishers, 1988.

The French composer's music for the film *Entr'acte* is discussed, 248–56.

Gimarc, George, and Pat Reeder.
>*Hollywood Hi-Fi: Over 100 of the Most Outrageous Celebrity Recordings Ever!* New York: St. Martin's Griffin, 1996.

Celebrity discography.

Gizzi, Peter.
>*Music for Films.* Providence, R.I.: Paradigm Press, 1992.

Title notwithstanding, this is a 36-page fragmented lyric poem by an American author.

Glinsky, Albert.
>*Theremin: Ether Music and Espionage.* Urbana and Chicago: Univ. of Illinois Press, 2000.

Biography of Leon Theremin examines the use of the theremin in popular culture. Film music topics include Miklós Rózsa's film scores and session musicians Dr. Samuel Hoffman and Paul Tanner. Author is a music professor and composer.

Goldberg, Halina, ed.
>*The Age of Chopin: Interdisciplinary Inquiries.* Bloomington: Indiana Univ. Press, 2004.

"Chopiniana and Music's Contextual Allusions," by Marianne Kielian-Gilbert, includes a discussion of Chopin's music in film, 162–200.

Goldberg, Isaac.
>*Tin Pan Alley: A Chronicle of the American Popular Music Racket.* New York: John Day, 1930. New York: F. Ungar Publishing, 1961.

"Bye, Bye, Theme Song" describes how Hollywood, through the early sound film, co-opted popular songs from Tin Pan Alley and Broadway, 297–319 (1930). "All song is theme song," writes the author, a magazine and newspaper editor knowledgeable in music theory and composition.

Goldberg, Justin.
>*The Ultimate Survival Guide to the New Music Industry: A Handbook for Hell.* Los Angeles: Lone Eagle Publishing, 2003.

"Those Golden Words: Film and Television" includes an interview with composer-agent Rich Jacobellis, 302–25.

Goldner, Orville, and George E. Turner.
>*The Making of* King Kong: *The Story Behind a Film Classic.* New York: A. S. Barnes, 1975.

On Max Steiner's score for the 1933 film, 189–91; and for its sequel, *The Son of Kong*, 210.

Gooch, Bryan Niel Shirley, and David Thatcher, eds.
>*A Shakespeare Music Catalogue.* 5 vols. Oxford: Clarendon Press, 1991.

Includes documentation of various types of incidental music for film and television productions. Each composition is cited, with information on its vocal and instrumental requirements and publication history.

Goode, James.
The Making of The Misfits. New York: Limelight Editions, 1986.
Material on the conception, recording, and dubbing of Alex North's score, 294–301; 306; 315–23.

Gordon, Douglas.
Feature Film: A Book. London: Artangel Afterlives, 2000.
Published in conjunction with *Feature Film*, a film by the author that incorporates Bernard Herrmann's score from Alfred Hitchcock's *Vertigo*. The book contains stills from both films and is accompanied by a compact disc of Herrmann's score and an eight-page pamphlet that contains the article "The Music of *Vertigo*," by Royal S. Brown.

Gordon, Eric A.
Mark the Music: The Life and Work of Marc Blitzstein. New York: St. Martin's Press, 1989.
Mentions film music by the New York-based composer.

Gorow, Ron.
Hearing and Writing Music: Professional Training for Today's Musician. Studio City, Calif.: September Publishing, 1999.
The author, a fixture at one of the leading film music copying services in Los Angeles, where he has served as a proofreader and take-down artist, passes on his knowledge and expertise in the field.

Gottesman, Ronald, ed.
Focus on Citizen Kane. Englewood Cliffs, N.J.: Prentice Hall, 1971.
"Score for a Film," by Bernard Herrmann, 69–72. Reprinted from the *New York Times*, May 25, 1941.

Gottesman, Ronald, and Harry Geduld, eds.
The Girl in the Hairy Paw: King Kong *as Myth, Movie, and Monster*. New York: Avon Books, 1976.
"*King Kong*: Music by Max Steiner," by Robert Fiedel, examines the creation of the music and analyzes the score, 191–97.

Gottlieb, Carl.
The Jaws *Log*. New York: Dell, 1975. 25th anniversary ed., New York: Newmarket Press, 2001. 30th anniversary ed., New York: Newmarket Press, 2005.
This "making of" book discusses John Williams in the context of producing the music for the 1975 film, 181–82 (2005).

Gottlieb, Robert, ed.
Reading Jazz: A Gathering of Autobiography, Reportage, and Criticism from 1919 to Now. New York: Pantheon Books, 1996.
"Johnny Green," by Fred Hall, 701–9. Interview covering songs by Green, excerpted from Hall's book, *More Dialogues in Swing* (1991).

Gottlieb, Sidney, ed.
> *Hitchcock on Hitchcock: Selected Writings and Interviews*. Berkeley: Univ. of California Press, 1995.

"On Music in Films: An Interview with Stephen Watts," by Alfred Hitchcock, 241–45. Originally appeared in *Cinema Quarterly* (Winter 1933–34).

Grainge, Paul, ed.
> *Memory and Popular Film*. Manchester, U.K.: Manchester Univ. Press, 2003.

"'Mortgaged to Music': New Retro Movies in 1990s Hollywood Cinema," by Philip Drake, examines the use of film music to evoke memories of the past in the present, 183–201.

Grant, Barry Keith, ed.
> *Film Genre Reader II*. Austin: Univ. of Texas Press, 1995.

Contains references to musicals.

Grau, Robert.
> *The Theatre of Science: A Volume of Progress and Achievement in the Motion Picture Industry*. New York and London: Broadway Publishing, 1914. Reprint, New York: Benjamin Blom, 1969.

Discusses the organ orchestra, the organ replacing or augmenting the live orchestra, and the Wurlitzer Unit Orchestra, 335–37.

Gray, Lois S., and Ronald L. Seeber, eds.
> *Under the Stars: Essays on Labor Relations in Arts and Entertainment*. Ithaca, N.Y.: ILR Press, 1996.

Includes material on the American Federation of Musicians (AFM) and film music; discusses the fact that in 1951 the AFM was the first union to obtain any form of supplemental compensation for motion pictures exhibited on television.

Green, Douglas B.
> *Singing in the Saddle: The History of the Singing Cowboy*. Nashville: Country Music Foundation Press and Vanderbilt Univ. Press, 2002.

"Western Music Rides to the Big Screen," 94–119. Contains extensive documentation of performers.

Green, J. Ronald.
> *With a Crooked Stick: The Films of Oscar Micheaux*. Bloomington: Indiana Univ. Press, 2004.

"The Sound Era: Signifying with Music," discusses black-cast musicals in early Hollywood sound films, 97–111.

Green, Paddy Grafton, and Gunter Poll, eds.
> *Music in Film, Television and Advertising*. Apeldoorn, The Netherlands: MAKLU Publishers, 1999.

Reports presented at a meeting of the International Association of Entertainment Lawyers, which took place at a 1999 international music industry trade show sponsored by MIDEM (Marché international de l'édition musicale) in Cannes, France.

Green, Richard D., ed.
    Foundations in Music Bibliography. New York: Haworth Press, 1993.
"'Perfuming the Air with Music': The Need for Film Music Bibliography," 59–104;
"Supplement to Steven D. Wescott's *A Comprehensive Bibliography of Music for Film
and Television*," 105–44. Both by Gillian B. Anderson, co-published simultaneously in
Music Reference Services Quarterly (1993).

Griffith, Richard.
    Anatomy of a Motion Picture. New York: St. Martin's Press, 1959.
"Scoring a Film" contains material on Duke Ellington's music for *Anatomy of a Murder*,
105–8.

Grove, Dick.
    Arranging Concepts: Complete: The Ultimate Arranging Course for Today's Music.
    Van Nuys, Calif.: Alfred Publishing, 1985.
This 433-page manual, popular among film and television composers, was developed
from the curriculum at the Dick Grove School in Los Angeles, a professional technical
school similar to the Berklee College of Music that attracted musicians and performers
pursuing a career in commercial music. All aspects of arranging are covered, including
working procedures, writing the arrangement, arranging concepts, and specific popular
musical styles. Author, in addition to founding the school, was a television music arranger, jazz musician, and music educator. Accompanying analog cassette contains numerous music examples by Grove. Material originally copyrighted by Grove in 1972.

Grover-Friedlander, Michal.
    Vocal Apparitions: The Attraction of Cinema to Opera. Princeton: Princeton Univ.
    Press, 2005. 186 pp.
Examines the correlation between several operas and films. Chapters include "*The Phantom of the Opera*: The Lost Voice of Opera in Silent Film"; "Brothers at the Opera," on
the Marx Brothers' *A Night at the Opera*; "*Otello*'s One Voice," on director Franco Zeffirelli's filmed opera; "*Falstaff*'s Free Voice," on director Götz Friedrich's film adaptation of the opera; "Opera on the Phone: The Call of the Human Voice"; and "Fellini's
Ashes." Author, a musicologist, is primarily concerned with opera-to-film adaptation and
its effect on the aesthetics of the original opera. Topics include the visualization of music
and conjured, disembodied, invisible, and migrating voices. Bibliography and index.

Grunfeld, Frederic V.
    Music and Recordings, 1955. New York: Oxford Univ. Press, 1955.
"Film Music," by Clifford McCarty, discusses the best and worst scores of the year, ret-
rogressive tendencies, and current trends, in particular the influence of Dimitri Tiomkin's
theme for *High Noon* (1952), 209–14.

Gunning, Annie.
    The Composer's Guide to Music Publishing. London: APC Publishing Limited,
    1987. 2nd ed., edited and produced by Richard Elen. London: Association of Profes-
    sional Composers, 1994. 329 pp.
Author is a longtime associate of the British music production firm Air-Edel Associates.
Her husband is the composer Christopher Gunning.

Guralnick, Peter, ed.
>   *Da Capo Best Music Writing 2000*. New York: Da Capo Press, 2000.

"Old Songs in New Skins," by Greil Marcus for *Interview* magazine, examines how the use of a popular song in a film can change the perception of the song, 374–76.

Hadleigh, Boze.
>   *Sing Out! Gays and Lesbians in the Music World*. New York: Barricade Books, 1997.

Includes entries on Marc Shaiman and a number of concert composers who wrote for film, such as Leonard Bernstein, Benjamin Britten, and Aaron Copland. Similar material appears in Hadleigh's *The Vinyl Closet: Gays in the Music World* (San Diego: Los Hombres Press, 1991).

Hal Leonard Publishing Corp.
>   *The Lyric Book: Complete Lyrics for Over 1000 Songs from Tin Pan Alley to Today*. Milwaukee: Hal Leonard, 2001.

"Songs from Musicals, Films, and Television," 29–31. Artist and songwriter indexes.

Halas, John, and Roger Manvell.
>   *The Technique of Film Animation*. New York: Hastings House, 1959. 2nd ed., New York: Hastings House; London: Focal Press, 1968. 3rd ed., London: Focal Press, 1971. 4th ed., London: Focal Press, 1976.

"The Music Track" touches on prerecording versus postsynchronization, on the rhythmic relationship between sound and image, and electronic music, 78–83; "The Composition and Recording of Music for Animated Films," by Francis Chagrin and Matyas Seiber, 237–53 (1959).

Hall, Ben M.
>   *The Golden Age of the Movie Palace: The Best Remaining Seats*. New York: Clarkson N. Potter, 1975. Rev. ed., New York: Da Capo Press, 1988. Previously published as *The Best Remaining Seats*, 1961.

"…The Peal of the Grand Organ, The Flourish of Golden Trumpets," on New York theater orchestras during the 1920s, 175–81; "The Apotheosis of the Mighty Wurlitzer," on organs and organists, 183–99 (all 1961 edition).

Hall, Charles J.
>   *A Chronicle of American Music, 1700–1995*. New York: Schirmer Books, 1996.

Year-by-year listings include film scores under "Other" in the "Representative Works" section. Composers are listed in the music index.

Halloran, Mark.
>   *The Musician's Business and Legal Guide*. Englewood Cliffs, N.J.: Prentice Hall, 1991. 2nd rev. ed., Upper Saddle River, N.J.: Prentice Hall, 1996. 3rd ed., 2001.

"Music Licensing for Television and Film: A Perspective for Songwriters," by Ronald H. Gertz, 342–49 (1991), 145–65 (1996); "Pop Music for Soundtracks," by Mark Halloran and Thomas A. White, 350–66 (1991), 166–80 (1996); "Motion Picture Soundtrack Songwriting and Performing" (2001).

Haltof, Marek.
> *Peter Weir: When Cultures Collide.* New York: Twayne; London: Prentice Hall International, 1996.

Contains numerous references to the use of music in Weir's films and to his frequent collaborator, Maurice Jarre.

Hammerstein, Oscar, II.
> *Lyrics.* Foreword by Stephen Sondheim, preface by Richard Rodgers. Milwaukee: Hal Leonard Books, 1985. 270 pp.

Revised and expanded edition by Oscar's son, William.

Hammonds, G. Roger.
> *Recorded Music for the Science Fiction, Fantasy and Horror Film.* 2 vols. New Holland, Penn.: Sound Track Album Retailers, 1982. Vol. 1: 690 films; vol. 2: new entries, plus corrections to the first volume.

Each volume lists composer, director, cast, and recordings issued, including foreign pressings. Compiled by a soundtrack collector and published by the soundtrack dealer.

Hammonds, G. Roger.
> *Recorded Music for the Western Film.* New Holland, Penn.: Sound Track Album Retailers, 1984.

Each volume lists composer, director, cast, and recordings issued, including foreign pressings. Compiled by a soundtrack collector and published by the soundtrack dealer.

Hampton, Benjamin.
> *History of the American Film Industry from Its Beginnings to 1931.* New York: Dover, 1970. Originally published as *A History of the Movies,* New York: Covici, Friede, 1931.

On the loss of employment of theater orchestra musicians due to the advent of sound films, written as the events unfolded, 363, 404–5.

Hanke, Ken.
> *Tim Burton: An Unauthorized Biography of the Filmmaker.* Los Angeles: Renaissance Books. 1999.

Contains many references to Danny Elfman's music in films directed by Burton.

Harcourt, Nic.
> *Music Lust: Recommended Listening for Every Mood, Moment, and Reason.* Seattle: Sasquatch Books, 2005.

"More Than Just Background Music: Movie Soundtracks" recommends ten rock and fifteen original score soundtracks (most from the 1960s and 1970s), 129–34. Author is a radio personality known for his passion for pop music.

Harmetz, Aljean.
> *The Making of* The Wizard of Oz. New York: Knopf, 1977. Reprinted as *The Making of* The Wizard of Oz: *Movie Magic and Studio Power in the Prime of MGM and the Miracle of Production 1060.* New York: Limelight Editions, 1984; New York: Dell Publishing, 1989; New York: Hyperion, 1998.

"The Brains, the Heart, the Nerve, and the Music," 61–100 (1977), includes material on the musical adaptation by Herbert Stothart; lyrics by E. Y. Harburg; music by Harold Arlen; arrangements and orchestrations by George Bassman, Murray Cutter, Paul Marquardt, and Ken Darby; and musical numbers. Author interviewed Bassman, Cutter, Darby, and Harburg.

Harmetz, Aljean.
   Round Up the Usual Suspects: The Making of Casablanca—*Bogart, Bergman, and World War II.* New York: Hyperion, 1992. Also published as *The Making of* Casablanca: *Bogart, Bergman, and World War II.* New York: Hyperion, 2002.
"Play It, Sam" offers a historical background on Max Steiner's music score and Herman Hupfeld's song, 253–64 (1992).

Harnell, Joe, and Ira Skutch.
   Counterpoint: The Journey of a Music Man. Philadelphia: Xlibris Corp., 2000.
Anecdotal memoir by the television composer covering his professional and personal life, including his lifelong battle with alcoholism.

Harpole, Charles, gen. ed.
   History of the American Cinema. New York: Charles Scribner's Sons; Toronto: Collier Macmillan Canada; New York: Maxwell Macmillan International; Berkeley: Univ. of California Press, 1990–2003.
A ten-volume set examining American films. Each volume includes comments on film music in some form.
   Musser, Charles. *The Emergence of Cinema: The American Screen to 1907.* Vol. 1. Reprint, Berkeley: Univ. of California Press, 1990, 1994. References to musical accompaniment for passion plays and Vitascope-projected films, as well as phonograph concerts and song films.
   Bowser, Eileen. *The Transformation of Cinema, 1907–1915.* Vol. 2. Reprint, Berkeley: Univ. of California Press, 1990. References to musical accompaniment.
   Koszarski, Richard. *An Evening's Entertainment.* Vol. 3. New York: Charles Scribner's Sons, 1990. "Going to the Movies" includes material on musical accompaniment, scores, orchestras, and film prologues, 41–53.
   Crafton, Donald. *The Talkies: American Cinema's Transition to Sound, 1926–1931.* Vol. 4. New York: Charles Scribner's Sons, 1997. "Musicians," on live versus recorded music, 218–221. Musicals are discussed, 313–17, 357–60. References to music and musicals throughout.
   Balio, Tino. *Grand Design: Hollywood as a Modern Business Enterprise, 1930–1939.* Vol. 5. New York: Scribner; Toronto: Collier Macmillan Canada; New York: Maxwell Macmillan International, 1993. Berkeley: Univ. of California Press, 1995. Includes analysis of one scene from *Charge of the Light Brigade,* including Max Steiner's music, 115–16. "Musicals," including MGM's domination of the genre, 211–35.
   Schatz, Thomas. *Boom and Bust: American Cinema in the 1940s.* Vol. 6. Berkeley: Univ. of California Press, 1995. Wartime musicals, 223–26; postwar musicals, 374–75; the MGM Freed unit, 375–77.
   Lev, Peter. *Transforming the Screen, 1950–1959.* Vol. 7. New York: Charles Scribner's Sons, 2003. "Musicals," including the Freed unit at MGM, 34–40, 219–22.

A section on musicians covers the 1958 strike and the transition from studio to freelance orchestras, 213–14.

Monaco, Paul. *The Sixties, 1960–1969.* Vol. 8. New York: Charles Scribner's Sons, 2001. Berkeley: Univ. of California Press, 2003. "Music in Film" includes material on Henry Mancini, Bernard Herrmann, the influences of jazz and folk music, and a summary of musical changes, 109–19.

Cook, David A. *Lost Illusions.* Vol. 9. New York: Charles Scribner's Sons, 2000. Music in blaxploitation and black action films, 260–62, 265–66. Musicals, 209–20. Many other references to cross-marketing music, rock music, and soundtrack albums.

Prince, Stephen. *A New Pot of Gold.* Vol. 10. New York: Charles Scribner's Sons, 2000. Material on marketing synergies (soundtrack tie-ins), 133–36; film scoring, 197–200; musicals, 306–9.

Harrell, Jean G.
Soundtracks: A Study of Auditory Perception, Memory, and Valuation. Buffalo, N.Y.: Prometheus Books, 1986.
"Film Music—Expression and Shallowness," 45–65. Adapted from "Phenomenology of Film Music," *Journal of Value Inquiry* (Spring 1980).

Harriman, Margaret Case.
Take Them Up Tenderly: A Collection of Profiles. New York: Knopf, 1944. Freeport, N.Y.: Books for Libraries Press, 1972.
Profiles previously published in the *New Yorker* include "The Wise Lived Yesterday" (Cole Porter); "Big-time Urchin" (Larry Adler); "Words and Music" (Rodgers and Hart); and "The Squarest Little Shooter on Vesey Street" (Oscar Hammerstein II).

Harris, Bernard, ed.
Integrating Tradition: The Achievement of Sean O Riada. Ballina, Ireland: Irish Humanities Centre & Keohanes, 1981.
"Film Making," by George Morrison, on the Irish composer's work related to films, 64–71.

Harris, Thomas J.
Children's Live-Action Musical Films: A Critical Survey and Filmography. Jefferson, N.C.: McFarland, 1989.

Harrison, Nigel.
Songwriters: A Biographical Dictionary with Discographies. Jefferson, N.C., and London: McFarland, 1998. 633 pp.
Entries on more than 1,000 songwriters and lyricists with birth and death dates, musical instruments played (if applicable), short biographies, and discographies. Some subjects worked primarily in film, such as Sammy Cahn, Marvin Hamlisch, Henry Mancini, and Dimitri Tiomkin. Compiled from secondary sources, including record company catalogs. Index.

Hasse, John Edward.
Jazz: The First Century. New York: William Morrow, 2000.

"Jazz and Film," by Krin Gabbard, 106–7; "Jazz on Television," by Larry Appelbaum, 132–33; "Worldwide Jazz Films," by Kevin Whitehead and Tad Lathrop, 182.

Hautamäki, Tarja, and Helmi Järviluoma, eds.
  Music on Show: Issues of Performance. Tampere, Finland: Department of Folk Tradition, Tampere University, 1998.
"Country Music Goes to the Movies," by David Brackett, in relation to *The Last Picture Show* (1971), 40–43; "Film and T.V. Music: Texts and Contexts," by Claudia Gorbman, proposes a cultural studies approach to film and television music studies, emphasizing topics related to economics, technology, and reception, 124–28; "Collage and Subversion in the Score of *Die Hard*," by Robynn J. Stilwell discusses Michael Kamen's score, 302–13.

Haver, Ronald.
  A Star Is Born: The Making of the 1954 Movie and Its 1983 Restoration. New York: Knopf, 1988. New York: Perennial Library, 1990. New York: Applause Theatre & Cinema, 2002.
Documents the creation of the songs by Harold Arlen and Ira Gershwin and the score by music director Ray Heindorf and arranger Skip Martin.

Havlice, Patricia Pate.
  Popular Song Index. Metuchen, N.J.: Scarecrow Press, 1975. First supplement, 1978. Second supplement, 1984. Third supplement, 1989. Fourth supplement (1988–2002), 2005.
A multivolume index of songbooks including songs from films.

Headley, Robert K.
  Motion Picture Exhibition in Washington, D.C.: An Illustrated History of Parlors, Palaces and Multiplexes in the Metropolitan Area, 1894–1997. Jefferson, N.C., and London: McFarland, 1999.
Material on music and musicians in the 1920s, 91–92, 112–14, 135–37.

Heilbut, Anthony.
  Exiled in Paradise: German Refugee Artists and Intellectuals in America, from the 1930s to the Present. New York: Viking Press, 1983. Boston: Beacon Press, 1984. Berkeley: Univ. of California Press, 1997.
Brief mention of Hollywood composers, including Erich Wolfgang Korngold; theorists Theodor Adorno and Hanns Eisler are discussed.

Heinsheimer, H. W.
  Menagerie in F Sharp. Garden City, N.Y.: Doubleday, 1947. Reprint, Westport, Conn.: Greenwood Press, 1979.
Anecdotal memoir of the émigré music publisher, long associated with a large Austrian music publishing company. Three chapters on film music: "An Old Friendship," on Heinsheimer's visit with George Antheil in Hollywood, 201–8; "Hollywood; or the Bases are Loaded," on his impressions of film music versus concert music, silent film music, Bernard Herrmann, Miklós Rózsa, Arnold Schoenberg, Max Steiner, and Franz Waxman, 209–35; "Deadlines, Click Tracks, and Stop Watches," on the process of creating music

for a mythical film, 236–56. Heinsheimer came to Hollywood in the 1940s hoping to become a champion of film composers but was not successful.

Heintze, James R., and Michael Saffle, eds.
> *Reflections on American Music: The Twentieth Century and the New Millennium: A Collection of Essays Presented in Honor of the College Music Society.* New York: Pendragon Press, 2000.

"The Sounds of Silents: An Interview with Carl Davis," by John C. Tibbetts, 107–18.

Heister, H.-W., ed.
> *Musik/Revolution: Festschrift für Georg Knepler zum 90.* Vol. 2. Hamburg, Germany: Von Bockel, 1997.

"*Aleksander Nevskij*: Renaissance and Transfiguration of a Masterwork," by Sergio Miceli, 279–99, analyzes Prokofiev's score for *Alexander Nevsky* in two restored versions of Sergei Eisenstein's film.

Herrmann, Irene, and Timothy Mangan, eds.
> *Paul Bowles on Music.* Berkeley: Univ. of California Press, 2003.

Includes Bowles's writings on film music, including its purpose. See, for example, "Film Scores by Copland and Tansman," reprinted from the *New York Herald Tribune* (November 1943), 127–29.

Higham, Charles.
> *The Films of Orson Welles.* Berkeley: Univ. of California Press, 1970.

Includes coverage of Bernard Herrmann's music for *Citizen Kane* and *The Magnificent Ambersons*, with passing references to Henry Mancini and other film music.

Hill, John, and Pamela Church Gibson, eds.
> *Film Studies: Critical Approaches.* Oxford: Oxford Univ. Press, 2000.

"Film Music," by Claudia Gorbman, offers an overview of aesthetics, aesthetic theory, and psychology, 41–47.

Hill, John, and Pamela Church Gibson, eds.
> *The Oxford Guide to Film Studies.* Oxford: Oxford Univ. Press, 1998.

"Film Music," by Claudia Gorbman, offers an overview of aesthetics, psychology, and history (writings about film music), 43–50.

Hines, William E.
> *Job Descriptions for Film, Video & CGI: Responsibilities and Duties for the Cinematic Craft Categories and Classifications.* 5th ed. Los Angeles: Ed-Venture Films/Books, 1999.

Standard job description handbook outlining the responsibilities and duties for the music rerecording mixer, 99–100; scoring mixer, 104; scoring recordist, 105; and music editor, 217–18. The composer is mentioned only in relation to these and other jobs.

Hirsch, Julia Antopol.
> The Sound of Music: *The Making of America's Favorite Movie.* Chicago: Contemporary Books, 1993.

Documents the adaptation of the music, songs, and music score; for the latter, see especially 160–62.

Hirschhorn, Joel.
   The Complete Idiot's Guide to Songwriting. Indianapolis: Alpha, 2001. 2nd ed., 2004.
"Movie Scoring and Songwriting," 159–70; "Live and Animated Musicals," 171–80 (all 2001). Includes practical tips from the Academy Award–winning songwriter.

Hitchcock, H. Wiley, and Stanley Sadie, eds.
   The New Grove Dictionary of American Music. 4 vols. New York: Grove's Dictionaries of Music, 1986.
Entries on William Axt, Elmer Bernstein, Joseph Carl Breil, Jack Elliott, Hugo Friedhofer, Jerry Goldsmith, John Green, Leigh Harline, Bernard Herrmann, Quincy Jones, Bronislaw Kaper, Henry Mancini, Cyril Mockridge, Jerome Moross, Alfred Newman, Alex North, Leonard Rosenman, Miklós Rózsa, Max Steiner, Herbert Stothart, Dimitri Tiomkin, Franz Waxman, Roy Webb, John Williams, and Victor Young. Contributors include Martin Marks, Clifford McCarty, Christopher Palmer, and Fred Steiner. The "Film Music" entry is by Steiner and Marks.

Ho, Allan, and Dmitry Feofanov, eds.
   Biographical Dictionary of Russian/Soviet Composers. New York: Greenwood Press, 1989.
Includes entries on Michel Michelet (born Mikhail Levin) and Dimitri Tiomkin.

Hochman, Steve, ed.
   Popular Musicians. 4 vols. Pasadena, Calif.: Salem Press, 1999.
Signed articles recap the careers, successes, and critical reputations of a wide range of contemporary artists, some of whom have worked in film, such as Phil Collins. Each profile begins with a summary listing the artist's musical style, first album release, and list of band members, and ends with a select discography, awards, and cross-references to other relevant articles.

Hodgson, Peter John.
   Benjamin Britten: A Guide to Research. New York: Garland, 1996.
For a film list, see pp. 83–88.

Hoedemaeker, Liesbeth.
   The Penguin Music Magazine, 1946–1949, Music, 1950–1952. Baltimore: NISC, 2005.
This reprint edition contains Ralph Hill's essay on film music and Scott Goddard's column "Music of the Film."

Hoffman, Henryk, comp.
   "A" Western Filmmakers: A Biographical Dictionary of Writers, Directors, Cinematographers, Composers, Actors and Actresses. Jefferson, N.C.: McFarland, 2000.
Entries on Jeff Alexander, Daniele Amfitheatrof, George Antheil, John Barry, Elmer Bernstein, David Buttolph, Ry Cooder, Adolph Deutsch, Frank DeVol, George Duning, Paul Dunlap, Jerry Fielding, Hugo Friedhofer, Dominic Frontiere, Joseph Gershenson,

Herschel Burke Gilbert, Ernest Gold, Jerry Goldsmith, David Grusin, Richard Hageman, Leigh Harline, Howard Jackson, Maurice Jarre, Bronislaw Kaper, Sol Kaplan, Fred Karlin, John Leipold, Cyril Mockridge, Jerome Moross, Ennio Morricone, Alfred Newman, Lionel Newman, Alex North, André Previn, David Raksin, Nelson Riddle, Heinz Roemheld, Laurence Rosenthal, Miklós Rózsa, Hans J. Salter, Paul Sawtell, Walter Scharf, Lalo Schifrin, Frank Skinner, Paul J. Smith, David Snell, Herman Stein, Max Steiner, Leith Stevens, Herbert Stothart, Dimitri Tiomkin, Franz Waxman, Roy Webb, John Williams, Victor Young.

Hoffmann, Frank, ed.
> *Encyclopedia of Recorded Sound.* 2nd ed. (Rev. ed. of *Encyclopedia of Recorded Sound in the United States*, ed. Guy Marco.) 2 vols. New York: Routledge, 2005.
Entry on "Motion Picture Sound Recordings" in vol. 2.

Hogan, David J.
> *Who's Who of the Horrors and Other Fantasy Films: The International Personality Encyclopedia of the Fantastic Film.* San Diego: A. S. Barnes; London: Tantivy Press, 1980.
Entries on a few composers, such as Bernard Herrmann and Hans Salter, consisting of selected film credits.

Højbjerg, Lennard, and Peter Schepelern, eds.
> *Film Style and Story: A Tribute to Torben Grodal.* Copenhagen, Denmark: Museum Tusculanum Press, 2003.
"A Reasonable Guide to Horrible Noise (part 2): Listening to *Lost Highway*," by Murray Smith, discusses the use of popular music in the David Lynch film, 153–70.

Holmes, Diana, and Alison Smith, eds.
> *100 Years of European Cinema: Entertainment or Ideology?* Manchester, U.K.: Manchester Univ. Press, 2000.
"Singing Our Song: Music, Memory and Myth in Contemporary European Cinema," by Wendy Everett, contemplates the popular song as a vehicle of memory in autobiographical films, 172–82.

Honegger, Arthur.
> *I Am a Composer.* Translated from the French by Wilson O. Clough, in collaboration with Allan Arthur Willman. New York: St. Martin's Press, 1966. Originally published as *Je suis compositeur*, 1951.
Scattered passing references to the author's film music.

Hopkins, Antony.
> *Beating Time.* London: M. Joseph, 1982. London and Sydney: Futura Publications / Macdonald & Co., 1983.
"Screen Themes," on the author's film scores, 189–96 (1983).

Hopkins, John.
> Shrek: *From the Swamp to the Screen.* New York: Harry N. Abrams, 2004.
In "Music," the film's director talks about the choice and role of music in the animated film and its sequel, and his idea of combining a "needle-drop" approach (using pre-

existing pop songs) with symphonic scoring by Harry Gregson-Williams and John Powell, 156–60.

Hove, Arthur, ed.
  Gold Diggers of 1933. Madison: Univ. of Wisconsin Press, 1980.
Discusses the relationship between the story line and musical segments of the film.

Howes, Frank.
  The Music of Ralph Vaughan Williams. London: Oxford Univ. Press, 1954.
"Film Music," 361–64.

Huff, Theodore.
  Charlie Chaplin. New York: Henry Schuman, 1951. Reprint, New York: Arno Press, 1972.
"Chaplin as a Composer," 235–41.

Hughes, Howard.
  Once Upon a Time in the Italian West: The Filmgoers' Guide to Spaghetti Westerns. London: I. B. Tauris, 2004.
Extensive commentary on music in individual films, particularly those scored by Ennio Morricone.

Hughes, Laurence A., ed.
  The Truth about the Movies, by the Stars. Hollywood: Hollywood Publishers, 1924.
"The Development and Importance of Motion Picture Music," by Ulderico Marcelli, 467–69. A brief biography of the Italian-born composer-conductor appears on page 526.

Hunter, William.
  Scrutiny of Cinema. London: Wishart, 1932.
Discusses scores by Edmund Meisel, 52–53.

Hyland, William G.
  The Song Is Ended: Songwriters and American Music, 1900–1950. New York: Oxford Univ. Press, 1995.
Some "film" songs are mentioned in the context of the Broadway musicals for which they were written. Title is taken from Irving Berlin's "The Song Is Ended but the Melody Lingers On." Author is a professor of foreign affairs.

Iger, Arthur L.
  Music of the Golden Age, 1900–1950 and Beyond: A Guide to Popular Composers and Lyricists. Westport, Conn.: Greenwood Press, 1998.
An annotated chronological listing of hit songs, including those from Hollywood musicals. Author is a retired marketing executive and amateur musician.

Inglis, Ian, ed.
  Popular Music and Film. London: Wallflower, 2003.
Twelve essays written by an international group of contributors.
    "Introduction: Popular Music and Film," by Ian Inglis, 1–7

"Score vs. Song: Art, Commerce, and the H Factor in Film and Television Music,"
   by Robb Wright, on the use of pre-recorded pop music, 8–21
"Music and the Body in Dance Film," by Lesley Vize, 22–38
"The Sting in the Tale," by Phil Powrie, 39–59
"The Music Is the Message: The Day Jimi Hendrix Burned His Guitar: Film, Musi-
   cal Instrument, and Performance as Music Media," by Anno Mungen, 60–76
"The Act You've Known for All These Years: Telling the Tale of the Beatles," by
   Ian Inglis, 77–90
"The Sound of a New Film Form," by Anahid Kassabian, on the textural use of
   sound/music and the trend toward soundtracks of aural and musical materials,
   91–101
"Case Study 1: Sliding Doors and Topless Women Talk about Their Lives," by Lau-
   ren Anderson, 102–16
"Ridiculous Infantile Acrobatics, Or, Why They Never Made Any Rock 'n' Roll
   Movies in Finland," by Antti-Ville Karja, 117–30
"Constructing the Future through Music of the Past: The Software in Hardware," by
   K. J. Donnelly, on the use of nonmodern music in science fiction films, 131–47
"'Music Inspired by—': The Curious Case of the Missing Soundtrack," by Lee Bar-
   ron, 148–61
"Case Study 2: *The Big Chill*," by Melissa Carey and Michael Hannan, 162–77
"Triumphant Black Pop Divas on the Wide Screen: *Lady Sings the Blues* and Tina:
   What's Love Got to Do with It," by Jaap Kooijman, 178–92

Inkster, Donald.
   Union Cinemas Ritz: A Story of Theatre Organs and Cine-Variety. Hove, East Sus-
   sex, U.K.: Wick, 1999.
A history of British picture palaces, in particular the Union Cinema chain, with an em-
phasis on the Wurlitzer and Compton organs and organists such as Robinson Cleaver,
Reginald Foort, Neville Meale, Phil Park, Harold Ramsay, Joseph Seal, Alex Taylor, and
Sidney Torch.

International Music Centre, comp. and ed.
   Films for Music Education and Opera Films: An International Selective Catalogue.
   Paris: UNESCO, 1962.
With a general introduction by Egon Kraus, and an introduction to opera films by Jack
Bornoff.

International Music Centre, comp. and ed.
   *Music in Film and Television: An International Selective Catalogue, 1964–1974:
   Opera, Concert, Documentation.* Paris: UNESCO Press; Vienna and Munich: Jugend
   und Volk, 1975.
Contains 223 entries for film and television productions of filmed operas, concerts, educational programs, and experimental programs. Each entry contains production credits
and a program summary. In German and English; English version by Erika Obermayer
and Silvia Kampas.

Irving, Ernest.
   Cue for Music: An Autobiography. London: Dennis Dobson, 1959.

"Music in Films," 161–66; "Rawsthorne, Walton, and Vaughan Williams," on the author's association with Ralph Vaughan Williams's film music, 172–77. Author, a British conductor, was music director at Ealing Studios from 1935 to 1953 and conducted film scores by Vaughan Williams and others.

Ivashkin, Alexander, ed.
 A Schnittke Reader. Translated by John Goodliffe. Bloomington: Indiana Univ. Press, 2002.
"On Film and Film Music (1972, 1984, 1989)," by Alfred Schnittke, 49–52.

Jacobs, Lewis.
 The Emergence of Film Art: The Evolution and Development of the Motion Picture as an Art, from 1900 to the Present. New York: Hopkinson and Blake, 1969. 2nd ed., New York: Norton, 1979.
"The Composer and the Motion Picture," by Hanns Eisler, 198–205 (1969, 1979). Reprinted from Eisler's *Composing for the Films* (1947).

Jacobs, Lewis.
 The Movies as Medium. New York: Farrar, Straus and Giroux, 1970.
"Music," on the role of music, in "Sound as Speech, Noise, Music," 254–60; "Music in the Movies," by Kurt Weill, 289–96 (reprinted from *Harper's Bazaar*, September 1946).

Jacobs, Lewis.
 The Rise of the American Film: A Critical History. New York: Harcourt, Brace, 1939. New York: Teachers College Press, 1968.
Musical accompaniment of silent films, 224–25 (1968); references to music in the chapter on sound, see pp. 14–18.

James, David.
 Scott of the Antarctic: *The Film and Its Production*. London: Convoy Publications, 1948.
"The Music," on the choice of Ralph Vaughan Williams for the 1948 film, 144–46; the book went to press before Vaughan Williams's score was completed. Author was the film's technical adviser.

James, Eric.
 Making Music with Charlie Chaplin: An Autobiography. Lanham, Md.: Scarecrow Press, 2000.
In this autobiography, the author, a pianist, documents his musical association with the filmmaker from the mid-1950s into the 1970s and offers insight into Chaplin's working method. Organized into two parts: the first three chapters are autobiographical, the remaining four are on working with Chaplin.

Jean, Stephane.
 The Robert Fleming Collection: Numerical List. Ottawa, Canada: National Library of Canada/Bibliothèque Nationale du Canada, 1998. 148 pp.
A guide to the papers of the Canadian composer, who served as a staff composer and music director at the National Film Board from the mid-1940s through the 1960s.

Jeromski, Grace, ed.
>	*The International Dictionary of Films and Filmmakers.* Vol. 4, *Writers and Production Artists.* 3rd ed. Detroit: St. James Press, 1997.

More than sixty entries on composers and lyricists, including William Alwyn, Malcolm Arnold, Burt Bacharach, John Barry, Richard Rodney Bennett, Irving Berlin, James Bernard, Elmer Bernstein, Nacio Herb Brown, Sammy Cahn, Hoagy Carmichael, Betty Comden and Adolph Green, Georges Delerue, Adolph Deutsch, Pino Donaggio, George Duning, Hanns Eisler, Arthur Freed, Hugo Friedhofer, Jerry Goldsmith, Johnny Green, Marvin Hamlisch, Bernard Herrmann, Arthur Honegger, Jacques Ibert, Maurice Jarre, Quincy Jones, Gus Kahn, Bronislaw Kaper, Erich Wolfgang Korngold, Francis Lai, Henry Mancini, Muir Mathieson, Alan Menken, Johnny Mercer, Darius Milhaud, Ennio Morricone, Alfred Newman, Jack Nitzsche, Alex North, Cole Porter, André Previn, Sergey Prokofiev, David Raksin, Leonard Rosenman, Nino Rota, Miklós Rózsa, Philippe Sarde, Lalo Schifrin, Dimitri Shostakovich, Carl Stalling, Max Steiner, Herbert Stothart, Toru Takemitsu, Mikis Theodorakis, Virgil Thomson, Dimitri Tiomkin, Vangelis, James Van Heusen, William Walton, Franz Waxman, John Williams, and Victor Young. Each entry includes a brief biography, filmography, and short essay. A dozen of the entries are written by Tony Thomas. Some entrants in the previous editions (1987 and 1993), such as Hans Salter, were not included in the third edition. A later edition by Tom and Sara Pendergast contains new entries.

Jezic, Diane Peacock.
>	*The Musical Migration and Ernst Toch.* Ames: Iowa State Univ. Press, 1989.

"The Hollywood Film Scores, 1935–1945," 78–83; "Filmography," compiled by Jack Docherty, 181–86. "Relating to Ernst Toch's Film Scores," with bibliographical references, 206–7.

Jinks, William.
>	*The Celluloid Literature: Film in the Humanities.* Beverly Hills, Calif.: Glencoe Press, 1971. 2nd ed., 1974.

"Appeal to the Ear: Sound," a historical survey with limited discussion of music, 87–105 (1971), 93–111 (1974).

Johnson, Julian.
>	*Who Needs Classical Music? Cultural Choice and Musical Value.* New York: Oxford Univ. Press, 2002.

Briefly discusses how exposure to classical music through film may result in a "failure to grasp the significance of materials in their original discursive context," 81–82.

Jones, Chris.
>	*The Guerilla Film Makers Movie Blueprint.* London: Continuum, 2003.

"Anatomy of a Cue Sheet" details the music process and includes material based on interviews with composer Domin Beeton and music contractor James Fitzpatrick.

Jones, Preston Neal.
>	*Heaven and Hell to Play With: The Filming of* The Night of the Hunter. New York: Limelight Editions, 2002.

The chapter on postproduction includes background information on the composition of Walter Schumann's score, taken from author's interview with Sonya Goodman, Schumann's widow, 337–43.

Jones, Reginald M., Jr.
  The Mystery of the Masked Man's Music: A Search for the Music Used on "The Lone Ranger" Radio Program, 1933–1954. Metuchen, N.J.: Scarecrow Press, 1987.
"Hooray for Hollywood" includes documentation on how music written for *The Lone Ranger* film serial, produced by Republic Pictures, was reused in the radio serial, 23–39. Short biographical sketches of the composers involved: Alberto Colombo, Cy Feuer, Karl Hajos, and William Lava.

Junchen, David L.
  The Wurlitzer Pipe Organ: An Illustrated History. Compiled and edited by Jeff Weiler. Indianapolis: American Theatre Organ Society, 2005.
Extensive documentation on the Wurlitzer organ and organists in motion picture theaters across the United States and in England.

Juslin, Patrik N., and John A. Sloboda, eds.
  Music and Emotion: Theory and Research. Oxford: Oxford Univ. Press, 2001.
"Music as a Source of Emotion in Film," by Annabel J. Cohen, 249–72.

Kallmann, Helmut, Gilles Potvin, and Kenneth Winters, eds.
  Encyclopedia of Music in Canada. Toronto: Univ. of Toronto Press, 1981. 2nd ed., 1992.
The second edition contains an article on film music as well as entries on Louis Applebaum, Michael Conway Baker, Maurice Blackburn, Robert Fleming, William McCauley, Eldon Rathburn, and Howard Shore.

Kander, John, and Fred Ebb, as told to Greg Lawrence.
  Colored Lights: Forty Years of Words and Music, Show Biz, Collaboration, and All That Jazz. New York: Faber and Faber, 2003.
"*Chicago*, the Movie," 208–18.

Kane, Henry, as told to.
  How to Write a Song. New York: Macmillan, 1962.
Includes interviews with Steve Allen, Hoagy Carmichael, Noël Coward, Duke Ellington, and Johnny Mercer.

Kaplan, Mike, ed.
  Variety International Showbusiness Reference. New York: Garland Publishing, 1981.
Many composers and songwriters—including Brad Fiedel, David Raksin, Nino Rota, Miklós Rózsa, Pete Rugolo, Fred Steiner, and Dimitri Tiomkin—are included among the 6,000 biographies. Each entry includes a paragraph-long biography and list of selected films.

Kasha, Al, and Joel Hirschhorn.
>*If They Ask You, You Can Write a Song.* New York: Simon & Schuster, 1979. New York: Cornerstone Library, 1984. New York: Simon & Schuster, 1986. First Fireside edition (updated), 1990.

This manual by the film songwriting team includes "Writing for Movies," 143–57, and "Writing a Movie Musical," 158–66 (all 1990).

Kasha, Al, and Joel Hirschhorn.
>*Jesus, Hollywood and Me.* Eastbourne: Kingsway, 1995. 222 pp.

Autobiographical, on Kasha's conversion from Judaism to Christianity.

Kashner, Sam, and Nancy Schoenberger.
>*A Talent for Genius: The Life and Times of Oscar Levant.* New York: Villard Books, 1994. Los Angeles: Silman-James Press, 1998.

The composer's biography includes documentation of his work at MGM and RKO studios and his film scores, 86–90, 145–46, 149–50, 157–59, 193–96.

Katz, Ephraim.
>*The Film Encyclopedia.* New York: Thomas Y. Crowell, 1979. New York: Putnam, 1982. 2nd ed., New York: HarperCollins, 1994. 3rd ed., rev., New York: HarperPerennial, 1998.

Includes biographical entries on prominent film composers.

Kaufman, Louis, with Annette Kaufman.
>*A Fiddler's Tale: How Hollywood and Vivaldi Discovered Me.* Madison: Univ. of Wisconsin Press, 2003.

Memoir of the prodigious violinist, one of the most sought-after soloists in Hollywood's studio era. "Hollywood: The Golden Years," on his experiences as a session musician and concertmaster, 115–47; "Bernard Herrmann—Another View," 160–69; "Return to Los Angeles," 330–39. Appendix with partial filmography organized by composer, 407–11. Erich Wolfgang Korngold, Alfred Newman, and Max Steiner are among those listed and are also covered in the chapter on Hollywood. Other composers mentioned include Robert Russell Bennett, Anthony Collins, Aaron Copland, Miklós Rózsa, William Grant Still, Franz Waxman, and Victor Young.

Kaufmann, Preston J.
>*Encyclopedia of the American Theatre Organ.* Vol. 3. Pasadena, Calif.: Showcase Publications, 1995.

Part one of the Wurlitzer organ story and its inventor, Robert Hope-Jones. "Developing a Theatre Market: Photoplayers Set the Stage," 126–55; "Accompaniment for the Silents: Entertaining Manhattan Audiences," 289–99. Author, an organ aficionado, amassed an enormous personal collection of movie theater memorabilia under the tutelage of organist Tom B'Hend. The collection is housed at the Margaret Herrick Library.

Kaufmann, Preston J.
>*Fox, the Last Word: ...Story of the World's Finest Theatre.* Pasadena, Calif.: Showcase Publications, 1979.

Covers the Fox Theatre in San Francisco, 258–72, including the Fox Grand Concert Orchestra; conductor Walter Roesner; prominent members of the orchestra, including a list of members in 1930; and arrangers, including a biography of Earl C. Sharp written by fellow arranger Melford Wesleder. Lavishly illustrated, with photographs of organs and organists, 287–95.

Kawin, Bruce F.
  How Movies Work. New York: Macmillan, 1987.
"The Role of the Music Track," on the responsibilities of the composer and music editor. Topics include cutting to music (particularly in regard to songs) and music's rhythm in relation to the film, 447–59. Aimed at general audiences seeking a better understanding and appreciation of movies.

Keller, Hans.
  Hans Keller: Essays on Music. Edited by Christopher Wintle, with Bayan Northcott and Irene Samuel. Cambridge: Cambridge Univ. Press, 1994.
"Film Music: The Harry Lime Theme," on the Anton Karas tune, 83–85, reprinted from *Music Survey* (1951). Wintle summarizes the author's perspective on film music in the introduction, xv.

Keller, Hans.
  Music and Psychology: From London to Vienna, 1939–52. Edited by Christopher Wintle with Alison Garnham. London: Plumbago Books, 2003.
Includes "The Psychology of Film Music," 157–60 (originally published in *World Psychology*, 1948); "Georges Auric at Film Music's Best," 160–63 (originally published in "Film Music and Beyond," *Music Review*, November 1954).

Kennedy, Joseph P.
  The Story of the Films: As Told by Leaders of the Industry to the Students of the Graduate School of Business Administration, George F. Baker Foundation, Harvard University. Chicago and London: A. W. Shaw, 1927. Facsimile reprint, New York: J. S. Ozer, 1971.
"Future Developments," by Harry M. Warner, on the possibilities of the Vitaphone providing music for pictures, including economic aspects and the attitude of organ manufacturers, 319–35; Cecil B. DeMille, on the use of music at rehearsals to inspire the actors, 143.

Kennedy, Michael.
  A Catalogue of the Works of Ralph Vaughan Williams. Rev. ed. London: Oxford Univ. Press, 1982. 2nd ed., 1996. 2003.
Documents the music and writings of the British composer, including all known published and unpublished works and the location of manuscripts and sketches. Originally published as part of *The Works of Ralph Vaughan Williams* (1964).

Kennedy, Michael, ed.
  The Concise Oxford Dictionary of Music. 3rd ed. London: Oxford Univ. Press, 1980. 4th ed., 2004.
"Film Music," 225–26 (1980), 251 (2004). Individual entries for some film composers, including Bernard Herrmann and Miklós Rózsa.

Kennedy, Michael, ed.
  The Oxford Dictionary of Music. Oxford: Oxford Univ. Press, 1985; 1991; 1994; 2002; 2003.
"Film Music," 458–60 (edited by Alison Latham, 2002); 298 (Kennedy, 2003).

Kennington, Donald.
  The Literature of Jazz. London: Library Association, 1970. Reprint, Chicago: American Library Association, 1971. 2nd rev. ed., Kennington and Danny L. Read, *The Literature of Jazz: A Critical Guide,* 1980.
Includes material on jazz in film.

Kerr, Cherie.
  Charlie's Notes: A Memoir. Santa Ana, Calif.: ExecuProv Press, 2004.
Chronicles the life of the author's father, jazz musician Charlie DePietro, who played background music for and sometimes appeared in numerous films.

Kiesling, Barrett C.
  Talking Pictures: How They Are Made, How to Appreciate Them. Richmond, Va.: Johnson Publishing, 1937. London: Spon, 1939.
"Music in Pictures," on MGM studios, 209–15.

Kildea, Paul, ed.
  Britten on Music. Oxford: Oxford Univ. Press, 2003.
This collection of Benjamin Britten articles and interviews includes "On Film Music" (ca. 1940–1941) and "Television and *The Turn of the Screw*" (1959).

Killiam Shows, Inc.
  The Killiam Collection. New York: Killiam Shows, 1974.
The one-page introduction for this 28-page film rental catalog is titled "Music for Silent Films." The more than thirty films listed were originally released between 1914 and 1932 and feature newly commissioned scores. The piano scores are by William Perry and Charles Hofmann, and the organ scores are by Lee Erwin, Gaylord Carter, and Jack Ward.

Kimball, Robert, ed.
  The Complete Lyrics of Cole Porter. New York: Knopf, 1983. 354 pp. New York: Da Capo Press, 1992. 501 pp.
Lyrics for all of Porter's film songs.

Kimball, Robert, ed.
  The Complete Lyrics of Ira Gershwin. New York: Knopf, 1993. 414 pp. New York: Da Capo Press, 1998. 414 pp.
Lyrics for all of Ira Gershwin's film songs.

Kimball, Robert, and Linda Emmet, eds.
  The Complete Lyrics of Irving Berlin. New York: Knopf, 2001. 530 pp. New York: Applause Theatre & Cinema Books/Hal Leonard, 2005. 530 pp.
Lyrics for all of Berlin's film songs.

Kimball, Robert, and Dorothy Hart, eds.
> *The Complete Lyrics of Lorenz Hart.* New York: Knopf, 1986. 317 pp. New York: Da Capo Press, 1995. 344 pp.

Lyrics for all of Hart's film songs, with an appreciation written by Alan Jay Lerner.

Kimball, Robert, and Steve Nelson, eds.
> *The Complete Lyrics of Frank Loesser.* New York: Knopf, 2003. 271 pp.

Lyrics for all of Loesser's film songs.

Kimberlin, Cynthia Tse, and Akin Euba.
> *Intercultural Music.* Bayreuth, Germany: E. Breitinger, 1995.

"Film Music: The New Intercultural Idiom of 20th Century Indian Music," by Subramaniyam Venkatraman, 107–12. From the first International Symposium and Festival on Intercultural Music, London, 1990.

King, Clyde L., and Frank A. Tichenor, eds.
> *The Motion Picture in Its Economic and Social Aspects.* The Annals, vol. 128, no. 217, November 1926. Philadelphia: American Academy of Political and Social Science, 1926.

"Music and Motion Pictures," by Hugo Riesenfeld, discusses program music performed before film screenings, synchronized scores, arranging and using scores, pay scales, and film music as a new field and training ground for composers and performers, 58–62.

King, Kimball, ed.
> *Woody Allen: A Casebook.* New York: Routledge, 2001.

"Song as Subtext: The Virtual Reality of Lyrics in the Films of Woody Allen," by Carol Goodson, 1–10; "Dissonant Harmonics: Classical Music and the Problems of Class in *Crimes and Misdemeanors*," by Thomas Fahy, 81–92.

Kingman, Daniel.
> *American Music: A Panorama.* New York: Schirmer Books, 1979. 2nd ed., New York: Schirmer Books; London: Collier Macmillan Publishers, 1990. Concise ed., New York: Schirmer Books; London: Prentice Hall International, 1998. 2nd concise ed., Belmont, Calif.: Thomson; New York: Schirmer, 2003.

"Hollywood and the Movie Song," a brief survey, 63–67; "Music with Film," on Virgil Thomson, Aaron Copland, and Leonard Bernstein, 387–96 (both 1979). "The Film Musical, 304–9; "Music with Film," 461–66 (both 1990).

Kinkle, Roger D.
> *The Complete Encyclopedia of Popular Music and Jazz, 1900–1950.* 4 vols. New Rochelle, N.Y.: Arlington House, 1974.

Volume 1 contains "Music Year by Year," a survey of popular music from 1900 to 1950 that includes songs and film musicals. Volumes 2 (A to K) and 3 (L to Z) offer short biographical entries for composers, songwriters, and arrangers, each followed by a list of movies and records (through the early 1970s). Frank Skinner and other popular musicians are listed among the usual Hollywood composers (Rózsa, Tiomkin, etc.). Volume 4 contains indexes for names, song titles, and "Movie Musicals," 2401–12. Numerical listings for nine major record labels—Brunswick, Columbia, and Victor, for example—from the mid-1920s through the early 1940s.

Kirstein, Lincoln, et al., eds.
> *Films: A Quarterly of Discussion and Analysis*. Reprint, New York: Arno Press, 1968.

A reprint edition in one volume of the original periodical issues, numbers 1–4, 1939–40. Includes "Music in Films: A Symposium of Composers" (Winter 1940).

Klamkin, Marian.
> *Old Sheet Music: A Pictorial History*. New York: Hawthorn Books, 1975.

"Movie Music of the Twenties, Thirties and Forties," a survey, 161–69; followed by sheet-music covers reproduced in black and white, 170–89.

Knight, Arthur (*aka* Arthur L. Knight III, b. 1960).
> *Disintegrating the Musical: Black Performance and American Musical Film*. Durham, N.C.: Duke Univ. Press, 2002.

Topics include black-cast musicals, jazz and jazz shorts, and the musical genre.

Knight, Arthur (1916–1991).
> *The Liveliest Art: A Panoramic History of the Movies*. New York: Macmillan, 1957. New York: New American Library, 1959. Rev. ed., 1978.

References to music in films and musical films, pp. 124–63 (1978).

Knox, Donald.
> *The Magic Factory: How MGM Made* An American in Paris. New York: Praeger Publishers, 1973.

This oral history narrative includes excerpts from interviews with Saul Chaplin, John Green, and Alan Jay Lerner.

Kobler, Helmut.
> *Anatomy of a Guerrilla Film: The Making of* Radius. Boston: Thomson Course Technology, 2005.

A first-time director offers tips to independent filmmakers. Includes "Music Composition," on the contributions of composer Jeremy Zuckerman and music supervisor Joe Fischer, 273–83.

Koepnick, Lutz P.
> *The Dark Mirror: German Cinema between Hitler and Hollywood*. Berkeley: Univ. of California Press, 2002.

Substantive discussion of music in German films. Topics include Westerns, 114–17, 121–25; film music, 146–50; Erich Wolfgang Korngold, 150–54; film noir, 170–72; and operatic music, 237–57.

Kohn, Al, and Bob Kohn.
> *Kohn on Music Licensing*. 2nd ed. Englewood Cliffs, N.J.: Aspen Law & Business, 1996. (Rev. ed. of *The Art of Music Licensing*. Englewood Cliffs, N.J.: Prentice Hall Law & Business, 1992.) 3rd ed., New York: Aspen Law & Business, 2002.

Although not focused specifically on film music, the material on sync licenses and music clearance is useful. Authors are leading authorities on music licensing.

Kolker, Robert Phillip.
   A Cinema of Loneliness: Penn, Kubrick, Coppola, Scorsese, Altman. New York: Oxford Univ. Press, 1980. *A Cinema of Loneliness: Penn, Kubrick, Scorsese, Spielberg, Altman.* 2nd ed., 1988. *A Cinema of Loneliness: Penn, Stone, Kubrick, Scorsese, Spielberg, Altman.* 3rd ed., 2000.
Numerous references to music in the films of directors Robert Altman, Stanley Kubrick, and Martin Scorsese.

Kostelanetz, Richard, and Robert Flemming, eds.
   Writings on Glass: Essays, Interviews, Criticism. New York: Schirmer Books, 1997.
"Philip Glass on Composing for Film and Other Forms: The Case of *Koyaanisqatsi*," by Charles Merrell Berg, 131–51.

Kracauer, Siegfried.
   Theory of Film: The Redemption of Physical Reality. New York: Oxford Univ. Press, 1960. London: Dobbson, 1961 (under the title *Nature of Film: The Redemption of Physical Reality*). Princeton, N.J.: Princeton Univ. Press, 1997.
"Music," on its physiological and aesthetic functions, as well as operatic performances, 133–56. Author's sociopsychological readings of film are written from personal experience and reflect his theory that the nature of film is to reproduce reality.

Kraft, James P.
   Stage to Studio: Musicians and the Sound Revolution, 1890–1950. Baltimore: Johns Hopkins Univ. Press, 1996.
"Boom and Bust in Early Movie Theaters" includes material on the practice of live music to accompany silent films, 33–58; "Playing in between the Wars," covers recording film music in Hollywood, including studio musicians, working conditions, and sideline musicians, 88–106. Draws on previous material written for *Labor History* and *Technology and Culture.* Author, a professor of history, wrote his dissertation on the subject.

Kramer, Lawrence.
   Musical Meaning: Toward a Critical History. Berkeley: Univ. of California Press, 2002.
Coverage on film and television music.

Krampert, Peter.
   The Encyclopedia of the Harmonica. Arlington Heights, Ill.: Tatanka Publishing, 1998.
An extensive listing of harmonica players, composers who have written for the instrument, and session musicians who played harmonica on film soundtracks. Entries for Larry Adler, Leo Diamond (possibly the only one of this group to receive a main title credit for his harmonica solos for *When Hell Broke Loose,* 1958), George Fields, Eddy Lawrence Manson, Tommy Morgan, Sonny Terry, Jean "Toots" Thielemans, Mike Turk, and groups such as the Cappy Barra Harmonica Ensemble and the Harmonica Rascals. Each short biography concludes with a list of selected movies (not indexed, however) featuring on- and off-screen performances in classical, rock, jazz, country, and other styles. Good starting point for those interested in compiling a harmonica filmography. Author is a Chicago-based freelance writer and harmonica player.

Krasilovsky, M. William, and Sidney Shemel.
> *This Business of Music: The Definitive Guide to the Music Industry.* 8th ed. New York: Watson-Guptill Publications, 2000. 9th ed., New York: Billboard Books, 2003.

A practical guide to the music industry for publishers, writers, record companies, producers, artists, and agents. "Music for Motion Pictures," on agreements, licenses, rights, royalties, and soundtracks, 259–68; "Licensing Recordings for Motion Pictures," 269–73 (2000). Other general topics include arrangements, copyright, demo records, mechanical rights, performing rights organizations, and songwriter contracts. Includes compact disc with ready-to-print contracts. First edition was published by Billboard in 1964 as *This Business of Music* by Sidney Shemel and M. William Krasilovsky, and included "Music and Movies," 162–69. Revised and enlarged editions, eventually under the expanded title, followed in 1971 (2nd), 1977 (3rd, including the Copyright Act of 1976), 1979 (4th), 1985 (5th), 1990 (6th), and 1995 (7th). *More about This Business of Music* was published in 1967, followed by revised and enlarged editions in 1974 (2nd), 1982 (3rd), 1989 (4th), and 1994 (5th).

Kratochvíl, M. V., and O. Vávra.
> John Huss: *A Screen Play.* Translated by Roberta Finlayson Samsour. Prague: Artia, 1957.

"On the Film Music for *John Huss*," by the composer Jiri Srnka, 172–74.

Krause, Bernie.
> *Into a Wild Sanctuary: A Life in Music and Natural Sound.* Berkeley, Calif.: Heyday Books, 1998.

The author and Paul Beaver, who cowrote the *Nonesuch Guide to Electronic Music*, championed the use of the Moog synthesizer in film and television scores in the late 1960s and early 1970s. This memoir contains anecdotes on Beaver and the Moog. Other topics include union concerns regarding the displacement of musicians by the Moog, 53–54; scoring *The Last Days of Man on Earth*, 87–89; and working as a session musician synthesist on *Apocalypse Now*, 94–95.

Krummel, Donald W., et al.
> *Resources of American Musical History: A Directory of Source Materials from Colonial Times to World War II.* Urbana: Univ. of Illinois Press, 1981.

In the index, entries under "Film Music" and "Silent Film Music" list institutions that hold thematic cue sheets and piano-conductor scores.

Kuhns, William, and Robert Stanley.
> *Exploring the Film.* Dayton, Ohio: G. A. Pflaum, [1968].

Brief comments on music, including a paragraph on *Loneliness of the Long Distance Runner* (1962), 98.

Kuna, Milan.
> *Zvuk a Hudba ve Filmu.* Prague: Panton, 1969.

This 266-page analytical essay on sound dramaturgy is written in Czech. "Sound and Musik in Film" is a three-page summary in English of the entire essay, 262–64.

Laird, Paul R.
   Leonard Bernstein: A Guide to Research. New York: Routledge, 2002.
"Film Score" lists eight books containing substantial material on Bernstein's score for *On the Waterfront*, 157–60.

Lambert, Constant.
   Music Ho! A Study of Music in Decline. London: Faber and Faber, 1934. New York: Charles Scribner's Sons, 1936. 2nd ed., London: Faber and Faber, 1937; 1941. Harmondsworth, U.K.: Penguin Books, 1948. 3rd ed., London: Faber, 1966. New York: October House, 1967.
Contains the essay "Mechanical Music and the Cinema," on composing for the microphone orchestra (similar to Kurt London's *Film Music* of 1936) and on opportunities specific to the film medium, such as surrealism, 256–68 (1937), 185–95 (1948).

Landon, John W.
   Behold the Mighty Wurlitzer: The History of the Theatre Pipe Organ. Westport, Conn.: Greenwood Press, 1983.
Frequent references to the use of the Wurlitzer to accompany silent films.

Landon, John W.
   Jesse Crawford, Poet of the Organ, Wizard of the Mighty Wurlitzer. Vestal, N.Y.: Vestal Press, 1974.
Biography of the theater organist.

Landy, Marcia.
   Italian Film. Cambridge: Cambridge Univ. Press, 2000.
On Ennio Morricone's music for Sergio Leone's films, 89–90; other references to music and musicals throughout.

Lange, Arthur.
   Arranging for the Modern Dance Orchestra. New York: A. Lange, 1926. 238 pp. New York: Robbins Music, ca. 1935. 238 pp.
Author is the noted dance-band arranger whose Hollywood composing career spanned 1929 to 1954. For his students, Lange also wrote *Arthur Lang's* [*sic*] *Spectrotone System of Orchestration* (Beverly Hills, Calif.: Co-Art, 1943), which included how to write double-stops for strings, and *A New and Practical Approach to Harmony* (Los Angeles, ca. 1954).

Lanza, Joseph.
   Elevator Music: A Surreal History of Muzak, Easy-Listening, and Other Moodsong. New York: St. Martin's Press, 1994. New York: Picador USA, 1995. Rev. and expanded ed., Ann Arbor: Univ. of Michigan Press, 2004.
"Emotional Archives: Background Music in the Movies," survey with examples drawn from a wide range of films, 55–66; "Elevator Noir" has material on Angelo Badalamenti (who at one time supplied arrangements for Muzak under the name Andy Badale), including an interview about his music for the television show *Twin Peaks*, 199–202 (1994). Other composers include Robert Farnon, Morton Gould, Francis Lai, and Michel Legrand. The Badalamenti interview does not appear in the revised edition, which contains new material on Stu Phillips, 199–201.

Larkin, Colin, comp. and ed.
>   *The Encyclopedia of Popular Music.* 3rd ed. 8 vols. London: Muze, 1998.

Brief biographical entries for Richard Addinsell, John Addison, William Alwyn, Harold Arlen, Malcolm Arnold, Burt Bacharach, John Barry, Les Baxter, Paul Beaver and Bernie Krause, Berklee College of Music, Irving Berlin, Elmer Bernstein, Leonard Bernstein, Nacio Herb Brown, Wendy Carlos, Hoagy Carmichael, Bill Conti, Carl Davis, George Duning, Duke Ellington, Percy Faith, George Fenton, Hugo Friedhofer, George and Ira Gershwin, Jerry Goldsmith, Ron Goodwin, Ron Grainer, Johnny Green, Dave Grusin, Richard Hayman, Neal Hefti, Victor Herbert, Bernard Herrmann, and many others, including Miklós Rózsa, Dimitri Tiomkin, and John Williams.

Larkin, Colin, ed.
>   *The Guinness Encyclopedia of Popular Music.* 4 vols. Enfield, Middlesex, U.K.: Guinness Pub.; Chester, Conn.: New England Pub. Associates, 1992.

Organized similarly to the author's *Encyclopedia of Popular Music* (see previous entry).

Larkin, Colin, ed.
>   *The Virgin Encyclopedia of Stage and Film Musicals.* London: Virgin Books, 1999.

More than 1,600 entries for musicals, composers, songwriters, lyricists, and performers. Culled from Larkin's *Encyclopedia of Popular Music* (see entry above) and previously published as two books, *The Who's Who of Stage Musicals* and *The Guinness Who's Who of Film Musicals and Musical Films*. Based largely on the personal collection of the author, a popular-music historian with a background in music and publishing.

Larsen, Arved M., gen. ed.
>   *Crossroads in Music: Traditions and Connections.* Belmont, Calif.: Thomson; New York: Schirmer Books, 2003.

This college-level music appreciation textbook devotes an entire chapter to film music. Discussion of music's role in films, some outstanding film composers, and the return to symphonic film scores, 239–47. Tan Dun's score for *Crouching Tiger, Hidden Dragon* is examined.

Larsen, Egon.
>   *Spotlight on Films: A Primer for Film-Lovers.* London: Max Parrish, 1950.

According to Wescott's *A Comprehensive Bibliography of Music for Film and Television*, this work includes a section on film music. However, a reference librarian at the Los Angeles Public Library confirms there is no such section.

Latham, Alison, ed.
>   *The Oxford Companion to Music.* New York: Oxford Univ. Press, 2002.

"Film Music," by Peter Gammond and Kenneth Chalmers, 458–60.

LaValley, Al, and Barry P. Scherr, eds.
>   *Eisenstein at 100: A Reconsideration.* New Brunswick, N.J.: Rutgers Univ. Press, 2001.

Analysis of the music for the opening credits sequence for *Ivan the Terrible*, 269–71; references to Sergey Prokofiev, 122–13; 194–95.

Lavery, David, ed.
> *Full of Secrets: Critical Approaches to* Twin Peaks. Detroit: Wayne State Univ. Press, 1995.

"'Disturbing the Guests with This Racket': Music and *Twin Peaks*," by Kathryn Kalinak, on music by Angelo Badalamenti, 82–92.

Lawson, John Howard.
> *Film: The Creative Process.* New York: Hill and Wang, 1964; 1967.

References throughout to music in film.

Lax, Roger, and Frederick Smith.
> *The Great Song Thesaurus.* New York: Oxford Univ. Press, 1984. 2nd ed., rev. and expanded, New York: Oxford Univ. Press, 1989.

Entries arranged alphabetically by song title and include composer and lyricist, year, and notes. Material related to film and television is indexed by title of production followed by song title(s), and can then be found by looking under individual song entry, 545–70. "Silent Films" lists seven songs, 545–46; "Musical Films" lists 906 films, 546–63; "Non-musical Films" lists 491 films, 563–69; "Radio and Television Shows and Programs" lists 68 productions, 569–70. The 1989 edition covers the same categories with new additions, 577–620. Authors are a songwriter and a special material writer for television, respectively.

Lee, Barbara.
> *Working in Music.* Minneapolis: Lerner Publications, 1996.

Aimed at juvenile readers seeking vocational guidance. "Composer" profiles independent film and television composer Carol Nethen (*America's Most Wanted*), 13–19.

Lees, Gene.
> *Arranging the Score: Portraits of the Great Arrangers.* London: Cassell, 2000.

Introduction discusses how band arrangers moved into film scoring in the 1950s and 1960s and the use of orchestral jazz in film, 9–11. "Mandelsongs: Johnny Mandel," 181–92; "Going Home: Henry Mancini," 193–221; "Bright Laughter: Billy May," 222–35. These essays first appeared in the author's publication *Jazzletter*.

Lees, Gene.
> *Friends along the Way: A Journey through Jazz.* New Haven, Conn.: Yale Univ. Press, 2003.

Chapters on Ralph Burns, 233–49, Allyn Ferguson, 212–32, and Hugo Friedhofer, 158–75. Personal reminiscences interspersed with biographical details.

Lees, Gene.
> *Singers and the Song.* New York: Oxford Univ. Press, 1987. *Singers and the Song II.* Expanded ed. New York: Oxford Univ. Press, 1998.

"Roses in the Morning—Johnny Mercer," on the lyricist and his conversations with Lees, 44–69; "The Hug—Hugo Friedhofer," on Lees's personal friendship with Hugo Friedhofer, 134–53 (1987), which appears in abridged form in Linda Danly's book, *Hugo Friedhofer* (1999). The expanded edition contains material on E. Y. Harburg, Arthur Schwartz, and Harry Warren.

Leigh, Janet, with Christopher Nickens.
  Psycho: *Behind the Scenes of the Classic Thriller.* New York: Harmony Books, 1995.
"Bernard Herrmann" includes quotes from Hitchcock's personal assistant, 165–68.

Leipold, John Max.
  The John Leipold Lessons in Counterpoint. 2 vols. N.p.: n.d.
One of several "self-education" books for musicians published by the author, who scored films throughout the 1930s and 1940s. Other titles include *The John Leipold Lessons in Harmony* and *The John Leipold Lessons in Composition,* both published before 1951. *Mathematics of Pitch* and *Harmony for the Accordionist* may have been published after 1951.

Leitch, Thomas M.
  The Encyclopedia of Alfred Hitchcock. New York: Facts on File, 2002.
Individual entries for Bernard Herrmann, Ron Goodwin, Miklós Rózsa, and Franz Waxman. Entries on specific films often mention Hitchcock's use of music.

Leonard, Harold L., ed.
  The Film Index: A Bibliography. Vol. 1, *The Film as Art.* New York: Museum of Modern Art and H.W. Wilson, 1941. Reprint, New York: Arno Press, 1970.
"Music," on the silent era, 202–7; on the sound era, 207–11; "Musical films," 468–72. With annotations.

Leopold, David.
  Irving Berlin's Show Business: Broadway-Hollywood-America. New York: Harry N. Abrams, 2005.
Three chapters cover Berlin in Hollywood: "I Ask You, Is That Nice?" (1927–31), 81–91; "Let's Face the Music and Dance" (1934–42), 121–41; "You Keep Coming Back Like a Song" (1945–54), 191–207.

Levant, Oscar.
  The Memoirs of an Amnesiac. New York: G. P. Putnam's Sons, 1965. Hollywood: Samuel French, 1989.
The songwriter's anecdotal memoirs mention many composers. "The Real Tinsel" concentrates on his experiences as an actor, 180–205.

Levant, Oscar.
  A Smattering of Ignorance. New York: Doubleday, 1940. Garden City, N.Y.: Garden City Publishing, 1942. Garden City, N.Y.: Doubleday, 1959.
Includes the essay "A Cog on the Wheel," on the author's experiences as a songwriter in Hollywood, on the music departments at RKO and MGM, on the state of Hollywood "picture music," and on Herbert Spencer and Max Steiner, 89–144 (1942). Essay previously published as "Movie Music" in *Town and Country* (December 1939) and reprinted in T. J. Ross, *Film and the Liberal Arts* (1970).

Levant, Oscar.
  The Unimportance of Being Oscar. New York: G. P. Putnam's Sons, 1968.
On songwriters, 37–48, 146–55, 158–67.

Levin, David J.
   Richard Wagner, Fritz Lang, and the Nibelungen: The Dramaturgy of Disavowal.
   Princeton, N.J.: Princeton Univ. Press, 1998.
This theoretical work contains discussion of music and film in the context of the book's
subject.

Levy, Edmond.
   Making a Winning Short: How to Write, Direct, Edit, and Produce a Short Film.
   New York: H. Holt, 1994.
Brief sections on music scoring and rights, 232–33, 241–42.

Lewine, Richard, and Alfred Simon.
   *Encyclopedia of Theatre Music: A Comprehensive Listing of More Than 4000 Songs
   from Broadway and Hollywood: 1900–1960.* New York: Random House, 1961.
"Motion Picture Songs" takes an interesting stance by listing only film songs written by
Broadway theater composers and/or lyricists, 137–50. Line listings include song title,
creators, film, and year.

Lewine, Richard, and Alfred Simon.
   *Songs of the American Theater: A Comprehensive Listing of More Than 12,000
   Songs, Including Selected Titles from Film and Television Productions.* New York:
   Dodd, Mead, 1973.
Uses criteria similar to those of the 1961 publication (see previous entry), only here the
film songs are not listed separately from theater songs, and television titles have been
added. Songs listed by production title, with song creators, title, and year.

Lewine, Richard, and Alfred Simon.
   Songs of the Theater. New York: H. W. Wilson, 1984.
Film and television titles are listed in an index, 861–70.

Leyda, Jay, ed.
   Voices of Film Experience: 1894 to the Present. New York: Macmillan, 1977. *Film
   Makers Speak: Voices of Film Experience.* Rev. ed. New York: Da Capo Press,
   1984.
Interview extracts, each preceded by a one-line bio, with Marc Blitzstein, 38; Benjamin
Britten, 47; Aaron Copland, 83–84; Hanns Eisler, 127–28; Bernard Herrmann, 198–200;
Maurice Jaubert, 226; Quincy Jones, 228–29; Henry Mancini, 296; André Previn, 369–
70; Miklós Rózsa, 409–10; Max Steiner, 441–42; Dimitri Tiomkin, 459; and Roy Webb,
496–97. Quotes are taken from books, newspapers, and magazines, including *Films: A
Quarterly of Discussion and Analysis* (1940) and various Christopher Palmer interviews.
A few directors mention music; for example, Jacques Demy on working with Michel
Legrand on *Les parapluies de Cherbourg* (1964), 106; and W. S. Van Dyke, 477 (all
1977).

Light, Alan, ed.
   The Vibe History of Hip Hop. New York: Three Rivers Press, 1999.
"Hip Hop in the Movies," by Gary Dauphin, 201–7.

Lindgren, Ernest.
  The Art of the Film: An Introduction to Film Appreciation. London: George Allen and Unwin, 1948. 2nd ed., New York: Macmillan, 1963.
"Film Music," 141–53 (1948), 134–45 (1963).

Lindner, Christoph, ed.
  The James Bond Phenomenon: A Critical Reader. Manchester: Manchester Univ. Press, 2003.
"Creating a Bond Market: Selling John Barry's Soundtracks and Theme Songs," by Jeff Smith, 118–34.

Lindsay, Vachel.
  The Art of the Moving Picture. New York: Macmillan, 1915; 1922. Reprint, New York: Liveright, 1970. New York: Modern Library, 2000.
One of the first books to equate film and art. Discusses musical accompaniment practice based on the author's observations as a filmgoer. Under the subheading "The orchestra, conversations and the censorship," the author, a painter-turned-poet, argues that there should be no music or other sound accompaniment, only the conversation of the patrons discussing the film, 189–198 (1915).

Lippy, Tod, ed.
  Projections 11: Film-Makers on Film-Making. London: Faber and Faber, 2000.
"Carter Burwell," interview, 36–52.

Litwak, Mark.
  Contracts for the Film and Television Industry. Los Angeles: Silman-James Press, 1994. Rev. ed., 1998.
"Soundtracks," buying pre-existing music, commissioning music, and distribution, along with sample contracts for composers on low-budget features, a television music rights license, and soundtrack recordings, 129–143 (1994). "Music," on same, 215–37 (1998).

Litwak, Mark.
  Dealmaking in the Film & Television Industry: From Negotiations to Final Contracts. Los Angeles: Silman-James Press, 1994.
"Music," on soundtracks and their distribution and the nature of music rights needed, 203–18.

Litwak, Mark.
  Litwak's Multimedia Producer's Handbook: A Legal and Distribution Guide. Los Angeles: Silman-James Press, 1998.
"Music," on licensing, 51–55.

Lochhead, Judy, and Joseph Auner, eds.
  Postmodern Music / Postmodern Thought. New York: Routledge, 2002.
"*Natural Born Killers*: Music and Image in Postmodern Film," by Jason Hanley, 335–59.

Lofman, Ron.
  Goldmine's Celebrity Vocals: Attempts at Musical Fame from 1500 Major Stars and Supporting Players. Iola, Wis.: Krause Publications, 1994.

Discography with many actor entries that include "sings on the following film sound-tracks" followed by title, record label, and record number. Goldmine is a magazine for record collectors.

London, Mel.
> *Getting into Film.* New York: Ballantine Books, 1977. Rev. ed., New York: Ballantine Books, 1985.

"Music," on location music, original scores, and library scores via a music editor, 51–57 (1977).

Lorenz, Juliane, ed.
> *Chaos as Usual: Conversations about Rainer Werner Fassbinder.* New York: Applause, 1997.

In "Peer Raben: Work without End," Raben, a composer and Fassbinder's most frequent collaborator, talks about working with the director, 29–39.

Lu, Sheldon H., and Emilie Yueh-yu Yeh, eds.
> *Chinese-Language Film: Historiography, Poetics, Politics.* Honolulu: Univ. of Hawaii Press, 2005.

"Shadow Opera: Toward a New Archaeology of the Chinese Cinema," by Mary Farquhar and Chris Berry, examines early opera films and revolutionary opera films from mainland China, 27–51.

Ludden, David, ed.
> *Contesting the Nation: Religion, Community, and the Politics of Democracy in India.* Philadelphia: Univ. of Pennsylvania Press, 1996.

"Film Music and Film Culture," by Peter Manuel, 129–38.

Lumet, Sidney.
> *Making Movies.* New York: Knopf, 1995.

In "The Sound of Music: The Sound of Sound," the author-director discusses the music-scoring process in the context of his own films and his collaborations with Quincy Jones, Richard Rodney Bennett, Mikis Theodorakis, and Paul Chihara, 170–85.

Lutyens, Elisabeth.
> *A Goldfish Bowl.* London: Cassell, 1972.

The British composer discusses her work in feature films, the horror genre, and documentaries, 150–51, 168–72, 255–56, 285–86, 293–94, with other passing references throughout.

Lyman, Darryl.
> *Great Jews in Music.* Middle Village, N.Y.: J. David Publishers, 1986.

Biographical sketches, including selected works, for George Antheil, Harold Arlen, Burt Bacharach, Leonard Bernstein, Marc Blitzstein, Aaron Copland, Philip Glass, Morton Gould, Jerome Kern, Erich Wolfgang Korngold, Frederick Loewe, André Previn, and Richard Rodgers. Thumbnail sketches for Larry Adler, Theodor Adorno, Elmer Bernstein, Henry Brant, Mario Castelnuovo-Tedesco, Hanns Eisler, Ernest Gold, Louis Gruenberg, Marvin Hamlisch, Bernard Herrmann, Friedrich Hollaender, Alfred Newman, Randy Newman, Sigmund Romberg, Albert Sendrey, Alexander Tansman, and Dimitri

Tiomkin. Lyman's criteria for inclusion follow the definition established by Jewish law: a Jew must be born to a Jewish mother or convert to Judaism (therefore Max Steiner is excluded).

Lynch, Richard Chigley, comp.
> *Broadway, Movie, TV, and Studio Cast Musicals on Record: A Discography of Recordings, 1985–1995.* Westport, Conn.: Greenwood Press, 1996. 254 pp.

Continuation of the series that began with *Broadway on Record* (1987) and *Movie Musicals on Record* (1989). Compiler is a retired assistant curator of the Billy Rose Theatre Collection at the New York Public Library. Introduction, discography, chronology, and performer and technical indexes.

Lynn Farnol Group.
> *Richard Rodgers Fact Book.* New York: Lynn Farnol Group, 1965.

"Stage, Film and Television Scores," 7–468; "Stage, Film and Television Songs and Themes," 469–76. Contains primarily production information and capsule reviews. Bibliography, discography, and index with film and television productions.

Lynn, Kenneth Schuyler.
> *Charlie Chaplin and His Times.* New York: Simon & Schuster, 1997.

This biography includes discussion of Chaplin's film music compositions and his collaboration with composer David Raksin, 382–84.

MacArthur, Sally, and Cate Poynton, eds.
> *Musics and Feminisms.* Sydney: Australian Music Centre, 1999.

"Women's Potential as Soundtrack Composers: Implications for Tertiary Educators," by Carol Biddiss, 29–34.

MacHale, Des.
> *The Complete Guide to* The Quiet Man. Rev. ed. Belfast: Appletree, 2001.

The running commentary on the film contains references to Victor Young's music score throughout.

MacMillan, Sir Ernest, ed.
> *Music in Canada.* Toronto: Univ. of Toronto Press, 1955. Reprint, St. Clair Shores, Mich.: Scholarly Press, 1978.

"Film Music," 167.

Madsen, Roy Paul.
> *The Impact of Film: How Ideas Are Communicated through Cinema and Television.* New York: Macmillan, 1973.

"Music," on the functions of music, including character and locale themes, moods, tempos, continuity, dramatic emphasis, premonition, and commentary, 115–20; "Musicals," 308–13.

Madsen, Roy Paul.
> *Working Cinema: Learning from the Masters.* Belmont, Calif.: Wadsworth, 1990.

"Music," on the functions of music, 302–4.

Maes, Francis.
    A History of Russian Music: From Kamarinskaya to Babi Yar. Translated by Arnold
    J. Pomerans and Erica Pomerans. Berkeley: Univ. of California Press, 2002.
"Theater, Film, and Ballet" includes a discussion of music for a few specific films, 324–
30.

Magill, Frank Northen, and Shawn Brennan, eds.
    Magill's Cinema Annual. Englewood Cliffs, N.J.: Salem Press, 1982–1994. Gale Re-
    search, 1995–2005.
Composers are included in the index for the films in each year-by-year survey. See "Music Director Index," 499–501 (2005).

Maltin, Leonard
    *The Great Movie Shorts: Those Wonderful One- and Two-Reelers of the Thirties and
    Forties.* New York: Crown, 1972.
"Musicals," a survey, 211–17.

Malvinni, David.
    *The Gypsy Caravan: From Real Roma to Imaginary Gypsies in Western Music and
    Film.* New York: Routledge, 2004.
"Gypsiness in Film Music: Spectacle and Act," 163–202.

Mantell, Harold, ed.
    *A Guide to Theme Music: A Complete Guide to Its Creative and Effective Use: From
    Spots to Features, Sitcoms to Documentaries, in the Classroom, over the Air, in the
    Theater.* Princeton, N.J.: Films for the Humanities, 1981.
This 99-page booklet accompanied the *Theme Music Library* of incidental music, issued
by Films for the Humanities on at least twenty-five LPs in the early 1980s. It contains a
numerical (by record number) and alphabetical index of the music on those discs. Also
includes "The Functions of the Film Score," by Mark Evans, 31–48, reprinted from
Evans's *Soundtrack: The Music of the Movies* (1975); "The Use of Music in In-House
Production," by Raymond J. Winter, on library music for audio-visual productions, 57–
64; "Tracking the Film Score," 75–79, and "A Glossary for Music Editors," 81–99, both
by Milton Lustig, reprinted from *Music Editing for Motion Pictures* (1980). Author also
wrote *The Complete Guide to the Creation and Use of Sound Effects for Films, TV and
Dramatic Productions* (Princeton, N.J.: Films for the Humanities, 1983).

Manuel, Peter Lamarche.
    Cassette Culture: Popular Music and Technology in North India. Chicago: Univer-
    sity of Chicago Press, 1993.
"Film Music and Film Culture," 40–46; "Film Music: Context and Content," 47–54; "The
Impact of Film Music on Folk Music," 55–57; "Parody in Film Music," 144; "Some
Recent Parodies in Film Music," 297.

Manvell, Roger.
    The Animated Film: With Pictures from the Film Animal Farm. London: Sylvan
    Press, 1954.
Short discussion of Matyas Seiber's score for the 1954 film, 35.

Manvell, Roger.
  Film. Harmondsworth, U.K.: Penguin Books, 1944. Rev. ed., 1946. Rev. ed., 1950.
"Essentials of Film Art: Sound," on the importance of film music, 70–76 (1946, 1950).

Manvell, Roger.
  The Film and the Public. Harmondsworth, U.K.: Penguin Books, 1955.
"Music and the Silent Film," 50–53; "Music and the Sound Film," 57–68.

Manvell, Roger, gen. ed.
  The International Encyclopedia of Film. London: Joseph; New York: Crown, 1972.
"Music and Film," by Manvell and John Gillett, on the silent and sound periods, including films of note and outstanding musicals from 1939 to 1972, 371–74.

Mapp, Edward.
  Directory of Blacks in the Performing Arts. Metuchen, N.J.: Scarecrow Press, 1978.
  2nd ed., 1990.
Includes biographical entries for Duke Ellington and Quincy Jones.

Mapp, T. J. A.
  The Art of Accompanying the Photo-Play. New York: Photo-Play Musical Bureau,
  1917.
A copy of this treatise can be found at the Library of Congress. No further information could be obtained.

Marco, Guy A., ed.
  Encyclopedia of Recorded Sound in the United States. New York: Garland Publishing, 1993.
"Motion Picture Music," on photoplayer and orchestrion manufacturers, 447–48; "Wurlitzer (Rudolph) Co.," on the 1913 "One-Man Orchestra" photoplayer, 777.

Marcus, Kenneth.
  Musical Metropolis: Los Angeles and the Creation of a Music Culture, 1880–1940.
  New York: Palgrave Macmillan, 2004.
A cultural history of music in Los Angeles; includes a discussion of music written for films.

Margolis, Harriet Elaine, ed.
  Jane Campion's The Piano. Cambridge: Cambridge Univ. Press, 2000.
"Music in *The Piano,*" by Claudia Gorbman, contains an analysis of Michael Nyman's score, 42–58. Additional references to the music for the film throughout.

Marill, Alvin H.
  Movies Made for Television: The Telefeature and the Mini-Series, 1964–1979.
  Westport, Conn.: Arlington House, 1980. *Movies Made for Television: The Telefeature and the Mini-Series, 1964–1984.* New York: New York Zoetrope, 1984. *Movies Made for Television: The Telefeature and the Mini-Series, 1964–1986.* New York: New York Zoetrope, 1987.
Most entries contain a music credit; however, composer names are not indexed, so access is by title only.

Markewich, Reese.
The Definitive Bibliography of Harmonically Sophisticated Tonal Music. New York: Author, 1970.
This 55-page pamphlet includes a few film songs by Henry Mancini, Michel Legrand, and others. Alphabetical listings by song title include composer and, if applicable, film title. Each composition was chosen for "harmonic richness" or for moving from one key center to another. Author, a New York jazz musician, compiled the material over a period of twenty years.

Marsh, James H., ed.
The Canadian Encyclopedia. Toronto: McClelland & Stewart, 2000.
"Incidental music," by Kenneth Winters, Patricia Wardrop, and Stephen Willis, includes discussion of film music. (Edition not confirmed.)

Martin, George, ed.
Making Music: The Guide to Writing, Performing and Recording. New York: William Morrow, 1983.
"Dave Grusin: Arranging," 84–85; "John Dankworth: Arranging," 86–88; "Carl Davis: Film Music," 89–93; "Hans Zimmer: Synthesizers," 118–25; "Bernard Krause: Electronic Music," 126–29; "Herbie Hancock: Playing Synthesizers," 130; "Quincy Jones: Producing Records," 286–88 (with material on synthesizers and analog synthesist Paul Beaver); "George Hamer: Session Musicians," 312–14. The Zimmer and Hancock pieces do not discuss film music.

Marvin, Elizabeth West, and Richard Hermann, eds.
Concert Music, Rock, and Jazz Since 1945: Essays and Analytical Studies. Rochester, N.Y.: Univ. of Rochester Press, 1995.
"Stylistic Competencies, Musical Satire, and *This Is Spinal Tap*," by John Rudolph Covach, 399–421.

Masson, Marie-Noëlle, and Gilles Mouëllic, eds.
Musiques et Images au Cinema. Paris: Rennes, 2003.
"Musical Subjectivities in Claude Sautet's *Un coeur en hiver*," by Julie A. Brown, on the use of Ravel's music, 37–48.

Mast, Gerald.
Can't Help Singin': The American Musical on Stage and Screen. Woodstock, N.Y.: Overlook Press, 1987.
Traces the evolution and history of the musical. Each chapter focuses on a specific composer, director, performer, studio, or time period: for example, Irving Berlin, Jerome Kern, George and Ira Gershwin, early sound musicals, Richard Rodgers and Lorenz Hart, Cole Porter, Arthur Freed, MGM. Author is a professor of English.

Mast, Gerald.
Film/Cinema/Movie: A Theory of Experience. New York: Harper & Row, 1977. Chicago: Univ. of Chicago Press, 1983.
"Music" contains a critical essay with an analysis of Herbert Stothart's score for *Camille*, 211–25 (1977).

Mathis, Jack.
   Republic Confidential. Barrington, Ill.: Jack Mathis Advertising, 1999.
A chapter profiling the music department at Republic Pictures (pp. 238–61) covers personnel, the studio orchestra, music department facilities, and music editors, accompanied by lavish visual documentation, including photographs of staff composers. Composers represented include George Antheil, R. Dale Butts, Alberto Colombo, Aaron Copland, Ross DiMaggio, Cy Feuer, Mort Glickman, Raoul Kraushaar, William Lava, Charles Maxwell, Gerald Roberts, Walter Scharf, Morton Scott, Stanley Wilson, and Victor Young.

Mathis, Jack.
   Valley of the Cliffhangers. Northbrook, Ill.: J. Mathis Advertising, 1975.
Sixty-six Republic Pictures serials from 1935 to 1955 are covered, with numerous references to the music—often to specific music cues—based on extensive research and documentation. These serials were twenty-minute chapter plays screened prior to feature films in a dozen or so installments. Most entries include the frames for the opening credits. A table of technical credits includes composers, 440–41. Composers and/or music directors represented include R. Dale Butts, Richard Cherwin, Alberto Colombo, Joseph Dubin, Cy Feuer, Mort Glickman, Harry Grey, Raoul Kraushaar, William Lava, Morton Scott, and Stanley Wilson. A 143-page supplement was published in 1995.

Mattfeld, Julius.
   Variety Music Cavalcade, 1620–1969: A Chronology of Vocal and Instrumental Music Popular in the United States. New York: Prentice Hall, 1952. Rev. ed., Englewood Cliffs, N.J.: Prentice Hall, 1962. 3rd ed. (updated), Englewood Cliffs, N.J.: Prentice Hall, 1971.
Film song titles listed alphabetically by year of publication. Each entry also includes the film title, composer, lyricist, publisher, and copyright date and owner. Brief summaries of political and social events of each time period. At one time published in serial form in *Variety*, and first published in its own right and in complete form in 1952, followed in 1962 by a second, enlarged edition. Compiled by a music arranger and librarian.

Matthew-Walker, Robert.
   From Broadway to Hollywood: The Musical and the Cinema. London: Sanctuary, 1996. 225 pp.
A film-by-film look at approximately thirty musicals written for the Broadway stage and subsequently made into Hollywood films. In three parts: the rise of the film musical, the Golden Age, and the future. The films discussed range from *Anything Goes* to *West Side Story*.

Maxford, Howard.
   Hammer, House of Horror: Behind the Screams. Woodstock, N.Y.: Overlook Press, 1996.
Contains references to the music of Hammer composer James Bernard.

Mayer, Michael F.
   The Film Industries. New York: Hastings House, 1973; 1978.
A "Music and Film" section covers music performing rights, 191–95 (1973), 205–9 (1978).

Maynard, Richard A., ed.
 The Black Man on Film: Racial Stereotyping. Rochelle Park, N.J.: Hatden, 1974.
"How Do We Stand in Hollywood?," a mostly nonmusical discourse by William Grant Still, contains two paragraphs on his experience in Hollywood and the accusation that his music was not authentically "black," 88–91. Reprinted from *Opportunity* (1945).

McBride, Joseph, ed.
 Filmmakers on Filmmaking: The American Film Institute Seminars on Motion Pictures and Television. 2 vols. Los Angeles: J. P. Tarcher, 1983.
Vol. 1 includes "The Composer," a transcription of seminars with Leonard Rosenman in 1975 and 1979, 111–24. Vol. 2 includes "The Composer," a transcription of seminars with Jerry Goldsmith in 1975, 1977, and 1978, 133–46.

McCarthy, Cameron, [et al.], eds.
 Sound Identities: Popular Music and the Cultural Politics of Education. New York: Peter Lang, 1999.
"'No Guarantees': Pedagogical Implications of Music in the Films of Isaac Julien," by Warren E. Crichlow, examines the use of music in *Soul Rebels* (1991) and *The Darker Side of Black* (1994), 363–90.

McClelland, Doug.
 Forties Film Talk: Oral Histories of Hollywood, with 120 Lobby Posters. Jefferson, N.C.: McFarland, 1992.
"David Raksin," interview, 146–50. Also contains anecdotal topical quotes from other composers, including Richard Rodgers, Dimitri Tiomkin, and Harry Warren.

McClelland, Doug.
 The Unkindest Cuts: The Scissors and the Cinema. New York: A. S. Barnes, 1972.
"MGMusical Chairs," on musical numbers and songs cut from films, particularly in foreign versions and, if applicable, subsequent reuse, 157–73.

McDougal, Stuart Y., ed.
 Stanley Kubrick's A Clockwork Orange. Cambridge: Cambridge Univ. Press, 2003.
"Rossini, Purcell, and Ludwig van," 93–103, in "Stanley Kubrick and the Art Cinema," by Krin Gabbard and Shailja Sharma, discusses music in *A Clockwork Orange* (1971) and other Kubrick films, including *Paths of Glory, Dr. Strangelove, Barry Lyndon, Full Metal Jacket,* and *Eyes Wide Shut.* Also discusses Kubrick's use of classical music. "'A Bird of Like Rarest Spun Heavenmetal': Music in *A Clockwork Orange,*" by Peter J. Rabinowitz, focuses on Wendy Carlos's electronic music for the film and how music is used to neutralize violence, 109–30.

McFarlane, Brian, and Anthony Slide, eds.
 The Encyclopedia of British Film. London: Methuen, 2003.
Entries for musicals as well as classical music, original scores, and popular music in British films, 471–74. Notable British composers such as Arthur Benjamin, Muir Mathieson, Stanley Myers, Michael Nyman, William Walton, and Ralph Vaughan Williams have entries consisting of a brief biography with milestone films followed by a list of other British films.

McGee, Mark Thomas.
   The Rock and Roll Movie Encyclopedia of the 1950s. Jefferson, N.C.: McFarland, 1990.
Includes a song-film reference list, 177–184, and a performer-song reference list, 185–194.

McParland, Stephen J.
   It's Party Time: A Musical Appreciation of the Beach Party Film Genre. Australia: John Blair, 1992.
Discusses songs and performers for some thirty films of the genre. Author is an Australian film expert and researcher.

Meeker, May Shaw.
   The Art of Photoplaying... In Operating Any Photoplayer or Double Tracker Piano Players for Theatres. St. Paul, Minn., 1916.
A copy of this treatise can be found at the Library of Congress. No further information could be obtained.

Meikle, Denis.
   A History of Horrors: The Rise and Fall of the House of Hammer. Lanham, Md.: Scarecrow Press, 1996.
Contains references to Hammer composer James Bernard.

Merritt, Greg.
   Film Production: The Complete Uncensored Guide to Independent Filmmaking. Los Angeles: Lone Eagle Publishing, 1998.
"Music," on composers, prerecorded songs, and licensing for low-budget films, 157–61.

Merschmann, Helmut.
   Tim Burton: The Life and Films of a Visionary Director. Translated by Michael Kane. London: Titan Books, 2000.
Discusses the director's collaboration with composer Danny Elfman.

Meyer, Leonard B.
   Emotion and Meaning in Music. Chicago: Univ. of Chicago Press [Phoenix Books], 1956.
"Notes on Image Processes, Connotations and Moods," 256–72. Even though this section does not discuss film music, the topic has practical applications to the art of scoring film. Thus the book is often cited by film studies scholars.

Meyer, William R.
   The Film Buff's Catalog. New Rochelle, N.Y.: Arlington House, 1978.
"Movie Soundtracks," aimed at the novice collector, contains a list of twenty recommended soundtracks with a brief description of each and a short list of soundtracks in print, 405–20.

Miceli, Sergio, Laura Gallenga, and Lena Kokkaliari, eds.
   Norme con ironie: Scritti per i settant'anni di Ennio Morricone. Milan: Suvini Zerboni, 1998.

"Tritonal Crime and 'Music as Music,'" by Philip Tagg, 273–309.

Michaels, Scott, and David Evans.
  Rocky Horror: From Concept to Cult. London: Sanctuary, 2002.
"I Really Love That Rock 'n' Roll," discusses the songs and score for *Rocky Horror Picture Show* and includes an interview with arranger Richard Hartley, 86–102. Also material throughout on songwriter Richard O'Brien and his music and lyrics.

Miell, Dorothy, Raymond MacDonald, and David J. Hargreaves, eds.
  Musical Communication. Oxford: Oxford Univ. Press, 2005.
"The Role of Music Communication in Cinema," by Scott D. Lipscomb and David E. Tolchinsk, 383–404.

Milhaud, Darius.
  My Happy Life. Translated from the French by Donald Evans, George Hall, and Christopher Palmer. London: M. Boyers, 1995.
Translation of the composer's autobiography *Ma vie heureuse* (1974). "Music for the Theater and the Cinema" contains brief material on Milhaud's film scores, 178–87.

Milhaud, Darius.
  Notes without Music. Translated from the French by Donald Evans, edited by Rollo H. Myers. London: Dennis Dobson, 1952. New York: Knopf, 1953. New York: Da Capo Press, 1970.
Translation of the composer's autobiography *Notes sans musiqué* (1949). "Music for the Theater and the Cinema" contains brief material on Milhaud's film scores, 240–42 (1953).

Millard, Andre.
  America on Record: A History of Recorded Sound. Cambridge: Cambridge Univ. Press, 1995.
The "Motion Picture Index" lists two dozen films mentioned in the text, usually in relation to their place in the history of sound, 413.

Miller, Don.
  Hollywood Corral. New York: Popular Library, 1976.
"Have Song—Will Warble," 127–36. Reprinted in Packy Smith and Ed Hulse, eds., *Don Miller's Hollywood Corral: A Comprehensive B-Western Roundup* (1993).

Miller, Marc H., ed.
  Louis Armstrong: A Cultural Legacy. Seattle and London: Queens Museum of Art, New York, in association with Univ. of Washington Press, 1994.
"Louis Armstrong: The Films," an essay by Donald Bogle, 147–79. This catalog accompanied the exhibition of the same name, organized by the Queens Museum of Art (a traveling version was organized and developed by the Smithsonian Institution Traveling Exhibition Service).

Miller, Maud M., ed.
  Winchester's Screen Encyclopedia. London: Winchester, 1948.

"Contemporary Trends in Film Music," by Muir Mathieson, 325–26; "Notable Film Music" and "British Film Music of 1947," compiled by John Huntley, contain line listings of films (title, composer, country, year), 327–29.

Miller, Paul Eduard.
   Miller's Yearbook of Popular Music. Chicago: PEM, 1943.
Aimed at jazz aficionados and those who listen to "hot music." The first part contains biographies on composers, arrangers, and musicians such as Oscar Levant, Billy May, Spud Murphy, David Rose, Raymond Scott, and Meredith Willson.

Mills, Margaret A., Peter J. Claus, and Sarah Diamond, eds.
   South Asian Folklore: An Encyclopedia: Afghanistan, Bangladesh, India, Nepal, Pakistan, Sri Lanka. New York: Routledge, 2003.
Contains an entry for "Film Music."

Mills, May Meskimen.
   The Pipe Organist's Complete Instruction and Reference Work on the Art of Photo-Playing. Philadelphia: Author, 1922.
This 80-page instruction manual attempts to associate individual actors with a particular type of music. A copy can be found at the Free Library of Philadelphia.

Milton, Joyce.
   Tramp: The Life of Charlie Chaplin. New York: HarperCollins, 1996. New York: Da Capo Press, 1998.
This biography includes some discussion of music in Chaplin's films, such as his collaboration with composer David Raksin, 343–45.

Minton, Eric.
   American Musicals, 1929–1933. Ottawa, 1969.
A 75-page collection of *New York Times* reviews of early sound musicals.

Misra, Susheela.
   Musical Heritage of Lucknow. Nai Dilli, India: Harman, 1991.
Survey of the Hindustani musical tradition in Lucknow; includes discussion of Indian film music.

Mitchell, Charles P.
   The Great Composers Portrayed on Film, 1913 through 2002. Jefferson, N.C.: McFarland, 2004.
Each of the sixty or so classical composer entries, arranged in alphabetical order, contains a summary of screen depictions, production credits, and noted documentaries. While most of the screen depictions relate to biographical films, some are for films the composer appeared in and scored, as in the case of Bernard Herrmann. Author is a librarian.

Mitchell, Donald.
   Britten and Auden in the Thirties: The Year 1936. Seattle: Univ. of Washington Press, 1981. London: Faber, 1981. Woodbridge, U.K.; Rochester, N.Y.: Boydell Press, 2000.
Includes a discussion of Britten's early film music, taken from a lecture at the University

of Kent at Canterbury in 1979.

Mitchell, Donald, comp. and ed.
  Benjamin Britten: Death in Venice. Cambridge: Cambridge Univ. Press, 1987.
"Aschenbach Becomes Mahler: Thomas Mann as Film," by Philip Reed, examines director Luchino Visconti's interpretation in the 1971 film, 178–83.

Mitchell, Donald, and Hans Keller, eds.
  Benjamin Britten: A Commentary on His Works from a Group of Specialists. New York: Philosophical Library, 1953.
"The Incidental Music," by William Mann, includes a discussion of Britten's film scores, 295–300. Filmography compiled by Eric Walter White, 312–13.

Mitchell, Tony, and Peter Doyle, eds.
  Changing Sounds: New Directions and Configurations in Popular Music. Sydney: Faculty of Humanities and Social Sciences, University of Technology, 2000.
"Film Songs, Film Singers, and Intertextuality in Hong Kong Popular Song and Cinema: Some Preliminary Observations," by J. Lawrence Witzleben, 416–17. From the International Association for the Study of Popular Music 10th international conference, Sydney, 1999.

Mitry, Jean.
  The Aesthetics and Psychology of the Cinema. Translated by Christopher King. Bloomington: Indiana Univ. Press, 1997. London: Athlone Press, 1998.
The French cinema theoretician discusses French avant-garde film music, image and music, impressionistic music, realism and music, rhythm of music, role of music, signification and music, and use of music in silent and sound films.

Mitsui, Toru, ed.
  Popular Music: Intercultural Interpretations. Kanazawa, Japan: Kanazawa University, 1998.
"The Allure of Sexuality in the Music of *The Jazz Singer* (1927): The Jewish Icon in Blackface Minstrelsy," by Yuko Sato Nakamura, 273–80. From the International Association for the Study of Popular Music's ninth international conference, Japan.

Mize, J. T. H., ed.
  The International Who Is Who in Music. 5th (mid-century) ed. Chicago: Who Is Who in Music, 1951.
Biographical entries for Nat Finston, Johnny Green, Alfred Newman, Richard Rodgers, and Miklós Rózsa, among others.

Monaco, James.
  How to Read a Film: The Art, Technology, Language, History, and Theory of Film and Media. New York: Oxford Univ. Press, 1977. Rev. ed., 1981. 3rd ed., completely rev. and expanded, 2000.
"Film and Music," 37–41 (1977), 54–60 (2000). Contains other references to music and musicals throughout.

Montagu, Ivor.
  Film World: A Guide to Cinema. Baltimore: Penguin Books, 1964.
The filmmaker and critic discusses music and the moving image, 59–61, 155–56, 168–70.

Moore, Dudley.
  Dudley Moore Off-Beat: My World of Music. New York: Arbor House, 1987. Also
  published as *Off Beat: A Musical Companion.* New York: St. Martin's Press, 1993.
Music anecdotes on classical music in "Movie Music," 96–97, and "Movie Madness,"
108–9 (1987).

Morgenstern, Sam, ed.
  Composers on Music: An Anthology of Composers' Writings from Palestrina to Cop-
  land. New York: Pantheon, 1956. New York: Greenwood Press, 1969.
"Films and Music," 525–26, excerpted from Carlos Chavez's *Toward a New Music* (New
York, 1937).

Morrison, Richard.
  Orchestra: The LSO: The London Symphony Orchestra: A Century of Triumph and
  Turbulence. London: Faber and Faber, 2004.
A history of the orchestra. "Film Work," 175–79.

Morros, Boris, as told to Charles Samuels.
  My Ten Years As a Counterspy. New York: Viking Press, 1959.
The Russian-born producer's memoir touches on his early career in film music and as
general music director at Paramount in the 1930s.

Morton, Brian, and Pamela Collins, eds.
  Contemporary Composers. Chicago: St. James Press, 1992.
A dozen entries on composers who have written film scores, including Malcolm Arnold,
Irwin Bazelon, Richard Rodney Bennett, Lennox Berkeley, Leonard Bernstein, Henry
Brant, Aaron Copland, John Corigliano, Philip Glass, Morton Gould, Gunther Schuller,
Stephen Sondheim, Toru Takemitsu, and Virgil Thomson. Brief biographies, comprehen-
sive lists of works (with instrumentation), and short essays. Selected bibliographies and
discographies. The entry for David Bedford lists three film scores, including *The Mission*
(1986), on which he served as choral coordinator.

Motion Picture News.
  Motion Picture News Blue Book. New York: Motion Picture News, 1929.
Includes biographies for music directors, such as Hugo Riesenfeld and Erno Rapée, in-
dexed under "Executives."

Motion Picture Producers and Distributors of America.
  The Men Who Write the Music Scores. Hollywood: MPPDA, 1943. Rev. ed., 1948.
Pamphlet. The Hollywood office of the MPPDA also distributed a five-page circular,
"Music in Films," by Boris Morros, ca. 1940.

Murphy, Spud. [Lyle Stephanovic, better known as Lyle "Spud" Murphy]
  Spud Murphy's Swing Arranging Method. New York: Robbins Music, 1937.

Author was a noted big-band arranger who turned to film music in the late 1930s. From the 1950s until his death in 2005, he promoted the Equal Interval System, a method of composition and arranging of his own device that he taught to students—a number of film composers among them—in the Los Angeles area. He authored a number of self-published books, including *The 12-Tone System: For Composing, Arranging, and Playing of New Creative Ideas and Sounds in Modern Music* (Hollywood, 1952–1957, 5 vols.) and *Advanced Theory: For Qualified Students* (ca. 1972).

Music Teacher's National Association.
> *Proceedings for 1942*. Series 37. Pittsburgh: Music Teacher's National Association, 1943.

"Some Functions and Problems of Film Music," an essay by Bruno David Ussher, in "Report of the Committee on Functional Music," 162–81. A subsequent publication, *Proceedings for 1946*, contains Walter H. Rubsamen's essay, "Descriptive Music for Stage and Screen."

Musiker, Reuben, and Naomi Musiker.
> *Conductors and Composers of Popular Orchestral Music: A Biographical and Discographical Sourcebook*. Westport, Conn.: Greenwood Press, 1998.

Biographical sketches, some with selected discographies, for Richard Addinsell, John Addison, William Alwyn, Harold Arlen, Malcolm Arnold, Burt Bacharach, Warren Barker, John Barry, Les Baxter, Robert Russell Bennett, Irving Berlin, Elmer Bernstein, Leonard Bernstein, Ronald Binge, Stanley Black, Sir Arthur Bliss, Luis Bonfa, Nicholas Brodszky, Nacio Herb Brown, Hoagy Carmichael, Hans Carste, Otto Cesana, Charlie Chaplin, Chappell Mood Music Library, Anthony Collins, Bill Conti, Aaron Copland, Frank Cordell, Alexander Courage, Carl Davis, Frank De Vol, Carmen Dragon, George Duning, Brian Easdale, Duke Ellington, Jack Elliott, Percy Faith, Robert Farnon, George Fenton, John Fox, Benjamin Frankel, Hugo Friedhofer, Rudolf Friml, Joseph Gershenson, George Gershwin, Ernest Gold, Jerry Goldsmith, Ron Goodwin, Morton Gould, Ron Grainer, Allan Gray, John Green, Philip Green, John Greenwood, Dave Grusin, Richard Hayman, Neal Hefti, Victor Herbert, Bernard Herrmann, Johnny Mandel, Muir Mathieson, Nelson Riddle, Raymond Scott, Jack Shaindlin, Wally Stott (Angela Morley), Dimitri Tiomkin, Stanley Wilson, and others. Also contains entries on notable performers who have recorded film arrangements, such as Herman Clebanoff and the Clebanoff Strings, Ray Conniff, Leroy Holmes, and the Hollywood Bowl Orchestra.

Musser, Charles.
> *Before the Nickelodeon: Edwin S. Porter and the Edison Manufacturing Company*. Berkeley: Univ. of California Press, 1991.

Musical accompaniment for the Kinetophone is discussed briefly, 53–55.

Myers, Rollo H., ed.
> *Twentieth Century Music*. London: John Calder, 1960. 2nd ed. (rev. and enlarged), London: Calder & Boyars; New York, Orion Press, 1968.

"Music and the Cinema," by Frederick W. Sternfeld, contains a historical survey of European, British, and American film music primarily composed by concert composers from the 1930s through the 1950s, 95–111 (1960), 123–39 (1968). Topics include Erik Satie's influence on film music. Selected chronological list of film scores, 1907–1958.

Nader, Jerome.
  A Guidebook to the Golden Age of Movie Musicals. N.p., 1972.
A twelve-page booklet on MGM musicals.

Natvig, Mary, ed.
  Teaching Music History. Aldershot, Hants, U.K.: Ashgate, 2002.
"Teaching Film Music in the Liberal Arts Curriculum," by Michael Pisani, 121–43, is an abridged version of his contribution to *Film Music 2* (Claudia Gorbman and Warren M. Sherk, eds.; see entry).

Naumburg, Nancy, ed.
  We Make the Movies. New York: Norton, 1937.
"Scoring the Film," a lengthy essay by Max Steiner on his approach to the film-scoring process written early in his career, 216–38, with Steiner biographical note, 279.

Navasky, Victor S.
  Naming Names. New York: Viking Press, 1980. New York: Penguin Books, 1981.
"The Reasons Why" contains information on David Raksin's testimony to the House Committee on Un-American Activities (HUAC), based on a 1975 interview, 249–52. A transcript of the testimony can be found in *Motion Picture Hearings*, pt. 4, 20 September 1951. Author is a journalist.

Neale, Steve, and Murray Smith, eds.
  Contemporary Hollywood Cinema. London: Routledge, 1998.
"The Classical Film Score Forever? *Batman, Batman Returns* and Post-Classic Film Music," by K. J. Donnelly, examines Danny Elfman's music, 142–55.

Nelmes, Jill, ed.
  An Introduction to Film Studies. London: Routledge, 1996. 2nd ed., London: Rout-
    ledge, 1999. 3rd ed., 2003.
"Music," 110–11 (1996), 77–78 (2003, with additional references to musicals).

Nelson, Thomas Allen.
  Kubrick: Inside a Film Artist's Maze. Bloomington: Indiana Univ. Press, 1982. Rev.
    and expanded ed., 2000.
Music in Kubrick's films, 51–52, 173–75 (1982).

Nestico, Sammy.
  The Complete Arranger. Carlsbad, Calif.: Fenwood Music, 1993.
Author, a career military musician, draws on his experience in commercial jazz and the educational market. He worked for and with television composer Earle Hagen in Hollywood after retiring from the military.

Nettl, Bruno, Ruth M. Stone, James Porter, and Timothy Rice, eds.
  The Garland Encyclopedia of World Music. 10 vols. New York: Garland Publishing,
    1998–2002.
Musicologists write about indigenous music around the globe. While most of the volumes contain only cursory mentions of film music, vol. 5 is particularly detailed in its coverage

of Indian and Bengal film music. The general index in the final volume includes an entry for "Film Music."

Vol. 1. *Africa.*

Vol. 2. *South America, Mexico, Central America, and the Caribbean.*

Vol. 3. *The United States and Canada.*

Vol. 4. *Southeast Asia.*

Vol. 5. *South Asia: The Indian Subcontinent.* "Film Music: Northern Area," by Alison Arnold, 531–41; "Film Music: Southern Area," by Paul D. Greene, 542–46.

Vol. 6. *The Middle East.* Egypt, 552–53; Turkey, 255–56.

Vol. 7. *East Asia: China, Japan, and Korea.* Japan, 749–51.

Vol. 8. *Europe.* Surprisingly few mentions of film music.

Vol. 9. *Australia and the Pacific Islands.*

Vol. 10. *The World's Music: General Perspectives and Reference Tools.*

Neveldine, Robert Burns.
  Bodies at Risk: Unsafe Limits in Romanticism and Postmodernism. Albany, N.Y.: State Univ. of New York Press, 1998.
"Music into the Body: Philip Glass," includes a reading of the music score for *Koyaanisqatsi*, 112–22.

Newcomb, Horace, ed.
  Encyclopedia of Television. Chicago: Fitzroy Dearborn, 1997. 2nd ed., New York: Fitzroy Dearborn, 2004.
"Music Licensing," by Peter B. Orlik, 1567–69; "Music on Television," by Tom McCourt and Nabeel Zuberi, 1569–78 (all 2004).

Newman, Kim, ed.
  Science Fiction/Horror. London: BFI, 2002.
Numerous references on the role of music in science fiction films, particularly those by director Stanley Kubrick.

Newquist, Roy.
  Showcase. New York: Morrow, 1966.
"Calvin Jackson," 211–23. Interview with the arranger, composer, and popular nightclub pianist who worked on MGM musicals in the 1940s and composed for a handful of films into the 1960s.

NewsBank, Inc.
  Film and Television. New Canaan, Conn.: NewsBank, 1975–1997.
This review of the arts contains index listings for "Music and Musicians" and "Musicals" (1980).

Newsom, Iris, ed.
  Wonderful Inventions: Motion Pictures, Broadcasting, and Recorded Sound at the Library of Congress. Washington, D.C.: Library of Congress, 1985.
"'A Sound Idea': Music for Animated Films," by Jon Newsom, 59–79 (reprinted from *Quarterly Journal of the Library of Congress*); "Threads of Melody: The Evolution of a Major Film Score—Walt Disney's *Bambi*," by Ross B. Care, analysis and music exam-

ples, 80–115; "David Raksin: A Composer in Hollywood," by Jon Newsom, 116–57 (reprinted from *QJLC*); "Life with Charlie," by David Raksin, 158–71 (reprinted from *QJLC*); "'A Bugle Call to Arms for National Defense!' Victor Herbert and His Score for *The Fall of a Nation*," by Wayne D. Shirley, 172–85 (reprinted from *QJLC*); "Golden Voices, Silver Screen: Opera Singers as Movie Stars," by David L. Parker, 186–96; "Music for *Star Trek*: Scoring a Television Show in the Sixties," by Fred Steiner, on his own music and that of his contemporaries Alexander Courage, George Duning, Jerry Fielding, Gerald Fried, and Sol Kaplan, 286–309.

Newsom, Jon, and Alfred Mann, eds.
  The Rosaleen Moldenhauer Memorial: Music History from Primary Sources: A Guide to the Moldenhauer. Washington, D.C.: Library of Congress, 2000.
"Arthur Honegger's *Les Ombres*: Fragment of a Lost Film Score," by Fred Steiner, 266–71.

Nicholls, David, ed.
  The Cambridge History of American Music. Cambridge: Cambridge Univ. Press, 1998.
"Popular Song and Popular Music on Stage and Film," by Stephen David Banfield, 309–44.

Nicoll, Allardyce.
  Film and Theatre. New York: Thomas Y. Crowell, 1936. London: Harrup, 1939.
"Musical Accompaniment," on the sound film, by a Yale professor of drama, 125–28.

Nisbett, Alec.
  The Sound Studio: Audio Techniques for Radio, Television, Film and Recording. 7th ed. Boston: Focal Press, 2003. Also published as *The Technique of the Sound Studio for Radio, Television, and Film.* New York: Focal Press, 1962. 3rd ed., rev., New York: Hastings House, 1972.
"Theme and Background Music," 235–36 (2003); except for a few pages on music in relation to production, the music topics here are peripheral to film. The material on music balance, while not limited to film music, may be of interest.

Noble, Peter, ed.
  British Film Yearbook, 1947–48. London: British Yearbooks, 1948.
"Music and the Film Script," by Ernest Irving, 47–52. The next yearbook (1949–1950) includes "Film Music in Britain," by John Huntley, 39–51. Subsequent yearbooks (into the 1980s) contain no music articles.

Noble, Peter.
  The Negro in Films. London: S. Robinson, 1948. Reprint, New York: Arno Press, 1970.
"Song," on black musicians and performers, 80–90.

Noblitt, Thomas, ed.
  Music East and West: Essays in Honor of Walter Kaufmann. New York: Pendragon Press, 1981.
"Bibliography of Walter Kaufmann's Works" includes a list of film scores, 381–86.

Kaufmann was a composer and conductor at Arthur Rank Films in the mid-1940s.

Nyman, Michael.
> *Experimental Music: Cage and Beyond.* New York: Schirmer Books, 1974. London: Studio Vista, 1974. New York: Schirmer Books, 1981. 2nd ed., Cambridge: Cambridge Univ. Press, 1999.

Contains no coverage of film music and is of interest only because few film composers have written books on general music topics. After the book's original publication, Nyman went on to found the Michael Nyman Band and forge a career as a film composer.

Oderman, Stuart.
> *Talking to the Piano Player: Silent Film Stars, Writers and Directors Remember.* Boalsburg, Penn.: BearManor Media, 2005.

Conversations with silent-film performers; however, none include the subject of music in their recollections. Author is a modern-day silent film accompanist.

Ohl, Vicki.
> *Fine & Dandy: The Life and Work of Kay Swift.* New Haven, Conn.: Yale Univ. Press, 2004.

Biography of the songwriter, who had a tangential relationship to film music.

Oja, Carol J., and Judith Tick, eds.
> *Aaron Copland and His World.* Princeton, N.J.: Princeton Univ. Press, 2005.

"Aaron Copland, Norman Rockwell, and the 'Four Freedoms': The Office of War Information's Vision and Sound in *The Cummington Story* (1945)," by Neil Lerner, 351–77.

Oland, Pamela Phillips.
> *The Art of Writing Great Lyrics.* New York: Allworth Press, 2001.

Contains anecdotes on writing on spec and on opening-title songs versus end-title songs, 204–13. Revised and expanded edition of *You Can Write Great Lyrics* (Cincinnati: Writer's Digest Books, 1989). Author is a film and television lyricist.

Oldham, Gabriella.
> *First Cut: Conversations with Film Editors.* Berkeley: Univ. of California Press, 1992.

Numerous references to film music.

Oliphant, Dave, and Thomas Zigal, eds.
> *Perspectives on Music: Essays on Collections at the Humanities Research Center.* Austin: Humanities Research Center, University of Texas, 1985.

"The Music for David O. Selznick's Production No. 103," by William Penn, on Dimitri Tiomkin's score for *Duel in the Sun*, 157–87.

Orledge, Robert.
> *Charles Koechlin (1867–1950): His Life and Works.* Chur, Switzerland: Harwood Academic Publishers, 1989.

Includes a discussion of the French composer's film scores. Author wrote his 1973 dissertation on Koechlin, then went on to become a leading scholar of early-twentieth-century French music.

Otfinoski, Steven.
　　The Golden Age of Rock Instrumentals. New York: Billboard, 1997.
Examines nonvocal popular music between 1955 and 1966, including motion picture and television series theme songs.

Parakilas, James, with E. Douglas Bomberger and others.
　　Piano Roles: Three Hundred Years of Life with the Piano. New Haven, Conn.: Yale Univ. Press, 1999.
"Preview: Silent Movies with Piano," by Michael Chanan, 324–27.

Parish, James Robert, and Michael R. Pitts.
　　Hollywood Songsters. New York: Garland, 1991. *Hollywood Songsters: Singers Who Act and Actors Who Sing: A Biographical Dictionary.* 2nd ed. 3 vols. New York: Routledge, 2003.
Second edition contains entries on more than 100 performers, with filmography and discography for each, documenting on- and off-camera musical performances. Index includes personal names and film titles, followed by a song and album index.

Parisi, Paula.
　　Titanic and the Making of James Cameron. New York: Newmarket Press, 1998.
On composer James Horner's collaboration with James Cameron, Horner's fee and soundtrack royalties, and the Academy Award-winning hit song, 163–66, 179–80, 193–96.

Parks, Gordon.
　　Voices in the Mirror: An Autobiography. New York: Doubleday, 1990. New York: Anchor Books, 1992. New York: Harlem Moon, 2005.
Author was involved with the music for several films, including *Shaft.*

Parlett, Graham.
　　A Catalogue of the Works of Sir Arnold Bax. Oxford: Oxford Univ. Press, 1999.
This chronology includes film music, with manuscript dates, makeup of the orchestra, performances, arrangements, adaptations, lengthy historical notes, and details from the manuscript, often including cue titles. Soundtracks listed in an appendix of recordings.

Parsons, Denys, comp.
　　Musical Appreciation: A List of Audio and Visual Aids. Pamphlet. London: British Film Institute, 1948. 15 pp.

Pasquariello, Nicholas.
　　Sounds of Movies: Interviews with the Creators of Feature Sound Tracks. San Francisco: Port Bridge Books, 1996.
Interviews with sound mixers on production and postproduction mixing. Interview with director Bertrand Tavernier and composer Ron Carter on their collaboration on *Beatrice* (1988).

Passman, Donald S.
　　All You Need to Know about the Music Business. Prentice Hall, 1991. 5th ed., rev. and updated. New York: Free Press, 2003.

"Motion Picture Music," on performer deals, songwriter deals, and composer agreements, 395–434 (1991), 383–417 (2003); "Music Supervisors," 418–20 (2003); "Sound Track Album Deals," 421–25 (2003).

Pasternak, Joe, as told to David Chandler.
   Easy the Hard Way. London: W. H. Allen, 1951. New York: Putnam, 1956.
The producer's autobiography. In the chapter "Music for Millions," Pasternak reminisces about music-related films at Universal, including music director Charles Previn, conductor Leopold Stokowski, and pianist Jose Iturbi, 184–98 (1951).

Patterson, Hannah, ed.
   Poetic Visions of America: The Cinema of Terrence Malick. London: Wallflower Press, 2003.
"Sound as Music in the Films of Terrence Malick," by James Wierzbicki, 110–22.

Paynter, John, and others, eds.
   Companion to Contemporary Musical Thought. 2 vols. London: Routledge, 1992.
"Music and Image on Film and Video: An Absolute Alternative," by David Kershaw, 466–99 (in vol. 1).

Pejrolo, Andrea.
   Creative Sequencing Techniques for Music Production: A Practical Guide for Logic, Digital Performer, Cubase and Pro Tools. Oxford and Boston: Elsevier/Focal Press, 2005.
"Elements of MIDI Orchestration" has practical applications related to film music.

Pendakur, Manjunath.
   Indian Popular Cinema: Industry, Ideology, and Consciousness. Cresskill, N.J.: Hampton Press, 2003.
Contains a chapter on film music with subheadings: "Pleasure and Popularity," 119–22; "Film Music Industry," 123–25; "Aesthetic of the Song," 126–30; "Major Types of Songs," 131–37; "Hybrid Music and National Consciousness," 138; "Background Score," 139–42; and "Conclusion" and "Endnotes," 143.

Pendergast, Tom, and Sara Pendergast, eds.
   The International Dictionary of Films and Filmmakers. 4th ed. Vol. 4, *Writers and Production Artists*. Detroit: St. James Press, 2000.
New to this edition are Richard Addinsell, Angelo Badalamenti, Richard Rodney Bennett, Carter Burwell, Bill Conti, Danny Elfman, Dave Grusin, Michel Legrand, Johnny Mandel, Thomas Newman, and Hans Zimmer. See the entry for the previous edition, edited by Grace Jeromski, for a full list of composers.

Pepperman, Richard D.
   The Eye Is Quicker: Film Editing: Making a Good Film Better. Studio City, Calif.: Michael Wiese Productions, 2004.
Brief discussion of music, including tempo, pacing, and use of rhythm in editing, 208–9.

Perriam, Chris, and Ann Davies, eds.
   Carmen: *From Silent Film to MTV*. Amsterdam: Rodopi, 2005.

Essays include "Space, Time and Gender in the Film d'Art *Carmen* of 1910," by Nicholas Till, 9–22; "Geraldine Farrar and Cecil B. DeMille: The Effect of Opera on Film and Film on Opera in 1915," by Gillian B. Anderson, 23–36; "*Carmen* and Early Cinema: The Case of Jacques Feyder (1926)," by Winifred Woodhull, 37–60; "Cinematic Carmen and the 'Oeil Noir,'" by Jeremy Tambling, 167–88.

Perry, Louis B., and Richard S. Perry.
    A History of the Los Angeles Labor Movement, 1911–1941. Berkeley: Univ. of California Press, 1963.
The chapter "Union Success in the Movie Industry" contains material on musicians.

Philip, Hans-Erik.
    The Filmsound as Means of Expression. Copenhagen: National Film School of Denmark, 1980.
This 85-page pamphlet contains an interview with Ennio Morricone from a seminar held at the school in December 1980.

Phillips, Gene D., and Rodney Hill.
    The Encyclopedia of Stanley Kubrick. New York: Facts on File, 2002.
Entries on the Chieftains (folk music), 44–46; Wendy Carlos, 40–42; Gerald Fried, 124–27; Alex North, 267–70; Nelson Riddle, 299–300; Jocelyn Pook, 292–93; Leonard Rosenman, 300–301. Film title entries often mention music.

Phillips, Mark.
    Heinemann GCSE Music. Oxford: Heinemann Educational, 2002.
British secondary school textbook. The chapter "Music for Film," 122–35, briefly discusses the use of a Rachmaninoff piano concerto in *Brief Encounter* (1945), Bernard Herrmann's music for *Psycho* (1960), Elmer Bernstein's music for *The Magnificent Seven* (1960), Michael Nyman's music for *The Draughtsman's Contract* (1982), and Ennio Morricone's music for *The Mission* (1986). Contains background on the film, music examples, and listening tasks.

Phillips, Ray.
    Edison's Kinetoscope and Its Films: A History to 1896. Westport, Conn.: Greenwood Press, 1997.
The chapter "Sound Is Added: The Kinetophone" includes a list, possibly the only surviving one of its type, of appropriate musical cylinders for specific Kinetophone films, 83.

Photoplay Research Society.
    Opportunities in the Motion Picture Industry, and How to Qualify for Positions in Its Many Branches. 3 vols. Los Angeles: Photoplay Research Society, Bureau of Vocational Guidance, 1922.
"Making Musical Adaptations," by Joseph Carl Breil, cites, as necessary traits, musical ability and improvisation combined with selecting music that fits the film emotionally, 85–87, in vol. 2.

Pickard, Roy.
    A Companion to the Movies: From 1903 to the Present Day. A Guide to the Leading Players, Directors, Screenwriters, Composers, Cameramen and Other Artistes Who

Have Worked in the English-Speaking Cinema over the Last 70 Years. London: Lutterworth Press, 1972. New York: Hippocrene Books, 1974. Rev. and updated ed., London: F. Muller, 1979.

"Famous Music Scores: A Check List," 257–64; "Musicals," 109–15, and who's who of musicals, 116–38 (all 1974); capsule biographies for composers appear in various sections.

Pinch, Trevor, and Frank Trocco.
   Analog Days: The Invention and Impact of the Moog Synthesizer. Cambridge, Mass.: Harvard Univ. Press, 2002.

Although this work is not directly related to film music, there is material on synthesists who worked in film, including Paul Beaver, Wendy Carlos, and Suzanne Ciani, and on the predigital machines of the 1970s, including the Moog, Minimoog, and ARP.

Pinne, Peter.
   Australian Performers, Australian Performances: A Discography from Film, TV, Theatre, Radio, and Concert, 1897–1985. Melbourne: Performing Arts Museum, Victorian Arts Centre, 1987.

According to FIAF, this book contains "fairly extensive essays on the use of music in Australian film and television." Author is an Australian composer who specializes in musical theater.

Pirie, David, ed.
   Anatomy of the Movies. New York: Macmillan, 1981.

"Film Music and Composers," by Colin Vaines, a historical overview with a section on symphonic scores in the 1970s, 192–97; "Musicals," by Geoff Brown, 252–61.

Pisani, Michael V.
   Imagining Native America in Music. New Haven, Conn.: Yale Univ. Press, 2005.

"Underscoring Ancestry: Music for Native America in Film," 292–332.

Pitts, Michael R., and Louis H. Harrison.
   Hollywood on Record: The Film Stars' Discography. Metuchen, N.J.: Scarecrow Press, 1978.

Lists recorded works of motion picture performers since 1948, with record title, label, and catalog number. Entries are alphabetical by performer and are further broken down into LPs, soundtracks, and compilation LPs. For example, the entry on pianist Jose Iturbi lists two soundtracks, three compilation LPs, and a dozen LPs. Excludes soundtrack albums consisting of background music.

Plantinga, Carl, and Greg M. Smith, eds.
   Passionate Views: Film, Cognition, and Emotion. Baltimore: Johns Hopkins Univ. Press, 1999.

"Movie Music as Moving Music: Emotion, Cognition, and the Film Score," by Jeff Smith, on the emotive use of music in *The Elephant Man* and *A Clockwork Orange*, 146–67.

Platts, Robin.
   Burt Bacharach & Hal David: What the World Needs Now. Burlington, Ontario, Canada: Collector's Guide Publishing, 2002. 232 pp.
Includes biographical information from archival research and interviews with the subjects, an annotated songography, and a selected discography. Author is a music journalist who lives in Canada.

Plummer, Mary.
   Soundtrack. Berkeley, Calif.: Peachpit Press, 2004.
On how to create original scores for video, DVD, and the Internet using the computer software Soundtrack, which allows the user to create "songs."

Polanski, Roman.
   Roman. New York: Morrow, 1984.
Numerous personal references to Christopher Komeda, the director's friend and musical collaborator.

Polish, Mark, Michael Polish, and Jonathan Sheldon.
   The Declaration of Independent Filmmaking: An Insider's Guide to Making Movies Outside of Hollywood. Orlando: Harcourt, 2005.
"Music" on collaborating with a composer, scoring the mood, low-budget scores, and licensing recorded music, 215–25. Contributions from British composer Stuart Matthewman.

Pollard, Elizabeth Watson.
   Teaching Motion-Picture Appreciation: A Manual for Teachers of High-School Classes. [Columbus]: Bureau of Educational Research, Ohio State University, 1933–1935.
"Sound and Music" contains a cursory look at music, 52–53.

Pratt, George C.
   Spellbound in Darkness: A History of the Silent Film. Greenwich, Conn.: New York Graphic Society, 1966. Rev. ed., 1973.
Contains some excerpts related to film music, reprinted from various periodicals. See "The Importance of the Musical Accompaniment" (*The New York Dramatic Mirror*, 1909), 63; "Comes Stravinsky to the Film Theater" (*Musical America*, 1921). Discussion of S. L. Rothapfel's compiled score for *The Cabinet of Dr. Caligari*, 358–59. Part of the chapter "'Thunder Drum for All Four Horsemen': Presentation" has material on musical accompaniment and musical presentation, 477–83 (all 1973).

Price, Michael H.
   The Big Country: *The Film.* N.p.: Screen Classics, 1990.
"The Music," by John Caps, 30–45; "The Composer," by John Caps, 46–62. May be considered liner notes, as it accompanied a CD of the soundtrack; however, this 63-page LP-size illustrated booklet looks at Jerome Moross and his score and lists the orchestra personnel.

Prokofiev, Sergei.
   Ivan the Terrible [title is in Russian]. Gamburg [Hamburg]: Sikorski, 1997.

Complete orchestral film score, with chorus and soloists, for Sergei Eisenstein's film. "Ivan the Terrible by Prokofiev—Eisenstein" contains historical notes, 26–31; "Commentary" for each musical number, 246–50; "Suggested Order for Concert Performances," 251–53; "The Manuscript Sources of *Ivan the Terrible*," 253–55. At the time of publication, this was the only extant example of a complete published film score, according to music librarian H. Stephen Wright.

Pudovkin, V. I.
> *Film Technique and Film Acting: The Cinema Writings of V. I. Pudovkin.* Translated by Ivor Montagu. New York: Bonanza Books, 1949. Rev. memorial ed., London: Vision Press, 1958.

The director discusses the music of Shaporin in one of his films, 93–95 (1949), 310–13 (1958).

Radic, Therese, ed.
> *Repercussions: Australian Composing Women's Festival and Conference, 1994.* Clayton, Australia: Monash University National Centre for Australian Studies, 1995.

"Where Eagles Dare: Aspects of the Documentary Film Music of Moneta Eagles," by Diane Napthali, 49–52.

Ramachandran, T. M., ed.
> *70 Years of Indian Cinema (1913–1983).* Bombay: Cinema India-International, 1985.

"Indian Film Song," by Bhaskar Chandavarkar, 244–51.

Ramsaye, Terry.
> *A Million and One Nights.* New York: Simon & Schuster, 1926. Reprint, London: Frank Cass, 1964.

An early history of Hollywood, including material on music director Hugo Riesenfeld, 723–25; and on Sam Katz, a nickelodeon pianist in 1906, 828–29.

Ramsey, Guthrie P., Jr.
> *Race Music: Black Cultures from Bebop to Hip-Hop.* Berkeley: Univ. of California Press, 2003.

Includes the chapter "Scoring a Black Nation: Music, Film, and Identity in the Age of Hip-Hop."

Ranson, P., comp.
> *"By Any Other Name": A Guide to the Popular Names and Nicknames of Classical Music, and to the Theme Music in Films, Radio, Television and Broadcast Advertisements.* 4th ed. North Shields: North Tyneside Libraries and Arts Department, 1978. 70 pp.

This 70-page mimeographed publication includes theme music for U.K. radio and television.

Rapf, Joanna E., ed.
> *On the Waterfront.* Cambridge: Cambridge Univ. Press, 2003.

"Leonard Bernstein and *On the Waterfront*: Tragic Nobility, A Lyrical Song, and Music of Violence," by Jon Burlingame, 124–47. An account, based on interviews and extensive research, of the scoring of Bernstein's only film score (for the 1954 film). Includes a cue-by-cue rundown of the music.

Rawlings, F.
  How to Choose Music for Amateur Films. London: Focal Press, 1955. 127 pp. 2nd ed., London: Focal Press, 1961. 128 pp.
This British handbook is similar in content to 1920s silent film performance manuals, except that the mood music is for sound films and the source is disc recordings. Music classifications such as "Romantic," "Pastoral," and "Water Scenes" and topics such as tempo, atmosphere, theme music, and timing parallel the earlier manuals. Chapters on background music, applying mood music, recorded mood music, and international music. Short list of incidental film music on record, including 78s and LPs. Aimed at amateur filmmakers seeking music for their productions.

Ray, Don B.
  Orchestration Handbook: Essential Guide to Every Instrument in the Orchestra. Milwaukee: Hal Leonard, 2000. 72 pp. Los Angeles: Periphera, 1983. 60 pp.
Information on every instrument in the orchestra, including clef, range, timbre, transposition, and special effects. Brief information on synchronizing film music, including film conversion charts and click tracks (information and tables). Author is a television composer and taught an influential UCLA Extension course in the early 1980s.

Raymond, Jack.
  Show Music on Record: From the 1890s to the 1980s. New York: F. Ungar, 1982.
Chronological listings include film and television productions of stage shows with songs.

Rayner, Jonathan.
  The Films of Peter Weir. London: Cassell, 1998.
Numerous references to the use of music in the director's films and to his frequent collaborator, Maurice Jarre.

Rebello, Stephen.
  Alfred Hitchcock and the Making of Psycho. New York: Dembner Books, 1990. New York: St. Martin's Griffin, 1998.
Bernard Herrmann's score is discussed in "Sounds and Music," 136–39. Contains other references to the score.

Recording Musicians Association, Los Angeles Chapter.
  Directory. Los Angeles: RMA, 1980s–present.
Provides contact information for studio musicians and recording industry support services. Published annually every June. The RMA was incorporated in 1983 to fight for effective representation within the American Federation of Musicians union regarding contract negotiations, pensions, and other issues affecting professional recording musicians. The 2003 directory lists more than 1,000 musicians and composers and includes National Recording Agreement summaries, music preparation charts, and a comprehensive list of Los Angeles-area scoring stages and recording studios. For a history of RMA, see Jon Burlingame's *For the Record* (1997).

Redepenning, Dorothea, and Annette Kreutziger-Herr, eds.
  Mittelalter-Sehnsucht? Texte des Interdisziplinären Symposions zur Musikalischen Mittelalterrezeption an der Universität Heidelberg. Kiel: Wissenschaftsverlag Vauk, 2000.
"Hearing Illusions: A Problem of Using Early Music in Period Films," by Linda Schubert, 57–70. From a 1998 symposium in Germany on medieval influences on music.

Reed, Rex.
  Valentines & Vitriol. New York: Delacorte, 1977.
"Marvin Hamlisch," a personal account by the film critic, 230–34.

Reed, Tom.
  The Black Music History of Los Angeles, Its Roots: 50 Years in Black Music: A Classical Pictorial History of Los Angeles Black Music of the 20's, 30's, 40's, 50's and 60's: Photographic Essays That Define the People, the Artistry and Their Contributions to the Wonderful World of Entertainment. Los Angeles: Black Accent on L.A. Press, 1992.
Material on composers and musicians, George "Red" Callender (studio musician), Benny Carter, Joe Greene, Jester Hairston, Quincy Jones, Oliver Nelson, William Grant Still, and Marl Young.

Reid, Mark A., ed.
  Spike Lee's Do the Right Thing. Cambridge: Cambridge Univ. Press, 1997.
"Polyphony and Cultural Expression: Interpreting Musical Traditions in *Do the Right Thing*," by Victoria E. Johnson, 50–72. Revision of an article published in *Film Quarterly* (Winter 1993–94).

Reinhart, Mark S.
  The Batman Filmography: Live-Action Features, 1943–1997. Jefferson, N.C.: McFarland, 2005.
Mentions music by Danny Elfman, Elliot Goldenthal, Neal Hefti, Nelson Riddle, and Lee Zahler, 76–77, 121–22, 125, 186.

Reis, Brian.
  Australian Film: A Bibliography. London; Washington, D.C.: Mansell, 1997.
Includes bibliographic entries for music, particularly for articles in *Cinema Papers*, 73–77.

Reis, Claire R.
  Composers, Conductors, and Critics. New York: Oxford Univ. Press, 1955. Reprint, Detroit: Detroit Reprints in Music, 1974.
History of the New York-based League of Composers. Reis was executive director. The chapter "Music and Electricity" contains a section on the league's programming of film music concerts in the 1940s, with references to George Antheil, Marc Blitzstein, Paul Bowles, Aaron Copland, Louis Gruenberg, Roy Harris, Bernard Herrmann, Werner Janssen, Douglas Moore, Virgil Thomson, and Ernst Toch, see pp. 126–31. Film music-related references to Robert Russell Bennett, Leonard Bernstein, and Lawrence Morton. Aaron Copland wrote an article on Reis for *Musical Quarterly* upon her death in 1978.

Reis, Claire R.
  Composers in America: Biographical Sketches of Contemporary Composers with a Record of Their Works. Rev. and enlarged ed. New York: Macmillan, 1947. New York: Da Capo Press, 1977.
Author is regarded as the first encyclopedist to introduce film music into the American mainstream. The biographical entries list approximately 375 films by seventy-five composers, with Hollywood films, art films, and documentaries fairly equally represented. Each short biographical sketch is followed by a selected list of concert works and film music, with concert suites or concert versions often noted. The 1947 edition includes entries on Daniele Amfitheatrof, George Antheil, Louis Applebaum, Richard Arnell, Stanley Bate, Marion Eugenie Bower, William Bergsma, Marc Blitzstein, Paul Bowles, Henry Brant, David Buttolph, Mario Castelnuovo-Tedesco, Aaron Copland, Henry Cowell, Paul Creston, Paul Dessau, Adolph Deutsch, David Diamond, Hanns Eisler, Lehman Engel, Amedeo de Filippi, Jerzy Fitelberg, Edwin Gerschefski, George Gershwin, Vittorio Giannini, Morton Gould, Johnny Green, Louis Gruenberg, Richard Hageman, Leigh Harline, Roy Harris, Charles Haubiel, Bernard Herrmann, Werner Heymann, Werner Janssen, Erich Wolfgang Korngold, Arthur Kreutz, Gail Kubik, Dai-Keong Lee, Oscar Levant, Robert Guyn McBride, Frances McCollin, Colin McPhee, Michel Michelet, Darius Milhaud, Cyril Mockridge, Douglas Moore, Jerome Moross, Alfred Newman, Alex North, David Raksin, Karol Rathaus, Earl Robinson, Bernard Rogers, Miklós Rózsa, Irving Schlein, William Schuman, Nathaniel Shilkret, Elie Siegmeister, Leo Smit, Willy Stahl, Max Steiner, Alexander Steinert, William Grant Still, Herbert Stothart, Alexandre Tansman, Virgil Thomson, Dimitri Tiomkin, Ernst Toch, John Verrall, Edward Ward, Franz Waxman, Roy Webb, Kurt Weill, Stefan Wolpe, Victor Young, and Eugene Zador. Contains previously published material from the author's *American Composers of To-Day*, 1930, and *American Composers: A Record of Works Written Between 1912 and 1932*, 1932, 2nd ed. A previous edition, *Composers in America: Biographical Sketches of Living Composers with a Record of Their Works, 1912–1937* (New York: Macmillan, 1938), listed only twenty-three films by eleven composers, including Antheil, Janssen, and Levant.

Rentschler, Eric, ed.
  West German Filmmakers on Film: Visions and Voices. New York: Holmes & Meier, 1988.
"Emotion Pictures (Slowly Rockin' On)," by director Wim Wenders, discusses the importance of music in American film, 42–44. Originally appeared in *Filmkritik* (May 1970).

Rhodes, Gary D.
  White Zombie: *Anatomy of a Horror Film*. Jefferson, N.C.: McFarland, 2001.
"Choosing *White Zombie*'s Music," discusses Abe Meyer, his Meyer Synchronizing Service, and the tracked music, 108–11.

Richards, Emil, comp.
  World of Percussion: A Catalog of Over 200 Standard, Ethnic, & Special Musical Instruments & Effects. [Los Angeles], 1970. 39 pp.
  World of Percussion: A Catalog of 300 Standard, Ethnic, and Special Musical Instruments and Effects. Sherman Oaks, Calif.: Gwyn, 1972. 94 pp.

A catalog for film and television composers. Includes a one-page biography of the author, a longtime session musician and percussionist. The 1970 edition was produced by Robert G. Bornstein, Paramount studios supervising music copyist.

Richards, Jeffrey.
   Films and British National Identity: From Dickens to Dad's Army. Manchester, U.K., and New York: Manchester Univ. Press/St. Martin's Press, 1997.
"Vaughan Williams, The Cinema and England," on the composer's place in British film music and a survey of his oeuvre, 283–325.

Riddle, Nelson.
   Arranged by Nelson Riddle: The Definitive Study of Arranging by America's #1 Composer, Arranger, and Conductor. Secaucus, N.J.: Warner Bros., 1985.
A primer for budding arrangers. "Personal and Musical Observations," 164–80, is a biographical career overview with references to the author's film and television music. "Music for Film," 143–63, contains a brief commentary and a Nelson music sketch and orchestration of a cue from the television series *Mickey Spillane's Mike Hammer.* Includes a three-page biography of Nelson.

Rieuwerts, Sigrid, and Helga Stein, eds.
   Bridging the Cultural Divide: Our Common Ballad Heritage. Hildesheim: Olms, 2000.
"Songs in *The Last Relic* and Their Visual Interpretation in Film," based on a paper delivered by Loone Ots at the 1998 International Ballad Conference in Germany, discusses songs composed by Uno and Tonu Naissoo for the 1969 film, 324–36.

Riley, Philip J., ed.
   MagicImage Filmbooks presents The Bride of Frankenstein. Universal Filmscripts Series, Classic Horror Films, vol. 2. Abesecon, N.J.: MagicImage Filmbooks, 1989.
The books in this series contain the film's shooting script and production background. References to Franz Waxman's score for the 1935 film, 33–34.

Riley, Philip J., ed.
   MagicImage Filmbooks presents Dracula. Universal Filmscripts Series, Classic Horror Films, vol. 13. Abesecon, N.J.: MagicImage Filmbooks, 1990.
"Music" contains material from William Rosar's article in the *Quarterly Journal of the Library of Congress* regarding the score compiled by music director Heinz Roemheld for the 1931 film, 69–71.

Riley, Philip J., ed.
   MagicImage Filmbooks presents Frankenstein Meets the Wolf Man. Universal Filmscripts Series, Classic Horror Films, vol. 5. Atlantic City, N.J.: MagicImage Filmbooks, 1990.
"Music," with conductor score excerpts of Hans Salter's music for the 1942 film, 41–43.

Riley, Philip J., ed.
   MagicImage Filmbooks presents The Ghost of Frankenstein. Universal Filmscripts Series, Classic Horror Films, vol. 4. Atlantic City, N.J.: MagicImage Filmbooks, 1990.

Foreword by Hans J. Salter, who composed the music for the 1942 film, 11–13; "Music Department" includes the conductor score for one cue, 43–45.

Riley, Philip J., ed.
> *MagicImage Filmbooks presents* House of Frankenstein. Universal Filmscripts Series, Classic Horror Films, vol. 6. Atlantic City, N.J.: MagicImage Filmbooks, 1991.

"Music" includes the conductor score for one cue by Hans Salter, 37–41.

Riley, Philip J., ed.
> *MagicImage Filmbooks presents* This Island Earth. Universal Filmscripts Series, Classic Horror Films, vol. 1. Atlantic City, N.J.: MagicImage Filmbooks, 1990.

Music is briefly covered, 37; with examples, 44–45.

Riley, Philip J., ed.
> *MagicImage Filmbooks presents* The Wolf Man. Universal Filmscripts Series, Classic Horror Films, vol. 12. Absecon, N.J.: MagicImage Filmbooks, 1993.

"The Music of *The Wolf Man*," by concert composer Joseph Marcello, contains analysis and extensive music examples of the music by Frank Skinner, Hans J. Salter, and Charles Previn for the 1941 film, 65–90. Includes a typeset short score of Jimmy McHugh's 1939 Universal signature logo.

Rivkin, Allen, and Laura Kerr.
> *Hello, Hollywood! A Book about the Movies by the People Who Make Them.* New York: Doubleday, 1962.

"I Can Still Hear the Music," an essay by Johnny Green, calls for the courageous use of music and laments the low-level dubbing of music, often at the producer's request, 329–32. Green is introduced by Rivkin and Kerr, 328.

Roach, Hildred.
> *Black American Music: Past and Present.* Boston: Crescendo, 1973. Rev. ed., 1976. Malabar, Fla.: R. E. Krieger, 1985. 2nd ed., 1992.

Biographical sketches of Duke Ellington, Jester Hairston, Herbie Hancock, Hall Johnson, Quincy Jones, John Lewis, and William Grant Still.

Robertson, Patrick.
> *Movie Facts and Feats: A Guinness Record Book.* New York: Sterling, 1980.

Film music firsts, primarily in the United Kingdom, are listed under "Music," 175–79. The same material with some updates can be found in the 2nd ed., *Guinness Film Facts and Feats* (1985), 150–53; 3rd ed., *Guinness Movie Facts and Feats* (1988), 156–59; and 4th ed., *The Guinness Book of Movie Facts and Feats* (1991), 162–65; *The Guinness Book of Movie Facts and Feats* (New York: Abbeville Press, 1993); and *Film Facts* (New York: Billboard Books, 2001), 178–82.

Robinson, Alice M.
> *Betty Comden and Adolph Green: A Bio-Bibliography.* Westport, Conn.: Greenwood Press, 1994.

"Films for Which Comden and Green Wrote the Screenplay and/or the Lyrics," 147–96.

Robinson, David.
:   *From Peep Show to Palace: The Birth of American Film.* New York: Columbia Univ. Press, 1996.
"Music," 1913, is documented, 171–74. Scattered references to music and musicians throughout.

Robinson, Earl, with Eric A. Gordon.
:   *Ballad of an American: The Autobiography of Earl Robinson.* Lanham, Md.: Scarecrow Press, 1998.
Documents Robinson's film work from 1938 to 1968, primarily on his songwriting (and on some of his underscores) and his struggle to get established in Hollywood. "Hollywood: Take 1" discusses his work on the war documentary *The Negro Soldier*, 159–73; "Hollywood: Take 2," 191–98; "Hollywood: Take 3," 313–31. "Films, Radio, and Television" lists his works, 443–44.

Robinson, Harlow, trans. and ed.
:   *Selected Letters of Sergei Prokofiev.* Boston: Northeastern Univ. Press, 1998.
"Prokofiev and Sergei Eisenstein," introduced by Robinson, 207–8, is followed by the correspondence between the composer and the director.

Rockwell, John.
:   *All American Music: Composition in the Late Twentieth Century.* New York: Knopf, 1983. New York: Vintage Books, 1984. New York: Da Capo Press, 1997.
The chapter on sound editor Walter Murch contains material on film music, primarily in relation to "serious" composers, 157–63; on commercial music and blandness, 231–32.

Rodgers, Richard.
:   *Musical Stages: An Autobiography.* New York: Random House, 1975. New York: Da Capo Press, 1995.
Includes the songwriter's take on working in musicals at MGM, Paramount, and United Artists from 1931 to 1934, 148–66 (1995).

Rodriguez, José, ed.
:   *Music and Dance in California.* Hollywood, Calif.: Bureau of Musical Research, 1940.
Anthology with articles on film music: "The Screen's Influence in Music," by Nathaniel Finston, 123–25; "Mechanical Aids in Films," by Roy Webb, 126–27; "Film Cartoon Music," by Albert Hay Malotte, 128–32; "Leitmotif in Film Scoring," by Gerard Carbonara, 133–36; "Some Experiences in Film Music," by Erich Wolfgang Korngold, 137–39, reprinted in *The Cue Sheet* (July 2004); "Screen Recording," by Ray Heindorf, 140–42; "Spirituals, Reels, Hoe Downs and Blues," by Hall Johnson, 170–76; "The Negro's Rise," by Clarence Muse, 177–82. Concludes with short biographies, some with photographs, including composers, arrangers, orchestrators, conductors, and musical directors such as Daniele Amfitheatrof, Leo Arnaud, George Bassman, Robert Russell Bennett, David Buttolph, Lucien Cailliet, Gerard Carbonara, Jay Chernis, Anthony Collins, Cecil Copping, Murray Cutter, Adolph Deutsch, Carmen Dragon, Cy Feuer, Nathaniel Finston, Lou Forbes, Hugo Friedhofer, Leigh Harline, W. Franke Harling, Ray Heindorf, Werner Heymann, Alex Hyde, Howard Jackson, Werner Janssen, Gordon Jenkins, Hall Johnson, Arthur Kay, Edward Kilenyi, Rudolph Kopp, Erich Wolfgang Korngold, Arthur Lange,

Louis Lipstone, Albert Hay Malotte, Paul Marquardt, Charles Maxwell, Felix Mills, Cyril Mockridge, Boris Morros, Arthur Morton, Alfred Newman, Maurice de Packh, Edward Powell, Charles Previn, Hugo Riesenfeld, Sigmund Romberg, Leo Shuken, David Snell, Herbert Spencer, Max Steiner, Franz Waxman, and Roy Webb. Session musicians represented include John Cave, Philip Kahgan, Louis Kaufman, Emanuel Klein, Ray Martinez, John Mayhew, Olga Mitana, Jack Pepper, Michel Perriere, Vincent de Rubertis, Raymond Turner, and others. This edition was preceded by Bruno David Ussher's *Who's Who in Music and Dance in Southern California* (1933) and followed by Richard Drake Saunders's *Music and Dance in California and the West* (1948).

Rodriguez, Robert.
   Rebel without a Crew, Or, How a 23-Year-Old Filmmaker with $7,000 Became a Hollywood Player. New York: Dutton, 1995.
The director-composer's diary includes material on the genesis and recording of the music for his film *El Mariachi*.

Rona, Jeffrey.
   Synchronization, from Reel to Reel: A Complete Guide for the Synchronization of Audio, Film & Video. Milwaukee: Hal Leonard, 1990.
Covers the technical aspects of synchronizing audio, including music, to film and video via SMPTE and MIDI. Author is a film music composer, longtime *Keyboard* magazine columnist, and onetime programmer who also wrote a complete text devoted to MIDI, *MIDI, the Ins, Outs & Thrus* (Milwaukee: Hal Leonard, 1987); rev. ed., *The MIDI Companion* (Milwaukee: Hal Leonard, 1994).

Rose, Cameron J.
   The Click Book: Timing Tables for 6 to 32-Frame Click Tempos at 24 Frames per Second. 2nd ed. Burbank, Calif.: CJR Music, 1997. Unpaged.
A volume of timing tables formulated for synchronizing music to film. The table for each tempo (120 beats per minute equals a 12-frame click, or 12–0) lists real-time values for each click (or musical beat) from 1 through 999. This translates into a four-minute cue at a fast tempo and a twenty-two-minute cue at a slow tempo. Professional composers using this book typically would consult the appropriate table to line up a musical "hit." For example, beat 52 would occur at exactly thirty-four seconds in a cue written with a metronome marking of 90 (16–0 click). Includes basic conversion formulas for SMPTE time code (the video standard). The 430-page first edition was titled *The Click Book: Comprehensive Timing Tables for Synchronizing Music to Film*.

Rosen, Jody.
   White Christmas: The Story of an American Song. New York: Scribner, 2002.
This history of Irving Berlin's song documents its creation and use in *Holiday Inn*, 104–19, and *White Christmas*, 171–73. Orchestrator Walter Scharf was interviewed.

Rosenberg, Bernard, and Deena Rosenberg.
   The Music Makers. New York: Columbia Univ. Press, 1979.
Interview-based profiles of harmonica player and composer Larry Adler, 297–310; and of concert manager and critic Lawrence Morton, 393–408.

Rosenberg, Bernard, and Harry Silverstein.
>   *The Real Tinsel.* New York: Macmillan, 1970.

"The Music Director," based on an interview with Max Steiner by the authors, 387–98.

Ross, Lillian.
>   *Picture.* New York: Rinehart, 1952. London: Victor Gollancz, 1953. New York: Avon, Discus Books, 1969; New York: Limelight Editions, 1984; New York: Garland, 1985; New York: Anchor Books, 1993; New York: Modern Library, 1997.

The chapter "Piccolos under Your Name, Strings under Mine," on the making of *The Red Badge of Courage,* contains material on the composing, recording, and dubbing of the 1951 music score by Bronislaw Kaper (see pp. 135–37, 144–46, 148–50, all 1952). Originally serialized in *The New Yorker.*

Ross, T. J., comp.
>   *Film and the Liberal Arts.* New York: Holt, Rinehart and Winston, 1970.

Textbook with the chapter "Film Music," 217–47, which has "A Cog in the Wheel," by Oscar Levant, 221–29 (excerpted from *A Smattering of Ignorance*); "Composing for Films," by Dimitri Tiomkin, 230–37 (reprinted from *Films in Review,* November 1951); "New Tendencies in Composing for Motion Pictures," by George Antheil, 238–43 (reprinted from *Film Culture,* Summer 1955); "Film Music as Noise," by critic Page Cook, 244–47 (reprinted from *Films in Review,* March 1968).

Ross-Russell, Noel.
>   *A Voice Within.* London: Open Gate Press, 1998. 205 pp.

The main character in this work of fiction—a love story revolving around film, music, and tennis—is a film music composer.

Rota, Nino.
>   *Fra cinema e musica del Novecento: il caso Nino Rota: dai documenti.* Florence, Italy: L. S. Olschki, 2000.

Some of the material—collected articles, interviews and letters—has been translated into English.

Rotha, Paul.
>   *Celluloid: The Film To-day.* London: Longmans, Green, 1931.

References to synchronized music and Edmund Meisel.

Rotha, Paul.
>   *Documentary Film.* London: Faber and Faber, 1936. 1939. 3rd rev. and enlarged ed. in collaboration with Road and Griffiths. New York: Communication Arts, 1952. Reprinted in 1963, 1966, 1968, and 1970.

Some references to music.

Rotha, Paul.
>   *Rotha on the Film: A Selection of Writings about the Cinema.* Fair Lawn, N.J.: Essential Books, 1958. New York: Garland, 1978.

Emphasizes that only source music is appropriate in realist (nonfiction) films, 22–23 (1958).

Rothel, David.
   The Singing Cowboys. South Brunswick, N.J.: A. S. Barnes, 1978.
Discusses a half dozen performers from Gene Autry to Jimmy Wakely. Includes discographies.

Rothwell, Kenneth S.
   A History of Shakespeare on Screen: A Century of Film and Television. Cambridge: Cambridge Univ. Press, 1999. 2nd ed., 2004.
"Spectacle and Song in Castellani and Zeffirelli," on specific films by the two directors, 119–35 (2004).

Rózsa, Miklós.
   An Evaluation of Progress in Music in Films. 1946. 13 pp.
An essay on the development of musical accompaniment of films in history through its natural evolution to the mid-1940s. Located in the pamphlet files at the Margaret Herrick Library and date-stamped March 8, 1946, this work appears never to have been published. Possibly intended for *Music Publishers Journal* (the title is similar to Franz Waxman's 1945 *Journal* essay, "Progress in Development of Film Music Scores").

Rubin, Steven Jay.
   The Complete James Bond Movie Encyclopedia. Chicago: Contemporary Books, 1990. Newly revised, 1995. Rev. ed., 2003.
"John Barry," 28–29 (1990).

Rubsamen, Walter H.
   Descriptive Music for Stage and Screen. Pamphlet. Los Angeles: UCLA Students' Store, 1949. 14 pp.
An essay with numerous film citations on descriptive music, including movement in the music complementing movement on the screen, deviation from the norm to depict the mysterious, imitation of natural (actual) sounds, and extramusical ideas. Reprinted from *Proceedings for 1946* of the Music Teachers National Association.

Rubsamen, Walter H.
   Music in the Dramatic Film. Pamphlet. Washington, D.C.: United States Information Service, 1957.
This essay, aimed at the layperson, discusses the role of background and descriptive music in film. A similarly titled article appeared in the *Juilliard Review* (1957).

Ruppert, Peter, ed.
   Ideas of Order in Literature and Film. Tallahassee: University Presses of Florida, 1980.
Selected papers from the Fourth Annual Florida State University Conference on Literature and Film in 1979, including "Music and Murder: The Association of Source Music with Order in Hitchcock's Films," by Elisabeth Weis, 73–83.

Ruppli, Michel, comp.
   The Decca Labels: A Discography. Westport, Conn.: Greenwood Press, 1996.
Vol. 1, "The California Sessions," includes listings related to session recordings of film music, circa 1950s. These are rerecordings, or "cover versions," of popular film music

released as single 45 rpm discs, performed by "Lionel Newman and His Orchestra" and "Henry Mancini and His Orchestra," among others. Listings are numerical by catalog number and include title(s), session date, and releasing record label and number. Artist index. Vol. 4, "The Eastern Sessions (1956–1973)," contains material related to film soundtracks.

Ruppli, Michel, and Ed Novitsky, comps.
> *The Mercury Labels: A Discography*. Westport, Conn.: Greenwood Press, 1993.

Vol. 1, "The 1945–1956 Era," includes listings related to session recordings of film music. These are rerecordings, or "cover versions," of popular film music released as single 45 rpm discs; "Alfred Newman and the 20th Century Fox Orchestra" is represented by *Captain from Castile* (1947). Listings are numerical by catalog number and include title(s), session date, and releasing record label and number. Artist index.

Ruppli, Michel, and Ed Novitsky, comps.
> *The MGM Labels: A Discography*. Westport, Conn.: Greenwood Press, 1998.

Vol. 1, "1946–1960," includes listings related to West Coast session recordings of film music. Includes rerecordings and music from soundtracks. Vol. 2, "1961–1982," includes "MGM Sessions" (1973–1975), 815–99. Vol. 3 has additional recordings and artist indexes. The MGM Studio Orchestra is well represented, as is conductor George Stoll. Listings are numerical by catalog number and include title(s), session date, and releasing record label and number.

Russo, Joe, and Larry Landsman.
> Planet of the Apes *Revisited: The Behind-the-Scenes Story of the Classic Science Fiction Saga*. New York: Thomas Dunne Books/St. Martin's Griffin, 2001.

Discusses Jerry Goldsmith's music for the film series, 82–84, 168–169; Leonard Rosenman, 135–37, 218–19; Tom Scott, 195–96.

Rust, Brian, and Allen G. Debus.
> *The Complete Entertainment Discography, from the Mid-1890s to 1942*. New Rochelle, N.Y.: Arlington House, 1973. 677 pp. 2nd updated and expanded ed. published as *The Complete Entertainment Discography, from 1897 to 1942*. New York: Da Capo Press, 1989. 794 pp.

Film songs are included in the performer listings, which are arranged alphabetically by name.

The RZA (Robert Diggs).
> *The Wu-Tang Manual: The RZA with Chris Norris*. New York: Riverhead Books, 2005.

"Hip-Hop Scoring," 112–14.

Sadie, Stanley, ed.
> *The New Grove Dictionary of Music and Musicians*. London: Macmillan; Washington, D.C.: Grove's Dictionaries of Music, 1980. 20 vols. Multiple reprints.

"Film Music," vol. 6, 549–56. Sections by Christopher Palmer on history, technique, functional music, realistic music, and the musical and animated film; and essays by John Gillett on Europe and the Far East. Biographical entries for Richard Addinsell, John Addison, George Antheil, Georges Auric, Arnold Bax, Richard Rodney Bennett, Elmer

Bernstein, Arthur Bliss, Georges Delerue, Hanns Eisler, Hugo Friedhofer, Bernard Herrmann, Maurice Jarre, Maurice Jaubert, Bronislaw Kaper, Erich Wolfgang Korngold, Michel Legrand, Henry Mancini, Muir Mathieson, Jerome Moross, Alfred Newman, Alex North, Leonard Rosenman, Nino Rota, Miklós Rózsa, Max Steiner, Robert Stolz, Herbert Stothart, Dimitri Tiomkin, Franz Waxman, John Williams, Victor Young, and others. (Herrmann, Korngold, and Rózsa are taken from a previous edition.) Palmer authored many of the biographical entries.

Sadie, Stanley, ed.
> *The New Grove Dictionary of Music and Musicians.* 2nd ed. 29 vols. New York: Grove, 2001.

Entries for nearly 100 film composers. "Film Music," by Mervyn Cooke in vol. 8, covers film music history, including Hollywood; developments outside the United States; early sound films; music for silent films; jazz, popular, and classical music; and techniques and functions, 797–809. See also "Film Musical," by Richard Traubner, Thomas L. Gayda, and John Snelson, vol. 8, 810–16. Consult the index for other subjects related to film music, such as electronics, and for a list of predominantly American or European film composers. Elliot Goldenthal is among the first-time entrants. Contributors include Kate Daubney, Martin Marks, and Clifford McCarty.

Saleski, Gdal.
> *Famous Musicians of Jewish Origin.* New York: Bloch, 1949.

Brief biographical sketches for Henry Brant, Mario Castelnuovo-Tedesco, Aaron Copland, Morton Gould, Bernard Herrmann, Jerome Kern, Erich Wolfgang Korngold, Michel Michelet, Elie Siegmeister, and Franz Waxman.

Salisbury, Mark.
> *Burton on Burton.* London: Faber, 1995. Rev. ed., 2000.

Numerous references to music in director Tim Burton's films regarding his frequent collaborator, Danny Elfman.

Sammon, Paul M.
> *Future Noir: The Making of* Blade Runner. New York: HarperPrism, 1996.

"Postproduction and the Music" contains material on Vangelis, the score, and the soundtrack, 267–77. An appendix contains a history of *Blade Runner* on disc, including a breakdown of music issued on various soundtracks and notes on miscellaneous music heard in the film, 419–25.

Sánchez-H., José.
> *The Art and Politics of Bolivian Cinema.* Lanham, Md.: Scarecrow Press, 1999.

"Conversations with Film Composers" includes Oscar Garcia, Cergio Prudencio, and Alberto Villalpando, 143–69.

Sandler, Kevin S., ed.
> *Reading the Rabbit: Explorations in Warner Bros. Animation.* New Brunswick, N.J.: Rutgers Univ. Press, 1998.

"From Vaudeville to Hollywood, from Silence to Sound: Warner Bros. Cartoons of the Early Sound Era," by Hank Sartin, 67–85.

Sandler, Kevin S., and Gaylyn Studlar, eds.
Titanic: Anatomy of a Blockbuster. New Brunswick, N.J.: Rutgers Univ. Press, 1999.
"Selling My Heart: Music and Cross-Promotion in *Titanic*," by Jeff Smith, discusses the form and function of the film's hit song, "My Heart Will Go On," 46–63.

Sanjek, Russell.
American Popular Music and Its Business: The First Four Hundred Years. Vol. 3, *From 1900 to 1984.* New York: Oxford Univ. Press, 1988.
Historical overview of the "pop" song interweaves commercial exploitation, business and economic aspects, performing rights, publishing, and technology. Film music is discussed primarily in terms of songs used in films. "Popular Songs and the Movie Business" (1921–1930), 47–56; "A Glut of Movie Music" (1921–1930), 91–114; "Music in Motion Pictures" (1931–1940), 147–58; "Television Music Licensing," (1981–1984), 617–23; other film music references, 476–77, 531–33. Voluminous material on ASCAP, BMI, the Composers and Lyricists Guild, and the Screen Composers Association. Author has been associated with BMI since 1940 and served as its vice president of public relations.

Sanjek, Russell, and David Sanjek.
American Popular Music Business in the 20th Century. New York: Oxford Univ. Press, 1991.
"Hollywood and Movie Music," covers the 1920s and 1930s, 33–46, abridged from vol. 3 of *American Popular Music and Its Business* (see above entry). Other references to the relationship between movies and music. David Sanjek is the son of Russell Sanjek.

Sanjek, Russell, updated by David Sanjek.
Pennies from Heaven: The American Popular Music Business in the Twentieth Century. New York: Da Capo Press, 1996.
This revised edition includes the entire contents of the third volume of *American Popular Music and Its Business* (see above entry), along with two new chapters that summarize the major events between 1985 and 1996. The new material mentions soundtrack and synergy trends, 658, 674.

Sarris, Andrew.
You Ain't Heard Nothin' Yet: The American Talking Film History & Memory, 1927–1949. New York: Oxford Univ. Press, 1998.
"Genres: The Musical," 31–67.

Saunders, Richard Drake, ed.
Music and Dance in California and the West. Hollywood: Bureau of Musical Research, 1948.
An enlightening collection of short essays by Hollywood practitioners. "What Price Culture," by Marlin Skiles, 32, 140; "Distinctly Different," by Leo Arnaud, discusses the differences between arranging and orchestrating, 43, 140; "Music by the Yard," by William Lava, on writing on demand, 76–77, 128; "Time Tells the Tale," by Nathaniel Finston, 78, reprinted in *The Cue Sheet* (July 2004); "The Growing Art," by Miklós Rózsa, 79, 133; "Drastic Decade," by Rudy de Saxe, 80, 132; "Select for Yourself," by Constantin Bakaleinikoff, 81, 143; "The Mood Comes First," by Rudolph Kopp, 82; "Where Seldom Is Heard an Encouraging Word," by Albert Sendrey, 83, 143; "Conducting on Cue," by Irvin Talbot, 84, 142; "Scissors Save the Score," by Roy Webb, 85, reprinted in

The Cue Sheet (July 2004), 144. Additional references to film music and the Hollywood Bowl. Earlier editions were edited by Bruno David Ussher (1933) and José Rodriguez (1940). The personalities section has brief biographies of some film composers; the Rodriguez edition contains a larger number of bios. Saunders, a Los Angeles area newspaper music editor and pianist-composer, also edited *A Guide to Music and Musicians in Greater Los Angeles and San Diego*.

Scanlon, J., and A. Waste, eds.
> *Crossing Boundaries: Thinking through Literature*. Sheffield: Sheffield Academic Press, 2001.

"Music to Desire By: Crossing the Berlin Wall with Wim Wenders," by Annette Davison, 161–68. Later published in Davison's *Hollywood Theory, Non-Hollywood Practice* (2004).

Schafer, R. Murray.
> *British Composers in Interview*. London: Faber and Faber, 1963.

Author, a Canadian composer and writer (his book on the sonic environment and the tuning of the world is remarkable), interviewed Malcolm Arnold, Elisabeth Lutyens, and others while studying in Britain. Unable to determine whether film music is discussed.

Schary, Dore, as told to Charles Palmer.
> *Case History of a Movie*. New York: Random House, 1950. New York: Garland Publishing, 1978.

A behind-the-scenes look at the making of *The Next Voice You Hear* (1950), for which Schary served as producer. The documentation of the music process for this sparsely scored film covers Schary's collaboration with David Raksin and the recording session conducted by Johnny Green, 195–201 (1950).

Schneider, Steve.
> *"That's All Folks!" The Art of Warner Bros. Animation*. New York: H. Holt, 1988.

The music of Carl Stalling is discussed, 52–56, including "The Music of Raymond Scott," on Stalling's use of Scott's novelty tunes, 54.

Schneider, Wayne, ed.
> *The Gershwin Style: New Looks at the Music of George Gershwin*. New York: Oxford Univ. Press, 1999.

"*Rhapsody in Blue*: A Study in Hollywood Hagiography," by Charlotte Greenspan, includes a discussion of the music selected for the film and a guide to the music cues, 145–59.

Scholes, Percy A.
> *The Oxford Companion to Music*. 9th rev. ed. London: Oxford Univ. Press, 1955. 10th ed., 1970.

"Cinematograph and Music," 186–87 (1955), 188–89 (1970). Brief entries for composers of concert music, such as Erich Wolfgang Korngold; however, no substantive information on film composers.

Schwam, Stephanie, selected by.
> *The Making of 2001: A Space Odyssey*. New York: Modern Library, 2000.

The testimonies chapter, compiled by Jerome Agel, contains "Alex North, Film Composer," in which North relates his experience of composing a score that ultimately went unused, 129–30.

Schwarz, David, Anahid Kassabian, and Lawrence Siegel, eds.
>   *Keeping Score: Music, Disciplinarity, Culture.* Charlottesville: Univ. Press of Virginia, 1997.

"At the Twilight's Last Scoring," by Anahid Kassabian, looks at gender, race, sexuality, and assimilation in the music for *The Hunt for Red October, Lethal Weapon 2,* and *Indiana Jones and the Temple of Doom,* 258–74. This essay also appears in Kassabian's book *Hearing Film.*

Scott, Evelyn F.
>   *Hollywood When Silents Were Golden.* New York: McGraw-Hill, 1972.

The child actor's autobiography includes the chapter "Background Music," 134–41, wherein a brief passage describing mood music played on set during the silent era appears on pp. 135–36.

Scott, Keith.
>   *The Moose That Roared: The Story of Jay Ward, Bill Scott, a Flying Squirrel, and a Talking Moose.* New York: St. Martin's Press, 2000.

"The Musicians" briefly describes the contributions of Frank Comstock, Fred Steiner, and Dennis Farnon, 336–39. Additional references throughout. Jerry Fielding is also mentioned.

Sebesky, Don.
>   *The Contemporary Arranger.* New York: Alfred, 1975. Definitive ed., Van Nuys, Calif.: Alfred, 1994.

Author has done music arrangements for films but is known primarily as a versatile arranger of jazz recordings.

Seger, Linda, and Edward Jay Whetmore.
>   *From Script to Screen: The Collaborative Art of Filmmaking.* New York: Henry Holt, 1994. 2nd ed., Hollywood: Lone Eagle Publishing, 2004.

"The Composer: Invisible Bridges" contains interview excerpts with Buddy Baker, Bill Conti, Maurice Jarre, Henry Mancini, David Newman, David Raksin, Don Ray, Shirley Walker, and Hans Zimmer, all interviewed for this book, 287–320. Topics include temp tracks, spotting sessions, writing themes and underscores, what music can convey, orchestration, communicating with the director, and whether the composer should read the script. Concludes with a close-up look at the score for *Dead Poets Society,* in which Jarre discusses the process, musical choices, and the final theme. The second edition replaces the Jarre material with "The Composer: Invisible Bridges," 201–18, a close-up with James Horner on the collaborative process for the score of *A Beautiful Mind.*

Seldes, Gilbert.
>   *An Hour with the Movies and the Talkies.* Philadelphia: J. P. Lippincott, 1929.

Music is mentioned several times in this essay, including a musical tonal center in the accompaniment for a silent film by director D. W. Griffith, 25; speculation on the role of music in the newly developed sound film, 27–28; and the idea that silent portions of sound films would be accompanied by music "because music has not yet been woven into the fabric of the talkie," 145–46.

Seldes, Gilbert.
> *The 7 Lively Arts*. New York: Sagamore Press, 1957.

"Say It with Music," 55–66, comments on popular songs and the objectivity of popularity but includes only a peripheral comment on music for movies. Originally written in 1923–1924, with new material written for this edition.

Seltzer, George.
> *Music Matters: The Performer and the American Federation of Musicians*. Metuchen, N.J., and London: Scarecrow Press, 1989.

Extensive documentation of the plight of Hollywood studio musicians, beginning in the 1950s, within the historical context of the AFM union and Los Angeles Local 47. Economic aspects, including pay scales, overdubbing, and synthesizers, are among the topics discussed. Author is a professor of economics and industrial relations.

Shales, Tom, and James Andrew Miller.
> *Live from New York: An Uncensored History of* Saturday Night Live. Boston: Little, Brown, 2002.

Includes interview material with composer Howard Shore.

Sheen, Erica, and Annette Davison, eds.
> *The Cinema of David Lynch: American Dreams, Nightmare Visions*. London: Wallflower Press, 2004.

"*Laura* and *Twin Peaks*: Postmodern Parody and the Musical Reconstruction of the Absent Femme Fatale," by John Richardson, 77–92; "'Up in Flames': Love, Control and Collaboration in the Soundtrack to *Wild at Heart*," by Annette Davison, 119–35. The ten remaining essays contain significant references to the music of Angelo Badalamenti and music in the films of David Lynch.

Shehan, Patricia.
> *Songs in Their Heads: Music and Its Meaning in Children's Lives*. New York: Oxford Univ. Press, 1998.

Contains an amusing interview with a third grader smitten with 1930s movie singers, a teacher who disapproves of popular music, and commentary on the place of American popular music in education, 119–22.

Shepherd, John, David Horn, Dave Laing, Paul Oliver, and Peter Wicke, eds.
> *Continuum Encyclopedia of Popular Music of the World*. London: Continuum, 2003.

"The Film Industry and Popular Music," by Jeff Smith, 499–504.

Sheth, Nirupama, and Ajita Setha.
> *Tagore: Indian Film & Film Music*. Bombay: Pankaj Mullick Music Research Foundation, 1994.

"[Rabindranath] Tagore's Impact on Indian Film Music," 33–51.

Shetler, Donald J.
    Film Guide for Music Educators. Pamphlet. Washington, D.C.: Music Educator's
    National Conference, 1961. 119 pp.
Lists 16mm educational films and filmstrips on the subject of music, including *Music
from the Mountains* (1951), a history of the Idyllwild School of Music and Arts, with
music composed by USC students under the direction of Miklós Rózsa.

Shipton, Alyn.
    A New History of Jazz. London: Continuum, 2001.
"Jazz on Film," a survey of the genre, 564–71.

Shlifstein, S., comp. and ed.
    S. Prokofiev: Autobiography, Articles, Reminiscences. Moscow: Foreign Language
    Pub. House, circa 1957.
"Music for *Alexander Nevsky*," 112–14, translated from material written in 1939.

Shorris, Sylvia, and Marion Abbott Bundy, eds.
    Talking Pictures: With the People Who Made Them. New York: New Press, 1994.
"Words and Music" contains brief interviews with Jule Styne, 211–17, and Sammy Cahn,
219–28, with partial filmographies for both.

Short, Marion.
    *From Footlights to "The Flickers": Collectible Sheet Music: Broadway Shows and
    Silent Movies*. Atglen, Penn.: Schiffer Publishing, 1998.
"Silent Movie Music" includes sheet music covers and historical notes, 88–93; "Early
Movie Companies," 94–107; "An Album of Silent Film Stars," 109–71; "Serial Photo-
plays," 172–79. Author also wrote *Hollywood Movie Songs,* on sound films.

Shusterman, Richard.
    Performing Live: Aesthetic Alternatives for the Ends of Art. Ithaca, N.Y.: Cornell
    Univ. Press, 2000.
"Affect and Authenticity in Country Musicals," 76–95.

Sibley, Brian.
    The Lord of the Rings: *The Making of the Movie Trilogy*. Boston: Houghton Mifflin,
    2002.
"Knowing the Score" documents the film's recording sessions, 173–81; "On the Theme
of Fellowship" explains Howard Shore's concept and use of a non-character-specific
theme for the trilogy, 182.

Siddons, James.
    Toru Takemitsu: A Bio-Bibliography. Westport, Conn.: Greenwood Press, 2001.
"Biography" contains a short section on the cross-pollination of the composer's film and
concert works, 10–11; "Film Scores," 107–18; "Discography," 119–45.

Sider, Larry, Diane Freeman, and Jerry Sider, eds.
    Soundscape: The School of Sound Lectures, 1998–2001. London: Wallflower Press,
    2003.

Drawn from symposium lectures that included directors, sound designers, theorists, critics, and composers. Composer contributions include "Music for Interactive Moving Pictures," by Stephen Deutch, 28–34; "Composing for the Coen Brothers," by Carter Burwell, 195–208. Many of the nonmusicians address music; for instance, director David Lynch talks about working with composers, director Mike Figgis gives his take on film music, screenwriter James Leahy discusses Dimitri Tiomkin's exemplary use of music in *Red River*, Shoma Chatterji discusses Indian film music, and sound designer Walter Murch talks about Henry Mancini's music for *Touch of Evil*. Editors founded the School of Sound to bring the personal expression of sound to an international listening audience.

Siefert, Marsha, ed.
  Extending the Borders of Russian History: Essays in Honor of Alfred J. Rieber. Budapest: Central European Univ. Press, 2003.
"Allies on Film: US–USSR Filmmakers and *The Battle of Russia*," by Siefert, 373–400, includes a page on Dimitri Tiomkin's score, 385. Editor is a CEU doctoral studies history tutor.

Siegmeister, Elie, ed.
  The Music Lover's Handbook. New York: William Morrow, 1943.
"Music in the Films," by Aaron Copland, from *Our New Music*, 628–35; "Morton Gould," by John Tasker Howard, 766; "Alex North," by Siegmeister, 769–71; "Other Americans," by Siegmeister, includes one-paragraph summaries on Louis Gruenberg, Bernard Herrmann, Douglas Moore, and Virgil Thomson, 774–80.

Silberman, Marc, ed. and trans.
  Brecht on Film and Radio. London: Methuen, 2000.
"On Film Music," 10–18. From an unpublished typescript written in 1942 at the request of Hanns Eisler in relation to a project he and Theodor Adorno were conducting at the New School for Social Research.

Silver, Alain, and James Ursini, eds.
  Film Noir Reader 2. New York: Limelight Editions, 1999.
"Dark Jazz: Music in the *Film Noir*," by Robert G. Porfirio, is based on his Yale University dissertation and includes material on aural effects in a sequence from *The Dark Corner* (1946), 177–87.

Silver, Alain, James Ursini, and Robert Porfirio, eds.
  Film Noir Reader 3: Interviews with Filmmakers of the Classic Noir Period. New York: Limelight Editions, 2002.
"Miklós Rózsa," interviewed by Porfirio in January 1977 in relation to his Yale dissertation, 163–76.

Silver, Alain, and Elizabeth Ward, eds.
  Film Noir: An Encyclopedic Reference to the American Style. Woodstock, N.Y.: Overlook Press, 1979. Rev. and expanded ed., 1988. 3rd ed., rev. and expanded, 1992.
Fifty composers are indexed by name, followed by film title, 349–52 (1979). The film entries contain credits and synopses and are arranged alphabetically.

Silverman, Kaja.
   The Acoustic Mirror: The Female Voice in Psychoanalysis and Cinema. Bloomington: Indiana Univ. Press, 1988.
This theoretical work focuses primarily on sound, not music. The chapter "Disembodying
the Female Voice" is of interest.

Silvester, Christopher, ed.
   The Grove Book of Hollywood. New York: Grove Press, 2000. Originally published
   as *The Penguin Book of Hollywood* (London: Viking, 1998).
Contains two extracts from Miklós Rózsa's autobiography *Double Life,* "A Haven for
European Refugees," on émigrés, 316–18; "Stravinsky in Hollywood," 327–28.

Sitsky, Larry, ed.
   Music of the Twentieth-Century Avant-Garde: A Biocritical Sourcebook. Westport,
   Conn.: Greenwood Press, 2002.
The selected works for composers often include film music (see Pierre Henry). Material
on Toru Takemitsu's film music, 512–13, 522.

Skinner, Frank.
   Frank Skinner's New Method for Orchestra Scoring. New York: Robbins Music,
   1935.
A course of study for amateurs and professionals, presumably based on the author's experience as a music arranger for Robbins, a major New York music publisher. The book
was published the same year that Skinner moved to Hollywood. An earlier book, possibly
titled *Frank Skinner's Book in Arranging*, was apparently published by Bibo Lang, ca.
1929. Skinner arranged the music for at least one silent film as early as 1915.

Skretvedt, Randy, and Jordan R. Young.
   *The Nostalgia Entertainment Sourcebook: The Complete Resource Guide to Classic
   Movies, Vintage Music, Old-Time Radio and Theatre.* Beverly Hills, Calif.: Moon-
   stone Press, 1991.
Lists a number of soundtrack and sheet music dealers across the United States.

Slide, Anthony.
   A Collector's Guide to Movie Memorabilia—With Prices. Des Moines, Iowa:
   Wallace-Homestead, 1983.
"Sheet Music" contains text accompanied by sheet music covers, 57–66.

Slide, Anthony.
   Films on Film History. Metuchen, N.J.: Scarecrow Press, 1979.
Subject index entries include "Composing for Films" and "Musicals." Includes an entry
for a little-known short film called "A Star for Max," on Max Steiner's star on the Hollywood Boulevard Walk of Fame, which features Elmer Bernstein and others.

Slide, Anthony.
   The New Historical Dictionary of the American Film Industry. Lanham, Md.: Scarecrow Press, 1998. Rev. and updated version of *The American Film Industry: A Historical Dictionary* (1986).
"Music," 135–36, and "Musicals," 136–37.

Slide, Anthony.
  Silent Topics: Essays on Undocumented Areas of Silent Film. Lanham, Md.: Scarecrow Press, 2005.
"Sheet Music of the Silent Stars," 85–91.

Slonimsky, Nicolas, ed.
  Baker's Biographical Dictionary of Musicians. 5th ed. New York: G. Schirmer, 1965. 8th ed. (revised by Slonimsky), New York: Schirmer Books; Toronto: Maxwell Macmillan Canada; New York: Maxwell Macmillan International, 1992. Centennial ed., New York: Schirmer Books, 2001.
Some composers who have written for film are included from the fifth edition on, as are film composers such as Miklós Rózsa who have written for the concert hall.

Slonimsky, Nicolas.
  Baker's Biographical Dictionary of Twentieth-Century Classical Musicians. New York: Schirmer Books, 1997.
Some film composers are included.

Small, Mark, and Andrew Taylor.
  Masters of Music: Conversations with Berklee Greats. Boston: Berklee Press, 1999.
A compilation of interviews with graduates of the Berklee College of Music, originally printed in *Berklee Today*, the alumni magazine. Topics include their Berklee training, breaking into the business, and lessons learned. Introduced by brief biographical sketches and quotes from the interviews. "Alan Silvestri: To *The Abyss* and Back," 30–39; "Abe Laboriel: High Style on the Low End" contains material on the bass player's session work for Quincy Jones, 75; "Branford Marsalis: Jazz Messenger," 108–13; "Jan Hammer: Beyond the Mind's Ear," 122–30; "John Robinson: A Place in Time" mentions the drummer's session work, 152–61; "Quincy Jones: The Best Is Yet to Come," 174–83; "Alf Clausen: Primetime Tunes" discusses scoring *The Simpsons*, 214–24; "Howard Shore: Subliminal Scores," 258–67; "Neil Stubenhaus: 'A Team' Player," contains material on the bass player's session work, 280–90.

Smith, Catherine Parsons.
  William Grant Still: A Study in Contradictions. Berkeley: Univ. of California Press, 2000.
Includes a discussion of the composer's film work from 1936 to 1942, 79–82. Author is a music professor.

Smith, Geoffrey-Nowell, ed.
  The Oxford History of World Cinema. Oxford: Oxford Univ. Press, 1996.
"Music and the Silent Film," by Martin Marks, 183–92; "The Sound of Music," by Martin Marks, covering the years 1930–1960, 248–59; "The Musical," by Rick Altman, 294–303; "Modern Film Music," by Royal Brown, 558–66.

Smith, Jim, and J. Clive Matthews.
  Tim Burton. London: Virgin, 2002.
Significant references to Danny Elfman's music in the director's films.

Smith, Joe.
    Off the Record: An Oral History of Popular Music. Edited by Mitchell Fink. New York: Warner Books, 1988.
"Henry Mancini," 53–54.

Smith, John M.
    Jean Vigo. London: November Books, 1972. New York: Praeger, 1972.
Discusses Maurice Jaubert's music for *Zero de Conduite* (*Zero for Conduct*, 1944).

Smith, Julia.
    Aaron Copland: His Work and Contribution to American Music. New York: E. P. Dutton, 1955.
Copland's film music is examined and discussed, 200–216, in this published version of an NYU dissertation by the author, a pianist-composer.

Smith, Packy, and Ed Hulse, eds.
    Don Miller's Hollywood Corral: A Comprehensive B-Western Roundup. Burbank, Calif.: Riverwood Press, 1993.
"Have Song—Will Warble," by Don Miller, 137–49 (originally appeared in *Hollywood Corral*, 1976); "The Singing Cowboy: An American Dream," by Douglas B. Green, 331–73 (reprinted from *The Journal of Country Music*, May 1978); "The Sons of the Pioneers: 'Guns on Their Hips, Songs on Their Lips,'" by Ken Griffis, 375–83; "Appassionato Dramatic: Music in the B Western," by composer-arranger James King, with additional material by Sam Sherman, 441–47.

Snow, Michael.
    Music/Sound, 1948–1993: The Performed and Recorded Music/Sound of Michael Snow. Toronto: Knopf Canada, 1994.
Includes a dialogue between the jazz/avant-garde musician and avant-garde filmmaker Bruce Elder, 217–50.

Snyder, Robert L.
    Pare Lorentz and the Documentary Film. Norman: Univ. of Oklahoma Press, 1968.
Information on the scores for the filmmaker's documentaries (see pp. 182–83), including *The Plow That Broke the Plains* (1936), music by Virgil Thomson, 33–36; *The River* (1938), music by Thomson, 58–61, 194–96; *The Power and the Land* (1940), music by Douglas Moore, 129–30; and *The Fight for Life* (1940), music by Louis Gruenberg, 109–12, 211.

Sobchack, Vivian Carol.
    Screening Space: The American Science Fiction Film. 1st ed. published as *The Limits of Infinity*, 1980. 2nd enlarged ed., New York: Ungar, 1987. New Brunswick, N.J.: Rutgers Univ. Press, 1997.
"Nonverbal Sound: The Music of the Spheres," on classical, electronic, and experimental music, with an emphasis on music in the films of Stanley Kubrick, 207–15 (1987).

Soifer, Rosanne.
    Music in Video Production. White Plains, N.Y.: Knowledge Industry Publications, 1991.

Topics include original music, music libraries, and public domain music. Discusses copyrights, licensing, and other legal aspects. Author is a musician and a columnist for *The Music Paper*.

Sonnenschein, David.
  Sound Design: The Expressive Power of Music, Voice, and Sound Effects in Cinema. Studio City, Calif.: Michael Wiese Productions, 2001.
Discusses how to use music for emotional impact. Examples include films such as *Star Wars* and *The Matrix*. Tables list the physical, mental, and emotional impact of musical genres and the emotional characteristic of harmonic intervals. Author is a sound designer with a background in music.

Spaeth, Sigmund.
  Fifty Years with Music. Westport, Conn.: Greenwood Press, 1977.
The chapter "Opportunities in Music" includes film composing, 214–15.

Spottiswoode, Raymond.
  Film and Its Technique. Berkeley: Univ. of California Press, 1951. Reprint, 1968.
"Film Music," 328–29. "The Liberation of Sound," on making music without instruments, 381–87.

Spottiswoode, Raymond.
  A Grammar of the Film: An Analysis of Film Technique. London: Faber and Faber, 1936. Berkeley: Univ. of California Press, 1950.
Discusses the commentative, contrastive, dynamic, evocative, and imitative role of music, 49–50, 190–95 (1936).

Staggs, Sam.
  All About All About Eve: *The Complete Behind-the-Scenes Story of the Bitchiest Film Ever Made.* New York: St. Martin's Press, 2000.
"And You, I Take It, Are the Paderewski Who Plays His Concerto on Me, the Piano?," on Alfred Newman's score and the onscreen pianist Claude Stroud, 174–80.

Staggs, Sam.
  Close Up on Sunset Boulevard: *Billy Wilder, Norma Desmond, and the Dark Hollywood Dream.* New York: St. Martin's Press, 2002.
Franz Waxman and his "sonata in noir" are discussed, as is the film's source music, 141–45.

Staggs, Sam.
  When Blanche Met Brando: The Scandalous Story of A Streetcar Named Desire. New York: St. Martin's Press, 2005.
"White Jazz" gives the back story on Alex North's score, 215–16.

Staines, Joe, and Duncan Clark, eds.
  The Rough Guide to Classical Music. 3rd ed. London: Rough Guides, 2001. 4th ed., rev. and expanded, 2005.
The 2001 edition contains an article on film music. *The Rough Guide to World Music*, a definitive reference source published since 1994, contains a discography for Indian film

music. Also, *World Music: The Rough Guide II: Latin and North America, Caribbean, India, Asia and Pacific* (Rough Guides, 2000) contains "India: Film Music—Soundtrack to a Billion Lives," by Ken Hunt, 102–8.

Stambler, Irwin.
> *Encyclopedia of Popular Music*. New York: St. Martin's Press, 1965.

Includes biographical entries for popular songwriters and composers such as Henry Mancini. Most entries are not specific to film music. Selected entries for musicals and songs.

Stanfield, Peter.
> *Hollywood, Westerns and the 1930s: The Lost Trail*. Exeter, Devon, U.K.: Univ. of Exeter Press, 2001.

"Blue Yodels: The Antecedents of the Singing Cowboy," on the emergence of the singing cowboy, 1931–1935, 60–73.

Starr, Kevin.
> *The Dream Endures: California Enters the 1940s*. New York: Oxford Univ. Press, 1997.

Includes a brief survey of émigré film composers, 361–62.

Steib, Murray, ed.
> *Reader's Guide to Music: History, Theory, Criticism*. Chicago: Fitzroy Dearborn, 1999.

"Film Music," by Jeongwon Joe, contains an overview of eight seminal books on film music, 235–36. The biographical entries for concert composers generally omit their film music credits, with some exceptions such as Philip Glass, 261–62, and Erich Wolfgang Korngold, 380–81.

Steen, Mike.
> *Hollywood Speaks! An Oral History*. New York: G. P. Putnam's Sons, 1974.

Contains a 1970 interview with John Green on his career as a composer, conductor, music director, and MGM music executive, 326–45.

Stephens, Michael L.
> *Gangster Films: A Comprehensive, Illustrated Reference to People, Films, and Terms*. Jefferson, N.C.: McFarland, 1996.

Brief biographical entries with representative film credits for Daniele Amfitheatrof, Hugo Friedhofer, Alfred Newman, David Raksin, Miklós Rózsa, Paul Sawtell, Max Steiner, Dimitri Tiomkin, Franz Waxman, Roy Webb, and others who contributed to the genre.

Stevens, Bertha, comp. and ed.
> *Bernard Stevens and His Music: A Symposium*. London: Kahn & Averill; White Plains, N.Y.: Pro/Am Music Resources, 1989.

"An Excursion into Film Music" is a discussion of Bernard Stevens's film scores with his widow, Bertha, 144–46.

Stites, Richard, ed.
> *Culture and Entertainment in Wartime Russia*. Bloomington: Indiana Univ. Press, 1995.

"Composing for Victory: Classical Music," by Harlow Loomis Robinson, includes a discussion of Prokofiev's score for *Ivan Grozniy* (*Ivan the Terrible*, 1944), 62–76.

Stokes, Jane.
> *On Screen Rivals: Cinema and Television in the United States and Britain*. New York: St. Martin's Press, 2000.

Contains "Pop and the Box: Youth, Television, Music and Movies in the 1950s and 1960s."

Stokowski, Leopold.
> *Music for All of Us*. New York: Simon and Schuster, 1943.

"Music and Motion Pictures" includes an example from *Fantasia* of balancing the orchestra for film recording versus concert performance, 241–47; "Music and Television" was written in the early days of the medium, with implications for music, 248–51.

Stone, Al, Jr.
> *Jingles: How to Write, Produce & Sell Commercial Music*. Cincinnati: Writer's Digest Books, 1990.

A veteran composer of television commercials gives pointers based on his experience. With examples, including a fully orchestrated commercial.

Stone, Desmond.
> *Alec Wilder in Spite of Himself: A Life of the Composer*. New York: Oxford Univ. Press, 1996.

"Adventures in Opera and Film" includes documentation on Wilder's scores for three Jerome Hill films in the late 1950s and early 1960s, 102–6.

Stone, Susannah Harris.
> *The Oakland Paramount*. Berkeley, Calif.: Lancaster-Miller Publishers, 1982.

"The Mighty Wurlitzer," 70–72.

Stratemann, Klaus.
> *Negro Bands on Film: An Exploratory Filmo-Discography*. Lübbecke, West Germany: Verlag Uhle & Kleimann, 1981.

This one-volume pamphlet covers the big-band era from 1928 to 1950 and includes music or song titles, performers, and music timing.

Straw, William, ed.
> *Popular Music: Style and Identity*. Montreal, Canada: Centre for Research on Canadian Cultural Industries and Institutions, 1995.

"Who Gets to Sound American in Hollywood Films?," by Anahid Kassabian, on Americanness in film music, 173–76.

Strock, Herbert L.
> *Picture Perfect*. Lanham, Md.: Scarecrow Press, 2000.

A guide to producing and directing films that includes "The Music Editor," 202–4. Author is a film and television director active from the 1950s through the 1970s.

Stuckenschmidt, H. H.
   Schoenberg: His Life, World and Work. Translated from the German by Humphrey Searle. London: Calder, 1977. New York: Schirmer, 1978.
On the composer's brief and unsuccessful interaction with Hollywood, 412–13.

Studlar, Gaylyn, and Matthew Bernstein, eds.
   John Ford Made Westerns: Filming the Legend in the Sound Era. Bloomington: Indiana Univ. Press, 2001.
"'The Sound of Many Voices': Music in John Ford's Westerns," by Kathryn Kalinak, focuses primarily on the music for *Stagecoach* (1939), 169–92.

Sullivan, Jack.
   New World Symphonies: How American Culture Changed European Music. New Haven, Conn.: Yale Univ. Press, 1999.
"Broadway, Hollywood, and the Accidental Beauties of Silly Songs," on the émigré experience in Hollywood, both successful and unsuccessful, focusing in particular on Erich Wolfgang Korngold and on the overall theme that film music is a legitimate outlet for composers, 161–78.

Suskin, Steven.
   Berlin, Kern, Rodgers, Hart, and Hammerstein: A Complete Song Catalogue. Jefferson, N.C.: McFarland, 1990.
Brief biographies of each songwriter, followed by exhaustive song listings, including songs from films.

Sutro, John, ed.
   Diversion: Twenty-Two Authors on the Lively Arts. London: Max Parrish, 1950.
"The Celluloid Plays a Tune," by Alan Rawsthorne, 25–34; and "The Orchestration of Movement," by Robert Helpmann, on ballet in films, 198–206.

Svehla, Gary J., and Susan Svehla, eds.
   Memories of Hammer. Baltimore: Luminary Press, 2002.
"James Bernard," interviewed by Bill Littman, 36–56; "Tribute to James Bernard," by Steve Vertlieb, 57–60; transcript of an audience Q&A with James Bernard and others, 229–54.

Tagg, Philip, ed.
   Film Music, Mood Music, and Popular Music Research: Interviews, Conversations, Entretiens sur la Musique de Film, de Sonorisation et sur la Recherche dans la Musique des Mass-Média. Göteborg, Sweden: Göteborgs Universitet, Musikvetenskapliga Institutionen, 1980.
This 90-page monograph includes interviews with representatives from prerecorded film music and television music, as well as an interview with a British film composer.

Tagg, Philip, and Bob Clarida.
   Ten Little Title Tunes: Towards a Musicology of the Mass Media. New York: Mass
   Media Music Scholars' Press, 2003. 898 pp.
Documents a research project in which test subjects listened to ten pieces of music without visual accompaniment. Extensive discussion of theory and methodology, as well as
an examination of the musical structure of the tunes. The ten pieces include Charles Williams's "The Dream of Olwen," music from *Sayonara* by Franz Waxman, *A Streetcar
Named Desire* by Alex North, and *Miami Vice* by Jan Hammer. Addresses interesting
questions (for example, Are pianos romantic?) and discusses the relationship between
minor key jazz and crime drama. Also includes the test subjects' written responses, test
session data, and an alphabetical list of verbal-visual associations. Authors are a musicologist specializing in popular music and a lawyer with a background in music scholarship, respectively.

Takemitsu, Toru.
   Confronting Silence: Selected Writings. 1995. Berkeley, Calif.: Fallen Leaf, 1995.
Essays translated from Japanese, with some discussion of the composer's film work.

Talmadge, William E.
   How to Play Pictures. N.p., 1914.
Advice in a folksy manner on accompaniment for silent films from a Northwestern musi-
cian, according to Martin Marks's bibliography in *Journal of the University Film and
Video Association* (Winter 1982).

Tanner, Paul.
   Conversations with a Musician: A Glenn Miller Trombonist Speaks... Tokyo: Cosmo
   Space, 1999.
Autobiography by the big-band trombonist, Hollywood session musician, UCLA jazz
professor, and author. Includes the chapters "Making Movies," on working with the
Glenn Miller Band in the early 1940s, 97–106, and "Hollywood Studios," on being a
freelancer in the 1950s, 155–69. Author also cowrote *"Every Night Was New Year's
Eve": On the Road with Glenn Miller* (Tokyo: Cosmo Space, 1992, 1998; Los Angeles:
Cosmo Space of America, 2000).

Tarasti, Eero, ed.
   Musical Semiotics in Growth. Bloomington: Indiana Univ. Press, 1996.
"Some Greimasian Concepts as Applied to the Analysis of Film Music," by Ennio
Simeon, 347–55, analyzes Ennio Morricone's music for *The Mission* using concepts
developed by Algirdas Julien Greimas, a Lithuanian linguist and semiotician.

Tasker, Yvonne.
   Working Girls: Gender and Sexuality in Popular Cinema. London: Routledge, 1998.
"Music, Video, Cinema: Singers and Movie Stars" includes some discussion of female
musical performance in films, 179–93.

Taylor, Deems.
   Some Enchanted Evenings: The Story of Rodgers and Hammerstein. New York:
   Harper, 1953.
Includes some discussion of films, 132–33, 148–40.

Taylor, John Russell.
  Hitch: The Life and Times of Alfred Hitchcock. New York: Pantheon Books, 1978.
  Hitch: The Life and Work of Alfred Hitchcock. London: Faber and Faber, 1978. Reprint, New York: Da Capo Press, 1996.
Contains some material on Bernard Herrmann.

Taylor, John Russell.
  Strangers in Paradise: The Hollywood Émigrés, 1933–1950. New York: Holt, Rinehart and Winston; London: Faber and Faber, 1983.
Includes material on the Hollywood experiences of Arnold Schoenberg, 80–81; Ernst Toch, 83; Erich Wolfgang Korngold, 84–89; Igor Stravinsky, 156; and Hanns Eisler, 157–58.

Taylor, Theodore.
  People Who Make Movies. Garden City, N.Y.: Doubleday, 1967.
"Music and the Musical," an overview of the scoring process, 119–32. Author had the cooperation of Henry Mancini.

Tedesco, Tommy.
  Tommy Tedesco: Confessions of a Guitar Player: An Autobiography. Fullerton, Calif.: Centerstream Publishing, 1993.
"Television and Films," 54–65. Includes quotes from Bill Conti, Frank DeVol, and Henry Mancini. Lists of films and television shows featuring the preeminent studio session guitarist.

Teetor, Henry C., and Herbert S. Mikesell.
  The Pipe Organ: Mechanics–Maintenance–Technic; Theatre and Church. Richmond, Ind.: Teetor-Mikesell Extension Training School, 1928.
A 57-page manual on the instrument, self-published by two Indiana locals.

Temple, Michael, James S. Williams, and Michael Witt, eds.
  For Ever Godard. London: Black Dog, 2004.
Of interest: "Sound and Music," 250–311; "Introduction," 250–51. "Recital: Three Lyrical Interludes in Godard," by Adrian Martin, on the use of songs in the films of director Jean-Luc Godard, 252–71; "JLG/ECM," by Laurent Jullier, on the difference between experiencing music while watching a Godard film versus hearing it on the soundtrack, 272–87; "Music, Love, and the Cinematic Event," by James S. Williams, on Godard's ideas of and for music, 288–311.

Terenzio, Maurice, Scott MacGillivray, and Ted Okuda.
  The Soundies Distributing Corporation of America: A History and Filmography of Their "Jukebox" Musical Films of the 1940s. Jefferson, N.C.: McFarland, 1991.
History of the filmed musical shorts that came to be known as "Soundies:" three-minute, black-and-white 16mm films with optical soundtracks that were rear-projected on a small, self-contained screen. The proprietary machine, a Panoram, was basically a video jukebox. The music covered genres from big band to country to jazz, with artists performing to a prerecorded music track. Musicians featured include Duke Ellington, Liberace, and Fats Waller.

Terrace, Vincent.
   The TV Theme Song Trivia Book: Mind-Boggling Questions about Those Songs and Themes You Can't Get Out of Your Head. Secaucus, N.J.: Carol Publishing Group, 1996.
This novelty book—technically not a true trivia book—asks the reader to guess the name of the theme song by providing a portion of the lyric. (Answers also given.)

Thomas, Allan, and Ross Clark, eds.
   Asia Pacific Voices: Selected Papers from the Asia Pacific Festival and Composers' Conference, December 1984, Aotearoa, New Zealand. Wellington: Victoria University, Composers' Association of New Zealand, 1986.
"Indian Film Music and the Classical Tradition," by Bhaskar Chandavarkar, 6–13.

Thompson, Frank.
   The Alamo: *The Illustrated Story of the Epic Film.* New York: Newmarket Press, 2004.
"Haunting and Tender: Composer Carter Burwell," 68.

Thompson, Frank.
   Tim Burton's Nightmare Before Christmas: *The Film, the Art, the Vision: With the Complete Lyrics from the Film.* New York: Hyperion, 1993.
On scoring the film with Danny Elfman's music, 159–60.

Thompson, Robert J., and Gary Burns, eds.
   Making Television: Authorship and the Production Process. New York: Praeger, 1990.
"Black Music and Television: A Critical Look at *Frank's Place,*" by Joe Moorehouse, examines music in the 1987–1988 situation comedy.

Thomson, John Mansfield.
   Biographical Dictionary of New Zealand Composers. Wellington, New Zealand: Victoria Univ. Press, 1990.
Contains references to composers who have written for film, including Gary Daverne, Russ Garcia, and Christopher Small.

Thomson, Virgil.
   American Music Since 1910. Vol. 1. New York: Holt, Rinehart; London: Weidenfeld and Nicolson, 1971.
Brief biographies on Aaron Copland (a short chapter on the composer offers insight on his transition from writing for ballets to scoring films), Hershy Kay, Ulysses Kay, Gail Kubik, and others.

Thomson, Virgil.
   The Musical Scene. New York: Knopf, 1945. New York: Greenwood Press, 1968.
"Processed Music" includes material on *Fantasia* and "Chaplin Scores," 249–66 (1945). Reprinted from the *New York Herald Tribune.*

Thomson, Virgil.
>   *The State of Music.* New York: William Morrow, 1939. 2nd ed. (rev.), New York:
>   Vintage Books, 1962. Reprint (of 1939 edition). Westport, Conn.: Greenwood Press,
>   1974.

"Music and Photography," an essay in the chapter "How to Write a Piece, Or Functional Design in Music," includes a discussion of the role of music in film, 173–90 (1974).

Tibbetts, John C.
>   *Composers in the Movies: Studies in Musical Biography.* New Haven, Conn.: Yale
>   Univ. Press, 2005.

Examines biopics of classical composers and also discusses specific films and directors, the creative process, and the use of classical music in film. Lengthy material on composer biopics in the studio era, 1930–1960; *A Song to Remember,* with music adapted from Frédéric Chopin; Hollywood's take on American popular songwriters; the composer films of directors Ken Russell and Tony Palmer; and recent composer biopics. Main focus is on the composer, the film and its production history, and the accuracy of the depiction, while the musical adaptation by Hollywood composers is underplayed. Author is a theater and film professor.

Towers, Harry Alan, and Leslie Mitchell.
>   *The March of the Movies.* London: Sampson Low, Marston & Co., 1947.

In "Music: Introducing Muir Mathieson," Mitchell interviews the Scottish film music conductor on getting started, aesthetics, and current trends, 54–62.

Tucker, Mark, ed.
>   *The Duke Ellington Reader.* New York: Oxford Univ. Press, 1993.

"Max Harrison on *Anatomy of a Murder,*" 313–15, reprinted from *The Jazz Review* ("Ellington's Music for *Anatomy of a Murder,*" November 1959); other references to Ellington's film music.

Turner, Adrian.
>   *The Making of David Lean's* Lawrence of Arabia. Limpsfield, U.K.: Dragon's
>   World, 1994.

"Enter Jarre," on the production of the music, including Maurice Jarre's score, 156–57.

Tyler, Parker.
>   *The Hollywood Hallucination.* New York: Creative Age Press, 1944. New York:
>   Simon & Schuster, 1970. Reprint (of 1944 edition), New York: Garland, 1985.

"Orpheus á la Hollywood" includes observations on Korngold's music for *Kings Row* (1942), 155–67. Author is a writer and poet.

USC Entertainment Law Institute.
>   *Conference Program on Legal Aspects of the Entertainment Industry.* 1 vol. Los An-
>   geles: University of Southern California School of Law and the Beverly Hills Bar
>   Association, 1962.

Contains a syllabus and forms on acquiring and using music for the eighth annual program on legal aspects of the entertainment industry.

Ussher, Bruno David, ed.
  Who's Who in Music and Dance in Southern California. Hollywood: Bureau of Musical Research, 1933.
"Music for Screen and Stage," by Edwin Schallert, focuses on musical films, 58–63. Biographical entries for some of the earliest musical figures active in Los Angeles film studios, including Constantin Bakaleinikoff, Louis de Francesco, Nathaniel Finston, Hugo Friedhofer, Alfred Newman, Max Steiner, and Morris Stoloff. Subsequent editions were edited by José Rodriguez (1940) and Richard Drake Saunders (1948).

Ustinov, Peter.
  Add a Dash of Pity. Boston: Little, Brown, 1959.

  Add a Dash of Pity and Other Short Stories. Amherst, N.Y.: Prometheus Books, 1996.
Both books include "The Man Who Took It Easy," a short story about a fictional film composer named Erhardt Von Csumlay, which also appeared in the *Atlantic Monthly* (January 1959).

Vaché, Warren W.
  The Unsung Songwriters: America's Masters of Melody. Lanham, Md.: Scarecrow Press, 2000.
Includes page-length biographies on songwriters such as Ray Heindorf, Bronislaw Kaper, Burton Lane, Henry Mancini, and Johnny Mandel, who also wrote songs for film. Entrants were active from about 1917 to 1950. Index. Author wrote a long-running column of the same name for the New Jersey Jazz Society.

Vail, Mark.
  Keyboard Presents the Hammond Organ: Beauty in the B. San Francisco: Miller Freeman, 1997.
History and development of various instruments utilized by film composers, including the Hammond B-3, Novachord, and Solovox.

Vail, Mark.
  Keyboard Presents Vintage Synthesizers: Groundbreaking Instruments and Pioneering Designers of Electronic Music Synthesizers. San Francisco: GPI Books, 1993. 2nd ed., updated and expanded, *Keyboard Magazine Presents Vintage Synthesizers: Pioneering Designers, Groundbreaking Instruments, Collecting Tips, Mutants of Technology.* San Francisco: Miller Freeman Books, 2000.
History and development of various instruments utilized by film composers, including the Moog, ARP, Minimoog, Oberheim, Prophet-5, Yamaha CS-80, Fairlight, E-mu Emulator, and Linn drum machine.

Vale, V., and Andrea Juno, eds.
  Incredibly Strange Music. Vol. 1. San Francisco: RE/Search Publications, 1993. Vol. 2. San Francisco: RE/Search Publications, 1994.
Interview with composer Gershon Kingsley, vol. 1, 82–91; "Robert Moog," two interviews with information on the Theremin, vol. 2, 132–41; "Bebe Barron," on her husband Louis Barron, their score for *Forbidden Planet*, and a list of projects scored by the Barrons, 194–202.

van den Berg, Harry, and Kees van der Veer.
   On the Structure and Function of Musical Discourse in Television Documentaries.
   Amsterdam: Vrije University, 1988. 16 pp.

van Dijk, Teun A., ed.
   Discourse and Communication: New Approaches to the Analysis of Mass Media.
   Berlin: Walter de Gruyter, 1985.
"Rhythmic Structure of the Film Text," by Theo van Leeuwen, contains peripheral mentions of music, 216–32.

van Hamersveld, Eric, comp.
   It Was Always the Music: A Celebration of Roy and Dale's Singing Cowboy B-Western Era of Country-Western Music. Brunswick, Victoria, Canada: R & R Publications Marketing, 2003.
Film-by-film, song-by-song look at music in the films of Dale Evans and Roy Rogers, primarily in the form of sheet music facsimiles and photographs.

van Leeuwen, Theo.
   Speech, Music, Sound. New York: St. Martin's Press, 1999.
This theory of sound includes a discussion of the communicative role of music in film and television soundtracks.

Van Vechten, Carl.
   Music and Bad Manners. New York: Knopf, 1916.
Contains "Music for the Movies," a lengthy essay by the famous photographer and novelist that is of interest due to its early publication date and judgmental stance, 43–54. The essay opens with: "Despite the fact that it would seem that the moving picture drama had opened up new worlds to the modern musician, no important composer, as far as I am aware, has as yet turned his attention to the writing of music for the films. If the cinema drama is in its infancy, as some would have us believe, then we may be sure that the time is not far distant when moving picture scores will take their places on the musicians' book-shelves alongside those of operas, symphonies, masses, and string quartets." Incidental music for spoken drama is discussed in the context of composers who have written music that has outlived the original production. Van Vechten bemoans that some music directors are more concerned with the musical program—such as fitting in an entire movement of a Beethoven symphony—than with performing an effective accompaniment to a film. The author calls for a new form of music for films: "It has occurred to no one that the moving picture demands a *new* kind of music." Discusses practices at the time, including the overuse of music with descriptive titles (in which the title may fit the scene but the music may not), orchestra leaders calling for "agits" (agitatos) for excitement, and that all pianists seem to play the same piece for Keystone comedies. Van Vechten predicts that excerpts of original film scores will be given to the Boston Symphony Orchestra to perform in concert but critics of film music in concert will say, "This music should never be played except in conjunction with the picture for which it was written." Book's title is taken from the lead essay, which is unrelated to the others. "Music for the Movies" was written in New York on November 10, 1915. Author was an assistant music critic at the *New York Times* and a New York drama critic.

Vasudev, Aruna, ed.
> *Frames of Mind: Reflections on Indian Cinema.* New Delhi: UBSPD, 1995.

Two chapters by Partha Chatterjee, "When Melody Ruled the Day," 51–65, and "A Bit of Song and Dance," 197–218.

Vaughan Williams, Ralph.
> *National Music and Other Essays.* London: Oxford Univ. Press, 1963, 1972. 2nd ed., Oxford: Oxford Univ. Press, 1987. New York: Clarendon Press, 1996.

"Composing for the Films," a 1945 essay on the composer's approach to scoring, 160–165 (1963). See entry below.

Vaughan Williams, Ralph.
> *Some Thoughts on Beethoven's Choral Symphony, With Writings on Other Musical Subjects.* London: Oxford Univ. Press, 1953. Reprint, Westport, Conn.: Greenwood Press, 1981.

In "Composing for the Films," written in 1945, the composer writes about time restraints, his preference for ignoring the details of the screen action in favor of intensifying "the spirit of the whole situation by a continuous stream of music," and the benefits of collaborating with filmmakers during preproduction, 107–15. Reprint of "Film Music" from *Royal College of Music Magazine.*

Vernon, Paul.
> *African-American Blues, Rhythm and Blues, Gospel and Zydeco on Film and Video, 1926–1997.* Aldershot, U.K.; Brookfield, Vt.: Ashgate, 1999.

Documents filmed performances of African American vernacular music by more than 2,000 artists. A resource for filmmakers and researchers to establish what exists and where it can be located. Organized alphabetically by artist name, then chronologically. Entries include location and date of recording, titles performed, source, and notes. Soundtrack material is included only if specifically written for a production. A number of entries are for Soundies and for television programs from *Jubilee Showcase* to *TV Gospel Time.* Preface provides a valuable brief history of African American vernacular music on film. Does not include jazz singers or blues-style material performed by non-African Americans. Eight appendixes include program, film title, and production company index; accompanists index; directors and producers index; resources; commercially available videotapes and laser discs; nonperforming interviewees; and soundtracks.

Vidor, King.
> *King Vidor on Film Making.* New York: David McKay, 1972.

"Film Music," 139–45. The director's thoughts on film music.

Viera, John David, and Robert Thorne, eds.
> *1986 Entertainment, Publishing and the Arts Handbook.* New York: Clark Boardman, 1986.
>> "Film Composing Agreements: Business and Legal Concerns," by Mark Halloran, on business and deal structures, including recent trends, 313–40. Adapted from an earlier article in the *Loyola Entertainment Law Journal* (1985).

1990 Entertainment, Publishing and the Arts Handbook. New York: Clark Board-
man, 1990.
  "Pop Music for Soundtracks," by Mark Halloran and Thomas A. White, 171–89.
  Reprinted in Halloran's *The Musician's Business and Legal Guide* (1991).

Volkov, Solomon.
  *Shostakovich and Stalin: The Extraordinary Relationship Between the Great Com-
  poser and the Brutal Dictator.* Translated from the Russian by Antonina W. Bouis.
  New York: Knopf, 2004. London: Little, Brown, 2004.
Film work, 130–35, 143–44.

Wagner, Walter, ed.
  You Must Remember This: Oral Reminiscences of the Real Hollywood. New York:
  Putnam, 1975.
"Silents Were Never Silent," interview with organist Gaylord Carter, 66–75.

Walker, Alexander.
  The Shattered Silents: How the Talkies Came to Stay. London: Elm Tree Books,
  1978. New York: William Morrow, 1979. New York: Morrow Quill Paperbacks,
  1980.
"The Music—That's the Big Plus about This," 15–27; "A Talkie Chronology (1925–
1929)," 207–9.

Walker, Dan, with Phil Shackleton.
  Recording & Film Scoring with SMPTE. Newbury Park, Calif.: Peter L. Alexander,
  1991. 80 pp.
A brief treatise for recording engineers on the use of the time code standard developed by
the Society of Motion Picture and Television Engineers (SMPTE) for synchronizing film
with sound and music. Topics include the history of SMPTE, equipment, syncing Musical Instrument Digital Interface (MIDI) to video, syncing MIDI to audio, and syncing
MIDI and audio to video. At the time of publication, SMPTE was making its way into
composers' home studios, where video was synced to sequenced music tracks via MIDI
and a computer.

Walker, Janet, ed.
  Westerns: Films through History. New York: Routledge, 2001.
"How the West Was Sung," by Kathryn Kalinak, 151–76; "Drums along the L.A. River:
Scoring the Indian," by Claudia Gorbman, 177–95 (originally published in slightly dif-
ferent form in Born and Hesmondhalgh's *Western Music and Its Others,* 2000).

Walker, John, ed.
  Halliwell's Who's Who in the Movies. 13th ed. (Rev. ed. of *Halliwell's Filmgoer's
  Companion.*) New York: HarperPerennial, 1999. 14th ed., London: HarperCollins
  Pub., 2001. 15th ed., rev. and updated. New York: HarperResource, 2003.
Includes film composer entries, with one-line biographies and selected credits.

Wallace, David.
  Hollywoodland: Rich and Lively History about Hollywood's Grandest Era. New
  York: St. Martin's Press, 2002.

"Movies' Music" contains several unattributed anecdotes and highlights some composers, notably Erich Wolfgang Korngold and Dimitri Tiomkin, 187–97. Author, a journalist, writes: "Today, many credit a third to a half of a film's success to its music."

Waller, Gregory A., ed.
   Moviegoing in America: A Sourcebook in the History of Film Exhibition. Malden, Mass.: Blackwell Publishers, 2002.
"What the Public Wants in the Picture Theatre," by music director Samuel L. Rothafel; "Where 'Movie Playing' Needs Reform," by K. Sherwood Boblitz, originally appeared in *Metronome* (June 1920); "Selections from Musical Presentation of Movie Pictures," by George Beynon, contains excerpts from his 1921 book; "Music," by John F. Barry and Epes W. Sargent.

Walter, Ernest.
   The Technique of the Film Cutting Room. London: Focal Press, 1969. 2nd rev. ed., London: Focal Press; New York: Hastings House, 1973.
"Music Editing," 185–205 (1969), 211–34 (1973).

Washburne, Chris, and Maiken Derno, ed.
   Bad Music: The Music We Love to Hate. New York: Routledge, 2004.
"Film, Music, and the Redemption of the Mundane," by Giorgio Biancorosso, 190–211.

Watts, Stephen, ed.
   Behind the Screen: How Films Are Made. New York: Dodge; London: Arthur Barker, 1938.
In "Film Music," Herbert Stothart writes about film music at MGM studios, 139–44; editor's note introducing Stothart, 138. Reprinted in *The Cue Sheet* (July 2004).

Weaver, Tom.
   MagicImage Filmbooks Presents Creature from the Black Lagoon. Atlantic City, N.J.: MagicImage Filmbooks, 1992.
"Post-production" includes information on music for the 1954 film, 30–31.

Webb, Michael, ed.
   Hollywood: Legend and Reality. Boston: Little, Brown, 1986.
"Scoring" strings together lengthy quotations from organist Gaylord Carter and composers Max Steiner, Bernard Herrmann, Miklós Rózsa, and Leonard Rosenman (all reprinted from other sources) alongside artifacts and photographs from a Smithsonian traveling exhibit, including the piano from *Casablanca* and a neon-edged violin from *Gold Diggers of 1933*, 149–61.

[Weiland, Frederik Christoffel, contributor.]
   Electronic Music Reports. 4 vols. Utrecht: Institute of Sonology, 1974.
"Relationships between Sound and Image," by Frederik Christoffel Weiland, includes a discussion of music, 66–92.

Weis, Elisabeth.
   The Silent Scream: Alfred Hitchcock's Sound Track. Rutherford, N.J.: Fairleigh Dickinson Univ. Press, 1982. London: Associated University Presses, 1982.

Music is mentioned peripherally in this analysis of the aural content of the director's films. See, for example, "Beyond Subjectivity: *The Birds*," 136–46.

Weis, Elisabeth, and John Belton.
> *Film Sound: Theory and Practice.* New York: Columbia Univ. Press, 1985.

"The Sound Track of *The Rules of the Game*," by Michel Litle [*sic*], 312–22; "Film Music," by Stephen Handzo, contains a useful glossary of terms, 408–11. Numerous additional references to film music throughout.

Weisbard, Eric, ed.
> *This Is Pop: In Search of the Elusive at Experience Music Project.* Cambridge, Mass.: Harvard Univ. Press, 2004.

"Interrupted Symphony: A Recollection of Movie Music from Max Steiner to Marvin Gaye," by Geoffrey O'Brien, 90–102.

Weissman, Dick.
> *Making a Living in Your Local Music Market: How to Survive and Prosper.* Milwaukee: Hal Leonard Publishing, 1990.

Some coverage of film music and songwriting.

Weissman, Dick.
> *The Music Business: Career Opportunities and Self-Defense.* New York: Crown, 1979. Rev. ed., New York: Crown, 1990. 2nd rev. ed., New York: Three Rivers Press, 1997.

"Composing, Arranging, and Film Music," 122–25 (1979).

Wells, H. G.
> *Things to Come.* New York: Macmillan, 1935. London: Cresset Press, 1936.

The film's script in novel form. "The Music," on pp. x–xi of the introduction, discusses Arthur Bliss's music for the film. This section does not appear in other editions of the novel.

Wenders, Donata.
> Buena Vista Social Club: *The Book of the Film.* London: Thames & Hudson, 2000.

Contains an interview with Ry Cooder.

Westerby, Herbert, ed.
> *The Complete Organ Recitalist.* London: Musical Opinion and the Organ, 1927.

"The Training of the Kinema Organist," by Quentin M. Maclean, 329–32; "New York and the Cinema," by T. Scott Buhrman, editor of *The American Organist*, has organist biographies and salaries, as well as other topics of interest, 347–54.

Westin, Helen.
> *Introducing the Song Sheet: A Collector's Guide, with Current Price List.* Nashville: T. Nelson, 1976.

"Songs of the Silents," 125–29; "Stars of the Radio, Records, and the Talkies," 129–34; "Shirley Temple and Walt Disney," 135–39.

Whitaker, Rod.
   The Language of Film. Englewood Cliffs, N. J.: Prentice Hall, 1970.
An influential textbook that includes "The Audio Content" (see "Local Music," 104, and "Background Music," 105–7). Author was a novelist who wrote under the names Trevanian and Nicholas Seare.

Whitcomb, Ian.
   Tin Pan Alley: A Pictorial History (1919–1939) with Complete Words and Music of Forty Songs. New York: Paddington Press, 1975.
"Movie Madness," 154–62.

White, Mark.
   "You Must Remember This...": Popular Songwriters, 1900–1980. London: F. Warne, 1983. New York: Charles Scribner's Sons, 1985.
Biographical sketches for hundreds of songwriters, a majority of whom contributed songs to films. Sammy Cahn and Johnny Mercer are the only film song lyricists represented. Indexes for song title, composer, performer, and film title.

White, Rob.
   The Third Man. London: British Film Institute, 2003.
Includes background on Anton Karas's score for the 1949 film, 33–35.

Whitney, John.
   Digital Harmony: On the Complementarity of Music and Visual Art. Peterborough, N.H.: Byte Books, 1980.
Author is a filmmaker who specialized in abstract and geometric computer animation. Discusses theoretical and practical aspects of visual music, with emphasis on the interaction of music and image in his films.

Whitworth, Reginald.
   The Cinema and Theatre Organ: A Comprehensive Description of This Instrument, Its Constituent Parts, and Its Uses. London: Musical Opinion, 1932. Reprint, Braintree, Mass.: Organ Literature Foundation, 1981.
This illustrated technical manual has a chapter on specific organs in theaters, primarily in London and New York. Concludes with a short treatise, "The Music of the Cinema Organ," 104–10.

Wiese, Michael.
   Film and Video Budgets. Studio City, Calif.; Stoneham, Mass.: Michael Wiese Productions and Focal Press, 1990. 2nd ed., with Deke Simon. Studio City, Calif.: M. Wiese Productions, 1995. 3rd ed., with Deke Simon and Michael Wiese. 2001.
"Sound and Music," an overview on creating a budget, 64–69 (1990).

Wilder, Alec.
   American Popular Song: The Great Innovators, 1900–1950. New York: Oxford Univ. Press, 1972.
Discusses the music of two dozen songwriters, many of whom wrote songs for film, including Harold Arlen, Irving Berlin, Hoagy Carmichael, Walter Donaldson, Vernon Duke, George Gershwin, John Green, Jerome Kern, Burton Lane, Hugh Martin, Jimmy

McHugh, Ray Noble, Cole Porter, Richard Rodgers, Arthur Schwartz, Jimmy Van Heusen, Harry Warren, Richard Whiting, and Vincent Youmans. Numerous music examples.

Wilk, Max.
> *They're Playing Our Song: From Jerome Kern to Stephen Sondheim—The Stories behind the Words and Music of Two Generations.* New York: Atheneum, 1973. Rev. ed., New York: New York Zoetrope, 1986. *They're Playing Our Song: The Truth behind the Words and Music of Three Generations.* Mount Kisco, N.Y.: Moyer Bell, 1991.

Engagingly written text by the gifted playwright, unlike any other on the subject. Songwriters and lyricists profiled include Harold Arlen, Irving Berlin, Sammy Cahn, Saul Chaplin, Betty Comden, Dorothy Fields, Ira Gershwin, Oscar Hammerstein (II), E. Y. Harburg, Lorenz Hart, Bert Kalmar, Jerome Kern, Frank Loesser, Johnny Mercer, Leo Robin, Richard Rodgers, Harry Ruby, Stephen Sondheim, Jule Styne, Harry Warren, Richard Whiting, and Vincent Youmans.

Williams, Linda Ruth.
> *The Erotic Thriller in Contemporary Cinema.* Bloomington: Indiana Univ. Press, 2005.

Discusses erotic musicals and sex scenes as production numbers.

Willian, Michael.
> It's a Wonderful Life: *The Essential Film Guidebook: A Scene-by-Scene Look at a Holiday Classic.* Kerpluggo Books, 2004.

"The Musical Score" on Dimitri Tiomkin's original score and the popular songs used, 119–21.

Willson, Meredith.
> *And There I Stood with My Piccolo.* Garden City, N.Y.: Doubleday, 1948. Reprint, Westport, Conn.: Greenwood Press, 1975.

The composer and playwright's reminiscences, told in a folksy manner. Followed in 1955 with *Eggs I Have Laid.*

Willson, Meredith.
> *"But He Doesn't Know the Territory."* New York: G. P. Putnam's Sons, 1959.

The playwright's autobiographical tales, primarily on the creation of the musical *The Music Man.* Scattered material on Willson's forays into film music, especially at MGM in the 1950s. Willson also wrote a forty-page treatise of his experience in radio, *What Every Young Musician Should Know: A Concise and Modern Volume Revealing the Inside of Radio Musical Technique*, published in New York by Robbins Music in 1938.

Wilson, Ivy Crane, ed.
> *Hollywood Album: The Wonderful City and Its Famous Inhabitants.* 3rd ed. London: S. Low, Marston, 1949.

"A Letter from Max Steiner," submitted by the composer in lieu of a promised article, 13–14; "Happy Times with Danny Kaye," by Johnny Green, 15–18.

Winder, Catherine, and Zahra Dowlatabadi.
Producing Animation. Boston: Focal Press, 2001.
Overview of the music production process, from spotting through postproduction; see "Songs," 204–6; "Music," 259–61.

Winkler, Martin M., ed.
Classical Myth & Culture in the Cinema. New York: Oxford Univ. Press, 2001.
Includes a discussion of music composed for films set in antiquity, particularly by Miklós Rózsa, 324–37.

Winkler, Max.
A Penny from Heaven. New York: Appleton-Century-Crofts, 1951.
Autobiography by the music publisher. Discusses his employment with Carl Fischer Music in New York, his account of his invention and development of the cue sheet (166–77, 221–29), and the formation of his company Cinema Music and its merger with S. M. Berg to form Belwin (230ff.). His personal account of the 1910s and 1920s from a publisher's perspective includes a discussion of music to accompany silent films and the effects of sound films on the publishing industry. Portions appeared in *Films in Review* (December 1951).

Witkin, Robert W.
Adorno on Popular Culture. London: Routledge, 2003.
"Film Music," by Theodor Adorno, 148–50.

Wlaschin, Ken.
Gian Carlo Menotti on Screen: Opera, Dance, and Choral Works on Film, Television, and Video. Jefferson, N.C.: McFarland, 1999.
Documents filmed operas by one of the best-known American opera composers in the post–World War II era.

Writers' Congress.
Writers' Congress: The Proceedings of the Conference Held in October 1943 under the Sponsorship of the Hollywood Writers' Mobilization and the University of California. Berkeley: Univ. of California Press, 1944.
"Music and the War" and "Song Writing and the War" contain the following: "The Obligation of Music," by Sol Kaplan, 241–47; "Collaboration between the Screen Writer and the Composer," by Adolph Deutsch, 248–50; "Humor in Music," by David Raksin, 251–55; "Music in the Documentary Film," by Gail Kubik, 256–59; "Prejudices and New Musical Material," by Hanns Eisler, 260–64; "Music in French Film," by Darius Milhaud, 272–76; "The Negro and His Music in Films," by William Grant Still, which calls for more realistic black music, 277–79; "Report on the American Theatre Wing Music War Committee," by Oscar Hammerstein II, 280–83; "War Songs of America," by Earl Robinson, 284–303.

Wyatt, Geoffrey.
At the Mighty Organ. Oxford: Oxford Illustrated Press, 1974.
This 98-page illustrated treatise includes references to the history and development of the cinema organ and its use in accompanying silent films in England.

Wyatt, Robert, and John Andrew Johnson, eds.
>   *The George Gershwin Reader*. New York: Oxford Univ. Press, 2004.
"Last Years: Hollywood, 1936–37" chronicles Gershwin's RKO scores, 237–68, and includes "Hollywood Ending (1938)," by Edith Garson, wife of Gershwin biographer and writer Edward Jablonski, 239–44.

Yavelow, Christopher.
>   *Macworld Music & Sound Bible*. San Mateo, Calif.: IDG Books Worldwide, 1992.
History of music and sound produced using the Macintosh computer. A chapter on film and video applications has information on music synchronization and cue sheet applications, with a foreword by Dominic Frontiere, 1108–10. Includes an interview with television composer Bruce Miller on computers and synthesizers, 1161–64. A chapter on music for multimedia has information on library music, specifically the Hollywood Film Music Library, 1233–34.

Zaimont, Judith Lang, ed.
>   *The Musical Woman: An International Perspective*. Vol. 3, 1986–1990. Westport, Conn.: Greenwood Press, 1991.
"Women Film and Television Composers in the United States," by Leslie N. Andersen.

Zhang, Yingjin, ed.
>   *Encyclopedia of Chinese Film*. London: Routledge, 1998.
"Music and Film," by Yingjin Zhang, on music in films from China, Taiwan, and Hong Kong, 243–44; "The Musical," by Yingjin Zhang, 244–46.

Zhang, Yingjin, ed.
>   *Cinema and Urban Culture in Shanghai, 1922–1943*. Stanford, Calif.: Stanford Univ. Press, 1999.
"Metropolitan Sounds: Music in Chinese Films of the 1930s," by Sue Tuohy, 200–221.

Zillner, Dian.
>   *Hollywood Collectibles*. West Chester, Penn.: Schiffer, 1991.
Includes numerous color photographs of sheet music and album covers related to twenty collectible actors, from Fred Astaire to John Wayne.
>   *Hollywood Collectibles: The Sequel*. Atglen, Penn.: Schiffer, 1994.
Includes numerous color photographs of sheet music and album covers related to two dozen collectible actors, from Jackie Coogan to Elvis Presley.

Zinsser, William.
>   *Easy to Remember: The Great American Songwriters and Their Songs*. Jaffrey, N.H.: David R. Godine, 2000.
"Made in Hollywood: 'As Time Goes By' and 'Laura'" offers a brief history of those songs, 165–69. Numerous other film songs are mentioned in chapters on specific composers. Film title and song title indexes.

Zollo, Paul.
   Hollywood Remembered: An Oral History of Its Golden Age. New York: Cooper
   Square Press, 2002.
In "David Raksin," the composer discusses his early years and working with Charlie
Chaplin, 69–74.

Chapter 6

Music for the Accompaniment of Silent Films

1909

Frelinger, Gregg A.

Motion Picture Piano Music: Descriptive Music to Fit the Action, Character, or Scene of Moving Pictures. Lafayette, Ind.: G. A. Frelinger, 1909.

This earliest known compilation of photoplay music has fifty-one short, simple pieces for piano with functional titles that refer to tempo, mood, character type, incident, or plot. Music was selected to fit the action, characters, and scenes of various motion pictures. A copy is at the Music Division of the Library of Congress. Author is a pianist.

1910

The Emerson Moving Picture Music Folio. Cincinnati: Groene Music, 1910.

A compilation of more than 125 piano pieces that is not known to survive. It was advertised for only one week in *Moving Picture World* (July 2, 1910, p. 36).

Orpheum Collection of Moving Picture Music. Chicago, 1910.

An anthology of melodramatic music, probably compiled by William E. King, music director of Chicago's Orpheum Theater. Not known to survive. Sold by Clarence Sinn in Chicago, according to an advertisement in *Moving Picture World* (October 1, 1910, p. 815). Sinn apparently published a reprinted edition from the original plates as late as 1917 (see *Moving Picture World*, October 20, 1917).

1911

Platzman, Eugene, arr.

F. B. Haviland's Moving Picture Pianist's Album. New York: Haviland, 1911.

Simplified arrangements of "familiar favorites," according to Rick Altman in *Silent Film Sound* (2004), by a Tin Pan Alley songwriter and arranger.

1912

Carl Fischer [Music].

Carl Fischer Moving Picture Folio, Especially Designed for Moving Picture Theatres, Vaudeville Houses, etc. New York: Carl Fischer, 1912.

An early effort by the publisher. Carl Fischer later started a motion picture service department addressing the musical needs of those in the field.

Zamecnik, John S.

Sam Fox Moving Picture Music. 4 vols. Cleveland: Sam Fox, 1912–1923.

For solo piano. Volumes 1 and 2 (1912–1913), volume 3 (1914), and volume 4 (1923). Author is a composer and conductor who served as music director of the Cleveland Hippodrome.

1913

Smith, George, comp.
>   *Carl Fischer Professional Pianist's Collection for Motion Picture Theatres, Vaudeville Houses, Theatrical Programs, and Dramatic Purposes.* New York: Carl Fischer, 1913.

1914

Lake, M. L., and Lester Brockton.
>   *Carl Fischer Loose Leaf Motion Picture Collection.* 3 vols. New York: Carl Fischer, 1914, 1916, 1918.

Volumes 1 and 2 composed by Lake, volume 3 by Brockton (pseudonym of M. L. Lake). The music was laid out in 32- and 64-bar sections purportedly to allow the performer to stop at any point or to repeat bars as needed to complete the scene. Lake was a music director who specialized in band music; he later helped Julius S. Seredy compile the *Motion Picture Music Guide to the Carl Fischer Modern Orchestra Catalogue* (1922).

Leo Feist [Publishers].
>   *Feist's Foto-Play Folio: Moving Picture Music.* New York: Leo Feist, 1914.

According to an advertisement, the music was printed on loose cards.

Levy, Sol P., comp.
>   *Gordon's Motion Picture Collection for Moving Picture Pianists.* 2 vols. New York: Hamilton S. Gordon, 1914.

Levy was a Chicago-born composer, songwriter, and clarinetist who wrote music for several films in the mid-teens before moving into music publishing with Belwin Music.

Martaine, G., arr. and comp.
>   *Album of Photo-Play Music.* 2 vols. New York: Academic Music, 1914.

After publishing *Famous Hymns, Famous Songs from Famous Operas,* and similar compilations, Martaine entered the motion picture field. A third volume, *Photo-Play Music Folio,* appeared the same year.

1915

G. Schirmer [Publishers].
>   *Schirmer's Photoplay Series: A Loose Leaf Collection of Dramatic and Descriptive Musical Numbers Especially Composed for Use with Motion Pictures Arranged for Small or Full Orchestra and Playable with Any Lesser Combination of Instruments Which Includes Violin and Piano.* 7 vols. New York: G. Schirmer, 1915–1929.

1916

Berg, S. M.
>   *Berg's Incidental Series.* New York: Belwin, 1916–1917.

Author was a music director who edited the "Music for the Picture" column in *Moving Picture World* in 1915 and 1916, and contributed cue sheets to the magazine for several years.

Carl Fischer [Music].
   Carl Fischer's Moving Picture Series of Incidental—Dramatic Descriptive and Characteristic Music. New York: Carl Fischer, n.d., ca. 1916.
Music by composers from Emil Ascher to Max Winkler.

Kerssen, Carl.
   Dramatic and Incidental Music: Comprising the Best and Most Practical Musical Accompaniments. 8 series. New York: [Carl Fischer], n.d., ca. 1916.
Author was best known for his arrangement of "The Animal Quartett" by J. Brixner. These numbers were composed and arranged specially for dramatic scenes, including murder, fights, riots, and sudden danger.

Ketèlbey, Albert William.
   New Moving Picture Music. London: Bosworth, 1916.
Author was a British composer and vaudeville music director famous for writing light popular music.

Roberts, Chas. J., arr.
   Carl Fischer Moving Picture Album. New York: Carl Fischer, ca. 1916.
A folio with musical numbers for a nine-piece ensemble. Roberts, a flutist, arranged or supervised the arrangement of the music. Born in Hungary, he was a staff arranger at a music publishing house and specialized in transcribing and arranging symphonic music for smaller orchestras. Advertisements praised Roberts's arrangements and claimed this was the only folio that could cover any reel of film from beginning to end. Roberts later collaborated with Julius S. Seredy on the *Motion Picture Music Guide to the Carl Fischer Modern Orchestra Catalogue* (1922).

1917
Breil, Joseph Carl.
   Joseph Carl Breil's Dramatic Music for Motion Picture Plays. New York: Chappell, 1917.
An original collection from the composer of *Birth of a Nation.*

Luz, Ernst.
   A.B.C. Feature Photo-Play Edition. 3 vols. New York: Photo Play Music, 1917–1919.
Author was a music director who wrote the "Picture Music" column in *Moving Picture News* in 1912 and 1913. He later developed a system for selecting music to accompany films, as explained in his monograph, *Motion Picture Synchrony* (1925).

Sam Fox Publishing.
   Sam Fox Concert Orchestral Folio. 2 folios. Cleveland: Sam Fox Publishing, 1917; 1923.
Original compositions specially adapted to the moving picture orchestra.

1918
Belwin.
   Cinema Incidental Series. New York: Belwin, 1918–1923.
At least thirty-eight different series of silent film music for orchestra.

Ditson.
> *Ditson's Music for the Photoplay.* At least 10 vols. Boston: Oliver Ditson, 1918.

Ditson's roots go back to 1783, when Batelle's Book Store (later the Oliver Ditson Company) started a music publishing business in Boston.

1919

Baker, Lacy.
> *Picture Music: A Collection of Classic and Modern Compositions for the Organ Especially Adapted for Moving Pictures with Practical Suggestions to the Organist.* 2 vols. New York: H. W. Gray, 1919.

An advertisement noted, "The Editor has also indicated when the piece can be cut so as to give the required length of performance."

Wilson, Mortimer.
> *Silhouettes from the Screen for Piano.* Opus 55. N.p.: Composers Music Co.

Author was an American composer who wrote incidental music for a handful of films in the 1920s. He also authored musical training books on harmony and orchestration.

Zamecnik, John S.
> *Sam Fox Photoplay Edition: A Loose Leaf Collection of High Class Dramatic and Descriptive Motion Picture Music.* 3 vols. Cleveland: Sam Fox Publishing, 1919; 1922; 1925.

Widely used music for orchestra.

1920

Swinnen, Firmin.
> *The Motion Picture Organist.* New York: G. Schirmer, 1920.

Twelve contemporary pieces transcribed by an experienced theater organist. Swinnen also composed twenty-five original compositions intended for films that were later published as *The Theater Organist* (J. Fischer, 1921).

West, George, comp. and ed.
> *Film Folio: Moods and Motives for the Movies.* Boston: Boston Music Co., 1920.

West cowrote a manual with Edith Lang, *Musical Accompaniment of Moving Pictures*, published the same year.

1921

Reeves, Ernest, arr.
> *Augener's Cinema Music for Piano, Violin & Violincello, to Which May Be Added Violin II, Bass & Harmonium.* London: Augener, 1921–1923.

1922

Hawkes.
> *The Hawkes Photo-Play Series.* 20 vols. London: Hawkes, 1922–1928.

Jungnickel, Ross, arr.
> *Photoplay Series.* Nos. 1–20. New York: Ross Jungnickel, 1922–1928.

1923
Capitol Photoplay Series. New York: Robbins-Engel, 1923–1928.
William Axt, music director and conductor at the Capitol Theatre in New York, contributed a number of orchestral compositions, as did his predecessor, Erno Rapée.

Gregory, Adam, comp.
Denison's Descriptive Music Book for Plays, Festivals, Pageants and Moving Pictures. Chicago: T. S. Denison, 1923.
Adam Gregory was the pseudonym of Chicago songwriter and arranger Henry S. Sawyer. Under the name Adam Gregory, he worked as a composer.

1924
Bosworth's Loose Leaf Film-Play Music Series. 12 vols. New York: Bosworth, 1924.
Piano conductor scores and parts, including music by Albert W. Ketélbey.

Rapée, Erno.
Motion Picture Moods for Pianists and Organists: A Rapid-Reference Collection of Selected Pieces Arranged by Erno Rapée; Adapted to Fifty-Two Moods and Situations. New York: G. Schirmer, 1924. 678 pp. Reprint, New York: Arno Press, 1970.
A massive volume of primarily classical and light classical music arranged for piano, organized alphabetically from Aëroplane to Wedding. Index of moods printed in the margin of each page for quick reference. Author was born in Hungary and was music director at New York's Capitol Theatre. Index of titles.

Savino, Domenico.
Descriptive and Dramatic Photoplay Series for Piano and Organ. New York: Robbins Music, 1924.
Author was an Italian composer, arranger, and longtime staff editor for Robbins Music who published numerous works under the pseudonym D. Onivas ("Savino" spelled backward).

1925
Bath, Hubert.
Feldman's Film Fittings. London: B. Feldman, 1925.
Author was a British composer who scored Alfred Hitchcock's film *Blackmail* (1929). He also wrote nineteen short piano pieces to accompany silent films (London: Cinephonic Music, 1929).

Belwin.
PianOrgan Film Books of Incidental Music: Extracted from the World Famous "Berg" and "Cinema" Incidental Series. 7 vols. New York: Belwin, 1925–.
Each volume contains half a dozen agitatos, furiosos, or "misterioses" [*sic*]; for example, "Book of Hurries" (vol. 1, 1925).

1927
Bierman, Emil.
Photo Play Music for Organ or Piano: A Collection of Original Music for Use in Moving Picture Theatres. New York: American Composers, 1927.

Author was a former Broadway music director who worked in near obscurity on a few films, most notably as an arranger on *Ramona* (1916).

Charles, Milton, comp.
   Robbins-Engel Series of Moviemusic for Piano or Organ. New York: Robbins-Engel, 1927.
Charles, a composer and organist, selected and compiled the music. Preceded by *Robbins-Engel Descriptive and Dramatic Series*, 1924–1927.

1928
Collins, W. R., ed.
   Ascherberg's Ideal Cinema Series. 4 vols. London: Ascherberg, Hopwood & Crew, 1928–1929.
This four-volume piano series shares the same title as an eight-volume series for orchestra. Collins is best known for writing the song "Laughing Marionette," which was popular at the time.

Hahn, Theodore, Jr., and Carl Hahn.
   Moods and Motives for Motion Pictures: For Orchestra. Cincinnati: John Church, 1928.
Authors were composers. Theodore served as musical director for the Capitol Theatre in Cincinnati; Carl was a conductor and orchestral composer in Indianapolis.

1929
Hastings, J. B., ed.
   Classified Catalogue of Sam Fox Publishing Co. Motion Picture Music. New York: Sam Fox Publishing, 1929.
Hastings was a music director and arranger in London. According to copyright records, the concert pianist Edward Kilenyi is associated with this volume of 185 musical numbers.

Sound Era (1930s–1950s)
The Sam Fox Publishing Company issued at least three books similar in content to the compilations listed above: *Incidental Music for News Reels, Cartoons, Pictorial Reviews, Scenics, Travelogues, etc.,* dating from 1931; Val Burton's *Eskimo Melodies and Incidental Music from the Motion Picture Igloo,* from 1932; and the *Sam Fox Variety Series: For Television, Radio, Film, and General Performance,* from 1955 and 1956. The *Sam Fox Variety Series* is a fourteen-volume set with music by Lucien Cailliet, L. E. DeFrancisco, and others.

Chapter 7

Film Music Periodicals

CinemaScore (US, 1979–1987)
CinemaScore was launched in January 1979 as an informal bimonthly journal devoted to the appreciation, analysis, and review of motion picture music. For the first two years it was an eight-page stapled fanzine with articles, analyses, and record reviews. Lawson W. Hill served as editor and co-publisher, and Lance H. Hill and Myrddin Press in Chicago handled the publication. Reviewers included Lawson Hill, Randall Larson, Gary W. Radovich, Tom Underwood, and others. Publication was suspended after the January–February 1981 issue for financial reasons. Randall Larson took over as editor and introduced an expanded format later that year with issue 9, published through his Fandom Unlimited Enterprises in Sunnyvale, California. Issue 10 introduced three new features: "Collector's Corner," by Gary W. Radovich and others; "Scoring Session," focusing on new scores, often with interview quotes from the composers and information on recording sessions; and letters to the editor. David Kraft's column "Technicalities" examined scoring from a technical perspective. Larson kept the "Fanfare" column created by Lawson Hill. *CinemaScore*'s content reflected Larson's personal interest in music for science fiction and fantasy films; during this time he researched, wrote, and published his 1985 book, *Musique Fantastique: A Survey of Film Music in the Fantastic Cinema*. Over the years Larson cultivated lasting relationships with composers, many of whom granted a number of interviews. Composers spoke with the magazine about current projects or about their work from earlier eras, particularly the 1950s. The interviews were often illustrated with production stills and photographs of the composers and scoring sessions. Later issues interviewed up-and-coming composers such as Alan Silvestri and James Horner—before the latter became famously reluctant to speak with fan magazines—and examined the careers and music of 1980s stalwarts such as Giorgio Moroder, David Shire, and Tangerine Dream. From 1979 to 1987, *CinemaScore* appeared more sporadically and was finally acquired by *Soundtrack* in 1989 (issue 16 is incorporated into *Soundtrack*, vol. 8, no. 31). The first eight issues of *CinemaScore* were reprinted as a special collector's edition in a stapled, reduced-size facsimile booklet in 1986. Issue 15, "Film Music around the World," was published as a stand-alone limited special edition. A predecessor to *Film Score Monthly*, *CinemaScore* served a growing American and European soundtrack collector fan base and coincided roughly with the founding of the Film Music Society and Intrada Records.

1:1 (January 1979)
Larson, Randall. "The Music for *Orca*: Tragedy of a Whale." 1–3. On Ennio Morricone's music.
Hill, Lawson. "Discography, 1975–1978." 3–6.

1:2 (March–April 1979)
Larson, Randall D. "The Story behind Starlog Records." 2–3.
Hill, Lawson. "The Music of *Citizen Kane*." 5–8. On Bernard Herrmann's score.

1:3 (May–June 1979)
Hill, Lawson. "For the Record: A Survey of *Citizen Kane* on Disc." 1–3.
Radovich, Gary. "The Cometa Morricone Releases." 6–8.

1:4 (July–August 1979)
Radovich, Gary W. "Collecting SF, Horror, and Fantasy LP's." 2–3.

1:5 (January–February 1980)
Reviews only.

1:6 (March–April 1980)
Larson, Randall. "The Story of Varese Sarabande." 2–5. With discography of film music
    albums.

1:7 (September–October 1980)
Fake, Douglass C. "Those Great Unrecorded Film Scores." 2–3.

1:8 (January–February 1981)
Larson, Randall. "Jerry Goldsmith: A Filmography/Discography." 5–7.

1:9 (October 1981)
Larson, Randall. "The Film Music of Pino Donaggio." 6–11.
Underwood, Tom. "*The Empire Strikes Back*." 12–16. Analysis and review of John Wil-
    liams's music.
Larson, Randall. "The Story behind Tony Thomas Productions." 16–19.

1:10 (Fall 1982)
Larson, Randall D. "The Music of *Conan*." 7–8. Review of *Conan the Barbarian*, includ-
    ing interview with Basil Poledouris.
Larson, Randall D. "James Horner and *Star Trek II*." 9–10. Review, with interview.
Larson, Randall D. "A Conversation with Ernest Gold." 12–19.
Underwood, Tom. "Film Music on Radio WQRS-Detroit." 22–23. Interview with host
    Jack Goggin.
Underwood, Tom. "Scoring with Electronics: *Halloween II*." 25–26. Review of John
    Carpenter's score.

1:11–12 (Fall–Winter 1983)
Larson, Randall D. "Jerry Goldsmith on *Poltergeist* and *NIMH*." 3–4. Interview regard-
    ing *Poltergeist* and *The Secret of NIMH*.
"Scoring Session: New Scores." Each includes interview quotes from the composers.
    Simak, Steven. "Another Pair of Summer Blockbusters from Jerry Goldsmith." 5. On
        Psycho 2 and *Twilight Zone–The Movie*.
    Larson, Randall D. "Arthur B. Rubinstein: On Working with Friedkin." 5–6.
    van Wouw, Martin. "Ennio Morricone: On Crowns and Things." 6. On *The Thing* and
        The Treasure of the Four Crowns.
    Larson, Randall D. "Trevor Jones and *The Dark Crystal*." 7.
    Larson, Randall D. "Gil Mellé Looks at *Voyeurs*." 7.
    Larson, Randall D. "Gerald Fried on Documentary Filmscoring." 7–8.
    Kraft, David. "Joe Harnell and *V*." 8. On the television miniseries.
Larson, Randall D. "Richard H. Band on *Metalstorm*." 9. Interview.
Larson, Randall D. "Bob Cobert on *The Winds of War*." 10–11. Interview-based article.

Larson, Randall D. "Lalo Schifrin on *Amityville*." 11–12. Interview regarding *The Amityville Horror* and *Amityville II: The Possession*.

Larson, Randall D. "Lee Holdridge of Beasts, Wizards and Warriors." 13–15. Interview regarding *The Beastmaster* and *Wizards and Warriors*.

"Announcing: The Society for the Preservation of Film Music." 15. Advertisement.

Wise, Peter J. "*Return of the Jedi*: The Score." 17–20. Analysis of John Williams's music.

Flanagan, Graeme. "A Conversation with Brian May." 21–25. Interview.

Kraft, David. "Technicalities: The Film Music Editor." 26–28. Interview with Dan Carlin.

Larson, Randall D. "The Vintage Score: *D.O.A.*: Music by Dimitri Tiomkin." 29–31. Analysis.

Larson, Randall D. "Scoring the B's: Fred Katz." 32–33. Interview.

Larson, Randall D. "The Sound of *Tron*." 34–42. Includes interview with Wendy Carlos.

Larson, Randall D. "A Conversation with James Horner." 51–54. Interview, with filmography from 1978 to 1983.

1:13–14 (Winter 1984–Summer 1985)

"Scoring Session: New Scores." Based on interviews, often with quotes from the composers.

Kraft, David. "Alan Silvestri: *Back to the Future*." 3.

Werba, Marco. "Ennio Morricone: *Once Upon a Time in America*." 3–4.

Carlin, Dan, Sr. "Film Music by Tangerine Dream." 4–5. On the group's approach to scoring.

Larson, Randall D. "Giorgio Moroder: *Metropolis*." 5–6. On his re-scoring of the 1926 silent film.

Thaxton, Ford A. "Amazing Music for *Amazing Stories*." 6. Music for Steven Spielberg's television series.

Larson, Randall D. "Trevor Jones: *Labyrinth*." 6.

Kraft, David. "Paul De Senneville and Oliver Touissaint: *Irreconcilable Differences*." 6–7.

Larson, Randall D. "Ernest Troost: *Dr. Desoto*, Scoring an Animated Short." 7.

Larson, Randall D. "Music for *Ghostbusters*: A Conversation with Elmer Bernstein." 9–11. Interview.

Werba, Marco. "Pino Donaggio on *Body Double*." 11. Interview.

Kraft, David, and Randall D. Larson. "Basil Poledouris on *Flesh and Blood*." 12–13.

Larson, Randall D. "Ernest Gold and *Wallenberg: A Hero's Story*." 14–15. Interview regarding the music for the television miniseries.

Simak, Steven. "James Horner on Scoring *Star Trek III: The Search for Spock*." 16–17. Interview.

Kraft, David. "*Heaven Help Us*: A James Horner Trilogy." 17, 19. Article.

Larson, Randall D. "John Harrison Scoring *Day of the Dead*." 18–19. Interview.

Simak, Steven. "Craig Safan's Music for *The Last Starfighter*." 20–21. Interview, with filmography.

Larson, Randall D. "Carl Davis on Scoring *Champions*." 22. Interview.

"Announcing a New Soundtrack Label: Intrada." 23. Advertisement.

Larson, Randall D. "The Universal Film Music of Herman Stein." 24–33. Interview, with filmography.

Kraft, David. "Technicalities: The Film Music Editor—Part II." 34–35.

Rosar, William H. "Notes on *Dragonslayer*: Music by Alex North." 36–40. Analysis.

Kraft, David. "The Sound of *2010*: Interviews with David Shire and Synthesist Craig Huxley." 41–44.

Larson, Randall D. "A Conversation with Arthur B. Rubinstein." 45–48.

Larson, Randall D. "The Film Music of Ronald Stein." 52–57. Interview, with filmography and discography.

1:15 (Winter 1986–Summer 1987)

"Scoring Session: New Scores." Most include interview quotes from the composers.

> Larson, Randall D. "Leonard Rosenman: Scoring *Star Trek IV: The Voyage Home*." 3–4. Interview.

> Kraft, David. "Carter Burwell: Music for the Bates Motel." 5–6. Interview regarding his score for *Psycho III*.

> Werba, Marco. "*Crawlspace*: A Conversation with Composer Pino Donaggio and Director David Schmoeller." 6. Interview.

> Larson, Randall D. "Basil Poledouris on Scoring *Amerika*." 7, 24. Interview.

> Thaxton, Ford A. "What Happened to the Real Score for *Invaders from Mars*: Christopher Young and the Invaders from Cannon." 8. Article.

> Rosar, William H. "The Original *Invaders from Mars* Score: A Case of Ghost Writing?" 9, 33. Article discussing the music score credited to Raoul Kraushaar, with possible contributions from Mort Glickman.

> Stoner, David. "Maurice Jarre Scoring Session for *Mad Max Beyond Thunderdome*." 10–11. Article.

> Douglas, Andrew. "The Color Grey: Quincy Jones and Georges Delerue." 12. Article on *The Color Purple*.

> Larson, Randall D. "Richard Band: *Re-Animator*." 13. Interview.

> "Music for Television Short Stories." 14–15.

> Kraft, David. "Bruce Broughton." 16.

> Larson, Randall D. "David Spear on Music for Expo Films." 17–18. Interview.

> "Notes and Quotes." 19–24. On John Barry, Elmer Bernstein, Georges Delerue, Richard Einhorn, Michael Hoenig (on the Synclavier), James Horner, Michael Kamen, Ennio Morricone, John Scott, Bruce Smeaton, and Ken Sutherland.

Larson, Randall D. "Henry Mancini on Scoring *Lifeforce* and *Santa Clause: The Movie*." 25–26.

Kraft, David. "David Shire on *Return to Oz*." 27–29.

Hershon, Robert. "Phil Aaberg and Windham Hill: Scoring *The Shape of the Land*." 29–30.

Werba, Marco. "Riz Ortolani on *Christopher Columbus*." 31–33.

Kraft, David. "Technicalities: The Film Music Orchestrator." 35–37. Interviews with Jack Hayes and Mark McKenzie.

"The Music for *Legend*." 38–45. Includes Jerry Goldsmith, interviewed by Jonathan Benair; Edgar Froese of Tangerine Dream, interviewed by Randall Larson; and comparative critique by Paul Andrew MacLean of the Goldsmith and Tangerine Dream scores.

"Film Music around the World." X–1 to X–74. Contents are listed under the following book entry: Larson, Randall D., ed. *Film Music around the World*.

Larson, Randall D. "The Vintage Score: *Seven Samurai*." 121–24. Analysis of Fumio Hayasaka's music for the 1954 film.

Lehti, Steven J. "*The Company of Wolves*: Notes on the Film and Its Score." 125–29.

Stoner, David. "*The Company of Wolves*: An Interview with George Fenton." 129–33. With filmography and discography.

The Cue Sheet (US, 1984–2005)
Quarterly journal of the Film Music Society (FMS). The society was born in 1974 during a meeting at composer-writer Fred Steiner's home. In attendance were Jon Newsom (Library of Congress), David Raksin, Clifford McCarty, Tony Thomas, Rudy Behlmer, John Hall (RKO archivist), George Korngold (son of Erich Wolfgang), and William Rosar. The meeting took place after it was learned that a major film studio had disposed of its music holdings to cut costs and conserve space. The Society for the Preservation of Film Music (SPFM) was formed as a nonprofit organization in 1982, with Rosar serving as president. Past presidents include composers Elmer Bernstein, David Raksin, and Christopher Young. The SPFM was renamed the Film Music Society (FMS) in 1997.

The Cue Sheet contains articles; interviews; material from and regarding the society's international film music conferences, news items on the society's activities, including the career achievement award dinner; coverage of film music concerts; obituaries; book reviews; and occasional lists of current recordings. Emphasis is on historical aspects, including composer interviews. Some issues, such as those on Richard Shores (2004) and Stanley Wilson (2001), provide career documentation that dwarfs any previously published material. Other issues are devoted to career achievement award recipients. Book reviewers have included Bruce Babcock, Rudy Behlmer, Royal S. Brown, Jon Burlingame, Phil Grayson, Clifford McCarty, Jeannie Pool, and Warren Sherk. The first four volumes (into 1987) were primarily eight to sixteen stapled pages. Beginning with vol. 4, no. 4 (November 1987), the issues were folded in half and stapled. Editors include Clifford McCarty, Kevin Fahey, Leslie T. Zador, Marsha Berman, Jon Burlingame, and Marilee Bradford.

The Cue Sheet newsletter became the society's journal in April 1989. The following year the society began publishing a bimonthly newsletter for members only. Compiled, written, and edited by Jeannie Pool, this was variously titled *News from the Executive Director* (August 1990 to January 1992), *SPFM Newsletter* (March–April 1992 to June–July 1996), and *The Film Music Society Newsletter* (September 1997 to September–October 2000). The newsletter contained timely information regarding society activities and film music news items, including occasional obituaries.

1:1 (January 1984)
Rosar, William H. "Herbert Stothart: A Biographical Sketch." 3–5. With filmography by Clifford McCarty.

1:2 (April 1984)
Zador, Leslie T. "Soundtracks, Copyright, and the A.F.M." 1–4.
"Former Head of MGM Music Editing Visits L.A." 4. Profile of Robert Wilson Stringer.

1:3 (July 1984)
Fry, Stephen M. "UCLA Music Library: Guide to the Archival Film and TV Music Collections." 4–5
Zador, Leslie T. "A Discussion of Matters Involving Copyright Law." 5–9.

1:4 (October 1984)
Behlmer, Rudy. "Film Scores at the Academy [of Motion Picture Arts and Sciences, Margaret Herrick Library]." 3–4.

2:1 (January 1985)
Behlmer, Rudy. "Film Scores at U.S.C. [University of Southern California]." 1–2.
Zador, Leslie T. "Bernard Herrmann Remembered." 2–4. Interview with Dorothy Herrmann, daughter of Bernard Herrmann.

2:2 (April 1985)
McCarty, Clifford. "Necrology." 10–13.

2:3 (August 1985)
Smith, Steven. "Bernard Herrmann Retrospective." 18–19, 27.
Zador, Leslie T., and Greg Rose. "Interview: Hugo Friedhofer." 24–26. Originally published in the *Los Angeles Free Press* in 1971.

2:4 (October 1985)
Rosar, William H. "President's Message: Preservation vs. Perpetuation." 34–35.

3:1 (January 1986)
Zador, Leslie T. "Interview." 3–5. Edited version of a 1971 conversation with André Previn.
Meyer, Nicholas. "Letters." 9–11. The director defends his decision not to use portions of David Raksin's adapted score for his television docudrama *The Day After*. Raksin's response to Meyer, pp. 11–13.

3:2 (April 1986)
"BMI Honors Lionel Newman." 17–18. John Williams's remarks excerpted from *BMI: The Many Worlds of Music* (1985, no. 4).
Zador, Leslie T., and Jack DeNault. "Fred Katz." 18–22. Background sketch and interview.
"Muir Mathieson Tells an Interviewer about His Early Days in Film Music." 28. Excerpted from *The March of the Movies* (1947).

3:3 (September 1986)
Behlmer, Rudy. "Alex North on *A Streetcar Named Desire*." 36–38. From a 1977 interview.
Smith, Steven. "Unheard Herrmann: Rare Scores by a Film Music Master." 39. On Bernard Herrmann.
Smith, Steven. "The Shape of Things to Come: Film Composers to Listen For." 40. On Geoffrey Burgon, Michael Kamen, and Craig Safan.

3:4 (October 1986)
Zador, Leslie T. "Gil Melle's Musical Toys." 46–48. Edited from a 1971 *Los Angeles Free Press* interview.

4:1 (January 1987)
Creason, Steve. "Arthur Honegger and the Films of Occupied France, 1940–1944." 23.

4:2 (April 1987)
Rosar, William H. "Directory of Film Music Researchers." 11–14.

4:3 (July 1987)
Darby, Ken. "Ken Darby's Hollywood." 31–32. Part 1. Transcription of radio commentaries broadcast in 1980 by the author, a choral director, regarding recording songs for *Call Me Madam*.

4:4 (November 1987)
Darby, Ken. "Ken Darby's Hollywood." 46–49. Part 2. On the song scores of *There's No Business Like Show Business* and *Carousel*.
D'Arc, James. "Film Music Collections at Brigham Young University." 56–57.

5:1 (January 1988)
Darby, Ken. "Ken Darby's Hollywood." 18–19. Part 3. Regarding *South Pacific*.

5:2 (April 1988)

Rosar, William H., and Leslie T. Zador. "An Interview with David Newman." 31–38. Regarding the Sundance Institute.

Hohstadt, Thomas. "American Film Music: Art or Entertainment?" 41–45. By a conductor of symphonic music.

Cohen, Allen. "Some Observations on Film Music Concerts." 46–48.

Rannie, Alex K. "Republic Pictures Music Rescued by SPFM." 50–51.

Wright, H. Stephen. "The Frank Skinner Collection at the University of Illinois." 54–56.

Thomas, Tony. "Composers on Camera or, the Lack Thereof." 59–60.

Countryman, John. "Jerry Goldsmith and Franklin J. Schaffner: A Study of Collaboration." 61–67.

5:3 (July 1988)

Caps, John. "An Interview with Jerome Moross." 73–80. Part 1. From a 1982 radio interview.

Thomas, Tony. "It Started with Saint-Saëns." 81–82. Article on recordings of the earliest original film scores.

Dawes, Scott. "Interview: Bruce Broughton." 86–94.

5:4 (October 1988)

Caps, John. "An Interview with Jerome Moross." 99–108. Part 2.

Silver, Martin, and Christopher Husted. "The Bernard Herrmann Archive at the University of California, Santa Barbara: A Short History and Guide to the Collection." 109–14. With a list of film score manuscripts.

D'Arc, James. "What's in a Name? The John Ford Music Collection at Brigham Young University." 115–19.

6:1 (February 1989)

Bernstein, Elmer. "Elmer Bernstein's Acceptance Speech." 7–11. For the society's career achievement award.

Thomas, Tony, and William Rosar. "Interview with Elmer Bernstein." 15–23.

Sherk, Warren M. "The Harry Sukman Collection at the Academy of Motion Picture Arts and Sciences." 30–32.

6:2 (April 1989)

Rosar, William H. "On Classifying Film Music Materials." 44–52.

Shropshire, Liz. "Where Are the Woman Composers?" 53–62. Includes profiles of Angela Morley, Nan Schwartz, and Shirley Walker.

Thomas, Tony. "Remembering Franz Waxman." 63–65.

6:3 (July 1989)

Thomas, Tony. "The Viennese Connection: Salter, Steiner, Korngold and Ernest Gold." 79–88. On Hans J. Salter, Max Steiner, Erich Wolfgang Korngold, and Ernest Gold.

Lewis, Edgar J. "The Archive Collections of Film Music at the University of Wyoming." 89–99. Part 1. Describes holdings relating to the careers of William Axt, Darrell Calker, Adolph Deutsch, Gerald Fried, and Jerry Goldsmith.

Behlmer, Rudy. "A Conversation with Jesse Kaye, the Producer of MGM Soundtrack Records from 1946 to 1973." 100–114.

6:4 (October 1989)

McCarty, Clifford. "Revising George Antheil's Filmography." 139–42.

Lewis, Edgar J. "The Archive Collections of Film Music at the University of Wyoming." 143–61. Part 2. Describes holdings relating to the careers of Dominic Frontiere, Maurice Jarre, Bronislaw Kaper, Gail Kubik, Alexander Laszlo, Hans J. Salter, Walter

Schumann, Nathan Scott, Richard and Robert Sherman, Marlin Skiles, Herman Stein, Oliver G. Wallace, and Eugene Zador.

7:1 (January 1990)

Rosar, William H., Leslie Zador, and Vincent Jacquet-Francillon. "Interview with Ernest Gold." 6–14.

Darby, Ken. "Ken Darby: Recollections of a Choral Director." 17–29. Introduction (containing biographical information) by Tony Thomas.

Rose, Greg. "Alex North." 30–35. Article.

7:2 (April 1990)

Larson, Randall D. "Computers and the Creation of Modern Movie Music." 3–11. Historical overview of synthesizers, including material from interviews with Richard Band, Wendy Carlos, Edgar Froese of Tangerine Dream, Alan Howarth, Ron Jones, Harry Manfredini, Gil Mellé, Alan Silvestri, and others.

Rosar, William H., and Vincent Jacquet-Francillon. "Maurice Jarre on *Lawrence of Arabia*." 13–23. Interview.

7:3 (July 1990)

Johnson, Carl. "Interview with Herbert Spencer." 83–104. A 1988 interview.

Schurmann, Gerard. "A Reply to Maurice Jarre about *Lawrence of Arabia*." 105–12. The orchestrator recalls his working relationship with Jarre.

7:4 (December 1990)

Gilbert, Herschel Burke. "An Appreciation: Arthur Lange." 123–27.

Bowling, Lance. "Arthur Lange: A Biographical Sketch." 128–43. With chronology.

Pool, Jeannie G., ed. and transcriber. "Interview with Arthur Lange and Ernst Klapholz Discussing Their Early Days in Hollywood." 144–60. From a 1954 interview.

McCarty, Clifford, comp. "Arthur Lange Filmography." 162–65. Followed by a one-page bibliography.

Bowling, Lance, comp. "Checklist: The Arthur Lange Collection at Lincoln Center, Library of the Performing Arts, New York Public Library." 167–74.

8:1 (March 1991)

Thomas, Tony. "John Williams: A Brief Biography." 3–5.

Thomas, Tony. "A Conversation with John Williams." 6–15.

Burlingame, Jon. "John Williams: The Television Work." 16–20.

Fry, Stephen M. "The Motion Picture Music of John Williams: A Selected Bibliography of the Literature." 22–27.

McCarty, Clifford. "John Williams Filmography." 28–30.

8:2 (July 1991)

Steiner, Fred. "Select Bibliography of Film Music." 40–49. This issue also contains film music resources such as sources for scores and recordings, organizations, journals, and film music on radio, pp. 50–72.

8:3 (September 1991)

Pool, Jeannie. "David Raksin Conducts Music of Alex North in Spain." 87–96. Interview.

Sherk, Warren M., transcriber. "Music from the Films: The Lawrence Morton–Maurice De Packh Interview." 97–109. Introduction by Warren M. Sherk. With De Packh filmography.

Caps, John. "John Williams: Scoring the Central Line." 110–17.

8:4 (March 1992)

Dinner program for the career achievement award honoring Henry Mancini in March 1992. Includes Mancini biography and a filmography by Clifford McCarty.

9:1 (January 1992)
Wright, H. Stephen, comp. "A Preliminary Directory of Film Music Collections in the United States." 4–44.

9:2 (April 1992)
Burlingame, Jon. "Henry Mancini: The Television Music." 9–13. With teleography.

Fry, Stephen M. "The Music for *The Pink Panther*: A Study in Lyrical Timelessness." 14–23.

Fry, Stephen M. "The Henry Mancini Collection at UCLA." 24–26.

Fry, Stephen M. "The Film and Television Music of Henry Mancini: A Selective Annotated Bibliography of the Literature." 27–33.

9:3 (July 1992)
Primarily reports on the SPFM's International Film Music Conference.

9:4 (October 1992)
Kranz, Jack. "The SPFM Union Catalog of Film Music." 6–10.

MacLean, Paul Andrew. "John Scott: An Interview." 11–26.

10:1–2 (1993–1994)
Raksin, David. "Music via a Devious Root." 4–6. Anecdotal recollection on the source of his theme for *Laura*.

Pool, Jeannie. "*Music for the Movies: Bernard Herrmann*: An interview with director Joshua Waletzky and composer David Raksin." 7–24.

Fry, Stephen M. "A Glossary of Film Music Terms." 25–30.

10:3–4 (1993–1994)
Raksin, David. "All Unquiet...on the Tiomkin Front." 4–7. Recollection of his work arranging Dimitri Tiomkin's score for *The Road Back*.

Kaufman, Annette. "Louis Kaufman." 9–11. On the death of her husband, the session musician.

Francillon, Vincent J. "An Interview with Jerry Goldsmith." 14–27.

Fry, Stephen M. "Jerry Goldsmith: A Selective Annotated Bibliography." 28–39.

11:1 (January 1995)
Provo, Walter. "Seminar: Film Music in Europe." 4–31. Excerpts from a roundtable discussion held at the Flanders International Film Festival in February 1993. Participants included Loek Dikker, Dirk Brossé, Frédéric Devreese, Pino Donaggio, Stanley Myers, David Raksin, and Philippe Sarde.

Pool, Jeannie. "Film Music Preservation in the United States." 32–42.

11:2 (April 1995)
Burlingame, Jon. "Ennio Morricone: A Filmography." 6–11.

Sherk, Warren M. "The Western Film Scores of Hans Salter." 12–18.

Danly, Linda. "Hugo Friedhofer's Westerns." 19–24.

Cochran, Alfred W. "*The Red Pony*." 25–35. Article on Aaron Copland's score.

11:3 (July 1995)
Pool, Jeannie, and Jon Burlingame, eds. "Issues Facing Contemporary Composers of Film and Television Music: A Panel Discussion." 2–25. Panelists Charles Bernstein, Alf Clausen, Fred Karlin, David Raksin, John Scott, and Christopher Young at the 1992 AFI Film Fest. Topics include getting started in the business, present-day issues, preserving film scores, and women composers.

Jacquet-Francillon, Vincent. "A Conversation with Maurice Jarre." 26–30. Interview on Jarre's education, early career, and the start of his work in American films.

11:4 (October 1995)
Bowling, Lance. "Carli Elinor: Master of the Compiled Scores." 24.
Elinor, Carli D. "From Nickelodeon to Super-Colossal: The Evolution of Music to Pictures." 5–15. Elinor's personal recollection of his early days in silent film, believed to have been written in the 1940s.
"The Carl Brandt Collection." 37–38. Acquired by the society.

12:1 (January 1996)
Kraft, William. "William Kraft on Toru Takemitsu." 6–9.
Shore, Howard. "Howard Shore on Toru Takemitsu." 10–11.
Raksin, David. "David Raksin on Toru Takemitsu." 12–13.
Nelson, Jack. "An Interview with George Duning."16–37. 1992 interview.

12:2 (April 1996)
Mauceri, John. "The Music Which Has No Name." 6–12. On the "historical and aesthetic roots of prejudice against composers of film music, based on the romantic, tonal quality of their work." Essay derived from a talk at an SPFM conference, first published in New York's Lincoln Center *Stagebill* (October 1995) and later in *Pro Musica Sana*.
Shoilevska, Sanya. "Alex North's Score for *The Misfits*." 13–27.

12:3 (July 1996)
Danly, Linda. "An Interview with Thomas Newman." 8–15.
Graubart, Jeffrey L. "GATT and U.S. Moral Rights." 16–29.

12:4 (October 1996)
Burlingame, Jon. "An Interview with John Barry." 3–15.
Clausen, Alf. "Advice to Young Musicians." 16–24.
Burlingame, Jon. "The Korngold Anthology: An Interview with Tony Thomas." 25–30.

13:1 (January 1997)
Danly, Linda. "Buddy Baker: An Appreciation." 4–20. Filmography.
Schnauber, George and Barbara. "The Louis B. Schnauber Silent Film Music Collection." 29–32.

13:2 (April 1997)
Herman, Sidney. "Music at Paramount." 4–10. Text of speech given by Herman, vice president of Famous Music Publishing Co., at the society's Fourth East Coast Film Music Conference.
Pool, Jeannie. "The Story of the Paramount Film Music Preservation Project." 11–30.
"Eldridge Walker Honored with Film Music Preservation Award." 31–34.

13:3 (July 1997)
Sciannameo, Franco. "From Grandfather to Godfather: A Biographical Profile of Nino Rota." 4–20.

13:4 (October 1997)
Tony Thomas tribute issue, with reminiscences by Rudy Behlmer, Jon Burlingame, Linda Danly, Ray Faiola, Danny Gould, John W. Morgan, Jeannie Pool, David Raksin, Nick Redman, and Leslie T. Zador. 4–29.
Burlingame, Jon, comp. "The Books of Tony Thomas," "The Documentaries," "The Recordings," and "The Compact Discs." 30–44.

14:1 (January 1998)
Burlingame, Jon. "An Interview with Brendan G. Carroll." 4–10. Interview with the Erich Wolfgang Korngold biographer.

14:2 (April 1998)
Steiner, Fred. "Part I: A Conversation between Composers Cyril J. Mockridge and Fred Steiner." 4–30. Edited transcription of a 1976 interview.

14:3 (July 1998)
Steiner, Fred. "Part II: A Conversation between Composers Cyril J. Mockridge and Fred Steiner." 4–35.

14:4 (October 1998)
Bradford, Marilee, transcriber, and Jeannie Pool, ed. "Elmer Bernstein: Opening Address." 10–23. Transcript of Bernstein's speech at the FMS's sixth International Film Music Conference.
Sherk, Warren M. "'The Dance of the Cuckoos': Music in the Films of Laurel and Hardy." 28–34. Survey of music by Marvin Hatley and LeRoy Shield.

15:1 (January 1999)
Castelnuovo-Tedesco, Mario. "Music and Movies." 4–29. Unpublished 1940 manuscript, edited by James Westby and translated from the French by Blair Sullivan.
"Elmer Bernstein Honored at Flanders Film Festival." 30–31.

15:2 (April 1999)
Westby, James. "Uno scrittore fantasma: A Ghostwriter in Hollywood." 4–46. On Mario Castelnuovo-Tedesco.

15:3 (July 1999)
Pool, Jeannie. "More Notes on the Society's Paramount Music Preservation Process." 3–17. Supplement to April 1997 article.
Kosovsky, Robert. "Introduction to the Plenary Session of the Music Library Association Los Angeles Meeting, March 18, 1999." 18–21.
"Elmer Bernstein and Film Music at Walnut High School [Walnut, California]." 22–23.
McCarty, Clifford. "*Miss Jerry*: A Pre-Film Picture Play with a Pre-Film Score." 24–29.
"Society Acquires Music from the Quinn Martin Television Shows." 30–31.

15:4 (October 1999)
Schubert, Linda. "Henry Vars in Hollywood: A Biography and Filmography." 3–13.
McDonagh, Michael. "Henry Brant on Alex North." 14–26. Interview with North's orchestrator.

16:1 (January 2000)
Allen, Clyde. "Joseph Carl Breil and the Score for *The Birth of a Nation*: A Commentary." 5–31.

16:2 (April 2000)
Burlingame, Jon. "Laurence Rosenthal: An Appreciation." 8–11.
"Laurence Rosenthal: A Filmography." 12–15.
Burlingame, Jon. "3,000 Attend Unveiling of Composer Stamps." 16–19.
Sherk, Warren. "Welcome to Hollywood: Alex North's Unused Score for *Distant Drums*." 20–30.

16:3 (July 2000)
McDonagh, Michael. "An Interview with Anna North." 4–19. Interview with North's widow.
D'Arc, James, and Lance Bowling. "An Interview with Annette Kaufman." 20–35. 1994 interview with the widow of studio violinist Louis Kaufman.

16:4 (October 2000)
Burlingame, Jon. "Clifford McCarty and *Film Composers in America*." 4–9.

17:1 (January 2001)
Burlingame, Jon. "Lalo Schifrin: An Appreciation." 8–11.
"Lalo Schifrin: Career Highlights." 11–12.
"Lalo Schifrin Filmography." 13–20. Includes concert works.
Behlmer, Rudy, and Ned Comstock. "Film Scores at USC." 30–32. Revised and updated
    version of an article in the *Cue Sheet* (January 1985).
Redford, John R. "The Paul Sawtell Collection: A Preliminary Inventory." 33–39.

17:2–3 (April–July 2001)
Burlingame, Jon. "Stanley Wilson: A Biographical Sketch." 4–14.
Shire, David. "Memories of Stanley Wilson." 15–18.
Murray, Lyn. "Eulogy for Stanley Wilson." 19–20. From 1970.
"Remembrances." 21–33. By Elmer Bernstein, Benny Carter, Sidney Fine, Gerald Fried,
    Billy Goldenberg, Jerry Goldsmith, Dave Grusin, Quincy Jones, Oliver Nelson Jr.,
    Pete Rugolo, Lalo Schifrin, John Williams, and Patrick Williams.
Burlingame, Jon. "Television Music by Stanley Wilson." 34–37.
McCarty, Clifford. "A Stanley Wilson Filmography." 38–41.
Burlingame, Jon. "A Selected, Annotated Discography [of Stanley Wilson]." 42–48.

17:4 (October 2001)
Snedden, N. William. "William Walton's Crowning Achievement for Film: The Music
    for Laurence Olivier's *King Henry the Fifth*." 2–13.
Maddren, Casey. "New Drama, New Music." 15–26. New trends in 1950s film scoring,
    as practiced by Kenyon Hopkins, Alex North, David Raksin, and Leonard Rosenman.

18:1–2 (January–April 2002)
Steiner, Fred. "A Conversation with David Buttolph." 3–20. 1977 interview.
Burlingame, Jon. "An Index to *The Cue Sheet*, 1984–2001." 21–49.

18:3–4 (July–October 2002)
Care, Ross. "Disney Music during the Classic Era: An Overview." 4–8.
Danly, Linda. "Frank Churchill." 9–15. Biographical essay.
Danly, Linda. "Leigh Harline." 17–21. Biographical essay.
Care, Ross. "Paul J. Smith." 23–27. Biographical essay.
Care, Ross. "Oliver Wallace." 29–33. Biographical essay.
Care, Ross. "George Bruns." 35–37. Biographical essay.
Burlingame, Jon. "An Interview with Buddy Baker." 39–49. 2001 interview.

2003
Publication suspended, no issues.

19:1 (January 2004)
Snedden, N. William. "Charles Gerhardt's Classic Film Score Recording Legacy." 3–10.
Benson, Robert E. "The Classic Film Scores Series." 11–23.
Gerhardt, Charles A. "Gerhardt on Classic Film Music." 25–27. Reprinted comments
    from the 1970s.
"Film Scores Conducted by Gerhardt." 29–32. Rerecordings listed alphabetically by
    composer.
"Gerhardt Film Music Discography." 33. Albums listed chronologically.

19:2 (April 2004)
Burlingame, Jon. "Richard Shores Remembered: A Look Back at the Life and Career of a
    Remarkable Composer." 3–17. With filmography, 18–21.

19:3 (July 2004)
Stothart, Herbert. "Film Music." 4–8. Reprinted from *Behind the Screen* (1938).

Korngold, Erich Wolfgang. "Some Experiences in Film Music." 9–12. Reprinted from *Music and Dance in California* (1940).

Finston, Nathaniel. "Time Tells the Tale." 13–15. Reprinted from *Music and Dance in California and the West* (1948).

Webb, Roy. "Scissors Save the Score." 16–19. Reprinted from *Music and Dance in California and the West* (1948).

Stravinsky, Igor. "Igor Stravinsky on Film Music." 20–26. Reprinted from *The Musical Digest* (1946).

Raksin, David. "Hollywood Strikes Back." 27–34. Reprinted from *The Musical Digest* (1946).

19:4 (October 2004)

In memoriam issue covering Elmer Bernstein, Fred Karlin, Jerry Goldsmith, and David Raksin, written by Jon Burlingame.

Newsom, Jon. "David: Remembrance of a Treasured Friend." 33–36. Reprinted from David Raksin's memorial service program.

20:1 (January 2005)

Burlingame, Jon. "Gil Mellé: Pioneer, Innovator, Maverick." 3–17. With filmography, 18–21.

Larson, Randall D. "An Interview with Gil Mellé." 23–46. 1983 interview.

20:2 (April 2005)

Arlen, Sam. "Foreword: The Gentle Gentleman." 5–6. By Harold Arlen's son.

Marotta, Sharon Zak. "Harold Arlen: A Lifetime in Music." 7–26.

"Harold Arlen in Hollywood: A Comprehensive List of Works Specifically Written for Motion Pictures." 27–33.

Fricke, John. "His Music and Her Voice: The Movie Musical Marriage Made in Hollywood." 34–52. On Judy Garland and Arlen.

20:3 (July 2005)

Bradford, Marilee. "Introduction: The Business of Film Music." 3–5.

Cartwright, Dorothea Hawley. "Tuning Up the Talkies: Watching the Music Departments Function." 6–12. Reprinted from *Talking Screen* (August 1930).

Brabec, Jeff, and Todd Brabec. "Music, Money, Success and the Movies." 13–29. Excerpted from *Music, Money and Success* (2004).

LeMone, Shawn, and Mike Todd. "Everything You Need to Know about Cue Sheets." 30–31.

Winogradsky, Steven. "Soundtrack Albums 101: A Brief Overview of the Legal and Business Aspects of Soundtrack Albums." 32–37.

20:4 (October 2005)

Burlingame, Jon. "In Memoriam: Clifford McCarty." 2–3.

Sherk, Warren. "Dimitri Tiomkin and the Army Orientation and Information Films (1942–1945)." 4–21.

Steiner, Fred. "About Alfred Newman: New Data (and Some Errata)." 22–33. Regarding Steiner's dissertation.

Film Music (US, 1998–2005)

Promoted as the professional voice of music for film and television, *Film Music*'s mission is to promote the free flow of information among composers as a resource for amateurs and professionals. Published in Glendale, California, by Mark Northam and Lisa Anne Miller, authors of *The Film and Television Composer's Resource Guide* and founders of Film Music Publications; the online Film Music Store; and Film Music Network, with chapters in Los Angeles, New York, and San Francisco. Dan Kimpel served as editor and Rudy Koppl as feature editor. Content was organized into features, columns, and departments; feature articles are listed below. News coverage includes Film Music Network events. Columns cover business and artistic aspects; departments included industry news and scoring notes. Columnists have included recording engineer Mick Stern; composers Peter L. Alexander, Mark Holden, Fred Karlin, and David Javelosa; music editor Christine Luethje; session musician Chris Tedesco (second cousin to Tommy Tedesco); attorney Steven Winogradsky; and soundtrack liner note specialist David Hirsch on new soundtrack releases. Illustrated with original photographs. Northam often contributes an editorial on current topics and is particularly interested in establishing communication among composers regarding pay for creative services and in reforming the practices of performing rights societies, particularly in the area of determining royalty payments. The magazine ceased publication temporarily after vol. 2, no. 3 (1999), when Kimpel left. Daniel O'Brien was named Focus Section editor, Koppl remained feature editor, and the magazine then became bimonthly. Publication was suspended again around 2000, with one issue circulated in 2002 and one in 2005. The latter two issues introduced a new design and were published solely by Northam. Similar in scope to *The Score*, the Society of Composers and Lyricists journal, *Film Music* caters to the interests and demographics of SCL members but lacks the support of a sponsoring member-based organization. This independence has perhaps hampered its ability to be self-sustaining. Its scope and tone set it apart from the fanzine *Film Score Monthly* and the more scholarly and journalistic *Cue Sheet*.

1:1 (July 1998)
Koppl, Rudy. "John Debney: Bringing the Music to Life." 12–16. Interview.
Northam, Mark. "Spotlight on Ira Hearshen." 17. Interview with the orchestrator.
Koppl, Rudy. "Linda Kordek: Innovative Agent Plays the Match Game." 18–19. Interview with the film music agent.
Koppl, Rudy. "Louis Febre: The Orchestra from Beyond." 20. Interview with the composer.
Northam, Mark. "Mike Lang." 21–23. Interview with the Los Angeles session keyboardist.

1:2 (August 1998)
Koppl, Rudy. "Inside the Filmharmonic: The Grand Experiment Begins." 13–17. Regarding a series of concert works accompanied by film, commissioned by the Los Angeles Philharmonic Orchestra, including an interview with composer David Newman.
Kimpel, Dan. "The Music of *Mulan*." 18–19. Includes brief interviews with composer Matthew Wilder and lyricist David Zippel on their collaboration.
Kimpel, Dan. "Camara Kambon: A Young Composer Gets Busy." 20.
Kimpel, Dan. "Modern Music: Concept Nouveau." 21–23. Profile of Modern Music, a music supervision company, with music supervisors Andy Hill, Alex Gibson, and Andrew Silver.
Stern, Mick. "John Richards: Scoring Mixer." 24–25.

1:3 (September 1998)
Koppl, Rudy. "Dennis McCarthy: Hot Rods to Hell." 12–16. Interview with the composer.
Stern, Mick. "Spotlight on O'Henry Studios." 17.
Kimpel, Dan. "On the Cutting Edge: Music Supervision with Sharon Boyle." 18–19. Interview with the music supervisor.
Koppl, Rudy. "Spotlight on Julia Michels." 20. Interview with the soundtrack consultant.

Tonks, Paul. "Anne Dudley: Winning BIG with *The Full Monty*." 22–23.
Miller, Lisa Anne. "1998 ASCAP Film Scoring Workshop." 42–43. Report.

1:4 (October 1998)
Koppl, Rudy. "David Newman: The Calm before the Storm." 11–14.
Kimpel, Dan. "*Titanic* Tunesmith." 16–17. Interview with lyricist Will Jennings.
Koppl, Rudy. "Robert Wise: The Legend Speaks." 18–19. Interview with the director's views on film music.
Kimpel, Dan. "Spotlight on ASMAC [American Society of Music Arrangers and Composers]." 20–21.

1:5 (November–December 1998)
"Special Focus on Soundtrack Labels." F1–F8. Overview, with brief interviews, of soundtrack labels: Atlantic Records, Capitol Records, Citadel, Hollywood Records, Intrada, Milan, Sonic Images (Christopher Franke and Brad Pressman), TVT Records, producer Ford A. Thaxton, Turner Classics Movie Music and Rhino, Varese Sarabande (Robert Townson), Virgin Records, and Warner Bros. Records.
Koppl, Rudy. "Mark Isham's Interactive Career: The Learning Experience." 17–21. Interview with the composer.
Kimpel, Dan. "The Sound of the Season: Julie Glaze Houlihan." 22–23. Interview with the music supervisor.
Koppl, Rudy. "John Ottman's Journey into Darkness: Scoring and Editing *Apt Pupil*." 24–26. Interview with the composer-film editor and the director Bryan Singer.
Kimpel, Dan. "Stephen James Taylor: Taylor-Making a New Musical Vocabulary." 28–29. Interview with the composer.
Kimpel, Dan. "Spotlight on Justin Wilde." 30. Interview with the songwriter-music publisher specializing in Christmas songs for films.

2:1 (January 1999)
"Special Focus on Orchestral Recording." F1–F9. Overview, including orchestra size, pricing, booking information, and contacts for Kiraly Music Network (Eastern Europe), L.A. East Studio (Utah), London Symphony Orchestra, Recording Musicians Association (Los Angeles), The Royal Philharmonic (London), Seattlemusic, Simon James Music (Seattle), Symphony Workshops Ltd. (Eastern Europe), and Trone Recording (Los Angeles).
Koppl, Rudy. "Graeme Revell: Lunatics and Insects: A Composer's Metamorphosis." 14–17. Interview.
Koppl, Rudy. "Elia Cmiral: The New Kid in Town." 19–21. Interview with Cmiral and director John Frankenheimer regarding *Ronin*.
Stern, Mick. "Alan Meyerson on Recording *The Prince of Egypt*." 22–23.

2:2 (February 1999) [Jerry Goldsmith tribute issue]
Romo, Ric. "An Inside Look at the Scoring World of Jerry Goldsmith." 6–10.
Romo, Ric. "Spotlight on Orchestrator Arthur Morton." 12.
Koppl, Rudy. "The Scoring Team." 15–20. Interviews with music editor Ken Hall, orchestrator Alexander Courage, and scoring mixer Bruce Botnick.
Kimpel, Dan. "The Musicians." 21.
Koppl, Rudy. "Spotlight on Sandy DeCrescent." 24–25. Interview with the music contractor.
Koppl, Rudy. "Composer Jerry Goldsmith: The Maestro Speaks." 26–32.
Koppl, Rudy. "Spotlight on Lois Carruth." 34. Interview with Goldsmith's personal assistant.

Romo, Ric, and Rudy Koppl. "The Directors." 36–40. Interviews with David Anspaugh, Stuart Baird, Joe Dante, Paul Verhoeven, and Jerry Zucker regarding Goldsmith.

Black, Edwin. "Jerry Goldsmith at Carnegie Hall: The Live Experience." 42–43.

Koppl, Rudy. "Spotlight on Robert Townson." 44. Interview with the Varese Sarabande vice president.

Tonks, Paul. "Edwin Paling, Leader of the Royal Scottish National Orchestra: Our Relationship with Jerry Goldsmith." 45.

Karlin, Fred. *"Film Music Masters: Jerry Goldsmith*: The Making of a Documentary." 47–48.

2:3 (circa March 1999)

"Special Focus on Tax and Financial Planning." F1–F8.

"Spotlight on Robert O. Ragland." 13. Interview with the composer.

Stern, Mick. "Shawn Murphy: Scoring Mixer at the Helm." 14–19.

Koppl, Rudy. "John Beal: Scoring in the Trailer Zone." 20–21.

McPherson, Andrew. "Phil Ayling: Inside Looking Out." 22–25. Interview with the Los Angeles session oboist.

Ottman, John. "Sound Off." 26–27. Guest editorial by the composer-editor on current trends in the test screening process.

(1999) [Laurence Rosenthal tribute edition, unnumbered]

Koppl, Rudy. "Laurence Rosenthal: Inside the Bright Shining Light." [1–5]. Interview.

3:1 (May 2000)

"Special Focus on Music Prep and Contracting." F1–F15.

O'Brien, Daniel, and Mark Northam. "Paramount's David Grossman: Shaping the Future of Television Music." 19–21, 43–45.

Mitchell, Robert. "Shelly Palmer: From Composer to Internet Developer." 23–24.

Northam, Mark. "Spotlight on Chris Walden." 25.

Stern, Mick. "Spotlight on the Village." 28–29. Article on the Los Angeles recording studio.

Deutsch, Didier. "Spotlight on Neil Norman: A&R Chief of GNP Crescendo Records." 30–31.

"Film and Television Music Salary and Rate Survey 2000" [insert].

4:1 (2002)

Derasse, Dominic. "New York and Film Music." 14.

"Film and Television Composer Studios." F1–F7.

Walker, Don. "Film Composing and the Composer Project Studio." F10–11.

Stern, Michael. "Skywalker Sound: Michael Stern Visits the Scoring Stage." 18–19.

Koppl, Rudy. "The Art, Craft and Business of Music Supervision: A Conversation with Bonnie Greenberg and Maureen Crowe." 22–27.

Winogradsky, Steven. "Adventures in Music Licensing." 28–31.

Rogers, Michael. "Music Supervision Here and Now: Inside the Business with Music Supervisor Chris Violette." 32–34.

Rogers, Michael. "Sundance and Slamdance: Film Directors on Music Collaboration." 35–40.

Tedesco, Chris. "Guitarist Roundtable." 48–49. On Los Angeles session musicians Dennis Budimir, George Doering, John Goux, Tim May, and Dean Parks.

Turnage, Neal. "Composer John Massari on Composing for the DVD Market." 50–51.

5:1 (September 2005)

Koppl, Rudy. "The Passion of Film Scoring with John Debney." 15–18. Interview.

Larson, Randall D. "Film Scoring and Modern Music Technology: A Conversation with Christophe Beck." 20–23. Interview.

Larson, Randall D. "Taking Notes from Aaron Zigman." 24–27. Interview.

Film Music Notebook (US, 1974–1978)

Publication of the Elmer Bernstein Film Music Collection, distributed quarterly to members. With each issue members also received an LP of rerecorded film music. Bernstein interviewed a fellow composer (often the composer of the accompanying LP) and wrote the "Collection News" column for each issue. Other contributors include John Caps, Christopher Palmer, Jay Alan Quantrill, William H. Rosar, and Fred Steiner. Its publication coincided with a growing awareness of film music, particularly in the number of soundtrack album releases. *Film Music Notebook* was succeeded by *CinemaScore, Film Score Monthly*, and other publications aimed at collectors. In 2004 the entire run of *Film Music Notebook* was reprinted in one volume by the Film Music Society, with an index and errata. As Jon Burlingame writes in the foreword to that edition, the conversations with Daniele Amfitheatrof and Leo Shuken are believed to be the only lengthy interviews those individuals ever gave.

1:1 (Fall 1974)

Bender, Albert K. "Max Steiner." 5–11.

Bernstein, Elmer. "An Interview with Hugo Friedhofer." 12–21.

Raksin, David. "Whatever Became of Movie Music?" 22–26. Reprinted from *Daily Variety*.

Steiner, Fred. "Herrmann's 'Black and White' Music for Hitchcock's *Psycho*—Part I." 28–36.

1:2 (Winter 1974–1975)

Scheff, Michael. "Elmer Bernstein." 5–9.

Bernstein, Elmer. "The Annotated Friedkin." 10–16. Excerpt from director William Friedkin's AFI seminar interview (annotated by Bernstein) regarding Lalo Schifrin's unused score for *The Exorcist*.

Bernstein, Elmer. "A Conversation with George Roy Hill." 17–23.

Steiner, Fred. "Herrmann's 'Black and White' Music for Hitchcock's *Psycho*—Part II." 26–46. Analysis of selected sequences.

1:3 (Spring 1975)

"Franz Waxman." 6–9.

Caps, John. "The Third Language: The Art of Film Music." 10–13.

Bernstein, Elmer. "A Conversation with Leo Shuken." 14–26. Interview with the orchestrator.

Frankenstein, Alfred. "Franz Waxman's Music for *The Silver Chalice*." 27–35.

1:4 (Summer 1975)

Steiner, Fred. "Bernard Herrmann: An Unauthorized Biographical Sketch." 4–9. Reprinted with a postscript in 3:2: 6–11.

Irving, Ernest. "Music and the Film Script." 10–13. Transcript of a lecture to the British Screenwriters' Association, reprinted from the *British Film Yearbook*, 1947–1948.

Bernstein, Elmer. "A Conversation with Daniele Amfitheatrof." 14–22.

Palmer, Christopher. "Focus on Films." 23–30. Classical music in films.

2:1 (1976)

Caps, John. "A Correspondence with Miklos Rozsa." 2–5.

Palmer, Christopher. "Miklos Rozsa Biography." 6–15. Excerpt reprinted from Palmer's 1975 Rózsa book.

Bernstein, Elmer. "A Conversation with Richard Rodney Bennett." 16–25.

Caps, John. "Serial Music of Jerry Goldsmith." 26–30.

Bernstein, Elmer. "Film Composers vs. The Studios: A Three Hundred Million Dollar Complaint." 31–39.

2:2 (1976)

Darby, Ken. "A Letter from Ken Darby." 3–4. Regarding the establishment of the Alfred Newman Memorial Library at the University of Southern California (USC).

Darby, Ken. "Alfred Newman Biography and Filmography." 5–13.

Bernstein, Elmer. "A Conversation with David Raksin [Part I]." 14–21.

Vaughan Williams, Ralph. "Film Music." 22–25. Article written in 1944, reprinted from *Film Music Notes*.

Steiner, Fred. "An Examination of Leith Stevens' Use of Jazz in *The Wild One* [Part I]." 2:2 (1976): 26–35.

2:3 (1976)

"David Raksin Biography and Filmography (with a personal note by Elmer Bernstein)." 3–8.

Bernstein, Elmer. "A Conversation with David Raksin (Part II)." 9–18.

Caps, John. "John Williams—Scoring the Film Whole." 19–25.

Steiner, Fred. "An Examination of Leith Stevens' Use of Jazz in *The Wild One* (Part II)." 26–34.

2:4 (1976)

"Happy 70th Birthday to Miklos Rozsa." 3–5. Notes from John Green, Bronislaw Kaper, David Raksin, and Elmer Bernstein.

Caps, John. "The John Barry Tryptych [*sic*]." 6–8.

Bernstein, Elmer. "A Conversation with John Green [Part I]." 9–21.

"John Green Biography and Filmography." 22–24.

Palmer, Christopher. "Miklos Rozsa on *The Thief of Bagdad*." 25–28. Interview.

3:1 (1977)

Palmer, Christopher. "Alex North." 2–8. Reprinted from *Crescendo* (April 1975).

Orowan, Florella. "A Look at Alex North's Use of Historical Source Music." 9–14.

Bernstein, Elmer. "A Conversation with John Green (Part II)." 15–31.

Maffett, James D. "*The Omen—Obsession*: Different Approaches to the Supernatural." 32–44.

3:2 (1977)

Quantrill, Jay Alan. "Current Assignments." 3–5.

Steiner, Fred. "Bernard Herrmann: An Unauthorized Biographical Sketch." 6–11. Reprinted from 1:4 (Summer 1975): 4–9, with a postscript.

Caps, John. "The Lyricism of Mancini." 12–17.

Bernstein, Elmer. "A Conversation with Jerry Goldsmith." 18–31.

Care, Ross. "The Film Music of Leigh Harline." 32–48.

3:3 (1977)

Quantrill, Jay Alan. "Current Assignments." 3–8. Also new recordings.

Quantrill, Jay Alan. "Jerry Fielding: A Biographical Sketch." 9–17.

Bernstein, Elmer. "A Conversation with John Addison." 18–32.

Quantrill, Jay Alan. "How Not to Be a Film Music Critic." 33–42.

Seydor, Paul. "Jerry Fielding: The Composer as Collaborator." 43–48. Comments made by Fielding while recording *Gray Lady Down*.

4:1 (1978)
Quantrill, Jay Alan. "State of the Art." 3–8.
Bernstein, Elmer. "A Conversation with Henry Mancini." 9–21.
Bernstein, Elmer. "The Aesthetics of Film Scoring: A Highly Personal View." 22–27.
Sharples, Win, Jr. "Motion Picture Music: A Select Bibliography." 28–32.

4:2 (1978)
Quantrill, Jay Alan. "State of the Art." 3–11.
Bernstein, Elmer. "Bronislaw Kaper Interview." 12–28.
Palmer, Christopher. "Dimitri Tiomkin: A Biographical Sketch." 29–33.
Palmer, Christopher. "Tiomkin as Russian Composer." 34–39.
Rosar, William H. "*Lost Horizon*: An Account of the Composition of the Score." 40–52.

Film Music Notes (US, 1941–1951)
Later titled *Film Music* (1951–1956), then *Film and TV Music* (1956–1958). Official publication of the National Film Music Council, published first in Hollywood and later in Connecticut and New York. Commonly known as *Film Music Notes*, it grew from a stapled newsletter into the premier film music periodical of its day. Grace Widney Mabee, founder and co-editor, chaired the Motion Picture Music Committee of the National Federation of Music Clubs (NFMC). Editors included Mabee, Constance Purdy, Margery Morrison (associate editor), Frederick W. Sternfeld, and Marie L. Hamilton. Noted author and critic Sigmund Spaeth served as advisory chairman and wrote an occasional informational column from 1944 to 1955 called "Afterthoughts." John Huntley wrote about British film music from 1944 and contributed the column "Notes from England" in the mid-1940s. In the early 1950s, Canadian Gerald Pratley wrote the columns "Canadian Film News" and "News from Canada." Stanlie McConnell, an elementary school superintendent of music, contributed to "Teaching Possibilities."

Film Music Notes' target audience was music clubs and the general public, although it was the educational market—colleges, schools, and libraries—that responded. In fact, it was published monthly from October to June to coincide with the school year. Each issue offered news and commentary on film music and capsule film reviews focusing on the music scores of films in current release. It often contained information and lists regarding the availability of publications and recordings of film music. News items were culled from Los Angeles area newspapers, such as the *Hollywood Citizen-News*. Scoring assignments and pictures in production were mentioned.

One bibliographer complained that the capsule reviews were nonselective and insufficiently critical of the music—not surprising considering the NFMC acted primarily as a booster club for film music. By the late 1940s, *Notes* had begun including articles by composers writing about their music, often accompanied by music examples. These unprecedented articles, written by Elmer Bernstein, Michel Michelet, David Raksin, Roy Webb, and many others, offered insight into the film scoring process. The first music example appeared at the end of the October 1943 issue. The examples were named and numbered, such as Portfolio No. 19. For the articles listed below, "with music excerpts" may include thematic material (usually on one or two staves), music sketches, conductor scores, or full scores.

Film Music Notes began featuring more articles and less filler, and *Notes* eventually was dropped from the title in 1951. Articles grew longer, fewer films were covered, and there was less in-depth coverage on films in current release. The capsule reviews were dropped entirely. In its incarnation as *Film and TV Music*, it attempted to embrace the emerging field of television music but featured no substantive articles on the subject prior to the periodical's demise in 1958.

News items and capsule reviews are not included herein. Early issues had no pagination; page numbers in brackets are from first page after the cover page. Entries marked "Reprinted in Limbacher" can be found in *Film Music: From Violins to Video* (1974).

Published as **Film Music Notes**

1:1 (October 1941)
Webb, Roy. "Things a Motion Picture Composer Has to Think About." 2.

1:2 (November 1941)
Hageman, Richard. 6. Comments on his music for *Paris Calling*.

1:3 (December 1941)
"*Suspicion*." 4. Review contains extensive quoted material from Franz Waxman.

1:4 (January 1942)
Haines, Chauncey, Jr. "The Orchestrator and His Importance to the Photoplay Score." 5.

1:5 (February 1942)
Bradley, Scott. "Cartoon Music of the Future." [5]. Reprinted from an article in the *Pacific Coast Musician*, June 1941. This same page contains a "Puppetoons" article regarding music scores for George Pal Puppetoons.

1:6 (March 1942)
"*Reap the Wild Wind*." 3–4. Review of Victor Young's score.

1:7 (April 1942)
"The Auroratone." [2].
Rózsa, Miklós. "Scoring *The Jungle Book*." [3].
Kaplan, Sol. "*Tales of Manhattan*." [5].
Rogers, Eleanore. "Musicians in Hollywood." [6]. Partial list of studio musicians, including many émigrés.

1:8 (May–June 1942)
Purdy, Constance. "Russian Music." [7]. Regarding an Academy of Motion Picture Arts and Sciences symposium on current Russian film music.
"Some Interesting Data on the Activities of Film Musicians Outside of the Studios." [8]. Concert works by Miklós Rózsa, Ernst Toch, Eugene Zador, and others.

2:1 (October 1942)
Spaeth, Sigmund. "The Importance of Motion Picture Music." [3].
Kubik, Gail. "Music in Government Films." [4]. With brief Kubik biography.

2:2 (November 1942)
"Musical Shorts." [4].
Rózsa, Miklós. "Notes on *Jacare*." [5]. With Sigmund Spaeth's review of the film and music.
"Constantin Bakaleinikoff." [6]. Biographical sketch with interview comments from the RKO music director. First in a series of articles on studio music department directors.

2:3 (December 1942)
"*Commandos Strike at Dawn*." [2]. Review includes quoted material from a screening with Louis Gruenberg.

2:4 (January 1943)
Schaindlin, Jack. "The Music Scoring of *The March of Time*." [2]. With brief Schaindlin biography.

"Max Steiner Comments on Music Scoring." [3].
Wolcott, Charles. "Music of the Americas." [6].

2:5 (February 1943)
Finston, Nat W. "Screen Music Assumes New Stature." [2–3].
"Notes from Mr. Louis Lipstone—Musical Director of Paramount as interviewed by
    Margery Morrison." [3]. Second in a series.
"Auroratone Motion Picture Productions." [7].

2:6 (March 1943)
Newman, Alfred. "Procedure of Preparing a Musical Score for a Picture" [2].
"Jose Iturbi Comes to the Screen." [3]. Regarding *Private Miss Jones.*
Leyda, Jay. "Shostakovich—Film Composer." [3–4].
"Albert Coates to Help Score *Russia.*" [4].

2:7 (April 1943)
Morrison, Margery. "A Visit to the Music Recording Stage at Warner Bros." [2].
Leftwich, Vernon. "What Music Arranging Does for the Pictures." [7]. With brief Left-
    wich biography.

2:8 (May 1943)
Reynolds, Naomi. "Meremblum's California Junior Symphony Orchestra Soon to Be
    Featured in M.G.M.'s *Russia.*" [3]
Shaindlin, Jack. "Motion Picture Music in the East." [4].

2:9 (June 1943)
Purdy, Constance. "Notes from a Talk Given to the Music Educators' Conference, West-
    ern Division, at Santa Barbara, May Sixth." [2]. On *Film Music Notes.*
Morrison, Margery. "An Afternoon in the Home of Erich Wolfgang Korngold." [3].
"Adolph Deutsch Comments on His Score for *Action in the North Atlantic.*" [5].
"Short Subjects Music." [9]. Includes mention of composers Max Terr and Howard Jack-
    son.

3:1 (October 1943)
Rudhyar, Dane. "Film Music for All Men." [3].
[Jones, Roger.] "*Phantom of the Opera*—A Daring Musical." [4].
Themes from Erich Wolfgang Korngold's score for *The Constant Nymph.*

3:2 (November 1943)
Morrison, Margery. "The Cinema Workshop–U.S.C." [2].
Spaeth, Sigmund. "Music in the Movies." [3–4].
Narodny, Ivan. "New Russian Film Music Born of War." [5].
"A Step in the Right Direction." [10]. Report on a meeting of a group of film composers
    that eventually became the Screen Composers Association.
"Miklos Rozsa." [12]. Biography. With themes from *Sahara.*

3:3 (December 1943)
Norton, Mildred. "Off Beat." [3]. Regarding Jose Iturbi and others.
"The Sixth Sense in Film Mechanics." [4–5]. Reprinted from *The American Cinematog-
    rapher*, October 1943.
"Notes on the Life and Works of Aaron Copland." With Copland's comments on his
    score for *The North Star*, with themes from the film.

3:4 (January 1944)
[Robert Stolz news item.] [1].
Purdy, Constance. "*Rhapsody in Blue*: A Day on the Gershwin Set." [3–4].
"Notes on Alfred Newman." [11]. With themes from *The Song of Bernadette.* [12].

3:5 (February 1944)
Hamilton, James Shelley. "Film Music." [3].
Jones, Isabel Morse. "Academy Award to Stress Progress in Film Scoring." [4].
Spaeth, Sigmund. "Upbeat in Music, *March of Time*—No. 5, January Release." [5].
Hampton, Ruth. "A Visit to New York University and the Museum of Modern Art." [6].
    Including material on Arthur Kleiner.
Stothart, Herbert. "The Orchestra—Hollywood's Most Versatile Actor." [12]. With brief
    Stothart biography and music examples from *Madame Curie* (1943).

3:6 (March 1944)
"Interview with Franz Waxman." [4]. Reprinted from "Tales of Hoffman," *Hollywood
    Reporter*.
Weldon, Ruth Parker. "Synchronization." [6–7].

3:7 (April 1944)
Huntley, John. "British Film Music." [5–6]. Reprinted from *Sight and Sound*, January
    1944.
"Notes on Victor Young." [11]. With "The Stella Song" from *The Uninvited*. [12].
Themes from *Heavenly Music* by Sam Coslow, adapted by Nathaniel Shilkret and Max
    Terr. [13].

3:8 (May 1944)
Morrison, Margery. "Visual Re-Creation of Music." [3].
Field, Alice Evans. "Scoring Film Drama." [4–5].
"Biography of Max Steiner." [11]. With music examples from *Mark Twain*.

3:9 (June 1944)
Kubik, Gail. "Film Music and Public Taste." [8].
"Biography of Gail Kubik." [13]. With music example from *The Memphis Belle*. [14].

4:1 (October 1944)
"Pictures Reviewed from October 1943 to June 1944." [19–20]. Index.
"Biography of Roy Webb." [21]; theme from *The Seventh Cross*. [22].
"Biography of Adolph Deutsch." [23]; themes from *The Mask of Dimitrios*. [24].

4:2 (November 1944)
Purdy, Constance. "A Few Words about the Music in the Film *Wilson*." 4–5. Music by
    Alfred Newman.
"Film Music Forum." Includes "Talk Delivered by the Composer, William Lava, on the
    Music Scoring for Warner Bros. Short Subject, *I Won't Play*." [6].
Reynolds, Naomi. "An Institute of Music in Contemporary Life." [7–8]. Report includes
    extensive coverage of Adolph Deutsch's talk on collaboration.
Article by Alfred Frankenstein of the *San Francisco Chronicle* on 12-tone music by
    Hanns Eisler in *White Floats*. [9].
"Biography of Edward Ward." [16]; themes from *The Climax*. [17].
"Biography of Bronislau Kaper." [18]; themes from *Mrs. Parkington*. [19].

4:3 (December 1944)
Kleiner, Arthur. "About Film Scores." [5].
Purdy, Constance. "Synchronization." [6].
Reynolds, Naomi. "An Institute of Music in Contemporary Life (conclusion)." [7–8].
Bradley, Scott. "Music in Cartoons." 4:3 (December 1944): [14–15]. Excerpt from a talk
    given at the Music Forum, October 1944. Bradley biography, [16]. Music example
    from *Tee for Two* (Tom and Jerry cartoon). Reprinted in Daniel Goldmark and Yuval
    Taylor, *The Cartoon Music Book* (2002), without the music example.

4:4 (January 1945)

Morrison, Margery. "How to Listen to Film Music." [6–7]. Adapted from a USC panel presentation.

Field, Alice Evans. "The Language of Music." [8–10].

"Biography of Werner Richard Heymann." [15]. Music example from *Together Again*.

4:5 (February 1945)

Hartshorn, William C. "Music of the Motion Pictures." [8–9].

Purdy, Constance. "Interview with Roy Webb." [10]. This is actually a summary, not an interview, of the author's lunch with Webb, and contains little substance.

Dill, Helen C., and Gordon E. Bailey. "Film Music as Viewed by Music Educators." [11].

"Biography of Alfred Newman." [18]. Music example from *The Keys of the Kingdom*.

4:6 (March 1945)

Webb, Roy. "Pattern for Mystery." [17]. Webb explains his approach to scoring mysteries. Music example from *I Walked with a Zombie*.

4:7 (April 1945)

Minor, Monachus. "A Music Library in a Motion Picture Studio." [9–10]. First in a series. Reprinted from *The Score*.

"Notes on the Life and Works of Max Steiner." [15]. Music example from *The Corn Is Green*.

Music example from *Guest in the House*, composer Werner Janssen.

4:8 (May 1945)

Mabee, Grace Widney. "National Film Music Council...Its [*sic*] Aims and Purposes." [1].

Alexandre Tansman (thumbnail sketch). [6–7]. News item.

Richard Korbel, RKO pianist. [7]. News item.

Spaeth, Sigmund. "Afterthoughts." [8–9].

Minor, Monachus. "A Music Library in a Motion Picture Studio." [10]. On a typical studio music reference library. Reprinted from *The Score*.

Jones, Isabel Morse. "Motion Pictures Seek New Musical Paths." [11–13]. Reprinted from *Musical America* (February 1945).

"Notes on Louis Gruenberg." [18]. With music sketch from *Counterattack*, 2 pages.

4:9 (June 1945)

Huntley, John. "Film Music News from Britain." [10].

Henderson, Charles. "Choral Music in Motion Pictures." [11].

"Film Music Appreciation in Junior and Senior High Schools of Greater Cleveland." [14].

Spaeth, Sigmund. "*Rhapsody in Blue* (The Story of George Gershwin): A Musical Study Outline of the Warner Bros. Motion Picture for Clubs and Classes." [15–16].

"Recent Films Containing Excerpts from Standard Works." [17–18]. Classical music used in films from October 1944 to June 1945.

"Best Pictures of the Year from a Musical Point of View." [19–20].

"Notes on Victor Young." [26]. Music example for *A Medal for Benny*.

5:1 (September 1945)

"A Message from the National Film Music Council." [2]. Includes a list of film music available for concerts.

News items include a report and program for a Hollywood Bowl film music concert. [3–6].

Spaeth, Sigmund. "Ann Ronell, George Gershwin, and Richard Rodgers." [16–17].

Waxman, Franz. "The New Music of Motion Pictures." [25–26]. Followed by theme from *Pride of the Marines*.

5:2 (October 1945)
Huntley, John. "Getting the Gen (A Course in Film Music)." [9–12]. With listening suggestions.
Minor, Monachus. "A Music Library in a Motion Picture Studio." [15–16]. Reprinted from *The Score*.
Rózsa, Miklós. "An Outline of University Training for Musicians in Motion Picture Work." [23–24].
"Biographical Notes on Miklos Rozsa." [25].

5:3 (November 1945)
Rubsamen, Walter H. "A University Course in Dramatic Music, Including Music for the Cinema." [11–12]. On a course at UCLA.
Gold, Ernest. "My First Movie Score." [22].
"Biography of Ernest Gold." [23]. Followed by theme from *The Girl of the Limberlost*.
"Note on Louis Applebaum. [25]. Followed by theme from *G.I. Joe*, written with Ann Ronell.

5:4 (December 1945)
Willson, Meredith. "Music...Not Catch Phrases." [13–14]. Reprinted from *Pacific Coast Musician*.
Barrymore, Lionel. "Music in Hollywood." [15]. Reprinted from *The Hollywood Reporter*.
Quinto, Lenard. "*Saratoga Trunk*." [19]. Analysis.
"Notes on Lennie Hayton." [26]. With themes from *Yolanda and the Thief*.

5:5 (January 1946)
Gold, Ernest. "Picture Music at the Concert Hall." [9].
Purdy, Constance. "Behind the Musical Scenes of *The Shocking Miss Pilgrim*." [10–11]. On recording Alfred Newman's score, with coverage of Charles Henderson, choral director.
Whitfield, Richard N. "Film Music for Music Appreciation." [12–13].
"Notes on Robert Emmett Dolan." [23]. Music excerpts from *The Bells of St. Mary*.

5:6 (February 1946)
Huntley, John, comp. "The Things They Say: British Film Composers, Directors, and Writers Comment on Their Specialized Branch of the Film Industry." 10–11.
Hautbois, Celeste. "Highs and Lows of Recent Scores." 12–13.
Darreg, Ivor. "The Place of Electronic Music in Films." 16–17.
Music examples from *Leave Her to Heaven* by Alfred Newman. [26].

5:7 (March 1946)
Hautbois, Celeste. "Highs and Lows of Recent Scores." 8–10.
Harford, Margaret. "Music's Film Value Recognized." 11–13. From *Hollywood Citizen-News* Academy Awards edition.
Michelet, Michel. "Craft Problems of the Realistic Film Seminar: Scenes with Dialogue and Music." 14–15. From an address by the author.
Deutsch, Adolph. "*Three Strangers*." 16–19. Reprinted from *Hollywood Quarterly*. On writing the score. Part 1 of 2.
"Notes on Michel Michelet." 24. With music examples from *Diary of a Chambermaid*. [25–26].

6:5 (April–May 1947)
"Academy Awards." 7–8. Report, with other scores deemed of merit by the National Film Music Council, 9–10.
Applebaum, Louis. "Hugo Friedhofer's score to *The Best Years of Our Lives*." 11–15. With music examples. Reprinted in Limbacher.
McConnell, Stanlie. "Teaching Possibilities in Current Films." 16. On Miklós Rózsa's score for *Song of Scheherazade*.

Special issue (1947)
McConnell, Stanlie. "*Carnegie Hall*: Its Music and Its Teaching Possibilities." 1–12. On the use of classical music in film, with music examples.

7:1 (September–October 1947)
McConnell, Stanlie. "Teaching Possibilities in Current Films." [3–12]. On Bronislaw Kaper's score for *Song of Love* and the use of classical music.
Morton, Lawrence. "The Music Makers." [13–18]. Profiles session musicians, including émigrés. [Continued next issue]
Knight, Arthur. "Planning a Film Music Program." [19–20].

7:2 (November–December 1947)
Raksin, David. "*Forever Amber*: Notes on the Musical Score." [3–4]. [Concluded next issue]
Applebaum, Louis. "David Raksin's Score for *Forever Amber*." [5–9]. With music examples.
Morton, Lawrence. "The Music Makers." [10–14]. More profiles of session musicians. [Continued next issue]
"Hollywood's Boy Choirs." [15]. On the St. Luke's Choristers and Robert Mitchell choir.
Alwyn, William. "*Odd Man Out*." [16].

7:3 (January–February 1948)
Rózsa, Miklós. "Teaching Composition for the Cinema." 3–4. On his course at USC.
Raksin, David. "*Forever Amber*: Notes on the Musical Score." 5–10. Conclusion.
Morton, Lawrence. "The Music Makers." 11–15. More profiles of session musicians.

7:4 (March–April 1948)
Michelet, Michel. "*Atlantis*." 7–10. With music examples.
Cohn, Arthur. "Film Music in the Fleischer Collection of the Free Library of Philadelphia." 11–13.
Mathieson, Muir. "Documentary Film Music." 14–15.

7:5 (May–June 1948)
"*Arch of Triumph*." 6–7. Music example by Louis Gruenberg.
Newman, Alfred. "*The Iron Curtain*." 19–23. On his use of music by Soviet composers, with music examples.

8:1 (September–October 1948)
Sternfeld, Frederick W. "*Louisiana Story*: A Review of Virgil Thomson's Score." 5–14. With music examples. Reprinted in Limbacher.
Spaeth, Sigmund. "Grand Opera on the Screen." 17.
"National Film Music Council." 15, 19–20. Report.

8:2 (November–December 1948)
Morton, Lawrence. "Composing for a Film Score." 4–10. On *Last of the Badmen*, with music examples by Roy Webb.
Hamilton, William. "*Macbeth*." 11–13. Review of Jacques Ibert's score, with music examples.

Applebaum, Louis. "Documentary Films." 19.

Index of personal names, films reviewed, feature articles, and music excerpts and analysis from September 1946 to September 1948.

Raksin, David. "A Note on the Music of *Force of Evil*." 6.

Morton, Lawrence. "*The Force of Evil*: A Review of David Raksin's Score." 7–10. With music examples.

Deutsch, Adolph. "Notes on the Score of *Whispering Smith*." 12–14. With music examples.

Stanley, Fred. "Film Tune Sleuths." 17–18. On music librarian George Schneider and clearing copyrighted music.

Morton, Lawrence. "*The Red Pony*: A Review of Aaron Copland's Score." 2–8. With music examples.

Walton, William. "The Music of *Hamlet*." [2]. See also Cross, *The Film* Hamlet (1948).

Kubik, Gail. "*The Red Shoes*." [8]. Review.

Bowman, Roger. "Music in Television and Its Problems." [9–10].

"Information on Film Music in the United States." [11–13]. Answers to questions submitted by the Department of State for an article. Responses detail the number of working film composers, foreign-born composers, and steps in the scoring process.

Dahl, Ingolf. "Notes on Cartoon Music." 3–13. On Scott Bradley's music for MGM cartoons, with music examples. Reprinted in Limbacher.

Shaindlin, Jack. "Stay East, Young Man! Stay East!" 14–15.

Hamilton, William. "*Champion*" and "*Home of the Brave*." 17. Reviews of two films scored by Dimitri Tiomkin. Reprinted in Limbacher.

Bowman, Roger. "Music for Films in Television." 20.

Applebaum, Louis. "Some Comments on the Score for *Lost Boundaries*." 5–6.

Adomian, Lan. "Louis Applebaum's Score for *Lost Boundaries*." 6–13. With music examples.

Morton, Lawrence. "Film Music Profile: David Raksin." 14–15.

Forrell, Gene. "Teaching Film Music." 16.

Duning, George. "*Jolson Sings Again*: Composer's Notes." 17.

Index for vol. 8, nos. 1–5.

Morton, Lawrence. "Film Music Profile: Adolph Deutsch." 4–5.

Bowman, Roger. "New Regulations Proposed for Music in TV Films." 6.

"Excerpts from the Score for *Hamlet*." 7–15. Music by William Walton.

Bliss, Arthur. "*Christopher Columbus*." 16. The composer on his score. Reprinted in Limbacher.

Bazelon, Irwin A. "*The Heiress*: A Review of Aaron Copland's Music Score." 17–18.

Hamilton, William. "*The Third Man* Music." 5–6. Review, with music example. Reprinted in Limbacher.

Morton, Lawrence. "*Prince of Foxes*: Some Comments of Alfred Newman's Score." 7–9. With music examples.

Morton, Lawrence. "Film Music Profile: Franz Waxman." 10–11.

Huntley, John. "The Music Mixer." 12–13. Reprinted in Limbacher.

Ronell, Ann. *"The Titan* and His Music." 14–15. Review of Alois Melichar's music.

Forrell, Gene. *"A Time for Bach."* 16–17. Reprinted in Limbacher.

"The Advisory Council [of the National Film Music Council]." 23–24. Brief biographies.

9:4 (March–April 1950)

Ronell, Ann. *"Love Happy:* Composer's Notes." 4–5.

Geller, Harry. "An Article on *Love Happy:* Part 1: Comments on Ann Ronell's Score." 5–10. With music examples.

Smith, Paul. "An Article on *Love Happy:* Part 2: On Precision Timing." 10–12.

Morton, Lawrence. "Film Music Profile: Leigh Harline." 13–14.

Duning, George. *"No Sad Songs for Me."* 15–17. With music examples. Reprinted in Limbacher.

Michelet, Michel. *"The Man on the Eiffel Tower."* 18–19. With music examples.

Livingstone, D. D. "The Dance in Films." 20–21.

Roggensack, Delinda. "Uses of Films in Music Education." 22–24.

9:5 (May–June 1950)

Raksin, David. *"The Next Voice You Hear."* 5–7. Brief introduction, with music excerpt.

Deutsch, Adolph. *"Annie Get Your Gun."* 10. On adapting Irving Berlin's music.

Antheil, George. "Notes on Music: *In a Lonely Place."* 11–13. Brief introduction, with music excerpts.

Brown, Harold. *"Daybreak in Udi."* 14. Review of the William Alwyn score.

Morton, Lawrence. "Film Music Profile: Alfred Newman." 15–16.

10:1 (September–October 1950)

Morton, Lawrence. "Film Music Profile: Hugo Friedhofer." 4–5.

Hamilton, William. *"Edge of Doom."* 6–15. On Friedhofer's score, with music excerpts. Reprinted in Limbacher.

Huntley, John. "The Music of *Treasure Island."* 16–17. On the score by Clifton Parker. Reprinted in Limbacher.

Deke, R. F. *"Glass Menagerie."* 17–18. On Max Steiner's score, with music excerpts.

Index from September 1949 to June 1950.

10:2 (November–December 1950)

Morton, Lawrence. "An Interview with George Antheil." 4–7. For the Canadian Broadcasting Corp.

Sternfeld, Frederick W. "Kubik's McBoing Score." 8–16. On Gail Kubik's score for *Gerald McBoing Boing*, with music.

Algar, James. "Film Music and Its Use in *Beaver Valley*." On Paul Smith's score.

Special bulletin (January 1951)

Bazelon, Irwin A. *"Cyrano de Bergerac:* A Review of Dimitri Tiomkin's Score." 2–8. With music excerpts. Reprinted in Limbacher.

10:3 (January–February 1951)

Morton, Lawrence. "Film Music Profile: Andre Previn." 4–5.

Huntley, John. "The Music in *The Mudlark*." 10–11. On the score by William Alwyn. Reprinted in Limbacher.

Cage, John. "A Few Ideas about Music and Films." 12–15. On his own experiences writing music for films, with music excerpts.

Thomas, Anthony. "Film Music Available on Disc." 16–19.

Bowman, Roger. "Notes on Music for Television." 19–20. On union negotiations.

10:4 (March–April 1951)

Morton, Lawrence. "Film Music Profile: Miklos Rozsa." 4–6.

Raksin, David. "Talking Back: A Hollywood Composer States Case for His Craft." 14–15. Reprinted from the *New York Times*.

Roggensack, Delinda. "The Scope of Film Music Education." 15–16.

Huntley, John. "Syllabus of a Course in Nine Lectures on Music and the Cinema." 18–20. Reprinted in Limbacher.

10:5 (May–June 1951)

Hepner, Arthur. "*The Emperor's Nightingale*." 7–8. On Vaclav Trojan's score for this puppet film.

Deke, R. F. "*The Emperor's Nightingale*." 8–9. Review, with music excerpts.

Huntley, John. "The Telekinema in London." 13–14. Report on music by Louis Applebaum and William Alwyn for the big-screen television.

Dill, Helen C. "Film Music on the Western Campus (UCLA)." 15–16.

Bowman, Roger. "New Radio and Television Prices and Conditions." 16–17.

Published as **Film Music**

11:1 (September–October 1951)

Morton, Lawrence. "Film Music Art or Industry." 4–6.

Applebaum, Louis. "Notes on the Music for *The Whistle at Eaton Falls*." 7–11. With music examples.

Simon, Alfred E. "*Strictly Dishonorable*." 12–13. Opera sequences by Mario Castelnuovo-Tedesco.

Deke, R. F. "*The Medium*." 13–15. On adapting Gian Carlo Menotti's music to the screen, with music examples.

Sykes, Wanda. "*Nature's Half Acre*." 16–19. With music examples.

Huntley, John. "*Oliver Twist*." 20–22. Reprinted in Limbacher.

Index to vol. 10, nos. 1–4.

11:2 (November–December 1951)

Rózsa, Miklós. "The Music in *Quo Vadis*." 4–10. With music examples. Reprinted in Limbacher.

Morton, Lawrence. "Rozsa's Music for *Quo Vadis*." 11–13.

Lewine, Richard. "*An American in Paris*." 14–16. On the movie musical, music by George Gershwin.

Applebaum, Louis. "Music in the Round." 17–19. On music in 3-D films seen in London.

Mathieson, Muir. "Documentary Film Music." 22.

11:3 (January–February 1952)

Denison, Alva Coil, and Ann Ronell. "*The River*." 4–10. On the ethnic Indian music in the film.

Hamilton, William. "*St. Matthew Passion*." 10–11. On illustrating paintings with classical music.

Lewin, Frank. "*A Street Car* [*sic*] *Named Desire*." 13–20. With music examples.

Knight, Arthur. "Movie Music Goes on Record." 21–23.

Bowman, Roger. "Television Survey." 24. On the cost of producing music.

11:4 (March–April 1952)

Adomian, Lan. "*Viva Zapata*." 4–14. On the music score by Alex North, with music examples.

Gray, Allan. "The Music of *The African Queen*." 19–21. With music examples by the composer.

Huntley, John. "*The African Queen*: The Composer and the Film." 22. On Allan Gray's music. Reprinted in Limbacher.

Schwartz, Elwyn. "Teaching Film Music." 23. On a music education course taught at the University of Idaho.

Lewin, Frank. "Pictura." 4–6. Music in films about painters.

Eaton, Quaintance. "*High Treason*." 7–8. On John Addison's music.

Mellot, Albert. "*The Two Mouseketeers*." 9–11. On Scott Bradley's music, with music examples.

Kremenliev, Boris A. "Can Film Composing Be Taught?" 12–15. With music examples.

Pratley, Gerald. "Music in the Films: Canada." 16–17. On Robert Fleming, Eldon Rathburn, Maurice Blackburn, William McCauley, and Louis Applebaum.

Index of names, films, and articles from September 1946 to May 1952.

Brown, Harold. "*The Miracle of Our Lady of Fatima*." 4–10. On Max Steiner's score for *The Miracle of Our Lady of Fatima*, with music examples.

Eaton, Quaintance. "*The Magic Box*." 12. On William Alwyn's score.

Raksin, David. "*Carrie*." 13–17. With music examples. Reprinted in Limbacher.

Hamilton, William. "*High Noon*." 19–20. On Dimitri Tiomkin's score. Reprinted in Limbacher.

Shindo, Tak. "Japanese Music Today." 21. On adapting Western music for Japanese films.

Gilbert, Herschel Burke. "*The Thief*." 4–12. With music examples. Reprinted in Limbacher.

Rózsa, Miklós. "More Music for Historical Films." 13–17. With music examples.

Hamilton, William. "*The Bad and the Beautiful*." 4–11. With music examples from David Raksin's score. Corrections posted in the next issue, page 14.

Forrell, Gene. "Re-editing a Score." 20. On changes made to a French film, including supplemental music.

Limbacher, James. "Film Music in the Air." 21–22. On a radio program, including a list of the music played.

Pockriss, Lee J. "*Moulin Rouge*." 4–7. On Georges Auric's score.

Duning, George W. "*Salome*." 8–12. With music examples. Reprinted in Limbacher.

Bute, Mary Ellen. "New Music for New Films." 15–18. On her music for abstract films. Reprinted in Limbacher.

Hamilton, William. "Music in Art Films." 19–23.

Bowman, Roger. "Television Notes." 23–24. On the paucity of live music.

Ronell, Ann. "So You Want to Be a Music Director? Notes on *Main St. to Broadway*." 3–9. With music examples.

Antheil, George. "*The Juggler*." 10–13. With music examples.

Parker, Clifton. "*The Sword and the Rose*." 14–15. By the composer. Reprinted in Limbacher.

Eaton, Quaintance. "Grand Opera Feature Films." 16–18.

Hamilton, William. "Music in Art Films: Part II." 20–23. Includes a list of films.

13:1 (September–October 1953)
Rózsa, Miklós. "*Julius Caesar*." 7–13. With music examples. Reprinted in Limbacher.
Morrison, Alen [*sic*]. "Film Music on Records." 14–16. Listed by composer.
Hickman, C. Sharpless. "Movies and Music." 21–22. On the scoring stage with Lucien Cailliet. Courtesy of *Music Journal*.
Index to vol. 12, nos. 1–4.

13:2 (November–December 1953)
Brown, Harold. "*The Robe*." 3–17. On Alfred Newman's score, with music examples.
Guernsey, Otis L., Jr. "The Movie Cartoon Is Coming of Age." 21–22. Reprinted in Limbacher.
Chamberlain, Gladys E. "Film Music and the Library." 23. New York Public Library holdings.

13:3 (January–February 1954)
Stevens, Leith. "*The Wild One*." 3–7. With music examples. Reprinted in Limbacher.
Manson, Eddy. "The Music for *Little Fugitive*." 8–14. With music examples.
Applebaum, Louis. "*The Best Years of Our Lives* (A Reissue)." 15–18. On Hugo Friedhofer's score, with music examples. Reprinted in Limbacher.
Mathieson, Muir. "Note on *Hamlet* (A Reissue)." 19. On recording the score. Reprinted in Limbacher.
Braslin, John E. "Motion Pictures: For Music Education." 20–23.

13:4 (March–April 1954)
Duning, George W. "*From Here to Eternity*." 3–10. With music examples. Reprinted in Limbacher.
Kremenliev, Boris. "*The Tell-Tale Heart*." 11–15. With music examples.
Eaton, Quaintance. "*Rhapsody*." 16–17. On the adapted score by Bronislaw Kaper.
Wheelwright, D. Sterling. "Classroom Needs for More Musical Films." 19.

13:5 (May–June 1954)
Scott, Tom. "*Summer Sequence*." 3–8. With music examples.
Shaindlin, Jack. "Of the Film and Music." 9–10. The writer is pictured standing behind a blown-up image of Morton Gould's theme for *Cinerama Holiday* in front of a movie theater.
Taubman, Howard. "Credit Overdue." 13–14. On recorded music used as background music and the lack of compensation to musicians. Lists many classical and contemporary works. Reprinted from the *New York Times*.
Haney, G. R., and George Vedegis. "Concerts on Film." 14–15.
Haney, G. R., and George Vedegis. "Musigraph: *Magic Fire*." 16–17. Regarding the Kerr Color Musigraph for visualizing music as animated color patterns.
Dickson, James P. "Film Music in a Public Library." 19.
Limbacher, James. "What Film Music Means to Me." 20.

14:1 (September–October 1954)
Hamilton, William. "*On the Waterfront*." 3–14. On Leonard Bernstein's score, with music examples. Reprinted in Limbacher.
Pratley, Gerald. "*The Stratford Adventure*." 15–17. On Louis Applebaum's score, with music examples.

14:2 (November–December 1954)
Raskin, David [*sic*]. "A Note on the Score of *Suddenly*." 3–11. With music examples.
Pratley, Gerald. "Ralph Vaughan Williams' *Sinfonia Antarctica*: A Radio Program in Two Parts." 12–16. Transcript of a Canadian Broadcasting Corp. program, including Ernest Irving interview quote.

Assum, Arthur L. "Cue-Sheet for *The General*." 21–22. Recorded music to be used with the 1927 film, prepared in 1953 by Assum.

14:3 (January–February 1955)

Vlad, Roman. "Notes on the Music for *Romeo and Juliet*." 3–5. With music examples.

Dubin, Joseph S. "*20,000 Leagues Under the Sea*." 6–15. By the film's orchestrator, with music examples.

Shaindlin, Jack. "Re *Cinerama Holiday* Music Score." 16–19. The film's music director on Morton Gould's score, with music examples. Reprinted in Limbacher.

Brown, Harold. "*The Silver Chalice*." 20–21. On Franz Waxman's score, with music examples.

14:4 (March–April 1955)

Brown, Harold. "*A Man Called Peter*." 3–9. On Alfred Newman's score, with music examples.

Linn, Robert. "The Story Tellers of *The Canterbury Tales*." 12–15. By the composer, with music examples.

Pratley, Gerald. "*High Tide in Newfoundland*." 16–18. On the music by Eldon Rathburn, with music examples.

Morrison, Alen. "Film Music on Record." 19–22.

Tanassy, Cornel. "Report on Music in Television." 23.

14:5 (May–June 1955)

Rosenman, Leonard. "Notes on the Score to *East of Eden*." 3–12. With music examples. Reprinted in Limbacher.

Duning, George. "*The Man from Laramie*." 13–18. With music examples.

Lewin, Frank. "*Land of the Pharaohs*." 19. On Dimitri Tiomkin's music, based on an interview with composer.

Joachim, Robin Jon. "Music at the Cannes International Film Festival." 20, 24. Report; Francis Polenc and Georges Auric were present.

Index of articles and reviews, 1946–1955. 21–23. Indispensable chronological list of music scores reviewed.

15:1 (September–October 1955)

Ronell, Ann. "*The Great Adventure*: Notes by Ann Ronell." 3–13. With music examples.

Schumann, Walter. "*The Night of the Hunter*." 13–17. With music examples.

Manson, Eddy. "*It's Always Fair Weather*." 18–19. On André Previn's score.

15:2 (Winter 1955)

North, Alex. "Notes on the Score of *The Rose Tattoo*." 3–15. With music examples.

Two films reviewed by Eddy Manson. 17–18.

Pratley, Gerald. "*Corral*." 20–23. On the music by Eldon Rathburn, with music examples.

15:3 (January–February 1956)

Duning, George. "*Picnic*." 3–16. With music examples.

Korngold, Erich Wolfgang. "The Music of Wagner in *Magic Fire*." 17. On adapting the music.

Manson, Eddy. "*Anything Goes*." 19.

Adler, Peter Herman. "TV in the Opera Picture." 23. The music director on special problems in adapting opera to television. Reprinted from *Theatre Arts*.

15:4 (Spring 1956)

Bernstein, Elmer. "*The Man with the Golden Arm*." 3–13. With music examples. Reprinted in Limbacher.

Manson, Eddy. "*Lovers and Lollipops*." 14–20. With music examples.
Walton, William. "Music for Shakespeare Films." 20. Reprinted in Limbacher.
Pratley, Gerald. "Composers at Work." 23. Report on his trip to Hollywood.

15:5 (Summer 1956)
Sainton, Philip. "The Music for *Moby Dick*." 3–6. With music examples.
Previn, André. "*Invitation to the Dance*: Ring around the Rosy Sequence." 8–16. On his original ballet music, with music examples.
Barron, Louis and Bebe. "*Forbidden Planet*." 18. On their electronic tonalities.
Scott, Tom. "Music for Television." 19–23. On his original music for television, with music examples.

Published as **Film and TV Music**

16:1 (Fall 1956)
Rózsa, Miklós. "*Lust for Life*." 3–7. With music examples.
Rota, Nino. "Background Music of *War and Peace*." 8–10.
McCarty, Clifford. "William Walton." 12–13. Biography and credits. First in a series of composer profiles.
Pratley, Gerald. "The Romance of Transportation." 16–19. With music examples.
Robin, Harry. "The State of Music in Television." 22–23.

16:2 (Winter 1956)
Bernstein, Elmer. "*The Ten Commandments*." 3–16. With music examples. Reprinted in Limbacher.
Bachmann, Gideon. "*8 x 8*: An Interview with Hans Richter." 19–20. The director on the use of Milhaud's music in his film.
McCarty, Cliff. "Leith Stevens." 21. Biography and credits.
Freedman, Lewis, and John McGiffert. "Music on Camera Three." 22. The producer and writer on the choice of music for the television program.
Young, Victor. "Confessions of a Film Composer." 23–24. Reprinted from *Music Journal*.

16:3 (Spring 1957)
North, Alex. "Notes on *The Rainmaker*." 3–16. With music examples.
Edens, Roger. "Labor Pains." 18–20. On the music for *Funny Face*.

16:4 (Summer 1957)
Antheil, George. "The Musical Score to *The Pride and the Passion*." 3–11. With music examples. Reprinted in Limbacher.
Glazer, Tom. "Notes on the Score of *A Face in the Crowd*." 13–19. With music examples.
Broekman, David. "Music and the *Wide Wide World*." 20–21.
Limbacher, James L. "Film and TV Scores on Long-Playing Records: Part I." 22–23.

16:5 (Late Summer 1957)
Duning, George. "Two Recent Scores: *3:10 to Yuma*, *Jeanne Eagels*." 3–11. With music examples. Reprinted in Limbacher.
Hopkins, Kenyon. "Notes on Three Scores: *The Strange One*, *Twelve Angry Men*, *Baby Doll*." 12–15. With music examples.
Bachmann, Gideon. "Composing for Films: Kenyon Hopkins Interviewed by Gideon Bachmann." 15–16.
Morrison, Alen. "*The Summoning of Everyman*." 19–20. With music examples by David M. Epstein.
McCarty, Cliff. "Victor Young." 21–22. Biography and credits.

Limbacher, James L. "Film and TV Scores on Long-Playing Records: Part II." 23–24.

17:1 (Fall–Winter 1957–1958)
Green, Johnny. "*Raintree County*: A Discussion of the Score by Its Composer." 3–12. With music examples. Reprinted in Limbacher.
Gallez, Douglas W. "The Music for *The Black Cat*." 16–18. On the film made at USC, with music examples.
McCarty, Cliff. "Johnny Green." 19–20. Biography and credits.
Limbacher, James L. "Film and TV Scores on Long-Playing Records: Part III." 22–23. Films with titles beginning with the letters R through Y, radio and television programs, and addenda.

Film Score Monthly (US, 1990–2005)

A leading voice in film music appreciation and soundtrack collecting for more than fifteen years. Founded as a one-page newsletter by editor-publisher Lukas Kendall in 1990, it evolved into a magazine and spawned a soundtrack label and Web site. Kendall is the Leonard Maltin of film music, a passionate fan who brought his enthusiasm for film music to the masses with strong opinions and an offbeat sense of humor that connected with other aficionados and collectors. Originally published in Massachusetts, *Film Score Monthly* moved west when Kendall relocated to Los Angeles in 1996 and began sporting a full-color cover the following year. The record label was launched in 1998 and to date has released more than 100 soundtrack recordings of classic film music from the 1940s through the 1980s. This venture gradually became the focus of Kendall's time and effort as his interest in more contemporary film scores waned. Managing editor Jeff Bond, as well as Joe Sikoryak and others, was brought in to run the magazine. By 2005, after more than 150 issues, publication ceased for financial reasons. The final print copy was distributed in December 2005; the magazine is now exclusively online. The end of the print version came a year after the end of another era marked by the deaths of icons Jerry Goldsmith and Elmer Bernstein, as well as senior statesman David Raksin.

In addition to articles and interviews, each issue featured soundtrack news; a record label round-up; "Collector's Corner," by Robert L. Smith; "The Adventures of Recordman," by R. Mike Murray; listings of film music concerts; soundtrack reviews; a lively letters section; and collector ads. Interviews with working composers usually highlighted their current projects and included at least one photo. In the regular feature "Downbeat," started around 2001, composers discussed their latest projects. The Margaret Herrick Library has an index of reviews that covers 1992 to 1996.

Issues No. 1 (1990) to No. 14 (October 1991)
The first fourteen issues were in the form of a monthly newsletter titled *Soundtrack Correspondence List*, also known as the *SCL Newsletter*.

Issues No. 15 (November 1991) to No. 21 (May 1992)
The next seven issues were titled *The Soundtrack Club*, or *STC*. Beginning with issue no. 15, *STC* incorporated *Score* (issue no. 10). *Score*, a fanzine published by Andy Dursin in Greenville, Rhode Island, contained soundtrack reviews and member questions such as, "Do you think it would be good or bad if John Williams ever scored *Star Trek*?" *STC* absorbed *Score* in May 1992. Dursin continued as editor of the "Score" section in *Film Score Monthly*.

Issue No. 22 (June 1992) to No. 29 (January 1992)
Issued as *Film Score Monthly*.

1:30–31 (February–March 1993)
Ford, Jeffrey. "Scoring the Silent Film." 9. Part 3.
Hubbard, Robert. "The Club Foot Orchestra." 10–11.
Ong, Augustinus. "The Ennio Morricone Soundtracks." 16–17.
Jahn, Wolfgang M. "The Elmer Bernstein Film Music Collection." 19–20.
Mathie, Brian. "An Interview with the Real Jerry Goldsmith." 23.
Cavanagh, Darren, and Paul Andrew MacLean. "An Interview with Basil Poledouris."
    24–25. Part 2.
MacLean, Paul Andrew. "A Conversation with Michael Lang, Session Keyboardist." 25–
    26.
Kendall, Lukas. "Jay Chattaway: Scoring *Star Trek: The Next Generation* and *Star Trek:
    Deep Space Nine*." 27–30.
MacLean, Paul Andrew. "An Interview with Maurice Jarre." 35–38.
Roth, Olivier. "Vangelis: Back to Film Scoring." 40. With filmography/discography.
Pacheco, Pedro. "Dave Grusin: One of a Kind." 41.
Ford, Jeffrey E. "Classic Corner: David Shire's *Return to Oz*." 42–45.
Pitkin, Shane. "Portrait of a Film Score: Bernard Herrmann's *Obsession*." 45.
Kendall, Lukas. "Christopher Young." 56–58. Interview.
Kendall, Lukas. "John Scott." 59. Interview.

1:32 (April 1993)
Harvey, Marshall. "Evolution of a Film Score: A Film Editor's Perspective." 7. On temp
    tracking Jerry Goldsmith's score for *Matinee*.
"Second Annual International Film Conference." Report on the Society for the Preserva-
    tion of Film Music conference.

1:33 (May 1993)
No feature articles or interviews.

1:34 (June 1993)
MacLean, Paul Andrew. "What Exactly Does an Orchestrator Do?" 6–7.
Taylor, Stephen. "The *Lost in Space* TV Scores (1965–68)." 7.
Pitkin, Shane. "Bernard Herrmann: Recycled Music." 7.
Kendall, Lukas. "New from Christopher Young." 13.

1:35 (July 1993)
"A Tribute to David Kraft." Reminiscences by Randall D. Larson, Jon Burlingame, and
    Nick Redman. 4–5.
Kendall, Lukas. "John Beal: Everything You Ever Wanted to Know about Scoring Trail-
    ers." 6–7. Interview. Part 1.

1:36–37 (August–November 1993)
MacLean, Paul Andrew. "Elmer Bernstein." 14–15. Interview.
MacLean, Paul Andrew. "The Fantasy Film Music of Elmer Bernstein." 15–17.
Kendall, Lukas. "John Beal: The Art (and Business) of Scoring Trailers." 18–19. Inter-
    view. Part 2.
Care, Ross. "Classical Connections: Some More Thoughts." 23.
Kendall, Lukas. "The Re-making of Alex North's *2001*: An Interview with Robert Town-
    son." 26.
Kendall, Lukas. "Richard Kraft and Nick Redman." 27–30. Interview. Part 1.
Ford, Jeffrey. "Classic Corner: Maurice Jarre's *Is Paris Burning?*" 31.

1:38 (October 1993)
Rixman, Joe. "John Debney: Scoring Steven Spielberg's *SeaQuest DSV*." 8–9. Interview.
Kendall, Lukas. "Richard Kraft and Nick Redman." 9–11. Interview. Part 2.

<u>1:39 (November 1993)</u>
Kendall, Lukas. "Richard Kraft and Nick Redman." 10–11. Interview. Part 3.
Szpirglas, Jeff. "30 Years of *Doctor Who* and Its Music." 14.

<u>1:40 (December 1993)</u>
Camuñas, Carlos Rafael. "Film Music in Puerto Rico." 4.
Kendall, Lukas. "Richard Kraft and Nick Redman." 8–9. Interview. Part 4.
Whitaker, Bill. "Conductor James Sedares: Re-Recording Classic Film Music." 10. Interview.

<u>1:41–42–43 (January–February–March 1994)</u>
Kendall, Lukas. "Elliot Goldenthal." 14–16. Interview.
Schweiger, Daniel. "Rachel Portman." 17. Interview.
Shivers, Will Davis. "James Newton Howard." 18–19. Interview.
Kendall, Lukas. "Randy Miller: Scoring *Heaven & Earth*." 20–21. Interview.
Ong, Augustinus. "A Survey of American Western Soundtracks." 21–23.
Kendall, Lukas. "*Star Wars*." 26–29. Article and cue sheet reconstruction.
Ford, Jeffrey. "Classic Corner: Hans J. Salter's *Frankensteins*." 29. On *House of Frankenstein* and *Ghost of Frankenstein*.
Dawes, Scott; editing, transcription, and introduction by Rich Upton. "Ken Darby: Alfred Newman's Right Hand Man." 30–32. 1987 interview.

<u>1:44 (April 1994)</u>
Büdinger, Matthias. "The Joel McNeely Chronicles." 12–13. Interview.
Kendall, Lukas. "*On Deadly Ground* (Basil Poledouris)." 13.

<u>1:45 (May 1994)</u>
Schweiger, Daniel. "Graeme Revell." 8–9. Interview.
Kendall, Lukas. "Randy Newman." 10–12. Interview.

<u>1:46–47 (June–July 1994)</u>
Whitaker, Bill. "John Morgan: Restoring the Classics." 8–10. Interview.
Hubbard, Robert. "Michael Nyman." 10–11. Article, with bibliography, discography, and concert works.
Schweiger, Daniel. "James Newton Howard." 12–13. Interview.
So, Mark G. "Patrick Doyle." 14–15. Interview.

<u>1:48 (August 1994)</u>
MacLean, Paul Andrew. "Does Classical Music Have a Place in Films?" 6. Part 1.
Kendall, Lukas. "Chuck Cirino and Peter Rotter: The Art and Craftiness of Scoring Low Budget Films." 8–10.
"So You Want to Be a Film Composer? Free Advice from Top Agent Richard Kraft." 11.
Kendall, Lukas. "Mark Mancina: New Composer *Speed*s His Way to the Top." 12–13. Article on *Speed*.
Wrobel, Bill. "Bernard Herrmann Archival Data." 17. Archives holding Herrmann scores.
Smith, Robert L. "Soundtracks for Cinerama." 20–21.

<u>1:49 (September 1994)</u>
Thomas, Tony. "Hans J. Salter: In Memorium [*sic*]." 7.
MacLean, Paul Andrew. "Does Classical Music Have a Place in Films?" 8. Part 2.
Derrett, Andrew. "Kubrick and Music." 9.
Kendall, Lukas. "Shirley Walker." 10–11. Interview.
Shivers, Will. "Hans Zimmer." 12–15. Interview.

1:50 (October 1994)
Schweiger, Daniel. "Mark Isham: Blowing His Horn." 10–11. Interview.
Dursin, Andy. "The Alan Silvestri Interview." 12–15.
Bender, John. "The Morricone Beat CDs." 19.

1:51 (November 1994)
Schweiger, Daniel. "Thomas Newman: Scoring *The Shawshank Redemption*." 8–9. Interview.
Kendall, Lukas. "J. Peter Robinson." 10–11. Interview.
Kendall, Lukas. "Howard Shore: *Ed Wood*." 12–13. Article.
Andres, Alan. The Music of *Heimat*." 19.
Bond, Jeff. "The Music of *Star Trek*." 20. Part 1. Bond went on to write the book *The Music of Star Trek* (1998).
Smith, Robert L. "Promo!" 21. On promotional soundtracks.

1:52 (December 1994)
Shivers, Will. "Marc Shaiman." 8–10. Interview, part 1.
Schweiger, Daniel. "Eric Serra: *The Professional*." 12–13. Interview.
Kremer, Jörg. "An Interview with Sandy De Crescent (music contractor)." 19.
Bond, Jeff. "The Music of *Star Trek*." 20. Part 2.

1:53–54 (January–February 1995)
Russ, Patrick. "Christopher Palmer." 5. Reminiscences by orchestrator Patrick Russ.
Upton, Rich. "Music and Oscar: An Uneasy Alliance." 8–9. Part 1.
Tonkens, Sijbold. "Sergio Bassetti, Jean-Claude Petit, Armando Trovajoli." 10–11. Interviewed at the Valencia Film Festival's third International Congress of Music of Cinema.
Shivers, Will. "Marc Shaiman." 12–14. Interview, part 2.
Bond, Jeff. "The Music of *Star Trek*." 18. Part 3.
Kelly, Peter. Dennis McCarthy: Scoring *Star Trek: Generations*." 19–21. Interview.

1:55–56 (March–April 1995)
Upton, Rich. "Music and Oscar: An Uneasy Alliance." 8–10. Part 2.
Dursin, Andy. "Joe LoDuca: From Jeep/Eagle to *The Evil Dead*." 10–11. Interview.
Schweiger, Daniel. "Alan Silvestri: Scoring *The Quick and the Dead*." 12. Interview.
MacLean, Paul Andrew. "Basil Poledouris: Scoring *The Jungle Book*." 13.

1:57 (May 1995)
Dursin, Andy. "Miles Goodman: Scoring Is Easy, Comedy Is Hard." 9–11.
Bond, Jeff. "The Music of *Star Trek*." 11. Part 4.
Adams, Doug. "Bruce Broughton's *Young Sherlock Holmes*." 12–14. Interview and analysis.

1:58 (June 1995)
Hubbard, Robert. "Royal S. Brown: Writing Real Film Music Criticism." 10–11. Interview.
Shivers, Will. "[Michael] Kamen Hard." 12–15. Interview, part 1.
Durnford, Mark J. "*Die Hard*: The Original." 16. Analysis.
Haupt, Art. "When Things Changed: Soundtracks and Their Fans in the 1960s and 1970s." 18–19. Part 1.

1:59–60 (July–August 1995)
Thomas, Tony. "Miklós Rózsa Remembered." 6.
Schweiger, Daniel. "Scoring on Air: Maurice Jarre Takes *A Walk in the Clouds*." 16–17. Interview.
Derrett, Andrew. "The Concert Hall: Film Music's Final Frontier." 18–19.

Kendall, Lukas. "The Film: Film Music's First and Greatest Frontier." 19–20.
Haupt, Art. "When Things Changed: Soundtracks and Their Fans in the 1960s and 1970s." 27. Part 2.

1:61 (September 1995)
Bond, Jeff. "The Music of *Star Trek*." 8–9. Part 5.
Shivers, Will. "Chris Lennertz." 9–11. Interview.
Adams, Doug. "Elliot Goldenthal." 12–15. Interview.
Shivers, Will. "[Michael] Kamen Harder." 16–19. Interview, part 2.
Pavelek, James. "Remembrance for Miklós Rózsa: September 3, 1995." 20. Report.

1:62 (October 1995)
Shapiro, Mike. "John Ottman: *The Usual Suspects*." 8–11. Interview.
Kendall, Lukas. "Danny Elfman: From *Pee-Wee* to *Batman* to Two Films a Year." 13–14. Article, part 1.
Walsh, Christopher. "Philosophy of Soundtrack Production, with Robert Townson, Inside Varese Sarabande." 16–18. Interview.

1:63 (November 1995)
Haupt, Art. "When Things Changed: Soundtracks and Their Fans in the 1960s and 1970s." 5. Part 3.
Kendall, Lukas. "*Goldeneye*: Eric Serra Tackles 007." 10–11. Interview.
Kendall, Lukas, and Andy Dursin. "Bondmania!" 11–14. Article on the John Barry scores, the non-Barry scores, and James Bond title songs.
Leonard, Geoff, and Pete Walker. "John Barry and James Bond: The Making of the Music." 15–18. Article.
Sutak, Ken. "DC 4 Decades." 19–21. *Davy Crockett* music by George Bruns and Tom Blackburn.

1:64 (December 1995)
Whitaker, Bill. "In the Recording Studio with *House of Frankenstein*." 4–5.
Shivers, Will. "[Michael] Kamen with a Vengeance." 8–9. Interview, part 3.
Kendall, Lukas. "Danny Elfman." 11–14. Article, part 2.
Kendall, Lukas. "Steve Bartek." 14–16. Interview with Elfman's orchestrator.
Murray, R. Michael. "The Blaxploitation Film Soundtracks." 18–20.
Walsh, Christopher. "Mark Banning: Inside GNP/Crescendo." 20–21. Interview.

1:65–66–67 (January–February–March 1996)
Adams, Doug. "Unstrung Newman: Thomas Newman Continues to Be Good and Interesting." 10–13. Interview.
Bateman, Tom. "*Robotech*: Composer Arlon Ober and Music Editor John Mortarotti Discuss the Scoring of the Popular 1985 Animated Series." 14–16. Interviews.
Walsh, John S. "The Ten Most Influential Film Composers." 18–22.
Kim, Kyu Hyun. "Toru Takemitsu." 26–27. Article.
MacLean, Paul Andrew. "Music for the Movies." 28–29. Documentary series review.
Gorbman, Claudia. "Aesthetics in the Age of *Gump*." 30–31. Amended version of a paper delivered at the 1995 SPFM conference.
Bond, Jeff. "The Music of *Star Trek*." 32–33. Part 6.
Walsh, Christopher. "Beauty and Philip Glass: Minimalist Composer Philip Glass Reworks Cocteau's 1946 *La Belle et la Bete* into a New Opéra Performed Live to Film." 33–34.
Whitaker, Bill. "Film Music Hikes Back to the Jungle—Literally: Alfred Heller Records Heitor Villa-Lobos's *Forest of the Amazon*, aka the Score to the 1959 Film *Green Mansions*." 35–36. Interview with Heller.

1:68 (April 1996)

Schweiger, Daniel. "Carter Burwell." 14–16. Interview.

Adams, Doug. "David Shire's *The Taking of Pelham One Two Three*." 18–20. Interview and analysis.

1:69 (May 1996)

Beacom, Michael. "Bernard Herrmann and Miklós Rózsa: Nationally Broadcast Radio Shows Pay Tribute to Two Masters." 10–11.

Mandell, Paul. "Forty-Year Mystery Solved: The Music behind *Plan 9 from Outer Space*." 12–13.

1:70 (June 1996)

Dursin, Andy. "Mark Mancina on *Twister* and a Steadily Rising Career." 7–10. Interview.

1:71 (July 1996)

"Michel Colombier." 8–11. Interviewed independently by Thomas Sanfilip and Jörg Kremer.

Schweiger, Daniel. "David Arnold: *Independence Day*." 12–14. Interview.

1:72 (August 1996)

Schweiger, Daniel. "*Escape from L.A.*" 6–7. Interview with John Carpenter and Shirley Walker, excerpted from the CD liner notes.

Merluzeau, Yann. "John Mauceri: Hollywood Bowl Conductor." 8–11. Interview.

Adams, Doug. "Thomas Newman's *The Player*." 16–18. Interview and analysis.

Kim, Kyu Hyun. "The Collected Works of Akira Ifukube." 22–23. Review, part 1.

1:73 (September 1996)

Whitaker, Bill. "David Schecter and Monstrous Movie Music." 8–10. Interview.

Murray, R. Michael. "A Late Night TV Guide to War Films, Their Composers and Recordings." 12–17. With lengthy list of titles.

Bender, John. "The Collected Works of Akira Ifukube." 22–23. Review, part 2.

1:74 (October 1996)

Howard, Jeffrey K. "Vic Mizzy." 8–9. Interview.

Hoshowsky, Robert. "Zhao Jiping." 11. Article.

Hoshowsky, Robert. "The Future of Film Music Scoring." 12.

Adams, Doug. "What's Wrong with This Picture?: Action Scores in the '90s." 13–19.

1:75 (November 1996)

Murray, R. Michael. "A Late Night TV Guide to War Films, Their Composers and Recordings." 8–12. Concluding list of titles.

Hoshowsky, Robert. "John Barry: The Gstaad Memorandum." 13–17. Transcription of a Cinemusic conference interview in Switzerland.

1:76 (December 1996)

Dursin, Andy. "The Randy Edelman Interview." 8–12.

Hoshowsky, Robert. "John Barry: Exclusive Interview." 13–15.

Schweiger, Daniel. "Partners in Crime: Composer Ry Cooder Teams Up Again with Walter Hill for *Last Man Standing*." 16–18. Interview.

2:1 (January–February 1997)

Matessino, Michael. "Return of the Trilogy." 9–12. Article on *Star Wars* trilogy special edition soundtracks.

Matessino, Michael. "The Comprehensive Reference for the John Williams Music Scores." 12–17.

Byrd, Craig L. "The *Star Wars* Interview: John Williams." 18–21.

Kendall, Lukas. "Did You Know There's No Theme for Han?" 22–26.

2:2 (March–April 1997)
Koppl, Rudy. "Inside the Industry: Promotional Soundtracks." 15–18. Part 1, Alan Silvestri, Hummie Mann, David and Eric Wurst, Mason Daring, Christopher L. Stone, Peter Manning Robinson, Richard Bellis, Mark McKenzie.
Tonkens, Sijbold. "The 5th International Film Music Congress in Valencia." 19–22. Report.
Adams, Doug. *"The Simpsons'* Secret Weapon: Alf Clausen." 24–33.

2:3 (May 1997)
Whitaker, Bill. "Michael Fine: Recording Miklos Rozsa." 14–16, 18. Interview.
Thomas, Tony. "[Miklós] Rozsa Noir." 17.
Whitaker, Bill. "Patrick Russ: Orchestrating Past and Present." 19–20. Interview.

2:4 (June 1997)
Koppl, Rudy. "Inside the Industry: Promotional Soundtracks." 15–18. Part 2, Ernest Troost, Nicholas Pike, Peter Rogers Melnick, Colin Towns, Craig Safan, Eric Allman, Stephen James Taylor, Laura Karpman, Randy Miller.
Adams, Doug. "Tales from the Black Side: An Interview with Danny Elfman." 20–26.
Byrnes, Kerry J. "Martin Denny and the Sounds of Exotica." 34–36. Article mentions Les Baxter and Arthur Lyman.
Salas, Randy A. "The Man behind the *Lady in White*: An Interview with Frank LaLoggia." 36–37.

2:5 (July 1997)
Adams, Doug. "Obligatory *Batman* Dept.: Elliot Goldenthal." 13–15. Interview.
Schweiger, Daniel. "Mark Mancina: Going Fast Again." 23–26. Interview.

2:6 (August 1997)
Kendall, Lukas. "Remembering Tony Thomas." 13–15. With sidebars by Jon Burlingame, Nick Redman, and Rudy Behlmer.
Kendall, Lukas. "John Powell and the Woo-Hans Clan: The British Composer and Media Ventures Associate Tackles His First Hollywood Film: John Woo's *Face/Off*." 16–18. Article.
Kendall, Lukas. "Lalo's Back and *Money Talks* Has Got Him!" 20–23.
Shivers, Will. "Marc of the Scoring Jungle." 25–27. Interview with Marc Shaiman regarding *George of the Jungle*.

2:7 (September 1997)
Bond, Jeff. "Curtis Hanson and the Secrets of *L.A. Confidential*." 18–19. Interview with the director.
Kendall, Lukas, and Jeff Bond. "[Hans] Zimmer Takes Aim…at FSM!" 21–24. Interview, part 1.
Adams, Doug. *"Scream* Away: Marco and *Mimic*." 25–28. Interview with Marco Beltrami.

2:8 (October 1997)
Follett, Jonathan. "The Men with the Junk Metal Instruments." 15–16. Article on the Alloy Orchestra, performing live for silent pictures.
Kendall, Lukas, and Jeff Bond. "The Final Confrontation: [Hans] Zimmer vs. FSM." 17–19. Interview, part 2.
Bond, Jeff. "Basil's [Poledouris] Battle of the Bugs." 20–24. Article on *Starship Troopers*.
Adams, Doug. "Playing *The Game* in ShoreLand." 27–31. Interview with Howard Shore.

2:9 (November–December 1997)

Tonks, Paul. "*Tomorrow Never Dies*, Yesterday Lives Again." 16–21. Article with interview quotes from David Arnold and John Barry.

Schweiger, Daniel. "In the Company of Aliens." 22–26. Interview with John Frizzell regarding *Alien Resurrection.*

Riordan, Paul M. "The Man Who Wrote the Bat." 42–45. Interview with Neal Hefti.

3:1 (January 1998)

Dursin, Andy, and Jeff Bond. "Williams' List." 24–33. CD guide. Part 1.

Adams, Doug. "Man of a Thousand Phrases." 34–40. Interview with Mychael Danna.

3:2 (February 1998)

Dursin, Andy, Jeff Bond, Jeff Eldridge, and R. Mike Murray. "Disasters, Downbeats, and Lil' Dogies: John Williams in the Pre-*Star Wars* Years." 16–21. CD guide. Part 2.

Bond, Jeff. "David Amram." 22–23. Article.

Adams, Doug. "Zen and the Art of Motion Picture Scoring." 24–30. Interview with Philip Glass regarding *Kundun.*

Marshall, Wes. "Raiders of the Lost Soundtracks." 34–37. Profile of Pendulum Entertainment Group.

3:3 (March–April 1998)

Lehman, Phil. "Cinerama Rides Again!" 18–20.

Marshall, Wes. "The Great McRitchie: The Man and His Music Remembered." 21–24. Profile of orchestrator Greig McRitchie.

Redman, Nick. "The Ship of Dreams: How *Titanic* Succeeds as Cinema." 36–37, 43.

Adams, Doug. "A Score to Remember? James Horner's Technique Critiqued." 38–43.

3:4 (May 1998)

Bond, Jeff. "Never Fear, Bruce Is Here." 20–24. Interview with Bruce Broughton regarding *Lost in Space.*

Bond, Jeff. "Music for a Force of Nature: David Arnold on Scoring the New *Godzilla*." 25–26. Article with interview excerpts.

Bond, Jeff. "Watch the Record Stores, Please: How the Score to *Close Encounters of the Third Kind* Finally Got the Album It Deserves." 27–32, 48.

Dursin, Andy, Jeff Eldridge, R. Mike Murray, and Jeff Bond. "Johnny Cool." 34–41. John Williams CD guide. Part 3. With sidebars on Williams's concert works and beginnings as a studio musician pianist.

3:5 (June 1998)

Bond, Jeff. "Anne Dudley and the Full Oscar." 17–18. Interview regarding *The Full Monty.*

Bond, Jeff. "Gojira! King of the Rubber Monsters." 22–26. Article on *The Best of Godzilla* CD, music by Akira Ifukube and others.

Comerford, Jason, Jeff Bond, and Doug Adams. "Bruce Broughton Buyer's Guide 1991–98." 27–29.

Adams, Doug. "Mark Spots the X." 30–32. Article on Mark Snow's *X-Files* scores.

Friede, David. "Jay Chattaway: Music for Maniacs." 33–37. Interview, introduced by Patrick Runkle.

3:6 (July 1998)

Freeth, Nick. "The Woman Went *Wilde*." 16–17. Article on Debbie Wiseman.

Bond, Jeff. "From Hell's Heart I Score at Thee! In Pursuit of Christopher Gordon's Music for *Moby Dick*." 18–19. Regarding the telefilm.

Bond, Jeff. "*Armageddon* Arrives." 20–21. Interview with Trevor Rabin by Lukas Kendall.

Redman, Nick. "The Beyondness of John Barry: A Concert Review and Life Reflection." 22–27.

Bond, Jeff. "Tru Tracks." 28–29. Interview with Burkhard Dallwitz regarding *The Truman Show*.

Kendall, Lukas. "The Soul of the Seventies: A Suite of New CD Releases Spark a Reappraisal of an Unfairly Dismissed Era in Film Music." 31–35.

3:7 (August 1998)

Bond, Jeff. "The Sound of Scuzzlebutt." 20–23, 47. Article regarding Adam Berry's music for *South Park*.

Bond, Jeff. "Game for Anything: Ira Newborn Makes His Play on *Basketball*." 22–23.

Bond, Jeff, Jason Comerford, and Doug Adams. "Bruce Broughton Buyer's Guide: Between Two Worlds." 29–33.

3:8 (September 1998)

Adams, Doug. "Schifrin Rushes In." 20–24. Article on Lalo Schifrin's score for *Rush Hour*.

Tonks, Paul. "The Emperor Jones." 25–29. Interview with Trevor Jones.

3:9 (October–November 1998)

Tonks, Paul. "Neither Shallow nor Grave: An Interview with Simon Boswell." 18–19, 45.

Whitaker, Bill. "Devotion." 22–28. Interview with Erich Wolfgang Korngold biographer Brendan G. Carroll.

Adams, Doug. "Composition Theory: Carter Burwell Interviewed." 29–33.

Marshall, Wes. "Storming the Citadel." 34–35. Profile of Citadel Records and Tom Null.

3:10 (December 1998)

Adams, Doug. "Scoring Shades of Gray: Composer Elia Cmiral on the Road to *Ronin*." 15. Profile.

Goldmark, Daniel. "Doing the Lord's Work: Finding Inspiration in *The Prince of Egypt*." 20–23. Article on Hans Zimmer's score.

4:1 (January 1999)

Adams, Doug. "The Evolution of Elfman." 20–23, 46. Danny Elfman interview.

Bond, Jeff. "Blood, Sweat, and Tunes." 24–29. Article on music for NFL Films by composers Sam Spence, Tom Hedden, and David Robidoux.

4:2 (February 1999)

Adams, Doug. "Window Treatment." 14–15, 47. Article on David Shire's music for *Rear Window* (television).

Bond, Jeff. "Jerry Goldsmith Buyer's Guide." 18–23. Part 1.

Park, George. "The Devil's Music: Lalo Schifrin, William Friedkin, and the Struggle to Score *The Exorcist*." 24–30.

Goldwasser, Dan. "For Promo's Sake! A Guide to Some High-Profile Limited Edition Compact Discs." 31–33.

4:3 (March 1999)

Bond, Jeff. "A Clockwork Composer: Wendy Carlos Switches Back on Soundtracks and Revisits Her Premiere Score." 18–23. Interview regarding *A Clockwork Orange*.

Bond, Jeff. "Jerry Goldsmith Buyer's Guide: Recording the Reagan-Bush Years." 30–38. Part 2.

4:4 (April–May 1999)

Adams, Doug. "A Valiant Effort: Franz Waxman Composing *Prince Valiant*." 22–29. Article with music examples.

Bond, Jeff. "Jerry Goldsmith Buyer's Guide: Super Hits of the Late '70s." 30–34. Part 3.

4:5 (June 1999)
Dyer, Richard. "Making *Star Wars* Sing Again." 18–21. Article on John Williams's score for *Star Wars: The Phantom Menace*, reprinted from the *Boston Globe*.

Adams, Doug. "Sounds of the Empire: Analyzing the Themes of the *Star Wars* Trilogy." 22–25, 47. Article regarding John Williams's music, with music examples.

Comerford, Jason. "Slicing and Dicing a Horror Score: The Rescoring of *Halloween* H20: An Investigative Report." 26–30. Article, including a music cue sheet with listed composers John Ottman, John Carpenter, and Marco Beltrami.

4:6 (July 1999)
Randall, Jasper. "Soundtrack 101: A Recent Graduate Answers Practical Questions about the USC Film Scoring Program." 18–21.

Bond, Jeff. "Shagging a Sequel Score: George S. Clinton and Director Jay Roach on *Austin Powers 2: The Spy Who Shagged Me*." 22–25. Article.

Bond, Jeff. "Wild Wild Elmer: The Master of the Western Returns to the Genre—Sort of: A Conversation with Elmer Bernstein." 26–28. Article regarding *Wild Wild West*.

Bond, Jeff. "Jerry Goldsmith Buyer's Guide: *Shaft*ed in the Watergate Era." 29–33. Part 4.

4:7 (August 1999)
Boris, Cynthia. "Fangs for the Melodies: A Chat with *Buffy the Vampire Slayer*'s Score-meister Christopher Beck." 17–18. Listed as Christophe Beck in the show's credits.

Adams, Doug. "Beat Guy." 19–21. Interview with session musician percussionist Emil Richards.

Bond, Jeff. "Tiny Tune Titans." 22–28. Article on music for Warner Bros. cartoons by composers Bruce Broughton, Richard Stone, Shirley Walker, and others.

Bond, Jeff. "Iron Mike." 29–31. Article on Michael Kamen's score for *The Iron Giant*.

Adams, Doug. "A Return, or a New Hope?" 32–34. Analysis of John Williams's score for *Star Wars: The Phantom Menace*, with music examples.

Lichtenfeld, Eric. "View from the Bridge: *Battlestar Galactica*'s Stu Phillips Talks about a Life in Music and the Music of a Saga." 35–38, 46. Interview.

4:8 (September–October 1999)
Bond, Jeff. "At the Top of His Game: Power Hitter Basil Poledouris Talks about His Score Lineup for the Current Season." 18–23. Interview, with sidebar on director Sam Raimi working with Poledouris.

Bond, Jeff. "Ears Wide Open." 24–25. Article on *Eyes Wide Shut* composer Jocelyn Pook.

Bond, Jeff. "Jerry Goldsmith Buyer's Guide: Swingin' in the Late Sixties, Baby!" 30–35. Part 5.

4:9 (November 1999)
Bender, John. "Also Sprach Peter Thomas." 20–23, 47. Article and interview.

Bond, Jeff. "Stamps of Approval: The Hollywood Composer Series." 24–27.

Tucker, Guy Mariner. "Float Like a Butterfly: Jerry Goldsmith's Score to *Papillon*." 28–34. Retrospective article.

4:10 (December 1999)
Annual review issue, 1999.

5:1 (January 2000)
Bond, Jeff. "Shore 'Nuff: Howard Shore Talks about *Dogma*, *Ed Wood* and Serial Killer Sounds." 20–23. Interview.

Lichtenfeld, Eric. "Super Rescues: The Story behind Rhino's Restoration of a Classic." 24–26.

Bond, Jeff. "Tale of the Cape: The Genesis of the Best Comic Book Film Ever." 27–28, 31.

Matessino, Michael. "*Superman*: The Cue Sheets." 29–31.

Bond, Jeff. "Strange Visitor from Another Channel: The Halcyon Sound of '50s TV— Coming to Your CD Player." 32–33.

5:2 (February 2000)
Redman, Nick. "Music by Jerry Fielding: A 20th Anniversary Reminiscence." 24–29. Article, with sidebar "Camille Fielding Remembers Jerry."

Bond, Jeff. "Any Given Composer: Oliver Stone Assembles a Crack Team of Musicians for His Football Epic *Any Given Sunday*." 30–32.

5:3 (March 2000)
Bond, Jeff. "The Sword and Sandal Sound: Hans Zimmer Scores Ridley Scott's Roman Opus." 17–18. Article regarding *Gladiator*.

Doctor Digital [Bond, Jeff?]. "*Phantom Menace* Mania." 24–31. Article with cue-by-cue annotations for John Williams's score.

Deming, Larry, and Jim Gustafson. "When Worlds Collide: Springfield Symphony Orchestra Music Director Mark Russell Smith Shares His Thoughts on the Unholy Convergence of Classical and Film Music." 32, 44. Interview.

5:4 (April–May 2000)
Bond, Jeff. "Ancient History X." 20–23. Article on the history of artists representation in film music, part 1.

Tucker, Guy Mariner. "Herrmann's Journey: *Journey to the Center of the Earth*." 24–29. Retrospective article.

Hall, Roger. "From Hitchcock to Harryhausen: Ten Essential Herrmann Scores." 30–33. Article with selected CD discography.

Kaplan, Jonathan Z. "The 'Rejected' Liner Notes from *Tora! Tora! Tora!*" 34–35.

5:5 (June 2000)
Bond, Jeff. "Ancient History X: The Evolution of Film Music Representation." 20–23. Part 2, with information on Carol Faith, Al Bart, and Richard Kraft.

Bond, Jeff. "Jerry Goldsmith Buyer's Guide: In the Beginning…" 26–31, 48. Part 6.

5:6 (July 2000)
Schweiger, Daniel. "The Nutty Composer." 22–23. Interview with David Newman regarding *The Klumps*.

Bond, Jeff. "Ancient History X: The Evolution of Film Music Representation." 30–33. Part 3, with information on Laura Engel and others.

5:7 (August 2000)
Comerford, Jason. "Finding Other Sounds: William Stromberg's Score for *Other Voices*." 13–14.

Lichtenfeld, Eric. "Hangin' with Mr. Elfman." 15, 19. Danny Elfman on the scoring stage for *The Family Man*.

Bond, Jeff. "Ancient History X: The Final Conflict." 16–19. Part 4.

Bond, Jeff. "Bruce's World." 20–23. Article on Bruce Broughton.

Adams, Doug. "Striking Gold in *Silverado*." 24–25. Retrospective article on Bruce Broughton's score.

Edwards, Timothy Andrews. "Immediate Impact: Jeffrey Fayman Talks about Writing Music for Coming Attractions." 29–33. Interview.

5:8 (September–October 2000)

Curran, Tim. "Springfield Symphonics: A Visit with Alf Clausen recording *The Simpsons*." 21.

Getlen, Larry. "He's Not Angry...Just Opinionated: An Interview with Randy Newman, Composer of *Meet the Parents*." 22–25.

Snedden, William. "Ahead of Its Time." 26–29. Article on a 1996 BBC Radio documentary on Arthur Bliss's score for *Things to Come*, possibly the world's first soundtrack album.

Foster, Jason. "Great Big Gobs of Greasy Grimy Grusin Cues: *The Goonies*." 30–34. Retrospective article.

5:9 (November–December 2000)

Bond, Jeff. "To Score or Not to Score?" 14–16. Article on Alan Silvestri's score for *Cast Away*.

Kaplan, Jon, and Al Kaplan. "Future Past Perfect." 16–21. Retrospective article on Alan Silvestri's music for the *Back to the Future* series, with thematic material.

Adams, Doug. "Set Free in *The Cell*." 22–25. Interview with Howard Shore.

Bond, Jeff. "Crouching Composer, Hidden Cellist." 45–48. Article on Tan Dun's score for *Crouching Tiger, Hidden Dragon*.

6:1 (January 2001)

Foster, Jason. "*Traffic*king in Atmosphere: Cliff Martinez Talks about His Score for Steven Soderbergh's Acclaimed Film." 15–16.

Leneker, Mark. "Small Town Sounds: An Analysis of Aaron Copland's Score to *Our Town*." 18–20, 48. With music examples.

Bond, Jeff. "Hail the *Hollow Man*: A Guide to Jerry Goldsmith's Complete Score and Commentary on DVD." 30–33, 48.

6:2 (February 2001)

Shutan, Bruce. "An Easy 3000 Miles: Graceland Hits Home for Composer Clinton." 15–16. On George S. Clinton's score for *3000 Miles to Graceland*.

Sikoryak, Joe. "Entering a Third Decade." 17–21. On Intrada's Douglass Fake.

Marmorstein, Gary. "Making the Scene." 22–23. Extended liner notes on Alfred Newman's score for *How to Marry a Millionaire*.

Bond, Jeff. "King of Outer (and Inner) Space: The Musical World of Irwin Allen." 24–27, 46. Part 1.

Kennedy, Steven A. "Copland on Celluloid." 28–30. Interview with conductor Jonathan Sheffer.

6:3 (March 2001)

Bond, Jeff. "Off-Kilter Comedy Cues: Rolfe Kent Blazes a Comedy Trail for the 21st Century." 15–16.

Harris, Scott. "Life in 13/8: The Odd-Metered Existence of Trumpeter and Composer Don Ellis." 18–22.

Harris, Scott. "Don Ellis Speaks: On Scoring *The French Connection*." 22.

Bond, Jeff. "That Hollywood Sound: The Art and Business of Being an L.A. Session Musician." 23–25.

Bond, Jeff. "Tales of Trouble, Days of Disaster: The Musical World of Irwin Allen." 26–29. Part 2, with discography.

Bond, Jeff. "The Michael Hennagin Story: A Favorite Composer Goes Undercover." 28. On Jerry Goldsmith's contribution to a score by Morton Stevens for *Voyage to the Bottom of the Sea*.

6:4 (April–May 2001)

Bond, Jeff. "Alan Silvestri: *The Mummy Returns*." 14–15.

Bond, Jeff. "Christopher Young: *Swordfish*." 16.

Kaplan, Jonathan Z. "Diving in Headfirst: On the Stage for James Newton Howard's *Atlantis* and Rolfe Kent's *Someone Like You*." 17–18.

Bond, Jeff. "Yabba Dabba Crew: Working with Hoyt Curtin at Hanna-Barbera." 20–23.

Karpinski, Gary J. "Bone Torture: A Conversation with Hoyt Curtin." 22.

Broxton, Jonathan. "King of the World: The James Horner Buyer's Guide." 24–30. Part 1.

6:5 (June 2001)

Hasan, Mark Richard. "Jeff Danna." 15–17. Interview-based article on *O, Green Dragon*, and *Higher Love*.

Leneker, Mark. "Ryan Shore." 17, 48. Interview-based article on *Vulgar*.

Danly, Linda. "[Hugo] Friedhofer and Fox." 18–20.

Kaplan, Jon, and Al Kaplan. "Egon, Your Music..." 22–25. On Elmer Bernstein's score for *Ghostbusters* (1984), with music examples.

Takis, John. "Sergei Prokofiev: The Man, the Music, the Legacy." 26–33.

6:6 (July 2001)

Adams, Doug. "Organic Sounds, Synthetic Worlds." 13–14. On Elliot Goldenthal's score for *Final Fantasy*.

Adams, Doug. "Assembling a Crack Team." 14–15, 47. On Howard Shore's score for *The Score*.

Broxton, Jonathan. "Clear and Present Melody: The James Horner Buyer's Guide." 16–23. Part 2. Includes a sidebar, "The Borrower: Those Nagging Accusations of Self-Plagiarism."

Bond, Jeff. "A Whole Different Animal." 24–28. On Danny Elfman's score for *Planet of the Apes* (2001).

Adams, Doug. "A.I.: Artistic Integrity." 29, 43. On John Williams's score for *A.I.: Artificial Intelligence*.

Bond, Jeff. "Hans Across America: The Affable Film Composer Faces Critics Once Again." 30–31, 48. Interview-based article on Hans Zimmer.

6:7 (August 2001)

Bond, Jeff. "Lalo Schifrin." 13–14. Interview-based article on *Rush Hour 2*.

Bond, Jeff. "Writing in a Family Way." 14–16. Interview-based article on a Ron Jones score for television's *The Family Guy*.

Foster, Jason. "Scoring on the Dark Side." 16. Interview-based article on Joel Diamond's score for *The Believer*.

Bond, Jeff. "There's Melody to His Madness." 17, 46. Interview-based article on John Debney's scores for *Spy Kids*, *Cats and Dogs*, and *The Princess Diaries*.

Wong, Cary. "A Spectacular Spectacular! How 20th-Century Songs Illuminate a 19th-Century Love Story in *Moulin Rouge*." 18–19.

Hasan, Mark Richard. "The King of Hip: A Quincy Jones Retrospective: Part One (1957–1967)." 20–25, 46.

Feigelson, Roger. "Sweating to the Classics: John Morgan Gets the Details Right for Marco Polo's Golden Age Reconstructions." 26–30. Interview-based article.

6:8 (September 2001)

Wright, Chris. "A Diamond in the Rough." 14–15, 23. On the film scoring program at North Carolina School of the Arts by an enrolled student.

Hasan, Mark Richard. "The King of Hip: A Quincy Jones Retrospective: Part Two (1968–2001)." 16–23.

Schweiger, Daniel. "The Madman and His Muse: Composer Angelo Badalamenti Takes Another Wild Ride with Director David Lynch for *Mulholland Drive*." 24–27, 44. Interview-based article.

Young-Groves, Deborah. "He Wrote the Book: Retired Composer and Author Earle Hagen Talks about His 40-Year Career Scoring for Film and Television." 30–33. Interview-based article.

6:9 (October–November 2001)
Wheaton, Mark. "*From Hell* to Eternity." 13, 48. Interview-based article on a Trevor Jones score.

Adams, Doug. "Danna in Demand: The Canadian Composer Reviews His Busiest Year Yet." 14–16, 48. Interview with Mychael Danna.

Takis, John. "Invasion of the Score Man: Ronald Stein: Unsung Hero of Hollywood's Golden Age." 18–21.

Adams, Doug. "Learning New Hobbits: Howard Shore Begins His Journey with *The Fellowship of the Ring*." 22–26. Interview.

Takis, John. "RRRAAAAAAGGGHHH! Tearing into the Score to *Jurassic Park*." 28–30. Analysis of John Williams's score with thematic examples.

6:10 (December 2001)
Bond, Jeff. "Downbeat Deluxe." 14–18. Composers Harry Gregson-Williams, Mark Isham, Rolfe Kent, and Christopher Young speak to FSM about their latest projects.

Bond, Jeff. "One of Us: Discussing Movies and Movie Music with Alejandro Amenabar, the Man behind *The Others* and *Open Your Eyes*." 20–21. Interview with the director-composer.

Takis, John. "The Other Lords of Middle-Earth." 22–23, 48. Article on Hobbit-themed music by Maury Laws and Leonard Rosenman.

7:1 (January 2002)
Bond, Jeff. "Facing the Prime Directive: Composer Velton Ray Bunch Discusses His Score for Enterprise's *Silent Enemy*." 11–12.

Joy, Nick. "Exporting Charm to the World: Yann Tiersen's Score de Force for *Amelie*." 13, 48. Interview.

Bouthillier, Paul. "Honey, I Copped the Theme: The James Horner Buyer's Guide." 14–18. Part 3.

Bond, Jeff. "Logan's Overrun." 20–23. Uncut liner notes discussing Jerry Goldsmith's score for *Logan's Run*.

Bond, Jeff. "The Best and the Worst of 2001." 24–26. With additional summaries from Jason Comerford, Jon and Al Kaplan, Nick Joy, and Doug Adams. 26–31.

Schweiger, Daniel. "In the War Zone: Hans Zimmer Goes to Battle for *Black Hawk Down*." 32–33, 48. Interview.

7:2 (February 2002)
Bond, Jeff. "Saints and Sinners: Checking in with the Composers of *John Q* and *Frailty*." 13–15. Aaron Zigman and Brian Tyler on their latest projects.

Hasan, Mark. "The Man with the Jazzy Sound: Elmer Bernstein's Cool Jazz: Part 1: The '50s." 16–19, 44.

Pavelek, Pav, ed. and transcriber. "His *Lust for Life*: Reminiscences by Miklos Rozsa." 20–23. With music examples.

Phillips, James. "A Touch of Elegance: The Film Music of Richard Rodney Bennett." 24–28.

Bettencourt, Scott. "How the Awards Were Won: The Secret History of the Film Music Oscars." 22–28. Historical overview of the music categories, largely researched from material available to the public at the Margaret Herrick Library.

Bond, Jeff. "Curse of the Sequel: The Motion Picture Academy Music Branch Debates the Eligibility of Film Score Sequels." 28–29.

Eppler, James. "Revelling in the Music: An Interview with Graeme Revell." 30–32.

8:3 (March 2003)

Schweiger, Daniel. "Battle Plans: John Frizzell and Randy Edelman Marshal Their Forces for *Gods and Generals*." 12–13, 18. Interview.

Bond, Jeff. "Take the Red Pill." 14–18. Interview with Don Davis regarding *The Matrix* franchise.

Bond, Jeff. "Arrakis Attack! Brian Tyler Tackles *Children of the Dune* and *The Hunted*." 19–21. With a sidebar on his score for a television episode of *Star Trek*'s *Enterprise*.

Bond, Jeff. "Call Forth the Mutants: John Ottman Steps aboard the X-Jet." 22–23, 32. On music for *X2: X-Men United*.

Kaplan, Jon, and Al Kaplan. "Magnificent Movie Music Moments." 24–31.

8:4 (April–May 2003)

Duff, Simon. "Nature into Music: George Fenton and *The Blue Planet* Live: A Concert of Harmony and Nature." 12–13. Interview.

Griffin, Mark. "Nobody Does It Better: An Interview with Marvin Hamlisch." 14–16.

"The New Stuff: A Conversation with Joey Santiago." 17, 48.

Kendall, Lukas. "From Lukas with Love." 18–23. Part 1. On his experience with soundtrack restoration and the EMI James Bond rereleases.

Bond, Jeff. "The Fine Line between Stupid and Clever." 24–29, 32. On the music for *This Is Spinal Tap*, *Waiting for Guffman*, and *A Mighty Wind*.

Bond, Jeff. "Brits and Babes: Ed Shearmur Goes Full Throttle on *Charlie's Angels* and *Johnny English*." 30–32.

8:5 (June 2003)

Kendall, Lukas. "From Lukas with Love." 12–17. Part 2.

Hasan, Mark. "To Miami and Beyond: There's More to Jan Hammer than Just *Miami Vice*." 18–21, 48. Continued from February 2003.

Bond, Jeff. "A Hulking Responsibility: Danny Elfman Plays the Hero Again, This Time with Ang Lee's *The Hulk*." 22–24.

Bond, Jeff. "Ex-Terminated: Marco Beltrami and the Rise of the Orchestra." 25–26. On *Terminator 3*.

Bond, Jeff. "The Big Combo: Alex Wurman Busts Out on *Hollywood Homicide*." 26–28.

Bond, Jeff. "Hitting It Big: Marc Shaiman Meets His Match in *Down with Love*." 28–29.

8:6 (July 2003)

Wong, Cary. "Practically Perfect in Every Way: Richard Sherman Talks about the Sherman Brothers' Extraordinary Career Writing Hit Songs for Stage and Screen." 18–22.

Bond, Jeff. "Shiver Me Timbers: Klaus Badelt Leads a Media Ventures Assault on Pirate Movie Scoring Traditions." 24–26.

Bond, Jeff. "Siren Song: Harry Gregson-Williams Scores *Sinbad: Legend of the Seven Seas*." 28–29, 48.

Bond, Jeff. "Taken with Her Music: Prolific Television Composer Laura Karpman Tackles Sci-Fi, Including an Online Videogame." 30–31.

8:7 (August 2003)
Adams, Doug. "Not Your Typical Chick Flicks: Rolfe Kent Scores *Legally Blonde 2* and *Freaky Friday*." 11, 48.
Bond, Jeff. "Earning His Spurs: Michael Kamen Tackles His First Western with Kevin Costner's *Open Range*." 12–14.
Griffin, Mark. "Better than a Dream: An Interview with Legendary Songwriter Betty Comden." 18–19, 48.
Joy, Nick. "Sex, Lions and Audiotape." 20–23. Interview with Patrick Doyle.
Sheffo, Nicholas. "Scores to Settle: In Search of the Perfect Union of Preservation, Aesthetic Appreciation and Technology in Film Music and Sound." 24–28. On remastering soundtracks.

8:8 (September 2003)
Takis, John. "Fortune and Glory: The Music of *Indiana Jones and the Temple of Doom*." 12–18, 48. On John Williams's score, with music examples.
"We Love the Boob Tube: A By-No-Means-Complete List of Fave TV Themes by the FSM Staff." 20–23.
Bond, Jeff. "Alive and Kicking." 24–29, 48. On television music by Jeff Beal, Michael Giacchino, Philip Giffin, Gary Stockdale, and Charles Sydnor.
Schmidt, Dennis. "On Leather Wings and Shiny Discs: An Interview with Writer/Director Matthew Robbins." 46–47. On Alex North's score for *Dragonslayer* and James Horner's score for **batteries not included*.

8:9 (October–November 2003)
Hasan, Mark. "Of Biblical Significance: Jeff Danna Scores a Decidedly Less Epic Retelling of Jesus' Life in *The Gospel of John*." 12–15.
Adams, Doug. "*The Matrix* Conclusions." 16–20. On Don Davis's music for *The Matrix Revolutions*.
Schweiger, Daniel. "Playing It...Cooler: Mark Isham Brings Back That 'Old Vegas' Jazz." 21–23. Interview regarding *The Cooler*.
Kaplan, Jon, Doug Adams, and Al Kaplan. "Dumped! Famous and Not-So-Famous Rejected Film Music." 24–31. On unused cues and altered or replaced scores.

8:10 (December 2003)
Joy, Nick. "Eighteen Months on a *Cold Mountain*: A Conversation with Gabriel Yared." 12–15.
Adams, Doug. "7 Days in September: A Trip to *The Return of the King* Recording Sessions." 16–26. On Howard Shore's score for *The Lord of the Rings*.
Bettencourt, Scott. "God Rest Ye Mr. Kamen: A Tribute to Maestro Michael (1948–2003)." 27–28.

9:1 (January 2004)
Bond, Jeff. "Silence and Light: Alexandre Desplat Paints Scarlett Johansson in *Girl with a Pearl Earring*." 12–13.
Adams, Doug. "Finding Newman: An Interview with the Overdubbing Prince of Hollywood Film Scoring." 14–17.
"Making the Best of the Worst: 2003 Edition." 18–29.
Lionnet, Leonard. "Mysteries of the Overlook: Unraveling Stanley Kubrick's Soundtrack for *The Shining*." 44–47. Examines the concert works used by the director, including a list of cues.

9:2 (February 2004)
Bond, Jeff. "Capturing a *Monster*: BT [Brian Transeau] Gets into the Mind of a Serial Killer." 10–11.

Bond, Jeff. "Act of Faith: John Debney Brings His Own Passion to Mel Gibson's Controversial Film." 12–14. On *The Passion of the Christ*.

Bond, Jeff. "Horner Revealed: The Oscar-Winning Composer Talks about His Recent Projects, His 'Sound' and the Mathematical Realities of Western Scales." 16–20. Interview.

Bouthillier, Paul. "James Then and Now: The Long-Awaited Conclusion to the Epic James Horner Buyer's Guide." 21–28. Part 4. Covers 1978–1985.

9:3 (March 2004)

Bond, Jeff. "The Future of Film Scoring." 10–17. On Tyler Bates, Jon Brion, and Brian Tyler.

Renick, Kyle. "For Christ's Sake: A Brief History of Music for Jesus Movies." 18–24, 48.

Miller-Phillips, Gabriel, and Scott Essman. "The *Bride* Revisited: Franz Waxman's Music Stands the Test of Time, One Way or the Other." 25–27. On *Bride of Frankenstein*.

Allina, John. "The RZA Makes His Own Breaks." 28–29. Interview with the *Kill Bill* hip-hop composer.

9:4 (April–May 2004)

Bond, Jeff. "Comment of the Apes: Jerry Speaks, We Listen." 10–13. Jerry Goldsmith's commentary on his *Planet of the Apes* score, transcribed from the DVD track.

Armstrong, Stephen B. "High above the Ground: A Conversation with David Shire." 14–17.

Bond, Jeff. "The Fall of *Troy*: Gabriel Yared and the Fate That Sank a Thousand Notes." 18–22. On the rejected score.

Long, Donald John. "Forbidden Film Score: The Life, Death and Rebirth of Music for a '50s Sci-Fi Classic." 23–25. On Louis and Bebe Barron's score for *Forbidden Planet*.

Rhodes, S. Mark. "A Sprig of Basil: Composer Basil Poledouris Takes a Brief Look at His Multi-Decade Career." 26–28. Interview.

9:5 (June 2004)

Bond, Jeff. "King-Sized Television: Two Large-Scale Stephen King Projects with Scores to Match." 12–15. On music by Gary Chang and Christopher Gordon.

Joy, Nick. "The Trouble with *Harry*: Lalo Schifrin Interviewed." 16–18.

Rugg, Karen. "In the Service of Two Masters: Singing the Praises of Williams and Shore." 19–21, 48. Interview with boys choir director Michael McCarthy.

Bond, Jeff. "Song Sung." 22–26. Interview with Gary LeMel, Warner Bros. president of Worldwide Music, on song compilation soundtrack albums.

Bond, Jeff. "When Harry Met *Shrek*...and Friends." 27–29. Interview-based article with Harry Gregson-Williams.

Marshall, Bruce R. "A Masterpiece Restored." 45–47. On Ennio Morricone's score for *The Good, the Bad and the Ugly*.

9:6 (July 2004)

Bond, Jeff. "I, Marco: Composer Beltrami Graduates to the Next Level." 11–12.

Bond, Jeff. "Taking Notes: Aaron Zigman Gets an Attractive Assignment." 12–13. On *The Notebook*.

Goldman, Charles. "George Bassman: Rhapsody in Black: A Golden Age Composer Profile." 14–16, 44.

Bond, Jeff. "Getting Real: Reality TV and the Guys Who Sort of Score It." 18–23. On Ken Douglas Berry, Russ Landau, Jeff Lippencott, David Vanacore, Mark Williams, and others.

Bond, Jeff. "Curious Klaus." 25–26. Interview with Klaus Badelt.

Morgan, John. "Re: Re-Recordings." 27–29. The master of the Marco Polo series speaks from experience.

9:7 (August 2004)

Bond, Jeff. "Quantifying Jerry Goldsmith's Contribution to Film Music Isn't Easy." 12–18.

Walsh, John S. "Goldsmith without Tears: Memories of an Imaginary Conversation." 19–22, 47.

Bond, Jeff, and Joe Sikoryak, collected by. "*Islands in the Stream*: Tributes from Friends, Peers and Colleagues." 24–27.

Takis, John. "Good as Goldsmith: The Goldsmith Method as Revealed in Four 1960s Masterpieces." 28–32. On *A Patch of Blue, The Blue Max, The Sand Pebbles*, and *Planet of the Apes*.

Kendall, Lukas. "Dear Jerry...The Letter I Never Wrote." 42–44.

Comerford, Jason. "A Soundtrack for Life: Jerry Unplugged." 45–47.

9:8 (September 2004)

Bond, Jeff. "Return of the Evil." 10, 27. On Jeff Danna's score for *Resident Evil: Apocalypse*.

Rhodes, S. Mark. "Brion of All Trades." 11–12, 44. Interview with Jon Brion.

Bond, Jeff. "Blast from the Past: Ed Shearmur and the *World of Tomorrow*." 13–15.

Hall, Roger. "Remembering [David] Raksin." 16–19.

Bond, Jeff. "Jerry Goldsmith Buyer's Guide: Part 7: The Final Conflict." 20–24.

Fake, Douglass. "Working for the Man: The Late, Great Orchestrator Arthur Morton Talks about His Decades Working for and with Jerry Goldsmith." 24–27. 1987 interview.

Coscina, David. "The Triumph of *Troy*: An Analysis of Gabriel Yared's Now-Famous Rejected Score." 28–31. With music examples.

9:9 (October 2004)

Bond, Jeff. "The Price of Payne: Rolfe Kent Goes to the Wine Country, *Sideways*." 10, 47. On the jazz aspect of the score.

Hasan, Mark. "Isn't It Incredible? Michael Giacchino's Score for *The Incredibles* Swings Like It's 1964 Again." 12–14.

Bond, Jeff. "Amazing Grace and Pluck." 16–18. Elmer Bernstein tribute.

Bond, Jeff, comp. "The Good Artist: Tributes from Friends, Peers and Colleagues." 19–21.

Care, Ross. "By Film Possessed: Elmer Bernstein's First Decade of Film Scoring: 1951–1961." 22–25.

Hall, Roger. "Elmer's Magnificent 7: Essential Elmer Bernstein Scores from the 1960s." 26–28, 47.

Hasan, Mark. "Musings of a Maestro." 30–31. On Elmer Bernstein.

9:10 (November–December 2004)

Rhodes, S. Mark. "Keeping Up with the Bluths: David Schwartz Talks about Composing for Television." 10–12. Interview.

Joy, Nick. "A Very Engaging Score: Composer Angelo Badalamenti Reteams with Director Jean-Pierre Jeunet." 16–19. Interview.

Bond, Jeff. "Elektra-fied: Buffy Alum Christophe Beck Scores a New Killer Female in *Elektra*." 20–21, 44.

Adams, Doug. "Howards of Different Hughes: Shore Soars with *The Aviator*." 22–26, 44. Interview-based article on Howard Shore's score.

Garcia, Teresa. "Keeping Time: The Bratislava Symphony Orchestra Balances Its Classical Repertoire with a Growing Demand for Its Film Music Recordings." 27–28.

FSM's Annual Best and Worst Awards (for 2004). 10–22.
Schreibman, Myrl A. "Memories of Max [Steiner]." 24–27, 46. Interview, circa 1967.
Bond, Jeff. "Composers of the Roundtable." 28–32, 48. Alejandro Amenabar, Carter Burwell, Alexandre Desplat, James Newton Howard, Jan A. P. Kaczmarek, Alan Menken, and Alan Silvestri look back at 2004.

Bond, Jeff. "The Americanization of Alexandre Desplat." 12–14.
Bond, Jeff. "I, *Palindromes*, I." Interview with Nathan Larson on his scores for independent films.
Allina, John. "Triplets in Sin: Robert Rodriguez Multiplies *Sin City*'s Score." 16–18. On the score by Rodriguez, Graeme Revell, and John Debney.
Schreibman, Myrl A. "Memories of Max, Part 2." 22–27. In the conclusion of this historic interview conducted with Max Steiner in 1967, the composer discusses music in general and his score for *Gone with the Wind* in particular.
Bond, Jeff. "*Major* Changes: A Restored Epic Gets a New Score 40 Years after Its Debut." 28–33, 52. On Christopher Caliendo's rescoring of *Major Dundee*, originally scored by Daniele Amfitheatrof.
Sikoryak, Joe. "Who Is Daniele Amfitheatrof..." 32.
Bettencourt, Scott. "1980: A Very Good Year." 34–40.

Bond, Jeff. "Harry, King of Scotts: Harry Gregson-Williams Enters the *Kingdom of Heaven*." 12–13. On the composer's collaborations with director Tony Scott.
Bond, Jeff. "Snow Season: Mark Snow Celebrates 30 Years in the Biz." 14–16.
Bond, Jeff. "Tight Situations: John Ottman Stretches with *Fantastic Four* and *Superman Returns*." 17–19.
Sikoryak, Joe. "World's Greatest Cartoon Soundtrack: Hoyt Curtin and *Fantastic Four*." 18.
Woolston, Stephen. "Psych Out: John Barry's Scores from the Hollywood Years, 1974–1980." 20–23.
Renick, Kyle. "Pet Sounds: A Serious Study of Cats and Dogs and the Music That Made Them Famous." 24–30.
Adams, Doug, Jeff Bond, Jon Kaplan, and Al Kaplan. "The Circle Is Complete." 31–35. On John Williams's music for *Star Wars Episode III: Revenge of the Sith*.
Lochner, James. "'You Have Cheated Me': Aaron Copland's Compromised Score to *The Heiress*." 36–39. With music examples.

Bond, Jeff. "*Crash* Course: Mark Isham Scores the Summer's Quietest Hit." 15–16.
Allina, John. "From the Fugees to the Flicks: Clef Is a Man of Many Musical Styles." 16–17. Interview with Wyclef Jean.
Bond, Jeff. "Put Up Your *Dukes*: Nathan Barr Gets His Neck Red." 17–18.
Schweiger, Daniel. "Run, Zombie, Run: Johnny Klimek and Reinhold Heil Give Their Groove to *Land of the Dead*." 19–21. Interview with the composers.
Essman, Scott. "What You Don't See Can Hurt You: A 30th Anniversary Retrospective of John Williams's *Jaws*." 22–24.
Scott, Nathaniel. "I Scored! An Aspiring Composer Documents the Journey of Scoring His First Feature Film." 25–27.

Kennedy, Peter F. "Fan Made Monster: An Interview with Hans J. Salter by Peter F. Kennedy Conducted May 8, 1980, at the Composer's Home, Studio City, California." 28–30.

Adams, Doug. "Mortality Plays: Danny Elfman Talks about *Charlie and the Chocolate Factory* and *The Corpse Bride*, and Looks Back on His 20 Years of Collaboration with Tim Burton." 32–39.

"Place Your Bets: Picking the Greatest American Film Scores." A list by composer of the 250 nominated scores for the American Film Institute's "25 Greatest American Film Scores."

10:5 (September–October 2005)

Bond, Jeff. "The Emperors Strike Back: Alex Wurman Walks the Walk on *March of the Penguins*." 12–13.

Bond, Jeff. "Darn the Defiant! John Frizzell Scores *The Prizewinner of Defiance, Ohio*." 13–14.

Bond, Jeff. "At Peace with Reese: Rolfe Kent's Assignment Is *Just Like Heaven*." 15, 62.

Trachtman, Mark. "A Voyage of Discovery: Tracking Down the Music for the National Geographic Television Specials." 16–18. Primarily on music by Elmer Bernstein.

Marshall, Bruce R. "*Vice*'s Verses: Getting Inside the 'Songs-as-Score' Stylings of the Groundbreaking TV Show." 19–21. On music in *Miami Vice*.

Hasan, Mark Richard. "Meet the Proglodytes: The Italian Progressive Rock Pioneers and Their Life at the Movies: A Goblin Buyer's Guide." 22–27. On the rock group Goblin.

Renick, Kyle. "The Poet of Paranoia: An Appreciation of the Late, Great Michael Small." 30–38. With a sidebar from his orchestrator, Christopher Dedrick.

Pincus, Saul, and Mike Petersen. "Remaking *Star Wars*." 40–44. On a concert performance, including an interview with conductor Erich Kunzel.

10:6 (November–December 2005)

Bond, Jeff. "*Serenity* Now!" 13–14. On David Newman's music.

Pincus, Saul, and Mike Petersen. "The Art of the Suite." 18–20. Interview with Cincinnati Pops conductor Erich Kunzel.

Haga, Thor J. "One of the Good Ones." 24–30. Danny Elfman buyer's guide covers 1996–2004.

Sikoryak, Joe. "The AFI's Top 25." 32–33. As presented by the American Film Institute.

Heintzelman, Michael. "The Dante/Goldsmith Project." 34–37. On the director and composer collaborations.

Lochner, James. "Not with the Eyes, but with the Ears." 38–41. Music for film versions of Shakespeare comedies.

Fistful of Soundtracks: The Movie Music Magazine (UK, 1980–1981)

Short-lived publication from Premiere Productions in London.

No. 1 (October 1980). Material on Henry Mancini and Dimitri Tiomkin. Composer guide, part 1 (Richard Addinsell to William Axt) includes William Alwyn, Malcolm Arnold, and Georges Auric.

No. 2 (May 1981). Includes a Henry Mancini article and discography, a conversation with John Addison, and a brief Pino Donaggio tribute. Composer guide, part 2 (Luis Bacalov to James Bernard) includes Burt Bacharach and John Barry.

No. 3 (July 1981). Composer guide, part 3 (Elmer Bernstein to Ken Cameron).

No. 4 (November 1981). Final issue. Bill Conti interview, and material on Mike Post and Dimitri Tiomkin. Composer guide, part 4 (John Cacavas to John Dankworth).

From Silents to Satellite (UK, 1990–1993)

Journal of British film and television music published in Bridport, Dorset, by editor John Williams (not the composer). Film director Ken Hughes contributed an occasional film music column from Hollywood. Contained articles, interviews, soundtrack reviews, book reviews, and some news. Incorporated *Hollywood Scores*. Williams went on to publish *Music from the Movies*, which absorbed *From Silents to Satellite* in its third issue.

No. 1 (February 1990)

No. 2
Interviews with Geoffrey Burgon and Ron Goodwin.

No. 3
Interview with E. Ashley.

No. 4
Ken Hughes on film music.

No. 5 (1991)
Palmer, Christopher. "Howard Blake: A Profile." 34–37.

No. 6 (1991)
Benjamin Frankel issue.

No. 7 (May 1991)
Belcher, John. "The Other Rawsthorne." 4–6. On Alan Rawsthorne, with filmography.
Williams, John. "A Conversation with Douglas Gamley." 22–26. Plus filmography.
"'Taking Risks': A Conversation with Rachel Portman." 30–33. Plus filmography.
Kent, Peter D. "Rachel Portman: An Appreciation." 36–38.

No. 8–9
Burt Bacharach.

No. 10 (Autumn 1991)
Malcolm Arnold issue.
Ritchie, Christopher. "The Arnold-Lean Trilogy." 26–32.

No. 11
Interviews with Debbie Wiseman, Denis King, and John Leach.

No. 14
Kent, Peter D. "[Stanley Myers]." Interview, reprinted in *Music from the Movies*, no. 5.

No. 15 (November 1992)
John Barry special issue, includes filmography, part 1.
Leonard, Geoff, and Pete Walker. "John Barry: The Early Years." 20–40.

No. 16 (1993)
Burlingame, Jon. "John Barry's Television Scores: An Overview." 34–8.

Hollywood Scores (UK, 1992)

Journal of American film and television music published quarterly by editor John Williams in Bridport, Dorset. Issue no. 1 was published in Winter 1992. Contains articles, interviews, and soundtrack news and reviews. Film director Ken Hughes contributed "The Ken Hughes Column" from Hollywood with his take on film music. Mark Trachtman wrote "USA Report: What's New in America." *Hollywood Scores* merged with *From Silents to Satellite*. Williams went on to publish *Music from the Movies*, which absorbed *From Silents to Satellite* in its third issue.

"John Sturges in Conversation with John Williams." 4–7. On music in the director's films and working with composers.

Kent, Peter D. "Man of the West: The Western Films of John Sturges." 12–17. Part 1.

Williams, John. "Enjoyable Diversions: The Adventure Films of John Sturges." 18–34.

"Elmer Bernstein Talks to Hollywood Scores." 36–38. Part 1.

"The Business of Film Scoring: Joe Curiale Talks to Mark Hasan." 42–50. With selected list of credits.

Kent, Peter D. "Georges Delerue (1925–1992): A Personal Tribute." 52–57.

Wooddell, Glenn. "The Franz Waxman Renaissance." 58–59.

The Journal of Film Music (US, 2002–2005)

Published by William Rosar, editor, with Leslie N. Andersen, managing editor, and Linda Schubert, reviews editor. Although announced as early as the 1990s, only two issues were published through 2005.

Rosar, William H. "Film Music: What's in a Name?" 1–18.

Stilwell, Robynn J. "Music in Films: A Critical Review of the Literature." 19–61.

Leinberger, Charles. "Thematic Variation and Key Relationships: Charlotte's Theme in Max Steiner's Score for *Now, Voyager*." 63–77.

Neumeyer, David. "Film Music Studies in the mid-1990s: George Burt's *Art* and Royal S. Brown's *Reading*." 79–97.

Devoted to studies of Bernard Herrmann's music.

Rosar, William H. "Bernard Herrmann: The Beethoven of Film Music?" 121–51. Editorial.

DeMary, Thomas. "The Mystery of Herrmann's Music for Selznick's *Portrait of Jennie*." 153–82.

Burbella, Ronald. "A Note on Commercial Recordings of Herrmann's 'Jennie's Song' from *Portrait of Jennie*." 183–84.

Fiegel, E. Todd. "Bernard Herrmann as Musical Colorist: A Musicodramatic Analysis of His Score for *The Day the Earth Stood Still*." 185–215.

Wierzbicki, James. "Grand Illusion: The 'Storm Cloud' Music in Hitchcock's *The Man Who Knew Too Much*." 217–38. On music by Arthur Benjamin.

Cooper, David. "Film Form and Musical Form in Bernard Herrmann's Score to *Vertigo*." 239–48.

Wrobel, William. "Self-Borrowing in the Music of Bernard Herrmann." 249–71.

Main Title (US, 1974–1977)

Quarterly newsletter of the Entr'acte Recording Society published in Chicago, edited by John Steven Lasher. Not to be confused with the French journal of the same name (1992–1994). *Main Title* covered news, events, and soundtracks of interest. Even though they are not well sourced, most of the non-Lasher articles previously appeared in print, primarily in *Film Music*.

Rózsa, Miklós. "Music for Historical Films (Part 1)." 2–5.

Lasher, John Steven. "David Raksin." 9. Profile.

Raksin, David. "The Music of David Raksin." 10–14. Part 1, *Forever Amber*.

Brown, Royal S. "Bernard Herrmann, Brian De Palma and *Sisters*." 15–17. Analysis.

<u>1:2 (Spring 1975)</u>
Rózsa, Miklós. "Music for Historical Films (Part 2)." (3 pages).
Raksin, David. "The Music of David Raksin." (4 pages). Part 2.
Lasher, John Steven. "Conversations with David Raksin." (2 pages,

<u>1:3 (Summer 1975)</u>
Raksin, David. "*Carrie*." (3 pages).

<u>1:4 (Fall 1975)</u>
Bazelon, Irwin. "*The Heiress*: A Review of Aaron Copland's Award-Wnning Score." (2 pages).

<u>2:1 (Spring–Summer 1976)</u>
Gilling, Ted. "Benny." (4 pages). On Bernard Herrmann.

<u>2:2 (Fall–Winter 1976)</u>
[Lasher, John Steven]. "The Mightiest Kong of All!" On the rerecording of Max Steiner's *King Kong* score. (2 pages).
"Early Film Music Collections in the Library of Congress." (1 page).

<u>2:3 (Spring–Summer 1977)</u>
Lasher, John Steven. "Daniele Amfitheatrof." (5 pages). Profile, filmography, and music excerpt.

<u>2:4 (Fall–Winter 1977)</u>
No articles.

Music from the Movies (UK, 1992–2005)

Quarterly fan magazine from England on British and American film music founded, edited, and published by John Williams (not the composer). Similar to its American counterpart, *Film Score Monthly*, it contained news, articles, interviews, CD reviews (edited by Mike Jenner), Varese Sarabande CD Club release news and reviews, soundtrack news, reports on scoring sessions, photo reportage, and scoring assignments for the United States, Europe, and Japan. The interviews in early issues were usually integrated into an article format, unlike the question-and-answer format found in *Soundtrack* and *Film Score Monthly*. Issues of *Music from the Movies* numbered around 100 pages; those from 1994 on, with slick covers, usually ran 48–60 pages. Williams also published *From Silents to Satellite* and produced a few limited-edition booklets. The first *Music from the Movies* issue is labeled "incorporating TV Music News" and features a brief rundown of scoring assignments around the globe, in this case, Australia, Canada, France, and Italy. The third issue incorporated *From Silents to Satellite*.

Paul Place served as co-editor and wrote a column in the late 1990s, "Main Title: Knowing the Score," which included news and scoring assignments. Director Ken Hughes contributed a column, as did Fred Karlin ("Behind the Screen"), and Mark Hasan ("Rare Vinyl"). Chris Cutter's "Welcome to the Session" included scoring news and assignments, and Kirk Henderson wrote a recurring series of articles on "Orphan Scores." The U.S. correspondent was Rudy Koppl. Koppl's articles often included Q&A interviews with the composer, the scoring team, and the director, and photos from the recording sessions. In 2000, Colin Bloom assumed the role of publisher, with editors Paul Place and Rudy Koppl. Mikael Carlsson, a frequent contributor, is a Sweden-based composer and journalist.

No. 1 (December 1992)

Matthew, Brian. "An Interview with John Barry." 3–6. Transcription of a BBC Radio interview.

Orr, Buxton. "*Battle of the Bulge*: Description and Discussion." 10–14. Orr conducted the Benjamin Frankel score.

"Jerome Moross in Conversation with Noah Andre Trudeau." 24–37. Transcribed from a U.S. radio broadcast.

"Ken Hughes from Hollywood." 46–48. The director's anecdotes on ghost writers.

"Dick DeBenedictis: Unsung Hero of Hollywood TV in Conversation with John Williams." 50–55.

Jenner, Mike. "*The Planet of the Apes*: A Retrospective." 66–73. On Jerry Goldsmith's score.

Williams, John. "Nicholas Pike: An Appreciation." 76–81.

No. 2 (April 1993)

Includes an article, "Synchronised Chaos," on Michael Winner and Jerry Fielding; interviews with Lee Holdridge, Maurice Jarre, and Craig Safan; analysis of Safan's music for *Remo Williams: The Adventure Begins*; and a Gerard Schurmann interview and filmography.

No. 3 (Summer 1993)

Mansell, John. "Trevor Jones: Speaking Personally." 2–5. Interview.

Wishart, David. "Recording *The Bride of Frankenstein*." 6–7. Report on rerecording Franz Waxman's score.

Williams, John. "Graeme Revell in Conversation with John Williams: *Boxing* Hollywood." 8–10. Interview, with filmography.

Redman, Nick. "In Memory of a Friend." 12–13. On David Kraft.

Williams, John. "Gerald Fried in Conversation with John Williams." 14–16.

Fake, Douglass. "Bruce Broughton at Intrada." 18–19.

Broughton, Bruce. "Composer-Speak: A Beginner's Guide for Studio Execs, Producers and Directors." 20.

Holz, Beatrice. "The Other Side of Bruce Broughton." 22–24. Interview.

Williams, John. "Michael J. Lewis: 'The Very Stuff of Genius.'" 26–31. Interview, with filmography.

Coleman, Todd. "Staying in Tune." 32–33. Article on tight recording schedules, with interview material from Terence Blanchard, Michael Kamen, Rachel Portman, and others.

Williams, John. "Philip Appleby: Pride and Passion." 46–50. Interview with the British composer, with filmography.

Williams, John. "Daniel Licht: Getting Ahead in Hollywood." 51–53. Interview, with filmography.

Williams, John. "Ken Wannberg in Conversation with John Williams." 56–57. Interview with the music editor.

Williams, John. "Ken Thorne Talks to John Williams." 58–59.

Williams, John. "Richard Lester." 60–61. Interview with the director on music in his films.

Williams, John. "Ken Thorne Talks to Brian Bennett." 62–64. Interview.

Williams, John. "David Hentschel Chats with John Williams." 65.

Mansell, John, and Colin Davies. "Brief Biography: Jerry Fielding." 80.

No. 4 (Winter 1993)

Frazer, Alan. "The Spielberg Williams Collaboration." 5–12.

Fitzpatrick, James. "Czeching It Out." 16–19. On recording in Prague.

Gleason, Alexander. "Dial M for Music, 1929–39." 20–21. Music in Hitchcock's early
    films.
Mansell, John. "Roy Budd: A Personal Tribute." 24–26.

No. 5 (Summer 1994)
Barth, Lori. "Rachel Portman: Wistful Melodies." 4–6. Interview, reprinted from *The
    Score* (1994).
Leonard, Geoff, and Pete Walker. "John Barry: Into the Sixties." 8–12. Adapted from
    their book.
Cavanagh, Darren. "David Newman: No Stranger in Paradise." 14–15. Interview.
Place, Paul. "Howard Shore: Between the Lines." 16–17. Interview-based article.
Gaydos, Steven. "Poles Apart." 18–19. Zbigniew Preisner interview, reprinted from the
    Hollywood Reporter.
Kent, Peter D. "Remembering Stanley Myers." 20–23. With filmography.
Kent, Peter D. "In Conversation with Stanley Myers." 24–25. Interview excerpts from
    previously published material in *From Silents to Satellite*, no. 14.
Williams, John. "Richard Bellis Talks to John Williams." 26–27. Interview.
"Tribute to Julian Wastall, 1959–1994." Interview with the British television composer.
Kent, Peter D. "Michael Fine of Koch International." 47. Interview.
Cavanagh, Darren. "Bruce Broughton: In Conversation with Darren Cavanagh." 48–50.
    Interview, part 1.

No. 6 (Autumn 1994)
Williams, John. "Robert Wise from *Citizen Kane* to *Star Trek*." 6–9. Interview.
Williams, John. "Technicalities: The Music Editor: Dan Carlin." 9–10. Interview.
Williams, John. "Small Talk: Elmer Bernstein." 10. Interview quotes.
Elley, Derek. "Miklos Rozsa in Conversation with Derek Elley." 14–18. Abridged, origi-
    nally published in *Films and Filming* (May 1977 and June 1977).
Mansell, John. "Full Moon [Productions]: Richard and Charles Band." 19. Company
    profile.
Williams, John. "Ed Welch: Beyond *The 39 Steps*." 20.
Williams, John, and Paul Place. "Jerry Goldsmith 65th Birthday Tribute." 21–25. In-
    cludes interview material from Saul David and Sid Sax.
Williams, John. "Small Talk: Stanley Kramer." 26. Interview quotes from the producer
    on film music and composers.
Williams, John. "Daemion Barry." 27. Interview with the British composer.
Williams, John. "John Sturges." 44–45. Interview with the director on music in his films.
Kent, Peter D. "The Man of the West: The Classic Westerns of John Sturges." 45–46.
Williams, John. "Joel McNeely: Beating on Doors..." 47–48. Interview.
Williams, John. "One of a Kind: Dave Grusin." 49–50. Interview.
Hasan, Mark R. "Oscar Peterson." 54–55. Interview regarding the jazz pianist's film
    work.
Williams, John. "Technicalities: Orchestrator/Composer Hummie Mann." 56–57. Inter-
    view.
Williams, John. "John Altman: Now We See Cosmonauts." 57, 62. Article and interview.
Williams, John. "Soundtrack Music Management." 58. Includes client list with brief
    credits.
Leonard, Geoff, and Pete Walker. "John Barry: Into the Seventies." 60–62. Part 1,
    adapted from their book.

No. 7 (Winter 1994–1995)
Leonard, Geoff. "John Barry: *The Specialist*." 6–8. Interview.
"The Pollyanna Company." 9. Profile of the European music supervision company.

Carlsson, Mikael. "Stefan the Conqueror: Stefan Nilsson." 10–11. Interview-based article on the Swedish composer, previously published in Swedish in *Movie Score*.

Tonks, Paul. "Patrick Doyle: Monster Maestro." 13. Interview-based article on *Frankenstein*.

Hasan, Mark. "*2001*: A Conflict Revisited." 14–15. On Alex North's unused score.

Cavanagh, Darren. "Technicalities: Music Editor Ken Hall." 16–17. Interview.

Williams, John. "John Rubinstein." 18–20. Interview.

Place, Paul. "David Arnold: *Stargate*'s Rising Star." 22–24. Interview-based article.

Place, Paul. "Colin Towns: Making a Difference." 25–27.

Maxford, Howard. "Just One of Those Things." 29. Interview with director Curtis Hanson on Maurice Jarre's rejected score for *The River Wild*.

Williams, John. "Geoffrey Burgon: Scoring *Martin Chuzzlewit*." 34–35.

Williams, John. "Christopher Gunning: Memories of *Middlemarch* and New Music for Poirot." 36.

Place, Paul. "A Fiddling Fixer Called Sax." 54. Interview-based article with music contractor Sidney Sax.

<u>No. 8 (Spring 1995)</u>

Needs, Jason. "Robert Folk: Out of the Shadows." 6–9. Profile and interview-based article.

Cavanagh, Darren. "A Refreshing Alternative: The Film Music of Thomas Newman." 10–13. Interview. The introduction used previously published (and unattributed) material written by Daniel Schweiger.

Cavanagh, Darren. "Crispin Merrill: Scoring Gerry Anderson's *Space Precinct*." 18–19. Interview-based article on scoring the British television series.

Williams, John. "The Sinfonia of London: From *Vertigo* to *Judge Dredd*." 24.

Carlsson, Mikael. "Second Summer: Scoring *House of Angels*." 26–28. Interview-based article on Björn Isfält's music.

Place, Paul. "Alan Silvestri: *Judge Dredd*." 30–31. Interview-based article.

Needs, Jason. "Robert Folk: *Lawnmower Man II*." 32. Scoring session report.

Williams, John. "Scoring *The Choir*: Stanislas Syrewicz." 34. On the BBC television series.

Maxford, Howard. "Panthers and Pitfalls." 46–50. On the partnership between Henry Mancini and director Blake Edwards.

Williams, John. "Guy Hamilton: Spitfires in the Night." 52–53. Interview with the British director on John Barry and Muir Mathieson.

Maxford, Howard. "Hammering Home the Music." 54–58. Hammer Film Production's musical legacy, with an A–Z guide to composers.

Orr, Buxton. "Benjamin Frankel's 12–note Serial Score for *Curse of the Werewolf*." 59–60. With music excerpts.

Maxford, Howard. "Small Talk: Brian Bennett." 61. Interview-based article.

Place, Paul. "Mike Ross-Trevor: Flying by the Seat of His Pants." 62–63.

Sutherley, Sue. "Jennie Muskett: Wildlife Film Composer." 64–65.

Rogers, Dave. "The Man with the Baton: Laurie Johnson." 70–72. Interview-based article reprinted from *Stay Tuned* (the Officially Authorised *Avengers* Magazine), vol. 2, no. 2.

Davis, Luke, and Ralph Titterton. "Symphony for Strings: Barry Gray." 74–77. Posthumous article on the British composer's life and career; originally appeared in *FAB* (the official Gerry Anderson Appreciation Society), no. 15.

Bergman, Vanessa. "Edwin Astley." 78–79. Interview-based article first published in *From Silents to Satellite*.

Cavanagh, Darren. "Simon Boswell." 80–82. Interview.

Leonard, Geoff, and Pete Walker. "John Barry: The Seventies." 84–86. Part 2, adapted from their book.

Williams, John. "Michael J. Lewis: The First 25 Years." 88–90. Interview-based article.

Walker, Mark. "Recording *Julius Caesar*." 92–93. Based on interviews with Bruce Broughton, Douglass Fake, and Daniel Robbins.

Williams, John. "Nic Raine: A Portrait in Music." 94–95. Interview-based article on the orchestrator-conductor.

Needs, Jason. "Michael Kamen: With a Vengeance." 7–9. Interview-based article.

MacLean, Paul Andrew. *"The Hollywood Soundtrack Story."* 13. On the airing of the documentary written by Tony Thomas.

Place, Paul. "Allan Wilson." 12. On the British conductor.

Williams, John. "The London Metropolitan Orchestra." 16.

Williams, John. "A New Recording of Victor Young's *The Quiet Man*." 18. Interview-based article with Joe Doherty and Philip Lane.

Place, Paul. "Martin Kiszko: A Monster Score for *Alien Empire*." 20–21. Interview-based article on scoring the British television series.

Place, Paul. "[Joel] McNeely Raises Herrmann." 22. Interview-based article.

Talouarn, Bruno. "John Ottman: *The Usual Suspects*." 24–25. Interview.

Maxford, Howard. "Richard Rodney Bennett." 36–37. Interview-based article.

Maxford, Howard. "[Alan] Menken's Midas Touch." 38–39. Interview-based article.

Williams, John. "John Frankenheimer." 40–41. Part 1. Interview-based article on music in the director's films.

Walker, Mark. "Monty Norman." 42–43. Interview, including the history behind the James Bond Theme.

Williams, John. "Michael English." 44–45. On the film use of the composer's production music.

Maxford, Howard. "Vangelis." 46. Interview-based article.

Carlsson, Mikael. "Elliot Goldenthal." 4–7. Interview-based article.

Williams, John. "Bond Is Back: John Altman on *Goldeneye*." 12. Interview-based article.

Williams, John. "Brian Easdale, 1909–1995." 1995 interview printed posthumously.

Appleby, Philip. *"Nothing Personal."* 16. The composer writes about his latest film.

Williams, John. "Art Phillips: Texture, Colour and Drama." 26–27. Interview with the American-born composer working in Australia.

Carlsson, Mikael. "Barrington's Visions." 28–31. Interview with Barrington Pheloung.

Maxford, Howard. "Small Talk: Rachel Portman." 31. Interview.

Maxford, Howard. "Andre Previn." 32–33. Interview-based article.

Place, Paul. "An Ear for a Score: Shawn Murphy." 34–35. Interview-based article with the recording engineer.

Williams, John. "John Cacavas." 36. Interview.

Williams, John. "Nick Bicat." 40–41. Interview.

Butterworth, Richard. "The Play It Again Story." On the British soundtrack label.

Includes interviews with Paul Bateman, Peter Best, Patrick Doyle, Joel McNeely, Irwin Kostal, and Mark Mancina (with filmography); analysis of Michael Kamen's music for *Die Hard*; and a Max Steiner biographical portrait.

Includes an article on Christopher Gunning; interviews with Nick Bicat, Trevor Jones, and Michael Kamen; interviews with Alan Menken, Stephen Schwartz, and others regarding *The Hunchback of Notre Dame*; and article, "John Barry: Into the Eighties," adapted from the book by Geoff Leonard and Pete Walker.

Carlsson, Mikael. "Howard Blake." 34–39. Interview.

No. 13 (Autumn 1996)
Includes interviews with David Arnold, Lee Holdridge, Fred Karlin, and Neil Smolar; an article on bootlegs; and a retrospective of Richard Harvey's music for *Shroud for a Nightingale*.

No. 14–15 (Spring 1997)
United Kingdom Film Music Seminar Special. Includes interviews with John Altman, Christopher Gunning, Rachel Portman, and Colin Towns; a tribute to Malcolm Arnold; and an article on film music and the Internet.

No. 16 (Summer 1997)
Carlsson, Mikael. "Mark Isham." 4–10. Interview.

Place, Paul. "Cool and Classic." 21. Interview with Fred Karlin.

Williams, John. "Gabriel Yared: Oscar-Winner for *The English Patient*." 22–23. Interview.

Cavanagh, Darren. "Essential Element." 24–27. Interview with Eric Serra on his score for *The Fifth Element*.

Cavanagh, Darren. "Bay Cities: The Rise and Fall of a Soundtrack Label." 28–30, 54.

Carlsson, Mikael. "Profundo Mansfield." 32–34. Interview with David Mansfield.

Place, Paul. "Getting Serious." 36–37. Interview with Mark Walker regarding his Gramophone film music book.

Carlsson, Mikael, and Peter Holm. "The Double Life of Zbigniew Preisner." 38–42. Interview.

Cavanagh, Darren. "Harry Garfield: Universal Music Man." 44–45. Interview with the MCA/Universal executive.

Hasan, Mark. "Bernard Herrmann's *Taxi Driver*." 46–48.

"Mario Nascimbene: Composer in Spite of Myself." 50–52. Extracts from his forthcoming autobiography.

Williams, John. "Sheldon Mirowitz." 53–54. Interview with the Boston-based composer.

No. 17 (Autumn 1997)
Place, Paul. "David Arnold: Bond Fever." 4–8. Interview regarding his score for *Tomorrow Never Dies*.

Place, Paul. "New Recordings: A Touch of Class from Nonesuch." 11. Interview with president Robert Hurwitz.

Koppl, Rudy. "Shirley Walker: Unrelenting Passion." 20–24. Interview.

Carlsson, Mikael. "Kendall Schmidt: The Copyist." 26–27. Interview with the copyist and trailer composer.

Carlsson, Mikael. "John Morgan: Restoring the Scores." 28–30. Interview.

Ritchie, Christopher. "Malcolm Arnold: A Celebration." 32–35. Part 2 of his tribute.

Holm, Peter. "Soren Hyldgaard: Eye of a Composer." 36–39. Interview.

Carlsson, Mikael. "Basil Poledouris: *Starship* Scorer." 40–43. Interview-based article on *Starship Troopers*.

Needs, Jason. "Michael Kamen's *Event Horizon*." 44. Scoring session report.

No. 18 (Winter 1997)
Carlsson, Mikael. "Revealing [Graeme] Revell." 4–9. Interview-based article.

Carlsson, Mikael. "Rykodisc: The MGM Deal." 13. Interview with Jeff Rougvie.

Koppl, Rudy. "Marco Beltrami: The Climb to the Top." 20–33. Interview; additional interviews with orchestrator Pete Anthony and directors Guillermo del Toro and Wes Craven.

Hasan, Mark. "For Promotional Purposes Only." 34–36. Survey of promo and demo CDs.

Barder, Oliver. "Animé Scores." 38–39.

Henderson, Kirk. "Orphan Scores: Raymond Leppard's *Lord of the Flies*." 40–41.

Leonard, Geoff, and Pete Walker. "The Essential Musical Guide to James Bond." 42–45.

No. 19 (Spring 1998)

"Biogs." 12–13. On composer Ilona Sekacz, composer Carl Vine, record producer James Fitzpatrick, and recording engineer Geoff Foster.

Place, Paul. "Debbie Wiseman: Wilde about Music." 14–18. Interview-based article.

Place, Paul. "Joel McNeely: Raising Herrmann." 19–21. Interview-based article.

Koppl, Rudy. "Mark McKenzie: *The Disappearance of Garcia Lorca*." 22–23. Interview-based article.

Koppl, Rudy. "J. Peter Robinson: From Rock to Film Scoring." 24–29. Interview.

Koppl, Rudy. "Christopher Young: A Life's Work: The Beginning and Today." 30–45. Part 1. Interview with the composer and others, including orchestrator Pete Anthony and synthesist Mark Zimoski.

Henderson, Kirk. "Orphan Scores: Mischa Spoliansky: *The Man Who Could Work Miracles*." 46–47.

No. 20 (Summer 1998)

Koppl, Rudy. "Stewart Copeland: From Rock to Film Scoring." 12–17. Interview.

Wagstaff, Ian. "Horns for Hollywood: A Transatlantic Tradition." 26–28. Includes interview material with James Thatcher and Hugh Seenan.

Koppl, Rudy. "Christopher Young: A Life's Work: Haunted or Humoured." 30–41. Part 2. Interview with the composer and others, including agent Lyn Benjamin, scoring engineer Bobby Fernandez, and music editor Tom Milano.

Henderson, Kirk. "Orphan Scores: Malcolm Arnold *1984*." 42–43. For the 1956 film.

Schweiger, Daniel. "Gabriel Yared: Touched by the *City of Angels*." 44–46. Interview.

Mera, Miguel. "Julian Nott." 47–51. On the British composer and his scores for Nick Park's Wallace and Gromit animated films.

Black, Edwin. "The Last Word: Too Much and Not Enough." 52–53. Essay on current trends.

No. 21 (Autumn 1998)

Koppl, Rudy. "Mark Snow: Scoring *The X-Files*: A Challenging Transition." 6–13. Interview; additional interviews with show creator Chris Carter, director Rob Bowman, and orchestrator Jonathan Sacks.

Henderson, Kirk. "Orphan Scores: Zdenek Liska's *The Fabulous World of Jules Verne*." 22–24.

Karlin, Fred. "Behind the Scenes." 25. First column (the remainder were titled "Behind the Screen"), on the language of film scoring, condensed from Karlin's book *Listening to Movies*.

Koppl, Rudy. "Inside the Filmharmonic: The Grand Experiment Begins." 26–31. Includes an interview with David Newman.

Phillips, Art. "The Mechanics of Composing for Production Music." 32–33. By the Australian composer.

Place, Paul, and Darren Cavanagh. "Robert Townson: Heart at Varese's Centre." 34–38. On the Varese Sarabande producer.

Schweiger, Daniel. "The Schifrin Sound: When It Comes to Scoring Asian Action Heroes, Lalo Schifrin Makes Our Day." 39–41. Interview.

Sutherley, Sue. "Carl Davis: The Creative Spirit behind His Spectacular Silent Movie Scores." 42–43.

Leonard, Geoff. "John Barry: A Personal Journey." 44–45.

Koppl, Rudy. "Michael Small: Scoring the Director's Vision." 46–53. Interview; additional interviews with directors Alan J. Pakula, Arthur Penn, Bob Rafelson, and John Schlesinger.

Place, Paul. "Biogs." 54. On composer Jane Livermore and writer Mark Walker.

No. 22 (Winter 1998) [erroneously labeled Winter 1999]

Black, Edwin. "Hans Zimmer: Scores and Scars." 6–10. Interview.

Hasan, Mark. "Vinyl Revival." 29–32.

Henderson, Kirk. "Orphan Scores: Richard Addinsell's *Waltz of the Toreadors*." 33–35.

Place, Paul. "Nicholas Dodd: The Big Picture." 36–37. Interview-based article on the orchestrator.

Koppl, Rudy. "Trevor Rabin: From Rock to Film Scoring." 38–43. Interview.

Keech, Andrew. "Rykodisc: The First Year." 44–47.

Carlsson, Mikael. "Howard Shore: Getting Inside the Drama." 48–52. Interview-based article, with filmography/discography.

Koppl, Rudy. "Marco Beltrami: Pushing the Envelope." 54–56. Interview.

Karlin, Fred. "Behind the Screen: *To Kill a Mockingbird* / *Casablanca*." 57–58. On the scores by Elmer Bernstein and Max Steiner.

Schweiger, Daniel. "A Newman's Life: Composer Randy Newman Fights to Be Heard in the Hollywood Anthill." 59–61. Interview.

No. 23 (Spring 1999)

Carlsson, Mikael. "From *The Brood* to *eXistenZ*: 20 Years of Film and Music by David Cronenberg and Howard Shore." 6–11. Interview-based article.

Black, Edwin. "Jerry Goldsmith." 17. Interview.

Karlin, Fred. "Behind the Screen: *Citizen Kane* / *Chinatown*." 28–30. On the scores by Bernard Herrmann and Jerry Goldsmith.

Henderson, Kirk. "Orphan Scores: Walter Scharf's *The Ladies' Man*." 32–34.

Hasan, Mark. "Rare Vinyl: A Consumer's Guide." 35–37.

Koppl, Rudy. "Elia Cmiral: Scoring *Stigmata*." 38–41. Interview.

No. 24 (Summer 1999)

Koppl, Rudy. "Don Davis: Downloading into *The Matrix*." 6–15.

"John Williams Scoring *Star Wars Episode I: The Phantom Menace*." 16–19. Interview.

Schweiger, Daniel. "Romancing the Star: Composer Trevor Jones Finds the Music of Love on *Notting Hill*." 20–21. Interview.

Schweiger, Daniel. "*Eyes Wide Shut*: Jocelyn Pook: Composing Kubrick's Last Avant-Garde Score." 22–23. Interview.

Schweiger, Daniel. "Wearing the Crown Again: Bill Conti: Returning to Big Budget Films with *The Thomas Crown Affair*." 24–25. Interview.

Leonard, Geoff. "Czeching Out *Raise the Titanic*." 36–37. Report on the rerecording session.

Karlin, Fred. "Behind the Screen: *East of Eden* / *Rebel without a Cause* / *A Streetcar Named Desire*." 38–39. On the scores by Leonard Rosenman and Alex North.

Koppl, Rudy. "David Newman: Juxtaposition." 40–45. Interview.

Koppl, Rudy. "Harald Kloser: *The Thirteenth Floor*." 46–51. Interview; additional interview with director Josef Rusnak.

Henderson, Kirk. "Orphan Scores: Daniele Amfitheatrof's *The Naked Jungle*." 52–55.

Barder, Oliver. "The Importance of Being Inglis." 56–57. Interview with conductor Anthony Inglis.

Aguirre, Paul. "I Dub Thee: Ghost Singers in Hollywood." 58–61. Includes an A–Z list of names with film titles.

Koppl, Rudy. "Theatre of Madness: Elliot Goldenthal." 6–28. Interview, part 1; additional interviews with composer John Corigliano and directors Neil Jordan, Barry Levinson, John Madden, Michael Mann, Joel Schumacher, Edward Shearmur, and Ron Shelton.
Carlsson, Mikael. "John Debney: Scoring *End of Days*." 29, 31. Interview-based article.
Hasan, Mark. "Jerry Goldsmith: *Alien*: 20th Anniversary Special." 46–50.
Henderson, Kirk. "Orphan Scores: Carmen Dragon's *Invasion of the Body Snatchers*." 51–54.
Karlin, Fred. "Behind the Screen: *Spellbound*." 55. On the score by Miklós Rózsa.
Goode, Rachel. "Richard Harvey." 56–59. Interview with the British composer.
Duff, Simon. "Maggie Rodford." 60–61. Interview with the managing director of the British music production company Air-Edel.

Koppl, Rudy. "Theatre of Madness: Elliot Goldenthal." 4–22. Interview, part 2; additional interviews with Julie Taymor; Goldenthal's scoring team, including orchestrator (Goldenthal), electronic music producer Richard Martinez, conductors Steven Mercurio and Jonathan Sheffer, recording engineer Joel Iwataki, and producer Teese Gohl.
Koppl, Rudy. "George Fenton: *Anna and the King*." 42–51. Interview; additional interview with director Andy Tennant.
Koppl, Rudy. "David Robbins: *Cradle Will Rock*." 52–58. Interview; additional interview with director Tim Robbins.
Karlin, Fred. "Behind the Screen: *Laura*." 59. On the score by David Raksin.
Carlsson, Mikael. "Richard Band: Out of the Darkness." 60–63. Interview.
Henderson, Kirk. "Orphan Scores: Rescued from Oblivion." 64–67. On what constitutes an orphan score.
Koppl, Rudy. "Randy Miller: Scoring *Amargosa*." 68–69. Interview-based article.

Koppl, Rudy. "Hans Zimmer: A Genre Awakes: Scoring *Gladiator* with Lisa Gerrard." 4–10. Interview.
Koppl, Rudy. "Lisa Gerrard: Scoring *Gladiator* with Hans Zimmer." 11–13. Interview.
Koppl, Rudy. "Elia Cmiral: Spontaneous Man Scores *Battlefield Earth*." 14–23. Interview; sidebar interviews with director Roger Christian, BMI's Linda Livingston, orchestrators Conrad Pope and Erik Lundborg, and John Travolta.
Koppl, Rudy. "Graeme Revell: A New Dawn in Animation Scoring *Titan: After Earth*." 24–35. Interview; sidebar interviews with Don Bluth and Gary Goldman.
Carlsson, Mikael. "Richard Gibbs: *28 Days* and Beyond." 52–53. Interview.
Dilivio, Lois. "Mason Daring." 54–58. Interview-based article.
Woolston, Stephen. "John Barry: In Form and Function." 59–61. An essay on film music style.
Carlsson, Mikael. "Mark Isham: *Rules of Engagement*." 62–63.

Carlsson, Mikael. "Now Showing: Inside Scores Currently on the Silver Screen." 8–13. Material on Joel Goldsmith, Hummie Mann, Jeff Rona, and Shirley Walker.

Koppl, Rudy. "The *X-Men* Project." 14–30. Interview with Michael Kamen; additional interviews with John Ottman, producer Lauren Shuler Donner, orchestrator Bob Elhai, and X-Men co-creator Stan Lee.

Koppl, Rudy. "John Ottman's *Urban Legends: Final Cut*." 31–39. Interview.

Woolston, Stephen. "David Arnold: *Shaft*." 40–42.

Koppl, Rudy. "Elliot Goldenthal: The Composer Incarnate." 44–49. Interview.

Kennaway, Dimitri. "Benjamin Frankel's *Battle of the Bulge*." 50–52. Analysis.

Carlsson, Mikael. "Internet: Film Music on the Web." 65.

No. 29 (October 2000)

Place, Paul. "[Jon] Burlingame's Vision." 6–7. Interview regarding Burlingame's book *Sound and Vision*.

Schweiger, Daniel. "Now Showing: Rolfe Kent Soap Opera." 8–10. Interview.

Woolston, Stephen. "Now Showing: Debbie Wiseman: *Tom's Midnight Garden*." 10–12. Interview-based article.

Carlsson, Mikael. "Now Showing: Carter Burwell: *Blair Witch 2*." 13–14. Interview-based article on *Book of Shadows: Blair Witch 2*.

Carlsson, Mikael. "Now Showing: Tyler Bates: *Get Carter*." 14–15. Interview-based article.

Henderson, Kirk. "Orphan Scores: Antony Hopkins' *Billy Budd*." 16–19.

Koppl, Rudy. "Goldsmith and Verhoeven: The Ultimate Seduction: Scoring *Hollow Man*." 20–41. Interviews, including an interview with programmer Nick Vidar.

Koppl, Rudy. "Rick Marvin: Going Deep with *U-571*." 42–47. Interviews with Richard Marvin and director Jonathan Mostow.

Koppl, Rudy. "Mr BT: Scoring *Under Suspicion* with Director Stephen Hopkins." 48–55. Interviews with Brian Transeau and Hopkins.

Koppl, Rudy. "Gloria Cheng and Don Davis: Recreating *Illicit Felicity*." 64–66. Interviews with the pianist and composer.

No. 30 (March 2001)

Duff, Simon. "Now Showing: *In the Nursery:* Hindle Wakes." 8–10. Interview.

Cavanagh, Darren. "Apollo 440: *Charlie's Angels*." 11–13. Interview with band members Howard Gray, Trevor Gray, and Noko.

Koppl, Rudy. "James Newton Howard: Scoring the Impossible: *Unbreakable* with Director M. Night Shyamalan." 14–23. Interviews.

Koppl, Rudy. "Edward Shearmur: Fast...Foxy...Fun...Scoring *Charlie's Angels* with Director McG." 24–31. Interviews.

Hasan, Mark. "Elmer Bernstein's Film Music Collections [*sic*]." 32.

Koppl, Rudy. "Christopher Young's Second Sight: Scoring *The Gift* with Director Sam Raimi." 34–39. Interviews.

No. 31–32 (Fall 2001)

Joy, Nick. "Once Upon a Time in the West End." 8–11. Article on Ennio Morricone.

Joy, Nick. "*Naked Lunch*: Live to Projection." 12–13. Interview with Howard Shore.

Koppl, Rudy. "*Final Fantasy: The Spirits Within* Elliot Goldenthal." 14–31. Interview; additional interviews with director Hironobu Sakaguchi, producer Teese Gohl, orchestrator Bob Elhai, conductor Dirk Brossé, electronic music producer Richard Martinez, engineer Joel Iwataki, and music editor Curtis Roush.

Koppl, Rudy. "Alan Silvestri: Doing the Imhotep Boogie: Scoring *The Mummy Returns*." 32–43. Interview; additional interview with director Stephen Sommers.

Koppl, Rudy. "Tan Dun: Scoring Ang Lee's Dream of China, *Crouching Tiger, Hidden Dragon* with Composer and Cellist Yo-Yo Ma." 44–53. Interviews.

Koppl, Rudy. "Ennio Morricone: The Italian Maestro Scores *Malena*." 54–59. Interview.

Koppl, Rudy. "Maurice Jarre: The Epic Master Scores *Sunshine*." 60–67. Interview.

Koppl, Rudy. "Cliff Martinez: Scoring on the Dark Side with *Traffic*." 68–75. Interview.

Hasan, Mark Richard. "Film Music on DVD: The Composer Speaks." 98–101. Survey of DVDs with composer commentaries.

<u>No. 33 (May 2002)</u>

Place, Paul. "It's Back: The Return of the Varese Sarabande CD Club." 8–11. Includes interview with Robert Townson.

Carlsson, Mikael. "Hans Zimmer: *Black Hawk Down*." 12–14. Interview.

Collins, Mark. "Kevin Sargent: *Crush*." 14–15. Interview.

Carlsson, Mikael. "Marco Beltrami: *I Am Dina*." 16–18. Interview.

Duff, Simon. "Scott Benzie: *Room 36*." 19–20. Interview.

Carlsson, Mikael. "David Newman: *Ice Age*." 20–22. Interview.

Carlsson, Mikael. "Howard Shore: *The Lord of the Rings: The Fellowship of the Ring* and *The Two Towers*." 24–33. Interview-based article.

Koppl, Rudy. "*Moulin Rouge*." 34–43. Interviews with Craig Armstrong and director Baz Luhrmann.

Koppl, Rudy. "Joshua Bell: *Iris*: The Virtuoso Violinist Talks to Rudy Koppl about His Collaboration with Composer James Horner." 44–45.

Koppl, Rudy. "*The Shipping News*: Christopher Young: Scoring Director Lasse Hallström's Journey of Self Discovery." 46–51. Interviews with the composer and director.

Koppl, Rudy. "Lisa Gerrard / Pieter Bourke: Scoring the Legend: *Ali*." 52–57. Interview with the composers; includes interview with director Michael Mann.

Joy, Nick. "Yann Tiersen: South of the River." 58–59. Interview with the French composer regarding his score for *Amélie*.

<u>No. 34 (July–August 2002)</u>

Collins, Mark. "The Art of the Film Score." 6–7. Interview with composer Martin Kiszko regarding his film scoring video.

Joy, Nick. "Fred Karlin: Look Who's Stalking." 9–11. Interview regarding *The Stalking Moon*.

Koppl, Rudy. "Brian Tyler: *Frailty*." 12–14. Interview, including an interview with director Bill Paxton.

Koppl, Rudy. "It's Austin Powers Baby! The Zany Musical Hybrid of *Goldmember* with George S. Clinton and director Jay Roach." 16–25. Interviews.

Place, Paul. "David Julyan: *Insomnia*." 26–29. Interview.

Lane, Peter. "The Best of British." 30–31. Interview with author Jan Swynnoe.

Koppl, Rudy. "Beware of Bio Hazards: *Resident Evil* with Marco Beltrami and Marilyn Manson." 32–41. Interviews with Beltrami, Manson, and director Paul S. W. Anderson.

Koppl, Rudy. "Cinema Realism Meets the Electronica of Asche and Spencer: *Monster's Ball* with Thad Spencer and Director Marc Forster." 42–45. Interviews.

Koppl, Rudy. "Through the Viewfinder: Richard Eyre's *Iris*: Inside the Musical Soul of a Film." 46–47. Interview with the director.

Koppl, Rudy. "Through the Viewfinder: Rod Lurie's *The Last Castle*: A Musical Homage by Jerry Goldsmith." 48–49. Interview with the director.

<u>Nos. 35–36 (2002)</u>

Place, Paul. "Three Decades of Classic British Television Themes." 6–7. Interview with Paul Lewis.

Hasan, Mark. "Disques Cinémusique: The Birth of a Record Label." 8–9. Interview with Clément Fontaine.

Place, Paul. "There's Something about Debbie [Wiseman]." 9–10. Interview.

Place, Paul. "Joby Talbot: The Race for Robbie!" 10–11. Interview-based article.

Hasan, Mark. "Jeff Danna: *The Kid Stays in the Picture*." 12–14. Interview-based article.

Duff, Simon. "Edwin Wendler: *Wrong Hollywood Number*." 16–17. Interview with the Austrian composer.

Place, Paul. "The World Soundtrack Awards at the Flanders Film Music Festival." 18–19. Report.

Lane, Peter. "The Sunset Also Rises." 20–23. Interview with Robert Townson on the new recording of Franz Waxman's score for *Sunset Boulevard.*

Place, Paul. "David Arnold: *Die Another Day*." 24–30. Interview.

Henderson, Kirk. "Orphan Scores: Maurice Jarre's *The Collector*." 30–33.

Koppl, Rudy. "Taking It to the *xXx*treme with Randy Edelman and Director Rob Cohen." 34–45. Interviews.

Koppl, Rudy. "When Dreams Become Reality: *Lathe of Heaven* with Angelo Badalamenti and Director Philip Haas." 46–51. Interviews.

Koppl, Rudy. "Through the Viewfinder: Robert Rodriguez: *Spy Kids 2*: Living on the Island of Lost Dreams." 52–59. Interview.

Joy, Nick. "Michael Nyman: From *Hours* to *Heures*: Rejected Scores and Upcoming Opportunities." 60–61. Interview.

No. 37 (2003)

Woolston, Stephen. "Bond 40th Anniversary: The Expanded Soundtracks." 7. Interview-based article with Lukas Kendall.

Hasan, Mark. "A Little Perseverance." 8. Interview with Robin Esterhammer regarding Perseverance Records.

Carlsson, Mikael. "New Kid on the Block." 10–11. Interview with Nathan Larson.

Koppl, Rudy. "*Daredevil* with Graeme Revell and Director Mark S. Johnson." 12–20. Interviews.

Special Awards section:

Koppl, Rudy. "Living the Score: *The Quiet American* with Craig Armstrong." 4–7. Interview.

Koppl, Rudy. "*25th Hour* with Terence Blanchard and Director Spike Lee." 8–17. Interviews.

Koppl, Rudy. "Philip Glass: *The Hours*." 18–21. Interview.

Koppl, Rudy. "*About Schmidt*: Self-Discovery in America with Rolfe Kent and Director Alexander Payne." 22–28. Interviews.

Hasan, Mark. "DVD Review." 29–32. DVDs with features of interest to the film music fan.

No. 38 (2003)

Place, Paul. "Richard G. Mitchell: *To Kill A King*." 10–15. Interview.

Lane, Paul. "Notes from the Golden Age: David Bahanovich: The History Man: Bringing the Past to Life through Music." 16–17. Interview with the "historical musical director" specializing in the authentic depiction and adaptation of period music.

Koppl, Rudy. "The Boys Are Back in Town: Christopher Young and Jon Amiel Scoring *The Core*." 18–27. Interview with the composer and director.

Koppl, Rudy. "United They Stand: *X2*: Ottman and Singer." 32–47. Interviews with John Ottman and director Bryan Singer on scoring *X-Men 2*.

No. 39 (2003)

A special issue on "Music from *The Matrix*" (*The Matrix* and *The Matrix Reloaded*) featuring interviews with Don Davis, Ben Watkins, and music editor Zig Grön.

No. 40 (2003)

Lane, Paul. "Re-recordings Versus Original Soundtracks: Technical Perfection or the Reel Thing?" 10–11.

Carlsson, Mikael. "Rachel Portman Smile." 12–14. Interview on *Mona Lisa Smile*.

Carlsson, Mikael. "Women in Film Music." 15–18. On Rachel Portman, Ilona Sekacz, Shirley Walker, and Debbie Wiseman, among others. With a quick guide to the ten most prolific female film composers, pp. 19.

Carlsson, Mikael. "*Under the Tuscan Sun*." 20–21. Interview with Christophe Beck.

Carlsson, Mikael. "From Tangerine Dream to *Underworld*." 22–23. Interview with Paul Haslinger.

Koppl, Rudy. "The Marconator on *Terminator 3: Rise of the Machines* with Marco Beltrami." 30–37. Interviews with Beltrami and director Jonathan Mostow.

No. 41 (2004)

Carlsson, Mikael. "The Passion of John Debney." 10–11. Interview-based article on *The Passion of the Christ*.

Carlsson, Mikael. "The Talented Mr. Tyler: *Timeline* composer Brian Tyler Is the Hottest Young Composer in Hollywood." 12–16. Interview-based article, with additional material from Rudy Koppl's interview with director Richard Donner, who discusses the circumstances behind the unused score by Jerry Goldsmith.

Carlsson, Mikael. "*Master and Commander* of the Scoring Stage." 17–19. Interview with Christopher Gordon.

Koppl, Rudy. "*Revolutions*: The Apocalypse Cometh." 20–43. Includes interviews with Don Davis, Ben Watkins, and the scoring team for *The Matrix Revolutions*.

No. 42 (2004)

A special issue on *The Lord of the Rings* (*The Fellowship of the Ring*, *The Two Towers*, and *The Return of the King*) featuring interviews with Howard Shore, writer-director Peter Jackson, writer-producer Fran Walsh, the scoring team, and many others.

No. 43 (2004)

Carlsson, Mikael. "Now Showing." 6–7. Interviews with Brian Tyler on *Paparazzi* and Jeff Danna on *Resident Evil: Apocalypse*.

Lane, Peter. "Philip Lane: Bringing British Film Music Back to Life." 10–12. On rerecording classic British film scores.

Joy, Nick. "Alex Heffes: Reaching beyond the Void." 13–15.

Koppl, Rudy. "Harald Kloser and Roland Emmerich: Visions of a Future Lost: *The Day After Tomorrow*." 16–20. Interviews.

Joy, Nick. "Captain Ed Shoots for the Skies." 21–23. Interview with Edward Shearmur on *Sky Captain and the World of Tomorrow*.

Koppl, Rudy. "*Van Helsing*: The Evolution of Horror: Stephen Sommers and Alan Silvestri." 24–29. Interviews with the director and composer.

Koppl, Rudy. "The Need for Nanites: *I, Robot* with Marco Beltrami and Alexis Proyas." 30–37. Interviews with the composer and director.

Koppl, Rudy. "The Behemoth Awakens: *Hellboy* with Marco Beltrami and Guillermo del Toro." 38–42. Interviews with the composer and director, and Theremin player Robby Virus.

Koppl, Rudy. "You Keep What You Kill: *The Chronicles of Riddick* with Graeme Revell and David Twohy." 44–49. Interviews with the composer and director.

Larson, Randall D. "John Van Tongeren's *Van Helsing*: The London Assignment." 50–51. On music for the direct-to-video animated short. Interview.

Hasan, Mark Richard. "The Restoration of William Walton's *The Battle of Britain.*" 64–66. Article on the DVD, based on interviews with James Fitzpatrick and the film's original music editor, Eric Tomlinson.

No. 44 (2005)

Larson, Randall D. "Report from the *Hollywood Reporter/Billboard* Film and TV Conference 2004." 7–8.

Carlsson, Mikael. "Now Showing." 9–15. Interviews with Howard Shore on *The Aviator*, Mychael Danna on *Being Julia*, Jan A. P. Kaczmarek on *Finding Neverland*, Christopher Young on *The Grudge*, and Debbie Wiseman (interviewed by Michael Beek) on *The Truth about Love.*

Koppl, Rudy. "Michael Giacchino and Brad Bird: The Guts and the Glory: Scoring *The Incredibles.*" 16–21. Interviews with the composer and director.

Koppl, Rudy. "*The Phantom of the Opera*: Through the Looking Glass of Love." 22–26. Interviews with Andrew Lloyd Webber and director Joel Schumacher.

Schweiger, Daniel. "i [heart symbol] jon brion: An Existential Composer Finds His Home at Huckabees." 27–29. Interview, on music for *I Heart Huckabees.*

Koppl, Rudy. "*Ray*: The Legend Lives with Craig Armstrong and Taylor Hackford." 30–35. Interviews with the composer and director.

Koppl, Rudy. "*Alexander*: As the Eagle Soars." 36–43. Interviews with Vangelis and director Oliver Stone.

Koppl, Rudy. "Itzhak Perlman: The Celluloid Transformation." 44–45.

Koppl, Rudy. "An Endurance of Faith: *A Very Long Engagement.*" 46–51. Interviews with Angelo Badalamenti and director Jean-Pierre Jeunet.

Nos. 45–46 (2005)

Carlsson, Mikael. "In Brief." 10–13. Interviews with Joseph LoDuca on *Boogeyman*, William Ross on *The Game of Their Lives*, and Teddy Castellucci on *The Longest Yard.*

Joy, Nick. "Hitchhiker and a Gentleman." 14–17. Interview with Joby Talbot on *The Hitchhiker's Guide to the Galaxy* and *The League of Gentlemen's Apocalypse.*

Parker, Jim. "Remembering [Jerry] Goldsmith." 18–21. Transcript of a 1974 interview.

Koppl, Rudy. "*Sin City*: All That Wicked Jazz." 22–33. Interviews with Graeme Revell, John Debney, and director-composer Robert Rodriguez.

Horace, Ben. "The Last of the Titans: Ennio Morricone." 34–65.

Horace, Ben. "A Man to Respect." 66–90. Interviews with Morricone experts and collectors.

Donga, Roy. "The Morricone Buyer's Guide." 92–93.

Koppl, Rudy. "Andrea Morricone and Yo-Yo Ma: Transcending the Picture—Live." 94–97. Interview with Ennio Morricone's son.

Care, Ross. "A Miracle of Modern Film Scoring: *The Robe.*" 98–101. On Alfred Newman's score.

Nick, Joy. "Beyond Kubrick." On Jocelyn Pook.

No. 47 (Winter 2005)

Carlsson, Mikael. "In Brief." 8–10. Interview with Dario Marianelli on *The Brothers Grimm.*

Beek, Michael. "Julian Nott and *The Curse of the Were-Rabbit.*" 14–16. Interview.

Koppl, Rudy. "Chasing the Light Fantastic: *Fantastic Four.*" 18–27. Interviews with John Ottman, director Tim Story, Fantastic Four co-creator Stan Lee, and producer Avi Arad.

Koppl, Rudy. "*The Greatest Game Ever Played*: A Flip of the Coin." 28–35. Interviews with Brian Tyler and director Bill Paxton.

Koppl, Rudy. "Wendy Carlos: Rediscovering Lost Scores." 36–45. Interview.
Koppl, Rudy. "Going *Sky High*." 46–52. Interviews with Michael Giacchino and director Mike Mitchell.
Johnson, Ian. "William Alwyn: Music in the Shadows." 53–55.

New Zealand Film Music Bulletin (New Zealand, 1973–1999)
Quarterly fanzine for film music enthusiasts and soundtrack collectors published by editor Colin A. Adamson. The first issue came out in February 1973 and the last in November 1999. Also known as *Film Music Bulletin*, it contains articles, interviews, soundtrack news and reviews, scoring assignments, and news. David Kraft wrote "The Kraft Report" from February 1985 to August 1988. "The Jeff Hall Report" contains news, notes on new recordings, and notes on other film music periodicals. Includes "Movies on NZTV," a list by Adamson of films shown on New Zealand television, with their music credits and available recordings. Includes some verbatim reprints of articles published outside of New Zealand.

(November 1980)
Article on John Green.

1:3 (September 1982)
Miklós Rózsa interview.
Jerry Goldsmith filmography/discography.

(November 1982)
Article on Miklós Rózsa.

(August 1983)
Article on Bronislaw Kaper.

(November 1983)
Article on Georges Auric.

(August 1985)
Article on Jerry Goldsmith.

No. 66 (May 1989)
Communicating with the director by David Kraft. 15–16. Reprinted from the *Hollywood Reporter* (January 17, 1989).

No. 83 (August 1993)
Kaufman, Louis. "Weeping and Laughing for Hollywood." 2–5. Kaufman is a studio violinist. Reprinted from *Classics* (November 1992).
Sotinel, Thomas. "No Jarring Notes." 7–9. Interview-based article.

No. 84 (November 1993)
Julier, Ian. "Scoring the Dream Factory." 1–5.

No. 85 (February 1994)
Werhand, Martin. "Georges Garvarentz Remembered." 1–3. With filmography for the French composer.

No. 90 (May 1995)
Interviews with Ron Goodwin and Phil Judd.

Reel Music (US, 2001–2002)
Magazine for film and television music enthusiasts published and edited by Martin A. Dougherty in Chula Vista, California. Written by Martin and his brothers, Michael and

Christopher, it contains news, interviews, and soundtrack reviews. The short-lived bi-monthly failed to make the transition from being a free publication to being a subscriber-based one. Issue no. 5 was announced as the last free issue. The Doughertys previously published a newsletter, *The Score List*.

No. 1 (2001)
Dougherty, Martin and Michael. [Don Davis interview, part 1]

No. 2 (November–December 2001)
Dougherty, Michael. "Eric Rigler: In His Own Words." 4–5. Interview with the session musician.
Dougherty, Martin and Michael. "The Don Davis Spectacular." 6. Interview, part 2.

No. 3 (January–February 2002)
Dougherty, Michael. "The Best of 2001." 6–7.
Dougherty, Martin. "The American Sound: Tim Morrison." 8–9. Interview with the session musician-trumpeter.

No. 4 (May–June 2002)
Dougherty, Martin. "FSM: Film Score Monthly." 5–7.
Dougherty, Martin. "Thad Spencer." 10–11. Interview with the *Monster's Ball* co-composer.

The Score (US, ASMA, 1944–1953)
Published by the American Society of Music Arrangers (ASMA) in Los Angeles, first monthly, then bimonthly (1944–1950), and finally quarterly (1953), with two breaks in publication: November 1946–1949 and June 1950–1952. As a professional organization, the Los Angeles chapter of ASMA was dominated by commercial musicians. *The Score* consists of members news (in film, symphonic, and radio fields), scoring assignments (listed in "The Scoreboard"), events, and membership lists. Editor Rudy de Saxe was assisted by associate editors Joseph Dubin, Albert Glasser, and Charles Maxwell. Dubin's "Pick-Ups" column was sprinkled with personal anecdotes from members. Lawrence Morton contributed book reviews and short articles. ASMA president Arthur Lange contributed a column, beginning with the first issue in January 1944. Herschel Burke Gilbert's column, "Asmantics," begins in vol. 4, no. 1 (January 1950). "The Scoreboard" continues into the 1950s; listings are by studio, with the composer and orchestrator(s) often listed.
Smith, Paul J. "Music in the Animated Cartoon." 1:3 (March 1944): 2, 4. Part 1.
Smith, Paul J. "Music in the Animated Cartoon." 1:4 (April 1944): 2. Part 2.
Smith, Paul J. "Music in the Animated Cartoon." 1:5 (May 1944): 2. Part 3.
"Strange Instruments Used in Pictures." 1:7 (July 1944): 1, 4. Native (Asian) instruments in recent MGM films.
Maxwell, Charles. "A Score Is Born." 1:7 (July 1944): 2, 4. Part 1.
Maxwell, Charles. "A Score Is Born." 1:9 (September 1944): 2, 4. Part 2.
Maxwell, Charles. "A Score Is Born." 1:10 (October 1944): 2, 4. Part 3.
Minor, Monachus. "A Music Library in a Motion Picture Studio." 2:3 (March 1945): 2, 4. Part 1.
Minor, Monachus. "A Music Library in a Motion Picture Studio." 2:4 (April 1945): 2, 4. Part 2.
Minor, Monachus. "A Music Library in a Motion Picture Studio." 2:5–6 (May–June 1945): 2, 4. Part 3.

De Saxe, Rudy. "Alfred Wallenstein Believes Film Music Has [a] Future." 2:11–12 (November–December 1945): 3, 6. Brief interview with the conductor.

De Saxe, Rudy. "Film Music and the Symphony Hall." 3:1–2 (January–February 1946): 3.

De Saxe, Rudy. "Musical Scores of the Month." 3:9–10 (September–October 1946): 3–4. Commentaries on recent film scores reprinted from "Matters of Note" in the *Hollywood Review*.

Maury, Lou. "Edward Powell." 4:2 (March 1950): 5. Profile.

Lange, Arthur. "The Epigrammatic Nature of Motion Picture Music." 4:2 (March 1950): 8–9.

Maury, Lou. "Joe Dubin." 4:3 (May 1950): 3. Profile.

Spirant, David. "Herschel Burke Gilbert." 5:2–3 (1953): 3, 15. Profile.

The Score (US, SCL, 1986–2005)

Published quarterly by the Society of Composers and Lyricists in Hollywood (later moved to Beverly Hills) to inform and educate members as well as to increase public awareness of their art and craft. The SCL serves members by organizing industry forums, seminars, and conferences, as well as disseminating information on performing rights, intellectual property rights, and contracts. Edited by Lori Barth, the first issue was published as a six-page newsletter. *The Score* grew into a premier resource featuring news, articles, and interviews. The interviews are often conducted by SCL members and therefore tend to be more candid than those meant for the general public. The articles reflect issues faced by members, including technology, performing rights, licensing, budgets, royalties, and copyright. Includes photo reportage of SCL events, dinners, and seminars. The president's message has been contributed by Richard Bellis, Bruce Broughton, Jay Chattaway, Ray Colcord, James Di Pasquale, Dan Foliart, Arthur Hamilton, and Mark Watters. Columns include "What's Happening" by Barth, "Musical Shares" by Charles Bernstein (compiled into a book, *Film Music and Everything Else!*, 2000), "Music and Technology" by Gary Woods, and "Composer's Corner" by Michael Isaacson. "Can You Top This" presents amusing stories from the trenches.

Quarter Notes, a precursor to *The Score*, was published by the Composers and Lyricists Guild of America (CLGA) from 1982 to 1985. It was edited by James Di Pasquale, then Sue Shifrin. The SCL also published a short-lived member newsletter, *Accent*, from around August 1994 to May 1995, that contains news and notes.

1:1 (undated, February 1986)
"Message from Arthur Hamilton."
Barth, Lori. "What's Happening."

2:1 (Winter 1987)
No articles.

3:1 (Winter 1988)
No articles.

4:1 (Spring 1989)
"Cynthia Weil on Lyric Writing for Film." 6–7. Interview.

4:2 (Summer 1989)
Bernstein, Charles. "Danny Elfman." 8–10. Interview.
Brabec, Jeffrey J., and Todd W. Brabec. "The Increasing Value of Film and Television Copyrights." 11–12. Part 1.

<u>4:3 (1989)</u>
Not consulted.

<u>4:4 (Winter 1989)</u>
Broughton, Bruce. "A Consumer's Guide to Agents: Bart/Milander, Gorfaine/Schwartz, ICM." 1, 8, 11. Part 1.
Brabec, Jeffrey J., and Todd W. Brabec. "The Increasing Value of Film and TV Copyrights." 4–5. Part 2, covers background score.
"Excerpts from a Dialogue between Henry Mancini and Jerry Immel." 6–7.

<u>5:1 (Spring 1990)</u>
Barth, Lori. "Where Old Film Scores Go to Die." 1, 12.
Di Pasquale, James. "The Cue Sheet: Chapter Two." 3, 12–13.
Broughton, Bruce. "A Consumer's Guide to Agents: The Carol Faith Agency and Robert Light Agency." 4–15. Part 2.
Spiegel, Dennis. "A Lyrical Dialogue: Alan and Marilyn Bergman." 8–10. Interview.

<u>5:2 (Summer 1990)</u>
Passman, Donald S. "How to Read Your Composer Contract." 1, 14–15.
Irwin, Ashley. "Scoring for Film in Australia." 5, 15.
Walker, Shirley. "Budgeting for Film." 6–8, 12.

<u>5:3 (Winter 1990)</u>
"Knowing Your Music Contractor." 1, 12. Sandy DeCrescent, Patti Fidelibus, Joe Soldo, and Ken Watson answer questions posed by *Score*.
Horunzhy, Vladimir. "Film Music in the USSR." 7.
"A Conversation with Gary LeMel and Lee Holdridge." 8–10, 12–13.

<u>6:1 (Spring 1991)</u>
Garfinkle, Craig Stuart. "Orchestrators: A Brief Overview." 1, 14–15. On Arthur Morton, Greig McRitchie, Jerry Grant, and Jack Eskew.
David Raksin in Conversation with James Di Pasquale: Reflections on a Creative Life." 4–6. Part 1.
"Score Interviews: Ralph Grierson." 8–10. Keyboard session player.
Lee, Spencer. "Fake Orchestras." 12. On the Fairlight sampler.

<u>6:2 (Summer 1991)</u>
Garfinkle, Craig Stuart. "Music Supervisors: A Guide for Composers." 1, 5, 12.
Barth, Lori. "John Bettis: On Lyric Writing for Film and TV." 8–10, 13.
Newton, Rodney. "Film and Television Composing in Great Britain Today." 17.

<u>6:3 (Fall 1991)</u>
"John Cacavas Talks with Morton Gould." 8–9, 11. Reprinted in Cacavas, *The Art of Writing Music* (1993).

<u>7:1 (Spring 1992) [erroneously labeled 6:5]</u>
Irwin, Ashley. "The Pros and Cons of Self-Publishing." 1, 4, 11–12.
Burlingame, Jon. "The History of SCL." 5–6.
Carlin, Daniel Allan. "Shirley Walker." 8–10. Interview.

<u>7:2 (Summer 1992)</u>
Kessler, Ralph. "Orchestration." 4.
Schyman, Garry. "A Talk with Harry Lojewski." 5, 12–13. MGM music executive.
Bellis, Richard. "The Dub: The Advantage of Being There." 6.
Barth, Lori. "Michael Kamen." 8–10. Interview.
Miller, Randy. "Raising 'Hell' in Moscow." 12. On recording *Hellraiser III* in Russia.

7:3 (Fall–Winter 1992)

May, David. "Soundtrack Album Deals: How They Can Work for Composers." 1, 13, 15.

Dreith, Dennis. "SCL/RMA: Some Common Ground." 4, 7.

Brockman, Jane. "The First Electronic Filmscore—*Forbidden Planet*: A Conversation with Bebe Barron." 5, 12–13.

Cochran, Scott. "Todd-AO/Glen Glenn Scoring Stage." 7.

Watters, Mark. "Alan Menken." 8–10. Interview.

8:1 (Spring 1993)

Cochran, Scott. "The Relationship between the Composer and the Scoring Mixer." 1, 10, 15.

Schyman, Garry. "Chris Montan Talks about Music at Disney." 4–5. Interview.

"John Williams: A Conversation about Film Composing with Charles Bernstein." 8–10.

Burlingame, Jon. "Why Critics Don't Seem to Know the Score." 11, 15.

8:2 (Summer 1993)

Broughton, Bruce, and Lori Barth. "Television Animation: The Good, the Bad, the Not-So-Hot." 1, 4–6, 12.

"Animation Music: Composers Discuss Different Approaches." 4–6, 10–12. Charlie Brissette, Alf Clausen, Hoyt Curtin, Thomas Jones Chase and Steve Rucker, Bruce Broughton, Richard Stone, and Shirley Walker.

Maltin, Leonard. "Cartoons and Music: Perfect Partners." 7.

Danly, Linda. "40 Years Ago at Disney: An Interview with Buddy Baker." 8–9.

8:3 (Fall 1993)

Brooks, Chris. "In Search of the New Film Music Editing Standard." 4–5.

Cochran, Scott. "The Relationship between the Composer and the Scoring Mixer: Dennis Sands Interviewed." 6.

Brockman, Jane. "Film and Music: Seeing and Hearing: An Interview with Leonard Rosenman." 8–10.

8:4 (Winter 1993)

Winogradsky, Steven. "Music Licensing: What Every Composer Should Know." 1, 14–15.

Barth, Lori. "Talking with Rachel Portman." 4–6.

Bernstein, Charles. "A Conversation with Maurice Jarre." 8–10.

Rhodes, Rick. "Composing for Production Music Libraries." 13.

9:1 (Spring 1994)

"Jazz Invades the Movies and TV." 8–12. Previously unpublished transcript of a CLGA panel discussion with moderator Mort Sahl and participants Elmer Bernstein, Henry Mancini, Johnny Mandel, André Previn, Pete Rugolo, Leith Stevens, and Bobby Troup.

9:2 (Summer 1994)

Bernstein, Charles. "An Interview with Ennio Morricone." 8–10, 15.

9:3 (Fall 1994)

Schonfeld, Richard. "Composers and the IRS." 1, 4.

Cochran, Scott. "The Relationship between the Composer and the Scoring Mixer: An Interview with Shawn Murphy." 5–6.

Shapiro, Alex, with Marc Parmet. "Some Unsolicited Advice on Electronic Orchestration." 7–8, 16.

Barth, Lori. "A Candid Talk with Bruce Broughton." 10–12, 18.

Special Edition (November 1994)
On performing rights, ASCAP, and BMI.

9:4 (Winter 1994)
Zimmitti, Patti. "What to Expect from Your Music Contractor." 5, 14.
Schyman, Garry. "A Word with David Grossman." 8–9, 12. Interview with Paramount vice president of television music.

10:1 (Spring 1995)
Kilian, Mark. "The Battle between Music and Sound Effects." 7–8, 20.
"Jerry Goldsmith Talks with Charles Bernstein." 10–11, 14, 19.

10:2 (Summer 1995)
Brockman, Jane. "*An Interview with the Vampire*'s Composer: Elliot Goldenthal." 10–13.

10:3 (Fall 1995)
"Theme Parks: Four Composers' Chronicles." 1, 4–8. Personal accounts of Richard Bellis, Bruce Broughton, Don Grady, and Steve Bramson.
Parmet, Marc. "An Interview with Alan Silvestri." 10–12, 16.

10:4 (Winter 1995)
Bernstein, Elmer. "The Great Tape Disaster." 7–8. On the increased use of demo tapes.
Barth, Lori. "A Word with James Newton Howard." 10–12.

11:1 (Spring 1996)
Bernstein, Charles. "Marc Shaiman Talks with Charles Bernstein." 10–12, 20.

11:2 (Summer 1996)
Barth, Lori. "Patrick Doyle." 10–12. Interview.

11:3 (Fall 1996)
Barth, Lori. "Stephen Schwartz: From Broadway to Hollywood." 10–12. Interview.

11:4 (Winter 1996)
Barth, Lori. "Music for Commercials." 1, 4–6, 8.
Bernstein, Charles. "Bill Conti Talks Film Music with Charles Bernstein." 10–12, 18.

12:1 (Spring 1997)
Barth, Lori. "The Many Sides of William Ross." 10–12, 16. Interview.

12:2 (Summer 1997)
Lawley, Linda, and Amy Horsting. "Scoring Cyberspace." 1, 4–7. Article on music for the Internet.
Chattaway, Jay. "Patrick Williams Interviewed." 12–14.

12:3 (Fall 1997)
Barth, Lori. "Hal David: The Many Sides of Lyric Writing." 10–12.

12:4 (Winter 1997)
Pelfrey, Danny. "My Teacher and Friend, Lyle 'Spud' Murphy." 7–8.
Barth, Lori. "Thomas Newman." 10–12. Interview.

13:1 (Spring 1998)
Barth, Lori. "Michel Legrand." 10–12. Interview.

13:2 (Summer 1998)
Miller, Robert. "Conducting for Film and Television." 1, 4, 6, 18–19.
Barth, Lori. "Anne Dudley: A Composer for All Seasons." 12–14. Interview.

13:3 (Fall 1998)
Miller, Rob. "Johnny Mandel." 10–13. Interview.

13:4 (Winter 1998)
Beal, John. "Welcome to Heart Attack City: The Business of Composing for Coming Attractions." 1, 4, 18–19. Article on scoring trailers.
Barth, Lori. "From the Rock and Pop World to Film and TV Composing." 5–8. Profiles of Stewart Copeland, Mark Mothersbaugh, Alexander "Ace" Baker, Ashley Irwin, Danny Lux, Camara Kambon, and Adrian Gurvitz.
Mothersbaugh, Mark. "Raymond Scott's Electronium." 8.
Barth, Lori. "A Look at Cliff Eidelman." 12, 14–15. Interview.
Barth, Lori. "Inside Chris Young." 13, 15–17. Interview.

14:1 (Spring 1999)
Barth, Lori. "Howard Shore." 10–12. Interview.

14:2 (Summer 1999)
Barth, Lori, and Linda Lawley. "Geared Up: Women, Music, and Technology." 1, 7–10, 19. Interviews with Charlyn Bernal, Julie Bernstein, Miriam Cutler, Sharon Farber, Lynn Kowal, Clair Marlo, Sophia Morizet, Lolita Ritmanis, Patrice Rushen, and Alex Shapiro.
McDaniels, Kevin. "An Interview with Lennie Niehaus." 12–14.

14:3 (Fall 1999)
McDaniels, Kevin. "The State of the Musical: Interviews with Leading Members of the Music Community." 1, 8–11.
Burlingame, Jon. "From SCA to CLGA to SCL." 4–7. The history of the Screen Composers Association, the Composers and Lyricists Guild of America, and the Society of Composers and Lyricists.
Bernstein, Charles. "An Afternoon with George Fenton." 12–14, 20.

14:4
Not issued.

15:1 (Spring 2000)
McDaniels, Kevin. "Electronic Sound Creation with Jeff Rona and Mark Snow." 5–6.
Bhatia, Amin. "Getting Started." 7–8, 12. On writing music.
Barth, Lori. "John Barry: Past, Present and Future." 14–16, 26. Interview.

15:2 (Summer 2000)
Barth, Lori. "Music Direction: Testimonials from the Pit." 1, 4–8. Interviews with Bill Conti, Jack Elliott, Ian Fraser, Ashley Irwin, and Mark Watters.
Halfpenny, James. "Tales of Heroism and Cosmic Flukes or...How I Got My First Gig." 9, 18–19. The career starts for Jerry Goldsmith, Trevor Rabin, Jonathan Wolff, Patrick Doyle, Bruce Broughton, Alf Clausen, John Debney.
McDaniels, Kevin. "An Interview with David Newman." 12–14.

15:3 (Fall 2000)
Bernstein, Charles. "The Evolution of Lalo Schifrin." 10–12, 16. Interview.
McDaniels, Kevin. "But Is It Art?" 13–14. Answers from John Corigliano, Alan Silvestri, and Dennis McCarthy.

15:4 (Winter 2000)
Barth, Lori, Laura Dunn, and Kevin McDaniels. "The Director/Composer Relationship: Casting Your Composer." 5–7, 18. Interviews with directors Mark Rydell, Norman Jewison, Wes Craven, Gary Ross, and François Girard.
McDaniels, Kevin. "The Business of Composing for TV: An Interview with Jonathan Wolff." 12–14.

16:1 (Spring 2001)

Halfpenny, James. "Recharging the Artful Battery." 7–8. On what Jay Chattaway, Alf Clausen, Ennio Morricone, Bennett Salvay, and W. G. "Snuffy" Walden do on their "down" time.

McDaniels, Kevin. "How AMPAS Decides Who Is Eligible for Oscar." 11, 20.

McDaniels, Kevin. "Composer Directions: An Interview with W. G. Snuffy Walden." 12–14.

16:2 (Summer 2001)

Dunn, Laura, and Kevin McDaniels. "From Cinema to Stage: Performing Film Music in Concert." 1, 4, 8.

McDaniels, Kevin. "MIDI Orchestration: Faking It." 5–7. Includes a sidebar, "Sampling the London Symphony Orchestra with Jeff Rona."

Morris, Trevor. "Taking the Giga Plunge." 7–8. On Nemesys's GigaStudio.

McDaniels, Kevin. "Keeping Up with John Debney." 12–14. Interview.

16:3 (Fall 2001)

Irwin, Ashley. "A Few Words with Lori Barth." 12–14, 16. Interview with the *Score* editor.

16:4 (Winter 2001)

Barth, Lori. "Industry Trends: A Look at Television Music for 2002." 1, 4, 8.

McDaniels, Kevin. "The Director/Composer Relationship: First Contact." 5–6. Four independent film directors talk about hiring and working with a composer.

Barth, Lori. "Behind the Scenes: *Bride of the Wind*: The Making of the Movie about Alma Mahler." 9, 20. On the film and Stephen Endelman's music.

McDaniels, Kevin. "MIDI Orchestration: Making Sample Sense with Shawn Clement." 15, 20.

17:1 (Spring 2002)

McDaniels, Kevin, and Steve Viens. "Sizing Up the Film Scoring Industry in 2002." 1, 4, 20.

Colcord, Ray. "The Working Composer: Under the Gun: Hans Zimmer and the Making of *Black Hawk Down*." 5–6, 18. Interview.

McDaniels, Kevin. "The Director/Composer Relationship: First Contact—Part II." 9–10.

McDaniels, Kevin. "An Interview with Basil Poledouris." 12–14.

17:2 (Summer 2002)

Barth, Lori. "Looking at Things from a Music Editor's Perspective." 1, 4, 20–23, 28.

Barth, Lori. "The Working Composer: Kurt Farquhar." 9–10. Interview.

Bernstein, Charles. "Sting Talks about the Dramatic Art of Writing Songs." 14–16, 18.

Gates, Pam. "The Recording Musicians Association." 17–18.

17:3 (Fall 2002)

Barth, Lori. "Package Deals: The Great Debate." 1, 4–5, 16–17, 19. With Mark Adler, Laura Karpman, agents Linda Kordek and Stan Milander, Mark Watters, and Pat Williams.

Costa, Ray. "The Composer...Does He Put the Songs in a Film? Educating the Media about Music in Film and Television." 9, 17. By a publicist specializing in representing composers.

Russ, Adryan. "Like Looking at a Diamond: A Chat with Arthur Hamilton." 12–14.

17:4 (Winter 2002)

Isaacson, Michael. "When No Music Is Better." 9, 24.

Parmet, Marc. "Personal Reflections with Elmer Bernstein." 12–14, 16. Interview.

18:1 (Spring 2003)
"Writing for Strings and Other Things: A Conversation between Composers/Arrangers Jorge Calandrelli and David Blumberg, January 10, 2003 at Musso and Frank Grill." 5–6, 18.
Isaacson, Michael. "The [Walter] Scharf Approach: Last Things First." 9. Writing for the film's finale first.
Cohen, Harvey R. "Reflections, Perceptions, Directions: A Conversation with the SCL's First President, James DiPasquale." 12–14.

18:2 (Summer 2003)
Mennella, Mary Jo. "An Inside Look: Fox Music Publishing." 5–6.

18:3 (Fall 2003)
Colcord, Ray. "Swingin' at Capitol." 1, 10–12, 23. Interview-based history of Capitol Records.
Russell, Sherry. "7 Lessons from Rejection's Autopsy." 7–9, 26. Includes personal advice on criticism and rejection from Charles Bernstein, Dan Foliart, and Jonathan Wolff.
Jacks, Larry. "Lunch with Leonard Maltin." 14–15, 21–22. The film buff's take on film music.
DiPasquale, Donna McNeely. "Can't Live with 'em, Can't Shoot 'em." 16–20. The spouses of Alf Clausen, Craig Stuart Garfinkle, Ron Grant, Bronwen Jones, and Mark Watters chat.

18:4 (Winter 2003)
Grant, Ron. "Film Scoring for Dummies." 1, 4, 10, 20. On Apple Computers' "Soundtrack" software.
Isaacson, Michael. "Musical Development in Film Scores." 7–8.
Babcock, Bruce. "Memoirs of a Famous Film Composer: An Interview with Earle Hagen." 12–17.

19:1 (Spring 2004)
Barth, Lori. "The Music World of Daytime Dramas." 1, 4, 10, 21–23. Gary Kuo, Dominic Messenger, and others relate their experiences scoring soap operas.
Barth, Lori. "Last Minute Revisions: Under the Gun." 5–6. Alf Clausen, Laura Karpman, and Tim Kelly on the subject.
Russ, Adryan. "Dan Foliart: Custom-Crafted and Off the Cuff." 14–16.

19:2 (Summer 2004)
Barth, Lori. "The Great Race: Composer and Songwriter Cattle Calls." 1, 10, 20–24. On submitting and pitching music and songs from the experiences of composers, songwriters, agents, and music supervisors.
Barth, Lori. "Mark Mancina." 14–16. Interview.

19:3 (Fall 2004)
DiPasquale, James. "Reflections on a Creative Life: David Raksin: A Conversation with David Raksin." 5–8. Reprint of a 1991 conversation previously published in vol. 6, no. 1.
Russ, Adryan. "John Cacavas: The Right Place at the Right Time." 12, 14–15, 19. Interview.
Barth, Lori. "Lee Holdridge: A Man of Many Styles." 13, 20, 22. Interview.

19:4 (Winter 2004)
DiPasquale, James. "Raksin, Bernstein, Goldsmith: A Living Legacy." 1, 8.
Barth, Lori. "An Afternoon with Alf Clausen." 12–14, 20. Interview.

20:1 (Spring 2005)
Barth, Lori. "Industry Trends: LibraryLand." 1, 8–10, 16–17, 20.
Barth, Lori. "Louisville via Los Angeles via Louisville: An Interview with Jonathan Wolff." 12–16.

20:2 (Summer 2005)
Barth, Lori. "A Candid Conversation with Rolfe Kent." 12–14, 24.

20:3 (Fall 2005)
Barth, Lori. "Industry Trends: What's Killing the Business." 1, 10–11, 20–22. Viewpoints from Richard Bellis, Chuck Fernandez, Jay Gruska, and others.
Barth, Lori. "John Morris: Then and Now." 14–17. Interview.

20:4 (Winter 2005)
Barth, Lori. "Agents." 1, 8–10, 20. Comments from Linda Kordek, Richard Kraft, Larry Marks, and Bob Rice.
Farrell, Christopher. "A Conversation with Michael Giacchino." 12–15, 22.

Sound Track: Music n' Movies, Music in Movies (US, 2005)

A fanzine published by "Captain America," the alias of a music enthusiast in Albuquerque, New Mexico, known for documenting the local music scene. For example, see no. 2 (May 2005).

Soundtrack! The Collector's Quarterly (Belgium, 1975–2002)

Quarterly newsletter published by Luc Van de Ven in Mechelen, Belgium, from 1975 to 2002. Familiarly known as *Soundtrack*, it began as *SCN: Soundtrack Collector's Newsletter* and was published under that title until 1980. (An unnumbered charter issue of *SCN* was distributed in December 1974.) International in scope, it contains articles, interviews, photo reportage, filmographies, discographies, lists of new recordings, letters, soundtrack reviews, book reviews, and reports on European film music concerts and film festivals. Discographies usually contain film title, release year, additional information (suite, rerecording, etc.), label and disc number, release format (LP, CD), and country of origin. Filmographies may include short films, documentaries, and rejected scores. Photo reportage is strong for European scoring sessions by European and American composers.

Interviews include European composers (often conducted in their native language and translated into English) and American composers (often in conjunction with European recording sessions). Discographies are compiled by collectors such as Ronald Bohn, David P. James, James Marshall, Jean-Pierre Pecqueriaux, and Luc Van de Ven, with additional research from John Caps, Tom DeMary, Daniel Mangodt, and others. Regular features and columns include "Cuttings," with excerpts of previously published interviews, "Deadline," which includes scoring assignments compiled by Van de Ven, David P. James, and Ford A. Thaxton, and "LP Checklist," with recent soundtracks listed by country of origin.

Around 1989 Van de Ven contributed background stories for his label, Prometheus Records. New releases were covered by Van de Ven and Forrest J. Ackerman. Roger Feigelson contributed "Crossfade" (also known as "Cross Fade"). David Hirsch wrote "Temp Track" from at least June 1995 to 2002. Jack Smith began writing "The Golden Age" in Summer 1999. British saxophonist Dirk Wickenden started contributing a series of articles on "The Golden Age" in 2000. Winter 2002 was the final print issue.

A new volume and issue sequence began in March 1982. *Soundtrack* absorbed *CinemaScore* in September 1989, including "Collector's Corner," by Gary W. Radovich, "Scoring Session" (resurrected in September 1997), and "The Vintage Score." Randall D.

Larson compiled a composer and film title index for issues from 1975 to 1990, "The S.C.Q. Index" (San Jose, Calif.: CinemaScore, 1989). After publisher Daniel Mangodt's death in September 1997, Van de Ven became editor and Larson contributing editor and, later, senior editor.

Published as SCN: Soundtrack Collector's Newsletter

1:1 (May–June 1975)

1:2 (July–August 1975)
Krasnoborski, W. F. "A Conversation with Bronislau Kaper." Part 1.

1:3 (September–October 1975)
Krasnoborski, W. F. "A Conversation with Bronislau Kaper." 3–8. Part 2.
Caps, John. "European Composer Series: Georges Delerue: Renaissance Man." 10–12.

1:4 (November–December 1975)
"A Conversation with Ron Goodwin."
Filmography: Georges Delerue. Part 1.

1:5 (January–February 1976)
Filmography: Georges Delerue. Part 2.
Filmography: Ennio Morricone. Part 1.

1:6 (March–April 1976)
Filmography: Ennio Morricone. Part 2.

2:7 (September 1976)
Caps, John. "In Conversation with Richard Rodney Bennett." Part 1.
Filmography: Ennio Morricone. Part 3.
Sutak, Ken. "*The Alamo* Remembered." Retrospective article and analysis of Dimitri Tiomkin's score, part 1.

2:8 (December 1976)
Sutak, Ken. "*The Alamo* Remembered." Part 2.
Filmography: Richard Rodney Bennett.
Filmography: Ennio Morricone. Part 4.
Caps, John. "In Conversation with Richard Rodney Bennett." Part 2.

2:9 (January 1977)
DeMary, Tom. "A Conversation with David Shire." 3–10. Part 1, with Filmography/ Discography.

2:10 (May 1977)
Caps, John. "Henry Mancini: On Scoring and Recording." 3–5.
Filmography: Carlo Rustichelli. Part 1.
DeMary, Tom. "A Conversation with David Shire." 17–22. Part 2.

3:11 (August 1977)
Cocumarolo, Enzo. "Carlo Rustichelli." 3–10, 13–16.
Filmography: Carlo Rustichelli. Part 2.
Filmography: Philippe Sarde. Part 1.

3:12 (November 1977)
Marshall, James. "European Composers: Mario Nascimbene." Part 1.
Filmography: Philippe Sarde. Part 2.
Sutak, Ken. "*The Alamo* Remembered." Part 3.

3:13 (March 1978)
Cardinaletti, Massimo. "Ennio Morricone: The Man and the Musician." 3–8. Interview, part 1.
Filmography/Discography: Nino Rota. 13–17.
Bryce, Allan. "TV Music: Intimate Themes." 18–19.
Marshall, James. "European Composers: Mario Nascimbene, Part 2." 20–22.

3:14 (June 1978)
Krasnoborski, William F. "Close Encounters of the Uncertain Kind." 3–7. On John Williams's score for *Close Encounters of the Third Kind.*
Filmography/Discography: John Barry. 13–17.
Cardinaletti, Massimo. "Ennio Morricone: The Man and the Musician." 18–23. Interview, part 2.

3:15 (October 1978)
Marshall, James, and Ronald Bohn, "Gerald Fried." 3–6. Article.
Filmography/Discography: Francesco Lavagnino. 13–16. Part 1.
Wright, John. "John Williams Lecture." 17–18. Report on a National Film Theatre program.
Sutak, Ken. "*The Alamo* Remembered." 22–27. Part 4.

3:16 (January 1979)
Bryce, Allan. "The Sound of Horror." 3–6.
Marshall, James. "European Composers: Francesco Angelo Lavagnino." 7–8. On Angelo Francesco Lavagnino.
Filmography/Discography: Francesco Lavagnino. 13–16. Part 2.
Orowan, Florella. "The Military Filmscore Examined." 18–23. Part 1.

4:17 (April 1979)
Wright, John. "Jerry Goldsmith Lecture." 3–7. Report on a National Film Theatre program.
Van de Ven, Luc. "Maurice Jarre on TV." 10–11.
Filmography/Discography: Mario Nascimbene. 12–16.

4:18 (July 1979)
Bohn, Ronald. "A Conversation with Gerald Fried." 3–7.
Filmography/Discography: Gerald Fried. 13–16.
Orowan, Florella. "The Military Filmscore Examined." 17–21. Part 2.
Bryce, Allan. "Jerry Goldsmith on *Star Sound.*" 23. Report on a radio interview.

5:19 (October 1979)
Caps, John. "The Ascent of Jerry Goldsmith." 3–8. Part 1.
Marshall, James. "Piero Piccioni." 9–12.
Filmography/Discography: Piero Piccioni. 13–16.

5:20 (January 1980)
Caps, John. "The Ascent of Jerry Goldsmith." 3–8. Part 2.
Filmography/Discography: Piero Piccioni. 13–16. Part 2.
Marshall, James. "Les Baxter." 17–21, 27. Article.

5:21 (April 1980)
Reali, Ezio. "A Conversation with [Angelo] Lavagnino." 3–8.
Filmography/Discography: Georges Delerue. 12–16. Part 1.

Published as **Soundtrack! The Collector's Quarterly**

5:22 (August 1980)
Bettens, Robert, "An Afternoon with Georges Delerue." 3–7.

Filmography/Discography: Georges Delerue. 13–17. Part 2.
Bryce, Allan. "The Music of the Macabre." 19–21, 11.

5:23 (November 1980)
Raksin, David. "A Conversation with Jerry Fielding." 3–10.
Filmography/Discography: Georges Delerue. 13–15. Part 3.
Filmography/Discography: Maurice Jarre. 16–17. Part 1.

5:24 (February 1981)
Reali, Ezio, and James Marshall. "A Conversation with Mario Nascimbene." 3–6.
Filmography/Discography: Maurice Jarre. 13–16. Part 2.
Crossland, Howard. *"The Overlanders."* 17–19. On John Ireland's score.
Bryce, Allan. "TV Music: The Mediocre Medium." 21–22, 10.

6:25 (May 1981)
Bryce, Allan. "A Conversation with Jerry Goldsmith." 3–8.
Filmography/Discography: Francesco DeMasi. 15–20.
Doherty, Jim. "The Overlooked Bernard Herrmann." 22–28.

6:26 (August 1981)
Bryce, Allan. "Film Music in Outer Space." 3–5.
Filmography/Discography: Elmer Bernstein. 7–12. Part 1.
Kraft, David, and Ronald Bohn. "A Conversation with Les Baxter." 14–24.

7:27 (December 1981)
Bryce, Allan. "Jerry Goldsmith at Abbey Road." 3–4.
Filmography/Discography: Elmer Bernstein. 5–7. Part 2.
Filmography/Discography: Vladimir Cosma. 9–12.
Kraft, David. "A Conversation with John Addison." 14–23, 4.

1:1 (March 1982)
Caps, John. "Keeping in Touch with John Williams." 3–7. Interview.
Filmography/Discography: Vladimir Cosma. 9–11.
Crossland, Howard. "Henry Mancini on the Parkinson Show." 13–14. Report.
Filmography/Discography: Roy Budd. 21–23.

1:2 (June 1982)
Filmography/Discography: Jerry Goldsmith. 3–8. Part 1.
Kraft, David. "European Composers: A Conversation with Georges Delerue." 11–16.

1:3 (September 1982)
Caps, John. *"E.T.: The Extra-Terrestrial."* 3–5. On John Williams's score.
Filmography/Discography: Jerry Goldsmith. 7–11. Part 2.
Kraft, David, and Richard Kraft. "A Conversation with Miklos Rozsa and Carl Reiner." 13–22. Part 1.
Doherty, Jim. "Kostal and the New Fantasia: Desecration of the *Temple*." 23–24.

1:4 (December 1982)
Macy, Tom. "Unrecorded Scores: *Raggedy Man*." 4–5.
Filmography/Discography: Carl Davis. 9–11.
Filmography/Discography: Alex North. 14–16. Part 1.
Kraft, David, and Richard Kraft. "A Conversation with Miklos Rozsa and Carl Reiner." 17–23. Part 2.

2:5 (March 1983)

Caps, John. "Dungeons and Dragons: Three Medieval Scores." 3–4. On music by Alex North for *Dragonslayer*; Basil Poledouris for *Conan the Barbarian*; and David Whitaker for *The Sword and the Sorcerer*.

Kraft, David, and Richard Kraft. "A Conversation with Carl Reiner." 4–5. The director talks about Miklós Rózsa.

Filmography/Discography: Alex North. 6–8. Part 2.

Williams, John. "A Conversation with Carl Davis." 10–15.

Filmography/Discography: Bruno Nicolai. 21–23. Part 1.

2:6 (June 1983)

Filmography/Discography: Bruno Nicolai. 10–12. Part 2.

Caps, John. "A Conversation with Elmer Bernstein." 14–22. Part 1.

Filmography/Discography: Lalo Schifrin. 24–25. Part 1.

2:7 (September 1983)

Caps, John. "A Conversation with Elmer Bernstein." 3–6. Part 2.

Filmography/Discography: Lalo Schifrin. 7–12. Part 2.

2:8 (December 1983)

Kraft, David. "Jerry Goldsmith: Entering Herrmann's Zone." 3–9. Interview with *Psycho II* director Richard Franklin regarding Jerry Goldsmith's score.

Filmography/Discography: Nicola Piovani. 10–11.

Larson, Randall. "Unrecorded Scores: Michel Legrand's License to Kill." 13–14. Regarding *Never Say Never Again*.

Filmography/Discography: John Barry. 21–23. Part 1.

3:9 (March 1984)

Filmography/Discography: John Barry. 3–7. Part 2, covers 1965–1974.

Lehti, Steven J. "*Brainstorm*." 10–12. On James Horner's score.

Caps, John. "Pipes of Pan." 14–16. On Jerry Goldsmith's score for *Under Fire*.

Santiago, Thom. "A Film Music Seminar." 18–23. Report on the Academy of Motion Picture Arts and Sciences 1983 seminar.

3:10 (June 1984)

Caps, John. "James Horner: Premature Plaudits?" 3–4.

Filmography/Discography: John Barry. 5–8. Part 3, covers 1974–1984.

Pugliese, Roberto. "A Conversation with Pino Donaggio." 18–26.

Filmography/Discography: Armando Trovaioli. 28–29. On the Italian composer, part 1, covers 1952–1961.

3:11 (September 1984)

Bryce, Allan. "A Conversation with Roy Budd." 3–7.

Filmography/Discography: Armando Trovaioli. 9–15. Part 2, covers 1961–1984.

Lehti, Steven J. "In the Valley of the Sequels." 16–20. Discusses music by James Horner, Basil Poledouris, and John Williams.

3:12 (December 1984)

Fitzpatrick, James. "A Conversation with Maurice Jarre." 6–10. Part 1.

Mangodt, Daniel. "Stelvio Cipriani." 11–15. Filmography/discography for the Italian composer, part 1.

4:13 (March 1985)

Kraft, David. "A Conversation with Alex North." 3–8. Part 1.

Mangodt, Daniel. "Stelvio Cipriani." 9–10. Filmography/discography, part 2.

Fitzpatrick, James. "A Conversation with Maurice Jarre." 16–18. Part 2.

Bohn, Ron, and others. "John Scott." 19–21. Filmography/discography.

4:14 (June 1985)
Pecqueriaux, Jean-Pierre, translated by Daniel Mangodt. "A Conversation with Philippe Sarde." 3–7. Part 1.
De Moor, John, Daniel Mangodt, Jean-Pierre Pecqueriaux, and Naoki Yoshijima. "John Williams." 9–12. Filmography/Discography. Part 1.

4:15 (September 1985)
Robley, Les. "*Jason and the Argonauts*." 3–5. Article on Bernard Herrmann's score.
Büdinger, Matthias. "Elmer Bernstein: Scoring *Marie Ward*." 7–9. With brief interview.
Pecqueriaux, Jean-Pierre, translated by Daniel Mangodt. "A Conversation with Philippe Sarde." 11–14. Part 2.
De Moor, John, Daniel Mangodt, Jean-Pierre Pecqueriaux, and Naoki Yoshijima. "John Williams." 19–21. Filmography/Discography. Part 2.
Mangodt, Daniel, Jean-Pierre Pecqueriaux, and John Wright. "Luis Enriquez Bacalov." 22–23. Filmography/Discography. Part 1.

4:16 (December 1985)
Tucker, G. M. "[Jerry] Goldsmith Explored." 3–4. Article.
Mangodt, Daniel, Jean-Pierre Pecqueriaux, and John Wright. "Luis Enriquez Bacalov." 19–22. Filmography/Discography. Part 2.

5:17 (March 1986)
Heimansberg, Udo. "An Interview with Elmer Bernstein." 3–5. Interviewed at the *Spies Like Us* recording sessions.
Bohn, Ronald, and Daniel Mangodt. "Lee Holdridge." 6–9. Filmography/Discography.
Van de Ven, Luc. "Philharmonic Productions." 10–13. Record producers Udo Heimansberg and Bernd-Jürgen Schlossmacher on rerecording Miklós Rózsa film scores.

5:18 (June 1986)
Kraft, Richard, and David Kraft. "An Interview with John Scott." 3–6, 17.
Bohn, Ronald L., Jim Doherty, and Luc Van de Ven. "Bernard Herrmann." 8–12. Filmography/Discography. Part 1.

5:19 (September 1986)
Bohn, Ronald L., Jim Doherty, and Luc Van de Ven. "Bernard Herrmann." 15–17. Filmography/Discography. Part 2.
Fuiano, Claudio. "An Interview with Nicola Piovani." 24–27.

5:20 (December 1986)
Tucker, Guy. "Retread City." 6–7. On sequels and remakes.
Fuiano, Claudio. "A Conversation with Mario Nascimbene." 9–14.
Pecqueriaux, Jean-Pierre, Daniel Mangodt, David Kraft, and Gerd Haven. "Bill Conti." 22–26. Filmography/Discography.

6:21 (March 1987)
Townson, Robert, and Kevin Mulhall. "Film Music 1986: A State of the Art." 4–5. Article on rejected scores.
Pecqueriaux, Jean-Pierre, Andrea Busi, David Kraft, and John Wright. "Nino Rota." 6–7, 10–12. Filmography/Discography. Part 1.
"A Conversation with John William Waxman." 13–15. Interview with Franz Waxman's son.
"A Short Conversation with Anton Garcia Abril." 28. Interview with the Spanish composer.
"Sevilla's First Film Music Convention." 30. Report.

Ritchie, Christopher. "Malcolm Arnold Just Writes What He Would Like to Hear." 5–9. Interview.

Kowalski, Alfons, and Christopher Ritchie, with Jack Docherty, Jean-Pierre Pecqueriaux, and David Kraft. "A Filmography/Discography of Ron Goodwin." 20–23.

Yagiyu, Sumimaro. "A Conversation with Dave Grusin." 25–27.

Van de Ven, Luc, and Daniel Mangodt. "A Conversation with Georges Delerue." 28–31.

Feigelson, Roger. "An Interview with Laurence Rosenthal." 4–10.

Schreurs, Thierry. "Meeting with a Remarkable Man." 18–19. Interview with Jerry Goldsmith's recording engineer Mike Ross-Trevor.

Mangodt, Daniël, revised by Bruce Broughton. "A Filmography/Discography of Bruce Broughton." 24, 26–27.

Fitzpatrick, James. "Jerome Moross' *The Big Country*." 28–31. Article on rerecording the score.

Büdinger, Matthias. "John Scott on Fire: The Third Time Around." 4–9. Interview.

Van de Ven, Luc. "An Interview with David Newman." 14–17.

Mangodt, Daniël, with Alfons Kowalski and Jean-Pierre Pecqueriaux. "A Filmography/Discography of Georges Delerue." 18–23. Part 1.

Büdinger, Matthias. "*The Adventures of Baron Munchausen*." 28–31. Interview with Michael Kamen.

Mangodt, Daniël, with Alfons Kowalski, Jean-Pierre Pecqueriaux, and Shoichi Uehara. "A Filmography/Discography of Georges Delerue." 6–11. Part 2.

Ritchie, Christopher. "A Conversation with Ron Goodwin." 21–24, 26–27.

Jacquet-Françillon, Vincent. "An Interview with Basil Poledouris." 28–31. Part 1.

First issue to incorporate Randall Larson's *CinemaScore*.

Jacquet-Françillon, Vincent. "An Interview with Basil Poledouris." 4–6. Part 2.

"Scoring Session." 18–20. Includes new scores by Wynton Marsalis, Stanley Myers, Laurence Rosenthal, and Lalo Schifrin.

Burlingame, John [*sic*]. "On the Scoring Stage with Bob Cobert Recording *War and Remembrance*." 21–22. Article on recording the television score.

Larson, Randall D. "Bob Cobert on *Dark Shadows* and *Night Stalkers*." 23–25. Interview regarding his television music.

Larson, Randall D. "Music for *Who Framed Roger Rabbit?*" 26–27. Interview with Alan Silvestri.

Einhorn, Richard. "The Musical Psychologies of *Sister Sister*." 28–30. Einhorn on his score.

Care, Ross. "Melody Time: Musicians for Disney Animation 1941–1955." 31–40. Article on the music of Frank Churchill, Jud Conlon, Joseph Dubin, Leigh Harline, Edward Plumb, Paul Smith, Oliver Wallace, Charles Wolcott, and others.

"Specialty Film Music Labels: Soundtracks on Disc: The State of the Art." 41–43. DRG Records, Intrada, Prometheus, Screen Archives Entertainment, Silva Screen, Southern Cross/Fifth Continent, Varese Sarabande, and Virgin responses to a *CinemaScore* questionnaire. Part 1.

Asch, Andrew. "Scoring *Rich Boys*." 44–45. The composer discusses his score.

Jones, Anthony R. "Scoring *Invasion Earth: The Aliens Are Here!*" 45–47. Jones on his score for the film.

Doherty, Jim. "Collaboration: The Film Music of Philip Glass." 48–53. Article and interview, with filmography/discography.

Mangodt, Daniël, with Alfons Kowalski, Jean-Pierre Pecqueriaux, and Shoichi Uehara. "A Filmography/Discography of Georges Delerue." 55–63. Part 3, covers 1971–1989.

8:32 (December 1989)

Sinclair, Duncan. "*E.T. The Extra-Terrestrial*: A Brief Guide to Its Musical Themes and Some Suggestions as to Their Origins." 6–7. Analysis of John Williams's score.

"Specialty Film Music Labels: Soundtracks on Disc, The State of the Art." 8–12. Part 2.

Burlingame, John [*sic*]. "John Barry and *U.S.A Today*." 13. Interview-based article.

Larson, Randall D. "Alan Silvestri: *Mac and Me*." 14. Interview.

Büdinger, Matthias. "Christopher Young." 25–31. Interview.

9:33 (March 1990)

"Bruce Broughton: An Interview." 4–7.

Feigelson, Roger. "A Look behind Crescendo Records." 9–11. Interview with Ford Thaxton, with comments about Christopher Young.

Mangodt, Daniël. "A Filmography/Discography of Laurence Rosenthal." 12–15.

Wooddell, Glenn. "In Memory of John Green: A Biographical Interview." 25–27. For Wooddell's New York radio program.

Büdinger, Matthias. "Georges Delerue: Scoring *Show of Force*." 30–31. Article and interview.

9:34 (June 1990)

Bergamino, Gianni, and Giuseppe Fenzi, translated from Italian by Mario Zargani. "The Apologetics of Film Music: A Conversation with Ennio Morricone." 4–6.

Larson, Randall D. "Gary Chang: Shocking the System." 7–9. Interview.

Werba, Marco. "Filmmusic by Michael Nyman." 10–11. Interview.

Elhaïk, Serge, and Daniël Mangodt. "A Filmography/Discography of Henry Mancini." 12–15. Part 1.

Gyffyn, Jenni. "Bruce Rowland: The Music from *Snowy River*." 25–27, 30–31. Interview regarding *The Man from Snowy River* and other projects.

9:35 (September 1990)

Büdinger, Matthias. "Carl Davis Unbound: Monsters over the Rainbow." 4–7. Interview.

Büdinger, Matthias. "Exploring *Mountains of the Moon* with Michael Small." 8–12. Interview.

Larson, Randall D. "From Aussie with Flames: Graeme Revell and *Spontaneous Combustion*." 17–19. Interview-based article.

Larson, Randall D. "Danny Elfman from Boingo to *Batman*." 20, 22–27. Interview.

Burlingame, Jon. "Danny Elfman on the Move." 21.

Larson, Randall D. "Misha Segal's *Phantom of the Opera*." 28. Interview-based article.

Burlingame, Jon. "John Addison's *Phantom of the Opera*." 29. Interview-based article.

Larson, Randall D. "Music from the Hammer Films." 36. Soundtrack review.

Elhaïk, Serge, and Daniël Mangodt. "A Filmography/Discography of Henry Mancini." 37–43. Part 2.

"*Star Trek*: Music for a Television Legend: Interviews with *Star Trek* Composers," includes:

Simak, Steven. "*Star Trek*: Alexander Courage." 44–45. Interview.

Larson, Randall D. "*Star Trek* and the Fantastic Film Music of Gerald Fried." 46–47. Interview.

Larson, Randall D. "*Star Trek*: George Duning." 49. Interview.

Larson, Randall D. *"Star Trek The Next Generation*: Ron Jones." 50–53. Interview. With sidebar listing music credits for the first three seasons, compiled by Ford Thaxton and David Hirsch.

Larson, Randall D. *"Star Trek The Next Generation*: Dennis McCarthy." 54–55. Interview.

Larson, Randall D. *"Star Trek*: Fred Steiner." 56–59. Interview. Steiner's music for *Twilight Zone* is also discussed.

Care, Ross. "Scoring the Short Film." 62–63. The composer's personal experiences.

9:36 (December 1990)

Jacquet-Françillon, Vincent. "Lee Holdridge." 5–8. Interview.

Büdinger, Matthias. "Eric Tomlinson." 9–11. Interview with the recording and mixing engineer.

Larson, Randall D. "The Vintage Score: *Cat People* (1942)." 12–14. Retrospective article and analysis of Roy Webb's score.

Büdinger, Matthias. "David Newman on the *Flower Planet*." 25–27, 30. Interview regarding Newman's score for the animated short film.

Burlingame, Jon. "David Raksin: Working in Television." 31. Interview-based article on *The Day After*.

10:37 (March 1991)

Larson, Randall D. "An Interview with Alan Silvestri: From Romances to Predators." 4–9.

Hauserman, Richard, Roger Feigelson, and Chris Young. "A Filmography/Discography of Christopher Young." 10–12.

Büdinger, Matthias. "Howard Shore's Music for *Silence of the Lambs*." 13–16. Interview.

Büdinger, Matthias. "Myers in Munich." 25–26. Interview with Stanley Myers regarding *Homo Faber*.

10:38 (June 1991)

Schweiger, Daniel. "An Interview with Thomas Newman." 4–7.

Larson, Randall D. "Hyper Reality: Alan Howarth's Synthesized Scores and Specialized Sound Effects." 8–11.

Mangodt, Daniel. "A Filmography/Discography of Michael Kamen." 12–13.

Feigelson, Roger. "The Story behind Bay Cities." 14–16.

10:39 (September 1991)

Schreurs, Thierry. "The Silva House." 5–8. Interview with James Fitzpatrick of Silva Screen Records.

De Moor, John, and Daniel Mangodt. "A Filmography/Discography of Philippe Sarde." 9–17.

Larson, Randall D. "Ragnar Bjerkreim: Film Music in Norway." 18–19. On the composer's film scores.

Kremer, Jorg. "An Interview with Dana Kaproff." 20–25.

Büdinger, Matthias. "Ira Newborn: Scoring the Contemporary Comedy." 26–29. Interview.

Larson, Randall D. "The Subtle Art of ReScoring: Kendall Schmidt and the World of Scoring Movie Trailers and Home Video Replacement Music." 41–43, 46–47. Interview.

Larson, Randall D. "Elliot Kaplan and the Rescoring of *Tentacles*." 43.

Powers, Philip R. W. "A Conversation with Bruce Smeaton." 48–53.

Werba, Marco. "A Conversation with John Scott." 60–62.

10:40 (December 1991)

Kraft, David, and Randall D. Larson. "Alex North Remembered." 4.

Larson, Randall D. "Alex North and *2001*: The Unused Score." 5. From an unpublished 1988 interview.

Mangodt, Daniel. "An Interview with Steven and Anne-Marie North." 6–7, 31. Reminiscences from Alex North's son and wife.

Schweiger, Daniel. "Cliff Eidelman Performs the *Enterprise*'s Swan Song for *Star Trek VI*." 8–10. Interview.

Schweiger, Daniel. "*Heavy Metal*: An Interview with Brad Fiedel." 19–21.

Schweiger, Daniel. "Flight of Fancy." 25–27, 30. Interview with James Horner on *The Rocketeer*.

Larson, Randall D. "Angelo Badalamenti: Anthony Asquith Award Report." 32.

11:41 (March 1992)

"James Horner's Melbourne Seminar." 4–7. Interview transcribed by Andrew Knipe, part 1.

Larson, Randall D. "The New *Addams Family*: An Interview with Marc Shaiman." 8–10.

Larson, Randall D. "The Original *Addams Family*: Vic Mizzy Interview." 11–12.

Schweiger, Daniel. "An Interview with Elmer Bernstein." 22–24. Includes discussion of his adaptation of Bernard Herrmann's original score for the remake of *Cape Fear*.

Van Wouw, Martin. "Bruno Nicolai Remembered." 25–27. Interview.

11:42 (June 1992)

Cavanagh, Darren. "Hollywood Has Been Zimmered: A Frank Conversation with Hans Zimmer." 4–7. Interview.

Cavanagh, Darren. "Shirley Walker Interview." 8–11.

Büdinger, Matthias, and Luc Van de Ven. "Georges Delerue Remembered." 12–16. With filmography, 1989–1992.

Schweiger, Daniel. "Basic Goldsmith." 25–27, 30. Interview regarding *Basic Instinct*.

11:43 (September 1992)

Werba, Marco. "Donaggio and De Palma: Together Again: Scoring *Raising Cain*." 4–7. Interview, with filmography/discography by Daniel Mangodt, 26–29.

Cavanagh, Darren, with Paul Andrew MacLean. "A Conversation with Bill Conti." 8–13. Interview.

Schweiger, Daniel. "Danny Elfman Returns." 17–20. Interview regarding *Batman* and *Batman Returns*.

Mansell, John. "In Conversation with James Bernard." 21–25. Interview.

Karban, Thomas. "An Interview with Michael J. Lewis." 35–36. Part 1.

Büdinger, Matthias, and David Schecter. "Days of Wine and Roses." 37–41. Reports on the Society for the Preservation of Film Music's first international film music conference.

Mülder, Günther. "A Welshman in Berlin." 42–43, 52. Interview with Brynmore Jones on his experience scoring films in Germany.

Fischer, Dennis. "Bernard Herrmann: Director Larry Cohen Talks about His Late Friend." 44–47.

"James Horner's Melbourne Seminar." 48–52. Interview transcribed by Andrew Knipe, part 2.

Kremer, Jörg. "An Interview with Gary Guttman." 53–56. On writing music for film studio theme parks.

"The Society for the Preservation of Film Music: A Conversation with William Rosar." 57–59, 62–63. Interview with Randall D. Larson (uncredited).

11:44 (December 1992)

Cavanagh, Darren. "Scoring *Wind*." 3. Interview with Basil Poledouris.

Cavanagh, Darren, and Paul Andrew MacLean. "A Conversation with Basil Poledouris." 4–7.

Karban, Thomas. "An Interview with Laurence Rosenthal: *The Young Indiana Jones Chronicles*." 8–10. On music for the television series, excerpted from a longer interview published in German in *FM-Dienst*.

Büdinger, Matthias. "Russell Garcia: A Man for All Seasons." 18–21. Interview concerning his Hollywood career and his relationships with other film music composers.

Merluzeau, Yann. "A Filmography of James Newton Howard." 22–24.

Bergamino, Gianni, and Dimitri Riccio. "Meeting Ennio Morricone Again." 25–27. Interview.

Büdinger, Matthias. "An Interview with Randy Miller." 28–29.

Doherty, Jim. "Herrmann, Sedares, and Koch International: A Coalescence of Vision." 30–31. Discusses conductor James Sedares's film music recordings.

12:45 (March 1993)

Mangodt, Daniel. "In the Shadow of Maurice Jarre." 4–8. Interview.

Büdinger, Matthias. "An Interview with Frank de Vol." 9–11.

Mangodt, Daniel. "A Filmography/Discography of Brian May." 16–17.

MacLean, Paul Andrew, and Darren Cavanagh. "A Conversation with Tim Boyle." 18–21. Interview with the recording engineer.

Larson, Randall D. "Scoring *Jennifer 8*: An Interview with Christopher Young." 25–26.

Blum, Gabriele. "Georges Delerue Remembered." 28–29. Comments from Bruce Beresford, Jack Clayton, Frederic Talgorn, and Fred Zinnemann.

Larson, Randall D. "Denmark: "Soren Hyldgaard Larsen." 30–31. Interview.

12:46 (June 1993)

MacLean, Paul Andrew. "The Society for the Preservation of Film Music's Tribute to Jerry Goldsmith." 4–7. Report.

Breyer, Wolfgang. "An Interview with Lalo Schifrin." 8–10.

Larson, Randall D. "Collector's Corner: The Story behind Alhambra Records." 14–15. Company profile.

Larson, Randall D. "A Conversation with Gerard Schurmann." 22–24. Interview.

Van de Ven, Luc. "Everything You Always Wanted to Know about Producing a Film Soundtrack...But Were Afraid to Ask." 25–31.

12:47 (September 1993)

Larson, Randall D. "Remembering David Kraft." 3.

Merluzeau, Yann. "An Interview with John Williams." 4–9.

de Klerk, Theo. "Barry Gray: Music with Strings." 10–13. Profile of the British composer, with discography, 17–18.

Larson, Randall D. "Barry Gray." 14–16. Previously unpublished interview from 1982, includes discussion of his use of electronics.

Fake, Douglass. "Murphy's Law." 20–21. On Intrada soundtracks, including the production and budget.

"A Filmography/Discography of Jerry Goldsmith." 22–42. Updated by Daniel Mangodt and Luc Van de Ven.

Vail, James B. "Alf Clausen and *The Simpsons*." 57–59. Interview.

Kremer, Jörg. "An Interview with Don Davis." 61–63.

12:48 (December 1993)

Büdinger, Matthias. "Interviewing Mister [Hans] Zimmer." 4–7.

Deutsch, Didier. "Danny Elfman." Interview. 8–10.

Mangodt, Daniel, and Luc Van de Ven. "The Society for the Preservation of Film Music: An Interview with Jeannie Pool." 14–16.

Neckebroeck, Kjell. "James Horner Tryptych [*sic*]." 16–17. Article on *Once Upon a Forest*, *In Country*, and *Project X*.

Mangodt, Daniel. "The Flanders International Film Festival—Ghent." 20–22. Report.

Larson, Randall D. "An Interview with John Cacavas." 26–27.

Mangodt, Daniel, and Luc Van de Ven. "Elmer Bernstein." 28–30. Interview, part 1.

13:49 (March 1994)

Mangodt, Daniel. "David Raksin." 4–7. Interview.

Mangodt, Daniel, and Luc Van de Ven. "Elmer Bernstein." 8–10. Interview, part 2.

Mangodt, Daniel, and Luc Van de Ven. "Pino Donaggio." 14–15. Interview.

Larson, Randall D. "*When the Whales Came*: An Interview with Christopher Gunning." 16–17.

Van de Ven, Luc. "Everything You Always Wanted to Know about Publishing a Fanzine...But Were Too Terrified to Ask." 26–29.

Henderson, Kirk. "Alex North's *2001* and Beyond." 30–31. An insider's view on the similarities between the situation Bill Conti faced for *The Right Stuff* and North faced for *2001: A Space Odyssey*.

13:50 (June 1994)

Büdinger, Matthias. "Once Upon a Time in America." 4–9. Report on the Film Music Society's third annual international film music conference in Los Angeles.

Blumenthal, Philippe. "An Interview with Robert Folk." 11–16.

Breyer, Wolfgang. "A Conversation with Akira Ifukube." 20–23. Interview topics include Japanese film music.

Büdinger, Matthias. "Henry Mancini." 24–26. Article.

Raynes, Doug. "A Filmography/Discography of Miklos Rozsa." 34–56.

"A Fistful of Soundtracks!...A Handful of Quotes." 60–63. Reprinted composer quotations from the first 50 issues.

13:51 (September 1994)

Büdinger, Matthias. "Henry Mancini Remembered." 3.

Blumenthal, Philippe. "An Interview with Bruce Broughton." 4–10.

Mansell, John. "David Whitaker." 11–13. Interview.

Schecter, David. "An Interview with Nick Redman." 16–21. The soundtrack producer discusses his job at Fox and the "Len Engel Collection" of film scores on open-reel tapes, part 1.

Büdinger, Matthias. "An Afternoon with Tony Thomas." 25–27. Interview, part 1.

Mansell, John. "A Hoosier in Hollywood: A Look at the Background of Composer George Duning." 28–29. Interview-based profile.

Büdinger, Matthias. "Ravel, Mahler, and Other Film Composers..." 30. Classical music in films.

13:52 (December 1994)

Mansell, John. "Trevor Jones: Scoring *Hideaway*." 4–5. Report on the recording of the score.

Mangodt, Daniel. "An Interview with Barrington Pheloung." 6–8.

Schecter, David. "An Interview with Nick Redman." 14–18. On Bay Cities and other topics, part 2.

Mangodt, Daniel. "Music Is My Life: An Interview with Fred Karlin." 19–21.

Büdinger, Matthias. "An Afternoon with Tony Thomas." 22–24. Part 2.

Mansell, John. "Creating Footsteps: An Interview with Patrick Doyle." 28–30.

Mangodt, Daniel. "Learning about Film Music at the Flanders International Film Festival—Ghent." 31. Report.

14:53 (March 1995)
Büdinger, Matthias. "Returning to David Shire." 4–7. Interview.
Hirsch, David. "Ken Wannberg Has No Regrets." 8–10. Interview with the music editor and sometime composer.
Neckebroeck, Kjell. "Alan Silvestri's Lego Set." 14–15.
Mansell, John. "Francesco de Masi." 25–27. Interview.
Larson, Randall D. "Music for Japanese Animation: Interview with Hiroshi Miyagawa." 28–31.

14:54 (June 1995)
Mansell, John. "Talking to Trevor Jones." 4–7. Interview-based article.
Hirsch, David. "Temp Track: Whither Film Music?" 8–9. Part 1. Article based on interviews with Don Davis, Joel Goldsmith, John Scott, and Ken Wannberg.
Larson, Randall D. "An Interview with Leonard Salzedo." 10–13. With filmography.
Neckebroeck, Kjell. "A Buff's Blues." 18–19. Editorial on soundtrack recordings.
Neckebroeck, Kjell. "Honey, I Shrunk the Score." 20–22. On James Horner's score for *Honey, I Shrunk the Kids*.
MacMillan, James. "A Filmography/Discography of Elmer Bernstein." 23–41.
Hirsch, David. "Joel Goldsmith: The Son Also Rises." 44–51. Interview.
Larson, Randall D. "Specialty Film Music Labels." 60–64. Survey of producers of soundtrack recordings.

14:55 (September 1995)
Breyer, Wolfgang. "Interview with Leonard Rosenman." 4–7. Part 1.
Doherty, Jim. "'We're Not Doing Linoleum': The Ongoing Bernard Herrmann Renaissance." 8–9.
Wendler, Edwin. "Film + Musik: A Film Music Symposium in Vienna." 10–11. Report.
Feigelson, Roger. "Crossfade." 12–13. On bootleg soundtrack recordings.
Hirsch, David. "Whither Film Music?" 25–27. Part 2. Article based on an interview with Richard Band on the history of film scoring.
Raynes, Doug. "In Memory of Miklos Rozsa." 28–29.
Mansell, John. "Original Ideas: An Interview with Franco Micalizzi." 30–31.

14:56 (December 1995)
Mangodt, Daniel. "Interview with Leonard Rosenman." 4–5. Part 2.
Mangodt, Daniel. "Listening to Movies." 6–7. Report on the third Film Music Workshop during the 1995 Flanders festival.
Neckebroeck, Kjell. "Christopher Young's *Species*." 8–11. With an interview excerpted from Peter Kelly's radio program SilverScore.
Hirsch, David. "Temp Track: Expect the Unexpected." 25–27. On reviewing soundtracks, particularly those of James Horner and Christopher Young.
Mansell, John. "Laurie Johnson." 28–30. Interview.
Reynolds, Robert D. "Max Steiner Re-Visited." 31. An appreciation.

15:57 (March 1996)
Breyer, Wolfgang. "Interview with Alan Menken." 4–6. Regarding his scores for Disney animated features.
Hirsch, David. "Temp Track: Preserving Film Music." 6–7. On bootleg soundtracks.
Breyer, Wolfgang. "A Conversation with Toru Takemitsu." 8–9. Interview.
Walker, Mark. "The Agony and the Ecstasy." 9–10. On the process of preparing his *Film Music Good CD Guide*.

Reynolds, Robert D. "Dimitri Tiomkin." 11. Profile.

Neckebroeck, Kjell. "Basil Poledouris's *White Fang*." 12–15. Article.

Feigelson, Roger. "Crossfade." 16. On Internet sites.

Kelly, Peter. "Silverscore." 29–30. David Arnold radio interview excerpt.

15:58 (June 1996)

Mangodt, Daniel, and Luc Van de Ven. "Bruce Broughton." 4–7. Interview.

Larson, Randall D. "Don Banks: A Profile." 12–13. With filmography.

Büdinger, Matthias. "Louis Kaufman: A Legendary Concertmaster in Hollywood." 14–16. Interview with the studio musician and violinist.

Larson, Randall D. "The Horror Film Music of Les Baxter." 17–20. Interview, with filmography.

Mangodt, Daniel. "John Barry." 21–23. Interview.

Mangodt, Daniel. "Leslie Bricusse." 24–25. Interview.

Delélée, Cédric. "Basil Poledouris." 26–31. Filmography/discography.

Hirsch, David. "Temp Track: Carl Davis' *City Lights*." 32–34. Interview.

Mangodt, Daniel. "Cinemusic International Music and Film Festival." 35. Report.

Büdinger, Matthias. "Marvin Hamlisch: The Way He Was." 44–45. Profile.

Walker, Mark. "Something Old, Something New." 46–47. On plagiarism.

Mansell, John. "The James Bernard Dossier." 48–53. Interview-based article.

Larson, Randall D. "James Bernard's *Nosferatu*." 54–56. Interview.

Hirsch, David. "Fred Karlin on Making the Film Music Masters Video Series." 57–59. Interview regarding his documentaries on Jerry Goldsmith and Elmer Bernstein.

Ruf, Patrick. "David Raksin." 60–63. Interview.

15:59 (September 1996)

Neckebroeck, Kjell. "Georges Delerue's *Joe Versus the Volcano*." 12–14.

Mangodt, Daniel. "The British and American Film Music Festival at the Royal Academy of Music." 15.

Buchsbaum, Tony. "A Conversation with David Arnold." 25–27. Interview.

Mansell, John. "A Performer, Not a Star." 30–31. Interview with Ennio Morricone's guitarist, Alessandro Alessandroni.

15:60 (December 1996)

Feigelson, Roger. "Crossfade." 3. On *CinemaScore* magazine.

Mangodt, Daniel. "Interview with Michael Kamen." 4–7.

Walker, Mark. "The Myth of the Original Soundtrack." 12–13. On "original" and new soundtracks.

Mangodt, Daniel. "Maurice Jarre." 21–23. Interview.

Larson, Randall D. "The Society for the Preservation of Film Music Conference Report." 24–26.

Larson, Randall D. "Michael Cimino: On Working with Maurice Jarre." 27. Transcript of remarks made at the 1996 SPFM conference.

Rusz, István. "Bootlegs? What Bootlegs?" 28–29.

Neckebroeck, Kjell. "Prime Examples of the 90s Action Score." 30–31. On the use of electronics and synthesizers, particularly by Hans Zimmer.

16:61 (March 1997)

Büdinger, Matthias. "Is Life Possible Without Film Music?" 3. Editorial.

Szebin, Frederick C., and Steve Biodrowski. "Interview with Danny Elfman." 4–7.

Neckebroeck, Kjell. "*Falling Down*." 12–15. On James Newton Howard's score.

Feigelson, Roger. "Crossfade." 22. Best of 1996.

Hirsch, David. "Temp Track: The Good, the Bad and the Boxed Set." 24.

Neckebroeck, Kjell. "The Myth of the Original Soundtrack: The Sequel." 25–27.
Larson, Randall D. "*Star Trek: Deep Space Nine*: Trials and Tribble-lations: Dennis McCarthy's Score for *Deep Space Nine*'s Return to the Enterprise." 28–31. Interview.

16:62 (June 1997)
Van de Ven, Luc. "Daniel Mangodt 1950–1977." 3. Remembering *Soundtrack*'s publisher.
Buchsbaum, Tony. "A Conversation with Composer Alan Menken." 4–5.
Mangodt, Daniel. "Film Music Archives at the Brigham Young University: Interview with James V. D'Arc." 13–17. The archivist discusses the BYU holdings, particularly the Max Steiner and Hugo Friedhofer collections.
Van de Ven, Luc. "The Good, the Bad and the Cranky." 18–19. The soundtrack dealer, on the conflict between his personal taste and his business interests.
Burlingame, Jon. "The Composer and His Director: A Workshop with Patrick Doyle and Régis Wargnier." 20.
Mangodt, Daniel. "Interview with Patrick Doyle." 21–22.
Piedesack, Gordon, and Jonathan Joseph. "Martin Böttcher." 23. Profile of the German-born film composer.
McClane, John. "The Secret Life of a Mailorder Dealer." 25–29. Interview with an anonymous dealer, primarily on selling bootlegs.
De Moor, John, and Gilles Loison. "François de Roubaix." 30–40. Filmography/discography.
Koppl, Rudy. "Christopher Franke: The New *Babylon 5*." 41–43. Interview.
Larson, Randall D. "*Hollywood Reporter* Film and TV Music Conference." 44–47. Report on the second annual conference.
Larson, Randall D. "Music in the Key of Nemo: Mark Snow and *20,000 Leagues under the Sea*." 48–52. Interview regarding the ABC television miniseries.
Russ, Steve. "Interview with John Steven Lasher." 60–62. The soundtrack producer discusses his Fifth Continent label and Bernard Herrmann.
Larson, Randall D. "Brian May: Road Warrior." 63. Remembrance.

16:63 (September 1997)
Larson, Randall D., and John W. Morgan "Tony Thomas Remembered." 3.
Larson, Randall D. "Catching Up with Mark Isham." 4–6. Interview.
Larson, Randall D. "Music for Mother Earth: Cliff Eidelman's *Free Willy 3*." 12–13. Interview.
Larson, Randall D. "Robert Folk: *Nothing to Lose*." 14–15. Interview.
Larson, Randall D. "Basil Poledouris on *Starship Troopers*." 16–17. Interview.
Larson, Randall D. "Making *Contact* with Alan Silvestri." 18–19. Interview.
Buchsbaum, Tony. "A Conversation with Alan Silvestri." 20–21. Interview.
Bordowitz, Hank. "David Newman: *Out to Sea*." 21. Interview.
Fake, Douglass C. "Projects that Fell Through." 25.
Koppl, Rudy. "John Scott: Interview with an English Gentleman." 28–31.

16:64 (December 1997)
Koppl, Rudy. "Basil Poledouris: A Man and His Music." 4–13. Interview, includes sidebars with director's interviews.
Woolston, Stephen. "Re-Discovering John Barry." 18–19.
Larson, Randall D. "Joel the Conqueror: Joel Goldsmith." 20–21. Interview.
Larson, Randall D. "Christopher Young: *The Man Who Knew Too Little*." 22–23. Interview.
Larson, Randall D. "Peter Bernstein and *Rough Riders*." 24. Interview.
Koppl, Rudy. "Mark McKenzie: *The Disappearance of Garcia Lorca*." 25. Interview.

Larson, Randall D. "John Debney: *I Know What You Did Last Summer*." 26–27. Interview.

Larson, Randall D. "Lee Holdridge: *The Long Way Home*." 27. Interview.

Neckebroeck, Kjell. "*Blown Away*: Score Analysis." 28–29. On Alan Silvestri's score.

Schweiger, Daniel. "Scoring, Not Sinking: Composer James Horner Steers His Way through *Titanic*'s Troubled Waters." 30–34. Interview.

Hirsch, David, and Roger Feigelson. "The Lost Boys." 40–42. Part 1, on Bruce Broughton, John Scott, Frederic Talgorn, and Christopher Young.

Larson, Randall D. "James Newton Howard: *Devil's Advocate*?" 44–46. Interview.

17:65 (March 1998)

Woolston, Stephen. "The Music of the Bruce Lee films." 3. On music by Joseph Koo and others.

Schweiger, Daniel. "Composer John Barry." 4–8. Interview.

Larson, Randall D. "Film Scoring with Robert Folk." 14–16. Interview.

Neckebroeck, Kjell. "Trevor Jones' *Loch Ness*." 18–21. Article.

Larson, Randall D. "David Michael Frank." 22–24. Interview.

Fake, Douglass. "Scoring *Holly vs. Hollywood*." 25. On his score for the film.

Koppl, Rudy. "The Film Music of Ernest Troost." 26–27. Interview.

Larson, Randall D. "David Amram." 28–29. Interview.

Larson, Randall D. "David Arnold Saves the World." 30–33. Interview.

Hirsch, David, and Roger Feigelson. "The Lost Boys." 38–43. Part 2, on Richard Band, Joel Goldsmith, Hummie Mann, Dennis McCarthy, Joel McNeely, Laurence Rosenthal, Arthur B. Rubinstein, and Craig Safan.

Koppl, Rudy. "Michael J. Lewis: The Great Welshman Commeth." 44–47. Part 1.

17:66 (June 1998)

Hirsch, David. "Temp Tracks: Ryko Speaks Before Going Silent!" 4–7. Interview with Ian Gilcrest.

Ruf, Patrick. "John Debney." 8–11. Interview.

Larson, Randall D. "Exchanging Bytes with Joel McNeely." 16–17. Interview.

Larson, Randall D. "Mark Snow: Scoring the *X-Files* Movie." 24–25. Interview.

Larson, Randall D. "Alf Clausen: On Scoring *The Simpsons* and *Half-Baked*." 26–28. Interview.

Buchsbaum, Tony. "Restoring *Close Encounters*." 29. Interview with filmmaker Laurent Bouzereau.

Larson, Randall D. "Joel McNeely on *Wild America* and *The Avengers*." 30.

Koppl, Rudy. "Ray Colcord: Scoring *Heartwood*." 32–33. Interview.

Larson, Randall D. "*Lost in Space* with Bruce Broughton." 34–37. Interview.

Koppl, Rudy. "Michael J. Lewis: The Great Welshman Cometh." 38–41. Part 2.

Bender, John. "Bava and Savina Render Death Exquisite." 42–43. On Carlo Savina's score for *Lisa and the Devil* (1975).

Larson, Randall D. "Shirley Walker's Ballsy Film Music." 44–48. Interview.

17:67 (September 1998)

Pavelek, James. "Miklos Rozsa." 5–9. 1977 Interview, part 1.

Kaufman, Jeff. "Day In and Day Out: The World According to a Film Music Agent." 10–11. Part 1.

Larson, Randall D. "Scoring Comedy with Craig Safan." 22–24. Interview.

Thaxton, Ford A. "Michael Kamen: Scoring *Lethal Weapon IV*." 24–26. Interview.

Larson, Randall D. "John Frizzell." 32–34. Interview.

Larson, Randall D. "Edward Shearmur." 34–36. Interview.

Walmsley, Simon. "Cinesonic Conference 1998." 37. Report on the first conference in Australia.

Van de Ven, Luc. "Projects that Fell Through." 38–39. On his experiences issuing soundtracks.

Koppl, Rudy. "John Ottman: The Wizard of Light and Sound." 46–51. Interview.

17:68 (Winter 1998–1999)

Rusz, Istvan. "Plagiarism? Give It a Rest." 4–6. Editorial.

Doherty, Jim. "Albert Glasser (1914–1998)." 7.

Broxton, Jonathan. "Debbie Wiseman Visits *Tom's Midnight Garden*." 8–9. Interview.

Pavelek, James. "Miklos Rozsa." 21–25. 1977 interview, part 2.

Kaufman, Jeff. "Day In and Day Out: The World According to a Film Music Agent." 34–35. Part 2.

Larson, Randall D. "Basil Poledouris: Looking Back on *Lonesome Dove*." 36–37. Interview regarding the music for the 1989 television miniseries.

Larson, Randall D. "Bill Whelan: *Dancing at Lughnasa*." 37–38. Interview.

Koppl, Rudy. "Mark Mancina: The Real Thing." 44–47. Interview.

Larson, Randall D. "Music for Atom Bombs: William Stromberg and John Morgan on *Trinity and Beyond*." 51. Interview-based article.

Larson, Randall D. "Catching Up with Christopher Young." 52–53. Interview.

Koppl, Rudy. "Trevor Rabin: *Armegeddon* and *Enemy of the State*." 56–59. Interview.

18:69 (Spring 1999)

Larson, Randall D. "Don Davis in *The Matrix*." 4–6. Interview.

Larson, Randall D. "James Bernard's Universal Horrors." 6. On music for the television documentary.

Kaufman, Jeff. "Day In and Day Out: The World According to a Film Music Agent." 9–10. Part 3.

Larson, Randall D. "John Debney." 11–12. Interview.

Kester, Gary. "'J.G. Confidential': A 70th Birthday Look Back at the Jerry Goldsmith Enigma." 23–28.

Fake, Douglass. "Jerry Goldsmith: Congratulations." 30.

Kester, Gary. "Jerry Goldsmith and *Lonely Are the Brave*." 35–37.

Townson, Robert. "Jerry Goldsmith at 70." 38–39.

Van de Ven, Luc. "Jerry Goldsmith Filmography, 1993–1999." 40–45.

Büdinger, Matthias. "A Patch of Goldsmith: An Appreciation in Honor of Jerry Goldsmith's 70th Birthday." 46–48.

Burbella, Ron. "Breakfast with Jerry Goldsmith." 49–51.

Larson, Randall D. "Joel McNeely's Infectious Music for *Virus*." 55. Interview.

Thaxton, Ford, and Randall D. Larson. "Barrington Pheloung." 60–61. Interview.

Smith, Jack. "The Golden Age." 62–63. Best new soundtrack releases.

18:70 (Summer 1999)

Dyer, Richard. "John Williams: Scoring *Star Wars: Episode I - The Phantom Menace*." 4–6.

Thaxton, Ford A. "Music Editor Ken Wannberg: *Star Wars Episode One: The Phantom Menace*." 8–9. Interview.

"John Williams: Scoring *The Phantom Menace*." 10–13. Media interview.

Kaufman, Jeff. "Day In and Day Out: The World According to a Film Music Agent." 14–15. Part 4.

Woolston, Stephen. "James Fitzpatrick on the Art of Reconstruction." 16–17. Interview.

Koppl, Rudy. "Composer Michael Hoenig: Television Scoring on the Cutting Edge." 22–25. Interview.

Koppl, Rudy. "George Clinton and the *Austin Powers* Phenomenon." 26–28. Interview.

Landry, Christopher. "Revisiting *Nineteen Eighty-Four*: An Interview with Dominic Muldowney." 40–41.

Thaxton, Ford A. "Gerald Fried on Stanley Kubrick." 42–43. Interview.

Thaxton, Ford A. "John Corigliano: *The Red Violin*." 46–47. Interview.

Broxton, Jonathan, and James Southall. "The Mighty Trevor Jones." 54–58. Interview.

18:71 (Fall 1999)
Koppl, Rudy. "Ears Wide Open: Jocelyn Pook Scoring Kubrick's *Eyes Wide Shut*." 4–7. Interview.

Thaxton, Ford A. "Michael Kamen Versus *The Iron Giant*." 10–11. Interview.

Larson, Randall D. "Discography of Hitchcock Films." 18–19.

Thaxton, Ford A. "*The Blair Witch Project*: Making a Soundtrack Where No Soundtrack Existed." 20. Interview with music supervisor Randy Gerston.

Larson, Randall D. "Mark Isham's *October Sky*." 22–24. Interview.

Koppl, Rudy. "From Shakespeare to Comic Book Super Heroes: The Flexibility of Film Scoring: Scoring *The Mystery Men* with Composer Steven Warbeck and Director Kinka Usher." 29–33. Interview with Stephen Warbeck.

Koppl, Rudy. "Additional Music by Shirley Walker: Rescoring the Changes to *Mystery Men*." 31.

Koppl, Rudy. "*Mystery Men*'s Director Kinka Usher." 33. Interview.

Koppl, Rudy. "Back to School with John Frizzell." 42–44. Interview. On scoring *Teaching Mrs. Tingle*.

Koppl, Rudy. "Director Kevin Williamson: On Working with John Frizzell." 45. Interview.

Kaufman, Jeff. "Day In and Day Out: The World According to a Film Music Agent." 46–47. Part 5.

Buchsbaum, Tony. "A Conversation with Bill Conti." 48–50. On scoring *The Thomas Crown Affair* remake.

18:72 (Winter 1999)
Thaxton, Ford A. "Don Davis on *House on Haunted Hill*." 4–5. Interview.

Kaufman, Jeff. "Day In and Day Out: The World According to a Film Music Agent." 6–7. Part 6.

Larson, Randall D. "Danny Elfman on *Sleepy Hollow*." 8–10.

Koppl, Rudy. "[John] Debney on *End of Days*." 23–27. Interview.

Koppl, Rudy. "Hyams on Debney." 28. Director Peter Hyams on John Debney.

Koppl, Rudy. "Entering the Eye of *The Hurricane*." 31–36. Interview with Christopher Young.

Mansell, John. "Unlocking the Vaults of Horror: A Conversation with G.D.I. Records." 44–45. Interview with Gary Wilson regarding releasing James Bernard's music for Hammer films.

Wickenden, Dirk. "*Commando*: Arnold Rocks to [James] Horner's Beat." 46–49. Article.

Buedinger, Matthias. "The Golden Age: Dimitri Tiomkin's 100th Birthday—Plus 5." 50–51. Guest column.

Feigelson, Roger. "If It's Not One Thing, It's Another..." 52–53. A brief history of how union reuse fees have affected soundtrack releases.

Larson, Randall D. "Mark Snow on *Harsh Realm*, *X-Files* and *Crazy in Alabama*." 54–56. Interview.

Broxton, Jonathan. "Patrick Doyle: Lost and Found." 57–59. Interview.

19:73 (Spring 2000)
Thaxton, Ford A. "Alan Silvestri: From *Stuart Little* to *Reindeer Games*." 4–5. Interview.

Thaxton, Ford A. "Rolfe Kent: A *Gun Shy* Composer." 6.

Buchsbaum, Tony. "Themes from *The Phantom Menace* and Other Film Hits." 10–11.

Thaxton, Ford A. "David Newman: *Galaxy Quest*." 18–19.

Larson, Randall D. "Contending with Larry Groupe." 20–21.

Leneker, Mark. "*Mission to Mars*: Scoring Session." 22–24.

Larson, Randall D. "*Mission to Mars*." 25.

Wickenden, Dirk. "The Golden Age of Movie Music." 26–27.

Koppl, Rudy. "Tuning in the Past to Change the Future: Scoring *Frequency*." 28–39.

Larson, Randall D. "Ernest Troost Enters the Beat Generation." 40.

Wickenden, Dirk. "Courageous Composer." 46–50. On the music of Alexander Courage, particularly his score for *Day of the Outlaw* (1959).

Broxton, Jonathan. "Simon Boswell: A Man Alone." 51–56.

Broxton, Jonathan. "1999: A Year in Review." 56–57.

Larson, Randall D. "Shirley Walker and *The Others*." 58.

19:74 (Summer 2000)

Thaxton, Ford A. "Underwater with Rick Marvin." 4–6.

Larson, Randall D. "Remembering George Duning." 7.

Larson, Randall D. "The Fantasy Film Music of George Duning." 7–9.

Larson, Randall D. "*Mission: Impossible 2*." 10.

Thaxton, Ford A. "Ryuichi Sakamoto." 18–19.

Southall, James. "Jerry Goldsmith at Barbican Centre." 20–22.

Koppl, Rudy. "Lalo Schifrin: Creating *Mission: Impossible*." 27–33.

Koppl, Rudy. "Hans Zimmer's Balancing Act: Scoring *M:I-2*." 34–35.

Larson, Randall D. "Danny Elfman: Expecting the Impossible." 36–37.

Koppl, Rudy. "Making It Rock." 38–39.

Thaxton, Ford A., and Randall D. Larson. "*Mission: Impossible*: Composer Alan Silvestri Disavowed." 39. Danny Elfman rescored the film.

Wickenden, Dirk. "Home Is Where the Heart Is: A Conversation with Mike Ross-Trevor." 40–47.

Larson, Randall D. "Patrick Williams: *Jesus and the Three Stooges*." 48–50.

19:75 (Fall 2000)

Larson, Randall D. "Mark McKenzie Confronts *Dragonheart II*." 4–5. Interview regarding *Dragonheart: A New Beginning*.

Azevedo, Daniel. "Normality with Irony: The Music of Ennio Morricone." 12–22. Part 1.

Buchsbaum, Tony. "Joe Kraemer's Score for *The Way of the Gun*." 23. Interview-based article.

Koppl, Rudy. "Inside *The Cell* with Composer Howard Shore and Director Tarsem Dhandwar." 24–27. Interviews.

Wickenden, Dirk. "A Simple Twist of Cliff Eidelman." 28–29. Article.

Hall, Roger. "Tip to Moviegoers: Take Off Those Earmuffs! Aaron Copland Talks about Film Music." 30–31. 1980 interview.

Neckebroeck, Kjell. "*Squanto*, The Last Great Warrior." 32, 47. Retrospective article and analysis of Joel McNeely's score.

Koppl, Rudy. "*What Lies Beneath*: The Supernatural Thrills of Alan Silvestri with Director Robert Zemeckis." 33–42. Interviews.

19:76 (Winter 2000)

Berkwits, Jeff. "Graeme Revell Journeys to *Dune*." 4–6.

Azevedo, Daniel. "Normality with Irony: The Music of Ennio Morricone, Part 2." 7–11.

Woolston, Stephen. "Preserving the Legacy of John Barry." 12–15.

Woolston, Stephen. "CD Micro Breweries Part 1: Fanderson Records." 16–17.

Hirsch, David. "*Supercar/Fireball XL-5.*" 17–18.
Hirsch, David. "*Space: 1999.*" 18. The first two years.
Koppl, Rudy. "Going to the *Vertical Limit.*" 19–27.
Thaxton, Ford A. "*Batman Beyond.*" 32–34.
Southall, James. "*Amanda.*" 35.
Koppl, Rudy A. "Dracula for the Millennium: Marco Beltrami Scoring *DK2.*" 45–50.
Wickenden, Dirk. "The Golden Age." 51–53.
Larson, Randall D. "*X-Files* Season VIII Music by Mark Snow." 54–56.
Larson, Randall D. "*Judas Kiss.*" 59–60.
Larson, Randall D. "*Highlander: Endgame.*" 60.
Larson, Randall D. "The Music of *Bagger Vance.*" 61–63.

20:77 (Spring 2001)
Thaxton, Ford A. "Hans Zimmer." 4–7.
Hirsch, David. "Film Score Monthly." 8–11.
Larson, Randall D. "Harry Manfredini Returns to *Friday the 13th.*" 12–14.
Wickenden, Dirk. "The Golden Age." 15–17.
Thaxton, Ford A. "*Crouching Tiger, Hidden Dragon.*" 18–19. On Tan Dun's music.
Koppl, Rudy. "*Enemy at the Gates.*" 27–41.
Koppl, Rudy. "Jean-Jacques Annaud." 41–42.

20:78 (Summer 2001)
Thaxton, Ford A. "Scoring Session: Graeme Revell: *Lara Croft Tomb Raider.*" 4–6.
    Interview.
White, Dave. "A Show of Hans: On Stage in Ghent: On *Lion King, Thin Red Line*, and
    Pearl Harbor." 8–11. Interview with Hans Zimmer.
Hall, Roger L. "The Magnificent One: 50 Years of Elmer Bernstein Film Scores." 12–13.
    Interview.
Koppl, Rudy. "The Behemoth Arise: Don Davis Scores *Jurassic Park III.*" 21–24, 29–31.
    Interviews with Davis and director Joe Johnston.
Wickenden, Dirk. "The Golden Age: Music by Van Cleave." 36–39. Profile.
Buchsbaum, Tony. "IMAX Film Scores: Composer Nigel Westlake, Director John
    Weiley, and *Solarmax.*" 42–45. Interview.
Larson, Randall D. "Christopher Young on *Swordfish.*" 48–50. Interview.

20:79 (Fall 2001)
Thaxton, Ford A. "Scoring Session: Danny Elfman Revisits the *Planet of the Apes.*" 4–6.
    Interview, transcribed and edited by Randall D. Larson.
·Thaxton, Ford A. "Lalo Schifrin on Scoring *Rush Hour 2.*" 6–7. Interview, transcribed
    and edited by Randall D. Larson.
Thaxton, Ford A. "Bombs and Romance: Hans Zimmer Invades *Pearl Harbor.*" 12. In-
    terview, transcribed and edited by Randall D. Larson.
Koppl, Rudy. "The Wings of Hans Zimmer: Music in the Key of Film." 13.
Thaxton, Ford A. "John Green: Film Music in the Extended Form." 14–17. Interview in
    1980.
Thaxton, Ford A. "Elliot Goldenthal's *Final Fantasy.*" 26–27. Interview, transcribed and
    edited by Randall D. Larson.
Larson, Randall D. "Media Bytes: Soundtracks: State of the Market: Robert Townson and
    Varese Sarabande Records." 28–30. Interview.
Thaxton, Ford A. "The Book Closes on Chapter III Records." 30.
Wickenden, Dirk. "The Golden Age: Alexander Courage: The Story of His Life." 36–41.
    Interview.
Larson, Randall D. "Lee Holdridge: Enhancing the *Mists of Avalon.*" 42–43. Interview.

Thaxton, Ford A. "The *Enigma* of John Barry." 44–46. Interview, transcribed and edited by Randall D. Larson.

20:80 (Winter 2001)
Thaxton, Ford A. "Scoring Session: *Zoolander* and *The Musketeer*: Catching Up with David Arnold." 4–7. Interview, transcribed and edited by Randall D. Larson.
Larson, Randall D. "Nott's Nice Music: Julian Nott Interviewed by Randall D. Larson." 8–10. On writing for Aardman Animation projects and British television.
Buchsbaum, Tony. "That's All Folks! Cartoon Songs from Merrie Melodies and Looney Tunes." 13.
Richter, Peter. "DVD: The Isolated Score: A Threat to the Soundtrack Album?" 16.
Koppl, Rudy. "The Emotional Touch: James Horner Scores *A Beautiful Mind*." 21–29. Interviews with Horner, director Ron Howard, and producer Brian Grazer.
Koppl, Rudy. "*The Lord of the Rings: The Fellowship of the Ring*: Composer Howard Shore Visits Middle-Earth." 28–37. Interviews with Shore and director Peter Jackson.
Larson, Randall D. "That 'Other' Williams: The Film Music by Alan Williams." 42–43. Interview.

21:81 (Spring 2002)
Koppl, Rudy. "On the Edge of Madness: Marco Beltrami Scores the Sci-Fi Cinematic Blood Fest *Blade II*." 4–8. Interview with Beltrami and director Guillermo del Toro.
Hall, Roger. "Bernard Herrmann: The Early Years." 9–11. An appreciation.
Thaxton, Ford A. "Scoring Session: Performing *Iris* Violinist Joshua Bell." 12. Interview, transcribed and edited by Randall D. Larson.
Thaxton, Ford A. "Scoring Session: Craig Armstrong." 13–14. Interview, transcribed and edited by Randall D. Larson.
Koppl, Rudy. "*Return to Never Land*: Joel McNeely's Symphonic Rebirth of Peter Pan." 20–27. Interview.
Koppl, Rudy. "IMAX Film Scores: The Western Wonder: Sam Cardon's IMAX Career." 40–43. Interview.

21:82 (Summer 2002)
Larson, Randall D. "Scoring Session: John Ottman: *Eight-Legged Freaks*." 4–7. Interview.
Cutter, Chris. "Onto the Action-Adventure Scoring Battlefield with Danny Elfman: *Spider-Man* and *Men in Black II*." 12–19. Interview.
Koppl, Rudy. "John Debney's Sword and Sorcery Spectacular." 20–27. Interview with Debney and director Chuck Russell regarding the score for *The Scorpion King*.
Wickenden, Dirk. "The Golden Age: Franz Waxman." 28–33. With comments from Waxman's son, John.
Larson, Randall D. "A New Enterprise for Dennis McCarthy." 42–44. Interview.
Hirsch, David. "Temp-track: Classic Japanese Sci-Fi, Fantasy, and Horror Scores. Part 1: 1954–1959." 45–47.

21:83 (Fall 2002)
Larson, Randall D. "Klaus Badelt." 4–7. Interview.
Larson, Randall D. "Scoring Session: Edward Shearmur." 8–11. Interview regarding his score for *Reign of Fire*.
Larson, Randall D. "'Scoring Session: Making It More Purple': The Film Music of Jeff Danna." 17–19. Interview.
Larson, Randall D. "Media Bytes: Screen Archives and Soundtrack Preservation." 20–21. Interview with Craig Spaulding.

Larson, Randall D. "*Iron Monkey* Versus MoJo Jojo: The Animated James Venable." 22–25. Interview.

Larson, Randall D. "The Film Music of Mychael Danna." 32–35. Interview.

Hirsch, David. "Temp-track: Classic Japanese Sci-Fi, Fantasy, and Horror Scores. Part 2: 1960–1965." 36–37.

Marshall, Greg. "Classical Guitarist John Williams." 38–41. Interview.

Larson, Randall D. "Fear and Laughter: The Film Music World of John Frizzell." 42–45. Interview.

Koppl, Rudy. "Going *Ballistic*: The Electronica of Don Davis." 51–54. Interview.

21:84 (Winter 2002)

Larson, Randall D. "Scoring Session: Christopher Young's Journey to the Center of *The Core*." 5–7. Interview.

Thaxton, Ford A. "Scoring Session: William Ross: Rising to the Occasion Adapting John Williams for *Harry Potter and the Chamber of Secrets*." 8–9. Interview.

Hall, Roger. "Dimitri Tiomkin's Golden Decade." 18–20. 1948–1958.

Cutter, Chris. "The Tricky Twisted World of *Red Dragon* with Danny Elfman." 21–24. Interview.

Koppl, Rudy. "*The Lord of the Rings: The Two Towers*: Climbing into Darkness: Scoring *The Two Towers* with Howard Shore." 31–37. Interviews with the composer, director Peter Jackson, and music editor Michael Price.

Larson, Randall D. "Christopher Lennertz: *Saint Sinner*." 40–41. Interview.

Wickenden, Dirk. "The Golden Age." 42–47. Interview-based article on Elmer Bernstein.

The Swiss Film Music Society Newsletter (Switzerland)

Published a German-language newsletter beginning in 1993 and a journal, *Das Fachmagazin für Filmmusik*, that includes some material in English. Editor Philippe Blumenthal cofounded the society.

Chapter 8

Composer Society Journals and Newsletters

ALBEDO: Vangelis International Appreciation Society (UK)
The international fan club, founded by Mark Griffin in 1997, published a newsletter edited by Griffin through at least 2000. Includes articles, interviews, news items, reviews, and letters.

No. 1 (1997)
Includes two reprinted interviews.

No. 2 (1997)
Includes a partial translation of a television interview, circa 1993, and an article on *Blade Runner* bootlegs.

No. 3 (April 1988)
Includes fan profiles, part 2 of a translated interview, circa 1993, a reprint of "Recording Vangelis," and an article by Mark Griffin on Vangelis reprinted from the *Record Collector*.

No. 4 (August 1998)
Includes a reprinted interview with Vangelis.

No. 5 (October 1998)
Includes a 1979 interview with Vangelis.

No. 6 (February–March 1998)
Includes interviews with Vangelis's engineer Frederick Rousseau.

No. 7 (October 1999)
Includes a corrected interview with Vangelis's engineer Frederick Rousseau.

No. 8 (circa December 1999)
Includes a transcription of an interview with Vangelis.

Bax Society Bulletin (UK)
Cronin, Kathleen. "[Arnold] Bax in the Modern Media." 1:4 (February 1969): 57–60.
Foreman, Ronald Lewis Edmund. "[Arnold] Bax and the Score of *Malta GC*." 2:8 (April 1970) 7–9. With music examples.

The Bernard Herrmann Society Journal (US)
Published by the Bernard Herrmann Society, established in 1981, in North Hollywood, California. Edited by Kevin Fahey. Includes articles on Herrmann, with material on other film composers and film music. Also referred to as the *Bernard Herrmann Journal*.

<u>Nos. 5–6 (Fall 1982)</u>
Harris, Steve. "An Afternoon with Bernard Herrmann." 16ff.

<u>No. 18 (198?)</u>
Daniel, Oliver. "A Perspective of Herrmann." 9–10. Reprinted from *Saturday Review* (1968).

<u>Nos. 28–29 (Winter 1989)</u>
Gray, Pat. "The Many Faces of Film Music." 1, 14. Herrmann interview reprinted from Bazelon, *Knowing the Score* (1975).
Gilling, Ted. "The Color of Music." 3–6, 14. Herrmann interview reprinted from *Sight and Sound* (Winter 1979).
Gilling, Ted. "The Player Lecture." 2, 7–13. Herrmann interviewed before a 1972 National Film Theater program.
Brown, Royal S. "Lots of Intuition." 2, 15–16. Herrmann interview reprinted from *High Fidelity* (September 1976).
Zador, Leslie, and Gregory Rose. "Herrmann at Home." 2, 17–31. Interview retranscribed from the original tapes for a 1970 interview in the *Los Angeles Free Press*.

The Bruce Broughton Society Journal (UK)
Published in Bridport, Dorset, by John Williams (not the composer), who also served as editor. Williams founded the society in 1992; Broughton served as honorary president. Contains news, scoring assignments, articles, interviews, and soundtrack reviews.

<u>No. 1 (May 1992) [Cover dated May, inside cover dated June]</u>
Hasan, Mark R. "An Analysis of Bruce Broughton's *Last Rites*." [4–7].
Cavanagh, Darren. "'I'm Just Doing It for the Fun': A Conversation with Bruce Broughton." [8–15]. Part 1.

Cantina Band (US)
Fan-based newsletter first published in 1987 by the John Williams Society in Los Angeles. The society was founded in France in 1989 by Yann Merluzeau to promote the composer's career and latest film scores. Contains news briefs, articles, and interviews.

<u>2:8 (July–August 1991)</u>
"A Conversation with Georges Delerue."

<u>2:9 (December 1992)</u>
Merluzeau, Yann. "John T. Williams: The Complete Work (to Date) from *Daddy-O* to *Jurassic Park*: A Filmography/Discography, Biography and Bibliography." 64 pp. Stand-alone issue sometimes referred to as *John Williams: The Complete Works*.

The Creel (UK)
Journal of the Friends of Alan Rawsthorne.

<u>1:4 (Spring 1991)</u>
Special film music section with an introduction and a list of Rawsthorne film scores.
Rawsthorne, Alan. "The Celluloid Plays a Tune." Reprinted from Peter Dickinson's *Twenty British Composers* (1975).
Belcher, John M. "Only Connect." See 1998 update, below.

<u>3:5 (Spring 1998)</u>
Cuckston, Alan. "*The Ladykillers*: Music from Those Glorious Ealing Films."
Lane, Philip. "Reconstructing Film Scores."
Belcher, John. "Only Connect: Alan Rawsthorne's Film Music in Context."

Belcher, John. "Rawsthorne Film Scores."

Dreams to Dreams (France)

Publication of the official James Horner Society, edited by Didier Lepretre. *Film Score Monthly* editor Lukas Kendall made no secret of his disdain for Horner's music, and the negative reviews, accusations of plagiarism, and Horner bashing in *FSM* were a catalyst for *Dreams to Dreams*. The first issue, in June 1995, is predominantly in French with some English translation. The subsequent issue was numbered vol. 2, no. 2 and was in English and French. Kjell Neckebroeck translated the French portions. Most of the contributors are Horner fans who discuss his music in broad, positive terms, often describing the drama and the music that accompanies it. Issues contain material on the latest Horner scores, upcoming projects, retrospectives of earlier scores, and soundtrack reviews. Interviews with other composers eventually found their way into the publication. By 1999 the magazine was published exclusively in French, had expanded its coverage, and had become the leading French magazine for film music, equivalent in size and substance to *Film Score Monthly*. Mark So published an unrelated newsletter, *The Horner Letter*, in Southern California.

Issue 1 (June 1995)
The first issue is the only one with the heading "Unofficial James Horner Society."

Issue 2 (December 1995)
Articles on *Casper, The Land Before Time,* and *Project X.* Interviews with directors Mel Gibson (*Braveheart*) and Ron Howard (*Apollo 13*).

Issue 3
Articles on *Jade* and *Star Trek II.* Interview with director William Friedkin (*Jade*).

Issue 4
Article on *Braveheart.* Interview with Luis Bacalov.

Issue 5
Article on *Willow.* Interviews with composer Jean-Claude Petit and Ron Howard (*Willow*).

Issue 6
Article on *Krull.* Interview with Alan Menken.

Issue 7 (Spring 1997)
Interviews with David Arnold, Maggie Boyle, Maurice Jarre, and Michael Kamen.

Issue 9 (Winter 1997–1998)
Interviews with John Debney, John Frizzell, Elliot Goldenthal, James Horner, Horner's bagpipe player Eric Rigler, and Mark Snow.

Erich Wolfgang Korngold Society Newsletter (UK)

The Korngold Society was formed by Brendan G. Carroll in 1982. Secretary/treasurer Konrad Hopkins and Carroll edited the newsletter, which consisted of editorial content, news, reviews, and a list of concert performances dubbed "Highlights of the Korngold Log."

No. 6 (January 1984). Includes "Korngold Raises Film Music to Its True Function in *Robin Hood*," by Joseph O'Sullivan, 10–12 [Originally appeared in the *Motion Picture Herald*, May 7, 1938]; "A Day on Stage Nine," on *The Adventures of Robin Hood* scoring session, by Rudy Behlmer, 12–16.

No. 7 (August 1985)

No. 8 (September 1985)
No. 9 (October 1985)
No. 13 (February 1986). Includes "A Tribute to William Alwyn," by Jack Docherty, 1–2.
No. 17 (June 1986). [Last issue]

International Filmusic Journal (UK)

Published by Robert Wood, founder of the Leeds, England-based John Barry Appreciation Society. Previously the society published a newsletter, *The Composer*, edited by Wood. Vol. 1, no. 1 was issued in 1978. This issue may contain composer Michael Perilstein's 1971 interview with John Barry. Three issues of the *International Filmusic Journal* were circulated: no. 1 (1979), no. 2 (1980), and no. 3.

No. 3 (1981, copyright 1982)
Hammonds, G. Roger. "Knowing the Score." 2–5. On the state of the art of film music.
Butterworth, David, and Martin Van Wouw. "Musing with Morricone." 7–9. Interview-based article on Ennio Morricone.
Wood, Robert. "John Barry Filmography." 10–12.
Heidecker, Tom. "Music from the Crypt: The Work of James Bernard." 13–14. Includes filmography.
Colon, David. "Miklos Rozsa: Hungarian Serenade." 15–24. Article with extensive concert music listings. The concert music is listed side by side with Rózsa's film scores for comparison and includes dedicatees, publishers, and more.
Wood, Robert. "That's Entertainment." 28. Finding soundtracks in London at That's Entertainment and similar shops.

Journal into Melody (UK)

Published by the Robert Farnon Society in England. Launched in 1956, it has featured extensive material on Farnon. It later began to include articles and lengthy obituaries on other composers of light music and is considered a preeminent source on the subject. Visits by American film composers to music festivals and concerts in Europe are often covered. Discographies often include film music; see David Rose (December 1984, part 3) and Victor Young (December 1984, part 2). "Keeping Track," a long-running feature, started as a list of music from films and television on LP and eventually included capsule reviews of CDs. A series on "British Recorded Mood Music Libraries" is of interest (EMI is in issue 145, December 2000). Editor David Ades also contributed entries on British film composers to the second edition of the *New Grove* (2000). Jeff Hall's column, "Film Music Bulletin," began in 2003, and Reuben Musiker was a regular contributor.

"Wally Stott / Angela Morley." 77 (December 1984): 20–24. Part 1, early life, continued in subsequent issues.
Elhaik, Serge. "Quincy Jones." 106 (February 1992): 15–18; Discography. 107 (April 1992): 22–23.
Elhaik, Serge. "The Frank de Vol Story." Part 1. 113 (September 1993): 12–13; Part 2. 114 (December 1993): 24–25; Part 3. 115 (February 1994): 51–53; Part 4. 116 (May 1994): 12–23; Part 5. 117 (July 1994): 50–52.
Friedwald, Will. "John Williams." 116 (May 1994): 4–5.
Friedwald, Will. "Johnny Mandel." 119 (December 1994): 37–39, through 128 (October 1996): 54–55. In ten parts.
Elhaik, Serge. "Les Baxter, 1922–1996." Part 1. 128 (October 1996): 34–35; Part 2. 129 (December 1996): 14–16; Part 3. 130 (March 1997): 14–16.
Noades, David. "Vintage Film Scores on Television." 131 (December 1997): 52.

Mandell, Paul. "Superman's Music of Mystery and Adventure." 135 (June 1998): 11–15.

Forster, John R. "What We Heard in the Cinemas." 139 (June 1999): 38.

Louis Levy biography. 139 (June 1999): 65–66.

Noades, David. "Hugo Montenegro: Love Themes from *The Godfather*." 144 (September 2000): 27–29. Part 1, documents the arranger's recordings of numerous film and television themes.

Taylor, Peter. "Elmer Bernstein: The Magnificent One." 148 (September 2001): 14–15.

Patten, Forrest. "Frank Comstock." 151 (June 2002): 17–26. Interview.

Hindley, Richard. "Conrad Salinger: M-G-M Arranger Supreme." 156 (September 2003): 8–15.

Edwards, Peter. "Carry On Composing! The Music of the *Carry On* Films 1958–78." 157 (December 2003): 24–29; 158 (March 2004): 28–34. On the low-budget film series, this is a shortened version of the author's undergraduate music dissertation at Durham University in Spring 2002.

Patten, Forrest. [Van Alexander interview.] 162 (March 2005): 55–60.

"Pete Candoli and Uan Rasey in Conversation with Forrest Patten." 164 (June–July 2005): 26–30.

Jessen, Richard. "Neal Hefti: The King of Cool." 166 (December 2005): 34–35.

Legend (UK)

The Jerry Goldsmith Appreciation Society was founded in 1982 by Roger Smith of Bedfordshire, England. Goldsmith was honorary president. Lyn Williams served as chairman. The society's first publication, called the *Journal*, appeared in April 1983. Written primarily by Smith, it was followed by several issues, newsletters, and bulletins for members. Special stand-alone articles were titled "M.G.M - Music from Goldsmith Movies." *Magic*, a booklet by members Rene Van Os and Arthur Yzendoom, is dated around 1985. A precursor to *Legend* called *Apollo* was published irregularly from 1983 through 1987, with news, information, and letters edited by Roger Smith.

Legend, the official Goldsmith Society journal, is published three times a year and contains articles, film music news, society news, letters, and soundtrack reviews. Late-breaking news comes in occasional supplements titled "Legend Extra" that are tipped into the journal proper. Although focused on Goldsmith, *Legend* also covers other composers. Gary Kester, a Goldsmith liner notes specialist, served as editor from 1992 to 1995. Other editors have included Barry Spence and Lyn Williams. Among the columnists are Tony Carty and Dirk Wickenden, who penned "Film + Music." Many of the contributors, such as Russell C. Thewlis, are active society members. No. 11 incorporates *Movie Music*. By 2005 some forty-four issues had been produced.

No. 12 (Spring 1993)
Williams, Lyn. "Profile: Alex North." 6–7. With filmography.

Kester, Gary. "Blood and Thunder: The War Film Scores of Jerry Goldsmith." 14–18. Part 2.

Spence, Barry. "Our Society: The First Ten Years, 1983–1987." 18–19. Part 1.

Mansell, John. "An Audience with Michael Kamen." 23. Report.

Winfrey, John. "Profile: Alfred Newman." 25–27.

No. 13 (Summer 1993)
Spence, Barry. "Love and Sex: The Gender Genre of Jerry Goldsmith." 18–19. Part 1.

Kester, Gary. "Charles the Great." 20–24. Profile of conductor Charles Gerhardt and capsule write-ups of his recordings for the RCA Classic Film Scores series.

Spence, Barry. "Our Society: The First Ten Years, 1988 to 1993." 26–27. Part 2.
Williams, Lyn. "Retrospective: *Planet of the Apes*." 28–29.
Kester, Gary. "Analysis: Notes of the Living Dead: A Look at George Romero's *Living Dead* Trilogy." 32–33. On music in Romero's *Living Dead* films, including library music and music by Goblin and John Harrison.
Kester, Gary. "Analysis: *A Patch of Blue*." 34–35.

No. 14 (Winter 1993)
Dietrichs, Klaus, based on biographical material by Jay Alan Quantrill. "Composer Profile: Jerry Fielding." 26–29. With filmography.
Kester, Gary. "Chaos Unleashed! The Filmed Science Fiction of Michael Crichton." 30–33. Music in filmed adaptations of Crichton's books.
Kester, Gary. "Hitting the Right Notes: [Erich] Kunzel, Telarc, & the Cincinnati Pops." 34–36.
Kester, Gary. "Franz Waxman: A Tribute to Genius." 38–41.
Spence, Barry. "Love and Sex." 42–43. Part 2, love scenes scored by Goldsmith in the 1970s.
Spence, Barry. "The *Unrecorded* Jerry Goldsmith." 44–45.
McLean, Jamie. "The 5 Greatest Orchestrators of All Time!" 46–47. On Jack Hayes, Greig McRitchie, Ennio Morricone, Arthur Morton, and Herbert Spencer.
Rischel, Aida. "Soeren Hyldgaard: In the Spirit of Chaplin." 48–49. Interview.
Wickenden, Dirk. "*Logan's Run*." 54–55. Article.
Spence, Barry. "Composed & Conducted By...NOT!" 58–60. A sampling of composers who do or do not conduct their own scores, including specific examples.

No. 15 (Spring 1994)
Wickenden, Dirk. "*Medicine Man*." 32–33. Article.
Tonks, Paul. "Interview: Patrick Doyle." 40–42.
Kester, Gary. "Knowing *The Score*." 47. On the 1971 BMI documentary.
Spence, Barry. "Love and Sex." 48–49. Part 3, love scenes scored by Goldsmith in the 1980s.
Kester, Gary. "Michael Whalen." 50. Mini-profile.

No. 16 (Summer–Autumn 1994)
Interviews with Christopher Gunning and Trevor Jones. Frederic Talgorn profile, Dimitri Tiomkin profile (part 1).

No. 17 (1995)
Lalo Schifrin profile and John Scott filmography-discography.

No. 18 (1995)
Basil Poledouris discography and Dimitri Tiomkin profile (part 2).

Max Steiner Music Society publications
The Max Steiner Music Society was responsible for three publications: *The Max Steiner Music Society News Letter* (1965–1976), *The Max Steiner Annual* (1967–1976), and *The Max Steiner Journal* (1977–1980). The society was founded by a fan, Albert K. Bender, in Connecticut in 1965. (Bender relocated to California the following year, eventually settling in Los Angeles.) It was the first film music society according to *Pro Musica Sana*. Steiner was honorary president, Page Cook served as assistant director, and foreign representatives included Britain's Jack Docherty. Brian A. Reeve took over in London after Bender retired in the early 1980s, and the society subsequently has been known as the Max Steiner Memorial Society and Max Steiner Film Music Society.

The Max Steiner Annual (US)
Published by the Max Steiner Music Society in Los Angeles from 1967 to 1976. Issues, averaging fifteen pages each, included news of interest; "Steiner Film Score Reviews," a

column by Cook focusing on one Steiner film each year; and occasional anecdotal material from Steiner himself. Britain's Philip J. S. Hammond served as special features editor. Superseded by *The Max Steiner Journal*.

1 (1967)
Chronology, filmography, songography. 3–8.
Cook, Page. "The Adventures of Don Juan." 13–14.

2 (1968)
Cook, Page. "Filmusic Basics." 3–5.
"Max Steiner Discography." 11.
Cook, Page. "*Death of a Scoundrel*." 13–14.

3 (1969)
Boller, Paul F., Jr. "Musical Notes on Max Steiner." 3–7. Excerpts of articles on or mentioning Steiner.
Schmidt, Edward A., and Clifford McCarty. "Max Steiner Bibliography." 8–10.
Cook, Page. "*Band of Angels*." 11–13.
Cook, Page. "A Basic Library of Film Scores." 13–17. On soundtracks.

4 (1970)
Hammond, Philip J. S. "Riding the Sagebrush Trail with Max Steiner." 2–3. On Westerns, partially reprinted from *Films and Filming* (December 1969).
Vertlieb, Steve. "The Horror and Fantasy Films of Max Steiner." 4–6.
Cook, Page. "*John Paul Jones*." 11–12.

5 (1971)
Hammond, Philip J. S. "Max Steiner's Music for the Errol Flynn Films." 2–6.
Thomas, Tony. "Flynn and Film Music." 12–13.

6 (1972)
Hammond, Philip J. S. "Max Steiner's Music for the Bette Davis Films." 3–14.
Steiner, Max. "My Association with the Great Victor Herbert." 15–16.

7 (1973)
Steiner, Max. "Max Steiner and the Birth of a Star." 3–4. On Rudolph Valentino.
Steiner, Max. "Jolson or Not Jolson." 4–5.
Lichtenberger, Robert S. "The Film Music of Sir William Walton." 6–9.
Hammond, Philip J. S. "The Career of Herbert Stothart." 10–12. Reprinted in the *Max Steiner Journal*.
Steiner, Max. "This Is Cinerama." 13–15.

8 (1974)
Hammond, Philip J. S. "Max Steiner's Music for *Little Women* (1933)." 10–14.
Steiner, Max. "Isn't That the Music You Used in Another Film?" 22–23.
Steiner, Max. "Scoring the TV Film." 23–24.
Steiner, Max. "My Father and the Masters." 24–26.

9 (1975)
Hammond, Philip J. S. "Max Steiner's Music for *Virginia City* (1940)." 3–9.
Morgan, John W. "Max Steiner Discography." 14–17. Update of the 1968 *Annual*. The number of recordings released from 1968 to 1975 outnumbered all combined Steiner recordings prior to 1968.

10 (1976)
Lazarou, George A. "Behind the Scenes of the *Gone with the Wind* Scoring." 3–5.
Morgan, John W. "Steiner's Epic Score for *Gone with the Wind*." 8–11.

"What Max Steiner Had to Say about the Film *Gone with the Wind*." 20.

Hammond, Philip J. S. "The Career of W. Franke Harling (1887–1958)." 25–26.

The Max Steiner Journal (US)

Published by the Max Steiner Music Society in Los Angeles from 1977 to 1980. Succeeded the *Max Steiner Annual* and *Max Steiner Music Society News Letter*. Includes "Rambling with Snell," by Mike Snell, branch news from society chapters around the world, and documentation of the organization's annual Max Steiner Award. One issue of an unrelated, similarly named journal, *The Max Steiner Journal*, was published by the South Jersey Better Film Council in cooperation with the Max Steiner Music Society in 1965. Edited by Jon F. Davison, it included news and a Steiner filmography.

1 (1977)

Snell, Mike. "Compliments to Kate." 3–9. Examines the eight Katharine Hepburn films scored by Steiner.

Snell, Mike. "Play the Part that I Like." 10–13. Examines films scored by Steiner in 1940.

Jordan, Robert. "Dimitri Tiomkin." 17–18. A collector looks at Tiomkin's soundtracks.

Bender, Albert K. "The Max Steiner Chronology." 27–30.

Filmography and songography. 31–33.

2 (1978)

Snell, Mike. "Out of the Blue: Max Steiner's Score for *Bird of Paradise*." 3–5.

Steiner, Max. "*Bird of Paradise*." 6.

Pavelek, James P. "Chaplin Remembered: The Enduring Popularity of Charlie Chaplin's Film Music." 7–8.

Snell, Mike. "*Now Voyager* Revisited." 9–11.

Pavelek, James P. "A Tribute to Alfred Newman." 15–16.

Snell, Mike. "Romance amid the 70's." 27–28. On music by John Barry.

3 (1978)

Snell, Mike. "The End of the Beginning: Max Steiner's Score for *She*." 3–6.

Hammond, Philip J. S. "The Career of Muir Mathieson." 7–15.

Snell, Mike. "Two of a Mind: A Tribute to Hugo Friedhofer and David Raksin." 22–25.

4 (1979)

Snell, Mike. "Symphony of Six Million." 3–9.

Pavelek, James. "Film Music Collection: An Appeal for Support." 19–20.

Stevens, John. "The Music from the Film *Superman*." 22–23. On John Williams's score.

Blackmore, Bob. "The Film Career of Stanley Black." 24–26.

Hammond, Philip J. S. "The Career of Herbert Stothart (1885–1949)." 31–41. Originally appeared in *The Max Steiner Annual*, includes addenda.

5 (1980)

Snell, Mike. "Music in Technicolor: Max Steiner's Score for *The Garden of Allah*." 3–5.

Burton, Geoff. "In Defense of Max Steiner." 7–9.

Hammond, Philip J. S. "Herbert Stothart: An Encore." 13–16, 31–32.

Snell, Mike. "From York to Roark: Max Steiner's Scores for Gary Cooper." 18–20.

Mitchell, Rick. "*China Gate*: A Rarity in Film Music History." 21–22.

Green, Stu. "Reflections on the *King Kong* Score." 23–25.

Pavelek, James. "Hans J. Salter: More Than a Master of Terror and Suspense." 27.

Special issue

The Max Steiner Centenary Journal, 1888–1988: A Tribute to Max Steiner, "The Dean of

Film Music." Los Angeles: Max Steiner Memorial Society, [1988?]. 19 pp. Tributes by Albert K. Bender, Philip J. S. Hammond, Ray Harryhausen, Henry Mancini, David Raksin, Mike Snell, Tony Thomas, and Hans-Paul Zimmer. Cover title: *The Max Steiner Centenary: A Celebration.*

The Max Steiner Music Society News Letter (US)
Published by the Max Steiner Music Society in Connecticut, then California, from 1965 to 1976. First issued as a one-page newsletter in October 1965, it contained news about, and of interest to, members. With issue 8 the format became a four-page foldover.

Steiner, Max. "My Scoring for *The Informer*." No. 24 (Autumn 1970): 1, 3.

Lasher, John Steven. "Elmer Bernstein." No. 31 (Summer 1972): 2–3.

Thomas, Tony. "Music and Film—The Odd Coupling." No. 31 (Summer 1972): 4. Part 1.

Thomas, Tony. "Music and Film—The Odd Coupling." No. 32 (Fall 1972). Part 2.

Collins, Red. "Sir Arthur Bliss and Malcolm Arnold." No. 33 (Winter 1972): 3–4.

Mann, John. "Dimitri Tiomkin." No. 34 (Spring 1973). 1–2. Profile.

Lasher, John Steven. "Ernest Gold." No. 37 (Winter 1973): 4–5.

Scofield, Tom. "Les Baxter." No. 42 (Spring 1975): 3–5.

The Miklos Rozsa Appreciation Music Society Journal (Australia)
Published irregularly by society founder and director John Stevens in New South Wales, Australia. Rózsa was honorary president. The Miklos Rozsa Cult, founded by Stevens in 1975, briefly became the Spellbound Music Society, then changed back to the original. In 1981 it became the BEN-HUR Miklos Rozsa Appreciation Music Society. Each issue includes a report from Stevens and letters from fans around the world.

BH1 (1981)

BH2 (April 1984)

BH3 (April 1992)
Includes a brief history of the society by Stevens on page 2.

BH4 (November 1993)
Dane, Jeffrey. "A Friday Morning Rehearsal." 10–11. Report on Rózsa's participation at a rehearsal of one of his concert works.

The Miklos Rozsa Cult Quarterly Newsletter (Australia)
Newsletter published irregularly by the Miklos Rozsa Society of Australia, in Albury, New South Wales. The society was founded by John Stevens in 1975. Nine of the newsletters, sometimes referred to as the MRC Newsletter, were published and numbered MRC1 to MRC9. A New York-based Miklos Rozsa Music Society was founded by David Colon in 1978. John Stevens printed that organization's newsletter, *Spellbound*, from Australia. Apparently two were published in 1978, and several in 1981–1982.

Vol. 1 (November 1975) MRC1
News.

Vol. 2 (January 1976) MRC2
News.

Vol. 2 (April 1976) MRC3
News.

Vol. 2 (July 1976) MRC4
Stevens, John. "The Making of *The Lost Weekend*." 3–4.

Rózsa, Miklós. "Scoring *The Lost Weekend*." 10–11.
Miller, Richard F. "*Ivanhoe*." 12–13.

<u>Vol. 3 (April–June 1977) (unpaged) MRC8</u>
Rózsa, Miklós. "*Spellbound*." Rozsa's take on his music. [2 pages]
Stevens, John. "*Ben-Hur* Revelations." Analysis. [3 pages]

<u>Vol. 4 (April 1980) MRC9</u>
Rózsa, Miklós. "Scoring *King of Kings*." August 1979. [1 page]
Stevens, John. "*King of Kings*." Analysis. [7 pages]
Stevens, John. "The Miracle of *Ben-Hur*." Analysis. [1 page]

Movie Music (UK)
Published by the Jerry Goldsmith Appreciation Society. Three issues were produced.
Material destined for no. 4 was published in *Legend*, nos. 11 and 12.

<u>No. 1 (Winter 1990)</u>
Interviews with James Campbell (orchestrator), Cliff Eidelman, Brian May, Alan Silvestri, Michael Small, Morton Stevens, and Christopher Young.

<u>No. 2 (Spring 1991)</u>
Interviews with Michael Kamen, Fred Karlin, Basil Poledouris, Arthur B. Rubinstein, Patrick Williams, and Hans Zimmer.

<u>No. 3 (Autumn 1991)</u>
Interviews with George Fenton and Jonathan Sheffer. Frank Skinner profile.

Musica sul Velluto (Holland)
Musica sul Velluto, also known as MSV, was founded by Martin van Wouw as a club for Ennio Morricone fans and soundtrack collectors. The newsletter is devoted to the music of Morricone and contains articles, interviews, and news.

<u>No. 1 (March 1980) 19 pp.</u>
van Wouw, Martin. "Cometa Something Special." 10–12. On the Italian soundtrack label.

Noise: Notes from Mark Isham (US)
Isham writes and distributes his own quarterly newsletter (1999–2005), with articles on his upcoming films, concert dates, information about his film seminar schedule, and so on.

Pro Musica Sana (US)
Quarterly, later semiannual, publication of the Miklós Rózsa Society (MRS). The journal was founded in 1972 by John Fitzpatrick in Bloomington, Indiana, while earning his doctorate at Indiana University. An ardent fan, he moved to New York in 1978 to pursue a career in the book publishing industry. Recurring items include society and general news; concert performances; recordings and soundtrack reviews by Fitzpatrick, associate editor Frank K. DeWald, Preston Neal Jones, Mark Koldys, and others; publications and book reviews; events of interest; European news from Alan Hamer; and analysis and documentation of Rózsa's concert music. Mary Peatman, Fitzpatrick's colleague from Indiana University, contributed articles. Ronald Bohn, the West Coast representative, joined as production editor in 1976, typing and preparing the layout for printing, with Koldys coordinating printing and mailing from Dearborn, Michigan. By 1976 society members numbered more than 300, and included core film music fans from Randall Larson to Luc van de Ven.
    The scope of the journal gradually broadened beyond Rózsa to include many of his

contemporaries, particularly Bernard Herrmann, as well as current scores and recordings. "Off the Beaten Track" contained brief notes on forgotten gems. In the 1970s, publication coincided with the RCA Classic Film Scores series conducted by Charles Gerhardt, which began an era of soundtrack rerecordings. The society distributed recordings, dubbed on member-supplied cassettes, of Rózsa original music tracks, studio recordings, concerts, and more. A 1981 catalog lists more than seventy items. The society and journal were reinvigorated after Rózsa's death and an emotional memorial service in Los Angeles was attended by the faithful. *Pro Musica Sana* is the cream of the crop of fan journals due mainly to Fitzpatrick's writing and editorial guidance and the quality of the contributions by John Caps, Derek Elley, Preston Jones, and Ken Sutak, among others.

1:1 (Spring 1972)
"The Origins." 1. Brief history of the organization.
"A Letter from Dr. Rozsa." 1–2.
Palmer, Christopher. "Miklos Rozsa." 2–5. Reprint of article in *Performing Right* (May 1971).
Fitzpatrick, John. "First Notes on *Young Bess*." 5–8.

1:2 (Summer 1972)
No articles.

1:3 (Fall 1972)
DeWald, Frank. "Filmusic and Film Music." 2–5. On the difference between film music on screen and in concert.
Bronfeld, Myron. "Rozsa on Disc. Part 1: The Concert Music." 5–9.

1:4 (Winter 1972–1973)
Doeckel, Ken. "The Four Concertos of Miklos Rozsa." 4–11.

2:1 (Spring 1973)
Palmer, Christopher. "Rozsa in London, October 1972." 2–3.
Wick, Ted. "The Birth of the *Spellbound* Concerto." 4–5.

2:2 (Summer 1973) (MRS 6)
Fitzpatrick, John. "Rozsa on Disc. Part 2: The Film Music." 11–21.

2:3 (Fall 1973) (MRS 7)
Gilling, Ted. "Herrmann in London." 20–21. Comments from the composer.

2:4 (Winter 1973–1974) (MRS 8)
Koldys, Mark. "The Power of *The Power*." 11–18. Analysis of Rózsa's television score.

3:1 (Spring 1974) (MRS 9)
Rózsa, Miklós. "Scoring *Sinbad*." 3–4.
Sutak, Ken. "The Return of *A Streetcar Named Desire*." 4–10. Part 1.
"Bernard Herrmann: A John Player Lecture (11 June 1972)." 10–16. Part 1.

3:2 (Summer 1974) (MRS 10)
"Bernard Herrmann: A John Player Lecture (11 June 1972)." 18–27. Part 2.

3:3 (Fall 1974) (MRS 11)
Koldys, Mark. "Miklos Rozsa and *Ben-Hur*." 2–20. Analysis.

3:4 (Winter 1974–1975) (MRS 12)
Sutak, Ken. "The Return of *A Streetcar Named Desire*." 9–15. Part 2.
"Miklos Rozsa: Lecture in London (October 1972)." 15–25. Interviewed by Alan Warner. Part 1.

4:1 (Spring 1975) (MRS 13)

Fitzpatrick, John. "The New Recording Societies." 11–14. On Elmer Bernstein's Film Music Collection (*Film Music Notebook*) and John Lasher's Entr'acte Recording Society (*Main Title*).

Fitzpatrick, John. "Into Our Fourth Year—An Assessment." 14–17.

"Miklos Rozsa: Lecture in London (October 1972)." 21–30. Part 2.

4:2 (1975) (MRS 14)

Fitzpatrick, John. "Rozsa on Tape." 7–18.

Sutak, Ken. "The Return of *A Streetcar Named Desire*." 18–24. Part 3.

"More on [Dum-da-Dum-Dum]." 24–25. Editorial notes on the musical similarities between *The Killers* (Miklós Rózsa) and *Dragnet* (Walter Schumann) and the resulting out-of-court settlement.

4:3 (1975) (MRS 15) [inadvertently labeled 3:3]

Reardon, Craig, with Preston Jones. "The Memorial Service." 2–4. Regarding Bernard Herrmann.

Reardon, Craig. "Film Music Collection: A Positive View." 11–12.

Fitzpatrick, John. "New Journals and Societies." 12–13.

Sutak, Ken. "The Return of *A Streetcar Named Desire*." 13–18. Part 4.

4:4 (1975) (MRS 16)

Peatman, Mary. "Prokofiev's Score for *Ivan the Terrible*." 6–19. Essay.

5:1 (August 1976) (MRS 17)

"News: Publications." 3. Actor-director Paul Henreid's comments on conversations with Franz Waxman and the music for *Battleshock* (1956) [*A Woman's Devotion*] eventually scored by Les Baxter, excerpted from *Media Montage*.

Koldys, Mark. "Composer of the Seventies." 6–8. On Jerry Goldsmith's score for *Logan's Run* (1976).

Fitzpatrick, John. "More Notes on *Young Bess*." 12–15.

5:2 (November 1976) (MRS 18)

Koldys, Mark. "[Dimitri] Tiomkin Reconsidered." 16–18.

5:3 (April 1977) (PMS 19)

Fitzpatrick, John, and Mark Koldys. "The Films of Miklos Rozsa: Checklist, Tapeography and Commentary." 11–25.

Bohn, Ronald. "UCLA/Filmex 'Filmmusic' Course." 29–32. Report on the class coordinated by Tony Thomas.

5:4 (July 1977) (PMS 20) [inadvertently labeled 5:3]

Koldys, Mark. "*Star Wars*." 4–6. On John Williams's score.

Peatman, Mary. "*Providence 1*: The Film." 9–18. Analysis.

6:1 (Winter 1978) (PMS 21)

Matz, Mary Jane. "Flesh-and-Blood Angel." 12–14. Nino Rota profile reprinted from *Opera News* (May 1977).

Fitzpatrick, John. "It's a Bird, It's a Plane, It's *Allegro molto agitato e tumultuoso*." 14–15. Appearances of Rózsa's concert music tracked in episodic television series.

6:2 (Spring 1978) (PMS 22)

No film music articles.

6:3 (Summer 1978) (PMS 23)
"Alain Resnais Interviewed by Bertrand Borie." 5–9. The director of *Providence* talks about Rózsa and the score. Originally appeared in the journal of the Miklos Rozsa Society of France, translated here by John Fitzpatrick.

6:4 (Fall 1978) (PMS 24)
"Martin [Morton?] Gould Interviewed by Mark Koldys." 12–14.
Fitzpatrick, John, and Martin Marks. "A Note on Film Music Scholarship." 17–19. Special supplementary guide to research in the field.

7:1 (Winter 1978–1979) (PMS 25)
Sternfeld, Frederick W. "Music and the Feature Films." 7–18. Analysis of Hugo Friedhofer's score for *The Best Years of Our Lives*. Reprinted from *Musical Quarterly* (October 1947).

7:2 (Spring 1979) (PMS 26)
Hannemann, Volker, and Wolfram Hannemann. "Overtures: A Checklist and Commentary." 4–8. Includes a list of overtures, intermezzi, and epilogues for films from 1939 to 1978 (not limited to the films of Rózsa).

7:3 (Summer 1979) (PMS 27)
Elley, Derek. "Miklos Rozsa Interviewed by Derek Elley." 4–19. Originally published in *Films and Filming* (May 1977 and June 1977).

7:4 (Fall 1979) (PMS 28)
"Miklos Rozsa Society Directory." 8-page insert.

8:1 (Winter 1979–1980) (PMS 29)
"Franz Waxman Interview." 4–9. Transcript of a radio interview with Lawrence Morton originally published as "Music from the Films: A CBC Broadcast," in *Hollywood Quarterly* (Winter 1950).

8:2 (Spring 1980) (PMS 30)
"Film Music in the 1970s: A Special Symposium."
Fitzpatrick, John. "Editor's Introduction." 4–6. Highlights of the 1970s.
DeWald, Frank. "A Backward Glance." 6–8. On style, film music on disc, and film music criticism.
Koldys, Mark. "The State of the Art." 9–11.
Quigley, Michael. "Renaissance?" 11–13.
Elley, Derek. "Re-Renaissance?" 13–14.
Sutak, Ken. "Categories." 14–16.
Bohn, Ronald. "Oscars for Dramatic Scores during the '70s." 16–19.
Hamer, Alan. "Roll of Honor." 19–21.
"The Best of the Decade: Some Additional Lists." 21–24.
Fitzpatrick, John. "Afterword." 24–28.

8:3 (Summer 1980) (PMS 31)
Kowalski, Alfons A. "William Alwyn." 4–11. Profile, with filmography and discography.

8:4 (Fall 1980) (PMS 32)
DeWald, Frank. "*Time after Time*: An Analysis." 3–19. With music examples.

9:1 (Summer 1981) (PMS 33)
Altman, Rick. "Cinema/Sound: An Introduction." 3–17. Preface to a special issue of *Cinema/Sound* (1980).
Hamer, Alan. "*Eye of the Needle*: The London Sessions." 18–19. Report.
Robbins, A. C. "Composer of the Eighties?" 20–21. On Jerry Goldsmith.

9:2 (Winter 1981–1982) (PMS 34)
Fitzpatrick, John. "Scoring *Altered States*: An Interview with John Corigliano." 4–9.
Caps, John. "A Word about Film Music Criticism." 9–12.

9:3 (Spring 1982) (PMS 35)
Jones, Preston Neal. "*Dead Men*'s Diary." 4–21. Report on recording *Dead Men Don't Wear Plaid*.

9:4 (Summer 1982) (PMS 36)
James, David P. "Modern Music that Works: John Corigliano and *Altered States*." 2–6.
Sutak, Ken. "A *Dragonslayer* Inquiry: From Two Heady Notes toward Some Hard Questions about the Score." 7–15. Examines Alex North's music.

10:1 (Fall 1982) (PMS 37)
Robbins, A. C. "Cinemascore." 4–5. On the fanzine.

10:2 (Spring 1983) (PMS 38)
Robbins, A. C. "The Rozsa Societies: A Survey." 4–6.
Fitzpatrick, John. "Some Reflections on *Double Life*." 6–9.

10:3–4 (Fall 1983) (PMS 39–40)
Archibald, John B. "Reunion with Old Friends." 3–9. On recurring thematic materials in Herrmann, Newman, and Rózsa.
Caps, John. "Discovering Patrick Gowers." 9–10. Profile of the British composer.
Brown, Royal S. "Herrmann, Hitchcock, and the Music of the Irrational." 15–25. Part 1. Reprinted from *Cinema Journal* (Spring 1982).

11:1 (Spring 1984) (PMS 41)
Brown, Royal S. "Herrmann, Hitchcock, and the Music of the Irrational." 6–13. Part 2.
Haupt, Arthur. "Kubrick's Canned Music." 13–18. Includes *2001: A Space Odyssey*.

11:2 (Fall 1984) (PMS 42)
Brown, Royal S. "Herrmann, Hitchcock, and the Music of the Irrational." 11–21. Part 3.

11:3 (Spring 1985) (PMS 43)
Caps, John. "Anatomy of a Film Score: The Example of *E.T.*" 7–16. On John Williams's score.

11:4 (Winter 1986) (PMS 44)
Elley, Derek. "*King of Kings*: An Analysis." 7–12. On Rózsa's score, with music examples. Part 1.
Chell, Samuel L. "Cinema, Sentiment, and the Soundtrack: *The Best Years of Our Lives*." 13–19. On Hugo Friedhofer's score. A longer version appeared in *Film Criticism*.
DeWald, Frank. "*A Christmas Carol* Found." 19–21. On Bernard Herrmann's television opera.

12:1 (Fall 1986) (PMS 45)
Elley, Derek. "*King of Kings*: An Analysis." 3–7. Part 2.
Bohn, Ronald L., and others. "The Film Music of Miklos Rozsa: A Checklist." 8–23. Parts 1 and 2, score and anthology disc recordings.

(Summer 1987) (PMS 46)
Elley, Derek. "*King of Kings*: An Analysis." 3–8. Part 3.
Bohn, Ronald L., and others. "The Film Music of Miklos Rozsa: A Checklist." 8–28. Part 3, anthology disc recordings.

(Winter 1989) (PMS 47)
DeWald, Frank. "On *The Private Files of J. Edgar Hoover*." 5–18. On Rózsa's score, with music examples.

Gideon, David. "Exploring with Goldsmith." 19–22. On Goldsmith's score for *Explorers*.

Viksten, Villu, with John Fitzpatrick. "The Film Music of Miklos Rozsa on Records: Supplement 1." 3–8.
"Film Music in the 1980s: A Symposium." 9–23. Contributions from Ronald L. Bohn, Royal S. Brown, John Caps, Frank DeWald, Derek Elley, John Fitzpatrick, Alan Hamer, Mark Koldys, Randall Larson, Ken Sutak, and Steve Vertlieb with their favorite scores of the decade.

No feature articles.

DeWald, Frank K. "The Song of *El Cid*: Singing the Praises of Miklos Rozsa's Greatest Achievement." 3–22. On Rózsa's score, with music examples. Part 1.

DeWald, Frank K. "The Song of *El Cid*." 3–11. Part 2.

"Collaboration." 11–16. A list of directors and actors for films scored by Rózsa.

Fitzpatrick, John. "Last Years and Leave-Takings." 3–9. Memorial issue with remembrances from director Nicholas Meyer, Jeffrey Dane, and others.

Mauceri, John. "The Music that Has No Name." 5–7. Previously published in the *Cue Sheet*.
DeWald, Frank K. "Restoring the *Cid*." 9–13. Article on the Koch *El Cid* rerecording, based on conversations with Nicholas Rozsa and Patrick Russ.

Heinle, Lothar. "The Teachers of Miklos Rozsa: A Closer Look." 14–17. On Theodor Kroyer and Hermann Grabner.

Fitzpatrick, John. "Rozsa in China: Rediscovering *The Seventh Sin*." 9–11.
"Bradford on *Ben-Hur*: A Correspondence." 11–13. Excerpts from correspondence between Rhino record producer Marilee Bradford and John Fitzpatrick.

DeWald, Frank K. "*Lust for Life*: An Impression." 3–17. On Rózsa's score, with music examples.

Heinle, Lothar. "Miklos Rozsa's *Thief of Bagdad*: A Study in Sources." 3–9.
Bush, Richard H. "*The Thief of Bagdad*: The Musical? (A Look at the Syracuse Manuscripts)." 10–18.

Wayne, John J. "*Scheherazade*'s Song Sublime: Film as Fantasy-Operetta." 3–17. On Rózsa's score for *Song of Scheherazade* (1947).
DeWald, Frank K. "Searching for the Rozsa-in-Rimsky." 17–18.

Komar, George. "*King of Kings*: Rediscovering the Film and the Score."

(Spring 2005) (PMS 61)
Erkelenz, Ralph. "*Ben-Hur*: A Tale of the Score." Part 1.

Chapter 9

Film and Media Periodicals

A&E Monthly (US)
Magazine and program guide for the Arts and Entertainment television network.
Sterns, David Patrick. "They Don't Get No Respect: The Tough, Unglamorous World of the Movie Composer." 9:2 (February 1994): 51–54.
Yakir, Dan. "The Men Who Score in Hollywood." 10:11 (November 1995): 34–37.

Action (US)
Published by the Directors Guild of America (DGA) in Hollywood.
Mancini, Henry. "Directors and Film Scores." 6:6 (November–December 1971): 18–21. On communicating with directors.
"The Film Musical Golden 13." 9:3 (May–June 1974): 4–9. The opening article of a film musicals issue, followed by articles on Busby Berkeley, George Sidney, and Bob Fosse.

After Dark (US)
Published monthly in New York.
Considine, Shaun. "The Music behind the Dialogue Steps Out." (October 1973): 45–47.
Delaunoy, Didier. "Michel Legrand Getting Grander." 6:12 (April 1974): 56–59.

Afterimage (UK)
From Afterimage Publishing in London.
Eisenschitz, Bernard. "The Music of Time: From *Napoleon* to *New Babylon*." No. 10 (Autumn 1981): 48–55. On scores by Carl Davis and Dimitri Shostakovich.

afterimage (US)
Published by the Visual Studies Workshop in Rochester, New York.
Djurica, Radmila. "Pula Film Festival." 32:1 (July–August 2004): 17. Interview with Yugoslavian composer Goran Bregovic.

American Cinematographer (US)
The journal of the American Society of Cinematographers (ASC), published in Hollywood.
Walker, Vernon L. "Rhythmic Optical Effects for Musical Pictures." 17:12 (December 1936): 504, 514. Fascinating look at the relationship between musical and visual rhythms in RKO musicals, dubbed "montage in swing-time."

Dane, Jeffrey M. "The Significance of Film Music." 42:5 (May 1961): 302–6. How film music tells the story in its own language, illustrated primarily through the music of Miklós Rózsa.

"Film Music." 43:4 (April 1962): 236–38. Pointers on adding music to 16mm films based on a series of articles relating to film music in *The Aperture* (the monthly journal of Calvin Productions, Kansas City, Missouri).

Kallis, Stephen A., Jr. "Background Music by Computer." 52:11 (November 1971): 1148–149. On the Muse, an early music generator (synthesizer) billed as a "virtually unlimited source of film music" that can be used without a license fee.

"350S 'Stylophone' Synthesizer for Electronic Music and Sound Effects." 57:12 (December 1976): 1354–55. Small enough to fit in a briefcase but can simulate the tones of almost all of the instruments of the orchestra.

Bolger, Ray. "*The Wizard of Oz* and the Golden Era of the American Musical Film." 59:2 (February 1978): 190–94.

Horning, Joseph. "Shooting a Live Symphony Orchestra Concert." 59:3 (March 1978): 264–65, 310.

Gold, Ron. "Untold Tales of *Koyaanisqatsi*." 65:3 (March 1984): 63–74. On editing the film to Philip Glass's music.

Robinson, Andrew. "Music: Music for *Jewel in the Crown*." 66:1 (January 1985): 83–96. Interview-based article on George Fenton's score.

Behlmer, Rudy. "[Douglas Fairbanks *The Black Pirate*] High Style on the High Seas." 73:4 (April 1992): 34–40. Brief mention of musicians on the set during filming and Mortimer Wilson's score, p. 36.

American Cinemeditor (US)

Official publication, previously titled *Cinemeditor*, of the American Cinema Editors, an honorary professional society.

Published as **Cinemeditor**

Lustig, Milton. "The Music Editor." 20:4 (Winter 1970–1971): 11–12. On the role and functions from a career music editor.

Published as **American Cinemeditor**

Perry, Alfred. "Contemporary Use of Background Music." 22:1 (Spring 1972): 8–9. Written by the music editor at Four Star International.

American Classic Screen (US)

Popular fan journal of American film heritage published by the National Film Society in Kansas. "Tracking the Score," a record review column by Charles Berg, ran from 1978 to 1980.

Articles

D'Arc, James, and the editors. "The Final Legacy of Max Steiner: Hollywood's Greatest Composer Finds an Archive Home." 5:5 (undated): 30–31. On the donation of the Steiner papers to Brigham Young University.

Parker, David L. "The Singing Screen: Remembering Those Movies that Not Only Talked but Sang." 7:2 (March–April 1983): 22–26. Opera on film.

Column, "Tracking the Score" by Charles Berg (selected)
2:5 (May–June 1978): 22. On the RCA Classic Film Score series.
3:1 (September–October 1978): 31. David Raksin profile.
3:3 (January–February 1979): 27. Record reviews.
3:4 (March–April 1979): 41. On *Soundtrack Collector's Newsletter*.

3:6 (June–August 1979): 22. News.
4:1 (Fall 1979): 21. Record reviews.
4:2 (Winter 1980): 22. Historical overview of music for Westerns.
4:3 (Spring 1980): 21. Record reviews.

American Film (US)

Journal of the film and television arts published by the American Film Institute in Washington, D.C. A short-lived "Sound Track" column written by various writers, including Robert Fiedel and Gene Lees, appeared in 1977 and 1978.

Articles

Wiener, Thomas. "The Rise and Fall of the Rock Film." 1:2 (November 1975): 25–29. Part 1.

Wiener, Thomas. "The Rise and Fall of the Rock Film." 1:3 (December 1975): 58–63. Part 2.

Sharples, Win [Jr.]. "Explorations: Love's Labour Found." 1:5 (March 1976): 68–70. On the Miklos Rozsa Society and Elmer Bernstein's Film Music Collection.

Lees, Gene. "Focus on Education: School for Scoring." 3:2 (November 1977): 68–69. On Patrick Williams's media orchestra for training young musicians in Denver, Colorado.

Mayer, Martin. "About Television: Music and the Medium." 3:4 (February 1978): 55, 79. On the power of television music.

Atkinson, Terry. "Scoring with Synthesizers." 7:10 (September 1982): 66–71. On the use of the synthesizer, primarily by Giorgio Moroder and Vangelis.

Occhiogrosso, Peter. "Reelin' and Rockin'." 9:6 (April 1984): 44–50. Rock music.

Kehr, Dave. "Can't Stop the Musicals." 9:7 (May 1984): 32–37. Contemporary musicals.

Murray, Lyn. "Chords and Discords." 11:8 (June 1986): 17–20. Excerpts from Murray's diary, published the following year in his book, *Musician*.

Woodard, Josef. "Sonata for Cello and Cherry Pie." 15:15 (December 1990): 13. On Angelo Badalamenti's music for director David Lynch.

Kennedy, Harlan. "The Harmonious Background." 16:2 (February 1991): 38–41, 46. Ennio Morricone interview.

Spheeris, Penelope, and Danny Elfman. "One on One: The Director and Composer Swap Tales." 16:2 (February 1991): 42–45.

Spotnitz, Frank. "Dialogue on Film: Alan Silvestri." 16:8 (August 1991): 14–17. Interview transcript from an AFI seminar.

Column, "Sound Track," by various writers

Fiedel, Robert. "And the Beast Goes On." 2:5 (March 1977): 71–72. Discusses Max Steiner's score for *King Kong* and recording and rerecording film music. He observes that "the single most difficult obstacle in recording film music is locating original source materials."

Brown, Royal S. "Changing the Score." 2:6 (April 1977): 62–63. Original chamber music in contemporary film scores.

Lees, Gene. "The Music Director: Good Step Backward." 2:7 (May 1977): 72–73. On the hiring of Dominic Frontiere as music director at Paramount.

Lees, Gene. "The Good Years of Hugo Friedhofer." 2:8 (June 1977): 77–78. Interview-based profile.

Fiedel, Robert D. "The Cornerstone Collection." 2:9 (July–August 1977): 62–64. The essential soundtrack collection in the opinion of the *Take One* film music critic.

Petric, Vlada. "Silence Was Golden." 2:10 (September 1977): 64–65. On the addition of new scores to silent films, often with unpleasant results.

Fiedel, Robert D. "Saving the Score—Wanted: A National Film Music Archive." 3:1 (October 1977): 32, 71. Preservation.

Lees, Gene. "In Memory of Mercer." 3:3 (December–January 1978): 64–65. Reminiscences of Johnny Mercer.

Rosenbaum, Jonathan. "Hollywood's Jazz." 3:5 (March 1978): 69–71.

Fiedel, Robert. "The Filmharmonic." 3:6 (April 1978): 64–65. On the rarity of concert performances of film music.

American Film Institute Report (US)

The *AFI Report* contains news for AFI members.

Shepard, David. "Silent Music." 3:1 (1972): 3–6.

Kleiner, Arthur. "The Re-Creation of a Lost Masterpiece: Edmund Meisel's Score for *Potemkin*." 3:1 (1972): 6–7.

American Premiere (US)

Motion picture industry trade magazine published in Los Angeles. Profiles of film composers and current projects appeared under "Filmusic" (1984–1985), "Soundtracks" (1989), and "Film Music" (1992–1994).

Feldman, Gail. "Filmusic." 5:3 (Summer 1984): 29. Georges Delerue profile.

"Filmusic." 5:4 (Fall 1984): 39. News.

Feldman, Gail M. "Filmusic." 6:1 (Winter 1985): 31. Bruce Broughton profile.

Feldman, Gail. "Filmusic." 6:2 (June 1985): 11. Bill Conti profile.

Feldman, Gail M. "James Horner: Serene on the Podium." 6:3 (September 1985): 28. Profile.

Birns, Debby. "Filmusic." 6:4 (December 1985): 31. Craig Safan profile.

Birns, Debby. "Filmusic." 8:2 (Summer 1986): 10. Jerry Goldsmith profile.

Singer, Barbara. "Cinemascore: A Technological Alternative." [8:3] [Winter 1986]: 7. On Tom Bahler's music production company.

"Movie Music Week." 8:6 (December 1988–January 1989): 32. News.

Roland, David. "Sound Tracks: Danny Elfman on Scoring *Batman* (1989)." 9:4 (August–September 1989): 7–8.

Roland, David. "Sound Tracks: Cliff Eidelman." 11:2 (March–April 1991): 15.

Slate, Libby. "Film Music: Composer Stephen Graziano." 12:4 (November–December 1992): 23. Profile of the scorer of film trailers.

Slate, Libby. "Film Music: Stanley Clarke." 13:1 (Spring 1993): 16–17. Profile.

Slate, Libby. "Film Music: Bruce Broughton." 14:2 (Summer 1994): 31. Profile.

Angles (US)

On women working in film and video.

Espinoza, Sheila. "Postscript: Composer Scores with Documentaries." 3:3–4 (1998): 34–35. By a Seattle-based composer.

Animation Journal (US)

An index to the first five volumes (Fall 1992 to Spring 1997) contains references to music.

Benshoff, Harry M. "Heigh-ho, Heigh-ho, Is Disney High or Low? From Silly Cartoons to Postmodern Politics." (Fall 1992): 62–85. Includes some discussion of music.

Corradini, Bruno Ginnani. "Chromatic Music." 4:2 (1996): 78–84. Written in 1912 on his experiments with music and color. Corradini was an Italian writer and futurist also known as Bruno Corra. The correct spelling is Bruno Ginanni Corradini.

Animation Magazine (US)

The business, technology, and art of animation.

Roger, Normand. "More Than the Music: Notes on Animation Sound Tracks." 2:4 (Spring 1989): 47–48. By the Canadian composer and sound designer.

Givens, Bill. "Say It with Music: On the Road with Restored Versions of *Fantasia* and *Allegro non Troppo*." 4:1 (Fall 1990): 26–28.

Chusid, Irwin. "50 Years of Musical Mayhem." 6:4 (Summer 1993): 43–47. Includes a list of Raymond Scott melodies used in Warner Bros. cartoons. Author is director of the Raymond Scott archives. This article and the next are under "Historical Perspectives" in *Animation Collection*, which forms part of *Animation* magazine yet has its own volume numbering, 1:4 and 2:6, respectively.

Chusid, Irwin. "Carl Stalling: Music to Toon By." 8:1 (October–November 1994): 74–75.

Kraft, Richard. "Music." 9:4–10:1 (January 1996): 74. On the peak of animation in the mid-1980s.

12:1 (January 1998): 57–59. The music and postproduction section includes material on Steve Rucker and Thomas Jones Chase.

Animation World Magazine (US)

Special issue, 2:1 (April 1997) ["Music, Sound, and Animation"]

Bhatia, Amin. "The Ink and Paint of Music." 8–10. A day in the life of a composer who writes music for animated television shows.

Martignoni, Andrea. "The Burgeoning of a Project: Pierre Hébert's *La Plante humaine*." 11–18. Marrying animation and music.

Moritz, William. "The Dream of Color Music, and Machines that Made It Possible." 20–24.

Kaufman, J. B. "Who's Afraid of ASCAP? Popular Songs in the Silly Symphonies." 25–27.

Goldmark, Daniel. "Carl Stalling and Humor in Cartoons." 28–30. On visual-musical gags.

Jackson, Wendy. "Desert Island Series." 52. Films and music that Alf Clausen and Danny Elfman would bring to a deserted island.

Animatrix (US)

Published by the UCLA Animation Workshop.

Raitt, Jason. "The Disney Animated Musical: The Future of the Animated Musical." No. 9 (1995–1996): 26–32.

Author and Composer (US)

A digest for songwriters, dramatists, scenario writers, and fictionists published in Hollywood.

Reid, Robert. "Max Steiner, Exclusive Interview." (October 1933): 9. The earliest known interview with Steiner in Hollywood.

Back Stage (US)

Vagnoni, Anthony. "Crossover Composers: Scoring for the Silver Screen." (April 27, 1990): 8B, 10, 12, 24. Music for television by Jonathan Elias, Rob Mounsey, and Cliff Eidelman.

The Big Trail (US)

This fan newsletter for the films of John Wayne featured a six-part article, "Dimitri

Tiomkin's Scores for John Wayne Films," by six different writers.

Kausler, Kurt. 14:1 (June 1997): 3–4, 15. On *Red River*.

Pugh, Greg. 14:2 (August 1997): 3–4, 15. On *The High and the Mighty*.

Lilley, Tim. 14:3 (October 1997): 3–4. On *Rio Bravo*.

Bryden, Bob. 14:4 (December 1997): 3–4, 18–19. On *The Alamo*.

Nohl, Phil. 14:5 (February 1998): 3–4, 19. On *Circus World*.

Doctor, Dustin. 14:6 (April 1998): 3–4, 23. On *The War Wagon*.

Blackhawk Film Digest (US)

Blackhawk Films was a leading seller of 8mm and 16mm films for home use in the days before video and DVD. Occasional articles on music appeared in their mail-order catalogs.

Shepard, David. "Music for Silents." [Date undetermined, circa 1970s.] The owner of Blackhawk explains the variety of approaches his company takes in scoring their releases of silent films.

Bann, Richard W. "Pipe Organ Music Tracks." [Date undetermined, circa 1970s.] On John Muri.

Carter, Gaylord. "Organ Scoring for Silent Motion Pictures." (Spring 1981 catalog): 4. Probably reprinted from *Theatre Organ*.

Boxoffice (US)

Business magazine of the global motion picture industry, largely devoted to exhibition. Published weekly from 1932 to 1980, then monthly, out of New York, later Chicago. Recurring section "Hollywood Boxoffice: News and Views of the Production Center" includes film music news, particularly scoring assignments. The latter are also in the "Cleffers" section under "Studio Personalities" from 1940 through 1956. The selections below provide a sampling of the news items.

"Film Music Council Is Exploitation Ally on Many Types of Pictures." 48:3 (November 24, 1945): 98. With quotes from chairperson Grace Widney Mabee.

"[Dimitri] Tiomkin to Get Top Salary for Scoring." 80:23 (March 26, 1962): SE6.

"Backstage with [Syd] Cassyd." 83:18 (August 26, 1963): W2. Dimitri Tiomkin on showmanship.

"Opera Series Earn Praise and Profits in All Seasons." 85:7 (June 8, 1964): 89–90. On a New Jersey theater's experience.

"Film Tunes Were Most Welcome Tonic to Depression-Harried Theatregoers." 102:22 (March 12, 1973): C25.

"Lalo Schifrin to Compose Score for *The Exorcist*." 104:5 (November 12, 1973): 8.

"Merle Anderson Has Been Nickelodeonist 71 Years." 104:5 (November 12, 1973): C2–C4.

"Lalo Schifrin to Write *Rollercoaster* Music." 110:9 (December 6, 1976): 4.

"Frontiere Resigns Para. Music Director Post." 112:2 (October 17, 1977): 4.

"*Star Wars* Music Battle Is Resolved." 112:2 (October 17, 1977): E6.

"Silent Era Anything but Silent, Organist Recalls." 113:5 (May 8, 1978): E8. Recollections of H. Arnold "Hap" Perkins reprinted from the *Baltimore Sun Magazine*.

"Silent Film Nostalgia Evokes Sounds of Music." 113 (July 17, 1978): ME4. An entertainment editor in Cleveland reminisces.

Linck, David. "Screen Stars a Fan Never Sees." 117:4 (April 1981): 16. On Charles Fox.

Klein, Judy E. "Violins or Vibes—Scoring Can Mean Money at the Boxoffice." 119:7 (July 1983): 26–27. Jerry Goldsmith, James Horner, and Jerrold Immel on current projects.

Karp, Alan. "Movies that Rock: Music Videos Rock the Silver Screen." 120:11 (November 1984): 10–11.

Karp, Alan. "A Brief History of Movies that Rock." 120:11 (November 1984): 12.

Karp, Alan. "*Footloose* in the Marketplace." 120:11 (November 1984): 14. On marketing rock music.

Richard, Julie. "Lalo Schifrin: Score One for the Composer." 122:3 (March 1986): SW30–32. Interview-based article.

Williamson, Kim. "Music Man." 131 (June 1995): 9. Alan Menken interview.

Allen, John F. "The Power of Music: A Critical Marketing Tool Remains Largely Unexploited." 136:11 (November 2000): 72, 74. On sound quality in theaters by a sound system specialist.

Reed, Jordan. "Scorekeeper: Christopher Young, *Swordfish*." 137:6 (June 2001): 30.

The British Film Academy Journal (UK)

Alwyn, William. "How Not to Write Film Music." 1 (Autumn 1954): 7–8.

British Film Review (UK)

Keller, Hans. "Benjamin Britten: Film Composer." 1:3 (May 1948). Reprinted in *Film Monthly Review*.

British Journal of Photography (UK)

Rawlinson, Harold. "Music and the Film." (March 16, 1945, and August 6, 1948).

Broadcast (UK)

Margolis, K. "Muskett Fife and Drum...and Synthesiser." (December 6, 1982): 13. Composer Jennie Muskett on the struggles women composers face.

Da Costa, P. "Electronic Twist to the Gothic." (April 25, 1986): 20. On composer Martin Kiszko's television music.

Felstein, Roma. "Pollyanna Masters Art of Noise on Film." (May 9, 1986): 22. On music supervision by Pollyanna Music & Film Company.

Harbord, Janet. "[George] Fenton's Air on a Film Screen." (May 15, 1987): 14. Profile.

White, I. "Record Brokers." (September 25, 1992): 24. On library music for British television.

Bulletin of the Academy of Motion Picture Arts and Sciences (US)

Hamilton, Arthur. "Changes: Forty Years of Film Music." 5 (Spring 1974): 6, 8. Brief overview of the music categories.

Business Screen (US)

Published in Chicago.

Velazco, Emil. "Film Music Ideas for the Making of a Good Music Track." 7:5 (1946): 28.

"Music for the Business Picture." 15:8 (1954): 48. On Richard Shores, Cavalcade Film Services, Chicago.

Meakin, Jack. "Music in the Business Film." 22:6 (October 21, 1961): 49–50.

Muscio, G. "Music Scoring: Editing Library Music." 21 (July 1978): 21.

Cahiers du Cinéma in English (US)

Hauduroy, Jean-Francois. "Writing for Musicals: Interview with Betty Comden and Adolph Green." No. 2 (1966): 43–50. With filmography.

Camera Obscura (US)

A journal of feminism and film theory published in Los Angeles.

Turk, Edward Baron. "Deriding the Voice of Jeanette MacDonald: Notes on Psychoanalysis and the American Film Musical." 25–26 (Spring 1991): 225–49.

Herman, Jeanette. "Memory and Melodrama: The Transnational Politics of Deepa Mehta's *Earth*." 20 (2005): 107–47.

Canadian Film Weekly (Canada)

"Our Film-Music Field Has Stature." 18:27 (July 8, 1953): 1, 6. On Canadian composers Louis Applebaum, Maurice Blackburn, Robert Fleming, William McCauley, and Eldon Rathburn.

Canadian Film Weekly Yearbook (Canada)

Published annually by Film Publications of Canada in Toronto from 1951 to 1971. Title varies: *Year Book of the Canadian Motion Picture Industry*; *Year Book, Canadian Motion Picture Industry*; *Year Book, Canadian Motion Picture Industry with Television Section*; *Year Book, Canadian Entertainment Industry*. Contains credits; for example, "Music" (1951, p. 174) lists ten background music composers and their credits.

Cantrills Filmnotes (Australia)

Wesley-Smith, Martin. "Intermedia—A Composer's View." No. 31–32 (November 1979): 48–52.

Moritz, William. "Towards a Visual Music." No. 47–48 (August 1985): 35–42. The history and development of visual accompaniments to music, including the color organ.

CBC Times (Canada)

Issued weekly by the Canadian Broadcasting Corporation in Toronto.

Pratley, Gerald. "Music for Films: A Special Craft." 4:37 (March 30–April 5, [1952]): 2. On the radio series.

Pratley, Gerald. "10 Years of *Music from the Films*." (April 4–10, 1959): 3. History of the radio program.

Channels of Communications (US)

Moore, F. "More Sound for Less." 9:8 (July–August 1989): 72. On computer-generated music for television.

CineAction (Canada)

Promoting the advancement of film studies through film criticism and theory.

Wei, Yanmei. "Music and Femininity in Zhang Yimou's Family Melodrama." No. 42 (February 1997): 18–27.

Austerlitz, Saul. "Music and Modernity in *A Brighter Summer Day*." No. 62 (October 2003): 67–71.

Clayton, Alex. "From Within: Music in the Style of Jean Renoir." No. 66 (Spring 2005): 61–72.

Cineaste (US)

America's leading magazine on the art and politics of the cinema, published in New York.

Articles

Rubenstein, Lenny. "Composing for Films: An Interview with John Addison." 8:2 (Fall 1977): 36–37, 59.

Auster, Al. "Gotta Sing! Gotta Dance! New Theory and Criticism on the Musical." 12:4 (1983): 30–35.

21:1–2 (February 1995). Special issue, contents listed below.

Hershon, Robert. "Film Composers in the Sonic Wars." 22:4 (March 1997): 10–13. On the difficulties of getting film music heard in the theater (due to other soundtracks, particularly sound effects) and getting a soundtrack released, as viewed through the experiences of Angelo Badalamenti, Elliot Goldenthal, Jerry Goldsmith, James Horner, and Mark Isham.

Hershon, Bob. "Off the Beaten Track: Harmonious Composer/Director Teams." 23:4 (1998): 38–41. On composers Carter Burwell, Stewart Copeland, Mark Isham, and Toru Takemitsu.

Hershon, Robert. "They're Playing Your Song: The Role of the Music Supervisor." 26:3 (Summer 2001): 24–26, 55. On how musical choices contribute to the drama and emotion of a film.

Special issue, 21:1–2 (February 1995): 34–page supplement ["Sound and Music in the Movies"]

Handzo, Stephen. "The Golden Age of Film Music." 46–55. Historical overview.

Weis, Elisabeth. "Sync Tanks: The Art and Technique of Postproduction Sound." 56–61.

Brown, Royal S. "Film Music: The Good, the Bad, and the Ugly." 62–67. Aesthetics.

Gorbman, Claudia. "The State of Film Music Criticism." 72–75.

Burlingame, Jon, and Gary Crowdus. "Music at the Service of the Cinema: An Interview with Ennio Morricone." 76–80.

CineFan (US)

Published biannually by Randall Larson and specializing in the analysis and review of science fiction, fantasy, and horror films, with emphasis on more obscure films.

No. 1 (1974). Max Steiner interview reprinted from a Max Steiner Music Society publication.

No. 2 (1980). Fantasy film music of Bernard Herrmann.

No. 3 (Winter 1984–Spring 1985). Les Baxter.

Cinefantastique (US)

A science fiction and horror film fan magazine published in Illinois. "The Score" column ran occasionally from 1970 to 1973 and from 1980 to 1988 (from the mid-1980s it documents upcoming releases and can be found in the section "Coming"), followed by a short-lived "Film Music" column. Noah Andre Trudeau occasionally reviewed soundtracks in 1989 and 1990. (The author of several books on the Civil War, Trudeau discusses film music on National Public Radio, where he's known as Andy.) The column "Soundtrax" contained some Randall Larson reviews from 1996 through 1998. Film music coverage seems to have ceased when the magazine began putting *CFQ* on the cover and sought a more trendy audience in early 2003.

Articles

Jones, Preston Neal. "The Ghost of Hans J. Salter." 7:2 (1978): 10–25. Interview, with music examples and filmography.

Siden, Hans. "The Music of *Star Trek*." 17:2 (March 1987): 35, 54. On Alexander Courage's music.

Counts, Kyle. "*The Little Mermaid*: Fantasy Songwriters." 20:5 (May 1990): 54–55. On Alan Menken's music.

Larson, Randall D. "The Man behind the Music." 22:3 (December 1991): 42. On Vic Mizzy.

Kendall, Lukas. "Scoring the Final Frontier." 23:2–3 (October 1992): 100–101, 124–25. On *Star Trek* music by Jay Chattaway, Ron Jones, and Dennis McCarthy.

Kendall, Lukas. "The Final Frontier's Musical Discord." 24:3–4 (October 1993): 84–86, 124. On *Star Trek* music by Jay Chattaway and Dennis McCarthy.

Garcia, Bob. "Batmusic." 24:6–25:1 (February 1994): 37, 61. On *Batman* music by Nelson Riddle.

Garcia, Bob. "Composing Music for Animation." 24:6–25:1 (February 1994): 108–110. On music by Shirley Walker.

Larson, Randall D. "*2001*: The Music: Composer Alex North on His Abandoned Score." 25:3 (June 1994): 40–42.

Vitaris, Paula. "*X-Files*: Music of the Night." 26:6–27:1 (October 1995): 79–81. Interview-based article on Mark Snow's music.

Bond, Jeff. "*Trek*'s Scrambled Music Credits." 28 (1996): 126. On *Star Trek*.

Montesano, Anthony P. "Horror's Anthem." 30:2 (June 1998): 6. On the use of the song "Don't Fear the Reaper," in *Halloween* and subsequent films.

Larson, Randall D. "*X-Files*: Dark Music." 30:7–8 (October 1998): 47–48. On Mark Snow's music.

Larson, Randall D. "The Horror of James Bernard." 30:7–8 (October 1998): 94–98.

Starita, Angela. "Sounds of Silents: Scoring Silent Era Horror Films: The Debate between Restoration and Reinterpretation." 30:7–8 (October 1998): 99, 101–3, 126.

Biodrowski, Steve. "Phantom of the Orpheum: Keeping the Tradition of Organ Accompaniment Alive." 30:7–8 (October 1998): 100–101.

Bassom, David. "Music: Composer Christophe Franke on Mixing Classical and Electronic." 31:12–32:1 (June 2000): 68. For the television series *Babylon 5*.

<u>Column, "Film Music" (selected)</u>

Larson, Randall D. "The Next Generation of Video Scores for *Star Trek*." 19:3 (March 1989): 46, 59. On music by Ron Jones and Dennis McCarthy.

Larson, Randall D. "Danny Elfman: Director Tim Burton's Rock Music Man." 20:1–2 (November 1989): 109, 120.

<u>Column, "Recordings" (selected)</u>

Trudeau, Noah Andre. "Scoring Sequels, Composers Who Can Top Themselves." 20:4 (March 1990): 1951.

<u>Column, "The Score" (selected)</u>

Stevens, Mark. 1:1 (Fall 1970): 40–41. Summary of current film scores.

Stevens, Mark. 2:3 (Winter 1973): 40–41. Last column by Stevens, with opinions on current scores.

Oatis, Greg. "John Williams Strikes Back, Unfortunately." 10:2 (Fall 1980): 8. Article on *The Empire Strikes Back*.

Oatis, Greg. "Only Kubrick's Soundtrack Manages to Shine." 10:3 (Winter 1980): 16. On the music for *The Shining*, including Wendy Carlos's score.

Gagne, Paul. "The Filming of *Altered States*." 11:2 (Fall 1981). Includes "What's a Nice Classical Composer Like John Corigliano Doing on a Film Like This?" 37.

Larson, Randall D. "The Beast within Les Baxter." 12:4 (May–June 1982): 8.

Larson, Randall D. "Electronic Music by [Wendy] Carlos." 12:5–6 (1982): 10.

Larson, Randall D. "Two from Jerry Goldsmith." 13:1 (1982): 14.

Gagne, Paul. "John Harrison's Creepmusic." 13:2–3 (1982): 10.

Larson, Randall D. "Some *Thing* New from Ennio Morricone." 13:4 (April–May 1983): 12.

Larson, Randall D. "He's a Low-Budget One-Man Band." 13:5 (June–July 1983): 14. Article on Richard Band.

Larson, Randall D. "Thunderous Blues and Score Games." 13:6–14:1 (September 1983): 16. Article on Arthur B. Rubinstein.

Lucas, Tim. "Cronenberg's Bioelectronic Composer." 14:2 (December 1983–January 1984): 12. On music by Howard Shore.

Larson, Randall D. "[Elmer] Bernstein Busts Ghosts, Knocks Rock." 15:1 (January 1985): 14, 52.

Larson, Randall D. "Craig Huxley's Musical Imagineering." 15:3 (July 1985): 20, 60.

Larson, Randall D. "Re-animating Bernard Herrmann. " 16:2 (May 1986): 12, 61. On music by Richard Band.

Larson, Randall D. "Tangerine Dream in the Shadow of a *Legend*." 16:3 (July 1986): 42, 61.

Larson, Randall D. "New Music for Star Fleet." 17:3–4 (June 1987): 30, 124–25. On Leonard Rosenman's music for *Star Trek IV*.

Larson, Randall D. "Christopher Young on *Hellraiser*." 18:4 (May 1988): 22, 58.

Column, "Soundtrax" (selected)
Larson, Randall D. "The X-Factor: Mark Snow." 29:4–5 (October 1997): 122.

Larson, Randall D. "Music to Crash To." 30:1 (May 1998): 60. On music by Howard Shore.

Cinegram Magazine (US)

Aldridge, Henry. "Film Music." 3:1 (Summer 1978): 32–34. Music's contribution for emotions, information, and rhythm.

Cinema (US, 1947)

A short-lived magazine for "discriminating movie-goers," published in Hollywood.

Stravinsky, Igor, and Ingolf Dahl. "Igor Stravinsky on Film Music: As Told to Ingolf Dahl." 1:1 (June 1947): 7–8, 21. On the function of film music and concert music in film. Reprinted from *Musical Digest* (September 1946).

Morton, Lawrence. "'Hollywood' Music." 1:3 (August 1947): 7–8, 19. On aesthetics and on being branded a Hollywood composer.

Cinema (US, 1962–1976)

Published by Spectator International and Jack Martin Hanson in Hollywood and Beverly Hills.

Hanson, Curtis Lee. "Three Screen Composers: Maurice Jarre, Dimitri Tiomkin, and Henry Mancini in Cinema Interviews on Writing Music for the Movies." 3:3 (July 1966): 8–10, 16, 33–34.

Reisner, Joel, and Bruce Kane. "An Interview with Alex North." 5:4 (1969): 42–45.

Cinema and Theatre (UK)

A monthly motion picture trade journal originally titled *Cinema and Theatre Construction*.

Huntley, John. "Stage One at Denham Studios." 13:6 (May 1947): 26–30. On the stage's conversion to music scoring.

Mathieson, Muir. "Background Music in British Films." 14:4 (September 1947): 7–9.

"Music Opens a Vast New Field for 16mm Films." 14:6 (November 1947): 46–47.

Huntley, John. "Music in New British Films." 15:1 (December 1947): 39–43.

Cinema Arts (US)

Short-lived magazine published in New York.

Garden, Mary. "Music Comes to Hollywood." 1:1 (June 1937): 19. Discovering and signing new singers from the world of opera.

Antheil, George. "Hollywood and the New Music." 1:2 (July 1937): 28–29. On Paramount's Boris Morros's signing of "modern" composers, including Stravinsky.

Cinema Canada (Canada)

Canada's leading film magazine, published in Toronto.

Special section, "Music for the Movies," no. 60–61 (December 1979–January 1980)

Paton, Robert. "Thriving on Variety." 14–17. Interview with jazz composer Paul Hoffert on the composer-director relationship.

Shragge, Lawrence. "Sounds behind the Scenes." 18–19. On the process of writing music for film.

Hahn, Richard, and Howard Knopf. "Film Music: Some Legal Notes." 20–25.

Costabile, Paul. "Different Schools Together." 26–29. On the collaborations of composers Paul Zaza and Carl Zittrer. Filmography.

Siegel, Lois. "Furey Knows the Score." 30–32. On composer Lewis Furey.

Paton, Robert. "Soundscape in Concert." 34–38. On composer R. Murray Schafer.

Hahn, Bob. "It's Mainly Because of the Music." 40–42. On Canadian film music.

Stone, Chris. "'Canned' Music: But Can You Tell?" 43–44. Stock music.

Morley, Glenn. "The Synthesizer: The Mockingbird of Instruments." 45–47.

Filletti, Connie. "The T.V. Composer's Untapped Potential." 48–50.

Morley, Glenn. "The Guild." 51–52. On the mandate of the Guild of Canadian Film Composers.

Morley, Glenn. "Professional Directory of Canadian Film Composers." 52–53.

Cinema Chronicle (USSR)

Published in Moscow by the USSR Society for Cultural Relations with Foreign Countries. Also appeared under the titles *Soviet Cinema Chronicle*, *Film Chronicle*, and *Soviet Film Chronicle*.

"New Soviet Feature Films: Cherevichki." No. 1 (January 1945): 1–7. On a Tchaikovsky filmed opera, *Christmas Slippers*, with comments from the directors.

"In the VOKS Film Section: New Sub-Section of Film-Composers and Film Musicians." No. 6 (June 1945): 27–28. News item on the newly formed group in Russia.

"In the VOKS Film Section: Meeting of the Film Music Composers Sub-Section." No. 11 (November 1945): 19. Brief report on a viewing of *Holiday Inn*.

Cinema in India (India)

Chandavarkar, Bhaskar. "The Tradition of Music in Indian Cinema: Birth of the Film Song." 1:2 (April–June 1987): 7–11. Part 1.

Chandavarkar, Bhaskar. "The Tradition of Music in Indian Cinema: Growth of the Indian Film Song." 1:3 (July–September 1987): 16–21. Part 2.

Chandavarkar, Bhaskar. "The Tradition of Music in Indian Cinema: Now It's the Bombay Film Song." 1:4 (October–December 1987): 18–23. Part 3.

Chandavarkar, Bhaskar. "The Tradition of Music in Indian Cinema: The Arrangers." 2:1 (January–April 1988): 20–23. Part 4.

Chandavarkar, Bhaskar. "The Tradition of Music in Indian Cinema: Song of the Instruments." 2:2 (April–June 1988): 22–27. Part 5.

Chandavarkar, Bhaskar. "The Tradition of Music in Indian Cinema: The Music Director Who Wasn't." 2:3 (July–September 1988): 6–10. Part 6. On Raj Kapoor.

Chandavarkar, Bhaskar. "The Tradition of Music in Indian Cinema: How Classical Is Filmi Classical?" 2:4 (October–December 1988): 18–23. Part 7.

Chandavarkar, Bhaskar. "The Tradition of Music in Indian Cinema: Youthtime!" 3:1 (January–March 1989): 16–21. Part 8.

Chandavarkar, Bhaskar. "The Tradition of Music in Indian Cinema: Those Were the Sixties!" 3:2 (April–June 1989): 22–28. Part 9.

Chandavarkar, Bhaskar. "Music a la Ilayaraja." 3:3 (July–September 1989): 22–29. On Raj Kapoor.

Chandavarkar, Bhaskar. "The Power of the Popular Film Song." 4:2 (April–June 1990): 20–24.

Shahani, Roshan. "Man of Music." 2:4 (April 1991): 15–22.

Saran, Sathya. "In the Mood: Composers Sharang Dev, Kuldeep Singh and Louis Banks Sound Off on the Importance of Background Music." 2:4 (April 1991): 23–27.

Vesuna, Sheila. "Young at Heart: An Interview with the Reclusive Music Composer, P. Navyar." 2:7 (July 1991): 26–33.

Gulzar, Meghna. "The Beat Goes On: An Interview with Music Composer, R. D. Burman, Who Says That He Has Opted Out of the 'Rat Race.'" 2:8 (August 1991): 14–19.

Gangar, Amrit. "The Music of Sound: An Interview with Music Underkind [*sic*], Rajat Dholakia." 2:8 (August 1991): 21–25.

Cinema Journal (US)

Journal of the Society of Cinematologists, formerly known as the Society for Cinema Studies.

Articles

Gallez, Douglas W. "Theories of Film Music." 9:2 (Spring 1970): 40–47. Pudovkin's aesthetic view, the viewpoint of composers, and toward a new functional synthesis.

Gallez, Douglas W. "Facing the Music in Scripts." 11:1 (Fall 1971): 57–62. Essay regarding musical indications in scripts.

Gallez, Douglas W. "Satie's *Entr'acte*: A Model of Film Music." 16:1 (Fall 1976): 36–50. On Erik Satie's score.

17:2 (Spring 1978). Special issue, contents listed below.

Brown, Royal S. "Herrmann, Hitchcock, and the Music of the Irrational." 21:2 (Spring 1982): 14–49. On the collaboration between director Alfred Hitchcock and Bernard Herrmann.

Kalinak, Kathryn. "The Text of Music: A Study of *The Magnificent Ambersons*." 27:4 (Summer 1988): 45–63. Analysis of Bernard Herrmann's score, with music examples.

Flinn, Carol. "The Most Romantic Art of All: Music in the Classical Hollywood Cinema." 29:4 (Summer 1990): 35–50. Aesthetics.

Darby, William. "Musical Links in *Young Mr. Lincoln*, *My Darling Clementine*, and *The Man Who Shot Liberty Valance*." 31:1 (Fall 1991): 22–36. Analysis of music by Alfred Newman and Cyril Mockridge in films directed by John Ford.

Ruoff, Jeffrey. "Conventions of Sound in Documentary." 32:3 (Spring 1993): 24–40. Includes "Music in Documentary," 32–34.

McLean, Adrienne L. "'It's Only That I Do What I Love and Love What I Do': Film Noir and the Musical Woman." 33:1 (Fall 1993): 3–16. Examines the contribution of song interludes.

Anderson, Tim. "Reforming 'Jackass Music': The Problematic Aesthetics of Early American Film Music Accompaniment." 37:1 (Fall 1997): 322. Covers roughly from 1907 to 1912.

Shumway, David R. "Rock 'n' Roll Sound Tracks and the Production of Nostalgia." 38:2 (Winter 1999): 26–51.

Stanfield, Peter. "An Excursion into the Lower Depths: Hollywood, Urban Primitivism, and St. Louis Blues, 1929–1937." 41:2 (Winter 2002): 84–108. On the use of the song "St. Louis Blues."

Yeh, Yueh-yu. "Historiography and Sinification: Music in Chinese Cinema of the 1930s." 41:3 (Spring 2002): 78–97.

Fay, Jennifer. "'That's Jazz Made in Germany!': *Hallo, Fraulein!* and the Limits of Democratic Pedagogy." 44:1 (Fall 2004): 3–24.

Special issue, 17:2 (Spring 1978)

Berg, Charles Merrell. "Cinema Sings the Blues." 1–12. Historical overview of the use of jazz in film.

Gallez, Douglas W. "The Prokofiev-Eisenstein Collaboration: *Nevsky* and *Ivan* Revisited." 13–35. History and analysis of Prokofiev's scores for *Alexander Nevsky* and *Ivan the Terrible*, with music examples.

Sharples, Win, Jr. "A Selected and Annotated Bibliography of Books and Articles on Music in the Cinema." 36–67. Includes listings for fan clubs, sources for soundtrack recordings, films on film music, and periodicals dealing with the subject of film music on a regular basis. It is similar in scope and content to but more extensive than the American Film Institute's *Film Music*, Factfile number 8, which Sharples helped compile the previous year.

Cinema Papers (Australia)

Australia's leading film publication, published in Melbourne. Australian film reviewer Ivan Hutchinson contributed an occasional column on soundtracks from 1975 to 1978 and from 1991 to 1994. The former tended to focus on individual composers and their music and the latter on soundtrack reviews of current releases.

Articles

Hutchinson, Ivan, and Peter Beilby. "Bruce Smeaton: Interview." No. 6 (July–August 1975): 165–67. With filmography.

Stanley, Raymond. "John Dankovitch Interview." No. 12 (April 1977): 332–35. With filmography.

Hutchinson, Ivan. "George Dreyfus." No. 13 (July 1977): 88. Profile.

Hutchinson, Ivan. "Brian May: Interview." No. 17 (August–September 1978): 32–33.

Ginnane, Anthony I., Leon Gorr, and Ian Baillieu. "Guide for the Australian Film Producer: Part 10, The Soundtrack Agreement." No. 17 (August–September 1978): 38. Including original music for feature films.

Beilby, Peter, Rod Bishop, and Cameron Allan. "Production Report: *Blue Fin*." No. 19 (January–February, 1979): 207–13, 242. Includes an interview with composer Michael Carlos.

"Scoring *The Earthling*." No. 26 (April–May, 1980): 119.

Hutchinson, Ivan. "Music." No. 40 (October 1982): 479. On current soundtracks.

Adler, Sue. "Ennio Morricone." No. 49 (December 1984): 425–27. Interview.

Koeser, Dorre. "Working Abroad: Two Composers: 1. Bill Conti." No. 50 (February–March 1985): 44–46, 88. Interview on working in Italy.

Hutchinson, Ivan. "Working Abroad: Two Composers: 2. Brian May." No. 50 (February–March 1985): 47–49, 88. Interview.

Grieve, Anna. "The Sounds of Martin." No. 61 (January 1987): 13. Profiles Australian film composer Martin Armiger.

Gyffyn, Jenni. "The Sound of Music." No. 69 (May 1988): 10–15. Interviews with Peter Best, John Clifford-White, Bruce Rowland, Paul Schütze, and Bruce Smeaton.

Brophy, Philip. "Film Music." No. 71 (January 1989): 50–51. Essay on the inseparable connection between music and film, specifically in the film music of Erik Satie and Brian Eno.

Silverton, Richard. "The Sound of Music: There's More Than Meets the Eye." No. 105 (August 1995): 53–54. Legal and copyright issues for soundtracks.

Murray, Scott. "Scoring *Babe*." No. 107 (December 1995): 12–13, 54. On Nigel Westlake's music.

Ross, Dina, and Deborah Niski. "Score!" No. 122 (December 1997): 18–21, 70. Ross interviews Australians Cezary Skubiszewski and David Hirschfelder; Niski interviews Eric Serra.

Ross, Dina. "In the Mix." No. 127 (October 1998): 50, 52. On the music group Supersonic.

Column, "Soundtracks" by Ivan Hutchinson
No. 6 (July–August 1975): 176. First column.
No. 7 (November–December 1975): 282. On John Williams.
No. 8 (March–April 1976): 375, 378. On Bernard Herrmann.
No. 9 (June–July 1976): 79. On British soundtracks.
No. 11 (January 1977): 277. On Jerry Goldsmith.
No. 13 (July 1977): 85. On Australian composer George Dreyfus.
No. 15 (January 1978): 271. Final 1970s column.
No. 84 (August 1991): 71. On soundtracks by Australian composers.
No. 89 (August 1992): 62–63. On soundtracks by Australian composers.
No. 90 (October 1992): 64–65. On current soundtracks.
No. 93 (May–June 1993): 56. On current soundtracks.
No. 94 (August 1993): 58–59. Reviews.
No. 95 (October 1993): 58–59. Reviews.
No. 99 (June 1994): 80–81. Reviews.
No. 100 (August 1994): 78–79. On compilations.

Cinema Quarterly (UK)

Published quarterly in Scotland from 1932 to 1935; absorbed by *World Film News* in 1936.

Hackenschmied, Alexandr [*sic*]. "Film and Music." 1:3 (Spring 1933): 152–155. The relationship between sound and image in the early sound film. Translated from the Czech by Karel Santar.

Watts, Stephen. "Alfred Hitchcock on Music in Films." 2:2 (Winter 1933–1934): 80–83. Reprinted in *Hitchcock Annual* (1994) and Sidney Gottlieb's *Hitchcock on Hitchcock* (1995).

Clark, G. R. "Films to Music." 2:4 (Summer 1934): 260–61. On original scores.

Leigh, Walter. "The Musician and the Film." 3:2 (Winter 1935): 70–74. Essay calling for composers to take greater advantage in writing music for film.

Cinema Studies (UK)

The journal of the Society for Film History Research, published in London.

Williams, David R. "The Development of Sound Films in Leicester." 1:7 (June 1963): 160–63. Documents the musical accompaniment of silent films from 1897 to 1914 (and, briefly, 1925 to 1929) through local newspaper accounts and interviews.

The Cinema Studio (UK)
Supplement to *The Cinema* and also known as *Cinema News and Property Gazette.* At the end of the section on current films in production is "Music Sessions," documenting film score recording sessions with such details as time spent, who was present, and instrumentation. Some issues contain film music-related news articles and report on the activities of British music director Louis Levy. Only 1948 issues are covered below; unable to access 1949 issues. Coverage of recording sessions appears to have ceased in 1950.

Articles (selected)
Huntley, John. "The Film Music of Arnold Bax: With an Ear to *Oliver Twist.*" 1:10 (June 2, 1948): 5.
"Music for the Ears of a Producer: But the Composer's Critic Didn't Hear a Note of It." 1:16 (July 14, 1948): 9–10. Interview-based article on Hans May.
"First Woman to Compose Feature Score: Grace Williams Uses Traditional Melodies." 1:17 (July 21, 1948): 5. Interview-based profile.
"Foxwell Says It with Music: With Hans May as Composer." 4:99 (February 15, 1950): 9–10.
Jones, Roger Railton. "It's Music…It's *Happy-Go-Lovely.*" 6:117 (January 1951): 13–15. On recording Mischa Spoliansky's score with Louis Levy conducting.
"Among My Souvenirs: Music from Films." 6:121 (May 1951): 35–36. On the latest records and sheet music.

Column, "Music Sessions" (selected)
1:5 (April 28, 1948): 20. On music by Allan Gray.
1:25 (September 15, 1948): 18. With profile of composer Edward Williams.
2:29 (October 13, 1948): 21. Including recording music for a TV program on British film music.

Cinema TV Today (UK)
Clarke, Sue. "Music Can't Bring a Rotten Film to Life—Miklos Rozsa." No. 10015 (January 20, 1973): 7.
Falk, Quentin. "[Jerry] Goldsmith on the Role of Film Music." No. 10141 (July 5, 1975): 12–13.

Cinema Vision India (India)
India's first professional cinema quarterly, established in 1980.

Special issue, 1:4 (October 1980) [on film music]
On the use of songs in Indian films; includes "The Rise of the Indian Film Song."

Special issue, 2:2 (January 1983) (selected) [on music in early sound films]
Sharma, K. C. "The Dentist Who Made Musical History." 34–38. On composer Ghulam Haider.
Bharatan, Raju. "The Final Touch Made All the Difference." 66–67. On composer S. D. Burman.
Burman, S. D. "Far Away from the World of Music." 68–69.
Kinikar, Shashikant. "Lasting Lady: Khurshid-Saraswati." 70–73. Interview with India's first woman film composer, Saraswati Devi.

Mahmood, Hameemuddm. "Music by Naushad [Ali]." 74–78. On the music director and composer.

Cinema Year Book of Japan (Japan)
Annual from the International Cinema Association of Japan.
Yamada, Kosçak. "Music and Motion Picture [*sic*]." (1936–1937): 36–39. The composer on scoring talkies and his score for *The New Earth.*

Cinemacabre (US)
For fans of the horror genre. A "Soundtrack" column with reviews by Steve Vertlieb, an East Coast-based historian and writer, appeared from 1979 to at least 1988. See no. 1 (1979): 48–54; no. 2 (1979): 54–62; no. 3 (1980): 56–62; no. 4 (1981): 55–62; and no. 5 (Fall 1982): 53–59.

Cinémas: Revue d'Etudes Cinematographiques (Canada)
Articles are in English and French.
Altman, Rick. "Reading Positions, The Cow Bell Effect, and the Sounds of Silent Film." 2:23 (Spring 1992): 19–31. Includes music.
Mettler, Peter. "Music in Films: Film as Music." 3:1 (Autumn 1992): 35–42. The Canadian director on his approach to making films.
Deslandes, Jeanne. "D'une Psychanalyse de la Musique au Cinema." 6:2–3 (1996): 189–97. Psychoanalytic analysis.

Cinemaya: The Asian Film Quarterly (India)
Singh, Madan Gopal. "If Music Be the Food of Love..." 39–40 (Winter–Spring 1998): 4–9.
Doraiswamy, Rashmi. "Mani Ratnam: The Way I Tell Stories." 56–57 (Autumn–Winter 2002): 70–81. Includes discussion of the Indian director's use of music.

Cinemusic and Its Meaning (US)
A series of articles by Bruno David Ussher, billed as "Photoplay Appreciation Study Material," distributed by the Public Relations Department of Fox West Coast Theatres as a public service. Ussher wrote program notes for the Hollywood Bowl from 1923 to 1945. Apparently issued concurrently with a similar publication, *Motion Picture Music and Musicians.* The Fox PR Department also distributed "Radio Talks," including a four-page pamphlet on "Music" that featured a transcript of a program involving a discussion of current film music, circa 1937.
"*The Private Lives of Elizabeth and Essex.*" (1939). First in a series. On Erich Wolfgang Korngold's score.
"Important Picture Scores of Tomorrow." (1939). Second in a series.
Ussher, Bruno David. "Hollywood's Magic Bullets of Sound." (1940). On notable scores, including Max Steiner's for *Dr. Ehrlich's Magic Bullet.*
Ussher, Bruno David. "Max Steiner Establishes Another Film Music Record." (1941). Study material, including background and thematic samples, for Steiner's score for *Gone with the Wind,* 8 pages.
Mehra, Lal Chand. "Hindu Music in Hollywood Motion Pictures." (1941). Includes "Hindu Music in *The Rains Came*" for which the author was musical adviser.
Mabee, Grace Widney. "Schubert's 'Quartette in A Major' Adapted to *Swiss Family Robinson.*" (circa 1942).

Classic Images (US)

Fan magazine initially for collectors of 8mm films, formerly known as *8mm Collector*, then *Classic Film Collector*, then *Classic Film/Video Images*. "Nostalgia Soundtrack," a column by Michael R. Pitts, documented a wide range of disc recordings and appeared in each issue from around June 1986 to November 1990. "Music in Films," a column by Harry H. Long, contained soundtrack reviews and appeared regularly from March 1999 to June 2002.

Published as **Classic Film Collector**

"Michael Merchant Interviews Arthur Kleiner." No. 41 (Winter 1973): 3ff.

Young, Robert R. "Music Makes the Difference in the Enjoyment of Silent Films." No. 47 (Summer 1975): 29–31. The writer supplies his own ideas for cues and musical selections (from pre-existing music) for *The Vanishing American*.

James, Neville. "Silent-Movie Orchestras Thrilled Fans in Early Flicker Days." No. 56 (Fall 1977): X8. Recollections of a New Zealander from around 1911.

Corneau, Ernest N. "Genius of Movie Music: Dimitri Tiomken [*sic*]." No. 57 (Winter 1977): 20, 37.

Published as **Classic Images**

Articles

Collura, Joe. "Dialogue in Los Angeles with David Raksin." No. 68 (March 1980): 24.

Oderman, Stuart. "Arthur Kleiner." No. 69 (May 1980): 49. Tribute.

Buchman, Chris, Jr. "Cinema Omnibus: Music for Silents." No. 70 (July 1980): 24–25. Primer on how to compile your own musical accompaniment for silent films.

McCarthy, John. "A Retrospective Look at Bernard Herrmann." No. 70 (July 1980): 27–28.

Collura, Joe. "Dialogue with Gaylord Carter." No. 70 (July 1980): 54–55. Interview.

Buchman, Chris, Jr. "Cinema Omnibus: Authentic Music vs. Contemporary Music for Silent Films." No. 71 (September 1980): 12. Essay.

Stewart, Norman. "The Korngold Society." No. 123 (September 1985): Center 16.

Johnson, Scott. "Ketelbey: A Notable Composer for Silent Film." No. 127 (January 1986): C8. Profile of British composer Albert W. Ketélbey.

Ward, L. E. "Make Mine Music: The Music of the Movies (1930–1960)." No. 186 (December 1990): 52–53. A historical overview.

Ward, L. E. "Make Mine Music: The Music of the Movies (1930–1960)." No. 187 (January 1991): C8, 57. Continued from above entry.

Ward, L. E. "Make Mine Music: The Music of the Movies (1930–1960): Part II." No. 188 (February 1991): 22–23, 28, 30, 37.

Ward, L. E. "Make Mine Music: The Music of the Movies (1930–1960): Part III." No. 189 (March 1991): 28–29, 45. Ending with two lists of twenty-five classic film scores, the second covering 1960–1990.

Reed, George. "The Paper Collector: Sheet Music—Double Pleasure." No. 207 (September 1992): C6, 58.

Reed, George. "The Paper Collector: Soundtracks, Memories/Images." No. 209 (November 1992): 52–53. Documents a 1928 film song released on disc at the time.

Rubin, Sam. "Classic Clinic: The Accompanists." No. 221 (November 1993): 45, 54. Documents contemporary silent film accompanists Rubin has known through Cinecon gatherings.

Phillips, Bob. "A Tip of the Stetson to the Cowboy Bands." No. 222 (December 1993): 30.

Crawford, Bruce. "Bernard Herrmann: Film Music Genius." No. 272 (February 1998): 30, 32. Career overview.

Column, "Music in Films" by Harry H. Long (selected)
"Masterpieces and Other Pieces of British Film Music." No. 289 (July 1999): C18.
"Western Film Scores and Anthologies of All Kinds." No. 292 (October 1999): C18.
"New Scores for Old Films." No. 294 (December 1999): C38–39. On silent films.

Close Up (UK)
Monthly international film journal published in Switzerland, then London.

Richardson, Dorothy M. "Continuous Performance: Musical Accompaniment." 1:2 (August 1927): 58–62. Eloquent essay on musical accompaniment of silent films, written in the waning days of the art.

Chowl, Hay. "Interview with Herr Meisel." 4:3 (March 1929): 44–48. Edmund Meisel interview.

Modern, Klara. "The Vienna of the Films." 9:2 (June 1932): 129–31.

White, Eric Walter. "The Music to *Harlequin*." 9:3 (September 1932): 164–71. Arranger White explains how he compiled the score.

Weiss, Trude. "The First Opera-Film." 9:4 (December 1932): 242–45. On Smetana's *The Bartered Bride*.

Blakeston, Oswell. "Teaching Music by the Abstract Film." 10:2 (June 1933): 161–62. Essay on the educational value of moving shapes combined with sound.

Howard, Clifford. "Symphonic Cinema." 10:4 (December 1933): 347–50. The challenges of recording a full symphony for such pictures as *Cavalcade*.

Contemporary Cinema (UK)
The monthly Christian review of film contains a film music column by Hans Keller in the last half of 1947. The columns are reprinted in *Film Music and Beyond*.

Articles
Albert, Harold A. "Music for the Movies." 1:4 ([May] 1947): 85–87.
Mathieson, Muir. "Background Music for British Films." 1:8 (September 1947): 213–17.

Column, "Film Music," by Hans Keller
"*Open City*." 1:7 (August 1947): 181.
"*Time Out of Mind*." 1:8 (September 1947): 229–31.
"Film-Musical Atmosphere." 1:9 (October 1947): 277–79.
"The Edinburgh Festival." 1:10 (November 1947): 307–11.
"Its Filmic Value." 1:11 (December 1947): 355–56.

Contemporary Theatre, Film, and Television (US)
Biographical guide published by Gale Research Co. in Detroit. Entries on composers and lyricists in the United States and Great Britain in volumes published annually, 1984–2005, each with a cumulative index. Personal data, career highlights, awards and honors, film and television credits, and recordings. Entrants include Paul Anka, Harold Arlen, David Arnold, Burt Bacharach, Angelo Badalamenti, John Barry, Richard Bellis, Marco Beltrami, Alan and Marilyn Bergman, Irving Berlin, Charles Bernstein, Elmer Bernstein, Leonard Bernstein, Terence Blanchard, David Byrne, Sammy Cahn, Stewart Copeland, John Corigliano, John Debney, Patrick Doyle, Fred Ebb, Danny Elfman, Ira and George Gershwin, Philip Glass, Ernest Gold, Elliot Goldenthal, Jerry Goldsmith, Dave Grusin, Marvin Hamlisch, Herbie Hancock, Otto Harbach, James Horner, James Newton Howard, Isaac Hayes, Bernard Herrmann, Joel Hirschhorn, Mark Isham, Quincy Jones, John

Kander, Mark Knopfler, Alan Jay Lerner and Frederick Loewe, Frank Loesser, Henry
Mancini, Branford Marsalis, Alan Menken, Johnny Mercer, Pat Metheny, Ennio Morri-
cone, David Newman, Randy Newman, Thomas Newman, Harry Nilsson, Michael Ny-
man, Basil Poledouris, Rachel Portman, André Previn, David Raksin, Miklós Rózsa,
Carole Bayer Sager, Paul Schütze, Ravi Shankar, Howard Shore, Alan Silvestri, Tom
Waits, Kurt Weill, John Williams, Paul Williams, Gabriel Yared, Neil Young, and Hans
Zimmer.

Cue (US)
New York area arts and entertainment guide, later absorbed by *New York Magazine*.
12:11–12 (August 14, 1943). On Max Steiner.
"Man Behind the Sound Track: He's Often Heard but Seldom Seen." (August 23, 1947):
    10. On Jack Shaindlin.
"Zither Dither: Anton Karas' Score for Movie Starts a New Vogue." (March 11, 1950):
    15. On *The Third Man*.
Scheuer, Philip K. "His Melodies Linger On." (March 23, 1957): 12, 15–16. Interview-
    based article on Dimitri Tiomkin.
Lewis, Emory. "A Salute to [Harold] Arlen." (March 20, 1965): 13, 48.
Wolf, William. "Wolf on Films: Facing the Music: Why Movie Scores Are Usually So
    Awful." 39 (December 5, 1970): 7. Reprinted in Limbacher.

Decision (US)
A review of free culture published in New York.
Diamond, David. "The Composer and Film Music." 1:3 (March 1941): 57–60. The young
    American concert composer had just written his first symphony when he wrote this
    essay on the plight of the modern composer in Hollywood. Focuses on Aaron Cop-
    land, with some observations on George Antheil, Ernst Toch, and others.

DGA News (US)
Published by the Directors Guild of America.
Redman, Nick. "Directors and Composers: Collaborators in Cinesthesia." 16:3 (July–
    August 1991): 7–13, 24. On Alfred Hitchcock, Bernard Herrmann, and others.

Dialogue on Film (US)
Published by the American Film Institute in Beverly Hills, California.
"Henry Mancini Seminar." 3:3 (January 1974): 2–24. Transcript of an AFI seminar, with
    filmography.

Disney Magazine (US)
Green, Amy Boothe. "Words and Music: The Sherman Brothers Have Scored Decades of
    Disney Hits, from *Tall Paul* to *The Tigger Movie*." (Summer 2000).

The Disney News (US)
Fanning, Jim. "Sherman Bros.: Got It Together." (Spring 1987): 26–27.

The Distributor (US)
Published weekly by the sales department of Metro-Goldwyn-Mayer Pictures, New York.
"Famous European Pianist Is Signed: Dimitri Tiemkin [*sic*] to Compose for M-G-M
    Musical Films." 5:12 (September 7, 1929): 1, 8. On the signing of Tiomkin.

"The Men behind the Product." (Culver City edition, May 18, 1930). Mentions Martin Broones, manager of the music department.

Documentary News Letter (UK)
Published by Film Centre.
Mathieson, Muir. "Film Music." 1:9 (September 1940): 17. On the possibilities of music for documentary films.

Dramatic Mirror (US)
Also known as the *New York Dramatic Mirror*. Featured a weekly column, "Preparing Music for Photoplay Accompaniments," by organist Montiville Morris Hansford aimed at the small exhibitor who could afford only a solo pianist or organist.

Articles (selected)
"Good Music or None." (March 4, 1915): 22.
Smith, Frederick James. "Chances of Escaping Tax for Use of Music Are Slim." (September 29, 1917): 10. Regarding the tax on the use of pre-existing music to accompany film. Unauthorized use of music was rampant and publishers were trying to crack down on offenders, much in the same way that music publishers today are fighting online music piracy.

Column, "Preparing Music for Photoplay Accompaniments" (selected)
(July 21, 1917): 11. Practical suggestions. First column.
(August 4, 1917): 10. "Preparing Programs for Photoplay Accompaniments."
(August 11, 1917): 10. Program suggestions.
(August 25, 1917): 14. A plea for less improvisation and more planned matching of pre-existing music to picture.
(September 1, 1917): 12. Using popular songs.
(September 8, 1917): 11. Using classical music.
(September 15, 1917): 12. Using classical music.
(September 22, 1917): 11. Using light classical music.
(September 29, 1917): 11. Using classical music.
(December 29, 1917): 12. Continues at least through the end of 1917.

Edison Kinetogram (US)
One of the earliest exhibitor publications to regularly publish musical suggestions for specific films. The suggestions were published bimonthly by the Edison Company from September 1909 to June 1910, and from September 1913 to at least January 1915 (the publication ended in January 1916). Each scene was assigned a category of incidental music such as march and Irish jig. "Incidental Music for Edison Pictures" first appeared in vol. 1, no. 4 (September 15, 1909), pages 12–13; continuing through "Music Cues for Edison Pictures" beginning in vol. 2, no. 9 (June 1, 1910), page 12. This resumed with "Music Cues for Edison Films Reviewed in This Issue" in vol. 9, no. 4 (September 15, 1913).
"The Use of Music as an Emotional Excitement." 11:12 (May 15, 1915): 4. News brief on an orchestra that played a selection from an opera to accompany a dramatic film scene.

Emmy (US)
The magazine of the Academy of Television Arts and Sciences, published in North Hollywood, California.

Freeman, Don. "A Touch of [Henry] Mancini." 4:6 (November–December 1982): 58–60. Article.

Slate, Libby. "Show Tunes: Notes on Television Theme Music." 5:4 (July–August 1983): 70–72, 74.

Burlingame, Jon. "Lament for the 'Lost' Scores." 8:1 (January 1986): 16. A plea for respect of television music.

Maurer, J. "A Computer that's Music to Your Ears." 8:2 (March 1986): 59–60. On using Auricle to synchronize music to film.

Burlingame, Jon. "The Music Men: Film Composers Strike a New Chord in TV." 9:4 (August 1987): 100–102. Mentions Bill Conti, Jerry Goldsmith, Michel Legrand, Henry Mancini, and Lalo Schifrin.

Burlingame, Jon. "Barry Scores Again." 10:6 (November–December 1988): 10–11. Article.

Rense, Rip. "Amen." 10:6 (November–December 1988): 11–12. Profile of Jester Hairston.

Burlingame, Jon. "[Billy] Goldenberg's World." 11:3 (June 1989): 20–22. Interview.

Burlingame, Jon. "*Peanuts* Takes Five." 12:1 (February 1990): 9–11. On the use of jazz in the Charlie Brown television specials.

Burlingame, Jon. "Post Production." 12:3 (June 1990): 14–16. On Mike Post's collaborations with producer Stephen J. Cannell.

Burlingame, Jon. "Piece of the Rock." 12:6 (December 1990): 9–10. On *Cop Rock*, television with musical numbers.

Burlingame, Jon. "For the Record?" 13:1 (February 1991): 9. On the lack of television soundtracks.

Burlingame, Jon. "[Ian] Fraser Hits the High Notes." 13:3 (June 1991): 92–93. Interview.

Burlingame, Jon. "Scoring Big." 13:4 (August 1991): 28–32. Patrick Williams profile.

Burlingame, Jon. "Tooning In." 14:1 (February 1992): 13–14. On Bruce Broughton's score for "O Pioneers!" on *Hallmark Hall of Fame*.

Burlingame, Jon. "Scoring a Record Renaissance." 16:1 (February 1994): 7–8. On television soundtracks.

Rense, Rip. "Zappa's Saucy Duck." 16:6 (December 1994): 12–13. On Frank Zappa's music for the animated series *Duckman*.

Entertainment Weekly (US)

Popular fan magazine published in New York.

Articles (selected)

Nashawaty, Chris. "Music to Their Ears." No. 260 (February 3, 1995): 51. Elliot Goldenthal, Thomas Newman, and Hans Zimmer reveal their favorite film scores.

Russo, Tom. "Score Tactics: The Unusual Passions of *Titan A.E.* Composer Graeme Revell." No. 546 (June 23, 2000): 70.

Gaslin, Glenn. "On the Track: A Web Guide to Movie Music." (June 29, 2001): 147.

Bierly, Mandi, Steve Daly, and Amy Feitelberg. "The Composer." (May 17, 2004): 50. Brief interview with Howard Shore.

European Journal of Communication (US)

van den Berg, Harry, and Kees van der Veer. "Musical Discourse in Television Documentaries: Structure and Functions." 5:4 (December 1990): 445–62.

Everyones (Australia)

A motion picture trade magazine published in Sydney.

Mumford, Fred G. "Music and the Photoplay: Their Combination as a Means of Effective Entertainment." (May 11, 1921).

"Mustel Organ Ideal for Picture Theatres." (March 7, 1927): 49.

"Organs As an Asset in Theatre Entertainment." 10:502 (October 2, 1929): 12.

"W. F. Wollaston Says Organ Music Is Essential." 10:503 (October 9, 1929): 20.

Exhibitors Daily Review (US)

Chandler, C. F. "Get In Tune with *Syncopating Sue*." 20:98 (October 25, 1926): 35–36. Suggestions for merchandising the picture through music.

Tiomkin, Dimitri. "Screen Music, Better, Dooms Concert Stage: International Authority on Film Music, Who Is Composing and Directing Twenty New Ballets for Hollywood Production." (November 30, 1929).

Exhibitors Herald (US)

A motion picture trade publication billed as "The Independent Film Trade Paper." Published in Chicago from 1919 to 1927, when it merged with *Moving Picture World* to become *Exhibitors Herald and Moving Picture World*. News items and articles on musicians, primarily organists, often herald the value of music for the benefit of exhibitors. In the section "Better Theatres" are music articles from 1925 to 1927, including a column, "Music in the Theatre," in 1926 and 1927. This column occasionally featured "How I Played the Picture," written by various organists. The music articles in "Better Theatres" continued after the merge.

Articles (selected)

"Synchronized Music Service to Be Available by April 1." 12:9 (February 26, 1921): 41. Announcement by the Synchronized Scenario Music Company of their intent to supply printed music scores to theaters nationwide. Carl Edouarde, James C. Bradford, and Joseph Carl Breil were to provide the arrangements.

Riesenfeld, Hugo. "Riesenfeld Traces Musical Development in Presentation Score for *Deception*." 12:20 (May 14, 1921): 53; 56–57.

Winkler, M[ax]. "Pictures Responsible for New Class of Music." 28:6 (January 22, 1927): 48–49.

Articles (selected, from "Better Theatres")

Keese, Alex. "Scoring Music to Picture Action." (January 31, 1925).

Vining, Iris Ethel. "Cueing Comedies." (February 28, 1925).

Vining, Iris Ethel. "Organ Accompaniment of Short Subject Reels." (May 23, 1925).

Vining, Iris Ethel. "Individuality in Organ Playing." (June 20, 1925).

Vining, Iris Ethel. "How the Organ Put Over a Sagging Short Feature with Audience." (August 15, 1925).

Vining, Iris Ethel. "Playing to the Psychology of an Audience." (September 12, 1925).

Wagner, Harry L. "Some 'Do's and Don't's' for the Theatre Organist." (October 10, 1925).

Wagner, Harry L. "Fitting the Music to the Action of the Picture." (November 7, 1925).

"Points Growing Popularity of Organ Music in Theatres." (December 5, 1925).

Wagner, Harry L. "Short Features Offer Opportunity for Organist to Demonstrate Versatility." (December 5, 1925).

Vining, Iris. "Mixing [Tom] Mix and Mixed Music." (December 26, 1925): 41–42. An organist's play-by-play account of accompanying a bad (in her view) film.

Column, "Music in the Theatre" (selected)

Cleaves, Edwin L. "How I Played the Picture: *Fine Manners*." 27:3 (October 2, 1926): 25, 36.

Juno, Irene. "How Stanley-Crandall Organists, Managers Achieve Better Music." 27:11 (November 27, 1926): 15. Report from a Washington, D.C., organist.

Crawford, Tim. "How I Played the Picture: *So's Your Old Man*." 28:6 (January 22, 1927): 18, 32.

Juno, Irene. "Martial Music: Its Use and Place in Theatre Programs." (June 11, 1927): 15, 17.

Lyon, Harold J. "Some Observations on Playing News Weeklies." (June 11, 1927): 17–18.

Exhibitors Herald and Moving Picture World (US)

In 1928 the independent film trade paper *Exhibitors Herald* merged with *Moving Picture World* to become *Exhibitors Herald and Moving Picture World* (later *Exhibitors Herald-World*). Superseded by *Motion Picture Herald* in 1931. From around April 1928 through December 1930 the weekly periodical included a "Music and Talent" section. This often included columns titled "Organ Solos" (primarily news on theater organists and their repertoire), "Sid Says about Songs" (best-selling songs and capsule reviews of songs by Sid Berman), "Up and Down the Alley" (featuring Tin Pan Alley publisher news from various writers including Larry Spier and Ed Dawson), "Theme Songs," and "Scoring" (with assignments). For example, see December 1, 1928, p. 53. "Madame Octave" wrote up scoring assignments, news, and tidbits in the late 1920s; see "Hollywood Tunes," October 19, 1929. The "Music in the Theatre" column ran from January 1928 through 1929 and focused on the coming of sound and the value of live organ music. The "Better Theatres" supplement contains occasional music articles for the exhibitor.

Articles (selected)

Brockman [*sic*], David H. "It's All a Fake." 92:7 (August 18, 1928): 43. Broekman was a synchronizing conductor for Recording Laboratories of America.

"Music and Talent: All Song Firms Making Film Tieups." (October 12, 1929): 45–46.

"Music and Talent: Screen Setting New Song Records." (November 2, 1929): 55–56.

Terry, Leo. "I Predict the Organ Solo's Come-Back." (August 2, 1930): 21. On the talkie crisis and his belief that there will always be live music in motion picture theaters.

Articles (selected, from "Better Theatres" supplement)

Lyon, Harold J. "The Organ in the Motion Picture Theatre—Its Use, Possibilities." (November 27, 1926): 17, 40.

"Organ vs. Orchestra." (March 17, 1928): 31, 48–49. A survey shows theater owners prefer an organ over a five-piece combo for economic reasons.

"The Organ as the Voice of the Silent Drama." (June 9, 1928): 61.

Gallo, A. Raymond. "Picture Songs Are Getting Popular: Music Publishers Learn Value of Screen Tieup." (July 21, 1928): 45–46.

"Making 'Music' Out of Colors with Lumitone." (July 6, 1929): 56.

"The Future of the Organ and Sound Pictures." (August 3, 1929): 60.

Melgard, Al. "The Place of Real Music in the Motion Picture Theatre." (August 31, 1929): 47.

Brown, Albert F. "Fitting the Organ Solo into the Deluxe Theatre Program." (December 21, 1929): 13; 57–58.

Column, "Music in the Theatre"

Terry, Leo. "Faking the Picture." (June 9, 1928): 30.

Cowdry, W. J. "How I Played the Picture." (September 29, 1928): 29. On *The Cossacks*.

Gallo, A. Raymond. "It All Depends on the Song." (February 16, 1929): 64, 66. On theme songs.

Meyn, Ted. "Advertising Advance Pictures through Organ Solos." (May 11, 1929): 53–54.

Pierson, Marie. "Cueing the Picture for a Non-synchronous Machine." (July 6, 1929): 55–56.

De Mars, Anita. "What I'm Doing at the Console in These Days of Sound." (August 3, 1929): 59–60.

Exhibitors Trade Review (US)

S. M. Berg wrote a column that included suggestions for musical settings from December 1916 through at least May 1917.

Column, "Music for the Photoplay" by S. M. Berg

"Selecting Appropriate Music for the Film Takes Skilled Musicianship and Experience." (December 16, 1916): 138.

"Symphony (Some Phony) Orchestra." 1:23 (May 12, 1917): 1610–11. On a theater claiming to have an "orchestra" of three musicians. With suggestions for musical settings for three films and music, "Agitato No. 6," by Carl Kiefert.

Exposure Sheet (US)

Schlesinger animation studio employee newsletter.

"Carl Stalling." 2:7 (April 15, 1940): unpaginated. Reprinted in Daniel Goldmark, *Tunes for 'Toons* (2005).

Fangoria (US)

Published for horror fans by *Starlog* in New York.

Curci, Loris, and Claudio Fuiano. "To Soothe the Savage Beast." No. 135 (August 1994): 20–25. Ennio Morricone interview, primarily regarding *Wolf*.

Gingold, Michael. "The Band Plays On." No. 142 (May 1995): 56–60, 82. Interview-based article on Richard Band.

Grey, Ian. "Dark Nights of Composing." No. 144 (July 1995): 56–60. Interview-based article on Elliot Goldenthal.

Weaver, Tom, and Michael Brunas. "Classic Com-Poe-Ser." No. 146 (September 1995): 70–75, 82. Interview with Les Baxter.

Ferrante, Anthony C. "All Hallowed Themes." No. 158 (November 1996): 19–23. On Alan Howarth's synthesized scores.

Film (UK)

Published by the British Federation of Film Societies. A "Soundtrack" column by Tom Vallance covered music in films from around vol. 32 (Summer 1962) to at least May 1975. Each column was usually devoted to a single topic. For example, vol. 39 [1964], pages 40, 42 are on Betty Comden and Adolph Green.

Hrusa, Bernard. "On the Musical." No. 14–15 (November–December 1957; January–February 1958).

McVay, Douglas, with Tom Vallance. "Gotta Sing! Gotta Dance!" No. 40 (circa 1964).

MacVay [*sic*], Douglas. "The Music of *Les Parapluies*." No. 42 (circa 1965): 31–32. On Michel Legrand's score.

Palmer, Christopher. "Dimitri Tiomkin: The Composer in the Cinema." No. 64 (Winter 1971): 19–21; No. 65 (Spring 1972): 13–20.

Film and Philosophy (US)

Published by the Society for the Philosophic Study of the Contemporary Visual Arts.

Wierzbicki, James. "Wedding Bells for *The Bride of Frankenstein*: Symbols and Signifiers in the Music for a Classic Horror Film." (Special horror edition, 2001): 103–16. On Franz Waxman's score for the 1935 film.

Film Careers (US)

McCarty, Clifford. "Notes on *Rhapsody*."1:1 (Fall 1963): 34. On the score, adapted from classical music, by Bronislaw Kaper.

Film Comment (US)

Published bimonthly by the Film Society of Lincoln Center in New York.

Schiffer, George. "The Law and the Use of Music in Film." 1:6 (Fall 1963): 39–43.

Broeck, John. "Music of the Fears: John Broeck on Bernard Herrmann." 12:5 (September–October 1976): 56–60. Overview and analysis.

Sarris, Andrew. "The Cultural Guilt of Music Movies and Other Early Film Musicals: *The Jazz Singer*, Fifty Years After." 13:5 (September–October 1977): 39–41.

Marsh, Dave. "Schlock around the Clock." 14:4 (July–August 1978): 7–13. Rock music.

Harvey, Steven. "Eine Kleiser Rockmusik." 14:4 (July–August 1978): 14–16. On the set of *Grease*.

Traubner, Richard. "The Sound and the Führer." 14:4 (July–August 1978), 17–23. German musicals and operettas.

Mariani, John. "Music to Cry to Movies By." 15:5 (September–October 1979): 37. Psychological effect of film music.

O'Toole, Lawrence. "Moving Music." 17:5 (September–October 1981): 13–20. Survey, with sidebar on Pino Donaggio.

Walsh, Michael. "*Prizzi's* Opera." 21:5 (September–October 1985): 4–6. Alex North's clever use of music in *Prizzi's Honor*.

Mitchell, Elvis. "Soundtrack: Cooder Been a Contender." 22:2 (March–April 1986): 76–78. Ry Cooder's score for *Streets of Fire*.

Walsh, Michael. "Sounds of Silents." 23:4 (July–August 1987): 66–69. Music scoring for silent films.

White, Armond. "Rock's Rebellion." 24:6 (November–December 1988): 32–36. On concert films.

Spence, Kenneth C. "Jazz Digest." 24:6 (November–December 1988): 38–43. On the taming of jazz.

Glicksman, Marlaine. "Citizen Artist: On Shostakovich and the Soviets." 24:6 (November–December 1988): 50–51. On *Testimony*.

White, Armond. "Celluloid Songs." 25:2 (March–April 1989): 36–39. Pop music (songs) written for films.

Klein, David Shawn. "Possession." 28:3 (May–June 1992): 79. Essay on the effect of film music underscoring on the author's everyday life.

Tebbel, John Robert. "Looney Tunester." 28:5 (September–October 1992): 64–66. On Carl Stalling.

Horton, Robert. "Music Man." 31:6 (November–December 1995): 2–4. Miklós Rózsa retrospective.

Hampton, Howard. "Scorpio Descending: In Search of Rock Cinema." 33:2 (March–April 1997): 36–42. Adapted from *The Last Great American Picture Show*, edited by Alex Horwath.

Thompson, Frank. "Songe de Titanic." 34:1 (January–February 1998): 64–67. Source music in Titanic films.

Norris, Chris. "Sound: Chris Norris on the *Bully* Soundtrack." 37:5 (September–October 2001): 14. On the dramatic use of popular music.

Kabir, Nasreen Munni. "Playback Time: A Brief History of Bollywood 'Film Songs.'" 38:3 (May–June 2002): 41–43. With a sidebar in which director Mira Nair recalls film songs of her youth, p. 44.

Norris, Chris. "Sound and Vision: Lalo Schifrin." 39:1 (January–February 2003): 16. Article.

Caps, John. "Sound and Vision: James Bond." 39:2 (March–April 2003): 16.

Chusid, Irwin. "Sound and Vision: *The 5,000 Fingers of Dr. T.*" 39:3 (May–June 2003): 16.

Caps, John. "Soundtracks 101: Essential Movie Music: A Listener's Guide." 39:6 (November–December 2003): 31–49. Part 1 of a series covers Hollywood movie music from 1933 to 2001. A chronological guide to 101 film scores beginning with *King Kong*. The first two pages encapsulate the history and evolution of the form. Editor Gavin Smith introduces the article in "The Sound of Music," p. 2.

Chang, Chris. "Guided by Voices." 41:4 (July–August 2005): 16. On music for *Last Days* by Hildegard Westerkamp.

Film Criticism (US)

Critical journal published from Allegheny College in Meadville, Pennsylvania.

Telotte, J. P. "Scorsese's *The Last Waltz* and the Concert Genre." 4:2 (1979): 9–20.

Chell, Samuel L. "Music and Emotion in the Classic Hollywood Film: The Case of *The Best Years of Our Lives*." 8:2 (Winter 1984): 27–38. Analysis of Hugo Friedhofer's score. Reprinted in *Pro Musica Sana*.

Neupert, Richard. "The Musical Score as Closure Device in *The 400 Blows*." 14:1 (Fall 1989): 26–32. Analysis of Jean Constantin's score.

Film Culture (US)

America's independent motion picture magazine, published in New York.

Hendricks, Gordon. "The Sound Track." 1:1 (January 1955): 55–60. On Leonard Bernstein's score for *On the Waterfront*.

Kracauer, Siegfried. "Opera on the Screen." 1:2 (March–April 1955): 19–21.

Hendricks, Gordon. "The Sound Track." 1:2 (March–April 1955): 45–47. On Roman Vlad's music for *Gate of Hell* and *Romeo and Juliet*.

Antheil, George. "New Tendencies in Composing for Motion Pictures." 1:4 (Summer 1955): 16–17. On prolonged dissonance and emotion, with a call for the use of smaller, more colorful combinations of instruments. Reprinted in T. J. Ross, *Film and the Liberal Arts*.

Croce, Arlene. "Film Musicals: A Crisis in Form." 2:8 (August 1956): 25–26.

Kubik, Gail. "Three Film Tunes Undergo a Metamorphosis." 4:3 (April 1958): 27. On adapting his symphony in three different films.

Cage, John. "A Few Ideas about Music and Films." No. 29 (Summer 1963): 35–37. Musical relevance and the collaborative process with sound engineers. Reprinted from *Film Music Notes* (1951).

Stern, Seymour. "The Film's Score." No. 36 (Spring–Summer 1965): 103–32. History, analysis, and the influence of Joseph Carl Breil's music for *The Birth of a Nation* (1915).

Weinberg, Gretchen. "The Backroom Boys." No. 41 (Summer 1966): 83–87. Interview with Arthur Kleiner on musical accompaniment of silent films.

Brick, R. "John Whitney Interview." Nos. 53–55 (Spring 1972): 39–73, 80–83. Some discussion of music.

Mesthus, Marie. "The Influence of Olivier Messiaen on the Visual Art of Stan Brakhage in *Scenes from under Childhood*, Part One." Nos. 63–64 (1977): 39–50. How the filmmaker was inspired by the music of Olivier Messiaen.

Brakhage, Stan. "Stan Brakhage on Music, Sound, Color, and Film." 67–69 (1979): 129–35.

Hackenschmied, Alexander. "Film and Music." Nos. 67–69 (1979): 238–41. The relationship between sound and image in the early sound film. Reprinted from *Cinema Quarterly* 1:3 (Spring 1933).

Ganguly, Suranjan. "Stan Brakhage: The 60th Birthday Interview." No. 78 (Summer 1994): 18–38. The filmmaker discusses the influence and use of music in his films.

The Film Daily (US)

Daily newspaper for the motion picture trade, published in New York from 1915 to 1970.

Ford, John. "Thematic Presentations: A Wish for the Future." 40:61 (June 12, 1927): 47. The director mentions music in D. W. Griffith productions.

Stothart, Herbert. "The Place of Film Music in the Motion Picture." (July 13, 1933): 23.

Shaindlin, Jack. "Of the Film and Music." 35th anniversary issue. (1953): 63, 183. On the viability of film music in concert.

Adams, Stanley. "Music and Motion Pictures, the Next Half Century." 50th anniversary issue. 133:79 (October 28, 1968): 109, 112, 163 (section 2). From ASCAP's president.

The Film Daily Yearbook of Motion Pictures (US)

Annual companion to *Film Daily*, with composer credits and songwriter credits from 1930 to 1970. The early 1930s are inconsistent. See listings, depending on the year, for "Music Composers," "Song Writers," "Composers" (beginning in 1937), or "Music Writers."

Mintz, M. J. "Thematic Music Cue Sheets Emphasize Music's Value." (1928): 868.

"Composers and Authors," lists those who are devoting or are considering devoting their talents to the film industry. A comparison of this list with that of 1937 shows the drastic personnel changes that occurred in the first decade of sound films when songwriters were supplanted by composers or "scorers." (1930).

"Song Writers and Their Recent Work." (1935): 518–23.

"Song Writers." (1936): 542–48.

Music composers, lyricists, and songwriters. (1937): 595–604.

"Music Credits." (1961): 426–33. For 1959 and 1960.

Credits for 1968 and 1969 and film and television soundtracks for 1969. (1970): 818–36.

Film Directions (UK)

Film magazine for Ireland.

McAlpin, C. "J.B. 007: John Barry That Is!" 9:34 (1988): 26. Interview.

Film Dope (UK)

Quarterly publication issued from 1972 to 1994 that includes an eclectic range of composers, primarily British and American. Each entry (listed alphabetically, below) is assigned a chronological number and contains a short biography, filmography, a brief assessment, and often a photograph. Filmographies often include short films, precomposed music and lyrics used in films, onscreen appearances, and other ephemera.

Yasushi Akutagawa, issue 39, entry 8 (March 1988): 6–7.

William Alwyn, issue 1, entry 27 (December 1972), unpaged; [additions and corrections, issue 39, entry 27 (March 1988), 16–17].

Philippe Arthuys, issue 39, entry 49 (March 1988): 28. Primarily commercials.

Georges Auric, issue 2, entry 61 (March 1973): 14–15; [additions and corrections, issue 39, entry 61 (March 1988), 35–36].

Burt Bacharach, issue 2, entry 71 (March 1973): 22l; issue 44, entry 71 (March 1990): 20a–20b.

Richard Rodney Bennett, issue 3, entry 118 (August 1973): 27–28. Additions and corrections in issue 12.

Elmer Bernstein, issue 3, entry 130 (August 1973): 37–38. Additions and corrections in issue 16.

Leonard Bernstein, issue 3, entry 131 (August 1973): 38.

Arthur Bliss, issue 4, entry 147 (March 1974): 9; Arthur Bliss interviewed by Peter Griffiths and David J. Badder, issue 5 (July 1974): 2–5.

Benjamin Britten, issue 5, entry 205 (July 1974): 22–23.

Betty Comden, issue 7, entry 312 (April 1975): 47–48.

Aaron Copland, issue 8, entry 322 (October 1975): 7–9.

Noël Coward, issue 8, entry 336 (October 1975): 27–29.

John Dankworth, issue 9, entry 358 (April 1976): 30–31.

Georges Delerue, issue 10, entry 379 (September 1976): 24–28 (includes list of scores Delerue conducted for other composers).

Hanns Eisler, issue 14, entry 448 (March 1978): 25–27 (includes information on the films and music for the Film Music Project at the New School for Social Research, 1940–1942).

Duke Ellington, issue 14, entry 451 (March 1978): 29–32.

Gerald Fried, issue 18, entry 540 (September 1979): 14–15.

Giovanni Fusco, issue 18, entry 546 (September 1979): 21–23.

George and Ira Gershwin, issue 19, entry 573 (December 1979): 20–24.

Jerry Goldsmith, issue 20, entry 595 (April 1980): 12–13.

Adolph Green, issue 21, entry 618 (October 1980): 2–3.

Hans Werner Henze, issue 24, entry 712 (March 1982): 21.

Bernard Herrmann, issue 24, entry 715 (March 1982): 24–25.

Arthur Honegger, issue 25, entry 735 (November 1982): 12–14.

Kenyon Hopkins, issue 25, entry 739 (November 1982): 18.

Jacques Ibert, issue 26, entry 771 (January 1983): 28–29.

Pierre Jansen, issue 27, entry 793 (July 1983): 38–39.

Maurice Jarre, issue 27, entry 794 (July 1983): 39–41.

Maurice Jaubert, issue 27, entry 796 (July 1983): 42–44.

Quincy Jones, issue 28, entry 811 (December 1983): 30–31.

Jerome Kern, issue 30, entry 852 (September 1984): 24–28.

Joseph Kosma, issue 31, entry 882 (January 1985): 35–37.

Krzysztof [Christopher] Komeda, issue 31, entry 875 (January 1985): 19–20.

Erich Wolfgang Korngold, issue 31, entry 879 (January 1985): 30–32; Korngold Society president Brendan G. Carroll's appreciation of Korngold, issue 32 (March 1985): 40.

Bruce Langhorne, issue 33, entry 917 (November 1985): 10. Session guitarist.

Michel Legrand, issue 34, entry 949 (March 1986): 20–23.

Maurice Le Roux, issue 35, entry 966 (September 1986): 4.

Walter Leigh, issue 21, entry 628i (October 1980): 32.

Alan Jay Lerner, issue 34, entry 963 (March 1986): 43–44.
Oscar Levant, issue 35, entry 970 (September 1986): 9–11.
Andrew Lloyd Webber, issue 36, entry 991 (February 1987): 3–4.
Henry Mancini, issue 38, entry 1058 (December 1987): 27–29.
Darius Milhaud, issue 43, entry 1141 (January 1990): 13–15.
Paul Misraki, issue 43, entry 1157 (January 1990): 42–44.
Burt Bacharach, issue 44 (March 1990): 20a–20b.
Jerome Moross, issue 45, entry 1181 (September 1990): 33–34.
Ennio Morricone, issue 45, entry 1182 (September 1990): 34–40.
Alfred Newman, issue 47, entry 1217 (December 1991): 17–23.
Jack Nitzsche, issue 47, entry 1231 (December 1991): 44.
Alex North, issue 48, entry 1236 (July 1992): 10–12.
Michael Nyman, issue 48, entry 1246 (July 1992): 28–29.

Film Heritage (US)
Published by the University of Dayton, Ohio.
Macklin, F. Anthony. "Welcome to Lion's Gate: Interviews with Director Alan Rudolph and Composer Richard Baskin." 12:1 (Fall 1976): 1–17.

Film History (US)
International journal published quarterly from 1987.

<u>Articles</u>
Denisoff, R. Serge, and George Plasketes. "Synergy in 1980s Film and Music: Formula for Success or Industry Mythology?" 4:3 (1990): 257–76. With notes on sources and filmography.
Merritt, Russell. "D. W. Griffith's *Intolerance*: Reconstructing an Unattainable Text." 4:4 (1990): 337–75. On Joseph Carl Breil's involvement with the music, 346–47.
Gitt, Robert. "Bringing Vitaphone Back to Life." 5:3 (September 1993): 262–74. Interview with the film preservationist regarding restoration and synchronization of Vitaphone films.
Carli, Philip C. "Musicology and the Presentation of Silent Film." 7:3 (Autumn 1995): 298–321. Silent film accompaniment.
Vance, Jeffrey. "*The Circus*: A Chaplin Masterpiece." 8:2 (1996): 186–208. Discusses the scores for the premiere of *The Circus* (1928) and for the 1970 reissue.
Asper, Helmut G., and Jan-Christopher Horak. "Three Smart Guys: How a Few Penniless German Émigrés Saved Universal Studios." 11:2 (1999): 134–53. Discusses musicals, classical music, and the studio's success at integrating music into the narrative flow.
Curtis, Scott. "'If It's Not Scottish, It's Crap!' Harry Lauder Sings for Selig." 11:4 (1999): 418–25.
Wedel, Michael. "[Oskar] Messter's 'Silent' Heirs: Sync Systems of the German Music Film 1914–1929." 11:4 (1999): 464–76. Synchronization.
Reynolds, Herbert. "Aural Gratification with Kalem Films: A Case History of Music, Lectures, and Sound Effects, 1907–1917." 12:4 (2000): 417–42. Silent film accompaniment.

<u>Special issue, 14:1 (2002) [on film music]</u>
Koszarski, Richard. "Introduction: Film/Music." 3–4.
Beynon, G. W. "Playing the Picture: Musical Directors." 5–10. Biographical sketches of music directors John Arthur, S. M. Berg, Carl Edouarde, Hugo Riesenfeld, Nat W. Finston, Francis J. Sutherland, Erno Rapée [Rappe, herein], and Alois Reiser.

Reprinted from *Musical Presentation of Motion Pictures*. New York and Boston: G. Schirmer, 1921, pp. 105–20.

Haggith, Toby. "Reconstructing the Musical Arrangement for *The Battle of the Somme* (1916)." 11–24. Music for silent films.

Patalas, Enno. "On the Way to *Nosferatu*." 25–31. Hans Erdmann's music score for the 1922 film is discussed, 30.

Koszarski, Richard. "Laughter, Music and Tragedy at the New York Pathé Studio." 32–39. Discusses musical shorts.

Hutchinson, Ron. "The Vitaphone Project: Answering Harry Warner's Question: 'Who the Hell Wants to Hear Actors Talk?'" 40–46. Includes material on the preservation and restoration of Vitaphone discs.

Hunt, Martin. "Their Finest Hour? The Scoring of *Battle of Britain*." 47–56. On William Walton's score for the 1969 film, preceded by an overview of British film composers.

The Film Index (US)

Published weekly in New York, it superseded *Views and Film Index* in 1908. Beginning in 1910, *Film Index* featured the first regular column on the topic of film music. During the time pianist Clyde Martin wrote the column he often traveled to various theaters around the United States, particularly in the Midwest, and reported on what he saw and heard in the way of musical accompaniment for films. His column offered advice on common problems encountered by soloists and answered letters from readers. *Film Index* was absorbed by *Moving Picture World* in July 1911.

"Il Trovatore—With Incidental Music: Pathe Freres Produce Famous Opera of Verdi in Colors with Music Score Specially Adapted to the Picture Portrayal." 7:1 (January 7, 1911): 1, 25.

"Picture Theatre Orchestras: Harry L. Barnhart Will Tell Film Index Readers about Orchestra Music for Pictures." 7:18 (May 6, 1911): 3.

Column, "Playing the Pictures" by Clyde Martin (selected)

6:15 (October 8, 1910): 30. First column.

6:18 (October 29, 1910): 7. Also a letter from George House, "Importance of Proper Music."

7:3 (January 21, 1911): 10. On handling short scenes.

7:25 (June 24, 1911): 14. On the use of mechanical organs and pianos. Last column.

Column, "Orchestral Music in Pictures" by H. L. Barnhart

7:20 (May 20, 1911): 15. Opening sentence of the first H. L. Barnard [*sic*] column: "I wish to state that pictures can be played successfully with an orchestra."

7:21 (May 27, 1911): 14. On following and playing a dramatic picture.

7:22 (June 3, 1911): 15. On playing operatic pictures.

Film Industry (UK)

A monthly from Film Press in London.

Huntley, John. "British Film Orchestras." 1:3 (September 1946): 4–5.

Huntley, John. "Stage One Music Theatre, Denham." 2:2 (1947).

Huntley, John. "Stage One at Denham." 2:11 (May 1947): 6–8.

Huntley, John. "The Year in Film Music." (December 30, 1948).

Film International (Iran)

Iranian Film Quarterly.

"Michael Nyman in Iran: Beyond Simplicity." 10:2 (Autumn 2003): 34–36. Interview.

Film International (Sweden)

Special issue, 13 (2005) ["Music and Moving Image"]
Gillian B. Anderson and Ronald H. Sadoff, guest editors.

Tagg, Philip. "Gestural Interconversion and Connotative Precision." 20–31. Includes examination of Charles Williams's music for *The Dream of Olwen*.

Anderson, Gillian B. "A Consummation and a Harbinger of the Future: Mortimer Wilson's Accompaniments for Douglas Fairbanks." 32–39.

Wallengren, Ann-Kristin. "Music in Children's Films—Empathy or Socialization?" 40–49. On music in children's films made in Sweden.

Film Library Quarterly (US)

Published by the Film Library Information Council in New York.

Hofmann, Charles. "Sounds for Silents." 2:1 (Winter 1968–1969): 41–43. An appeal to keep the tradition of live musical accompaniment for silent films from becoming a dying art.

Ascher, Felice. "An Interview with Teo Macero." 2:2 (Spring 1969): 9–12. Macero's experiences composing music for documentary films.

Oderman, Stuart. "The Next Tremolo You Hear..." 4:1 (Winter 1970–1971): 54–56. Oderman relates his experiences providing musical accompaniment for silent films.

Film Monthly Review (UK)

Published in London from 1942 to 1950; formerly titled *Monthly Film Review* (1942–1946). Music critic Hans Keller was a regular contributor from 1948.

Mathieson, Muir. "Music for Crown." Original publication date undetermined. Music for Britain's Crown Film Unit. Reprinted in *Hollywood Quarterly* (Spring 1948).

Keller, Hans. "Film Music: Theme Song and Leading Motif." 6:4 (January 1948).

Keller, Hans. "The Simple Tune." 6:5 (February 1948): 13. On melody in film music. Reprinted in *Film Music and Beyond*.

Keller, Hans. "Film Music: Variations." 6:6 (March 1948): 10–11.

Keller, Hans. "Films and Opera." 6:6–7 [7–8?] (April–May 1948). On music for the film *Hamlet*.

Keller, Hans. "Benjamin Britten: Film Composer." 6:9 (June 1948). Reprinted from *British Film Review* (1948).

Keller, Hans. "Films and the Ballet." 6:11 (August 1948): 4–5. Reprinted in *Film Music and Beyond*.

Keller, Hans. "Another Filmed Opera." 6:14 (December 1948): 16–17. On Verdi's *Rigoletto*. Reprinted in *Film Music and Beyond*.

Column, "Film Music: Record Review" by John Huntley

7:9 (October 1949): 32. On disc recordings with film music.

7:10 (December 1949): 38–39. On music by Mischa Spoliansky and others.

8:1 (January 1950): 43–44. On Anton Karas's music for *The Third Man*.

Film News (US)

Shaindlin, Jack. "Scoring for the Film." 7:5 (February–March 1946): 16–17. Reprinted in *Film Music Notes* (May 1946).

Film Quarterly (US)

Published as *Hollywood Quarterly* from 1945 to 1951; *Quarterly of Film, Radio and Television* from 1952 to 1957; and *Film Quarterly* from 1958 to 2005. Initially published by the University of California and the Hollywood Writers Mobilization, later by the

University of California Press. Often contains reviews of books on film music.

Published as **Hollywood Quarterly** (1945–1951)
In "Film Music of the Quarter" Lawrence Morton reviewed music from current films from 1947 through 1951. In addition to Morton's column virtually every issue included a substantial article on film music, many with copious music examples. Morton headed the advisory board, which included a handful of film composers, and contributed occasional book reviews on film music.

<u>Articles</u>
Morton, Lawrence. "Chopin's New Audience." 1:1 (October 1945): 31–33. On *A Song to Remember*.
Kubik, Gail. "The Composer's Place in Radio." 1:1 (October 1945): 60–68.
Deutsch, Adolph. "*Three Strangers*." 1:2 (January 1946): 214–23. Deutsch follows the process of creating the score for the film and emphasizes his collaboration with the screenwriter.
Forrest, David. "From Score to Screen." 1:2 (January 1946): 224–29. The veteran music mixer on music's place in the mix.
Zissu, Leonard. "The Copyright Dilemma of the Screen Composer." 1:3 (April 1946): 317–20. Zissu was legal counsel for the newly formed Screen Composers Association.
Jones, Chuck. "Music and the Animated Cartoon." 1:4 (July 1946): 364–70. The cartoon director's take on music and its potential. Reprinted in Daniel Goldmark and Yuval Taylor, *The Cartoon Music Book* (2002).
Morton, Lawrence. "The Music of *Objective Burma*." 1:4 (July 1946): 378–95. Analysis of Franz Waxman's score.
Leyda, Jay. "Music." Supplement 1 (1946): 4–5. Part of the annual communications bibliography on film technique.
Nelson, Robert U., and Walter H. Rubsamen. "Literature on Music in Film and Radio." Supplement 1 (1946): 40–45. Annotated bibliography.
Nelson, Robert U. "Film Music: Color or Line?" 2:1 (October 1946): 57–65. Essay.
Sternfeld, Frederick W. "The Strange Music of Martha Ivers." 2:3 (April 1947): 242–51. Analysis of Miklós Rózsa's score for *The Strange Love of Martha Ivers*.
Sternfeld, Frederick W. "Preliminary Report on Film Music." 2:3 (April 1947): 299–302. On the need for study scores.
Potter, Ralph K. "Audivisual [*sic*] Music." 3:1 (Fall 1947): 67–78. The title refers to audible visual music.
Mathieson, Muir. "Music for Crown." 3:3 (Spring 1948): 323–26. Music for Britain's Crown Film Unit reprinted from the *Monthly Review*, with supplementary material.
Rubsamen, Walter H. "Literature on Music in Film and Radio Addenda (1943–1948)." 3:4 (1949): 403–4.
Kremenliev, Boris. "Background Music for Radio Drama." 4:1 (Fall 1949): 75–83. Includes material on composers who worked in film: Cy Feuer, Lucien Moraweck, and Fred Steiner.
Sternfeld, Frederick W. "Gail Kubik's Score for *C-Man*." 4:4 (Summer 1950): 360–69. Analysis.
Pratley, Gerald. "Furthering Motion Picture Appreciation by Radio." 5:2 (Winter 1950): 127–31.
Morton, Lawrence. "Music from the Films: A CBC Broadcast." 5:2 (Winter 1950): 132–37. Transcript of Franz Waxman radio interview.

Zuckerman, John V. "A Selected Bibliography on Music for Motion Pictures." 5:2 (Winter 1950): 195–99. Revision of his 1949 bibliography in his *Music in Motion Pictures: Review of Literature with Implications for Instructional Films.*

<u>Column, "Film Music of the Quarter" by Lawrence Morton</u>
3:1 (Fall 1947): 79–81. First column.
3:2 (Winter 1947–1948): 192–94. On David Raksin's score for *Forever Amber.*
3:3 (Spring 1948): 316–19. On Max Steiner's score for *The Treasure of Sierra Madre* and Richard Hageman's for *The Fugitive.*
3:4 (1949): 395–402. On Hugo Friedhofer's score for *Joan of Arc*, Aaron Copland's for *The Red Pony*, and Leigh Harline's for *The Boy with Green Hair*, with music excerpts for the latter.
4:1 (Fall 1949): 84–89. On anti-Hollywood bias in the listings and omissions in *The Gramophone Shop Encyclopedia of Recorded Music* (1948), discrimination by film critics, and on Virgil Thomson's score for *Louisana Story.*
4:3 (Spring 1950): 289–92. On the need for film music criticism.
4:4 (Summer 1950): 370–74. On opera on screen.
5:1 (Fall 1950): 49–52. On Anton Karas's score for *The Third Man.*
5:2 (Winter 1950): 178–81. On Hugo Friedhofer's score for *Broken Arrow* and Franz Waxman's for *The Furies.*
5:3 (Spring 1951): 282–88. On the International Music Congress in Florence, Italy.
5:4 (Summer 1951): 412–16. On current scores.

Published as **Quarterly of Film, Radio and Television** (1952–1957)
Lawrence Morton's column "Film Music of the Quarter" ran 1951–1953. Gerald Pratley's column "Film Music on Records" ran 1951–1955, at which time his column "Recorded Filmusic" began appearing in *Films in Review.*

<u>Articles</u>
Morton, Lawrence. "Composing, Orchestrating, and Criticizing." 6:2 (Winter 1951): 191–206.
McLaren, Norman. "Notes on Animated Sound." 7:3 (Spring 1953): 223–29.
Paulu, Burton. "Televising the Minneapolis Symphony Orchestra." 8:2 (Winter 1953): 157–71. An early case of music on television.
Cantrick, Robert. "Music, Television, and Aesthetics." 9:1 (Fall 1954): 60–78. On telecasting musical performances and the ability to "see" music.
Helm, Everett. "Gail Kubik's Score for *C-Man*: The Sequel." 9:3 (Spring 1955): 263–82.

<u>Column, "Film Music of the Quarter" by Lawrence Morton (selected)</u>
5:3 (Spring 1951): 282–88. On the International Music Congress, Florence, Italy.

<u>Column, "Film Music on Records" by Gerald Pratley</u>
6:1 (Fall 1951): 73–97. First annual column. Lists (alphabetically by composer) many of the first 78 rpm discs that contained music from films.
7:1 (Fall 1952): 100–107. Additional listings.
8:2 (Winter 1953): 194–205. Lists more than three dozen composers.
9:2 (Winter 1954): 195–208. Additional listings.
10:2 (Winter 1955): 186–207. Last column.

Published as **Film Quarterly** (1958–2005)
Field, Sidney. "*Outrage.*" 18:3 (Spring 1965): 13–39. In "The Composer," Alex North writes about his score for the film, pp. 31–34.

Johnson, William. "Face the Music." 22:4 (Summer 1969): 3–19. Essay on the aesthetics of film scoring, including the use of concert music in film, primarily in the 1930s–1950s. The examples cited go farther afield than typical.

Gorbman, Claudia. "Music as Salvation: Notes on Fellini and Rota." 28:2 (Winter 1974–75): 17–25. Primarily an analysis of Nino Rota's music for *Le notti di Cabiria*.

Warshow, Paul. "More Is Less: Comedy and Sound." 31:1 (Fall 1977): 38–45. Essay on the addition of realistic sound to *The General* and the resulting effect, including the impact on the music.

Gentry, Ric. "Clint Eastwood: An Interview." 42:3 (Spring 1989): 12–23. Includes a discussion of adapting jazz saxophonist Charlie Parker's music for *Bird*.

Allan, Blaine. "Musical Cinema, Music Video, Music Television." 43:3 (Spring 1990): 2–14. Compares filmed musicals with music videos.

Johnson, Victoria E. "Polyphony and Cultural Expression: Interpreting Musical Traditions in *Do the Right Thing*." 47:2 (Winter 1993–1994): 18–29. On William Lee's music and the role of rap and other music in the film. Later revision published in Mark Reid's *Spike Lee's* Do the Right Thing (1997).

Merritt, Russell. "Recharging *Alexander Nevsky*: Tracking the Eisenstein-Prokofiev War Horse." 48:2 (Winter 1994–1995): 34–47. On performing a live score with the film, with music examples.

Tobias, James. "Cinema, Scored: Toward a Comparative Methodology for Music in Media." 57:2 (December 2003): 26–36.

Film Reader (US)

Published annually by the Northwestern University Film Division in Evanston, Illinois.

Bartush, Jay. "*Citizen Kane*: The Music." No. 1 (1975): 50–54. Analysis of Bernard Herrmann's score.

Mitry, Jean. "Music and Cinema." No. 3 (1978): 136–49. The French director on musical and visual rhythm, particularly in his films. Translated from *Le Cinéma Expérimental* (Paris, 1974).

Kalinak, Kathryn. "The Fallen Woman and the Virtuous Wife: Musical Stereotypes in *The Informer*, *Gone with the Wind*, and *Laura*." No. 5 (1982): 76–82. On using musical stereotypes to depict female sexuality on screen.

Film Review (UK)

Annual film yearbook, published in London beginning around 1944. Compiled and edited by F. Maurice Speed, followed by James Cameron-Wilson. Each volume contained a one-year retrospective (as indicated by the first year given, below) and a look at future releases (the second year). Derek Elley wrote narrative articles; Cameron-Wilson tended to contribute capsule reviews.

Mathieson, Muir. "Music in British Films." (1948): 18–20.

Everson, William K. "The History of the Musical." (1957–1958): 17–21.

Elley, Derek. "Soundtrack!—Cinema on Disc." (1975–1976): 49–51.

Elley, Derek. "Soundtrack!—The Year's Soundtrack Highlights." (1976–1977): 56–58.

Elley, Derek. "Soundtrack!—The Year's Releases on Record." (1977–1978): 168–70; (1978–1979): 184–86.

Elley, Derek. "Soundtrack!—The Year in Film Music." (1979–1980): 168–70.

Cameron-Wilson, James. "Film Soundtracks." (1996–1997): 165–67; (1997–1998): 165–67; (1998–1999): 165–67; (1999–2000): 166–68; (2000–2001): 166–68; (2001–2002): 158–60.

Cameron-Wilson, James. "Soundtracks." (2002–2003): 163–65; (2003–2004): 152–54; (2004–2005): 165–68.

Film Spectator (US)
Biweekly magazine with film reviews, published in Los Angeles in the late 1920s. Editor Welford Beaton had much to say about the sound revolution and didn't believe "talkies" would survive. Succeeded by *Hollywood Spectator*.
"Something about the Proper Way to Present Theme Songs" 7:6 (February 23, 1929): 7.
"Synchronized Scores." 9:4 (February 1, 1930): 3. Beaton's editorial calls for more synchronized scores.
"Synchronized Score Helps Some of the Scenes in *Laughing Lady*." 9:4 (February 1, 1930): 6.

Film Studies (UK)
Published by Manchester University Press.
"Dossier: Hans Keller: Essays on Film Music." No. 5 (Winter 2004): 106–31. This selection comes in advance of the publication of Keller's collected writings on film edited by Christopher Wintle, *Film Music and Beyond: Writings on Music and the Screen, 1945–59*, published by Plumbago Books in 2006.

Film West (Ireland)
Ireland's film quarterly.
O'Connor, Derek. "Music in Similar Motion: Philip Glass." No. 35 (1999): 44–45. Interview.
Fielder, Miles. "Angelo Badalamenti: Damn Fine Music." No. 46 (Winter 2001): 24–25. Interview.

Filmfax (US)
Magazine of unusual film and television, catering to fans of science fiction. The "Hi-Tek HiFi" column from 1996 to 2004 contains soundtrack reviews, often of esoteric material on Albert Glasser, the Hammer films, Hans J. Salter, Republic serials, film noir, and so on. Written primarily by David J. Hogan from 1996 to 1999, and Harry H. Long from 1999 to 2005, with occasional contributions from Jeff Berkwits. "Wax Museum," a column with news and reviews of record collectibles by Jay Alan Henderson, ran from 1989 to 1992.
Littman, Bill. "Masters of the Quick Score: Bargain Basement Music from Those Untouched Toscaninis of Gower Gulch." No. 15 (May–June 1989): 52–55. On music from Monogram Pictures and Edward Kay.
Weaver, Tom, and Michael Brunas. "Opus for Musical Oddities: Albert Glasser: A Noteworthy Interview with the Composer and Conductor of a Grab Bag Full of B-Movie Biggies." No. 25 (February–March 1991): 74–82.
Sanford, Jay Allen. "Boris Karloff's Classic TV Series *Thriller!*" No. 29 (October–November 1991): 65–71. Music by Jerry Goldsmith and Pete Rugolo is mentioned, 70–71.
Hawk, Wayne. "Carl Stalling: Master of the Merrie Melody." No. 34 (August–September 1992): 74–77. Profile.
Stanley, John W. "Legacy of a Hollywood Maestro: Music to the Max: The Max Steiner · Story." No. 36 (December–January 1992–1993): 78–82. Profile.

Rappaport, Frederick. "Prolific Pragmatist: The Musical Career of Paul Dunlap." No. 40 (August–September 1993): 36–41; 96–97. Interview.

Fischer, Dennis. "A World of Childhood Delights: *The Thief of Bagdad*." No. 60 (April–May 1997): 59–63, 70–75. Retrospective look at the 1940 film, including Miklós Rózsa's score, pp. 70–74.

Long, Harry H. "*Metropolis* Reborn! The Reconstruction and Restoration of Fritz Lang's Silent Classic!" No. 95 (February–March 2003): 56–60, 82–83. Including the discovery of Gottfried Huppertz's music manuscript for the film.

Bradley, Matthew R. "He Shoots, He Scores! The Career of Hollywood Producer and Music Man Igo Kantor!" No. 99–100 (October 2003–January 2004): 66–73, 130–32. Contains music references by the music editor of horror genre films.

Bamber, George. "The Amazing Music of Vic Mizzy." No. 103 (July–September 2004): 86–89, 129. Interview.

Filmmaker (US)

The magazine for independent film.

Bonin, Liane. "Spin Control." 4:2 (Winter 1996): 18–22. Music licensing.

Martin, Reed. "Line Items: For a Song." 10:3 (Spring 2002): 35–40, 67–72. Music licensing.

Martin, Reed. "Line Items: How and When to Score." 10:4 (Summer 2002): 35–40. The roles of composer and music supervisor.

Filmmakers Newsletter (US)

A clearinghouse for bringing information to filmmakers, published in New York and Massachusetts.

Moore, Richard. "Music, Films, Computers." 4:6 (April 1971): 26–30. On the possibilities of using computers to synchronize sound and for synthesizer scoring.

Amarasingham, Indiran. "Film-Sound-Space: The OSS (Optical Sound Synthesizer)." 4:6 (April 1971): 35–38.

Valentino, Thomas, Jr. "Music for Films: The Music Library." 4:6 (April 1971): 42–43. By an executive of a music library company.

Petric, Vlada. "Sight and Sound: Counterpoint or Entity?" 6:7 (May 1973): 27–31. Includes a graphic with film frames and notated music to illustrate the counterpoint between the movement of images and Prokofiev's music in *Alexander Nevsky*.

Scott, Duncan. "Filmmaker's Notebook: Rx for Stock Music Blues." 7:9–10 (Summer 1974): 79–80. Suggestions for using stock music.

Sharples, Win, Jr. "CineScenes: Bernard Herrmann, 1911–1975." 9:12 (October 1976): 12. Memorial service report.

Filmplay Journal (US)

A monthly fan magazine published in Indiana.

Holman, Russell. "Music with Their Reels." 1:8 (February 1922): 38–39, 56. On the practice of performing music on the set to aid acting.

Opdycke, Mary Ellis. "What the Movies Have Done to Music." 2:1 (July 1922): 16–17. Essay on the relationship between music and the screen, particularly on associating classical music with film scenes.

Films: A Quarterly of Discussion and Analysis (US)

Focuses on film as art, not casual entertainment, and published in New York. Reprinted by Arno Press (1968).

London, Kurt. "Film Music of the Quarter." 1:1 (November 1939): 76–80. Discussion of significant scores by Korngold, Copland, and Prokofiev.

London, Kurt. "Film Music of the Quarter." 1:2 (Spring 1940): 43–48. On filmed concerts and documentary films.

"Music in Films: A Composer's Symposium." 1:4 (Winter 1940): 5–20. With Marc Blitzstein, Paul Bowles, Benjamin Britten, Aaron Copland, Hanns Eisler, Karol Rathaus, Lew Schwartz, Dimitri Shostakovich, William Grant Still, and Virgil Thomson.

"Composers on Film Music: A Bibliography." 1:4 (Winter 1940): 21–24.

London, Kurt. "Film Music of the Quarter." 1:4 (Winter 1940): 25–29. On Hanns Eisler and the New School for Social Research, scores by Copland, Gruenberg, and the film *Fantasia*.

Films and Filming (UK)

The magazine combines popular and serious views of film and is published in London. A "Film Music" column by Derek Elley ran from 1981 to 1989. (From 1989 until the magazine's demise in 1990, the column was called "Score" in the table of contents and "Music" in the body of the magazine.) Initially it contained reviews of music on disc and as heard in American and British films; in later years it focused more on soundtrack reviews, with some news. It appears irregularly in some years, including 1983 to 1984; 1986, and in every issue in other years, such as 1985. Pre-dating Elley's column was an occasional series of film composer interviews conducted in 1977. A "Filmusic" column by Lionel Godfrey ran from 1966 to 1969. The "Records" column by Alan Warner then takes over and is more "pop" oriented, with soundtrack reviews and occasional film composer profiles. Some columns end with soundtrack news ("Music Notes").

<u>Articles</u>

Freed, Arthur. "Making Musicals." 2:4 (January 1956): 9–12, 30. In a special issue, "Twenty Five Years of Musicals."

Levy, Louis. "Britain *Can* Make Good Musicals." 2:4 (January 1956): 13, 30.

Green, Philip. "The Music Director." 3:9 (June 1957): 12–13. Behind the scenes with the British music director.

Alwyn, William. "Composing for the Screen." 5:6 (March 1959): 9, 34. Reprinted in Thomas, *Music for the Movies*.

Fothergill, Richard. "Putting Music in Its Place." 5:6 (March 1950): 10–11, 33. On the strengths and weaknesses of contemporary film music.

Godfrey, Lionel. "The Music Makers." 12:12 (September 1966): 36–40. Article on Elmer Bernstein and Jerry Goldsmith.

Warner, Alan. "Musicals and Comedies or Thanks for the Memory." 18:1 (November 1971): 18–33.

Elley, Derek. "Versatility." 22:7 (April 1976): 44–46. Interview with Wilfred Josephs.

Elley, Derek. "The Film Composer: 1 Miklós Rózsa." 23:8 (May 1977): 20–24. Interview.

Elley, Derek. "The Film Composer: 1 Miklós Rózsa." 23:9 (June 1977): 30–34. Interview.

Elley, Derek. "The Film Composer: 2 Elmer Bernstein." 24:6 (March 1978): 20–24. Interview, in one part only.

Elley, Derek. "The Film Composer: 3 John Williams." 24:10 (July 1978): 20–24. Interview.

Elley, Derek. "The Film Composer: 3 John Williams." 24:11 (August 1978): 30–33. Interview.

Elley, Derek. "The Film Composer: 4 Jerry Goldsmith." 25:8 (May 1979): 20–24. Interview.
Elley, Derek. "The Film Composer: 4 Jerry Goldsmith." 25:9 (June 1979): 20–24. Interview.

<u>Column, "Filmusic" by Lionel Godfrey (selected)</u>
"Hitch-break." 13:3 (December 1966): 44–45. Possibly the first column.
13:7 (August 1967): 63–64. On Dimitri Tiomkin and others.
14:3 (December 1967): 31–32. On his visit to composers in Hollywood and New York.
"Hand and Glove." 14:7 (April 1968): 34–37. On musicals.
"Master of All Trades?" 14:8 (May 1968): 41–42. On André Previn.
14:11 (August 1968): 50–51. Lalo Schifrin profile.
"Morals and Minis." 15:6 (March 1969): 74–75.
15:10 (July 1969): 74–75. Final column.

<u>Column, "Film Music" by Derek Elley (selected)</u>
325 (October 1981): 50–51. Appears to be the first column.
328 (January 1982): 43–45. On music by Pino Donaggio.
336 (September 1982): 43. On music by John Williams.
340 (January 1983): 41. On music by Carl Davis.
398 (November 1987): 40. Soundtrack reviews.
414 (April 1989): 18. Includes news.
418 (August 1989): 48. Soundtrack update. Last column titled "Film Music."
425 (March 1990): 64. Final column and final issue of the magazine.

<u>Column, "Records" by Alan Warner (selected)</u>
15:11 (August 1969): 66. First column.
"Six-Gun Scoring." 16:1 (October 1969): 72. On Westerns.
"Rapid Recognition." 16:9 (June 1970): 122. On Miklós Rózsa.
"The Creative Force of Walter Scharf." 16:10 (July 1970): 66. Profile.
17:2 (November 1970): 66. On Henry Mancini.
18:6 (March 1972): 66. On Max Steiner, with quotes from George Korngold.
20:9 (June 1974): 68. On Marvin Hamlisch.
"A Choice of Forty." 23:7 (April 1977): 46–47. Favorite LPs from 1975 to 1977, followed by "Music Notes."
"Disco around the Clock." 23:10 (July 1977): 46.
23:12 (September 1977): 50. With "Music Notes." This appears to be the final column.

Films Illustrated (UK)
Mark Whitman reviewed soundtracks during the 1970s. See, "Soundtracks," vol. 1, no. 16 (October 1972): 28–29, and "Records" (March 1979).
Thompson, Kenneth. "Why *Jaws* Scores." 5 (April 1976): 318.

Films in Review (US)
Published by the National Board of Review of Motion Pictures in New York. Superseded *New Movies* and *National Board of Review Magazine*. "An Index to *Films in Review*," by Marion Fawcett (New York: National Board of Review, 1961), includes "Filmusic" and "Titles of Films Discussed in the Sound Track and Recorded Filmusic," for the years 1950 to 1959 (see pp. 18–20). A long-running column titled "The Sound Track" reviewed music in films. Often, other story items related to film music appeared on the page of, or after, the column. Gordon Hendricks, who wrote several letters to the editor on the subject of film music in the early 1950s, penned the first column in December 1952, and

went on to supply the column through 1954. Edward Connor wrote a number of columns between 1955 and 1960. During this time "The Sound Track" section included a separate column on "Recorded Filmusic" by Gerald Pratley, host of a Canadian radio show on film music. (This followed on the heels of his column "Film Music on Records" in *Quarterly of Film, Radio and Television*.) Pratley discussed the music from major releases and often included unusual choices, such as short films.

"The Sound Track" is now synonymous with writer/critic Page Cook. His thirty-year reign as a leading advocate in print for soundtracks extended from 1963 to 1993. (Royal S. Brown's "Film Musings" column in *Fanfare* began its near twenty-year run in 1983.) Charles Boyer, writing as Page Cook, did not have a background in music or film; however, his passion for symphonic film scores is apparent. His critiques reflect his personal taste in composers and music and are opinionated. Each column often covered several topics, even if only one topic or film is listed herein. By the 1980s columns often concluded with several capsule reviews of current film scores. One issue each year, often in February, reviewed the best scores of the previous year, and another annual issue included a survey of current scores. Cook compiled a discography for *Films in Review* of the best film music available on disc, which was sold to readers around 1977. In its early years the column critiqued current film scores. As soundtrack LPs proliferated in the 1970s and 1980s, Cook featured soundtrack reviews and eventually covered music on CD and laserdisc. By the time Jack Smith took over the column in 1993, it was wholly devoted to soundtrack reviews, with comments from composers on rerecorded scores. The magazine has been online since March 1997. Perhaps it is fitting that one of the last print issues (March–April 1996) was a special issue devoted to "Filmusic."

Huff, Theodore. "Chaplin as Composer: His Unique Gift for Scoring His Films." 1:6 (September 1950): 1–5.

Jablonski, Edward, and Milton A. Caine. "Gershwin's Movie Music." 2:8 (October 1951): 23–28.

Tiomkin, Dimitri. "Composing for Films: It's Easier When You Invent Than When You Borrow." 2:9 (November 1951): 17–22. Reprinted in T. J. Ross, *Film and the Liberal Arts*, and Derek Elley, *Dimitri Tiomkin*.

Winkler, Max. "The Origin of Film Music." 2:10 (December 1951): 34–42. Primarily on cue sheets for silent films. Reprinted in Limbacher.

Hendricks, Gordon. "*Quo Vadis* Music." 2:10 (December 1951): 62–63. On authenticity in Miklós Rózsa's score.

Hendricks, Gordon. "Film Music Comes of Age: It Is an Art within an Art and Should Be Written by Our Best Composers." 3:1 (January 1952): 22–27. Reprinted in Limbacher.

Hendricks, Gordon. "*Rashomon*'s Music." 3:2 (February 1952): 94–95. Letter to the editor.

Hendricks, Gordon. "Music and Nature's Sound." 3:6 (June–July 1952): 301. On Allan Gray's score for *The African Queen*.

Hendricks, Gordon. "*Ivory Hunter*'s Music." 3:7 (August–September 1952): 342–45. On Alan Rawsthorne's music.

Embler, Jeffrey. "The Structure of Film Music: A Knowledge of It Enriches Movie-Going for Even the Non-Musical." 4:7 (August–September 1953): 332–35. Reprinted in Limbacher.

Griggs, John. "The Music Master: The Days of the Piano and the Grand Organ Are Recalled by One Who Played Them." 5:7 (August–September 1954): 338–42. Recollections of accompanying silent films in Illinois.

Jablonski, Edward. "Filmusicals: Are a Form of Entertainment That Sometimes Touches Art." 6:2 (February 1955): 56–69.

Tozzi, R. V. "Jerome Kern." 6:9 (November 1955): 452–59. Profile.

Thomas, Anthony. "Erich Wolfgang Korngold." 7:2 (February 1956): 89–90.

Connor, Edward. "The Composer on the Screen." 7:4 (April 1956): 164–70. Music for screen biographies.

Green, Stanley. "Richard Rodgers' Filmusic." 7:8 (October 1956): 398–405, 420.

Dunham, Harold. "Music for *Intolerance*." 8:1 (January 1957): 44.

McCarty, Clifford. "Filmusic for Silents." 8:3 (March 1957): 117–18, 123.

McCarty, Clifford. "Victor Herbert's Filmusic." 8:4 (April 1957): 183–85.

McCarty, Clifford. "Filmusic Librarian." 8:6 (June–July 1957): 292–93. On studio librarians, including MGM's George Schneider.

Belinsky, Dmitri. "Boris Morros." 8:8 (October 1957): 418–19.

Scher, Saul N. "Irving Berlin's Filmusic." 9:5 (May 1958): 225–34.

Beams, David. "Soviet Filmusic." 10:5 (May 1959): 306–8.

Jacobs, Jack. "Alfred Newman: One of the Earliest Composers of Filmusic Has Also Been One of the Foremost Conductors of It." 10:7 (August–September 1959): 403–14.

Haun, Harry, and George Raborn. "Max Steiner." 12:6 (June–July 1961): 338–51.

Jablonski, Edward, and William R. Sweigart. "Harold Arlen: His Filmusic Has Consisted Exclusively of Songs." 13:10 (December 1962): 605–14.

Thomas, Anthony. "David Raksin." 14:1 (January 1963): 38–41.

Thomas, Anthony. "Hugo Friedhofer." 16:8 (October 1965): 496–502.

Doeckel, Ken. "Miklos Rozsa." 16:9 (November 1965): 536–48.

Behlmer, Rudy. "Erich Wolfgang Korngold Established Some of the Filmusic Basics Film Composers Now Ignore." 18:2 (February 1967): 86–100.

Uselton, Roi A. "Opera Singers on the Screen." 18:4 (April 1967): 193–206; 18:5 (May 1967): 284–97; 18:6 (June–July 1967): 345–59.

Cook, Page. "Bernard Herrmann." 18:7 (August–September 1967): 398–412.

Cook, Page. "Franz Waxman." 19:7 (August–September 1968): 415–30.

Cook, Page. "Ken Darby Has Specialized in the Cinematic Use of the Singing Human Voice." 20:6 (June–July 1969): 335–56.

Stothart, Herbert, Jr. "Herbert Stothart Was a Pioneer of Filmusic Who Helped Its Technique to Evolve." 21:10 (December 1970): 622–30.

Ripley, John W. "Song-Slides: Helped to Unify US Communities and Sell Sheet Music." 22:3 (March 1971): 147–52.

Peeples, Samuel A. "The Mechanical Music Makers: Brought Sound to the Silents." 24:4 (April 1973): 193–200. On the Photoplayer and similar instruments for the music accompaniment of silent films.

Peeples, Samuel A. "Films on 8 and 16." 27:8 (October 1976): 493–94, 99. On the use of music to accompany silent films.

McClelland, Doug. "'Dubbing' *The Jolson Story*." 32:5 (May 1981): 278–85. On ghost singing by Virginia Rees and Paul Silverman.

Haun, Harry. "Franz Waxman." 42:10 (October 1991): 325–27. Article based on a interview with John Waxman.

Tanner, Louise. "Who's in Town." 44:7–8 (July–August 1993): 245–46. Includes "*Musica* by an Old Pro," on Henry Mancini's music for *Tom and Jerry: The Movie*.

Younger, Richard. "Song in Contemporary Film Noir." 45:7–8 (July–August 1994): 48–50.

47:3–4 (March–April 1996). Special issue, contents listed below.

Column, "Recorded Filmusic" by Gerald Pratley (selected)

5:10 (December 1954): 546–47. On the new era spawned by William Walton's *Henry V* score.

6:6 (June–July 1955): 293–94. On the use of jazz.

6:7 (August–September 1955): 351–53. On music for three short films from director George K. Arthur.

6:8 (October 1955): 416–17. Interview-based article on Ray Heindorf.

7:2 (February 1956): 88–89. On a Doreen Carwithen (later Mary Alwyn, wife of William) scored short.

9:8 (October 1958): 469–70. On a recording of *The Big Country*.

Column, "Recorded Filmusic" by Don Miller (selected)

10:8 (October 1959): 498–500. On British film music.

11:10 (December 1960): 626–27. Year-end reviews.

Column, "The Sound Track" by various writers (selected)

Page numbers may include the entire "Sound Track" section, which incorporated "Recorded Filmusic." Other topics may be covered in addition to those included herein.

3:10 (December 1952): 531–33. First column. Gordon Hendricks on *High Noon*, *Limelight*, and *This Is Cinerama*.

4:2 (February 1953): 87–90. Gordon Hendricks; and Jeffrey Embler on *A Streetcar Named Desire*.

4:5 (May 1953): 243–47. Gordon Hendricks on UPA cartoons; Leith Stevens on composing for films.

6:2 (February 1955): 88–90. Edward Connor on quoting classical music.

6:3 (March 1955): 135–37. Edward Connor on film scores of 1954.

6:7 (August–September 1955): 350–53. Edward Connor on the availability of film scores.

6:8 (October 1955): 416–19. Edward Connor on music for historical films.

7:1 (January 1956): 37–39. Edward Connor on the classics as background music.

7:2 (February 1956): 87–89. Edward Connor on music for early sound films.

7:4 (April 1956): 181–83. Edward Connor on original concert music written for films (as in original classical music used as source music).

8:5 (May 1957): 228–29, 233. Channing T. Miller on "Scoring Silent Films" using records.

8:9 (November 1957): 471–73. Edward Connor on horror film scores and Edward Jablonski, "Recorded Filmusic."

10:2 (February 1959): 114–15. Robert B. Kreis on jazz scores.

10:7 (August–September 1959): 431–34. Edward Connor on the use of Gregorian chant and Don Miller editorial on opinions expressed by others in previous issues of the magazine.

11:2 (February 1960): 109–12. T. M. F. Steen on music for thrillers, including the use of jazz and fugues.

11:3 (March 1960): 175–76. T. M. F. Steen on war films.

11:4 (April 1960): 242–44. T. M. F. Steen on French film composers, Georges Auric, Jean Constantin, Philippe Gerard, and Paul Misraki.

11:7 (August–September 1960): 436–37, 440. T. M. F. Steen on poor music.

11:8 (October 1960): 497–99. T. M. F. Steen on music for short films.

11:10 (December 1960): 623–26. T. M. F. Steen on quoting classical music.

12:1 (January 1961): 43–45. Edward Connor on quoting classical music and T. M. F. Steen on poor music.

12:2 (February 1961): 116–18. T. M. F. Steen on music in early sound cartoons.

12:3 (March 1961): 180–81. Bill McCutcheon on best film scores of 1960 and Bernard Herrmann's music for *Psycho*.

12:5 (May 1961): 303–5. T. M. F. Steen on Yugoslav cartoon music.

13:3 (March 1962): 177–80. Anthony Thomas on Erich Wolfgang Korngold and Bill McCutcheon on best film scores of 1961.

13:6 (June–July 1962): 369–70. T. M. F. Steen on Jean Prodromidès's music.

13:7 (August–September 1962): 435–36. T. M. F. Steen on Richard Rodney Bennett.

13:8 (October 1962): 495–96. T. M. F. Steen on films with two scores (domestic and foreign versions).

14:3 (March 1963): 181–83. Bill McCutcheon on film scores of 1962.

14:7 (August–September 1963): 429–30. Anthony Thomas on music in the films of producer David O. Selznick.

15:5 (May 1964): 295–97, 300. Frank Verity (Clifford McCarty's pseudonym) on the Academy Awards for music.

Column, "The Sound Track" by Page Cook (selected)
Other topics may be covered in addition to those included herein.

14:9 (November 1963): 556–57. First column, on Nino Rota and Miklós Rózsa.

14:10 (December 1963): 622–23. On spectacle films.

15:1 (January 1964): 42–43. On comedies.

15:6 (June–July 1964): 363–64, 367. On film scores of 1963.

15:9 (October 1964): 567–69. Page Cook on music in current films and Anthony Thomas on pop-oriented scores.

16:2 (February 1965): 105–6. On film scores of 1964.

17:2 (February 1966): 111–12. On film scores of 1965.

17:3 (March 1966): 177–78. On Sol Kaplan's music.

18:2 (February 1967): 107–8, 111. On film scores of 1966.

19:2 (February 1968): 99–100. On film scores of 1967.

19:3 (March 1968): 162–63, 166. On film music as noise. Reprinted in T. J. Ross, *Film and the Liberal Arts*.

20:2 (February 1969): 110–11. On film scores of 1968.

20:3 (March 1969): 169–70. On the increased use of popular music.

20:4 (April 1969): 244–46. On television music.

21:2 (February 1970): 110–12. On film scores of 1969.

22:2 (February 1971): 98–99, 102. On film scores of 1970.

22:8 (October 1971): 501–5. Extensive discussion of David Raksin's score for *What's the Matter with Helen?* Reprinted in Limbacher.

22:10 (December 1971): 631–34. On Elmer Bernstein's score for *See No Evil* and Georges Delerue's score for *Women in Love*.

23:2 (February 1972): 102–4. On film scores of 1971.

23:6 (June–July 1972): 362–66. On replacement scores.

Vol. 24 (1973)
2 (February): 107–10. Best and worst film scores of 1972.

5 (May): 298–300. On Phillip Lambro and his score for the horror film *Hannah: Queen of the Vampires*.

6 (June–July): 365–68. Brief history of soundtrack albums.

Vol. 25 (1974)
2 (February): 104–7. Best film scores of 1973.

3 (March): 171–74. Conductor Paul Howarth Asmussen on the relationship between film music and classical music; report on film music in concert.

4 (April): 235–37, 240. Comments on writing film music (from a BMI documentary film) by Hugo Friedhofer, Jerry Goldsmith, Earle Hagen, and Quincy Jones.

5 (May): 294–97. Documentary film music.

6 (June–July): 362–66. Miklós Rózsa's comments on his score for *The Golden Voyage of Sinbad*.

8 (October): 494–97. On Bernard Herrmann's music.

9 (November): 560–63. On Phillip Lambro's unused score for *Chinatown*.

Vol. 26 (1975)
2 (February): 113–15. Best film scores of 1974.

Vol. 27 (1976)
2 (February): 116–18. Best and worst film scores of 1975.

3 (March): 175–78, 180. On the late Bernard Herrmann.

4 (April): 234–37. On Bernard Herrmann's film music, particularly *The Ghost and Mrs. Muir* and *Psycho*.

6 (June–July): 369–72; 76. On the establishment of the Alfred Newman Memorial Library at the University of Southern California.

8 (October): 495–99. On the role of music in film.

Vol. 28 (1977)
1 (January): 44–46, 55. On Elmer Bernstein's "Film Music Collection."

2 (February): 112–15. Best film scores of 1976.

4 (April): 239–41, 244. Young film music composer Rennie Dawson discusses his career.

5 (May): 307–9. On recent film scores by Jerry Goldsmith.

10 (December): 617–20. On film scores written for director Fred Zinnemann.

Vol. 29 (1978)
2 (February): 102–5, 114. Best film scores of 1977.

7 (August–September): 426–29, 433. Account of a 1968 lecture by Ken Darby and Alfred Newman.

8 (October): 489–90. On sequels.

9 (November): 559–63. On Jerry Goldsmith.

10 (December): 627–30. On Miklós Rózsa's career.

Vol. 30 (1979)
1 (January): 38–41. On the increased interest in soundtracks.

2 (February): 105–7, 124. Best film and television scores of 1978.

3 (March): 167–70. On Varese Sarabande.

4 (April): 225–28. Rennie Dawson interview.

6 (June–July): 358–61, 366. On Miklós Rózsa's score for *Fedora*.

7 (August–September): 416–19. On Miklós Rózsa's career.

8 (October): 484–86. On John Williams's score for *Dracula*.

9 (November): 551–53. On Miklós Rózsa's score for *Time after Time*.

10 (December): 613–15, 624. On Scott Lee Hart's score for *Salderaladon*.

Vol. 31 (1980)
1 (January): 35–37, 44–45. Interview with John Steven Lasher of Entr'acte Records.

2 (February): 99–101,105. Best film scores of 1979.

3 (March): 163–65, 184. On Jerry Goldsmith's score for *Star Trek: The Motion Picture*.

4 (April): 230–32, 238. On Alfred Newman's score for *Anastasia* (1956), first in a series of retrospectives of distinguished scores of the past.

8 (October): 483–85. On Alex North's score for *Carny*.

9 (November): 551–52, 572–73. Article on composer Edward David Zeliff.

10 (December): 615–17, 639. Various film scores by Bernard Herrmann.

1 (January): 38–39, 45. Music critic Donald Bishop Jr. on the higher quality and quantity of soundtrack recordings.
2 (February): 108–10, 115. Best film scores of 1980.
3 (March): 165–70, 176. Interview with record producer Lesley Anderson-Snell regarding soundtrack marketing.
4 (April): 230–32. On John Morris's score for *The Elephant Man*.
5 (May): 298–300, 304. On Jerry Goldsmith's score for *Masada* and Lee Holdridge's score for *East of Eden*, both television miniseries.
6 (June–July): 365–67, 372. On David Raksin's score for *Separate Tables*, including written comments from the composer. Second in a series of retrospectives of distinguished scores of the past.
7 (September–August): 436–38. Tribute to Hugo Friedhofer.
8 (October): 499–500, 502. On Miklós Rózsa's score for *Eye of the Needle*.
9 (November): 567–69. Article on composer Edward David Zeliff.

1 (January): 52–54, 57. On Miklós Rózsa's score for *A Double Life*.
2 (February): 115–19. Best and worst film scores of 1981.
3 (March): 180–85. 1950s film scoring, emphasis on Hugo Friedhofer, Frank Skinner, and Dimitri Tiomkin.
4 (April): 249–51. On the lack of musical scoring in recent films with emphasis on Leonard Rosenman.
5 (May): 311–13. Recent film scores by Elmer Bernstein, Johnny Mandel, and Henry Mancini.
6 (June–July): 371–73, 383. Friedrich Brock's score for *La Sonorité*.
8 (October): 500. Music by Wendy Carlos, Harry Manfredini, David Whitaker, and Christopher Young.
9 (November): 561–65. Music in the films of Ingrid Bergman and Grace Kelly.

2 (February): 118–22. Best film scores of 1982.
3 (March): 178–80. Film music by Canadian composer Stephen Cosgrove.
4 (April): 245–47, 249. Film festival report.
5 (May): 311–13, 318. On Fred Steiner's research on Alfred Newman.
6 (June–July): 375–78. On Bronislaw Kaper.
9 (November): 559–65. On music for *The Twilight Zone* (TV) and *Twilight Zone—The Movie*.

1 (January): 48–50. On Jerry Goldsmith's score for *Under Fire* and James Horner's for *Brainstorm*.
2 (February): 118–20. Best film scores of 1983.
3 (March): 184–86. On Bronislaw Kaper's score for *Lili* and Alex North's for *Cheyenne Autumn*.
4 (April): 246–48. On John Morris's score for *To Be or Not to Be*.
6 (June–July): 372–74. On Piero Della Corte's score for *Notte Senza Luminiro (Night without Light)*.
10 (December): 632–34. Music in the films of Bette Davis.

2 (February): 122–24. Best film scores of 1984.
3 (March): 186–88. On Rennie Dawson's score for *Trionfo della Morte*.
4 (April): 251–53. On electronic music.

6 (June–July): 378–81. On Alex North's score for *Spartacus* and other films.
10 (October): 504–7. Ernest Gold on his career and composing for film and television.

Vol. 37 (1986)
3 (March): 187–89. Best film music of 1985.
5 (May): 314–17. On David Shire's career.
6–7 (June–July): 377–81. On Alex North's career.
8–9 (August–September): 440–43. On Elmer Bernstein's Western film scores.
12 (December): 632–35. On Stephen Cosgrove's score for the Canadian film *The Praying Mantis*.

Vol. 38 (1987)
3 (March): 183–86. Best film music of 1986.
12 (December): 622–23. On John Scott's career. Part 1.

Vol. 39 (1988)
1 (January): 56–58. On John Scott's career. Part 2.
4 (April): 249–50. Best film scores of 1987.
12 (December): 630–33. On John Scott's career.

Vol. 40 (1989)
3 (March): 184–86. Report on the "Film Music Symposium" sponsored by the New York Film and Television Library Society.
4 (April): 250–53. Best film scores of 1988.
8–9 (August–September 1989): 437–40. On Alfred Newman's score for *All about Eve*.
12 (December 1989): 633–37. On John Morris's score for *The Wash*.

Vol. 41 (1990)
1–2 (January–February): 58–61. On Miklós Rózsa's score for *El Cid*.
10 (October): 502–6. On Alfred Newman's score for *The Diary of Anne Frank*, part 1.
11–12 (November–December): 570–74. On Alfred Newman's score for *The Diary of Anne Frank*, part 2.

Vol. 42 (1991)
7–8 (July–August 1991): 282–84. On Richard Robbins.

Vol. 43 (1992)
5–6 (May–June): 209–11. On the resurgence of interest in Bernard Herrmann's film music.

Vol. 44 (1993)
2 (March–April): 138–41. Final Page Cook column.
5–6 (May–June): 206–8. First Jack Smith column.

Special issue, 47:3–4 (March–April 1996) ["Filmmusic"]
Eder, Bruce. "Miklos Rozsa." 2–21. Career profile.
"Isolated Scores." 22–23. Isolated music tracks on laserdisc, listed by distribution company.
Eder, Bruce. "Of Music and Movies." 24–27. Film music concert review.
Potter, Nicole. *"The Passion of Joan of Arc/Voices of Light."* 28–30. Review of the concert presentation of *Le passion de Jeanne d'Arc* with live oratorio composed by Richard Einhorn. "Conversation with Richard Einhorn," pp. 31–33.
Oderman, Stuart. "The Sound of Silents: Lillian Gish Encouraged the Author in His Dream to Be a Silent Film Pianist." 37–39.

Films of the Golden Age (US)
Magazine for film lovers.

Crawford, Bruce. "Miklos Rozsa: Musical Interpreter of the Ancient World." No. 12 (Spring 1998): 92–94.

Films on Screen and Video (UK)
British monthly motion picture trade magazine that featured a column on film music from 1981 to 1983 by Derek Elley, later by David Stoner. Some of the columns include "News" at the end. The Stoner columns often had one-word thematic titles, such as "Partners," "Pleasures," or "Concepts." The final column appeared in November 1983.

Column, "Film Music" by Derek Elley (selected)
"Cultural Gaps." 1:6 (March 1981): 44–45. On soundtrack reissues.
"Hungarian Harmony." 1:7 (June 1981): 42–43. Music in contemporary Hungarian films.
"Movement and Moments." 1:8 (July 1981): 44. On Australian composer Brian May.
"Nuggets of Value." 1:10 (September 1981): 42. Last Elley column.

Column, "Film Music" by David Stoner (selected)
"Partnerships." 2:11 (October 1982): 22. On the latest collaborations between Henry Mancini and Blake Edwards; and Ennio Morricone and Sergio Leone.
"Operas without Voices." 2:12 (November 1982): 4041. Carl Davis interview.
"Contrasts." 3:1 (December 1982): 22. Primarily on British television scores.

Flickers Magazine (UK)
Levy, Louis. "Background Music Is a Help." (1935).

Focus on Film (UK)
Published quarterly by Tantivy Press in London. The film review credits section often lists the composer, with a brief bio and additional credits. "On Record," a column by Tom Vallance that surveyed new records of historic and nostalgic interest, ran from no. 22 (Autumn 1975) to no. 31 (November 1978).
Vallance, Tom. "Melody Always Wins." No. 21 (Summer 1975): 14–26. Jule Styne interview, with filmography.
Amata, Carmie. "Scorsese on *Taxi Driver* and Herrmann." No. 25 (Summer–Autumn 1976): 5–8. Director Martin Scorsese interview, with brief Bernard Herrmann biography and credits, 10.
Atkins, Irene Kahn. "The Melody Lingers On: Source Music in Films of the American Past." No. 26 (1977): 29–37.

Focus on Fox (US)
20th Century-Fox employee newsletter, published in Los Angeles from around 1976 to 1994, featuring corporate news, promotions, and department and employee profiles.
5:1 (1980). On Chris Montan.
6:6 (June–July, 1981). On the retirement of music librarian Paul Sprosty.
Baker, Marj. "Newman Cues Music for Fox Productions." 6:8 (September 1981). On Lionel Newman.

Funnyworld (US)
Amateur magazine devoted to comic books, comic strips, and animated cartoons edited by Mike Barrier.
Barrier, Mike. "An Interview with Carl Stalling." 13 (Spring 1971): 21–27. The only extensive interview with Stalling known to exist actually combines two interviews, one conducted by Barrier and Milton Gray and the other by Gray and Bill Spicer,

supplemented by correspondence from Stalling. Reprinted in Daniel Goldmark and Yuval Taylor, *The Cartoon Music Book* (2002).

Care, Ross. "Symphonists for the Sillies: The Composers for Disney's Shorts." 18 (Summer 1978): 38–48. On Frank Churchill, Leigh Harline, Carl Stalling, and their music, with filmography.

Care, Ross. "Mickey Mouse Music." 22 (1981): 47–49.

G-Fan (Canada)

Quarterly fanzine devoted to coverage of Godzilla and other Japanese monsters.

Akira Ifukube interview. No. 18 (November 1995).

Gore Creatures (US)

Horror fanzine. After issue no. 25 it became *Midnight Marquee*.

Littman, Bill. "The *King Kong* Score." No. 23 (1974).

Littman, Bill. "*Jaws*: Music to Digest By." No. 24 (October 1975): 33–36.

Littman, Bill. "Music for the *Bride*." No. 25 (September 1976).

Griffithiana (Italy/US)

Journal of film history, published in conjunction with the annual Pordenone Silent Film Festival in Italy. Articles are in Italian and English. David Robinson's *Music of the Shadows* was issued as a supplement to the October 1990 issue; see entry under "Books on Film and Television Music."

Anderson, Gillian B. "'No Music until Cue': The Reconstruction of D. W. Griffith's *Intolerance*." 13:38–39 (October 1990): 158–69. Article with illustrations, 154–57, regarding *Intolerance* (1916).

Cherchi Usai, Paolo. "Silent Film Music." 13:38–39 (October 1990): 279–80.

Bassetti, Sergio. "Silent Film Music on Record." 14:40–42 (October 1991): 146–56. Annotated discography, including original music and compilations.

Merritt, Russell. "Opera without Words: Composing Music for Silent Films. An Interview with Carl Davis, Kevin Brownlow and David Gill." 14:40–42 (October 1991): 168–81. With Carl Davis filmography.

Tsivian, Yuri. "Dziga Vertov's Frozen Music: Cue Sheets and a Music Scenario for *The Man with the Movie Camera*." 18:54 (October 1995): 92–121. Material regarding the 1929 film from Russia's State Archive of Literature.

Lanchbery, John. "Recreating the Music for *The Birth of a Nation*." 20:60–61 (October 1997): 31. On preparing to perform the Joseph Carl Breil score.

Harlequinade (US)

Jones, Isabel Morse. "Photographed Music." 1:1 (April 1931): unpaged.

Historical Journal of Film, Radio, and Television (UK)

An interdisciplinary journal published quarterly.

Article

Tibbetts, John C. "Shostakovich's Fool to Stalin's Czar: Tony Palmer's *Testimony* (1987)." 22:2 (June 2002): 173–96. Material on Dimitri Shostakovich.

Special issue, 18:4 (October 1998) ["Hanns Eisler and Film Music"]

Culbert, David. "Introduction. Hanns Eisler (1898–1962): The Politically Engaged Composer." 493–502.

Betz, Albrecht. "A Source Is Revealed: A Conversation with Joris Ivens about Hanns Eisler (1972)." 503–7.

Fasshauser, Tobias. "Hanns Eisler's *Chamber Symphony Op. 69* as Film Music for *White Flood* (1940)." 509–21.

Helbing, Volker. "Hanns Eisler's Contribution to the New Deal: *The Living Land* (1941)." 523–33.

Hufner, Martin. "*Composing for the Films* (1947): Adorno, Eisler and the Sociology of Music." 535–40.

Heller, Berndt. "The Reconstruction of Eisler's Film Music: *Opus III, Regen* and *The Circus*." 541–59.

Weber, Horst. "Eisler as Hollywood Film Composer, 1942–1948." 561–66.

Schebera, Jürgen. *Hangmen Also Die* (1943): Hollywood's Brecht—Eisler Collaboration." 567–73.

Dümling, Albrecht. "Eisler's Music for Resnais' *Night and Fog* (1955): A Musical Counterpoint to the Cinematic Portrayal of Terror." 575–84.

Weinstein, Larry. "*Solidarity Song: The Hanns Eisler Story* (1996): Some Comments from the Filmmaker." 585–90.

Eisler, Hanns. "Film Music—Work in Progress (1941)." 591–94.

Eisler, Hanns. "Final Report on the Film Music Project on a Grant by the Rockefeller Foundation (1942)." 595–98.

Hitchcock Annual (US)

Watts, Stephen. "Alfred Hitchcock on Music in Films." (1994): 149–57. Originally published in *Cinema Quarterly* (Winter 1933–1934).

Hollywood (US)

Manfort, Jerome. "Ann Harding's Romance with Werner Janssen." (September 1937): 35, 69.

Hollywood Creative Directory (US)

Published by the Hollywood Creative Directory in Santa Monica, California, then by IFILM Publishing in Hollywood, from 1987 through 2005. Probably the most popular directory in use among composers for contact information on motion picture and television studios and production companies.

Hollywood Daily Screen World (US)

Published in Hollywood at a time when similar dailies were often published in the Midwest or East, thus the claim "Today's Motion Picture News Today."

"Dimitri Tiomkin, Composer, to Universal Writes Music for Carewe Production of *Resurrection*." (August 1, 1930).

"'Musicals Can Stage Comeback,' Says [Arthur] Lange, Mus. Dir." 4:73 (July 8, 1931). On the need for spontaneity in musicals.

Hollywood Filmograph (US)

Weekly film news published in Los Angeles from 1922 to around 1936. Previously known as *Filmograph* (1922–1925). A rich source of information concerning the transition to sound films in the late 1920s and for musicals in the early 1930s. A column, "Along Music Row" by Herman Pincus contained news. "Lyrics and Music," debuting in the April 12, 1930, issue, assisted producers in searching for suitable lyrics and melodies. Valcour Verne edited the column that included brief news items regarding music and songs in films. The column was inaugurated on behalf of those who "suffered annoyance bordering on agony by being compelled to listen to boresome renditions of decidedly inane verses being sung to the accompaniment of music of such puerile quality that the whole picture left a dark brown taste in one's system." An occasional 1930s column, "Music and Song: Stage and Screen Reviewed," was penned by the magazine's music editor, Laurence A. Lambert, who also wrote feature articles. The 1930s issues are a good source for news items regarding songwriters, musical films, and scoring and music assignments. The news items document the careers of a wide range of composers, including Louis Gottschalk, Erno Rapee, Max Steiner, and Dimitri Tiomkin. The influx of composers of light and comic opera to Hollywood, including Sigmund Romberg, Rudolf Friml, and Oscar Straus, is likewise documented. A "Vitaphone Notes" column also appeared.

Cherniavsky, Josef. "Restrictions Harm to Scores." 9:20 (May 18, 1929): 55.
Baravalle, Victor. "Music in Sound Films." (June 15, 1929): 18.
"Let's See—Who's Who." 9:26 (June 29, 1929): 4. Constantin Bakaleinikoff biography.
"[Heinz] Roemheld Made Musical Director at Big U." (August 9, 1930): 21.
"John Boles Praises Dimitri Tiomkin's Music." (November 15, 1930): 7. Regarding *Resurrection*.
"Arthur Lange." (June 27, 1931). On the "Lange Process" for recording and dubbing music with singers.
Lange, Arthur. "The Music Situation." (August 22, 1931): 4.

Hollywood Movie Music Directory (US)
Published annually by the Hollywood Creative Directory in Santa Monica, California, from 1993 to 1996. Includes companies involved with the licensing, production, clearance, publishing, and scoring of movie and television music, and their staffs. With contact information on songwriters, composers, music supervisors, performing rights organizations, and major studio and network music executives. No. 1 (1993); No. 2 (1994); No. 3 (1995); No. 4 (1996).

Hollywood Music Industry Directory (US)
Published annually by the Hollywood Creative Directory in Santa Monica, California. This "insider's guide to the insiders" includes contact information for agents, film and television composers, managers, music supervisors, recording studios, and soundtrack executives. Name index. First edition, 2004.

The Hollywood Reporter (US)
One of two perennial daily trade papers (the other is *Variety*) that cover the film industry. Contains music business coverage of film and television scoring, publishing and licensing, composers and recording artists, music representation and unions, and obituaries. Articles listed below are only a representation of the vast range of material. A long-running column, "The Note Book," contains music news briefs in the Friday issue from at least 1944 to 1966. "Soundtrack" by Dianne Bennett appears at least in 1973. In the late 1980s the *Reporter* began publishing special reports on film and television music, first in one issue per year, later in multiple issues per year, including an update issue commencing in November 1996. Contributing writers include Ray Bennett, Jon Burlingame, Steven C. Smith, and later Jeff Bond, Chuck Crisafulli, and Alan Waldman. "Eye on Oscar" includes material focusing on potential nominees and films for music score (see January 15, 1997). It was followed by "Oscar Watch Song and Score" (see February 15–21, 2005).

"No More MGM Music." 1:47 (November 6, 1930): 1, 3. On the abolishment of the music department.

Stoloff, Morris. "New Day in Music." (October 8, 1940): section two (unpaged).

Cameron, Sue. "Being a Background Writer Not Enough Today: [Dominic] Frontiere." (June 12, 1970).

Knight, Arthur. "Knight at the Movies: Tune Detecting at Filmex." (March 21, 1980): 12–13. On Fred Steiner, Lyn Murray, and John Morgan's reconstruction of a silent film score.

Robinson, Ruth A. "Film Composers: An Independent Breed." (August 13, 1982).

Schwartz, Sam, and Ruth Robinson. "The Musical Score: An Afterthought?" (August 13, 1982).

Stone, Christopher. "Film Scoring Comes of Age." 273:7 (August 13, 1982).

Robinson, Ruth A. "Film Composers: An Independent Breed." 273:7 (August 13, 1982): S83 and S84.

Meyer, Constance. "Temp Track: Battling for the Score." (August 12, 1986): S26, S28.

Dawn, Randee. "Carter Burwell." (September 14, 1999). Gotham Award honoree.

Conniff, Tamara. "Execs Who Really Know the Score." (October 17, 2002): 12–13. Discussion with Burt Berman, Robert Kraft, Chris Montan, Kathy Nelson, and Lia Vollack.

Richmond, Ray. "Harry Gregson-Williams: Composer of the Year." (October 17, 2005): S–14. Brief profile.

Longwell, Todd. "Ethnic Fare." (December 13, 2005): S6. On the current use of ethnic instruments.

Special issues: Anniversary issues (selected)

Frontiere, Dominic. "Film Music–'70–'Taking a Stand.'" (40th anniversary edition, December 4, 1970): D3. If a picture needs dramatic underscore a producer should budget for it.

Stern, Mark. "Movie Music: Emotion Pictures." (41st anniversary edition, 1971): K8.

Barrett, Charles A. "Recording Artists Scoring TV Films." (46th anniversary edition, 1976): 103–11.

Special issues: Film and Television Music

Most issues contain lists of who's who in composing, composers who score prime-time shows, and film studio music executives.

January 23, 1987

Electronic music; Georges Delerue interviewed by Jeffrey Ainis; clearances and copyright; scoring low-budget films (Lyn Benjamin); music production companies; music licensing; Alan Silvestri on film scoring workshops; and source licensing.

January 22, 1988

Recent trends; Nan Schwartz; Lee Holdridge; European royalties; Synclavier advertisement; tax reform; music software; source licensing; session musicians; "Thoughts on Composing" by Earle Hagen; how it works (chart and terminology); Alex North interviewed by David Kraft; and focus on British film music: APRS, soundtrack labels, recording studios, and production houses.

January 17, 1989

Ennio Morricone (interview); Al Kasha and Joel Hirschhorn on songwriting; scoring and music supervising in the United Kingdom; music editors; communicating with the director (David Kraft talks to Stewart Copeland, Jerry Goldsmith, Dennis McCarthy, Alan Silvestri, Shirley Walker, and Christopher Young); cue sheets and royalties; Saban Productions (music for television animation); music supervisors, including credits; a call for improved conditions by Bruce Broughton; the studios versus the composer, with fee structures for film and television; and music publishing and licensing.

<u>August 29, 1989</u>

Television music; the Sundance Institute film music program; publishing soundtrack divisions sidebar on Warner/Chappell and EMI; per-program licensing; soundtracks; Steven C. Smith on animated films and on new faces, including Wendy Blackstone, Jim Campbell, Carl Dante, Cliff Eidelman, Jay Gruska, Cliff Martinez, James Stemple, Frederic Talgorn, and Nathan Wang; hit song royalties; Randy Edelman profile; writing for sound systems; George Fenton's *Dangerous Liaisons* score step by step; temp tracks excerpt from *On the Track* by Fred Karlin and Rayburn Wright; television theme songs; and top-selling soundtracks.

<u>January 16, 1990</u>

Rock musicians scoring as crossover artists, with a list of the latter; crossovers from advertising music; 1980s soundtracks sidebar, with *Billboard*'s top ten soundtracks from 1980 to 1989; W. G. "Snuffy" Walden on *thirtysomething*; agency who's who sidebar; and MIDEM 1990 record industry.

<u>August 24, 1990</u>

Independents; television music; cable, including company contacts; case study of *The Doors*; minorities, including Wendy Blackstone, Stanley Clarke, and Shirley Walker; case study of Angelo Badalamenti's music for *Twin Peaks*; case study of *thirtysomething*; electronic scoring and the Synclavier; cable music rights; MRI: music tracking system; music software; and musicals.

<u>January 15, 1991</u>

Runaway production for soundtrack recordings; shortage of recording studios; eastern Europe recording facilities; foreign composers; U.S.S.R.; where to score: Germany [sidebar]; profiles of John Barry, Gary Chang, Joel Hirschhorn, Al Kasha, and Leonard Rosenman; *Mermaids*; network television music; Mike Post; Fricon Entertainment music services; MIDEM; licensing music; *Rear Window* court decision; and songs between 1963 and 1978.

<u>August 27, 1991</u>

Rekindling the musical; *Newsies*; production music; television composers; breaking in, on Laura Karpman, Nicholas Pike, Nan Schwartz, and others; elimination of ICM music division (Richard Kraft, Charles Ryan); the British scene; cue sheet revenue; classes and workshops; point of view with David Foster, Michael Gore, Bill Lee, Henry Mancini, Lalo Schifrin, Tom Scott, and Howard Shore; list of production music companies; and Society of Composers and Lyricists (SCL).

<u>January 14, 1992</u>

Copyright; commercials; profiles of Chris Boardman, Stanley Clarke, Frankle Twins (Jennie and Terrie), Herbie Hancock, Bob Israel, Marc Shaiman, and Shirley Walker; soundtracks; and television networks.

<u>August 25, 1992</u>

On the synergy between corporate film and music units; contemporary rhythm and blues; Recording Musicians Association (RMA), AFM Local 47; film production and soundtrack guide; music for animated films; Alan Menken, *Aladdin*; profiles of James Patrick Dunne, Dave Koz, Lennie Niehaus, Tommy Vig, and Paul Williams; Hollywood and country music; David Wheatley on hiring a composer; music for film trailers; royalties; and music via computer.

January 18, 1993
Scoring a job; house music with Mark Chosak, Stanley Clarke, George Duke, Danny Elfman, Charles Fox, Billy Goldenberg, David Kurtz, Tom Scott, Mark Snow, Marc Tanner, and Jonathan Wolff; compact discs; composer-speak with Bruce Broughton; Danny Elfman interview; preservation of soundtracks; America Online: Taxi; specialty labels; profiles of Benny Carter, Marcos Loya, and Randy Miller; and Euro talent.

August 24, 1993
Soundtracks; television music; music supervision; Ry Cooder interview; equipment; agents; Zbigniew Preisner; director David Lynch; late-night talk shows; publishers; soundtrack collectibles; licensing; rock music; and profiles of Mark Isham and Ennio Morricone.

January 26, 1994
Scoring and music supervising for nonstudio projects; Kitaro; Rachel Portman profile; compact disc vending machines; the Latino market; Patrick Doyle interview; copyrights; budgets; women composers; soaps; dubbing; and the Alfred Hitchcock–Bernard Herrmann collaboration.

August 23, 1994
Soundtracks; classic rock (*Forrest Gump*); classic songs; television themes; electronic equipment wish lists; Cuban music (*The Perez Family*); profiles of Terence Blanchard, Stewart Copeland, Tito Larriva, John McEuen, Eric Sadler, and Cassandra Wilson; rock documentaries; licensing (*Strawberry Fields*); interviews with Maurice Jarre and Gary LeMel; and cue sheets.

January 26, 1995
Elliot Goldenthal interview; recording studios of the world; session musicians; song plugging; synthesized television music; profiles of Laura Karpman and Cynthia Millar; and music representatives.

August 29, 1995
Hans Zimmer interview; directors on music; and profile of Tom Hiel.

January 16, 1996
"The Scoring Life," by Joshue Mooney; Oscar contenders; Jon Burlingame on television themes; James Newton Howard interviewed by Jon Burlingame; Ray Bennett on soundtracks; temp tracks; preservation; roundtable with Robert Folk and others; and sound systems.

August 27, 1996
George Fenton interview; Stewart Copeland; "Great Cues: Filmmakers' Favorite Movie Music Moments," compiled by Scott Chernoff; hit songs roundtable with Miles Goodman, Mark Watters, Jonathan Wolff, and Gary Woods; top soundtrack singles; interview with James Cameron and Brad Fiedel from an SCL seminar.

November 8, 1996
"And Now for a Song," by Jon Burlingame; and "Musical Franchise," by Jon Burlingame on music for *Star Trek*.

January 1997
"*Star Wars* Revisited," by Jon Burlingame; ten film composers discuss the year's best scores; Randy Newman interview; a rock version of *All about Eve*; Jay Chattaway interview; Randy Edelman on scoring and recording; the year's hot composers and hot soundtracks; "Filmharmonic," by Jon Burlingame, on the Los Angeles Philharmonic's program

to commission short films performed with live scores.

<u>August 21, 2001</u>
Prime-time music; labor relations; Lalo Schifrin interview; movie music pipeline; hip-hop soundtracks; working relationships; John Williams in concert; and Flanders festival.

<u>November 13–19, 2001</u>
"Pitch-Slapped," by Jeff Bond examines the shortening window for scoring summer blockbusters.

<u>January 2002</u>
Soundtracks from 2001; John Barry interview; and a behind-the-scenes look at promotional music. Includes a special section, "Oscar Watch Song and Score," with material on contenders and hopefuls.

<u>April 23–29, 2002 (Film and Television update)</u>
"Sound Trackers," by Chuck Crisafulli on music libraries.

<u>August 20–26, 2002</u>
Randy Newman profile; Elliot Goldenthal; the new breed of composers; movie music pipeline; session life; and Flanders festival.

<u>November 12–18, 2002</u>
"Soundtrack of Life," by Chuck Crisafulli on documentary film scores; "One from the Heart," by Jeff Bond on Elmer Bernstein's score for *Far from Heaven*; "Music Libraries Redux," by Chuck Crisafulli; "'Dream' Factory," by Dylan Callaghan on Daniel Pelfrey; "Keeping the Score," by Dylan Callaghan contains capsule interviews with Stanley Clarke, George S. Clinton, Philip Glass, James Newton Howard, Christopher Lennertz, Drew Neumann, Conrad Pope, John Powell, and John Williams on their latest projects; and "Themes Like Old Times," by Ray Richmond on television series title songs.

<u>January 14, 2003</u>
Popular soundtracks; "Civil Score," on the set of *Gods and Monsters*; music publisher peermusic; movie music pipeline; composer spotlight; John Williams spotlight; MIDEM; and Howard Shore tribute.

<u>April 22–28, 2003</u>
"Master of *The Matrix*," by Jeff Bond on Don Davis's score; and "Dialed In," by Ada Guerin on L.A. radio station KCRW's airplay of soundtracks for independent films.

<u>August 19–25, 2003</u>
Jeff Bond on recent rejected scores; "Composer in a Can," by Chuck Crisafulli on digital scoring; movie music pipeline; cue tips; and Flanders festival.

<u>November 11–17, 2003</u>
"Meet the Independents," by Jeff Bond on Jeff Danna, Mychael Danna, Rolfe Kent, and Christopher Lennertz; director Quentin Tarantino interview; "Bursting into Song," on musicals; "Keep Your Composer," by Chuck Crisafulli on the benfits of a strong composer-director relationship.

<u>January 2004 (supplement)</u>
Music department heads; the year's most prolific composers; and a retrospective look at Michael Kamen. A special "Oscar Watch Song and Score" section contains "Settling the Score: 15 Oscar Contenders Discuss the Process Behind This Year's Most Memorable Film Music," with Christophe Beck, Mychael Danna, Don Davis, Alexandre Desplat, Danny Elfman, James Horner, James Newton Howard, Mark Isham, Mark Mancina, Thomas Newman, Rachel Portman, Howard Shore, Stephen Trask, Gabriel Yared, and Hans Zimmer.

<u>April 20–26, 2004</u>
Licensing; current movie music; and Marco Beltrami on his score for *Hellboy.*

<u>August 17–23, 2004</u>
Flanders Film Festival; and cue tips.

<u>November 16–22, 2004</u>
Music for religious-themed films; Elmer Bernstein; and an interview with Vangelis.

<u>January 2005</u>
"Breaking the Sound Barrier," by Chuck Crisafulli on composers of color and a review of 2004 soundtracks. A special "Oscar Watch Song and Score" section contains a virtual roundtable and other articles, including "Changing of the Guard," by Jeff Bond on emerging composers.

<u>April 19–25, 2005</u>
Technology and how computers are changing the composing process; and preservation and sound restoration for soundtracks.

<u>August 16–22, 2005</u>
Music supervision; "The Sound of Music," by Jeff Bond on seventy-five years of film music; "Going the Distance," by Bond on television miniseries; in the pipeline.

<u>November 15–21, 2005</u>
Jeff Bond on trailer music; song licensing fees; and Oscar hopefuls.

Hollywood Review (US)
Rudy de Saxe's "Matters of Note" column from 1946 contains music news. See, for example, vol. 38, no. 4 (October 1, 1946), page 2. Miklós Rózsa was "Personality of the Week" in vol. 36, no. 17 (December 31, 1945).

Hollywood Spectator (US)
Editor Welford Beaton's weekly recognized music as an indispensable element of screen entertainment. Dr. Bruno David Ussher's articles on music in motion pictures in 1937 (see October 9, for example) evolved into a column first titled "Music in Current Pictures" (1937–1939), later "Film Music and Its Makers" (1939–1940). The columns often had a leading topic, such as opera in films, and capsule paragraphs, or "constructive discussions," about music in current films as well as news coverage and the composers involved. A "Studio Music and Musicians" column by Abe Meyer ran in 1942 and included news and notes. *Hollywood Spectator* was formerly titled *Film Spectator.*
10:7 (September 13, 1930): 10. On David Broekman's music for *All Quiet on the Western Front.*
Roemheld, Heinz. "Music and Motion Pictures." 10:12 (November 22, 1930): 87. The composer's thoughts on the role of music in film.
"Music's Place in Motion Pictures." 15:4 (February 15, 1941): 4.

<u>Column, "Music in Current Pictures" by Bruno David Ussher (selected)</u>
12:24 (December 4, 1937): 14–15. First column.
12:30 (January 15, 1938): 10–11. On opera and more.
12:31 (January 22, 1938): 11–13. On Disney short films.
12:38 (March 12, 1938): 10–12. On film songs and their singers.
13:4 (May 7, 1938): 11–12. On Erich Wolfgang Korngold's music for *The Adventures of Robin Hood.* Reprinted and distributed by Fox West Coast Theatres.

Column, "Film Music and Its Makers" by Bruno David Ussher (selected)
14:1 (April 15, 1939): 11–12. First column.
14:3 (May 13, 1939): 21–22. On Erich Wolfgang Korngold's music for *Juarez*.
14:4 (May 27, 1939): 13–14. On recent scores.
14:17 (December 9, 1939): 11–12. On Albert Sendrey's music for *Whirlpool of Desire*.
14:23 (March 15, 1940): 15, 17. On the Academy Awards in the music category.
14:25 (April 15, 1940): 12–13. On recent scores.
15:1 (May 15, 1940): 15, 17, 19. On current films and events.
15:2 (June 1, 1940): 12–13. On Herbert Stothart's music for *Edison, the Man*. This appears to be the final column.

Column, "Studio Music and Musicians" by Abe Meyer
17:1 (September 1, 1942): 9–11. First column.
17:2 (September 15, 1942): 10–11, 15. On recent film scores and events.
17:3–4 (October 15, 1942): 8–10. Includes Charles Previn biography.

Hollywood Studio Magazine (US)
Popular journal for film buffs published in Studio City, California.
Collins, Pat. "The Man Responsible for Bringing Animated Films to Life." 6:12 (April 1972): 12–13. On Hoyt Curtin.
Carle, Teet. "The 'Voice' of a Silent Screen." 11:4 (1977): 8–10. The film publicist recalls the musical accompaniment of silent films in the waning years from 1927 to 1930.
Hughes, Mike. "Those Glorious Screen Musicals." 15:9 (June 1982): 23–25. General interest article.
Owens, Gary. "Gary Owens' Musical Memories: Bogart's Movie Music." 17:2 (March 1984): 11, 40. The radio show host discusses Max Steiner's score for *Casablanca*.

Hollywood Who's Who (US)
Published by Dell Publishing Company in New York.
Stothart, Herbert. "Scoring: Music Makes Moods." 1:1 (1941): 60.

Image (US)
Journal of the International Museum of Photography at the George Eastman House in Rochester, New York.
Iredale, Jane. "The Loneliness of the Long Distance Pianist: A Talk with the Musical Director of Channel 13's 'The Silent Years.'" (1970s): 3–5. On William Perry.
Hunsberger, Donald R. "Orchestral Accompaniment for Silent Films." 25:1 (March 1982): 7–16. Historical survey.
Pratt, George C. "Cue Sheets for Silent Films." 25:1 (March 1982): 17–24. Titles in the Eastman House cue sheet collection listed alphabetically.

Indian Cinema (India)
Chandavarkar, Bhaskar. "Film Music." (1982–1983). 35–39.

Inside Facts of Stage and Screen (US)
Published in Los Angeles from 1924 to 1931, this periodical includes news items and listings for area theaters concerning conductors, organists, songwriters, and other musicians, notably during the transition to sound.

International Documentary (US)

The magazine of the International Documentary Association published in Los Angeles.

Fairweather, Kathleen. "How to Score with Your Documentary Composer: An Interview with Richard Fiocca." 18:11 (November 1999): 53–54.

McTurk, Craig. "Music Rights Clearance: What You Don't Know *Can* Hurt You." 19:1 (January–February 2000): 34, 36.

Pray, Doug. "Doc Score: Composer Patrick Seymour on Writing Music for Nonfiction." 20:5 (June 2001): 8–9.

Powell, David. "All Clear? A Basic Primer on Music Clearance." 22:4 (May 2003): 16–20.

Cutler, Miriam. "You Shoot, They Score: A Film Composer's Tips for Finding the Right Musical Accompaniment." 22:4 (May 2003): 22–25.

International Film Annual (US)

Published by Doubleday in New York from 1957 to 1959, superseded by the *International Film Guide*.

Manvell, Roger. "The Composer's Role." 1 (1957): 84–89. Brief essay that begins, "The largest chain of concert halls in the world is the cinemas."

International Film Festival Magazine

"Makin' the Rounds: *Rounders'* Composer Christopher Young." No. 6 (1998): 40. Interview-based article.

International Motion Picture Almanac (US)

Published annually by Quigley Publications from 1929 through 2005. Titled *Motion Picture Almanac* from 1929 to 1935. "Composers" are listed in the 1929 through 1932 editions; "Songwriters" added in 1930. "Song Hits from Pictures" are listed in 1930 and 1931. From 1933 through 2005, the "Who's Who" section contains brief biographical details for composers, songwriters, and music directors, with selected film and television credits.

International Review of Educational Cinematography (Italy)

Published by the International Institute of Educational Cinematography, League of Nations, in Rome. Of interest for its international perspective on music in early sound films.

Giovannetti, Eugenio. "Must We First Educate the Film Director? Music for the Centaurs." 5:5 (May 1933): 324–27. On aesthetics pertaining to music and image, translated from the Italian.

London, Kurt. "Music and Film." 6:4 (April 1934): 289–91.

Malipiero, G. Francesco. "Cinema Music of Tomorrow." 7 (August 1935): 138–42. Translated from the Italian.

International Television and Video Almanac (US)

Published annually by Quigley Publications from 1956 through 2005. Titled *International Television Almanac* from 1956 to 1986. The "Who's Who" section contains brief biographical details for composers, songwriters, and music personnel.

Iris (US and France)

A journal of theory on image and sound.

Altman, Rick. "Film Sound: All of It." No. 27 (Spring 1999): 31–48. Includes some discussion of music.

Stockfelt, Ola. "Classical Film Music." No. 27 (Spring 1999): 81–94. On the literature of film music.

Thain, Alanna. "Sound Is Overlooked: History, Technology and Aesthetics of Music and Sound in Motion Pictures." No. 27 (Spring 1999): 169–71. Report on a Duke University conference.

Jones' (US)

A movie magazine by moviemakers, published in Los Angeles.

"Let's Get Acquainted with Universal Music Department." 2:7 (February 1938): 48–49, 66.

Phelps, Russell. "Maestro Werner Janssen." 2:12 (July 1938): 23, 67–68.

Journal of Communication (US)

Siefert, Marsha. "Image/Music/Voice: Song Dubbing in Hollywood Musicals." 45:2 (June 1995): 44–64.

Journal of Film and Video (US)

Aimed at campus filmmakers and teachers, sometimes referred to as the University Film Association Journal. Former titles include *Journal of the University Film Producers Association* (1949–1967), *Journal of the University Film Association* (1968–1981), and *Journal of the University Film and Video Association* (1982–1983).

Published as Journal of the University Film Producers Association

Lavastida, Bert, and Pete Stallings, Norman Phelps, and Glen Gould. "Music for Motion Pictures." 7:2 (Winter 1954): 12–16. Conference presentation transcript.

Driscoll, John. "Music Is for Beauty." 13:1 (Fall 1960): 2–4.

Published as Journal of the University Film Association

Raksin, David. "Raksin on Film Music." 26:4 (1974): 68–70, 79. Excerpts from a 1974 UFA conference using examples from his film scores.

Bernstein, Elmer. "On Film Music." 28:4 (Fall 1976): 7–9. Transcript of a 1976 UFA conference.

Raksin, David, with Charles M. Berg. "Music Composed by 'Charlie Chaplin': Auteur or Collaborateur?" 31:1 (Winter 1979): 47–50. With an explanatory letter from Raksin to Berg.

Cocking, L. "Ode to a Composer." 33:1 (Winter 1981): 49–57. Interview with Lyn Murray, 49–52.

Published as Journal of the University Film and Video Association

Marks, Martin. "Film Music: The Material, Literature, and Present State of Research." 34:1 (Winter 1982): 3–40. Revision of MLA Notes article.

Published as Journal of Film and Video

Fink, Edward J. "Television Music: Automaticity and the Case of Mike Post." 50:3 (Fall 1998): 40–53.

Journal of Film Preservation (Brussels)

Published by the International Federation of Film Archives (FIAF).

Anderson, Gillian. "Preserving Our Film Heritage or Making Mongrels? The Presentation of Early (Not Silent) Films." 57 (December 1998): 19–24. Text of a paper delivered at an Italian workshop on music for film.

Journal of Popular Film and Television (US)

An academic journal with a sociocultural perspective, edited at the College of Arts at North Michigan State and the Department of Popular Culture at Bowling Green State University, Ohio. Prior to 1979 it was titled *Journal of Popular Film.*

Published as Journal of Popular Film

Landon, John W. "Long Live the Mighty Wurlitzer." 2:1 (Winter 1973): 3–13. On the use of organs to accompany silent films.

Scheurer, Timothy E. "The Aesthetics of Form and Convention in the Movie Musical." 3:4 (Fall 1974): 307–24.

Hodgkinson, Anthony W. "*Forty-Second Street* New Deal: Some Thoughts about Early Film Musicals." 4:1 (1975): 33–46.

Berg, Charles M. "The Human Voice and the Silent Cinema." 4:2 (1975): 165–177.

Published as Journal of Popular Film and Television

8:1 (Spring 1980): Special issue on Hollywood musicals, contents listed below.

Shout, John D. "The Film Musical and the Legacy of Show Business." 10:1 (Spring 1982): 23–26.

Grant, Barry K. "The Classic Hollywood Musical and the 'Problem' of Rock 'n' Roll." 13:4 (Winter 1986): 195–205.

Gabbard, Krin, and Glen O. Gabbard. "Play It Again, Sigmund: Psychoanalysis and the Classical Hollywood Text." 18:1 (Spring 1990): 6–17. Regarding *Casablanca.*

Scheurer, Timothy E. "Henry Mancini. An Appreciation and Appraisal." 24:1 (Spring 1996): 34–43.

25:4 (Winter 1998): Special issue on "Popular Film, Television, and Music," contents listed below.

Ritter, Kelly. "Spectacle at the Disco: *Boogie Nights*, Soundtrack, and the New American Musical." 28:4 (Winter 2001): 166–75.

Wierzbicki, James. "Weird Vibrations: How the Theremin Gave Musical Voice to Hollywood's Extraterrestrial 'Others.'" 30:3 (Fall 2002): 125–35.

Chadwell, Sean. "Inventing that 'Old-Timey' Style: Southern Authenticity in *O Brother, Where Art Thou?*" 32:1 (Spring 2004): 2–9.

Plasketes, George. "*Cop Rock* Revisited: Unsung Series and Musical Hinge in Cross-Genre Evolution." 32:2 (Summer 2004): 64–73. Musical narrative in the television show.

Scheurer, Timothy E. "'You Know What I Want to Hear': The Music of *Casablanca*." 32:2 (Summer 2004): 90–96. Analysis of Max Steiner's score for the 1942 film.

Scheurer, Timothy E. "The Best There Ever Was in the Game": Musical Mythopoesis and Heroism in Film Scores of Recent Sports Movies." 32:4 (Winter 2005): 157–66. On the Randy Newman and Jerry Goldsmith scores for *The Natural* (1984), *Hoosiers* (1986), and *Rudy* (1993).

Special issue, 8:1 (Spring 1980) [on Hollywood musicals]

Telotte, J. P. "A Sober Celebration: Song and Dance in the 'New' Musical." 2–14.

Schultz, Jacques. "Categories of Song." 15–25. On the role songs in musicals.

Scheurer, Timothy E. "'I'll Sing You a Thousand Love Songs': A Selected Filmography of the Musical Film." 61–67.

Special issue, 25:4 (Winter 1998) ["Popular Film, Television, and Music"]

Donnelly, K. J. "The Perpetual Busman's Holiday: Sir Cliff Richard and British Pop Musicals." 146–54.

Fink, Edward J. "Episodic's Music Man: Mike Post." 155–160. Interview.

Scheurer, Timothy E. "Kubrick vs. North. The Score for *2001: A Space Odyssey*." 172–82. Compares Alex North's unused score with the score assembled from classical music that Kubrick used.

Jump Cut (US)

A review of contemporary cinema published in Berkeley, California.

Bruce, Graham. "Music in Glauber Rocha's Films." 22 (May 1980): 15–18. Analysis.

Kinematograph Weekly (UK)

Published in London and popularly known as *Kine Weekly*. Covers all aspects of the British film industry. Advertisements in the mid-1910s cover film music. Soundtrack recordings are reviewed from 1956 to 1959.

Byng, F. D. [Title undetermined.] (March 25, 1915): 81–83. On the use of Mozart's music to accompany films.

Crowhurst, Cyril. "How a Music Recording Theatre Was Made from a Sound Stage." (September 26, 1946).

Irving, Ernest. "British Film Music." (December 19, 1946).

Huntley, John. "Music Recording Stage." (July 10, 1947): 11–12.

Huntley, John. "Sixty Years of Film Music: The Films Were Never Silent." (May 3, 1956): 67ff.

Kinematograph Year Book, Film Diary and Directory (UK)

Published in London by Kinematograph and Lantern Weekly.

Wortham, L. "Kinema Music During 1917." (1918): 83–84.

LA 411 (US)

A motion picture industry directory published in Los Angeles since 1982. The annual volume includes professional references to commercial film production, including line listings for composers, music libraries, and music production.

The Last Word (US)

Published weekly in New York in 1930 and 1931 by Fox Theatres Corp. as a successor to *Now*. Its purpose was to aid theater owners in selling pictures by sharing exploitation, creative publicity, and tie-ins with theaters across the country. There were Eastern and Western editions, the latter often included a "music cue" section that lists pre-film prologue music performed by pit orchestras in Los Angeles theaters. Some volumes include an index with music news; for example, see the July 4, 1931, issue. An example of these brief news items includes, "Famous Composers Write Music," on page 17 in vol. 4, no. 47 (November 29, 1930), on songwriters Sam Messenheimer and Val Burton.

Leonard Maltin's Movie Crazy (US)

The film critic's newsletter for people who love movies.

Maltin, Leonard. "Biography of a Song: Don't Fence Me In." No. 5 (Summer 2003): 1, 12–13. On the film use of Cole Porter's cowboy anthem.

Maltin, Leonard. "The Story of Soundies." No. 6 (Autumn 2003): 1, 8–11. Incorporates material from Maltin's 1970s interview with songwriter Sam Coslow.

Maltin, Leonard. "Conversations: Alexander Courage." No. 7 (Winter 2004): 2–7. Interview.

Maltin, Leonard. "Conversations: Alexander Courage, Part 2." No. 8 (Spring 2004): 2–6. Interview.

Lion's Roar (US)

The lavish bimonthly in-house journal of Metro-Goldwyn-Mayer (MGM) Studio, prepared by the publicity department from 1941 to 1947. Most of the articles are on films in production, including musicals, and the music or songs are often mentioned. Articles listed below without page numbers are in unpaged issues and are usually one or two pages long.

"The New Musical Method." 1:1 (undated; circa 1941). On the importance of story over set pieces.

"Names Make Music." 1:1 (undated; circa 1941). On the Gershwins' and Roger Edens's music for *Lady Be Good.*

"Master Music." 1:3 (undated; circa late 1941). On Nathaniel W. Finston, MGM's music department head, and George Schneider, musical research chief.

"College Professor Goes Musical." 1:3 (undated; circa late 1941). Background article on Herbert Stothart.

"Songs that Never Die." 3:1 (September 1943). On the songs in *Girl Crazy.*

"Hollywood, World's Music Capital." 3:1 (September 1943). On Nathaniel Finston, Herbert Stothart, and conductor Albert Coates.

"[Jose] Iturbi, By a Knockout." 3:2 (January 1944).

"Song Hits Sell Theatre Tickets." 3:2 (January 1944).

"Meet the Maestro." 3:2 (January 1944). On Albert Coates.

"Jesters in Tail Coates." 3:3 (May 1944 supplement). On Jose Iturbi and Albert Coates.

"One Finger Virtuoso." 3:3 (May 1944 supplement). On actress Gracie Allen's piano playing.

Mayer, Mary. "Music and the Movies." 3:4 (July 1944). Profile of the music department, including material on the art of timing, scoring problems, cue sheets, and theme songs.

Stothart, Herbert. "Telling History with Music." 3:5 (December 1944). Brief article.

"The Nation Sings—Words and Music by M-G-M." 4:5 (November 1945): 56–57. On the studio's publishing arms and music exploitation.

"G.I. Means 'Get Iturbi.'" 5:4 (August 1946): 7. Profile of pianist Jose Iturbi.

Literature/Film Quarterly (US)

Academic journal published from Salisbury State College in Maryland.

Rothwell, Kenneth S. "Zeffirelli's *Romeo and Juliet*: Words into Picture and Music." 5:4 (Fall 1977): 326–31. On Nino Rota's score.

Fawell, John. "The Musicality of the Filmscript." 17:1 (January 1989): 44–49. Music as refrain, dialogue as music.

Brown, Royal S. "Serialism in Robbe-Grillet's *l'Eden et aprés*: The Narrative and Its Doubles." 18:4 (October 1990): 210–20.

Mosley, Philip. "Literature, Film, Music: Julien Gracq's 'Le roi Cophetua' and André Delvaux's *Rendezvous à Bray.*" 20:2 (April 1992): 138–45. Cinema as music.

Berg, Charles. "Music on the Silent Set." 23:2 (April 1995): 131–36. Documents the use of mood music performed during filming to assist actors.

Everett, Wendy. "Director as Composer: Marguerite Duras and the Musical Analogy." 26:2 (April 1998): 124–29. The use of music in films directed by Duras as well as the argument that her films function as music.

Walker, Elsie M. "When Past and Present Collide: Laura Rossi's Music for *Silent Shakespeare* (1999)." 33:2 (2005): 156–67. Music for a British Film Institute video compilation of silent films.

Lumiere (Australia)

Shirley, G. "Sound of Film." 24 (June 1973): 9–11. Interview with Murray Schafer regarding background music in films.

The Media Project, Inc. (US)

Newton, Jon. "Scoring for Features in Oregon." No. 21 (December 1982): 1–3. On two recent features.

Metro (Australia)

A long-running film and media magazine covering Australia and New Zealand.

English, Elizabeth. "Use of Music and Sound in *Strikebound*." Nos. 9–10 (Study Guide 1984).

Hamilton, Peter, Janet Bell, Bryan Williams, and Michael Simons. "Who the Hell Are You?" No. 43 (Autumn 1978): 26–27. Interview with Charles Wayne about scoring director Peter Weir's film *The Last Wave*. Reprinted in "Australian *Film Special*," (Mediagraph, 24), Victoria, Education Department, Curriculum and Research Branch, 1979.

Robinson, Sue. "Iva Davies and Fairlight." No. 64 (1984): 40–41.

Considine, Michael. "Music and Society: A Teaching Framework." No. 70.

Schütze, Paul. "A Day in the Life: Composer Paul Schütze." No. 89. Written by the film composer.

Bruce, Graham. "Double Score: Bernard Herrmann's Music for *Cape Fear* 1961 and 1991." No. 96 (Summer 1993): 10–14.

Danks, Adrian. "Verite Jukebox." No. 112 (1997): 99–100. On documentary film music.

Armiger, Martin. "My Side of the Picture." No. 123 (2000). Written by the film composer.

Brophy, Philip. "Local Noise: Australian Film Sound and Music." Nos. 127–128 (2001): 58–62. On the state of film music in Australia.

Davey, John. "A Foot in Both Worlds." Nos. 129–130 (2001): 226–31. Interview with David Hirschfelder.

Dzenis, Anna. "This Is My Land or This Land Is Me?" Nos. 131–132 (2002): 114–17. Analysis of *One Night the Moon*, a filmed story told in song.

Jobling, David. "Functional Harmonies: Interviews with Music Creators." No. 133 (2002): 44–54. Film music composers, including Michael Nyman, speak.

Maddox, Sarah. "From Little Things Big Things Grow: A Revival of the Film Music." No. 133 (2002): 38–43. On a perceived worldwide revival of film musicals.

Sandars, Diana. "*Ally McBeal* Brings the Hollywood Musical to Television." No. 133 (2002): 150.

Caputo, Raffaele. "Very Sound: Philip Brophy." No. 136 (2003): 112–17. Interview with the Australian composer and founder of Cinesonic.

O'Shaughnessy, Michael. "*Walkabout*'s Music: European Nostalgia in the Australian Outback." No. 140 (Spring 2004): 82–86.

Coyle, Rebecca. "Pop Goes to Music: Scoring the Popular Song in the Contemporary Sound Track." No. 140 (Spring 2004): 94–98.

Hancock, Matthew. "Soundscape: Reverberations of Hope, Loss and Nostalgia: The Beauty and Filth of *Little Fish*." No. 146–147 (2005): 180–84. Interview with composer Nathan Larson.

Metro-Goldwyn-Mayer Studio Club News (US)

Published for members at the studios in Culver City, circa 1936 to 1947. The "Music Notes" column by F. H. Kruger contains items of personal interest regarding music department personnel, such as birthday parties and home purchases. For example, see vol. 1, no. 12 (January 15, 1937). News items, including contract signings, may also appear in *MGM Studio News*, published bimonthly from 1935 through at least 1947.

The M-G-M Record (US)

Publicity newsletter published in Beverly Hills for M-G-M Records, a division of Metro-Goldwyn-Mayer that released music tracks from the studio's films.

"M-G-M Records *Pirate* Album Taken Direct from Sound Track of Film!" 2:88 (July 3, 1948): [3].

Midnight Marquee (US)

This long-running fanzine focuses on science fiction, fantasy, classic horror, suspense, and film noir. Superseded *Gore Creatures*.

Doherty, Jim. "The Herrmann Zone." No. 31 (Fall 1982): 10–13. Herrmann's music for *Twilight Zone* (TV).

Doherty, Jim. "The Musical Brainstorms of James Horner." No. 33 (Fall 1987).

Larson, Randall D. "*The Gorgon*: Music by James Bernard." No. 38 (Spring 1989).

Larson, Randall D. "Roy Webb's Fantasy Scores." Nos. 40–41 (1990–1991).

Larson, Randall D. "Scoring Val Lewton: The Quiet Horror Music of Roy Webb (The Robert Wise Films)." No. 44 (1992).

Vertlieb, Steve. "The Reinvention of Miklos Rozsa." No. 52.

DiLeonardi, Vincent A. "Music for Frankenstein." No. 55.

Vertlieb, Steve. "Hitchcock and Herrmann." Nos. 65–66 (2002): 82–95.

Millimeter (US)

Originally billed as the magazine for and about film and videotape people; later as the magazine of the motion picture and television industries.

Cook, G. Richardson. "Scoring with Composer Michael Small." 3:9 (September 1975): 18–22, 45.

Smith, David R. "The Sorcerer's Apprentice: Birthplace of *Fantasia*." 4:2 (February 1976): 18–24, 64–67. Recording the music for Disney's animated feature.

Stamelman, Peter. "Film Composer David Shire: Shuffling Off from Buffalo." 4:4 (April 1976): 20–24, 46–47. Interview-based article.

Powell, Stephen. "The Mighty Musical Makes Its Comeback." 7:1 (January 1979): 24–40, 166.

Zimmerer, Teresa. "Close-Ups: Suzanne Ciani." 7:1 (January 1979): 92.

Curley, Joseph. "A Few Easy Pieces: Interviews with Composers Bill Conti and Jerry Goldsmith." 7:4 (April 1979): 34–35, 38–46.

Levy, Barry. "Michael Crichton Discusses His Directing of *The Great Train Robbery*." 7:5 (May 1979): 158–160, 162. Includes the director's comments on Jerry Goldsmith's music for this film and for *Coma*.

Curley, Joseph. "Nobody Does It Better: Composers Marvin Hamlisch and Henry Mancini Discuss Their Work." 7:6 (June 1979): 26–31, 35–38, 176–77.

Curley, Joseph. "Elmer Bernstein: How Rock Has Rolled over Film Scoring." 8:8 (August 1980): 134–39. Interview.

Rodman, Howard A. "Scoring with Auricle." 13:11 (November 1985): 98–99. On Ron and Richard Grant's software for synchronizing music to picture.

Padroff, Jay. "Rock 'n' Reel: Today's Knockout Movies Often Rely on Punchy Songs and Music Department Maestros." 13:11 (November 1985): 142–46. With a sidebar on "The New Conductors: Engineers."

"Music Composers." 14:13 (December 1986): 194–99. Contact listings.

"Music Composers." 15:12 (December 1987): 204–9.

Monthly Film Bulletin (UK)

Published by the British Film Institute in London.

"Checklist 72: Bernard Herrmann." 37 (November 1970): 238–39.

Palmer, Christopher. "The Music of Bernard Herrmann." 43:513 (October 1976): 224. Article.

Palmer, Christopher. "The Music of Miklós Rózsa." 45:530 (March 1978): 60. Article.

Palmer, Christopher. "Write It Black: Roy Webb, Lewton and Film Noir." 48:571 (August 1981): 168. Article on Webb's film noir and horror music at RKO. Reprinted in *Twentieth-Century Literary Criticism*, vol. 76.

Motion (Canada)

Published bimonthly by Motion Canada Media Productions in Toronto in the 1970s.

Special section, 4:2 (1975) ["Film and Music"]

"Introduction to Film and Music." 6.

Runnells, Rory. "Music Sense." 7. On Bob McMullin and his music for documentaries.

McLarty, James. "Silence Really Is Golden." 8–10. On Harry Freedman's score for *Lies My Father Told Me*.

Charent, Brian. "The Silents with Charles Hofmann and Horace Lapp." 4:2 (1975): 10–12. Lapp was an organist.

Jacques, Arthur O. "Law and Music." 13.

McLarty, James. "Appointment with Agostini." 14–15. On composer-conductor Lucio Agostini.

Charent, Brian. "A Kind of Awareness." 16–18. Interview with composer William McCauley.

Motion Picture Classic (US)

Fan magazine published monthly in New York.

Dittmar, Maud Waters. "The Language of the Silent Drama." 4:5 (July 1917): 52, 64. Essay on the state of the art.

Motion Picture Herald (US)

Motion picture trade paper published in New York from 1931 to 1972. It superseded *Exhibitors Herald*, *The Film Index*, *Motography*, and *Moving Picture World*. Music critic Joseph O'Sullivan regularly wrote about film music throughout the 1930s. Each article usually dealt with a specific film and usually incorporated music excerpts. O'Sullivan, a musician and composer, often selected films related to opera, an area he specialized in.

Gorney, Jay. "A New Ratio for Dialogue in Films." 109:6 (November 5, 1932): 24. The composer calls for more music underscore.

Meehan, Leo. "Musicomedy Comeback." 110:4 (January 21, 1933): 28.

Burt, Francis L. "Publishers Charge Films with Prompting Need of Music Code: 'Plugging' of 'Inferior' Songs to Advertise New Films Is Blamed at Trade Practice Conference." 129:2 (October 9, 1937): 14.

Lazarus, Charles J. "Music Hath Charms to Catch Patron Dollar: Companies Promote Songs as Means to Increase Grosses of Pictures." 176:12 (September 17, 1949): 30.

Buchanan, Loren G. "The Art of Composing Music Scores for Films: Alex North, an Expert, Comments on His Craft." 234:8 (October 13, 1965): 12, 36. Reprinted in Limbacher.

Articles by Joseph O'Sullivan (selected)

"Music as the Narrator." 103:2 (April 11, 1931): 14, 38. On Hugo Riesenfeld's score for *Tabu*.

"A Contrast in Musical Treatment." 104:2 (July 11, 1931): 25, 35. On *Svengali* and *Der Grosse Tenor*.

"Four M's of German Production." 107:7 (May 14, 1932): 18. Coordinating music with action (Musical Movie Motivation Methods) as exemplified in *Congress Dances*.

"Music Texture in Romantic Drama." 108:5 (July 30, 1932): 18. On *Fire in the Opera* and *Schubert's Dream of Spring*.

"Opera—A Neglected Film Source." 109:6 (October 15, 1932): 27. Includes a biography of O'Sullivan.

"Music as a Spiritual Symbol." 109:12 (December 17, 1932): 17. On Rudolph Kopp's score for *Sign of the Cross*.

"*Madame Butterfly* as Music-Film." 110:4 (January 21, 1933): 19.

"An Appreciation of the Musical Treatment of *Cavalcade*." 110:7 (February 11, 1933): 20–21. On Louis De Francesco's score.

"When the Music Tells the Story." 110:10 (March 4, 1933): 11. Correlating music, dialogue, and action in Alfred Newman's score for *Hallelujah, I'm a Bum*.

"A Music Lesson for Hollywood." 111:6 (May 6, 1933): 14. On *Be Mine Tonight*.

"Screen Can Make Opera Pay If—" 112:2 (July 8, 1933): 15.

"Experiment in Music and Narration on *Famous Scenes from Pagliacci*." 115:3 (April 14, 1934): 23.

"Notable Screen Music Adventure." 118:13 (March 30, 1935): 12. On Herbert Stothart's score for *Naughty Marietta*.

"A Symphony of the Emotions." 119:8 (May 25, 1935): 14. On Max Steiner's score for *Break of Hearts*.

"Russians Draw Music Instead of Playing It." 120:7 (August 17, 1935): 34.

"Music as a Narrative Element of *The Crusades*." 120:9 (August 31, 1935): 33. On Rudolph Kopp's score.

"Don't Shoot the Piano Player! He Gave Clue to Modern Screen." 120:13 (September 28, 1935): 195–98.

"Mendelssohn's Melody Interprets Shakespeare's *Dream* on Screen." 121:2 (October 12, 1935): 32–33. On Erich Wolfgang Korngold's score for *A Midsummer Night's Dream*.

"Diversion along the Beaten Path in Music of *Metropolitan*." 121:5 (November 2, 1935): 15.

"[Lily] Pons Film, New Musical Recipe at Start, Returns to Formula." 121:10 (December 7, 1935): 39. On Max Steiner's score for *I Dream Too Much*.

"Arrival of the Screen Operetta Found Confirmed in *Rose Marie*." 122:8 (February 22, 1936): 23. On Herbert Stothart's score.

"Current of Song Moves Story in *Give Us This Night*." 122:11 (March 14, 1936): 18. On Erich Wolfgang Korngold's score.

"Motif Music Adds Strength to Screen in *Anthony Adverse*: Korngold's Score Gives Visual Scenes Eloquence without Disturbing Spoken Word." 124:8 (August 22, 1936): 15. Analysis with musical examples.

"Virginia Ham and Caviar Blend Musically in *Maytime*: Liaison of Opera and Symphony in Motion Picture Called New Achievement." 126:13 (March 27, 1937): 15. On music by Herbert Stothart.

"100 Musicians Can't Be Wrong; New Film Breaks with Tradition." 128:12 (September 18, 1937): 29. On Frank Skinner's score for *100 Men and a Girl*.

"Voice Comes into Its Own in Music of *Snow White*." 130:7 (February 12, 1938): 12. On Frank Churchill's score for *Snow White and the Seven Dwarfs*.

"Korngold Raises Film Music to True Function in *Robin Hood*." 131:6 (May 7, 1938): 25. On *The Adventures of Robin Hood*.

"*Alexander* Carries Berlin's Genius from Dirty Eddies to Carnegie Hall." 132:5 (July 30, 1938): 32. On *Alexander's Ragtime Band*.

"Music Paces Action as Screen Widens Scope of *The Mikado*." 135:7 (May 20, 1939): 27.

Motion Picture Magazine (US)

Billed as the "quality magazine of the screen," this fan magazine for general audiences was published monthly in New York.

Cook, Burr C. "Fitting Music to the Movie Scenes: Screen Opera the Latest Thing in Filmdom." 12:9 (October 1916): 111–14. On the trend toward writing specific music for a film; mentions many practitioners. Title reference to opera is not meant in the traditional sense of the word but refers to the emerging art form of live music accompanying screen drama.

Lachenbruch, Jerome. "The Marriage of the Muses." 20:7 (August 1920): 42–43, 114–18. An extensive history of the use of music to accompany silent films.

Denbo, Doris. "A Tune for a Tear." 28:10 (November 1924): 36–37, 94–95, 104–5. Actors on the influence of music on the set to create emotion.

Denbo, Doris. "A Tune for a Tear—Part II: What the Directors Think of the Business of Acting to Music." 28:11 (December 1924): 52–53, 92–93.

Denbo, Doris. "A Tune for a Tear—Part III: What the Musicians Think of the Business of Acting to Music." 28:12 (January 1925): 61–62, 114–15.

Motion Picture Mail (US)

Music critic Sigmund Spaeth wrote a "Music and the Movies" column that first appeared in vol. 2, no. 18 (January 13, 1917), page 10. The column was on the present state of the art. This weekly periodical, published in New York, began and ceased publication in 1917; it is unclear whether there were any additional Spaeth columns.

Motion Picture Music and Musicians (US)

A series of articles by Vernon Steele, billed as "Photoplay Appreciation Study Material," distributed by the Public Relations Department of Fox West Coast Theatres as a public service. The study guides were usually four pages in length and are not dated, although the films date from 1939 and 1940. It was apparently issued concurrently with *Cinemusic and Its Meaning*.

"Discussion of the Musical Scores in *We Are Not Alone* and *First Love*." Music by Max Steiner, Hans Salter, and Frank Skinner from 1939.

"Discussion of the Musical Score to *Rulers of the Sea*." Music by Richard Hageman.

"A Discussion of the Musical Scores in *Hunchback of Notre Dame, Gulliver's Travels,* and *Balalaika.*"

"Discussion of the Musical Score to *Pinocchio* and *Abe Lincoln in Illinois.*" Fourth in series.

Motion Picture News (US)

Trade paper published in New York, preceded by *Moving Picture News* (1908–1913). *Motion Picture News* continued the "Music and the Picture" column introduced by John M. Bradlet in *Moving Picture News* in September 1913. It was intended to answer exhibitors' questions regarding the use of music in photoplays and to suggest suitable music for current pictures. The column was edited by E. A. Ahern, H. S. Fuld, Charles D. Isaacson, Ernst Luz, E. M. Wickes, and others. Brief news items and letters from readers sometimes appeared on the same page spread. Music plots, cue sheets, or musical suggestions were found after the editorial content. After Luz left in the mid-teens the length of the editorial content is subsumed by the increased space devoted to the musical suggestions and reviews of music intended for film accompaniment. "Music and the Picture" usually appeared near the back of the paper in the "Accessory News" section alongside other technical topics such as cameras.

Hawkins, John M. "Union Musicians Cause Trouble in Elizabeth." 10:3 (July 25, 1914): 36. On the hiring of a non-union pianist in New Jersey.

"The Revolution in Photoplay Music." 10:6 (August 15, 1914): 39–40. Followed by news briefs on organs, fotoplayers, and other instruments, and "Drums for Picture Houses," on Leedy instruments.

Burton, Alice S. "A Woman's Suggestions for Musical Scores." 12:2 (July 17, 1915): 191. From a pianist in Hawaii.

"Musical Program for Its Pictures Is Paramount Plan." 12:13 (October 2, 1915): 76. George W. Beynon to arrange orchestra settings.

Holway, B. A. "A Picture without Music Is Almost Like Soup without Salt." 13:22 (June 3, 1916): 3450, 3462.

Isaacson, Charles D., ed. "Special Music Supplement." 23:8 (February 19, 1921): 1501–24. Contains extensive documentation of the state of the art of film music and its practitioners in honor of the first national conference of the Association of Motion Picture and Music Interests. Includes membership list, text of speeches, and discussion of topics, including the kind of music to be used, the perfect motion picture score, cue sheets, the use of classical and popular music, musical directors, the Federation of Women's Clubs music department, and the history of the organ. Includes comments from Ernst Luz, Erno Rapee, Hugo Riesenfeld, Samuel Rothapfel, and Max Winkler, among others.

"Premiere Presentation of *Sin Flood.*" 25:5 (January 21, 1922): 658. Special article with editorial comments on the musical presentation of the film.

"Special Course Inaugurated for Motion Picture Organists." 26:20 (November 11, 1922): 2455, 2469. At the Eastman School of Music.

Powell, A. L. "Color Lighting as an Aid to Music in the Motion Picture Theatre." (June 2, 1928): 1861, 1863, 1878.

Column, "Music and the Picture" (selected)

The page numbers include the entire "Music and the Picture" section, which may include editorial content, news briefs, musical suggestions, and so on.

10:8 (August 29, 1914): 39. On cooperation between the projectionist and pianist.

10:10 (September 12, 1914): 39. "Getting the Best Out of the Music and the Pictures," by E. A. Ahern.

10:11 (September 19, 1914): 35. "Following the Pictures, Not the Music," by E. A. Ahern.

10:18 (November 7, 1914): 73. "Popularity of Wurlitzer on the Increase," by H. S. Fuld.

10:19 (November 14, 1914): 80. "Effective Playing for Comedies," by E. A. Ahern.

10:19 (November 14, 1914): 81. "Music for the Modern Photo-Playhouse," by H. S. Fuld. First in a series describing musical instruments adaptable to the motion picture theater.

10:22 (December 5, 1914): 114. "Fitting the Words of a Song to the Picture" and "'Piano-Orchestrions' Versus Orchestras," by H. S. Fuld.

10:23 (December 12, 1914): 114. "Using the Resources of an Orchestra to Interpret a Photoplay," by H. S. Fuld.

10:26 (January 2, 1915): 115. "Using Judgment in Playing to Pictures," by E. A. Ahern.

12:2 (July 17, 1915): 190–92. "The Exhibitor and Music," and "The One-Man Orchestra Is Best for the Picture," both by Ernst Luz.

12:20 (November 20, 1915): 159–60. "The One-Man Orchestra Possesses Many Advantages," by E. F. Licome.

13:15 (April 15, 1916): 2256–57. Column, followed by news item, "Paramount Arranges with Schirmer for Musical Scores to Accompany Features."

13:18 (May 6, 1916): 2778–79. By Ernst Luz, includes "In *Ramona* Is a Theme for Every Character; It Is Varied According to the Character's Mood," on the score by Emil Bierman, with mention of music director Carli Elinor.

13:26 (July 1, 1916): 4114–19. "Musical Synchronization to Dramatic Photoplays," by Ernst Lux [*sic*].

14:1 (July 8, 1916): 135–39. Ernst Luz on musical advancements evident by scores for *Birth of a Nation*, *Fall of a Nation*, and *Ramona*.

14:8 (August 26, 1916): 1267, 1276. "A Musician's View of Motion Picture Music."

14:9 (September 2, 1916): 1435–36. "Programming Music for Photoplay Synchronization," by Ernst Luz.

14:17 (October 28, 1916): 2738. "A Convincing Brief Held for the Pipe Organ," by Ernst Luz.

14:18 (September 4, 1916): 2896, 2900. "Orchestra Interpretation of Motion Pictures," by Ernst Luz.

14:26 (December 30, 1916): 4281–83. "Romantic and Dramatic Motion Picture Situations," by Ernst Luz.

15:1 (January 6, 1917): 145–47. "Poor Music Drives Away Patronage," by Ernst Luz.

15:9 (March 3, 1917): 1445–47. "Music for Oriental Pictures," with suggestions by the editor.

15:26 (June 30, 1917): 4134–35. "Musical Review of Latest Compositions Suited for Picture Playing." This became a recurring feature.

16:18 (November 3, 1917): 3151–52. "Playing the Pictures."

17:13 (March 31, 1918): 1944–47. "Ideal Usefulness of the Organ for Motion Pictures," by E. M. Wickes.

19:1 (January 4, 1919): 133–35. "Phrasing."

21:14 (March 27, 1920): 2079–81. "A Progressive Orchestra Leader."

24:4 (July 16, 1921): 458. "The Fool-Proof Picture," by Charles D. Isaacson, who contributed other articles around this time.

25:4 (January 14, 1922): 552. "Why Do We Need Music with Pictures?" with commentary from Hugo Riesenfeld. Ironically, this was one of the last essays before the column went to a news format.

25:6 (January 28, 1922): 792. Short news articles.
25:11 (March 4, 1922): 1420. "Music for Non-Atmospheric Dramas," on Joseph Sainton's working method.
25:12 (March 11, 1922): 1536. "Synchronized Music Company Reorganized."

Motion Picture News Studio Directory (US)
This *Motion Picture News* annual companion, later known as the *Motion Picture News Studio Directory and Trade Annual*, contains composer biographies from 1916 to 1924. Eight issues: January 29, 1916; October 21, 1916 (see, for example, Joseph Carl Breil); April 12, 1917; 1918; 1919; 1920; 1921; and 1923–1924.

Motion Picture Review Digest (US)
Published weekly by the H. W. Wilson Co. from 1936 to 1940. The "Music" index lists composers, music directors, and songwriters with film titles. The annual and quarterly indices contain cumulative lists. For example, the music index in vol. 2, no. 52 (December 27, 1937) begins with Harry Akst and ends with Victor Young.

Motion Picture Story Magazine (US)
Whitney, Todd S. "The Motion Picture and Grand Opera." 3:1 (February 1912): 156.

Motion Picture Studio Insider (US)
Trade and technical magazine published in the interest of motion picture studio artisans in Los Angeles.
Rivard, Leio [*sic*] J. "Royalty Rights of Music Composers Are Protected by ASCAP." 1:1 (April 1935): 21, 46. Inside look at the relationship between the performing rights organization and Hollywood songwriters.
Steiner, Max. "How to Appreciate Music in Motion Pictures." 1:6 (May 1936): 21, 56.

Motography (US)
A trade paper published in Chicago for exhibitors that merged with *Exhibitors Herald* in 1918.
"Music for Cines Subject." 7:4 (April 1912): 179–80.
"Music Versus Pictures." 7:5 (May 1912): 197–98. Report on the battle for audiences between movies and music concerts in Chicago.
"Music for the Theatre." 8:13 (December 21, 1912): 499. On the Peerless Orchestrion.
"Music with Their Pictures." 10:13 (Christmas 1913): 491. On a Wurlitzer organ.
Manhood, Orville. "Dramatic Music and the Big Picture." 15:6 (February 5, 1916): 305–6. From the conductor of the orchestra accompanying *The Birth of a Nation*.
Fitz Patrick, Mildred Maginn. "Playing in the Picture House: Helpful Ideas for Musicians and Exhibitors." 17:2 (January 13, 1917): 71–72. Billed as the first in a series. Reprinted in *Theatre Organ* (April 1973).
Harris, Genevieve. "Setting *Hearts of the World* to Music: An Interview with Carli D. Elinor." 19:19 (May 11, 1918): 893; 911. On working with director D. W. Griffith.

Movie (UK)
Special issue, no. 24 (Spring 1977) [on musicals]
Dyer, Richard. "Entertainment and Utopia." 2–13. Musicals as entertainment. Reprinted in Dyer's *Only Entertainment* (1992, 2002); and in *Hollywood Musicals: The Film Reader* (2002).

Giles, Dennis. "Show-Making." 14–25. Reprinted in *Genre, The Musical: A Reader* (1981).

Belton, John. "The Backstage Musical." 36–43.

Paul, William. "Art, Music, Nature and Walt Disney." 44–52. On the function of music.

Movie Collector Magazine (UK)

Aimed at consumers who buy films on video. Contains "Soundtracks News," with new releases and scoring assignments; and "Soundtrack Reviews," by soundtrack editor David Stoner and others. Due to limited access, only selected issues appear below.

1:1 (September–October 1993)

"*Much Ado about Nothing.*" Patrick Doyle interview.

"*Son of the Morning Star.*" Craig Safan interview on the made-for-TV film.

John Scott interview.

1:2 (November–December 1993)

"2001: Alex North's Odyssey." 63–67. Jerry Goldsmith, Matthew Peak, and Robert Townson on North's unused score for *2001: A Space Odyssey*.

1:7 (July–August 1994)

"Basil Poledouris: Robocomposer." 62–63. Interview-based article.

Willsmer, Trevor. "Gerard Schurmann." 64–68. Interview.

1:8 (September–October 1994)

"Blood Counts the Most: James Newton Howard on *Wyatt Earp*." 75–76.

"Christopher Young." 78–83. Interview.

2:1 (December 1994)

Rimmer, Dave. "Music in Motion: *The War Lord*." 100–101. On music by Jerome Moross and Hans J. Salter.

"Danny Elfman's Christmas Nightmare." 103–9, 130. Interview regarding *The Nightmare Before Christmas*.

"Patrick Doyle on *Mary Shelley's Frankenstein*." 110–11.

Masheter, Philip. "John Barry on *The Specialist*." 113–15. Interview.

2:2 (January 1995)

Stoner, David. "Music in Motion: *Jaws*." 95–97. On John Williams's music.

"David Arnold: Through the *Stargate*." 99–103, 110. Interview-based article.

Wishart, David. "Christopher Palmer." 104–5. Tribute.

2:3 (March 1995)

Article on David Arnold's music for James Bond.

Movie Maker (UK)

Aimed at amateur filmmakers.

Cleave, Alan. "Let's Make Music for Our Movies." 9:1 (January 1975): 30–31. In seven parts, through July 1975. Cleave also reviewed at least one soundtrack; see the August 1975 issue.

Satariano, Cecil. "This Way to Better Movies: Lesson Nine—The Soundtrack." No. 15 (January 1981): 32–33.

Movie Pictorial (US)

The National Movie Publication published bimonthly in Chicago. A column by Mabel Bishop Wilson, "The Music Story: A Department for Musical Interpretation of Moving Pictures," was an early attempt to raise the standards of movie music accompaniment. The initial column appears in vol. 1, no. 22 (October 15, 1914), pages 9, 20, and was introduced on the cover. Wilson, a practitioner herself, claims that "the public is gradually demanding better music." Regarding this new art form, she adds, "The ideal accompaniment to the photoplay is the result of a capable musician's well directed efforts to combine character and length of selection in a way that it may perfectly fit the picture and thereby add realism and sincerity to the action on the screen." The column, which drew largely on readership participation, apparently continued into 1915, although further occurrences could not be documented.

Movieline (US)

An entertainment magazine devoted to the movies. Steve Pond wrote a column variously titled "Soundtracks" and "Soundtracks and Scores" from around 1993 to 1998. The column began as early as 1990 with contributions by Chris Morris and Cary Darling.

Rebello, Stephen. "Danny Elfman's Nightmare." 5:3 (November 1993): 54–58; 86–87.

MovieMaker (US)

A quarterly chronicle of the art and business of independent movies.

Gaspard, John, and Dale Newton. "Making Beautiful Music: Finding and Working with Your Composer." 6:31 (November–December 1998): 58–60. On indie films and composer David Reynolds.

Sterling, Mark. "On the Set: The Importance of the Music Editor." 6:31 (November–December 1998): 62–63. A music editor explains his job.

Essman, Scott. "Profile: John Ottman: [Bryan] Singer's Secret Weapon." 6:31 (November–December 1998): 64–65.

Williams, Phillip. "On the Right Track: Movie Music Experts Talk about Finding Just the Right Sound." 11:55 (Summer 2004): 78–81.

Movies Now (US)

Published by the National Association of Theatre Owners (NATO) for theater patrons.

Moss, Robert. "Rock Isn't Raucous…It's Revolutionary! Reflections on the Impact of Rock Music and Musicians on the Movies." 1:1 (1970): 28–29. On the changing shape of film scores.

Movietone News (US)

Published by the Seattle Film Society.

Cumbow, Robert C. "Morricone Encomium." No. 40 (April 13, 1975): 22–26. Survey of Ennio Morricone's music for Sergio Leone Westerns.

Moving Image (US)

A magazine for Super 8mm and video filmmakers, published in San Francisco.

Karman, Mal. "Carmine Coppola: Scoring with Sound." No. 5 (March–April 1982): 30–33. Interview.

Hubbert, Julie. "The Music from *More Treasures from American Film Archives, 1894–1931.*" 5:2 (Fall 2005): 154–57. Discusses the musical accompaniment by Martin Marks.

Moving Picture News (US)

Trade paper published in New York from 1908 to 1913, superseded by *Motion Picture News* in October 1913. "Our Music Column" answered letters and offered suggestions to musicians in 1911 and 1912. From October 1912 through August 1913 Ernst J. Luz wrote the column "Picture Music," which contained topical articles, suggestions, and responses to reader inquiries. The columns often concluded with "Musical Plots," cue sheets by Luz with music suggestions for specific films preceded by practical suggestions or "a few rules governing their use."

"Moving Picture Pianists Becoming More Skillful." 4:14 (April 8, 1911): 11.

MacDonald, M[argaret]. I. "The Musician in the Moving Picture Theater." 4:41 (October 14, 1911): 8.

Grau, Robert. "Advent of the One-Man Orchestra and Its Significance to the Silent Drama." 4:52 (December 30, 1911): 8.

Grau, Robert. "The Evolution of the Organ into the One-Man Orchestra." 5:5 (February 3, 1912): 12.

"The Pictures and Their Music." 6:7 (August 17, 1912): 18. On procuring music.

Simon, Walter C. "Musical Suggestions for *Caprices of Fortune*." 6:14 (October 5, 1912): 23.

Bradlet, John M. "Music and the Picture." 8:13 (September 27, 1913): 25. Column, subsequently carried in *Motion Picture News*.

Column, "Our Music Column" (selected)

4:45 (November 11, 1911): 23; 26. Playing suggestions by C. W. Long.

"Our Music Page." 5:17 (April 27, 1912): 10. Playing suggestions by C. W. Long.

Column, "Picture Music" by Ernst Luz (selected)

6:15 (October 12, 1912): 20–21. Introductory column by Luz, titled "The Musician and the Picture," outlining his goals for elevating picture music.

6:17 (October 26, 1912): 29. On "toning" the picture.

6:21 (November 23, 1912): 19. On improving picture music. Followed by "Musical Plots," 19–20.

7:7 (February 15, 1913): 14–15. On the possibilities of music.

7:8 (February 22, 1913): 22. On selecting music.

7:9 (March 1, 1913): 20–21. On cooperating with the exhibitor.

7:11 (March 15, 1913): 29. On suggestive playing.

7:12 (March 22, 1913): 18–19. More on suggestive playing.

Moving Picture World (US)

Independent weekly trade paper for motion picture exhibitors, published in New York from 1907 to 1927, when it merged with *Exhibitors Herald*. A good source for articles on music accompaniment for silent films, particularly for 1910 and 1911. The column "Music for the Picture" appeared roughly bimonthly from November 26, 1910, through March 8, 1919, and was edited by S. M. Berg, George W. Beynon, and Clarence E. Sinn. It included suggestions for music to accompany current releases for pianists and organists and articles on technique, aesthetics, current practice, and working conditions. It also incorporated comments, suggestions, and reports from musicians in the field.

"New Musical Wonder: A One-Man Orchestra Combination." 3:25 (December 19, 1908): 498.

"The Musical End." 5:1 (July 3, 1909): 7–8. Editorial calling for more attention to music by exhibitors.

"Musical Accompaniments for Moving Pictures." 5:17 (October 23, 1909): 559. Editorial.

"The Music Question: The Piano-Orchestra: An Instrument Specially Adapted for Moving Picture Places." 5:23 (December 4, 1909): 804–5.

"Motion Picture Music: Gregg A. Frelinger Compiler of Valuable New Work." 5:25 (December 18, 1909): 879. On his book of descriptive piano music for moving pictures.

Sinn, Clarence E. "The Music and the Picture—I." 6:15 (April 16, 1910): 590–91. This article was the catalyst for Sinn's similarly named column later in the year.

"Feature Films for Feature Music." 6:15 (April 16, 1910): 591. Editorial.

Rothapfel, S. L. "Music and Motion Pictures." 6:15 (April 16, 1910): 593.

Pilar-Morin. "Silent Drama Music." 6:17 (April 30, 1910): 676. Mlle. Pilar-Morin was a French actress.

Sinn, Clarence E. "The Music and the Picture—II." 6:19 (May 14, 1910): 772.

Bradlet, John M. "The Pipe Organ." 7:10 (September 3, 1910): 526–27. Decries an instrument associated with sacred music being used to accompany films.

Hafner, John. "Automatic Special Music." 8:2 (January 14, 1911): 76. Regarding player pianos.

Harrison, Louis Reeves. "Jackass Music." 8:3 (January 21, 1911): 124–25. Critical of current film music accompaniment. A letter from Wm. H. McCracken in response is in the next issue, vol. 8, no. 4 (January 28, 1911), p. 176.

Sinn, Clarence E. "*Il Trovatore* Begins Lyric Reform." 8:9 (March 4, 1911): 474.

Bush, W. Stephen. "Giving Musical Expression to the Drama." 9:5 (August 12, 1911): 354–55.

Bush, W. Stephen. "Possibilities of Musical Synchronization." 9:8 (September 2, 1911): 607. Syncing music and picture has so far been impossible.

McQuade, James S. "The Belasco of Motion Picture Presentations." 10:10 (December 9, 1911): 796–98. On S. L. Rothapfel and how to select a musical program for a picture.

"Splendid Kalem Feature—*A Spartan Mother* Combines Pathos and Patriotism with Stirring Effect—Presented with Special Music." 11:9 (March 2, 1912): 770–71. Film review with comments on Walter C. Simon's score.

"Some Suggestions for Pianists." 11:10 (March 9, 1912): 853.

Powell, [?]. "A Criticism of Picture Music." 13:7 (August 17, 1912): 639.

Blaisdell, George. "Dramatizing the Song." 20 (June 13, 1914): 1523.

"Music for the Picture: The Photoplayer, Its Inventors and the Manufacturing Plant." 25 (July 10, 1915): 267.

"Music for Equitable Players." 27:4 (January 22, 1916): 605. On music played on the set while filming.

Leavitt, Guy. "Every Picture Needs Good Music." 40:12 (June 21, 1919): 1759. On orchestra leader Robert Cuscaden's methodology for selecting musical motifs for actors.

"Erno Rapee, Conductor at Capitol, Joins Synchronized Music Company." (June 4, 1921): 526.

Ferrell, MacCullum. "Playing Tunes for the Cutting Room." 85 (March 27, 1927): 361, 440.

Column, "Music for the Picture" (Clarence E. Sinn, 1910–1915)

The column was introduced by John M. Bradlet in the November 26, 1910, issue (see p. 1227). The Sinn columns from December 3, 1910, to December 18, 1915, are listed in Steven D. Wescott's *Comprehensive Bibliography of Music for Film and Television* (1985). The December 31, 1910, column in vol. 7 (pp. 1518–19) discusses the use of sheet music for *Il Trovatore*. Beginning in 1913, music suggestions for films in current release were included. Sinn was billed as the "Cue Music Man."

Column, "Music for the Picture" (S. M. Berg, 1915–1916)
The Berg columns from December 25, 1915, to July 8, 1916, are listed in Wescott. The last column was cowritten with Walter C. Simon, and the five prior columns with Norman Stuckey. Clarence Sinn coedited some columns with Berg from January to August 1916.

Column, "Music for the Picture" (Clarence E. Sinn, 1916–1918)
The Sinn columns from December 16, 1916, to January 26, 1918, are listed in Wescott. S. M. Berg coedited some columns from January to August 1916. From January to May 1917, Norman Stuckey was coeditor; in June and July 1917, Frank E. Kneeland served in that capacity.

Column, "Music for the Picture" (George W. Beynon, 1918–1919)
The Beynon columns from February 2, 1918, to March 8, 1919, are listed in Wescott. Beginning in August 1918, cue sheets prepared by George W. Beynon, S. M. Berg, James C. Bradford, Louis Gottschalk, Harley Hamilton, and others accompanied the articles.

Column, "Music Cue Sheets for Films of Current Release" (1919)
When the "Music for the Picture" column ended in March 1919, this cue sheet column continued from April 5, 1919 (for example, see pp. 96–97). The cue sheets were prepared by S. M. Berg, James C. Bradford, Louis Gottschalk, Harley Hamilton, Joseph O'Sullivan, Max Winkler, and others. Appeared irregularly (twelve times in 1919).

National Board of Review Magazine (US)
Published monthly from 1926 to 1942 in New York. Superseded by *New Movies*. The board later published *Films in Review*.

Kuttner, Alfred B. "Movie Music." 3:5 (May 1928): 3, 6. Editorial arguing imitative music is better than no music.

Branscombe, Gena. "The Creative Power of the Sound Film." 4:5 (May 1929): 3–4. The American composer editorializes on the sound film as art.

Moore, Douglas. "The Motion Picture and Music." 10:8 (November 1935): 4–9. From a National Board of Review conference presentation on literalness; includes a survey of film music. Reprinted from *Harper's Magazine* (July 1935).

Tibbett, Lawrence. "The Motion Picture's Part in America's Changing Musical Appreciation." (June 1936).

The New Hungarian Quarterly (Hungary)
An international journal of the arts and society, preceded and superceded by the *Hungarian Quarterly*.

Berlasz, Melinda. "Laszlo Lajtha and T. S. Eliot." 33 (Fall 1992): 163–69. On Lajtha's music for *Murder in the Cathedral* (1952).

The New Movies (US)
Monthly publication of the National Board of Review from 1942 to 1949. Continues the *National Board of Review Magazine*. Superseded by *Films in Review*.

Quinto, Capt. Lenard. "Are You a Film Music Critic?" 20 (December 1945): 8–9.

The Nickelodeon (US)
"America's Leading Journal of the Motograph," absorbed by *Motography*.

"Musicians in Nickelodeons." 1:2 (February 1909): 69.
"Music in Picture Theatres." 2:1 (July 1909): 4. Editorial.
"The Musical Accompaniment." 5:3 (January 21, 1911): 69–70. Editorial.
"Musical Program for Gaumont Film." 5:5 (May 1911): 104. Musical suggestions in the
    form of a cue sheet.

Now (US)

Late 1920s weekly, published by West Coast Theatres in Los Angeles and aimed at ex-
hibitors of Fox Theatres Corp. films. It contained occasional articles on music in the
waning days of silent films. Superseded by *The Last Word*.
"Explanation of Organization Chart." 1:1 (June 10, 1927): [6]. A paragraph on "Produc-
    tion and Music" explains the position of the music department in the organization.
Lanterman, Frank. "The Organist as Salesman." 1:2 (June 25, 1927): 6. By the organist at
    the Alexander Theatre in Glendale, California.
Selfridge, H. Gordon. "The Music of *Beau Geste*." 1:2 (June 25, 1927): 6. Reprinted from
    Artland Magazine.
Jones, Samuel. "Martial Music—Its Use and Place in Theatre Programs." 1:3 (July 15,
    1927): 10. Interview with Captain Taylor Branson, U.S. Marine Band leader.
"Music Is a Big Factor in Movie Success." 1:4 (August 1, 1927): 12.
"The Organist." 1:4 (August 1, 1927): 12.
Lanterman, Frank. "Psychology, the Organist, and the News Reel." 1:6 (September 1,
    1927): 14.
"For the Baton Wielder: Are There Sure Fire Overtures?" 1:7 (September 15, 1927): 5.
Elinor, Carli. "'Keep Your Music Simple' This Expert Advises." 1:10 (October 31,
    1927): 12.
Lyons, Al. "Music Should Influence the Box Office." 1:11 (November 14, 1927): 10. By
    the music director of Loew's Theatre, San Francisco.
"Wurlitzer Tieup Materially Helps *Student Prince*." 2:4 (February 20, 1928): 12.

Onfilm (New Zealand)

Chun, Mike. "Face the Music." 11:6 (July 1994): 15, 22. Copyrighting film music in
    layperson's terms.

On Location (US)

Motion picture industry magazine published bimonthly, later monthly, in Hollywood.
Feldman, Linda. "Sound Notes Scooped from the Cutting Room's Floor." 2:5 (May–June
    1979): 52–53. On music editors, scoring, and tracking.
Esser, Carl. "Scoring." 4:9 (February 1981): 90–91, 93. Michael Small profile.
"Microchip Arms Industry with Rhodesystems II." 7:12 (April 1984): 114. News item on
    Roger Rhodes's invention that aids in synchronizing music and images, via computer.
Eller, Claudia. "Audio: Evergreen Recording Studios…Conceived with the Musician in
    Mind." 8:1 (May 1984): 88–89. Includes a film and television client and project list
    for the popular Los Angeles recording studio.

On Writing (US)

Published by the Writers Guild of America, East.
"Michael Small and Carter Burwell." Vol. 5 (June 1996): 1–9. Joint interview.

Outre (US)

Entertainment magazine from Filmfax.

Satola, Mark. "Raymond Scott." No. 15 (1999): 58–62ff. Biography.

Paramount Artcraft Progress-Advance (US)

Published weekly by Paramount Pictures in New York from 1914 to 1920 for the motion picture exhibitor. From January 1918 to at least January 1919, each issue regularly included music suggestions for two or three films in current release, broken down by timing, title or description, tempo, and music selection. These were supplied primarily by Louis F. Gottschalk and James C. Bradford, with occasional contributions from George Beynon, Harley Hamilton, Max Winkler, and Filmusic Studios. The latter, located in Los Angeles, provided pipe organ rolls to theaters. The "Music Suggestions" page occasionally contained unrelated music news items.

Beynon, George W. *"Fires of Faith* Lends Itself to Music: It Calls for Big Melodic Presentation." 5:25 (May 1, 1919): 589, 601. Mentions that Paramount offers a musical service composed of a special orchestra score, cue sheet, a fine ballad, song slides, phonograph records, and piano rolls.

"This New Song Is a Direct Ad for Your Theatre When You Play *Oh, You Women!*" 5:22 (May 1, 1919): 596. Topical song tie-in.

"Music Suggestions" (selected)
4:8 (January 17, 1918): 152. By Louis F. Gottschalk.
4:10 (January 31, 1918): 192. By Louis F. Gottschalk.
4:51 (November 21, 1918): 1172. By Filmusic Studios.
4:52 (November 28, 1918): 1195. By Max Winkler, James C. Bradford, and George Beynon.
5:8 (January 23, 1919): 188. By Harley Hamilton and Filmusic Studios.

Special issue, 4:22 (April 25, 1918) ["Music Number"]
"Striking the First Note: Two Pioneers in Combining Good Music with Good Pictures, and a Survey of Their Methods and Accomplishments." 429, 438. On Hugo Riesenfeld and S. L. Rothapfel, with material on Carl Edouarde.
Gottschalk, Louis F. "The Importance of a Musical Synopsis." 434.
"Photoplay Music of the Future: By a New York Musician." 439.
Maitland, Rollo F. "Organ and Orchestra." 441. By a Philadelphia organist.

Paramount Progress (US)

Published weekly by Paramount Pictures in New York in 1914 and 1915. Beginning in the summer of 1915, "Musical Selections for Paramount Releases," by James C. Bradford, director of the Broadway Theatre in New York, appeared to aid exhibitors. Musical suggestions, each with title and composer, were given for current films that were broken down by screen action. For examples, see vol. 1, no. 36 (August 5, 1915), p. 7; and vol. 1, no. 43 (September 23, 1915), pp. 8–11.

Paramount Studio News (US)

Published weekly by Paramount Studios in Hollywood from 1924 to 1928. Vol. 1, no. 42 (March 14, 1928) contains a news item on Hugo Riesenfeld on page 4. Later in-house journals include *Paramount around the World* (1928–1932); *Paramount International News* (1933–1938; 1943–1955); *Paramount Parade* (1936–1960); *Paramount News* (1941; 1949–1952); *The Paramounteer* (1954–1955); *Paramount World* (1955–1960s); and *Paramount Pictures Corporation News* (1982–). Although these publications cover sales and marketing of films in current release, they occasionally carry news items related to music.

Penguin Film Review (UK)

An international survey of film published monthly by Penguin Books. John Huntley's column contained a critical survey of primarily British film music. Roger Manvell was executive editor of a two-volume reprint, *The Penguin Film Review, 1946–1949* (London: Scolar Press, 1977).

Huntley, John. "Notes on Film Music." No. 1 (August 1946): 35–37. Reprinted in Manvell.

Dickinson, Thorold. "Search for Music." No. 2 (January 1947): 9–15. The director goes to Africa in search of authentic music for his film.

Huntley, John. "Film Music." No. 2 (January 1947): 21–24. Reprinted in Manvell.

Huntley, John. "Notes on Film Music." No. 3 (August 1947): 15–17. Reprinted in Manvell.

Huntley, John. "Film Music." No. 4 (October 1947): 17–20.

Mathieson, Muir. "Developments in Film Music." No. 4 (October 1947): 41–46.

Huntley, John. "Film-Music Orchestras." No. 5 (January 1948): 14–18. On British orchestras, including a list of films. Reprinted in Manvell.

Huntley, John. "British Film Music." No. 6 (April 1948): 91–96.

Huntley, John. "The Music of *Hamlet* and *Oliver Twist.*" No. 8 (January 1949): 110–16. On music by William Walton and Arnold Bax.

The Perfect Vision (US)

The journal for "High End Video."

Eder, Bruce. "Epic Scores." 6:22 (July 1994): 105–10. Historical overview concentrating on a few specific scores from *Birth of a Nation* to *Doctor Zhivago*.

Photoplay (UK)

Fan magazine published monthly in London.

"How to Score a Movie." 31:6 (June 1980): 61–62. May contain excerpts from interviews with Miklós Rózsa and Marvin Hamlisch by Mike Munn.

"Where You'll Find the Soundtrack Specialists." 31:7 (August 1980): 20.

Photoplay (US)

Fan magazine published monthly in New York.

"Shooting the Music." 13:4 (March 1918): 41. On the method used by Joseph O'Sullivan to develop cue sheets for Mutual films, including describing the plot, action, timings, and music moods.

Cohn, Alfred A. "What Makes Them Cry." 13:5 (April 1918): 50–56, 120. Music on the set.

Riesenfeld, Hugo. "Who Made America Musical?" 15:3 (February 1919): 49. Argues music performed with films has enlightened audiences.

"Rare Atmosphere for Eddie Polo." 16:3 (August 1919): 79. Photo caption regarding music on the set for sympathetic acting.

Handy, Truman B. "Owed to the Pictures." 17:5 (April 1920): 52–54, 119. On the shift from solo pianos to orchestras for the accompaniment of silent films.

Van Vranken, Frederick. "With Music By—." 20:5 (October 1921): 54, 105. On Louis Silvers, whom the author considered the first full-time composer and arranger for motion pictures.

Larkin, Mark. "The Truth about Voice Doubling." 36:2 (July 1929): 32–33, 108–10.

"Music of the Films." 36:5 (October 1929): 100, 108. *Photoplay*'s Record Review Department discusses songs used in films and released on disc.

Fenton, Maurice. "The Birth of the Theme Song: A Musician Tells How Music Came to the Films and What It Did for the Shadows on the Screen." 36:6 (November 1929): 66, 136.

Fenton, Maurice. "The Best Music of the New Pictures." 37:3 (February 1930): 84. Primarily discusses song tunes in films.

Fenton, Maurice. "The Best Music of the New Pictures." 37:4 (March 1930): 80.

Hamilton, Sara. "Sing, Hollywood, Sing!" 45:4 (March 1934): 52–53, 105–6. Tongue-in-cheek essay on the overabundance of songwriters in town.

Reeve, Warren. "Song Hits Make Stars and Stars Make Song Hits." 48:6 (November 1935): 28.

Friedman, Joel. "Hollywood's Music Craze." 52:3 (September 1957): 37. On popular singers in film.

Photoplay Studies (US)

Group discussion guides published by Educational and Recreational Guides in Newark, New Jersey, beginning in 1935.

"*Music for Madame*" 3:6 (1937). Includes "Music Information" on songs in the film, 14.

"*Moonlight Sonata*" 5:14 (1939). Includes "Music in the Film," 3–4.

Picture Show (UK)

Popular British fan magazine.

"Classical Music in Films." (1945).

The Picturegoer (UK)

Huntley, John. "That Background Music." (April 26, 1947): 8.

Polish Film (Poland)

"Krzysztof Penderecki on Soundtrack." No. 1 (1989): 16–17. Interview with the Polish composer regarding his film work and on the relationship between music and film.

Post Script (US)

A scholarly journal of film and the humanities, published in Jacksonville, Florida.

Dagle, J., and Kathryn Kalinak. "The Representation of Race and Sexuality: Visual and Musical Construction in *Gone with the Wind*." 13:2 (Winter–Spring 1994): 14–27. On Max Steiner's score.

Yeh, Yueh-yu. "A Life of Its Own: Musical Discourses in Wong Kar-wai's Films." 19:1 (Fall 1999): 120–36. Popular music in the director's Hong Kong films.

POV: Point of View Magazine (US)

Published by the Producers Guild of America in Beverly Hills.

Hirschhorn, Joel. "A New Golden Age for Scoring." 10 (Spring 1999): 13ff.

Pratfall (US)

A Laurel and Hardy fan magazine.

Shadduck, Jim. "The Ku-ku Song Man!" 1:6 (issue 7, 1972). On Marvin Hatley and his music for Laurel and Hardy. Reprinted in Limbacher.

Premiere (US)

Published monthly in New York. The pop-oriented "Movie Music" column and "Cameos" section include occasional material on film composers.

Articles

Clark, John. "Filmographies: Ennio Morricone." 2:12 (August 1989): 112.

Lehman, Susan. "Birthday Blues." 3:4 (December 1989): 32. On paying to use the song "Happy Birthday" in films.

Hoberman, J. "Cartoon Cultism Zaps America." 4:4 (December 1990): 42–43. On a CD of Carl Stalling's music.

Medich, Rob. "It's the Same Old Song." 4:7 (March 1991): 19. On the practice of naming movies after song titles.

Kuhn, Eleonore. "The Hollywood Food Chain." 8 (June 1995): 26. On Carter Burwell, Elliot Goldenthal, and Thomas Newman.

Potter, Maximillian. "Black by Popular Demand." 9:5 (January 1996): 39–40. On rap music.

Goldstein, Gregg. "Vanguard All-Stars: Music Supervisor Randall Poster." 14:6 (February 2001): 67.

"Cameos"

Rosenbluth, Jean. "Soundtrack Producer Gary LeMel." 3:5 (January 1990): 48. Profile.

Phinney, Kevin. "Composer Elmer Bernstein." 4:2 (October 1990): 52. Profile.

Burlingame, Jon. "Composer John Barry." 4:4 (December 1990): 65–66. Profile.

Rubin, Rosina. "Composer Danny Elfman." 4:5 (January 1991): 42. Profile.

Kimble, Christopher. "Composer Hans Zimmer." 4:9 (May 1991): 46. Profile.

Column, "Movie Music" by various writers (selected)

Fagen, Donald. "[Henry] Mancini's Anomie Deluxe." 1:2 (October 1987): 97–99.

Fagen, Donald. "The Big Rattle." 1:9 (May 1988): 91–92. On synthesizers.

Geller, Lynn. "The Key to Scoring *Big*." 1:10 (June 1988): 107–8. On Howard Shore's score.

Morrison, Mark. "Finding Hollywood's Lost Music." 1:11 (July 1988): 91–92. On David Newman.

Bowermaster, Jon. "Wonderful World, Beautiful Music." 2:5 (January 1989): 102–3. On reggae soundtracks.

Rensin, David. "Coupla White Guys Sitting Around Talking." 2:10 (June 1989): 137–39. Interviews with Mark Knopfler and Randy Newman.

Geller, Lynn. "For Cool Scores, Go to the Source." 3:4 (December 1989): 50–52. Profile of music supervisor Gary Goetzman.

Pareles, Jon. "The Ethnic 'Passion' of Peter Gabriel." 3:6 (February 1990): 102–3. On the score for *The Last Temptation of Christ*.

Publix Opinion (US)

Published biweekly by Publix Theatres Corporation in New York from 1927 to 1932. (Publix became Paramount Publix Corporation in 1930.) "Paramount Music Notes" covers musical activities related to films. Topics include sheet music sales and tie-ins. The activities of Publix music head Boris Morros are often documented. Some Volume 2 issues include lists of bandleaders. Some Volume 3 issues include "Songs in Features," featuring songs from Paramount and other studios.

"Announce New Assignments for Stage Band Leaders." 2:29 (June 30, 1928): 9. Lists Publix theaters by city with musical directors, organists, and pit conductors.

"'Low' Volume Deadly Evil, Says Expert." 2:49 (April 13, 1929): 1–2. Irvin Talbot of the Paramount music department.

"Publix Music Department Scores Again! Novelties and Records Can Now Be Played on Regular Equipment." 3:1 (September 14, 1929): 4. Brief news item on organist Jesse Crawford is also on this page.

"How to Score Paramount Newsreel." 3:10 (November 15, 1929): 7. Boris Morros explains.

"Boris Morros, Musician by Heritage." 3:22 (February 7, 1930): 7. Profile.

Quarterly Review of Film and Video (UK)

Kovacs, Katherine S. "Parody as 'Countersong' in Saura and Godard." 12:1–2 (May 1990): 105–24. On the directors' film versions of the opera *Carmen*.

Celeste, Reni. "The Sound of Silence: Film Music and Lament." 22:2 (April–June 2005): 113–23.

Tibbetts, John C. "Elgar's Ear: A Conversation with Ken Russell." 22:1 (January–March 2005): 37–49. The director discusses his films about music and musicians.

Quarterly Review of Film Studies (US)

Academic journal published in New York from 1976 to 1989, superseded by *Quarterly Review of Film and Video*.

Geduld, Harry. "Film Music: A Survey." 1:2 (May 1976): 183–204. Lists books and records.

Gorbman, Claudia. "Teaching the Soundtrack." 1:4 (November 1976): 446–52. Some discussion of music.

Gorbman, Claudia. "Film Music." 3:1 (Winter 1978): 105–13. On recent books.

Brown, Royal S. "Music and *Vivre sa vie*." 5:3 (Summer 1980): 319–33.

Norden, Martin F. "Society for Cinema Studies Conference: April, 1981." 6:4 (Fall 1981): 457–62. Includes "Session: Bernard Herrmann: Aspects of His Work," 458–60, with participants Royal S. Brown and Kathryn Kalinak; "Session: Music/Sound and the Individual Film," 460–61.

Radio Personalities (US)

A pictorial and biographical annual published by Press Bureau in New York from 1935. Includes brief biographies of some composers who worked in film, including Johnny Green, Lennie Hayton, Erno Rapee, Bert Shefter, Frank Skinner, and Victor Young. (Consulted 1936 edition, edited by Don Rockwell.)

Reel Life (US)

House organ of the Mutual Film Corporation, published in New York.

Rothapfel, Samuel L. "Dramatizing Music for the Pictures." 4:25 (September 5, 1914): 23.

Reel West (Canada)

On Western Canada's film, video, and television industries.

Baker, Michael Conway. "Michael Conway Baker, Composer." 14 (August–September 1999): 34.

Caddell, Ian. "Immortal Melodies." 16 (June–July 2001): 24–27ff. On Schaun Tozer.

RKO Studio Club News (US)

Official publication of the RKO Studio Club published monthly, later bimonthly, in Hollywood from 1935 to 1956. "The Music Box" included scoring assignments and music department news from the late 1930s. "Tuneups from the Music Dept." by employee Pat Hertzog includes scoring assignments, anecdotes, news of personnel travel, business, and concerts away from the studio, from April 1941 (initial column is in vol. 3, no. 9, pp. 6, 11) through December 1953. The war years have the most extensive coverage, particularly

for department head and music director Constantin Bakaleinikoff and chief composer
Roy Webb. The December 1941 issue (vol. 4, no. 5) contains a list of fifteen music department personnel, including Alfred Newman. Other in-house journals that may contain
news items related to music include *Radio Flash* (1930s–1950s), *The New RKO Radio
Flash* (1950s), *Flash* (1977), and *Show News* (1920s–1950s).

"RKO Music Heads Conduct." 3:12 (July 1941): 7. On Constantin Bakaleinikoff, Roy
     Webb, and Louis Gruenberg.

Verr, B. "Music and SFX." 8:1 (December 1945): 37. On music and sound effects.

Rob Wagner's Script (US)

On arts and entertainment in the Southwest, published weekly in Beverly Hills. Music
critic Lawrence Morton wrote an untitled column beginning with the January 20, 1940,
issue; by the end of the year it was called "Music Notes." Although the column primarily
covered concert music, film music is discussed, usually in the form of critiques of specific film scores or concert reviews, such as the Motion Picture Academy Nights at the
Hollywood Bowl.

Corwin, Emil. "Movie Music, Shadow or Substance." (October 1947): 9–10, 56–57. On
     the trend toward Hollywood's use of prominent composers.

<u>Column, "Music Notes" by Lawrence Morton</u>

"About Aaron." 24:559 (June 15, 1940): 18–19. On Copland's first two film scores.

"Louis Gruenberg's *Fight* Music." 24:569 (October 5, 1940): 19. On *The Fight for Life*.

"Music Notes." 25:603 (June 14, 1941): 26. On Leo Shuken's symphonic jazz concerto
     heard in *Our Wife*.

"Music Notes." 27:628 (May 9, 1942): 24. On an event organized by the music branch of
     the Academy of Motion Picture Arts and Sciences on effective film scoring for Rus-
     sian films with music by Prokofiev and Shostakovich; guests included Daniele Am-
     fitheatrof, [Constantin] Bakaleinikoff, Nathaniel Finston, and Dimitri Tiomkin.

"Music Notes." 29:646 (January 23, 1943): 24. By guest columnist Hugo Friedhofer;
     does not discuss film music.

"Music Notes." 30:683 (July 15, 1944): 22. On Michel Michelet's music for *Voice in the
     Wind*.

"Music Notes." 31 (August 25, 1945): 20. On the quality of film music, based on a Hol-
     lywood Bowl concert.

"Music Notes." 32:730 (May 25, 1946): 18–19. On the Screen Composers Association.

"Music Notes." 32:744 (December 7, 1946): 20–21. On Hugo Friedhofer's score for *The
     Best Years of Our Lives*.

"Music: Mr. Selznick's Debussy." (March 1949): 36. On Dimitri Tiomkin's adapted
     score for *Portrait of Jennie*.

Roxy Theatre Weekly Review (US)

Official organ of the Roxy Theatre in New York.

Stewart, Thomas. "The Story of Erno Rapee." 1:17 (July 2, 1927): 6–7, 22. Profile.

Scarlet Street (US)

This magazine of mystery and horror often carries reviews of genre-related soundtracks.
Although it does not appear in every issue, Ross Care's long-running "Record Rack"
column appears from 1993 (no. 12) to 2003 (no. 49).

Savello, Danny. "Horrors! Hammer's Music Man Is Back!" No. 18 (Spring 1995): 30. On
     James Bernard's return to scoring.

Scrivani, Richard. "A Little Nightmare Music: John Morgan Interviewed by Richard Scrivani." No. 18 (Spring 1995): 82–87. Discusses rerecording the music of Hans Salter, with William Stromberg.

Scrivani, Richard. "A Little More Fright Music." No. 21 (Winter 1996): 38–39. On John Morgan and William Stromberg's rerecording of music from Universal horror films.

No. 22 (1996): Special issue, contents listed below.

Amorosi, Tom, and Richard Valley. "He Plays the Violin: Sherlock on CD." No. 23 (1996): 24, 26–27. A compilation of music from Sherlock Holmes films.

Mandell, Paul. "The Music behind *Plan 9 from Outer Space*." No. 23 (1996): 55–58. On the music for the 1959 film. Reprinted from *Film Score Monthly*.

Care, Ross. "The Music of Sound: Alfred Hitchcock *Rear Window*." No. 37 (2000): 60–63, 76. On music by Franz Waxman and others.

Scrivani, Richard. "Not His Last Bow." No. 38 (2000): 52–54, 76, 78. On film music rerecordings by John Morgan and William Stromberg.

Long, Harry H. "Scoring *The Fly*." No. 48 (2003): 70. Sidebar on music by Paul Sawtell and Bert Shefter.

Valley, Richard. "Music to Die For! Jeepers Creepers." No. 49 (2003): 42–46, 72. On songs from horror films related to a compilation disc.

Special issue, No. 22 (1996)

Madison, Bob, and Drew Sullivan. "He Who Must Be Replayed! James Bernard Hammers It Home." 23. On the present-day recording of Bernard's music.

Sullivan, Drew. "Over the Rainbow and Under the Desert." 27, 98. Replacing music for copyright reasons for *Dr. Phibes* video releases.

Scrivani, Richard. "SciFi Serenade." 34–36, 39. On David Schecter's and Kathleen Mayne's rerecording of 1950s science fiction films for their label, Monstrous Movie Music.

Scrivani, Richard. "The Gertzenstein Monsters!" 37–41, 96–97. Irving Gertz and Herman Stein interviews.

Care, Ross. "Forever Raksin." 60–65. David Raksin interview.

Screen (UK)

The journal of the London-based Society for Education in Film and Television.

Amsden, Peter C. "Composing for Films." 11:2 (March–April 1970): 80–86. Interview with Michael J. Lewis.

Higson, Andrew. "Sound Cinema." 25:1 (January–February 1984): 74–78. Report.

25:3 (May–June 1984). Special issue, contents listed below.

Flinn, Carol. "The 'Problem' of Femininity in Theories of Film Music." 27:6 (November–December 1986): 56–72.

Gorbman, Claudia. "Hanns Eisler in Hollywood." 32:3 (Autumn 1991): 272–85.

Knight, Arthur. "Silent Screen, Live Sounds: A Symposium on Music and Silent Film, University of Chicago, 6 February 1993." 34:3 (1993): 287–89. Report.

Stilwell, Robynn. "Symbol, Narrative, and the Musics of *Truly, Madly, Deeply*." 38:1 (Spring 1997): 60–75. On Barrington Pheloung's score.

MacRory, Pauline. "Excusing the Violence of Hollywood Women: Music in *Nikita* and *Point of No Return*." 40:1 (Spring 1999): 51–65. On music for action heroines.

Stilwell, Robynn J. "Film Music Conference, University of Leeds, 11 July 1998." 40:1 (Spring 1999): 100–102. Report.

Garwood, Ian. "Must You Remember This? Orchestrating the 'Standard' Pop Song in *Sleepless in Seattle*." 41:3 (Autumn 2000): 282–98. On transforming the pop song into film music.

Link, Stan. "Sympathy with the Devil? Music of the Psycho Post-*Psycho*." 45:1 (March 2004): 1–20.

Special issue, 25:3 (May–June 1984)

King, Norman. "The Sound of Silents." 21–25. With references to music.

Batchelor, Jennifer. "From 'Aïda' to 'Zauberflöte': Jennifer Batchelor Considers the Opera Film." 26–38.

Merck, Mandy. "Composing for the Films: Mandy Merck Asks Lindsay Cooper about Scoring the Independents." 40–54. Interview.

Levin, Tom. "The Acoustic Dimension: Notes on Cinema Sound." 55–68. With references to silent film music.

Lang, Robert. "Carnal Stereophony: A Reading of *Diva*." 70–77. References to nondiegetic music in the film.

Frith, Simon. "Mood Music: An Inquiry into Narrative Film Music." 78–87.

The Screen (US)

A Journal of Motion Pictures for Business School Church.

Riesenfeld, Hugo. "How Music Lends Voice." 2:1 (July 1921): 12–15.

Screen Education (UK)

The journal of the London-based Society for Education in Film and Television.

Frith, Simon, and Angela McRobbie. "Rock and Sexuality." 29 (Winter 1978–1979): 3–19. With some discussion of musicals.

Colley, Iain, and Gill Davies. "*Pennies from Heaven*: Music, Image, Text." 35 (Summer 1980): 63–78. On the function and effectiveness of songs in the television play.

Screen Facts (US)

The magazine of Hollywood's past, published in New York.

McCarty, Clifford. "Miklos Rozsa." 1:1 (1963): 41–51. Profile.

Screen International (US)

Motion picture and entertainment industry trade publication, published in London and later in Los Angeles. Often contains news related to music in films in current release.

Articles (selected)

Summers, Sue. "It's an Equal Partnership and the Composer Should Be Given His Due." No. 81 (April 2, 1977): 23. Interview with Marvin Hamlisch.

Vaines, Colin. "Batt Strikes Out to Score a Hit." No. 225 (January 26, 1980): 12. Mike Batt interview.

Beer, Carol. "The Beat Goes On for Nitzsche." No. 297 (June 20, 1981): 6. Interview-based article on Jack Nitzsche.

Newport, David. "[Bruce] Smeaton Completes Score for *Eleni*." No. 504 (July 13–16, 1985): 20. Interview.

Brown, Colin. "Soundtracks: Harmony and Discord." No. 1036. (December 1, 1995): 10–11.

Brown, Colin. "Pop Goes the Score." No. 1036. (December 1, 1995): 12.

"Close Up: Ian Neil." (September 15, 2000): 23. Profiles of the music consultant and publishing exec.

"Close Up: Angelo Badalamenti." No. 1331 (November 2, 2001): 15.

Goodridge, Mike, and Jeremy Kay. "Oscar Players." No. 1441 (February 20, 2004): 24–25. Profiles of Howard Shore, Thomas Newman, and Gabriel Yared.

Kay, Jeremy. "Word of Mouth: Duets for One." No. 1507 (July 8, 2005): 6. When two composers collaborate on scoring one film.

The Screen Writer (US)
Published by the Screen Writers Guild in Hollywood.
MacDougall, Ranald. "Sound—and Fury." 1 (September 1945): 1–7. Includes a plea for collaboration between writers and composers.

Screenland (US)
Fan magazine published in New York.
Gebhart, Myrtle. "The Silent Orchestra." 3:3 (November 1921): 14. On music played during the shooting of silent films to inspire actors.

Shadowland (US)
Monthly fan magazine published in New York.
Scheffauer, Herman George. "The Visible Symphony." 5:1 (September 1921): 36–37, 59, 62. On the use of music by director Walter Ruttman.

Showtime in Walthamstow (UK)
Occasional publication from the Walthamstow Antiquarian Society, edited by William Gregory Sidney Tonkin.
Manning, Clifford S. "Organs in Walthamstow Cinemas: Showtime Memories by Local Residents: A Collection of Advertisements and Programme Extracts." No. 9, supplement (1967): 1–12.

Sight and Sound (UK)
Independent critical magazine published by the British Film Institute in London. Excluding trade papers, this is arguably one of the longest continuously published film periodicals offering occasional coverage of film music. The "Music" column by composer and critic Antony Hopkins from 1949 to 1951 contains some film music coverage. John Huntley's column, "The Sound Track," ran from 1950 to 1954. Mark Kermode's "End Notes" column from 1994 to at least 1996 sometimes featured film music topics.
Raybould, Clarence. "Music and the Synchronised Film." 2:7 (Autumn 1933): 80–81.
Popper, Paul. "Synthetic Sound." 2:7 (Autumn 1933): 82–84. Producing music by drawing directly onto the film.
Borneman, Ernest J. "Sound Rhythm and the Film: Recent Research on the Compound Cinema." 3:10 (Summer 1934): 65–67. On musical montage, pictorial music, and synthesis. Argues that sung music weakens the visual image.
"Notes of the Quarter: Music and the Film." 3:11 (Autumn 1934): 98–99. Clarence Raybould's score for *Rising Tide*.
Grierson, John. "Introduction to a New Art." 3:11 (Autumn 1934): 101–4.
Calvocoressi, M. D. "Music and the Film: A Problem of Adjustment." 4:14 (Summer 1935): 57–58. On the function of music in relation to film, written by a music critic.
Danilova, Alexandra. "Classical Ballet and the Cinema: Filming the Russian Ballet." 4:15 (Autumn 1935): 107–8.
Solev, V. "Absolute Music." 5:18 (Summer 1936): 48–50. Producing music by drawing directly onto the film.
Cross, Elizabeth. "Plain Words to the Exhibitor." 10:39 (Autumn 1941): 44–45. Includes "Incidental Music." Response to Cross's article, "Sound Recordist Ken Cameron Protests." 10:40 (Spring 1942): 75–76.

Huntley, John. "Film Music." 12:48 (January 1944): 90–93. Overview of British film music, the *Fantasia* effect, and Russian influences. Omissions from Huntley's article "Film Music: A Letter from Darrel Catling." 12:49 (May 1944): 19.

Keen, Stuart. "Music for Silent Classics." 13:50 (July 1944): 43–44. Synchronized musical accompaniment using gramophone records.

Kleiner, Arthur. "New Yorker Arthur Kleiner Writes about Film Scores." 13:52 (January 1945): 103–4. On the cue sheet and first original score.

Huntley, John. "British Film Music and World Markets." 15:60 (Winter 1946–1947): 135. Film music at film festivals and in the concert hall.

Keller, Hans. "Film Music—Some Objections." 15:60 (Winter 1946–1947): 136. Reprinted in *Film Music and Beyond.*

Keller, Hans. "Revolution or Retrogression?" 16:62 (Summer 1947): 63–64. On a filmized opera, *The Barber of Seville.* Reprinted in *Film Music and Beyond.*

Thomas, Anthony. "Hollywood Music." 16:63 (Autumn 1947): 97–98. Overview, with Miklós Rózsa's score for *Spellbound* as example.

Keller, Hans. "Hollywood Music—Another View." 16:64 (Winter 1947–1948): 168–69. Response to Thomas article. Reprinted in *Film Music and Beyond.*

Winge, John H. "Cartoons and Modern Music." 17:67 (Autumn 1948): 136–37. On the music of Scott Bradley.

Lindgren, Ernest. "The Composer: William Alwyn." Special Issue (July 1951): 19–20. BFI special publication, *Films in 1951: Festival of Britain.*

Alwyn, William. "The Composer and Crown." 21:4 (April–June 1952): 176–77. On opportunities regarding music for Britain's Crown Film Unit, Muir Mathieson, music director.

Newton, Douglas. "Poetry in Fast and Musical Motion." 22:1 (July–September 1952): 35–37. On musicals.

Jacobs, Arthur. "*The Front Page*: Looking Back: Musical Cinerama." 24:3 (January–March 1955): 117.

Vaughan, David. "After the Ball." 26:2 (Autumn 1956): 89–91, 111. On musicals.

Johnson, Albert. "Conversation with Roger Edens." 27:4 (Spring 1958): 179–82. Interview with the MGM songwriter.

Gilling, Ted. "The Colour of the Music: An Interview with Bernard Herrmann." 41:1 (Winter 1971–1972): 36–39.

Gilling, Ted. "The *Citizen Kane* Book." 41:2 (Spring 1972): 71–73. George Coulouris and Bernard Herrmann with Ted Gilling.

Kemp, Jeffery [*sic*]. "Write What the Film Needs: An Interview with Elisabeth Lutyens." 43:4 (Autumn 1974): 203–5, 248.

Care, Ross. "Cinesymphony: Music and Animation at the Disney Studio, 1928–42." 46:1 (Winter 1976–1977): 40–44. Overview, with material on Carl Stalling and others.

Ellis, Mundy. "In the Picture: Crowd Music." 50:4 (Autumn 1981): 224. Regarding Carl Davis's score for *The Crowd* (1928).

Milne, Tom. "Jazz in the Movies." 51:2 (Spring 1982): 130–31. Regarding David Meeker's book and film jazz research.

Pulleine, Tim. "Lelouch." 52:3 (Summer 1983): 150–51. Director Claude Lelouch on collaborating with Francis Lai.

Palmer, Christopher. "Tiomkin: A Phenomenal Dramatic Instinct." 55:2 (Spring 1986): 78–79.

Stanbrook, Alan. "The Sight of Music." 56:2 (Spring 1987): 132–35. Film versions of operas.

Gillett, John. "Nevsky Live." 58:4 (Autumn 1989): 220. A sound film, *Alexander Nevsky* (1938), with live orchestral accompaniment.

Dodd, Philip. "Requiem for a Rave." [new series] 1:5 (September 1991): 8–13. A sidebar, "Sounds New," explains how Charlie Gillett chose music for *London Kills Me*, 13.

Priestley, Brian. "Beating Time." 1:12 (April 1992): 27. On the use of jazz music in John Cassavetes's films.

Christie, Ian. "Sounds and Silents." 3:3 (March 1993): 18–21. Historical overview of music for silent films.

Penman, Ian. "Juke-Box and Johnny Boy." 3:4 (April 1993): 10–11. On music in *Mean Streets*.

Dargis, Manohla. "Hard and Fast." 5:3 (March 1995): 24–27. Interview with director Mike Figgis; sidebar, "Figgis on His Film Scores," 27.

Boswell, Simon. "Neither Mozart nor Hendrix." 5:4 (April 1995): 37, 62. On collaborating with directors. With filmography by Mark Kermode.

Meeker, David. "Cherokee to Madison County." 5:9 (September 1995): 26–28. Lennie Niehaus interview. With filmography by Meeker and Markku Salmi.

"Elmer Bernstein: Composer." 6:5 (May 1996). On Cecil B. DeMille. In "Movie Times" supplement under "Inside Movies," pp. 1.

Jones, Chris. "RoboComposer." 7:2 (February 1997): 31. Creating music using a personal computer.

MacNab, Geoffrey. "Sensitive to Nature." 12:2 (February 2002): 70. Interview with Maurice Jarre.

Bracewell, Michael. "Tunes of Glory." 14:9 (September 2004) 26–29. On the relationship between pop music, electronics, and film. Article is followed by interview quotes from directors and musicians answering specific questions: how can music best enhance film, 30–31; favorite scores, 32–40; "The Talented Mr. Rota," a Richard Dyer article based on an interview with Nino Rota, 42–45; the most effective use of music in your own film, 46–47; what would you rescore, 48–49.

Column, "End Notes" by Mark Kermode (selected)
4:6 (June 1994): 71. Scoring trends.
4:10 (October 1994): 63. On Ennio Morricone, particularly *Wolf*.
4:12 (December 1994): 63. Music in *Forrest Gump*.
5:9 (September 1995): 71. On rock soundtracks.
5:11 (November 1995): 62. On Michael Nyman's score for *Carrington*.
6:[6] (July 1996): 62. Soundtrack reviews.

Column, "Music" by Antony Hopkins (selected)
"Music." [18] (December 1949): 23.
"Music." 19:1 (March 1950): 32.
"Music." 19:3 (May 1950): 127.
"Music: Congress at Florence." 19:6 (August 1950): 243–44. With a list of papers read at the conference in Italy.
"The Music of Copland." 19:8 (December 1950): 336.
"Letter from an Unknown Critic." 19:10 (February 1951): 416.
"Orchestration Run Riot?" by Lawrence Morton, with Antony Hopkins's reply. 20:1 (May 1951): 21–23, 30. The Lawrence essay previously appeared in *Hollywood Quarterly*.

Column, "The Sound Track" by John Huntley (selected)
19:5 (July 1950): 223. On recent recordings.
19:7 (November 1950): 301–2. On theme songs and *Dream of Olwen*.
19:9 (January 1951): 381. On music in Michael Powell's productions.
19:10 (February 1951): 417, 422. On sound effects and music.
21:2 (October–December 1951): 95. On new recordings.

21:3 (January–March 1952). On the MGM Studio Orchestra.
22:2 (October–December 1952): 94. On music in director John Ford's films.
22:3 (January–March 1953): 145. "Chaplin's Film Music."
22:4 (April–June 1953): 202–3. On music by Georges Auric.
24:2 (October–December 1954): 107. On a film about the London Symphony Orchestra.

The Silent Picture (UK/US)

Hofmann, Charles. "There Were Always Sounds for Silents." No. 13 (Winter–Spring 1972): 27.

Silver Screen (US)

Fan magazine published by Screenland Magazine.

Williams, Whitney. "Hollywood Answers the Critics." 9:6 (April 1939): 28–29, 75–76. Filmmakers and actors defend the use of music in films, specifically in respect to scenes in which no orchestra is present.

The Silver Sheet (US)

Published by the Thomas H. Ince Corp. in Culver City in the 1920s. Each issue was often devoted to a single film. The news items in "On the Ince Lot" occasionally relate to music, such as the reference to Lee Zahler playing music on the set of *Playing with Souls* (1924) in a 1925 issue for that film (p. 24).

"Music and Prologues: Suggestions for *Homespun Folks*." (September 1920): 14.
"Mischa Guterson Writes Special Score for *The Woman*." (December 1921): 19.
"*Lorna Doone* Told in Song." ([October] 1922): 17. On sheet music tie-in.

SMPTE Journal (US)

Monthly journal of the Society of Motion Picture and Television Engineers. Previously published under other titles, including the *Journal of the Society of Motion Picture Engineers*.

Wagner, Victor. "Scoring a Motion Picture." 25 (May 3–6, 1926): 40–43. Observations from the music director of the Eastman Theatre in Rochester, New York.
Previn, Charles. "Setting Music to Pictures." 29:4 (October 1937): 372–73. From "How Motion Pictures Are Made," a 1937 symposium at Universal Studios, at which Previn, the music director, was a presenter.
Wetzel, Edwin. "Assembling a Final Sound-Track." 29:4 (October 1937): 374–75. From the Universal symposium (see previous entry). Wetzel was a dubbing mixer.
Lootens, C. L., D. J. Bloomberg, and M. Rettinger. "A Motion Picture Dubbing and Scoring Stage." 32 (April 1939): 357–80. On the new music recording and rerecording building at Republic studios. Includes diagrams and photographs. The authors were representatives of Republic and RCA.
Brown, Bernard B. "Prescoring and Scoring." 39 (October 1942): 228–31.
Goldsmith, L. T. "Re-Recording Sound Motion Pictures." 39 (November 1942): 277–83.

Soviet Film (Russia)

Monthly national film journal published in several languages. Entries below are from the English-language edition.

Eisenstein, Sergei. "PRKFV." No. 167 (April 1971): 35–37. The director talks about collaborating with Sergei Prokofiev. Reprinted in Limbacher.
Belyavski, Oleg. "Two-Way Process: Reflections on a Profession: Composer Andrei Petrov." No. 206 (July 1974): 35–36. Interview.

Roshal, Grigory. "Dimitri Kabalevski." No. 211 (December 1974): 38–39.

Zlotnik, Olga. "Arno Babajanian: The Cinema Is My First Love." No. 230 (July 1976): 27–28. Interview with the Armenian composer.

"Dimitri Shostakovich: We Get Along Well Together." No. 232 (September 1976): 11. The composer's remarks on cinema.

Petrov, Andrei. "Talking about My Profession: The Secrets of Music in Films." No. 233 (October 1976): 24–25.

Zulfikarov, Timur. "A Word about My Colleague: Rumil Vildanov—Listening to the Singer's Voice." No. 261 (February 1979): 7. On the Uzbek composer.

Frolova, Galina. "Music Is My Profession: Composer Raymond Pauls." No. 277 (June 1980): 40–41. Interview.

Abdrashitov, Alexander. "Music and Cinema." No. 308 (January 1983): 15. On Konstantin Lopushansky.

Podorzhansky, Mikhail. "Hearing the Past." No. 309 (February 1983): 23. Interview with Alexei Rybnikov.

Matveyev, Evgeny. "A Word about a Colleague: Composer Evgeny Ptichkin." No. 312 (May 1983): 31.

Varzhapetian, Vardvan. "Solo for Composer." No. 333 (February 1985): 32–33. On Alfred Snitke [*sic*].

Malukova, Larissa. "Marriage of Music and Drawing." No. 334 (March 1985): 34–35. Animator Inessa Kovalevskaya talks about music in her films.

Ognev, Kirill. "Composer Evgeni Doga." No. 343 (December 1985): 28–29.

Ovchinnikov, Boris. "Julian Grunberg: 'Blend of Film and Music.'" No. 363 (August 1987): 32–33. Interview with the chief musical editor of Gorky film studios.

Vasilkova, Natalia. "Film Music by Mikhail Meerovich." No. 372 (May 1988): 30. Profile.

Vasiliev, Andrei. "Alfred Schnittke Hits the Bull's Eye." No. 385 (June 1989): 26–27. Interview.

Kichin, Valerie. "Do We Have Musical Films?" No. 392 (January 1990): 2–8.

Gurchenko, Lyudmila. "May There Be More Music." No. 392 (January 1990): 8–11. The actress on her work in musicals.

Vasiliyev, Andrei. "Untapped Bonanza." No. 392 (January 1990): 14–16. On the role of rock music in Soviet cinema.

Spaghetti Cinema (US)
Mid-1980s fanzine published by William Connolly in Hollywood.

"A Prolific Composer." 2:2 (February 1985). 27–32. Filmography for Ennio Morricone.

"Ennio Morricone." 2:4 (February 1985): 15–17. Interview from *Cinema Papers* (December 1984).

Connolly, William. "[Francesco] De Masi's Music." 2:4 (July 1985): 18–23. Filmography.

"The Brothers DeAngelis." 3:3 (April 1986). 17–19. Filmography for Guido and Maurizio DeAngelis.

Bahn, Bob. "Is Soundtrack Collecting Dying?" 3:6 (August 1986): 10.

Star Trek: The Next Generation (US)
Starlog publication aimed at fans.

"Music of the Stars." No. 14 (April 1991): 5. Article on Dennis McCarthy's music.

"Sounds in Space." No. 14 (April 1991): 16. Article on Ron Jones's music.

No. 18 (April 1992): 32. Article on Jay Chattaway's music.

Star Trek Voyager (US)
Starlog publication aimed at fans.
"The Music of *Star Trek: Voyager*." No. 4 (October 1995).

Star Wars Insider (US)
Doughton, K. J. "Skyrockers: *Star Wars* in Popular Music." No. 69 (August 2003): 40–43. Music inspired by John Williams's score for the 1977 film.

Starlog (US)
Fan magazine covering "the Science Fiction Universe," published first by O'Quinn Studios, later by Starlog Communications International.
Squires, Frank, and David Huston. "The Music of the Spheres." No. 2 (November 1976): 57–59, 65. On sci-fi soundtracks.
O'Quinn, Kerry. "An Invisible Man." No. 10 (December 1977): 63. On Albert Glasser.
Houston, David. "Miklos Rozsa." No. 31 (February 1980): 47–49. Interview.
Ahrens, Dennis. "John Williams Strikes Back! or, The Soundtrack Continues." No. 37 (August 1980): 29–30.
Maronie, Sam. "Jerry Goldsmith: Science Fiction's Hottest Film Scorer Prefers to Let His Music Do the Talking." No. 51 (October 1981): 52–54. Interview-based article.
Hutchison, David. "Music for a Barbarian." No. 62 (September 1982): 24–25, 65. Basil Poledouris interview regarding *Conan the Barbarian*.
Sciacca, Tom. "James Horner: New Melodies for the Starship 'Enterprise.'" No. 63 (October 1982): 22–23.
Bates, Cary. "John Barry: Scoring James Bond: A Personal View." No. 94 (May 1985): 68–71. Interview.
Clement, Thom. "Composer Elmer Bernstein: Scoring Fantasy Films." No. 103 (February 1986): 68–71. Interview-based article on Bernstein's score for *The Black Cauldron*.
Larson, Randall. "Alan Silvestri: Tunes for Toons." No. 135 (October 1988): 19–23, 44.
Shapiro, Marc. "Music of the Dark Knight." No. 147 (October 1989): 62–66, 96. Interview-based article on Danny Elfman's score for *Batman*.
Hirsch, David. "Composer of the Fantastic." No. 172 (November 1991): 56–60, 72. On Leonard Rosenman.
Hirsch, David. "Music for *RoboCop*." No. 196 (November 1993): 58–63. Basil Poledouris interview.
Soter, Tom. "License to Score." No. 199 (February 1994): 41–45. On John Barry.
Warren, Bill. "Martian Melodies." No. 235 (February 1997): 48–51. Interview-based article on Danny Elfman's score for *Mars Attacks*.
DeMain, Bill. "Fear's Accomplice." No. 237 (April 1997): 52–55. On Mark Snow's music for the TV series *The X-Files*.
Hirsch, David. "Musician of Myth." No. 243 (October 1997): 54–57. On Joseph LoDuca.
Weaver, Tom. "Heavier Metal: Michael Kamen Is Happy Making Music for Fantasy Films." No. 268 (November 1999): 66–70.
Spelling, Ian. "Music of Middle-Earth." No. 297 (April 2002): 25–29. Interview-based article on Howard Shore's music for *Lord of the Rings: The Fellowship of the Ring*; also discusses the composer's collaborations with director David Cronenberg.

Starlog Science-Fiction Explorer (US)
Issue no. 7 (June 1995) contains an extensive section on film music, "Fantasy Music Thrills: From *The X-Files* to *Beauty & the Beast*," according to the cover.

Step (US)

On music, film, new media, and beyond, published in Glendale, California.

Hearn, Michael. "The Voice behind the Music." No. 4 (July–August 1999): 6–10, 14–15. Interview with Christopher Young.

Stills (UK)

"Bad Vibes from Virgin." [14] (November 1984): 12. On the controversy surrounding the two music scores for *1984*, one by Dominic Muldowney and the other by the Eurythmics.

Take One (Canada)

Billed as "The Film Magazine" and "The Magazine of the Movies." Published in Montreal. Featured columns by Robert Fiedel in 1977 and Ross Care in 1979.

Medjuck, Joe. "Frank Zappa." 2:2 (1968): 8–9. Interview on the music for the surrealistic documentary *Uncle Meat*.

De Palma, Brian. "Remembering [Bernard] Herrmann." 5 (May 1976): 39–41. Originally appeared in *The Village Voice* (October 11, 1973) as "Murder by Moog: Scoring the Chill."

Conway Baker, Michael. "A Composer's Experience with Philip Borsos." 11:38 (July–August 2002): 20–28.

Column, "Scoring" by Ross Care (selected)

"Scoring: Into Orbit: The Scores of Ferde Grofe." 7:2 (January 1979): 40–41.

"Scoring: Nino Rota." 7:6 (May 1979): 46–47. On Rota's collaborations with Fellini.

Column, "Sound Tracks" by Robert Fiedel (selected)

"Recordings: Mystic Romanticism and Tudor Pomp." 5:6 (January 1977): 27–28.

"Digging for Goldsmith." 5:8 (March 1977): 32–33. Apparently the first "Sound Track" column. On *Logan's Run* and *The Omen*.

"A Citadel of Soundtrack Riches." 5:12 (November 1977): 39–40. On releases by Tony Thomas's record label.

Talking Screen (US)

Published monthly by Dell Publishing in New York.

Cartwright, Dorothea Hawley. "Tuning Up the Talkies: Watching the Music Departments Function." 1:6 (August 1930): 54ff. On Nathaniel Finston, Erno Rapée, and others. Reprinted in the *Cue Sheet* (July 2005).

TCI (US)

Theatre Crafts International. Covers entertainment technology and design.

Boepple, Leanne. "tomandandy." 31:5 (May 1997): A10. Profiles Tom Hajdu and Andy Millburn and their company, which specializes in electronic music for films.

Technical Bulletin (US)

Technical credits for films issued by the Academy of Motion Picture Arts and Sciences from 1929 to 1940. Music mixers are among the technicians included. Listed by production title and individual name.

Television and New Media (US)

International journal devoted to recent trends in television and new media studies, with some articles on music television (MTV).

Forman, Murray. "Soundtrack to a Crisis: Music, Context, Discourse." 3:5 (2002): 191–204.

Television Quarterly (US)
Hanser, Richard. "Robert Russell Bennett: A Sound for All Seasons." 18:4 (Winter 1981–1982): 43–55. Tribute from the television writer and cowriter of *Victory at Sea*.

Theatre Arts (US)
Published monthly by Theatre Publications in New York. Previously published as *Theater Arts Monthly* from 1924 to 1939.

Bakshy, Alexander. "The Movie Scene: Notes on Sound and Silence." 13:2 (February 1929): 97–107.

Isaacs, Hermine Rich. "New Horizons: *Fantasia* and Fantasound." 25:1 (January 1941): 55–61.

Isaacs, Hermine Rich. "Face the Music: The Films in Review." 28:12 (December 1944): 718–27. On the state of the art, followed by film reviews.

Milhaud, Darius. "Music for the Films." 31:9 (September 1947): 27–29. On the challenges facing composers.

Moor, Paul. "Composers and the Music Track." 33:6 (July 1949): 49, 93. On mediocrity.

Knight, Arthur. "All Singing! All Talking! All Laughing!" 33:8 (September 1949): 33–40. On 1929, the year of transition.

Spolar, Betsey [*sic*], and Merrilyn Hammond. "How to Work in Hollywood and Still Be Happy." 37:8 (August 1953): 80, 96. Profile of Alex North.

Adler, Peter Herman. "TV in the Opera Picture." 40:1 (January 1956): 32–33, 95–98. The music director discusses special problems in adapting opera to television.

Bennett, Robert Russell. "From the Notes of a Music Arranger." 40:11 (November 1956): 24–25, 88–89. Some film work is mentioned.

Today's Film Maker (US)
"The Magazine for the Contemporary Cinematographer," published by American Film Makers Magazine.

Lewin, Frank. "Motion Picture Music: New Ways of Viewing = New Ways of Listening." 1:4 (May 1972): 43, 64. Essay by the composer mentions the advent of video cassettes for private viewing.

The Triangle (US)
Published weekly in New York for exhibitors by Triangle Film Corporation. The articles by William Furst usually discuss the musical treatment of one or two specific Triangle films.

Furst, William. "Composer Talks on Triangle Music: Explains How Varying Combinations of Instruments Should Be Handled to Get Best Results." 1:1 (October 23, 1915): 6.

Furst, William. "Triangle Director Aids Conductors." 1:2 (October 30, 1915): 5.

Furst, William. "Hints from Triangle Musical Director." 1:3 (November 6, 1915): 5.

Furst, William. "Suggestions from Musical Director." 1:4 (November 13, 1915): 4.

Furst, William. "Suggestions from Musical Director." 1:5 (November 20, 1915): 5.

[Furst, William.] "Musical Hints and Expert Advice." 1:6 (November 27, 1915): 5.

Furst, William. "Director of Music Gives Orchestra Hints." 1:8 (December 11, 1915): 4.

Furst, William. "Orchestra Hints on Playing to the Pictures." 1:9 (December 18, 1915): 6.

Furst, William. "Playing Feature Pictures in Most Approved Style." 1:10 (December 25, 1915): 5.
Furst, William. "Tells How Pictures Should Be Played." 1:11 (January 1, 1916): 5.
Furst, William. "Suggestion for the Picture Accompaniment." 1:12 (January 8, 1916): 5.
"Pictures Give Striking Themes to Composers: Writing for the Screen and Adapting Appropriate Scores—a New Profession That Pays Well." 1:14 (January 22, 1916): 3.
"Victor Schertzinger, Composer Inspired by *Hell's Hinges*." 1:17 (February 12, 1916): 7.
"Adaptation of Scotch Songs in *Peggy* Scores." 1:18 (February 19, 1916): 5. With comments by Hugo Riesenfeld.
"Music Cues and Hints to Orchestra Leaders." 2:6 (May 27, 1916): 8. Music cue suggestions for two films.
"Stories and Music Cues for Current Pictures." 2:9 (June 17, 1916): 6.
"Synopses and Music Cues for Current Films." 2:10 (June 24, 1916): 6. The music cues for current films continues through at least vol. 2, no. 26.

T.V. Guide (US)

Program guide to television listings, published in Pennsylvania.
Barber, Rowland. "Could Dr. Welby Practice without Music? A Noted Composer-Conductor Explains What It Adds to TV Drama." (May 19, 1973): 52–56. Interview-based article on Leonard Rosenman.
Wolf, Jeanne. "John Williams Scored 'Em." 41:27 (July 3, 1993): 28. Profile.

24 Images (Canada)

Vallerand, Francois. "An Interview with Miklos Rozsa." No. 12 (April 1982).
Privet, G. "'This Film Should Be Played Loud': Quelques Notes sur la Musique dans les Films de Martin Scorsese." No. 67 (Summer 1993): 36–39. On the use of music in the director's films.

Twilight Zone Magazine (US)

Sullivan, Jack. "Music." (June 1983): 15–17.

Universal City Studios Club News (US)

Monthly studio publication, published from 1927 to around 1965 under various titles, including *Universal City Club News, Universal International Studio Club News*, and *Revue Studios Club News*. May contain occasional news items on composers or music. Superseded by *Universal City News* (1976–1983). A monthly employee newsletter, *MCA Ink*, was published from 1982 to 1986, followed by *MCA Newsletter* (1989–1991) and *MCA News* (1991–1995).

The Universal Weekly (US)

Studio trade publication, published from 1912 to 1936, with occasional news items on music for Universal productions. Also known as *The Moving Picture Weekly*. Filled with publicity coverage aimed at exhibitors. Music suggestions were published as early as 1915. See, for example, "Appropriate Music for Every Picture," featuring a list of films with one or more music suggestions for each, in vol. 6, no. 1, January 2, 1915, p. 2. Though not as comprehensive as a cue sheet, these lists were printed in advance of a film's release so that the music could be obtained. See also "Music to *The Target*," vol. 2, no. 10, February 26, 1916, p. 39. A good source of information for 1930s musicals (though there is a break in publication between June 1930 and October 1932).
"Noble Kreider Composes Special Music for *Samson*." 3:25 (December 13, 1913): 9.

"'Estrellita' Is Theme Song Hit of *Señor Americano.*" 30:22 (January 4, 1930): 12.
"*Showboat* Has More Popular Songs Than Any Other Picture." 38:9 (March 28, 1936): 24–25.

University Film Study Center Newsletter (US)

Herrmann, Bernard. "The Contemporary Use of Music in Film: *Citizen Kane, Psycho, Fahrenheit 451.*" 7:3 (February supplement, 1977): 5–10. Condensed version of Herrmann's paper, "The Effects of the Coming of Sound on the Writing of Music for American Films," delivered at a symposium sponsored by the University Film Study Center Research Program held at the George Eastman House in 1973. Bibliography.

Variety (US)

One of two perennial daily trade papers, along with the *Hollywood Reporter*, that cover the film industry. Contains music business coverage of film and television scoring, publishing and licensing, composers and recording artists, music representation and unions, and obituaries. Since 1999, many of the obituaries have been contributed by journalist Jon Burlingame. *Variety Obituaries: Including a Comprehensive Index* (New York: Garland Publishing, 1988–) stands at 15 volumes and covers 1905 to 1994. A column dating back as early as 1944 lists music business news items, including scoring assignments and activities of Hollywood composers. Date ranges given for columns have been verified; however, some columns may appear outside these ranges. A "Record Reviews" section in the 1950s includes some soundtrack capsule reviews; for example, Al Scharper writes about *A Streetcar Named Desire* in the September 14, 1951, issue, p. 8. Howard Lucraft wrote "Record Roundup" in the early 1970s. *Daily Variety* is published in Hollywood; *Variety Weekly* is published in New York. The weekly edition contains a business-oriented music section with financial figures related to popular music and the record business. Two annual issues focusing on film music were first issued in 1997, the same year that Jon Burlingame joined the staff. Burlingame has written many articles for "Film and TV Music Spotlight" and "Eye on the Oscars: Music." The Oscar issue discusses potential nominees in the music categories of song and scores. Articles below give a hint of the scope of the news items.

"[Ray] Heindorf Backs Quality of O'seas Filmusic Sound over Hollywood." 101:8 (September 17, 1958): 1, 4.

Foreman, Carl. "Tiomkin by Foreman." (July 31, 1961): 6–7. The writer-director on the composer.

Roth, Henry. "Hollywood and the Negro Musician." (February 17, 1964). Claims that a black composer has yet to receive screen credit. Advertisement, reprinted from *Frontier* magazine, January 1964.

"[John] Barry's Off-Beat Film Scoring Technique Is to Do the Soundtrack Album First." (January 24, 1967): 4.

Kirk, Cynthia. "Composer [Leonard] Rosenman Finds New Respect for Film Work." (May 5, 1983).

[Film and TV music] 234:1 (December 6, 1991): 32-page insert.

"American Music Legend: Jerry Goldsmith." (September 8, 1995): 41–66. Special section honoring Jerry Goldsmith.

Hindes, Andrew. "Composers Wax Melodic on a Movie Music Master." (September 8, 1995): 57–58. On Jerry Goldsmith, part of the section in the preceding entry.

Gallo, Phil. "Local Jazz." (July 15, 1997): 28–32. Includes some discussion of film music.

Burlingame, Jon. "L.A. Music's First Family." (July 15, 1997): 35–36, 41. On the Newman family: Alfred, David, Lionel, Maria, Randy, and Thomas.

Koehler, Robert. "Thomas [Newman] Finds His Own Way." (July 15, 1997): 40.

Burlingame, Jon. "Range, Versatility David's [Newman] Hallmark." (July 15, 1997).

Matsumoto, Jon. "The Last Outposts of Film's Golden Age, Scoring Stages Preserve History, Jobs." (July 15, 1997).

Bennett, Ray. "Big Score." (November 25, 1997): 70.

Burlingame, Jon. "Tunesmiths to Get Stamps of Approval." 261:55 (November 20, 1998): 8, 42. On United States postage stamps honoring Bernard Herrmann, Erich Wolfgang Korngold, Alfred Newman, Max Steiner, Dimitri Tiomkin, and Franz Waxman.

Burlingame, Jon. "The Maestro Scores Again." (August 26, 1999). On Maurice Jarre.

Burlingame, Jon. "Composers Curry Kudos." (November 8, 1999): A10. On women film and television composers.

Burlingame, Jon. "Sony Classical Corners Film Score Marketplace." (April 7, 2000).

Burlingame, Jon. "Theme Songs Provide Perfect Ambience." (August 31, 2001): 45. Special television and Emmy issue.

Burlingame, Jon. "Laura Karpman." (November 14, 2001): A14. In "Women in Showbiz" issue.

Burlingame, Jon. "Scoring Pros Reveal Their CD Trays." (January 9, 2002): A23. What Elliot Goldenthal, Harry Gregson-Williams, James Newton Howard, Lolita Ritmanis, Christopher Young, and Hans Zimmer listen to.

Burlingame, Jon. "Composers Make Music with Upstarts." 277: 41 (December 3, 2002): A4. Alexander Janko, Shirley Walker, and Christopher Young on mentoring young composers.

McCarthy, Todd. "What's the Film Score? Loud and Overblown." 277: 42 (December 4, 2002): 16, 34.

"Legends & Groundbreakers." (December 4, 2003): A1–A20. Special section on Hans Zimmer.

Mermelstein, David. "Gospel According to Debney." (December 8, 2004). On John Debney.

Burlingame, Jon. "Resettling an Old Score." (March 10, 2005). On Christopher Caliendo's new score for *Major Dundee* (1965).

Burlingame, Jon. "'Lost' Art of Real Players." (August 17, 2005). On television scores such as the music for *Lost*.

Burlingame, Jon. "Behind the Curtain: *Kong*'s Dueling Scores." (November 29, 2005). On music by Howard Shore and James Newton Howard's replacement score for *King Kong*.

<u>Column, "Studio Doings" (February–March 1944)</u>
The "Cleffing" subheading contains scoring assignments; see March 6, 1944.

<u>Column, "Short Shorts" (April–December 1944)</u>
The "Assignments," "Music," and "Cleffing" subheadings document music scoring assignments and other news. For example, the September 19, 1944, column includes mention of Mischa Bakaleinikoff, Ann Ronell, and Nathaniel Shilkret.

<u>Column, "Out of the Horn's Mouth" (March 1946–February 1947)</u>
For example, see April 9, 1946.

<u>Column, "Music Notes" (June–December 1947; 1950)</u>
Mostly documents popular music happenings.

Column, "Clef Dwellers" by Eddie Kafafian (1956–1961)
Scoring assignments for composers and songwriters. Appeared from around October 1956, through January 11, 1961. May have appeared sporadically thereafter.

Column, "What's the Score" by John G. Houser (1961–1962)
Contains scoring assignments, newsbriefs, interview quotes, and recording news. This Wednesday column was often on a page titled "Music," with other industry coverage. Appeared from January 18, 1961, through at least May 1962.
February 15, 1961. On Dimitri Tiomkin and George Duning.
April 26, 1961. On Max Steiner, based on a recent conversation with Houser.
June 14, 1961. On Jerry Fielding.

Column, "Music Notes" (1962–1963)
Appeared from December 12, 1962, through December 1963.

Column, "Clef Dwellers" by Mike Kaplan (1964)
For example, see July 29, 1964.

Column, "On the Beat" by Joe X. Price (1963–1966)
Appeared from December 11, 1963, through January 24, 1966. (In the Tuesday edition beginning in January 1964.)

Column, "On the Music Beat" by Marvin Fisher (1968–1969)
January 25, 1968, through January 23, 1969.

Column, "High and Low Notes" by Elizabeth Murphy (1972)

Column, "On the Music Beat" by Steve Toy (1975–1976)
For example, see January 26, 1976.

Column, "Music Notes" (1975; 1979; 1986)
For example, see April 30, 1979; March 8, 1986.

Special issues: Anniversary editions
These were issued in a separately bound "section 2" for each indicated date.
Gilbert, L. Wolfe. "Music Moves to Picture Makers." 3rd annual. 13:15 (September 24, 1936): 97–98. On fellow songwriters.
"Screen Music Strikes Bold Niche; Public Accepts Wider Appeal." 4th annual. 17:27 (October 7, 1937): 9.
Haynes, Gene. "Pick of the Nation's Songs." 4th annual. 17:27 (October 7, 1937): 163. Six out of ten of the year's most played songs were from Hollywood films.
"Pop Songs Top Picture Tunes." 5th annual. 21:42 (October 24, 1938): 58.
Gilbert, L. Wolfe. "Studio Music Purge." 5th annual. 21:42 (October 24, 1938): 294, 298. Claims five teams of songwriters write the majority of songs for the entire film industry.
Haynes, Gene. "Music's in the Air Again: Tunes, Action and Comedy Are '41 Film Trends." 7th annual. 29:32 (October 21, 1940): 9.
"Studios Have Mastered 'Know How' of Filmusicals." 9th annual. 37:30 (October 19, 1942): 39.
Joy, Jack E. "Music and the War." 10th annual. 41:39 (October 29, 1943): 14.
McHugh, Jimmy. "How to Write a Song." 11th annual. 45:29 (October 16, 1944): 29.
"Music Biz Takes on Martial Air." 12th annual. 49:38 (October 29, 1945): 411. On the state of the business, including the hiring of the first studio "music coordinator."
"Pic Music Upbeat on Wax." 20th annual. 81:40 (November 2, 1953): 66.
North, Alex. "Film Music." 27th annual. 109:37 (October 25, 1960): 18.

"Film Music Credits." 27th annual. 109:37 (October 25, 1960): 308. For 1959. This feature continued in several subsequent annuals.

Green, John. "Don't Stop the Music." 30th annual. 121:97 (October 29, 1963): 41, 182.

Tiomkin, Dimitri. "Oscar Night—1984." 31st annual. 125:37 (October 27, 1964): 14, 64. A take-off on his famous acceptance speech at the Academy Awards.

Bernstein, Elmer. "Beware the Siren Songs of Film Scoring." 32nd annual. 129:37 (October 26, 1965): 218.

Jarre, Maurice. "Music and Films." 35th annual (October 29, 1968): 81. Retrospective look at the year 1933.

Rosenman, Leonard. "Composers and Film Producers Not Always in Harmony." 36th annual. (October 28, 1969): 196. What film music can and cannot do.

Lucraft, Howard. "Pop Music Sounds and Personalities." 37th annual. (October 27, 1970): 150, 156–58. On Burt Bacharach and others.

Bernstein, Elmer. "Music in Films Has Changed Dramatically, Not in All Ways for the Better, During Last 20 Years; It's Big Biz—and Hot Antitrust Issue." 39th annual. (October 31, 1972): 20.

Klein, Doreen North. "Rock Revolution Shatters Film Music Traditions." 40th annual. (October 30, 1973): 230–32.

41st annual. (October 29, 1974). Contains credits directory for composers.

Stewart, Mike. "Usually Pix Boost Soundtrack Sales." 43rd annual. (October 26, 1976): 192, 202. The chairman of United Artists Music Group makes prescient remarks about Bill Conti's music for *Rocky*.

Tisch, Steve. "H'wood Hops on Pop Music Bandwagon: Awakens to Fact that Film and Tune Markets Cater Mostly to the under 30 Age Group." 44th annual. (October 25, 1977): 220.

Cornyn, Stan. "'Unless the Film Is a Success the Soundtrack Will Not Be Meaningful' as Disk Seller." 45th annual. (October 31, 1978): 222–24. From a Warner Bros. Records executive.

Lucraft, Howard. "Livingston and Evans Know the Magic of Academy Awards Night, and the Rocky Road to Melodious Acclamation." 48th annual. (October 27, 1981): 231.

Lucraft, Howard. "Film Composers Change the Score: Rather Than Advancing, Screen Music Is Digressing to Variations on a Song." 49th annual. (October 26, 1982): 120.

Lucraft, Howard. "[Pete] Rugolo's 'How's' of Arranging-Composing." 50th annual. (October 25, 1983): 415. Listed in contents, not printed in consulted issue.

Allen, Al. "Composing with Computers: Doesn't Obviate Talent but Can Make It Easier for Film Tunesmiths." 51st annual. (October 30, 1984): 206.

Di Pasquale, James. "Synthesizers, Composers Almost Inseparable." 52nd annual. (October 29, 1985): 245, 248–49.

LeMel, Gary, and Robert E. Holmes. "Soundtrack Albums: Looking Back and Looking Forward." 52nd annual. (October 29, 1985): 286, 366, 375.

Moore, Phil. "Things I Forgot to Tell You." 53rd annual. (October 28, 1986): 140–42. Excerpts from a proposed book by one of the first black musicians hired by a major studio, with anecdotes from his experiences interacting with the MGM music department in the 1940s.

Schipper, Henry. "Pop Soundtracks Sales Booming." 53rd annual. (October 28, 1986): 242, 244, 247–48.

Lucraft, Howard. "Special Treatment for [Charlie] Parker's Music by [Lennie] Niehaus for *Bird*." 55th annual. (October 25, 1988): 174, 190.

Lucraft, Howard. "[Alex] North, Man of Music and Conscience." 55th annual. (October 25, 1988): 176.

Haring, Bruce. "Against the Wind." 58th annual (October 29, 1991): 24. On marketing music.

Special issues: "Oscars: Music"
(January 23, 1997). Includes "Bending Tradition: Unorthodoxy Bonds Classic, Modern Scores," by Robert Koehler; "Singing Oscar's Praises," on what winning an Academy Award meant to John Barry, Elmer Bernstein, Maurice Jarre, and Hans Zimmer, by Jerry Roberts; and articles on repurposing rock and pop music for film and on Disney songs.
(January 22, 1998). Includes "Less Is More: Minimalist Music at Film Forefront," on Philip Glass and others, by Robert Koehler.
(January 26, 1998). Includes "Fanfare for the Uncommon Score" and "Labels View Film Composers as the New Classicists," by Jon Burlingame; "Best Scores of 1997."
(January 20, 1999). Includes "Sweet Sounds of Success: Rookies Out to Be Heard by Academy," by Jon Burlingame; "[Lalo] Schifrin's Mantra Is Hard Work during *Rush Hour*," by Robert Koehler; an article on Hans Zimmer's company, Media Ventures.
(January 21, 2000). Includes articles by Jon Burlingame, "Tunes Steal the Scene: Films Focus on Musicians' Art," on Elliot Goldenthal and Thomas Newman; "Spotlight: Thomas Newman;" and "The Family Business: On Scoring Stage that Bears His Name, [Thomas] Newman Follows in His Father's Footsteps."
(January 19, 2001). Includes "Scoring Stages Offer Distinct Features," by Jon Burlingame.
(January 23, 2002). Includes "Successful Scores Breathe Life into Animated Worlds" and "Composer's *Rhapsody* Lies in Small Films," on Cliff Eidelman, both by Jon Burlingame; "Helmer Hyphenates Direct Films Down to the Score," on filmmakers who also compose film music, by Robert Koehler.
(January 6, 2003). Includes "Elmer Bernstein [*Far from Heaven*]: Where Melody Rules the Day," by Jon Burlingame; "Mychael Danna [*Ararat*]: Seeing the World through Music," profile by Robert Koehler.
(December 5, 2003). Includes "Musical Interlude," on Clint Eastwood's score for *Mystic River*, by Jon Burlingame; articles on James Horner, Howard Shore, and rock singers.
(December 8, 2004). Includes "Le Divorce: Rejected Scores, Even by Oscar Winners, a Continuing Refrain," by Jon Burlingame; "Leonard Bernstein Hits High Note: Maestro Produced a Classic *Waterfront*, His First and Only Original Film Score," by David Mermelstein.
(February 14, 2005). Includes "Call of the Masses: Classical Icons Created Some of Their Most Compelling Work for the Screen" and "Beat of a Different Drummer: Many of Today's Hottest Talents Avoided Traditional Route to Scoring," both by Jon Burlingame.
(November 30, 2005). Includes "Harry Gregson-Williams," a brief profile by Anthony D'Alessandro; "Master Class: [John] Williams Earns Himself a Spot in Pantheon of Composers," by Jon Burlingame.

Special issues: "Spotlight: Film and TV Music"
(October 15, 1997): 17–43. Includes "Preservation Key in Growing Original Score Market" and "Re-recording Classic Scores," by Jon Burlingame.
(October 21, 1998): A1–A26. Includes articles on Elia Cmiral, Christopher Gunning, and John Ottman, and a special section on Burt Bacharach.
(October 15, 1999). Includes "Big Sound, Small Screen," by Jon Burlingame on television miniseries; articles on John Powell, Stephen Sondheim, W. G. "Snuffy" Walden, and Christopher Young. "Top Composers of the '90s" ranks listed composers by total box office, and "Top Music Supervisors of the Decade" lists names and soundtracks.

(September 13, 2000): A1–A11. "Soundtracks and Scores" section with articles by Jon Burlingame on bootleg soundtracks, the Emmy music branch, and Lalo Schifrin. Also, profiles of Tan Dun, Rolfe Kent, John Lurie, and Stephen Warbeck; chart with top composers and music supervisors of the 1990s.

(July 29, 2002): A49–A55. Includes articles on music supervision, technology, and alternative rock music; and Jon Burlingame on scores for small films.

Variety Weekly (selected articles)
"Music" section with news, activities, and so on dates back to 1929.

"The Theme Song." 93:12 (January 2, 1929): 28.

Gallagher, Frank. "The First Theatre Organist." 93:12 (January 2, 1929): 29. On his experience beginning in 1908.

Gilbert, L. Wolfe. "Song-Writing for Pictures." (January 8, 1930): 119.

Swigart, Bill. "Studio Music." (January 8, 1930): 121. The past year in review and the present state of film music. Topics include music written to fit the picture, staff musicians, and more.

Swigart, Bill. "Along the Coast." (May 21, 1930): 56. On the activities of song and film composers.

Steiner, Max. "Setting Emotions to Music." (July 31, 1940): 41.

"First Entirely Jazz Background on a Pic Set on Coast by Stevens." 195:10 (August 11, 1954): 45. On Leith Stevens's score for *Private Hell 36*.

"Tiomkin's Plea: Give Film Music More 'Liberty.'" 205:9 (January 30, 1957): 4, 63.

Tiomkin, Dimitri. "The Maturity of Music for Motion Pictures." 213:6 (January 7, 1959): 212.

"Composing-for-TV Emerging as New Art Form: Elmer Bernstein's Status." 214:1 (March 4, 1959): 22, 42.

"New Film Directors Accenting Music as Potent Dramatic Angle: Alex North." 220 (October 12, 1960): 59.

Tiomkin, Dimitri. "On Motion Picture Music." 221 (January 4, 1961): 207.

Tiomkin, Dimitri. "Don't Underestimate Filmusic." 229 (December 5, 1962): 42.

"Elmer Bernstein Warns of Hazards in Trying to Write Pic Tunes as Pop Hits." 237 (February 10, 1965): 55.

Shaindlin, Jack. "Don't Shoot the Piano Player." 241:7 (January 5, 1966): 205. Reprinted in Limbacher.

275:1 (May 15, 1974). Includes a "Film Music" section with articles on British composer John Cameron, Philippe Sarde, and "Gold Albums from Film Soundtracks" from 1958 to 1974.

Beaupre, Lee. "Pic Scores' Dissonant Theme." 275:1 (May 15, 1974): 58, 68. On the dumping of the original score for *The Exorcist* in favor of prerecorded music.

"[David] Raksin Raps State of Art." 275:1 (May 15, 1974): 59, 70.

Goldsmith, Jerry. "Vital Dialog in Film Making between Director and Composer." 275:1 (May 15, 1974): 61.

"[Jerry] Fielding Tells Everybody Off: Coast Film Composer Raps Film Academy, Producers, Directors, Rock and Our Epoch." 294:7 (March 21, 1979): 90.

Schipper, Henry. "Don't Call Al Bart 'The Grand Old Man.'" (July 1, 1985): 9, 25. On the agent.

Zimmerman, Kevin. "Gotham's Film-Scoring Scare." 349:5 (November 23, 1992): 60. On the closing of BMG studios in New York.

Rooney, David. "Work of Notes: Composer Considers Contribution to Films." 361:11 (January 22, 1996): 89ff. Ennio Morricone interview.

Koehler, Robert. "Five Composers Spawn 'New Golden Era' of Film Music." (July 16, 1996): 16. On David Arnold, Danny Elfman, Elliot Goldenthal, Michael Kamen, and Thomas Newman.

Burlingame, Jon. "Studio Musicians Have Meaty Chops." 369 (November 17–23, 1997): 33–34.

Burlingame, Jon. "Indie Scores Offer Creative Leeway." (July 16, 1998): 6.

Burlingame, Jon. "The Reel Thing: Popularity of Live Film Music Spans Country." (July 30, 1998): A8, A11.

Burlingame, Jon. "The Maestro Scores Again." 376 (August 30–September 5, 1999): A20ff. On Maurice Jarre.

Burlingame, Jon. "Melody Makers." 377 (November 15–21, 1999): N12.

Burlingame, Jon. "Music Mentor Ties Hollywood's Greats." 380 (2000): 24. On Mario Castelnuovo-Tedesco.

Burlingame, Jon. "Jeff Beal." 384 (August 27–September 2, 2001): 59. On Beal's score for *Pollack*.

Burlingame, Jon. "Joel Diamond." 384 (August 27–September 2, 2001): 60ff.

Burlingame, Jon. "Reinhold Heil and Johnny Klimek." 384 (August 27–September 2, 2001): 62.

VLIFE (supplement to *Variety*)

Burlingame, Jon. "You Shoot, They Score." (December 2003): 85–86. Brief profiles on Mark Mothersbaugh, Van Dyke Parks, Heitor Pereira, The RZA, and Stephen Trask.

Burlingame, Jon, as told to. "Where the Art Is: Thomas Newman, Composer for *Angels in America* and *Lemony Snicket*, Talks about His Favorite Place to Work—Home." (August–September 2004): 46.

Variety International Film Guide (UK)

British film guide, annual review of world cinema edited by Peter Cowie and others, published since 1964 in New York by A. S. Barnes, and in London by Tantivy Press. Title was changed from *International Film Guide* in 1989. Articles on film music include "25 Leading Composers: An Index," by Felix Bucher, containing a brief survey of the foremost living film composers in the world from Georges Auric to Franz Waxman, 37–42 (1967); "Film Music," by Tony Thomas, outlining the state of the art and including Thomas's ten best soundtrack LP list, 79–85 (1973); "Hugo Friedhofer," by Page Cook, containing a biographical sketch with filmography and discography, 398–404 (1974). Tom Vallance wrote a yearly column on soundtrack albums (1974–1981). The 1996 annual contains a section on film music with the following articles: "The Year in Review," by John Williams (editor of *Music from the Movies*), 61–64; "Ennio Morricone: A Profile," by John Mansell, 64–66, with discography; additional composer profiles (with selective discographies) by Mansell include Luis Enriquez Bacalov, Elmer Bernstein, Francesco De Masi, Patrick Doyle, Jerry Goldsmith, James Horner, Maurice Jarre, Trevor Jones, Riz Ortolani, Zbigniew Preisner, and Hans Zimmer, 67–76; "CAM: Profile of a Pioneer in Soundtrack Recordings," by Mansell, 77–78. "Film Music Annual Roundup," by Andy Kline, 57–59 (1997); "Luis Enriquez Bacalov, composer," 59–60, 100 (1997); "A Zeitgeist Thing: The Music Supervisor and Modern Soundtracks," by Andrew Poppy, 67–71 (1998); "Mason Daring: Bending the Music," by Philip Kemp, 71–72 (1998); "Jerry Goldsmith: Boldly Scoring for 40 Years," by Jon Burlingame, 57–62 (1999); "Filmusic," a listing of soundtrack dealers around the globe, 58–61 (2000).

The Velvet Light Trap (US)

Critical journal of film and television published by the University of Wisconsin Press;

good source for reviews of books on film music.

Gomez, Joseph A. "*Mahler* and the Methods of Ken Russell's Films on Composers." 14 (Winter 1975): 45–50. Music in Russell's biographical films, including *Mahler* (1974).

Gorbman, Claudia. "The Drama's Melos: Max Steiner and *Mildred Pierce*." 19 (1982): 35–39. Analysis.

Yanc, Jeff. "'More Than a Woman': Music, Masculinity and Male Spectacle in *Saturday Night Fever* and *Staying Alive*." 38 (Fall 1996): 39–50.

Special issue, 51 (Spring 2003) ["Sounding Off: Film Sound/Film Music"]

Smith, Jeff. "Black Faces, White Voices: The Politics of Dubbing in *Carmen Jones*." 29–42.

Jha, Priya. "Lyrical Nationalism: Gender, Friendship, and Excess in 1970s Hindi Cinema." 43–53.

White-Stanley, Debra. "'God Give Me Strength': The Melodramatic Sound Tracks of Director Allison Anders." 54–66.

"An Interview with Rick Altman." 67–72. Interviewed by the editors.

"Panel Discussion on Film Sound/Film Music: Jim Buhler, Anahid Kassabian, David Neumeyer, and Robynn Stilwell." 73–91. Transcription of an online chat room.

Venice (US)

Magazine covering the Los Angeles arts and entertainment scene since 1988, named after the funky beach neighborhood. Often contains interviews of film composers by contributing editor Daniel Schweiger, a music editor specializing in temp-tracking films. (Schweiger is married to composer-orchestrator Penka Kouneva.) While the lengthy interviews often focus on the composer's latest project, other topics and previous films are often discussed. Schweiger also reviews soundtracks in his "On the Score" column.

Schweiger, Daniel. "James Newton Howard Is on Target with His First Western Score for *Wyatt Earp*." (July 1994): 40–42. Interview.

Schweiger, Daniel. "Blowing His Horn." (September 1994): 43–47. Mark Isham interview.

Schweiger, Daniel. "Memoirs of a Visible Composer." (March 1992): 42–43. Interview with Shirley Walker.

Schweiger, Daniel. "The Newman Redemption: Thomas Newman's Music Breaks through *Shawshank*'s Prison Bars." (October 1994): 44–47. Interview.

(August 1995). Maurice Jarre interview.

Schweiger, Daniel. "Carter and the Coens: From Blood Simple to Fargo, No One Plays Murder and Madness for the Coen Brothers Like Carter Burwell." (March 1996): 36–38. Carter Burwell profile and interview.

Schweiger, Daniel. "Arnold's Day." (July 1996): 51–53. David Arnold profile and interview.

(August 1996). Shirley Walker and John Carpenter interview on *Escape from L.A.*

Schweiger, Daniel. "The Nutty Composer: Composer David Newman's the King of Comedy, but After *The Klumps*, He's Looking to Step Off the Throne." (August 2000): 62–64. Interview.

Schweiger, Daniel. "Angelo Badalamenti: The Madman and His Muse." (October 2001): 68–73. Interview.

Schweiger, Daniel. "Playing It *Cooler*: Mark Isham Brings Back that Old Vegas Jazz." (November 2003): 54–57. Interview.

Schweiger, Daniel. "Harry Gregson-Williams: From Venice to *Narnia*." (December 2005–January 2006): 18. Profile.

Vertigo (UK)
Wood, Jason. "Song of Innocence and Experience." 2:9 (Autumn–Winter 2005): 10–11. Includes a discussion by director Lucile Hadzilhalilovic on the use of music in her film *Innocence*.

Video Magazine (US)
Roman, Shari. "Tarquin Gotch, Soundtrack Specialist." 13:2 (May 1989): 18. Profile of the music supervisor.

Videomaker (US)
Alldrin, Loren. "Do-It-Yourself Music." 14 (March 2000): 131–34. Alldrin contributed other articles in 1999 and 2000 on the topic of audio that often mentioned various aspects of music.

Views and Film Index (US)
Weekly publication from New York dedicated to the trade interests of moving pictures. In 1906 this became the first American trade paper devoted exclusively to motion pictures. Succeeded by *The Film Index* in 1908.
"The Demand for Realistic Exhibitions: Music an Important Factor." 1:25 (October 13, 1906): 3. Offers the early commentary, "Many exhibitors are prone to overlook the importance of music as an essential to the success of the show."

Vitagraph Bulletin (US) and **Vitagraph Life Portrayals** (US)
Published by the Vitagraph Company of America to aid exhibitors, these periodicals included announcements and descriptions of Vitagraph films. According to musicologist Martin Marks's *Music and the Silent Film* (1997), the *Bulletin* began publishing suggestions for appropriate music for individual films in the first half of October 1910. The *Life Portrayals* were published semi-weekly beginning in July 1911, and by the third issue included "Incidental Music Suggestions for Vitagraph Films." By 1916 this had been shortened to "Music Suggestions." The paragraph-long suggestions could include specific musical compositions and/or generalizations, such as "play Western music."

Articles (selected)
"Special Music for Special Features." 3:4 (June 1913): 4, 6.
"Do You Use Vitagraph Special Music?" 3:7 (September 1913): 4.
"Something New in Music Cues." 4:10 (January 1915): 4, 6.

Vitaphone News (US)
News from the Vitaphone Project in New Jersey, from project director Ron Hutchinson since 1992. Documents early sound shorts, including restoration and preservation efforts and found discs.

Warner Club News (US)
Published for Warner Club members (Warner Bros. employees) at the studios in Burbank from 1933 to circa 1961. Little specific coverage of the music department.
Forker, Jack. "Scoring a Picture." (Thanksgiving 1939): 1, 13. A staffer follows a Max Steiner score through production.
Goedeck, Eddie. "Musicalities." (January 1944): 24. Profiles music department staffer Jaro Churain, longtime secretary to Erich Wolfgang Korngold.

"This Month's Thumbnail Sketch." (March 1948). On Carl Stalling. Reprinted in Daniel Goldmark, *Tunes for 'Toons* (2005).

What's Happening in Hollywood (US)

Published by the Motion Picture Association of America in Hollywood from 1943 to 1949. Alice Evans Field, the publication's director, apparently wrote most of the articles.

"Scoring Dramatic Pictures at M-G-M." No. 30 (April 13, 1946): 2–3. On David J. Chatkin, head of the music department, and comments on scores by Scott Bradley, Bronislaw Kaper, Nathaniel Shilkret, and Herbert Stothart. Reprinted in *Film Music Notes* (May 1946).

"*Film Music Notes*." No. 31 (April 20, 1946): 2–3. History of the publication.

"With Music and Lyrics." 5:15 (April 5, 1948): 2–3. On studio musicals in production.

"Music Scoring." 5:17 (May 3, 1948): 2–3. On current assignments and so on.

Wide Angle (US)

Academic quarterly journal of theory, criticism, and practice, published by Ohio University and the Athens Center for Film and Video in Ohio.

Altman, Charles F. "The American Film Musical: Paradigmatic Structure and Mediatory Function." 2:2 (1978): 10–17. Emphasis on *New Moon* (1940) and *Gigi*.

Lehman, Peter, and Jonathan Rosenbaum. "Filmmaking: Film Music: An Interview with Jerry Fielding and Dan Carlin." 4:3 (1980): 64–68. Transcribed from the Sound and Music in Cinema Workshop held at the Appalachian Regional Media Center in Athens, Ohio, October 1979.

Gorbman, Claudia. "*Cleo from Five to Seven:* Music as Mirror." 4:4 (1981): 38–49. Analysis of the music for the 1962 film.

Hamand, Carol. "Sound and Image." 6:2 (1984): 24–33. A three-page section on music includes musical accompaniment for silent films and the early sound film.

Creekmur, C. K. "The Space of Recording: The Production of Popular Music as Spectacle." 10:2 (1988): 32–40.

Doty, Alexander. "Music Sells Movies: (Re)New(ed) Conservatism in Film Marketing." 10:2 (1988): 70–79. Historical (1950s–1970s) and current trends in marketing.

World Film News (UK)

Published monthly in London from 1936 to 1938. Many issues devote a page to "Music," with articles of current interest. Absorbed *Cinema Quarterly*.

Hughes, Spike. "Music in Films." 1:1 (April 1936): 26. Essay on functional music and the melodic line.

"Milhaud to Work for Toeplitz." 1:1 (April 1936): 26. On Darius Milhaud.

Eisler, Hans [*sic*]. "Music and Film: Illustration or Creation?" 1:2 (May 1936): 23. On his film composing experiences.

Jaubert, Maurice. "Music and Film." 1:4 (July 1936): 31. Criticism of current practice.

Leigh, Walter. "Music and Microphones." 1:5 (August 1936): 40.

"Weill Scores *Pirate Fantasy*." 1:5 (August 1936): 40. On Kurt Weill's score for *A High Wind in Jamaica*.

"French Composers Work on Royalty System." 1:6 (September 1936): 46. Regarding SACEM.

"Renaissance by Radio: Milhaud Wants Decentralisation." 1:7 (October 1936): 46. Darius Milhaud criticizes film producers.

Britten, Benjamin. "*As You Like It*: Walton's Music." 1:7 (October 1936): 46.

Perkoff, Leslie. "Music: Notes and Theories." 2:1 (April 1937): 41.

"Music Can Provide Only Interior Rhythm, Says Alberto Cavalcanti." 2:4 (July 1937): 26–27. The director discusses music.

"Wagner, Verdi and the Film by Darius Milhaud." 2:4 (July 1937): 27. Translated from the Italian magazine *Cinema*.

Chapter 10

Music Periodicals

The Absolute Sound (US)
High-end journal of audio and music.
8:31 (September 1983). Jerry Goldsmith interview.

Acoustic Guitar (US)
Dick, Stephen. "American Dream, The Musical Odyssey of Laurindo Almeida, from Bossa Nova to Jazz to Hollywood Film Scoring." No. 20 (September–October 1993). Interview.
Simmons, Michael. "A.G. at the Movies." No. 43 (July 1996). Anachronistic guitars in the movies.
Miller, Dale. "Ry Cooder, Evocative Scores from a Master of Slide." No. 43 (July 1996). On *Paris, Texas*.
Quinones, Sam. "Local Gold, Ry Cooder Uncovers a Scintillating World of Cuban Music with *Buena Vista Social Club*." No. 65 (May 1998).
Bergman, Julie. "Ax Tracks, Mark Mancina Brings Acoustic Guitar to the Movies." No. 88 (April 2000). Profile.
Kotapish, Paul. "Big Little Music: The Weird and Wonderful World of String Wizard David Lindley." No. 90 (June 2000): 48–63. An interview with the session musician and Ry Cooder collaborator.
Carnahan, Danny. "Ry Cooder: Cultural Ambassador." No. 91 (July 2000).
Bergman, Julie. "Acoustic Guitar Goes to the Movies." No. 91 (July 2000). The acoustic guitar in soundtracks, commercials, and television.

Acta Musicologica (Switzerland)
Published by the International Musicological Society.
Lek, Robbert van der, translated from Dutch by Mick Swithinbank. "Concert Music as Reused Film Music: E.-W. Korngold's Self-Arrangements." 66:2 (July–December 1994): 78–112. Korngold's reworking of film music from 1935 to 1946 in his concert works from 1946 to 1957.
Stilwell, Robynn J. "*Sense & Sensibility*: Form, Genre, and Function in the Film Score." 72:2 (2000): 219–240. Reprinted with minor changes in Claudia Gorbman, *Film Music 2*.
Bick, Sally. "Political Ironies: Hanns Eisler in Hollywood and behind the Iron Curtain." 75:1 (2003): 65–84.

African Music (South Africa)

Kubik, Gerhard. "Transcription of African Music from Silent Film: Theory and Methods." 5:2 (1972) 28–39. The author shares his experiences and methods, which include watching films in slow motion in order to write out the music being played on the screen.

American Composer's Alliance Bulletin (US)

Previously known as the *Bulletin of American Composers Alliance*.

Antheil, George. "George Antheil on Tom Scott." 6:2 (Winter 1957): 3.

Ringo, James. "Some Notes on Tom Scott's Music." 6:2 (Winter 1957): 4–12. Biography, concert music survey, and discussion of Scott's music style, with only passing references to his film career; however, the "Catalogue of Compositions" lists his film, television, and radio scores.

Whittenberg, Charles. "Ussachevsky's Film Music." 11:1 (June 1963): 5. Vladimir Ussachevsky's electronic music score for *No Exit* (1962), realized in the Columbia-Princeton Electronic Music Center in New York. This pre-Moog synthesizer score is unusual for its use of synthesized sound/music in a non-science fiction setting.

American Harp Journal (US)

Published by the American Harp Society.

Stockton, Ann Mason, and Dorothy Remsen. "Motion Picture Recording." No. 2 (1967): 8–9.

Smith, Eric J. "The Hollywood Studio Trio: Ann Mason Stockton, Catherine Gotthoffer and Dorothy Remsen on the Harp in Film." 17:2 (Winter 1999): 7–15. Biographies, reminiscences, and war stories from these session musicians active from the 1950s to the present. The three harpists were gathered by Russell Wapensky for a filmed interview related to a book project.

American Music (US)

Journal devoted to all aspects of American music, from the Sonneck Society and the University of Illinois Press.

Rosenberg, Neil V. "Image and Stereotype: Bluegrass Sound Tracks." 1:3 (Fall 1983): 1–22. Bluegrass music in film and television, including its symbolic use and associations.

Shapiro, Anne Dhu. "Action Music in American Pantomime and Melodrama, 1730–1913." 2:4 (Winter 1984): 49–72. Silent film accompaniments, such as *hurry music*, share common elements with stage melodrama (see pp. 66–69).

Nisbett, Robert F. "Louis Gruenberg's American Idiom." 3:1 (Spring 1981): 25–41.

Hubbard, Preston J. "Synchronized Sound and Movie-House Musicians, 1926–29." 3:4 (Winter 1985): 429–41. On the displacement of musicians from movie theaters, including attempts to prevent the use of recorded music in movie houses.

Gabbard, Krin. "Race and Reappropriation: Spike Lee Meets Aaron Copland." 18:4 (Winter 2000): 370–90. On the director's use of Copland's music in his film *He Got Game* (1998).

Brackett, David. "Banjos, Biopics, and Compilation Scores: The Movies Go Country." 19:3 (Fall 2001): 247–90. Examines music in *Five Easy Pieces* (1970), *The Last Picture Show* (1971), *Tender Mercies* (1983), and *Sweet Dreams* (1985).

Jenkins, Jennifer R. "'Say It with Firecrackers': Defining the 'War Musical' of the 1940s." 19:3 (Fall 2001): 315–39.

Hubbert, Julie. "'Whatever Happened to Great Movie Music?' *Cinéma Vérité* and the Hollywood Film Music of the Early 1970s." 21:2 (Summer 2003): 180–213. Reexamines music of the time, including the displacement of traditional music and Hollywood composers. The title is a reference to articles by David Raksin and Elmer Bernstein that bemoaned the rise of popular music in film.

22:1 (Spring 2004). Special film music issue; contents listed below.

Patterson, David W. "Music, Structure, and Metaphor in Stanley Kubrick's *2001: A Space Odyssey*." 22:3 (Fall 2004): 444–74. Detailed analysis of the use of pre-existing music in the film.

Bick, Sally. "*Of Mice and Men*: Copland, Hollywood, and American Musical Modernism." 23:4 (Winter 2005): 426–72.

Mazullo, Mark. "Remembering Pop: David Lynch and the Sound of the '60s." 23:4 (Winter 2005): 493–513. On the director's use of American popular songs.

Special issue, 22:1 (Spring 2004)

Special issue on music and the moving image, with an introduction by coeditors Gillian B. Anderson, Thomas Riis, and Ronald Sadoff. Selected papers from conferences at New York University and the University of Colorado, Boulder, 2001.

Gorbman, Claudia. "Aesthetics and Rhetoric." 14–26.

Herzog, Amy. "Discordant Visions: The Peculiar Musical Images of the Soundies Jukebox Film." 27–39.

Greenspan, Charlotte. "Irving Berlin in Hollywood: The Art of Plugging a Song in Film." 40–49.

Swayne, Steve. "So Much 'More': The Music of *Dick Tracy* (1990)." 50–63. On the use of pre-existing music and music by Stephen Sondheim.

Sadoff, Ronald H. "Composition by Corporate Committee: Recipe for Cliché." 64–75.

Link, Stan. "Nor the Eye with Seeing: The Sound of Vision in Film." 76–90.

Clague, Mark. "Playing in 'Toon: Walt Disney's *Fantasia* (1940) and the Imagineering of Classical Music." 91–109.

Russett, Robert. "Animated Sound and Beyond." 110–21.

Neumeyer, David. "Merging Genres in the 1940s: The Musical and the Dramatic Feature Film." 122–32.

Knapp, Raymond. "History, *The Sound of Music*, and Us." 133–44.

Morris, Mitchell. "*Cabaret*, America's Weimar, and Mythologies of the Gay Subject." 145–57.

American Music Research Center Journal (US)

Sauer, Rodney. "Photoplay Music: A Reusable Repertory for Silent Film Scoring." 8–9 (1998–1999): 55–76. Includes references to the music of Gaston Borch, Erno Rapée, and John Zamecnik.

John, Antony. "Songs and the Audience in Early Movie Musicals." 11 (2001): 35–45.

American Music Teacher (US)

Fink, M. "How Music Functions in Films." 40:2 (1990): 24–25.

The American Organist (US)

Leading resource for musical presentation, repertoire, and score suggestions for accompanying silent films, published monthly in New York, 1919–1930. Articles; biographical sketches, often with photographs; news ("Los Angeles Notes"); reviews ("Critiques"); music suggestions; and more are well documented and indexed in Anderson and Wright, *Film Music Bibliography I* (1995), from which a selection appears below. Topics include the debate concerning the unit organ versus the console organ and the displacement of organists with the advent of sound films in the late 1920s. Documents organs in theaters; schools and theater organ departments, including the American Conservatory and the Del Castillo Theater School; and groups including the Society of Theatre Organists and the Los Angeles Organists Club. Contributors include Frank Stewart Adams, T. Scott Buhrman, and Roy L. Medcalfe. In 1967 the American Guild of Organists resurrected the magazine.

Webbe, William Y. "Cinema and the Organist." 2:3 (March 1919): 113.

Taylor, Edwin Lyles. "Photoplay Accompanying." 2:8 (August 1919): 333–35.

Hamrick, George Lee. "Photoplaying." Series from 2:12 (December 1919): 489–91 through 3:6 (June 1920): 209–11. Topics include playing the drama.

Maitland, Rollo F. "Photoplaying in the Stanley." 3:4 (April 1920): 119–22.

Buhrman, T. Scott. "Photoplays Deluxe." 3:5 (1920): 157–75. On Hugo Riesenfeld.

Adams, Frank Stewart. "Photoplaying, Dramatic Potentialities of Photoplay Music." 3:9 (September 1920): 324–27.

Hansford, Montiville Morris. "Pictures and Picture Playing." 3:10 (October 1920): 368–70.

Cooper, J. Van Cleft. "Concerning Comedies." 3:12 (December 1920): 443.

Swinnen, Firmin. "The Theater Organ." 3:12 (December 1920): 444–47.

Nason, Ruby Belle. "Improvising for Picture Work." 4:8 (August 1921): 276.

Borch, Gaston. "A Repertoire Suggestion." 4:9 (September 1921): 315.

"S. G. del Castillo [*sic*]." 4:10 (October 1921): 351. On L. G. del Castillo.

Medcalfe, Roy L. "Synchronizing the Organist." 4:12 (December 1921): 409–10.

"Roy L. Medcalfe." 4:12 (December 1921): 417–18. Profile.

Berentsen, Robert. "Qualifications of the Theater Organist." 5:1 (January 1922): 30–34.

Adams, Frank Stewart. "Evolution of Theatre Organ Playing." 5:2 (February 1922): 70–72.

Buhrman, T. Scott, and Latham True. "The Kinema Organ—Los Angeles." 5:7 (July 1922): 261–64.

Lang, Edith, and J. Harold Weisel. "Cue Sheets: Two Discussions." 5:7 (July 1922): 289–91.

"Wurlitzerizing in the Rialto." 5:7 (July 1922): 292–94.

del Castillo, L. G. "Cue Sheets and Something Better." 5:10 (October 1922): 452–53.

Medcalfe, Roy L. "When Organist and Conductor Meet: What Constantin Bakaleinikoff Does about It." 6:1 (January 1923): 40–41.

Berentsen, Robert. "Impressions from a European Trip." 6:1 (January 1923): 45–47.

Lang, Edith. "The Theater Organist." 6:2 (February 1923): 74–76.

Naftel, H. St. John. "Comedy Playing." 6:4 (March 1923): 243.

Riesenfeld, Hugo. "Jazz Goes to the Congressional Library." 6:7 (July 1923): 455.

Audsley, George Ashdown. "How to Write an Organ Specification." Parts 14–16: "The Motion Picture Theater Organ." 6:12 (December 1923): 723–28; 7:1 (January 1924): 10–17; 7:2 (February 1924): 74–80.

Riesenfeld, Hugo. "European Impressions." 7:2 (February 1924): 96–97.

"The Loew Music System: How Ernst Luz Manages the Complicated Routine of Orchestral Scores and Film Circuits." 7:6 (June 1924): 332–35.

"Miss Edith Lang." 7:11 (November 1924): 638–39. Profile.

Medcalfe, Roy L. "Chauncey Haines." 8:5 (May 1925): 201. Profile.

D'Or, Edmund Mie. "Worser Music for Worser Films." 8:12 (December 1925): 424–26.

Medcalfe, Roy L. "Stunt the Picture or Your Income." 9:4 (April 1926): 111–12.

Medcalfe, Roy L. "Scores of Scores but Little Art." 9:5 (May 1926): 148–50.

Hopkins, Henry Patterson. "Photoplaying—An Art." In five parts from 9:7 (July 1926): 206–7 through 9:11 (November 1926): 325.

Frise, Sallie. "Never the Twain Shall Meet." 9:12 (December 1926): 361. Claims that the first organ used in a movie theater was in Chicago in 1913, according to Anderson, *Film Music Bibliography I* (1995).

Cooper, J. Van Cleft. "They Still Like Pictures: Music May Be Sweet and Beautiful but the Picture Is Inane and What Could Empty Heads Like Better Than That? It's Your Own Fault If You're a Photoplayer." 10:6 (June 1927): 153–55.

"Where Is It?" 10:9 (September 1927): 232–33. On Ernst Luz and his *Symphonic Color Guide*.

Simpson, G. Criss. "Paris as I Saw It." 10:10 (October 1927): 262.

"Mr. Frank Lanterman." 11:7 (July 1928): 252. Profile.

"Vitaphone et al.: An Examination of the Results of Filmized Music and a Few Reflections on the Whole Pack of Inventions." 11:10 (October 1928): 442–43.

"Mr. L. G. Del Castillo." 11:10 (October 1928): 449–50. Profile.

"A Genuine Opportunity: Filmized Music Makes the Organ Sound as a Pleasant Relief Whereas the Orchestra Makes It Sound as a Letdown—Who Says This Is Not to Our Advantage?" 11:12 (December 1928): 568.

"Another Solution: The Tone-Picture Film in the Paramount with Organ Accompaniment." 12:4 (April 1929): 228.

Buhrman, T. Scott. "A Photoplayer's Delight: The Moller Organ in the Met Theater of Philadelphia Where Organists Have All They Can Want." 12:8 (August 1929): 35–37.

Buhrman, T. Scott. "Here We Are." 13:1 (January 1930): 34. On the demise of the magazine's Photoplaying Department.

Smith, Rollin. "Firmin Swinnen." 53:6 (November 1970): 28–31.

American Record Guide (US)

Independent journal of critical opinion, primarily covering classical music. Soundtrack reviews by Mark Koldys, Milton A. Caine, and others from 1979 to 2005. A short-lived "Soundtracks" column by Noah Andrew Trudeau appeared in the early 1990s; see, for example, vol. 56, no. 2 (March–April 1993), pp. 202–3. Film music articles often tie in with recent record releases.

"Sir William Walton's Shakespeare Film Scores." 30:9 (May 1964): 881–83. Review.

Ellis, William. "A Chat with Michael Nyman." 60:2 (March–April 1997): 32–34. Brief interview.

Tibbetts, John C. "Giving Sound to the Silents: Carl Davis—Master Film Composer." 60:4 (July–August 1997): 11–14.

Koldys, Mark. "Film Music." 61:2 (March–April 1998): 51–68. Survey of music on compact disc by Elmer Bernstein, Jerry Goldsmith, Bernard Herrmann, Erich Wolfgang Korngold, Alfred Newman, Alex North, Miklós Rózsa, Max Steiner, Dimitri Tiomkin, Franz Waxman, John Williams, and others.

Raykoff, Ivan. "Seeing Is Hearing." 61:3 (May–June 1998): 11–13. Report on a group seeking to promote more filmed music.

Grove, Jeff. "The Saga of *The Red Violin*." 62:4 (July–August 1999): 19–21. On the collaboration between John Corigliano and violinist Joshua Bell.

Sullivan, Jack. "Sounding the Unconscious: Hitchcock's Film Music Probed the Psyche." 63:2 (March–April 2000): 20–22.

ASCAP in Action (US)

Published by the American Society of Composers, Authors and Publishers in New York, primarily for its membership. Print and photo coverage of ASCAP events, including awards to film and television composers and film scoring workshops. Preceded by *ASCAP Today* and superseded by *Playback*.

Duning, George. "Scoring with the Click Track." 1:1 (Fall 1979): 46.

Addison, John, and others. "Getting Started in Film and TV Scoring." (Fall 1981): 36–38.

Mancini, Henry. "Music in Motion." (Fall 1984): 21–22.

Scoppa, Bud. "The Marriage of Film and Music." (Fall 1988): 50. Panel discussion.

Diesenhouse, Susan, and Bill Bernstein. "Film on Film." (Fall 1991): 16–21. Short bios and interview quotes for Angelo Badalamenti, Carter Burwell, Stewart Copeland, Cliff Eidelman, Brad Fiedel, Richard Gibbs, James Horner, Mark Isham, Ira Newborn, Randy Newman, Marc Shaiman, and Howard Shore.

ASCAP Today (US)

Published by the American Society of Composers, Authors and Publishers in New York. Contains good coverage on songwriters. Published from 1967 to 1978; superceded by *ASCAP in Action*.

Adams, Stanley. "Music and Motion Pictures." 1:2 (June 1967): A.

"It All Started with *Ramona*." [5?]:1 (1971): 32–33.

Paisley, Tom. "Henry Mancini: Doin' It Right." 9:1 (Spring 1978): 6–10.

Asian Music: Journal of the Society for Asian Music (US)

Marcus, Scott. "Recycling Indian Film-Songs: Popular Music as a Source of Melodies for North Indian Folk Musicians." 24:1 (Fall 1992–Winter 1993): 101–10.

Arnold, Alison E. "Aspects of Production and Consumption in the Popular Hindi Film Song Industry." 24:1 (Fall 1992–Winter 1993): 122–36.

Stock, Jonathan. "Reconsidering the Past: Zhou Xuan and the Rehabilitation of Early Twentieth-Century Popular Music." 26:2 (Spring–Summer 1995): 119–35. Some discussion of Chinese film songs.

Manuel, Peter. "Music, Identity, and Images of India in the Indo-Caribbean Diaspora." 29:1 (Fall 1997–Winter 1998): 17–35. Includes some discussion on film music influences.

Gibbs, Jason. "Spoken Theater, La Scène Tonkinoise, and the First Modern Vietnamese Songs." 31:2 (Spring–Summer 2000): 1–33. Includes some discussion of its influence on film music.

Booth, Gregory D. "Pandits in the Movies: Contesting the Identity of Hindustani Classical Music and Musicians in the Hindi Popular Cinema." 36:1 (Winter–Spring 2005): 60–86.

Australasian Music Research (Australia)

Kouvaras, Linda. "The Semiotic and the Symbolic in Music in Two Sweets-Smearing Scenes." 6 (2001). Examines music in *Life Is Sweet* (1990).

Australian Musical News (Australia)

Waters, Thorold. "Music's Winning Chance in the 'Talkies': Cine-Opera the Most Natural Development." 18:11 (June 1, 1929): 3–4.

Band Wagon (UK)

Huntley, John. "Music by Appointment: Sir Arnold Bax and *Oliver Twist*." 7:2 (August 1948): 26–27.

BBC Music Magazine (UK)
Duchen, Jessica. "Composer of the Month: Erich Wolfgang Korngold." 59 (May 1997): 36–40.

Beethoven Forum (US)
Published by the University of Illinois Press.

Wierzbicki, James. "Banality Triumphant: Iconographic Use of Beethoven's Ninth Symphony in Recent Films." 10:2 (Fall 2003): 113–38. Notably for *The Man Who Wasn't There.*

Brown, Kristi A. "*Pathétique Noir:* Beethoven and *The Man Who Wasn't There.*" 10:2 (Fall 2003): 139–61.

Stilwell, Robynn J. "Hysterical Beethoven." 10:2 (Fall 2003): 162–82.

Beckerman, Michael. "A Dialogue Concerning the Pond Scene in *Immortal Beloved.*" 10:2 (Fall 2003): 233–46.

Berklee Today (US)
Alumni magazine for Berklee College of Music in Boston. Occasionally features profiles and interviews with film-scoring graduates. Class of 1973 alumnus Mark Small asks interviewees about their Berklee training, breaking into the business, lessons learned, and current projects. Berklee was founded by Lawrence Berk, who named the school after his son, Lee. It is one of the leading schools outside of the Los Angeles area to offer professional training, with a popular music bent, to aspiring film composers.

Taylor, Andrew. "Alan Silvestri: To *The Abyss* and Back." 1:3 (Spring 1990): 12–16. Interview with Silvestri '70.

Taylor, Andrew. "High Style on the Low End." 3:1 (Summer 1991): 16–20. Interview with session musician bassist Abraham Laboriel '72.

Small, Mark L. "*The Tonight Show*'s Jazz Messenger: Saxophonist Branford Marsalis '81 Talks about Calling the Tunes for Jay Leno." 4:2 (Fall 1992): 12–16. Interview.

Small, Mark L. "Beyond the Mind's Ear." 5:1 (Summer 1993): 12–16. Interview with Jan Hammer '69.

Small, Mark L. "A Place in Time." 6:1 (Summer 1994): 12–16. Interview with session musician drummer John Robinson '75.

Small, Mark L. "The Best Is Yet to Come." 6:3 (Spring 1995): 12–16. Interview with Quincy Jones '51.

Small, Mark L. "Primetime Tunes: Composer Alf Clausen '66 Is Riding High Underscoring *The Simpsons.*" 8:1 (Summer 1996): 14–18. Interview.

Small, Mark. "Subliminal Scores." 9:2 (Fall 1997): 16–20. Interview with Howard Shore '69.

Small, Mark. "'A Team' Player." 10:1 (Summer 1998): 16–20. Interview with session musician bassist Neil Stubenhaus.

Small, Mark. "Alum Profile: Kevin Kaska '94: Taking the High Road to Hollywood." 14:3 (Winter 2002).

Small, Mark. "Alum Profile: Curt Sobel '78: A Film Tribute to an American Icon." 16:2 (Fall 2004). On his score for *Ray.*

Billboard (US)
International newsweekly of music and home entertainment. In the late 1940s and early 1950s, the "On the Sound Track" or "Hollywood" subheadings of "Music as Written" contained music assignments; see September 23, 1950, p. 28. In 1996 David Sprague wrote a column on soundtracks and film score news called "The Reel Thing" and later

"Nothin' Like the Reel Thing." From around March 1998 to March 2000 Catherine Applefeld Olson contributed a column, "Soundtracks and Film Score News." Charles Karel Bouley took over from Olson in 2000, and the column was once again named "The Reel Thing" in 2001. Carla Hay wrote "Soundtracks" in 2003 and 2004 and "Movies&Music" in 2003. "Words&Music" on songwriting, sometimes for film, was written by Irv Lichtman in 1997 and by Jim Bessman from 2003 to 2005. Selections below give a hint of the scope of the news items.

"Screen Composers' Beef to Gov't." (May 7, 1949): 18.

"Switch of Film Song Titles Is New Exploitation Twist." (June 6, 1953): 1, 16.

"Making a Movie? Gotta Have a Song." (November 12, 1955): 34.

"Don't Abuse, Stevens Warns on Electronic Synthesizer." (March 29, 1959): 15.

"Soundtracks Should Be Sold Separately—[Neal] Hefti." (July 18, 1964): 4.

"Big 3 and Its Technicolor Ties." (September 2, 1967): RFM17. On the dominance of Robbins-Feist-Miller as a publisher of film songs.

Oliver, Dick. "Soundtrack LP's from Vintage Movies Enjoy a Renaissance with or without Impetus of the Nostalgia Wave." (May 4, 1974): N6, N34, N48.

McCullaugh, J. "Film Composer's Lot Not Easy: [Bill] Conti Considers Himself Lucky." 89 (August 20, 1977): 18.

Harrison, Ed. "A Day in the Life of Quincy Jones." 90 (July 15, 1978): 75.

Sippel, John. "Film Music Creators Finally Making a Buck." (March 17, 1979): 14, 110.

Peterson, Susan. "Selling a Hit Soundtrack: Key Label Executives Analyze Their Approach to the Marketing of Movie Music." (October 6, 1979): ST3.

Forrest, Rick. "The Creative Dilemma: Schifrin, Hamlisch, Jabara, Williams, Mancini and More Offer Insight." (October 6, 1979): ST3, ST4.

Manson, Eddy Lawrence. "Composer without Portfolio." (May 26, 1984). On the lack of royalties for arrangers.

Henderson, Richard. "Keeping the Scores on the Soundtracks: Are Song-Based Movie CDs Losing Track of the Instrumental Compositions?" (September 9, 1995): 58–60.

Henderson, Richard. "Don Was: Keeping Track of the Scores: The Artist's Vision Applies to Film As Well As Music." (March 1, 1997): DW16.

Lichtman, Irv. "[John] Barry Makes Movies' Music Matter." (February 6, 1999): 41, 44.

Smith, Steve. "Philip on Film: Glass Continues to Score." (July 21, 2001): 13, 100.

Hay, Carla. "The Last Word: A Q&A with Kathy Nelson." (July 26, 2003): 88.

Bessman, Jim. "[Clint] Eastwood Dives into Scoring for *Mystic River*." (November 15, 2003): 58.

Morris, Chris. "Eastwood Discusses Film Music." (November 29, 2003): 8, 67.

Hay, Carla. "Breaking into the Big Screen: More Recording Artists Are Scoring Films." (January 29, 2005): 5, 46.

Issues with special sections on soundtracks

"Soundtracks." (May 7, 1994): 47–56.

"Sound Tracks." (April 29, 1995): 54–56. Articles on radio airplay of soundtracks and music supervision.

"The Reel Thing." (May 9, 1998): 19–28. Articles by Catherine Applefeld Olson, Carrie Bell, and others on increased demand for soundtracks, soundtrack news from around the world, and profiles of music supervisors Sharon Boyle, John Houlihan, Randy Gerston, Kathy Nelson, and Alex Steyermark.

Black Music Research Journal (US)

Murphy, Paula. "Films for the Black Music Researcher." 7 (1987): 45–64. A list of 16mm educational, documentary, or instructional short films.

Black Perspective in Music (US)
"New Music (1970–72)." 1:1 (Spring 1973) 97–100. Lists premieres and/or publication data for various categories of black music, including music for films, and musical films (films depicting musical activities).

Bluegrass Unlimited (US)
Knopf, Bill. "Songs from the Stage and Screen." 14 (June 1980): 54. On banjo music.

BMI Bulletin (US)
Bimonthly newsletter for members of Broadcast Music Inc. John Tynan, a frequent contributor, worked on the West Coast edition of *Down Beat*.
"John Lewis." (October 1962).
Wilson, John S. "Jack Shaindlin." (November 1962): 31–33.
"Johnny Richards." (May 1963): 36–37. Profile.
"Jerry Goldsmith." (September 1963): 28–30. Profile.
Tynan, John. "Profile: Lionel Newman." (October 1963): 30–33.
Tynan, John. "Fred Steiner." (February 1964): 36–39.
Tynan, John. "Profile: Dominic Frontiere." (March 1964): 35–36.
Tynan, John. "Profile: Jerry Fielding." (June 1964): 28–30.
Korall, Burt. "Profile: Frank Lewin." (June 1964): 30–31.
Tynan, John. "Johnny Williams." (date undetermined): 36–38.

BMI: The Many Worlds of Music (US)
Prepared by the Broadcast Music Inc. public relations department in New York for members of BMI. Published monthly from 1964 to 1972 and quarterly from 1973 to 1987. Russell Sanjek, who wrote a book on popular music, was vice president of BMI. News, honors, and documentation of the organization's events, including good coverage of television music. Superseded by *MusicWorld*.
Wilson, John. "Jacques Belasco." (October 1967): 17. Profile.
Siders, Harvey. "Earle Hagen." (April 1969): 6. Profile.
Tynan, John. "Billy May." (May 1969): 22.
"The Williams Way." (June 1969): 11–12. On John Williams.
Siders, Harvey. "Leith Stevens." (June 1969): 18. Profile.
Wilson, John. "Frank Lewin." (October 1969): 18. Profile.
Siders, Harvey. "Quincy Jones." (November 1969): 16. Profile.
"John T. on Films." (March 1970): 10. On John Williams.
Shaw, Arnold. "Stanley Wilson." (April 1970): 5. Profile.
Orloff, Kathy. "Randy Newman." (April 1970): 6. Profile.
"How to Play a Movie." (April 1970): 14. On Arthur Kleiner.
Siders, Harvey. "Kenyon Hopkins." (December 1970): 18. Profile.
Siders, Harvey. "Benny Golson." (January 1971): 10. Profile.
Tynan, John. "Gil Melle." (February 1971): 21. Profile.
Siders, Harvey. "Warren Barker." (May 1971): 15. Profile.
Tynan, John. "Charles Fox." (Summer 1971): 19. Profile.
Tynan, John. "Fred Karlin." (October 1971): 19. Profile.
Tynan, John. "Duane Tatro." (January 1972): 16. Profile.
Shaw, Arnold. "John T. Williams." (February 1972): 6. Profile.
Siders, Harvey. "Pat Williams." (March 1972): 21. Profile.
Chapin, Louis. "Walter Carlos." (April 1972): 6. Profile.
Tynan, John. "Joel Hirschhorn." No. 3 (1972): 35. Profile.

Tynan, John. "Sherman Brothers." No. 5 (1972): 28. Profile.
"*The Score*: BMI's Film Documentary." No. 1 (February 1974): 4–13. Transcript for
   Earle Hagen's documentary on film music.
"*The Score*: The Writers in Profile." No. 1 (February 1974): 14–33. Brief biographies
   (and photos) for BMI-affiliated composers, with prime-time television composers of
   the time particularly well represented: Charles Albertine, Warren Barker, Ian Bernard,
   Elmer Bernstein, Harry Betts, Carl Brandt, Leslie Bricusse, Emil Cadkin, Robert Co-
   bert, Irwin Coster, Alexander Courage, Jack Elliott, Ray Ellis, Charles Fox, Hugo
   Friedhofer, Dominic Frontiere, Harry Geller, Billy Goldenberg, Jerry Goldsmith,
   Benny Golson, George Greeley, Dave Grusin, Earle Hagen, Dick Hazard, Guy Hem-
   ric, Bernard Herrmann, Kenyon Hopkins, J. J. Johnson, Quincy Jones, Fred Karlin,
   Frank Lewin, William Loose, Peter Matz, Billy May, Gil Melle, Hugo Montenegro,
   Arthur Morton, Joseph Mullendore, Oliver Nelson, Lionel Newman, John Parker, Stu
   Phillips, Robert Prince, Don Ray, Nelson Riddle, Milton "Shorty" Rogers, Leonard
   Rosenman, George Roumanis, Pete Rugolo, Lalo Schifrin, Jack Shaindlin, Robert and
   Richard Sherman, David Shire, Duane Tatro, John Williams, Pat Williams, and Marl
   Young.
"*The Score*: On the Record." No. 1 (February 1974): 34–43. Discography.
Siders, Harvey. "Jerry Goldsmith." (Spring 1975): 39. Profile.
Shaw, Arnold. "Nelson Riddle." (Spring 1975): 40. Profile.
Tynan, John. "John Williams." (Spring 1975): 43. Profile.
Kirk, Cynthia. "Billy Goldenberg." (Summer 1975): 33. Profile.
Kirk, Cynthia. "Elmer Bernstein." (Spring 1975): 47. Profile.
"The Sound of Jazz on TV." (Winter 1976): 4–8. Article on BMI composers.
Siders, Harvey. "Leonard Rosenman." (Spring 1976): 42. Profile.
Siders, Harvey. "Bill Conti." No. 2 (1977): 35. Profile.
Hunt, Dennis. "Paul Jabara." No. 1 (1979): 37. Profile.
Siders, Harvey. "Charles Fox." No. 1 (1979): 41. Profile.
Siders, Harvey. "Giorgio Moroder." No. 2 (1979): 23. Profile.
Hunt, Dennis. "Joe Renzetti." No. 2 (1979): 25. Profile.
Siders, Harvey. "David Shire." No. 2 (1980): 20. Profile.
Siders, Harvey. "Norman Gimbel." No. 2 (1980): 22. Profile.
Campbell, Mary. "Michael Gore and Dean Pitchford." No. 2 (1981): 24. Profile.
Schifrin, Lalo. "Them and Us." No. 2 (1982): 22. On new technology.
"Television, 1981–1982: BMI Music on the Home Screen." No. 2 (1982): 23–26.
"Television, 1982–1983: BMI Music on the Home Screen." No. 4 (1982): 29–32.
Siders, Harvey. "John Williams." No. 1 (1983): 24–25. Profile.
Goodman, Fred. "Dave Grusin." No. 1 (March 1984): 24–25. Profile.
Dexter, Dave, Jr. "Nelson Riddle." No. 1 (March 1984): 26–27. Profile.
"BMI Honors Lionel Newman." No. 4 (December 17, 1985): 42. John Williams's re-
   marks were excerpted in the *Cue Sheet* (April 1986).
"Profile: John Barry." No. 1 (1986): 20.
Siders, Harvey. "Profile: Jerry Goldsmith." No. 2 (November 15, 1986): 34–35.
Manna, Sal. "Profile: [Earle] Hagen." No. 2 (November 15, 1986): 38–39.
Manna, Sal. "Profile: [Dean] Pitchford and [Tom] Snow." No. 2 (November 15, 1986):
   62–63.
"Profile: Earle Hagen." (Summer 1987): 38.
Sheff, Victoria. "Alan Silvestri: Composing for the 'Long Concept.'" (Fall 1987): 42–45.

Brio (UK)
Published by the U.K. branch of the International Association of Music Libraries.

Burnand, David. "Reasons Why Film Music Is Held in Low Regard: A British Perspective." 39:1 (Spring–Summer 2002): 26–32.

British Journal of Ethnomusicology (UK)
Morcom, Anna. "An Understanding between Bollywood and Hollywood? The Meaning of Hollywood-Style Music in Hindi Films." 10:1 (2001): 63–84.

British Music: Journal of the British Music Society (UK)
Legard, John. "Music for a Documentary Film Unit, 1950–1980." 15 (1993): 4–14. On scores for British Transport Films, many conducted by Muir Mathieson. Composers include Kenneth V. Jones, Elisabeth Lutyens, Humphrey Searle, and Edward Williams.

Shenton, Kenneth. "From A to B: Kenneth Alford (1881–1945) and Hubert Bath (1883–1945)." 17 (1995): 49–60. Discusses their work related to films.

Youdell, Andrew. "Storm Clouds: A Survey of the Film Music of Arthur Benjamin." 18 (1996): 19–27.

British Music Society News (UK)
Smith, Steven C. "Bernard Herrmann—Anglophile." No. 100 (December 2003): 85–95. Excerpt from Smith's book *A Heart at Fire's Center* (1991).

British Music Yearbook (UK)
Survey and directory with statistics and reference articles, published annually by R. R. Bowker from 1975 to 1998. Yearly reports on film and television music summarize noteworthy contributions.

1975
Palmer, Christopher. "Musicals and Film." 160–65.

"Film Music." 167–72. Month-by-month list of films released from January 1973 to June 1974 and their composers.

Spence, Keith. "Television." 193–97.

1976
Palmer, Christopher. "On Stage and Screen." 137–41.

"Film Music." 143–46. Month-by-month list of films released from July 1974 to June 1975 and their composers.

Last, Richard. "Television." 163–71.

1977–1978
"Films and Their Music." 186–90. Month-by-month list of films and their composers.

1984
Hepple, Peter. "Music for Television." 80–84. Survey in "Incidental Music for Stage and Television."

British Musician (UK)
D'Esterre, Neville. "Music and Talk in the Picture Theatre." 6:2 (February 1930): 38–41.

Cadenza (US)
From Boston music publisher Walter Jacobs.

Harding, Henry J. "The Evolution of the Picture House." (January 1915): 3–4.

Harding, Henry J. "Pictures and Picture Playing." 21:8 (1915): 2–4.

"Organ Music and the Movies." 21:8 (1915): 8–10.

Cambridge Opera Journal (UK)

Leicester, H. Marshall, Jr. "Discourse and the Film Text: Four Readings of *Carmen*." 6 (1994): 245–82.

Grover-Friedlander, Michal. "*The Phantom of the Opera*: The Lost Voice of Opera in Silent Film." 11:2 (July 1999): 179–92.

The Canadian Composer (Canada)

Published by the Society of Composers, Authors and Music Publishers of Canada, in English and French. Superseded by *Words & Music*.

Morgan, Kit. "Original Music...The Difference Between an Excellent Film and an Outstanding Film." (October 3, 1965).

Flohil, Richard, and Michael Schulman. "Interview! Lou Applebaum." No. 87 (January 1974): 10–19.

Pratley, Gerald. "The Ups and Downs of Creating Music for Canadian Feature Films." No. 104 (October 1975).

Timmerman, Nicola. "Music for Film Is Ron Harrison's Job." No. 147 (January 1980).

"This London Composer Keeps Active." No. 181 (May 1983): 38. On Kem Murch in London, Ontario.

Spurgeon, C. Paul. "Musical Scores, Film and Video Media and the Canadian Composer: Facts to Consider." No. 181 (May 1983): S1–[S28].

Shopsowitz, Karen. "Lights, Action, Music." No. 211 (May 1986): 8–[12]. Composing for Canadian films.

Laurier, Andree. "Francois Dompierre." (May 1986): 12–[16].

Baragon, Ellen. "Vancouver Film Composer Says His Art Is 'Bloody Hard Work.'" No. 228 (March 1988) 18–[22]. On Michael Conway Baker.

Powis, Tim. "They Shoot: He Scores!" 4:1 (1993): 20–21. Interview-based article on Paul Zaza.

Jones, Christopher. "Focus on Film Music." 4:4 (Fall 1993): 10–12. With comments by Michael Conway Baker, Miles Goodman, Hagood Hardy, Glenn Morley, Fred Mollin, and Ian Thomas.

Canadian Folk Music Bulletin (Canada)

Lyon, George W. "Folk Music in NFB Films." 22:2–4 (December 1988): 10–12. National Film Board of Canada filmography.

Canadian Musician (Canada)

Taylor, Chris. "Synchronization Licensing for Film and Television." (January 2004).

Canadian Review of Music and Art (Canada)

Rooke, Peggy. "Film Music." 6:1–2 (February–March 1974): 25.

Canadian University Music Review (Canada)

Marks, Martin. "The Well-Furnished Film: Satie's Score for *Entr'acte*." No. 4 (1983): 245–77. On Erik Satie's music for the 1924 film.

Flinn, Carol. "Male Nostalgia and Hollywood Film Music: The Terror of the Feminine." 10:2 (1990): 19–26. Analysis of music in *Detour* (1945).

Deaville, James, and Simon Wood. "Synchronization by the Grace of God? The Film/Music Collaboration of Jean Cocteau and Georges Auric." 22:1 (2001): 105–26.

Magdanz, Teresa. "The Celluloid Waltz: Memories of the Fairground Carousel." 23:1–2 (2003): 62–83. Based on material from her University of Toronto dissertation.

The Canon: A Musical Journal (Australia)
Rath, Maximilian. "On Film Music." 8 (June 1955): 426–29.

Capitol News (US)
Published by Capitol Records along with *Capitol Record* (for disc jockeys and reviewers) and *The Capitol: News from Hollywood.* Some coverage of soundtrack music among the three, but primary focus is on Capitol artists—writers and performers of popular music.
Capitol News
"Max Steiner OK's Wax Pact: He Has Composed for 208 Movies." (1949).
"Jazz Is Native Folk Music Sez *Streetcar* Composer." 9:10 (October 1951): 11. On Alex North.

Capitol Record
"*Streetcar* Music Recorded." 2:286 (October 1, 1951): 1. On Alex North's score.

Cassettes and Cartridges (UK)
Jones, Peter. "Henry Mancini: The Movie Music Maestro." (January 1975).
Britt, Stan. "EMI Sound Tracks." (July 1975): 138–40.

Centerstage (US)
Branch, Clifford, and John Grassadonia. "An Afternoon with Henry Mancini." (July 1978): 22–29.

Chinese Music (US)
Sin-yan, Shen. "The Erhu: 1900–2000, Part II." 24:1 (2001): 4–15. Discusses use of the Chinese *erhu*, a fiddle-like folk instrument, in film music.
Ying, Shao. "Centennial of Xian Xinghai and Liu XueAn." 28:4 (2005): 64–67. Profile of the composers, who have done some film work.

Church Music (UK)
Palmer, Christopher. "Music in the Hollywood Biblical Spectacular." 3:18 (1972): 5–9.

Cine-Technician (UK)
Huntley, John. "The Music Mixer." 14:73 (July–August 1948): 114–17.

Cinema Organ Society Newsletter (UK)
Published by the Cinema Organ Society in London since 1977. News items, articles, and reviews of recordings.

Civiltà Musicale (Italy)
Anderson, Gillian. "Musical Missionaries: 'Suitable' Music in the Cinema 1913–1915." 19: 51–52 (January–August 2004): 173ff.

Classic CD (UK/US)
Some soundtrack reviews, often for films that incorporate classical music or for rerecordings of classic film music.
"Composing for the Prophet." No. 57 (January 1995): 6. On Barrington Pheloung's music for *Nostradamus.*
Davey, Peter. "Music in the Movies: A Very Special Relationship." No. 61 (May 1995): 24–27.

Beadle, Jeremy. "The Music Guide to Today's Top Movies." No. 61 (May 1995): 30–32.

"The Top 50 Films that Use Classical Music." No. 61 (May 1995): 28.

"Composing for Jane Austen." No. 72 (April 1996): 8. On Patrick Doyle's music for *Sense and Sensibility.*

Hayes, M. "Hollywood's Last Romantic." No. 90 (October 1997): 38–42ff. On film music composers.

Davey, Peter. "Music for the Silver Screen." No. 90 (October 1997): 46–54.

Barry, John. "My Dream Music." No. 97 (April 1998): 98.

Webster, Jonathan. "*Kundun*'s Three Wise Men." No. 99 (June 1998): 28–34. Includes an interview with Philip Glass.

Rohan, Michael Scott. "Music of the Movies." No. 100 (July 1998): 82–85.

"Making Music for *Jackie.*" No. 108 (February 1999): 42–43.

"Romanticising Shakespeare." No. 109 (March 1999): 61.

Funnell, Mark. "In Pursuit of Eternity." No. 109 (March 1999): 66–67. On Eleni Karaindrou.

Hayes, M. "William Walton: Casualty of *Battle of Britain.*" No. 113 (July 1999): 80–82.

Classical Music (UK?)

Kennicott, Philip. "What's Opera Doc? Bugs Bunny Meets the Musical Masters." 3:1 (January 1991): 18–24.

Classics (UK)

Featuring the best buys in classical recordings.

Passy, Charles. "You Oughta Be in Pictures! A Short History of Music in the Movies." 7:2 (1987): 8–11. Includes a sidebar from Aaron Copland, "I Had a Great Deal to Learn," on writing music for *Of Mice and Men.*

Kaufman, Louis. "Masters of the Bow: Weeping and Laughing for Hollywood." (November 1992): 12–16. The studio violinist writes about his career in Hollywood. Reprinted in *New Zealand Film Music Bulletin*, no. 83.

Clavier (US)

Sanucci, Frank. "So You Want to Be a Film Music Director." 6:6 (1967): 54–55.

CLGA's Report (US)

Published from at least 1958 to 1963 by the Composers and Lyricists Guild of America (CLGA) for members. News, meetings, events, and honors. Presidents included Leith Stevens and David Raksin (who contributed a "From the President" column).

Kaper, Bronislau. "CLGA's Roving Reporter Series No. 1." 8 (December 29, 1961): 9.

Courage, Alexander. "Music from Hollywood." 10:9 (December 24, 1963): 11–12. News, including a report on the CLGA concert at the Hollywood Bowl.

Co-Art Turntable (US)

Published by Arthur Lange in Beverly Hills, California, from 1941 through 1943, to promote recordings of advanced thought in musical creativity by the Co-Art label. Lange contributed the columns "Off the Cuff" and "I Grew Up in Tin Pan Alley," the latter featuring autobiographical installments.

2:4 (April 1942). [Article by Hugo Friedhofer.]

Tremblay, George. "Co-Art Forum No. 7." 3:1 (January 1943): 7–11. Transcribed interviews with Maurice de Packh and Marlin Skiles, largely unrelated to film music.

College Music Symposium (US)
Published annually by the journal of the College Music Society, originally from State University of New York.
Mulligan, Mary Ann. "College Music Educators: Their Concerns." 16:1 (Spring 1976): 102–4. Introduction of film and television scoring into college music curriculum is briefly mentioned.
Brody, Elaine. "Music and the Mass Media: An Informal Report from the Twelfth Congress of the IMS." 18:1 (Spring 1978) 192–96. Mention of Roy Prendergast's paper describing "the apathy and ignorance of most musical scholars with regard to film music" (quoting Brody) and his call for a historical archive of film music, p. 193. Prendergast's paper "Music in Films" was published in the International Musicological Society's *IMS Report* (1977).
Sun, R. F. "The Esthetics of Film Music." 19:1 (Spring 1979): 216–20. On the lack of respect for the genre ("Film music is still considered the bastard child").
Warren, Alicyn. "The Camera's Voice." 29 (1989): 66–74. Includes discussion of Bernard Herrmann's opera excerpt in *Citizen Kane*.
Neumeyer, David. "Source Music, Background Music, Fantasy and Reality in Early Sound Film." 37:1 (1997): 13–20. Follows on David Bordwell's components of narration, with expansion of film music into "cinematic musical codes." Examples drawn from Fritz Lang's *Liliom*, music by Franz Waxman.

Composer (UK)
Penn, William. "The Celluloid Image and Mixed Media." No. 4 (1970): 179.
Arnell, Richard. "Composing for Animation Film." No. 73 (Summer 1981): 8. On an electronic score for a short film.

The Consort: The Journal of the Dolmetsch Foundation (UK)
Mera, Miguel. "Representing the Baroque: The Portrayal of Historical Period in Film Music." 57 (Summer 2001): 3–21.

Contemporary Keyboard (US)
Billed as "the magazine for all keyboard players" from 1975 to 1981. Superseded by *Keyboard*.
Barrett, David. "Theatre Organ: Its History, From Silent-Movie Houses to Pizza Parlors." 3:10 (October 1977): 16–18, 42.
Lyons, Len. "Michel Legrand: Pianist, Songwriter, Film Composer." 3:10 (October 1977): 20, 51.
Siders, Harvey. "Henry Mancini: Film Composer Extraordinaire." 4 (August 1978): 12, 50, 52. Interview.
Aiken, Jim. "Mike Lang: First-Call Keyboardist for Movies & Television." 5:11 (November 1979): 30–38.
Darter, Tom. "Keyboards in the Movies." 6:4 (April 1980): 46–57. Includes composer biographies and musicians in the movies.
Darter, Tom, and Bob Doerschuk. "Ralph Grierson: Reflections of a Studio Heavyweight." 6:7 (July 1980): 56–60. On the session keyboardist.
Hyman, Dick. "Synchronizing with Films." 7:2 (February 1981): 64.
Hyman, Dick. "Synchronizing Piano Music to Films." 7:3 (March 1981): 53.

Contemporary Music Forum (US)
Music theory journal from Bowling Green State University's MidAmerican Center for

Contemporary Music.

Bargar, Robin. "Composition and Synchronized Sound: From Opera and Cinema to the Computer." 2 (1990): 21–33. Paper by a composer and technology wizard on mapping music to image, from the proceedings of the university's New Music and Art Festival.

Contemporary Music Review (UK)

Forum for new tendencies in composition, published by Routledge, part of the Taylor & Francis Group.

Cohen, Annabel J. "Associationism and Musical Soundtrack Phenomena." 9:1–2 (1993): 163–78.

Dart, William J. "Dorothy Buchanan." 11:1–2 (1994): 47–54. The New Zealand composer talks with the editor of *Music in New Zealand* about her contemporary scores for silent films.

Neumeyer, David. "Performances in Early Hollywood Sound Films: Source Music, Background Music, and the Integrated Sound Track." 19:1 (Spring 2000): 37–62.

Richie, Donald. "Notes on the Film Music of Takemitsu Toru." 21:4 (Fall 2002): 5–16.

Context: A Journal of Music Research (Australia)

International music journal.

Robinson, Suzanne. "'You Absolutely Owe It to England to Stay Here': Copland as Mentor to Britten, 1939–1942." No. 8 (Summer 1994): 3–11.

Arthur, Bronwen. "'Ban the Talkies!': The Musicians' Union of Australia 1927–1932." No. 13 (Winter 1997): 47–57. Examines the loss of orchestral jobs due to the introduction of sound films.

Crawdaddy (US)

Rock music criticism magazine. Some soundtrack record reviews, such as *Close Encounters of the Third Kind* in no. 82 (March 1978), p. 73.

Somma, Robert. "Movie Music & Manfred Mann." 1:18 (September 1968): 46–48.

Creem (US)

Monthly rock 'n' roll magazine.

Lababedi, Iman. "John Barry: The Man with the Golden Baton." 19:2 (October 1987).

Aoki, Guy. "Soundtracks: From *Top Gun* to *Dirty Dancing*." 19:8 (April 1988).

Crescendo International (UK)

Numerous articles by Christopher Palmer and Les Tomkins. Howard Lucraft, a member of the Hollywood Foreign Press representing the United Kingdom, began interviewing composers in November 1987 in "The Hollywood Film Composers" (Alex North was the first). Continued by *Crescendo & Jazz Music*.

Mancini, Henry. "You Have to Know How to Deal with Film People—That's the Secret, Says Henry Mancini." (September 1970): 22, 24.

Horwood, Wally, and Jack Carter. "Music as a Visual Art: Johnny Green Concludes His Story." 10 (September 1971): 12.

Palmer, Christopher. "The Changing World of Film Music." 10 (April 1972): 8ff.

Palmer, Christopher. "Dimitri Tiomkin: Master of the Symphonic Film Score." 10 (July 1972): 18–19.

Palmer, Christopher. "The Function of Film Music." 11 (August 1972): 26–27.

Palmer, Christopher. "A True Composer for the Screen: Miklos Rozsa." 11 (January 1973): 12–13.

Palmer, Christopher. "Roy Webb: Film Score Veteran." 11 (March 1973): 12ff. Interview.

Palmer, Christopher. "American Film Music's Bernard Herrmann." 11 (April 1973): 23–24. Part 1.

Palmer, Christopher. "American Film Music's Bernard Herrmann." 11 (May 1973): 23. Part 2.

Palmer, Christopher. "Popular Appeal Plus Musical Purpose: The Film Music of Jerome Moross." 11 (June 1973): 25–27.

"The Art of Silent Film Accompaniment." 12 (November 1973): 18.

Francis, Harry. "As I Was Playing." 12 (December 1973): 10. Composer biographies on film.

Palmer, Christopher. "Music from the Golden Age." 12 (March 1974): 26–27.

Palmer, Christopher. "Whatever Happened to Hollywood Music?" 12 (April 1974): 8–10.

Tomkins, Les. "The Continuing Musicianship of Henry Mancini." 12 (August 1974): 22–24. Interview.

Tomkins, Les. "Henry Mancini Talking to Les Tomkins." 13 (September 1974). Conclusion of interview.

Tomkins, Les. "From the Bands to the Films: Jerry Fielding Tells His Outspoken Story." 13 (September 1974): 22–24. Interview.

Palmer, Christopher. "Christopher Palmer Continues His Survey of Hollywood Music." 13 (October 1974): 26–27.

Tomkins, Les. "Film Composer Jerry Fielding Speaking His Mind." 13 (November 1974): 6–7. Interview.

Palmer, Christopher. "The Rozsa Touch." 13 (January 1975): 26–27.

Palmer, Christopher. "Satisfaction and Scores: Miklos Rozsa." 13 (February 1975): 26–27. Interview.

Palmer, Christopher. "Film Music Profile: Alex North." 13 (April 1975): 28–29ff. Interview. Reprinted in *Film Music Notebook* 3:1 (1977).

Fielding, Jerry. "Jerry Fielding on the Architecture of the Film Score." 13 (May 1975): 23–24.

Palmer, Christopher. "Leonard Rosenman and the James Dean Sound." 14 (September 1975): 26–27.

Palmer, Christopher. "The Remembrance of Things Past." 14 (October 1975): 26–27.

Palmer, Christopher. "Dimitri Tiomkin in London." 14 (January 1976): 24–25.

Palmer, Christopher. "Bernard Herrmann, 1911–1975: A Personal Tribute." 14 (February 1976): 24. Part 1.

Palmer, Christopher. "Bernard Herrmann, 1911–1975: A Personal Tribute." 14 (March 1976): 8–9. Part 2.

Palmer, Christopher. "Aaron Copland as Film Composer." 14 (May 1976): 24–25.

Palmer, Christopher. "Hollywood in London." 14 (July 1976): 10–11. Rerecording Miklós Rózsa.

Schifrin, Lalo. "My Approaches to the Film Score." 15 (September 1976): 8–10.

Tomkins, Les. "It's Exciting to Be a Musical Alchemist, Says Lalo Schifrin." 15 (October 1976): 15–16.

Palmer, Christopher. "Max Steiner and the Original *King Kong*." (circa 1976): 10, 12.

Palmer, Christopher. "Film Composing and Prokofiev." 15 (March 1977): 10–11.

Tomkins, Les. "Music Gives the Meaning to a Film, Says Richard Rodney Bennett." 20 (June 1982): 16–17. Interview.

Tomkins, Les. "John Cacavas: The Changeable World of Film Scoring." 25 (January 1988): 20–23.

Tomkins, Les. "Scoring the Right Sounds: John Cacavas." 25 (March 1988): 12–13.

Column, "The Hollywood Film Composers" by Howard Lucraft
"'I Like to Relate to a Story.'" 24 (November 1987): 10–11. Interview with Alex North.
"Lennie Niehaus." 25 (February 1988): 8–9.
"Leonard Rosenman." 25 (May 1988): 10.
"Lalo Schifrin." 26 (June–July 1989): 19.
"Walter Scharf." 27 (January 1990): 13.

Crescendo & Jazz Music (UK)

Continues *Crescendo International*. Howard Lucraft, a Hollywood Foreign Press member representing the United Kingdom, jazz band leader and arranger, and radio show host, continues his interview series, variously known as "Hollywood Film Composer" (as in "Pete Rugolo: Hollywood Film Composer") and "Hollywood Film Composers." Only the name of the interviewee is given below.

Ades, David. "Robert Farnon at Eighty." 34:3 (June–July 1997): 22–23.

Levinson, Peter. "Lalo Schifrin Forms a New Record Label." 35:3 (June–July 1998): 14.

Simmonds, Ron. "The Prolific John Keating." 36:4 (August–September 1999): 14–15.

Column, "The Hollywood Film Composer(s)" by Howard Lucraft
"Van Alexander." 29:4 (1992): 16.
"Allyn Ferguson." 29:5 (1992): 6.
"Hugo Friedhofer." 29:6 (1992–1993): 22.
"Lennie Niehaus." 30:1 (1993): 12.
"Pete Rugolo." 30:3 (1993): 7.
"Henry Mancini." 30:4 (1993): 9.
"John Scott." 30:5 (1994): 6.
"Herschel Burke Gilbert." 31:2 (1994): 5.
"Johnny Mandel." 31:4 (1994): 18.
"Elmer Bernstein." 31:5 (1994): 13.
"Lalo Schifrin Today." 31:5 (1994): 26.
"Buddy Baker." 32:1 (1995): 19.
"Dominic Frontiere." 32:3 (1995): 24.
"Mark Isham." 32:4 (1995): 23–24.
"Jerry Fielding." 32:5 (1995): 24.
"Shirley Walker." 33:2 (1996): 6.
"Pete Myers." 33:3 (1996): 18.
"Lee Holdridge." 33:5 (1996): 22.
"Angela Morley." 34:1 (February–March 1997): 18–19.
"Patrick Williams." 34:2 (April–May 1997): 18.
"Elliot Goldenthal." 34:3 (June–July 1997): 11.
"John Barry." 34:4 (August–September 1997): 22.
"Jerry Goldsmith." 34:5 (October–November 1997): 11.
"Alex North." 34:6 (December 1997–January 1998): 25.
"James Horner." 35:1 (February–March 1998).
"Alf Clausen." 35:2 (April–May 1998): 28.
"Burt Bacharach." 35:5 (October–November 1998): 4.
"Russ Garcia." 35:6 (December 1998–January 1999): 11.
"David Rose." 36:1 (February–March 1999): 6.
"Hans Zimmer." 36:2 (April–May 1999): 16.

"Jeremy Lubbock." 36:3 (June–July 1999): 6.

"Ernest Gold." 36:4 (August–September 1999): 9.

"John Williams." 36:5 (October–November 1999): 8.

"Thomas Newman." 36:6 (December 1999–January 2000): 11.

"Howard Shore." 37:1 (February–March 2000): 28.

"Lennie Niehaus: Hollywood Film Composer Re-Visited." 37:2 (April–May 2000): 19.

"Hugo Friedhofer, Jerry Goldsmith, Bronislaw Kaper: Hollywood Film Composers." 37:3 (June–July 2000): 7.

"Tak Shindo." 37:4 (August–September 2000): 25.

"Arturo Sandoval Hits the Movies." 37:6 (December 2000–January 2001): 11.

"Randy Newman." 37:6 (December 2000–January 2001): 12.

"Tan Dun." 38 (April–May 2001): 16.

"Alan Silvestri." 38 (June–July 2001): 25.

"Jimmie Haskell." 38 (October–November 2001): 19.

"Michael Kamen." 38 (December 2001–January 2002): 16.

"Klaus Badelt." 39 (June–July 2002): 14.

"Mike Melvoin." 39 (August–September 2002): 13.

"John Altman." 39 (October–November 2002): 18.

"Hollywood Film Composers: Developments and Directions." 39 (December 2002–January 2003): 22–23.

"Hollywood Film Composers Golden Globe Award." 40 (February–March 2003): 22.

"Stephen Endelman." 40 (October–November 2003): 22.

"Hollywood Film Composers: *Chicago* Portends New Musicals!?" 40 (April–May 2003): 5.

"Hollywood Film Composers: Styles and Directions Today." 40 (June–July 2003): 12.

"Lalo Schifrin." 40 (August–September 2003): 6.

"Cole Porter." 41 (February–March 2004): 27.

"Mark Isham." 41 (April–May 2004): 34.

"Cole Porter *De-Lovely*." 41 (June–July 2004): 30–31.

"John Debney." 41 (August–September 2004): 27–28.

"John Scott." 41 (December 2004–January 2005): 9–10.

"Alan Silvestri." 42 (April–May 2005): 24–25.

"Aldemaro Romero." 42 (June–July 2005): 7–8.

"John Williams." 42 (August–September 2005): 28.

"Walter Scharf." 42 (October–November 2005): 12.

"Hugo Friedhofer." 42 (December 2005–January 2006): 10.

Cum Notis Variorum (US)

Newsletter of the music library at the University of California, Berkeley.

Anderson, Gillian. "Music and Silent Film: A Festival." 126 (October 1988): 3–6. Frankfurt festival report.

Anderson, Gillian B. "Silent Film Scores and Cue Sheets: Sources in the United States." 131 (April 1989): 19–21. Abbreviated version of material in Anderson's book *Music for Silent Films 1894–1929: A Guide* (1988).

Current Musicology (US)

Published under the aegis of the music department at Columbia University.

Nisbett, Robert F. "Louis Gruenberg: A Forgotten Figure of American Music." No. 18 (1974): 90–95.

Neumeyer, David. "Melodrama as a Compositional Resource in Early Hollywood Sound Cinema." No. 57 (January 1995): 61–94. Speech accompanied by music as a compositional source for underscoring dialogue, illustrated by the practice of Alfred Newman, Max Steiner, Herbert Stothart, and others.

Wanner, Dan. "Leaving the Ivory Tower." No. 67–68 (Fall–Winter 1999): 443–51. Topics include film music.

Czech Music (Czech Republic)
Vicar, Jan. "Vaclav Trojan (1907–1983)." No. 1 (1997): 1–3. Tribute.

The Diapason (US)
International monthly devoted to the organ since 1909. Official publication of the Organ Builders' Association of America from 1918 to 1927. Contains a column billed in an ad from January 1920 as an "Excellent Department for the Moving-Picture Organist by Wesley Kay Burroughs." See, for example, "With the Movie Organist," vol. 7 (February 1916), p. 3.

Spong, Jon. "Firmin Swinnen: An American Legend." (December 1999): 16–17. On the organist.

Discourses in Music (Canada)
Canadian graduate student journal.

Magdanz, Teresa. "Classical Music—Is Anyone Listening? A Listener-Based Approach to the Soundtrack of Bertrand Blier's *Too Beautiful for You* (1989)." 3:1 (Fall 2001).

Down Beat (US)
Jazz magazine, often carrying reviews of soundtracks, also known as *Downbeat*. In 1940 *Down Beat*, published in Chicago, bought *Tempo,* a Los Angeles-based music magazine, and brought its editor, Charles Emge, on board. Emge became the magazine's Hollywood correspondent and his column, "Movie Music," appeared from at least 1943 through 1953. Reviews of films that incorporate jazz predominate, alongside news items and observations. Emge also reviewed films for the column "On the Beat in Hollywood"; see December 1, 1944, p. 6. In the 1950s Hal Holly wrote film reviews for both "The Hollywood Beat" and "Filmland Up Beat." In the late 1950s John Tynan worked the West Coast edition and may have been responsible for bringing Henry Mancini in to write the column "On the Soundtrack" in 1957 and 1958. The magazine's annual movie poll included several soundtrack categories; see, for example, the sixth annual poll in the March 17, 1960, issue, p. 5. Coverage of music on television through reviews, news items, and columns is particularly strong in the 1950s. In the 1970s Leonard Feather wrote a column, "TV Soundings." Harvey Siders, a television producer and writer, contributed articles in the early 1970s.

"New Employment Field Opens Up in Hollywood." 18:11 (June 1, 1951): 9. On rescoring theatrical films for television, particularly by Bert Shefter.

"Little of Jazz Interest in 25 Years of Sound Films." 20:17 (August 26, 1953): 3. Survey of jazz in film since 1928.

Emge, Charles. "Composer Tries Out Theory in *Wicked Women* Score." 20:22 (November 4, 1953): 5. On Buddy Baker's use of jazz for the film.

"How Songs Are Written to Fit Action in Movies." 21:1 (January 13, 1954): 32. On Paul Francis Webster.

Emge, Charles. "Some Real Progress in Film Music during 1953." 21:3 (February 10, 1954): 5.

"RKO First Major Studio to Drop Staff Orchestra." 21:8 (April 21, 1954): 1.

"Composers Seek Union." 22:17 (August 24, 1955): 7.

Green, Johnny. "Johnny Green Tells Duties, Functions, and Details of Motion Picture Musical Director." 23:17 (August 22, 1956): 13, 41.

"Republic Films Lops Bandsmen." 24:3 (February 6, 1957): 11. On the demise of the studio orchestra.

Tynan, John. "Film Flam." 25:12 (June 12, 1958): 35. On the increased use of jazz underscores.

Tynan, John. "Take Five." 26:1 (January 8, 1959): 42–43. Johnny Mandel and Dimitri Tiomkin give their opinions of jazz underscores.

Tynan, John. "Take Five." 26:4 (February 19, 1959): 40–41. More of Johnny Mandel and Dimitri Tiomkin on jazz underscores.

Stevens, Leith. "Storm over Hollywood." 26:21 (October 15, 1959): 16–17, 43. On the growing schism between composers and songwriters.

"Hip Hitch." 27:1 (January 7, 1960): 16. On jazz in crime programs, such as Alfred Hitchcock's television show (in section on music news).

Lees, Gene. "The Great Wide World of Quincy Jones." 27:3 (February 4, 1960): 16–21.

Siders, Harvey. "Keeping Score on Schifrin: Lalo Schifrin and the Art of Film Music." 36:5 (March 6, 1969): 16–17, 35.

Siders, Harvey. "Warren Barker." (early 1970s): 15. Interview-based profile.

Binkley, Fred. "[Henry] Mancini's Movie Manifesto." 37:5 (March 5, 1970): 16–17. Interview-based article on jazz-oriented music in films.

Siders, Harvey. "Oliver's New Twist." 37:14 (July 23, 1970): 17. On Oliver Nelson's use of the Moog for television music; mentions Paul Beaver.

Siders, Harvey. "Studios: Bread, Sweat & Ulcers." 38:5 (March 4, 1971): 16–17, 33. On studio musicians, including Benny Golson and Carol Kaye.

Siders, Harvey. "Meet Pat Williams." 38:5 (March 4, 1971): 20, 32.

Siders, Harvey. "The Jazz Composers in Hollywood: A Symposium with Benny Carter, Quincy Jones, Henry Mancini, Lalo Schifrin, Pat Williams." 39:4 (March 2, 1972): 12–15, 34.

Siders, Harvey. "The Mancini Generation: No Gaps." 40:4 (March 1, 1973): 14–15.

Tolnay, Thomas. "The Renaissance of Michel Legrand." 41:10 (May 23, 1974): 15–16.

Berg, Charles. "Henry Mancini: Sounds in the Dark." 45:20 (December 7, 1978): 14–15, 36, 44. Interview-based article.

Terry, Kenneth. "John Williams Encounters the Pops." 48:3 (March 1981): 20–22, 64.

Tiegel, Eliot. "Frankly, Patrick Williams." 48:9 (September 1981): 19–21.

Grusin, Dave, with Gene Kalbacher. "Film Scoring: An Inside Look." 52:3 (March 1985): 59–61. Pro Session column.

Mandel, Howard. "Terence Blanchard/Donald Harrison: Young, Gifted, and Straight Ahead." 53:12 (December 1986): 22–4.

Santoro, Gene. "Music through Blank Eyes." 55:1 (January 1988): 60ff. On Les Blank's films.

Bourne, Michael. "Stu Gardner: Music Director." 55:7 (July 1988): 22ff. On music for Bill Cosby productions, including *The Cosby Show*.

Yanow, Scott. "Dave Grusin: Scoring It Big." 56:7 (July 1989): 24ff. On Grusin's score for *The Milagro Beanfield War*.

Self, Wayne K. "Back from Frustration: Terence Blanchard." 59:8 (August 1992): 30–33. Interview.

Tiegel, Eliot. "Scoring in Hollywood." 60:10 (October 1993): 24ff. On jazz in films, with comments from Tom Scott and Dave Grusin.

Bourne, Michael. "In Tribute to Lady Day." 61:5 (May 1994): 16–21. On Terence Blanchard.

Binkley, Fred. "[Henry] Mancini's Movie Manifesto." 61:7 (July 1994): 80. Reprinted for the 60th anniversary issue; originally appeared March 5, 1970.

Gallo, Phil. "Mark Isham: Miles, Movies and the Muse." 62:11 (November 1995): 30–31. Interview.

Enright, Ed. "Perpetuating the Groove: Clint Eastwood's Latest Evokes Drama through Jazz." 65:1 (January 1998): 10–11. Interview with the director regarding *Midnight in the Garden of Good and Evil.*

Hadley, Frank-John. "Groovy Film Music." 65:2 (February 1998): 61. On recently released film and television soundtracks from the 1960s and early 1970s.

Macnie, Jim. "John Lurie: Go Fish." 65:10 (October 1998): 38–40. Interview.

Stewart, Zan. "Triple Threat: Lalo Schifrin Dwells in a Genre-Blind Bliss." 67:2 (February 2000): 48–51. Profile.

Tiegel, Eliot. "Making *Sweet and Lowdown.*" 67:5 (May 2000): 52. On jazz guitarist Howard Alden.

Panken, Ted. "Bernie Wallace Forgets Hollywood." 67:9 (September 2000): 44–45. On the saxophonist.

Jackson, Michael. "Backstage with…Denny Zeitlin." 71:9 (September 2004): 18. With comments on his score for *Invasion of the Body Snatchers* (1978).

Column, "Movie Music" by Charles Emge

(April 15, 1943): 5. May be the first "Movie Music" column.

11:4 (February 15, 1944): 7. On sideline musicians.

"Hoagy [Carmichael] Gives Song Writer Slant on Film Tune Job." 17:2 (June 16, 1950): 8.

"Showing of Jazz Movies Arouses Big Storm in L.A." 17:23 (November 17, 1950): 9. On jazz musical shorts.

"Jazz Influence Is Strong in Score from *Streetcar.*" (November 16, 1951). On Alex North's score for *A Streetcar Named Desire.*

"Movies' 'Musician DPs' Shifting to TV Studios." 20:23 (November 18, 1953): 5.

Column, "On the Soundtrack" by Henry Mancini

24:16 (August 8, 1957): 30. First column is confusingly titled "Off the Soundtrack."

24:20 (October 3, 1957): 51–52. On his approach to scoring.

24:26 (December 26, 1957): 48. On pre-scoring techniques.

Ear (US)

Monthly journal of new and experimental music.

Weidenaar, Reynold. "Down Memory Lane: Forerunners of Music and the Moving Image." 9:5–10:1 (Fall 1985): 3.

Weidenaar, Reynold. "So You Want to Compose for the Moving Image." 9:5–10:1 (Fall 1985): 28, 35.

Hulser, Kathleen, and Reynold Weidenaar. "The Composer and the Moving Image." 9:5–10:1 (Fall 1985): 40.

Kuipers, J. Dean. "Beyond the Bubble Machine: William Schimmel." 12:10 (February 1988): 8–11. On the accordionist, who has performed on numerous film soundtracks.

Electronic Age (US)

Television trade magazine from Radio Corp. of America in New York.

(Autumn 1968). Henry Mancini interview.

Electronic Musician (US)

Aimed at the home studio musician; popular among film composers with home studios.

Levitin, Daniel. "A Day in the Life: Homicidal Maniac, Doug Cuomo's Scoring for Television." 11:9 (September 1995): 70–6. On music for *Homicide*.

Seidel, Jennifer. "Keeping Score." 11:11 (November 1995). On Laura Karpman.

Decker, Duane. "Know the Score." 14:9 (September 1998): 78–85, 88.

Cleveland, Barry. "Fast Moving Music: Pioneering Synthesist Larry Fast Looks Back on His Career." 15:3 (March 1999): 30–32, 36–37, 40–43.

The Elgar Society Journal (UK)

Lace, Ian. "Bernard Herrmann's Admiration and Appreciation of Elgar." 13:4 (March 2004): 29–33.

Empire (UK)

Clark Collis reviewed film music for this British movie magazine; see the March 1995 issue, for example.

Heath, Chris. "For Your Ears Only." No. 1 (June–July 1989): 42–45. The history of the James Bond theme and music by Monty Norman and John Barry. With previous Bond title songs and performers.

"There's Things I'd Like to Do While You Play..." No. 61 (July 1994): 78–79. On Michael Nyman's music.

Jeffries, Neil. "They Shoot, He Scores." No. 108 (June 1998): 88–92. John Barry interview. Topics include choosing projects, taking charge, importance of first impressions, music timings, and doing the work yourself.

Freer, Ian. "[*Revenge of the Sith*.]" No. 189 (February 2005). Freer discusses John Williams's music.

Ethnomusicology (US)

From the Society for Ethnomusicology.

Zemp, Hugo. "Filming Music and Looking at Music Film." 32:3 (Fall 1988): 393–428.

The Etude (US)

Music publisher Theodore Presser founded this music magazine, published in Philadelphia and best known for its printed music for piano players of all levels. Surprising number of articles related to film music and several columns, including "Worth While Music in the Movies" and "Music of Worth in the Movies," both by pianist Verna Arvey, a Russian Jew who later married William Grant Still, and "Current Films with Worth While Music" by Donald Martin.

Weller, Alanson. "For the Movie Organist." 44 (July 1926): 538.

"New Musical Marvels in the Movies." 44 (October 1926): 781. Editorial regarding *Don Juan* and the future of music.

Weller, Alanson. "A Movie Player's Stock." 47 (May 1929): 380–81.

Rapée, Erno. "The Future of Music in Moviedom." 47 (September 1929): 649–50, 669. Article may be attributed to "Erno Rappe."

Arvey, Verna. "Present Day Musical Films and How They Are Made Possible." 49:1 (January 1931): 16–17, 61–72.

Arvey, Verna. "How Music Has Helped the Stars." 50:10 (October 1932): 693–94, 747.

"Music on the Films." 53:11 (November 1935): 682. "Announces the inauguration of a department for the review of musical films," according to Anderson and Wright, *Film Music Bibliography I* (1995).

Martini, Nino. "And Now the Movies." 54:6 (June 1936): 349–50. On opera films.

Stokowski, Leopold. "My Symphonic Debut in the Films." 54:11 (November 1936): 685–86.

Arvey, Verna. "Composing for the Pictures: By the Noted Austrian Master Erich Korngold: An Interview Secured Expressly for *The Etude Music Magazine*." 55:1 (January 1937): 15–16 Article based on an interview at Warner Bros. studios.

"Bringing the Symphony Orchestra to Moving Picture Patrons." 55:11 (November 1937): 710.

Laine, Juliette. "Operetta and the Sound Film." 56 (June 1938): 359–60.

Smith, Paul J. "The Music of the Walt Disney Cartoons." 58:7 (July 1940): 438, 494.

Jeffrey, Arthur. "The Sound Track of Yesterday and Today." 58:8 (August 1940): 516.

Lessner, George. "So You Want to Try Hollywood." 61:11 (November 1943): 712.

Laine, Juliette. "There's No Substitute for Knowledge! How Motion Picture Music Is Written, an Interview with Victor Young." 63:2 (February 1945): 67–68.

Heylbut, Rose. "Background of Background Music: How NBC's Experts Fit Music to Dramatic Shows." 63 (September 1945): 493–94.

Rózsa, Miklós. "University Training for Motion Picture Musicians." 64 (June 1946): 307, 360.

Rubsamen, Walter H. "Fortunes in Movie Music." 65:7 (July 1947): 420. Letter to the editor.

"Singing in the Movies." 70:11 (November 1952): 16, 59. From an interview with Kathryn Grayson, as told to Gunnar Asklund.

Epstein, Dave A. "Back Stage with the Film Music Composer." 71:2 (February 1953): 19, 60–61. Interview with Dimitri Tiomkin.

"If You Hope for a Film Career." 71:11 (November 1953). Interview with Jeanette McDonald, secured by Rose Heylbut.

Elias, Albert J. "Background Music in Radio and TV." 73:11 (November 1955): 18, 45, 64.

Elias, Albert J. "TV Music by Contemporary Composers." 74:11 (November 1956): 22, 47–51. On *Air Power*, with music by George Antheil, Paul Creston, Norman Dello Joio, and Frank Smith.

Heylbut, Rose. "Disney Fun with Music: The Musical Background of the Walt Disney Productions Has Much to Do with Their Success." 74:8 (October 1956): 23, 57, 59–60.

Column, "Worth While Music in the Movies" by Verna Arvey

56 (August 1938): 496.

56 (December 1938): 786.

57 (February 1939): 82.

57 (March 1939): 152.

57 (May 1939): 304.

Column, "Music of Worth in the Movies" by Verna Arvey

57 (June 1939): 372.

57 (July 1939): 434.

57 (August 1939): 498.

57 (September 1939): 562.

57 (October 1939): 632.

57 (November 1939): 706.

57 (December 1939): 776.

<u>Column, "Current Films with Worth While Music" by Donald Martin</u>
"Current Films with Worth While Music." 58:1 (January 1940): 14, 20.
"Fine Scores for New Musical Pictures." 58:2 (February 1940): 85, 88.
"Moviedom Turns to Musical Pictures." 58:3 (March 1940): 157.
"Current Films with Worth While Music." 58:5 (May 1940): 300.
"Some Recent Tuneful Films." 58:6 (June 1940): 375.
"Singing Films Advance." 58:7 (July 1940): 446.
"Film Music for the New Season." 58:8 (August 1940): 519.
"A Preview of the Year's Musical Films." 58:9 (September 1940): 589.
"News of the New Autumn Musicals." 58:10 (October 1940): 661.
"Music in Film-Land." 58:11 (November 1940): 735.
"Two Outstanding Films with Music." 58:12 (December 1940): 805.
"New Films with Notable Music." 59:1 (January 1941): 13.
"Musical Films and Their Makers." 59:2 (February 1941): 84.
"Movie Music of High Merit." 59:3 (March 1941): 157.
"Schubert Again Enters the Films." 59:4 (April 1941): 228.
"Screen Music." 59:5 (May 1941): 305.
"Musical Films for Early Summer." 59:6 (June 1941): 373.
"Film Music that Musicians Like." 59:7 (July 1941): 445.
"Gay Musical Films Open the Season." 59:8 (August 1941): 518.
"New and Lavish Musical Films." 59:9 (September 1941): 594.
"Music of the Silver Screen." 59:10 (October 1941): 663.
"Musical Films Widely Acclaimed." 59:11 (November 1941): 741. Including *Dumbo*.
"Music Films of Primary Interest." 59:12 (December 1941): 811.
"Disney's New Musical Picture Does It Again; Music Takes a Stellar Role in *Bambi*." 60
    (September 1942): 588.

European Meetings in Ethnomusicology (Romania)
Malvinni, David. "Gypsy Music as Film Music: Spectacle and Act." 10 (2003): 45–76.

Ex Tempore (US)
Journal of compositional and theoretical research in music.
Rollin, Robert. "A Conversation with Multifaceted Film Composer Johnterryl Plumeri."
    12:1 (Spring–Summer 2004): 124–28.

Fanfare (US)
Royal S. Brown's "Film Musings" column ran every other month for nearly twenty years, from 1983 through 2001. As a film and music critic, Brown's consideration of the filmic text sets him apart from many contemporary soundtrack reviewers. His column covered original soundtrack LPs and CDs and focused on scores from films in current release as well as on new recordings of music from the 1930s to 1970s. Elmer Bernstein, Jerry Goldsmith, Bernard Herrmann, Miklós Rózsa, Howard Shore, Franz Waxman, John Williams, and Gabriel Yared are well represented. *Film Musings: A Selected Anthology from Fanfare Magazine* was published by Scarecrow Press in 2006.

<u>Articles (selected)</u>
"Is There Music after Death?" 3:3 (1980): 186–89. On horror films.
Silber, Frederic. "The State of the Art: The Film Soundtrack as Contemporary Music;
    Contemporary Music as Film Score." 4:1 (1980): 309–17.

James, David P. "Between the Frames: John Corigliano and *Altered States*." 5:4 (March–April 1982): 62–68ff.

Silber, Frederic. "America in the Movies: Soundtracks Lost and Found." 5:4 (March–April 1982): 347–51. On *Pennies from Heaven*, *Reds*, and other contemporary scores.

Silber, Frederic. "Sing a Song of Broadway: The State of the Contemporary Musical on Stage, Screen and Record." 6:1 (1982): 494–501.

Silber, Frederic. "Danny Elfman: Wunderkind of Film Music." 13:2 (1989): 568–73. Profile.

Articles by Royal S. Brown (selected)

"*North by Northwest*: by Hitchcock by Hermann [*sic*]." 3:6 (1980): 12–15.

"The Best Film Scores of the 1970s." 5:1 (1981): 44–45.

"Oscar's Tin Ear." 5:6 (1982): 50–55ff.

"A Treasure Trove for Soundtrack Collectors." 6:4 (1983): 368–72.

"An Interview with Miklos Rozsa." 11:6 (1988): 406–14.

"An Interview with Henry Mancini." 14:3 (January–February 1991): 60–81.

"Quadruple Life: An Interview with Lalo Schifrin." 14:4 (March–April 1991): 108–17.

"A Major Film/Music Collaboration: Richard Robbins and Merchant/Ivory." 15:6 (July–August 1992): 69–81.

"Bay Cities: Film Music, the Classics...and Somewhere in Between." 16:1 (September–October 1992): 135–41.

"The 20th Century Fox Film Scores Series: An Interview with Nick Redman." 17:6 (July–August 1994): 26–37.

"A New Source of Film Music: Edel America." 20:1 (September–October 1996): 64–66.

"An Interview with Erich Kunzel." 22:5 (May–June 1999): 47–54.

"Restoring the Golden Age of Film Music: An Interview with John W. Morgan and William T. Stromberg." 22:6 (July–August 1999): 40–52.

Column, "Film Musings" by Royal S. Brown (selected)

7:2 (November–December 1983). First column.

[11:2] (January–February 1987). Includes a brief interview with Angelo Badalamenti on *Blue Velvet*.

19:3 (January–February 1996): 425–26. Includes an interview with John Ottman on *The Usual Suspects*.

19:4 (March–April 1996): 396–98. Includes an interview with Howard Shore on *Se7en*.

20:4 (March–April 1997): 400ff. Includes an interview with David Raksin regarding *The Bad and the Beautiful*.

21:6 (July–August 1998): 316ff. Includes material on Rykodisc.

24:6 (July–August 2001). Final column.

Film and Television Music Guide (US)

Published annually since 1996 by the Music Business Registry in Los Angeles. Aimed at those active in the industry, it contains contacts for agents and managers; composers; film studio, television network, and production company music departments; music clearance companies; music editors; music libraries; music preparation; music publishers; music supervisors; performing rights societies; record labels; and scoring stages. Name index.

Film and TV Music Yearbook (UK)

Compiled by John Williams.

Film and TV Music Yearbook 1998. Dorset: Variations, 1998. 140 pp. Directory of composers, agents, recording studios, record labels, societies, periodicals, and so on. With special features on Roger Bolton, Geoffrey Burgon, Howard Goodall, Ron Grainer,

Richard Harvey, Nigel Hess, Martin Kiszko, Jane Livermore, Stephen McKeon, Michael Omer, John Scott, Patrick Williams, and Debbie Wiseman.

Film and TV Music Yearbook 1999. Dorset: Variations, 1999. 164 pp. With special features on John Barry, Warren Bennett, Christopher Gunning, Jerry Goldsmith, Michael Kamen, Stanley Myers, Jim Parker, and Debbie Wiseman.

Finnish Music Quarterly (Finland)

Jalkanen, Pekka. "Musical Character Spotting: The Leitmotiv in Finnish Film Music." 9:3 (1993): 51–56.

Kuusisaari, Harri. "Music Invades the Silver Screen." No. 3 (March 1999): 2–9.

Folk Roots (US)

Irwin, Colin. "July Jigging." 13:1 (July 1991): 15, 17. An interview with Paddy Moloney of the Chieftains.

Hunt, Ken. "Ravi Only." 14:4 (October 1992): 26, 29. Interview with composer and sitarist Ravi Shankar.

Crane, Joe. "The Flawless Piper." 14:12 (June 1993): 27, 29, 45. On uilleann piper Liam O'Flynn.

Vernon, Paul. "On All Cylinders." 15:5 (November 1993): 19, 21, 23. On Indian soundtracks.

Scott, Iain. "Rahman Empire." 18:9 (March 1997): 25–27. On Indian film music composer and director A. R. Rahman.

Vernon, Paul. "Ethno-Talkies: Paul Vernon Chronicles the History of Roots Music on Film." 20:10 (April 1999): 51–53. Videography.

The Gramophone (UK)

Monthly journal focused on sound recordings.

Green, Alice. "Picture-House Beethoven—and Then the Gramophone." 6:63 (August 1928): 101–2.

Chapple, Stanley. "Film Synchronization." 11:97 (June 1931): 8–9.

Culshaw, John. "Film Music and the Gramophone." 24:280 (September 1946): 45.

Webster, Jonathan. "The Composer's Contract." 72:863 (April 1995): 14, 17. Interview-based article on Michael Nyman.

"Film Music." 74:880 (September 1996): 122ff. Expanded review section edited by Mark Walker includes "*Frankenstein* in Moscow," on John Morgan and William Stromberg rerecording Hans Salter's music; "Something Psychological," with Joel McNeely on rerecording Bernard Herrmann.

"Film Music." 76:909 (December 1998): 120–40. Expanded review section edited by Mark Walker includes material on Varese Sarabande rerecordings of music by Alex North and related interviews with Henry Brant, Jerry Goldsmith (with Paul Tonks), and Robert Townson.

Walker, Mark. "sex, death, and lunch: Mark Walker Spends Three Days with Film Composer Debbie Wiseman." 76:909 (December 1998): 120–22.

Walker, Mark. "Happily Ever After." 76:909 (December 1998): 130–32. Interview-based article on George Fenton.

Quinn, Michael. "Jerry Goldsmith: The Modernist Past of a Hollywood Composer." 80:956 (August 2002): 11. Interview-based article.

Guitar Player (US)

In his "Studio Log" column, which ran from around 1983 to 1991, Tommy Tedesco, a Los Angeles session guitarist, wrote about his studio recording sessions and the composer, wages, and instruments used. A lead sheet of his guitar part is often included. The column may have appeared as early as 1979; unable to confirm.

Forte, D. "L.A. Studios' First-Chair Guitar: Tommy Tedesco." 14 (February 1980): 98–105ff.

Mulhern, Tom. "Mitch Holder: Studio Playback." 16 (July 1982): 32ff.

Obrecht, Jas. "Al Hendrickson: The Way We Were." 22 (March 1988): 18. On the session guitarist.

Sievert, Jon. "Snuffy Walden: Of *thirtysomething* and *The Wonder Years*." 24:3 (March 1990): 42–48.

Rule, Greg. "Gary Hoey: Shred Sails in the Sunset." 28:11 (November 1994): 16. Interview with the guitarist regarding his score for *Endless Summer II.*

31:4 (April 1997). Special issue ("Guitar in the Movies"), contents listed below.

Ellis, Andy. "One-Two Punch." 35:2 (February 2001): 68. Interview with Mark Knopfler.

Column, "Studio Log" by Tommy Tedesco (selected)

"Aging of a Studio Player." 17 (March 1983): 101.

"*Twilight Zone* Mystery Solved." 17 (July 1983): 133.

"*Indiana Jones and the Temple of Doom*." 18 (May 1984): 106. Music by John Williams.

"Six Decades Later." 18 (November 1984): 120ff. With guitar transcription of John Williams's theme for *The River.*

"Miscellaneous Instruments, Part I." 19 (January 1985): 100.

"In a Time Capsule." 21 (January 1987): 187. Television music for *Green Acres* and *Bonanza.*

"Things You Don't Learn in School." 21 (July 1987): 125. On music for *Raw Deal.*

"Recording *Ironweed*—with an Audience." 22:11 (November 1988): 126. On John Morris's music.

"*Bird* Jazz." 23:1 (January 1989): 103.

"*Breaking Home Ties*." 23:2 (February 1989): 119. On the made-for-television movie.

"Returning to the Cocoon." 23:3 (March 1989): 98ff. On James Horner's music for *Cocoon: The Return.*

"Doubling for Indiana Jones." 23:5 (May 1989): 109. On John Williams's music for *Indiana Jones and the Last Crusade.* Part 1.

"*Indiana Jones* and the Temple of Guitars." 23:6 (June 1989): 133. Part 2.

"Shoeless Joe." 23:11 (November 1989): 118ff. On James Horner's music for *Field of Dreams.*

"Three for Three." 24:1 (January 1990): 110. On James Horner's music for *In Country.*

"Stay Loose." 24:2 (February 1990): 114. On Garnet Brown's music for *Harlem Nights.*

"A Little '60s Folk Picking." 24:5 (May 1990): 118. On James Horner's music for *Dad.*

"Nylon-String *Revenge*." 24:6 (June 1990): 115. On Jack Nitzsche's music.

"Party Time at the Corral." 24:7 (July 1990): 101. On Michel Colombier's music for *Lover Boy.*

"Banjo Polka." 24:8 (August 1990): 121. On Thomas Newman's music for *Men Don't Leave.*

"*Goodfellas* and Goodbye." 25:1 (January 1991): 106. Final column.

Special issue, 31:4 (April 1997) ["Guitar in the Movies"]

Obrecht, Jas. "From Talkies to TV: The Guitarists of Hollywood's Golden Age." 45–54. On session guitarists George M. Smith (1930s), Bob Bain, and Al Hendrickson (both 1950s and 1960s), and on the introduction of the electric guitar in the 1960s.

Gore, Joe. "The Good, the Great and the Godly: Ennio Morricone's Miraculous Soundscapes." 57–60. Interview regarding the guitar in Morricone's scores.

Gore, Joe. "The Man with the Golden Pen: Composer John Barry Takes Stock of Bond." 63–68. Interview.

Obrecht, Jas. "Ry Cooder: *Last Man Standing*: Scoring for the Silver Screen." 70–78. Interview.

Gore, Joe. "Dream Theater: Daniel Lanois Goes to the Movies." 80–86. Interview with the composer-guitarist regarding his score for *Sling Blade*.

Ellis, Andy, and James Rotondi. "You Oughta Be in Pictures: Soundtrack Savvy from Marc Bonilla and Mason Daring." 89–96. Interview with the guitarists turned film composers.

Gress, Jesse, and Joe Gore. "Technicolor Twang: A Guide to the Great Guitar Scores." 99–115. Selected guitar transcriptions from film scores with prominent guitar parts.

High Fidelity (US)

Billed as the magazine for music listeners. Published under various titles: *High Fidelity Incorporating Musical America*, (1965–1969), *High Fidelity and Musical America* (1970–1979), and *High Fidelity* (1980–1986). In 1987 *High Fidelity* and *Musical America* parted company. In 1989 *High Fidelity* was absorbed by *Stereo Review*. Most of the articles and reviews related to film music discuss phonograph records and soundtracks. A column by Royal S. Brown, "Theater and Film," contains soundtrack reviews and ran from as early as April 1975 through 1986.

"New Sounds in Film Music from India." 16:10 (October 1966): 68.

Lees, Gene. "The New Sound on the Soundtracks." 17:8 (August 1967): 58–61. On the emergence of jazz-trained composers in Hollywood.

Hiemenz, Jack. "Music to Commit Violence By." 22:5 (May 1972): 76–77. Music in *A Clockwork Orange*.

Lees, Gene. "The Making of a Film Composer." 22:6 (June 1972): 16. On Lalo Schifrin.

22:7 (July 1972). Special issue devoted to film music, contents listed below.

Brown, Royal S. "The Korngold Era: Sumptuous, Romantic Film Music by a Master." 23:2 (February 1973): 66, 68.

Kreuger, Miles. "Extravagant! Spectacular! Colossal! Movie Musicals in the Thirties." 24:4 (April 1974): 66–73. Reprinted in *Performing Arts* (August 1974).

Ramin, Jordan. "Oscar's Songs." 25:4 (April 1975): 54–60.

Lees, Gene. "Hugo Friedhofer: Still Striving at the Periphery." 25:6 (June 1975): 20ff.

Lees, Gene. "[Henry] Mancini at Fifty—Mr. Lucky." 25:7 (July 1975): 11–12. Interview-based article.

Brown, Royal S. "Soundtrack Albums: Why?" 25:7 (July 1975): 49–52.

Brown, Royal S. "Bernard Herrmann and the Subliminal Pulse of Violence." 26:3 (March 1976): 75–76.

Wick, Ted. "Creating the Movie-Music Album." 26:4 (April 1976): 68–71.

Brown, Royal S. "An Interview with Bernard Herrmann (1911–1975)." 26:9 (September 1976): 64–67. 1975 interview published after Herrmann's death.

Caps, John. "An Interview with Richard Rodney Bennett." 27:6 (June 1977): 58–62.

Fiedel, Robert. "Theater and Film: Film Music by Alex North." 28:2 (February 1978): 102. Review.

Brown, Royal S. "Herrmann and Hitch." 28:4 (April 1978): 80–81.

Fiedel, Robert D. "It's *Superman*!" 29:6 (June 1979): 75–76. On John Williams.

"Revisiting *The Twilight Zone*." 35:4 (April 1985): 64. Marius Constant on his theme for the television anthology.

Column, "Theater and Film" by Royal S. Brown (selected)

27 (April 1977): 119. On Elmer Bernstein's music for *To Kill a Mockingbird*.

27 (July 1977): 126. On Bill Conti's music for *Rocky*.

27 (November 1977): 137. On John Williams's music for *Star Wars*.

28 (March 1978): 112. On Franz Waxman's music for *The Spirit of St. Louis*.

29 (November 1979): 122. On Hugo Friedhofer's music for *The Best Years of Our Lives*.

Special issue 22:7 (July 1972) [on film music]

Lees, Gene. "When the Music Stopped." 20. On the musicians' strike.

Kreuger, Miles. "The Birth of the American Film Musical." 42–48.

Kreuger, Miles. "Dubbers to the Stars." 49–54.

Bernstein, Elmer. "What Ever Happened to Great Movie Music?" 55–58. Reprinted in *Crossroads to the Cinema*, compiled by Douglas Brode.

Margolis, Gary. "Why Soundtrack Albums Don't Sound Better." 59–61.

Sutak, Ken. "The Investment Market in Movie Music Albums." 62–66. Includes a list of rarities, with prices.

Hinrichsen's Musical Year Book (UK)

Published by Max Hinrichsen of the Hinrichsen family, founders of the music publisher Peters Edition.

Huntley, John. "Film Music." 4–5 (1947–1948): 382–88. With a list of major film scores by contemporary composers.

Nelson, Robert U., and Walter H. Rubsamen. "Classified Bibliographies: Bibliography of Books and Articles on Music in Film and Radio." 6 (1949–1950): 318–31. Ends with "Writings by John Huntley Contained in Books and Periodicals."

Rubsamen, Walter H. "Descriptive Music for Stage and Screen." 7 (1952): 559–69. Reprint of a 1949 pamphlet in turn reprinted from the Music Teachers National Association's *Volume of Proceedings* (1946).

The Horn Call (US)

Journal of the International Horn Society.

Hilliard, Howard. "Horn Playing in Los Angeles from 1920 to 1970." 30:2 (February 2000): 33–43.

The Hymn Society of Great Britain and Ireland Bulletin (UK)

Routley, E. "Hymns by Accident." 10:3 (1982): 79–81. On the use of hymns in film and television.

Indian Musicological Society (India)

Myers, Helen. "The Process of Change in Trinidad East Indian Music." 9:3 (September 1978): 11–16. On the film orchestra.

Dixit, Pradip. "Influence of Thumri and Dadra on Film Music." 19:1–2 (1988) 78–83.

Indiana Theory Review (US)

Scholarly journal with two significant issues devoted to film music.

Berry, David Carson. "The Popular Songwriter as Composer: Mannerisms and Design in the Music of Jimmy Van Heusen." 21 (Fall–Spring 2000): 1–51.

Special issue, 11 (Spring–Fall 1990) [Film Music Pedagogy]

Neumeyer, David. "Film Music Analysis and Pedagogy." 1–27. Covers teaching film music, analytic methods, development of a canon, and the relationship of the pedagogy to traditional music theory and musicology.

Kalinak, Kathryn. "Music to My Ears: A Structural Approach to Teaching the Sound-track." 29–45.

Penn, William. "Music and Image: A Pedagogical Approach." 47–63.

Cochran, Alfred W. "The Spear of Cephalus: Observations on Film Music Analysis." 65–80.

Mathiesen, Thomas J. "Silent Film Music and the Theatre Organ." 81–117.

Covach, John Rudolph. "The Rutles and the Use of Specific Models in Music Satire." 119–44. The Rutles are a fictitious 1960s musical group.

Burt, George. "*East of Eden*: Climactic Scene." 145–164. Analysis of Leonard Rosenman's music, with music examples.

Special issue, 19 (Spring–Fall 1998) [Film Music]

Cochran, Alfred W. "The Functional Music of Gail Kubik: Catalyst for the Concert Hall." 1–11.

Cox, Helen, and David Neumeyer. "The Musical Function of Sound in Three Films by Alfred Hitchcock." 13–33.

Davison, Annette. "Playing in *The Garden*: Sound, Performance, and Images of Persecution." 35–54. On Derek Jarman's *The Garden*.

Latham, Edward. "Physical Motifs and Concentric Amplification in Godard/Lully's *Armide*." 55–85.

Neumeyer, David. "Tonal Design and Narrative in Film Music: Bernard Herrmann's *A Portrait of Hitch* and *The Trouble with Harry*." 87–123.

Rodman, Ronald. "There's No Place Like Home: Tonal Design and Closure in *The Wizard of Oz*." 125–43. Analysis of Herbert Stothart's music.

Institute for Studies in American Music Newsletter (US)

Published semiannually by the Institute, located at the Conservatory of Music, Brooklyn College of the City University of New York. Frequently cited as the *ISAM Newsletter*.

Anderson, Gillian B. "*The Thief of Bagdad* and Its Music." 14:1 (November 1984): 8–10. On Mortimer Wilson's score.

Ramsey, Guthrie P., Jr. "The Muze 'n the Hood: Musical Practice and Film in the Age of Hip Hop." 29:2 (Spring 2000): 1–2, 12. On music in *Do the Right Thing* (1989).

Oja, Carol J. "Filming the *Music of Williamsburg* with Alan Lomax." 33:1 (Fall 2003): 1–2, 12–13. Discusses Lomax's role in coordinating the traditional music for a 1960 tourist film.

Goldmark, Daniel. "Jungle Jive: Race, Jazz, and Cartoons." 34:2 (Spring 2005): 1–3. Revised excerpt from Goldmark's *Tunes for 'Toons*.

The Instrumentalist (US)

Aimed at school band and orchestra directors and instrumental music teachers. Published in Evanston, Illinois.

Broughton, William. "Studio Musicians in Hollywood." 33:2 (September 1978): 43–45.

Dobroski, Bernie, and Claire Greene. "Pass the Popcorn: An Interview with John Williams." 38:12 (July 1984): 6–9.

Baker, Lida Belt. "Henry Mancini: Making Film Score Magic." 41 (March 1987): 10–15.

Karlin, Fred. "Scoring Success in Hollywood with Lalo Schifrin." 45 (February 1991): 37–50.

Meloy, M. "Michael Kamen: Chameleon Composer." 46 (April 1992): 44–47.

Interdisciplinary Humanities (US)

Wierzbicki, James. "Raiders of the Lost Arc: Hollywood's Appropriation of Operatic Narrative Structure." (Fall 2002).

Interdisciplinary Studies in Musicology (Poland)

Buhler, James, and David Neumeyer. "Music–Sound–Narrative: Analyzing *Casablanca.*" 5 (2005): 277–91.

International Journal of Music Education (US)

From the Australian-based International Society for Music Education.

Brand, Manny. "Reel Music Teachers: Use of Popular Films in Music Teacher Education." 38 (November 2001): 5–12. Identifies popular films that depict music teachers.

International Journal of Musicology (Switzerland)

Sheer, Miriam. "Western Classical Compositions in Kurosawa's Films." 7 (1998): 355–73.

International Music Guide (UK/US)

The 1978 edition, edited by Derek Elley, included a section on film music and a Miklós Rózsa appreciation as a musician of the year, with interview quotes.

International Musician (US)

Journal of the American Federation of Musicians of the United States and Canada, published monthly in New York. Articles on union business affairs, including union recording of film scores, and agreements with producers. Occasional articles on or interviews with film and television composers. Jazz musician and critic Leonard Feather wrote a column, "From Pen to Screen," from around May 1968 to October 1974.

Siders, Harvey. "Nelson Riddle: Arranger-Composer-Conductor." (June 1973): 18.

Backer, Thomas E., and Eddy Lawrence Manson. "In the Key of Feeling." 77 (November 1978): 14ff. Previously published in *Human Behavior* (1978).

King, Marshall. "Getting Your Foot in the Door: A Talk with Composer Don Ray." 82 (January 1984): 7ff.

"AFM Protests Use of Foreign Players to Score Oscar Nominee." 85 (April 1987): 1. Related to Jerry Goldsmith's music for *Hoosiers*.

Lipton, Michael. "Lennie Niehaus on *Bird*." 87 (March 1989): 6–7.

Gabriel, Dick. "Jammin': Working as a Sideline Musician." 94:11 (May 1996): 16. On onscreen musicians.

Kane, Jo Ann. "Jammin': Film Composers Face Double Dilemma." 94:11 (May 1996): 16. The supervising music copyist discusses MIDI transcriptions (in which a composer's computer-generated music sketch is transcribed for use by the orchestrator).

Schnackenberg, Karen. "Voices: The Music behind *Mr. Holland's Opus*." 94:11 (May 1996): 17–18. On the use of non-AFM musicians to record the music for the film.

"The Tale of *Dumb and Dumber*." 98:15 (September 2000): 8. On film musicians who worked without a union contract.

"W. G. Snuffy Walden: Settling the Score." 99:4 (April 2001): 16–17.

DeCrescent, Sandy. "Always a Bridesmaid...and Finally a Bride." 100:5 (May 2002). On Randy Newman's Academy Award.

"AFM Attends Cannes to Promote Motion Picture Scoring under AFM Agreements." 100:7 (July 2002): 5.

"From Cowboy to Composer: Clint Eastwood Takes the Reins in Hollywood and Makes His Mark in Music." 101:10 (October 2003): 16–17.

"Composer Lectures on Future of Movie Music at Berklee." 103:1 (January 2005): 24. On Gary Chang.

Nelson, Florence. "Official Reports: Keeping Film Scoring on Our Shores." 103:6 (June 2005): 4.

"Peake's Career Contains Few Valleys." 103:6 (June 2005): 16. Career profile of the film and television composer Don Peake, best known as a session guitarist.

"Alf Clausen: Life with *The Simpsons*." 103:6 (June 2005): 18–19.

Millner, Chris. "Space Saga's Ending Caps Decades of Recording Work for AFM Musicians." 103:6 (June 2005): 20. On the *Star Trek* franchise, 1966–2005.

"John Williams: Writing the Soundtrack to Our Lives." 103:7 (July 2005): 14–15.

Column, "From Pen to Screen" by Leonard Feather (selected)
(May 1968): 10, 24. On Lalo Schifrin.
67:4 (April 1969): 6–7. On John Williams.
69 (August 1970): 11. On Stanley Wilson.
69 (September 1970). On Burt Bacharach.
69:4 (October 1970): 7. On Henry Mancini.
69 (December 1970): 4. On Jerry Goldsmith.
70 (April 1971). On Mort Lindsay.
70 (September 1971): 7ff. On Kenyon Hopkins.
70 (December 1971): 5ff. On Fred Karlin.
70 (June 1972): 3. On Don Ellis.
72:4 (October 1973): 9, 22. On Tom McIntosh.
73:4 (October 1974): 7, 32. On Fred Werner.

International Review of the Aesthetics and Sociology of Music (Republic of Croatia)
Published by the Croatian Musicological Society.

Premuda, Noemi. "Luchino Visconti's 'Musicism.'" 26:2 (December 1995): 189–210. The influence of music on the director's films. For errata, see 27:1 (June 1996): 95–98.

Paulus, Irena. "Music in Krzysztof Kieslowski's Film *Three Colors: Blue*: A Rhapsody in Shades of Blue—The Reflections of a Musician." 30:1 (June 1999): 65–91.

Paulus, Irena. "[John] Williams Versus Wagner or an Attempt at Linking Musical Epics." 31:2 (December 2000): 153–84.

International Who Is Who in Music (US)
Dictionary of musicians, published in Chicago and New York.

The 1929 edition (published as *Who Is Who in Music*) includes "Synchronization of Music for Motion Picture," by Hugo Riesenfeld, pp. 30–31. The 1941 edition (4th, published as *Who Is Who in Music*) includes "Music in the Films," a historical survey and contemporary view by Bruno David Ussher, pp. 552–54. The biographical entries are somewhat esoteric and include Nat Finston, Alfred Newman, Victor Young, and Eugene Zador. The 1951 edition (5th, *The International Who Is Who in Music*, J. T. H. Mize, editor in chief) contains biographical entries, with small photos, for approximately seventy composers who wrote music for films.

International Who's Who in Classical Music (US)
John Williams and other film composers who write concert music are in the 21st edition (2005).

International Who's Who in Popular Music (US)
James Newton Howard, Thomas Newman, David Shire, Howard Shore, and others are in the 7th edition (2005). Good source of basic biographical data on living film composers, including education and compositions. Previously issued as *International Who's Who in Music and Musician's Directory*. Past issues have included Ernest Gold and Lee Holdridge (10th edition) and John Williams (17th edition).

Irish Musical Studies (Ireland)
Published in association with the Society for Musicology in Ireland.
Whittle, David. "The Decline and Fall of Bruce Montgomery." 4 (1996): 247–54. On film music by the British crime writer (who also wrote fiction under the pen name Edmund Crispin), including music for films in the Carry On series.

Jacobs' Orchestra Monthly (US)
Progressive band orchestra journal from New York music publisher Walter Jacobs. Apparently included the column "Interpretive Music for the Movies" by Joseph Fox from around 1922 to 1924. Some columns were reprinted in *Melody* magazine, also published by Jacobs.

Jazz Educators Journal (US)
Published by the National Association of Jazz Educators.
Berg, Charles. "Henry Mancini: A Man for All Seasons." 17 (December–January 1985): 20–23. Interview-based article, including Mancini's working methods.
Gaber, Brian. "Getting in Sync." 33:2 (September 1998): 37–39. Synchronizing music with visual images.

Jazz Journal International (UK)
Contains a column, "Jazz on the Screen" by Peter Vacher (previously by Reg Cooper and Liam Keating), from at least the early 1990s.

Jazz Magazine (US)
Maltin, Leonard. "Unearthing Jazz Heritage You Can See and Hear." 1:2 (Fall 1976): 36–41.
Heckman, Don. "Sound Tracks: How Hollywood Buried Jazz." 1:2 (Fall 1976): 41–43.

Jazz Research Proceedings Yearbook (US)
Compilation of research papers presented at annual conferences of the International Association for Jazz Education.
Cochran, Alfred W. "Leith Stevens and the Jazz Film Score: *The Wild One* and *Private Hell 36*." 10 (1990): 24–31.
Fisher, L. "A Conversation with Johnny Mandel Concerning His Compositions and Arrangements for Hollywood Films, Television, and Recordings." 22 (2002).

The Jazz Review (US)
Harrison, Max. "Ellington's Music for *Anatomy of a Murder*." 2:10 (November 1959): 35–36. Reprinted in Mark Tucker's *The Duke Ellington Reader* (1993).

Jazz Times (US)
Milkowski, Bill. "Terence Blanchard: He May Still Consider Himself a Novice When It Comes to Writing Film Music, but the Trumpeter Is Fast Becoming a Master of the Art Form." 29:4 (May 1, 1999): 64. Profile.

Jazziz (US)
Since 1984 this jazz monthly has profiled and/or interviewed a number of jazz artists with connections to film scoring, from Dave Grusin to Lalo Schifrin (see February 2005). The October 2003 issue covered jazz on television, including "Wither Jazz on TV," by Bill Milkowski and an article on "The Golden Age."
Hershon, Bob. "Cinemusic." 13:11 (November 1996): 34–35. On Lalo Schifrin.
Yanow, Scott. "Watching Jazz." (February 2005). Excerpted from his book, *Jazz on Film: The Complete Story of the Musicians and Music Onscreen* (2004).

JEMF Quarterly (US)
Published by the John Edwards Memorial Foundation to promote American folk music of the 1920s through 1940s.
Smyth, William. "A Preliminary Index of Country Music Artists and Songs in Commercial Motion Pictures (1928–1953)." 19:70 (Summer 1983): 107–12; 19:71 (Fall 1983): 188–96; 19:72 (Winter 1983): 241–47; 20:73 (Spring–Summer 1984): 8–18. Indexed by film title, with songs, performer, dates of recording and release, and studio.

Journal of the American Musicological Society (US)
Buhler, James, and David Neumeyer. "Film Studies/Film Music." 47:2 (1994): 364–85.
Sheppard, W. Anthony. "An Exotic Enemy: Anti-Japanese Musical Propaganda in World War II Hollywood." 54:2 (Summer 2001): 304–57. Analyzes the adapted use of Igor Stravinsky's music, pp. 312–21.

Journal of the Association for Recorded Sound Collections (US)
Parker, David L., and Burton J. Shapiro. "The Phonograph Movies." 7:1–2 (July 1975): 6–20.

Journal of the Cinema Organ Society (UK)
Published in Leeds from around 1952 to 1994. Historical articles, profiles, and news.
Manning, Clifford S. "The Theatre Organ in the British Isles." 21:100 (December 1973): 50–57. Part 1.
Manning, Clifford S. "The Theatre Organ in the British Isles." 22:100 [*sic*] (March 1974): 24–30. Part 2.
"The Theatre Organ in Germany." 25:116 (December 1977): 16–19.

The Journal of Country Music (US)
Green, Douglas B. "The Singing Cowboy: An American Dream." 7:2 (May 1978): 4–61.

Journal of Music Therapy (US)
Smith, David S. "An Age-Based Comparison of Humor in Selected Musical Compositions." 31:3 (Fall 1994): 206–19. Cartoon music is included in the discussion.

Journal of Musicological Research (UK)
Focuses on study and teaching.

Joe, Jeongwon. "Don Boyd's *Aria*: A Narrative Polyphony between Music and Image."
    18:4 (1999): 347–69.
Marks, Martin M. "Music and the Silent Film: Contexts and Case Studies, 1895–1924."
    19:2 (2000): 182–90.

The Journal of Musicology (US)
Anderson, Gillian B. "The Presentation of Silent Films, or, Music as Anaesthesia." 5:2
    (Spring 1987): 257–95. Essay, with *The American Organist* providing much of the
    source material.
Sheer, Miriam. "The Godard/Beethoven Connection: On the Use of Beethoven's Quartets
    in Godard's Films." 18:1 (Winter 2001): 170–88.
Citron, Marcia J. "Subjectivity in the Opera Films of Jean-Pierre Ponnelle." 22:2 (Spring
    2005): 203–40. On the director's opera films for television.

Journal of Popular Music Studies (US)
Biannual, interdisciplinary, peer-reviewed journal devoted to a wide range of approaches
to popular music. Good source for book reviews.
Ferriano, Frank. "Did He Write That? America's Great Unknown Songwriter Harold
    Arlen." 3:1 (December 1990): 8–17.
Sieving, Christopher. "Super Sonics Song Score as Counter-Narration in *Super Fly*." 13:1
    (March 2001): 77–91.
Mera, Miguel. "Is Funny Music Funny? Contexts and Case Studies of Film Music Hu-
    mor." 14:2 (September 2002): 91–113.

Journal of the Royal Musical Association (UK)
One of the major international refereed journals in its field. Established in 1986; suc-
ceeded the *Proceedings of the Royal Musical Association*. The proceedings included
papers (or lectures) read to the association.
Proceedings of the Royal Musical Association
Irving, Ernest. "Film Music." 76 (1949–1950): 35–45.
Orledge, Robert. "Charles Koechlin and the Early Sound Film 1933–38." 98 (1971–
    1972): 1–16. Discusses Koechlin's compositions with cinematic associations.
Kennedy, Michael. "The Unknown Vaughan Williams." 99 (1972–1973): 31–41.

Journal of the Royal Musical Association
Brown, Julie. "*Ally McBeal*'s Postmodern Soundtrack." 126:2 (2001): 275–303. Includes
    a discussion of "music's contribution to the show's controversial representations of
    contemporary gender politics."
Rogers, Holly. "Fitzcarraldo's Search for Aguirre: Music and Text in the Amazonian
    Films of Werner Herzog." 129:1 (Spring 2004): 77–99.

Journal of the United Kingdom branch of the International Association of Music
   ### Libraries, Archives and Documentation Centres (UK)
Burnand, David. "Reasons Why Film Music Is Held in Low Regard: A British Perspec-
    tive." 39:1 (Spring–Summer 2002): 26–32. The name of the journal is *Brio*.

Juilliard Review (US)
Rubsamen, Walter H. "Music in the American Dramatic Film." 4:2 (Spring 1957): 20–28.
    Appeared the same year as his similarly titled pamphlet, "Music in the Dramatic
    Film."

Kastlemusick Monthly Bulletin (US)

Monthly magazine for collectors of recordings.

Kamen, Stan. "Henry Mancini: A Review of the Last 25 Years." No. E-27 (February 1977): 1, 12.

Keyboard (US)

Aimed at popular music and freelance musicians, with extensive coverage of electronic keyboard instruments, synthesizers, commercial music, and home studios. Jeff Rona, a respected home studio film and television composer, contributed a column from 1992 to 2005, "Reel World Notebook," later "Reel World." In addition to Rona's own projects, the column documents technology changes and scoring trends related to composing and synchronizing film and television music. Superseded *Contemporary Keyboard*.

(December 1984). On Mark Isham.

Darter, Tom. "Jerry Goldsmith." (February 1985): 19–26.

Darter, Tom. "Jerry Goldsmith." 11 (April 1985): 44ff.

Milano, D. "The Fine Art of Programming Synthesizers: Programming in Action; Michael Boddicker's Ultra-Tech Soundtrack for *The Magic Egg*." 11 (June 1985): 34–37.

Darter, Tom, and Greg Armbruster. "Dave Grusin: A Top Film Composer and Record Producer Goes Back Out on the Road." 11 (July 1985): 36–41. Interview.

Armbruster, Greg. "Mark Isham: A Bulletin from the Frontiers of Film Scoring." 11 (November 1985): 46.

"First Electronic Film Score." (February 1986).

(April 1986). On Brad Fiedel.

(August 1986). On agent Robert Kraft.

Greenwald, Ted. "The Self-Destructing Modules behind the Revolutionary 1956 Soundtrack of *Forbidden Planet*." 12:2 (February 1986): 54–65.

(May 1986). On session musician Ralph Grierson.

(October 1986). On Frank Serafine.

(December 1986). On Michele Rubini.

(April 1987). On Philip Glass.

(September 1987). On Danny Elfman.

(February 1988). On Stewart Copeland.

Dery, Mark. "James Horner: Bringing Sound Colors to the Big Screen in *Aliens, Commando*, and *Willow*." 14 (July 1988): 58–64. Interview.

di Perna, A. "Craig Safan: The Improvisational Score." 14 (September 1988): 28.

Doerschuk, Bob. "Randy Newman: Dreams of the Piano Player." 15 (February 1989): 58–59ff.

Doerschuk, Bob. "The Art of Noise: An Interview with Anne Dudley." 15 (February 1989): 82–84ff.

Marans, Michael. "Hans Zimmer." 15:6 (June 1989): 74–81. Interview.

Milano, D. "Peter Gabriel Identity." 15 (October 1989): 32–36ff. On *Passion*, music from the film *The Last Temptation of Christ*.

Doerschuk, Robert L. "Danny Elfman: The Agony and the Ectasy [*sic*] of Scoring *Batman*." 15 (October 1989): 82–83ff.

16:3; issue 167 (March 1990). Special issue, see page 519 for contents.

Widders-Ellis, A. "World View: Under the Gun with *Days of Thunder*." 16 (June 1990): 24–25.

Combs, J. "Wrapped in Plastic: Kinny Landrum Explains What Really Went On at the *Twin Peaks* Soundtrack Sessions." 16 (November 1990): 68–69ff.

Doerschuk, Robert L. "World View: Gary Chang—Art Meets Legs on *Perfect Weapon* and *A Shock to the System*." 16 (December 1990): 16–17.

Riesman, Michael. "Silent Films Never Had It So Good; A Live Six-Keyboard Pit Orchestra (The MIDI Wurlitzer?) Goes on Tour with Philip Glass's Scores for *Koyaanisqatsi* and *Powaqqatsi*." 17 (September 1991): 34–38ff.

Doerschuk, Robert L. "World View: Michel Colombier Bats Three-for-Three with *Hit Man*, *Dark Wind*, and *Go Natalie*." 17 (October 1991): 28–29.

Doerschuk, Robert L. "World View: Cliff Martinez and Jeff Rona: Seeking Cimbalomism in *Kafka*." 17 (November 1991): 28–29.

Doerschuk, Robert L. "Brad Fiedel." 18 (April 1992): 18–19ff. Interview.

Doerschuk, Robert L. "Hold On to Your Face: Score in the Depths of *Netherworld*." 18 (May 1992): 40–46ff.

Hurtig, B. "Making Tracks: So You Want to Be in Pictures..." 18 (November 1992): 127–28.

(January 1993). On session musician Mike Lang.

Foster, A. "World View: Full Moon Mania with Richard Band." 19 (August 1993): 21.

Doerschuk, Robert L. "Michael Kamen." 19 (September 1993): 56–65.

Doerschuk, Robert L. "*The Firm*: Dave Grusin Battles Soundtrack Conformity with a Taut Solo Piano Score." 19 (October 1993): 72–78.

Kirk, A. "First Steps in Film Scoring: Insights and Advice from Academy Award Winner Ernest Gold." 19 (November 1993): 32–33ff.

Tingen, P. "Michael Nyman: Inside *The Piano*." 20 (October 1994): 62–63ff.

Doerschuk, Robert L. "World View: Sessions Datebook—Michael Lang, Part 1." 21 (April 1995): 15.

Stewart, D. "Inside The Music: Towards *McGroggan*." 21 (May 1995): 132–33. On television scoring.

Vail, Mark. "World View: Starr Parodi and Jeff Fair—Life after *Arsenio*." 21 (June 1995): 14.

Leiter, Richard. "Composing: David Schwartz: Write from the Gut." 21 (October 1995): 132–33. On *Magic in the Water*.

Leiter, Richard. "Composing: Trailer Secrets Revealed!" 21 (November 1995): 134.

Miller, J. "The Dream Never Ends: Tangerine Dream's Edgar Froese Reflects on 25 Years of Visionary Electronic Music." 22 (January 1996): 48–51ff.

Rule, Greg. "A Day in the Life of the *X-Files*: Mark Snow." 22:3 (March 1996): 24–28, 33–34.

Alberts, R. "World View: Wayne Sharpe: Scoring for the Biggest Screens." 22 (May 1996): 14. Composing for IMAX films.

Leiter, Richard. "Composing: Emotional Noise." 22 (May 1996): 132–33. On *The Player*.

Rule, Greg. "Arnold...David Arnold...The New Sound of James Bond." 24 (April 1998): 26–33. Interview.

Leiter, Richard. "Composing: Micro-Meddling." 24 (August 1998): 124ff. The author's experiences with the arranger of his music for a film trailer.

Leiter, Richard. "Composing: Through the Looking Glass." 25:3 (March 1999): 134–35. On Indian tabla player Zakir Hussain and his approach to film scoring.

Gallagher, Mitch, and Greg Rule. "Movie Music Magic! Inside Media Ventures with Hans Zimmer and Company." 25:4 (April 1999): 30–40. Sidebars profile staff composers such as Harry Gregson-Williams.

Rovito, M. "411: John McEntire; Jack-of-All-Trades Makes His First Big Score." 25 (May 1999): 22. On *Reach the Rock*.

"Michael Whalen." 25:10 (September 1999): 72. Profile.

Northam, Mark, and Lisa Anne Miller. "Film and Television Composer's Resource Guide: The Complete Guide to Organizing and Building Your Business." 25 (November 1999): 8.

Leiter, Richard. "Composing: Feedback Ripped My Flesh (Distinguishing Uncritical Reviews from Creative Feedback)." 25 (November 1999): 148–49.

Anderton, Craig. "Record Multimedia: The Big Score: The Sequel." 26 (November 2000): 72ff.

Krogh, John. "James Newton Howard: Master of MIDI Orchestration." 26:1 (December 2000): 34–36.

Busch, Robbie. "Spotlight: *Dream* Team: Composer Clint Mansell and Sound Designer Brian Emerich behind the Scenes on *Requiem for a Dream*." 26:1 (December 2000): 60, 62.

Krogh, John. "Five Questions with BT [Brian Transeau]." 27 (January 2001): 17.

Hughes, Ken. "Ed Goldfarb: Synthesizing the *Apocalypse*." 27 (September 2001): 54–56.

Krogh, John. "Electronic Producer/Composer: Brian Transeau." 27 (November 2001): 30–32ff.

Hughes, Ken. "Spotlight: Joe Hogue and Dan Haseltine; Scoring *Hometown Legend* with a Virtual Orchestra." 28: (March 2002): 54.

"Behind the Scenes of ABC's *Alias*: Composer Michael Giacchino Blends Orchestral Music and Electronica for One of the Hottest Shows on TV." 28 (July 2002): 38. Interview.

Busch, Robbie. "Kevin Shields: *Lost* and Found." 30 (January 2004): 12. Interview with the songwriter for *Lost in Translation*.

Prager, Michael. "The Unreal Orchestra, Part 1: The Virtual Film Score." 30 (February 2004): 26–28ff.

Rideout, Ernie. "Musicmakers: Steve Horowitz Supersized." 30 (September 2004): 12. Interview with the composer of *Super Size Me*.

Gennet, R. "Keytracks: Album: *A Clockwork Orange* Soundtrack; Keyboards: Wendy Carlos." 31 (January 2005): 14.

Column, "Reel World Notebook" by Jeff Rona (selected)

"Client: Hans Zimmer; Project: *Green Card* Soundtrack." 18 (February 1992): 118.

"Music with Muscles; Client: Arthur Kempel; Project: *Double Impact.*" 18 (May 1992): 107–9.

"Tempi, Tempi; Client: Pat Leonard; Project: *Nameless*." 18 (June 1992): 113–15.

"Client: David Frank; Project: *Poison Ivy*." 18 (July 1992): 123–24. Part 1.

"Client: David Frank; Project: *Poison Ivy*." 18 (August 1992): 126ff. Part 2.

"Client: David Michael Frank; Project: *Poison Ivy.*" 18 (September 1992). 131ff. Part 3.

"Project: *Tom and Jerry*—The Movie." 18 (December 1992): 163–64.

"Misfit Sounds and Other Found Objects." 19 (January 1993): 115.

"Client: Hans Zimmer; Project: *Toys* (Part 1)." 19 (February 1993): 115ff.

"Project: *Toys*, Part 2; Client: Hans Zimmer." 19 (March 1993): 109ff.

"Project: *Toys*, Part 3; Client: Hans Zimmer." 19 (April 1993): 117–18.

"The Level Playing Field; Project: *The Lipstick Camera*." 20 (February 1994): 171ff. Part 1.

"The Level Playing Field; Project: *The Lipstick Camera*." 20 (March 1994): 147ff. Part 2.

Column, "Reel World" by Jeff Rona (selected)

"The Art of Documentary Project: *The Art of Survival;* client: Harlan Steinberger." 21 (January 1995): 138ff.

"Enough Is Enough." 21 (May 1995): 135. On selecting studio gear.

"Fired." 21 (October 1995): 130–31.

"Sync Up." 21 (December 1995) : 176. On synchronizing with SMPTE.
"Letting Go." 22 (January 1996): 138–39.
"Are You Up to Speed?" 22 (February 1996): 143–44. On meeting deadlines.
"House of Style." 22:4 (April 1996): 121ff.
"Three Sheets to the Wind." 22 (May 1996): 129–30. On *White Squall.*
"*White Squall,* Part 2: The Hard Part." 22 (June 1996): 128ff.
"Going to London." 22 (July 1996): 130ff. On recording *White Squall.*
"*White Squall,* Part 4: The Big Finish." 22 (September 1996): 130–31.
"Breaking In." 22 (October 1996): 111–12.
"Learning by Doing." 22 (December 1996): 167–68. On composing cohesive film scores.
"More Learning by Doing." 23 (January 1997): 129ff. On determining musical cues.
"'Do Me a Favor.'" 23 (February 1997): 151–52ff. On scoring low-budget features.
"Sundance? *Yes!*" 23 (May 1997): 118ff. On scoring *The House of Yes.*
"The Politics of Dancing." 23 (August 1997): 136ff. On personality conflicts.
"Get to Know Me." 23 (September 1997): 122ff. On getting hired.
"Money Matters." 23 (October 1997): 136ff. Part 1.
"Money Matters." 23 (November 1997): 126ff. Part 2.
"Time Keeps on Ticking." 23 (December 1997): 130ff. On rhythm-based scores.
"Smells Like Team Spirit." 24 (May 1998): 122–23. Interview with music editor Adam
    Smalley.
"Art and Motion." 24 (June 1998): 116–17. On aesthetics.
"Sounds Good to Me." 24 (July 1998): 136ff. Interview with recording engineer Alan
    Meyerson.
"Staying Ahead of the Curve." 24 (October 1998): 152ff. On the importance of keeping
    up with technology.
"Expand and Contract." 24 (November 1998): 136ff. On budgets for recording with live
    players.
"Walk Like an Egyptian." 24 (December 1998): 144ff. On music for *The Prince of Egypt.*
"Agents of Change, Part 1." 25:4 (April 1999): 132–33. First of a three-part article on
    agent Cheryl Tiano and marketing composers.
"Agents of Change, Part 2." 25:5 (May 1999): 120.
"Agents of Change, Part 3." 25:6 (June 1999): 112.
"The Executive Suite: An Interview with Robert Kraft, Part 1." 25:8 (August 1999): 132–
    33. First of a three-part article with the Fox music department head.
"The Executive Suite, Part 2." 25:9 (Fall 1999): 116–17.
"The Executive Suite, Part 3." 25:10 (September 1999): 118–20.
"Demonstrative: Just as Actors Audition for a Role, Composers Must Audition by Sub-
    mitting a Demo." 25:11 (October 1999): 148–49.
"According to Basil: As Expectations and Approaches Have Changed in Film Music,
    Basil Poledouris Has Stayed on the Cutting Edge." 25:12 (November 1999): 144.
"Conduct Yourself Accordingly." 25 (December 1999): 126–27. On conducting film
    scores.
"The Door: Pop Tunes Rely on Hooks to Set Them Apart; the Way to Write a Good Film
    Score Is Through a Door." 26:2 (February 2000): 144.
"Making Soundtracks, Part 1: Those Pesky Songs that Show Up in between Your Cues—
    Who Puts 'em There, Anyway?" 26:3 (March 2000): 118. Interview with music su-
    pervisor Chris Douridas.
"Making Soundtracks, Part 2: More on the Differences between the Score and the Sound-
    track." 26:4 (April 2000): 138–39.
"Out with *The In Crowd*: Fusing Electronica Techniques with Traditional Film Scoring."
    26:5 (May 2000): 130–31.

"Making the Cut; How to Keep Up with Recuts, Rating Changes, and Fader Finger." 26:6 (June 2000): 130. On editing film music.

"Aye, There's the Dub; The Dubbing Stage Is Where Your Film Score Dukes It Out with the Other Sonic Elements of the Film." 26:7 (July 2000): 150–51.

"Raising Carter Burwell, Part I." 26:8 (August 2000).

"Raising Carter Burwell, Part II." 26:9 (September 2000): 134.

"The Song Remains the Same…But How Do I Transpose This Track?" 26:10 (October 2000): 144–45.

"Watching Movies; It's Not Just for Kicks…It's Your Job!" 27 (January 2001): 152.

"Heavy *Traffic*." 27 (April 2001): 142ff. On synergy between sound design and composition for the 2000 film with music by Cliff Martinez.

"This Is Gonna Hurt—No One Emerges Unscathed from *Exit Wounds*." 27 (May 2001): 140.

"*Exit Wounds* 2: Time and the Promise of New Work Heals Wounds." 27 (June 2001): 140.

"Film Music, Voxels, Walking, and Chewing Gum—It's All Part of the Discussion at Aspen." 27 (October 2001): 142ff.

"Making a Scene; Boost Your Career with Scene-Specific Demos." 27 (November 2001): 130.

"*Black Hawk* Sound: It's Not the Sound of One Person Composing." 28 (May 2002): 124ff. On working with Hans Zimmer on *Black Hawk Down*.

"Flex! With Film Music, Your Most Valuable Muscle Is Invisible." 28 (August 2002): 126. On adaptability.

"As the Studio Turns…Keeping Up with the Joneses." 29 (February 2003): 114. On the use of Emagic software for film scoring.

"*Shelter Skelter*: A Move to a New Studio Solidifies a New Method." 29 (April 2003): 122. On scoring a film solely with computer software.

"Playing in *Traffic*, Part 2: Mixing the Real and the Unreal." (May 2004): 98. On Rona's score for the television miniseries.

"*A Thousand Roads* Led to Collaboration in Australia." 31 (March 2005): 54. On working with Lisa Gerrard.

"All Mixed Up." 31 (October 2005): 56. On Rona's score for *Slow Burn*.

Special issue, 16:3; issue 167 (March 1990) [Film Scoring]

Doerschuk, Robert L. "Top Guns: Trends, Frustrations, Artistic Skills, and the Impact of Electronics." 43–62. Interviews with Bruce Broughton, James Newton Howard, Michael Kamen, David Newman, and Alan Silvestri on the state of the art.

"An Open Letter from Danny Elfman." 47, 62, 64. Regarding his musical abilities.

Lehrman, Paul D. "Hit Lists." 67–73, 77–78. Computer synchronization software from Auricle to Cue.

McRae, Bill. "Breaking In." 83–88. Career strategies.

Doerschuk, Robert L. "Back to the Past: Steve Bernstein Revives Forgotten Classic Soundtracks." 86. Preparing scores for rerecording.

Lehrman, Paul D. "Time Code." 91–97. Using MIDI and SMPTE to synchronize music to film.

Keyboard Classics (US)

See also *Classics* (UK).

Passy, Charles. "You Oughta Be in Pictures! A Short History of Music in the Movies." 7:2 (1987): 8–11.

Copland, Aaron. "I Had a Great Deal to Learn." 7:2 (1987): 9. On *Of Mice and Men*.

Kurt Weill Newsletter (US)

Keller, Hans. "Drops in the Dreigroschen Ocean." 9:2 (Fall 1991): 10–11. Reprint of "Film Music: The Harry Lime Theme" from *Music Survey* (1951).

Sherry, Peggy. "David Raksin Remembers Weill, *Where Do We Go from Here*, and 'Developing' Film Music in the 1940s." 10:2 (Fall 1992): 6–9. Interview.

Latin American Music Review/Revista de Musica Latinoamericana (US)

Pedelty, Mark. "The Bolero: The Birth, Life, and Decline of Mexican Modernity." 20:1 (Spring–Summer 1999): 30–58. Includes a discussion of the bolero's role in Mexican film and television.

Parker, Robert Leroy. "Revueltas in San Antonio and Mobile." 23 (Spring–Summer 2002): 114–30. On Silvestre Revueltas's involvement conducting at an Alabama movie theater in the final days of silent films, circa 1928.

Thompson, Donald. "Film Music and Community Development in Rural Puerto Rico: The DIVEDCO program (1948–91)." 26:1 (Spring–Summer 2005): 102–14. History of the film music component of the program, which turned out original scores for approximately 100 films.

Leonardo Music Journal (US)

Journal of the International Society for the Arts, Sciences and Technology.

Sauer, Matthias. "International Theremin Resource Directory." 6 (1996): 78–82. Includes film scores that incorporate the Theremin in an issue devoted to the instrument.

Life with Music (US)

Published in Hollywood, California.

Starr, June. "Movie Music Makers." (May–June 1950): 15–16. On Leith Stevens's score for *Destination Moon*.

Listen to Norway (Norway)

Published by the Norwegian Music Information Center.

Haddal, Per. "Film Music: Hidden Cultural History." 2:1 (1994). A history of film music in Norway by journalist Haddal, translated by Virginia Siger.

Living Music (US)

Journal of the Living Music Foundation for the promotion of new music.

"Jack Elliott and the New American Orchestra." 1:3 (Spring 1984). The orchestra performed film music in Los Angeles-area concerts.

Parker, Robert. "Carlos Chavez and Music for the Cinema." 4:3 (Spring 1987): 1–2.

The Los Angeles Record (US)

Member newsletter from the Los Angeles chapter of NARAS, the National Academy of Recordings Arts and Sciences (the "Recording Academy"). Profile of Eddy Lawrence Manson in vol. 4, no. 1 (February 1984). See also *NARAS Journal*.

Mechanical Music (US)

Since 1954 this journal of the Musical Box Society International has included numerous articles on the PianOrchestra, Orchestrions, and so on.

Bowers, Q. David. "Theatre Photoplayers." 16:5 (1970): 202–14.

Baxter, Joan. "Musical Mechanisms in the Movies." 22:2 (1976): 146, and 22:3 (1976): 211. The series continued with parts 3 and 4 (1977) and parts 5 and 6 (1979).

Bopp, Ronald. "Fotoplayers, Films, Follies." (1980).

Walker, Charles. "Mechanical Musical Instruments in Television Movies." 31:1 (1985): 10–11.

Bowers, Q. David. "Photoplayer, Reminiscences, and Theater Organs." (1986).

Bopp, Ronald. "Mechanical Music in the Movies." (2004). On films that depict mechanical music.

Melody (US)

Monthly magazine, aimed at photoplay organists and pianists and lovers of popular music, from music publisher Walter Jacobs. Lloyd G. del Castillo, a leading organist who ran a theater organ school in New York, wrote a column, "The Photoplay Organist and Pianist" from 1924 through at least 1929. The "Speaking of Photoplay Organists" column ran from 1925 through at least 1927. A short-lived "Playing the Picture" column can be found in 1921 and perhaps other issues.

Fox, Joseph. "Interpretive Music for the Movies." 6:1 (January 1922): 24–25.

McGill, Maude Stolley. "A Ten-Lesson Course in Motion-Picture Playing." 6:2 (February 1922): 7. Lesson 1, with general advice. Reprinted from her book, *Ten Lesson Course in Moving Picture Piano Playing* (1916).

Fox, Joseph. "Interpretive Music for the Movies." (April 1923). "No. 10: Thematic Music Cue Sheets." Reprinted from sister publication *Jacobs' Orchestra Monthly* (the progressive band orchestra journal).

Schonemann, A. C. E. "The Organ in Picture Playing: An Interview with Miss Hazel Hirsh, Organist, State-Lake Theatre, Chicago." (August 1923).

Schonemann, A. C. E. "My Method of Scoring Pictures: An Interview with L. Carlos Meier, Organist at the Capitol Theatre, Des Moines, Iowa." 7:10 (October–November 1923): 6.

"Irene Juno, Photoplay Organist." 8:5 (May 1924): 4, 22. Profile.

Fox, Joseph. "And Now Try Your Hand at Prologue Production." 8:5 (May 1924): 5–6.

Fox, Joseph. "Interpreting Music for the Movies." 8:10 (October–November 1924): 7–8. Reprinted from *Jacobs' Orchestra Monthly*.

del Castillo, L. G. "What's Good in New Music." 10:1 (January 1926): 6–7. A somewhat regular feature in which the organist reviews orchestra, photoplay, organ, and popular music. Photoplay music is listed by name, with publisher, playing difficulty, brief description, and capsule review. For example, the music for *Flick and Flock*, in scenes with crowds, bustle, and excitement, "defeats its purpose by being in the minor key, which makes the agitato element predominate." This series may be the most extensive contemporary review of music published for motion picture accompaniment of the era.

Juno, Irene. "The Peter Pan of Organists." 9:5 (May 1925): 5–6. Otto Beck profile.

"Music and the Cinema." 9:5 (May 1925): 6–7.

Juno, Irene. "Among the Washington [D.C.] Organists." 9:5 (May 1925): 26–27. Became a somewhat regular feature.

Juno, Irene. "Among Washington Organists." 10:1 (January 1926): 32. Lists and discusses more than a dozen theater organists.

Parks, Henry Francis. "Chicago's Maestro of the Movie Symphony Orchestra." 10:11 (November 1926): 6. Profile of M. Adolphe Dumont.

Parks, Henry Francis. "Seven Chicago Cinema Synchronizers." 10:11 (November 1926): 12–14. On Henri A. Keates, Mrs. Jesse Crawford, and others.

Barnard, J. D. "Northwestern Movie Musicians." 10:11 (November 1926): 22.

Juno, Irene. "Bits of Blue." 13:1 (February 1929): 7, 51. On the lack of work for organists due to mechanical music (synchronized sound films).

Juno, Irene. "R.K.O. Organists." 13:4 (April 1929): 13, 49. Profiles of organists at the theater chain.

Column, "The Photoplay Organist and Pianist" by L. G. del Castillo (selected)

[No title.] 8:5 (May 1924): 6–7. Tips on novelties and classifying music.

"A Vacation Tour of Theatre Organs in New York." 8:9 (September 1924): 5–6.

10:1 (January 1926): 5, 25. On mechanical aids to cueing pictures.

"First Aid to the Photoplayer." 12:1 (January 1928): 12–13. Installment no. 44.

"Where Do We Go From Here?" 13:9 (September 1929): 13, 15. Installment no. 64. On the revolution of synchronized sound pictures and its effect on theater organists.

"The Disease Is Organic." 13:10 (October 1929): 8–9. Installment no. 65. Follow-up to previous column.

Column, "Playing the Picture" (selected)

"Not Enough Musicians." 5:5 (May 1921): 24–25.

Jay, Alice Smythe. "The Cue-Sheet and Synchronizing." (September 1921). Claims to have originated the cue sheet in 1913.

Column, "Speaking of Photoplay Organists" (selected)

9:2 (February 1925): 26. Second installment. George Allaire Fisher profile of Lloyd G. del Castillo.

9:5 (May 1925): 5. George Allaire Fisher profile of Lewis Bray.

10:1 (January 1926): 7. Ward Allen profile of Frank Richter.

10:2 (February 1926): 6. Irene Juno profile of Robert Machat.

11:6 (June 1927): 20–21. M.V.F. and Avelyn M. Kerr profiles of Henry Francis Parks, R. Wilson Ross, and others.

Melody Maker (UK)

Weekly British newspaper aimed at popular music and musicans.

Mathieson, Muir. "The British Film Musical." (January 1947).

Houston, B. "[Lalo] Schifrin: Instinct Alone Is Not Enough." (October 16, 1965): 6. On scoring *The Liquidator*.

"[Pink] Floyd Write Major Film Score." 44 (December 13, 1969): 3. On songs for *Zabriskie Point* by the British rock band Pink Floyd.

Jones, M. "Bringing Jazz to the Screen." 45 (June 13, 1970): 10. On Pete Rugolo.

The Metronome (US)

Monthly journal from New York music publisher Carl Fischer, aimed at orchestra and band leaders and devoted to the interest of music in general. Also known as *The Metronome Band Monthly* and *The Metronome Orchestra Monthly*; can be considered a sister publication to *The Musical Observer*. Frank Edson edited a column, "The Movies," in 1915 and 1916. Around 1916 *Metronome* advertised the Carl Fischer Moving Picture Service Department, which provided music suggestions and cue sheets selected and compiled by a staff of experts.

Shaw, L., Jr. "The Motion Picture Pianist." 30:11 (1914): 32.

"The Movies: A Moving Picture Score by Victor Herbert." 32:6 (June 1916): 16. Interview.

Boblitz, K. Sherwood. "Moving Picture Music and How It Impresses the Child." 32:8 (August 1916): 42. Originally appeared in *Musical Observer* (1916).

Breil, Joseph Carl. "Moving Pictures of the Past and Present and the Music Provided for Same." 32:11 (November 1916): 42. On his scores for a number of films.

O'Sullivan, Joseph. "Adaptation of Music to Motion Pictures." 33:7 (1917): 58.

"How Motion Pictures Have Helped Good Music in America." (August 1920): 19.

Van Broekhoven, J. "Musical Opportunities in the Movies." (September 1920): 51.

Lachenbruch, Jerome. "The Motion Picture as the Press Agent for Good Music." (January 1921): 76.

Lachenbruch, Jerome. "Pitfalls of Popular Music in the Photoplay Theatre." (March 1921): 78.

Lachenbruch, Jerome. "Jazz and the Motion Picture." 38:4 (April 1922): 94. An early mention of jazz in connection with film.

"Where Music of the Theatre Will Be Studied." (December 1922): 66–67.

Antrim, Doron K. "The Growing Tendency to Popularize the Classics." (January 1923): 59.

"J. S. Zamecnik, Editor, Composer, Arranger, Executive." (September 1923): 153.

Wallace, Harry. "The Business of Scoring and Syncronizing [*sic*] the Motion Pictures." (June 1925): 51.

Beck, Bernard N. "Popular Music for Motion Picture Work." (October 15, 1925): 52.

Hyman, Edward L. "Choosing Picture Music that Pleases the Patrons." (February 1, 1926): 55.

Antrim, Doron K. "Possibilities of Movie Music—Present and Future." (February 15, 1926): 20.

Beck, Bernard N. "Popular Music in Pictures." (May 15, 1926): 17.

Lyon, Harold J. "The Organ in the Motion Picture Theater." (September 1926): 23.

Lyon, Harold J. "The Organ in the Motion Picture Theater, II." (November 15, 1926): 22, 41.

Whyte, Gordon. "J. S. Zamecnik." (September 1927): 41; 62.

Crawford, Tim. "What Is Required of the Theatre Organist." (September 1927): 56.

Crawford, Tim. "The Use and Misuse of Themes." (May 1, 1927): 24.

Sidney, L. K. "What Modern Music Has Done to the Motion Picture Theaters." (January 1928): 26.

Lyon, Harold J. "Organist Versus Sound Films." 45:3 (March 1929): 41–42.

"General Musical Director of Publix Theatres." 45:3 (March 1929): 42–43. Profile of Boris Morros.

Channing, Leroy L. "Are We Downhearted? A Survey of Conditions after Three Years of Talkies." (September 1929): 47–48.

Kelly, Fran. "Leith Stevens: Unsung Hero." 71 (September 1955): 20–27.

Mix Magazine (US)

Professional audio and music production magazine. Interviews and articles on all aspects of sound mixing, including music, and news items related to recording studios. Articles on specific films in the section "Sound for Picture" occasionally mention music.

"Interview with Henry Mancini." (November 1988).

Michie, Chris. "Scoring on the Road." 21:4 (April 1997): S38–S40.

Droney, Maureen. "Brad Fiedel: Scoring at Home." 21:6 (June 1997): 83.

Kenny, Tom. "Carter Burwell: An Ironic Twist on Film Scoring." 21:10 (October 1997): 269, 272–76.

Eskow, Gary. "Film Score Introductions: Two Composers on the Right Track." 21:11 (November 1997): 109, 118, 120.

Lambert, Mel. "An Industry Legend Revitalized." 21:12 (December 1997): 171, 181.

"The Newman Scoring Stage at 20th Century Fox." 22:4 (April 1998): S3.

Clark, Rick. "Scoring for Film." 23:2 (February 1999). Insights from interviews with Danny Elfman, Michael Kamen, John Ottman, and Trevor Rabin.

Flans, Robyn. "Sound for Film: Scoring for the Biggest Screen." 23:11 (November 1999): 149, 154–60. On Steve Wood and his scores for *Everest* and *The Living Sea*.

Eskow, Gary. "Composer Spotlight: Irwin Fisch." 23:12 (December 1999). On the New York-based composer and his score for the television series *Aftershock*.

Chun, Kimberly. "Composer Spotlight: Anne Dudley." 24:2 (February 2000): 151, 157–64.

Michie, Chris. "Scoring *The Patriot*." 24:7 (July 2000). On John Williams's music.

Chun, Kimberly. "Composer Spotlight: Ryuichi Sakamoto: Emperor of Technopop." 24:9 (September 2000): 29–38.

Lambert, Mel. "The Interview: Composer Snuffy Walden—From *The Wonder Years* to *The West Wing*." 25:2 (February 2001): 81–84.

Farinella, David John. "Scoring to Survive." 26:3 (March 2001). On Russ Landau and his music for the television show *Survivor*.

Verna, Paul. "Composer Spotlight: Carter Burwell." 26:10 (October 2001).

Clark, Rick. "Composer Spotlight: Gary Chang." 26:11 (November 2001).

Farinella, David John. "Composer Spotlight: Richard Wolf." 27:1 (January 2002). On scoring the animated television program *Static Shock*.

Reesman, Bryan. "Composer Spotlight: Mychael Danna, Globe-Trotting Visionary." 27:5 (May 2002).

Reesman, Bryan. "Composer Spotlight: Christopher Young." 27:8 (August 2002).

Walker, Chris J. "Paramount Scoring Stage M." 27:10 (October 2002).

"Special Report: Music and Sound Effects Libraries." 27:12 (December 2002). Includes profiles on the Hollywood Edge, Killer Tracks, and Megatrax Music.

"Sound for Picture: Lisa Gerrard: The Color of Sound." 28:2 (February 2003).

Droney, Maureen. "Sound for Picture: A Day in the Life of a Scoring Stage." 29:4 (April 2004). Documents a visit to the Clint Eastwood Stage at Warner Bros. to record Jerry Goldsmith's score for *Looney Tunes: Back in Action*.

Hurwitz, Matt. "Sound for Picture: Recording the Score for *Troy*." 29:7 (July 2004). On recording James Horner's score.

Hurwitz, Matt. "*Christmas with the Kranks*." 30:1 (January 2005). On recording John Debney's score.

Hurwitz, Matt. "Sound for Picture: *Fantastic* Score." 30: 7 (July 2005). On recording John Ottman's score for *Fantastic Four*.

Hurwitz, Matt. "The Sound of Silents." 30:12 (December 2005). On Robert Israel and creating scores for silent films.

Hurwitz, Matt. "Bringing in New Blood." 30:12 (December 2005). On scoring mixer Dan Blessinger and TCM's Young Film Composers Competition.

Modern Music (US)

Published in New York by the League of Composers from 1924 to 1946. Articles in the early to mid-1930s often discuss the developing art of scoring sound films, many by well-known composers of concert music with modernist tendencies. Topics include musical style, dialogue scoring, and the challenge of recording music. Composer George Antheil wrote a column, "On the Hollywood Front" from 1936 through 1939, that included references to music in films in current release. Paul Bowles and Leon Kochnitzky continued the column as "On the Film Front" through 1942. "On the Hollywood Front" then returned from 1944 to 1946, written by Lawrence Morton. The "Films and Theater" column by Paul Bowles and Elliott Carter often mentioned film music. For additional articles, see "Film Music," pp. 71–72, in Wayne D. Shirley's *Modern Music, Published by The League of Composers, 1924–1946: An Analytic Index* (New York: AMS, 1976).

Riesenfeld, Hugo. "Film Music." 3:2 (January–February 1926): 30–31. On the lack of "modern" in motion picture music.

Petit, Raymond. "Forecast and Review: Music Written for French Films." 3:3 (March–April 1926): 32–36.

Fried, Alexander. "Forecast and Review: For the People." 4:2 (January–February 1927): 33–37.

Milhaud, Darius. "Experimenting with Sound Films." 7:2 (February–March 1930): 11–14. On his early attempts at film scoring, translated from *La Revue du Cinema*, 1929.

Closson, Hermann. "The Case against 'Gebrauchsmusik.'" 7:2 (February–March 1930): 15–19. On utility music (*Gebrauchsmusik*), including early sound films.

Heinsheimer, Hans. "Film Opera: Screen vs. Stage." 8:3 (March–April 1931): 10–14. Film as operatic substitute.

Hammond, Richard. "Forecast and Review: Pioneers of Movie Music." 8:3 (March–April 1931): 35–38. On experimental scores by Marc Blitzstein, Colin McPhee, and Darius Milhaud.

Einstein, Alfred. "Forecast and Review: [Arnold] Schönberg's Super-Film Musik." 8:3 (March–April 1931): 45–46.

Thomson, Virgil. "A Little about Movie Music." 10:4 (May–June 1933): 188–91. On aesthetic problems with film music.

Weatherwax, John. "Forecast and Review: On the Pacific Coast." 11:2 (January–February 1934): 106–9. Mention of Desider Vecsey and a paragraph on Hungarian film music.

Antheil, George. "Composers in Movieland." 12:2 (January–February, 1935): 62–68. On the demand for original scores composed by a single composer.

Blitzstein, Marc. "Theatre-Music in Paris." 12:3 (March–April 1935): 128–34. On the "hipness" of movies and film music as an antecedent to stage music, 130–33.

Eisler, Hanns. "Reflections on the Future of the Composer." 12:4 (May–June 1935): 180–86.

[Engel, Lehman]. "[Dimitri] Shostakovich 'Accompanies' a Film." 12:4 (May–June 1935): 207. Brief article by "L.E." on *The Youth of Maxim*.

Toch, Ernst. "Sound-Film and Music Theatre." 13:2 (January–February 1936): 15–18.

Antheil, George. "Good Russian Advice about Movie Music." 13:4 (May–June 1936): 53–56. On Leonid Sabaneev.

Antheil, George. "Breaking into the Movies." 14:2 (January–February 1937): 82–86.

Thomson, Virgil. "Films Seen in New York." 14:4 (May–June 1937): 239–40. Including Silvestre Revueltas's score for *The Wave*.

Blitzstein, Marc. "On Writing Music for the Theatre." 15:2 (January–February 1938): 81–85. Includes music for films.

Gutman, John A. "Casting the Film Composer." 15:4 (May–June 1938): 216–21. On France and Britain.

Copland, Aaron. "Second Thoughts on Hollywood." 17:3 (March–April 1940): 141–47. On the scoring process and the need for effective music.

Thomson, Virgil. "Chaplin Scores." 18:1 (November–December 1940): 15–17. Regarding *City Lights*.

Cowell, Henry. "The League's [League of Composers] Evening of Films." 18:3 (March–April 1941): 176–78.

Eisler, Hanns. "Film Music—Work in Progress." 18:4 (May–June 1941): 250–54.

Moross, Jerome. "Hollywood Music without Movies." 18:4 (May–June 1941): 261–63. On concert music by "film" composers.

Herrmann, Bernard. "Four Symphonies by Charles Ives." 22:4 (May–June 1945): 215–22.

Kubik, Gail. "Composing for Government Films." 23:3 (Summer 1946): 189–92. Kubik served as director of music for the Office of War Information.

Column, "On the Film Front" (selected)
19:3 (March–April 1942): 192–94. Leon Kochnitzky on music for World War II short films.

Column, "On the Hollywood Front" by George Antheil (selected)
14:1 (November–December 1936): 46–49. First column.
14:2 (January–February 1937): 105–7. On the current state of film music. Reprinted in *Perspectives of New Music* (1964).
16:2 (1939): 278–80. Last column.

Column, "On the Hollywood Front" by Lawrence Morton
21:2 (January–February 1944): 116–18. On Alfred Newman's music for *The Song of Bernadette*.
21:3 (March–April 1944): 184–86. On Bernard Herrmann's music for *Jane Eyre*.
21:4 (May–June 1944): 264–66. On Robert Russell Bennett's music for *Lady in the Dark* and Gail Kubik's scores for *Earthquakers* and *Memphis Belle*.
22:1 (November–December 1944): 63–65. On Leigh Harline's music for *Baggage Busters* and Hanns Eisler's 12-tone music for *White Floats*.
22:2 (January–February 1945): 135–37. On the state of the art.
22:3 (March–April 1945): 205–6. On Franz Waxman's music for *Objective Burma*.
22:4 (May–June 1945): 274–75. On Dimitri Tiomkin's score for the war documentary *San Pietro*, film music as propaganda, and Ben Machan's score for *Power Unlimited*.
23:1 (Winter 1946): 75–76. On costume dramas and Hugo Friedhofer's score for *Marco Polo*.
23:2 (Spring 1946): 141–43. On folk songs.
23:3 (Summer 1946): 220–22. On William Walton's score for *Henry V*.
23:4 (Fall 1946): 313–15. On music by Georges Auric.

Monthly Musical Record (UK)
Scott, Cyril. "The Cinema and Programme Music." 63:752 (December 1933): 225.
King, A. Hyatt. "Looking Back on Film Music." 70:820 (October 1940).

Motion Picture and Television Music Credits Annual (US)
The Belgische Filmmuziek Society in Mechelen, Belgium, published this 176-page annual, compiled and edited by Ronald L. Bohn, in 1984. Lists film and prime-time television credits for 1983. Sources include trade papers, film periodicals, newspaper reviews, print ads, and viewing of screen credits. Supplemented by information on European films from several correspondents. The 1,256 entries are in random order, with indexes by name, film title, and name of television program.

MP/TV Music Credits Bulletin (US)
Quarterly publication compiled and edited by Ronald L. Bohn in Los Angeles. Original correspondents were James Marshall (Great Britain) and Luc Van de Ven (Belgium), later joined by Jean-Pierre Pecqueriaux, Julius J. C. Wolthuis, and David Kraft. Intended as a reference tool for researchers and those interested in film music and composers. In two sections: current theatrical releases and television programs, with an emphasis on television films and pilots. Composer credits, director, cast, and running time included.

Sources included trade papers, ads, film studios and television stations, and actual viewing. Publication ceased after the fourth issue. Bohn compiled a similar annual in 1983 (see next entry). A fan of film music, Bohn worked in the physics department at UCLA. In the 1970s he edited the "Cinema Buffs Newsletter"; see, for example, "*Cimarron* and Max Steiner," vol. 2, no. 3 (January 1974), p. 1.

1:1 (January–March 1980)
1:2 (April–June 1980)
1:3 (July–September 1980)
1:4 (October–December 1980)

Music Analysis (UK)
Published in association with the Society for Music Analysis.

Krims, Adam. "What Does It Mean to Analyse Popular Music?" 22:1–2 (March 2003): 181–209.

Davison, Annette. "Music and Multimedia: Theory and History." 22:3 (October 2003): 341–65. Film music is included in this discussion, which draws on the writings of Nicholas Cook.

Music and Letters (UK)
Leading British journal of music scholarship, known for fostering a dialogue between musicology and other disciplines. Some reviews of books on film music.

Austin, Cecil. "Cinema Music." 5:2 (April 1924): 177–91. On the state of the art.

Evans, Edwin. "Music and the Cinema." 10:1 (January 1929): 65–69.

Sabaneev, Leonid. "Music and the Sound Film." 15:2 (April 1934): 147–52.

Irving, Ernest. "Music in Films." 24:4 (October 1943): 223–35.

Avery, Kenneth. "William Walton." 28 (1947): 1–11.

Smith, Richard Langham. "Debussy and the Art of the Cinema." 54:1 (January 1973): 61–70. Focuses on Debussy's writings alluding to the cinema.

Stilwell, Robynn J. "'I Just Put a Drone Under Him…': Collage and Subversion in the Score of *Die Hard*." 78:4 (November 1997): 551–80. On Michael Kamen's score, with music excerpts.

Crisp, Deborah, and Roger Hillman. "Verdi and Schoenberg in Bertolucci's *The Spider's Stratagem*." 82:2 (May 2001): 251–67.

Music and Musicians (UK)
Monthly music guide devoted to serious music and opera. Superseded by *Music and Musicians International* in 1987.

Arnold, Malcolm. "I Think of Music in Terms of Sound." 4:11 (July 1956): 9.

"Richard Rodney Bennett." 19 (January 1971): 18–19. Brief mention of Bennett's film music class in the United States.

Palmer, Christopher. "Composer in Hollywood." 21:4 (December 1972): 15–16. Miklós Rózsa interview, reprinted in Jay Leyda's *The Voices of Film Experience* (1977).

Palmer, Christopher. "St. Petersburg to Hollywood." 21:8 (April 1973): 18–20. On Dimitri Tiomkin's music for *Tchaikovsky*.

Music and Musicians International (UK)
Continued *Music and Musicians* from 1987. During the 1990s Geoffrey Crankshaw occasionally wrote about music on television (see August 1990, p. 25).

Giffuni, Cathe. "A Bibliography of the Film Scores of Ralph Vaughan Williams." 37:2 (October 1988): 24–31.

Palmer, Christopher. "Prokofiev and Eisenstein." (November 1989): 6–10.

Palmer, Christopher. "The Music of Metro-Goldwyn-Mayer." 38:7 (March 1990): 8–12.

Music and the Arts (US)

Kellow, Brian. "George Duning and *Picnic*." 1:4 (circa 1996): 32–35.

Music Clubs Magazine (US)

Antheil, George. "Music Takes a Screen Test." 18:2 (November–December 1938): 7–10, 22. Originally appeared in *American Scholar* (Summer 1937).

Music Connection (US)

Music industry trade magazine aimed at the professional and semipro musician. Published biweekly since 1977. Dan Kimpel and Jonathan Widran profiled and interviewed numerous composers under a variety of headings, including "Composer Crosstalk" and "Songwriter Profile."

Widran, Jonathan. "Arranger Crosstalk: Steve Bartek." 12 (1995).

"Composer/Arranger Crosstalk: Patrick Williams." 21:7 (March 31, 1997–April 13, 1997): 17.

Widran, Jonathan. "Composer Crosstalk: Thomas Jones Chase and Steve Rucker." 21:13 (June 23–July 6, 1997).

Widran, Jonathan. "Luis Bacalov." 21:14 (July 7–20, 1997): 17.

"Composer Profile: Camara Kambon." 21:16 (August 4–17, 1997): 15.

Widran, Jonathan. "Composer Crosstalk: Graeme Revell." 21:18 (September 1–14, 1997): 17.

Widran, Jonathan. "Film Scorer Crosstalk: Alan Silvestri." 21:20 (September 29–October 12, 1997): 19.

Widran, Jonathan. "Composer Crosstalk: Dennis McCarthy." 21:22 (October 27–November 9, 1997).

Widran, Jonathan. "Film Composer: Zbigniew Preisner." 21:23 (November 10–23, 1997): 17.

Widran, Jonathan. "Mychael Danna." 22:1 (January 5–18, 1998): 17.

Widran, Jonathan. "Harry Gregson-Williams." 22:3 (February 2–15, 1998): 17.

Baur, Bernard. "Composer Crosstalk: Robyn Miller." 22:11 (May 25–June 7, 1998).

Widran, Jonathan. "Composer Crosstalk: Lou Forestieri." 22:14 (July 6–19, 1998): 17.

Widran, Jonathan. "Composer Crosstalk: Roger Bellon." 22:16 (August 3–16, 1998): 17.

Baur, Bernard. "Composer Crosstalk: Richard Gibbs." 22:18 (August 31, 1998–September 13, 1998): 17.

Kimpel, Dan. "Songwriter Profile: Will Jennings." 22:22 (October 26, 1998–November 8, 1998): 15.

Widran, Jonathan. "Composer Crosstalk: Cliff Eidelman—This Veteran Film Scorer Continues to Search for Magical Moments in His Work." 22:23 (November 9–22, 1998): 17.

Kimpel, Dan. "Songwriter Profile: Peter Himmelman—Scratching the Five Year Itch." 23:8 (April 12–25, 1999): 15.

Widran, Jonathan. "Producer Crosstalk: Stephen Warbeck." 23:9 (April 26, 1999–May 9, 1999): 17.

Kimpel, Dan. "Newman's Own—Randy Flies Solo after 10 Hectic Years." 23:14 (July 5–18, 1999): 28, 31, 37.

Widran, Jonathan. "Producer Crosstalk: Mark Snow." 23:15 (July 19, 1999–August 1, 1999): 17.

Widran, Jonathan. "Songwriter Profile: Mark Mancina—Me Tarzan, You Phil Collins." 23:16 (August 2–15, 1999): 19.

Kimpel, Dan. "Songwriter Profile: Ennio Morricone—A Movie Maestro's Voyage to 1900." 23:22 (October 25, 1999–November 7, 1999): 19.

Widran, Jonathan. "High Profile: Tangerine Dream." 23:25 (December 6, 1999–January 2, 2000): 73.

Kimpel, Dan. "Songwriter Profile: Michael Tavera—*Drowning Mona*'s Composer Breaks the Surface." 24:7 (March 27, 2000–April 9, 2000): 19.

Kimpel, Dan. "Artist Profile: Ryuichi Sakamoto—Imagining the Music." 24:7 (March 27, 2000–April 9, 2000): 53.

Kimpel, Dan. "Songwriter Profile: From Bloodbaths to Blockbusters." [25]:15 (July 16–29, 2001). On Christopher Young.

Kimpel, Dan. "Songwriter Profile: Coen Bros. and the Sonic Shadows." [25]:22 (October 22–November 4, 2001). On Carter Burwell.

Music Educators Journal (US)

Peer-reviewed journal with scholarly and practical articles on teaching, published by the National Association for Music Education. Served at one time as the official magazine of the Music Educators National Conference (MENC). Oldest academic journal in music education. In 1934 superseded *Music Supervisors' Journal*.

"The Use of Standard Musical Compositions in Motion Pictures." 25:2 (October 1938): 56.

Ussher, Bruno David. "Film Music and School Music." 26:4 (February 1940): 18–19. Calls for film music in public school education.

Hartshorn, William C. "Music of the Motion Pictures." 30:6 (May 1944): 30, 35.

Rózsa, Miklós. "The Cinderella of the Cinema." 32:3 (January–February 1946): 15–17, 58. Brief history of film music.

Rodriguez, José. "Music of the Animated Pictures." 32:5 (April 1946): 18–19.

Bradley, Scott. "Personality on the Sound Track: A Glimpse behind the Scenes and Sequences in Filmland." 33:3 (January 1947): 28–30. Reprinted in Daniel Goldmark and Yuval Taylor, *The Cartoon Music Book* (2002).

McConnell, Stanlie. "Can Film Music Be Used Educationally?" 33:4 (February–March 1947): 30–31.

Braslin, John E. "Motion Pictures for Music Education." 35:5 (April 1949): 30, 33.

Wall, Dorothy. "Let's See a Movie!" 36:6 (June 1950): 25–26. Schoolchildren's responses to *The Schumann Story*, an MGM short subject film.

Ress, Etta Schneider. "Audio-Visual Forum." 38:2 (November–December 1951): 40, 42. On Arthur Honegger's score for *Pacific 231*.

"The Handwritten Sound Track." 55:3 (November 1968): 114.

Creston, Paul. "Music and the Mass Media." 56:8 (April 1970): 35–36, 101–6. The composer touches on film music.

63:7 (March 1977). Special issue, contents listed below.

Newlin, Dika. "Music for the Flickering Image: American Film Scores." 64:1 (September 1977): 24–35. On the functions of film music. Includes an excerpt, "Composing for Films," from a transcript of Earle Hagen's documentary film *The Score*, reprinted from *BMI: The Many Worlds of Music* (1974), and an article by Tom Shales, "Scoring One for the Movies," on Jerry Goldsmith, reprinted from the *Washington Post*. Introduced by John Aquino; see "Overtones," 5.

Kennedy, Evelyn. "Film Music Editor." 69:2 (October 1982): 54. On her job duties. Revision of her March 1977 article.

Spaeth, Jeanne. "Alan Menken on Music's Many Forms." 84:3 (November 1997): 39–40, 48. Interview.

Special issue, 63:7 (March 1977) ["Careers in Music: Broadcasting/Recording/Film Careers"]

Lindsay, Mort. "TV Music Director." 62–63. Lindsay was music director for the *Merv Griffin Show*.

Griffith, David. "TV Music Producer." 63–64.

Kennedy, Evelyn, as told to Robert Osborne. "Film Music Editor." 71.

Pemberton, Roger. "Studio Musician." 80.

Reed, Alfred. "Music Editor." 110–11.

Music in Art (US)

International journal for music iconography.

Dapena, Gerard. "Spanish Film Scores in Early Francoist Cinema, 1940–1950." 27:1–2 (Spring–Fall 2002): 141–51. Part of an issue devoted to music in Iberian art and film.

Music in Education (UK)

"Film Music: A Teacher's Aspect." (July 1946).

Green, Derick M. "*Oliver Twist*: Music for the Film." (September–October 1948): 123.

Cockshott, Gerald. "Twenty-Four Films." 29: 313 (1965): 137–38. Reference to Ralph Vaughan Williams.

Music Journal (US)

Monthly educational magazine dedicated to the advancement of music in America. Published in New York from 1946 to 1987; previously published as *Music Publishers Journal* from 1943 to 1946. Columns by C. Sharpless Hickman include "Heard While Seeing" from November 1951 to May 1952, followed by "Movies and Music" from September 1952 to at least April 1955. Later, "Cinema Music" by Joel Reisner appeared from 1968 to 1970.

Waxman, Franz. "Action on the Frontiers of American Composition." 2:1 (January–February 1944): 7ff.

3:5 (September–October 1945). Special film music issue, contents listed below.

Shilkret, Nathaniel. "Some Predictions for the Future of Film Music." 4:1 (January–February 1946): 29, 47–49.

McConnell, Stanlie. "Music Teachers and the Challenge of Film Music." 4:4 (1946): 15.

Saxe, Rudy De. "Views on the Function of Film Music." 4:4 (1946): 34.

Hendricks, Gordon. "Hollywood Film Music." 8:3 (May–June 1950): 11–12.

Shavin, Norman. "Them Days Is Gone Forever." 12:3 (March 1954): 13, 74–75. On piano accompaniments for silent film.

Young, Victor. "Confessions of a Film Composer: Victor Young." (September 1956): 16. Interview. Reprinted in *Film and TV Music*.

Tiomkin, Dimitri. "Writing Symphonically for the Screen." 17:1 (January 1959): 26, 106.

Spaeth, Sigmund. "In and Out of Tune." 20:4 (April 1962): 72. On dubbing.

Tiomkin, Dimitri. "The Music of Hollywood." 20:8 (November–December, 1962): 7, 87.

Amram, David. "The Five Keys to the Composer's Kingdom." 21:4 (April 1963): 27. Amram writes: "Most film composers (how can one write for films exclusively and be considered a composer?) in the process of selling out, hire ghostwriters and orchestrators who write ninety-five per cent of the music that appears in the film. Hollywood is a graveyard for serious composers."

Schnee, Charles. "Hollywood Plots with Music." 21:4 (April 1963): 48, 92.

Gustafson, Dwight L. "Composing for a Celluloid Taskmaster." 21:8 (November 1963): 56-57ff. On a student film.

Mann, Anthony. "Music and the Cinema." 22:3 (March 1964): 66.

Gold, Ernest. "For Whom Do You Write?" 22:12 (December 1964): 29.

Epstein, Dave A. "Flicker Flashback: Music Still Hath Charm." 23:4 (April 1965): 42–43, 99.

Cummings, Jack. "Music: Hollywood's Star Salesman." 23:4 (April 1965): 97.

"Shostakovich's Film Music: New *Hamlet* Released." 24:3 (March 1966): 54.

Mascott, Laurence E. "Documentary Film Music." 25:3 (March 1967): 36, 77.

Lippert, Robert L. "Film Music in the Mainstream." 25:9 (November 1967): 40.

Nelson, Gene. "Values of Film Music." 26:6 (June 1968): 24.

Column, "Cinema Music" by Joel Reisner (May 1968–1970) (selected)

"Kaper's Film Capers." 26:4 (April 1968): 71, 77. On Bronislaw Kaper.

26 (November 1968). On Bernard Herrmann.

Column, "Heard While Seeing" by C. Sharpless Hickman

9:7 (November 1951): 19. First column.

9:8 (December 1951): 32–33. On experiments in film music.

10:1 (January 1952): 36–37.

10:2 (February 1952): 38–39. On film scores of 1951.

10:3 (March 1952): 70. On Miklós Rózsa's score for *Quo Vadis*.

10:4 (April 1952): 46–47. On the MGM music department and library.

10:5 (May 1952): 30–32. On the MGM music department.

Column "Movies and Music" by C. Sharpless Hickman

10:6 (September 1952): 38. On current scores.

10:7 (October 1952): 36–37. On dubbing.

10:8 (November 1952): 28–29. On *Limelight*.

10:9 (December 1952): 32. On Miklós Rózsa.

11:1 (January 1953): 63. On opera and film.

11:2 (February 1953): 28–29. On Alex North.

11:3 (March 1953): 34. On current scores.

11:4 (April 1953): 38. On current scores.

11:8 (August 1953): 26–27. On George Antheil.

11:10 (October 1953): 30–31. On Frederick Hollander.

11:11 (November 1953): 26–27. On UPA animated films.

11:12 (December 1953): 26–27. On True-Life films.

12:1 (January 1954): 31, 53–54. On MGM's music department and John Green.

12:3 (March 1954): 60. Best scores of 1953.

12:4 (April 1954): 21. On UCLA student films.

12:6 (June 1954): 18–19. "Music School for Movies."

12:7 (July 1954): 18–19. On USC student films.

12:9 (September 1954): 46–47. On the Roger Wagner Chorale.

12:10 (October 1954): 78, 80. On film music research.

12:11 (November 1954): 45–46. On Leo Arnaud.

13:2 (February 1955): 36, 38. On David Raksin.

13:4 (April 1955): 46–47. Interview-based article on Dimitri Tiomkin.

Special film music issue: 3:5 (September–October 1945)

Waxman, Franz. "Progress in Development of Film Music Scores." 9, 66–67. Optimistic essay.

Spaeth, Sigmund. "Film Music and the Public." 10, 58–59.

"Composers Portrayed in Motion Pictures." 11, 48.

Kubik, Gail. "Music in Documentary Films." 13, 54–56.

Leinsdorf, Erich. "Some Views on Film Music." 15, 53–54.

Herrmann, Bernard. "Music in Motion Pictures—A Reply to Mr. Leinsdorf." 17, 69.

Burke, Johnny. "The Quiet Life of Film Song Writers." 19.

Evans, Lawrence. "Motion Picture Roles and Careers of Concert Artists." 21, 72.

Browning, Mortimer. "Establishing Standards for Evaluation of Film Music." 23, 63–64.

Maxwell, Charles. "A Score Is Born." 25, 50–53. Follows a film score from inception to scoring.

Quinto, Lenard. "Some Questions for Music Educators on Film Music." 27, 60–63.

Janssen, Werner. "Visualization of Music on the Screen." 29, 70.

Mabee, Grace Widney. "Work and Purposes of the National Film Music Council." 31, 67.

Thomson, Virgil. "Processed Music." 33, 60.

Minor, Monachus. "Music Library in the Film Studio." 35, 67–69.

Morrison, Margery. "Getting Acquainted with Some Film Music Scores." 38, 49.

De Saxe, Rudy. "Studio and Symphony Players." 40, 69.

"Milestones in History of Film Music." 57. From the files of the Museum of Modern Art, New York City.

Music Journal Annual (US)

Anthology, published as the July issue of *Music Journal* from 1961 to 1971.

Davis, Curtis W. "Television Puts Music in the Home." (1961): 66.

Chiusano, Michael. "The Year in TV." (1962): 52–53.

Spaeth, Sigmund. "The Year in Film Music." (1963): 60–64.

Spaeth, Sigmund. "The Year in Film Music." (1964): 129–30.

Spaeth, Sigmund. "The Year in Film Music." (1965): 76, 80.

Whitaker, Rod. "The Role of Movie Music." (1966): 68, 70.

Tiomkin, Dimitri. "Music for the Films." (1967): 29, 52.

Music News (US)

Published in Chicago.

"Concerning the New Art of Movie Music." (circa summer 1916).

"Movie Music and Joseph Carl Breil." (September 26, 1919): 16. Interview.

Previn, Charles. "Schillinger's Influence on Film Music." (March 1947): 13–16. The music director discusses Joseph Schillinger and his Schillinger System of Musical Composition. Herbert Spencer, Edward Powell, Lennie Hayton, and Frank Skinner are mentioned as students of the system; Nathan Van Cleave is listed in an ad as an authorized teacher.

Wheelwright, D. Sterling. "An Interview with Miklos Rozsa." 44 (October 1952): 15.

Music Parade (UK)

Illustrated miscellany for the music lover, published in London from 1946 to 1952. A "British Film Composers" series profiled at least nine composers. Most of the individual issues are undated.

Unwin, Arthur. "Music of the Cinema." 1 [1946].

Alwyn, William. "The Music in the Background." 1 [1947].

Mathieson, Muir. "William Walton." 1:6 [1948]: 11–12. No. 1 in a series.

Huntley, John. "William Alwyn." 1:7 [1948]: 7–9. No. 2 in a series.

Huntley, John. "Ralph Vaughan Williams." 1:8 [1948]: 7–9. No. 3 in a series.
Huntley, John. "Benjamin Frankel." 1:10 [1948–1949]: 10–11. No. 4 in a series.
Huntley, John. "Arthur Bliss." 1:11 [1948–1949]: 9–11. No. 5 in a series.
Huntley, John. "Clifton Parker." 1:12 [1948–1949]: 15–16. No. 6 in a series.
Huntley, John. "Arthur Wilkinson." 1:13 [1949]: 15–16, 18. No. 7 in a series.
"Young Veteran of Film Music: Muir Mathieson." 2:1 [1949]: 1.
Huntley, John. "Richard Addinsell." 2:1 [1949]: 19–21, 23. No. 8 in a series.
Huntley, John. "Alan Rawsthorne." 2:2 [1950]: 12–13. No. 9 in a series.
Arnell, Richard. "Richard Arnell Discusses His 'Opus 65.'" 2:12 (December 1952): 6–8.

Music Perception (US)

Interdisciplinary journal published by University of California Press.

Marshall, Sandra K., and Annabel J. Cohen. "Effects of Musical Soundtracks on Attitudes toward Animated Geometric Figures." 6:1 (Fall 1988): 95–112. Results of a study with university psychology students.

Boltz, Marilyn G. "Musical Soundtracks as a Schematic Influence on the Cognitive Processing of Filmed Events." 18:4 (Summer 2001): 427–54. A study of film music's effect on story comprehension, including a viewed scene from *Cat People* (1982) and *Vertigo* (1958) with positive and negative music (neither by the original composers).

Music Reference Services Quarterly (US)

Devoted to the needs of reference librarians at music libraries.

Miletich, Leo N. "Celluloid Serenades: Hollywood's Oscar-Winning Songs, Composers, and Nominees, 1934–1991." 1:4 (1993): 3–25.

Wright, H. Stephen. "Film Music in America: An Essay and Bibliography." 1:4 (1993): 101–13.

Anderson, Gillian. "'Perfuming the Air with Music': The Need for Film Music Bibliography." 2:1–2 (1993): 59–103. This entry and the following entry were copublished simultaneously in *Foundations in Music Bibliography* (1993), edited by Richard D. Green.

Anderson, Gillian. "Supplement to Steven D. Wescott's *A Comprehensive Bibliography of Music for Film and Television*." 2:1–2 (1993): 105–44. Shorter, preliminary version of Anderson's bibliographic additions to Wescott.

Krishan, Bal. "Film Music of India: An Essay and Bibliography." 3:1 (1994): 11–18.

Krishan, Bal. "Movie Music Mania: The Intense Popularity of Indian Film Music in the 1990s." 3:4 (1995): 39–43.

Wright, H. Stephen. "Bernard Herrmann: A Selected Secondary Bibliography." 4:1 (1995): 49–68.

Music Research Forum (US)

Published by the University of Cincinnati College–Conservatory of Music.

Joe, Jeongwon. "Hans Jürgen Syberberg's *Parsifal*: The Staging of Dissonance in the Fusion of Opera and Film." Vol. 13 (1998): 1–21.

Rooney, Kim. "Parlor Music in Film Adaptations of Jane Austen's Novels." Vol. 20 (2005): 39–54.

The Music Review (UK)

Published quarterly in Cambridge from 1940 to 1994. Music critic Hans Keller's column "Film Music," later "Film Music and Beyond," appeared from 1948 to 1959 and mostly covered British composers and music in films in current release. "The Half-Year's Film

Music" from 1953 to 1955 was a midyear review. Most of the articles are reprinted in *Film Music and Beyond*.

Carter, Ian. "Train Music." 54:3–4 (August–November 1993): 279–90. On music inspired by trains, including some film music.

<u>Column, "Film Music" / "Film Music and Beyond" by Hans Keller (selected)</u>

"Walton's *Hamlet*." 9:3 (August 1948): 197–99. Includes Arnold Bax's *Oliver Twist*. The Bax portion was reprinted in the *Bax Society Bulletin* (vol. 2, no. 2, 1970).

"Film Music and No Film Music." 10:1 (February 1949): 50–51.

10:2 (May 1949): 138. On Ralph Vaughan Williams's music for *Scott of the Antarctic*.

"Nine Swiss Shorts." 10:3 (August 1949): 225–26.

"Bliss—Frankel—Larson—Berg." 10:4 (November 1949): 303. On Arthur Bliss, Benjamin Frankel, and others.

"Arnell—Frankel." 11:1 (February 1950): 52–53. On Richard Arnell and Benjamin Frankel.

"William Alwyn: Bad and Great Work." 11:2 (May 1950): 145–46. On the "bad."

"William Alwyn: Bad and Great Work." 11:3 (August 1950): 216–17. On the "great."

"Roman Vlad (b. 1919)." 12:2 (May 1951): 147–49.

"The Dragon Shows His Teeth." 12:3 (August 1951): 221–25. Essay on film music criticism in response to recent articles by Lawrence Morton and Antony Hopkins.

"From Auden to Hollywood." 12:4 (November 1951): 315–17. On being aware of film music.

"Continental, British and American." 13:1 (February 1952): 54–56.

"Noisy Music and Musical Noise." 13:2 (May 1952): 138–40.

"World Review." 13:4 (November 1952): 310–12.

"Tales from the Vienna Hollywoods." 15:2 (May 1954): 140–42.

"Georges Auric at Film Music's Best." 15:4 (November 1954): 311–13.

"Carmen *à la* Hollywood." 16:2 (May 1955): 153–55. On *Carmen Jones*.

"[Georges] Auric–[Arthur] Benjamin–[Francis] Chagrin–[Alan] Rawsthorne–[Mátyás] Seiber–[William] Walton." 17:2 (May 1956): 154–56. Reviews.

"Malcolm Arnold Oscarred." 19:2 (May 1958): 150–51.

20:4 (November 1959): 301. This brief two-paragraph entry is the last appearance of "Film Music and Beyond." Keller's column "The New in Review" began around this time.

The Music Scene (Canada)

A monthly music magazine published in English and French by La Scène Musicale.

Kirkland, Bruce. "Writer Combines Styles for Final Lighthouse Sound." (November–December 1972). On Howard Shore.

Landry, Jacques. "More Film-Scoring Jobs Available When Conditions Change." No. 312 (March–April 1980).

"Music Cue Sheets: A Film and Television Composer's Route to Royalties." No. 361 (May–June 1988).

Music Supervisors' Journal (US)

Continued by *Music Educators Journal* in 1934.

Oberndorfer, Mrs. Mary E. "The Influence of the Visual in Music Appreciation." 12:2 (December 1925): 8–16.

Harley, Alexander M., and Louis A. Astell. "Music Appreciation through Visual Aids." 19:2 (November 1932): 20–21.

Music Survey (UK)

Coedited by music critic Hans Keller from 1949 to 1952. Columns are reprinted in *Film Music and Beyond*. Vols. 2–4 reprinted in book form as *Music Survey, New Series, 1949–52*, ed. Donald Mitchell and Hans Keller (London: Faber Music, 1981).

Column, "Film Music" by Hans Keller and others (selected)

1:6 (1949): 196–97.

2:1 (Summer 1949): 25–27. "The Question of Quotation," on classical music quotations.

2:2 (Autumn 1949): 101–2. On Virgil Thomson's score for *Louisiana Story*.

2:3 (Winter 1950): 188–89. On Virgil Thomson's score for *Louisiana Story*.

2:4 (Spring 1950): 250–51. On Benjamin Britten.

3:1 (Summer 1950): 42–43. Clarifications re "The Question of Quotation."

3:2 (1951): 101–2. [Written by guest columnist Bernard Stevens.]

3:3 (1951). Written by guest columnist Donald Mitchell.

3:4 (June 1951): 283–85. "The Harry Lime Theme." On Anton Karas's music for *The Third Man* and the influence of Kurt Weill.

4:4 (1952). Written by undetermined guest columnist.

Music Teacher (UK)

Milne, A. Forbes. "Good Music and the Kinema." 14 (1922): 297, 302.

Green, Christopher. "Composers for the Silver Screen." 60 (June 1981): 20–21.

Music Theory Spectrum: The Journal of the Society for Music Theory (US)

Leydon, Rebecca. "Debussy's Late Style and the Devices of the Early Silent Cinema." 23:2 (Fall 2001): 217–41.

Music Tracks Newsletter (US)

Serving the filmmaker with informative interviews and articles on music and film. Edited by music supervisor Richard R. McCurdy.

McCurdy, Richard. "Albert Sendrey: Adventures in Orchestrating Film Music." 1:4 (Summer 1980): 1–7; 1:5 (Summer 1981). Interview.

McCurdy, Richard. "Albert Sendrey on Orchestrating Film Music." 10 (Spring 1987): 1–5. Reprint of 1980–1981 interview.

Music Trade News (US)

Schertzinger, Victor. "The Composer of *Marcheta* Talks about the Talking Pictures." 8:4 (September 1929): 15–16.

The Music Trade Review (US)

"The Organ, the Organist, and the Motion Picture." 67:13 (September 28, 1918): 15.

Music U.S.A. (US)

Lucraft, Howard. "First Jazz Score: *The Wild One*." 76 (June 1959): 7. On Leith Stevens's music.

"Jazz Is Heard at the Movies." (July 1959): 38ff.

The Music World (US)

Cadman, Charles Wakefield. "The Musical Enigma of the Soundies." 1:4 (September 1930): 9, 20; 1:5 (October 1930): 6, 21.

Musica e Storia (Italy)

Bortolozzo, Roberta. "The Music in Woody Allen's Film *A Midsummer Night's Sex Comedy*." 6:2 (December 1998): 463–74. Discusses the director's use of music by Mendelssohn.

Musical Advance (US)

Schaff, Edward. "Jazz and the Picture House." 16:10 (May 1929): 3.

Musical America (US)

New York's weekly music magazine, incorporated into *High Fidelity* in 1965.

"Practical Way to Uplift 'Movie' Music." 22:18 (1915): 4.

Greenland, Blanche. "'Faking' in 'Movie' Music Corrupting Public's Taste." 22:22 (1915): 12.

Grant, J. P. "Popular Opera via the Movies." 24:9 (1916): 36–37.

29:2 (May 13, 1916): 43. Interview with Victor Herbert on *The Fall of a Nation*. See also an article on the film (June 17, 1916): 39.

Baldwin, Ruth Ann. "Motion Pictures Fertile Field for Composers." (July 1917): 3.

"On Motion-Picture Ideals in the Realm of Music." 29:18 (March 1, 1919): 24.

"Making Motion Picture Palaces Homes of Best Music." 30:3 (May 17, 1919): 9.

Crain, Hal. "Leaders of Joint Interests United under the Motto 'Finer Film-Music.'" 33:14 (January 29, 1921): 1, 3–4.

Isaacson, Charles. "Specialized Knowledge Is Need of Moving Picture Musicians." 33:18 (February 26, 1921): 37.

Kilenyi, Edward. "Fitting Music to the Films an Exacting Task." (September 15, 1923): 4.

Rogers, Bernard. "Is the Screen a Sesame to Opportunity for Our Composers?" 40:7 (June 7, 1924): 5, 32.

Arvey, Verna. "The Composer in Hollywood." (November 10, 1936).

Korngold, Julius. "About the Fate of Film Music." (February 10, 1942): 23. By Erich Korngold's father. A photo spread, "Some Composers Who Have Gone Hollywood," appears in the same issue.

Keefer, Lubov. "Soviet Film Music Plays Leading Role." 63 (September 1943): 6–8, 34.

Jones, Isabel Morse. "Golden Anniversary: Music a Willing Handmaiden in 50 Years of Film-Making." 64 (May 1944): 4–5, 10.

Jones, Isabel Morse. "Motion Pictures Seek New Musical Paths." 65 (February 1945): 23, 220. Reprinted in *Film Music Notes* (May 1945).

Clifford, Hubert. "British Film Music Comes of Age." 66 (January 10, 1946): 29, 34.

Deutsch, Adolph. "The Composer: Forgotten Man of the Movies." 66 (June 1946): 5, 38.

Jones, Isabel Morse. "Film Music: The Composer Emerges: A Man of Importance in New Hollywood Releases." 67 (February 1947): 19, 362.

Musical Courier (US)

Weekly journal from New York devoted to music and the music trades. A column, "Musical Comedy–Motion Pictures–Drama," ran from around 1923 to 1927 under this and various titles such as "Musical Comedy, Drama, and Motion Pictures." See vol. 87, no. 5 (August 2, 1923), p. 40, for an example by May Johnson. The column, often unattributed, included reports and reviews of music performed at New York motion picture theaters such as the Capitol, Rialto, and Rivoli. Music directors and conductors involved are often named. A column by Josephine Vila, "Music and the Movies," appears in 1927; beginning with vol. 94, no. 11, it is titled "Music and the Movies: Musical Comedy and

Drama." Vila's column documents the activities of Hugo Riesenfeld and the exhibition of *King of Kings,* and covers New York theaters such as the Roxy and Strand. By September 1928 the column was unattributed and contained only brief theater reports. Henry W. Levinger's column, "Radio, Television," ran from at least 1952 to 1954 and often mentions music on television.79 (October 2; 1919): 20. News item on Joseph Carl Breil's film scoring activities.

Gilbert, Henry F. "My Summer in the Movies," 86:3 (January 18, 1923): 6, 46–47. On the American composer's experience writing music to accompany a film in 1922.

Klemm, Gustav. "Music and the Movies." 86:11 (March 15, 1923): 7. The composer and music critic on the state of the art.

Hinrichs, Gustav. "A Plea for the Musician Who Creates the Musical Score for Feature Pictures." 86:25 (June 21, 1923): 7. A letter from the American conductor and composer.

Whithorne, Emerson. "Music and the Movies." 93:6 (August 5, 1926): 6, 31. On William Frederick Peters, on how the successful presentation of film depends on music, and the educational benefits of the symphonic orchestra in the movie theater.

Hadley, Henry. "Henry Hadley Talks on Writing Music for the Movies." 93:24 (December 9, 1926): 23. On his synchronized score for *When a Man Loves.*

Vila, Josephine. "Hugo Riesenfeld Tells How He Scores a Film." 94:7 (February 17, 1927): 48–49.

"Tiomkin under Contract with Metro-Goldwyn-Mayer." (October 19, 1929).

Saunders, Richard Drake. "Fitting the Music to the Film." 121:1 (January 1, 1940): 5, 25.

Saunders, Richard Drake. "'Rhythm Sheet' Aids in Hollywood Film Composition." 121:5 (March 1, 1940): 7. On click tracks, with a sample rhythm sheet.

Hickman, C. Sharpless. "Musicians in Films." 146:7 (November 15, 1952): 17. On Warner Bros. choral director Norman Luboff.

Hickman, C. Sharpless. "Musicians in Films." 147:1 (January 1, 1953): 15. General news.

[Post, Carl]. "Musicians in Films." 147:4 (February 15, 1953): 26. On George Antheil; also, Walter Scharf defends Hollywood.

Column, "Music and the Movies" by Josephine Vila

94:9 (March 3, 1927): 48–49. Subheading, "John Murray Anderson Enthusiastic about Paramount Theater Presentations."

94:10 (March 10, 1927): 44–45, 48. Subheading, "Samuel L. Warner Tells of the Plans of the Vitaphone Company," and discussion of music at the Capitol and Paramount theaters.

94:11 (March 17, 1927): 44–45, 48. On Paramount theater organist Jesse Crawford, May Dolin's invention for synchronizing pictures and music, and Jacques Grunberg's special music compositions for the Mark Strand theater.

94:14 (April 7, 1927): 44. Subheading, "The Cue Man for Fox Films," on Michael P. Krueger.

94:21 (May 26, 1927): 44–45. Guest article by William H. Denk, "Do You Take Your Ears to the Movies?"

Column, "Radio, Television" by Henry W. Levinger

"[Bohuslav] Martinu Opera for TV Premiere." 147:2 (January 15, 1953): 21.

Column, "Sound Track" (unattributed)

146:5 (October 15, 1952): 25. First column. On symphonic reworkings of film music by Miklós Rózsa and Franz Waxman. It is unclear if this column continued.

The Musical Digest (US)

Eaton, Quaintance. "Reading Music from Shadows: The 'Sound Track' on a Movie Film Is Not Yet an Open Book to Technicians." 14:9 (1929): 15–16.

Stravinsky, Igor, and Ingolf Dahl. "Igor Stravinsky on Film Music: As Told to Ingolf Dahl." (September 1946): 4–5, 35–36. On the function of film music and concert music in film. Reprinted in *Cinema* (June 1947) and the *Cue Sheet* (July 2004).

Raksin, David. "Hollywood Strikes Back: Film Composer Attacks Stravinsky's 'Cult of Inexpressiveness.'" 30:1 (January 1948): 5–[7]. Reprinted in the *Cue Sheet* (July 2004).

Marlott, Harry. "Music in the Movies." 30:2 (February 1948).

Musical Express (UK)

Mathieson, Muir. "Background for British Pictures." (January 3, 1947).

Huntley, John. "The Studio Orchestra." No. 56 (January 1, 1948): 2.

Huntley, John. "The Film Music of Sir Arnold Bax." No. 90 (June 25, 1948): 2.

Huntley, John. "Composer at the Barrel Organ." No. 95 (July 30, 1948): 3.

Musical Leader (US)

Bauer, Marion. "Interview with Dimitri Tiomkin." (October 31, 1929). Interview-based article. Publication date unverified.

Musical News (UK)

"Music at Cinemas." 48 (1915): 271–72.

Welsh, W. H. "Orchestras in Cinemas." 51 (1916): 313–14.

Davison, A. E. "Picture Music." No. 1423 (December 7, 1918): 163.

Musical News and Herald (UK)

"Music and the Films." 62:1554 (January 7, 1922): 19.

Henry, Leigh. "The Filming of Music." 62:1563 (March 11, 1922): 314, 316.

The Musical Observer (US)

Each issue included music for pianists. Advertisements claimed every musician who plays for the movies should subscribe. Sister publication was *The Metronome*.

Weisel, J. H. "The Moving Picture Organist; Ideal Usefulness of the Organ for Moving Pictures; Requirements of a Successful Organist; Selection and Timing of Numbers." 13:3 (March 1916): 177–78.

Boblitz, K. Sherwood. "Moving Picture Music and How It Impresses the Child." 14 (1916): 319, 353. Reprinted in *Metronome* (1916).

Van Broekhoven, J. "Hugo Riesenfeld, Concertmaster, Composer, and Director of the Rivoli, Rialto and Criterion Theatres." 19:5 (May 1920): 18, 28.

Tiomkin, Dimitri. "A New Field for Composers." 20:7 (July 1930): 5, 16.

Musical Opinion (UK)

Quarterly music trade periodical. Music critic Hans Keller wrote four articles in 1954 and 1955 and contributed a monthly column, "Television Music," from January to September 1959 (all reprinted in *Film Music and Beyond*).

Klein, John W. "Recent Film Music." 66 (June 1943).

Capell, Richard. "*Fantasia*: or the New Barbarism." 66 (November 1943): 41.

Kubik, Gail. "Music in the Documentary Film." 67 (September 1944): 379–80. Reprinted from *Writers' Congress* (1944).

"'Opus 65': An Essay in Film Music." 76 (November 1952): 105. On Richard Arnell's music.

Keller, Hans. "Music on Everest." 77 (January 1954): 213–15.

Keller, Hans. "*West of Zanzibar*: Some Problems of Film Music." 77 (July 1954): 585–87.

Keller, Hans. "*Lease of Life*: A New Formal Principle of Dramatic Music." 78 (December 1954): 151–52.

Keller, Hans. "The Arthur Benjamin Annual." 78 (September 1955): 721–22.

Column, "Television Music" by Hans Keller, 1959

"Lunch with Lionel Salter." 82 (June 1959): 597–99. Reprinted in *Film Music and Beyond*.

The Musical Quarterly (US)

Scholarly musical journal first published by New York music publisher G. Schirmer, later by Oxford University Press.

Potamkin, Harry Alan. "Music and the Movies." 15:2 (April 1929): 281–96. Argues that there is no absolute justification for the use of music to accompany film and that to date, film music has been interpretive and, therefore, in principle, identical. Calls for smaller orchestras because "symphonic music is too grand to be submissive to the movie."

Winter, Marian Hannah. "The Function of Music in Sound Film." 27:2 (April 1941): 146–64. Covers territory missing from Kurt London's *Film Music* (1936), including a survey of French and German avant-garde films and Russian and American film music.

Sternfeld, Frederick W. "Music and the Feature Films." 33:4 (October 1947): 517–32. Lengthy analysis of Hugo Friedhofer's score for *The Best Years of Our Lives* with music examples. Reprinted in *Pro Musica Sana* (Winter 1978–1979).

Sternfeld, Frederick W. In "Current Chronicle." 35:1 (January 1949): 115–21. Analysis of Virgil Thomson's score for *Louisiana Story*.

Sternfeld, Frederick W. In "Current Chronicle." 36:2 (April 1950): 274–76. On Gail Kubik's score for *C-Man* (1949).

Goldbeck, Frederick. In "Current Chronicle: France." 36:3 (July 1950): 457–60. On Yves Baudrier.

Sternfeld, Frederick W. "Copland as a Film Composer." 37:2 (April 1951): 161–75. Analysis with music examples.

Rubsamen, Walter. "Schoenberg in America." 37:4 (October 1951): 469–89. See pp. 471–72.

Schwarz, Boris. "Karol Rathaus." 41:4 (October 1955): 481–95. Mentions his film music, and a list of works includes "Film Music," 494.

James, Richard S. "Avant-Garde Sound-on-Film Techniques and Their Relationship to Electro-Acoustic Music." 72:1 (Winter 1986): 74–89.

Citron, Marcia J. "A Night at the Cinema: Zeffirelli's *Otello* and the Genre of Film-Opera." 78:4 (Winter 1994): 700–41.

Nisbett, Robert F. "Pare Lorentz, Louis Gruenberg, and *The Fight for Life*: The Making of a Film Score." 79:2 (Summer 1995): 231–55.

Altman, Rick. "The Silence of the Silents." 80:4 (1996): 648–718. Altman's reexamination of silent film sound and musical accompaniment challenges standard histories and offers evidence that silence was a regular practice of silent film exhibition.

Marshall, Robert L. "Film as Musicology: *Amadeus*." 81:2 (Summer 1997): 173–79.

Lockwood, Lewis. "Film Biography as Travesty: *Immortal Beloved* and Beethoven." 81:2 (Summer 1997): 190–98.

Kallberg, Jeffrey. "Nocturnal Thoughts on *Impromptu*." 81:2 (Summer 1997): 199–203.

Shelemay, Kay Kaufman. "'What's Up, Doc?' A View of 'Reel' Musicologists." 81:2 (Summer 1997): 204–9.

Feisst, Sabine M. "Arnold Schoenberg and the Cinematic Art." 83:1 (Spring 1999): 93–113. On Schoenberg's unsuccessful foray into film music—including documentation of his meeting with producer Irving Thalberg at MGM—and his subsequent influence on film music.

Burke, Richard N. "Film, Narrative, and Shostakovich's Last Quartet." 83:3 (1999): 413–29.

Lerner, Neil. "Copland's Music of Wide Open Spaces: Surveying the Pastoral Trope in Hollywood." 85:3 (Fall 2001): 477–515.

John, Antony. "'The Moment that I Dreaded and Hoped For': Ambivalence and Order in Bernard Herrmann's Score for *Vertigo*." 85:3 (Fall 2001): 516–44.

Citron, Marcia J. "Operatic Style and Structure in Coppola's *Godfather* Trilogy." 87:3 (Fall 2004): 423–67. On Nino Rota's music.

Hubbert, Julie. "Modernism at the Movies: *The Cabinet of Dr. Caligari* and a Film Score Revisited." 88:1 (Spring 2005): 63–94.

Musical Standard (UK)

Donaldson, Leonard. "Bioscope Music: A Plea for the Picture-Pianist." 37 (1912): 148–49, 166–67, 193–95.

Chelsey, John. "Cinema Music." New series, 9 (1917): 151–52.

James, Leslie W. "The Organ in the Cinema." 10 (August 18, 1917): 109–10.

Florian, Felix. "Picture Theater Music." 12: 283 (July 20, 1918): 28.

Chatterton, Julia. "The Liaison of Music and Cinema." (February 25, 1922): 65.

Bowen, Arthur Lloyd. "Music in Films." 38 (July 1932): 121. On music by Edmund Meisel.

The Musical Times (UK)

The United Kingdom's oldest classical music journal. A number of letters to the editor in the 1920s concerned music in the cinema. Music critic Hans Keller wrote a film music column in 1955–1956 (reprinted in *Film Music and Beyond*). In the 1970s Christopher Palmer, Keith Spence, and others reviewed films with a bent toward music.

Salmon, Arthur L. "Music at the Cinema." 61 (December 1, 1920): 803–4.

Holt, Richard. "Music and the Cinema." 65:975 (May 1, 1924): 426–27.

Chuckerbutty, S. W. Oliphant. "What's Right with Cinema Music?" 68 (July 1, 1927): 611–12. By the British cinema organist Soorjo Alexander William Oliphant Chuckerbutty, who performed as "Wilson Oliphant."

Sabaneev, Leonid. "Music in the Cinema." 70:1032 (February 1, 1929): 113–15.

Newman, Frank. "These Cinema Organs—and Organists." 72:1055 (January 1, 1931): 45–46. This article by an organist drew heated letters of response—on the church organ versus the cinema organ—for the next nine issues.

Benjamin, Arthur. "Film Music." 78:1133 (July 1937): 595–97.

Chuckerbutty, S. W. "To Be or Not to Be—a Cinema Organist." 79:1147 (September 1938): 662–63; 79:1149 (November 1938): 817–19; 80:1151 (January 1939): 21–22.

Fisher, Trevor. "Opera into Film." 90:1276 (June 1949): 204–6.

Keller, Hans. "London Music: Twelve-note Music on Television." 95:1332 (February 1954): 92.

Huntley, John. "Music in Films." 98:1378 (December 1957): 662–63. Survey.

Maw, Nicholas. "Richard Rodney Bennett." 103:1428 (February 1962): 95–97.

Wright, Basil. "Britten and Documentary." 104:1449 (November 1963): 779–80.

Palmer, Christopher. "Walton's Film Music." 113:1549 (March 1972): 249–52. With music excerpts.

Keller, Hans. "Television." 123:1669 (March 1982): 200.

Palmer, Christopher. "Prokofiev, Eisenstein and Ivan." 132:1778 (April 1991): 179–81. On Prokofiev's score for *Ivan Groznyj* (*Ivan the Terrible*).

Mellers, Wilfrid Howard. "Platform: Are Musicals Musical?" 132:1782 (August 1991): 380.

Column, "Film Music" by Hans Keller, 1955–1956

"Recent Film Music." 96:1347 (May 1955): 265–66.

"Problems of Integration." 96:1349 (July 1955): 381–82.

"Frankel—Blomdahl—Arnold." 96:1350 (August 1955): 435.

"Speech Rhythm." 96:1351 (September 1955): 486–87. Reprinted in Roger Manvell's *The Technique of Film Music* (1957).

"The Operatic Problem." 96:1352 (October 1955): 549.

"Rawsthorne's *Leonardo.*" 97:1355 (January 1956): 29.

The Musical Woman: An Interdisciplinary Perspective (US)

Andersen, Leslie N. "Women Film and Television Composers in the United States." 3 (1986–1990): 353–70. Profiles of Suzanne Ciani, Anne Dudley, Nicky Holland, Nan Schwartz, Elizabeth Swados, and Shirley Walker.

The Musician (US)

Published in Boston.

Lovewell, S. Harrison. "A New Field of Activity for Organists." 20 (1915): 346–47.

Miller, George. "The Organ in the Theatre." 20 (1915): 414–15.

Gerwig, H. C. "The Photo-Play Organist." 21 (1916): 54–55.

Sterns, Theodore. "Music for the Movies." 21 (April 1916): 203.

"'Movie' Organs." 21 (1916): 246–47.

Maitland, Rollo F. "Some Difference between Church and Motion Picture Organ Playing." 22 (1917): 226.

Hansford, Montiville Morris. "Motion Picture Playing: An Outlook." 24:11 (1919): 8, 10.

Smith, Warren Storey. "Music for the Moving Pictures, a New Art and a New Profession." 25:12 (March 1920): 12.

Boblitz, K. Sherwood. "Where 'Movie Playing' Needs Reform." 25 (June 1920): 8, 29. Reprinted in *Moviegoing in America* (2002).

Riesenfeld, Hugo. "The Picture Drama, a New Field For Composers." 29 (July 1924): 11.

"What Chance Has the Church Organist to Make Good in the Moving Picture Theatre?" 29 (November 1924): 41. Written under the pseudonym of De Profundis.

"Choir and Organ: In Which We Forsake the Choir Loft Temporarily to Investigate the Duties of the Moving Picture Organist." 29 (December 1924): 41. Written under the pseudonym of De Profundis.

"Arranging Synchronized and Special Music Scores for Sound Pictures." 34 (June 1929): 32.

"Music in the Movies Wins New Place." 40:1 (January 1935): 14. On the establishment of an Academy Award for music.

"Opera via Talkies." 40 (June 1935): 4.

Morros, Boris. "Motion Pictures Turning to Music: The Dramatic Possibilities of Music Other Than as a Mere Background Are Just Becoming Realized by the Movie Magnates." 43 (September 1938): 154.

De Vore, Nicholas. "Film Music Attains Artistic Stature." 51 (November 1946): 150–51.

Musicologica (Czechoslovakia)

Vicar, Jan. "Vaclav Trojan's Film Music." No. 1 (1993): 65–77.

Musicology (Australia)

Hillman, Roger. "Beethoven, Mahler, and the New German Cinema." 20 (1997): 84–93.

MusicWorld (US)

Published quarterly by the Broadcast Music, Inc. (BMI) Corporate Relations Department in New York. News, member events, film and television awards, and photo reportage for the performing rights organization. Journalist Jon Burlingame wrote a column tracking the latest projects of BMI composers; the first was titled "The Scorekeeper: A Round-Up of What's Happening in the World of Film and Television Composers" (Spring–Summer 1999, page 40). The column ran through at least Fall 2001. Also known as *BMI Musicworld*, *MusicWorld* continues *Many Worlds of Music*.

Sheff, Victoria. "Profile: Steve Dorff." (Spring 1988): 47–50.

Robinson, Julius. "Profile: Danny Elfman." (Fall 1988): 37–39.

Sheff, Victoria. "Profile: Thomas Newman." (Winter 1988): 51–53.

Robinson, Julius. "Profile: Dave Grusin." (Spring 1989): 41–44.

White, Adam. "Profile: Michael Kamen." (Summer 1989): 39–41.

Sheff, Victoria. "Profile: Lalo Schifrin." (Winter 1989): 53–55.

Robinson, Julius. "Profile: Hans Zimmer: The Team Approach to Film Scoring." (Winter 1993): 32–35. Interview-based article.

Clay, Jennifer. "Profile: David Arnold: Celebrating His Independence." (Fall 1996): 42–44.

Robinson, Julius. "Profile: Mark Mancina." (Winter 1996): 38–41.

Kronke, David. "Profile: Miles Goodman." (Summer 1996): 36–38.

Clay, Jennifer. "Profile: David Arnold." (Fall 1996): 42–45.

Clay, Jennifer. "[Profile]: Rachel Portman." (Spring 1997): 26–29.

Burlingame, Jon. "Profile: Patrick Williams." (Fall 1997): 48–51.

Clay, Jennifer. "Profile: William Ross." (Winter 1997): 24–27.

Stone, Adrianne. "On the Scene: Mychael Danna." (Spring–Summer 1999): 9. Profile.

Clay, Jennifer. "Sitting on Top of the Tube: Snuffy Walden." (Spring–Summer 1999): 39. Interview-based article.

Burlingame, Jon. "Lalo Schifrin: A Man with Multiple Missions." (Spring–Summer 1999): 41.

Clay, Jennifer. "On the Scene: John Ottman." (Fall 1999): 8. Profile.

Burlingame, Jon. "John Williams: Altering the Course of Film Scoring." (Fall 1999): 30–31.

Burlingame, Jon. "A Career Shift Puts Trevor Rabin in High Gear." (Fall 2001): 21. Interview-based article.

NARAS Journal (US)

The National Academy of Recordings Arts and Sciences (the Grammys), now known as the Recording Academy, published this semiannual journal for members in the 1990s. NARAS also published a member newsletter, *The Los Angeles Record*.

Larson, Randall D. "Computers and the Creation of Modern Movie Music." 1:2 (Fall 1990): 53–64. Reprinted from the *Cue Sheet* (April 1990). On synthesizers.

The New Music Review and Church Music Review (US)
Official organ of the American Guild of Organists, published by H. W. Gray Co. in New York.
12 (February 1913): [55–56]. Includes an abstract of an article in the *New Bedford Sunday Standard* of January 5 on "The Art of Moving Picture Playing."

New Sound (Yugoslavia)
The international magazine for music.
Kulezic, Danijela. "The Audio-Visual Structure of Film and the Influence of the Poetics of Myth on Its Maturing." No. 9 (1997): 59–64. Discusses music in the films of Jean Cocteau and Sergei Eisenstein. Translated from the Serbian.

New Zealand Listener (New Zealand)
Jenkin, Douglas. "Music by." 121:2524 (July 1988): 36–37. Interviews with New Zealand women composers Michelle Scullion, Sue Alexander, and Jenny McLeod.
Morrison, J. "Calling the Tune." 124:3188 (October 25, 1990): 10. On selecting title music for a television news program.

Notes: Quarterly Journal of the Music Library Association (US)
Aimed at specialized music libraries and libraries with music holdings. Articles and reviews largely written by MLA members. One of the few scholarly journals that consistently offers in-depth reviews of books on film music. Many reviews are by H. Stephen Wright, coordinator of the organization's "Film Music" roundtable for many years.
McDonald, Gerald D., comp. "A Bibliography of Song Sheets—Sports and Recreations in American Popular Songs: Part IV—Songs of the Silent Film." Second series, 14:3 (June 1957): 325–52.
Marks, Martin. "Film Music: The Material, Literature, and Present State of Research." 36:2 (December 1979): 282–325. See Marks's update in the *Journal of the University Film and Video Association* (Winter 1982).
Wright, H. Stephen. "Film Music Web Sites (SoundtrackNet; Film Score Monthly; Classical Music Used in Films; Classics from the Silver Screen)." 59 (September 2002): 128–30.
Turner, Charles. "Jerome Moross: An Introduction and Annotated Worklist." 61:3 (March 2005): 659–727.

On Tape (US)
Bennetts, Leslie. "Mancini." 1:2 (Summer 1972): 4–8.

Opera (US)
"Hollywood Chatter: Music in the Films." 2:5 (May 1946): 13, 33.

Opera, Concert, and Symphony (US)
Stevens, Leith. "The Promotion of Film Music in the Concert Hall." 12:8 (August 1947).
Stevens, Leith. "Radio vs. Movie Underscoring." 13:1 (January 1948).

Opera News (US)
Published by the Metropolitan Opera Guild in New York. Ernest Gold was a frequent

contributor; although many of his articles are not related to film music, they are of interest for having a film composer's perspective on opera. Composer Harper MacKay, long associated with the Los Angeles Civic Light Opera Music Theater Workshop, wrote a number articles in the 1990s. Contains occasional news of opera on film and reviews of movies with opera elements.

Gold, Ernest. "Salome: A Musical Paradox." (January 24, 1955): 3ff.

Gold, Ernest. "Wagner: Alchemist of Folklore." (January 24, 1955): 4ff.

Gold, Ernest. "A Rondo at the Momus." (March 21, 1955).

Gold, Ernest. "The Mystic Abyss." (February 25, 1957): 8ff.

Gold, Ernest. "Notes from the Cutting Room." 26 (December 23, 1961): 8–13. Overview of the film scoring process.

Beckley, Paul V. "Divas in Movieland." 29:6 (December 19, 1964): 8–13. Historical overview of opera on film documents how opera singers have left their mark on Hollywood.

Rizzo, Francis. "Shadow Opera: Hollywood Has Come Up with Some Spectacular Musical Fakes." 32:14 (February 3, 1968): 9–12. Reprinted in Limbacher.

Pleasants, Henry. "The Screen and the Voice." 34:12 (January 17, 1970): 9–13. Should singers be heard and not seen?

Matz, Mary Jane. "Flesh-and-Blood Angel." (May 1977). Nino Rota profile. Reprinted in *Pro Musica Sana* (Winter 1978).

MacKay, Harper. "Going Hollywood." 55:15 (April 13, 1991): 10ff. On opera stars in film.

MacKay, Harper. "Reel Sound." 56:11 (February 15, 1992): 12ff. On film composers who wrote opera.

Scherer, Barrymore Laurence. "The Flickering Light." (December 11, 1993): 42–43, 60. On silent opera films.

MacKay, Harper. "On the Double." 59:4 (October 1994): 16–18, 20, 22. On vocal dubbing.

Kellow, Brian. "The Last Metro Girls: MGM Had Gable and It Had Garland—and It Also Had Three of the Most Popular and Talented Sopranos to Come Out of the Movie Musical's Golden Age." 67:2 (August 2002): 38–44. Interview-based article on Ann Blyth, Kathryn Grayson, and Jane Powell.

The Opera Quarterly (UK)
Abbate, Carolyn. "Wagner, Cinema, and Redemptive Glee." 21:4 (Autumn 2005): 597–611.

Optic Music (US)
Published monthly in Los Angeles from 1984 to 1987 as *Optic Music*, then *Opticmusic's Film and Video Production*. Covered the burgeoning field of popular music videos.

The Organ (UK)
Hallowes, Malcolm. "Organs in Cinema." 1:1 (July 1921): 26–30.
Audsley, George Ashdown. "The Cinema Organ." 4:13 (July 1924): 45–51. By a pipe organ designer and builder.

Organised Sound (UK)
International journal of music and technology.

Cipriani, Alessandro, Fabio Cifariello Ciardi, Luigi Ceccarelli, and Mauro Cardi. "Collective Composition: The Case of Edison Studio." 9:3 (December 2004): 261–70. On contemporary soundtracks for silent films at Edison Studio in Rome, Italy.

Ovation (US)

Hemming, Roy. "Musical Magic at the Movies." 5 (November 1984): 10–12ff. Classical music and films in the 1930s and 1940s.

Deutsch, Didier. "Opera Gives Its Regards to Broadway." 7 (September 1986): 30–32. Includes opera singers in films.

Shear, Nancy. "*Alexander Nevsky*: A Masterwork Restored." 8 (November 1987): 20–22. On Prokofiev's music.

Kennicott, Philip. "When Opera Goes Pop: An Elitist's Lament." 10:7 (August 1989): 18–21, 67.

Overture (US)

Official publication of Professional Musicians, American Federation of Musicians (Local 47), Los Angeles. Dating from at least 1925 (the earliest issue in Local 47's archives), when it was a biweekly newsletter, it has been issued monthly since the 1930s. All union recording of motion picture music in Los Angeles is contracted through Local 47. "Final Notes," with death notices and colloquial memories submitted by members with biographical information and anecdotes, is a good source of information on lesser-known musicians. For example, an entire page is devoted to Irwin Coster's career (February 2005, p. 10). "Manson on Music," a column by Eddy Lawrence Manson, ran from 1975 to 1983. Casually written, it brought an arranger's perspective to film scoring and was based on his vast experience in the studios. Light on content, it usually denounced current trends, such as the use of electronics. A few columns were titled "The Arranger's Corner."

"A Producer Looks at Music." (February 1946): 19. Text of an address by the MGM producer.

Hall, Hal. "Los Angeles Musicians and Eighteenth Academy Awards." (April 1946): 8–9.

"Story of...Filmworld Music." (October 1946): 14–15. Includes "Screen's Hot Men of Music" (*hot* meaning "in demand," not sexy).

"It's on the Sound Track." (November 1946). Erich Wolfgang Korngold interviewed.

"M-G-M Musicians." (November 1946): 18. List of players in the studio orchestra, first installment of a series.

"RKO Recording Orchestra." (October 1951): 20–21. Photo spread, with some players identified in the captions.

Schneider, George. "Functions of a Film Music Library." (May 1953): 10–11, 37. On his work at MGM.

Blumberg, David. "Spotlight on ASMAC's Lyle 'Spud' Murphy." (October 1995): 3. Interview regarding his Equal Interval System and his students.

Plowman, Charles. "Vince De Rosa: The Man with a Golden Horn." 81:6 (October 2001): 10, 13. On the session musician.

"Composer Shirley Walker Scores *Willard*." (May 2003): 14.

Levin, Charles. "Where's the Orchestra? *Simpsons* One of a Handful of Shows Still Using Live Musicians to Record Its Weekly Score." 83:9 (January 2004): 1, 11.

Column, "Manson on Music" by Eddy Lawrence Manson
(December 1975). On spotting a film.
(January 1976). On spotting a film.
(May 1977). Scoring music under dialogue.

(June 1977). Psychology of film music.
(July 1977). Psychology of film music.
(August 1977). Psychology of film music.
(October 1977). On arranging.
(December 1977). On orchestration.
(January 1978). On orchestration.
(February 1978). On orchestration.
(March 1978). On the relationship between orchestration and drama.
(April 1979). On the audible range of hearing.
(June 1979). On scoring between the lines.
(July 1979). On characterization.
(September 1979). On originality.
(December 1979). On session musicians.
(January 1980). On session musicians.
(February 1980). On agents.
(March 1980). On stress.
(April 1980). On stress.
(May 1980). On stress.
(June 1980). On music editing.
(August 1980). On avant-garde music.
(September 1980). On avant-garde music.
(November 1980). On music for comedies.
(December 1980–January 1981). On music for comedies.
(February 1981). On current scoring trends.
(April 1981). On getting started in a career in film music.
(June 1981). On technology versus humanity.
(August 1981). On *Napoleon*.
(September 1981). On *Napoleon*.
(May 1982). On melody.
(June 1982). On melody.
(July 1982). On melody.
(August 1982). On melody.
(September 1982). On electronic music.
(October 1982). On source music.
(November 1982). On source music.
(January 1983). On twelve-tone music.

Pacific Coast Musician (US)

Billed as "The Oldest Musical Magazine in the West," the magazine covered concerts, opera, and motion pictures. At one time it was the only weekly musical magazine published west of Chicago. Although published from 1911 to 1948, serious film music coverage commenced in the mid-1930s and diminished around World War II. Published semimonthly in Los Angeles by Frank H. Colby, significant coverage of film music by business manager R. Vernon Steele began in 1937. Steele contributed a four-page spread, variously titled "Motion Picture Music and Musicians," "Screen and Radio Music and Musicians," and "Sound Track and the Movie Musician." The section featured interviews, two or three capsule film music reviews, and news, including film music performed at the Hollywood Bowl. Coverage of radio music was initiated in April 1938, branching off into "Screen and Radio" a few months later. "Sound Track," a subheading under "Motion Picture Music and Musicians," contains news briefs from 1937 to 1948. In addition to interviewing composers and studio personnel, Steele often spoke with actors and actresses who also were singers, such as Nelson Eddy. Prior to Steele's tenure, news items often featured news and reviews of concerts with Alfred Newman (February 4, 1933, p. 7), Victor Young, and others.

Breil, Joseph Carl. "Motion Picture Music." (November 1916).

"Personals." (July 27, 1929): 10. On Charles Wakefield Cadman.

"Prestissimo Cadman." (August 31, 1929): 7. On Charles Wakefield Cadman.

"Personals." (November 16, 1929): 11. On Charles Wakefield Cadman.

Romberg, Sigmund. "Screen Operetta." 19:18 (May 3, 1930): 16.

"Will Film Music Productions Stage Come-Back?" 20:10 (March 7, 1931): 4.

"Nathaniel W. Finston." 22:12 (March 25, 1933): 6. With biographical details.

"Jack Chertok." 22:26 (July 1, 1933): 9. The MGM music department head calls for a music division of the Academy of Motion Picture Arts and Sciences.

"Nathaniel W. Finston." 23:16 (April 21, 1934): 8. With biographical details.

"Nathaniel Finston." 23:41 (October 13, 1934): 10. With biographical details.

"Shilkret Comes West." 25:1 (January 4, 1936): 6. On Nathaniel Shilkret.

Sacerdote, E. [Edoardo]. "Music and the Films." 25:11 (June 6, 1936): 3–4. The opera singer and American Conservatory voice department head discusses the possibilities of opera and music drama and film.

"Stoloff at Columbia." 25:13 (July 4, 1936): 6. On Morris Stoloff.

[Victor Young.] 25:15 (August 1, 1936): 1. Profile.

Stokowski, Leopold. "My Symphonic Debut in the Films." 25:17 (September 5, 1936): 3.

[Boris Morros]. 25:23 (December 5, 1936): 1. Profile.

"Music in the Pictures." 26:3 (February 6, 1937): 4. This editorial coincides with the first appearance of "Motion Picture Music and Musicians," a four-page spread of interviews, articles, news, and reviews.

Arvey, Verna. "The Significance of Composers in Hollywood." 26:8 (April 17, 1937): 3. On Joseph Achron, George Antheil, William Grant Still (who married Arvey two years later), and Ernst Toch.

Colby, Frank H. "Prospective Film Opera." 27:1 (January 1, 1938): 2. Prospects at MGM.

"Robert Mitchell Boy Choir." 28:24 (December 16, 1939): 6. Documents the film work and repertoire of the Los Angeles-based St. Brendan's Boy Choir.

Steele, Vernon. "Film Music Begins to Grow Up." 29:20 (October 19, 1940): 16. On the trend of signing serious composers, including Mario Castelnuovo-Tedesco and Eugene Zador.

Korngold, Dr. Julius. "Letters to the Editor." 31:24 (December 19, 1942): 2. Claims his son Erich Korngold's score for *Kings Row* is one of the best of 1942. Korngold wrote several articles for *Pacific Coast Musician* in the two years following this letter; however, none apparently discusses film music.

"[Constantin] Bakaleinikoff at [Hollywood] Bowl." 33:13 (July 1, 1944): 28. With biographical details.

"Franz Waxman." (August 19, 1944): 9.

Column, "Motion Picture Music and Musicians" by Vernon Steele

"Korngold and Picture Music." 26:3 (February 6, 1937): 12. Interview with Erich Wolfgang Korngold.

"Stokowski in Pictures." 26:4 (February 20, 1937): 10. Interview.

"The American Music to Come through Motion Pictures, Says George Antheil." 26:4 (February 20, 1937): 12. Interview.

"Academy Awards." 26:5 (March 6, 1937): 10, 13.

"Magnitude of Music Department of Pictures." 26:5 (March 6, 1937): 12–13. Interview with James O'Keefe, music department business manager for 20th Century-Fox.

"Dimitri Tiomkin." 26:6 (March 20, 1937): 12, 15. Interview regarding *Lost Horizon.*

"Gruenberg Here." 26:6 (March 20, 1937): 15. On Louis Gruenberg.

"Screaming Fiddles and Braying Brasses." 26:7 (April 3, 1937): 10, 12–13. On Arthur Lange and 20th Century-Fox.

"Opera in Motion Pictures." 26:8 (April 17, 1937): 10, 13. Interview with William von Wymetal, director of opera at MGM studios.

"Interview with Oscar Straus." 26:8 (April 17, 1937): 11.

"Hugo Friedhofer." 26:9 (May 1, 1937): 10, 13. Interview.

"Scoring for Cartoons: An Interview with Scott Bradley." 26:10 (May 15, 1937): 12–13.

"Director vs. Conductor: An Interview with Al Colombo." 26:11 (June 5, 1937): 12. The Republic Pictures music director talks about communicating with directors.

"National Music, Opera and the Movies: An Interview with Kurt Weill." 26:13 (July 3, 1937): 12–13.

"Opera Training and Pictures: An Interview with Frank Forrest." 26:14 (July 17, 1937): 10.

"Sound and Fury: An Interview with Nathaniel Shilkret." 26:14 (July 17, 1937): 12.

"Inspiration Not Purchasable: An Interview with Dr. Howard Hanson." 26:15 (August 7, 1937): 10. The American composer muses about film music.

"Don't Call It Music: An Interview with Russell Bennett." 26:15 (August 7, 1937): 12.

"An Authority Speaks: An Interview with Paul Kerby." 26:20 (October 16, 1937): 10. Includes discussion of opera and film. Kerby was a composer signed by MGM.

"First Ten Years Are the Hardest." 26:21 (November 6, 1937): 10. Recollections of Vitaphone shorts and a report from Leo Forbstein on the music personnel for Warner Bros.' *The Jazz Singer.*

"Thirty Years of Lyric Writing: An Interview with Gus Kahn." 26:21 (November 6, 1937): 12–13.

"Fairyland Goes Hollywood: An Interview with Leigh Harline." 26:22 (November 20, 1937): 10. On *Snow White and the Seven Dwarfs.*

"Ghost Composers." 27:1 (January 1, 1938): 8. Interview with John Kurucz regarding his gypsy music.

"An Authority Speaks." 27:2 (January 15, 1938): 10, 13. Interview with Richard Hageman.

"From Broadway to Vine Street." 27:2 (January 15, 1938): 10, 13. Interview with Emil Gerstenberger.

"West from Lisbon, New Hampshire." 27:3 (February 5, 1938): 10, 13. Interview with Cecil Copping, a New York-based composer since 1914.

"Sound Track and the Movie Musician." 27:3 (February 5, 1938): 12. Interview with J. W. Gillette of the American Federation of Musicians.

"Some Observations on the Academy Awards." 27:4 (February 19, 1938): 12.

"Korngold Returns." 27:5 (March 5, 1938): 10.

"And This Is Hollywood." 27:5 (March 5, 1938): 12–13. Interview with Elton Koehler, 20th Century Fox music librarian.

"A Native (?) from Brooklyn." 27:6 (March 19, 1938): 10, 13. Interview with Charles Previn.

"Let's Concertize Picture Music." 27:6 (March 19, 1938): 12.

"An Interview with Irving Berlin." 27:7 (April 2, 1938): 10, 18.

"Twenty-four Years!" 27:7 (April 2, 1938): 12–13. Interview with former silent film composer Harry Cockayne, who had moved to RKO.

"Picture Music of Tomorrow." 27:8 (April 16, 1938): 10, 13. Interview with Alfred Sendrey.

"A Discovery." 27:9 (May 7, 1938): 10. On singer Margaret Carlisle.

"Watching the Wheels Go 'Round." 27:10 (May 21, 1938): 10. Arthur Lange on the Fox lot.

"A New Singing Star." 27:10 (May 21, 1938): 12. On Miliza Korjus.

"Watching the Wheels Go 'Round—Literally." 27:11 (June 7, 1938): 10. On Heinz Roemheld.

Column, "Screen and Radio Music and Musicians" by Vernon Steele

"'Unheard' Picture Music." 27:12 (June 18, 1938): 12. Interview with Arnold Schoenberg.

"Doing His Best—Always." 27:12 (June 18, 1938): 14–15. Interview with Meredith Willson.

"Day at a Motion Picture Studio." 27:13 (July 2, 1938): 8. On a visit to MGM.

"Cinema Music under the Stars." 27:15 (August 6, 1938): 8. Hollywood Bowl concert review.

"Making Popular Music Good and Good Music Popular: An Interview with David Broekman." 27:20 (October 15, 1938): 30–31.

"Hackworkers? Trash?" 27:21 (November 5, 1938): 10. Defending film music against comments published by Richard Drake Saunders in a Hollywood newspaper.

"Music for *A Christmas Carol*." 27:23 (December 3, 1938): 10, 13. On Franz Waxman's score.

"Making Good Pictures Better." 27:24 (December 17, 1938): 8. On Max Steiner.

"'Experts' Not Always Expert." 28:2 (January 21, 1939): 10. On the supposed waning popularity of musicals.

"A Prophet with Honor." 28:3 (February 4, 1939): 10, 13. On Russell Bennett.

"Manhandle *The Mikado*? Never! An Interview with Victor Schertzinger." 28:5 (March 4, 1939): 10.

"Screen Opera Inevitable: An Interview with Walter Damrosch." 28:11 (June 3, 1939): 10–11.

"Hindustan Comes to Hollywood." 28:13 (July 1, 1939): 12, 15. On Lal Chand Mehra.

"Louis R. Lipstone." 28:14 (July 15, 1939): 7. Profile of the new director of music at Paramount Pictures.

"How a Briton Does It: An Interview with Anthony Collins." 28:14 (July 15, 1939): 8.

"Interesting As Well As Great: An Interview with Albert Coates." 28:15 (August 5, 1939): 8.

"A Prophet Honored in His Own Country: An Interview with Werner Janssen." 28:16 (August 19, 1939): 8.

"N.F.M.C. and Motion Picture Music: An Interview with John Warren Erb." 28:18 (September 16, 1939): 8. On the National Federation of Music Clubs, from which *Film Music Notes* would soon blossom.

"Stone Started Something." 28:20 (October 21, 1939) 20. On the producer-director Andrew Stone's influence on using music dramatically in musical pictures.

"A 'Busman's Holiday': An Interview with Julian Brodetsky." 28:21 (November 4, 1939): 8. On the extracurricular activities of the studio violinist.

Column, "Motion Picture Music and Musicians" by Vernon Steele

Around this point the original heading of "Motion Picture Music and Musicians" returns, consisting of the subheading "Sound Track" and film reviews. By February 1940, film music coverage is limited to one page.

"A Backward Glance." 29:1 (January 6, 1940): 8. On the best scores of 1939.

"Radio, Railways and Recording." 29:2 (January 20, 1940): 8. Profile of organist Eddie Dunstedter.

"Seven-League Boots." 29:3 (February 3, 1940): 8. Interview with arranger Felix Mills.

Hageman, Richard. "Composing for Films: Some Problems—A Solution—A Suggestion." 30:12 (June 21, 1941): 26, 37. Guest columnist.

Bradley, Scott. "Cartoon Music of the Future." 30:12 (June 21, 1941): 28. Guest columnist. Reprinted in Daniel Goldmark, *Tunes for 'Toons* (2005).

Steele, Vernon. "Sound Track." (July 5, 1941): 11. On the National Federation of Music Clubs convention and associated Hollywood Bowl concert.

Column, "Sound Track" by Vernon Steele
Appears sporadically from 1943 to 1948.
(July 3, 1943): 13. On music for *Phantom of the Opera*.
(July 17, 1943): 9. On Gail Kubik.
(January 1, 1944)
(March 4, 1944)
(April 1, 1944)
34:5 (March 3, 1945). On screen opera.
(July 7, 1945)
35:5 (March 2, 1946)
(July 20, 1946)
(April 17, 1948)
(September 4, 1948)

Column, "Rhyme, Rhythm and Song" by Eleanore Rogers Hageman
34:3 (February 3, 1945): 12. On grand opera on the screen.
34:5 (March 3, 1945): 14. On grand opera on the screen, with commentary on Hearst newspaper columnist Hedda Hopper's article "Films Set Public Whistling Opera."
34:6 (March 17, 1945): 35.

Penguin Music Magazine (UK)
Published three times a year from December 1946 to July 1949. Editor Ralph Hill contributed an essay on film music in vol. 5 (1948). A column by Scott Goddard, "Music of the Film," discusses film scores and the role and function of film music. Published in book form, prepared by Liesbeth Hoedemaeker (2005).

Perfect Beat (Australia)
The journal of research into contemporary music and popular culture. The January and July 2003 issues (vol. 6, nos. 2, 3) were replaced by a double issue published as an anthology, *Off the Planet: Music, Sound and Science Fiction Cinema*. This was subsequently published in book form in 2004.

Valtwies, Meret. "Success Is in the Air: The Soundtrack, Music and Marketing of *Strictly Ballroom*." 1:3 (July 1993): 38–49.

Performing Arts (US)
Regional editions were published monthly from 1965 to 2002 by Performing Arts Network in Los Angeles for California theatergoers. Each issue contained various articles; the program information varied according to the venue.

Jablonski, Edward. "Top Tunes, White Lies, No Tales." 3:7 (July 1969): 6–10. American musicals in the 1930s.

Barkin, Haskell. "If You Can Hear the Music, It's Too Loud." (October 1973): 8[–19]. On the state of television music.

Kreuger, Miles. "Extravagant! Spectacular! Colossal! Movie Musicals in the Thirties." (August 1974): 9ff. Reprinted from *High Fidelity* (1974).

Wilson, Eric. "A Conversation with David Raksin." (December 1979): 32, 35–36, 38.

Sherk, Warren M. "Keeping Track: Looking Back at 100 Years of Film Music." 3:2 (August 1995): 16–22. Companion article to a Hollywood Bowl concert.

Performing Arts Annual (US)

Issued by the Library of Congress in Washington, D.C. The 1986 edition includes material on Alex North; see "Memoirs of a Movie Childhood in Harrisburg's [Pennsylvania] Film Palaces," by Ross Care, pp. 95–97. The 1989 edition, edited by Iris Newsom, includes "Hot Spells: Alex North's Film Score for *A Streetcar Named Desire*" by Ross Care.

Performing Arts at the Library of Congress (US)

Issued by the Library of Congress in Washington, D.C. The 1992 edition, edited by Iris Newsom, includes "Hot Spells: Alex North's Southern Gothic Film Scores" by Ross Care, pp. 10–25, with an analysis of *The Sound and the Fury*; *The Rose Tattoo*; *The Long Hot Summer* (continues "Hot Spells: Alex North's Film Score for *A Streetcar Named Desire*" by Care in *Performing Arts Annual 1989*); "Lillian on the Rocks: D. W. Griffith's *Way Down East* in Italy" by Gillian B. Anderson, 86–107, with material on William Frederick Peters and Louis Silvers, a cue sheet, and piano score excerpts; "Performances at the Library of Congress: Music" regarding Aaron Copland and Leonard Bernstein with a page from Bernstein's pencil piano score for *West Side Story* and a page from his score for *On the Waterfront*.

Performing Arts: Broadcasting (US)

Annual issued by the Library of Congress in Washington, D.C. The 2002 edition includes "Production Music in Television's Golden Age: An Overview" by Paul Mandell on library music and CBS, Capitol Hi-Q, Lud Gluskin, David Gordon, Langlois Filmusic, Mutel Music Service, World Broadcasting System, and composers Jack Beaver, Trevor Duncan, Herschel Burke Gilbert, Jerry Goldsmith, Ronald Hammer, Bernard Herrmann, Leon Klatzkin, Bill Loose, Mahlon Merrick, Joseph Mullendore, Don B. Ray, David Rose, Rudy Schrager, Jack Shaindlin, Fred Steiner, Morton Stevens, and Herb Taylor, 148–69; "Jazz on Television at the Library of Congress," by Krin Gabbard, 170–85.

Performing Arts: Motion Pictures (US)

Continues *Performing Arts at the Library of Congress*. Annual, issued by the Library of Congress in Washington, D.C. The 1998 edition, edited by Iris Newsom, includes "The Great (Almost) American Novel Becomes the Great American Film Score: Johnny Green's Music for *Raintree County*" by Ross Care; "Heaven and Hell to Play With: The Filming of the *Night of the Hunter*" by Preston Neal Jones; "Jazz on Film in the Collections of the Library of Congress" by Patrica Willard; "Twilight's Last Gleaming: The Americanization of Hollywood Film Music, 1950–1965" by Ross Care.

Performing Right (UK)

Published by the Performing Right Society in London.

Palmer, Christopher. "Profile: Dimitri Tiomkin." No. 53 (May 1970): 24–26, 32.

Palmer, Christopher. "Miklos Rozsa." No. 55 (May 1971): 11–15. Profile.
Palmer, Christopher. "British Composers for the Screen: Ron Goodwin and John Addison." No. 56 (November 1971): 20–28. Profiles.
Palmer, Christopher. "British Composers for the Screen: Frank Cordell." No. 58 (December 1972): 13–19. Profile.

Perspectives of New Music (US)

Independent international professional journal for composers of new music and those interested in new music, published biannually.

"From *Modern Music*: Some Representative Passages." 2:2 (Spring–Summer 1964): 26–27. Reprint of a George Antheil "On the Hollywood Front" column from 1937.
Rosenman, Leonard. "Notes from a Sub-Culture." 7:1 (1968): 122–35.
Raksin, David. "A Note for Aaron Copland." 19 (1981): 47.
Miller, Patrick. "Music and the Silent Film." 21:1–2 (Fall–Winter 1982 and Spring–Summer 1983, double issue): 582–84.

Piano & Keyboard (US)

Mangan, Timothy. "MIDI and Me: Composer's Cut." No. 172 (January–February 1995): 19–20. Marc Shaiman interview.
George, K. A. "MIDI and Me: Grand Illusion." No. 173 (March–April 1995): 20–21. Cliff Eidelman interview.

Piping Times (UK)

Vaughan Williams, Ralph. "Composing for the Films." 4:1 (October 1943): 4–5. Basis for "Film Music," published the following year in the *Royal College of Music Magazine*.
Cameron, Ken, and Muir Mathieson. "Film Music." 4:2 (1944).
Smith, Alexander Brent. "Music and the Cinema." 4:3 (1944).

Playback (US)

Published by the American Society of Composers, Authors, and Publishers (ASCAP) in New York, for its members. Covers ASCAP activities and events, including articles and photo reportage of the annual Film and Television Music Awards and the ASCAP Foundation Film Scoring Workshop. Many articles are by editor in chief Erik Philbrook and director of media relations Jim Steinblatt. First issued in Autumn 1990. Preceded by *ASCAP in Action* and *ASCAP Today*. Other publications include the *ASCAP Journal*, circa 1937–1938; *Notes from ASCAP*, 1950s; and *ASCAP News*, circa 1963. *ASCAP Click-Track*, a short-lived newspaper for the organization's film and television members, debuted in February 1984. The first issue included a who's who of studio music directors, "Finding Work as a Film Composer" by Don Ray, and a profile of Varese Sarabande.

Philbrook, Erik, and Jim Steinblatt. "The Reel Life Adventures of Today's Top Film Composers." 2:6 (November–December 1995). Brief profiles, with interview excerpts, of Elliot Goldenthal, James Horner, James Newton Howard, Mark Isham, and Howard Shore.
Steinblatt, Jim. "Yip Harburg: The Man Who Put the Rainbow in *The Wizard of Oz*." 3:5 (Winter 1997). Ernie Harburg shares his thoughts on his father's legacy.
Philbrook, Erik. "Hans Zimmer: They Shoot, He Scores." 4:2 (March–April 1997). Profile, with interview excerpts.
Steinblatt, Jim, and Erik Philbrook. "Newman's Own." 6:1 (January–February 1999). Interview with Randy Newman.

Steinblatt, Jim. "The Man with the Golden Score." 8 (July–August 2001). Elmer Bernstein interview.

Steinblatt, Jim. "John Debney and the Art of the Film Score." 10:1 (February–March 2003): 20–21. Interview.

Steinblatt, Jim. "A Shore Thing." 11:3 (Summer 2004). Howard Shore interview.

Steinblatt, Jim. "Henry Mancini's Enduring Legacy." 11:3 (Summer 2004).

Steinblatt, Jim. "When We Were Young." 11:4 (Fall 2004): 56–57. Interview with Harold Arlen's son.

Playon (US)

Publication of the Henry Mancini Institute. Included news on the institute's film music concerts. Ceased publicaton with the closure of the organization in 2006. Institute conductor Jack Elliott is remembered in vol. 14, no. 2 (Fall–Winter 2001).

Popular Music (UK)

International multidisciplinary journal.

Manuel, Peter. "Popular Music in India: 1901–86." 7:2 (May 1988): 157–76. Survey of film music.

Arnold, Alison. "Popular Film Song in India: A Case of Mass-Market Musical Eclecticism." 7:2 (May 1988): 177–88.

Banerji, Sabita. "Ghazals to Bhangra in Great Britain." 7:2 (May 1988): 207–13. Discusses the use of the ghazal in film music.

Huckvale, David. "*Twins of Evil*: An Investigation into the Aesthetics of Film Music." 9:1 (January 1990): 1–36. On Harry Robertson's score for the 1971 Hammer film.

Tagg, Philip. "Analyzing Popular Music: Theory, Method, and Practice." 9:1 (January 1990): 37–67. On the importance of a serious study of popular film music.

Lapedis, Hilary. "Popping the Question: The Function and Effect of Popular Music in Cinema." 18:3 (October 1999): 367–79.

Booth, Gregory D. "Religion, Gossip, Narrative Conventions and the Construction of Meaning in Hindi Film Songs." 19:2 (April 2000): 125–45.

Special issue, 21:3 (October 2002) ["Music and Television"]

Negus, Keith, and John Street. "Introduction to 'Music and Television' Special Issue." 245–48.

Foreman, Murray. "'One Night on TV Is Worth Weeks at the Paramount': Musicians and Opportunity in Early Television." 249–76.

Frith, Simon. "Look! Hear! The Uneasy Relationship of Music and Television." 277–90.

Lury, Karen. "Chewing Gum for the Ears: Children's Television and Popular Music." 291–305.

Stahl, Matthew. "Authentic Boy Bands on TV? Performers and Impresarios in *The Monkees* and *Making the Band*." 307–29.

Donnelly, K. J. "Tracking British Television: Pop Music as Stock Soundtrack to the Small Screen." 331–43. Some material appears in Donnelly's *The Spectre of Sound: Music in Film and Television* (2005).

Brownrigg, Mark, and Peter Meech. "From Fanfare to Funfair: The Changing Sound World of UK Television Idents." 345–55.

Corner, John. "Sounds Real: Music and Documentary." 357–66.

Chanan, Michael. "Middle Eight: Television's Problem with (Classical) Music." 367–74.

Popular Music (US)

Popular Music: An Annotated Index of American Popular Songs was edited by Nat

Shapiro; later volumes were edited by Bruce Pollack and Gary Graff. The 27-volume series from Adrian Press in New York began in 1964 with decade and half-decade retrospective volumes (vol. 1 covered 1950–1959; vol. 3 covered 1960–1964). From 1985 to 2002 it was issued annually. Songs from motion pictures are included in each volume's entries. Entries listed alphabetically within each year and include composers, lyricists, and publishers; some include information on a song's introduction along with the performers identified with it. Miles Kreuger's essay "Theater and Film Music" is in vol. 5, 1920–1929 (1969), pp. 21–30. There is a revised cumulation volume for 1920–1975 (Detroit: Gale Research, 1985).

Popular Music & Society (US)
Scholarly journal founded in 1971. Articles include historical, theoretical, critical, sociological, and cultural approaches to popular music.
Woll, Allen L. "From 'Blues in the Night' to 'Ac-cent-tchu-ate the Positive': Film Music Goes to War, 1939–1945." 4:2 (1975): 66–76.
Condren, R. "Abstract for 'Let It Bleed': The Music for *Goodfellas*." 15:3 (1991): 131–36.
Lunde, Nanette G. "Tiptoe through the Tulips with Me: The Life and Songs of Joseph A. Burke." 19:1 (Spring 1995): 133–55. Profile of the Tin Pan Alley and Hollywood songwriter.
Evans, Jeff. "Something New: Music as Re-vision in Jonathan Demme's *Something Wild*." 19:3 (Fall 1995): 1–17.
Stilwell, Robynn J. "'In the Air Tonight': Text, Intertextuality, and the Construction of Meaning." 19:4 (Winter 1995): 67–103. Discusses the use of the Phil Collins song in film and television.
Scheurer, Timothy E. "John Williams and Film Music Since 1971." 21:1 (Spring 1997): 59–72. Essay on John Williams's rise and the return of the establishment composer after 1960s pop music scores. With annotated list of twenty-five soundtracks from the past twenty-five years.
Plasketes, George M. "The Long Ryder: From Studio Sessions to Solo Artist to Score and Soundtrack Specialist: Ry Cooder's Musicological Quest." 22:2 (Summer 1998): 49–65. Cooder's approach to film scoring is explored in this essay by a film professor. Annotated discography, pp. 56–64.

Psychology of Music (US)
Vitouch, Oliver. "When Your Ear Sets the Stage: Musical Context Effects in Film Perception." 29 (2001): 70–83. On the influence of film music, based on a study.
Rickard, Nikki S. "Intense Emotional Responses to Music: A Test of the Physiological Arousal Hypothesis." 32 (2004): 371–88. On the power of music with film.

Psychomusicology (US)
Research journal on music cognition. A 1994 issue was devoted to the psychology of film music.
Thayer, Julian F., and Robert W. Levenson. "Effects of Music on Psychophysiological Responses to a Stressful Film." 3:1–2 (1983) 44–52.
Ellis, Robert J., and Robert F. Simons. "The Impact of Music on Subjective and Physiological Measures of Emotion While Viewing Films." 19:1 (Spring 2005): 15–40.

Special issue, 13 (Spring–Fall 1994)
Taylor, J. A. "Preface." 1.

Cohen, A. J. "Introduction to the Special Volume on the Psychology of Film Music." 2–8.

Thompson, William Forde, Frank A. Russo, and Donald Sinclair. "Effects of Underscoring on the Perception of Closure in Filmed Events." 9–27.

Bolivar, V. J., A. J. Cohen, and J. C. Fentress. "Semantic and Formal Congruency in Music and Motion Pictures: Effects on the Interpretation of Visual Action." 28–59.

Lipscomb, Scott D., and Roger A. Kendall. "Perceptual Judgement of the Relationship between Musical and Visual Components in Film." 60–98.

Bullerjahn, Claudia, and Markus Güldenring. "An Empirical Investigation of Effects of Film Music Using Qualitative Content Analysis." 99–118.

Sirius, George, and Eric F. Clarke. "The Perception of Audiovisual Relationships: A Preliminary Study." 119–32.

Iwamiya, S. "Interaction between Auditory and Visual Processing When Listening to Music in an Audio Visual Context." 133–53.

Rosar, William H. "Film Music and Heinz Werner's Theory of Physiognomic Perception." 154–65.

Pulse! (US)

Free monthly magazine published by Tower Records from 1983 to 2002.

Gourse, Leslie. "When Jazz Greats Score." (May 1985): 26.

Weidenbaum, Marc. "Orchestral Maneuvers: Many 'Contemporary Instrumental' Composers Have Found Receptive Audiences in Hollywood, Scoring Movies." 87 (July 1992): 87, 89.

Freeman, Paul. "Guys, Can You Disney-fy It? The Chim Chim Cher-ee Days of Richard and Robert Sherman." (December 1992): 103–4.

Levy, Shawn. "The Director as DJ: Giving a Fresh Listen to Your Favorite Movies." (September 1993): 44–46. Survey of several directors, including John Carpenter, Jonathan Demme, and John Hughes.

The Ragtimer (Canada)

"Ragtime and Marvin Hamlisch Put *The Sting* on Movie Director George Roy Hill." (March–April 1974): 13–16.

Recording Engineer/Producer (US)

"Film Scoring Sessions: Danny Wallin's Wide Range of Experience." (October 1983). The recording engineer discusses room layout, section miking, rock versus film scores, and synth versus live strings.

Records and Recording (UK)

Included a column by Derek Elley with reviews of film music, circa 1978 to 1980.

Rock and Roll in the Movies (US)

Short-lived magazine edited by Alan Clark focusing on 1950s rock films, with plot summaries and poster art. Published from 1986 to 1993, first by Alan Lungstrum, then by the National Rock and Roll Archives in West Covina, California. Five issues: no. 1 (1986), no. 2 (1987), no. 3 (1988), no. 4 (1989), and no. 5 (1993). Clark also produced at least one issue of *Country Music in the Movies*: no. 1 (1993).

Rolling Stone (US)

Covers rock music in film and television, with occasional soundtrack reviews.

Miller, Debby. "Rock Is Money to Hollywood Ears." 407 (October 27, 1983): 102–3, 105.

"Hollywood and Vinyl: 1986." (December 18, 1986–January 1, 1987): 66, 68. On soundtracks.

Malan, Rian. "In the Jungle." (May 25, 2000): 54–66, 84–85. The story of how music by a Zulu tribesman made it into *Ace Ventura: Pet Detective.*

Royal College of Music Magazine (UK)
Mathieson, Muir. "Film Music." 32:3.
Vaughan Williams, Ralph. "Film Music." 40:1 (February 1944): 5–9.
Jones, Kenneth V. "Music for Films." 63:2 (1967): 55–56.
Arnell, Richard. "Composing for Animated Films." 80:1 (1984): 19–20.
Hawkins, B. "Film Music: RCM and RCA Collaboration." 91:1 (1994): 41.

RTS Annual (US)
Published by Ron T. Soeda, a mail-order soundtrack dealer in Santa Ana, California (later in Costa Mesa, California). Established in 1970 and billed as "the only publication of its kind." At least five annual issues were published through 1978.

The 1st RTS Annual (September 1974)
Includes information and services from RTS, information on collecting and market values, some brief composer biographies, and "Scoring the 'B' Movie" by Edward Rose, pp. 23–24.

The 2nd RTS Annual (September 1975)
Includes information on collecting and market values, some brief composer biographies, and "Stylists in Film Music" by Edward Rose, p. 12; "The Music for Television," p. 14; "The 'Ins and Outs' of John Barry," p. 28.

RTS Music Gazette (US)
Newsletter for collectors of rare records, published by Ron T. Soeda, a mail-order soundtrack dealer in Costa Mesa, California (previously in Santa Ana, California. News items and material of interest to soundtrack collectors, including "Insider's Report." Its timely publication coincided with a dearth of information for film music aficionados. The simple, staple-bound newsletter included interviews with film composers; reports on film music at Filmex, a Los Angeles film festival; and plentiful information related to collecting. Known as *Music Gazette* from 1976 to 1978, *RTS Music Gazette* from 1978 to 1994, and again as *Music Gazette*, 1994. Debuted in 1973 according to vol. 6, no. 3. The first six volumes (prior to July 1978) stand out because everything is in uppercase letters. Issued monthly from 1978 to August 1985, bimonthly (slightly irregular) from September 1985 to around 1991, and monthly from 1991 to 1994. Related publications include *The Best of Music Gazette: The First Five Years* (a compilation of the best articles from 1973 to 1978) and a *Film Music Buyer's Guide.* The 1978 issue lists some 1,300 soundtracks with market values. Its competitor, Sound Track Album Retailers (STAR) in Pennsylvania, which also specialized in vinyl soundtrack LPs, published a similar item, *Price Guide for Sound Track Records* around 1984.

3:9 (January 1976)
"Film Scores: Nino Rota." 5, 13.
"A Forum on Film Music." 13. Part 1.

<u>4:3 (July 1976)</u>
"A Forum on Filmmusic, Part VI." Quincy Jones, Jerry Goldsmith, Alfred Newman; Oakland Report: Part III; history of film music by Fred Steiner.

<u>August 1976</u>
"The Influence of Black Film Composers."; "Film Music Forum, Part VII." Lalo Schifrin, Hugo Friedhofer, Quincy Jones, Jerry Goldsmith, Alfred Newman; Oakland Report: Part IV. Ernest Gold.

<u>September 1976</u>
Alex North interview in five parts. (September 1976–January 1977); Oakland Report: Part V. Ernest Gold and David Raksin. "Film Music Forum, Part VIII." Quincy Jones, Jerry Goldsmith, Aaron Copland, Max Steiner, William Alwyn, Bernard Herrmann.

<u>1977–1979 (selected)</u>
Crosthwaite, Martyn. "The Exclusive Lalo Schifrin Interview." 5:1 (May 1977): 2.
Crosthwaite, Martyn. "Our Maurice Jarre Interview." 5:4–5:8 (August 1977–December 1977). In five parts.
Crosthwaite, Martyn. "The Exclusive John Addison Interview." 6:4–6:7 (September 1978–November 1978). In four parts.
Crosthwaite, Martyn. "The Exclusive Roy Budd Interview." 6:9–6:11 (January 1979–March 1979). In three parts.
Crosthwaite, Martyn. "Film Score Notes from Jerry Fielding." 6:11 (March 1979), 6:12 (April 1979). Excerpts from a 1978 interview.
Crosthwaite, Martyn. "The Exclusive John Barry Interview." 7:4–7:8 (August 1979–December 1979). In four parts.

Sangeet Natak: Journal of Indian Music, Dance, Theatre (India)
Formerly the *Journal of the Sangeet Natak Academy.*
Ranade, Ashok. "Music and Music Films." No. 39 (January–March 1976): 23–29.
Mitra, Manab. "Salil Chowdhury: A Phenomenon in Modern Bengali Music." No. 91 (January–March 1989): 39–49.

The School Music News (US)
Published by the New York State School Music Association.
LaBalbo, Anthony C. "Solo Concerto in Film Music." (January 1983): 31.

Schwann Opus (US)
Published quarterly since 1991, this directory lists classical recordings.
Thomas, Tony. "Music for a Golden Age." (Summer 1996): 8A–15A.
Raksin, David. "Miklos Rozsa: A Composer for All Seasons." (Summer 1996): 16A–23A. With sidebar, "A Last Waltz," by conductor John Mauceri.
Smith, Steven C. "Bernard Herrmann and the Politics of Film Music." (Summer 1996): 24A–31A.
Swed, Mark. "Toru Takemitsu." (Summer 1996): 32A.

The Score and I.M.A. Magazine (UK)
Keller, Hans. "*On the Waterfront.*" No. 12 (June 1955): 81–84. On Leonard Bernstein's score. Reprinted in *Film Music and Beyond.*
Gold, Ernest. "The New Challenge." (December 1955): 36–40. First of a series in which young composers discuss problems they face and the many systems of composition in vogue.

Screen Songs (US)
Published monthly by Charlton Publications from circa 1945 to 1948, with lyrics to "songs the screen stars sing." During the same period Charlton published a similar lyrics magazine, *Best Songs*, that included movie songs. See also *Song Hits Magazine*.

Selected Reports in Ethnomusicology (US)
Published by the Department of Ethnomusicology and Systematic Musicology, UCLA.
Crespo, Francisco Javier. "The Globalization of Cuban Music through Mexican Film." 11 (2003): 225–31.
Cohen, Annabel J. "How Music Influences the Interpretation of Film and Video: Approaches from Experimental Psychology." 12 (2005): 15–36.
Lipscomb, Scott David. "The Perception of Audio-Visual Composites: Accent Structure Alignment of Simple Stimuli." 12 (2005): 37–67.

Show Music (US)
Musical theater magazine published first by Max O. Preeo in Las Vegas, later by the Goodspeed Opera Company in Connecticut, from 1981 to 2002. Contained two film music-related columns: "Music from the Silver Screen" by Preeo, covering soundtrack releases related to musical films and personalities (see 3:1, October 1983), and "'Reading' the Compact Discs" by Didier C. Deutsch, which had soundtrack reviews but was not limited to musicals. Deutsch's first column (3:4, October 1984, pp. 16–19) surveys soundtracks released on the (then) new compact disc format. Other columns, including "The Sheet Music Scene" by Glen D. Hunter, "Composers' and Lyricists' Corner," and "Between the Covers," while focused on musicals, occasionally contain references to film music or film composers.

Sheet Music Magazine (US)
Shanaphy, Ed. "The Man Who Was *Laura* and the Golden Age of Film Music." (January–February 1995). On David Raksin.

The Sinfonian (US)
Mehr, Sheldon. "Reel Music Appreciation." (Winter 1992): 7. On using symphonic music from films to teach music appreciation.

Sing Out (US)
Folk song magazine published in New York.
Badeaux, Ed. "Folksongs in Films." 10:2 (Summer 1960): 30–31.

Song Hits Magazine (US)
Published monthly by Song Lyrics, Inc., in New York from 1937 to 1979. Contains song lyrics for popular songs of the screen, stage, and radio, with brief publicity-driven articles on recording artists. There were a number of similar publications, all published in New York, including *Songs and Themes for the Screen, Radio and Stage*, circa 1937; *Songs and Music: New Popular Song Smashes from Radio, Stage, Screen*, circa 1941; and *Screen Songs*, circa 1945 to 1948.

Songwriter Magazine (US)
Published in Hollywood.

Baratta, Paul. "Henry Mancini: Music with a Sense of Drama." 2:6 (March 15, 1977): 24–29. Interview.

Baratta, Paul. "A Closeup on Film Scoring." 3 (December 1977): 36–39. Interview with agent Al Bart.

Baratta, Paul. "Bill Conti: He Put the Musical Punch in *Rocky* and *F.I.S.T.*" 3 (August 1978): 24–31.

Wiseman, R. "Charley Fox." 4 (June 1979): 28–33. Interview with Charles Fox.

Delamater, M. "Richard and Robert Sherman: Walt Disney's Dynamic Duo." 5 (September 1980): 34–36. Interview.

Songwriters Guild of America News (US)

Quarterly newsletter serving American songwriters. Previously known as *The Songwriters Guild News*; the "Quarter Notes" column in that publication (based on Spring 1984 issue) contains member news.

Songwriter's Market (US)

Resource book aimed at aspiring and unaffiliated songwriters. Published annually since 1989 by Writer's Digest Books, Cincinnati, Ohio. Filled with articles, contacts, information on preparing demo tapes, and so on. "Film and TV Index" lists companies that place music in motion pictures and television, excluding commercials. The 1999 edition contains material on film and television music supervisors, pp. 23–24; and a sidebar on versatility as the key to success by Danny Benair, vice president of film and television at Polygram Music Publishing, pp. 92–93.

Songwriters Musepaper (US)

Braheny, John. "Interview: Mark Isham." (November 1995): 7–11, 16, 19.

Kimpel, Dan. "Lights! Camera! Music! A Short Arbitrary History of Hollywood Music." (August 1997): 14, 19, 24.

Sonneck Society Newsletter (US)

Published by the Sonneck Society for American Music.

Anderson, Gillian B. "*The Circus*." 20:1 (Spring 1994): 5–9. On restoring the original accompaniment for the 1928 film.

Schubert, Linda. "Bringing the Dead to Life: Scores for Romantic Supernatural Films of the 1940s." 23:2 (Summer 1997): 33–37.

Sound Illustrated (UK)

Heppner, Sam. "Background Music to the Fore." (December 1944). By a music journalist.

Huntley, John. "Music and World News." (December 1944).

Huntley, John. "Tchaikovsky, Walton, Addinsell." (May 1945).

Goehr, Walter. "Fitting the Music to the Picture." (October 1946). By the German-born conductor.

Huntley, John. "Music for the Olympic Games Film." (September 1948).

Sound Waves (US)

Devoted to articles and news items on all aspects of sound and music, including the conversion of theaters to sound. Some information on the activities of studio music directors and composers, such as Victor Schertzinger. Published bimonthly from August 1928 (1:1) to June 1929 (2:11).

Reay, Neville. "About Those Sound Stages on the Universal Lot." 2:3 (February 15, 1929): 6.

Darte, [?]. "Joseph Cherniavsky Hailed as Music Talker Genius: Pollard Epic Gets Marvelous Score." 2:7 (April 15, 1929): 8. On *Show Boat*.

Darte, [?]. "Hollywood to Be World Music Center States Italian: Opera Films Seen as 'Permanents.'" 2:10 (June 1, 1929): 9.

"Gets Film Job." 2:10 (June 1, 1929): 12. On Pietro Cimini.

Sounds Australian (Australia)
Journal of the Australian Music Centre.

Burt, Warren. "Interview with Bruce Smeaton." No. 19 (Spring 1988): 6–8.

Special issue, No. 61 (2003)

"Australian Screen Music: The Art and Craft of Composing to Moving Image," edited by Art Phillips and Yantra de Vilder.

Phillips, Art, and Yantra de Vilder. "Editorial."

Phillips, Art. "The History and Mechanics of Screen Music: The Early Days." Includes some notable Australian films with music credits between the 1930s and 1950s.

Hartl, Phillip and Coralie. "Contracting an Orchestra for the Soundstage."

Tyson-Chew, Nerida. "Beyond the Music: A Film Composer's Challenges."

de Vilder, Yantra. "In Depth with David Hirschfelder and Burkhard Dallwitz."

Libaek, Sven. "Hanna Barbera Telemovies: Set on the Australian Soundstage."

Gross, Guy. "Mickey Mousing: The Techniques of Scoring to Animation."

Atherton, Michael. "Educating the Screen Composer in Australia."

Curtis, Leah. "Scoring Opportunities in Los Angeles."

Miller, Peter. "That String Ringing Sound."

The Soundtrack Collector
Bimonthly publication started in 1995; covers vinyl records only. Issue 2 contains an article on biker film soundtracks.

The Southern California Music Record (US)
Arvey, Verna. "Who Writes Movie Music?" (August 1, 1940).

Sruti: India's Premier Music and Dance Magazine (India)
Jayaraman, P. C. "G. S. Mani's Lecdems on Art and Film Music." No. 136 (January 1996): 27–30. Interview with the Indian film singer.

Stereo Review (US)
Frequent source of soundtrack reviews by Steve Simels and others. Absorbed *High Fidelity* with October 1989 issue.

Kresh, Paul. "Is There Any Music at the Movies?" 23:3 (September 1969): 75–80. Reprinted in Limbacher.

Windeler, Robert. "André Previn: Who Wants Me in May 1978?" 27:3 (September 1971): 48–57.

Jablonski, Edward. "American Songwriter: Harold Arlen." 31:5 (November 1973): 54–65. Survey.

Kresh, Paul. "Bernard Herrmann: In a Class by Himself." (January 1976).

Goodfriend, James. "Movies I Heard with You." 44 (June 1980): 56.

Garland, Phyl. "Early Jazz in Film Shorts." 45 (October 1980): 104.

Simels, Steve. "Movie Music: From *Kings Row* and *King Kong* to *Miami Vice*, Music from the Movies and TV Sounds Better Than Ever on CD." 52 (April 1987): 59.

Livingstone, William. "Center Stage: John Williams." 53:7 (July 1988): 110–11. Interview.

Simels, Steve, and Gerald Carpenter. "Elmer Bernstein: The Dean of American Movie Music." 58:9 (September 1993): 73–75. Interview.

Simels, Steve. "The Soundtrack Boom: More and More Hit Albums Are Coming Out of the Movies." 59:5 (May 1994): 62ff.

"Dracula Revived." 64:8 (October 1999): 146. On a new score by Philip Glass.

The Strad (UK)
Monthly classical music magazine for strings enthusiasts, including violinists, violists, and cellists.

Dale, S. S. "Contemporary Cello Concerti: Korngold and Penderecki." 87:1036 (August 1976): 277–89. On the Korngold concerto first heard in *Devotion*.

Dale, S. S. "Contemporary Cello Concerti: Miklos Rozsa, Hendrik Herman Badings." 87:1041 (January 1977): 735–45.

Swedish Journal of Musicology [Svensk tidskrift för musikforskning] (Sweden)
Tagg, Philip. "An Anthropology of Stereotypes in TV Music." (1989): 19–42.

Symphony (US)
Magazine of the American Symphony Orchestra League, published in Washington, D.C.

Steinberg, Michael. "Celluloid Schoenberg: Cinematic Imagery from the Viennese Master." 44:1 (1993): 5–6.

Lane, Chester. "No Sin in Cinema." 46:1 (January–February 1995): 32–34ff. On film music in concert, with conductor John Mauceri and music by Franz Waxman and others.

Mauceri, John. "Moving Music: Film Scores Fit for the Concert Stage." 47:6 (1996): 9–10. The conductor of the Hollywood Bowl Orchestra weighs in with his choices.

Symphony News (US)
Lasher, John Steven. "Film Music in the Concert Hall." (February–March 1974): 9–13.

Tempo (UK)
Newsletter from music publisher Boosey & Hawkes. Columns by Hubert Clifford and Ernest Irving in the mid-1940s contain discussions of film music and reviews of music in current British films in release. Some soundtrack reviews in the 1980s; for example, Paul Chipchase's "Walton Film Music" (December 1987).

Clifford, Hubert. "British Film Music." No. 8 (September 1944): 14–15.

Mathieson, Muir. "Aspects of Film Music." No. 9 (December 1944): 7–9.

Clifford, Hubert. "Walton's *Henry V* Music." No. 9 (December 1944): 13–14. Critical essay.

Clifford, Hubert. "British Film Music." No. 12 (September 1945).

Anderson, Lindsay. "*This Sporting Life*." 139 (December 1981): 33–34. On Roberto Gerhard's score.

Davies, Hugh. "Roberto Gerhard: A Survey: The Electronic Music." New series, no. 139 (December 1981): 35–38. On Gerhard's techniques for film.

Morton, Lawrence. "An Autobiographical Sketch." New series, no. 164 (March 1988): 29–31. Reprint of a 1979 essay, introduced by Peter Heyworth.

Mellers, Wilfrid Howard. "Jean Wiener Redivivus." New series, no. 170 (September 1989): 24–29. Includes some discussion of his film music.

Pace, Ian. "Music of the Absurd? Thoughts on Recent Kagel." No. 200 (April 1997): 29–34. Discusses film music by Mauricio Kagel.

Column, "Music from the Films" by Hubert Clifford

No. 10 (March 1945): 10–11.

No. 11 (June 1945): 13–14.

No. 13 (December 1945): 11–12.

No. 15 (June 1946): 12–13. Written by Ernest Irving; his new column starts with the next issue.

Column, "Film Music" by Ernest Irving

New series, no. 1 [No. 16] (September 1946): 31–32.

New series, no. 2 [No. 17] (December 1946): 26–27. On Dimitri Tiomkin's music.

New series, no. 3 [No. 18] (March 1947): 26–27.

Tempo (US)

The "Modern Musical Newsmagazine," edited by Charles Emge and published in Los Angeles from 1933 to 1940.

Mertz, Paul. "Recording a Musical Performance: The 'How' and 'Why' of Different Methods of Recording Music for Motion Pictures." (August–November 1938).

Theatre Organ (US)

Journal of the American Theatre Organ Society (ATOS), published from 1959 to 2002. In addition to extensive biographical material and historical articles written by organists, the journal documents present-day performances and recordings and other news regarding the musical accompaniment of silent films with theater organs. ATOS previously published *The Tibia* (1955–1958). The succeeding journal was subsequently titled *Theatre Organ* (1959–1963), *The Bombarde* (1964–1966), *Theatre Organ Bombarde* (1967–1969), and back to *Theatre Organ* (1970–2002). Index compiled by Jack Moelmann is available from ATOS.

The Tibia

"Profile Number 2: George Wright." 1:2 (Summer 1956): 8–9, 16.

Walton, Judd. "Famous Organs: The San Francisco Fox Wurlitzer." 1:2 (Summer 1956): 10–13.

Hare, Frank. "The Theatre Organ in Britain." 1:3 (Fall 1956): 15. Part 1.

Hare, Frank. "The Theatre Organ in Britain." 1:4 (Winter 1956): 18. Part 2.

Hare, Frank. "The Theatre Organ in Britain." 2:1 (Spring 1957): 14. Part 3.

Blakely, Clealan. "The Theatre Organ in Canada." 2:2 (Summer 1957): 21, 24.

Theatre Organ

"The Only Wurlitzer on TV: Leonard Leigh Profile." 1:2 (Summer 1959): 5–8.

Vining, Iris Ethel. "Organ Accompaniment of Motion Pictures." 5:3 (Fall 1963): 12–13.

Theatre Organ Bombarde

George Tootell's *How to Play the Cinema Organ: A Practical Book by a Practical Player* (1927) was partially reprinted (April–October 1967).

Klos, Lloyd E. "The Life and Times of Gaylord Carter." 9:5 (October 1967): 36–40. Transcript of a 1966 radio interview. Reprinted in the March–April 2001 issue.

Jenkins, Col. Harry J. "Silent Movie Accompaniment." (October 1968): 24; 11:4 (February 1969): 17; (August 1969): 12–13; (April 1970): 14–15. By a 1920s theater organist. In four parts, with various titles.

Jenkins, Harry J. "Koko and His Bouncing Ball." (October 1969). The history of the bouncing ball sing-alongs at the movies.

Marion, Douglas. "The *Real* Crawford Special." 11:6 (December 1969): 22–25. Jesse Crawford interview regarding the organ at the Paramount Theatre in New York.

Crawford, Jesse. "What Is Required of the Theatre Organist." (February 1971): 28ff.

"Musical Accompaniment for Motion Pictures (Lang and West)." (August 1971): 11ff.

Theatre Organ

Higgins, Esther, and Mary Bowles. "Everything You Always Wanted to Know about Cueing a Silent Movie and How to Get the Information." 15:1 (February 1973): 5–11.

Fitz Patrick, Mildred Maginn. "Playing in the Picture House: Helpful Ideas for Musicians and Exhibitors." 15:2 (April 1973): 11–12. Reprinted from *Motography* (January 13, 1917).

Muri, John. "Playing the Film." Part 1. 16:2 (April–May 1974): 21. Part 2. 16:3 (June–July 1974): 28–29. Part 3. 16:4 (August–September 1974): 45.

Sauls, Randy. "Zamecnik: Forgotten Composer of the 'Silent' Era." 16:5 (October 1974): 29–32.

Muri, John. "An Outline for a Course in Theatre Organ." 17:2 (April 1975): 22. First installment in a series. Part 7, "Playing the Film," 18:2 (April–May 1976): 17–18.

"The Movie Organist." (December 1975–January 1976): 62. Poem.

Carter, Gaylord. "Organ Scoring for Motion Pictures." 23:3 (June–July 1981): 42.

Twitchell, Elsie R. "Silent Movie Days—at the Piano." 37:1 (January–February 1995): 25. Memories of musical accompaniment in Thornton, Illinois.

Elliot, Tim. "The Mighty Wurlitzer." 37:1 (January–February 1995): 36–37.

Wright, George. "Straight Talk about Crawford." 37:6 (November–December 1995): 9–13. The writer reminisces about Jesse Crawford.

Gates, Robert. "The Sounds of the Silent Movies." 41:1 (January–February 1999): 12. Some material on organist Ken Rosen and the Fotoplayerist, played by Robert Israel.

Elliott, Chris. "Gaylord Carter: The 'Flicker Fingers' Who Brought *The Perfect Song* to Life." 43:2 (March–April 2001): 14–16.

Klos, Lloyd E. "The Life and Times of Gaylord Carter." 43:2 (March–April 2001): 17–21. Transcript of a 1966 radio interview. Reprinted from *Theatre Organ* (October 1967).

"Working for the Mouse: A Day in the Life of a Working Organist." (January–February 2005): 24–26.

Theatre Organ Review (UK)

Published by the Theatre Organ Club, Leeds, England, in the 1950s and 1960s; edited by organist Frank Hare. Historical articles, profiles, news.

Owen, A. W. "The Evolution of the Theatre Organ." 5:17 (March 1951): 8–9.

Three Oranges (UK)

Published by the Serge Prokofiev Foundation.

Morrison, Simon. "*Tonya*." No. 9 (May 2005): 12–17. On Prokofiev's music for an unreleased film from 1942.

Riley, John. "Soviet Wartime Films." No. 9 (May 2005): 18ff. On Prokofiev's music.

Twentieth-Century Music (UK)
Bundler, David. "Views from William Bolcom." 6:10 (October 1999): 1–7. Interview, with some information on his film-composing activities.
Brown, Julie A. "Listening to Ravel, Watching *En Coeur en Hiver*: Cinematic Subjectivity and the Music-Film." 1:2 (September 2004): 253–75.

21st Century Music (US)
McDonagh, Michael. "North by North's Wife." 7:4 (April 2000): 1–5. Interview with Alex North's widow, Anna.
Feisst, Sabine. "Serving Two Masters: Leonard Rosenman's Music for Films and for the Concert Hall." 7:5 (May 2000): 18–25.

Vierundzwanzigsteljahrsschrift der Internationalen Maultrommelvirtuosen-genossenschaft (VIM) (US)
Semimonthly journal of the International Society of Trump Virtuosi. *Trump* is the British term for the instrument variously known as the Jew's harp, jaw harp, or mouth harp.
Crane, Frederick. "The Trump in the Movies." No. 6 (1997): 114–147. Contains a list of nearly 100 films.

The Violinist (US)
Published in Chicago from 1900 to 1937.
Riesenfeld, Hugo. "Music and the Movies." 35:6 (December 1924): 211.

Wagner (UK)
Huckvale, David. "Wagner and the Mythology of Film Music." 9:2 (April 1988): 46–67.

Women & Music (US)
Journal of gender and culture, published annually by the University of Nebraska Press.
Sherinian, Zoe C. "Re-presenting Dalit Feminist Politics through Dialogical Musical Ethnography." 9 (2005): 1–12. Includes a discussion of Indian film music.

Words & Music (Canada)
Published by the Society of Composers, Authors and Music Publishers of Canada, preceded by *The Canadian Composer*.
MacMillan, Rick. "Learning from the Greats: Mentor Program a Boon for Budding Film Composers." 11:2 (Summer 2004): 30.
Simon, Martin. "Want to Make Music for Movies? The Guild of Canadian Film Composers Is Here to Help." 12:3 (Fall 2005): 11.

The World of Music (Germany)
Journal of the ethnomusicology department, Otto-Friedrich University of Bamberg. Previously the quarterly journal of the International Music Council.
Pleasants, Henry. "Jazz and the Movies." 10:3 (1968): 38–47.
Howard, Keith. "Different Spheres: Perceptions of Traditional Music and Western Music in Korea." 39:2 (1997): 61–67. Discusses the film music of Soo-chul Kim.

Yearbook of the International Folk Music Council (US)
Skillman, Teri. "The Bombay Hindi Film Song Genre: A Historical Survey." 18 (1986): 133–44. Survey from 1930 to 1980.

Chapter 11

General Interest and Other Periodicals

The Advocate (US)
Walters, Barry. "Celluloid Sounds." 745 (October 28, 1997): 55ff. On queer soundtracks of the 1990s.

Africa Today (US)
Henderson, Clara. "'When Hearts Beat Like Native Drums': Music and the Sexual Dimensions of the Notions of 'Savage' and 'Civilized' in *Tarzan and His Mate*, 1934." 48:4 (Winter 2001): 90–124. The film was scored by Herbert Stothart.

American (US)
"Arthur [Kleiner] and the Keystone Kops." 148 (October 1949): 112. Profile of the pianist.

American Hebrew (US)
Riesenfeld, Hugo. "The Advancement in Motion Picture Music." 116 (April 3, 1925): 632. Traces music from the past ten years and the use of classical music.
Mendoza, David. "The Theme Song." 124 (March 15, 1929): 664. On collaborating with William Axt on synchronized scores. Mendoza writes, "Most of the silent films made in Hollywood are sent East for synchronization."
Ewen, David. "Welcome to a Beloved Composer." 126 (January 24, 1930): 399. On Oscar Straus's arrival at Warner Bros.

American Heritage (US)
Boller, Paul F., Jr. "The Sound of Silents." 36:5 (August–September 1985): 98–107. Article with emphasis on Joseph Carl Breil's score for *Birth of a Nation* (1915). With sidebar, "In the Pit: An Old Pro Tells What It Was Like to Play for the Silents" by New York pianist Abraham Lass.
Sheed, Wilfrid. "The Songwriters in Hollywood." 44:6 (October 1993): 82–93. On Irving Berlin, Hoagy Carmichael, George and Ira Gershwin, Jerome Kern, Cole Porter, Richard Rodgers, and Harry Warren.

American Journal of Psychoanalysis (US)
Diaz de Chumaceiro, Cora L. "Induced Recall of Film Music: An Overlooked Mirror of Transference-Countertransference Interactions." 58:3 (September 1998): 317–27. Discussion of psychotherapy and popular film music, including the unintentional or induced recall of film songs (one case involved a song from *The Alamo* by Dimitri Tiomkin and Paul Francis Webster; another involved music from *Exodus* by Ernest

Gold). Written by a clinical psychologist in Venezuela whose doctoral dissertation focused on induced song recall in psychotherapy.

American Scholar (US)

Antheil, George. "Music Takes a Screen Test." 6:3 (Summer 1937): 354–64. Reprinted in *Music Clubs Magazine* (November–December 1938).

Zinsser, William. "From Natchez to Mobile, from Memphis to St. Joe: Songwriters Hoagy Carmichael, Harold Arlen and Johnny Mercer." (Spring 1994).

Annali di Sociologia (Italy)

Fattore, Luciano, translated by Ralph Raschen. "The Profession of Film Music Composition in Contemporary Italy." 5:1 (1989): 325–49. Thirteen Italian film composers discuss their field of work in this sociology yearbook.

Annals of the American Academy of Political and Social Sciences (US)

Riesenfeld, Hugo. "Music and Motion Pictures." 128 (November 1926): 58–62. Brief history of silent film music.

ARSC Journal [Association for Recorded Sound Collections] (US)

Shaman, William. "The Operatic Vitaphone Shorts." 22:1 (Spring 1991): 35–94. History (1926–1932) and filmography, with extensive notes.

Arts (US)

Converse, Frederick S. "Music and the Motion Picture." 4 (October 1923): 210–12. The American composer, best known for his concert music, on his music for *Puritan Passions*.

Arts and Architecture (US)

"Music in the Cinema," a column by Walter Rubsamen on music in films in current release, ran circa June 1944–July 1946.

Rubsamen, Walter H. "A Modern Approach to Film Music: Hanns Eisler Rejects the Cliches." 61:11 (November 1944): 20, 38.

Whitney, James and John. "Color Music – Abstract Film – Audio-Visual Music." 61:12 (December 1944): 25, 42.

Rubsamen, Walter. "Contemporary Music in Films." 62:7 (July 1945): 34, 46. On the dearth of contemporary music in films, with dissonance reserved for sinister moments. Reprinted in *Film Music Notes* (May 1946).

Rubsamen, Walter. "Music as Dramatic Device." 62 (October 1945): 46, 52. On filmed opera.

Rubsamen, Walter H. "The Devices of Descriptive Music." 63:1 (January 1946): 10, 19, 51–54.

Column, "Music in the Cinema" by Walter Rubsamen

62 (August 1945): 24, 50, 52. Compares Prokofiev's *Alexander Nevsky* score and cantata.

63 (February 1946): 22–23, 59. On Miklós Rózsa's music for *The Lost Weekend*.

Arts and Decoration (US)

Spaeth, Sigmund. "Music and the Movies: It's Growth and a Prophecy." 13:36 (May 25, 1920): 36.

Arts Magazine (US)
Bach, Steven. "The Hollywood Idiom." (December 1967): 16–17.

Atlantic (US)
Kindschi, Lowell. "Twilight Furioso." 181 (May 1948): 95–96. Memories of a theater organist.

Atlantic Monthly (US)
Antheil, George. "Hollywood Composer." 165 (February 1940): 160–67. Reprinted in the book *College Prose* by Gates and Wright.
Elliot, Paul. "Musical and Low." 176 (July 1945): 109, 111–12.
Ustinov, Peter. "The Man Who Took It Easy." (January 1959): 43–49. Short story by the actor about a fictional film composer named Erhardt Von Csumlay.

Asian Art and Culture (US)
Cheng, Shui-cheng. "'I Heard a Voice from My Memory': Chinese Opera and Film." 7:2 (1994): 81–95.

Audience (US)
Published from 1968 to 1998; soundtrack reviews in the "Aural Fixations" column.

Audio Magazine (US)
Lawrence, Harold. "Silent Film Music-Making." 45:1 (January 1961): 58–59.
Diliberto, John. "The Audio Interview: Mark Isham." 80:5 (May 1996): 36ff.

Ballet Review (US)
Croce, Arlene. "Music for Astaire and Rogers: A Conversation with Hal Borne." (1972): 50–60. Behind-the-scenes look with the rehearsal and recording pianist. Croce drew on some of this material for *The Fred Astaire & Ginger Rogers Book*, published the same year.

BAM [Bay Area Magazine] (US)
Darling, Cary. "Mark Isham: Sensitive Soundtrack: A Human in a Mechanical World." (January 31, 1986): 13.

Black Creation (US)
Murray, James P. "Black Movies and Music in Harmony." 5 (Fall 1973): 9–11. On connections between black music and black film.

Booklist (US)
Monthly magazine published by the American Library Association; often includes reviews of books on film music.

Bookman (UK)
Marshall, Norman. "Music in the Talkies." 84 (1933): 191–92.

Boston Magazine (US)
Baird, Susanna. "The Perfect Score." 40:12 (December 2002): 181–[82]. Interview with Toru Takemitsu.

California Arts and Architecture (US)
Schoenberg, Arnold. "Art and the Moving Picture." (April 1940): 12.

California Life (US)
Pietschmann, Patti. "Henry Mancini...Knows the Score." (June 1977): 42–43.

Callaloo (US)
Journal of Afro-American and African arts and letters.
Ramsey, Guthrie P. "Muzing New Hoods, Making New Identities: Film, Hip-Hop Culture, and Jazz Music." 25:1 (Winter 2002): 309–20. Discusses jazz and rap music in *Do the Right Thing* and other films.

Canadian Psychology (Canada)
Frye, Northrop. "Music in the Movies." 22 (December 1942): 275–76. By the Canadian literary critic.
Cohen, Annabel J. "Music Cognition and the Cognitive Psychology of Film Structure." 43:4 (1997): 215–32.

Canzona (New Zealand)
Farquhar, David. "Applied Music." 3:10 (November 1981): 50–59. Survey of film and television music by New Zealand composers.
Kerr, Elizabeth. "Arrangement for Score of *La Passion de Jeanne d'Arc.*" 10:30 (1988): 11–12. On the arrangement and expansion by Dorothy Buchanan of the original score by Victor Alix and Leo Pouget for the 1928 silent film.

Carte Blanche (US)
Bernstein, Elmer. "Secret World of the Movie Composer." (Spring 1967): 30, 45.

Catholic Digest (US)
Legler, Henry M., Jr. "The Robert Mitchell Boychoir." 11:4 (February 1947): 57–61.

The Chesterian (UK)
Lajtha, Laszlo. "Music and Films." 23:155 (July 1948): 4. From a BBC lecture on aesthetics by the Hungarian composer at the time of his first film score.

Christian Science Monitor Magazine (US)
Daugherty, Frank. "Music for the Millions: Some of the Foremost Contemporary Composers Help Make Motion Picture Backgrounds of Sound, Melodious and Otherwise, Which Accent the Photoplay's Emotional Values." (April 27, 1938): 8.
"Thriller with a Zither Theme." (February 25, 1950): 14. On Anton Karas's music.
Shipp, Richard. "Setting Hollywood to Music." 72 (November 30, 1979): B8–9.

The Chronicle of Higher Education (US)
O'Neill, C. "Making Music for the Movies." 18 (July 9, 1979): B14–15.
Harries, Martin. "In the Coen Brothers' New Film, the Dark, Utopian Music of the American South." 47:21 (February 2, 2001): B14–[15]. On the use of American folk music in *O Brother, Where Art Thou?*
Sullivan, Jack. "Musical Redemption in Hitchcock's *Rear Window.*" 50:39 (June 4, 2004): B18–19.

Collier's (US)

Churchill, Sir Winston. "Everybody's Language." (October 26, 1935): 24.

McLeod, Norman Z., as told to Kyle Crichton. "Gamble with Music." 117 (March 23, 1946): 22–23. The director talks about filming a musical production.

Hartwell, D. "Masses Go for Music." 119 (May 24, 1947): 14–15ff. On classical music in films.

Commentary (US)

Pechter, William. "Movie Musicals." 53:5 (May 1972): 77–81.

Teachout, Terry. "I Heard It at the Movies." 102:5 (November 1996): 53ff. Article on renewed interest in film scores.

Teachout, Terry. "The Double Life of Miklos Rozsa." 112:5 (December 2001): 62–65. A reevaluation of Rózsa's place in music history.

Commonweal (US)

Varese, Edgar. "Organized Sound Film." 33 (December 13, 1940): 204–5.

Contemporary Review (UK)

Green, Laurence. "The Impact of Music on Film." 260:1515 (April 1992): 214–16.

Coronet (US)

Carroll, Sidney. "Music Works for Alfred Newman." (November 1944): 46–50.

Cosmopolitan (US)

Affelder, P. "Sound-Track Favorites on Discs." 141 (October 1956): 6.

Wood, Michele. "Recordings: Music from the Movies." (March 1964): 22–23. On Henry Mancini.

Creative Art (US)

Abbott, Jere. "Films and Music." 8:283 (April 1931).

Critical Inquiry (US)

Kramer, Lawrence. "Recognizing Schubert: Musical Subjectivity, Cultural Change, and Jane Campion's *The Portrait of a Lady*." 29:1 (Autumn 2002): 25–52.

Current Biography (US)

H. W. Wilson quarterly publication from the 1940s to the present. Entries include David Amram (November 1969); George Antheil (July 1954); Harold Arlen (July 1955); Burt Bacharach (October 1970); John Barry, 61:3 (March 2000): 9–13; Richard Rodney Bennett (March 1992); Irving Berlin (May 1942, May 1963); Elmer Bernstein, 64:6 (June 2003): 5–12; Leonard Bernstein (February 1944, February 1960); Aaron Copland (September 1940); Hanns Eisler (May 1942); Jerry Goldsmith, 62:5 (May 2001): 56–61; James Horner, 58:3 (March 1997): 23–26; Quincy Jones, 38:2 (February 1977): 34–37; Alan Menken, 62:1 (January 2001): 52–56; Ennio Morricone, 61:10 (October 2000): 64–67; Alfred Newman (July 1943); Randy Newman (October 1982); Miklós Rózsa (February 1992); Max Steiner (September 1943): 732–35; Harry Warren (June 1943); John Williams (October 1980); Paul Williams (June 1983); Hans Zimmer, 63:3 (March 2002): 83–89.

Current Opinion (US)
Bernard, Gabriel. "The Movies as a Source of Musical Inspiration." 65 (August 1918): 95–96. On improvisation; originally appeared in a French magazine.

Details (US)
Allman, Kevin. "A Little Nightmare Music." (December 1993): 182–83. Profile of Danny Elfman.

Direction (US)
Siegmeister, Elie. "Music for Films." 3:4 (April 1940). In Hollywood issue.

Discovery (US)
Daum, Raymond W. "[Gloria] Swanson and Music." 10:1 (1985): 15–19. On the actress's interest in music and a 1929 film waltz she commissioned from Franz Lehar.

Dynamics (US)
Soifer, Alex. "A Music Student in Soviet Russia." (April 5, 1935): 6–7. The future Alex North writes about his Russian experience for the Juilliard Student Club magazine.

The Economist (US)
"A Tune Is Worth 1,000 Pictures: The Neglected Craft of Film Music." 343:8018 (May 24, 1997): 82.

Eighteenth-Century Life (US)
Knapp, Elise F., and James Pegolotti. "Music in Kubrick's *Barry Lyndon*: 'A Catalyst to Manipulate.'" 19:2 (May 1995): 92–97.

Empirical Studies of the Arts (US)
Cohen, Annabel J. "Understanding Musical Soundtracks." 8:2 (1990): 111–24.

Entertainment, Publishing and the Arts Handbook (US)
Annual published by the Clark Boardman Co., New York (1983–). Continuation of the *Entertainment Law Journal*, published by the Entertainment Law Journal Association.
Brabec, Jeffrey J., and Todd W. Brabec. "Life after the Motion Picture Release: Movie Songs—a Lifetime Annuity." 6 (1988): 205–24. Documents sources of money for movie and television songs in addition to the fee paid for their inclusion in a film. Covers past hit songs, soundtracks, and royalty sources, including advertising, video, mechanical, foreign, sheet music, and Academy Awards show performances.

The Epigram (US)
"ERPI's Music Right Department Is Operated on Non-Profit Basis as Service to Producers: Has Made Available for Sound Picture Use the Music of the World." 2:9 (May 1, 1930): 4–5. Discusses the problems wrought by worldwide copyright as it relates to films with synchronized music. Published by Electrical Research Products in New York.

Esquire (US)
"Hollywood's Frustrated Music Makers." (September 1946). Reprinted in *Reader's Digest* (October 1946).
Lawrenson, Helen. "Mamma Mia, That'sa Some Musical Meatball!" 76:1 (July 1971): 94–97, 40–47. Interview-based article on André Previn.
"Mark Isham: Composer." 111:6 (June 1989): 91.

The European Legacy (US)
Landy, Marcia. "Opera, Cinema, Melodrama, and History: The Case of Italian Cinema."
  1:4 (July 1996): 1597–1601.

Everyweek Magazine (US)
Tildesley, Alice. "How Songs Hits Are Born." (August 4, 1940): 6. Overview of Hollywood songwriters and the process of creating film songs in a newspaper supplement.

The Force of Vision: Inter-Asian Comparative Literature (Japan)
Neumeyer, David. "Hayasaka's Music for *Rashomon*." 6 (1996): 477–86. From the proceedings of the 13th Congress of the International Comparative Literature Association.

Friends of the Harold B. Lee Library Newsletter (US)
"From Silents to Stereo: Film Music Archives at the Harold B. Lee Library." 2:1 (Fall
  1995): 3–5. Brief descriptions of the collections of John Addison, Ken Darby, Jerry
  Fielding, Hugo Friedhofer, Max Steiner, and Republic Pictures.

Frontier (US)
Morton, Lawrence. "Music: Reflections on Film Scores." (July 1951): 20, 25.
Morton, Lawrence. "Music: Confession." (May 1955): 21. On Dimitri Tiomkin's accep-
  tance speech at the Academy Awards ceremony.

Good Housekeeping (US)
Robson, Mark. "Why You Hear What You Do at the Movies." (July 1955): 99–102.

GQ (Gentlemen's Quarterly) (US)
Ryan, Rob. "The Score Keeper." 65:10 (October 1995): 118–20. On Michael Nyman.

Grand Street (US)
Burlingame, Jon. "Scoring Hitchcock." 13:1 (Summer 1994): 234–35. On Bernard
  Herrmann's music.

Harper's Bazaar (US)
Weill, Kurt. "Music in the Movies." (September 1946): 257, 398–400.

Harper's Magazine (US)
Moore, Douglas. "Music and the Movies." 171 (July 1935): 181–88. Historical survey
  followed by present conditions.

Harvard Library Bulletin (US)
Marks, Martin. "The First American Film Scores." Old series, 2:4 (Winter 1991): 78–
  100. Discusses scores by Walter Cleveland Simon for two 1912 Kalem films. With
  music examples.
Shirley, Wayne D. "Response to 'The First American Film Scores.'" Old series, 2:4
  (Winter 1991): 101–3.

Health (US)
Setterberg, Fred. "How They Make Movies Moving: Soundtrack Composers Use a
  Whole Bag of Psychological Tricks to Provoke Tears—and Terror." 9:7 (November–
  December 1995): 62, 64. On musical associations.

Holiday (US)

Hine, Al. "Movies: Once Unheralded and Almost Unheard, Movie Music Now Has Plenty of Listeners, Gets Recorded and Wins Oscars." 6 (July 1949): 22.

McNulty, John. "'Come Quick. Indians!' A Piano Player of the Silent Movies Recalls an Old Thrill." 13 (January 1953): 22–23, 106.

Human Behavior (US)

Backer, Thomas E., and Eddy Lawrence Manson. "In the Key of Feeling." (February 1978): 63–67. Cowritten by a psychologist and an arranger, with functions and examples of how music works in a film. Reprinted in *International Musician* (1978).

The Illustrated London News (UK)

Orme, Michael. "Music and the Talking Pictures." 176:514 (March 29, 1930): 5–14.

Orme, Michael. "Music—the Screen's Natural Ally." 180 (April 9, 1932): 540.

International Journal of Instructional Media (US)

Cooper, B. Lee. "Dracula and Frankenstein in the Classroom: Examining Theme and Character Exchanges in Film and Music." 19 (Winter 1992): 339–47.

Interview (US)

Schrader, Paul. "Giorgio Moroder." 12 (March 1982): 56–58. Interview.

Ehrlich, Dimitri. "Hopper's Hot Spot." 20:10 (October 1990): 58. On Miles Davis's music for *The Hot Spot*.

Mizrahi, Isaac. "Burt Bacharach." 26 (February 1996): 84–87. The New York fashion designer, a fan of Bacharach, interviews the composer.

Kornreich, Jennifer. "Who's Pricking Up Our Ears." (April 1996): 42. On popular composers.

ITA Journal (US)

Broussard, George L. "A Musician's Odyssey: The Life and Times of Leo Arnaud." 13:2 (1985): 26–28.

The Journal of Aesthetics and Art Criticism (US)

Milano, Paolo. "Music in the Film: Notes for a Morphology." 1:1 (Spring 1941): 89–94.

English, H. B. "*Fantasia* and the Psychology of Music." 2:7 (1943): 27–31.

Journal of American Culture (US)

Denisoff, R. Serge, and William David Romanowski. "The Pentagon's Top Guns: Movies and Music." 12:3 (Fall 1989): 67–78. Examines the relationship between films and the military through popular songs in *Top Gun* and other films.

MacDonnell, Francis. "'The Emerald City Was the New Deal': E. Y. Harburg and the Wonderful *Wizard of Oz*." 13:4 (December 1990): 71–75.

Reitinger, Douglas W. "Paint It Black: Rock Music and Vietnam War Film." 15:3 (Fall 1992): 53–59.

Cooper, B. Lee. "Terror Translated into Comedy: The Popular Music Metamorphosis of Film and Television Horror, 1956–1991." 20:3 (Fall 1997): 31–42.

Journal of Australian Studies (Australia)

Clancy, Jack. "Music in the Films of Peter Weir." 41 (1994): 24–34.

Journal of European Studies (UK)

Hillman, Roger. "Cultural Memory on Film Soundtracks." 33: 3–4 (2003): 323ff. Addresses issues of cultural memory arising from the use of classical music on film soundtracks.

Journal of General Psychology (US)

Karwoski, T. F., H. S. Odbert, and C. E. Osgood. "Studies in Synthetic Thinking: II. The Role of Form in Visual Responses to Music." 26 (April 1942): 199–222.

Journal of Popular Culture (US)

Feuer, Jane. "The Themes of Popular Versus Elite Art in the Hollywood Musical." 12:3 (Winter 1978).

Shrubsall, Wayne. "Banjo as Icon." 20:1 (Summer 1986): 31–59. Including its use in film and television.

Arora, V. N. "Popular Songs in Hindi Films." 20:2 (Fall 1986): 143–66.

Romanowski, William David, and R. Serge Denisoff. "Money for Nothin' and the Charts for Free: Rock and the Movies." 21:2 (Fall 1987): 63–78.

Burns, Gary. "Popular Music, Television, and Generational Identity." 30:3 (1996): 129–41.

Fahy, Thomas. "Killer Culture: Classical Music and the Art of Killing in *Silence of the Lambs* and *Se7en*." 37 (August 2003): 28–42.

Journal of the Copyright Society of the U.S.A. (US)

Colby, Richard. "Music in Motion Pictures." 30 (October 1982): 34–37.

Brylawski, E. Fulton. "Motion Picture Soundtrack Music: A Gap or Gaff[e] in Copyright Protection?" 40 (Spring 1993): 333–48.

The Journal of Value Inquiry (US)

Harrell, Jean G. "Phenomenology of Film Music." 14 (Spring 1980): 23–34. Later adapted in Harrell's *Soundtracks: A Study of Auditory Perception, Memory, and Valuation* (1986).

Keynote (UK)

Maffery, George. "This Concerto Business." (1947).

L.A. Weekly (US)

"Score Sheet: A Who's Who of Film Composing." (July 10–16, 1987): 24?–26, 28. On the early careers of Mark Isham and James Horner.

Labor History (US)

Kraft, James P. "The 'Pit' Musicians: Mechanization in the Movie Theaters, 1926–1934." 35 (Winter 1994): 66–89.

Ladies Home Journal (US)

"A Woman to Watch: Rachel Portman." 118:3 (March 2001): 22.

Liberty (US)

Feuer, Cy. "Stop-Watch Composers." 22 (September 15, 1945): 34–35, 80, 82–83.

Library of Congress Information Bulletin (US)

Anderson, Gillian B. "The Music of *The Circus*: LC Specialist Conducts Original Accompaniment to Film." 52:17 (September 20, 1993): 341–48.

Library of Congress Newsletter (US)

Parker, David L. "Golden Voices and the Silver Screen: The 'Singer' Films." 4:3 (1973): 92–96, 4:4 (1973): 93–96.

The Listener (UK)

Frank, Alan. "Music and the 'Cellulose Nitwit.'" 18:468 (December 29, 1937): 1444–445.

Donat, Misha. "Music in the Cinema." (October 28, 1971).

Literary Digest (US)

"How Music Is Made to Fit the Films." 56:58 (January 26, 1918): 58.

"Sound-proof Studios for Talkies." (January 12, 1929): 19.

Delehanty, Thornton. "The Film Cycle from Music to Guns to Music." 116 (July 8, 1933): 27.

The Lone Hand (Australia)

Cross, Zora. "The Music at the Movies." (February 1, 1918): 128. The writer weighs in on live versus mechanical music accompaniment of motion pictures.

Look (US)

"Alfred Newman." (February 19, 1946): 86–89.

Los Angeles Magazine (US)

Pietschmann, Richard J. "Sound and Music: Hey Kids, Let's Put on a Soundtrack! How the Record Mavens Are Rediscovering Song-and-Dance." 25:5 (May 1980): 258–63.

Manna, Sal. "Roll over Tiomkin." 29:8 (August 1984): 192ff. Soundtracks featuring popular recording artists.

Lasky, Jane E. "A Day in the Life: Jimmie Haskell: Music Scorer." 30:8 (August 1985): 2.

Manna, Sal. "Heard Any Good Movies? How Mike and Sam Got a Lucrative Lock on the Sound Track Market." 30:10 (October 1985): 124ff. Profile of agents Michael Gorfaine and Sam Schwartz.

Marx, Arthur. "Rhapsody in Orange." 35:12 (December 1990): 162–68. On Hollywood's golden age songwriters.

Logan, Michael. "Uncle Walt's Boys." 37:5 (May 1992): 86. On Richard and Robert Sherman.

"Close-Up: Hep Cat." 39:8 (August 1994): 36–41. Profile of Benny Carter.

Mitchell, Sean. "Isham's Blues." 40:10 (October 1995): 74–75. On Mark Isham.

Leibowitz, Ed. "One-Track Mind: Finding Friends and Foes among the Film-Score Obsessed." 46:7 (July 2001): 20–21. On Lukas Kendall and *Film Score Monthly*.

Erickson, Steve. "Low Fidelity." 46:9 (September 2001): 134. On film music.

Maclean's (Canada)

Canadian national weekly current affairs magazine.

Abel, E. "He Makes Movie Music." (May 1946). On Louis Applebaum.

Macworld (US)

Yavelow, Christopher. "Top of the Charts." (August 1987): 138–45. Using the Apple Macintosh computer for film music and sound design.

Holsinger, Erik. "Film Scoring Simplified." 4 (September 1987): 158–60.

Magazine of Art (US)

Pollack, Robert. "Hollywood's Music." (September 1938): 512–13.

Marketing Theory (US)

Holbrook, Morris B. "Ambi-diegetic Music in Films as a Product-Design and -Placement Strategy: The *Sweet Smell of Success.*" 4:3 (2004): 171–85.

Meanjin (Australia)

McMahon, Elizabeth. "Lost in Music." 59 (June 2000): 166ff. On film adaptations.

Memory and Cognition (US)

Boltz, Marilyn, Matthew Schulkind, and Suzanne Kantra. "Effects of Background Music on the Remembering of Filmed Events." 19:6 (1991): 593–606.

Boltz, Marilyn. "The Cognitive Processing of Film and Musical Soundtracks." 32:7 (2004): 1194–1205.

The Mentor (US)

Rothafel [*sic*], S. L. "Making the Program." 9:6 (July 1921): 33. General article on music for motion pictures in an issue devoted to motion pictures.

Michigan Academician (US)

Elworth, Steven B. "Sounds of the Green World: Ideology, Music, and Color in *The Quiet Man.*" 31:2 (1999): 135.

Michigan Quarterly Review (US)

Marks, Martin. "Music, Drama, Warner Brothers: The Cases of *Casablanca* and *The Maltese Falcon.*" 35:1 (Winter 1996): 112–41.

Military Chaplains' Review (US)

Butler, Ignatius W. "Can You Imagine *Kings Row* without Music: Erich Wolfgang Korngold's Classic Film Scores." 16:1 (Spring 1987): 89–113.

The Mississippi Quarterly (US)

McCraw, Harry W. "Tennessee Williams, Film, Music, Alex North: An Interview with Luigi Zaninelli." 48 (Fall 1995): 763(13). Zaninelli, a composer, discusses North's score for *A Streetcar Named Desire*.

Mosaic (Canada)

Journal for the interdisciplinary study of literature.

Powis, Tim. "How to Get Your Music on Television." 365 (January–February 1989).

Brown, Monika. "Film Music as Sister Art: Adaptations of *The Turn of the Screw.*" 31:1 (March 1998): 61–81. Includes discussion of music by Georges Auric, Benjamin Britten, Robert Cobert, and J. Peter Robinson.

Kehler, Grace. "Still for Sale: Love Songs and Prostitutes from *La Traviata* to *Moulin Rouge.*" 38:2 (June 2005): 145–62. On the use of popular music.

Nation (US)

Bakshy, Alexander. "Films: With Benefit of Music." 132 (April 1, 1931): 359–60. On the irrelevancy of music by noted composers, including Darius Milhaud, in several early sound films.

Haggin, B. H. "Music for Documentary Films." 152:7 (February 15, 1940): 194. By music critic Bernard H. Haggin.

National Identities (UK)

Burnand, David, and Benedict Sarnaker. "The Articulation of National Identity through Film Music." 1:1 (March 1999): 7–13.

The New Criterion (US)

Simon, John. "The Other Rota." 19:1 (September 2000): 53–59. On Nino Rota.

The New Republic (US)

Seldes, Gilbert. "Theory about Talkies." (August 28, 1928): 305–6.

Josephson, Matthew. "Modern Music for the Films." (April 1, 1931): 183.

Ferguson, Otis. "Love Me Some Other Time." 83:1077 (July 24, 1935): 308. Survey of musical films.

Ferguson, Stanley. "Gone with the Soundtrack: Pit Orchestras." 106:13 (March 30, 1942): 426–27.

New Statesman and Nation (UK)

Turner, W. J. "Music in the Cinema." 18 (January 14, 1922): 419–20.

"Music and the Film." (April 13, 1940).

Turner, W. J. "Music for the Films." 19: 477 (April 13, 1940): 490. Music by "serious" composers.

Whitebait, William. (August 29, 1942): 140. On William Walton's *The First and the Few*.

Clinch, Dermot. "Always Playing Second Fiddle." 125:4292 (July 12, 1996): 37–38. On John Williams, honored by the Royal Academy of Music, and the status of film music.

Cook, Richard. "Screen Writer: Richard Cook on Film Music." 128:4421 (January 29, 1999): 37. Profile of Greek composer Eleni Karaindrou.

Johnson, Phil. "Sight and Sound." 129:4426 (March 5, 1999): 43. On Roy Budd.

Tennant, Neil. "Diary: 'Is This Tony Banks?' I Asked James Fox. 'No,' He Remonstrated. 'Tony Blair.' Three and a Half Years Later, I Was Invited to the Notorious 'Noel Gallagher' Victory Party." 133:4705 (September 13, 2004): 9. The Pet Shop Boys were invited to write a new soundtrack to the classic silent *Battleship Potemkin*.

New Theatre (US)

Antheil, George. "Music in the Film." 2 (October 1935): 14–15.

New West Magazine (US)

Meyer, Nicholas. "Miklos Rozsa: The Maestro Scores Again." 4:20 (September 24, 1979): 50–55. The director Nicholas Meyer discusses the score for his film *Time after Time*.

New York (US)

Shaw, Daniel. "The Sound of Silents." Vol. 20 (March 2, 1987): 22. On orchestral music for silent films.

New York Times Magazine (US)

Stang, Joanne. "Making Music: Silent Style." 110 (October 23, 1960): 83–84. On Arthur Kleiner.

Copland, Aaron. "A Tip to Moviegoers: Take Off Those Ear-Muffs." (November 6, 1949): 28–32. Advice on listening to the soundtrack. This article appeared one month after the composer's suite from *The Red Pony* was performed by the New York Philharmonic.

Maremaa, Thomas. "The Sound of Movie Music." (March 28, 1976): 40–48. "Audiences have changed—they want the music to work on them, to wipe them out. And that's what the new film scores are all about." John Williams talks about his score for *Jaws* (1976) on the eve of the Academy Awards ceremony.

Hooland, Bernard. "Highbrow Music to Hum." (January 31, 1982): 24–25, 56–57, 65–66, 70. On John Corigliano's music for *Altered States*.

Schoemer, Karen. "Frank DeVol." (January 2, 2000): 37. On television themes.

New Yorker (US)

Leamy, Edmund. "The Talk of the Town: Theme Songs." (January 5, 1929): 13.

Johnston, Alva. "Profiles: American Maestro-1." (October 20, 1934): 26–30; "Profiles: American Maestro-2." (October 27, 1934): 23–26. On conductor and composer Werner Janssen, two years before he scored his first film.

Heggie, Barbara, and Robert Lewis Taylor. "Profiles: Idea Flourisher." (February 5, 1944). Profile of Erno Rapee, with mention of composer Richard Mohaupt.

McCarten, John. "The Talk of the Town: Music by the Frame." 25:24 (August 6, 1949): 13. Based on an interview with Arthur Kleiner.

Wind, Herbert Warren. "Profiles: Another Opening, Another Show." (November 17, 1951): 46–71. Lengthy, detailed profile of Robert Russell Bennett that touches briefly on his foray into Hollywood.

Kahn, E. J., Jr. "Profiles: The Hit's the Thing." (January 14, 1956): 33–55. Second of two parts. Profile of Cy Feuer, including his career in Hollywood.

Rodgers, Richard. "Profiles: You Can't Force It." (November 18, 1961). On his music for television.

Clyde, Amy. "The Talk of the Town: Accompany Man." (April 18, 1994): 35. On Steve Sterner, piano accompanist for silent films.

Griffiths, Paul. "Screening the Music: What Happens When Movie Scores Become Live Performances?" 71:22 (July 31, 1995): 86–87.

Lahr, John. "Profiles: The Lemon-Drop Kid." 72:29–30 (September 1996): 68–74. Profile of E. Y. Harburg.

Ross, Alex. "Scoring for Oscar: The Thrills and Chills of Composing in Hollywood." 74:3 (March 9, 1998): 82–86. On how the popularity of James Horner's score for *Titanic* is raising the profile of orchestral film music.

Mead, Rebecca. "The Talk of the Town: The Musical Life." 75:19 (July 19, 1999): 30. Profile of Marc Shaiman.

Smith, Giles. "Arts and Crafts: Composer Symphony in See." (October 20, 2003). On Howard Shore.

Ross, Alex. "The Ring and the *Rings*." 79:40 (December 22, 2003): 161ff. On music by Howard Shore for *Lord of the Rings*.

Ross, Alex. "Sound and Vision: [Philip] Glass's *Koyaanisqatsi* and the Art of Film Scoring." (June 27, 2005): 102–4.

Lahr, John. "Come Rain or Come Shine: The Bittersweet Life of Harold Arlen." (September 19, 2005): 89–94.

News from the Fleischer Collection (US)
The Edwin A. Fleischer Collection of Orchestral Music is at the Free Library of Philadelphia.
Cochrane, Keith. "[George] Antheil's Music to a World's Fair Film." No. 4 (June 1993): 1–3.

Newsday (US)
Burlingame, Jon. "Themes Like Old Times Are Rare Today." (April 5, 1992): 18. Vic Mizzy and others comment on the current state of television themes.
Burlingame, Jon. "The Sound of (TV) Music: The *Friends* Sound Track Might Be Hot Right Now, But Will It Ever Really Be As Good As *I Spy*?" (November 19, 1995): 20.
Burlingame, Jon. "Playing Off the Sounds of Success: TV Themes Revamped for the Movies." (January 17, 1996): B60ff.
Burlingame, Jon. "The Dream Themes: Not Only Can You Hum Them, but These Top 10 TV Tunes Have Stood the Test of Time." (December 22, 1996): C16ff.
Burlingame, Jon. "Answering the Call: John Debney Was Known for Scoring Comedy Films—until Mel Gibson Came Along and Offered Him *The Passion of the Christ*." (March 7, 2004): C27ff.

Newsweek (US)
"Is It Bad to Be Good?" (July 9, 1945): 93. The Bernard Herrmann–Erich Leinsdorf debate, originally published in the *New York Times*.
"Man behind the Tune." (July 20, 1953). On Robert Russell Bennett's score for *Victory at Sea*.
"The Melody Lingers On." 44:10 (September 6, 1954): 50–51. On theme songs and Dimitri Tiomkin.
"Music: Melody in the Courtroom." (January 5, 1959). On Dimitri Tiomkin's score for *The High and the Mighty*.
"Allegro, Presto, Whee!" 60 (August 13, 1962): 83. Profile of silent film accompanist Arthur Kleiner.
"Music: Lights...Camera...Music!" (July 24, 1967): 77–78. On the new breed of composers.
McGuigan, Cathleen, with Peter McAlevey. "Rock Music Goes Hollywood." (March 11, 1985): 78.

North American Review (US)
Mermey, Maurice. "The Vanishing Fiddler: The Talkies Threaten Calamity." 227 (March 1929): 301–7.
Rose, Donald. "Silence Is Requested." (July 1930): 127–28.
Berchtold, William E. "Grand Opera Goes to Hollywood." 239 (February 1935): 138–46.

The Observer Magazine
Wigglesworth, Angela. "Howard Blake, Mixed Media Music Man." (June 10, 1979).

The Open Space Magazine (US)
Missiras, Michael. "The Transformative Power of Film Music: Non-Diegetic Musical Considerations in the Film *East of Eden*." No. 1 (Spring 1999): 97–103.

Opportunity (US)
Arvey, Verna. "Hall Johnson and His Choir." (May 1941): 151, 158–59.

Still, William Grant. "How Do We Stand in Hollywood?" 13:2 (Spring 1945): 74–77.

Orange County Illustrated (US)

Mancini, Henry. "Go Where the Action Is." (February 1966): 40–41. Advice to young composers.

Our Time (UK)

Silverman, Edward. "Putting in the Sound Track." (October 1946). A British studio violinist describes a film music recording session. Reprinted in John Huntley's *British Film Music* (1947) as "A Film Recording Session."

The Outlook (US)

"Music and the Movies." 108 (September 16, 1914): 158–59.

Buchanan, Charles L. "Music and the Movies." 144 (November 3, 1926): 307–8. On musical accompaniment and on opera on film.

The Pacific Spectator (US)

Literary journal published in Stanford, California, by the American Society of Learned Societies and the Pacific Coast Committee for the Humanities.

Huntley, John. "Notes on Film Music." 1 (August 1946): 35–37; 2 (January 1947): 21–25.

Nelson, Robert U. "The Craft of the Film Score." 1:4 (Autumn 1947): 435–46. On music's subservience to film. This article was read at the 1947 University of Oregon Festival of Contemporary Music. Discusses film scores of the time, including Bernard Herrmann's music for *Anna and the King of Siam*, with music examples.

Mathieson, Muir. "Developments in Film Music." 4 (October 1947): 41–46.

Huntley, John. "Film Music Orchestras." 5 (January 1948): 14–18.

Huntley, John. "British Film Music." 6 (1948).

Huntley, John. "The Music of *Hamlet* and *Oliver Twist*." 8 (1949).

PC/Computing (US)

"PC's Go Hollywood: Auricle...Making Beautiful Music." (May 1989). Includes a discussion of Alan Silvestri's synchronization of music via computer.

Peanuts Collectors Club Newsletter (US)

Bang, Derrick. "Vince Guaraldi: He Worked for More Than *Peanuts*." (Summer 1993). Extensive profile.

People (US)

Carlson, Peter, and Carl Arrington. "As It Ponders *The Color Purple*'s Sound Track, Hollywood Hums, 'I've Heard That Song Before.'" (March 31, 1986): 38, 41. On the similarity between Quincy Jones's score and the film's temp track by Georges Delerue.

Jerome, Jim. "Blues Guitarist Ry Cooder Turns into Rock 'n' Reel Star as a Hot Hollywood Composer." 2 (June 1986): 127–30.

Abrahams, Andrew. "His Haunting Mood Music Makes Composer Angelo Badalamenti the Lynch-Pin of *Twin Peaks'* Success." (September 10, 1990): 117–18. Interview-based article.

People Weekly (US)
Rizzo, Monica. "Water under the Bridge." 49:6 (February 16, 1998): 26. Brief interview-based article on James Horner.

Philosophy and Literature (US)
Leibowitz, Flo. "Pianists in the Movies." 21:2 (October 1997): 376–81. Written on the heels of the popular success of *Shine*.

Playboy (US)
"On the Scene: Henry Mancini: Swinging Sultan of the Sound Track." (March 1963).

Popular Culture in Libraries (US)
Hendricks, Leta. "Viewing the Hip: An Overview of Rap Music in Film." 5:1 (January 1998): 1–19. Examines the use of rap music in films from 1989 through 1995.

Pynchon Notes (US)
McLaughlin, Robert L. "Movie Music in *Gravity's Rainbow*." No. 28–29 (Spring–Fall 1991): 143–45. On film music references in Thomas Pynchon's novel.

Q (US)
Cooper, M. "Heard Any Good Films Lately?" 35 (August 1989): 16–19.

Quadrant Magazine (Australia)
Australia's independent review of literature and ideas.
McDonald, Neil. "Music, Opera and Film." 47: 9 (September 2003): 60–63.

Quarterly Journal of the Library of Congress (US)
Published as a supplement to the Annual Report of the Library of Congress. Many articles were written or influenced by LC archivist Jon Newsom, a friend of David Raksin's, in the days after their involvement in the formation of the Film Music Society. Newsom later reprinted some of the articles in his book, *Wonderful Inventions* (1985).
Waters, Edward N. "Music." 15 (November 1957): 22–23; 17 (November 1959): 25–26; 20 (December 1962): 31; 26 (January 1969): 43, 45.
Shirley, Wayne. "Another American in Paris: George Antheil's Correspondence with Mary Curtis Bok." 34 (January 1977): 2–22.
Newsom, Jon. "David Raksin: A Composer in Hollywood." 35:3 (July 1978): 142–72. On *Force of Evil* (1948), *Carrie* (1952), *Separate Tables* (1958), and *The Redeemer* (1966), with music examples. Includes two 7-inch discs of music. Reprinted in Newsom, pp. 117–158.
Newsom, Jon. "'A Sound Idea': Music for Animated Films." 37:3–4 (Summer–Fall 1980): 279–309. Survey, including Disney's composers and United Productions of America (UPA). Includes one 7-inch disc of music. Reprinted in Newsom, pp. 59–80.
Parker, David L. "Golden Voices, Silver Screen: Opera Singers as Movie Stars." 37:3–4 (Summer–Fall 1980): 370–86.
Steiner, Fred. "Keeping Score of the Scores: Music for *Star Trek*." 40:1 (Winter 1983): 4–15. Documents who wrote original music for the television series.
Shirley, Wayne D. "A Bugle Call to Arms for National Defense! Victor Herbert and His Score for *The Fall of a Nation*." 40:1 (Winter 1983): 26–47. Reprinted in Newsom, pp. 173–186.

Care, Ross. "Threads of Melody: The Evolution of a Major Film Score—Walt Disney's *Bambi*." (Spring 1983): 76–98. Reprinted in Newsom. Discusses Frank Churchill, Charles Henderson, Edward Plumb, Paul Smith, Alexander Steinert, and Charles Wolcott.

Raksin, David. "Life with Charlie." 40:3 (Summer 1983): 234–53. Raksin discusses his collaboration with Charlie Chaplin on *Modern Times*. Reprinted in Newsom, pp. 159–172.

Rosar, William H. "Music for the Monsters: Universal Pictures' Horror Film Scores of the Thirties." 40:4 (Fall 1983): 390–421. Well-documented survey of music composed by David Broekman, James Dietrich, Karl Hajos, Bernhard Kaun, Heinz Roemheld, Clifford Vaughan, and Franz Waxman. Rosar interviewed Dietrich, Kaun, Roemheld, and Vaughan, and the widows of Broekman and Hajos. Excerpted in *MagicImage Filmbooks presents* Dracula (1990).

Radio Pictorial

Levy, Louis. "Music from the Movies Radio Programme." (January 21, 1938).

Radio Times (UK)

Journal of the BBC.

Hill, Ralph. "The Story of British Film Music." (December 31, 1937).

RCA News (US)

"The Theremin Wins Famous Musicians and Stars for Stars on Tour." (September 1930): 24–25. On the attention the Victor Theremin received in Hollywood from film studios and actors.

Readers Digest (US)

White, E. B. "Mood Men: Playing for Silent Pictures." 33 (July 1938).

Recorded Sound (UK)

Arnold, Malcolm. "Film Music." No. 18 (April 1965): 328–34.

The Reporter (US)

Not to be confused with the *Hollywood Reporter*.

Hentoff, Nat. "Movie Music Comes into Its Own." (June 12, 1958): 28–30.

Research in African Literatures (US)

Higginson, Francis. "The Well-Tempered Savage: Albert Schweitzer, Music, and Imperial Deafness." 36:4 (Winter 2005): 205–22. Examines the use of music in *Le Grand Blanc de Lambaréné* (1995).

Ritz (UK)

Burlingame, Jon. "Spotlight: John Barry: Echoes." No. 7 (Winter–Spring 2003): 16–21. Interview-based article for the London magazine.

The Sackbut (UK)

Fletcher, Stuart. "Two Arts that Meet as One." (June 1929): 374.

Salmagundi (US)

Schwartz, Lloyd. "Movie Tunes." 148–149 (Fall 2005): 211–22.

Saturday Review (UK/US)

Published as **Saturday Review** (UK)

Baughan, E. A. "Moving Pictures and Music." 133 (January 14, 1922): 33–34. On the use of classical music with film.

Lambert, Constant. "Music in the Kinema." 147 (April 13, 1929): 498–99.

Published as **The Saturday Review of Literature** (US)

Sobel, Bernard. "Let the Audience Think." 28 (November 10, 1945): 30.

Herrmann, Bernard. "From Sound Track to Disc." 30 (September 27, 1947): 42.

Canby, Edward Tatnall. "Music for Background." 32 (January 8, 1949): 29.

Kolodin, Irving. "Have *Gunn...*" 42 (April 11, 1959): 55. Review of the *Peter Gunn* television series soundtrack.

Published as **Saturday Review** (US)

Hedlund, Oscar. "Ingmar Bergman, The Listener." 47:9 (February 29, 1964): 47–49, 61. The director discusses the relationship between film and music.

Williams, Martin. "Jazz at the Movies." 50:28 (July 15, 1967): 49. Reprinted in Limbacher.

Daniel, Oliver. "A Perspective of [Bernard] Herrmann." 51:28 (July 13, 1968): 49.

Knight, Arthur. "A Chat with the Composer." 55:28 (July 8, 1972): 71. John Barry interview.

Kolodin, Irving. "The Wide Screen World of Bernard Herrmann." 3:11 (March 6, 1976): 35–38.

Kolodin, Irving. "Sounds for the Silver Screen." 5:4 (November 12, 1977): 44–46.

School and Society (US)

Tindall, Glenn M. "Music and the Movies." (December 3, 1938): 721.

Science Digest (US)

Heinsheimer, H. W. "Hollywood's Musical Doctors." (August 1947): 52–56.

Scientific American (US)

"Making the Movie Film Give the Music Cues: With This Invention the Orchestra Leader Need Never Look at the Screen." (October 1925): 232.

Yates, Raymond F. "A Technician Talks about the Talkies." (November 1930): 384–85.

Peck, A. P. "What Makes *Fantasia* Click: Multiple Sound Tracks and Loud-Speakers Give Auditory Perspective to Sound Movie Screen." 164 (January 1941): 28–30.

Levinson, Nathan. "What Sound Hath Wrought." (August 1946): 101–9; (September 1946): 176–90.

Scone (US)

Newsletter from the New England soundtrack dealer; see no. 19 (November 1979). Discography no. 1 (August 1982) is an eight-page newsletter listing current soundtrack releases.

Scop (US)

Swanson, Jane. "Movie Music." 1:1 (Summer 1945): 23–26. Essay published in the Associated Students of UCLA literary publication; according to editor's note, it won an honorable mention in an *Atlantic Monthly* contest.

Seven Arts (US)
Van Vechten, Carl. "Music and the Electrical Theatre." 2 (May 1917): 97–102. On overtures played before films.

Shakespeare Quarterly (US)
Hurtgen, Charles. "The Operatic Character of Background Music in Film Adaptations of Shakespeare." 20:1 (Winter 1969): 53–64.

SIGUCCS Newsletter (US)
From the Association for Computing Machinery (ACM) Special Interest Group on University and College Computing Services.
Zivkovic, Brane, and David Frederickson. "Scoring Films on Cue and Online: The Future Is Here." 25:1–2 (June 1995): 37–38.

South Atlantic Quarterly (US)
Lerner, Neil. "'Look at that Big Hand Move Along': Clocks, Containment, and Music in *High Noon*." 104:1 (Winter 2005): 151–73.

The Southern Quarterly (US)
Austin, Wade. "Hollywood Barn Dance: A Brief Survey of Country Music in Films." 22:3 (Spring 1984): 111–23.

Southwest Review (US)
Boller, Paul F., Jr. "Music by Max Steiner." 51:3 (Summer 1966): 256–71. Profile by a history professor.

The Spectator (UK)
Hussey, Dyneley. "Music in the Cinema." 154 (February 15, 1935): 247.

Stage: The Magazine of After-Dark Entertainment (US)
Antheil, George. "More Melody, Please!" (January 1, 1935): 14–15.
Davenport, Marcia. "Gelatine on the High C's." (February 1936): 35–37.
Davenport, Marcia. "Source-Spring for New—and Good Music: The Motion Picture Is Becoming an Important Source of Original and Significant Musical Composition." 14:4 (January 1937): 60–62.
Churchill, Douglas W. "Music to My Ears." 15:5 (February 1938): 57–59.

Stanford Humanities Review (US)
Corbett, John. "Siren Song to Banshee Wail: On the Status of the Background Vocalist." 3:2 (Fall 1993): 91–101.

Stanford Magazine (US)
Oxfeld, Jesse. "Getting in Synch." (May–June 2004): 70–71. Profile of alumnus Christopher Tin in this issue of the Stanford University Alumni Association magazine.

Studies in the Literary Imagination (US)
Carroll, Noël, and Patrick Carroll. "Notes on Movie Music." 19:1 (Spring 1986): 73–81.

Style (US)
Berliner, Todd, and Philip Furia. "The Sounds of Silence: Songs in Hollywood Films Since the 1960s." 36:1 (Spring 2002): 19ff.

Talkabout (UK)
Mathieson, Muir. "Dramatists in Music." (1945).

TASCAM User Guide (US)
"Studio Report: 488 Scores Movie Hit." 11 (Autumn 1993): 15. Recording Eric Guthrie's score for *El Mariachi* on a TASCAM Portastudio.

Teaching Music (US)
Reninger, Rosemary D. "James Newton Howard JAMS with TRI-M." 8:3 (December 2000): 42–45. Interview on Howard's work with junior ASCAP members.

Technology and Culture (US)
Kraft, James P. "Musicians in Hollywood: Work and Technological Change in Entertainment Industries, 1926–1940." 35 (April 1994): 289–314.

The Theatre (US)
Russell, Alexander. "A Scholarly Musician Examines Sound Films." 50 (August 1929): 21, 60–62.
Straus, Oscar. "And So to Hollywood: Notes on a Pilgrimage to the Sound Studios." 51 (April 1930): 40, 62.

The Thousand Eyes Magazine (US)
Magliozzi, Ron. "Starting a Soundtrack Collection." 2:6 (February 1977).

Time (US)
"Music: Movie Music." (September 3, 1923). On Victor Herbert conducting a cinema orchestra.
"Music: Movie Music." (April 15, 1940). On the occasion of Arthur Honegger's film music played on radio.
"Music: Hollywood Music." (March 9, 1942). On a special Academy Award to conductor Leopold Stokowski.
"Music: Sound-Track Concertos." (September 16, 1946): 61. On Miklós Rózsa.
"Music: Here Come the Zithers." (January 16, 1950): 75. On the sudden popularity of the instrument after the release of *The Third Man* (music by Anton Karas).
"Cinema: Theme Song." 62 (September 14, 1953): 108. On Dimitri Tiomkin.
"Music: They Write the Songs." (March 26, 1956). Includes interview quotations from Dimitri Tiomkin.
"Music: Never Too Much Music." 79 (May 25, 1962): 70ff. On Henry Mancini.
"Music: Composers: To Touch a Moment." (January 17, 1964): 70. On the greater range of emotion available to Hollywood composers.
"Music: Composers: Cool Hand in Hollywood." (July 25, 1969): 52. On Lalo Schifrin.
Jones, Robert T. "Movie Time at the Opera." 96 (July 27, 1970): 56. A festival of opera films.
"Music: Reels of Sound." (September 8, 1975): 31.
Cocks, Jay. "The Lyrical Assassin at 5 a.m.: Got a Favorite Movie Theme? This Man Probably Wrote It." 129 (March 16, 1987): 83. On Ennio Morricone.
Zoglin, Richard, and Patrick E. Cole. "Music from the Darkside." (October 11, 1993): 80–81. On Danny Elfman.
Thigpen, David E. "Music: Jazz Goes to the Movies." (May 16, 1994). On Terence Blanchard's film music.

Walsh, Michael. "Running Up the Scores." (September 11, 1995). On the new crop of composers, including James Horner, Michael Kamen, and Elliot Goldenthal.

Time Out (UK)
Grant, Steve. "Angelo Badalamenti: Mood Awakening." (October 17, 1990): 21. Interview-based article.

Time Out (US)
Bennett, Bruce. "Key Players: MoMA's Seasoned Accompanists Make Silent Pictures Sing." 226 (January 20–27, 2000). Interview-based article on Stuart Oderman and Ben Model.

Today (US)
Taubman, H. Howard. "Maestros in the Movies." 6:18 (August 22, 1936): 12–13, 28. The New York critic on opera singers, virtuosos, choirs, and conductors headed for Hollywood.

Town and Country (US)
Levant, Oscar. "Movie Music." (December 1939): 90–91, 130–33. Reprinted as "A Cog in the Wheel" in Levant's book, *A Smattering of Ignorance*.

Twentieth Century (UK)
Wilson, Sandy. "From Broadway to Hollywood: A Revaluation of the Light Composers of the 1930's." 177:1042 (1969): 35–38.

UCLA Librarian (US)
"That's Entertainment: A Survey of the Hollywood Motion Picture Musical." (July–August 1983). Posters, photographs, disc recordings, and memorabilia from 1930 to the present on display at the UCLA Rubsamen Music Library.

University of Hartford Studies in Literature (US)
Grant, Barry Keith. "'Jungle Nights in Harlem': Jazz, Ideology, and the Animated Cartoon." 21:3 (1989): 3–12.

Urban Life (US)
Faulkner, Robert R. "Dilemmas in Commercial Work: Hollywood Film Composers and Their Clients." 5 (April 1976): 3–32.

Vanity Fair (US)
Moss, Nathaniel. "Vanities: Silent Partners." (April 1977). On the Boston-based Alloy Orchestra.

Woman's Home Companion (US)
Downes, Olin. "The Music of the Movies." (September 1940): 10.

World Psychology
Keller, Hans. "The Psychology of Film Music." 3:3 (March 1948): 23–26.

Yale French Studies (US)
Published by Yale University Press. Rick Altman served as special editor of a *Cinema/Sound* issue in 1980 that includes four essays on music, introduced by Altman, and

Claudia Gorbman's bibliography on sound in film, which includes a section on music.

Special issue: *Cinema/Sound* 60 (1980)
Bordwell, David. "The Musical Analogy." 141–56.
Rosen, Philip. "Adorno and Film Music: Theoretical Notes on *Composing for the Films*." 157–82.
Gorbman, Claudia. "Narrative Film Music." 183–203.
Insdorf, Annette. "Maurice Jaubert and Francois Truffaut: Musical Continuities from *L'Atalante* to *L'histoire d'Adele H.*" 204–18.

Index

482, 483, 489, 493, 498, 501, 521–23, 535, 538, 540, 541, 544, 562, 563, 567; as salesmen, 450; Australian, 397; biography, 131; church v. theater, 540, 541; Compton, 23, 169; console, 482; development of cinema organ, 245; displacement of, 482; effects, 23, 51, 117, 130; evolution into one-man orchestra, 447; evolution of playing, 482; German theater, 513; Hammond, 136; imitating animal sounds, 11; in Britain, 60, 136; installations, 136; lack of work, 522; manual for, 234; mechanical, 405; musical effects, 11, 36; orchestra and, 451; organ orchestra, 158; pipe, 11, 117, 172, 180, 195, 234, 380, 443, 448; pipe and console, 23; pipe organ orchestra, 125; pipe rolls, 451; playing from odd parts, 60; playing with orchestra, 60; replacing or augmenting orchestra, 158; salaries, 242; solo playing, 60; specifications, 136; synchronized sound films effect on, 522; synchronizing, 482; technical manual, 243; theater, 11, 473, 509, 523; theater organ encyclopedia, 173; theater, evolution of, 563; theater, in Britain, 562; theater, in British Isles, 513; theater, in Canada, 562; training, 242; unit organ, 482; Walthamstow Cinemas, 459
Orgatron, 136
Orledge, Robert, 77, 202, 514
Orlik, Peter B., 200
Orloff, Gene, 128
Orloff, Kathy, 487
Orme, Michael, 572
Orowan, Florella, 272, 337
orphan scores (series of articles), 312, 318–21, 323
Orpheum Theater, 249, 384
Orr, Buxton, 313, 315
Ortolani, Riz, 6; interview, 258; profile, 474
Os, Rene van, 363
Osborne, Jerry, 47, 48
Osborne, Robert, 530
Oscar. *See* Academy Award
Osgerby, Bill, 45
Osgood, C. E., 573
O'Shaughnessy, Michael, 437
O'Shea, Helen, 14
O'Sullivan, Joseph, 361, 439, 440, 449, 452, 523
Otfinoski, Steven, 203
O'Toole, Lawrence, 400
Ots, Loone, 212
Otter, Kelly Joyce, 77
Ottman, John, 121, 270, 297, 304, 308, 320, 472, 524; interview, 269, 292, 316, 321, 323, 325, 352, 356, 504; profile, 446, 542
Our Time, 579
Outlook, The, 579
Outre, 450
Ovation, 545
Ovchinnikov, Boris, 463
overdubbing, 223

Overture, 545
overtures, 583; list of, 371
Owen, A. W., 563
Owens, Gary, 431
Oxfeld, Jesse, 583

Pace, Ian, 562
Pacheco, Pedro, 289
Pacific Coast Musician, 154, 546
Pacific Spectator, The, 579
pacing, 204
Padroff, Jay, 439
painters, music in films about, 284
Paisley, Tom, 484
Pakula, Alan J., 319
Paling, Edwin, 270
Pallmeyer, Karl, 303
Palmer, Charles, 221
Palmer, Christopher, 48, 57, 93, 96, 137, 166, 184, 194, 218, 271–73, 291, 310, 369, 399, 439, 445, 460, 489, 491, 494, 495, 527, 528, 540, 541, 551, 552; interview, 341
Palmer, Shelly, 270
Palmer, Tony, 236, 422
Panken, Ted, 500
Panuccio, Alessandro, 36
Paolo, Cherchi Usai, 422
Papadimitriou, Lydia, 45
Paramount Artcraft Progress-Advance, 451
"Paramount Music Notes," 454
Paramount Pictures, 43, 101, 106, 107, 146, 149, 197, 264, 265, 331, 377, 386, 428, 451; music department, 275; music director, 549; musicals, 214; studio publication (*Publix Opinion*), 454
Paramount Progress, 451
Paramount Publix Corp., 454
Paramount Publix Theatres. *See* Publix Theatres
Paramount Studio News, 451
Paramount Theatre, 131, 537, 563
Pareles, Jon, 454
Parish, James Robert, 48, 203
Parisi, Paula, 203
Park, George, 296
Park, Nick, 318
Park, Phil, 169
Parker, Charlie, 409, 471
Parker, Clifton, 38, 39, 282, 284; profile, 533
Parker, David L., 201, 376, 513, 574, 580
Parker, Jim, 64, 325, 505
Parker, John, profile, 488
Parker, Robert, 520
Parks, Dean, 270
Parks, Gordon, 203
Parks, Henry Francis, 521; profile, 522
Parks, Van Dyke, 153; profile, 474
Parlett, Graham, 203
parlor music, 533
Parmet, Marc, 330, 331, 333
Parodi, Starr, 516
parody, 188, 223, 455

About the Compiler and Editor

Warren M. Sherk is the special collections database archivist and music specialist at the Academy of Motion Picture Arts and Sciences' Margaret Herrick Library. As music and recorded sound specialist, he has cataloged the library's music holdings, which include sheet music, scores and manuscript material, disc and tape recordings, and compact discs, as well as the papers of Jerry Goldsmith, Alex North, Harry Sukman, Sammy Cahn, and the Screen Composers Association. He holds a bachelor's degree in music composition from the University of Arizona, where he studied with Robert Muczynski, and a master's from UCLA, where he studied with Roger Bourland and Paul Reale. He also works extensively in music preparation for motion pictures, providing orchestrations for such films as *Dragonheart: A New Beginning* and *101 Dalmatians II: Patch's London Adventure*. His orchestral reconstructions of classic film music can be heard on Koch, Naxos, Silva Screen, Tadlow Music, and Varese Sarabande.

Sherk is currently secretary of the Film Music Society and oversaw the publication of *Film Music 2: History, Theory, Practice* and *Elmer Bernstein's Film Music Notebook* for the society. His writings on film music appear in the Society's *Cue Sheet*, the second edition of the *Grove Dictionary of American Music* (forthcoming), *Wagner & Cinema* (Indiana University Press, 2010), and on www.dimitritiomkin.com. In addition, he co-edited the *Dimitri Tiomkin Anthology*, the largest collection of the composer's film songs ever assembled (Hal Leonard, 2009). He lives with his wife and two sons in Culver City ("the Heart of Screenland"), California, on a former backlot of MGM.